C0-AWQ-943

JAMES K. POLK
A POLITICAL BIOGRAPHY

JAMES K. POLK
A POLITICAL BIOGRAPHY

BY

EUGENE IRVING McCORMAC, Ph.D.

NEW YORK
RUSSELL & RUSSELL · INC

0772262

FIRST PUBLISHED IN 1922
REISSUED, 1965, BY RUSSELL & RUSSELL
A DIVISION OF ATHENEUM PUBLISHERS, INC.
BY ARRANGEMENT WITH THE UNIVERSITY OF CALIFORNIA PRESS
L. C. CATALOG CARD NO: 64-66402
ISBN: 0-8462-0131-3
PRINTED IN THE UNITED STATES OF AMERICA

TO
THE MEMORY OF
MY MOTHER

PREFACE

In the two standard sets of American biographies—namely, the *American Statesmen Series* and the *American Crisis Biographies*—the name of James K. Polk does not appear in the list of titles. Evidently the editor of the first set did not consider Mr. Polk to have been a statesman worthy of serious consideration, and the editor of the second set seems to have been unaware that Polk had played a conspicuous part in any of the crises of American history.

Although it is not my purpose to criticize the selection made by these editors, I believe that the character and success of Polk's political career entitled him to a place in either series. I believe that the following pages will show Mr. Polk to have been a constructive statesman—a statesman possessed of vision, sound judgment, and unusual executive ability. Surely he was a "crisis" President. He extended our national boundaries to the Pacific Ocean and determined the political destinies of the future population of the vast area lying west of the Louisiana Purchase. His request for an appropriation with which to conduct negotiations with Mexico called forth the Wilmot Proviso; and this proviso precipitated the "irrepressible conflict," which was one of the greatest crises in American history.

When nominated for the Presidency in 1844, Polk was neither unknown nor inexperienced in national affairs. He had been selected to conduct Jackson's bank war in the House of Representatives, and he had performed this task to the entire satisfaction of the President and the Democratic party. As Speaker of the House of Representatives, he had displayed alertness of mind, sound judgment, and ability as a party leader. And when, in 1844, Van Buren announced his opposition to the annexation of Texas, General Jackson urged that Polk be nominated, for, as he said, Governor Polk was the ablest exponent of Democratic doctrines and the one who would be most capable of carrying them into successful operation. The General did not overrate the political ability of his protégé. As President, Polk formulated his policies with precision and confidence; and despite many obstacles, he succeeded in carrying them into effect.

It has not been my purpose to write a personal biography. Therefore this volume deals almost entirely with Polk's political career. In the discussion of the events of his administration I have attempted to show the part played by the President in formulating the policy of the nation. In the field of foreign relations I have been concerned mainly with the President's foreign policy and with the motives, viewpoints, and exigencies which led to the adoption of that policy. For this reason the history, policies, and motives of other countries concerned have been treated incidentally only. Polk's policies were influenced by what he believed to be the facts concerning those countries, and not by the facts which have subsequently been found to be true. For example, I did not feel that a biography of President Polk called for an exhaustive discussion of conditions in Mexico, either before or during our war with that nation. For similar reasons, the discussion of the Oregon question is confined to the official acts of Great Britain and to the interpretation of those acts by the government of the United States.

The material used in the preparation of this volume has been gathered mainly in the University of California Library, the Tennessee State Library, and the Library of Congress. I am indebted to Dr. John W. Jordon, Librarian of the Historical Society of Pennsylvania, for placing at my disposal the Buchanan Papers, and to Professor St. George L. Sioussat for assistance

[vi]

of various kinds. I am under especial obligation to Dr. Gaillard Hunt and Mr. John C. Fitzpatrick, of the Manuscripts Division of the Library of Congress. Their never-failing courtesy and valuable suggestions facilitated my research work in many ways.

Dr. Justin H. Smith's valuable work entitled ''The War with Mexico'' was published soon after the manuscript of my volume had been completed. Although it appeared too late to be used in the preparation of my manuscript, I am gratified to note that on most points covered by the two works we have arrived substantially the same conclusions.

BERKELEY, CALIFORNIA,
December, 1919.

CONTENTS

[ix]

0777262

78619

[x]

CHAPTER I

ANCESTRY AND EARLY LIFE OF JAMES K. POLK

The pedigree of the Polk family has been traced back to 1075—to Fulbert, who was born in the reign of Malcolm III, of Scotland. In 1153 Fulbert was succeeded by his son Petrius, who took the surname Pollok from the estate which he inherited. In 1440 Sir Robert de Pollok, a "younger son" of the family, inherited an Irish estate and removed to Ireland. By common usage the name of this branch was soon contractd into Polk. Sometime between 1680 and 1687[1] Robert Bruce Polk, or Pollok, second son of Sir Robert II, left Ireland with his wife, six sons, and two daughters, and settled in Somerset County, Maryland. Their oldest son, John Polk, married Joanna Knox and established that branch of the family whence came our subject, James K. Polk.

William Polk, the only son of John and Joanna, after living for a time in Carlisle, Pennsylvania, removed with his family to Mecklenburg County, North Carolina. Colonel Ezekiel Polk, the seventh child of William, married Mary Wilson, and the fourth child of this union was Samuel Polk, the father of the future President. The President's mother was Jane Knox, a great-grandniece of John Knox, of Scotland. Her father, James Knox, of Iredell County, North Carolina, was a captain in the Revolution. Mrs. Polk was a rigid Presbyterian, and a woman of keen intellect and high character. From her James inherited many of his well-known traits. She lived to witness the whole of his successful career, and to assist, during his last moments, in preparing him for "a future estate."[2]

---

[1] Authorities differ as to the date.

[2] Garrett, *Pedigree of the Polk family.* Richardson, *Messages,* IV, 371. Nelson, *Memorials of Sarah Childress Polk,* 150 and *passim.* Chase, *History of the Polk Administration,* 475.

James Knox Polk, oldest of the ten children of Samuel and
Jane Knox Polk, was born on November 2, 1795, in Mecklenburg
County, North Carolina.[3] The Polk family had settled in this
frontier region some time before the Revolution, and tradition
has credited Polk's ancestors with a leading part in promulgat-
ing the much-mooted Mecklenburg Declaration of Independence.
His grandfather, Colonel Ezekiel Polk, whom the Whigs in 1844
accused of Toryism, was an officer in the Revolutionary army.

James's father, Samuel Polk, was a plain but enterprising
farmer. At an early age he had been thrown upon his own
resources and had met with the hardships incident to frontier
conditions. With the hope of improving his fortunes, he followed the trend of emigration westward, and in the autumn of
1806 settled in the valley of the Duck River, Tennessee. He was
one of the first pioneers in a region then a wilderness; but the
valley proved to be fertile and Mr. Polk in time was rated as a
prosperous farmer. He was an ardent supporter of Jefferson,
and his faith in the soundness of Republican doctrines was inherited by his son James. The correspondence in the Polk Papers
indicates that the entire family, including the President's mother,
took a keen interest in politics and that all of them were firm
believers in the maxims of Jefferson.

James was but eleven years old when his father located in
Tennessee. Had he possessed a strong physique, doubtless he
would have shared the fate of the average eldest son and have
been trained to cultivate the family estate. But he was not
strong[4] and his first years in Tennessee were spent in making

---

[3] On November 2, 1846, Polk noted in his diary: "This is my birthday.
According to the entry in my father's family Bible I was born on the
2nd day of Nov., 1795, and my mother has told me that the event occurred,
as near as she could tell about 12 o'clock, Meridian, on that day." (*Diary*,
II, 216.)

[4] "I closed my education at a later period of life than is usual, in
consequence of having been very much afflicted and enjoyed very bad health
in my youth. I did not commence the Latin Grammar until the 13th of
July, 1813." (Polk, *Diary*, IV, 160.)

good use of such limited educational advantages as were afforded in a pioneer community.

Young Polk was studious and ambitious, but Fate seemed determined to deprive him of the opportunity for satisfying his desire for an education. His health did not improve, and his father, believing that a more active life than that of a student would be conducive to health, determined to make a business man of his son. Accordingly, much to the son's disgust and over his protest, he was placed with a merchant to learn the business. After remaining but a few weeks with the merchant, however, the earnest appeals of the son overcame the resistance of the father, and in July, 1813, James was permitted to continue his education under the guidance of Reverend Robert Henderson at a small academy near Columbia, Tennessee. For about a year Polk "read the usual course of latin authors, part of the greek testament and a few of the dialogues of Lucian," and, according to the testimony of his preceptor, he "was diligent in his studies, and his moral conduct was unexceptionable & exemplary."[5] After spending nine months at Murfreesborough Academy, where his "literary merit and moral worth" won the approval of the rector, Samuel P. Black,[6] James entered the University of North Carolina at Chapel Hill in the autumn of 1815. He was naturally drawn to the university of his native state, and the fact that his cousin, Colonel William Polk, had for many years been one of its trustees, may have been an additional reason for selecting this institution.

At college Polk manifested those peculiar traits which later characterized his career as a statesman. Eschewing the less profitable, but usually more attractive, side of college life, his time was occupied with hard and well directed study. "His ambi-

---

[5] A recommendation dated December 31, 1814. MS in Tenn. Hist. Soc. Library.

[6] Recommendation dated October 5, 1815. MS in Tenn. Hist. Soc. Library.

tion to excel," wrote one of his political friends,[7] "was equalled by his perseverance alone, in proof of which it is said he never missed a recitation nor omitted the punctilious performance of any duty." Numerous remarks in the diary written while he was President show that, in Polk's own opinion, time spent in mere pleasure was so much time wasted. He seems to have been equally serious-minded during his college days. Neither at college nor at a later time did Polk deceive himself or attempt to deceive others by assuming great native brilliancy. He never posed as one whose genius made it easy for him to decide great questions offhand. He never attempted to conceal the fact that his conclusions were reached as the result of unremitting labor. And if his conclusions were sometimes attacked as unsound, he was, on the other hand, spared the embarrassment of ridicule, which often fell to the lot of his more brilliant competitors during his long political career.

Polk was graduated from the university in 1818 and enjoyed the distinction of being awarded first honors in both mathematics and the classics. He was very fond of both subjects, as each appealed to his taste for industry and precision. Of his classical training he retained the substantial and discarded the ornate. "So carefully," wrote the friend above cited, "has Mr. Polk avoided the pedantry of classical display, which is the false taste of our day and country, as almost to hide the acquisitions which distinguished his early career. His preference for the useful and substantial, indicated by his youthful passion for mathematics, has made him select a style of elocution, which would perhaps be deemed too plain by shallow admirers of flashy declamation."

After his graduation Polk returned to Tennessee with health impaired by close application, and early in 1819 began the study of law in the office of Judge Felix Grundy. A warm personal and political friendship resulted, which was severed only by the death

---

[7] *Democratic Review*, May, 1838. Polk says that this sketch was written by J. L. Martin, later *chargé d'affaires* to the Papal States (*Diary*, IV, 132).

of Grundy in 1840. The pupil studied hard, and late in 1820 he was admitted to the bar. He immediately began the practice of law at Columbia, in his home county of Maury, among friends and neighbors whose confidence in his ability assured him, from the beginning, a profitable practice. "His thorough academic preparation, his accurate knowledge of the law, his readiness and resources in debate, his unswerving application to business, secured him, at once, full employment, and in less than a year he was already a leading practitioner."[8] His account books show that he continued to enjoy a lucrative practice although much of his time was spent in public service.[9]

For three years the young attorney's time was occupied exclusively in the practice of his profession. His only active participation in politics was to serve for one term as clerk of the state senate. In 1823, however, he was chosen to represent his county in the state legislature, and, having thus entered the political arena, he continued in a very active, and for the most part successful, political career to the close of his term as President. He spent two years in the legislature, where he soon established a reputation for business capacity and for superiority in debate. He took an active interest in all measures for developing his state and gave special attention to the providing of better educational advantages. He enjoyed the personal and political friendship of General Jackson, and it afforded him much pleasure to assist by his vote in sending that military hero to Washington to represent the state in the Senate of the United States. Few acts of his life gave him, in later years, greater pride than his participation in launching Jackson in his political career; and, as the General was ever mindful of the welfare of his political supporters, this incident was no impediment to Polk's own political advancement. His friendship for Jackson was natural, although the two men differed widely in personal characteristics and in

---

[8] *Dem. Rev., sup. cit.*

[9] His account books are in the Library of Congress.

their attitude toward authority. From early youth Polk had been an ardent advocate of republicanism. He was a firm believer in the teachings of Jefferson and shared with his patron an unbounded faith in individual freedom. Pioneer conditions also are conducive to a strong belief in practical democracy, and Jackson seemed to be a leader who understood the people's desires and sympathized with them.

On January 1, 1824, Polk married Sarah Childress, whose father was a prosperous farmer near Murfreesborough, Tennessee.[10] Mrs. Polk was a lady of refinement and ability. Her sound sense and personal charm aided materially the political fortunes of her husband and later caused her to be regarded as one of the most popular ladies of the White House. Many who rated her husband as inferior, even contemptible, joined in the unanimous verdict that Mrs. Polk was a lady of culture and attractive personality. This fact is attested by numerous private letters. Judge Story was "thunderstruck" to hear of Polk's nomination in 1844, but he admired Mrs. Polk. When her husband was leaving Washington in 1839 to enter the campaign for the governorship of Tennessee, Story expressed his admiration for Mrs. Polk in a poem written in her honor.[11]

One of the young men who attended Polk on his wedding day was his law partner, Aaron V. Brown, later United States senator and governor of Tennessee. Their friendship continued to the end, and to no one else, except Cave Johnson, did Polk more frequently confide his usually well concealed political plans.

Two years in the state legislature increased the young attorney's natural taste for politics, and his success in that field made him determine to seek a wider opportunity for satisfying his political ambitions. In 1825 he offered himself as a candidate, and in August of that year was chosen to represent, his district in Congress. When elected, he was not quite thirty years of age,

---

[10] Nelson, *Memorials of Sarah Childress Polk*, 17.
[11] *Ibid.*, 54.

and on entering Congress, he was, with one or two exceptions, the youngest member of that body.

Mrs. Polk did not accompany her husband on his first trip to Washington. The journey was made on horseback, in company with several other members of Congress. At Baltimore they took the stagecoach, leaving their horses until their return in March.[12] On his second journey to Washington, Mrs. Polk accompanied him in the family carriage. The money paid to members as mileage in those early days was small compensation for the hardships encountered on a journey from remote western states. Still, the pioneer statesmen endured such hardships without complaint; they even extracted pleasure from these tedious overland journeys.

There was little ostentation in Washington in this early period. The life of the average congressman's family was extremely simple. It was customary for two or more families to rent a single house for the season and "mess" together.[13] Among the "messmates" of the Polks were Hugh L. White, of Tennessee, and John C. Calhoun, of South Carolina, both of whom later became Polk's bitter political enemies.

Although in politics a disciple of Jefferson and an ardent supporter of Jackson, Polk was wholly unlike either man in personal peculiarities. Jefferson was a born leader of men, and his exuberant optimism and personal charm attracted hosts of disciples. He advertised his democracy by extreme informality and slovenly garb; and he delighted in shocking the "well born" by disregarding the rules of social etiquette. Jackson, also, was a born leader of men. He commanded the multitude because he insisted upon doing so,[14] but the "plain people" approved him

---

12 *Ibid.*, 27–28. 13 *Ibid.*, 30–31.

14 Judge Catron has given such an excellent description of Jackson's will to command that it seems desirable to rescue his letter from oblivion in spite of its length. It was written on the day after the General's funeral.

"One thing may be safely said of Gen¹ Jackson—that he has written his name higher on the Temple of fame, than any man since Washington,

mainly for the reason that they regarded him as one of themselves. Polk, on the contrary, had few intimate friends. His
associates recognized his ability, but he lacked that magnetism
which alone can attract a wide personal following. He was
naturally formal and punctilious, and he seldom sacrified his
dignity in the pursuit of popular applause. While he was

---

of those belonging to History in this country. And what is more remarkable in him than any other American is, that he maintained his power
from seventy to *eighty*, when he had nothing to give. This he did by the
force of will and courage, backing his thorough out & out honesty of
purpose. His intuitive faculties were quick and strong—his instincts
capitally good. The way a thing should be done struck him plainly—&
he adopted the plan. If it was not the best, it would still answer the purpose, if well executed. Then to the execution he brought a hardy industry,
and a sleepless energy, few could equal—but this was not the best quality
he brought to the task. He cared not a rush for anything behind—he
looked ahead. His awful *will*, stood alone, & was made the will of all he
commanded; & command it he would and did. If he had fallen from the
clouds into a city on fire, he would have been at the head of the extin-
guishing host in an hour, & would have blown up a palace to stop the fire
with as little mis-giving as another would have torn down a board shed.
In a moment he would have willed it proper—& in ten minutes the thing
would have been done. Those who never worked before, who had hardly
courage to cry, would have rushed to the execution, and applied the match.
Hence it is that timid men, and feeble women, have rushed to onslaught
when he gave the command—fierce, fearless, and unwavering, for the first
time. Hence it is that for fifty years he has been followed, first by all
the timid who knew him—and afterwards by the broad land, as a match-
less man—as one they were ready to follow wherever he led—who with
them never was weary—and who could sweep over all opposers abroad or
at home, terrible and clean as a prairie fire, leaving hardly a smoke of the
ruin behind. Not even death could break the charm. The funeral yesterday was a great mass meeting—of women, children, men, black, white
colored—of every grade, mixed up by the acre outside—the House crammed
within. There was not a loud word nor a smile so far as I heard or saw.
See him they would and did—nay they would see the cof[f]in cased in
lead. It was just possible to have room for the soldiers, (a rather tedious
process) they claimed it as a *right* to see the thing done. The [illegible]
crowd followed him to the Tomb; a stone grave by the side of Mrs.
Jackson's—laid there in 1828—covered with a copper roofed canopy some
ten feet high resting on stone pillars. He was tediously put in, and the
tomb-stone left off, so all could look once more. It was a scene for a
painter to see the dense crowd at the particular spot—the slave women
in an agony of grief laying their heads on the shoulders and backs of the
lady friends of their old master; leaving laces wet with tears—nor did
the circumstance elicit a single remark so far as I heard. Death did not
make all equal, more completely than did this funeral'' (Catron to
Buchanan, Nashville, June 11, 1845, *Buchanan Papers*).

Speaker of the House, a press correspondent gave the following sketch of his personal appearance:

> I have never seen a man preside over a popular legislative body with more dignity and effect than Mr. Polk. In person he is rather below the middle size, and has a firm and upright carriage which gives great self-possession and command to his manner. His head is finely formed, with a broad and ample forehead, and features indicative of a character at once urbane and decided. He is scrupulous in his dress and always appears in the chair as if he were at a dinner party.[15]

[15] *United States Magazine,* quoted by Nashville *Union,* July 17, 1839.

CHAPTER II

OPPOSITION MEMBER OF CONGRESS

On questions of governmental policy which divided the people of his day Polk entered the political field, as he left it, a consistent Jeffersonian Republican. Like his illustrious patron, however, he found, when entrusted later with the highest executive responsibilities, that theories, however good, must sometimes yield to the practical solution of the problem in hand. On such occasions, as in his expansion policy, he did as Jefferson had done; he assumed far-reaching power for the executive branch of the central government, leaving himself thereby open to the same criticisms which he and Jefferson had hurled at the Federalists.

Polk began his career in Congress as an opponent of the existing administration, and republicanism is always most vigorous when relieved of responsibility. During his first years in Congress his republicanism could have free play. He took a definite stand at once on the side of the states and the people, and vigorously assailed the autocratic powers alleged to have been assumed by President Adams, as well as the centralizing tendencies of that administration.

At a later day Polk's political opponents ridiculed him as being Jackson's *alter ego* and asserted that he had ascended the political ladder on the coat-tails of the "old hero." However effective such allegations may have been as campaign arguments, the fact remains that as early as 1825 Polk's political views were already freely promulgated in Congress, while those of Jackson on most questions were yet unformulated, or at least unannounced. As to the tariff, the only important question on which the General seems at that time to have formed a definite idea, the two men differed widely. That Polk, like others, humored the whims of General Jackson for political reasons need not be denied, that he profited by his friendship is beyond question; but priority in advocating measures later championed by both men would seem to absolve Polk from the charge that his opinions were derived ready-made from his more conspicuous chief. It does not appear that he gripped more firmly to the General's coat-tails than did others of his party.

Since the Tennessee land question was the theme of Polk's first formal speech in Congress, and since this subject was destined to acquire great political significance, it seems desirable to give a summary of its history in order to show its political importance.[1]

North Carolina, the former owner of Tennessee, when ceding this territory to the United States, had reserved the right to dispose of certain lands included in the ceded area. Other tracts were reserved for the Indians. These reservations necessarily limited the amount of land left at the disposal of Tennessee. Under the so-called compromise agreement of 1806, much of the Indian land was procured for the state, and one-sixth of it was to be reserved for educational purposes. In 1821, however, the provision relating to school lands was found to be invalid. As a result, the Tennesseans decided to ask Congress for certain government lands (in Tennessee) which might be disposed of for educational purposes. As the lands in question were those which settlers had declined to purchase at the price asked by the federal government, they were commonly called "waste" lands, although they were far from being worthless.

Although the legislature considered the subject as early as 1821, no definite action was taken until 1823, when it was referred to a select committee of which Polk was made chairman. From

---

[1] For a more detailed account, see Professor Sioussat's interesting article, "Some Phases of Tennessee Politics in the Jackson Period," *Am. Hist. Rev.*, Oct., 1908.

this committee the chairman reported resolutions which, in addition to asking Congress to grant the lands in question, requested the senators and representatives from Tennessee to work for this end.[2]

In 1825, Polk was transferred from the state legislature to the federal House of Representatives. Realizing that the school land question was of prime importance to the people of his state[3] he embraced the earliest opportunity (January 23, 1826) to call up the Tennessee memorial—which he had prepared in 1823—and moved that it be referred to a select committee rather than to the Committee on Public Lands; and despite considerable debate this course was followed. Polk was made chairman of the new committee.[4] The bill which he reported soon afterward failed to pass the House. As will appear later, however, this Tennessee land question was revived from time to time by both Polk and "Davy" Crockett, and it was one of the rocks on which the Jackson party in Tennessee split into fragments.

Questions less local in character soon presented themselves. All of Jackson's supporters asserted, and doubtless many of them believed, that their hero had been virtually, even if not legally, cheated out of the Presidency in 1824 by "bargain and corruption" on the part of Adams and Clay. The well-known fact that the House of Representatives, whenever it might be called upon to select the chief magistrate, was intended by the Constitution to

---

2 Printed copy of the resolutions in *Colonel Wm. Polk Papers*.

3 "You cannot be too industrious," wrote one of his constituents a year later, "in endeavoring to effect the object contemplated in your Report of the last session on the subject of those govr n ment lands. To get this matter through 'is a consumation devoutly to be wished' for it will in a great measure disarm the opposition." The writer told Polk that the press did not tell the people very much about his work in Congress, and he advised Polk to send personal communications to many friends to counteract any assertions by enemies that he is inefficient. He also urged Polk to make a "thundering speach" against Haynes' bankrupt bill. "I do not know what your sentiments are on this subject but I think I know what your *interest* is" (Jim R. White to Polk, Dec. 30, 1826, *Polk Papers*).

4 *Register of Debates*, 19 Cong., 1 sess., 1075–1077.

have a free choice, irrespective of the popular vote, did not in the least appease their wrath. They resolved at once on two lines of policy—to alter the Constitution of the United States in order to deprive the House of the privilege of choosing a President in any case, and in the meantime to make it as uncomfortable as possible for the one who had been so chosen. It is not easy to determine the degree of their sincerity in the first part of their program, but in the second part they were in deadly earnest.

The first move toward altering the Constitution was made by McDuffie, of South Carolina. On December 9, 1825, he offered resolutions which were referred to the Committee of the Whole House. His resolutions declared that the Constitution ought to be so amended that in electing the President and Vice-President of the United States "a uniform system of voting by Districts shall be established in all the States," and in no case should the choice of these officers devolve upon the respective houses of Congress. The resolutions provided also that the subject should be referred to a select committee "with instructions to prepare and report a joint resolution embracing the aforesaid objects."[5] On December 29, Cook, of Illinois, offered resolutions much like those of McDuffie, but providing in addition that the voters in the districts should vote directly for both officers. If by employing this method no election resulted, the choice should "be made by States" from the two highest on the list.[6] The last part was not clear, for it did not specify the manner in which the states should make the choice.

The resolutions of McDuffie and Cook caused considerable debate, and afforded an opportunity for others to air their views on constitutional questions. Some thought that the people were already intrusted with more power than they could use with intelligence, while others vigorously expounded the doctrine of *vox populi vox dei*. McDuffie was not, he said, "one of those visionary

---

[5] *Register of Debates*, 19 Cong., 1 sess., 797.
[6] *Ibid.*, 866.

advocates of the abstract rights of man, that would extend the power of the people further than is conducive to the happiness of the political society.'' Patriotic intentions, he admitted, would furnish no adequate security for the wise selection of a chief magistrate, in the absence of sufficient intelligence. ''It would be a vain and delusive mockery, to invest them with an elective power, which they could exercise to the destruction of that which is the end of all government—the national good.''[7]   Although McDuffie himself believed that the people were sufficiently intelligent to make a proper choice, the conservatives could not be convinced that he was not playing with fire.

Polk spoke to the resolutions on March 13, 1826.[8]   He apologized for departing from his usual custom of giving a ''silent vote,'' and for extending a debate already prolonged.   But as the subject was national in scope and vital in character, he could no longer remain silent.   He attempted no flights of oratory, but he displayed at once more than ordinary ability as a debater. His remarks were clear and incisive, both in declaring his own views and in refuting the arguments of others.   Jefferson himself never gave more unqualified endorsement to the doctrine of majority rule.   The resolutions involved, said Polk, the question of the people's sovereignty.   *''That this is a Government based upon the will of the People; that all power emanates from them; and that a majority should rule;* are, as I conceive, vital principles in this Government, never to be sacrificed or abandoned, under any circumstances.''   In theory, all ''sound politicians'' admit that ''the majority should rule and the minority submit,'' but the majority, in his opinion, did not always prevail under the existing system of elections.

In his zeal for the popular cause Polk attempted to refute an assertion made by Storrs, of New York, that it was not intended by the framers of the Constitution to intrust the choice of

---

7 Feb. 16, 1826.   *Abridg. of Debates,* VIII, 992.

8 *Abridg. of Debates,* IX, 8–16.

dent and Vice-President to direct popular vote. He made the rather astonishing statement that, if Storrs were right, "I am free to admit that I have been wholly mistaken, and totally wrong, in my conceptions upon this subject." With a shade of sophistry he held that it was not reasonable to suppose that the people, having "recently broken the chains of their slavery, and shaken off a foreign yoke," should in drafting their Constitution have voluntarily disfranchised themselves. In spite of well-known facts to the contrary, he tried to prove his contention by quoting parts of the preamble,[9] and rather unsuccessfully from the *Federalist*, Randolph, and Monroe, to show that election by the people had been intended by those who framed the Constitution. He was on surer ground when he asserted that it mattered little whether Storrs were right or wrong, inasmuch as the question before them did not concern elections under the present provisions of the Constitution but an amendment for changing the present method of selecting a President.

In Polk's opinion, there were several good reasons why the President should never be chosen by the House of Representatives. He is not an officer of the House. He is the chief magistrate of the whole people and should therefore be responsible to them alone, and dependent upon them for reëlection. Election either by the House or the Electoral College always makes choice by a minority possible, and there is danger that such elections will become more frequent. Representatives are chosen a long time before, and not for the purpose of selecting a President. A Representative may be ignorant of the wishes of his constituents, or he may willfully ignore their preference. The long period between the election of Representatives and their choice of a President affords ample time to influence their votes by bribery or by executive patronage.

Election by districts, as proposed in the resolutions, was, Polk believed, better than a continuation of the present system under

---

[9] "We, the People etc. do ordain and establish this Constitution."

which some electors were chosen by state legislatures, others by districts, thereby making it possible for one-fourth of the people to elect a President. But he concurred with Livingston, of Louisiana,[10] who preferred to dispense with electors altogether. "Let the people vote directly for the President without their intervention . . ." then ". . . . there can be no division between contending candidates for elector, in favor of the same candidate, and the majority of the people of each district can control and give the vote of that district . . . the sentiment of each mass of the community throughout the Union, composing a district, is fairly elicited, and made to have its due and proportional weight in the general collected sentiment of all the districts in the Union."

Although he offered no resolution embodying his ideas he suggested one[11] for the committee's consideration. His suggestions were more explicit and covered the ground more completely than the resolutions already before the House. Some of his arguments on this subject were partisan and sophistical; but in no case did he indulge in such absurdities as did one of his opponents, Edward Everett, who tried to convince his fellow-members that any attempt to amend the Constitution was itself unconstitutional. Each member, said the sage from Massachusetts, had taken an oath to support the Constitution as it is, and could not propose to alter it without violating that oath.[12] Neither George III nor John Tyler could plead a more tender conscience nor display a greater respect for oaths of office than Everett did on this occasion. No wonder Polk asked if "the gentleman [were] serious in this puerile conception?"

---

[10] McDuffie favored this also.

[11] Each state was to be divided into as many districts as it had members in both houses of Congress. The people in each district were to vote directly for President and Vice-President, without the intervention of electors, and a plurality in each district was to count as one vote. If no election should result, the matter was to be referred back to the people, who were then to select from the two highest on the list (*Abridg. of Debates,* IX, 16).

[12] *Ibid.,* 18.

In attempting to show that members of the House were not the proper persons to elect a President, Polk supported the extreme democratic view which would divest a member of Congress, even as a legislator, of his representative character and make him a mere delegate. "It has been openly avowed upon this floor," said he, "that there is no connection between the Representative here, and his constituent at home; that the Representative here is not bound to regard or obey the instructions of those who send him here. For myself, I have never entertained such opinions, but believe, upon all questions of expediency, that the Representative is bound to regard and obey the known will of his constituent." Any other view would intrust the rights of the people to "the accidental interest, or capricious will of their public servants." He no doubt had Jefferson's inaugural in mind when he added: "Shall *we* assume to ourselves the high prerogative of being uncontaminated and incorruptible, when the same attributes are denied to all the rest of mankind? Is immaculate purity to be found within these walls and no other corner of the earth?" Whether representatives endowed with "immaculate purity" or "angels in the form of kings"[13] can be intrusted with the government of their fellows may be open to question, but both Jefferson and Polk must have known that the framers of the Constitution had consciously placed more reliance on the discretion of the public officials than on the efficacy of a count of heads.

A remark made by Everett gave Polk an opportunity to pay tribute to General Jackson as the champion of the people. If the government were ever destroyed, said Everett, "it would not be by a President elected by a minority of the people, but by a President elected by an overwhelming majority of the people; by some 'military chieftain' that should arise in the land." "Yes, sir," answered Polk, "by some 'military chieftain,' whose only crime it was to have served his country faithfully at a period

---

[13] See Jefferson's inaugural address.

when that country needed and realized the value of his services.''
If the government were ever destroyed, it would be, in his opinion,
by ''the encroachments and abuse of power and by the alluring
and corrupting influence of Executive patronage.'' This was
intended, of course, as a thrust at President Adams; but in lending his support to the elevation of the ''old hero,'' Polk was helping to hasten the demoralizing influence of patronage which he
so much feared.

Some of the northern members objected to the proposed
amendment on the ground that under it slaves would be represented. During his whole political career, slavery was a subject
which Polk avoided whenever possible. It is interesting to note,
however, that his opinions now expressed for the first time in
Congress were never substantially modified. He regretted exceedingly ''that scarcely any subject of general concern can be
agitated here, without having this important subject of slavery,
either collaterally, or incidentally, brought into view, and made
to mingle in our deliberations.'' His views now expressed were
reiterated in substance when he had to deal with the Wilmot
Proviso. Both now and later he was unable to see why this
irrelevant topic should be dragged into discussions of public
policy.

In answering his opponents Polk declared his firm belief in
state rights. Storrs and others had alleged that the proposed
amendment would tend to consolidate the people of the Union.
Polk denied this and said that he would oppose the amendment
if he had any idea that it would produce any such result. ''No
man,'' said he, ''deprecates more than I do, any violation of
rights secured to the States by the Federal Constitution,'' and
no one more fears ''the yawning gulf of consolidation.''[14]

Polk always referred to himself as a Republican, but it is
plain that he was not a believer in true representative govern-

---

[14] ''When I speak of State rights, I mean, as I understand the constitution to mean, not the rights of the Executives of the States, but I mean
the rights of the people of the States.''

ment, and was in fact a democrat.[15] His remarks show clearly the influence of Jefferson's teaching. He was an admirer of General Jackson, and used his influence both publicly and privately[16] to promote the General's interests, but there is no evidence that he relied on Jackson for political opinions. On the contrary, Jackson read with approval Polk's speech on the constitutional amendment and assured him that it was well received by his constituents and would give him a strong claim to their future confidence. "I agree with you," wrote the General,[17] "that the District System is the true meaning of the Constitution, but as this cannot be obtained any uniform System ought to be adopted instead of leaving the election of President to Congress."

As a critic of the Adams administration Polk did not rise above the political claptrap of the day. All that can be said in his favor in this respect is that he spoke less frequently than did some of his colleagues. Even his private letters are tinctured with a bias and a bitterness that do him no credit. A letter written to Colonel William Polk concerning the subserviency of the Speaker and of congressional committees is of special interest, for in it Polk makes the same charges which were later made against himself when he became the leader of the administration forces. "The 'factious opposition' as they are termed," said the letter,[18]

who really consist of the friends of the Constitution, & who do not support upon the fashionable doctrine of *faith* every measure emanating from the administration, merely because it is an administration measure, are to the extent of the power of the administration, and its friends literally proscribed."

Senate committees have been "arranged for effect," although there is but a small administrative majority in that body.

---

[15] There was, of course, no Democrat party at this time.

[16] For example, in a letter to Colonel William Polk, Dec. 14, 1826, he urged the latter to induce the legislature of North Carolina to give some public expression in favor of Jackson on January 8 (*Colonel Wm. Polk Papers*).

[17] Jackson to Polk, May 3, 1826, *Polk Papers*.

[18] Polk to Col. Wm. Polk, Dec. 14, 1826, *Colonel Wm. Polk Papers*.

"Studied majorities in favor of the administration have been placed on each, regardless, it would seem in some instances, of qualifications, talents, or experience. The selections were no doubt made, in conformity to a previous secret understanding, among the favorites at Court.''

In the House, also, ''some remarkable changes have been made in committees by the Speaker. They too have all been arranged for effect.'' The power of patronage, he continued, is corruptly used to ''sustain an administration, who never came into power by the voice of the people.'' How could a man who felt thus, within three short years, give his unqualified support to the administration of General Jackson? The answer is simple. Polk was, despite his ability and generally sound judgment, above all a party man.

At the close of his first term in Congress, Polk, in his appeal to his constituents for reëlection, laid special stress on his opposition to the Panama mission. Soon after taking his seat, he said it became his duty to act upon a proposition emanating from the executive, ''as novel in its character as it was believed to be in consequences.''[19] Not believing in entangling alliances, ''I was opposed to the Mission in every possible shape in which it could be presented, believing, as I did, that the United States had nothing to gain, but much to lose, by becoming members of such an extraordinary Assembly.'' The administration, lacking popularity, was trying to extend the powers of the federal government ''to an inordinate and alarming extent . . . and substitute patronage for public will.'' He was reëlected without difficulty and was, at the beginning of the next session of Congress, made a member of the Committee on Foreign Affairs.[20]

Throughout the Adams administration Polk corresponded with General Jackson. He not only supplied the hero of the Hermitage with information on passing events, but offered welcome suggestions and advice. ''I feel greatly obliged to you,'' wrote

---

[19] Polk's circular letter to his constituents, dated March 4, 1827. Printed copy in *Colonel Wm. Polk Papers*.

[20] *Jour. of H. R.*, 20 Cong., 1 sess., 25.

Jackson on one occasion,[21] "for the information contained in your letter [on internal improvements] . . . and I truly appreciate those feelings of friendship which dictated the communication."

When, in the spring of 1828, the subject of Jackson's execution of the six militia men was under investigation in Congress, Polk and Judge White procured and published a statement from General Gaines and a copy of Governor Blount's orders to Jackson.[22] It was Polk who first notified Jackson of his vindication by a committee, and it was to Polk that the General forwarded additional documents to be used in case it should become necessary.[23] Jackson approved Polk's advice that the attack of the opposition relating to this subject should be met by an active campaign of refutation, but that there should be no defense on the Burr episode until there had been some definite charge.[24] To another letter from Polk offering advice on political matters, Jackson answered: "I have read your letter with great interest & attention—the reasons therein contained leaves no reason to doubt of the correctness of your conclusions, it is such as I had long since concluded to pursue."[25] It is evident that the General already recognized the soundness of Polk's judgment and his shrewdness as a practical politician.

During the session of 1828–29 the Tennessee land bill again became the subject of animated discussion in the House. When he first introduced it, in 1825, Polk had the unanimous support of the people of Tennessee, and of the entire delegation in Congress from that state. But it now met with opposition from an

---

[21] Jackson to Polk, Dec. 4, 1826, *Polk Papers*.

[22] Polk to Jackson, April 13 and 15, 1828, *Jackson Papers*.

[23] Jackson to Polk, March 23, 1828, *Polk Papers*.

[24] The six militia men are made a hobby by the opposition, said Jackson, by which they "can impose upon the credulity of the ignorant. . . . The plan there that you have suggested is the only one that can fairly meet, and effectively put down their hobby." "I think your reflections on the Burr business is correct, no defence, without a charge" (Jackson to Polk, May 3, 1828, *ibid.*).

[25] Jackson to Polk, Sept. 16, 1828, *ibid.*

unexpected quarter—an opposition which resulted in a bitter political feud. The eccentric David Crockett, for reasons best known to himself, had come to the conclusion that the "waste" lands, instead of being sold at a higher price for the support of schools, should be given or sold at a nominal price to poor settlers. He therefore offered an amendment to effect this purpose, and thus assumed the rôle of champion of the poor, as opposed to the rich who, as he said, could alone afford to take advantage of schools. Whatever his motives may have been, his opposition to a bill which he had ardently supported at the last session was at once attributed to the influence of Jackson's political enemies. The Tennessee delegation, wrote Polk,[26] were mortified to think that Crockett "should have coöperated with some of our bitterest and most vindictive political enemies, men, some of them of 'coffin hand bill' and 'six militia men' memory, and joined them in denouncing the Legislature of his state on the floor of Congress." Gales and other "Adamsites," Polk continued, are urging him on and reporting speeches that he never made, while he, it is said, will vote for Gales and Seaton for public printers and against Duff Green. They are making a tool of Crockett in order to deal a blow at Tennessee. Other members of the Tennessee delegation, said Polk, will furnish evidence against Crockett, but prefer not to do so, because the people might regard such action as persecution.

Crockett differed from his colleagues not merely on the land question; he opposed, also the attempt made by the Jackson party to introduce *viva voce* voting in the House so that they might brand the unfaithful. Several members, including Polk, Judge White, R. Desha, and J. C. Mitchell prepared statements concerning the boasts and the conduct of Crockett, and addressed them to Pryor Lea, one of their colleagues. The statements were based largely on assertions made by Crockett at White's lodgings in the presence of the men who had prepared them. Crockett

---

[26] Polk to McMillan, Jan. 16, 1829, *ibid.*

there produced his amendment and boasted that it would be adopted. When asked if he were willing to imperil the entire land bill by insisting upon his amendment, he replied in the affirmative. His constituents, he said, wished the land bill to be killed, for so long as the land continued to be property of the United States the people might use it free of charge. He went so far as to avow that, regardless of his instructions from the legislature, he would support the measures of any man who would vote for his amendment. All agreed that he had been fraternizing with Adams men in an effort to procure their votes. To Mitchell, Crockett openly admitted that Gales had printed— under Crockett's name—a speech which had never been delivered, so that the latter might distribute it among his constituents.

As a result, it was thought, of Crockett's opposition, the House laid the entire land bill on the table. Not satisfied with his victory, however, the incorrigible "Davy," after returning to his district in western Tennessee, continued his attacks upon his colleagues. In public addresses he told the people that the land bill, had it passed, would have sacrificed the interests of the poor settlers. He was especially enraged by what he termed Polk's "officious interference" in the affairs of West Tennessee.[27] Apparently, Polk retaliated by publishing articles hostile to Crockett in a local paper of the latter's congressional district.[28]

Although Crockett did not succeed in his efforts to obtain cheap land for his constituents, he nevertheless had the pleasure of blocking the attempt made by his colleagues to procure school

---

[27] Adam R. Alexander to Polk, April 25; Polk to Alexander, May 1, 1829; *ibid.*

[28] In volume 80 of the *Polk Papers* is a series of five undated articles in Polk's handwriting headed "Col. Crockett & his course in Congress." They are signed "Several voters," and as Crockett is spoken of as "our immediate representative," it is evident that they were to be understood as coming from his constituents. They were probably written for publication in some West Tennessee newspaper. They point out that Crockett had been elected as a friend of General Jackson, but that he has been supporting the old Adams-Clay party, "under the orders of Daniel Webster" and other Hartford Convention Federalists. He has been absent from duty in the House and has done "literally nothing" for the poor settlers of his district.

lands for their state.[29] Until his defeat by Adam Huntsman in 1835 he remained in Congress and continued to oppose all measures championed by the followers of Jackson. The importance of his defection lies in the fact that it was the first breach in the solidarity of the Jackson party in Tennessee. One of the chief critics of Crockett's apostasy in 1829 was Judge White, a man destined ere long to become the center of a political storm that would overthrow Jackson's supremacy in his state and seriously weaken it in the nation. For the time being Crockett stood practically alone. Tennesseans generally were proud to uphold the standard of their warrior hero.

As General Jackson entered the White House the specter of executive usurpation vanished through the window and Polk, like other critics of President Adams, now became a loyal supporter of executive policies. In a letter to his constituents, dated February 28, 1829,[30] Polk congratulated them on the recent political victory, and dwelt at length on the significance of that victory. The contest had been "between the virtue and rights of the people, on the one hand and the power and patronage of their rules [rulers] on the other." The people, said he, have spoken with a voice of warning to future aspirants who may seek to elevate themselves by bargain and intrigue. The country is still destined to be divided into political parties, and already there is evidence that the partisans of Adams and Clay are preparing under the leadership of the latter to oppose the incoming administration. But Jackson has nothing to fear from his enemies. "He is expected to produce reform, correct abuses, and administer the Constitution in its purity, and upon Republican principles contemplated by its wise framers." He has been chosen by the people, and his administration will be both prosperous and popular.

---

[29] By the acts of 1841 and 1846 Congress finally granted these lands to Tennessee (Sioussat, "Some Phases of Tennessee Politics in the Jackson Period," *Am. Hist. Rev.*, 1908, 58).

[30] Pamphlet in Tenn. State Library.

Having pronounced this encomium on the new régime, Polk reminded his constituents that he had contributed his "feeble aid" to the Jacksonian cause because he believed the General's principles to be orthodox and his purpose to be to serve the whole Union. According to others, however, the aid which he had contributed was not so *feeble* as his modesty had led him to assume. The Adams men in Tennessee gave him "grate credit" for compassing their mortifying defeat, and resolved, on that account, to defeat him if possible at the next election.[31]

Despite efforts of his enemies Polk was re-elected by a large majority. On his return to Washington he soon became leader of the administration forces in the House and, as will appear in the following chapter, acted as Jackson's aide-de-camp in the war on the Bank of the United States. With his customary discretion he declined to join with those who felt impelled to give unsolicited advice to the President regarding his social and his executive duties. Toward the end of Jackson's first year in office, and after political Washington had been arrayed in hostile camps by the crusade against Mrs. Eaton,[32] certain members of Congress met, by invitation of C. A. Wickliffe, of Kentucky, for the purpose of discussing the situation. Some of those who attended proposed that the President should be urged to remove Eaton from the cabinet, and that he should be advised to hold regular cabinet meetings. When consulted, Polk, White, Grundy, and other members from Tennessee declined to participate. They even refused to enter into a correspondence with Wickliffe concerning the subjects which had been discussed at the meeting.[33] By thus declining to assume the rôle of guardian over the President, Polk and his associates retained his confidence and good will. While each did his part in supporting Jackson's legislative program, Polk, more than any other, aided in his war against the Bank of the United States.

---

[31] Yell to Polk, Sept. 9, 1829, *Polk Papers.*

[32] See Parton, *Life of Andrew Jackson*, III, chap. xvii.

[33] Letters from Wickliffe to White, Grundy, Polk *et al.*, Dec. 24, 1831. Also other letters on this subject in the *Polk Papers.*

CHAPTER III

POLK AND THE BANK OF THE UNITED STATES

In the bank controversy of Jackson's administration, which Sumner has called ''one of the greatest struggles between democracy and the money power,''[1] Polk bore a prominent and difficult part. It was a part which required a thorough knowledge of the subject, alertness of mind, industry, and sound judgment. It required, also, an intimate knowledge of the plans and purposes of the President, and a certainty on Jackson's part that his confidence would not be misplaced. As this is a biography of Polk, not of Jackson, no attempt will be made to treat the bank war in all of its phases. Yet it seems necessary to consider certain aspects of this controversy in order to make clearer the part played by Polk as a member of the Committee of Ways and Means.[2]

It is generally held by historians that Jackson, when he became President in 1829, harbored no special hostility to the Bank of the United States, but that he was later won over by his friends, who had grievances of their own against the bank. But if Jackson's memory may be relied upon, this belief is contrary to the facts in the case. In 1833, in reply to a letter of inquiry from Polk, Jackson stated that the original draft of his inaugural address, written at the Hermitage, contained a paragraph giving his views on the bank, and another, his views on surplus revenue. After he had reached Washington, he said, he was persuaded by friends to omit both of these paragraphs, as it was thought that the subjects were better suited to an annual message to Congress.

---

[1] Sumner, *Andrew Jackson*, 227.

[2] The summary of the beginnings of the bank war, unless otherwise noted, is drawn largely from Sumner.

"Every one knows," he added, "that I have been always opposed to the U. States Bank, nay all Banks."[3]

In his first annual message Jackson questioned both the constitutionality and the expediency of the existing bank, and vaguely suggested the desirability of a bank "founded on the credit of the government and its revenues." This part of the message was referred by each house to a regular committee. In the Senate, Smith, of Maryland, reported from the Committee on Finance in favor of the bank. In the House, April 13, 1830, McDuffie, of South Carolina, reported from the Committee of Ways and Means, also in favor of the bank. McDuffie declared that the constitutionality of the bank had already been settled by decisions of the Supreme Court, that its expediency was beyond question, and that a bank modeled on the President's suggestions would be both inexpedient and dangerous. On May 10, the House, by a vote of eighty-nine to sixty-six, tabled resolutions which declared that the House would not consent to renew the charter of the bank, and on May 29 it likewise tabled resolutions calling for a report of the proceedings of the bank. It was evident that Congress would not support the President in his opposition to the bank. The defection of McDuffie, who had taken a leading part in the attack of the Jackson forces on the Adams administration, made it necessary for the President, when the time came for forcing the bank question to an issue, to look elsewhere for a leader on whom he could rely.

In his message for 1830, Jackson again proposed a bank as a "branch of the Treasury Department." This seemed to indicate a desire for something like the sub-treasury which was later recommended by President Van Buren. But Jackson's suggestions were vague and Congress gave them little serious consideration. An attempt of the Secretary of War, in July, 1831, to remove the pension funds from the New York branch of the bank,

---

[3] Polk to Jackson, Dec. 23, 1833. Jackson's reply is undated and written on the back of Polk's letter (*Polk Papers*).

met with opposition and failure. By the end of 1831 the President's message was more pacific in tone, and the report of his Secretary, McLane, even spoke in favor of the bank.

The tone of the message only encouraged his political opponents, who were already making plans for the next Presidential election. The bank took the initiative by addressing a memorial to Congress, asking that the bank be rechartered. On January 9, 1832, this memorial was presented in the Senate by Dallas and in the House by McDuffie, both ''bank Democrats.''[4] The committees of the two houses to which the subject was referred both reported in favor of a new charter, but with certain modifications. The Jackson supporters now determined to fight a recharter with every possible weapon and demanded a searching investigation of the bank's conduct. On February 23, Clayton, of Georgia, presented a motion in the House asking for the appointment of a select committee to conduct the investigation. Technical objections were raised by friends of the bank, but Polk met their objections point by point and defeated them with their own weapons.[5] In a speech delivered on this occasion, Polk condemned the bank for having the audacity to ask for a charter and then trying to prevent an investigation. The inference to be drawn from such shrinking from scrutiny, said he, was that there was something ''rotten in the state of Denmark.'' In justification of his motion for a select committee, Clayton presented two lists of charges, which had been prepared for the purpose by Benton.[6] The first specified seven instances of charter violation, involving forfeiture; the second gave fifteen instances of abuse, which required correction, though not involving forfeiture. The investigating committee which the Speaker selected submitted three reports (that of the majority unfavorable to the bank), but our present purpose does not warrant a discussion of either the reports or the charges.

---

[4] *Register of Debates,* 22 Cong., 1 sess., 54.

[5] Benton, *Thirty Years View,* I, 236.

[6] *Ibid.,* 237. The charges are given on the next page.

In the Presidential campaign of 1832, Clay, seeing the *availability* of the bank question, made it a leading issue. In so doing he acted contrary to the better judgment of many friends of the bank, including its president, Nicholas Biddle. A bill passed Congress, providing for a recharter of the bank, and Jackson must now either admit defeat or kill the bill by his veto. He accepted the challenge, vetoed the bill, and appealed to the people to sustain him. He was reëlected by a large majority. Jackson's triumph at the polls was not in reality an endorsement of his veto, but he so regarded it and resolved to exterminate the "monster."

When the bank question first became prominent, the opinions of the administration party were not yet clearly defined. This party "was still only that group of factions which had united in opposition to Adams."[7] A large number of Jackson's most enthusiastic supporters were friends of the bank. Some of the political leaders, including Van Buren, had even signed petitions for the establishment of branch banks. Many politicians, as Niles said, had to "turn a short corner," when Jackson came out against the bank. More independent spirits, like McDuffie, refused to see the light and braved the executive wrath. Opposition in Congress made Jackson only the more determined to wage a relentless war upon the "corrupt institution," but his success would depend, to a considerable degree, on the orthodoxy and ability of the leaders of the administration forces in that body. Obviously the administration program could not be intrusted to the recently converted, whose past record would surely be held up to embarrass them. The fight must be led by those whose record was unassailable. Such was James K. Polk, of Tennessee, the friend and neighbor of the President. He gave to the administration his unqualified support, and, to quote his eulogist,[8] "in

---

[7] Sumner, *Andrew Jackson,* 248.

[8] Eulogy delivered at the time of Polk's death, by L. M. Smith, Newman, Ga. (*Papers of Mrs. Polk,* I).

the hour of darkness and danger, was unquestionably its chief reliance.''

When Congress convened in December, 1832, Polk was transferred from the Committee on Foreign Affairs to the Committee of Ways and Means. A confidential letter written by Jackson to Polk on December 16 discloses the temper of the President as well as the intimate relations of the two men:

> The president with his respects to Col. J. K. Polk, of Congress, encloses him a note from Mr. Page of Philadelphia, a man of high character & in whom confidence may be placed. This is done to add to the information heretofore given the Col. *to show* him that the hydra of corruption is only *scotched, not dead,* and that the intent is thro' Wolf's recommendation, to destroy the vote of the people lately given at the ballot boxes & to rally around the recharter the present Session of Congress *two thirds.* . . . Call upon the Sec. of the Treasury who must agree with me that an investigation by Congress is absolutely necessary.

A postscript instructed Polk to have Sullivan, a government director, brought before the committee, and ended with a peremptory order ''Attend to this.''[9] Polk did ''attend'' to it, and the Secretary of the Treasury seems to have been persuaded that an investigation was necessary.

Though Jackson in his annual message, December 4, 1832, informed Congress that the report of the Secretary of the Treasury ''will exhibit the national finances in a highly prosperous state,'' nevertheless he advised the sale of all corporation (bank) stocks held by the government. He also urged that the safety of public deposits in the Bank of the United States was worthy of ''serious investigation'' by Congress. In response to these suggestions, the Committee of Ways and Means, of which Polk was a member, undertook an investigation of the charges which had been brought against the bank. The directors were summoned to Washington and examined upon oath,[10] and other testimony was taken to supplement the information which had

---

[9] *Polk Papers.*
[10] *Dem. Rev.,* May, 1838.

been gathered by the President. Reuben M. Whitney, the political scavenger of the administration, wrote to Polk from Baltimore, February 9, 1833, urging him to hasten the investigation,
and warning him that Adams and Sergeant had been consulting
with members of the committee. On February 11 Whitney
wrote from Philadelphia advising Polk that the bank relied much
on the ability of Verplanck[11] to outgeneral his opponents on
the committee. While the investigation was in progress, Polk, on
February 13, reported a bill to sell the bank stock owned by the
government, but it failed in the House by a vote of one hundred
and two to ninety-one. On March 1, Verplanck, for the majority
of the Committee of Ways and Means, reported the bank to be
sound and the public deposits safe, although it was admitted that
in interfering with the plan of the government to pay off the
three per cent securities the bank had exceeded its lawful powers.
This report was adopted by the House. The *Globe* charged the
majority with forcing the adoption of its report without having
considered or presented the evidence which had been collected
by its minority members. Many members, it said, who were not
in favor of the bank had voted for adoption because, on the showing of the majority report, they could not conscientiously say
that the bank was *not safe*.[12] Anticipating the character of the
majority report, Polk prepared and submitted a minority report
for himself and two other members of the committee. After
criticizing the majority of the House for wishing to force the
adoption without adequate consideration of evidence, and inti-
mating with some justice that the committee had passed lightly
over certain damaging testimony, Polk went with considerable
detail into the question of the "three per cents." These were
securities bearing three per cent interest issued by the government

---

[11] Chairman of Ways and Means Committee and a friend of the bank.
Whitney urged Polk to see that Gilmore, another member of the committee,
should not be tampered with. Verplanck, he said, was not to be trusted
and should not be permitted to have access to the testimony already
taken, unless accompanied by "one of our friends" (*Polk Papers*).

[12] Washington *Globe*, March 6, 1833.

in 1792 for accrued interest on the Revolutionary debt. The government had decided to pay off about $6,500,000 of these, and on March 24, 1832, the Secretary of the Treasury notified the bank of his intention to pay this amount on the first of July. Biddle requested the government to postpone payment until October 1 and agreed to reimburse the treasury for the extra three months' interest. To this the government agreed. When asking for postponement, Biddle based his request largely on two special reasons, neither of which implied that the bank wished any accommodation for itself. The assigned reasons were: (1) that $9,000,000 of duty bonds would be payable on July 1, and merchants would be inconvenienced should the three per cent debt also fall due on that date; (2) should the much feared cholera appear, business would be deranged, and if, in addition, the bank should have to call in its money loaned to merchants, in order to pay off the three per cents, great distress would result.

The government having agreed to delay payment, the bank made secret but unsuccessful attempts to arrange with Thomas W. Ludlow, New York agent of foreign holders, to postpone payment of part of this debt. It then sent General Cadwallader, a director of the bank, to Europe. He made an agreement with Baring Brothers & Co., of London, by which the Barings were to arrange with certificate holders to postpone payment for one year. The Barings were to pay all holders who were unwilling to wait and themselves to assume the debt to that amount. As a result of Cadwallader's agreement adjustments were made to the extent of nearly five million dollars. Every effort was made to keep the transaction a secret, but it leaked out, and an account of it was published in a New York paper. Biddle then disavowed the arrangement.

In his minority report Polk showed conclusively that the real reasons for the bank's desire for postponement could not have been those assigned by its president. He gave a very clear analysis of the evidence which had been collected by the committee and made it plain that the bank had no intention of applying any of its money to the purpose for which it had said it desired these funds. He reached the inevitable conclusion that the bank had desired postponement because of its own weakness.

In his entire report, but especially in his arraignment of Biddle, Polk displayed those qualities which ever distinguished him in debate, and which fully justified the confidence reposed in him by General Jackson. His preparation was exhaustive and his arguments clear cut and logical. His language was well chosen and dignified, but at the same time scathing and merciless. "When the President of the Bank," said Polk, "not only induces the board to act for reasons unknown to themselves, but conceals even from the committees acts done in their names, something stronger than doubt almost seizes on the mind. When, to the consideration that the committees know little of the proceedings had in their names, is added the fact that every Government director is excluded from even that little, by being excluded from every committee, the Government at least has grounds to doubt whether its interests are safe in such keeping. When a show of the strength of the Bank is made, consisting of sums in specie and amounts in exchange, while the debts are secretly contracted, which have enabled the Bank to accumulate these funds, are concealed even from those who make the exhibition, there is just ground to doubt whether there be soundness in the institution, or proper precaution and responsibility in its management."[13]

When, in the spring of 1832, Benton prepared his catalogue of charges against the bank for Clayton to present in the House, he strained his imagination in order to make his list as long and as formidable as possible. Such a course may have been effective for campaign purposes, but many of Benton's charges were easily shown to be exaggerated or unfounded. For this reason his arraignment lost force and failed to convince the doubtful. Polk, on the contrary, confined his denunciation to points on which the

---

[13] *Reports of Committees*, 22 Cong., 2 sess., No. 121.

bank could offer no legitimate defense of its conduct. His arguments were then, and are today, unassailable.[14] Polk well knew
that neither his report nor his arguments on the floor would have
much weight in the House, as a majority of the members were
resolved to stand by the bank in spite of its faults. He was
speaking to a wider audience and may have been already seeking
popular support for the impending executive assault on the bank.
However this may have been, he significantly pointed out that
the institution might be reached by the executive without any
assistance from Congress. "Whether the existing facts," said
Polk in his report,

are sufficient to justify the Executive in taking any steps against the
Bank, authorized by its charter, is a matter for the decision of the proper
officers, acting upon their own views and responsibility: any opinions by
Congress can make it neither more nor less their duty to act. Whatever,
therefore, the opinions of the members of this committee might be as to
the justice or policy of any Executive action, they deem it unauthorized
and improper to express them officially.

In other words, it was for the executive alone to determine
whether the bank had violated its charter or had been guilty of
mismanagement, and, if so, to apply the remedy.

Whether, at the time Polk made his report, Jackson had resolved upon a removal of the deposits from the bank as a proper
remedy, we are unable to say.[15] If he had, Polk, who was certainly in his confidence, was doubtless aware of the fact. Polk's
remarks on executive responsibility and his indifference to the
opinions of Congress seem to indicate that such was the case.
He may even have suggested removal of the deposits to the President, but of this there seems to be no direct evidence. It is

14 "Its facts and reasonings," said the *Globe* (March 6, 1833), "are
perfectly irresistible. It exposes the subterfuges and self-contradicted
testimony under which that corrupt and corrupting institution has shel-
tered itself, in a manner so clear and convincing, that it must satisfy
every honest man who reads it, of the utter profligacy of its management."

15 To quote Sumner on this point: "Lewis says that he does not know
who first proposed the removal of the deposits, but that it began to be
talked of in the inner administration circles soon after Jackson's second
election" (Sumner, *Jackson*, 297).

worthy of note, however, that the well-known paper of September 18, 1833, in which Jackson announced to his cabinet his intention to remove the deposits, makes use of many of the same facts and employs much the same reasoning that Polk had already used in his minority report.

The minority report arrayed against its author all the power and the venom of the bank party, and measures were taken to prevent his reëlection to Congress. Friends of the bank held a meeting at Nashville and denounced his report. He was accused of destroying credit in the West by proclaiming that the people were unworthy of mercantile confidence. Handbills signed "Muhlenging" were circulated, alleging that Polk as a member of Congress had been opposed to pensioning Revolutionary soldiers.[16] Polk met the issue squarely as a foe of the bank, and during the campaign stress was laid on the bank affiliations of Bradford, his opponent. Under the circumstances, Polk's success or defeat was regarded as of more than local importance. "Your friends here," wrote Donelson from Washington, "take a deep interest in your election and are all well apprised of the instruments which are employed to defeat you."[17] Donelson showed his own interest by inclosing in his letter evidence to be used against Bradford. In 1827 Bradford had applied to Adams for an appointment as marshall. His friends had sent letters of recommendation representing him to be a friend of Adams and an opponent of Jackson. From the files in the State Department, without the knowledge of the Secretary, Donelson had copied extracts, and now sent them to Polk, to be used at his discretion so long as Donelson's name was not mentioned. A speech made by Bradford in the Tennessee Senate in 1831, in favor of rechartering the bank, was also reprinted and circulated among his constituents. It was a spirited contest, but Polk was reëlected by a majority of over three thousand votes.

---

[16] *Dem. Rev.*, May, 1838. Polk's "Circular Letter" to his constituents.

[17] A. J. Donelson to Polk, May 30, 1833, *Polk Papers*. The letter was marked "*Private and for your eye alone.*" There is nothing to indicate whether Jackson was cognizant of Donelson's act.

As soon as he was safely elected, Polk, with the assistance of Cave Johnson, began a quiet campaign for the Speakership.[18] He received encouragement from his political friends, but the expected vacancy[19] did not occur and he continued his labors as a floor member.

The adoption by Congress of Verplanck's report did not in the least alter Jackson's opinion of the character of the bank. On August 31, 1833, he[20] sent Polk a confidential letter in which he inclosed a report of the bank directors. Polk was authorized to use the facts contained in the report, but not to divulge that they had come from the President. Jackson regarded these facts as proof positive that Biddle had been using the people's money for purposes of corruption.

By September Jackson was ready to carry into effect his plan to deprive the bank of the use of government money. Duane had in May succeeded McLane in the Treasury Department and was expected to do the bidding of the President. On September 18, Jackson read to his cabinet the well-known paper in which he asserted that the deposits ought to be removed. Among the reasons assigned for the proposed action were the political activities of the bank, its attempt to postpone payment of the three per cents, and the fact that it had come into existence by an unconstitutional law. He would not, he said, dictate to the Secretary, but the President himself, assuming all responsibility, had

---

[18] This subject will be considered at length in another place.

[19] Stevenson was expected to accept a foreign mission and not be a candidate for reëlection. He resigned later for this purpose.

[20] The signature is cut off, but the letter is in Jackson's unmistakable hand. He says: ''You will find from the inclosed that I have at last thro the Government Directors got a *Small peep* into their expense account, and the corruption on the morals of the people.

''In two years $80 odd thousand expended to corrupt the people & buy a recharter of that mamoth of corruption. I think when these scenes of corruption are made known to the people and that by an order of the board of directors, the whole funds of the Bank are placed at the disposal of Mr. Biddle to appropriate as he pleases [cut out with signature] most bold specious of corruption ever practiced by any body of people in the most corrupt governments'' (*Polk Papers*).

decided that, after October 1, government money should no longer be deposited in the bank, and that all money there on that date should be drawn out as needed. Duane declined to give the necessary order to effect Jackson's purpose and later refused to resign. He was dismissed and Attorney General Taney commissioned to take his place, September 23, 1833.[21] Taney gave the order, and the "hydra of corruption" was at last more than "scotched."

Jackson's high-handed act produced much excitement throughout the country. The bank issued a paper[22] in reply to the President's charges, and a bitter conflict was inevitable as soon as Congress should assemble. "At such a crisis it became important to have at the head of the Committee of Ways and Means a man of courage to meet, and firmness to sustain, the formidable shock. Such a man was found in Mr. Polk, and he proved himself equal to the occasion."[23]

Congress met on December 2, 1833, and, as a result of the recent election, the administration forces were in unequivocal control of the House. Jackson's message, dealing among other topics with his removal of the deposits, and accompanied by a report of the Secretary of the Treasury on the same subject, was sent to Congress on the third of December. A contest at once arose over the reference of both message and report. Friends of the bank wished them referred to the Committee of the Whole House, where the enormity of the President's conduct might be discussed without limit. The Jackson supporters, on the other hand, wanted them referred to the Committee of Ways and Means, of which Polk had recently been made chairman. On the tenth, McDuffie succeeded in carrying a resolution to refer Taney's report to the Committee of the Whole. On the eleventh, Clay, of Alabama, presented a resolution to refer that part of the President's message relating to finance to the Committee of Ways and Means, but to this McDuffie and others offered vigorous

21 Mosher, *Executive Register*, 113.
22 *Niles' Reg.*, XLV, 248.   23 *Dem. Rev.*, May, 1838.

objections. On the same day, Polk moved a reconsideration of
the vote which had referred Taney's report to the Committee of
the Whole, and he was at once accused by the opposition of aiming to have it referred to his own committee so that he could
smother the question. Chilton, of Kentucky, who was especially
opposed to a reconsideration, did not wish to see "the whole
weight of this massive Government imposed on the shoulders of
his friend from Tennessee,"[24] and urged that the question ought
to be left with the larger committee so that all might discuss it.

Discussion was the last thing which Polk desired, and precedent supported his contention that the reference made under
McDuffie's resolution had been entirely irregular. Never before,
he said, had a great subject of national policy been referred, in
the first instance, to the Committee of the Whole on the state of
the Union. The course which he advocated was simply the usual
one. In the argument Polk was the equal of any of his opponents.
When they told him that the Secretary's reasons had been stated
in his report, thereby making investigation by a committee unnecessary, Polk replied that the report contained various statements of fact which might involve the bank's charter, and that
these facts should be carefully investigated. He also reminded
them of their assertions that the state banks in which the President had deposited public money were unsafe, and that the public
faith had been violated. "Is it not proper, then, for a committee
of the House to inquire by which party the contract was violated?"[25] After much discussion the House, on December 17,
decided, by a yea and nay vote of one hundred and twenty-four
to one hundred and two, to reconsider its vote on McDuffie's
resolution.

Having won on the question of reconsideration, Polk now
fulfilled Chilton's prophecy by moving that Taney's report be

---

24 *Cong. Globe,* 23 Cong., 1 sess., 24. All arguments made in the House,
unless otherwise noted, are taken from the *Globe,* and may be found under
dates mentioned in the text.

25 *Ibid.,* p. 25, Dec. 12, 1833.

referred to the Committee of Ways and Means. McDuffie immediately moved that Polk's committee be instructed to "report a joint resolution providing that the public revenue hereafter collected be deposited in the Bank of the United States, in conformity with the public faith pledged in the charter of the said bank." It is not at all likely that McDuffie expected his motion to carry, but he gained what was doubtless his main object—an opportunity for a discussion of all phases of the question. This move on the part of the opposition brought from the President a letter instructing Polk to make a short reply and then to call for the previous question ;[26] but two long months of debate had yet to elapse before Polk's committee would be able to consider the Secretary's report, unhampered by annoying instructions.

Binney, of Pennsylvania, interrupted the discussion on December 18 by presenting a memorial from the bank. The substance of this document was a declaration that the bank was entitled to the deposits unless Congress should decide otherwise. On Polk's motion, the memorial was referred to his committee. On the same day, Chilton moved to instruct the Committee of Ways and Means to report a joint resolution directing the Secretary of the Treasury to restore the deposits to the bank, but, on the request of McDuffie, this motion was withdrawn.

On the main question of referring the Secretary's report with instructions to Polk's committee, McDuffie made the opening speech (December 19). The gist of his remarks was that removal of the deposits was illegal because the President had usurped authority in performing it. Even the President, he said, had admitted that the authority rested with the Secretary, and, if so, Jackson could not lawfully assume it. On December 30, Polk replied in defense of the administration. As usual he had thoroughly prepared himself for his task. He was ready with authorities and precedents to support his own contentions as well as to refute those of his opponents. So thorough and

---

[26] Jackson to Polk, Dec. 18, 1833, *Polk Papers*.

inclusive was his array of facts and arguments that, although
the debate lasted nearly two months longer, there was little for
any other administration member to add. Every opposition member who spoke to the question devoted most of his time to answering the arguments of Polk. He was regarded by all as the
chief supporter, in the House, of the President and his policies.
Jackson himself, on his next visit to Tennessee, told the people
of Nashville that "Polk for the hard service done in the cause
deserves a Medal from the American people."[27]

So far as a reference of Taney's report to the Committee of
Ways and Means, as well as the attempt to instruct that committee, were concerned, Polk showed without difficulty that the
opposition members were clearly in the wrong. The memorial of
the bank setting forth its grievances, and likewise the charges of
the government directors against the bank, had, after full deliberation, been referred by the House to the Committee of Ways
and Means; there was consequently no good reason why the Secretary's report should not be sent to the same committee. Polk
intimated that the real reason for this attempt to interrupt the
normal procedure was the desire of his opponents to "flood the
country with inflammatory speeches," telling the people that
panic must result from the removal of the deposits. Should the
committee be compelled, said Polk, to act under the instructions
proposed by McDuffie, it would be prejudging the question;
investigation would be superfluous, and a report made under
such instructions would be absurd. The task of justifying the
arbitrary conduct of the President was more difficult. By many,
Polk's argument on this subject may not be regarded as convincing.[28] But whether Jackson had acted within his rights or had

---

27 Robert M. Burton to Polk, Aug. 27, 1834, *Polk Papers*. Polk's speech
may be found in *Cong. Deb.*, X, 2.

28 When Polk was a candidate for the Presidency, the *National Intelligencer* (Sept. 21, 1844) said: "Throughout the whole of Mr. Polk's
course in Congress in relation to the Bank of the United States, there was
exhibited a zeal not only without knowledge, but often, we must think,
against conviction."

been guilty of gross usurpation, no one could have defended his course more ably than did the chairman of the Committee of Ways and Means. A slightly new turn was given to the discussion by the motion of Jones, January 14, 1834, to substitute instructions for those submitted by McDuffie. McDuffie's instructions, as Polk had pointed out, prejudged the whole question, and were mandatory as to the findings of the committee. Those now offered by Jones simply instructed the committee to "inquire into the expediency of depositing the revenues hereafter collected," not in the Bank of the United States, but in state banks.[29] It was now a question of compulsory restoration of the deposits, on the one hand; on the other, discretion for the committee as to its findings, after the expediency of deposit in state banks had been investigated.

While the question of reference with instructions was being debated, memorials from groups of individuals, some for and some opposed to the bank, were sent to the House. One came from the Maine legislature, upholding Jackson and pronouncing the bank unconstitutional. Efforts were made to refer some of the memorials to select committees, but, usually, on Polk's motion, they were all sent to the Committee of Ways and Means. Polk and his committee were therefore the objects of much criticism and even abuse. The sole purpose of both Taney and Polk, according to Binney, was to sustain the administration, without thought of the country's welfare. Polk's object in wishing to get possession of Taney's report, in the opinion of Moore, of Virginia, was to stifle debate, to put the stamp of approval on the report, and then to send it forth to deceive the people and prejudice them against the bank. A motion made by Hubbard to refer to Polk's committee the President's message on the re-

---

[29] On February 19, Mardis, of Alabama, offered a resolution, "That the Committee of Ways and Means be instructed to inquire into the expediency of reporting a bill requiring the Secretary of the Treasury to deposit the public moneys of the United States in State banks." There was much debate on this resolution, but, as it was later withdrawn by the mover, it will not be considered in the present discussion.

fusal of the bank to surrender its books and papers as pension agent, caused Watmough, of Pennsylvania, to think that "the Committee of Ways and Means have got a voracious appetite, and seem desirous to devour all that comes before the House." It was a question of law, he said, and should be referred to the Judiciary Committee. He was supported by Barringer, of North Carolina, who asserted that Polk's committee was trying to grasp all important legislation so that it might be shaped in the administration mold. But oppositon was futile; the message went with the memorials to appease the "voracious appetite" of Polk and his colleagues. There, too, went Taney's report, the main subject of discussion. On February 18, 1834, the two months' debate was closed by invoking the previous question, and Polk's original motion (of December 17, 1833) to refer to his own committee Taney's report on the removal of the deposits was at last carried by a yea and nay vote of one hundred and thirty to ninety-eight. All motions to instruct the committee had already been voted down, and the House now refused to hear new resolutions for this purpose. The victory of the committee was complete, and it could proceed, unhampered, to perform its part in the executive program. Polk's successful defense of the administration brought him letters of commendation from all parts of the country, and especially from his own state. Governor Carroll wrote from Nashville to compliment Polk on his "temperate, able and successful vindication of the President," and added that "this is almost the universal sentiment here."[30] Polk's services

---

[30] Governor Carroll to Polk, Jan. 23, 1834, *Polk Papers*. John H. Dew, member of the Tennessee legislature, wrote to Polk, Jan. 21: "Your argument in defence of the Executive for the exercise of an ordinary power, expressly conferred on him by the Constitution of the U. S. and fully sanctioned by precedent & custom evinces a most intimate acquaintance with the multifarious movements that have been made upon the great American political *Chess board* from the organization of the Government to the present *Crisis*. You have shown most incontestibly, from laborious research into public records and documents that the President and his Cabinet have in all things acted strictly within the sphere of their Constitutional duty and rule of action." There are many similar letters among the *Polk Papers*.

as guide in the proposed constitutional convention of his state were eagerly sought, and he was much talked about as a desirable candidate for Governor of Tennessee, and for Speaker of the national House of Representatives. Even your enemies say, said a letter from his home town, that "you could be elected for anything in Maury."[31]

Before the vote on the reference of Taney's report had been taken, the Committee of Ways and Means had already made it quite clear that nothing favorable to the bank might be expected from them. On February 11, Polk reported for the committee on Jackson's message against the bank—the message in which the bank was denounced for not surrendering the books and money held by it in its capacity as pension agent. Polk fully sustained the President and refuted every contention of the bank. "The committee," so read the report, "cannot condemn, in terms too strong, the conduct of the bank in this transaction." He reported a bill to the effect that, in future, pensions should be paid by officers of the government, and not left in "the hands of an irresponsible corporation."

By March 7, the committee was ready to submit its opinions on the removal of the deposits. These opinions were placed before the House on that date, and it was generally understood that they had been drawn up by the chairman. They held that both the removal of the deposits and the placing of this money in state banks were unquestionably legal. The committee believed the bank to be unconstitutional, but, even if it were not, its conduct had been such that it ought not to be rechartered, and therefore, the deposits ought not to be restored. They expressed full confidence in the competence of state banks to perform all necessary services for the government, and revived Jefferson's well-known arguments to prove that such an institution as the Bank of the United States had never been contem-

31 T. H. Cahal to Polk, Jan. 2, 1834, *Polk Papers.* Maury was Polk's county.

plated by the framers of the Constitution. For his own reputation, Polk might well have stopped here; but he repeated the
arguments of the day that "none can doubt the power of the
bank to create embarrassment," and he proceeded to show that
this had been done by loaning money at a given place during one
month, and then calling it in during the next. Such action may,
indeed, have been within the power of the bank, but banking
institutions seldom resort to that form of amusement. This may
have been one of the occasions noted by the *National Intelligencer*[32] on which Polk's zeal was not supported by either
"knowledge" or "conviction." However this may be, Polk had
not been found wanting in his defense of the President. His
services as a party leader of the House were none the less efficient because history may pronounce some of his arguments
untenable.

The House, on March 12, suspended the rules so that Polk
might have his report made a special order and thereby hasten
its adoption. This action was denounced by Adams, who said
that Polk, acting under royal prerogative, would soon close all
debate by the previous question and deprive the minority of its
constitutional right of discussion. But Adams could not very
well complain, as Polk pointed out, because Adams himself had
voted for the previous question when the bill to recharter the
bank had been forced through the House.

Polk did not, however, immediately call for the previous question, and his critics made the most of the opportunity afforded
them. Instead of reporting on Taney's reasons for removing the
deposits, said Wilde, of Georgia (March 19), the committee had
reported an argument—that the bank ought not to be rechartered. They had "gone beyond the President and the Secretary,
in claiming power for the Executive." Harden, of Kentucky,
admired the "master-stroke of policy" of the committee in pronouncing against recharter when that question was not before it,

---

[32] *National Intelligencer*, Sept. 21, 1844. See above, note 28.

but it had given no information except a reëcho of Taney's report. McDuffie criticized Polk for shutting off debate, but he gave him full credit for acting "with a tact and skill and zeal worthy of a better cause."[33] McDuffie concluded his argument on April 4, Mason called for the previous question, and the debate on Polk's report was closed. Resolutions prepared by the committee, providing among other things for a select committee to investigate the bank, were quickly adopted. The new committee, appointed by the Speaker on the seventh, repaired at once to Philadelphia whence Mason, one of its members, kept Polk informed of its proceedings by confidential letters.[34] But the bank refused to submit its books for examination, and the special committee soon (May 22) reported that it had been unable to perform the duty assigned to it by the House. While investigation thus ended in failure, nothing was left undone which in any way depended upon the vigilance or activity of Polk. On June 13, he succeeded in sending to the table two joint resolutions from the Senate: one, disapproving of the removal of the deposits; the other, directing that the deposits be restored to the Bank of the United States.

By adopting Polk's report the House had put its stamp of approval on the President's act in removing the deposits, but the question of depositing this money in state banks had still to be considered. Jackson's opponents had always contended that, without the authority of Congress, the President had no right to intrust public money to such banks. On April 22, 1834, Polk reported from his committee a bill for regulating these state deposit banks. It was based on the report of the Secretary of

[33] McDuffie said he had criticized Jackson in the hope of bringing out Jackson's supporters. "The honorable member from Tennessee did come out boldly and manfully, took his position, and, whatever views I may entertain of his generalship, I am ready to bear testimony that the position which he has assumed is the only one he could assume, without leaving unprotected and undefended the very part which it was his duty to defend" (April 3, 1834). I have converted this into direct discourse. It is reported *indirectly* in the *Cong. Globe.*

[34] Mason to Polk, May 5 and May 10, 1834, *Polk Papers.*

the Treasury. Adams (June 7) attempted to filibuster by moving a resolution to call on the Secretary of the Treasury to lay before the House the names of officers and stockholders of such banks, as well as numerous unimportant details. Polk promptly met this by moving an amendment which required a similar statement from the Bank of the United States. A request made by Adams (June 13) that Polk should withdraw his amendment gave the latter an opportunity, not only to defend the administration, but to employ that sarcasm and scorn which ever made him feared as a debater. It was far more necessary, Polk believed, to require information from the old bank than from the new banks, because the government was a stockholder as well as a depositor in the Bank of the United States. It was also more necessary, he said, because that bank

had set itself up in antagonistic position to the Government, had denounced the Executive as a tyrant, usurper, and despot, and more ʻrecently, had denounced and insulted the representatives of the people, because they had sustained him in his measures. But, according to the gentleman, this immaculate and inoffensive Bank of the United States must not be looked into, though the affairs of the State banks must be thoroughly probed.[35]

Polk's bill for regulating the deposits in state banks passed the House, June 24, 1834, by a vote of one hundred and twelve to ninety, but it was now near the end of the session and the Senate at its last meeting, June 30, laid the bill on the table. In the House, at least, the friends of the bank had been defeated on every point, and the acts of the President had been fully vindicated. The completeness of this vindication was due, in no small measure, to the industry and vigilance of the chairman of the Committee of Ways and Means.

---

[35] Polk here read from the *National Gazette* an article in which the bank directors had denounced Jackson and the House.

CHAPTER IV

POLK-BELL CONTEST FOR THE SPEAKERSHIP

During his canvass for reëlection to Congress in 1833, Polk seems to have decided to become a candidate for the Speakership in the event of his success at the polls. Public attention had recently been called to this office by a rumor that the Speaker of last session, Andrew Stevenson, was to be given a diplomatic appointment and would therefore not be a candidate for re-election.

Whether Polk's idea of becoming a candidate originated with himself or was suggested to him by friends is uncertain. There are among his papers letters which show that, soon after his election early in August, he began to sound his friends on the subject. Other letters make it equally clear that he was being considered for the office by men who knew nothing of his own initiative in the matter. Cave Johnson, his most intimate friend, aided him by soliciting the support of their political associates.

His first campagn for the Speakership was soon abandoned, for Stevenson did not go abroad as soon as had been expected. However, his aspirations met with some encouragement. In answer to a letter from Polk on the subject, C. C. Clay, of Alabama, wrote: "Should the vacancy, of which you speak, occur, I know of no other member, whose election to fill it would be more agreeable to my own feelings than yours." On the same day Clay said in a letter to Cave Johnson: "I am pleased with your suggestion of Polk as the successor of Stevenson, and hope we may be able so to manage, as to effect the object."[1] A week later Leavitt, a member from Ohio, informed Polk of Stevenson's

---

[1] Clay to Polk, Aug. 19, 1833; same to Johnson, same date, *Polk Papers*.

rumored appointment to a foreign mission. He did not know, he said, whether Polk had been approached, but he hoped that he would be chosen to fill the vacancy.[2] Other letters of similar import were received; one from Cave Johnson[3] said that he had been writing letters to members of the House in an effort to bring about concerted action in Polk's behalf.

At this early date Jackson seems to have taken no special interest in Polk's political promotion, although he was ready to give it his approval. Having corresponded with the President on the subject, Grundy informed Polk[4] that he had "received an answer from the highest quarter of the most satisfactory & encouraging character." He advised Polk to induce his friends to write to members of the House, but to avoid writing such letters himself. James Walker, a brother-in-law of Polk, went to Washington in October in quest of a mail contract. After an interview with the President in relation to Polk's aspirations, Walker reported that *"he gives in to them I think decidedly and frankly."*[5] Jackson told Walker that some persons believed it would not "look very modest" to solicit the Speakership for Tennessee, as well as the Presidency. The President himself ridiculed this objection and assured Walker that Polk's election would in no respect embarrass the administration. Walker got the impression, however, that William B. Lewis was in favor of Bell. Here may have been the beginning of Polk's intense dislike for Lewis. Another interview with Jackson convinced Walker that the President was not only willing but eager to have Polk chosen Speaker of the House. He was charmed with the Vice-President and advised Polk to make it known to Van Buren that he would support him for the Presidency.[6]

---

2 H. H. Leavitt to Polk, Aug. 26, 1833, *ibid.*

3 Johnson to Polk, Aug. 26, 1833, *ibid.*

4 Grundy to Polk, Sept. 13, 1833, *ibid.*

5 Walker to Polk, Oct. 22, 1833, *ibid.*

6 Walker to Polk, Nov. 7, 1833, *ibid.* From Yell, also, came a letter (Dec. 1) stating that in his opinion Van Buren could throw the Speakership to whom he pleased.

The twenty-third Congress convened on December 2, 1833, and Stevenson was reëlected Speaker on the first ballot—virtually without opposition. As Polk's candidacy had been contingent upon Stevenson's refusal to stand for reëlection he accepted the party program without evidence of disappointment. The committees were announced on the ninth, with Polk at the head of the Committee of Ways and Means—the appointment having been made, it was said, upon the suggestion of General Jackson. The chairmanship of this committee is an important position under normal conditions. At this time, when the President was preparing for his last and greatest contest with the bank, it was undoubtedly the most responsible position in the House. But Polk was not the man to shirk responsibility, and his success in outgeneraling the bank party soon demonstrated that the administrtaion had been fortunate in its choice of a leader.

Polk had scarcely accepted his new appointment when letters came from friends at home urging him to become a member of the proposed Tennessee constitutional convention. "A great number of people," wrote James Walker,[7] "will be satisfied in no other way than for you to be in the Convention."

While there seems to have been a general desire for Polk's services in the convention and a feeling that he of all men in the state was best fitted to draft a new constitution, yet some, even among his friends, appear to have doubted his ability to cope with his new duties in Congress. His brother-in-law, A. C. Hayes, wrote from Columbia, Tennessee, that Polk's friends were pleased, and his enemies mortified, by his elevation to the chairmanship of the Committee of Ways and Means. But he added: "I have, however, heard it suggested by some of your *good friends,* that you may not leave the present congress with the same reputation with which you entered—'they fear, that there is too great weight of talent against you on the Bank Question.' "[8]

---

[7] Walker to Polk, Dec. 18, 1833, *Polk Papers.*
[8] Hayes to Polk, Jan. 10, 1834, *ibid.*

Polk himself had no such fears, for self-confidence was one of his chief characteristics; difficulties never appalled him when party services were to be performed. He was already occupied with his committee and therefore declined to serve in the convention.

On June 2, 1834, Speaker Stevenson presented to the House his long expected resignation. On the same day John Bell, of Tennessee, was chosen to succeed him. On the first ballot Polk received forty-two votes to Bell's thirty. Both men gained as the balloting proceeded, but Bell's gains—due to accessions from the anti-Jackson camp—were larger than those of his rival. When the tenth ballot was counted the tellers reported that Bell had received one hundred and fourteen votes—more than enough to elect—while his nearest competitor, Polk, had received but seventy-eight.

The brief official record of this day's proceedings which one finds in the *Congressional Globe* gives not the slightest hint of the heartburnings and bitterness which were associated with this choice of a Speaker. From this election, however, resulted a political feud which split the Jackson party in Tennessee, and materially weakened it in other states. From this day forth Polk and Bell were uncompromising enemies—each determined to overthrow the political power of the other. As the opponents of the President had helped to elect Bell, the new Speaker was forced to ally himself more and more with this element. His endorsement of Judge White's candidacy aroused the ire of the President. Regarding both men as apostates and traitors, Jackson resolved to employ every means at his disposal for the purpose of crushing them. Polk profited much by this new turn of affairs. He was already fighting the battles of the President in the war on the bank. He had always enjoyed the confidence and good opinion of Jackson; but Bell's defection still more identified the Speaker's rival, Polk, with the party of the President. In a greater degree than ever was Polk now regarded as the administration leader of the House.

The antecedents of the Speakership election and the attitude of Polk and Bell toward adhering to a party program are told in a statement prepared, at Polk's request, by Cave Johnson. Johnson was, of course, one of Polk's closest friends, but his statement seems credible and is corroborated by the testimony of other members of the House. It reads as follows:

> It was supposed many months before the vacancy actually happened, that it would take place & several individual friends of the administration were spoken of as suitable to fill the vacancy, among the number you & Col. Bell were esteemed the most prominent. None seemed to doubt that if so many friends of the administration were run, that the election would be finally settled by the votes of the opponents of the administration, who would of course cast their votes upon the man least acceptable to the President & his friends. This was a result the friends of the administration wished to evade—and therefore it was proposed, that the friends of the administration should have a meeting that the strength of the several candidates should be ascertained, that the strongest should be run as the candidate of the administration party & the others should yield their pretensions & support him. You unhesitatingly determined, that you was willing to have the election submitted to the friends of the administration & let them decide who should be the candidate & that you would support the man thus selected. You was considered I believe finally by all parties as the administration candidate & so far as I knew, heard or believe every vote which you received except one was given by the friends of the administration. . . . I understood, from members who conversed with Col. Bell upon the subject whose names I can give if necessary, that he refused to submit his claims to the Speakers chair to the friends of the President, & in consequence of his refusal no such meeting was holden. He received the votes of the opponents of the administration & was elected by them in conjunction with a few votes received by him among the friends of the administration.[9]

In a similar statement,[10] John McKintry, of Alabama, charged Bell with having refused to submit his claims to Jackson's friends and with having stated "that he did not expect to be elected by the administration party in the House, that he did not expect to get of that party more than 25 or 30 votes, [and] that he was supported by the opposition & elected by them." McKintry was

---

[9] Johnson to Polk, Sept. 12, 1834, *ibid.*

[10] McKintry to Polk, Aug. 13, 1834, *ibid.* C. C. Clay, of Alabama, in a letter to Polk (Sept. 13) says that Bell was generally considered to be an opposition candidate.

equally positive that Polk had readily consented to submit his claims to his party friends and to abide by their decision.

Up to the time that Bell became a candidate for Speaker, he was considered to be a loyal supporter of General Jackson. He was so regarded in his own state as well as in the House of Representatives. When the rumor that Stevenson would not be a candidate for reëlection was first circulated, it will be remembered that Jackson was consulted as to his attitude toward Polk's candidacy. Although the President was willing to give his approval, he did not appear to have any special interest in Polk's elevation. There is no evidence that the General, at that time, harbored any ill feeling toward Bell. Indeed, James Walker gathered from various conversations that Major Lewis preferred Bell for Speaker. But Bell's conduct during his recent campaign for the office changed all this. He was first distrusted, then openly denounced, by the President and his friends.

Congress adjourned shortly after the election of a Speaker, and in the final rush of legislation little attention was given to the contest between the two candidates. It was not apparent at the time that the controversy would have any vital significance in national politics. The first important result of the victory of Bell over Polk was its effect upon the influence of the two men in their home state.

For some time past Polk had been considered a desirable candidate for governor, and after his defeat by Bell his friends in Tennessee renewed their offer to support him for this office. His ever loyal brother-in-law, James Walker, began on his own initiative to agitate Polk's claims to the office and to assure him of the certainty of success. He informed Polk[11] that he had not lost prestige on account of his recent defeat, and that he could beat any man in Tennessee if he would consent to run. Letters offering support and encouragement came from Cave Johnson and other party leaders of the state. James Standifer assured

---

[11] Walker to Polk, June 30, 1834, *Polk Papers.*

Polk that he had not "seen the first man but what says they would rather have James K. Polk's standing than John Bell's Speaker's place and all, the people are for the man that stands up boldly for the President and his measures, they are for no other sort of man these times."[12] The sentiment expressed in this letter was becoming general in Tennessee, namely, that Polk and Grundy were the administration leaders in the state, and that Bell had deserted to the enemy. This view was impressed upon the President, who was then spending his vacation at the Hermitage, and it was about this time that he declared Polk to be deserving of a medal for "the hard service done in the cause."

Much resentment was aroused in Middle Tennessee by a speech delivered by Bell at Murfreesborough on October 6, 1834. The circuit court was then in session and Bell took advantage of the occasion to address the people there assembled. There are conflicting reports as to the substance of this speech, but in general the account of it given to Polk in a letter from his brother-in-law, John W. Childress, seems to be corroborated by the testimony of many who heard the speech delivered. According to this letter[13] Bell was very severe in his criticism of all who had questioned the propriety of his course in Congress, particularly during his contest for the Speakership. He asserted that all his competitors except one had treated him in a gentlemanly manner, leaving it to be inferred that Polk had not. "He vaunted greatly," said Childress,

his adherence to principle, his unwavering support of the president, and said distinctly, and in these words, that had he not been true and firm to the administration, he could have changed the small majority in the house upon the Bank question by going over and taking his friends with him and thereby have defeated all the measures of the President.

His enemies, he said, had managed to delay Speaker Stevenson's appointment to a foreign mission in the hope of weakening his

---

12 Standifer (member of Congress from Tennessee) to Polk, Aug. 25, 1834, *ibid.*

13 Childress to Polk, Oct. 7, 1834, *ibid.*

(Bell's) prospects and strengthening their own (i.e., Polk's), but of this the President was of course not aware. He alleged that although other tricks had been employed in an effort to defeat him, he still had the confidence of the entire party except six or seven individuals. He said

that he was willing to give Jackson's experiment [state banks] a fair trial and if it did not answer the wants of the people, that then he *might* be in favor of a National Bank. That he had no idea that a metalic currency would answer the purpose of a circulating medium and almost said it was Demagoguic in any one that would say so.

W. R. Rucker, another brother-in-law, said in a letter[14] that the speech was "most intemperate and ill advised" and that many of Bell's friends did not approve such "abuse" of Polk and General Jackson.

Under the circumstances, Bell's speech was certainly ill advised, even if every assertion made in it had been true. Moreover, even though reports of the speech may have exaggerated its abusive character, yet certain remarks attributed to the speaker were of such a nature that, if skillfully used, they would arouse the ire of General Jackson against the man who had uttered them. Protestations of loyalty to the administration had an unwelcome ring in the General's ears when accompanied by boasts of Bell's great influence over party members and of the ease with which he might have defeated administration measures in the House. The truth of such an assertion would make it all the more galling to a man of Jackson's temperament. One can imagine his exclaiming: "By the Eternal, I'll show John Bell!" Then, too, Bell's remark concerning the President's *experiment,* and his *quasi* endorsement of a national bank, were most unfortunate for any man who wished to retain the friendship of "the old hero."

Polk's answer to Rucker indicated clearly the use that was to be made of Bell's speech. If the address has been accurately reported, said Polk, "it places him clearly and unequivocally at

---

[14] Rucker to Polk, Oct. 12, 1834, *ibid.*

issue with the policy of the administration.''[15] He wished the speech to be reported accurately and published to the world; then he would be fully prepared to meet its author on the issues which it had raised.

Before Bell's Murfreesborough speech had been delivered, Polk, as we have seen, had already been collecting statements from his friends concerning Bell's conduct in Congress. Both men had also been exerting themselves to get control of the press in Middle Tennessee. Local newspapers at that time wielded great influence, and the success of a politician depended in a great measure on his control over the reading matter of his constituents.

Polk's home was in Columbia; therefore the *Observer*, a local paper of that place, supported its townsman and criticized Bell's maneuvering in the late Speakership election. The two leading papers of Nashville at that time were the *Republican* and the *Banner*. The *Republican* defended Bell, and many of Polk's friends promptly administered the customary punishment of canceling their subscriptions to that paper. One of these was Colonel Archibald Yell, an ardent admirer of Polk and an orthodox party man. In answer to his protest, Allan A. Hall, editor of the *Republican*, defiantly predicted that Polk would soon lose the friendship of Jackson, Grundy, and Governor Carroll, and would be driven from power if he should dare to persist in his opposition to Bell.[16]

Bell succeeded in getting control of the *Banner*, also. Until the middle of September, 1834, this paper had been edited by

---

[15] Polk to Rucker, Oct. 16, 1834, *ibid.*

[16] Yell to Polk, Sept. 25, 1834, *ibid.* One part of Hall's letter, as quoted by Yell, read: ''and now mark me Yell for a prophet in less than six months there will be a split between Carroll & Polk nay there will be a split between Polk & the President!! Coming events cast their shadows before. Col. Polk by no earthly possibility can continue to maintain his present *position*, in the event of Certain future Contingencies which are *obliged* to take place.'' Yell took this to mean that Polk was to be driven from the chairmanship of the Committee of Ways and Means. Carroll denied that he was hostile to Polk (Carroll to Polk, Dec. 19, 1834).

Samuel H. Laughlin, a friend of Polk, but who, unfortunately for both men, had been made extremely unreliable by a passion for strong drink.[17] His contract as editor expired at this time and the proprietor, Hunt, formed a partnership with Bell. A new editor was installed and the paper henceforth championed the cause of the Speaker.[18] For the time being Polk had to rely mainly on the support of the Columbia *Observer* and the Murfreesborough *Monitor*.

Bell seems to have become somewhat alarmed at the result of his Murfreesborough speech, for both of his Nashville papers maintained that he had been misquoted, and that he was still a loyal follower of General Jackson. Thereupon, William Brady, of Murfreesborough, set about collecting statements from various persons who had heard Bell deliver the address. These Brady published in an extra number of the *Monitor*. Copies of this number were sent to the President, to members of Congress, to leading political journals, and to prominent individuals, for the purpose of removing the "veil which now covers the political hypocrite [Bell]."[19]

Polk and his associates saw the necessity of establishing in Nashville a paper which would promulgate their own views. "I think it more desirable," wrote A. C. Hays, of Columbia,[20]

that a Newspaper should be established in Nashville, that will fearlessly speak the sentiments of the people of the State, at this time than it has ever been, because I believe that the Press is at this time more under the influence of the *Bank & Bell & Foster* faction than it has *ever been*.

Laughlin had offered to serve as editor of an administration journal, but Brady[21] was not alone in thinking that "poor Sam" had already proved himself to be a total failure. "The trouble

---

17 One becomes accustomed to reading in private letters: "Laughlin has been drunk for a week."

18 John W. Childress to Polk, Sept. 18; Wm. Brady to Polk, Dec. 26, 1834, *Polk Papers*.

19 Brady to Polk, as cited above.

20 Hays to Polk, Dec. 24, 1834, *Polk Papers*.

21 Brady to Polk, as cited above.

is,'' said he, ''Sam lacks moral courage; and when the sound of the Bugle is heard—and the enemy shall appear in force—Sam's in the straw.'' In Brady's opinion, some editor ought to be found who would be ''wholly *de Nashvilleized,*'' who would stand by the President and support Van Buren as his successor.[22] For his own purposes, said Brady, Bell is putting Judge White forward to succeed Jackson, with the hope of succeeding White in the Presidential chair.

Bell's success in getting control of the Nashville papers was disconcerting enough to Polk's Tennessee friends, but they were still more chagrined because the Washington *Globe* seemed also to be lending its support to the Speaker. ''How is it with the Globe?'' wrote Brady in the letter above cited,

if that print is with the President and his friends, to me it has an awkward way of shewing of it. It is true that Blair sanctions the President personally, and in the main the measures of his administration; but how is it, that every apologetic article, which has appeared in the Nashville papers or elsewhere, in relation to Bell's election to the Speaker's chair, or his Murfreesboro Speech have found their way into the columns of the Globe?

Brady thought that Blair ought to give both sides or neither; Polk should compel him to show his colors by presenting for publication in the *Globe* the account of Bell's speech which had appeared in the extra *Monitor.* ''Why is the Globe either silent— or giving support to Bell?'' asked Childress.[23] People in Tennessee, he added, are beginnig to believe that the President prefers Bell to Polk; this is what Bell's adherents claim, and the attitude of the *Globe* lends color to their assertions. By all means, urged Childress, Polk must have his side of the argument published.

By courting the enemies of the administration and by subsequent indiscretions, Bell had engendered feelings of distrust

---

[22] On December 28 General Samuel Smith, in a letter to Polk, dwelt on the necessity of starting a new paper. Many in Tennessee, said he, whom Jackson believes to be his friends are in reality against him.

[23] Childress to Polk, Dec. 20, 1834, *Polk Papers.* Polk received other letters of similar character.

and hostility that were destined to involve others in serious political difficulties. Polk was a man who did not easily forget, and by lending aid to Bell in 1834 Blair was paving the way for his own downfall, when Bell's rival became President ten years later. Polk's friends believed that they saw the sinister as well as successful influence of the Speaker in every quarter. Polk himself alleged that Bell's exertions in behalf of Judge White were not due to any love for the judge, but for the sole purpose of promoting his own political advancement.[24]

The project of founding an administration newspaper in Nashville now absorbed the attention of party leaders. As no really suitable man could be found to edit such a paper, Laughlin was considered, although not without misgivings.[25] Many politicians who had hitherto shouted for Jackson had deserted to White, and nearly all of the papers of Middle Tennessee, including even the Columbia *Observer,*[26] had come out for the judge. This fact made it all the more necessary to have an orthodox journal which would *enlighten* the people, and Laughlin, despite his weaknesses, was a loyal party man. After many tribulations capital was collected, an outfit purchased, and in March, 1835, Laughlin was installed as editor of the Nashville *Union.* Polk and Grundy were the guiding spirits of the new paper, and to them and Cave Johnson "poor Sam" appealed for aid in increasing his subscription list. He reported to Polk that the editor of the *Banner* was "wallowing in the mire," entirely under the influence of Bell and Foster; and that efforts were being made to retard the progress of the *Union.*"[27]

During the excitement which was created by Bell's Cassedy letter, Laughlin—being "himself again"[28]—with his "sharp pen"

[24] Polk to James Walker, Dec. 24, 1834, *Polk Papers.*

[25] Sam'l G. Smith to Polk, Jan. 6, 1835, *ibid.*

[26] James Walker to Polk, Jan. 17, 1835, *ibid.*

[27] Laughlin to Polk, April 17, 21, 1835, *ibid.*

[28] Grundy to Polk, June 25, 1835, *ibid.* For the Cassedy letter, see p. 84.

did effective service for Polk by heaping odium upon Bell. ''That Cassedy letter,'' wrote Grundy to Polk, ''will make you Speaker, I think.''[29] It did, indeed, contribute to this result, but in Tennessee the combined influence of Bell and White could not be overcome. In spite of heroic efforts on the editor's part, the *Union* could not pay expenses, and the list of political ''apostates'' was steadily growing. Although Laughlin labored without salary, he was not without hope,[30] and his pungent editorials undoubtedly aided Polk in his campaign for reëlection.

President Jackson viewed with alarm the disintegration of the administration party in his home state. He was especially interested in the election of members of Congress. From his retreat at the ''Rip Raps'' he asked Polk[31] for reliable information concerning the political situation, and directed him to coöperate with Grundy and Cave Johnson in combating the schemes of Judge White and John Bell. He was able to get some news from the *Union,* although it came irregularly; ''the other Nashville papers, like base coin, circulate freely, but they have become the mere echo of Duff Green & other opposition prints.''

White's candidacy had irrevocably split the Jackson party in Tennessee. The President now considered White, Bell, and all their supporters to be his political and personal enemies. Polk, Grundy, and Johnson were to a greater degree than ever looked upon as the administration leaders in the state. It was certain that Polk would have the President's backing in his next contest with Bell for the Speaker's chair. From Washington, Donelson[32] wrote to congratulate Polk on his triumphant

[29] *Ibid.*

[30] ''I am now fairly in a State of belligerancy with my worthy neighbors. I have them, I think, in a good way if I can keep them so. A gradual but sure work of reformation in public sentiment is in progress here, and I hope the same work is going on throughout the State'' (Laughlin to Polk, July 5, 1835, *ibid.*).

[31] Jackson to Polk, Aug. 3, 1835, *ibid.*

[32] Donelson to Polk, Aug. 28, 1835, *ibid.*

reëlection in spite of the "intrigues" of Bell, and he reported the President to be in good spirits, notwithstanding the defeat of Governor Carroll. Donelson had, he said, conversed with many politicians, all of whom wished Polk to be chosen Speaker.

In Nashville, Laughlin, through the columns of the *Union* and by letters to individuals, was doing his utmost to discredit Bell and to present Polk's claims to reward for his loyalty to General Jackson. Polk had been the intended victim of Bell's "treachery," wrote Laughlin, and therefore "ought to be made the instrument of his defeat."[33]

While the rivalry between White and Van Buren was of greater interest in national politics, yet administration leaders in all parts of the Union had come to feel that Bell—the alleged instigator of the party schism—was, after all, more guilty than White, and consequently deserving of punishment. Polk, on the other hand, was clearly entitled to the support of the administration forces in Congress. As chairman of the Committee of Ways and Means he had borne, in the House, the brunt of the President's war on the bank. In his home state he had done more than any other, with the possible exception of Grundy, to oppose the Bell-White coalition and to uphold the standard of General Jackson.

When Congress convened in December, Polk's election to the Speaker's chair was practically assured, and he was chosen on the first ballot by a majority of thirty-nine votes. His triumph over Bell was regarded by all as a distinct party victory. A

---

[33] Laughlin to Polk, Aug. 30, 1835, *ibid.* He quoted several reasons which he had assigned when urging Polk's election, among them:

"That your election will prostrate Bell and the White influence in this State, by showing to the people the true position of Bell, and how his position is received by the Republican party every where else, and that they are only sustained now by the false opinion which prevails that they are friends of Gen. Jackson.

"That your election will unmask the White party and exhibit them as the opponents of the Administration.

"That much is due to you. That you have stuck when others failed. . . . That your confidential relation to the President ought to be considered both as a merit and as a necessary qualification in a Speaker &c &c."

"White" member of the Tennessee legislature, when writing to congratulate Polk on his election,[34] said that, although Bell's own friends hardly expected him to win, they did not think that he would be beaten so badly; they "attribute Mr. Bell's defeat to the influence of the President." Although a White supporter, the writer said that Polk had gained by his firm stand and that he was now stronger in his district than either White or Van Buren. "The election of Speaker," wrote Judge Catron,[35] "had an uncommonly great effect on the country people. They had been lead to believe great strength existed elsewhere—this is now admitted to be a mistake, and what must follow [defeat of White] is certain, as I believe." Bell himself had not been sanguine. He predicted his defeat by Polk before Congress had convened.[36]

Before proceeding with Polk's career as Speaker of the House of Representatives it seems desirable to retrace our steps in order to consider, in the following chapter, Judge White's unsuccessful campaign for the Presidency. The rivalry between White and Van Buren was the dominant factor at the time in both state and national politics. It played an important part in making Polk the presiding officer of the House, and it helped to shape many of the issues with which Polk, as Speaker, had to deal.

---

[34] H. M. Watterson to Polk, Dec. 21, 1835, *Polk Papers*.

[35] Catron to Polk, Jan. 8, 1836, *ibid.* "The effect of the news [Polk's election] upon the White cause," wrote Nicholson, December 20, "has been blighting." Many White men, said he, now think that their candidate should be withdrawn.

[36] W. H. Polk to J. K. Polk, Dec. 21, 1835, *Polk Papers*. He had seen a letter written by Bell to Judge Kennedy before the opening of Congress.

CHAPTER V

JUDGE WHITE AND THE PRESIDENCY

No biography of a statesman of the thirties—particularly of a prominent Tennessean—would be complete that did not include a chapter on the far-reaching effect of Judge White's decision to become a candidate for the Presidency. The importance of this decision lay in the fact that General Jackson had made other plans. In the parlance of the day, "King Andrew" had decreed that the "little magician" must be his successor, regardless of the will of the subjects—the "consent of the governed." When, therefore, the friends of White brought him forward as a rival to Van Buren, harmony in the Jackson camp was at first threatened, and finally destroyed. "Davy" Crockett had driven the first wedge into the solidarity of the Jackson domination of Tennessee; the White movement split it asunder. The result was the birth of the Whig party and a national political realignment.

When White was first mentioned in connection with the Presidency, Jackson's feelings were those of regret that his old friend should have been deluded by designing politicians; but when the judge was found to be a willing victim—independent even to the point of defying the President's wishes—the old-time friendship changed to bitter hatred. It was soon made apparent to politicians that they could not support Judge White without forfeiting all claim of loyalty to General Jackson. Assurances on their part that the two things were not incompatible availed nothing; all were forced to choose between the two men.

It is not easy to determine just when and by whom Judge White was first brought forward as a candidate for President, but his nomination for that office was considered by the Tennessee legislature as early as December, 1833. Up to this time, so far as Tennessee politics were concerned, Judge McLean, of Ohio, seems to have been regarded as Van Buren's most formidable rival. Some of the local papers had hoisted the McLean banner, with either Governor Carroll or Judge White for Vice-President.[1] But before adjourning in early December, 1833, the legislature seriously considered the feasibility of presenting a Presidential candidate from their own state. A resolution to nominate White was actually drawn up; but it was made known by a member that White opposed such a proceeding, and the matter was dropped. None of the members manifested any interest in nominating either Van Buren or McLean.[2]

Several causes coöperated in fixing the attention of politicians on White as a possible candidate. It was well known that Jackson had decreed that the Vice-President should succeed him; in spite of this, however, Van Buren had never been popular in Tennessee. Many of the President's most loyal supporters did not, and could not, share his admiration for the "heir apparent." State pride caused many to feel that, if possible, another Tennessean should be chosen to fill the office, and, next to Jackson, White was generally conceded to be the most able and popular son of the state. It is probable that Jackson's preference for Van Buren would have been sufficient to cause a split in the party as soon as the White movement assumed serious proportions, but the rivalry between Polk and Bell, and the support of White by the latter, lent an added bitterness and political significance to White's candidacy. The plan to nominate White was alleged to have been conceived by Bell for the purpose of advancing his own political fortunes in both state and national politics. Whether this allegation was true or false is a matter difficult to determine; but whatever Bell's motives may have been,

---

[1] Yell to Polk, Dec. 1, 1833, *Polk Papers.*
[2] A. O. P. Nicholson to Polk, Dec. 5, 1833, *Polk Papers.* Orville Bradley to White, Aug. 23, 1836 (Scott, *Memoir of Hugh Lawson White*, 302).

it seems clear that White's conduct was at all times aboveboard and commendable. He was too honest to seek political preferment by underhand methods, but he was, also, too brave and independent to step aside simply because General Jackson willed that he should do so.

Up to the time when White and Van Buren had been formally nominated and party lines definitely drawn, there was quite a diversity of opinion in Tennessee, even among Jackson's friends. On December 22, 1833, A. V. Brown wrote to ask Polk "the signs as to the 'successorship to the throne,'" and spoke of McLean's popularity. "Personally," said Brown, "I like McLean myself but *politically* I fear he is *too far off* from us in the South—and how will Van Buren help that matter in the least?" Between Clay and Van Buren, he continued, "might not one find refuge in the personal worth & virtue of McLean, although he would prefer some other than either, if chance or destiny had not thrown him too far in the rear of probable success?"[3] Other passages in the letter indicate that it was Calhoun to whom he referred. Generally, however, those of Polk's correspondents who were "not satisfied" with Van Buren were of opinion that White was the only man who would bring success to the party.[4]

On June 2, 1834, Bell defeated Polk in the contest for the Speakership. He was supported by many who were openly opposed to the administration. In the House Polk had, during the entire session, been leading the battle against the bank, and when Congress adjourned on June 30 he had won a signal victory for the administration. In his defeat by Bell, Polk could easily be made to assume the rôle of a martyr who had suffered for his loyalty to the President and the party. He seems sincerely to have regarded himself as a victim of the treachery of Bell, who had solicited opposition votes.

---

3 *Polk Papers.*

4 E.g., John W. M. Breazeale to Polk, March 21, 1834, *Polk Papers.*

As soon as Congress had adjourned, both men returned to Tennessee to air their grievances on the platform and in the public press. Polk, as we have seen, applied to his congressional friends for statements which would prove the perfidy of Bell, while Bell proceeded to get control of the Nashville papers, the *Republican* and the *Banner,* in order to defend himself and to overthrow the influence of Polk. Many of Polk's friends were desirous of nominating him for Governor, but he preferred to continue in national politics.

General Jackson, also, spent his summer vacation in Tennessee. The bank question was uppermost in his mind, and in a speech delivered in Nashville he made it clear that any new federal bank would be quite as objectionable as the one now in existence. As yet he seems to have taken no active interest in the quarrel between Bell and Polk, but he naturally felt grateful to the latter for his loyal support of the administration during the last sesssion. It was at this time that he declared Polk to be deserving of a medal from the American people for his services in Congress. Bell had not yet broken with the party and gave the President new assurances that he would continue to support the administration.[5] Indeed after Jackson's return to Washington there was, as we have seen, complaint in Tennessee that the *Globe* seemed to show a preference for Bell.[6] But during the fall of 1834 the political situation in Tennessee became such that the interests of Polk and the President were closely identified, while Bell cast his lot with the opponents of the administration. The main cause of the party cleavage was the renewed effort to nominate Judge White for the Presidency.

While Jackson was still in Nashville a caucus was held in that city—by friends of the bank, it was said—for the purpose of considering the nomination of White.[7] White was informed that

---

[5] Gen. Sam'l Smith to Polk, Sept. 20, 1834, *Polk Papers.*

[6] See above, p. 57.

[7] Burton to Polk, Aug. 27, 1834, *Polk Papers.*

the President threatened. to denounce him should he express a willingness to become a candidate.[8]   Jackson doubtless noted many evidences of the popularity of White and of the unpopularity of Van Buren, but at this time it is probable that he had hopes of preventing disaffection.

While the President was passing through East Tennessee on his way to Washington, Orville Bradley, a member of the legislature, told him of the attempt made by the assembly in 1833 to nominate White — an attempt which Bradley, acting under White's directions, had been able to defeat. He told the President, also, that two-thirds of the legislature had been unfavorable to Van Buren. Jackson vigorously defended Van Buren. He said "that White could hardly get a vote out of Tennessee, and that Tennessee must not separate from the rest of his friends." He was willing to compromise by supporting White for Vice-President, and it would be time enough for White to run for President after Van Buren had retired.[9]

Jackson did not at this time harbor bitter feelings toward White, personally. These did not come until later, and even then, as will appear, he regarded the judge more as a dupe of political intriguers than as his personal enemy. His feeling in 1834 was one of annoyance that White should be made the instrument in an attempt to thwart the plans he had made for Van Buren.

White and Jackson had long been close personal friends. The judge had loyally supported the "old hero" in his campaigns for the Presidency and during the first part of his administration was regarded as one of his most able advisers.[10]   But White was no sycophant, and he was too independent to follow any man's program, even though the man might chance to be

----

[8] White to Polk, Aug. 26, 1834 (Scott, *Memoir of Hugh Lawson White,* 254).

[9] Bradley to White, Aug. 23, 1836 (Scott, *Memoir of Hugh Lawson White,* 302).

[10] See letters of Jackson, Overton, Coffee, Polk *et al.,* in Scott, *Memoir of Hugh Lawson White,* 267–269.

General Jackson. As early as 1831, when Jackson was recon-
structing his cabinet so that Van Buren might, under the President's own rule,[11] be made eligible to succeed him, he had invited
White to become Secretary of War, while Eaton, the outgoing
Secretary, was to have White's place as Senator from Tennessee.[12]
The judge declined the offer, and although no breach between
the two men resulted, White was henceforth made to feel that
he was no longer in good standing in administration circles.[13]

Jackson was irritated by various manifestations of White's
independence, and especially so by his disregard of the President's wishes when Clay's compromise tariff bill was before the
Senate in 1833. The Senate had voted to refer Clay's bill to
a select committee. Before White, their presiding officer, had
appointed the committee, he was invited to a conference with
the President. Preferring Clay's bill to one which had been sent
to the House by the Secretary of the Treasury, and anticipating
that Jackson had sent for him for the purpose of dictating the
membership of the committee, White, before going to see the
President, selected a committee which he thought would support
Clay's measure. A majority, which included Clayton, of Delaware, were rated as anti-administration men.[14] The President
was much ''mortified'' and told Grundy in a letter that ''it is an
insult to me, & the Sec. of the Treasury that such a man as

---

[11] This rule was that none of his cabinet should succeed him if he
could prevent it.

[12] White's testimony before the House Committee (Scott, *Memoir of
Hugh Lawson White*, 299; Washington *Globe*, May 25, 1831).

[13] ''The true reason why nothing I have said is noticed in the Globe,
I have no doubt is, because I have never assured any man that as soon as
Gen. Jackson's terms of service are at an end, I will use all my endeavors
to elect the favorite of those who direct the operations of the paper. I am
for Gen. Jackson; but am not either a Calhoun Jackson man, or a Van
Buren Jackson man, and therefore it is pleasing to the Globe and Tele-
graph not to notice favorably anything I can say or do; and as I am
opposed to Mr. Clay, his papers will of course speak disrespectfully of
me.'' White to F. S. Heiskell, editor of the Knoxville *Register*, May 18,
1832 (Scott, *Memoir of Hugh Lawson White*, 269).

[14] Testimony of Judge White before the House Committee (Scott,
Memoir of Hugh Lawson White, 299).

Clayton should be upon it [the committee]."[15]   Nevertheless,
Jackson held White in high esteem, and, despite this "insult"
and other similar vexations, the two men continued amicable
relations.   White was still rated as a Jackson man, and, in the
judge's opinion, it was not until the President visited Tennessee
in 1834 that he became convinced that White would not support
his political program.[16]   Jackson was willing to compromise by
letting White have the Vice-Presidency, but the judge must not
stand in the way of Van Buren.

Up to the time that Polk returned to Washington for the
opening of Congress, there is nothing in his correspondence,
except his letter to White, to indicate that he took an active interest in the movement to nominate Judge White.   His thoughts
were centered on Bell, and the suggestion made by C. C. Clay[17]
to *"take good care to put your adversary in the wrong"* was
entirely superfluous.   His task was made comparatively easy by
the indiscretions of the adversary himself.   Bell's Murfreesborough speech[18] proved a boomerang to its author, for in it he
had criticized the President and given quasi support to the
national bank.   Then, too, Hall, of the Nashville *Republican,* had
boasted that there would be "a split between Polk and the President," and that Polk would be driven from power[19] by the
political influence of Bell.   Such arrogance, when duly reported
to the President, was sufficient to arouse his resentment, and,
when it soon developed that Bell was one of the most ardent supporters of White, he was denounced as a political apostate.

The determination of White's Tennessee friends to nominate
him, and Jackson's strenuous opposition to such a nomination,
placed Polk in an awkward position.   White's friends have always

---

[15] Jackson to Grundy, Feb. 13, 1833, *Am. Hist. Mag.,* V, 137.

[16] "He no doubt believed that whenever he and those he could control
changed their creed, I would change my creed likewise, and he was never
convinced to the contrary, until after his attempt upon me through Mr.
Bradley, which was in the autumn of 1834." White to the "Freemen of
Tennessee" (Scott, *Memoir of Hugh Lawson White,* 320).

[17] Clay to Polk, Sept. 23, 1834, *Polk Papers.*

[18] See above, p. 53.   [19] Yell to Polk, Sept. 25, 1834, *Polk Papers.*

assumed that Polk treacherously turned against White simply to please General Jackson, and White himself appears to have held this view. Even now, after Polk's entire correspondence has become available, it is difficult to determine to what extent this charge is true. His friendship for Judge White he never attempted to conceal, and that he desired the support of Jackson is beyond question; but after his defeat by Bell the political situation, both in Tennessee and in Congress, was such that for reasons of his own, and irrespective of Jackson's wishes, he could not support a candidate whose chief sponsor was his rival, John Bell. He liked White and, like many of his Tennessee friends, he probably did not share the President's admiration for Van Buren; but he was a firm believer in party loyalty; and besides, the men who were taking the lead in promoting White's interests were at the same time endeavoring to undermine Polk himself.

Polk's habitual reticence adds to the difficulty of determining his thoughts and motives. If possible, he always avoided controversies which did not immediately concern himself, and to his best friends he was guarded in expressing his opinions. When, in 1831, there was discord in Jackson's cabinet, Polk discreetly declined to participate in the effort to force Eaton from the cabinet, or even to discuss the matter in writing.[20] When the break between Jackson and Calhoun occurred, he forwarded Calhoun's "defense" to his friends, but without disclosing his own views. One of his closest friends complained that " I write you my opinions freely as I am not disposed with you to conceal my views, but I must acknowledge that you have been more *prudent* with yours for I am not able to even conjecture how your feelings are after all your long letters."[21]

---

[20] Several letters to C. A. Wickliffe declining to discuss the subject (*Polk Papers*).

[21] A. Yell to Polk, March 13, 1831, *Polk Papers*. Yell expressed his own opinions freely enough. He believed Calhoun's defense to be honest and sincere, and that Crawford was a scoundrel. He had a "bad impression" of Van Buren and hoped that he would not be nominated as Jackson's successor. The attempt to force Van Buren on the people would only aid "Prince Hal."

Polk and White had long been personal and political friends. There is nothing to indicate that their friendship had been in any degree affected by the coolness between White and the President. To this White's comments on Polk's defeat by Bell in 1834 bear witness. "Both are to me like children;" he wrote[22] "therefore I took no part in the contest." Polk's expression of "surprise and astonishment"[23] in September, 1834, when informed of Jackson's threat to denounce White, should he consent to become a candidate, was no doubt unfeigned. He was frequently evasive or noncommittal, but he was not given to flattery.[24]

Polk returned to Washington to assume his duties in the House in December, 1834. Up to this time there appears to have been no connection between his quarrel with Bell and Jackson's opposition to White. But he had not been in Washington long before these two controversies became merged by an effort on the part of Polk's opponents to bring White out as a candidate. Polk's own version of his attitude toward the judge's nomination is stated in a *"confidential"* letter to his brother-in-law, James Walker. As his motives in opposing White have often been questioned, it seemes desirable to insert this letter in spite of its length.

I have been so busily engaged in preparing the appropriation bills—and those connected with the Banks that I have not heretofore taken leisure to write to you. I have had nothing to do with the management—and undercurrents which I understand have been going on here in regard to the next Presidency. I have considered that it was my first duty to attend to the important measures committed to the committee of which I am a

---

[22] To editor of Knoxville *Register* (Scott, *Memoir of Hugh Lawson White*, 253).

[23] Polk to White, Sept. 2, 1834, *ibid.*, 254.

[24] White's biographer in commenting on this letter (of *September, 1834*) makes the rather astonishing statement that as soon as Polk ascertained "the sentiments of Gen. Jackson in regard to his successor" he shaped his "course according to the President's wishes, although motives of personal policy . . . decided him not to define his position until after his reëlection the ensuing August." She then goes on to show that Polk and Cave Johnson "had determined to pick a quarrel" with White in February, 1835!

member. This I have done and shall continue to do, and I am sure my constituents will appreciate my services more than if I were engaged in the intrigues of politicians with a view to my own personal advancement. I have no doubt that my constituents feel and think as I do, upon the subject of the succession,—but still they have not commissioned me here— either to engage their votes, to commit them upon the subject or to express their opinions. As a citizen I shall have a right to my own opinion,—and whenever there shall be occasion shall certainly exercise it. In regard to our countryman Judge White I have said this,—that there was no man to whom personally—I have ever had kindlier feelings, and that if he was brought forward, or taken up and run by our political party, it would give me pleasure to support him,—but at the same time I think that the party now dominant in the country, who have recently achieved so signal a victory, have fought the battle to little purpose, if in the moment of this triumph, they permit themselves to be divided & distracted about men, and thereby perhaps enable our political adversaries to take advantage of our divisions,— throw the election into the House, when there is danger that the money of the Bank and the patronage of the Government,—would corrupt & purchase votes enough to carry the election against us. It must certainly be the desire of our party, who are emphatically—from the policy we advocate, the party of the country,—if possible to continue united and not divide about men. I think the party should unite if it be possible and run but one man, and it would assuredly give me pleasure should Judge White be that man. Suppose we divide and select more than one candidate,—and suffer the friends of our respective candidates to become irritated & exci[ted] against each other; may not the opposition, and will they not take advantage of such a state of things, and at a moment when it shall be too late for us to retrace our steps, and re-unite our friends in favor of any one, suddenly push out a candidate of their own, defeat an election before the people, throw the election into the House and thus stand a fair chance to come into power against the popular will. To meet such a state of things I repeat we should continue united and if possible run but one man. Should Judge White be the man upon whom the party unite, none would support him with more pleasure than myself. Upon this subject, the present moment may be an important crisis. As soon as Congress assembled,—many of the opposition members expressed wishes that Judge White should be brought out and announced their intention to support him,—if he was &c. Their motive for this, the game they will play hereafter or the subject they hope to effect, I know not except—that they would doubtless do any thing in their power to divide & scatter us. That portion of our delegation in W^t Tennessee, who manifested such unprovoked hostility to me during the past summer—I mean the Speaker, Dickinson &c. probably think they can make something out of this state of things to my prejudice, and for their own purposes,—have been zealous, or pretended to be so, to bring Judge White

out at once, and at all events, without waiting to consult any portion of
the democratic party—residing in other states with whom we have so
long acted,—and who have so long acted with us in supporting the administration of the present Chief Magistrate. Ought they not to be at least
consulted before such a step is taken? But that portion of our delegation
probably think that by taking this course they will gain an advantage of
me in Tennessee and that by uniting with the opposition Mr. B[ell] may be
enabled to retain his place here at the next Congress, in the same way he
originally obtained it. The East Tennessee part of our delegation very
honestly and sincerely desire to see Judge White elected. On the day before
yesterday I was informed by Col. Standifer that there was to be a meeting
of the delegation,—on the night following (last night) upon the subject
and was requested to attend. On yesterday Mr. Lea spoke to me on the
subject & told me the meeting was to be at *Peyton's* room and urged us to
attend. I told him that my attending or not attending was a matter of no
consequence;—that neither my own opinions or that of my constituents of
Judge White would be changed,—whether I attended or not; that I had no
commission from my constituents to speak for them; that, that was a matter
they would attend to for themselves, when the time came for them to act;
that I was very laboriously engaged in the discharge of my public duty as a
member of the House; and that I did not regard the proposed meeting as
any part of that duty. I told him furthermore that I could not but suspect
that, that portion of our delegation who are, without cause given by me so
exceedingly hostile to me, were prompted in this movement more in the hope
of injuring me, than for any love they had for Judge White. And furthermore I told him, that what was conducive against my attendance was this—
that I could not without losing all self-respect go into a consultation upon
any subject,—(unless public duty required it,) with that portion of our
delegation,—who had during the past summer through their organs and
tools so unjustly and wantonly assailed me, and especially when I was
informed that the meeting was to take place at the room of a colleague[25]
who was certainly unfriendly in his feelings towards me, and had never
invited me to come to it. For these reasons I declined and did not attend.
The meeting was held, Grundy, Blair & myself absent. Johnson attended—
but will probably communicate to the delegation his views in writing; they
entirely accord with mine. I understand that *Dunlap* (though I have not
talked to him) agrees in his views with Johnson and myself. I write you
very confidentially—that you may be apprised of what is going on here.
From the unfairness with which I have been treated in other things I have
reason to suspect that letters may be written home misrepresenting me upon

---

[25] Peyton, who was White's nephew, had opposed Polk in the Speaker-
ship election and had given as his reason, according to Cave Johnson, that
Polk had worked with the Nullifiers! (Johnson to Polk, July 15, 1834,
Polk Papers).

this;—probably representing from my absence from the meeting, that I am unfriendly to Judge White &c.—and I look for nothing else than to see some misinformation in regard to it, through the Nashville papers. I write you to put you in possession of the facts,—that you may in the proper way, and without using my letter publicly be enabled to put the matter right. I wish you to take so much of your time from your business—which I know to be pressing upon your time, as to write me your opinion fully & freely upon the subject;—and whether you think I have acted prudently or not. I have acted upon my convictions of what was proper,—and with feelings of most perfect friendship for Judge White. Can I be affected by it?

James Walker, Esq.,
    Columbia, Tenn.
                Very sincerely,
                  Yr friend,
                    James K. Polk[26]

This letter seems to give ample reasons why a man of Polk's well-known belief in party loyalty should not support the apparently hopeless cause of Judge White. It is not fair to assume, as the friends of White have done, that those who did not come out for the judge were necessarily the abject creatures of General Jackson. There was only one man whose support could, by any possibility, have elevated White to the Presidential chair. That man was Jackson himself; and neither Polk nor those who acted with him could hope, even if they had so desired, to alter the President's determination to aid Van Buren. To support White, as Polk pointed out, would result in splitting the party and endangering its success, without benefiting the judge in any particular. It was too much to ask of Polk to coöperate with men whom he both distrusted and despised as he did Bell and Peyton in supporting a candidate who would inevitably be defeated. There is no reason for questioning the sincerity of Polk's belief that Bell was flirting with the opposition, as he had done when he was a candidate for Speaker. The assertions made by Polk, Grundy, and Johnson that they would gladly support White if he could procure the party nomination were said by their opponents to be pure cant and of course there was no possibility of his

---

[26] The letter is dated Dec. 24, 1834, *Polk Papers.*

procuring such a nomination unless Jackson should change his mind—but there is nothing in their private correspondence to indicate that they did not really prefer White to Van Buren.

On the day after the above letter was written Polk wrote[27] another *"confidential"* letter to Walker. Alluding to the former letter he said:

Since then the fact that a meeting took place and the objects of it has been communicated to ——— ———[28] and my course is highly approved. The meeting has attracted attention and things as they *really are in Tennessee*, are beginning to be well understood here. He says that if Judge White should be united upon and be a candidate of the party—that then he should be supported by the party—but any portion of those professing to be the friends of the administration who would bring him or any one else out—without consulting the wishes of the friends of the administration in other States, will eventually not only destroy him but themselves. The storm I apprehended is to burst upon us, and we in Tennessee must be prepared to meet it. Whatever our personal preferences for men may be, as patriots we should go for the good of the country,—and to that end should avoid divisions—and preserve if possible the integrity of the party.

The portion of the letter just quoted clearly indicates that Polk declined to attend the meeting without having a consultation with the President. Continuing, he told Walker that the person to whom he has alluded (Jackson ?)

says he has already heard that it has been dropped out by some one of the opposition, that the plan of their operation, is upon the *Bell* system, alluding to the Speaker's election. I will not be hasty or imprudent in this matter,—but may venture to communicate what is passing *to you.*[29]

He wished to know whether Tennessee would probably send delegates to the national convention of the party. He instructed

---

27 Polk to Walker, Dec. 25, 1834, *Polk Papers.*

28 Blanks in the copy in the Polk collection, but evidently mean Jackson.

29 Cave Johnson, Polk told Walker, had written to the Tennessee delegation stating that he would not support White "if he is to be run by the opposition Nationals and Nullifiers,—aided by a small portion of the Jackson party." Polk, Dunlap, and Blair felt the same way, and "Grundy is more excited than I have almost ever seen him,—and seems almost ready to come out and denounce the whole movement,—as calculated to divide and destroy the party."

Walker to prevail upon the Columbia *Observer* to support the regular nominee in case its favorite should fail to procure the nomination. To this Walker replied[30] that he preferred White if he could be nominated by the party, but he feared that a split would make success doubtful. He promised to induce the *Observer*, if possible, to support the national ticket whoever might be nominated.

In a formal statement prepared by Polk[31] several items concerning the meeting of the Tennessee delegation in Washington are related which are not mentioned in his letters to Walker. According to this account, on the Sunday night before Congress convened, while Polk was calling on Grundy, Duff Green came in and urged that the Tennessee members should come out for White. Green expressed his own readiness to support the judge. Polk remained silent, but Grundy replied that he was not prepared to act on this subject. Although Polk had declined to meet with the other delegates, Lea, of Tennessee, came to the House a few days after the meeting had been held and handed Polk a letter which the delegation had prepared to send to Judge White. There were no signatures attached and Lea explained that the delegation had desired to have Polk sign it first. Polk replied

---

[30] Jan. 12, 1835 (*Polk Papers*). Walker had already written on January 7 that it had been reported in Tennessee that Bell and others intended to run White whether he is chosen by the national convention or not. "I believe Judge White is the most popular man in Tennessee except Gen. Jackson, but I do not think it is certain that even he can get the vote of Tennessee in opposition to the regular nomination of the Republican party—it looks like suicide—and how can we mix with such men as Poindexter and others of the same stamp?" He hopes that White will not lend his name to the scheme.

[31] It is addressed to J. B. & Co. (John Bell & Co.), but is changed into a letter to Cave Johnson. It is dated January 20, but relates to events that occurred as late as March 26. It probably is the first draft of his statement addressed to Johnson under date of March 26. In another letter to Johnson, dated March 28, Polk gives his reason for addressing him instead of Bell. Bell's criticisms of Polk had been contained in a letter written to Johnson, and, as Polk had received no communication directly from Bell, he could not write to him; or, if he should do so, Bell would not publish the letter. So it was sent to Johnson for publication at the proper time.

that he had nothing against White, but would not act with a portion of the party. A few days later Hubbard, of New Hampshire, informed Polk that Green was trying to interest members of Congress in the establishment of a White paper in Washington. Bell had tried to convince Hubbard that it would benefit New Hampshire to join with the South and West in forming a new party, but Hubbard declined to coöperate with him. May, of Illinois, told Polk that he had "stumbled on a caucus" composed of Bell, Peyton, and other Tennessee members. To May's protests against dividing the party, Bell replied that he saw no sacrifice of principle in winning opposition votes. In all of this Polk saw—or, at least, pretended to see—a plot of Bell, Green, and Crockett[32] to use Judge White for the purpose of overthrowing the Republican party.

The other side of the story is told in letters written to Cave Johnson by other members of the Tennessee delegation. These, White's biographer has published for the purpose of showing the "duplicity of Johnson and Polk."[33] The essential difference between these letters and those of Polk above quoted is that they state that Polk and Johnson had expressed a preference for White over any other man and had agreed to support him "under any circumstances that he, Judge White, would permit his name to be used," while Polk maintained that he had promised support only in case White should be nominated by the party. Which of the two statements is correct we are unable to determine with absolute certainty, but Polk's version accords with his invariable practice of conforming to the party program.[34]

While Polk was declining to meet with Bell, his friend Brady was sending to Jackson and to members of Congress copies of the

[32] Crockett had signed the letter to White.

[33] Scott, *Memoir of Hugh Lawson White*, 259–262.

[34] Standifer asserted that the meeting of the delegation held for the purpose of considering White's nomination "was a project of my own without being prompted by any one." Both Polk and Grundy, he said, after ascertaining that Bell would be there, declined to attend the meeting (*ibid.*, 260–262).

Murfreesborough *Monitor* containing Bell's Murfreesborough speech. He also urged upon Polk the necessity of establishing an administration paper in Nashville.[35] The plan of the bolters, he said, was White for eight years, and then "the Speaker will graciously condescend to take upon himself the burthens of State."

There is abundant evidence that Polk's Tennessee friends really believed that Bell and his adherents were plotting to divide the party. Daniel Graham of Murfreesborough wrote[36] that, while he preferred White to any other man, he distrusted his supporters. "No one here doubts," wrote Polk's brother-in-law, W. R. Rucker, "that he [Bell] is a thorough Bank man and at heart (though a dissembling hypocrite) one of Gen[l] Jackson's bitterest enemies."[37] In the opinion of James Walker, another brother-in-law, Van Buren was the only man who could lead the party to victory. "We justly esteem and appreciate Judge White, but cannot consent to become the tools of the opposition, or to be associated in political feeling with such as Poindexter & others."[38] A. V. Brown, one of Polk's closest friends, preferred White as a successor to Jackson but asked the question,

Do the Whigs really mean to do something finally for him—or is it a part of their policy to make a *present shew* in his favor to effect division in the Jackson ranks & so weaken Mr. Van Buren & then finally press some favorite of their own & so throw the Election in the House?[39]

Childress informed Polk[40] that it was rumored in Nashville that Bell and his friends were confident of throwing the election into the House, where White would have a majority, and that they

---

[35] Brady to Polk, Dec. 26, 1834, *Polk Papers.*

[36] Graham to Polk, Jan. 2, 1835, *Polk Papers.*

[37] Rucker to Polk, Jan. 5, 1835, *Polk Papers.* "Don't misunderstand me," he added, "I like White as well as any of these people, but I don't like these intriguing friends of his." He urged Polk to inform Jackson of the intrigues.

[38] Walker to Polk, Jan. 15, 1835, *Polk Papers.*

[39] Brown to Polk, Jan. 15, 1835, *Polk Papers.*

[40] Childress to Polk, Jan. 23, 1835, *Polk Papers.* Childress was Mrs. Polk's brother.

were equally confident of defeating Polk and Cave Johnson at the coming election.

The anomalous situation in Tennessee was aptly put by another of Polk's correspondents.

The more I reflect on the posture of affairs, the more am I provoked at the success of iniquity. Almost every man in the community who takes part in or cares for public doings, finds himself occupying a false position which he is compelled to defend. I shall find myself opposed to Judge White, which is not true, so of Doct Rucker & thousands of others—whilst thousands will find themselves opposed to Genl Jackson who are sincerely with him. Furthermore Genl Jackson & Judge White will find themselves in hostile attitude before the scene closes, whatever may be their hopes and expectations now.[41]

All agreed that John Bell was the man who had created this embarrassing predicament.

No doubt the intriguing of White's supporters was greatly exaggerated, but it seemed real enough to those who were striving to preserve party solidarity. Jackson's determination to force upon the people an unpopular candidate was after all the main cause of the difficulty, for many could not pass White by and support Van Buren without sacrificing their principles. Party loyalty alone kept others from espousing White's cause, and for some time many of Jackson's friends had hopes that he might yet drop Van Buren and acquiesce in White's nomination.[42]

The President, however, had no thought of abandoning his favorite. He vehemently condemned the activities of the Tennessee delegation, and he was beginning to regard Bell as an enemy.[43] Back of the encouragement given to White by political opponents was seen the hand of Henry Clay, who was believed to be ready to seize any advantage that might result from throwing the election into the House.[44]

---

[41] Daniel Graham to Polk, Jan. 29, 1835, *Polk Papers*.

[42] Gen. Sam'l G. Smith to Polk, Feb. 3, 1835, *Polk Papers*.

[43] Polk to Walker, Jan. 18, 1835, *Polk Papers*.

[44] Copy of a letter from Polk to somebody in Tennessee, dated February 7, 1835, *Polk Papers*. The letter was probably written to James Walker; see Walker to Polk, Feb. 24, *ibid.*

After the meeting of the Tennessee delegation, White of course realized that the members had divided on the question of supporting him. He regretted the discord that had arisen but nevertheless declined to forbid the use of his name.[45] On December 29, 1834, the delegation had addressed him a letter asking if he would accept a nomination, and he replied in the affirmative.[46] He said afterwards that he would never have consented to become a candidate but for Jackson's threat to make him "odious to society" if he did.[47]

Outwardly, at least, the judge remained on friendly terms with the Tennessee members of Congress who had opposed his nomination until a controversy arose over a question of patronage. Polk and Johnson had recommended, and Jackson had appointed, a district attorney for West Tennessee without consulting Senator White. In a letter to the two men[48] White intimated that there had been "secret contrivance" to bring about the appointment. If, as White's biographer asserts, these two Tennesseans "had determined to pick a quarrel with Judge White," they now had their opportunity—and they certainly made the most of it. They replied in a very caustic letter in which they repelled what they regarded as insinuations against themselves and the President. White's rejoinder was equally caustic, and the break was complete.[49]

It is quite possible that Polk may have welcomed such an excuse for openly breaking with the judge. The time had arrived when he must take a definite stand for one side or the other, inasmuch as it was now certain that the opposition intended to

[45] White to Alexander, Jan. 12, 1835 (Scott, *Memoir of Hugh Lawson White*, 255).

[46] Correspondence in Scott, *Memoir of Hugh Lawson White*, 329–331.

[47] Speech at Knoxville, Aug. 1, 1838 (Scott, *Memoir of Hugh Lawson White*, 359).

[48] Dated Feb. 24, 1835 (*Polk Papers*).

[49] The correspondence may be found in the *Polk Papers* under dates of February 24–26. Part of it is printed in Scott, *Memoir of Hugh Lawson White*, 256–259.

use White for the purpose of defeating the nomination of an administration candidate—that is a regular Republican nomination.[50] Such being the case, both self-interest and party loyalty beckoned in the same direction, for he could expect no favors from the men who were promoting the campaign for White's nomination. Bell was his personal enemy and political rival; many letters warned him that the White adherents were scheming, as one put it, "to get White & the people upon one side & Van Buren & my friend Col. Polk on the other."[51] Having made the inevitable choice, Polk endeavored, through James Walker and other local leaders, to hold his constituents in line for the administration, but White's popularity was already playing havoc with party solidarity.[52] At a political meeting held in Columbia on February 12, Walker, by resolution, tried to pledge the meeting to the "party candidate." The resolution was defeated by the aid of many who had hitherto been averse to White's nomination.[53] Not long after this Walker felt certain that White would carry Tennessee and he cautioned Polk that "non interference may be your true position."[54]

Nearly all the newspapers in Tennessee favored White's nomination. Bell controlled both Nashville papers, and late in February F. K. Zollicoffer, of the Columbia *Observer*, hoisted the White banner. Polk and his friends in Middle Tennessee were without an organ of influence until they established, a month later, the Nashville *Union*, which White, in a speech in the Senate,

---

[50] Polk to —— (probably Walker), Feb. 7, 1835, *Polk Papers*.

[51] James H. Thomas to Polk, Feb. 12, 1835, *Polk Papers*. J. W. Childress wrote (Jan. 23) that Polk and Johnson had been marked for defeat. Similar information came from Gen. Smith (Feb. 13), W. G. Childress and James Walker (both Feb. 14), *ibid*.

[52] Some in Tennessee, said W. G. Childress in his letter of February 14, "seem to think or to say that Jackson, the Jackson party and Jackson administration will soon be no more, that the whole will be swallowed in the White party."

[53] "The small politicians are all on the scent and expect to rise on the White excitement" (Walker to Polk, Feb. 24, 1835, *Polk Papers*).

[54] Walker to Polk, Feb. 28, 1835, *ibid*.

called a "vehicle of slanders and falsehoods, gotten up in this city [Washington]" for the purpose of distorting the truth.[55] This paper was edited by Samuel H. Laughlin; its policy was directed by Polk, Grundy, and Judge Catron, who were mainly responsible for its financial support.

Polk returned home after Congress had adjourned, only to find White's prospects daily growing brighter. In a speech delivered at Columbia, April 20, he justified his refusal to join other members of the delegation in asking White to run on the ground that he had not been sent to Washington for the purpose of making presidents. His personal preference had been for White, he said, if he could have been nominated by the Republican party.[56] Grundy approved this speech, but as to any further discussion of the subject his advice to Polk was that "the judicious course is a plain one—say nothing."[57]

In Washington, General Jackson was eagerly awaiting news from Tennessee. He was now fully convinced of Bell's "perfidy," but apparently he did not yet realize the strength of the White movement. In a long letter[58] he expressed a fear that Polk's promised communication had been delayed by illness, " for I am sure the little noise, and various meetings, got up by the instrumentality of Mr. Bell and Co. cannot have alarmed you." After delivering a homily on the iniquity of abandoning principles, and citing Clay, Calhoun, and Burr as horrible examples, he said that "Mr. Bell, Davy Crockett & Co. has placed Judge White in the odious attitude of abandoning principle & party for office," and with the association of the nullifiers

The eyes of the people soon were opened to this wicked plan, to divide and conquer the Democracy of the union, prostrate the present administration by making it odious by crying out corruption and misrule, and being supported by office holders, and corruption, thereby to bring into power the

---

[55] Scott, *Memoir of Hugh Lawson White*, 292.
[56] Speech printed in the Washington *Globe*, May 29, 1835.
[57] Grundy to Polk, May 11, 1835, *Polk Papers*.
[58] Jackson to Polk, May 3, 1835, *ibid*. The letter was marked "private for your own eye—it is wrote in haste."

opposition, recharter the United States Bank, destroying the republican government & substitute in its stead, a consolidated government under the controle of a corrupt monied monopoly.

After scanning this doleful picture of a future possibility, Polk must have felt relieved when he read further on that "Mr. Bell & Co. have not succeeded—Virginia is erect again." "Surely," continued the President, "Tennessee will never put herself in the false position of joining the piedbald opposition of Whiggs, nullifiers, blue light federalists, and Hartford convention men. It cannot be—heaven and every principle of virtue and republicanism forbid it." Had White remained with his party, said Jackson, he might have procured the Vice-Presidency, but

he has been placed by Mr. Bell & Co. as the candidate of the opposition under the odious imputation of abandoning his old republican principles & party, for office, and whether he has or not the world has taken up that opinion, and he never can regain the confidence of that party again. The opposition never intended that he should be elected, they meant to divide, that they might conquer for Mr. Clay who, you may rely, is to be their candidate at last.

He had hopes that "judge White's eyes may be opened and he will *now* see that he is in a false position and abandon Bell, Davy Crockett & Co., and withdraw himself from the odious attitude intriguing apostates have placed him [in]."

It was doubtless pleasing news that Jackson thus fixed the blame for disrupting the party upon Polk's own enemies, Bell and Crockett. Equally pleasing must it have been to read that

You and Grundy, (by the true Republicans in Congress) are looked to, to take a firm and open stand in favour of the republican principles, a *national convention* by *the people*, and in toto, against nullification & disunion—and against *little* caucuses, of a few apostate members of congress, & preserve Tennessee from the disgrace of uniting with the piebald opposition to put down my *administration, and my fame* with it, and give the reigns of Government into the hands of those who have recently conspired to recharter the Bank.

In this fight for principles, said the President, all must take a definite stand; "do your duty (as you have done here) *at home,* and you will stand high with the republicans everywhere.'' Saving Tennessee proved to be a more difficult task than Jackson had anticipated, but, by attempting to do so, Polk and Grundy earned his undying gratitude.

In the President's opinion, two mutually antagonistic factions had joined forces for the purpose of destroying the Republican party. While Bell and Clay were aiming at consolidated government, Calhoun and his friends were using White's name ''to build up a Southern confederacy and divide the union.'' The President still spoke of White with regret more than anger. He did not charge him with being either a consolidationist or a nullifier, and he still had hopes that the judge would free himself from the influence of evil associates.

Jackson was much encouraged by the success won by his party in Virginia, Rhode Island, and Connecticut. As to Tennessee he had fears, but he also had hopes. ''Can it be,'' he said in closing his letter,

that Tennessee will abandon republican principles and be ranked with apostates, nullifiers & bluelight Federalist—Tristam Burges says she will—*forbit it virtue, forbit it heaven*—Tennessee has sustained me thus far, and I trust she never will abandon her principles for any person.

In another long letter written to Polk on May 12, Jackson vented his wrath upon those who held political control of the state for their refusal to participate in the national nominating convention.[59] ''How it is,'' he asked, ''that there is no man in the Republican ranks to take the stump, and relieve Tennessee from her degraded attitude?'' This question may have been intended as a hint for a more aggressive stand on Polk's part. ''If I was a mere citizen of Tennessee again,'' he continued, ''and wanted

---

[59] For example, the Nashville *Banner,* denouncing the national convention, said: ''So long as we live and breathe American air, we will resist the insidious proposition (whensoever and wheresoever it may originate), to lay at the feet of village politicians and placemen, who most usually fill *conventions,* the inestimable privilege of thinking and acting for ourselves in the choice of our rulers.'' Quoted in *Niles' Register* (March 28, 1835), XLVIII, 58.

everlasting fame, I would ask no other theatre to obtain it than
before the people of Tennessee."[60]   In this letter Jackson spoke
of the seceders as "White Whiggs," and although both White
and Bell still claimed membership in the Republican party, the
press of both parties was beginning to class them as Whigs.[61]
It was becoming the custom to apply this name to the National
Republicans, of whom Clay was a recognized leader; they, with
the White supporters, constituted the new Whig party.[62]

The desire of the Jacksonites to identify White and Bell with
the Clay faction of the Whigs was aided materially by the discovery of Bell's "Cassedy" or "Bedford" letter of May 11,
1835.[63]   There is nothing particularly damaging to either man
in the letter itself, but as construed and placed before the people
by their opponents, it was said to be a pledge that White, if
elected, would not veto any law for rechartering the bank.   The
latter part of it was construed as a suggestion that Polk's

[60] In *Polk Papers*. Jackson's signature has been cut from this letter.

[61] "Elected, if elected at all, by the votes of the Whigs, he [White]
will naturally and necessarily select his councillors from their ranks, and
modify his measures according to their views."   Richmond *Whig*, quoted
by Richmond *Enquirer*, and reprinted in Washington *Globe*, May 4, 1835.

[62] In his letter of May 3 to Polk, above quoted, Jackson spoke of
"modern Whiggs."   He often omitted the h, and invariably used the
double g.

[63] It was written to Charles Cassedy of Bedford County, Tennessee,
and read as follows:

"Dear Sir: You will receive enclosed, the manifesto of the White
cause and party.   I think it contains our principles and the argument upon
which they may be sustained briefly set forth.

"You will see by my letter all I know of Judge White's views about
the Bank.   He doubtless never will swerve from them, but it would be
most unprecedented, and do him, and very justly too, a great injury, to
be declaring before hand, that he would put his veto upon any measure
whatever.   It would be said to be an electioneering declaration, and besides Mr. Van Buren has given no such pledges.

"To defeat me for the Speaker's chair, is the main interest which
Mr. Polk and Johnson have in this whole contest, as I believe.

"It would not do to ask Polk to vote for me against himself, but he
might be made to pledge himself to go for me against any other candidate.
My course in appointing him chairman of the Committee of Ways and
Means could be used to show that I have not been influenced by personal
considerations against him, when the country is concerned.

"Yours truly,   "JOHN BELL."

Printed in Nashville *Union*, April 5, 1839.

constituents should pledge him to cast his vote for Bell in the election of a Speaker. Between the lines there was seen a threat to defeat Polk in his campaign for reëlection to Congress unless he should give such a pledge. The rumored contents—before its publication—were far worse than the letter itself, and its appearance in print failed to counteract the effect which the rumors had produced.[64]

Knowing that the people still believed in Jackson despite their loyalty to Judge White, Bell, who was himself a candidate for reëlection, published a long letter in the Nashville *Republican* denying that he had "brought White out" in the sense and for the reasons claimed by the Democrats. "I am not against Jackson or his administration," he wrote, "but I am opposed to Mr. Van Buren."[65] As a blow at Polk, however, he published in a McMinnville paper extracts from the correspondence which had passed between Cave Johnson and the Tennessee delegation at the time that White had been invited to become a candidate. Bell's adversaries now published the entire correspondence in the Nashville *Union,* and that journal highly commended the course which had been pursued by Polk, Grundy, and Johnson. From T. J. Pew, of Kentucky, Laughlin, the editor, learned that during the previous autumn Bell had urged Col. R. M. Johnson to become a candidate on the bank ticket[66] and this paper now claimed to have conclusive proof of Bell's affiliations with the bank. His "Cassedy" letter was published in the *Union* on June 26, and Grundy confidently assured Polk that "that letter will make you Speaker, I think."[67]

During this same month (May 20) Van Buren was nominated for the Presidency by the Baltimore convention, and a bitter

---

[64] A similar letter was written by Bell to a man in Giles County (Kincannon to Polk, June 1, 1835, *Polk Papers*). Kincannon said that he had seen the letter.

[65] Copied by the Washington *Globe*, May 28, 1835.

[66] Laughlin to Polk, May 30, 1835, *Polk Papers*. Pew said that he had seen Bell's letter to Johnson.

[67] Grundy to Polk, June 25, 1835, *ibid*.

national campaign was waged in Tennessee simultaneously with the contest for supremacy between Polk and Bell. Although Jackson had, in his "Gwin letter,"[68] asserted that it was to be a convention "fresh from the people" to whose will all in the party ought to submit, it was well known that this body had been called together for the sole purpose of ratifying the "appointment" already made by the President. His letter to Gwin had failed to produce the desired effect, for Tennessee did not even send delegates to the convention at Baltimore. Still unwilling to believe that the people of his state could fail to do his bidding, Jackson caused a statement to be circulated to the effect that the contest was really between himself and White, and not between the judge and Van Buren.[69]

There was much vituperation on either side during the months which preceded the congressional elections in Tennessee. Both parties seemed to realize that, if elected, Polk would be chosen Speaker of the House. Polk was popular in his district and many of the "White Whigs" remained loyal to him. Toward the close of the campaign, the Bell forces became more moderate in their criticisms, for it had become apparent that by indulging too freely in denunciations they had strengthened both Polk and Van Buren.[70]

Confident of victory, Jackson, from his retreat at "Rip Raps," was already planning work for Polk to do as soon as he had been reëlected.[71] Polk, Grundy, and Johnson were to get up meetings which would instruct Representatives in Congress to vote against the chartering of any bank. They were also to induce the state legislature to instruct the Senators from Tennessee to vote

---

[68] *Niles' Register*, XLVIII, 80–81.

[69] Scott, *Memoir of Hugh Lawson White*, 335.

[70] Polk to Jackson, Aug. 14, 1835, reporting his victory at the polls, *Polk Papers*.

[71] Clay, said the President, is the real candidate of the opposition, and Bell will sacrifice White and try to get votes for himself in the Speakership election. "The Judge will be left politically prostrate as ever Aron Burr was, and as few to sympathize with him on his downfall."

for Benton's expunging resolution and against a bank charter. In order to preclude the charge of persecution, he advised that the local meetings should draft their instructions before the legislature had convened and before either Bell or White had been nominated for reëlection as members of Congress. In any event, Bell's ''Cassedy letter'' would be a sufficient answer to any such charge.[72] And yet the man who wrote this letter vehemently denied that he ever interfered with the free choice of the people!

Some of the party politicians[73] were inclined to doubt the wisdom of having the members of Congress instructed by local meetings. They were not given much choice, however, in the matter of instructing Senators, for the President himself prepared an outline of instructions, which he sent to Governor Carroll. Major Guild was selected to present the instructions in the legislature. Jackson sent to Carroll, also, two volumes of the *Extra Globe* which contained Benton's speeches and other materials that might be useful for reference. He instructed Polk to repair to Nashville before the meeting of the legislature for the purpose of arranging everything for prompt action.[74] He also urged Polk to be in Washington a few days before the opening of Congress, and ''there must be a meeting of the friends of the administration & select the candidate for Speaker and elect him the first ballott.'' He did not state explicitly that Polk would be that candidate, but his assurance that ''the New England states will sustain you'' indicates that Polk was the President's own choice for the office.[75]

---

[72] Jackson to Polk, Aug. 3, 1835, *Polk Papers.*

[73] For example, A. V. Brown (Brown to Polk, Aug. 27, 1835, *Polk Papers*).

[74] ''You must be in Nashville some days before the Assembly meets, every arrangement ought to be made, and as soon as the House is formed the resolutions ought to be offered, or the opposition will forestall you by a set prepared for their own pallate be prompt and do not permit yourselves to be outgeneraled, the first blow is half the battle, and as they are preparing to elect a Senator, these resolutions will strike terror & confusion in their ranks—produce a panic, and blow up all their digested arrangements, and will add all the doubting members to your ranks.''

[75] Jackson to Polk, Sept. 15, 1835, *Polk Papers.* ''When you read & note burn this'' was his final instruction.

Even if there had not already existed a strong personal friend-ship between Polk and the President, their common desire to overthrow the Bell-White faction was sufficient to identify their political interests.

For the next two months Polk kept Jackson well informed on passing events in Tennessee. With Donelson, also, he kept up a separate correspondence, concerning which they did not always take the President into their confidence.[76] Donelson did not share Jackson's belief that the legislature would adopt the Guild resolutions to instruct the Senators from Tennessee.[77]

In October, while the legislature was in session, Judge White visited Nashville and other nearby towns, where public dinners were given in his honor. Without assigning any reasons, Polk curtly declined to attend any of these, but he reported to the President that White had taken advantage of the occasions to electioneer for himself and to censure Polk, Grundy, and other supporters of the administration. Jackson was much incensed by this information, but he still believed that the effect of the judge's speeches would be counteracted by the debate in the legislature on the expunging resolutions. "Mark these words," he wrote to Polk, "have the yeas & nays taken upon them, and all who votes against them will be taught by the people of Tenn-essee that they have misrepresented them."[78] White, in Jack-son's opinion, could not be too severely condemned for attacking Polk and other members of Congress; "rouse Grundy & Johnson into action, and I will vouch for the virtue of the people."[79]

The President's wish for prompt action on the expunging resolutions was doomed to disappointment; a wearisome discussion

---

[76] Both suspected that Bell had a spy in the President's household by whom he was supplied with administration secrets, but they give no clew as to whom they suspect (Donelson to Polk, Sept. 24, 1835, *Polk Papers*).

[77] Donelson to Polk, Oct. 20, 1835, *ibid.*

[78] "I cannot yet believe," he continued, "that the democratic repub-licans of Tennessee can be so unjust to me, as to unite with Clay & the opposition in condemning me for preserving the constitution."

[79] Jackson to Polk, Oct. 20, 1835, *Polk Papers*.

followed the introduction of the subject. On the other hand, the legislature very promptly nominated White for the Presidency, even before Jackson's above-quoted letter had reached Tennessee. In his letter of acceptance, White declared emphatically that his political principles had undergone no change; that the administration forces, and not he, had deserted the traditional party standards and become "a mere *faction*."[80] After the formal nomination had been made the people regarded the campaign as a contest between Jackson and White, and the Presidency was the principal topic of discussion at every local gathering. The country people generally stood loyally by the President, while those living in towns were more apt to favor White.[81]

After the congressional delegation had set out for Washington—Polk to be elected Speaker over his arch enemy, Bell, and Johnson to frighten his friends by his near approach to a duel with the much hated Bailie Peyton[82]—the legislature continued the acrimonious debates on Jackson's expunging resolutions. To add variety, the White supporters in the legislature were accused by their opponents of fraud in connection with the public printing. While the debate was in progress, Jackson sent appeals for support to members of the legislature, and it was said that Polk had prepared the list to be thus solicited. White, also, corresponded with some of the members. He made no attempt to influence their votes, but his exposure of the methods employed by the President to defeat him undoubtedly brought him support. Strong language was used by both sides, and members did not hesitate to call General Jackson a "dictator" or to accuse him of trying to appoint his successor.[83]

[80] The documents relating to White's nomination are printed in Scott, *Memoir of Hugh Lawson White*, 331–334.

[81] J. W. Childress to Polk, Nov. 22, 1835, *Polk Papers*.

[82] Laughlin to Polk, Dec. 1; J. W. Johnson to Polk, Dec. 9, 1835, *Polk Papers*.

[83] A. O. P. Nicholson to Polk, Feb. 4, 1836, *ibid*. "It is declared every day & by the leaders, that to Mr. Van B's personal character they do not object—but their great objection is, to Pres^t Jackson nominating his successor" (Catron to Polk, Jan. 8, 1836, *ibid*.).

Both Jackson and Bell were said to have flooded the state with "franked" political literature for the purpose of influencing both the legislature and the people. But the command of the "old hero" was no longer as of yore. The legislature which had so recently nominated Judge White now declined to instruct him to vote for Benton's expunging resolution[84]

Polk was elected Speaker of the House by a large majority, and both in Washington and in Tennessee the defeat of Bell for that office was expected to injure White's prospects in his own state. "It was urged by the faithful," wrote White,

> that by the election of Polk, the vote of Tennessee would be changed. The course of Alabama,[85] it was said, will be followed by the legislature of Tennessee, and in a very short time my name will be dropped everywhere. . . . Everything which can be done to my injury, within their power, is done by Grundy and Johnson, from my own State, and probably by Polk, also.[86]

Party leaders in Tennessee undoubtedly believed that White would now withdraw from the race, or that in any case Van Buren would carry the state. Polk received many letters expressing this opinion.[87] Their hopes of defeating the judge were somewhat disturbed by the refusal of the legislature to instruct him on the expunging resolutions, but they were revived by the expected effect of White's votes against some of Jackson's appointments and by his arguments and vote in favor of Clay's land distribution bill.[88]

---

[84] E. H. Foster to White, Feb. 26, 1836 (Scott, *Memoir of Hugh Lawson White,*. 337).

[85] The legislature of Alabama nominated White, but on the condition that he should be "the choice of the republican party throughout the Union."

[86] White to Geo. W. Churchwell, Jan. 3, 1836 (Scott, *Memoir of Hugh Lawson White*).

[87] Among the rest Nicholson wrote (January 22) that since Polk's election the White men had practically given up the struggle; "all excitement here has subsided, and the election of V. B. is given up by all but Gen. Barrow."

[88] Walker to Polk, April 11, 1836. White's vote on the land bill "must seal his fate," wrote Laughlin to Cave Johnson on May 9. One of White's admirers said at a political meeting that he "had followed White to his grave when he [White] voted for the land bill—and that he could not stand to be buried with him" (Herndon to Polk, May 25, 1836). All in *Polk Papers.*

One of the most serious handicaps of the administration party in Tennessee was the weakness of their press. The Bell-White faction had procured control of the leading newspapers in Nashville and elsewhere. The Nashville *Union* was the main Democratic organ and Polk was in constant receipt of letters from Laughlin, its editor, which stated that the paper was approaching bankruptcy. Laughlin himself was enthusiastic but unreliable. Many a letter from Nashville politicians reported to Polk that "Laughlin has been drunk for a week." Near the close of the campaign he became so untrustworthy that Judge Catron was obliged to edit the *Union*.[89]

For our present purpose it is unnecessary to follow in detail the remainder of White's campaign for the Presidency. By splitting the Democratic party and by bringing to Polk the powerful support of General Jackson, it was one of the principal factors in elevating Polk to the Speaker's chair. In his attitude toward White, Polk may have in some degree played the "unscrupulous partisan" which Parton says he was,[90] but the political situation which resulted from White's candidacy left him very little choice.[91] He could not coöperate with Bell, and it would have been political suicide to break with the President.

With the remainder of this campaign Polk's political welfare was not so intimately connected. It will therefore be treated incidentally only, in connection with his career as Speaker of the House.

---

[89] Catron to Polk, Sept. 6, 1836, *Polk Papers*.

[90] Parton, *Life of Andrew Jackson*, III, 617.

[91] That partisan Democrats really believed Judge White to have been made the tool of designing politicians and his own ambition is well indicated by Laughlin's entry in his diary on hearing of the death of White. "So, here is the end of ambition—of the ambition of an old politician who had been betrayed and deceived by his pretended friends, John Bell and others, into a course of intrigue and tergiversation, which had cast him from the Senate, had lost him the esteem of all good men in his state, and had embittered his latter days, and probably shortened his life. What a warning his example ought to afford to all thinking and candid men!" (*Diary*, April 14, 1840). As White carried the state by an overwhelming majority, there must inded have been a dearth of "good men" and a surplus of rascals!

CHAPTER VI

SPEAKER OF THE HOUSE UNDER JACKSON

Following Jackson's advice Polk went to Washington late in November, 1835, in order to prepare the way for his election as Speaker.[1] The twenty-fourth Congress assembled on December 7, and, as the President had planned, Polk was elected on the first ballot. The coveted office was his reward for party loyalty, but he soon discovered that he must also pay the penalty of his success by being the object of more heckling and abuse than had fallen to the lot of any of his predecessors. The Democrats had a substantial majority in the House and were able to carry their measures; but the knowledge of this power only made their opponents more determined to goad the majority by obstructive tactics and by personal vituperation.

The entire period of Polk's speakership was one of political unrest, sectional discord, and personal animosity. Those who had so recently been friends and relentless in pursuing the common enemies, Adams and Tobias Watkins, hated one another all the more cordially now that the party was disintegrating, for each faction believed the other treacherously to have abandoned traditional party principles. On his own account, Polk had to suffer the slings and arrows of his brilliant but censorious rival, and of Peyton, Crockett, and other personal enemies. In addition, all who harbored grudges against the "military chieftain"— whether Nullifiers or Whigs—took keen delight in vitriolic attacks upon the administration, and in making it personally uncomfortable for the Speaker, whom they charged with being the President's creature and obedient slave. To this potpourri of

---

[1] Jackson to Polk, Sept. 15, 1835, *Polk Papers.*

discord was added the battle between Adams and the southern fire-eaters over the abolition petitions. Each side accused the Speaker of unfairness and harrassed him with hairsplitting questions of parliamentary procedure. Fortunately for himself his knowledge of detail, his methodical mind, and his habitual coolness under the most trying ordeals, enabled him to preside over the exciting debates with dignity and success when many a more brilliant man would have met with failure.

The disposition to humiliate Polk was manifested even before he had been elected. As soon as the House had been called to order, the clerk announced the first business to be the election of a Speaker by ballot. To this customary procedure Patton and others objected, and insisted upon a *viva voce* election. Except for showing a disposition on the part of the opposition to resort to annoying tactics whenever possible, this attempt to alter the mode of election was of little importance, for the House proceeded to ballot as usual, and Polk received one hundred and thirty-two votes to eighty-four for Bell—a vote which Benton says "was considered a test of the administration strength, Mr. Polk being supported by that party."[2]

The President's message was sent to Congress on the second day of the session. Evidently descrying the gathering war clouds, Jackson called attention to the dangers that would result from internal dissensions. He again recommended the adoption of an amendment to the Constitution which would prevent the election of a President from devolving upon the House. It is unlikely, however, that he had much hope that his suggestion would be followed.

The standing committees were announced by the Speaker on the fourteenth of December. In forming them, Polk followed the usual custom of placing safe party majorities on those which would have the shaping of important legislation. In so doing he simply followed precedent; but he had, when a minority

---

[2] Benton, *Thirty Years' View*, I, 569.

member, condemned the practice, and by adhering to precedent now he became the object of criticism and abuse.

The first difficult problem which confronted the new Speaker was the disposition of abolition petitions. On December 18, 1835, Jackson, of Massachusetts, presented a memorial in which citizens of his state asked Congress to abolish slavery in the District of Columbia. Hammond, of South Carolina, moved that the petition "be not received," but Polk ruled that such a motion had never before been presented to the House and that under the rules it was not in order. When Hammond offered another motion to "reject" the petition, Polk ruled that any petition might be rejected after it had been received. Although his rulings were logical and fair, they were assailed by the contestants on either side. The Speaker's motives were impugned and appeals were taken to the House, but even John Bell admitted that Polk had made the best disposition of a new and debatable question. This particular petition was sent to the table on Decemcember 21; but others like it soon appeared, and the "right of petition" became one of the most heated topics of debate. The *Globe* upheld the cause of the petitioners. Should the House, it said, yield to the demands made by Hammond and Wise and refuse to receive such petitions, it would be violating one of the most sacred constitutional guaranties.[3]

Nearly all of the northern members held that all petitions from American citizens must be received and that, after reception, Congress might dispose of them as it pleased. Southern members did not deny the right of petition, in the abstract; they were willing, they said, to receive *"bona fide"* petitions. But radicals from that section argued that, inasmuch as the petitioners in question were asking something which did not fall within the power of Congress to perform, there could be no obligation to receive requests to do the impossible.

---

[3] Washington *Globe,* Jan. 1, 1836.

On February 8, Pinckney, of South Carolina, presented a resolution which prescribed a method for dealing with anti-slavery petitions. After its passage by Congress it was popularly known as the ''gag rule.'' It directed that all memorials, already presented or to be presented, praying for the abolition of slavery in the District of Columbia should be referred to a select committee. By the same resolution the committee was instructed to report that Congress possessed no power to interfere with slavery in states and ought not to interfere with it in the District. Regarded as a compromise, the resolution was passed by a large majority, but its provisions did not win the approval of extremists on either side. Slavery restrictionists condemned a measure which to them seemed a combination of cowardice and tyranny, while southern hotspurs like Hammond and Wise were dissatisfied because Congress would not reject all petitions relating to this subject. The recalcitrant members raised endless technical objections and appealed repeatedly from the decisions of the chair, but only in one instance did the House fail to sustain the rulings of the Speaker. Of all the objectors, Wise was the most abusive and unfair. Among other things he accused Polk of trying to force members to ''vote like mules'' without affording them an opportunity to consider the questions to be decided.

Pinckney's resolution did not succeed in precluding further debate on the subject of slavery. Briggs, of Massachusetts, presented another petition on February 15, and, in response to a question put by Wise, Polk decided that the Pinckney resolution applied only to petitions which had already been received. Thereupon Wise moved that the Briggs petition ''be not received,'' and the Speaker ruled the motion to be in order. The ruling was clearly an error on Polk's part, and his decision was overruled by a vote of the House. His apparent concession to Wise was severely criticized by both northern and southern men. Among the latter, Manning, of South Carolina, said that the effect of the Speaker's decision would be to renew the angry

sectional debates which the supporters of the Pinckney resolution
had hoped to obviate; in addition, it was an arbitrary setting
aside of the will of the House. "If the Speaker," continued
Manning, "can by his decision reverse this resolution . . . then
he has power to suspend, alter, or change, any deliberate act of
this House, intended as a rule for its governance."[4] The vote
of the House settled the question for the session at least. The
effect of the reversal of Polk's decision was to apply the "gag
rule" to all petitions that might appear, and to refer them automatically to the select committee. It was, of course, well understood that they would not be considered or reported back by the
committee.

The Nashville *Republican* criticized Polk for being unable to
keep order in the House. It contrasted him unfavorably with
Bell, and *proved* his incompetence by citing numerous appeals
that had been taken from his decisions. The *Globe* replied that
the disorder and appeals were machinations of Bell's henchmen,
who had been purposely trying to discredit the Speaker. It
pointed with pride to the fact that only one of his decisions—a
new rule which Polk had construed in favor of the Bell men—
had been reversed by the House.[5]

The twenty-fourth Congress had not been long in session before the candidacy of Judge White entered into the debates of
the House. On January 2, 1836, the *Globe* charged that Nullifiers, like Wise, and Abolitionists were supporting White for no
other reason than to draw votes from Van Buren. For the same
reason, it said, Webster was urged to run on a ticket of his own.
In turn, Wise embraced every opportunity to attack the President and administration members, including the Speaker, and
to accuse them of engaging in political intrigues.

---

[4] *Cong. Globe*, 24 Cong., 1 sess., App., 145.

[5] "The truth is, Mr. Polk has deserved the confidence of the House by
a firm, faithful, industrious, and able discharge of his duties." This paper
denied that Polk desired or had been offered a place in the cabinet, for
the administration wished him to remain in the Speaker's chair (Washington *Globe*, March 16, 1836).

Such an opportunity was presented when Adams moved that a certain passage of the President's message be referred to a select committee. During the last days of the twenty-third Congress the House had passed, as part of the general appropriation bill, an item of $3,000,000 to be expended for national defense by order of the President. As the two houses had been unable to agree on certain details, the measure was defeated in the Senate. The President in his message deplored the failure of Congress to pass this necessary measure, and again recommended the appropriation. Adams moved that the subject be referred to a select committee for the purpose of ascertaining by whose fault the appropriation had been lost.[6] While debating the question, Wise sarcastically remarked that it was a most important subject, for "the fate of the presidential canvass is in part made to depend upon it." The President, he said, had intended to use the money as a secret service fund; had Cambreleng not refused to accept the reasonable amendments proposed by the Senate, the measure would have carried. He charged Polk with having solicited votes for the appropriation on the plea that the President desired it, and with having requested the members solicited to refrain from mentioning this fact.[7] Scarcely a measure came before the House that was not made by Wise the motif for an assault upon the administration. His criticisms of the Speaker were many and bitter, and frequent though futile were his appeals from the decisions of the chair. Polk's friends thought that Wise and Peyton were trying to provoke the Speaker into fighting a duel; even his own family feared that blood might be shed.[8]

---

[6] The *National Intelligencer* had asserted that the House, not the Senate, had been at fault—a charge which Adams resented.

[7] Jan. 21, 22, 29. *Cong. Globe*, 24 Cong., 1 sess.

[8] James Walker advised Polk to treat their abuse with contempt. No one, he said, would doubt the Speaker's physical courage. The whole matter was, in his opinion, a scheme of Bell to disgrace Polk by drawing him into a duel with either Wise or Peyton (Walker to Polk, March 14, 1836, *Polk Papers*).

Although Bell was less abusive than either Wise or Peyton, he frequently questioned the justice of the Speaker's rulings and accused him of partisan bias.[9] On February 3, 1836, during a debate on the reference of a Senate bill for limiting the terms of certain officers, Bell said that never before had so many things of importance been excluded from the discussions of the House "by forms and decisions upon the rules." His principal speech of the session was delivered while the naval appropriation was being discussed in the House. He had little to say on the subject under consideration, but, having avowed his intention "to indulge the privilege of debate to the utmost limit of parliamentary license," he launched into an extended discussion of "the general policy of the present Administration, as lately developed."[10] He employed the present occasion, he said, because those who were in control of the House took good care to exclude any resolution to which such remarks as he desired to make would be really germane. After twitting the Speaker with having changed his opinions on the subject of patronage,[11] he arraigned the administration party for having abandoned the principles on which General Jackson had been chosen President. It was not surprising, he said, that strange doctrines should appear, inasmuch as the single principle which is common to the present majority is unlimited devotion, not to any particular creed, but to *the party*. He pointed out with remarkable precision the evils of abject partyism, and the inevitable abuses which result from

---

[9] Perhaps, as was later suggested by the Boston *Age* (Aug. 17, 1836), prudence led Bell to refrain from leading the assault and to delegate this function to his two associates. Still, Wise needed little urging, and the fact that Bailie Peyton was a nephew of Judge White was sufficient to account for his animosity.

[10] March 16, 22, 25, 1836. *Cong. Globe*, 24 Cong., 1 sess., App., 722 ff.

[11] "It was, I believe, a private scheme [earlier] of my colleague, who is now the presiding officer of this House [Mr. Polk] to take from the Secretary of State the power of designating the publishers of the laws, and to vest it in the House of Representatives; so important at that day was the purity of the public press regarded by the Jackson party."

personal government by a popular hero.[12] His own speech was
no doubt intended for campaign purposes, but the picture which
he drew of existing evils was none the less accurate on that account. If it lacked in any particular, it was in being too charitable to the President himself, for after all Jackson was the
individual most responsible for perpetuating those evils in the
interest of party discipline. There were other critics of the

---

[12] "How has it happened that these abuses have not only been suffered
to exist, but even to increase, under an Administration so decidedly popular and powerful? When this problem shall be solved to the satisfaction
of the public, the remedy will be supplied. The true answer to the question, how these abuses came to exist under such an Administration, is,
because the *Administration is such* as it is, because it is *popular*. Every
man of sound mind and lawful age knows that the President, nor any
other being of created existence, can exercise a personal inspection and
superintendence over all, or even a tenth part of the most important details of the public service. Yet every important transaction connected
with the public service is so managed by the subordinate officers, as to
throw the responsibility upon the President. If the delinquent officers
do not do this themselves, their defenders in Congress and out of Congress
do not fail, in effect, to fix the responsibility there. Whether in Congress,
or in the country, complaint is made of abuse in any branch of the public
service, the answer is, eternally, that the charge is meant as an attack
upon General Jackson! His great name and popularity are the shield and
buckler of every official delinquent, whether from incompetency or infi-
delity, from a clerk to the head of a Department—from the register or
receiver of a land office, or an Indian agent, to a Minister Plenipotentiary!
The name and services of General Jackson, I repeat, are invoked to shield
and cover, as with a mantle, every official transgression or omission, from
the highest to the lowest, whenever it suits the interest of party to avail
themselves of them.

"And the people are called upon to rally round—to stand by and
defend—not the individual arraigned—not the delinquent department, but
the President himself, who it is asserted through a thousand channels, is
intended to be struck at and stabbed through the sides of the accused
officer or Department. The people cannot at once detect the artifices of
party. They are jealous of everything which savors of an attack upon
General Jackson, and they in general act upon that suspicion. Those,
therefore, who dare, here or elsewhere, to find fault with the course of
affairs, upon any ground, instead of finding countenance from those in
power, or from the dominant party—instead of being cheered on in the
ungracious task of reform, are met on the threshold, with the charge of
secret and sinister motives—with anti-Jacksonism! They are told, that
their object is to assail the character of the hero of New Orleans, and the
conqueror of the United States Bank; as if either one or the other of
those victories could be of any worth now or hereafter, except to protect
the Constitution, the country, and its liberties—as if those victories could
be of any value, if as the price of them we are to surrender that very
Constitution, those very liberties—those rich and glorious prizes for which

administration,[13] but none covered the whole ground so thoroughly and so accurately as did Bell.

The attacks made by Wise on the Speaker and the administration were capricious and, to his associates, extremely entertaining. His assertions, however, were more irritating than convincing. His own resolution, which called for an investigation of the method by which state banks of deposit had been selected, gave him an opportunity to vent his wrath upon Reuben M. Whitney, and upon those who had employed Whitney. His time was ill spent; assailing Whitney's reputation was like slaying the dead.

Throughout the session the Presidential campaign was a topic of absorbing interest. Few questions came before the House that did not elicit a discussion of the approaching election. This was natural, perhaps, for Van Buren had been nominated for the avowed purpose of continuing the policies of the present administration, and it was from these very policies that the White element of the party had revolted. On this subject personal animosity increased as the end of the session approached. As

those battles were fought and won. If those who venture to make charges against any department of the public service are not met precisely in this way, they are, at all events, told that General Jackson is the head of the Government—that he is responsible for all the executive branches of the public service, and no attack can be made upon any branch of the public service, therefore, without attacking him, and everybody knows that he does his duty. A most shameful, egregious, and pernicious flattery. But the absurdity of the argument does not prevent it from being constantly interposed. The argument is, that because General Jackson is able, faithful, and patriotic, in the discharge of all his duties, therefore all the subordinate officers of the Government are so likewise. But more: if anyone shall reply to all this, and that he means no attack upon General Jackson, that he is willing to exonerate him from any agency in the abuses which are alleged to exist, he is forthwith denounced as a hypocrite—as a dastardly assailant, who wants the courage and independence to make a direct attack. He is dared to come forward like a man, and assail General Jackson as the author of all these abuses—his pride is appealed to—his feelings are chafed to draw him on to utter the fatal denunciation; and the moment he does so, the myrmidons of the party stand ready to hack him to pieces! These, sir, are the true *causes* of the continued abuses in the public service.''

[13] Robertson, of Virginia, when speaking (April 5) on the same bill, asserted that the administration desired a large appropriation for the navy so that there might be no surplus to distribute among the states.

if to make amends for the moderation displayed in his speech on the naval appropriation bill, Bell, when discussing the river and harbor bill on June 23, severely castigated both the Speaker and the administration. He charged the administration with deliberate extravagance, and said that the Committee of Ways and Means had been purposely organized by Polk "upon a principle of extravagance."[14] His purpose was to show, as Robertson, of Virginia, had tried to show when discussing the naval appropriation bill on April 5 that the administration hoped to nullify the effect of Clay's "distribution bill" by leaving no surplus for distribution among the states. However, it is difficult to see how Polk could have anticipated the passage of this bill when he appointed the Committee of Ways and Means.

Bell had little reason to complain of Polk's committees, for, as Gillet, of New York, pointed out (June 24), they were substantially the same as those appointed by himself.[15] In selecting his committees Polk had given no greater advantage to the majority than was customary, yet it is interesting to recall in this connection that he, too, during the Adams administration, had complained because "studied majorities" had been placed on committees, "in conformity to a previous secret understanding,

---

[14] "I have said that I regard this bill as the result of a deliberate system of extravagance—of a plan for increasing the wants of the Government, and exhausting the Treasury. . . . I affirm that your Committee of Ways and Means of this House was organized upon a principle of extravagance. Look at the composition of that committee, sir, and then tell me it was not constituted with a deep design, and expressly with a view to the largest expenditure for which a pretext could be found, in every branch of the public service. Was there ever such a Committee of Ways and Means appointed in this House? Was there ever a more palpable desertion of the principle of representation—a more shameful abandonment of the interests of the entire interior of the country?" (*Cong. Globe*, 24 Cong., 1 sess., App., 745).

[15] Gillet scathingly denounced Bell's attitude toward Polk. He twitted Bell with not having defended his constituent (the President) when during the last Congress he had been called a *toothless tyrant* by a member of the opposition party. Repelling such attacks upon the President and declining to attend a caucus of the Tennessee delegation were the only crimes, said Gillet, of which Polk could be convicted, and as Speaker, "even his political opponents bear testimony to his capacity, honesty, and impartiality."

among the favorites at Court."[16]   Both men advocated majority
rule, yet neither accepted it with good grace when he chanced to
be numbered with the minority.

In this same speech Bell reverted to the caucus of the Tennessee delegation, which had been called to consider the nomination of Judge White.   He said that the main object of the
meeting had been to test the sincerity of certain members and
that two of these gentlemen, Polk and Grundy, "are at this
moment in the enjoyment of the rewards of their hypocrisy and
their treachery to their colleagues."   He still spoke with respect
of General Jackson and denied that he had ever called the President a tyrant or a crouching sycophant.   "He may be the master
of *slaves* and *menials*," said Bell, "but nature has disqualified
him from becoming one himself."

The first session of the twenty-fourth Congress terminated
on July 4, 1836.   Among its legislative acts were the admission
to statehood of Arkansas and Michigan, and the reorganization
of the general post-office along lines advocated by Amos Kendall.
Another law approved the President's order for removing public
deposits from the Bank of the United States, and regulated for
the future the method of depositing public money in state banks.
As a result of the payment in full of the national debt, Clay
introduced in the Senate his well-known measure for distributing
among the states the surplus revenue of the federal government.
As it was made to assume the guise of a deposit rather than a
gift, the bill passed both houses of Congress and was signed—
but with reluctance—by the President.   On June 7, while the
bill was before the House, an attempt was made to refer it to the
Committee of the Whole, for the purpose, said the *Globe,* of pro-
longing the debate and thereby defeating the admission of Arkansas and Michigan.   Polk blocked such a reference by casting
his ballot in the negative and making it a tie vote.[17]

---

[16] Polk to Colonel Wm. Polk, Dec. 14, 1826, *Col. Wm. Polk Papers.*
[17] Washington *Globe,* June 10, 1836.

Although the Speakership is the most important and responsible position in the House, and although the Speaker's influence upon legislation is surpassed by few other officers of the federal government,[18] yet, from the very nature of his position, that influence is difficult to trace. By the personnel of his committees, by his decisions, by his control over debate by recognizing or refusing to recognize members who may desire to speak, one may trace in a general way the part played by the Speaker; but necessarily he takes little part in the discussions of the House. Polk did not even avail himself of the privilege of participating in debate when the House had resolved itself into a Committee of the Whole. For this reason his views on the various measures are not readily ascertained, and during this particular period his private correspondence affords little assistance. That he satisfied the party which elected him, there is abundant evidence in the records of the House, and in the public press. That he possessed the necessary knowledge and coolness of temperament to avoid the pitfalls prepared by his adversaries, is equally clear. ''Never,'' said the editor of the Boston *Age,*

was man more rigidly and constantly assailed by a pack of untiring pursuers, than was Mr. Speaker Polk by his uncompromising assailants. They left no stone unturned that could be moved to his disadvantage. . . . But notwithstanding all the efforts that were made to destroy Mr. Polk, he passed the ordeal unscathed, and ultimately triumphed.

The editor said that he did not like Polk personally, and that he had preferred Bell for Speaker, still ''it is but an act of justice to say of him, that he discharged his duties with great ability, promptness, and throughout the session was popular with an immense majority of the members,'' and self-respect compelled

---

18 Mrs. Polk probably voiced her husband's sentiments when she said, years afterward: ''The Speaker, if the proper person, and with a correct idea of his position, has even more power and influence over legislation, and in directing the policy of parties, than the President or any other public officer.'' Conversation with Samuel J. Randall. Quoted in Nelson, *Memorials of Sarah Childress Polk,* 206.

northern Whigs to support the Speaker in putting down Wise and his friends.[19]

After the adjournment of Congress on July 4, the great problem to be solved by the administration forces was not so much how to elect Van Buren, for that seemed certain, but how to save Tennessee. The prospect of losing the vote of the President's own state was most humiliating to himself and to the entire party. At first Jackson could not believe such a calamity possible; but, as the campaign proceeded, even he began to realize that, if the state could be saved at all, it could be done only by heroic efforts.

As usual, Jackson spent his vacation at the Hermitage, and during the summer he was honored with public dinners at various places. The people of Nashville entertained him with a barbecue to which "all creation" was invited.[20] The press and the platform of the respective parties vied with each other in regaling the people with political gasconade and personal abuse of the opposing politicians. On the President's side were Polk, Grundy, Cave Johnson, and Judge Catron, assisted by many lesser lights who followed their directions. Opposed to them were White, Bell, Peyton, and Foster, aided by a much longer and much abler list of second-rate assistants than could be rallied to the Jackson standard.

The most serious handicap with which the administration leaders had to cope was the want of an influential press. The Nashville *Union,* which had been founded after Bell had obtained control of the other Nashville papers, had never prospered, and was now in the final stages of bankruptcy. Long, the proprietor, had given up in despair and gone to Athens in East Tennessee to edit an obscure Van Buren sheet of precarious existence.[21] Due to drink, Laughlin, the editor of the *Union,* had become so unreliable that Catron, in the heat of the campaign, was forced

---

[19] Boston *Age,* Aug. 17, 1836; copy among *Polk Papers.*
[20] Laughlin to Polk, Aug. 8, 1836, *Polk Papers.*
[21] Long to Polk, Aug. 21, 1836, *ibid.*

to come to the rescue and edit the paper himself.[22] The Washington *Globe* devoted considerable space to political affairs in Tennessee. It tried to convince the people of the state that White could not by any possibility be elected, and that his nomination had been the work of instruments of Clay and Calhoun, who were conspiring against Jackson and Van Buren and attempting to deceive the people of Tennessee.[23] Bell, of course, was charged with being the chief conspirator. "It is painful," said the *Globe* on October 7,

> to a fair mind to deal with petty tricks—the offspring of low cunning— of a man educated as a pettifogger, and improved into a political Machiavel by a persevering study of the arts of deception in a seven years' apprenticeship in Congress. John Bell has arrived at a point which entitles him to a diploma as a political imposter

who is trying to deceive the people of Tennessee. As examples of Bell's hypocrisy, it cited his original opposition to White and his attempt to induce R. M. Johnson to run for President on a bank platform.

Much emphasis was placed on White's alleged affiliation with friends of the United States Bank. Bell's "Cassedy letter" was said to have pledged White, in the event of his election, to sign a bill for rechartering the bank. In several letters, Van Buren had already stated his unalterable opposition to such an institution, and by so doing furnished an excuse for the catechizing of his rival. In a letter addressed to him by one of the local Democrats, White was asked the definite question whether he, if elected, would sign a bill to establish a bank of discount and deposit, or one of deposit only. It was hoped that the letter would place the judge in an embarrasing position, but this hope was not realized. He met the issue squarely by stating that, while he considered the bank question to be obsolete, he would nevertheless give his

---

[22] After the campaign was over Catron, in a letter to Polk (Nov. 24) said that, while he hated to desert a man for "that infirmity," they must have a reliable èditor.

[23] Washington *Globe*, Aug. 27 and Sept. 5, 1836.

views on the subject. He had always believed, he said, that Congress did not possess the power to authorize any bank to transact business within the states; moreover, even if the power existed, it should not be exercised. This was still his opinion.[24]

In a speech delivered at Knoxville in August, White had already given a very complete statement of the principles for which he stood. He enumerated the doctrines which had been advocated by himself and the President at the time of the latter's first election. For advocating these same doctrines, said he, the President is now "openly denouncing me as a 'red hot Federalist,' having abandoned his Administration and being as far from him as the poles are asunder." The judge claimed to uphold the Republican creed of Jefferson, while the President is on "that side which leads directly to monarchy, although I hope he does not so intend it."[25]

Not even Jackson could shake the faith of Tennesseans in the ability and the integrity of Judge White. Even though the motives of his leading supporters may have been somewhat questionable, nothing that was ignoble or equivocal could be traced to White himself. He carried the state in spite of the misrepresentations of his traducers, and never again during the life of the "hero of New Orleans" was Tennessee to be found in the Democratic column at a Presidential election—although one of her own sons was the candidate in 1844.

The President was greatly mortified by the loss of his state. He declared that White had always been a hypocrite, and that the "morals of society" demanded his exposure.[26] But the mote in

---

[24] Andrew A. Kincannon to White, Sept. 14; White to Kincannon, Sept. 19, 1836, *Polk Papers.*

[25] Speech printed in Scott, *Memoir of Hugh Lawson White*, 346 ff. Excerpts in Washington *Globe*, Sept. 23, 1836.

[26] "Nothing but falsehood appears to be the weapons of our modern new born White Whigs of Tennessee in their late political crusade. White, Bell, Peyton, Murray & Co. appear to have abandoned truth, and now when the election is over, does not wish to be held accountable for their falsehoods . . . should I live to get home, a duty I owe to truth & the morals of society will induce me to expose Judge White, Mr. Bell, Mr. Peyton,

his brother's eye obscured the huge beam in his own own; his unfair treatment of White had been the determining factor in making the Judge a candidate and in winning for him the electoral vote of the state.

Congress reassembled on December 5 and, on the following day, received the last annual message of General Jackson. This document criticized the operation of the deposit act passed at the last session and advised the adjustment of revenue to the actual needs of the government. It informed Congress of the promulgation of the "specie circular" and asked that the policy therein adopted be made permanent by legislative enactment. It urged that the finances of the government should be put on a hard money basis. The tone of the message was optimistic, and indicative of the satisfaction felt by the President with the results of his administration. It contained no hint that he even suspected the country to be already on the verge of one of its most disastrous industrial and financial crises.

To carry the administration program through the House was a task of little difficulty for the Speaker. Polk arranged his committees on a political basis, and there was a safe majority in that body to insure the passage of desired measures. It required both skill and patience, however, to preserve order and to render harmless the assaults of an opposition whose animosity had not been lessened by their recent defeat at the polls.

Early in the session there appeared a new avalanche of memorials in which Congress was asked to abolish slavery in the District of Columbia. Generally, but not always, they were presented by John Quincy Adams. Polk decided that the "gag rule" had

---

Mr. Murray, and their falsehoods, so that the moral part & truth loving portion of the citizens of Tennessee may judge what credit can be reposed in those men, when they make assertions as to the acts & doings of others. I now believe that Judge White has been acting the hypocrite in politics, all his life, and individually to me—that he is unprincipled & vindictive I have full proof—that he will willfully lie, his Knoxville speech amply shows. I can forgive, & will, but I never can forget hypocrisy, or the individual capable of it'' (Jackson to Rev. H. M. Cryer, Nov. 13, 1836, *Am. Hist. Mag.*, IV, 242–243).

expired with the last session, and so the whole question was once more open for discussion. After several heated debates, the rule was reënacted in an aggravated form which sent all such petitions to the table as soon as presented, without even the courtesy of a reference to a committee. Southern members looked upon these petitions as the work of fanatics[27] whose sole purpose was malicious mischief. They failed to realize that abolition was simply one among the many manifestations of the birth of a public conscience and of a desire to reform the world. The old idea that governments should not abridge personal privileges, even by eradicating admitted evils, was, during this period, rapidly giving way to a new belief that society as well as individuals possesses rights, and that governments are in duty bound to protect them. It was a period among which "isms" of various sorts flourished, and among the number, *abolitionism*. The most important and permanent product which resulted from this social unrest and striving for the ideal was the emergence of a public conscience and a determination to adjust individual conduct to the standards of public opinion. A feeling of responsibility for existing evil led the troubled conscience to seek power to eradicate it, and in seeking the necessary power the reformers naturally turned to the federal government. Calhoun understood the changed viewpoint far better than did his contemporaries. He realized that, on the subject of slavery, a national conscience had developed, although he may have exaggerated the part played in this development by the Nullification proclamation of General Jackson.[28]

---

[27] "Abolition," said Bynum, of North Carolina, Jan. 9, 1837, "is priestcraft [i.e. New England clergy], concocted and brought into existence by their unholy alliance with the superstitious and ignorant of both sexes."

[28] Speaking in the Senate on the Oregon bill, Aug. 12, 1849, Calhoun said: "The abolition of African slavery in its old form in the British West India Islands, and the long and violent agitation which preceded it, did much to arouse this feeling at the North, and confirm the impression that it was sinful. But something more was necessary to excite it into action,—and that was, a belief, on the part of those who thought it sinful, that they were responsible for its continuance.

"It was a considerable time before such a belief was created, except to a very limited extent. In the early stages of this Government, while

The enactment of gag rules resulted in more harm than good to the cause which they were intended to benefit. Many who had little sympathy with abolitionists disapproved of this drastic method of stifling public opinion. They regarded the gag laws as a fatal blow to the right of petition, although it is difficult to see why the southern members were not right in their contention that this right extended only to those who would petition about their own grievances, and not those of other persons. The right of the people to petition for a redress of their own grievances was never questioned by the most belligerent of the southern fire-eaters.

Polk was a slaveholder, but he did not let this fact influence his decisions. When objections were raised because Adams insisted upon presenting petitions from states other than Massachusetts the Speaker decided, on February 6, 1837, that "every member had a right to present a petition, come from what quarter it might." Adams thereupon informed the Speaker that he had a petition purporting to have come from slaves and asked if it would fall within the regular rule. The character of the petitioners presented a new point in procedure, which Polk did not attempt to decide; instead, he asked for a ruling by the House. Without seeking to ascertain the nature of the petition—which

it was yet called, and regarded to be, a federal Government, slavery was believed to be a local institution, and under the exclusive control of the Governments of the States. So long as this impression remained, little or no responsibility was felt on the part of any portion of the North, for its continuance. But with the growth of the power and influence of the Government, and its tendency to consolidation,—when it became usual to call the people of these States a nation, and this Government national, the States came to be regarded by a large portion of the North, as bearing the same relation to it, as the counties do to the States; and as much under the control of this Government, as the counties are under that of their respective State Governments. The increase of this belief was accompanied by a corresponding increase of the feeling of responsibility for the continuance of slavery, on the part of those in the North who considered it so. At this stage it was strengthened into conviction by the proclamation of General Jackson and the act of Congress authorizing him to employ the entire force of the Union against the Government and people of South Carolina." Having discovered the extent of *national* power, said Calhoun, the abolitionists have, since 1835, been striving to bring it into operation (Calhoun, *Works*, IV, 517–521).

turned out to be a hoax, and asked for the expulsion of Adams—southern members wasted much time in an intemperate tirade against the venerable ex-President. They at first demanded his expulsion, and, failing in this, asked that he should be censured "for giving color to an idea" that slaves might address a communication to Congress. After Adams had riddled their arguments with sarcasm and ridicule, the House finally ended the matter by deciding simply that slaves had no right to petition. The charge made by Adams that Polk had exercised arbitrary authority in his decisions on the subject of petitions seems to have been wholly unwarranted, for the Speaker accorded him every privilege which the rules of the House permitted.[29]

The Speaker's enemies tried on many occasions to confuse him by propounding unusual and complicated questions, but in this they were invariably disappointed. His thorough knowledge of parliamentary procedure, and his ability to anticipate their designs and to prepare for them, enabled him to render his decisions promptly and correctly. Never frustrated, he was quick to see the bearing of an unusual proposition.[30] Although he safeguarded the interests of the administration whenever possible, yet his rulings were sustained—almost without exception, by a considerable number of his political opponents.

The most severe charge which was brought against Polk during the session arose out of the investigation of Reuben M. Whitney's connection with the Treasury Department. It was alleged that Whitney had given out advance information to speculators

---

[29] Polk's opinion of Adams' conduct and his complaints is recorded in an undated manuscript in the *Polk Papers*. It is an answer to letters written by Adams to the Quincy *Patriot*. "The Speaker carries out and enforces the decisions of the majority & therefore he represents in his letter that the 'Speaker and the majority of the House' have undertaken to exercise 'arbitrary authority.' If Mr. Adams is unwilling to submit to the decisions of the majority of the House, he is unfit to be a member of that body. . . . His complaints that his petitions were not read,—shows either a total ignorance of the rules of the House, or is an attempt to impose on the public" (*Polk Papers*, undated, vol. 80).

[30] For example, Bell's motion of January 10 for leave to bring in a bill to secure freedom of elections.

regarding the purport of Jackson's specie circular, and that he had been a partner in the resulting speculations. It was said, also, that he had levied blackmail upon the state banks which had been selected as depositories for government funds. A majority of the committee which Polk appointed to investigate these charges exonerated Whitney, but, in a minority report, Peyton, of Tennessee, accused the Speaker and the majority of the committee with having deliberately covered the fraud out of subserviency to the President. Nothing better, he said, could be expected from a Speaker who had crawled up to his office and had exchanged principle for power.[31] Even if these charges had been true, Peyton was not the man to throw stones. Hamer, of Ohio, forced him to admit that he had himself solicited for Bell the support of the President on the plea that Bell was a good party man and that Polk had been seeking votes from the Nullifiers.

The short but stormy session was adjourned by the Speaker on March 3, 1837. Although Polk had been severely criticized by some of his enemies, no one—as was done two years later—refused to join in extending to him the customary vote of thanks. The administration and its defenders had been denounced in violent language for alleged interference in elections, abuse of the power of patronage, and derangement of the finances of the country. Investigations had been demanded, and in some cases undertaken, but the charges had not been sustained. Indeed, so long as Polk had the selection of committees, there was small danger that any malfeasance would be *officially* unearthed.

For good or for evil, General Jackson had triumphed over all opposition. Van Buren had been chosen to succeed him, Taney

---

[31] ''The *price*, in *these days*, which must be paid for *power*, is the *sale* and *prostration* of *every principle* of *honor*, *patriotism*, *independence;* and I fear, sir, the day is distant when we shall see the *Speaker* of an *American Congress* dare to appoint investigation committees, a majority of which will be in favor of inquiry, how important soever it may be to the *preservation* of the *institutions* and *liberties* of *this country*. . . . Any man who *crawls* up to that point [Speakership] in *these days*, will never hazard the *consequences* of a *patriotic*, a *generous*, or a *noble* action; it would be fatal to him.'' March 1, 1837 (*Cong. Globe*, 24 Cong., 2 sess., App., 349–359).

had been confirmed as Marshall's successor, the mortifying censure of the Senate had been expunged, and the Bank of the United States no longer existed as a federal institution. On the last day of the session Congress passed an act which not only carried out another of the President's wishes, but which affected materially the future career of the Speaker of the House. Incorporated in the civil appropriation bill was a clause providing for the outfit of a minister to Texas, which meant, in effect, a recognition of Texan independence. The already approaching financial crisis made Congress unwilling to continue by law the policy of the specie circular, as Jackson had recommended in his message; instead, that body sent him, on the last day of the session, a bill which would virtually annul the celebrated circular. But even in this, "Old Hickory" had his way. He declined to sign the bill on the ground that its provisions were obscure and contradictory.[32]

---

[32] Richardson, *Messages*, III, 282.

CHAPTER VII

SPEAKER OF THE HOUSE UNDER VAN BUREN

Judge White's victory in Tennessee humiliated, and for the time being discouraged, the Democrats of that state. Before the winter had passed, however, their hopes revived and they began to lay plans for the future. They were encouraged by the belief that White would never again be a candidate and that the main cause of defection would therefore be removed. In a letter to Polk, Nicholson said that the opposition leaders were determined to hold the state, and would do all in their power to injure Van Buren. But the people, said he, had gone over to White for purely personal reasons and would return to the Democratic fold.[1] Childress, also, had hopes that the people would renew their allegiance. He believed, on the other hand, that the leaders of the White party would vote for "Theodore Dwight himself" if he were run on the opposition ticket.[2] Still another informant discovered that the White faction was plotting to get control of the legislature for the purpose of ousting Grundy from the federal Senate. They were planning, he thought, to run Bailie Peyton for Governor; and should this be done, no one except Polk or Jackson could defeat him.[3] At the Hermitage Jackson was busily engaged in repelling slanders invented and circulated by the Whigs. One of these slanders was that, as a result of endorsing notes for relatives, the General had become financially ruined and now wanted a national bank. Protesting that he never had and never would favor a bank, Jackson announced his intention

---

[1] Nicholson to Polk, Jan. 22, 1837, *Polk Papers*.

[2] Childress to Polk, Feb. 17, 1837, *ibid*.

[3] J. H. Talbot to Polk, April 21, 1837, *ibid*.

to prepare an article on the subject which he desired Polk to see before its publication.[4]

Democrats were united in their desire to regain control of the state, but opinions differed as to the better method of procedure. Grundy advocated a conciliatory attitude toward the White supporters; this policy was adopted, and was voiced by John O. Bradford, the new editor of the Nashville *Union*.[5] But the seceders did not respond to kind treatment. Dunlap was badly beaten in his campaign for reëlection to Congress, and his district sent only bank supporters to the state legislature.[6] Cave Johnson was likewise unexpectedly defeated by an opponent who was as "bitter and malignant" as John Bell.[7] The result of the election caused a tempest at the Hermitage. Still blind to the real cause of the dissensions within his party, Jackson, in characteristic fashion, denounced the temporizing policy of Grundy and the *Union*.[8]

The outcome of the state elections and the fact that the sub-treasury plan was unpopular in Tennessee[9] led Catron and

[4] Jackson to Polk, May 22, 1837, *ibid.*

[5] Catron to Polk, July 7, 1837, *ibid.*

[6] Dunlap to Polk, Aug. 7, 1837, *ibid.*

[7] Johnson to Polk, Aug. 7, 1837, *ibid.* One gets an interesting glimpse of the prevailing professional ethics from his remark that he is going to Mississippi to practice law, for "I cannot charge my friends & my enemies will not employ me." In another letter to Polk, August 14, Johnson tells a story which indicates that election methods in his day were not unlike those of our own: "I was beaten in the last two days by the almost united action of the merchants & iron makers—who as if by concert upon my leaving a county for the last time went to work, under the pretence of collecting their debts, telling the people that they would be compelled to collect in gold & silver if I were elected—the price of property be reduced to almost nothing and the people ruined. Some of the iron makers, told their workmen, that they could not be employed if I was elected."

[8] "Davidson [County] has resulted as I expected, from the imbecile councils, of the Nashville politicians. The Union has been Muzzled by some unseen hands, and has been a great help to the enemy instead of benefit to the republican party. Mr. Grundy will feel the effects, of the combination, which has been produced by supineness & want of courage" (Jackson to Polk, Aug. 6, 1837, *Polk Papers*).

[9] James Walker informed Polk on August 27 that if the Van Buren administration should adopt the sub-treasury plan, it would find itself in

other prominent Democrats to believe that the state could never be regained by pursuing Grundy's conciliatory policy. It was a battle of numbers against wealth, said Catron,[10] and war to the knife was therefore the true Republican policy. He favored the sub-treasury plan, for "the Treasury is the arm of power" and must not be placed in private hands; the possession of government money by private banks "will convert the keepers into Federalists in principle & practice in a few years." Unlike Jackson and Van Buren, he advocated the emission of paper money by the Treasury, for the people want it and "numbers will govern in fact, in Congress, & out of it." Although he approved in general the idea of a sub-treasury, still, after reading the new President's message on the subject, he pronounced the plan there suggested to be sound in principle, but hardly possible in practice. The people, he said, demanded something more tangible, and unless provision were made for issuing paper money, the party would surely go down to defeat.[11] "Strike boldly," was his advice to Polk, "it is your habit, & the means of your elevation; it is expected of you."[12]

The echo of Jackson's farewell address had scarcely died away before the long-gathering financial storm burst upon the country, leaving in its wake the wrecks of shattered banks, ruined business enterprises, and a panic-stricken people. So desperate were

---

the minority in Tennessee, as the plan was too unwieldy and costly. White, he said, had announced that he was not opposed to a bank located in the District of Columbia, with branches in the states. Walker thought that this idea would win in Tennessee if states instead of individuals were made stockholders (*Polk Papers*).

10 "Open war, & to the knife, has ever been the course for the Republican side—no other position is left for it, nor has there been, since the days of Jefferson. It is the contest of Wealth against numbers; sapped by the statutes of descents when wealth consisted of Estates: but the European policy is here basing itself upon *incorporated* & merchantile wealth" (Catron to Polk, Sept. 2, 1837, *ibid.*).

11 Catron to Polk, Sept. 10, 1837, *ibid.*

12 "Go in for 30 or 40 millions, to be circulated fast as may be by the Govt—go for 20ties & over in gradations of tens. Strike out the interest feature—boldly declare that the farmers will hoard the notes bearing 5 per cent" (Catron to Polk, September 27, 1837, *ibid.*).

financial conditions that Van Buren felt constrained to convene the twenty-fifth Congress in extra session on September 4, 1837, for the purpose of laying before that body his plans for relief. His principal recommendation was the establishment of a sub-treasury; for experience had shown, he said, that depositing public money in state ·banks was little better than leaving it in the hands of the federal bank. The only safe custodian of the public funds was, in his opinion, the government itself. As a temporary remedy, he advised Congress to withhold further deposits with the states under the distribution act, and to authorize the emission of treasury notes. Although his recommendations were straight-forward and sensible, they were, for that very reason, unlikely to be followed. Even the members of his own party were divided in opinion concerning the cause of the trouble, consequently they did not agree on remedies to be applied. Catron, as we have seen, was an advocate of paper money, while Jackson and the President still believed in hard money. Jackson received advance information concerning the character of the message and was delighted with the news that the President would recommend a separation of government finances from all banks, and the collection of public revenues in gold and silver coin.[13]

The members of Congress who had striven so hard to defeat Van Buren at the polls were not disposed to aid him now by sympathetic coöperation. In the House they were far more intent upon making life uncomfortable for the Speaker and the President than they were on relieving the financial stress of their fellow-citizens. It was known, of course, that Polk would be reëlected, and before the ballot had been taken, Mercer, of Virginia, proposed to transfer from the Speaker to the House itself the power to appoint committees. While the suggestion was not adopted, Mercer had the satisfaction of insulting Polk by imply-ing that he could not be trusted. On the other hand, Patton, of Virginia, wished to have the rules so amended that the Speaker

---

13 Jackson to Polk, Aug. 6, 1837, *ibid.*

might have a vote on all questions, but his amendment was rejected by the House. As most of the business of the session would necessarily pass through the hands of the Committee of Ways and Means, Polk safeguarded the interests of the administration by selecting seven of its nine members from the ranks of his own party.

Although the President, when convening Congress, had definitely limited the scope of legislation, Adams was more terrified by the possible annexation of Texas than he was by the magnitude of the financial crisis. On September 13, he moved to ask the President whether Texas had offered to join the United States, and, if so, what had been the reply made by our government. Any proposition to annex it, declared Adams, would be unconstitutional—one which neither the President nor Congress "had any right to receive, entertain or consider." It was his firm opinion that "a very large portion of the people of this country, dearly as they loved the Union, would prefer its total dissolution to the act of annexation of Texas." The House, on September 18, curtailed his dissertations on the subject by passing a rule which limited discussions to questions included in the President's message. Adams tried by various devices to inject the subject of Texas into later discussions, but Polk rigorously enforced the rule just adopted.

The rule for limiting discussion did not deter Wise from offering a resolution which provided that a committee be chosen by *ballot* to investigate the causes, delays, and failures of the Florida war. Adams approved this method of selecting committees, for, said he, experience had proved that no real investigation would be prosecuted by any committee selected by the present Speaker.

Having failed in his attempt to deprive the Speaker of the power to make appointments, Wise welcomed the appearance in the House of the Senate bill for creating a sub-treasury. This subject gave him an opportunity to vent his wrath and sarcasm not only upon the "Greatest and Best," as he called General

Jackson, but upon Van Buren and Polk as well. The late and
present administrations, he said, "have deliberately and wickedly,
with malice aforethought, wrought this mischief" and should be
indicted by the people for their crimes. He took special delight
in reading one of Jackson's messages which had incorporated a
part of Polk's report—as chairman of the Committee of Ways
and Means—highly commending the safety and efficiency of state
banks. And now we read in the message of Van Buren, shouted
Wise, "that *the experiment has failed*"—the great chief, whom
all had been taught to regard as a god, was after all a weak
mortal whose wisdom was as fallible as that of other men.[14]

Little was accomplished during this brief session. The sub-
treasury bill was defeated, and Congress contented itself with
the enactment of emergency measures. The first three installments paid out under the operation of the distribution act were
permitted to remain with the states, but the fourth was postponed
and never paid. To meet the immediate needs of the government, the President was authorized to prepare interest-bearing
treasury notes to be issued to an amount not exceeding ten million dollars. Having failed to agree upon any permanent financial
policy, Congress, on October 19, adjourned until the regular
session in December.

Before Congress had adjourned, the Tennessee legislature met
in regular session. Governor Cannon assailed with some vehe-
mence both Jackson and his successor. The Whigs began at once
to formulate plans which they hoped might insure Polk's political downfall and prevent the reëlection of Grundy. Some of
the Democrats were in favor of silently ignoring their critics, but
Polk, who was still in Washington, urged the adoption of an
aggressive course and the prevention of the election of a Senator,
for the present at least.[15] Before he set out for Tennessee, Polk
was authorized by Grundy to withdraw his name, as candidate

14 *Cong. Globe*, 25 Cong., 1 sess., App., 318.
15 Jonas E. Thomas to Polk, Oct. 5; Polk to Nicholson, Oct. 9, 1837;
Polk Papers.

for Senator, should it develop that the interests of the administration might be promoted by so doing.[16] Grundy was reëlected, but not without difficulty, for the ranks of the Whigs were steadily increasing.

The Democrats were alarmed but not disheartened. A new editor, Cunningham, was put in charge of the *Union;* for to the moderation of Bradford, under Grundy's guidance, had Jackson attributed the recent defeats.[17] Most hopeful of all was Jackson himself; he prophesied that Tennessee would be "herself again" in less than two years, in spite of Bell's New England tour, which was designed to transfer the state to Webster and the Federalists.[18]

When the twenty-fifth Congress met in December for its second session, a rather unusual problem was presented to the House for solution. It was a question of settling a contested election of members from Mississippi, and, as the decision ultimately devolved upon the Speaker, Polk incurred the enmity of Sergeant S. Prentiss, a man quite as venomous as Wise or Peyton, and far more able than either.

In July, 1837, the Governor of Mississippi had called a special election in order that the state might send members to the extra session of Congress which had been proclaimed by President Van Buren. Claiborne and Gholson, the men chosen at the special election, were, at the extra session, declared by the House to be members for the entire term of the twenty-fifth Congress. Notwithstanding this decision of the House, Mississippi held another

---

16 Grundy to Polk, Oct. 17, 1837, *ibid.*

17 Although removed for the *moderation* of his editorials, Bradford was, on the other hand, dropped from the roll of divinity students by the Whig bishop for being so ardent a Democrat. The incident well illustrates the political intolerance of the period.

18 "The course of Mr. Bell in attending the aristocratic, federal & shin-plaster meetings in Boston & New York, & his speeches at those meetings, which is a transfer of Tennessee to Mr. Webster & the blue lights, abolitionists and vagrants, is working well here—it has opened the eyes of the democracy of Tennessee, and none of his Whigg friends here will guarantee the sale." Jackson to Grundy, Dec. 16, 1837 (*Am. Hist. Mag.*, V, 138–139).

election in November and chose for Representatives S. S. Prentiss and T. J. Ward. Claiborne and Gholson were supporters of the administration, and their friends in Mississippi, relying on the decision made by the House, took no part in the November election. As a result, Prentiss and Ward were easily elected. Each side now claimed its representatives to have been lawfully elected and appealed to the House for a decision. After prolonged debate the House reversed its former decision and pronounced the election of Claiborne and Gholson void. It then proceeded to ballot on the validity of the second Mississippi election at which Prentiss and Ward had been chosen. On this question the vote stood 117 to 117. Polk cast his ballot in the negative, and the whole matter was referred back to the people of the state, who later reëlected Prentiss and Ward. The "glorious infamy" which attached to the Speaker's vote against him, Prentiss never forgot. In a flight of oratory he told the people of Mississippi that "the still small voice of James K. Polk deprived you of that which a hundred thousand bayonets could not have forced upon you."[19] On his return to Congress he had the supreme satisfaction, not only of harassing the Speaker on every possible occasion, but of opposing the ordinary vote of thanks to Polk on his retirement from the Speakership.

Slade, of Vermont, precipitated a stormy debate on slavery by presenting, on December 20, two memorials which asked for the abolition of slavery in the District of Columbia. After moving that the memorials be referred to a select committee, he entered into a prolonged and scathing discussion of the slavery question in its various phases. Having recognized the member from Vermont, Polk found it difficult to prevent his continuing, since Slade for some time was careful to keep within the bounds of parliamentary rules. When he finally launched into a discussion of slavery in Virginia, a member entered a protest and

---

[19] Clipping from some Philadelphia paper, dated Feb. 7, 1838 (*Polk Papers*).

Polk ordered Slade to his seat.[20] Wise, Rhett, and other southern radicals were choking with rage. Several exhorted their colleagues to leave the hall in a body. After adjournment a meeting was held, and, although threats of disunion were freely made, few members were ready for so drastic a procedure.

On the following day Patton, of Virginia, introduced, as a "concession . . . for the sake of peace, harmony, and union," a gag rule more drastic than its predecessor. It directed that all petitions on the subject of abolition should be laid on the table "without being debated, printed, read or referred," and that no further action should be taken thereon. The rules were suspended, the previous question invoked, and the vote hurriedly taken. When his name was called, Adams shouted that the resolution violated the federal Constitution, whereupon the Speaker forced him to take his seat. Polk then ruled to be out of order the demand made by Adams that his reason for not voting should be entered in the journal. A few days later, Polk even extended the new "gag-rule," by deciding that a resolution of the Massachusetts legislature asking for a repeal of the gag rule also came under the rule itself and could not therefore be considered.[21]

Sectional feeling was still more embittered during this session by the killing, in a duel, of Jonathan Cilley, of Maine, by another member of the House, William J. Graves, of Kentucky. The demands made upon Cilley by Graves and his second, Wise, were held by many to have been extremely unreasonable. By such members the killing of Cilley was regarded as little better than premeditated murder. The appointment of a committee to investigate the circumstances of the duel with a view to punishing members who had taken part, led to a strange alignment in

---

[20] Polk said that, while his position would not permit him to state his own opinions on such agitation of this question, "they might readily be inferred by the House."

[21] January 3, 1838. Polk seems, however, to have felt that he had gone too far in this matter, for on February 5 he ruled to be in order a petition of similar purport from citizens of Massachusetts.

defense of the participants. Friends of Graves and Wise charged that Polk had "packed" the committee to the prejudice of the defendants; while Adams, declaring the investigation to be "an administration measure," not only condemned the committee for having prepared an opinion, but objected to receiving their report. So intense was partisan feeling that Sawyer, of North Carolina, objected to receiving a message from the President which arrived while the clerk was reading the report of the committee, but Polk promptly decided that the constitutional right of the President to send a message to the house at any time transcended the rule which required unanimous consent to its reception.

Hectoring of the Speaker continued to the end of the session. On June 23, Adams reached the climax of absurdity by demanding that Polk should reduce to writing some irrelevant remarks which Adams had made and which the Speaker had declared to be out of order. On Polk's refusal, Adams appealed from the decision. Needless to say, the House sustained the Speaker.

While Polk was successfully parrying the shafts of his enemies in Congress, his friends in Tennessee were compassing the downfall of Bell, as well as formulating new plans for the Speaker himself. Donelson was indefatigable in his efforts to *expose* Bell's *treachery*. From his retreat at the Hermitage "the chief" forwarded documents to the Speaker and requested him to answer Bell's charges against himself [Jackson], either in Congress or through the *Globe*.[22] Desirous of representing Polk's district in Congress, Nicholson saw in the Speaker excellent Vice-Presidential timber, but Polk was inclined to agree with other friends that he might be able to accomplish more good in the governor's chair. Ex-Governor Carroll had announced to Polk his willingness to become once more a candidate for the office, and promised to handle Cannon "without gloves";[23] but the politicians, fearing that he would be defeated, did not rally to his support.

<hr/>

22 Doneldson to Polk, Jan. 4; Jackson to Polk, Feb. 2, 1838; *Polk Papers.*
23 Carroll to Polk, Feb. 17, 1838, *ibid.*

Even before Polk had consented to run for governor, each party was striving to strengthen its own position in the state and to weaken the hold of its opponent. In Boston, C. G. Greene, under Polk's direction, collected evidence to prove that Bell, on his New England tour, had been entertained by Hartford Convention Federalists;[24] while in Tennessee, the Whig legislature instructed Grundy to vote against any sub-treasury bill that might come before the Senate. Although the purpose of this move was to force his resignation, he disappointed the Whigs by promptly announcing that he would obey his instructions. Much Whig literature was franked from Washington. White and Bell scattered widely the speech in which Wise had castigated Polk and the President.

From many sources Polk was importuned to accept the gubernatorial nomination, for it was believed that he could regain the state for the Democratic party.[25] Apparently the office was not attractive to him, yet duty to his party seemed to point in that direction. Late in the summer, after mature consideration, he finally consented to become a candidate. Many letters told him of the good effect which his acceptance had produced. One from Cave Johnson reported that in many places "whole neighborhoods" had returned to the Democratic party.[26]

The Democrats were still embarrassed by the weakness of their local papers, for Cunningham had proved to be quite as unsuccessful a journalist as Bradford. When seeking a more competent editor for the *Union,* Polk offered the position to

---

[24] Green to Polk, Jan. 18, 1838, *ibid.*

[25] One correspondent intimated that prospects of success might be better in the state than in Congress. Polk, he said, would redeem the state if any one could, and "If there is any possible chance of the opposition getting the upper hand in the ensuing Congress, perhaps this course might be the prudent one; as your friends would as soon be annihilated at once, as to see that *most* INFAMOUS OF ALL INFAMOUS PUPPIES, John Bell, triumph over you in a contest for the Speaker's chair. Should the opposition succeed in their views, this must and will be the result, as you are now the most dreaded and consequently the most hated by them" (W. S. Haynes to Polk, July 24, 1838, *ibid.*).

[26] Johnson to Polk, Nov. 2, 1838, *ibid.*

several persons in succession. Among the number were Edmund
Burke[27] and C. G. Greene, of Boston. It was Greene, who, when
declining the offer, suggested Jeremiah George Harris, then editor of the *Bay State Democrat*.[28] For the Democrats this proved
to be a most fortunate suggestion. In Harris they found a man
in every way suited to Tennessee politics—one who was more
than a match for his adversaries of the quill, with the possible
exception of Parson Brownlow. The *Union* was enlarged, and
on February 1, 1839, the proprietor, J. M. Smith, introduced the
new editor to the people of Tennessee. In the same issue Harris
announced his policy: namely, to fight for the principles of
Jefferson and his Republican successors, and for the overthrow
of "Federalism" in the state.[29] A week later Smith reported
to Polk that a war of words with Hall, editor of the *Banner,* had
already begun and that he [Smith] was much pleased with
Harris.[30]

The proprietor of the *Union* had no reason to revise his
opinion. Harris launched at once into a campaign of vituperation and merciless denunciation of the Whigs which endeared him
to his friends and made him dreaded by his opponents. He was
the type of editor in whom the people of the West delighted. He
and General Jackson became fast friends, but, in the main, it was
to Polk that he looked for counsel and guidance. He plunged
with zeal into the campaign against Governor Cannon and announced that "Tennessee has not seen so proud a day since the
election of her own Jackson to the Presidency as will that on

---

[27] Burke was later a Representative from New Hampshire. In 1845,
Polk put him in charge of the General Patent Office.

[28] Greene to Rives of the *Globe,* Dec. 3, 1838, *Polk Papers.*

[29] "That tory federalism of 1798, Hartford convention federalism
of 1814, and 'whig' Federalism of this day are identical, so far as they
relate to the two grand party divisions of the country, is too susceptible
of the clearest letter of proof to admit of a doubt."

[30] "Mr. Hall of the Banner has commenced the war with the new
editor of the 'Union' and if I am not mistaken he will find that he will
have a little more to do than he at present imagines" (Smith to Polk,
Feb. 7, 1839, *Polk Papers*).

which the sovereigns of her soil shall by their unbought suffrage call Mr. Polk to the gubernatorial chair.''[31]

This is not, however, the place for a prolonged discussion of Polk's gubernatorial campaign. Reserving this for another chapter, we may follow his career through his last session as Speaker of the House. Selected by the Democrats for the avowed purpose of bringing Tennessee back into the party fold, Polk, as he called to order the third session of the twenty-fifth Congress, was more cordially hated than ever by Bell, Wise, Prentiss, and other enemies of the administration.

Van Buren's message, which reached the House on December 4, 1838, was optimistic in tone. He informed Congress that the rapid improvement of financial conditions and the resumption of specie payment by the principal banks had proved beyond question that a federal bank is not indispensable. Reiterating the belief that a sub-treasury would prove to be the best agency for collecting and disbursing the public revenue, he again recommended its creation by law. He alluded to Swartwout's defalcation and asked for legislation which would make such peculation in future a felony.

The lawmaking body of the nation paid little heed to the President's recommendations. Jockeying for position suited their present mood far better than constructive legislation. Having made gains in recent political contests, the Whigs had high hopes of carrying the next Presidential election. Without as yet announcing any program for themselves, they employed all of

---

[31] Nashville *Union*, Feb. 8, 1839. In the same issue Harris quoted an article from the Pennsylvania *Reporter* in which that paper urged that Polk should be made Vice-President. Concerning Polk's record the *Reporter* said: ''Knowing that the Bank of the United States was about to bring the whole of its mighty influence to bear against the administration of Gen. Jackson, it was deemed of the highest importance to be well fortified at the point where the attack was to be made, and the chairman of the Committee of Ways and Means, as the financial organ of the administration, became the most important position in the House. Col. Polk's known position in opposition to the re-charter of that institution, his intimate acquaintance with its history and transactions, and his powers as a ready and able debater, recommended him for its occupancy. And well did he justify the confidence so reposed in him.''

their energies in heaping odium upon the administrations of Van Buren and his predecessor. In the House the session was stormy from the beginning. When they could enlist the votes of the so-called conservatives, the Whigs were able to outvote the Democrats, and the task of the Speaker was made still more difficult.

On the second day of the session, and before the President's message had been received, Adams fanned the flame of sectional discord by moving that all petitions, remonstrances, and resolutions, for or against the annexation of Texas, should be referred to a select committee. His resolution was laid on the table by a vote of 136 to 61. His solicitude on this subject proved to be unwarranted, for the President in his message assured Congress that all proposals for annexation had been withdrawn. Adams then submitted a resolution which called for a committee to investigate the controversy of Andrew Stevenson, late Speaker of the House and present minister to England, with Daniel O'Connell, a member of Parliament. This also was sent to the table, but it had accomplished its intended purpose of attaching odium to the administration.

Abolition petitions again made their appearance. The persistence of the reformers aroused the fears as well as the wrath of southern members, and slaveholders required guaranties for the protection of their "peculiar institution." On December 11, Atherton, of New Hampshire, submitted a series of resolutions the purport of which was to declare unconstitutional any interference with slavery either in the states or the District of Columbia, and to reënact the gag rule regarding petitions. After a brief debate these resolutions were adopted by the House. The adoption of the gag rule did not, however, eliminate the slavery question. On the thirteenth, Adams tried to introduce a resolution to the effect that no enactment of Congress could add to or deduct from the powers of Congress which had been conferred by the Constitution. On the same day, Wise offered a series of resolutions which were designed to deprive Congress of all power to interfere with slavery. In both cases permission to introduce the resolutions was denied by the House. While Polk applied the gag rule whenever possible, Cushing, of Massachusetts, won applause from the reformers by forcing the Speaker to decide that a protest against the constitutionality of the gag rule, although itself out of order, must be inserted in the *Journal*, if brought up on the following day in the form of a correction of the minutes.[32]

For the Whigs, the news of Swartwout's defalcation was an unusually sweet morsel, for it gave them an excuse to explore with telescope and microscope the administrations of Jackson and Van Buren. And, as the Democrats no longer had a majority in the House, it incidentally gave them a chance to humiliate Polk by depriving him of the power to appoint the investigating committee. In disposing of the questions mentioned in the President's message, Cambreleng had moved that the part relating to the defalcation be referred to the Committee of Ways and Means, of which he was chairman. On December 21, Garland, of Virginia, moved to amend by referring the question to a select committee of nine to be chosen by *ballot*. In a scurrilous tirade, Wise asserted that any committee appointed by the present Speaker would conceal rather than disclose the facts. He had, he said, been chairman of another committee selected by Polk to investigate the affairs of the General Post Office, and all his efforts to ascertain the truth had been defeated. Kendall, the Post Master General,[33] had declined to furnish information on the

---

[32] Dec. 21, 1838. *Cong. Globe*, 25 Cong., 3 sess., 59.

[33] Wise called Kendall "the President's *thinking* machine, and his *writing* machine—ay, and his *lying* machine! Sir, if General Jackson had been elected for a third term, one great good would have come of the evil—*Amos Kendall would have been worked to death!* Poor wretch, as he rode his Rosinante down Pennsylvania avenue, he looked like Death on a pale horse—he was chief overseer, chief reporter, amanuensis, scribe, accountant general, man of all work—nothing was well done without the aid of his diabolical genius." Shielding Kendall, said Wise, was the more reprehensible because Jackson had so relentlessly pursued Tobias Watkins: "When the *indictments*, the *prosecutions*, were pressed unrelentingly against poor Watkins—when the Administration was crying,

ground that he was responsible to the President alone, and the majority of the committee had excluded everything that might reflect upon the administration. "Now, sir," said Wise to the Speaker,

I propose to show that *your* committee obeyed the will of their master. Yes, as you had done, by *packing* and stocking the committee. It was *your* committee—peculiarly and emphatically *yours*—its *appointment*, its *conduct*, its honor or *infamy*, will forever attach itself, sir, to *your name*. In illustrating the conduct of that committee, I could consume days to show how the plainest and most obvious and undeniable propositions were voted down; how resolution after resolution, question after question to witnesses, going into the very vitals of inquiry, were unblushingly rejected and stifled by the majority of the committee . . . *you*, the Speaker, the President of the United States, the heads of Executive Departments, *your* committee, and your whole party, combined and conspired to stifle investigation.

Some of Wise's friends asked him to yield the floor for a motion to adjourn. He declined on the plea that he might never get it again, for, said he to the Speaker, "I distrust you, sir."[34] Polk bore the onslaught with dignity and composure, and without interference until Wise referred to Benton as the "monster" who was to perpetuate the present dynasty. On January 8, 1839, he again assailed the Speaker and compared him to a gambler who plays with loaded dice.[35]

It was believed by the Speaker's friends that Wise, Peyton, and Clay were trying to provoke him into sending a challenge,[36] for the "murder" of Jonathan Cilly had not been forgotten.

Shylock-like, 'my bond, my bond!' against one of Mr. Adams's defaulters, then 'general and minute inquiries' were not only lawful, but a duty; but, sir, the moment the band of investigation touched one of *his* 'little ones,' then inquiry was worse than a 'Spanish Inquisition.' "

[34] Dec. 21, 1838. *Cong. Globe*, 25 Cong., 3 sess., App., 386–387.

[35] "My colleague," said he, "wants the committee appointed by ballot, in order to avoid imputations on the *Speaker;* I want it appointed by ballot, to avoid the Speaker himself."

[36] According to a story printed in the *Globe*, August 21, 1844, on the authority of General Jackson, Clay at one time appeared at the bar of the House and said to Speaker Polk: "Go home, *G–d d–n you, where you belong!*" In 1844 this ejaculation was made the theme of a campaign song. During a heated debate in the House, Wise shouted to Polk: "*You are a damned little petty tyrant; I mean this personally—pocket it!*"

But Polk treated their insults with silent contempt, and by so doing did much to establish a new precedent in such "affairs of honor." His personal bravery was questioned by none except his bitter enemies, and even the impetuous Jackson commended him for ignoring such flagrant indignities.[37]

The committee was chosen by ballot, and, needless to say, a majority of its members were opposed to the administration. The Democrats asked for the privilege of selecting the minority members, but their request was denied. Both majority and minority reports were tabled by the House on February 27, 1839. The investigation had been successful only in intensifying political discord. In a letter to Polk, Jackson asked for an account of the investigation, and expressed the belief that Swartwout could not have invested all of the million and a quarter which he had taken. "Where is the balance?" he asked, "The Whiggs have it."[38] To Grundy he suggested that William B. Lewis and Daniel Jackson, if put on oath, might tell how Swartwout had invested some of his money.[39]

Defalcations had been both frequent and brazen, and their cause, as Underwood, of Kentucky, pointed out,[40] could be traced to Jackson's policy of filling offices with those "whose subserviency to the will of the President, and devotion to the interests of party, constituted their principal recommendation." But undoubtedly Bynum's statement was equally true—that, when demanding that the select committee be chosen by ballot, the Whigs were less interested in political purity than in blasting Polk's prospects in his gubernatorial campaign.[41]

---

[37] Jackson to W. P. Rowles, Aug. 24, 1840. Printed in Washington *Globe,* July 19, 1844.

[38] Jackson to Polk, Feb. 11, 1839, *Polk Papers.*

[39] "I have no doubt," he continued, "if the truth can be reached, that the Whigg merchants of New York hold in their hands of the revenue chargeable to Swartwout, from $600,000 to $800,000 if not more, and it is suggested that he loaned to our little Whigg printer, Hall of the Banner, some thousands." Jackson to Grundy, Feb. 20, 1839 (*Am. Mag. of Hist.,* V, 141–142).

[40] *Cong. Globe,* 25 Cong., 3 sess., App., 375.

[41] *Idem,* 125.

Unquestionably disintegration of the Jackson party was due in part to the jealousy of ambitious politicians who had failed to obtain what they considered to be an adequate reward for services rendered. But there was a deeper cause for defection—one based on the nature and ends of government itself. For example, a man of Bell's type—one who believed in constitutional government, and one whose penetrating mind enabled him so clearly to see the inevitable results of administering the government according to Jacksonian methods—never logically belonged in the ranks of the party which followed so loyally the dictates of the "old hero." Bell, and all others who viewed things as he did, were constitutionalists, and they gravitated naturally to the party which accepted the precepts of Hamilton, Marshall, and Webster. During Jackson's first term, and to some extent during his second, there was much confusion of thought on governmental principles and functions. Admiration for the man had obscured the vision of many who would otherwise have been quick to detect the inherent evils of Jacksonism. By the time Van Buren became President, the personal element had, to a considerable degree, disappeared from politics. In the party realignment which resulted, personal qualities were not entirely ignored; but of far greater importance was the attitude of statesmen and their supporters toward the fundamentals of government itself. On this question the issue was clear cut.

Several speeches delivered during this session show that their authors fully understood the nature of Jacksonism and its paralyzing influence upon constitutional government. The President in his message had attributed the success of our institutions to the "constant and direct supervision by the people over every public measure." With this as a text, Bell assailed the "democratic tendencies" of which the administration boasted, and made an ardent plea for a return to constitutional government:

The People are told that our ancestors, who framed the Constitution in 1789, were half a century in the rear of the improvements of the present age; that they had not the benefit of the new lights which experience has shed upon the subject of government since that time, and which are now in full blaze around us. The science of government, we are told, has made great strides since our Constitution was framed; and, in deed, that instrument is beginning to be looked upon by many rather as a device of bad men, to advance the interests of the few at the expense of the many, and forming an actual obstruction to that full tide of happiness and prosperity which awaits us when the inventions of modern democracy shall be substituted for it. At all events, it is proclaimed to be the duty of every man who would improve the condition of the human family to strengthen the democratic tendencies of the Constitution, and to disrobe or rather strip it of those limitations and restrictions upon the popular will, with which our unimproved ancestors have thought it necessary to encumber it. . . . In truth, sir, it cannot be disguised that there are a class of politicians in the country at this moment, whose aspirations it does not suit that any restriction, any limitation whatever, shall exist in the practice of the Government upon the will or absolutism of the majority; and, in the estimation of all their followers, our Constitution is defective.[42]

Deploring the attempt to bring about more immediate control by the people, Bell boldly asserted that

according to our system, the People do not, and cannot, exercise any *direct* supervision over any public measure. Their power, their influence, their supervision, can be constitutionally exercised only by petition and remonstrance, and by the utterance of their voice at the ballot-box.

This was but a simple statement of facts; nevertheless, it required temerity to proclaim such a truth in the face of clamor for the exercise of popular will. To Van Buren's declaration that the extension of practical democracy had strengthened the Union, Bell replied that never before had there been such a relaxation of all ties which bind society together.[43] The power of the people, he said, had not in reality been increased, for party discipline had deprived them of all voice in public affairs.[44] The

---

[42] Dec. 26, 1838. *Cong. Globe,* 25 Cong., 3 sess., App., 360–361.

[43] ''At no former period has so general a spirit of opposition to legal restraints or requirements manifested itself throughout the country, when they stand in the way of wilful passions or purposes of any kind. Slight regard for the Constitution and laws, commencing with the Government itself and its administrators, has gradually diffused itself over society.''

[44] ''Such is and has been the power of party discipline—such the despotic principle of party association for years, that the mass of the community have rather stood in the relation of subjects to be governed than the controlling elements of power.''

truth of this statement, however, only made more deplorable the fact that the party which Bell himself had helped to organize should keep up the fiction of popular sovereignty, and even outdo their opponents in catering to the passions of the multitude.

When discussing an appropriation bill, on February 19, 1839, Kennedy, of Maryland, diverged from his subject to give a critical analysis of Jacksonism and to point out its disastrous consequences. Jackson, he said, had been singularly unlucky as a reformer, although he had been an innovator "in the broadest and worst sense":

> His administration was one ceaseless change: change, sometimes stealing along in noiseless advance, sometimes bursting forth in bold, open-day achievement; one while sweeping with the breath of spring, at another with the rage and havoc of the tornado. We had ever change of men, change of measures, change of principles. . . . The pervading characteristic of that most anomalous and extraordinary administration was mutation—uncertainty—experiment. It lived in perpetual motion, defying all hope of repose; it rejoiced in turmoil, and revelled in paradox. . . . The idea of political consistency never entered the President's head—he had no perception of the meaning of the term.

Jackson's idol, continued Kennedy, was popularity, and whatever sustained popularity constituted the theory of his conduct. It was not that wholesome popularity based on services rendered, "but a domineering, wayward, arrogant popularity—an impatient, hectoring assumption of the right to lead, which repudiates all law, despises all observance, and maintains its supremacy by personal and party force." Jackson, said he, used his popularity to increase his power; and, in turn, he used that power to increase his popularity.[45]

---

[45] "The very boldness of his designs seemed to fascinate the public admiration: he dazzled the popular mind by that fearlessness which we were, for a time, accustomed to interpret as a proof of his honesty and uprightness of purpose. . . . . He flattered the People with the address of a practiced courtier, startled and amused them by the thunderclaps of his policy, identified his success with the gratification of their favorite passions, grappled himself with wonderful adroitness to the predominant sentiments, wishes, and prejudices of the great and massive majority—

On February 22, Slade, of Vermont, obtained the floor for the purpose of discussing the general appropriation bill. His time was mainly occupied, however, in a masterful arraignment of Jackson and Van Buren, and of their methods. He attributed the gift of prophecy to Benton, Van Buren, and R. M. Johnson, who, in 1826, had reported to the Senate on the evils of executive patronage. Patronage, they said, would inevitably lead to one man power. By exchanging patronage for votes the President would soon control not only both houses of Congress, but the entire country.[46] "What was prophecy in 1826," said Slade, "has become history in 1839."

Under the caption of the "Pretensions of Democracy," he contrasted the now obsolete Republicanism of Jefferson with

and became a monarch, an autocrat, by the sheer concentration of republican suffrage."

Having discussed in detail the methods by which Jackson had arrogated all authority to himself while professing reverence for the Constitution, Kennedy depicted most admirably the effect of Jacksonism, not alone upon the character of the government, but upon society itself. It led not merely to corruption in official circles, but it demoralized the masses, as well. "We lived," said he, "in the midst of convulsions. The public taste was vitiated and fed by the stimulous of constantly recurring political eruptions; it delighted in strange conjectures—the heavings and spasms of that capricious power which displayed itself in such fantastic action at the capital. A spirit of insubordination, of misrule and riot became diffused through the community. Wild and visionary theories of political duty were disseminated abroad and showed themselves, in the most mischievous forms, in the proceedings of the State Legislatures. The most abstruse and difficult problems of political economy—questions of currency, finance, constitutional power—were summarily but authoritatively disposed of by the shallowest pretenders to statesmanship; and the oldest and best institutions of the country attacked and beaten down by political charlatans. Knowledge, deliberation, experience, all were obliged to give way to this newly-inspired intuition; and the greatest pains were taken by party leaders and demagogues to deceive the people into the belief that the profoundest questions of government might be consigned to the decision of men of the lowest scale of qualification in political science" (*Cong. Globe,* 25 Cong., 3 sess., App., 410–412). The whole speech is well worth reading.

[46] "We must look forward to the time when the nomination of a President can carry any man through the Senate, and his recommendation can carry any measure through the two Houses of Congress; when the principle of public action will be open and avowed—the President wants my vote, and I want his patronage; I will vote as he wishes, and he will give me the office I wish for. What will this be but the government of one man? and what is the government of one man, but a monarchy?" Quoted from their report by Slade.

the madness of Jacksonian Democracy—*"the* Democracy," as it is called. Its chief characteristic, said he, is sham, and it relies for its success upon fomenting class prejudice.[47] He read the well-known letter to Monroe in which Jackson urged the President to crush the "monster, party spirit," and contrasted the sentiments expressed in that letter with the practice of the administration of its author. Hypocritical as had been the pretensions to political virtue of those who had brought General Jackson forward for the Presidency, Slade did not believe that even they had fully realized the political debauchery upon which they were entering.[48]

The Speaker, to whom this merciless, but for the most part well-merited, arraignment of Jacksonism was officially addressed, listened, undismayed by the perils which were being depicted. None believed more thoroughly in party discipline than he, and few had been more closely identified with the administrations of Jackson and Van Buren. He had effectively served his party in many capacities, from conducting the bank war in the House down to establishing local party newspapers. His enemies fully recognized his skill as a political strategist, even though they denounced him as the tool of those whom he served.

---

[47] "Thus, the rich are made an object of jealousy to the poor. The laborer is excited against the capitalist—the indolent and improvident against the industrious and frugal—the ignorant against the learned and intelligent—and even the vicious and abandoned against the virtuous and upright. Associated wealth, no matter how widely it may embrace men of small means, is declared to be monopolizing and dangerous. Banks, however prudently and safely managed, are denounced as the money making machines of the wealthy, designed only to make the rich richer and the poor poorer. Factitious distinctions are created. Jealousies are excited. An imaginary aristocracy is raised up in the midst of every community; and nothing can be heard but the war-cry—down with monopolies, and down with the aristocracy."

[48] "It seems impossible they should have dreamed that General Jackson, the author of the noble sentiments I have quoted, could ever be brought to enact, in his own administration, an utter falsification of every profession they contained—a falsification so complete, that there should not be, as in truth, there is not, found a single one of his friends whose face does not crimson with blushes at an exhibit of the contrast" (*Cong. Globe,* 25 Cong., 3 sess., App. 323 ff).

Jacksonism was not without its defenders, although they failed to match their opponents in oratorical powers or in logical arguments. Crary, of Michigan, saw in the Supreme Court a political body "of the worst character," and he commended Jackson for having assumed the right to construe the Constitution as he pleased. As soon as men are elevated to that court, said Crary, they apply themselves to the study of British law and British precedents, and "they cannot be operated upon by the healthy influence of a sound public opinon."[49] Rhett, of South Carolina, said that the country had always been divided into two great political parties—one which feared government and another which feared the people. Inasmuch as strength in the government could be attained only at the expense of popular freedom, he believed, like Jefferson, in restricting the functions of government within the narrowest possible limits.[50]

The entire session was characterized by intense party and personal recrimination. The Democratic party was no longer omnipotent. It was reaping the harvest of its own misdeeds, and, in addition, it was held accountable for the distressed condition of the country, although this had resulted from causes economic rather than political. Hope of success added boldness to the attacks of its opponents. Twelve years earlier, an attack upon Jackson and his policies would have meant political suicide for the assailant; it was now one of the surest means of acquiring popularity.

More than any other member of the House, Polk was given credit by one party, and blame by the other, for the success of the legislative part of the Jackson program. Consequently his adversaries were unwilling to permit him to withdraw from national politics without making one more attempt to humiliate him in the eyes of the nation. They had been unsuccessful in their efforts to confuse him in the complexities of parliamentary

---

49 *Cong. Globe,* 25 Cong., 3 sess., App., 154.
50 *Idem,* 134.

procedure. Their insulting invectives and their invitations to
personal combat had been received with a dignity and composure
that did credit to the Speaker. Unable to gratify their desire
to injure the Speaker in a more effective manner, his enemies
resorted to the petty and unprecedented course of opposing the
ordinary vote of thanks on his retirement from office. Prentiss,
who had, at a previous session, been deprived of a seat in the
House by Polk's casting vote, was chief actor and stage manager
in this puerile *opera bouffe*. The resolution which thanked the
Speaker for "the able, impartial, and dignified manner" in which
he had presided over the House, Prentiss moved to amend by
striking out the word *impartial*. Prentiss did not "deny the
capacity of the *Speaker,* his dispatch of business, or his full and
thorough knowledge of parliamentary law," but he could not
agree that he had been *impartial*. He argued that the House
had expressed its distrust of the Speaker by taking from him the
appointment of the Swartwout committee. On the other hand,
he frankly admitted that his main objection to the resolution
was the favorable effect it would have upon Polk's gubernatorial
canvass in Tennessee. The Speaker, he said, was "playing a
political game," in which this resolution would constitute an
important part. Reviewing the personnel of the House committees, he condemned the Speaker for having put on all "political
committees" a greater number of administration men than the
small majority of that party would justify. He charged Polk
with being a tool of the President and of the party. "A more
perfectly party Speaker," said he, "one who would be more disposed to bend the rules of the House to meet the purposes of his
own side in politics, never had pressed the soft and ample cush-
ions of that gorgeous chair."[51]

There was little justification for this intemperate arraignment
and for the conduct of the other fifty-six members[52] who cooperated with Prentiss in opposing the customary vote of thanks.

[51] *Cong. Globe,* 25 Cong., 3 sess., 251–252.
[52] The vote stood 94 to 57.

When forming his committees, Polk had simply followed precedent. Many Whigs bore testimony to the justness of his decisions. And yet, he could hardly complain because of this partisan attack, for he had himself, on a former occasion, quite as unjustly accused a Speaker of subserviency to "the throne."[53]

Polk's farewell address to the House, in response to the resolution of thanks just passed, did much to destroy the effect of the shafts which had been hurled at him, and to elevate him in the opinion of fairminded men of all parties. He did not descend to answer the charges made against him or to indulge in recrimination. Without boasting, he alluded to his record of "constant and laborious" service,[54] and to the peculiar difficulties which attach to the office of Speaker. All Speakers. said he, have borne testimony to the impossibility of giving entire satisfaction to all, but

it has been made my duty to decide more questions of parliamentary law and order many of them of a complex and difficult character, arising often in the midst of high excitement, in the course of our proceedings, than had been decided, it is believed, by all my predecessors, from the formation of this Government.

Ignoring the minority, he thanked the majority for the evidence of their approbation. With good-tempered adroitness, he belittled the effect of the negative vote by declaring that he regarded the resolution just passed "as the highest and most valued testimony I have ever received from this House," because, under the circumstances, it was not a mere and a meaningless formality.[55] Many who, for partisan reasons, had voted against the resolution, as soon as Congress had adjourned, hastened to assure the late Speaker of their personal good will.[56] Instead of discrediting

---

[53] See pp. 19–20.

[54] "I can, perhaps, say what few others, if any can—that I have not failed to attend the daily sittings of this House a single day since I have been a member of it [14 years], save on a single occasion, when prevented for a short time by indisposition."

[55] *Cong. Globe,* 25 Cong., 3 sess., 252–253.

[56] The Nashville *Union,* March 22, 1839, quoted a letter from a person who had been present when Polk made his farewell address: "I

the Speaker, the minority had really made him an object of
interest throughout the Union. Their conduct was generally condemned, while his dignified reply raised him in the estimation
of all except the most zealous partisans.[57] His ability as a presiding officer was made still more apparent during the following
session by contrasting him with his successor, R. M. T. Hunter,
of Virginia. In the opinion of Cave Johnson, Hunter displayed
"ignorance of rules and a want of energy & power to command";
he feared that the House had chosen a boy to do the business of
a man.[58] J. W. Blackwell likewise reported that Hunter was
too young for the position. "While you were Speaker," said
he, "your friends praised, and your enemies abused you, but it
is now admitted, on all sides, that Jas. K. Polk was the best presiding officer that we have had for many years, and some say—
the best we ever had."[59]

At the close of the session Polk set out for Tennessee to
engage in an active campaign for the governorship. After fourteen years of service in the House of Representatives, his party
had assigned him duties in a new field of labor. Whatever his
success in the new field might be, no one even dreamed that the
retiring Speaker would next appear in Washington as President-
elect.

---

never witnessed more enthusiasm than the Speaker's admirable reply to
the vote elicited. Many of those who had voted in the negative expressed
their admiration of it, and gave evident signs of shame and regret at
the partisan course they had pursued. Even Mr. Graves, of Kentucky,
declared to a friend at his elbow that the Speaker had done as well as
any one could do under such circumstances, and stepping forward took
manly leave of him—as also did most of the members, a few bitter and
envious partisans excepted."

[57] For example, the Worcester (Mass.) *Palladium*, an independent
paper, said: "The disreputable conduct of the opposition members of
Congress, towards the Speaker of the House, at the close of the session,
makes that gentleman an object of peculiar interest, at the present
moment, to the whole democratic party of the Union. An effort was
made, as violent as it was uncourteous, to prevent the passage of the
usual complimentary resolution to the Speaker on his retiring from the
Chair. But it was an unavailing effort." Quoted by Nashville *Union*,
April 8, 1839.

[58] Johnson to Polk, Dec. 21, 1839, *Polk Papers*.

[59] Blackwell to Polk, Dec. 30, 1839, *ibid*.

CHAPTER VIII

POLK VERSUS CANNON, 1839

In May, 1838, shortly before he consented to become a candidate for the governorship of Tennessee, Polk was examined by a phrenologist, who, unless he had made a thorough study of his client beforehand, made some exceedingly shrewd *guesses*.[1] "He is very quick of perception"; so reads the prepared statement,

when he enjoys, he enjoys remarkably well, and when he suffers, he suffers most intently. . . . His is a remarkably active mind, restless unless he has something of importance to do; cannot be idle for a moment, is by nature one of the most industrious of men; loves mental labour & hard study as he does daily food; . . . and is throughout a *positive* character.

The traits pointed out in another part of the statement are manifest throughout Polk's public career, but especially so during the four years of his Presidency: He

thinks well of himself; often asks advice, & does just as he pleases; is one of the firmest of men; slow in committing himself, but once committed, does all in his power to carry through his measures . . . has many acquaintances, few bosom friends . . . has an astonishing command of *facts* and can call to mind with great precision what occurred long ago.

To those who are familiar with Polk's career in national politics only, one part of the phrenologist's statement might seem very wide of the mark. In it, the phrenologist says that Polk would have succeeded on the stage, for he has ability in the use of pungent sarcasm and ridicule and "could 'take off' the peculiarities of others if he would indulge this propensity." During the campaign which followed, Polk indulged this propensity to the full—especially against his opponent and Bailie Peyton—for ridicule and mimicry were among the chief weapons

---

[1] The phrenologist's name was O. S. Fowler, and the statement which he prepared bears the date of May 30, 1838 (*Polk Papers*).

used in assailing his adversaries. He is usually regarded as "a man who never smiled"; however this may have been, he was very successful in the art of amusing others.

There was rejoicing among the Democrats of Tennessee when, in September, 1838, Polk announced that he would enter the contest with Governor Newton Cannon for the highest office of his state. He received many letters in which the writers expressed their delight, promised support, and assured him of victory. It was the general opinion that he alone could restore the state to the Democratic party. It was, indeed, this belief that induced him to abandon his career in the national legislature. The unholy work of White and Bell must be undone; Old Hickory's state must be redeemed.

While he was still in Washington, presiding for the last time over the House of Representatives, Polk received many letters from Tennessee friends urging him to put the chief emphasis of his gubernatorial campaign on national issues and state internal improvements. It was pointed out that the Whigs would confine themselves almost exclusively to an attack upon the national administration and that the people of the state were much interested in internal development. The advice seems to have accorded with his own views. At any rate the topics suggested were the ones on which he placed the most emphasis.

As stated elsewhere, one of the most important events of Polk's campaign against Cannon was the advent of Jeremiah George Harris as editor of the Nashville *Union*. In response to the popular taste of the period, the press of the state had been notorious for extravagance of statement and personal abuse. It now entered upon a campaign of scurrility and abandon that has seldom been equaled ; Mark Twain's employer could scarcely have made his editorials more "peppery and to the point."[2] Equipped with a style that was cutting without descending to mere ribaldry, and with a pen dipped in wormwood, Harris goaded his

---

2 See Mark Twain, "Journalism in Tennessee," in *Sketches New and Old*.

opponents to a frenzy that was unprecedented. Lacking the
ability to imitate his style, his enemies often resorted to coarse
and vulgar abuse. No Whig editor in the state, except the in-
imitable Parson Brownlow, could cope with him in picturesque
invective. Harris had a spread-eagle woodcut prepared, large
enough to cover a considerable portion of the front page of his
paper. As its appearance in the *Union* was always accompanied
by news of Democratic victory, the Whigs expressed their contempt by calling it "Harris's buzzard."[3]

When Harris took charge of the *Union*, February 1, 1839,
A. A. Hall, of the Nashville *Banner*, was already making capital
of the charge made in Congress, by Wise and others, that Polk
had "packed" the committees of the House. The new editor
plunged at once into a vigorous defense of the Speaker and attributed the charges to jealousy of Polk's success and to a desire
to injure him in Tennessee. When the House voted to select the
Swartwout committee by ballot, the *Banner* exultingly heralded
the event as proof positive that the House, having learned by
experience that "Speaker Polk could not be trusted, proclaimed
the fact to the world."[4]

Some of the other Whig papers were even more scurrilous
than the *Banner*. For example, an article in the Knoxville
Register, signed "Curtius," spoke of Polk as "lost to a sense
of honesty, decency and integrity, laboring under insanity and
disgrace, pliant tool, traitor, apostate and tory."[5] The Memphis
Enquirer called him "a crouching sychophant" who lacked even

---

[3] It was said that a leading Whig, who had gone to the Murfreesborough post-office in quest of election news, saw through the window a
package of "*Unions*" and exclaimed in disgust: "It's all over; there is
Harris's infernal buzzard in the mail" (Phelan, *Hist. of Tenn.*, 381).

[4] "He has been tried by his peers and found wanting. A brand is
upon him that no time can efface. He may cry 'Out d—d spot,' but it
will abide with him for life" (Quoted in Nashville *Union*, February 8,
1839.) When criticizing a speech made by Dr. Duncan, candidate for
Congress, the *Banner* called it "the roaring, staving, bellowing, howling
Doctor's fanfaronade of bombast and nonsense" February 13, 1839.

[5] Quoted in *Union*, March 4, 1839.

the sense of shame.[6] A friend had written to Polk that "your election is dovetailed into that of every candidate for Congress in the State."[7] The Whigs apparently believed this, also, and were resolved at all hazard to defeat him.

In April, 1839, Polk formally opened his gubernatorial campaign by publishing a long and argumentative "Address to the People of Tennessee."[8] The address deals almost entirely with national issues, the nature of the government, and the principles of the two great political parties. It was pronounced by the *Banner*[9] to be "a poor enough concern"; but Phelan, with sounder judgment, has called it "the ablest political document which appeared in this State up to the time of the war."[10] For the student of history, it is one of the most interesting documents ever penned by its author, for in it he has stated fully and with clearness the principles and doctrines which he considered to be essential to all just government. It was evidently prepared with great care, and nowhere else does he give so full a statement of his views on so varied a list of subjects.

---

6 "Condemned and spit upon by a majority of the U. S. House of Representatives, in taking from him [Mr. Polk] the power of appointing committees, freely entrusted to all of his predecessors, but which he basely prostituted for the benefit of the party—of locofocoism—plainly told in language of thundering indignation that has been heard even to the shores of the seas, that he was no longer worthy of the confidence of Congress, like a crouching sychophant, instead of resigning his narrowed trust with shame, and disdaining tamely to see his integrity assailed by even those who exalted him, he submits, ignobly bears the rankling contumely, and in hope of political reward for 'self-sacrifice' upon the altar of loco-focoism, he still patiently ministers at its shrine reeking in corruption with a zeal that can only be inspired by a hope of reward.'' When quoting this, the *Union* replied in the same issue that "the raving of Mr. Prentiss, the ranting of Mr. Wise, and the management of Mr. Bell in reference to the appointment of the 'Swartwout Committee,' were all calculated for *effect* in Tennessee,'' and would be so regarded by the people (Nashville *Union*, March 4, 1839).

7 A. Balch to Polk, February 21, 1839, *Polk Papers.*

8 A copy in pamphlet form may be found in the *Polk Papers*, vol. 83. It is printed in full in the Nashville *Union*, April 10, 12, 15, 1839, as well as in other papers.

9 Nashville *Banner*, April 11, 1839. On April 17 the *Banner* called it "an elaborate and ingenious production, but characterized by a want of manliness, candor and sincerity.''

10 Phelan, *Hist. of Tenn.*, 381.

In stating his reasons for confining his address so largely to national questions, Polk asserted that the chief objections urged against him were based on the principles and policies which he had upheld as a member of Congress. He gave a historical summary[11] of the perennial contest between those who distrusted and ignored the will of the people and those who believed that government should carry into effect the popular will. The popular party, he said, had triumphed in the convention which drafted the Constitution, but Hamilton and his adherents soon procured by construction what they had failed to have embodied in the Constitution. Democracy triumphed under Jefferson, but under J. Q. Adams the

latitudinarian doctrines, with all the consolidating tendencies of the Hamilton school, as practiced under the administration of the elder Adams, were resuscitated and revived. It was publicly proclaimed that the wholesome restraints of the public will on the action of the servants of the people were to be disregarded, and that the 'Representative was not to be palsied by the will of his constituents.' It was declared by the Chief

---

[11] "In the origin of the Government there were two parties. In the Convention that framed the Constitution one party distrusted the power and capacity of the people for self-government, and wished a strong central government. They admired the British Constitution—they were in favor of a President and Senate for life—they were for forming a strong government, far removed from the popular control; they wished to abstract from the power of the States—to restrict the right of suffrage, and to create other influences than the will of the people to control the action of their public functionaries. This party was not successful in the convention, and a constitution was formed which invested the new government with a few delegated and well defined powers, leaving all others to the States and the people, to exercise according to their sovereign will. The parties in the convention were the germ of the two great political divisions, which afterwards contended, and are still contending for the mastery in the Government.

"No sooner was the government put in operation under the Constitution, than the enemies of popular control over public authority, attempted by a latitudinous construction of the Constitution, to make the government in practice what they had in vain attempted to make it in principle and form. Alexander Hamilton, a professed monarchist in principle, and in the Convention the leading advocate of a strong central government, was the first Secretary of the Treasury, and immediately began, by strained and unwarranted constructions of the Constitution, to enlarge the power and influence of the Federal Government, with the view of diminishing the power of popular will over the administration of the Government.'' Jefferson himself could scarcely have penned a more telling indictment against the Federalists.

Magistrate to be ineffably stupid to suppose that the Representatives of the people were deprived of the power to advance the public weal, thereby substituting the unrestrained discretion of Congress and of the Federal Government for the specific grants of power conferred by a Constitution of limitations and restrictions.

Polk's recital of historical occurrences was accurate and well put; but it was begging the question to imply, as he did, that the framers of the Constitution had intended that representatives should divest themselves of all judgment and become mere automatons for registering the popular will. Custom and a desire for reëlection may prevent members of Congress from exercising their own judgment, but undoubtedly Adams rather than Polk reflected the views of those who drafted the Constitution.

It was thought by many politicians of both parties that Clay would be the candidate of the Whigs at the approaching Presidential election. Polk, therefore, devoted a considerable portion of his address to Clay and the policies which he advocated. The principal achievements of the Federalist administrations were, in Polk's opinion, the grasping of power by the general government and the creation of the money power. Their successors, the Whigs, likewise stood for these evils, and in addition, had adopted Clay's "miscalled 'American System' of high tariff and internal improvements, the result of which combination would oppress the poor and increase the evils of executive patronage.

The administration of Jackson he eulogized without stint. The adherents of White were told that they had supported the judge because he had been represented to be a better "Jackson man" than Van Buren, consequently there was no reason now why they should not return to the party of the people. It was untrue, said he, that Jackson had changed since his elevation to power; his detractors, not he, had deserted to the enemy. "I," continued Polk,

in common with the whole Republican party, am represented to you as one of these changelings. In what have I changed? I opposed Henry Clay on account of his odious Federal doctrines, and his coalition with

Mr. Adams, and I oppose him still. I opposed the high tariff policy, and I oppose it still. I opposed Internal Improvements by the General Government, and I oppose them still. I supported the removal of the deposits, and I have not changed my language or my opinions in relation to that great measure. In fine, what single point is there, involving the principles of the great Republican party, in which my course has not been uniform since 1825, when I was first honored with a seat in Congress, down to the present day?

From a man who had a reputation for concealing his views, this was certainly a most unequivocal declaration. Moreover, it was a true declaration, and it required courage to make it under the existing political conditions in Tennessee. Whether right or wrong, Polk had not swerved from his original political platform, although many of the policies for which he stood had become unpopular in his state. He may have broken with Judge White for personal as well as political reasons, but on national issues he had been consistent. He pinned his faith now, as he had always done, on government by the will of the majority; and however chimerical this may be in practice, his most private correspondence indicates that his belief in its practicability was sincere. Passing lightly over state issues, he asked for approval or condemnation on his record in national politics—a record which was being grossly misrepresented by the Whig papers of the state.[12]

At Murfreesborough, on April 11, 1839, Polk made his first speech of the campaign. Governor Cannon attended and was invited by Polk to speak first, on account of his age and office. This he declined to do, saying that, although he had not come prepared to speak, he might make a reply. Polk talked for two and a half hours, mainly on national issues and in commendation of the Jackson party. He said little on state issues, of which the *Banner* (April 15) ungenerously credited him with knowing "very little more than the man in the moon."

---

[12] "For months past I have been the unceasing and almost exclusive object of their calumnies and misrepresentation."

Cannon in reply said that *he* had never "clung to the coat tail" of General Jackson, and when "danger approached, jumped into his pocket," but, instead, he had had to "stem the buffetings of his wrath." Before the Creek war, according to his own story, Cannon was a member of a jury selected to try one Magnus on the charge of having murdered Patton Anderson, a personal friend of Jackson. When Cannon voted for acquittal, Jackson, pointing his finger at the young juror, exclaimed, "I'll mark you, young man!" Cannon insinuated, also, that, in fulfillment of this promise, Jackson had, during the Creek war, purposely exposed Cannon and a small detachment of troops to almost certain death, while the General himself remained in safety on the other side of the river. He was a "tyrant by nature and education," and no one could be his follower "who would not be his tool and his slave."[13]

In a brief rejoinder Polk, according to the *Union* (April 12), made the "roof ring" with his "power of ridicule." The *Banner,* on the other hand, reported that "the locomotive candidate seemed to feel deeply that he had caught a *Tartar,*" and that Governor Cannon "triumphantly overthrew" him.[14]

Polk's superiority, both in intellect and debating powers, was apparent from the beginning of the campaign. Cannon was slow and prosaic—lacking in force and personal magnetism. He was unable either to hold the attention or to arouse the sympathy of the multitude. He had until recently professed loyalty to Democratic doctrines, and he still seemed uncertain as to whether he had become a full-fledged Whig.[15] There was, on the contrary,

---

[13] Nashville *Rep. Banner,* April 16; Nashville *Union,* April 12, 1839.

[14] The *Banner* made much sport of Polk's "grins and grimaces" in imitation of Bailie Peyton and Henry Clay. "James K. Polk, the narrow minded, superficial, little, grimacing politician attempting to expand his outward man, gesture and voice into something his hearers might take for *Henry Clay!*" He tried, also, it said, to imitate Webster (*Banner,* April 13, 1839).

[15] In his reply to Polk, Cannon said: "I Le.ieve I have always been a Democrat. Indeed, they used to call me an Ultra Democrat, a Radical." He claimed to be a Democrat still, but not in favor of Van Buren (*Banner,* April 16, 1839).

no uncertainty about Polk's views, and he knew how to state them
most effectively. He was, says Phelan,[16]

the first great "stump speaker" . . . always full of his subject, ready at
retort, sophistical, quick to capture and turn the guns of the enemy against
him, adroit in avoiding an issue whose result must be unfavorable, thoroughly equipped with forcible illustrations, humorous anecdotes, and a
ridicule which ranged through all the changes from burlesque to wit.

With no pretensions to oratory, his strength lay in his ability to
state the issues clearly and forcibly, and to argue these issues in
language that was simple and convincing.

On April 13, the candidates met again at Lebanon. On state
issues they were in substantial agreement, and once more their
time was occupied mainly with a discussion of national affairs.
At the close of the debate Governor Cannon, pleading important
state business, set out for Nashville. Polk informed his wife
that the Governor and himself got on "very harmoniously," but
there was little harmony in his relations with Bell.

Polk and Cannon had consumed the entire afternoon, and
Bell, who was not expected to take part, took the stump at 5:30
in a "rage of passion." He talked until sunset, and then an-
nounced that he would continue at the courthouse after supper.
His first address, as reported, was most abusive in character.[17]
Polk wrote home that even Bell's friends were disgusted by the
speech, and that he had no difficulty, in his reply, in putting
Bell in the wrong and winning tremendous applause.[18]

Governor Cannon resumed the debates, at McMinnville, on
April 18, but shortly after he retired from the stump entirely.
At McMinnville, having been taunted with indecision, he at last

---

[16] *Hist. of Tenn.*, 377.

[17] He said that Hopkins L. Turney, Representative from Tennessee,
"was not good enough for the Penitentiary—that Amos Lane was a
scoundrel—that Dr. Duncan was a moral pestilence—that these were the
tools which Col. Polk set forward to make speeches in Congress, instead
of coming out and answering him [Bell] on the floor of Congress face to
face" (*Union*, April 17, 1839).

[18] Polk to Mrs. Polk, April 14, 1839, *Polk Papers.*

came out squarely for Clay, in the event of his nomination.[19] Because Polk had declared here and elsewhere that he and Cannon differed little in their views on state questions, the *Banner* called Polk a "Government emissary" and regarded it as extremely impudent in him to try to depose the Governor for his dislike of Van Buren.[20]

The people in those days took keen delight in political campaigns. They attended in large numbers, and no debate was long enough to be tedious if it were spiced with personal recrimination and with what passed for witty retorts. The popular ear in Tennessee of that day was not attuned to a very high grade of humor, while, in argument, pungent thrusts rather than logic won the sympathy of the audience. The festal side of a campaign was quite as important as the forensic, consequently political debates were usually held in open air, accompanied by a banquet or a barbecue. When Polk reached East Tennessee, the Whig section of the state, special pains were taken by the Democrats to give his journey the appearance of a triumphal procession.[21] Even though he could not hope to gain many votes in this section, the appearance of popularity in a Whig stronghold might aid him in other parts of the state.

---

[19] Nashville *Union,* April 22, 1839.

[20] "Is it not a most impudent, unheard of request, then, on his part, to the people of Tennessee, that they should turn Governor Cannon out and put *him* in, all because the Governor is opposed to Mr. Van Buren's election? Is it not apparent that he is a Government emissary, traversing the State, county by county, with the sole view of revolutionizing it on the subject of national politics?" (*Banner,* April 19, 1839). On May 22, the same paper called Polk a deserter from genuine republican doctrines, "a political changeling—a weather cock, pointing ever in the direction from whence comes the breath of the President's nostrils—a devourer, eater-up of his own sentiments, formerly proclaimed in tones of self-gratification—a palace slave laborer for his master at Washington."

[21] The *Tennessee Sentinel* thus described a Polk meeting at Jonesborough on May 17, 1839: "As a means of enhancing the enjoyments of the day, suitable arrangements were made for a dinner, free to all of each party, without distinction, who might think proper to participate." After dinner there were toasts to Washington, Jackson, Van Buren, Polk, Amos Kendall, *et. al.,*—and one to "*Newton Cannon*—the friend and supporter of Henry Clay for the next Presidency. Will the freemen of Tennessee be thus transfererd by *dictation* from the mouth of any *Cannon?* Cries of No! No!" Quoted in Nashville *Union,* June 3, 1839.

The political contest was by no means confined to the stump and the platform. Wherever a group of people gathered, issues and candidates were freely discussed. Personal encounters not infrequently resulted[22] when arguments had failed to convince. Despite his surroundings, however, Polk always maintained his own dignity; although his language on the stump was often scathing and exasperating, he never descended to vulgarity or mere personal abuse.

Accuracy was not a desideratum in a political newspaper. That editor was most popular who could hurl grotesque epithets at his opponents and who always reported as well as prophesied victory for his own side. Harris of the *Union* fully measured up to the Democratic ideal,[23] and for this reason his paper wielded great political influence.

In June, A. A. Hall, of the *Banner,* caused consternation in Democratic ranks by quoting anti-slavery articles which had been written by Harris while he edited the New Bedford (Massachusetts) *Gazette.*[24] By befogging the issue and heaping abuse upon his accusers, Harris was quite successful in extricating himself from the difficulty. Nevertheless, the charge that Harris had been an abolitionist did Polk some injury in the canvass, for it was he who had been mainly responsible for bringing the editor to Nashville.[25] In order to divert attention from his own past record and to give new impetus to Democratic enthusiasm Harris

---

[22] For example, Polk's brother-in-law, Dr. Rucker, is reported to have thrashed a "bully" whom the Whigs had brought to Murfreesborough to provoke a quarrel with him (John W. Childress to his sister, Mrs. Polk, May 27, 1839, *Polk Papers*).

[23] For example, in reporting a debate between Bell and his opponent, Burton, the *Union* said that Bell abused Van Buren, eulogized Clay and called Polk "the travelling missionary," but Burton "literally dissected his opponent who has been schooled in the sophistries of partizanship, and laid the diseased limbs of Modern Whigism bare to the bone" (May 27, 1839).

[24] One of them, dated May 13, 1836, in opposing the annexation of Texas, called slavery "the blackest, the foulest, blot on our national escutchen," and said that it would be "the height of madness" to extend it over more territory (*Banner,* June 11, 1839).

[25] John W. Childress to Mrs. Polk, June 18, 1839, *Polk Papers.*

printed in the *Union* (June 24) the "Mecklenburg Declaration of Independence" and suggested its ratification on the Fourth of July. He dilated at length on the fact that Polk had been born in Mecklenburg county—a fact which proved that he had come from pure Democratic stock.

The Whigs hoped for good results from a speech made by Judge White in Knoxville, on the Fourth of July. He still professed adherence to Jeffersonian Republicanism, but denounced the Democrats, whose whole creed consisted in "always acting with the *same man*, or set of men." Far from being democrats they were, said he, "in reality *monarchists.*"[26] Harris was horrified because White had talked politics on the Fourth of July, but concluded from the "claptrap" which the judge had uttered that he must be in his "dotage."[27]

White's warning against monarchists did not produce the effect which the Whigs had anticipated, for Polk succeeded in winning back a considerable number of those who had supported the judge in 1836. Before the close of the campaign he received many letters telling of the good results which his canvass had achieved.[28]

Cannon was easily vanquished, and he retired from the stump, but Bell dogged Polk's footsteps, bringing into full play his great ability and oratorical powers. On July 17 he spoke at Nashville "from early candle-lighting until midnight" in an effort to defeat Polk in Middle Tennessee. He was, however, doomed to disappointment. On August 1 Polk was elected by a majority of three thousand votes, and Harris got out his "buzzard" to adorn the front page of the *Union* along with the election returns. The result of the campaign was justly regarded as a great

---

[26] Copied from Knoxville *Times* in Nashville *Banner*, July 18, 1839.

[27] Nashville *Union*, July 19, 1839.

[28] C. W. Hall, writing from Kingsport on July 12, told him that "one of my neighbors said the other day, 'Sir, I did not understand my political position, until I heard Col. Polk, and I then discovered most clearly, *that I was acting with men, who are opposed to my principles,* and I instantly resolved to quit their company'. . . . This is a common observation" (*Polk Papers*).

personal victory for Polk, inasmuch as the Whigs elected seven members of Congress and the Democrats only six.[29] The Democrats elected a majority of the state legislature, which gave them the power to get rid of the Whig Senators by hampering them with obnoxious instructions.

Up to the very last the Whigs of the state seemed confident of victory. They were reluctant to admit defeat even after the election had been held. But the *Banner,* on August 9, mournfully informed its readers that owing to a lack of proper organization in Middle Tennessee[30] the ''Spoilsmen for a season will have the management of affairs in the State.'' Two days before this, prominent Whigs held a meeting in Nashville. Resolutions were passed urging the organization of committees in every county for the purpose of retrieving the state. They invited Clay to visit Tennessee, but he was unable at the time to accept the invitation. Although the *Banner* from time to time reported enthusiastic Whig meetings, it was several weeks before there were signs of recovery from the shock of the recent defeat.

In their elation over Polk's election, the Democrats rather overrated its significance. It has already been noted that they regarded the result as a personal victory for Polk over his enemies; but, in addition, they interpreted it to mean that Tennessee had returned, or at least was returning, to the party of Jackson and Van Buren. Polk had been nominated for the avowed purpose of regaining the state for the national administration; he had made his canvass almost entirely on national issues; and Bell, as well as others, had opposed him on his record as an administration member of Congress. As his friend Maclin said in a letter, more importance was attached to Polk's success than to the election of any other candidate. There was, in his

---

[29] One of these was Cave Johnson. Writing to Polk on August 11 he said that he had been elected by a majority of 1300 votes, and, as he had entered the race only on account of Polk and Grundy, he expected to retire from politics at the end of his term (*Polk Papers*).

[30] On August 13 the same paper attributed the result to bribery and illegal voting.

opinion, but one thing lacking to make the triumph complete—
namely, the success of Burton over John Bell.[31]

To no one did the national effect of Polk's victory appear of
greater importance than to General Jackson. As soon as the
news reached him, he hastened to congratulate Polk and the
country on his election and ''the return of old democratic Tennessee to the republican fold again.'' With customary hyperbole
he predicted that ''it will be at least a century before she will
permit herself to be again duped into her late false position by
such jesuitical hypocrites & apostates as Bell, White & Co.''[32]
Polk was doubtless well aware of the program that was to be
carried into effect in the event of his election, and presumably
he aided in formulating it; therefore Jackson did not allude to
it in the letter just quoted. In a letter to Van Buren, however,
the General outlined the party plans in characteristic fashion.
As the Democrats have elected both governor and legislature,
said he,

of course Mr. Foster[33] & his gagg law will not any more trouble the U.
States Senate—Judge White must resign, or he will feel the weight of
instructions & a Senator elected over his head—the precedent set by our
last Legislature will justify this proceedure. My own opinion is, White
will resign—Bell being disappointed in going into the Senate to fill White's
vacancy, which was the price of his apostacy, if he is disappointed in getting into the Speaker's chair, will resign or *cut his throat* in despair &
disappointment; and this catastrophy will end the existance of bluelight
federalism in Tennessee.

For so great a triumph, he gave the principal credit to Colonel
Polk and General Robert Armstrong.[34] As will appear in the

---

[31] Sacfield Maclin to Polk, August 10, 1839, *Polk Papers*.

[32] Jackson to Polk, August 13, 1839, *ibid*.

[33] E. H. Foster was elected to the Senate when Grundy resigned.

[34] Jackson to Van Buren, August 12, 1839, *Van Buren Papers*s ''I
hope,'' wrote Richard Warner to Polk, September 29, ''we shall be able
to adopt such measures as will compel Foster to give up the seat he and
his friends usurped at the last session.'' The legislature should instruct
the Senators to vote for the sub-treasury bill. If this does not bring
''poor old White'' to his senses, it should then be ascertained whether
he is a Senator at all. (On account of ill health, White had tendered his
resignation to Governor Cannon, but it had not been accepted.)

following chapter, the program here outlined, except the suicidal rôle assigned to Bell, was carried into successful operation.

When the election took place, the "old hero" was sojourning at Tyree Springs, in Sumner County. After it had been ascertained beyond question that the state had been redeemed, the leading Democrats of Middle Tennessee, including Polk, Attorney-General Grundy, Judge Campbell, and General Armstrong, reported, with their ladies, to that place in order to join with the General in celebrating the victory. Burdens of state as well as the infirmities of age were, for the time being, forgotten, and the company once more indulged in the frivolities of youth. Each morning, after breakfast, a mock court was held, of which Grundy was Chief Justice and General Jackson, Associate. From fines levied by this "court," provisions for the day were supplied—a proceeding which seems to have added much to the enjoyment of the company.[35]

Polk did not remain long within the jurisdiction of this improvised court. He soon returned to his home in Columbia to complete his plans for ousting the Whig Senators, and to prepare for his inauguration. Unlike many who offered him advice, Cave Johnson believed that the program of persecution would do the Democrats more harm than good, and therefore urged Polk to oppose it. "It is essential," he wrote,

to the existence of our party that every selfish consideration be laid aside & act in concert & no man can do so much to effect this as yourself. . . . It has struck me with some force, that *our friends* should go to work & do the business of the State without the slightest interference with Federal politics—let White and Foster take their course—go to Washington if they choose—if Foster adopts that course he is forever disgraced—toward the conclusion of the Session we can instruct.

He did not "wish our party to have the semblance of coercing either until it is absolutely necessary." He believed that Foster would resign even without instructions, but however that might be, "by all means let the necessity for interference be manifest

---

[35] Nelson, *Memorials of Sarah Childress Polk,* 60–63.

before it is done, rather let it be urged upon the Legislature by
the people rather than upon the people by the Legislature.''[36]
Johnson's advice may have been prompted by political sagacity
rather than by a sense of justice, but whatever the motive his
recommendations were good.

As will appear in the following chapter, other counsels prevailed, and the Democrats elected to make the most of their
political power. Their choice gave them a temporary advantage,
although eventually their unfair treatment of the Whig Senators
helped to transfer votes from their own party to that of their
opponents.

---

[36] Johnson to Polk, Clarksville, September 28. The year is not given.
The letter has been put with the *Polk Papers* for 1838, but evidently it was
written in 1839.

CHAPTER IX

GOVERNOR OF TENNESSEE

In accordance with an absurd custom, a governor of Tennessee, in the closing hours of his administration, enacted the solemn farce of submitting to the legislature a message in which he made elaborate recommendations for its consideration. This was done with a full knowledge that within a few days a new governor would be inaugurated and that he, in turn, would present entirely different recommendations.

On October 8, 1839, Governor Cannon submitted his final message to a legislature composed of thirteen Democrats to ten Whigs in the Senate, and forty-nine Democrats to thirty-three Whigs in the lower house. It is unnecessary to dwell on his suggestions concerning state affairs, for, needless to say, no heed was paid to them. For political reasons, however, the Democratic majority in the new legislature felt that his severe condemnation of the national administration merited both consideration and rebuke. Unanswered, the Governor's remarks might tend to influence the wavering, and a refutation would afford another opportunity to herald the glorious achievements of the "party of the people."

Among other things the retiring Governor had expressed a hope that "the country will ere long be delivered from the maladministration of the present rulers, with its pernicious train of experiments and spoliations." This part of his message was referred by the legislature to a "Committee on Federal Relations" which was created early in the session. The most active member of the committee was Samuel H. Laughlin, former editor of the Nashville *Union* and a personal friend of both Polk and

Jackson, and it was easy to foretell what the verdict would be. On January 29, 1840, Laughlin reported that his committee had been

wholly unable, from anything contained in said message, or in the past action of the Federal Government, executive, legislative or judicial, during the late or present administrations, which can, in the slightest degree, even by implication, afford the least warrant of authority for the imputations contained in that portion of said message.[1]

The verdict of the committee was approved by the legislature, and little attention was paid to a minority report which upheld the contentions of the former Governor. Laughlin's report served as a vindication of the national administration. In addition, it served as the basis for one of the instructions given to the federal Senators from Tennessee—the instruction to vote against the bill to prevent interference in elections by certain federal officers.

On October 14, 1839, Polk was inaugurated as governor of Tennessee. Among those present to witness the ceremony it gave Harris of the *Union* "great pleasure to notice ex-President Jackson, with health apparently improved." The inaugural address, according to the same writer, was "an effort of great happiness on the part of Gov. Polk." "It was," wrote Old Hickory, "a great address well suited to the occasion—there was a great contrast betwen his and Mr. Cannon's."[2]

On account of its supposed influence on national politics, more importance was attached to Polk's inauguration than is usually the case when a state executive is installed. Levi Woodbury voiced the sentiment of most Democrats when he wrote: "I have seldom known the result of any election to be more triumphant & gratifying over the whole Union than that of yours."[3]

---

[1] *Tenn. Sen. Jour.*, 1839–40, 7, 504.

[2] Jackson to Van Buren, Oct. 18, 1839, *Van Buren Papers.*

[3] Woodbury to Polk, October 20, 1839, *Polk Papers.*

The new Governor's first message was submitted to the legislature on October 22, and the subjects most emphasized in it were banks and internal improvements. He expressed the belief that there had been no necessity for the suspension of specie payments by the banks of Tennessee. On the assumption that they had suspended such payments simply because eastern banks had done so, he urged the enactment of measures which would compel resumption, for "like individual debtors, they should meet their liabilities honestly and promptly as long as they are able to pay." Banks often, said he, do their most profitable business during suspension, while the loss is borne by labor. He denied that the federal government had been responsible for derangement of the currency or that a national bank could have prevented it. The main cause of financial distress, he said, was speculation on borrowed capital. For remedy, therefore, he did not seek new legislation, but suggested something far more sensible—a remedy which in no degree depended on governmental action. "The only substantial and permanent relief," said the Governor,

is to be found in habits of economy and industry, and in the productive labor of our people. By the observance of these, another crop would more than liquidate our eastern debt. We must bring our expenses within our income. Our merchants and traders must cease to indulge in hazardous and wild speculations which they are unable to meet.

This was very sound advice, far too sound to be widely accepted in a period when most people believed that the government was able to dispense or withhold prosperity at will, regardless of their own reckless speculative ventures.

Another recommendation was that the legislature should, by law, prohibit the Bank of Tennessee from emitting notes under twenty dollars, because excessive issues of paper tended to drive out metal money, and in addition, to facilitate speculation.

Polk declared himself to be strongly in favor of internal improvements made by the state. He asked, however, that existing

laws on that subject should be so modified as to prevent extravagance. For example, the legislature at the preceding session had
enacted a law which required the state to subscribe for one-half
of the capital stock of all railroads, macadamized turnpikes,
graded turnpikes, and sanded turnpikes for which acts of incorporation "have heretofore been granted or for which acts of
incorporation may be hereafter granted." Such a law had great
possibilities for evil, and under it worthless enterprises had
already been undertaken. Polk now urged that the law should
be so modified that subscriptions in future must be limited to
works of real improvement, and that a board of public works
should be created to authorize and supervise such enterprises.[4]

On the whole the Governor's message was a creditable document, although it lacked the vigor and elaboration which usually
characterized his written productions. It was evident that his
interests were national rather than local. His recommendations
were duly considered by the legislature, but even the members
of that body seemed to be more interested in "doing practical
politics" for the national party than in enacting laws for the
good of the state. At any rate practical politics was given first
place on their program.

It was well known to all that the main reason for making Polk
the gubernatorial candidate was the belief that he alone could win
the state back to Democratic allegiance. For this same reason
he had consented to make the race. The question which soon
presented itself was: What does he expect as his reward, if he
succeeds? During the campaign the Whigs made the charge that
Polk did not care for the governorship, and that his nomination
had been simply a ruse to win Tennessee for Van Buren and the
Vice-Presidency for himself at the approaching federal election.
In such an event he would, of course, resign in the middle of his
term. The charge was repelled by Polk's friends, but the probability of its truth was so great that many, especially in East

---

[4] *Tenn. Sen. Jour.*, 1839–40, 64–68.

Tennessee, declined to vote for him under the circumstances. He was urged[5] to make an emphatic denial of the charge, but he followed his usual policy of keeping silent. When, therefore, the state senate, within forty-eight hours after his inauguration, began to consider the question of nominating Polk for Vice-President, the *Banner* charged that this had been the sole purpose of making him governor, and that the people had been grossly deceived.[6]

The senate with little opposition passed a resolution nominating Van Buren and Polk, and on October 22, the same day on which it received the Governor's message, the house proceeded to consider this senate resolution. Two amendments were offered by the opposition—one to require the candidates to support a federal bank, another to strike out the name of Polk—but both were promptly rejected. After prolonged and animated debate the house, on November 4, concurred in the senate resolution and formally nominated the two candidates.[7] Until the question had been decided, the local newspapers kept up a war of words on the subject, each trying to surpass its rival in vulgar abuse, which doubtless pleased the readers but which made few converts in the legislature.[8]

In Washington the Democratic members of the Tennessee delegation in Congress were busily engaged in an effort to procure for Polk the second place on the national ticket. His principal competitor was the incumbent, Colonel Richard M. Johnson, of Kentucky. Johnson had the support of the conservative

---

[5] H. W. Anderson, of Brownsville, to Polk, September 10, 1839, *Polk Papers.*

[6] Nashville *Banner,* Oct. 19, 1839. One enthusiastic friend urged Polk not to leave the governorship for the Vice-Presidency: "The plan that I had laid off was for you to be our Governor six years and then Senator Six and at the end of Benton's eight years make you President" (Amos Kirkpatrick, of Meigsville, to Polk, Oct. 17, 1839, *Polk Papers*).

[7] *Tenn. House Jour.,* 1839–40, 68–69.

[8] To quote one sample of their ability in vivid description: The *Union,* on October 16, informed its readers that John B. Ashe, a state senator, "came very near bursting his boiler and collapsing his flue on yesterday," in condemning the *Union.*

element of the party—of the class of people whose main rule of action is leaving well enough alone. But a portion of the party desired a more vigorous candidate, a man who would conduct a more energetic campaign, and a man who would be more acceptable to the southern states. These qualities were especially desired in the candidate for Vice-President in order to offset the want of them in Van Buren, their candidate for President.

The supporters of Polk fully realized that it would be difficult to procure for him the coveted nomination. They knew that there was little genuine enthusiasm for Johnson in any quarter, still they feared that he might be nominated by the national convention simply because that body would not know how to get rid of him. Their only hope seemed to lie either in preventing the calling of a national convention, or in preventing any nomination of a Vice-Presidential candidate if such a convention should be held. A letter outlining the situation was sent to Polk by six Democratic members of Congress from Tennessee.[9] It stated that a national convention had been recommended by New Hampshire, and that it now seemed to be a certainty. If so, it was their opinion that Johnson would probably be nominated, although New England, New York, Virginia, North Carolina and other states preferred Polk. Johnson was a "dead weight" on the party, they said, but it was hard to drop him. It was possible, they believed, that the convention might fail to nominate any one, and break up in confusion, but at all events Tennessee should be fully represented in the convention. In a separate letter (dated February 4) Brown tells Polk that Calhoun is for him on the ground of "your *position,* your *abilities* & your *principles.*"

A few days after the receipt of the above-mentioned letter Polk informed Hubbard, a member of the House from New Hampshire,[10] that his position was "passive"—that he would accept

---

[9] The letter was dated at Washington, February 3, 1840, and was signed by Felix Grundy, A. McClellan, H. M. Watterson, H. L. Turney, C. Johnson, and A. V. Brown (*Polk Papers*).

[10] Polk to Hubbard, February 7, 1840, *Polk Papers.*

the nomination at the hands of his party, but would not seek it. Such at attitude was in line with his usual adherence to party unity. His passive attitude, however, seems to have been somewhat affected by his unanimous nomination by a Virginia convention. This nomination was made, it was said[11] at the instance of the friends of Calhoun. In response to Polk's letter, Hubbard strongly urged Polk to put aside all delicacy and run. Johnson, he said, was in favor of both tariff and internal improvements, and was unpopular with many in the party. For these reasons, said Hubbard, Democrats should oppose a national convention, and should nominate Polk in some other way; Virginia had done so, and why should other states not follow her example? Should the election eventually devolve upon the Senate, he was certain that Polk would be chosen.[12] In Washington, A. J. Donelson was using his influence to procure Polk's nomination. On March 4 he wrote that, although the South was unequivocally for Polk, yet he feared that the convention would choose Johnson instead.[13]

Polk was willing enough to run, but being a firm believer in party solidarity, he was reluctant to become the candidate of a portion of the party unless it should develop that the party as a whole could not agree upon a choice. Writing to Cave Johnson on March 27, he said that "up to now" he had maintained that he would not run unless nominated by the undivided party. But, said he, the refusal of Virginia and South Carolina to send delegates to the Baltimore convention had changed the situation by making unanimity in any case out of the question; consequently if the convention should fail to make a nomination, in other words, in the event of there being no party nominee, he might in that case consent to run.[14]

---

11 Theophilus Fisk to Polk, Richmond, February 21, 1840, *Polk Papers.* In reporting the news to Polk, Fisk added: "Wherever my paper, the Old Dominion, circulates, and it has a very wide one, the people will hear of no candidate but yourself."

12 Hubbard to Polk, February 23, 1840, *Polk Papers.*

13 Donelson to Polk, March 4, 1840, *ibid.*

14 *Polk Papers.* He wrote a similar letter to Hubbard on April 5, 1840.

Ready as ever to aid his friends, General Jackson used his influence in an attempt to procure Polk's nomination by the national convention. In a letter to Van Buren he said that

A man ought to be chosen that all the republicans in every state would cheerfully unite on, and if this is not done it will jeopardise your election—it ought to be a man whose popularity would strengthen you, not one that would be a dead weight upon your popularity.

Polk, in his opinion had double the popularity of Johnson, and his nomination by the party would insure victory. He was pained to learn from Major Donelson that many in Congress believed it advisable to make no nomination for the Vice-Presidency; "surely our friends have not taken a common sense view of the whole subject."[15]

Before leaving Tennessee, Laughlin and some of the other delegates to the Baltimore convention held a conference in Nashville with Polk, Jackson, and other political leaders. The General was firm in his belief that candidates ought to be nominated for both President and Vice-President, and that Van Buren and Polk should be the nominees. Polk, he repeated, would add strength to the ticket, while Colonel Johnson would be an encumbrance. On the other hand, Polk made it clear to the delegates that in no event would he run as a sectional candidate, as Judge White had done in 1836; should Johnson be nominated, he would earnestly support him. Should no nomination be made at Baltimore, and if within a reasonable time a sufficient number of states had not indicated a preference for himself, he would then take field in support of Colonel Johnson or any other candidate that seemed most likely to bring success to the party.[16]

Laughlin arrived in Washington on April 25, and three days later, after conferences with Tennesseans, he recorded in his diary that "all were now agreed that Gov. Polk could not be nominated—that Johnson could not without New York, and that

---

[15] Jackson to Van Buren, April 3, 1840, *Van Buren Papers*.

[16] S. H. Laughlin, "Diary," April 14, 15, *Tenn. Hist. Mag.*, March, 1916, 45–47.

the best way, if possible, was to make no nomination. This matter
was in treaty between Mr. Grundy and Mr. Wright.'' On the
day following, Laughlin reported to Polk that Benton and
Buchanan were secretly in favor of Johnson and that ''such
creatures as Walker and Sevier are only fit to do mischief,'' but
that Calhoun was heartily in favor of Polk's nomination.[17] At
a meeting held in Grundy's room on May 1 it was agreed that
Polk's only hope lay in preventing any nomination by the convention, and some believed that a refusal by delegates to attend
would be the most effective way of procuring the desired result.[18]
This plan was not followed, however, and a few days later Laughlin wrote from Baltimore that the convention had nominated
Van Buren but, by a vote of one hundred and thirty-two to
ninety-nine, had declared it inexpedient to nominate a candidate
for Vice-President.

After the convention had adjourned without naming a candidate for Vice-President, Polk prepared a statement in the form
of a letter to Grundy and requested him to have it published in
the Washington *Globe*.[19] It had been his wish, he said, that the
Baltimore convention might nominate a candidate, but, as it had
not done so, he still hoped that the opinions of the majority could
in some way be ascertained. In that event he would cheerfully
support the choice, but, as he had been nominated by some of the
states, he would let the party decide whether to settle on one or
more. He hoped that some one would be chosen by the electoral
college. In answer, Grundy told him[20] that no doubt he would
have won if there had been no convention, but as matters now

[17] S. H. Laughlin, ''Diary,'' April 28, 29, *op. cit.* Laughlin to Polk,
April 29, 1840, *Polk Papers.* In his diary for May 4, Laughlin recorded
that ''Mr. Buchanan from hostility to Gov. Polk's future prospects had
allied himself to King, and by contrivance, their friends were trying first
to effect a compromise with the friends of Johnson and Polk and thereby
get King nominated upon the half-way house principle; but if they could
not get this done, they united and were to unite with Johnson's friends
and press for a nomination.''

[18] Laughlin to Polk, May 2, 1840, *Polk Papers.*

[19] Polk to Grundy, May 27, 1840, *ibid.*

[20] Grundy to Polk, June 1, 1840, *ibid.*

stood, he thought that Johnson would be elected. The Nashville *Union,* he said, had injured rather than aided Polk by calling on the states to declare their preference. As it would not look well to withdraw formally from the race, Grundy advised Polk simply to do nothing.

The contest between Polk and Johnson for second place on the Democratic ticket was more than a rivalry between the two men. Back of it was a party cleavage which four years later was to land Polk in the White House. Despite Jackson's loyalty to Van Buren, many of the General's best friends did not like the "little magician"; they supported him only from a sense of party duty. Still less did this wing of Democracy like Colonel Johnson, and, if they must support Van Buren, they wished at least to have a Vice-Presidential candidate for whom they could willingly vote. There seems to be no evidence that Polk himself had, up to this time, been opposed to Van Buren, nevertheless he was on very intimate terms with the insurgent faction of the party. This wing of the party was impelled mainly by a desire to promote southern interests, although a revolt against "old fogyism" was already becoming a political factor. Its adherents regarded Polk as sound on southern questions, while they had doubts in the case of both Van Buren and Johnson. Party cleavage had existed before Polk had been suggested for the Vice-Presidency, but the apparent hostility of the administration to his candidacy aided in widening it. Although the President himself seems to have expressed no preference, those who were in his confidence and who were supposed to voice his wishes were directly or indirectly supporting Colonel Johnson. Among them were Benton, Buchanan, Kendall, and Blair.[21] For a second time[22] Blair appeared reluctant to give aid to Polk when he was sorely in need of it. These instances alone furnish a very good reason

---

[21] Jackson's attitude toward the candidates had no connection with this party split. He favored Van Buren and Polk, and opposed Johnson, purely for personal reasons.

[22] The first time was when Polk was a candidate for Speaker of the House.

why Polk, when he became President, declined to adopt the *Globe* as his official organ.

Shortly after the Democratic convention had adjourned, Cave Johnson informed Polk[23] that a *Life of Van Buren and Johnson* had appeared and that he believed it had been published at the office of the *Globe*. Blair, he said, had declared himself to be impartial as to Colonel Johnson and Polk, but "I have no faith in that establishment so far as your interests are concerned." For this reason he (Cave Johnson) and his friends were not eager to extend the circulation of Kendall's *"Extra Globes,"* which had been prepared especially for campaign purposes. On May 25, five of the Tennessee delegation[24] addressed a letter to Kendall himself. In it they stated that while they were anxious to advance the cause of the administration, they were unwilling to prejudice the cause of their favorite candidate, and therefore, "before we undertake the circulation of the *Extra Globe,* we are desirous of being informed, whether the *Extra* will take any part, & if any what part, in the election of Vice President." Kendall gave a rather evasive reply[25] in which he stated that, while he thought well of their "favorite candidate," he would attempt to promote the cause of the party by speaking well of any or all candidates as the occasion might require. With this reply, which was regarded as a virtual endorsement of Johnson, they had to be content, but the hostility to Kendall and Blair by no means abated. The element that supported Polk became more and more alienated from Van Buren and his intimates until, in 1844, they succeeded in preventing his nomination.

The other question of a purely political nature that engrossed the attention of the Tennessee legislature was that of forcing White and Foster out of the United States Senate by the use of humiliating instructions.

---

[23] Johnson to Polk, May 24, 1840, *Polk Papers.*

[24] Cave Johnson, A. V. Brown, H. L. Turney, A. McClellan, and H. M. Watterson.

[25] June 9, 1840. Both letters are in the *Polk Papers.*

In White's case another method was first attempted, for the judge was still popular in the state, and, if he could be eliminated without resorting to instructions, less odium would attach to his adversaries. In the fall of 1838 White had, on account of ill health, tendered his resignation to Governor Cannon. The Governor suspended action in the hope that White's health might improve. As it did improve sufficiently to enable him to make the journey to Washington, the resignation, at Cannon's request, was withdrawn without having been accepted.

Rumors of White's letter of resignation had found their way to Democratic ears and suggested the possibility of disposing of the judge by maintaining that by his own action his seat had become vacant. Accordingly, when the legislature convened in October, 1839, the senate by resolution asked Governor Cannon for copies of the correspondence which had passed between himself and White relative to the latter's resignation. Cannon replied that White's resignation had never been accepted and that his letter had been returned; all other correspondence had been personal, not official, and had not been preserved. Attorney-General Grundy wrote[26] from Washington urging that White's successor should be chosen without delay, and expressing the opinion that Foster would resign if instructed to vote for the sub-treasury bill. Such a program, if successful, would give the Democrats an opportunity to choose both Senators, one of whom was to be Grundy himself.

Notwithstanding Grundy's advice, the difficulty of proving that White's seat had become vacant seemed to be so great that, on October 25, Levin H. Coe introduced in the state senate a series of resolutions which instructed the Senators and requested the Representatives to carry out the wishes of the legislature on certain enumerated subjects.[27] While the resolutions were being

---

[26] Grundy to Polk, October 17, *Polk Papers.*

[27] (1) To vote against the chartering of a United States bank. (2) To vote for the sub-treasury. (3) To vote against any bill for the prevention of interference in elections by certain federal officers, as such a bill would

discussed by the legislature, Judge White wrote to one of the members of the lower house stating that he would resign rather than support the sub-treasury bill.[28] His letter was read to the legislature, and soon afterwards that body, by a strict party vote, passed the resolutions. General Jackson's program was thereby successfully carried into effect, and once more he had the satisfaction of humiliating the man who had dared to run for President against his wishes. It was a contemptible transaction, and those who participated in it are deserving of nothing but condemnation. It remained to be seen, of course, whether the Whig Senators would repudiate their instructions, but there was little doubt that White at least, would resign.

On his way to Washington, early in November, John Bell stopped at Knoxville to deliver a public address in which he scathingly denounced the administration and its supporters. In response to a call from the audience, White addressed the same meeting in language which was reported to have been violently intemperate.[29]

While White was yet on his journey to Washington, Polk, in a letter to Van Buren, congratulated him on recent Democratic victories, and pointed out that they were a good omen for 1840. "Judge White," said Polk, "forgetting the dignity of his station, as well as the former character of which he boasted, descended into the political arena, and became an active partisan and travelling electioneer." He told Van Buren that the legislature

---

violate the Constitution of the United States. (4) To vote against distribution among the states of revenue derived from the sale of public lands—and for reducing the price of such lands. (5) To vote for a repeal of the duty on salt. (6) To support in good faith the leading measures of the present administration (*Tenn. Sen. Jour.*, 1839–40, 77–79; Scott, *Memoir of Hugh Lawson White*, 370).

28 White to Jacobs, September 5, 1839 (Scott, *Memoir of Hugh Lawson White*, 371).

29 Lewis P. Roberts to Polk, Nov. 11, 1839, *Polk Papers*. Roberts doubtless exaggerated in reporting that White "characterized the whole of the V. B. party as gamblers and blacklegs" and accused Van Buren of pocketing the money which the people had lost from a derangement of currency.

had instructed the Senators to support the President's measures, and expressed the belief that Foster would resign and White obey the instructions. Grundy, he said, would be the best man to succeed Foster; he therefore urged the President to give up his Attorney-General for the good of the cause.[30]

Foster promptly resigned on November 15, thus leaving one seat in the Senate at the immediate disposal of the Democrats. Catron, who was holding court in Louisville, believed that White, too, would soon be forced to resign. Tennessee, he wrote, must be held loyal to the administration, and the best way of insuring this was to make Polk the candidate for Vice-President.[31]

The legislature by a party vote chose Grundy to fill Foster's unexpired term. As soon as the news reached Washington, however, one of his friends, H. C. Williams, pointed out to him that he was not eligible for the office.[32] The constitution required that a Senator, at the time of his election, must be a local resident, and it was thought that Grundy was not such a resident so long as he remained in the cabinet. He therefore resigned his seat in the Senate, and the technicality was obviated by his reëlection after his return to Tennessee.[33]

On receiving his instructions from the legislature, White decided that instead of resigning at once he would wait until some question had been presented which would compel him either to vote contrary to his principles or to violate his instructions. The Democrats, therefore, hastened to bring forward an obnoxious measure. On January 13, 1840, Silas Wright called up the sub-treasury bill and thereby forced the issue. White rose and explained to the Senate the embarrassment of his position, and then read the letter of resignation which he was about to send

---

[30] Polk to Van Buren, Nov. 11, 1839, *Van Buren Papers.*

[31] Catron to Polk, Nov. 19, (1839 ?), *Polk Papers.*

[32] Williams to Polk, Nov. 28, 1839, "*Most strictly confidential.*" On December 1 Cave Johnson gave a similar opinion, and said that Grundy would go to Nashville to look after the matter *(Polk Papers).*

[33] *Niles' Register,* Jan. 11, 1840.

to the Tennessee legislature.[34] Grundy and others had expected
from the persecuted Senator a bitter arraignment of the administration party. They had come prepared to answer him, but
Grundy himself admitted that White's letter to the legislature
had been "drawn with some ability" and was too respectful to
call for a reply.[35]

While no one questioned the legal right of a state to instruct
its Senators, it was generally felt that the legislature had used
its power for the unworthy purpose of punishing White and gaining a political advantage to which the Democrats were not entitled. A dinner was given in the deposed Senator's honor at
which all of the prominent Whigs were present. His public career
and his loyalty to principle were exalted in toasts and addresses
made by Clay, Preston, and many others.[36] It was his last public
appearance. An attack of pneumonia before his departure from
Washington and the fatigue caused by the journey home greatly
impaired his vitality, and his death occured on April 10, 1840.

White's resignation gave the choice of his successor to the
Democratic majority in the legislature. As the judge was from
East Tennessee, custom required that his successor should be a
resident of the same section of the state. The legislature selected
Alexander Anderson, a lawyer of fair ability but a man without
national reputation.

As noted above, the principal recommendations made by
Governor Polk in his message dealt with banks and internal improvements. To these topics the legislature gave its attention
when it was not too busily engaged with *practical politics.* Like
most banks in the Union those of Tennessee had suspended specie
payments. In response to the Governor's suggestion Yoakum, on
October 28, 1839, presented a resolution which, if adopted, would

---

[34] Both explanation and letter are printed in Scott, *Memoir of Hugh
Lawson White,* 375 ff.

[35] Grundy to Polk, Jan. 13, 1840, and other letters on the same subject in the *Polk Papers.*

[36] An account of this dinner is given in Scott, *Memoir of Hugh Lawson
White,* 395 ff.

compel the Bank of Tennessee and its branches forthwith to resume and continue specie payments on all notes of and under ten dollars. Another resolution moved by Jennings, an opposition member, required the committee on banks to interrogate the president and directors of this bank as to whether financial accommodations were made on the basis of political sentiments. On November 11, Jennings presented a bill which embodied and made more explicit the ideas included in his resolution. The bill required the committee on banks to call on the Bank of Tennessee for the following items of information: (1) whether the choice of officers of the branch banks was influenced by politics; (2) whether contracts were so influenced; and (3) whether politics was considered in making loans. Another bill was proposed by Wheeler the purpose of which was to compel all banks of the state to resume specie payments within thirty days on penalty of forfeiture of their charters. On January 15, 1840, Jennings proposed an amendment to the state constitution the intent of which was to prevent the state in future from becoming the sole proprietor of, or a partner in, any bank, and from raising money on the credit of the state, except for defense.[37]

None of these proposals was enacted into law. The Democrats easily disposed of the political measures of their opponents, but, with the exception of a few minor remedial regulations, they were unable to carry their own. Toward the close of the session Laughlin submitted a report from the committee which had been appointed by the senate to investigate the banks. It stated that no evidence of politics in bank transactions had been discovered and that specie payments would, in the opinion of the banks, be resumed by July 1, 1840.[38] This belief, however, proved to be erroneous.

In response, also, to suggestions made in the Governor's message, the legislature undertook to modify existing laws on the

[37] *Tenn. Sen. Jour.*, 1839–40, 85–86, 109, 156–157, 407.
[38] *Ibid.*, Appendix.

subject of internal improvements. Yielding to a popular clamor for state aid, the legislature under Cannon's administration had made it obligatory for the state to become a partner in all improvement ventures regardless of the nature of the enterprise. Wholesale extravagance had been the result; nevertheless it was not an easy matter to eliminate the abuses without doing injury to those who, relying on continued support from the government, had invested capital in various projects.[39] The secretary of state reported to the senate that, under the act of 1836, $2,732,541⅔ had been subscribed by the state to improvement enterprises, and under the act of 1838, $889,500 had been subscribed for turnpikes and river improvements, $65,000 to the Louisville, Cincinnati, and Charleston Rail Road Company, and a similar amount to the Hiawassee Rail Road Company.[40]

In order to save the state in future from such ruinous expenditures, the legislature repealed all laws which had required the governor to subscribe for stock in improvement corporations. In the repealing act provision was made for the withdrawal, so far as possible, from partnerships already formed. By another act, passed on January 28, 1840, the legislature recalled $150,000 in state bonds which had been placed with banks to be sold and the proceeds invested in stocks of improvement companies. This legislation was substantially what the Governor had recommended, and, although there was no remedy for the waste that had already

---

[39] In responding to a vote of thanks at the close of the session, Speaker Coe, of the Senate, stated very clearly the difficulty which confronted the legislature: "In 1836 and 1838 laws were passed for the encouragement of Internal Improvement and works of the most extensive character have been commenced, and are now in progress of erection. If we continued to advance under the law as we found it, many saw in it the germ of a disordered and bankrupt treasury, and a people loaded down with taxes, levied to pay the interest on an onerous State debt—whilst it was asserted by others, with much reason, that the State had voluntarily tendered the right hand of assistance to large bodies of our fellow citizens, and had invited enterprises, having for their object the cultivation and improvement of our common country; and under such circumstances the sudden withdrawal of all aid, would involve individuals in private ruin and consign public works to dilapidation" (*ibid.*, 545–546).

[40] Reports of Luke Lea, secretary of state, Oct. 25 and Nov. 23, *Tenn. Sen. Jour.*, 1839–40, 74, 142.

occurred, so long as Polk remained in the governor's chair care was taken to restrict expenditures and to reduce the state debt.

During Polk's first year as governor of his state, the people of the nation were engaged in the whirlwind Presidential campaign of 1840—the first and most boisterous of its kind. In every state in the Union the contest was waged with unprecedented fury, and especially so in Tennessee. Reason and logical argument were cast to the winds, while noise and caricature became the order of the day. The "stump speech" played a less important part than usual; while both sides, but especially the Whigs, expended their energies in fantastic processions. The greater the din of deafening and discordant noises, the more spectacular or grotesque the banners and other devices designed to excite the emotions of the crowd, the more successful was the pageant considered.

For sentimental reasons, as well as for the importance of her electoral votes, the contest in Tennessee was regarded as of national significance. Failure to redeem "Old Hickory's state" was thought by Democratic politicians to be nothing short of disgrace, while the hope of thus humiliating their opponents spurred the Whigs to untiring effort. But the Whigs had the advantage from the outset. The rank and file of the Democrats did not share the feeling of the party leaders; they could not wax enthusiastic over Van Buren. In the Whig camp, on the contrary, there was unity.

In 1839, as soon as it became known that Polk had been elected, prominent Whigs held a convention in Nashville and arranged for the appointment of local committees throughout the state. These committees were effective engines of agitation, and the *Union* promptly denounced them as "new and strange fermentations in the body politic to be put down by all lovers of peace and social order."[41] Clay was invited to visit Tennessee by a delegation sent to Kentucky for that purpose by the Nashville

---

[41] Phelan, *Hist. of Tenn.*, 384.

convention, but, the sage of Ashland, pleading illness and pressure of private business, declined to make a definite promise
to accept.[42]   It was expected, of course, that the legislature
would instruct the Whig Senators and force their resignation,
and the *Banner* was certain that such a course would be of
great advantage to the Whigs in the Presidential campaign.
This paper urged the Senators to remain in office until forced
to resign.   In such an event their names were to head the Whig
electoral ticket, and the state was to be "thoroughly and ably
canvassed, in every county and every neighborhood and victory
would be assured."[43]

The national convention of the Whig party met at Harris-
burg, Pennsylvania, on December 4, 1839.   Due to prejudice
against national conventions, the Whigs of Tennessee refused to
send delegates, for it will be remembered that opposition to the
convention which nominated Van Buren was a chief factor in the
creation of the "White Whig" party.   As their hearts were set on
Clay, they were disappointed, and at first somewhat discouraged,
when Harrison received the nomination.   They soon rallied,
however, and throughout the campaign their loyalty and energy
were not surpassed by the Whigs of any other state.   Bell was
their most eloquent speaker, although Foster, who canvassed the
entire state, was more successful in winning votes.   In this campaign the Whigs appealed more to the eye than to the ear.   They
relied more on banners and processions than on oratory or arguments.   "The fact is," wrote one of Polk's Democratic friends
after the election, "the people like coonery and foolery better
than good argument."[44]

The great event of the campaign was the Whig convention
held in Nashville on August 17, 1840.   Delegations came from
surrounding states, each joining in the spectacular procession

---

[42] *Niles' Register*, October 12, 1839.

[43] Nashville *Banner*, quoted in *Niles' Register*, September 7, 1839.

[44] Isaac Goladay to Polk, November 9, 1840, *Polk Papers*.

and each bearing aloft banners fantastically decorated and adorned with mottoes designed to win popular applause.[45] The procession wended its way to a grove in the outksirts of the city, where the multitude was entertained by speeches made by prominent Whigs of Tennessee and other states. Foster, who was chairman of the meeting, made the opening address, but the lion of the occasion was Clay himself, whose personal magnetism and oratorical flights electrified the audience, although his address was rather commonplace.

The Democrats were not so well organized as the Whigs and their speakers were decidedly inferior to those of their opponents. Their most effective debater, Polk, was prevented by his office from actively entering into the canvass, although he made a few speeches in favor of Van Buren, which led to his presentment as a ''nuisance'' by the grand jury of Sevier county,[46] and the Whig papers circulated the story that the Governor's grandfather had been a Tory during the Revolution.[47] Nicholson met Bell in debate; Cave Johnson, A. V. Brown, and H. L. Turney did their utmost to stem the Whig tide; Jackson wrote letters in which he lauded Van Buren, and denounced Harrison as a Federalist, but the people would not listen as of yore. On the eve of the election the Democrats tried to brand Harrison as an abolitionist. At the last moment, they distributed handbills on which they had printed a letter which Harrison was alleged to have written to Arthur Tappan declaring himself to be such. But the plot had been discovered, and the *Whig* was ready with Harrison's denial as soon as the handbills appeared.

Tennessee refused to be ''redeemed''; the vote for Harrison was 60,391, while Van Buren polled but 48,289. It was a signal victory for the Whigs, and, unlike four years earlier, it could not be said that voters had supported the Whig candidate simply because he was a favorite son of the state. Undoubtedly one of

---

45 The parade is described in some detail by Phelan, *Hist. of Tenn.*, 387 ff.
46 *Ibid.*
47 Edwin Polk to Polk, August 27, 1840, *Polk Papers.*

Polk's correspondents was right in saying[48] that many Democrats had refrained from voting because they "could not be rallied to Van Buren," and that the Democratic loss was much greater than the Whig gain. Still, any hopes built on such calculations were illusive, for in national politics the state was irretrievably lost to the Democrats.

Not realizing the real strength of the Whigs, the leading Democrats, almost before the smoke of battle had lifted, began to formulate plans for winning the next state election. First of all, Harrison and his administration must be vigorously assailed, regardless of the course he might pursue. The difficulty of finding anything of sufficient importance to attack caused them no little anxiety. A. O. P. Nicholson put the case frankly in a letter to Polk, written before it had been definitely ascertained that Harrison had been elected. The Democrats, he said, must

keep up a raking fire upon the whole of Harrison's inconsistent and imbecile history. It is unfortunate for us that Harrison's administration (if elected) will not be developed before our August elections, but still enough will probably have transpired to present available points of attack.[49]

And yet the politicians who uttered such sentiments claimed to be followers of Jefferson, one of whose cardinal principles was "absolute acquiescence in the decisions of the majority."[50]

Although the Democrats were hopeful and even confident, the Whig victory of 1840 made them realize that Polk's defeat in 1841 was within the realms of possibility. When, therefore, in December, 1840, it was reported in Washington that Grundy could not live, the Democratic members of Congress from Tennessee counselled together and decided that Polk ought to succeed him as Senator from his state. In a letter to Polk,[51] Hopkins L.

---

[48] Samuel P. Walker to Polk, November 4, 1840, *Polk Papers.*

[49] Nicholson to Polk, November 6, 1840, *Polk Papers.* Other letters to Polk also expressed regret that there would probably be little to attack.

[50] See Jefferson's first inaugural address.

[51] Turney to Polk, December 21, 1840. On the same day A. V. Brown wrote a letter of similar purport. Both in *Polk Papers.*

Turney pointed out to the Governor that his reëlection was doubtful and, even if such were not the case, he would stand a better
chance of promotion if elected Senator. Both Cave Johnson
and A. V. Brown, he said, concurred in this view. Before this
letter had reached its destination, however, Polk had appointed
Nicholson to succeed Grundy, whose death had occurred on the
nineteenth of the month. So gratified was Nicholson by his
appointment that, on his arrival in Washington, he saw visions
of his benefactor's certain elevation to the Presidential chair.
After telling the Governor of his popularity in Washington and
of the anxiety for his reëlection, he added: "I shall be disappointed if your success in this contest does not lead on certainly
to your elevation to the Presidency."[52]

While the politicians on either side were speculating on the
probability of Harrison's calling an extra session of Congress,
considerable excitement was caused in Nashville by the shooting
of J. George Harris, editor of the *Union,* by Robert C. Foster,
a son of the deposed Senator. Harris quickly recovered, but the
affair furnished Democrats with something to denounce while
they were awaiting further political developments.

In case Harrison, after his inauguration, should call Congress
together in extra session, Tennessee would have no representation in the House[53] unless the Governor should see fit to call a
special election. Anderson, who had been chosen to fill Foster's
unexpired term, would cease to be Senator on March 4, and the
official term of Nicholson, who was serving on the governor's
appointment, would be automatically terminated should Polk
decide to call an extra session of the legislature. Should no
extra session be called, Nicholson would continue in office until
the regular session which would open in October, 1841. As the
probability of a called session of Congress increased, the Democrats differed as to whether it would be wiser to convene the

---

[52] Nicholson to Polk, Jan. 13, 1841, *ibid.*

[53] The terms of present members would expire on March 4 and a regular
election would not be held until autumn.

legislature and attempt to elect two Senators, or to be contented with one Senator, Nicholson, leaving the other seat vacant.

When sounded on the subject, Polk expressed himself as opposed to convening the legislature. He gave, as his reasons, economy, and the fear that the Whigs would make political capital of such a procedure. On the other hand, Jackson, who had lost none of his political zeal, strongly favored an extra session in order that two Senators might be chosen and instructed as to how they should cast their votes. ''If it can be done with propriety,'' he advised Governor Polk,

if there is a called session of congress, the Legislature should be convened to give us a full representation in the Senate; and to instruct our senators & request our representatives to vote against a high Tariff, a distribution of the Public Funds, against a national Bank of any kind, or deposits in the State banks, and against a repeal of the sub-treasury act, and, altho last not least, to pass a law to compell our Banks to resume specie payments or wind up.[54]

From Washington, Anderson urged the necessity of a full representation in the Senate.[55] Turney seconded this appeal and once more tried to induce the Governor to become a candidate. Polk, he said, could do much good in the Senate, for since Grundy's death there was no one able to cope with the Whigs. On this same subject Polk received what appears to be his first letter from Andrew Johnson.[56] In it Johnson advises the Governor to convene the legislature for the purpose of electing members of Congress whose terms, unless he is ''rong,'' expire on the fourth of March.

While Nicholson was in Washington, still worrying for fear there would be little in the Harrison administration to assail,[57]

---

[54] Jackson to Polk, Feb. 8, 1841, *Polk Papers*.

[55] Anderson to Polk, Feb. 17, 1841, *ibid.*

[56] At least it is the first letter from Johnson in the Polk collection. It seems that Polk had written to Johnson, stating that either he or Blair must run for Congress. Johnson declined to become a candidate (Johnson to Polk, March 4, 1841, *Polk Papers*).

[57] ''I do not calculate that we will be able to make any capital out of the Inaugural; but the Cabinet will be enough for our purposes, if we use

the much-reviled administration of Van Buren passed into history.[58] Ignoring his critics, the "little magician" remained unperturbed and courteous to the end. When his successor arrived in Washington, an invitation to dine was extended by Van Buren and accepted by Harrison, and the Nashville *Union* marvelled that Harrison could take "vermacilla soup from those horrible gold spoons!"[59] The Whig newspapers never tired of contrasting the democratic simplicity and generous hospitality[60] of Harrison with the royalistic pomp and cold exclusiveness of Van Buren. It was unkind of the Whigs thus to purloin from their opponents the very arguments—almost the exact phrases—which had done such effective service in winning popular support for General Jackson. Such utter disregard for the proprietary rights of others fully justified J. George Harris in trying to render harmless the stolen implements of war. Shortly after

it with skill." It is rumored, he said, "that Webster will be Secretary of State; Granger, Post-Master-General; Ewing, Secretary of the Treasury; Bell, Secretary of War; Preston, Secretary of the Navy; and Crittenden Attorney-General. What think you now of the Cabinet! I think you may set it down as settled that we are to have an anti-war fed. for Secretary of State, an abolition fed. for Post-Master-General, a uniform fed. for the Treasury, a gag-bill Clay fed. for Atty. Gen., a gag-bill-no party-White Whig fed. for the War, and a Nullification fed. for the Navy. Will not this open the eyes of Tennesseans! If not, then may we surrender at discretion" (Nicholson to Polk, Feb. 12, 1841, *Polk Papers*).

58 "Tomorrow night, at twelve o'clock," said the *Madisonian*, "the administration of Martin Van Buren terminates. That administration, accidental in its beginning, and unfortunate and profitless in its career, will then have gone, with all its powers, its prerogatives, its follies, its malign influence, and with whatever streak of virtue may have been possibly mingled in its texture, to control us, to agitate us, to injure us, no more. Four years it has lived, and its principal achievement has been the passage of the sub-Treasury, by trampling with contempt upon the broad seal of a sovereign State. What good it has done, we are unable to point out. What harm it has accomplished, we may possibly conceive of, by considering the present condition of the Treasury, of our foreign relations, of our Navy, of the Army and the defences, of the Post Office, and of the public morals, and the condition of the people. But we congratulate the country that it has at last come to an end. It is gone" (The *Madisonian*, March 3, 1841).

59 *Union*, March 4, 1841.

60 Under the heading "Hospitality at the White House" an article in the New Haven *Palladium* said: "He [Harrison] keeps his house open to all comers. . . . The servants at the White House find more difficulty

his inauguration, the President had directed Webster to issue a most wholesome order stating that any interference in elections, state or federal, by federal officers, would be regarded as cause for removal. The plain farmer of the Whigs was promptly branded by Harris as a usurper of royal powers and a violator of the rights of states, for "the Autocrat of all the Russias never issued an *Ukase* more potent."[61] But before these unjust charges against the President had been put in type, the career of the "autocrat" had been cut short, and the same issue of the paper which contained them chronicled, also, the news of Harrison's death.

As Polk's campaign for reëlection began as soon as his competitor had been nominated on March 5, 1841, the incidents of the remainder of his gubernatorial term will be treated in the succeeding chapter, which deals primarily with that spirited political contest and with the transfer of Tennessee to the Whigs.

---

in adapting themselves to the change of Administration than any other officeholders. He breaks in on all the elegant aristocratic usages of the palace, and plays the mischief with that systematic courtly etiquette which with the Sub-Treasury constituted the two great radical reforms of the late President. He gets up at sunrise, like a plain farmer as he is, and wants his breakfast within an hour after, (the vulgar man!)—and eats with an appetite of a common day laborer. He gave one of his servants a regular 'blowing up' the other day, for leaving a visitor dripping wet and muddy in a cold 'ante-chamber,' because the President was at breakfast and could not be disturbed, and because the carpet would be injured by the muddy feet of one who came on foot! The President brought the visitor into the breakfast parlor, and insisted on making him comfortable at the fire at once. At all these things the *democracy* are much shocked, and look aghast at this desecration of the 'palace!'" Quoted in Nashville *Banner*, April 5, 1841.

[61] Harris quoted from the *Evening Post:* "this document has added the last insult that can be given to a free and independent people, and will be held up to popular execration by every man who is not disposed to yield his neck to the yoke of party, or who is not a base and degraded slave. It is so insolent in spirit and dictation, breathes an air so vile and debasing, that it is difficult to speak of it without subjecting one's self to an unwonted excitement" (Nashville *Union*, April 12, 1841).

CHAPTER X

DEFEATED BY JONES IN 1841

From the day of their defeat in 1839 the Whigs of Tennessee had been marshalling their forces for the next gubernatorial contest, and the great national victory of 1840 gave them reason to hope for success. It had also, by example, indicated the type of campaign that would be most likely to win that success. Cannon's main weakness as a candidate had been his inability to adjust himself to the guerrilla variety of campaign by which many a less brilliant politician had endeared himself to the people. Capable but painfully serious, Cannon was a shining mark for the shafts of wit and ridicule which Polk had hurled with unerring aim whenever they had met in joint discussion. On the contrary, Polk had demonstrated his adaptability to a degree that surprised his closest friends. Distinguished for his dignified and learned discussions in the national House of Representatives, Polk had, in 1839, discomfited his rival and won the people by a most skilful use of mimicry and sarcasm. The Whigs were therefore familiar with the campaign methods of the Governor as well as the predilections of the people, and the convention which assembled at Murfreesborough on March 5, 1841, displayed political wisdom by nominating the one man in the state who was thought to be capable of ''beating the governor at his own game.'' This man was Major James C. Jones,[1] a ''horny-handed'' farmer from Wilson County, who had represented his county in the legislature, served as a Presidential elector, and acquired a local reputation as an effective ''stump speaker.'' Tall and ungainly in appearance, Jones possessed many of those grotesque personal

---

[1] Jackson declined to call Jones, major, ''for he never was a corporal'' (Jackson to Polk, March 20, 1841, *Polk Papers*).

qualities which had made John Randolph famous. Even the sobriquet "Lean Jimmy," with which his admiring friends had christened him, served as a valuable asset in a contest so closely following the "great whirlwind campaign" of 1840. Realizing that, in knowledge and debating powers, he was no match for his adversary, Jones resorted to hectoring tactics and relied more on amusing than on convincing his audience. Nevertheless he was a man of considerable ability, and he displayed a fair knowledge of the political issues of the day. In spite of the picture drawn by Phelan and others, there was a serious side to the campaign of 1841. Jones did not devote all of his time to "coonery and foolery," but at times displayed alertness and skill as a debater.

As in 1839 the canvass dealt principally with national issues. In his "Address to the People," Polk stated that his views on national questions had been given in detail in his address of 1839, and that nothing had since occurred to alter them. He had, he said, been forced to begin the campaign early because of the untiring efforts of the Whigs to defeat him.[2]

Each side accused the other of being Federalists, and Harrison's "autocratic" order against interference in elections, and Van Buren's regal splendor, were offered as evidence to prove the opposing contentions. The death of Judge White nearly a year before did not prevent his name from being dragged into the contest. Jackson, in exhorting Polk to answer the "falsehoods" of Bell and Foster regarding Van Buren's extravagance in furnishing the executive mansion, provided him with a statement that it was Bell's disappointment at not being made a member of Jackson's cabinet, on White's recommendation, that had caused Bell to desert the party and to bring White out for

---

2 "From the moment of my election in 1839, it had been manifestly an object of no minor importance with my leading political opponents in the State, to prostrate and destroy me. Their attacks were constant. Their presses kept up an incessant war upon me. No calumny or misrepresentation of my political opinions and course had been too gross to fill their columns" (Nashville *Union*, March 29, 1841).

the Presidency.[3] A friend in Albany[4] furnished Polk with several letters written by Granger, the Postmaster-General which were to be used for the purpose of proving him to be an Abolitionist. Jones and other Whigs tried to counteract the effect produced by these by asserting that Polk's grandfather had been a Tory.

Early in March Jones published a list of his speaking appointments. He opened the campaign at Murfreesborough, where he boasted that he could tell a greater number of anecdotes than the Governor himself.[5] He promptly accepted an invitation from Polk to meet in joint debate whenever possible,[6] and they met for the first time at Murfreesborough on the twenty-seventh of March.

Polk opened the discussion with a spirited attack upon the Harrison administration. He denounced Granger as an Abolitionist, and Webster as a Federalist who, in 1835, had been so unpatriotic as to declare that he would not support a certain bill to appropriate money for defense ''though the *enemy* were battering down the walls of the Capitol.'' Unfortunately for himself, Polk tried, as he had done in the canvass with Cannon, to weaken his opponent by making him an object of ridicule. Among other shafts of sarcasm, he said that his friend Jones was a ''promising young man,'' but ''as for his being Governor, that's all a notion.''[7] As soon as Jones took the platform, he referred repeatedly to Polk as ''my venerable competitor.'' This he continued to do whenever they met in debate, much to the amusement of the audience, for Polk at that time was only forty-six years of age.

Before the candidates met again, Governor Polk issued a public statement in which he gave his reasons for not convening

3 Jackson to Polk, March 20, 1841, *Polk Papers*.

4 E. Crowell to Polk, March 19, 1841, *ibid*.

5 Yoakum to Polk, March 15, 1841, *ibid*.

6 Polk to Jones, March 15; Jones to Polk, March 18, 1841, *ibid*.

7 Nashville *Union*, March 29, 1841.

the legislature in extra session so that Senators might be chosen in time for Harrison's called session of Congress. He had already called a special election for the purpose of choosing members of the House of Representatives. In declining to convene the legislature, Polk, as we have already noted, disregarded the wishes, not only of General Jackson, but of nearly all of the leading Democrats of the state. It was thoroughly characteristic of Polk to follow his own judgment rather than the wishes of his friends, even of "Old Hickory," and yet he was often charged with being a weak tool of General Jackson.

The main reasons assigned in his public statement for not convening the legislature were unnecessary expense and the impropriety of taking advantage of an accident to strengthen his own party in the federal Senate. The members elected to the legislature in 1839 had not, he said, been chosen with the selection of Senators in view, and "my opinion is that the frank, fair, and honest course, is to leave the choice open for the decision of the people at the next August election." Harrison, he said, had given him an opportunity to disregard the popular will, for it is

certain that if I had availed myself of them that the present General Assembly, if convened, would choose two Democratic Senators. If, however, the President under the influence and control of inflamed partisans, maddened with their late success . . . has committed a capital political blunder, it is no reason why I should commit one also.

He denounced the President for unnecessarily convening Congress, for, as there was plenty of money in the Treasury, the call must have been made for purely political reasons.[8]

---

[8] "Large and extravagant promises which can never be redeemed had been made to the people, and it was doubtless deemed to be necessary to do something, or to *appear* to do something to keep up the public expectation, and thereby possibly to operate upon the elections which are to take place in States during the present year. . . . They probably fear to let the public mind sober down to a state of calm reflection, lest peradventure they may not succeed in their favorite measures of Federal policy, at the next regular session of Congress." Printed in Nashville *Union*, April 1, 1841.

Whether the Governor was influenced solely by a spirit of fairness, no one but himself could know, but, whatever his motives were, he received no thanks from the Whigs for his magnanimity. The *Banner* bitterly assailed him for impugning the motives of the President, and for praising himself. It pronounced his action hypocritical and declared that his forbearance had been due to a knowledge that the legislature would not dare to choose two Democrats in the face of the late election, and to fear that an attempt to make such a choice would injure his own prospects of reëlection.[9] At a debate held at Lebanon shortly after the publication of Polk's statement, Jones won applause by reminding the Governor that his solicitude for the popular will had not prevented him from appointing Nicholson Senator after the people had repudiated him (Nicholson) by refusing to make him a Presidential elector. The Whig paper of the town commended Polk's wit and added that "he makes as much of it with his face as with his tongue."[10] Most effective of all were his impersonations of Bailie Peyton, the chief feature of which was what the Whigs called "Polk's horrible grin."

The candidates visited the principal towns of the state. From the press notices, one would be led to believe that their time was occupied almost entirely with the relation of humorous anecdotes and the coining of witty remarks. Nevertheless, their printed speeches show that a serious discussion of political issues was by no means omitted. Polk, especially, displayed great power as a debater. He thoroughly understood the questions under

---

[9] Nashville *Banner*, April 5, 1841. The most abusive of all papers was Parson Brownlow's Jonesborough *Whig*. In an article addressed to Polk, the editor said that the Governor while "under the influence of *liquor* or opium, being *half drunk*" had denounced the *Whig* for criticising his ancestors who had been lying in the tomb for forty years. Brownlow reminded Polk that he had criticized both White and Harrison since their death, and then continued: "You canting, cringing hypocrite—you demagogue and time-serving politician, you advise mankind as to prudence and moderation!" Undated in *Polk Papers*.

[10] Lebanon *Chronicle*, quoted by Nashville *Banner*, April 5, 1841.

discussion, and few could excel him in clear and logical presentation. Had his opponent attempted to meet the Governor's arguments by a frank and fair discussion, he would have been easily vanquished, for his knowledge of political questions was superficial and limited. To Jones, however, ignorance of the subject was never a cause of embarrassment. By substituting bold assertion for knowledge, he was able to discuss any topic without hesitation, and, so far as his audience was concerned, he had disproved every contention of his adversary. It availed Polk little to demolish these assertions by clear presentation of historical data. Like Douglas in his debates with Lincoln, Jones would calmly reiterate his assertions, no matter how often they had been refuted, or else he would divert the attention of the audience by a humorous anecdote or by a dissertation on the beauties of coon fur. In either case the effect of Polk's argument was entirely lost, while his adversary succeeded in winning the vociferous applause of an uncritical audience. No wonder that a Democrat who heard their debate at Somerville exclaimed in disgust: "Mr. Polk made an ass of himself, talking sense to a lot of d—d fools," and urged that the Governor "ought to get a stick and crack Jones's skull, and end this tomfoolery!"[11]

One of Jones's most exasperating characteristics was his never-failing good humor. As he had declined to become embarrassed by the most complete demonstration of his ignorance, so, also, he refused to be angered by sarcasm or ridicule. At times Polk tried to crush his opponent by belittling his abilities and by holding him up to scorn. In reply, Jones would solicit the compassion of the hearers for his "irascible but venerable competitor." Polk said that he had tried to discuss questions of state in a serious manner and that his opponent had wisely made jest of things which were beyond his comprehension. When he asserted that Jones was better suited to the circus ring than to the Governor's chair, Jones good-naturedly admitted that they

---

[11] Phelan, *Hist. of Tenn.*, 403.

would both do well in the ring—himself as a clown, and the Governor as "the little fellow that is dressed up in a red cap and jacket and who rides around on a poney."[12] The Governor wearied of the travesty, and would gladly have abandoned joint meetings, but, as they had been undertaken upon his own invitation, there was no way of breaking gracefully with his trifling antagonist.

The debates attracted attention in all parts of the state, and everywhere large audiences greeted the speakers. Much importance was attached to their meeting at Nashville, which was not only the capital, but the political headquarters of the state. Here, on May 19, they were greeted by a large and enthusiastic concourse of people, and each candidate according to agreement spoke for two and one-half hours. "Polk," as Phelan has well said, "made a speech that would have swept from the stump any man who had ever been Governor of Tennessee before him, and any man who was Governor after Jones until Andrew Johnson came forward."[13] It was a forceful and logical presentation of the issues, replete with historical data and spiced with humorous illustrations. Jones's address was a compound of sophistry and nonsense. Intead of answering Polk's arguments he constructed innumerable "men of straw" and then demolished them to the entire satisfaction of his audience. He misquoted and distorted everything that the Governor had said, after which he amused the crowd by poking fun at his opponent and by relating preposterous stories.[14] No man of Polk's training and dignity could cope with such politcal bushwhacking.

Had the people been really interested in political issues, Jones could not have commanded a hearing. But since 1840,

---

[12] *Ibid.*, 402.   [13] *Ibid.*, 404.

[14] The *Union* of May 24 thus described him: "Maj. Jones is a floater; amusing at times, but superficial as a bubble. He drifts along on the surface of today and plays with the uppermost passions and prejudices of his hearers; trifles with important matters and converts important matters into trifles. . . . In a word, he is quite possible as an electioneer for his party—good of the kind, but the quality is none of the best."

the Whigs had abandoned serious discussion and had staked everything on an appeal to the emotions. For this reason Polk's training and success were used to prejudice the people against him. Not only had his grandfather been a Tory, but the Governor himself was said to be an aristocrat, who, at heart, held the people in contempt. Ignorance, uncouth appearance, and slovenly dress were regarded as attributes of honest statesmanship, and Jones always emphasized the fact that he had followed the plow.[15] The Governor, however, deserved little sympathy on account of these misrepresentations, for with similar weapons he had aided in "putting down" the able and upright John Quincy Adams.

Up to the close of the canvass, no one could predict, with any degree of certainty, what the result would be. The Whigs did most of the shouting. They made extravagant claims, but many Democrats could not believe that a majority of the people would be willing to cast out a man of Polk's ability and reputation and put in his place a man whose sole claim to fame rested on a grotesque personal appearance and low-grade wit. The Democrats, however, had overrated the people's sense of propriety, and on that account were doomed to disappointment. At the election, which was held on August 5, Polk was defeated by a majority of over three thousand votes, but the *Union* congratulated the Democrats on their "signal TRIUMPH OF PRINCIPLE in sweeping away TEN THOUSAND of the last year's majority."[16] It was generally conceded, even by the Whigs, that no other man in the party could have polled so many votes, and instead of losing prestige, Polk was credited by his party with

---

[15] The Knoxville *Register* in contrasting the candidates said that Jones was "free, manly, undisguised, plain, and carrying conviction with every sentence." Polk was "hidden, dissembling, artful, shrinking and hypocritical in the extreme" Quoted in Nashville *Banner*, August 2, 1841.

[16] "Never," said Harris, the editor, "did Gov. Polk win for himself more laurels than he has won in this contest. The Democracy of the whole Union will appreciate his Herculean efforts at the expense of health to maintain the principles that he has uniformly supported, the principles of Jefferson and Jackson" (Nashville *Union*, August 12, 1841).

having won a great personal victory. In a letter to Van Buren, General Jackson rejoiced in the reduction of the Whig majority and said that ''Gov. Polk deserves the thanks of the Democracy of the whole union, he fought the battle well and fought it alone, I may say.'' Strange to say, Jackson commended rather than criticized Polk for having disregarded his advice about convening the legislature. He pointed out to Van Buren that, had the legislature been called, two Democratic Senators would have been elected, but ''the Governor threw aside policy, and adopted the real republican creed—that a majority have the right to rule.''[17]

In the legislature which was elected with Jones, the Whigs had a majority of three in the lower house. In the senate the Democrats still had a majority of one. But one of their number, Samuel Turney, was regarded as rather independent in politics, and, when the time came for him to take a definite stand with his colleagues, he proved to be weak and vacillating. Nominally, however, the Democrats had a majority of one and thereby possessed the power to block any measure of the lower house that required their separate approval. But on any question which required the joint vote of the two houses the Whigs, by virtue of their majority of three in the lower house, were in a position to outvote their opponents.

In Tennessee, politics had precedence over legislation. Therefore the defeated party began at once to devise ways and means of preventing their opponents from filling the two vacant seats in the United States Senate. The term for which Judge White had been elected, and which since his resignation had been filled by Alexander Anderson, had expired. The other vacancy had been caused by the death of Senator Grundy, and had been filled temporarily by A. O. P. Nicholson, by virtue of the Governor's recess appointment.

Following the election, Polk received many letters, the main object of which was to congratulate him for having reduced the

---

17 Jackson to Van Buren, Aug. 16, 1841, *Van Buren Papers.*

Whig majority. In these letters several of his friends expressed the opinion that the Democrats ought to demand the privilege of choosing one of the Senators, and that Polk himself should be the man. Among others, Hopkins L. Turney advised such a course. He assured Polk, also, that his brother, Samuel Turney, would vote with the Democrats.[18]

When plotting to force the Whigs to concede them one Senator, Democratic leaders tried to ease their conscience by asserting that in 1840 Whig members of the legislature had threatened, in the event of Polk's convening the legislature, to remain at home and thus prevent an election of Senators. It was further alleged that these threats had been made on the advice of Henry Clay.[19] It was said, also, that, during the recent campaign, when it was believed that the Democrats would elect a majority of the legislature, Jones had boasted that the Whig members would not permit the Democrats to hold an election for Senators.[20] Polk at first was noncommittal, but he soon made it known that he was not a candidate for the office. The reason which he gave for not permitting the use of his name was that he would not accept any office except one conferred upon him by a vote of the people.[21] With Polk out of the race, the politicians turned their attention to other candidates, but nothing could be done, of course, until the meeting of the legislature and the inauguration of a new governor.

---

[18] Turney to Polk, Washington, Aug. 24, 1841 (*Polk Papers*). Laughlin, Huntsman, and others assured Polk that some of the Whigs had agreed to vote for him.

[19] H. L. Turney to Polk, Jan. 2, 1842, *ibid.*

[20] Alex. Anderson to Polk, Aug. 20, 1841, *ibid.* Anderson urged that the Democrats should now practice this plan upon those who had invented it.

[21] Geo. W. Smith, of Memphis, advised Polk not to permit the use of his name for two reasons: (1) possibility of defeat and loss of prestige; (2) it would lend color to the Whig charge that he had never cared for the governorship, and had wished it only as a stepping-stone to a higher office. (Smith to Polk, Sept. 2, 1841, *ibid.*) Polk may have been influenced by considerations of this kind.

As soon as the legislature had convened, Polk, on October 7, submitted his final message as governor.[22] It was a long document and filled with detailed information on various topics, but mainly on banks and internal improvements. For a man who had only a week longer to serve, Polk was surprisingly free with advice and suggestions for the future. He expressed satisfaction with the degree of prosperity which had been enjoyed by the people during the last two years, and he attributed it to corrective legislation and the consequent elimination of extravagant speculation. He regretted that banks had not been compelled by law to resume specie payments, and once more recommended the enactment of such a law. "There is," said he, "no sound principle of ethics or of public policy which should exempt Banks from the moral and legal obligations which rest upon individuals to pay their debts." He pointed out that the bank note circulation amounted to about three million dollars and that the average rate of depreciation was eight and one-half per cent; this unnecessary burden was borne by the people, while the banks were prosperous—even paying dividends. He reported that the law recently enacted which provided for "the reduction of the State debt" had enabled him to recall and to cancel fifteen hundred state bonds of one thousand dollars each. The outstanding internal improvement bonds amounted to $1,816,916.66⅔, while, so far, only one company had paid a dividend to the state—the small sum of $1620. The currency, he said, had been much improved by the law which prohibited the emission of notes under ten dollars; as a further remedy for financial ills, he recommended that commercial houses and improvement companies should be prevented by law from issuing checks designed to circulate as money. The internal improvement board had, in his opinion, accomplished much good by requiring various companies to reduce their stock and to conduct their affairs in a more economical manner. Among other things the retiring Governor

---

[22] *Tenn. Sen. Jour.*, 1841–42, 22–42.

recommended that improvements be made in hospitals for the insane, that sexes be segregated in penitentiaries, and that the governor be given power to commute the death penalty to life imprisonment.[23] His recommendations were salutary and sensible. Some of his suggestions indicated grave need for improvement in social conditions.

One paragraph in the Governor's message is especially interesting, for in it Polk expressed his views on the slavery question, a subject which he usually avoided. He informed the legislature that he had, during the past year, received two communications from friends of negroes convened in London, on June 12 to 20, 1840, in which they had asked for the abolition of slavery and the slave trade. Viewing these communications "as an impertinent and mischievous attempt on the part of foreigners to interfere with one of the domestic institutions of the State," he had declined to enter into any correspondence with this convention. Doubtless he was governed more by his belief in state rights than by an interest in the institution of slavery itself; still, he was ready to resent outside interference with the "peculiar institution."

On October 14 Polk delivered his valedictory, and on the same day James C. Jones was inaugurated as his successor.[24] While it is true that Polk's interests were national rather than local, yet the state was indebted to him for causing the enactment of beneficial laws. Under his leadership the state had been freed from a ruinous internal improvement policy, and he had done much to check currency inflation and to reduce the debt of the state. His reform measures were all in the line of sound statesmanship, and, if we may judge from the suggestions made in his final message, the people might have profited by continuing him in office.

---

[23] He could now pardon only.
[24] *Tenn. Sen. Jour.*, 1841–42, 78.

CHAPTER XI

POLK IN RETIREMENT

On October 14, 1841, James C. Jones became governor of Tennessee, and on the nineteenth his first message was sent to the legislature.[1] His recommendations differed little from those which had already been submitted by his predecessor,[2] and, also like Polk, he attributed most of the distress of the people to their own fault—to buying more than they could reasonably hope to pay for. In one respect only did Jones differ radically from the former governor. The crisis in the monetary affairs of the country, he said, had been produced by the destruction of the Bank of the United States. Such a statement was naturally to be expected, for some part of a Whig governor's message must needs indicate the change of administration, and the bank was a subject of general interest.

As usual the legislature was far more interested in ''practical politics'' than in the less sportive business of lawmaking. The paramount question was the election of United States Senators, but first of all, the opinions of both legislators and constituents must be molded so as to accord with those of the leaders. The Democrats were most active in the senate, for in this branch they had, counting Samuel Turney, a majority of one. The leaders in the senate were Samuel H. Laughlin, former editor of the *Union,* and Andrew Johnson, who, at the recent election, had been promoted to the upper house. Johnson had ability and force, but Laughlin excelled him in political cunning and effectiveness as a manipulator. In the Polk-Bell contest, Johnson

---

[1] *Tenn. Sen. Jour.,* 1841–42, 116–125.

[2] Jones was accused of having *borrowed* from Polk's inaugural of 1839, and to prove the claim the *Union* published the two addresses in parallel columns (Laughlin, *Diary,* Oct. 21, 1843).

had supported the latter. Laughlin had ever been subservient and therefore enjoyed the entire confidence of Polk and other prominent Democrats.

On October 18, Laughlin, as chairman of the committee on federal relations, submitted a series of eight resolutions to which four more were added on the fifth of November.[3] The preamble recited the Virginia and Kentucky Resolutions of 1798 and declared that many of the laws enacted by Congress at the late extra session violated the spirit of the Constitution quite as much as did the laws against which those historic resolutions had protested. The first resolution reaffirmed those of 1798 and asserted that they were "universally true at all times and especially applicable to the present crisis and state of affairs." The succeeding seven resolutions condemned the convening of Congress by Harrison and, also, the various measures[4] proposed or enacted by the Whigs at that session. This indictment of the Whigs was intended to prepare public opinion for the items which were to follow—the four resolutions that were added on the fifth of November. The first of these, the ninth of the entire list, declared that the legislature had full power to instruct Senators chosen to represent the state in Congress, and that it was the duty of these officials to obey or resign. The second asserted that it was the duty of candidates for legislative offices to give explicit answers to queries made by citizens or members of the legislature concerning their views on public questions. The third affirmed the right of the people to instruct members of the legislature. The fourth formally instructed the Senators (not yet chosen) and requested the Representatives from Tennessee to conform their votes to the opinions expressed by the foregoing resolutions.

The last four resolutions displayed far more shrewdness than principle. On their face they contained nothing which any

---

[3] The resolutions may be found in *Tenn. Sen. Jour.* under the dates given.

[4] For example, the "bankrupt bill" and the tariff, distribution, and bank bills.

advocate of representative government could very well decline to support. But they were designed, as every one knew, for the purpose of harassing the Whig candidates with embarrassing interrogations and for rendering them ineligible should they decline to answer. By asserting the right of the people to instruct their representatives in the legislature, the Democrats hoped to hold in line their own members who might be inclined to follow their individual judgments. Their party had nothing to lose by obstructive tactics, and, by blocking their opponents at every turn, they might worry the Whigs into conceding one seat in the Senate.

Ephraim H. Foster and Spencer Jarnagin were selected as the Whig candidates and on November 16 the lower house sent to the senate a resolution urging the immediate election of two United States Senators lest delay "may lead to bargain, intrigue, and management, to the detriment of the public interest." As soon as the resolution was read in the senate, Andrew Johnson moved to amend by making it read that delay "may lead to bargain, intrigue, and management, to the great detriment of E. H. Foster and Spencer Jarnagin, and thereby promote and advance the public interest, by keeping them out of power for the next four and six years."[5] The Democratic majority in the senate soon came to be called "the immortal thirteen" and except for an occasional desertion by Samuel Turney they voted as a body on all questions of party politics.

The customary method of electing Senators in Tennessee was by a joint "convention" of the two houses. As the Whigs had a majority of three in the lower house and the Democrats a majority of but one in the senate, it was obvious that if the usual method were to be followed the Whigs would outnumber their rivals in the convention. The Democrats now made the discovery that the usual method was unconstitutional, for, as they alleged, the constitution of the state required that each house should vote

---

[5] Protests against the amendment were made, but it passed the senate by a vote of 13 to 12 (*Tenn. Sen. Jour.*, 1841–42, 227, 232–233).

separately for Senators. For their own purposes it was an important discovery; by no other method could they hope to prevent an election until the Whigs were ready to compromise on choosing one Senator from each party.

Up to November 22 the Democrats were confident of their ability to prevent an election unless the Whigs would yield to their terms. A few days before, Turney had introduced a resolution calling for an election by convention, but he had subsequently voted with the Democrats on the above-mentioned Johnson resolution. On the twenty-second, however, Turney caused consternation in Democratic ranks by announcing that he would call up and support his resolution in favor of a convention election.[6] According to William H. Polk, Turney had, for the last two weeks, "been shivering in the wind," due to the fact that the Whigs had "brought every influence to bear on him within the range of human ingenuity."[7] On November 22 Gardner moved to amend Turney's resolution by fixing the following Saturday as the date on which the Senate would vote *separately* for federal Senators. Turney accepted the amendment, but it was the younger Polk's opinion that, after one trial, Turney would revert to the convention plan. The Democrats offered another *compromise* resolution the purport of which was to declare elected Hopkins L. Turney and Thomas Brown, a Whig from East Tennessee. It was hoped that, having passed the senate, this resolution could be forced through the lower house.[8] On the twenty-third Gardner modified his amendment.

---

[6] "On Saturday last the '13' were safe against the world, and the Whigs considered themselves as beaten. Guess then, what our astonishment was, when coming into the Senate on Monday morning [November 22], Sam Turney announced that he had changed his mind, and would call up and vote for his own resolutions to bring on the Senatorial election at an early day on joint vote in Convention." Turney said that his change of mind was due to letters from his constituents (Laughlin to Polk, November 24, 1841, *Polk Papers*).

[7] W. H. Polk to J. K. Polk, November, 22, 1841, *ibid.*

[8] "My own impression is, that if the resolution passed the Senate, as now amended, declaring Turney and Brown the Senators elect—we *can force* it through the House, by lashing the doubtful men into a redemption of their former pledges . . . . can at least produce a tie" (*Idem*).

The legislature was now asked to choose one Senator from each party on the ground that the popular vote at the recent election had been nearly equally divided. Other modifications were suggested, but these, as well as Gardner's resolution, were rejected. The Democratic majority in the senate succeeded in passing a resolution which named Hopkins L. Turney as Grundy's successor, but, on December 1, the lower house refused to concur in its adoption. On the same day Speaker Samuel Turney joined the Whigs of the senate in making an agreement with the lower house to meet in joint convention on the second and third of December for the purpose of electing Senators. It was understood that each of those days would be devoted to filling one of the vacancies.

On December 2, therefore, Speaker Turney and the twelve Whigs proceeded, according to agreement, to the chamber of the lower house to join with that body in choosing one of the Senators. The other twelve Democratic senators declined to attend the election. When summoned by the doorkeeper, they sent written notice to their speaker (Turney) that they were in the senate chamber, ready for "constitutional business."[9] The joint convention, for want of a quorum, was forced to adjourn. On the morning of the third the lower house again notified the senate that it was ready to receive the senators and to proceed to the election of one of the federal Senators. It had already been arranged to hold the other election in the afternoon and for this reason Speaker Turney deemed it to be unnecessary to join the house in convention twice in one day, inasmuch as both elections could be held during the same half-day. He therefore voted with the Democrats in declining to attend the forenoon session of the convention. This vote so angered the Whig senators that they left the senate chamber in a body. By so doing they gave a distinct advantage to the Democrats, who now adjourned to the following day, thereby nullifying the original

9 *Tenn. Sen. Jour.*, 1841–42, 280.

resolution which had designated December 2 and 3 as the days on which elections by *convention* should be held.

By seceding from the senate the Whigs had committed the tactical blunder of releasing Turney from his agreement. He now blamed them for the failure to elect Senators, and once more became one of the "immortal thirteen."[10] Five of the twelve Democratic senators submitted a written statement of reasons why they had refused to participate in the proposed election. The proposed method of election, they asserted, would violate the Constitution of the United States, which vests the election of Senators in the legislature of the state—not in a convention. It would violate, also, the state constitution, which says that Senators shall be chosen by the concurrent vote of the two houses *"sitting separately"*—not together. Both statements were untrue, and besides, the convention method had been thoroughly established by custom, and up to this time its validity had never been questioned. This new-born solicitude for constitutional limitations was simply a clever bit of pettifogging.

Before any attempt to elect Senators had been made, two interesting resolutions for dividing the state were offered in the senate. The first was introduced by Andrew Johnson, on December 7, and provided that a joint committee of the two houses should be appointed to consider the expediency and the constitutionality of ceding East Tennessee to the United States so that it might be made an independent commonwealth and called the "State of Frankland." The resolution directed Governor Jones to correspond with the governors of Georgia, North Carolina, and Virginia with a view to procuring portions of those states for inclusion within the limits of "Frankland." On December 15, Gardner offered a similar resolution which provided for the

---

10 Turney's explanation, *ibid.*, 304–305. On December 13, J. Geo. Harris informed Polk by letter that there was no prospect of an election. "Thank God and the immortal thirteen Ephraim's [Foster] fiddle is broke. No more will its dulcet strains minister to the desponding faculties of faction" (*Polk Papers*).

creation of the state of "Jacksoniana." It was to include the "Western District" of Tennessee and portions of Kentucky and Mississippi.[11] The senate rejected Gardner's proposal by a vote of eleven to fourteen. Johnson's resolution passed the senate by a vote of seventeen to six (January 18), but after considerable discussion and many futile attempts to amend, this too was finally rejected by the lower house.

In accordance with the Laughlin resolutions,[12] Democratic members of the legislature had addressed queries to all senatorial candidates concerning their views on public questions. Foster and Jarnagin treated these queries with silent contempt. Hopkins L. Turney, the Democratic aspirant, gave satisfactory answers as a matter of course, and so, also, did Thomas Brown, a Whig of Roane County, East Tennessee. On December 20, Laughlin offered in the senate a resolution which differed little from the one previously submitted by Gardner. Whereas, in choosing Senators, the popular will should be consulted, so read the preamble, and, as the recent election had shown the people to be about equally divided in politics, and as neither party was able to choose Senators without the coöperation of the other, it was therefore resolved that Turney and Brown, having responded to all interrogatories, be declared the Senators to represent the state in the Senate of the United States. Turney was to fill the unexpired term of Grundy, and Brown was to have the full term of six years.[13] The resolution passed the senate but failed in the other house, and that body once more invited the senate to join them in an election by convention. The Whigs of both houses refused to coöperate with the Democrats in electing a

---

[11] *Tenn. Sen. Jour.*, 1841–42, 288, 345.

[12] Those which he had introduced on Nov. 5, relating to the interrogation of candidates for office. See above.

[13] *Tenn. Sen. Jour.*, 1841–42, 366–67. "Some of our friends here are of opinion—that after all our Senators should be elected—if the Whigs can be brought 'to elect one and one'" (A. V. Brown to Polk, Washington, Dec. 23, 1841, *Polk Papers*). This seems to indicate that the Democrats had counted more on preventing an election than on effecting a compromise.

comptroller and a treasurer unless the Democrats would agree to choose Senators by a joint vote. Of this refusal the Democrats tried to make political capital;[14] by exploiting it they endeavored to divert the attention of the people away from their own obstructive tactics.

Polk kept in close touch with the contest that was being waged at Nashville and from time to time gave directions to his political friends. He was one of the first to doubt the loyalty of his old friend A. O. P. Nicholson, and to suspect him of courting an alliance with Foster for the purpose of procuring their election to the Senate.[15] He was most severe in his denunciation of Nicholson and predicted that he would follow in the footsteps of John Bell.[16] Hearing that some of Bell's friends had made overtures offering to settle the senatorial deadlock by choosing Bell and some Democrat, Polk stated to Senator Maclin[17] that it would never do ''to elect *Bell* by Democratic votes. It would not only be placing him in a position to do mischief but it would be rewarding his apostacy.'' He had heard also, he said, that similar overtures had been made by Foster's friends. ''To no man in the State,'' he continued, ''would it be more grating than to myself to be driven to the necessity of making a compromise by which he might obtain a seat in the Senate, and yet it is not

---

[14] ''Our whole object is,'' wrote Wm. H. Polk, who was a member of the lower house, ''to place them [the Whigs] in the position of refusing to elect State officers, necessary and essential to the proper administration of our State Government, because we prevent them from placing in the Senate men who stand *Mum*'' (W. H. Polk to J. K. Polk, Jan. 6, 1842, *Polk Papers*).

[15] In answer to one of Polk's letters, J. P. Hardwick wrote from Nashville that ''I have no doubt a great effort is being made to carry out an unholy alliance between F. & N.'' (Hardwick to Polk, Jan. 16, 1842, *ibid.*)

[16] ''Every day convinces me more and more that he [N] is now travelling in the broad road—that John Bell travelled for several years before his apostacy—whilst he was making *loud professions* of his adhesion to our principles. We all know where *John Bell* now is, *and mark what I now say to you*, that five years, perhaps not one will pass—before he is where *Bell* now is, unless it shall be his personal interest shall make him *seem* otherwise. *I am not mistaken*'' (Polk to State Senator Sackfield Maclin, Jan. 17, 1842, *Andrew Johnson Papers*, vol. 1).

[17] *Ibid.*

impossible that our *safety as a party* in the State might require
such a sacrifice.''[18] Should an agreement with Foster be made,
Polk believed that the Democrat ought to be chosen from East
Tennessee; but if any western Democrat was to be selected, it
should be Hopkins L. Turney. He preferred a Whig Senator
to Nicholson, because he had ''more respect for an open opponent
than a hypocritical friend.''[19] Some of the ''immortal thirteen,'' however, were unwilling to accept any compromise which
did not eliminate both Foster and Bell.

On February 7, the last day of the session, Laughlin, probably acting under instructions from Polk, offered a new resolution ''in the spirit of harmony, concession and compromise.''
This resolution authorized the Whig members of the legislature
to choose a Senator from any of the three divisions of the state
(east, middle or west), and provided that the Democrats should
then select a Senator from one of the other divisions. The resolution passed the senate by a strict party vote, but not until an
amendment had been added which required that both Senators
must be ''selected from men who have not been in public life for
the last four years.'' Such a limitation had not been contemplated by either Laughlin or Polk, but some of the *thirteen*
would accept nothing less. The lower house would not, of course,
agree to the resolution; all hope of compromise was at an end;
and the legislature adjourned without having filled either vacancy. On the same day the *thirteen* had the satisfaction of

---

18 ''It would be a *bitter pill*,'' said Polk, ''to take Mr. F. even upon a
compromise, and yet if nothing else can be done I have been brought very
seriously to doubt, whether we had not better take him with *some good and
true Democrat* than to have the State unrepresented in the Senate and thus
raise up a perplexing troublesome issue of *Senators or no Senators* in the
State, which may and probably will be the test question in our elections in
1843.   Before you can compromise at all with him or any other Whig—
they must yield to *your mode of elections and agree to obey instructions.*
If they will do this and agree to give us a Democratic Senator with him—
my conviction is, that it is the course of safety to yield to it.''

19 Polk to James Walker, Jan. 17, 1842, *Polk Papers.* Whether well
founded or not, the belief in Nicholson's disloyalty was quite general.
H. L. Turney wrote from Washington to Polk, April 25, 1842: ''I think
A. O. P. N. has put his foot in it. Can it be possible that he can longer
deceive the democracy of Tennessee?''

rejecting for a second time a list of persons whom Governor Jones had nominated to be directors of the Bank of Tennessee, and as a result, the Democratic incumbents retained their positions.

In their game of obstruction the Democrats had won a decided victory—much greater than they had any reasonable hope to expect. Had any of the "immortal thirteen" failed them, everything would have been lost, and more than once Samuel Turney had threatened to desert to the enemy. By bad management, the Whigs had failed to take advantage of his willingness to coöperate with them, while the Democrats spared no effort to hold him in line. The tactics employed by the senate to attain its ends were as unscrupulous as they were successful. The aid given by Polk and Jackson was something of which neither man had reason to be proud, but politicians are seldom overscrupulous when party interests are at stake.

Just as the Democrats were rejoicing over their success in thwarting the Whigs, their own party suffered a real loss in the retirement of J. George Harris from the editorship of the *Union*.[20] He had taken charge of the paper when it was bankrupt and impotent, and under his management it had become one of the most influential papers in the state. His style was not always elegant nor his assertions true, but he was peculiarly fitted to perform the task to which he had been assigned. After his retirement the *Union* rapidly deteriorated, until Polk and his associates had to take its rehabilitation in hand during the campaign of 1843.

After the adjournment of the legislature, the thoughts of politicians turned to plans for the future. Although it was an open secret that Polk would, in 1843, again be the candidate for governor, both he and his friends were ever on the alert to promote his prospects for the Vice-Presidential nomination in 1844.

---

[20] In the issue of March 31 Harris announced that he was going to Europe for a few months and that the owners, Hogan and Heiss, would conduct the paper themselves.

The more apparent it became that Van Buren would again head the Democratic ticket, the more necessary it seemed to be to find a running mate that would be acceptable to the South and West. Maclin, of the Tennessee senate, voiced the general sentiment when he told Polk that ''Our friends intend to fight the battle with you, and keep Van Buren as much out of sight as possible.'' In these two sections of the Union, influential leaders fully appreciated Polk's great services to the party and looked with favor upon his nomination for the Vice-Presidency, but, as Maclin frankly told him, it had been urged that he was not well known to the people in other parts of the country.[21]

Politicians of both parties attached much importance to Van Buren's visit to the Hermitage in the spring of 1842. Knowing Jackson's warm friendship for Polk, the Whigs expected and many Tennesseans hoped that the visit would result in a formal agreement between Van Buren and Polk. But, despite the efforts of Polk's friends in his behalf, the New Yorker remained noncommittal to the point of exasperation[22] and left Tennessee without having mentioned to Polk the subject of the Vice-Presidency.[23]

Although Van Buren declined to take any part in promoting Polk's candidacy or even to discuss it, and even though his indifferent attitude during his visit had still further alienated the supporters of Polk, yet both the Whigs and the Calhounites were

---

21 Maclin to Polk, May 4, 1842, *Polk Papers.* Maclin had just returned from Mississippi, where he had been sounding Polk's praises and urging the people to call a convention for the purpose of nominating Van Buren and Polk.

22 ''I am at a loss to know what to say to you, I can learn nothing. . . . Mr. Van Buren seems disposed to say nothing on the subject we spoke of when I last saw you. I made an effort through Donelson again this evening but it was all *Mum.* . . . It may be that he will say to you what he will not say to another person. The old Genl will *tell him before leaving the Hermitage,* to have a conversation with you'' (Gen. R. Armstrong to Polk, May 4, 1842, *Polk Papers*).

23 Polk himself said in a letter that during Van Buren's visit neither had ''mentioned verbally or in writing'' the subject which the Whigs say brought him to Tennessee (Polk to Elmore, of South Carolina, June 13, 1842, *Polk Papers*).

certain that an agreement between the two candidates had been effected and that one of its objects was to crush Calhoun.[24] Van Buren was not popular in Tennessee, and many Democrats felt that Polk's election would be more certain if some other than the New Yorker could be nominated for President.[25] Cass was most frequently mentioned by those who held this belief. Others were inclined to await developments. Benton, like Van Buren, had declined to commit himself in Polk's favor, but his denunciation of Richard M. Johnson was regarded by Tennesseans in Washington as a hopeful sign.[26] Realizing the general indifference toward Van Buren in southern states, friends of Calhoun began to entertain hopes that he would be nominated for the Presidency in 1844;[27] but, believing, as they did, that Polk was in agreement with Van Buren, they did not, it appears, seek assistance from his friends. Then, too, the adherents of the great nullifier could hardly hope for the coöperation of a man who was thought to be under the dominating influence of General Jackson.

When the Tennessee legislature convened in the autumn of 1842, another futile attempt was made to fill the vacant seats in the federal Senate. J. George Harris, who had returned to Nashville, reported to Polk that Bell's supporters had offered to make an agreement whereby Bell was to answer the queries which had

24 "It is thought," wrote Dixon H. Lewis, "Van has effected his purpose with Polk," while according to Gentry, of Tennessee, no one doubted that Van Buren and Polk would be the Democratic candidates (Lewis to Richard Crallé, May 31, and June 10, 1842, *Crallé Papers*).

25 "I assure you, sir," wrote J. P. Hardwicke, "there is a disinclination to take up Van Buren again. I have taken some pains to arrive at this conclusion at our little caucuses" (Hardwicke to Polk, Nov. 13, 1842, *Polk Papers*).

26 Cave Johnson to Polk, Jan. 29; H. L. Turney to Polk, Jan. 31, 1843, *Polk Papers*.

27 One of the hopeful was Duff Green. He thought that, if the Van Burenites' plan of an early nominating convention could be thwarted, Calhoun would be nominated. "It has now narrowed down," he wrote, "to a choice between Calhoun and Van Buren and the demonstrations are becoming more decided for Mr. Calhoun so that, in my opinion, the concentration in his favor will become so apparent as public opinion develops that the convention will indeed become obsolete" (Green to Crallé, February 8, 1843, *Letters of Duff Green* in Library of Congress).

been ignored by Foster and Jarnagin. Having done this, he was
to be elected as one of the Senators, and the Democrats were to
fill the other vacancy with a candidate of their own choice.
Harris was in favor of such an agreement if Polk would consent
to be the Democratic Senator; Foster would be killed, politically,
while Bell if properly instructed would be less powerful than at
present.[28] Nothing, of course, resulted from the suggestion.
Polk had already declined to make any compromise with Bell,
and besides, the overtures of Bell's friends were probably made
without his knowledge. During this session the Democrats made
little attempt to force a compromise, but simply contented themselves with blocking the Whigs from electing their candidates.
Their greatest fear seems to have been that Nicholson, by some
treacherous agreement with the Whigs, would attempt to promote his own selfish interests.[29]

Feeling that both his own and his party's interests could be
best served by defeating Governor Jones, Polk once more entered
the race. The campaign was opened by a joint debate at Spring-
field, March 25, 1843. Jones scathingly denounced the conduct
of the "immortal thirteen." Polk retorted by charging that
Jones had originated the idea which they had put into practice.
The *Union*[30] published letters from Whigs who claimed to have
heard Jones boast that, in case the Democrats should have a bare
majority on joint ballot, the Whigs would prevent a choice of
Senators by refusing to participate in the election. Throughout
the campaign the *Union* defended the thirteen for preventing
the election of men who refused to be bound by the wishes of
their constituents. The refusal of the state senate to confirm
Jones's list of bank directors was purely for political reasons.
The truth was reprehensible enough, but on the stump Jones

---

28 Harris to Polk, Dec. 11, 1842, *Polk Papers.*
29 W. H. Polk to J. K. Polk, February 14, 1843, *Polk Papers.* Andrew
Johnson, fearing that his known friendship for Nicholson might be misinterpreted, wrote to Polk that "you have always been my first choice for
anything" (Johnson to Polk, February 20, 1843, *ibid.*)
30 March 31, 1843.

won applause by asserting that the Polk directors were corrupt and time-serving partisans who, for fear of exposure, did not dare to relinquish their offices.

In many respects the campaign was a repetition of that of 1841. There was, perhaps, more argument and less burlesque, although both candidates made use of anecdotes and sarcastic retorts. Polk was not unmindful of his own powers of wit. When writing to his wife of a debate held at Jackson with Milton Brown, he said that his opponent tried to turn the "occasion into a frolic . . . but I turned the laugh upon him & almost laughed him out of the Court House."[31]

In his "Letter to the People"[32] Polk, as usual, emphasized national issues such as the tariff, the national bank, and the general extravagance of the Whigs. Once more Tennessee was regarded as the pivotal state—the index to the approaching Presidential campaign. As it was practically certain that Clay would be the Whig candidate, much of Polk's time on the stump was devoted to Clay and his policies. Incensed by a revival of the old "bargain and corruption" charge of 1825, Clay challenged Polk to a discussion of this question at a time and place to be fixed by the Tennessean himself.[33] Apparently the challenge was not accepted.

Early in the campaign a group of persons in Memphis submitted to the two candidates a list of questions on political topics. Jones replied at once, and among other things expressed the following views. He favored a national bank, but was not fully satisfied with Clay's bill that had been vetoed by Tyler. He believed in a tariff for revenue, with incidental protection to home industries. In his opinion the legislature had full power to choose Senators in any manner which it saw fit. The last

31 Polk to Mrs. Polk, April 4, 1843, *Polk Papers.*

32 It bore the date of May 17, 1843, and was printed in the *Union*, May 23 and 26.

33 Typewritten copy of a letter from Clay to Polk dated Ashland, May 20, 1843, *Polk Papers.*

answer did not harmonize very well with his condemnation of
the Democratic senate for insisting that each house should vote
separately.[34]

In answer to the same queries Polk stated that he believed
in the sub-treasury, and in metal money for the nation supplemented by a limited amount of paper issued by state banks.
He opposed direct taxes and endorsed tariff for revenue only.
Like Jones, he thought that the legislature possessed the right
to elect Senators in any manner agreeable to itself. He held,
on the other hand, that all candidates for office were under obligation, when called upon, to express their views before election
on all public questions. "The chief, if not the only value of the
right of suffrage," said he,

consists in the fact, that it may be exercised *understandingly* by the
constituent body. It is so, whether the immediate constituency consists
of the Legislature, as in the case of the election of United States Senators,
or of the people in their primary capacity, in the election of their Executive or Legislative agents. In either case the constituent has a right to
know the opinions of the candidate before he casts his vote.[35]

Except on the bank question the views expressed by the two
men were very much alike. Indeed, the paramount issue was:
Shall Tennessee be returned to the Democratic column in national
politics?

Throughout the campaign the Democrats were handicapped
by the weakness of their party press. Since Harris's resignation
the *Union* lacked both spirit and influence, and was rapidly drift-
ing into bankruptcy. On the other hand, the Whigs had several
vigorous papers, the most invincible of which was Brownlow's
Jonesborough *Whig*. Polk was condemned for the part he had
taken in the administrations of Jackson and Van Buren, and
again it was said that he sought the governorship merely as
a stepping-stone to the Vice-Presidency. Polk's "Tory"

---

[34] Jones's reply is dated April 24, 1843, and is printed in the Memphis
American Eagle, May 2, a copy of which is among the *Polk Papers*.

[35] The answer is dated May 15, and is printed in the *Union*, June 2, 1843.

grandfather was again held up to scorn, while a Chattanooga paper charged the Democratic candidate with being an aristocrat who had "refused to eat with some wagoners who were stopping at the same tavern with him some years ago."[36]

Although Polk made a thorough canvass and demonstrated his superiority over his rival, Jones was reëlected by a majority of nearly four thousand votes. This time the Whigs elected a majority of the legislature as well as the governor, and the power of the "immortal thirteen" had been broken. Polk attributed the victory of the Whigs to their success in drawing the attention of the people to local questions and away from great national issues. He was still confident that his party would carry the state in the federal election of 1844.[37]

Soon after the election the defeated candidate's friends once more turned their attention to procuring for him the Vice-Presidential nomination. They were interested of course in his personal advancement, and besides, they had hopes that, with their favorite on the ticket, Tennessee might be restored to the Democratic party. On September 5 the *Union,* in a series of editorials, urged his nomination and declared him to be "one of the ablest men in the democratic party in the Southwest." In a letter to Van Buren, General Jackson expressed the belief that the former President would be nominated—and elected, also, if Polk were put on the ticket with him. Such a ticket, he said, would surely carry Tennessee; Polk would add strength to the party in all of the states, while Colonel Johnson would weaken it.[38]

The new legislature met on October 2, 1843. In the senate the Whigs had fourteen members, the Democrats, eleven; in the lower house the Whigs numbered forty, the Democrats, thirty-five. The two main political questions which confronted the

---

[36] Both articles and a denial are in the *Union,* June 27, 1843.

[37] Polk to Van Buren, August 8, 1843, *Van Buren Papers.*

[38] Jackson to Van Buren, September 22, 1843, *ibid.*

legislature were fixing a permanent location for the state capital, and the election of federal Senators. Although now in the minority, the Democrats planned to prevent the election of Foster and Jarnagin by supporting two other Whigs, A. R. Alexander, of West Tennessee, and Joseph L. Williams, of East Tennessee. Some of the Whigs, especially the Rutherford delegation, were eager to have the capital removed from Nashville to some more central location. The Democrats therefore concocted a scheme by which they hoped to procure a sufficient number of Whig votes to elect Alexander and Williams by offering to vote for the removal of the capital. Polk was then in Nashville and gave his support to the plan.[39] Their plotting was in vain. On October 7 both houses voted to retain the capital at Nashville, and on the seventeenth Foster and Jarnagin were elected Senators, the former to fill Grundy's unexpired term, the latter to succeed Anderson.[40]

Repeated defeats annoyed but did not discourage Democratic leaders. Harmony within their own ranks was the first desideratum, and Laughlin undertook the task of bringing Nicholson and his adherents back into the fold.[41] The task did not seem hopeless, for since the seats in the Senate had been filled by the Whigs there was no reason why Nicholson should not coöperate with his former associates. The "little magician" was the chief cause of embarrassment. Democrats, generally, were ready to support Polk, but from all parts of the state came reports of indifference or hostility to Van Buren.

Laughlin's "missionary" work was not confined to the Nicholson faction. As soon as the question of locating the capital had been settled, it was a foregone conclusion that Foster and Jarnagin would be elected. Freed from the responsibility of

---

[39] S. H. Laughlin, "Diary," October 1–4, 1843.

[40] *Ibid.*, Oct. 17. "*Jonakin* has gone home a Senator—and Ephe is running about, grinning and jumping like a pleased monkey—with just about the dignity of one, at best" (Laughlin to Polk, Oct. 20, 1843, *Polk Papers*).

[41] Laughlin to Polk, Oct. 12, 1843, *Polk Papers*.

manipulating the scheme to defeat this election, Laughlin could devote his entire energy to procuring for Polk the nomination for Vice-President. In letters to influential leaders and newspaper men, he almost demanded that Polk should be taken up by "the press and the People." He proposed that the former Governor should be nominated by the state convention which was to meet in November, and that the Tennessee delegation should go to the national convention "supporting his claims, and uncommitted as to Presidential candidate, but committed to abide its nomination." He told his correspondents that if Polk were put on the ticket with Van Buren or any other good Democrat the party would surely win, "but without Polk's name we would be beaten and tied down in federal chains in Tennessee for the next six or ten years."[42] His remark concerning the national convention seems to be the first indication of the plan, later adopted, to nominate Polk, and to remain noncommittal as to the Presidential candidate. The determination to make no nomination for President was strengthened, no doubt, by a letter written from New York by Harvey M. Watterson to A. O. P. Nicholson. Van Buren was Watterson's own choice, but, fearing that his favorite could not be elected, he did not believe it wise to nominate him. Cass, in his opinion, was the most *available* candidate. He said that "the Van Buren party intend to give Polk the *go by* as to a nomination for the Vice Presidency," and that Johnson would be nominated by the national convention.[43] On October 18, two days after the receipt of Watterson's letter, Laughlin conversed with A. V. Brown. Brown advised serving notice on the New Yorkers that the Tennesseans would support Van Buren if his adherents would agree to support Polk; otherwise they would go for Cass. To this Laughlin and Armstrong assented, and Donelson was selected to state their views to Silas Wright and other friends of Van Buren.[44] Probably this threat

---

[42] S. H. Laughlin, "Diary," Oct. 9, 1843.
[43] *Ibid.*, October 16, 1843.
[44] *Ibid.*, October 18, 1843.

was not carried into effect. At any rate Polk later disclaimed
any knowledge of a project to drop Van Buren for Cass.[45] In
January, 1844, he asked Heiss to place Van Buren's name along
with his own at the head of the political columns of the *Union*,[46]
but, for the time being, the editor refused to comply.

The State convention met at Nashville on November 23, 1843.
Polk was nominated for Vice-President by a unanimous vote,
but no one was named for the Presidency. The convention simply agreed to support whatever candidate the Baltimore convention might see fit to nominate. The reason assigned for not
nominating Van Buren, as stated to him in letters from both
Polk and Jackson,[47] was a fear that the Cass supporters might
resist such action, and that a breach in the party would result.

On hearing from Cave Johnson and A. V. Brown that Van
Buren was stronger in Washington than Cass and that he would,
in all probability, be nominated at Baltimore, Polk advised the
editors of the *Union* to come out for the ex-President.[48] His
real feeling toward Van Buren is not easy to determine, but
from his silence rather than his words, one always gets the impression that his support of the New Yorker was based, as in
this case, on expediency instead of admiration for the man. It
was quite natural that this should have been so, for Van Buren
had more than once shown indifference when Polk needed his aid.

Realizing that the party had suffered from the want of a
vigorous newspaper, Polk turned his attention to rehabilitating
the Nashville *Union*. Since its purchase by Hogan and Heiss,
it had been edited by the senior partner. He had never been a
forceful writer, and of late his health had become so impaired
that the paper was practically without an editor. With the consent of the owners, Polk asked Laughlin to take charge of the

---

[45] Polk to Cave Johnson, March 18, 1844, ''Polk-Johnson Letters.''

[46] Polk to Heiss, Jan. 21, 1844, ''Heiss Papers.''

[47] Jackson to Van Buren, Nov. 29; Polk to Van Buren, Nov. 30, 1843,
Van Buren Papers.

[48] Polk to Heiss, Dec. 21, 1843, ''Heiss Papers.''

paper and promised him financial support from the party. Fearing, however, that he might jeopardize his chances of being elected to Congress (from his home district), Laughlin at first declined to accept the position.[49] His subsequent acceptance and his editorial services to his party will be considered in the following chapter.

[49] Polk to Heiss, Dec. 21, 1843, ''Heiss Papers.'' Laughlin to Polk, Dec. 7; Heiss to Polk, Dec. 19, 1843, *Polk Papers.*

CHAPTER XII

SELECTION OF CANDIDATES, 1844

The campaign of 1844 may be said to have opened with the new year. From early in January announcements from prospective candidates, declarations of principles, and notices of nominations made by local bodies, began to occupy leading places in the columns of the party journals. There was little doubt that Clay would be chosen to head the Whig ticket, although, in response to an inquiry from friends, Webster announced his willingness to accept a nomination at the hands of the Whig convention. Tyler had been read out of the Whig party, and, since the Democrats had not shown a disposition to adopt him as their own, it seemed likely that he would enter the contest as an independent candidate. Van Buren's nomination by the Baltimore convention was fully expected by all parties not so much because any considerable portion of his party wanted him, as because there seemed to be no one who had a better claim. He had been left by General Jackson as a legacy to the party, the position he had occupied gave him prestige, and, as Dixon H. Lewis remarked, he had the advantage of *"being considered the candidate of the party."*[1] These influences combined would insure him the nomination unless something should happen before the meeting of the convention to change indifference into active hostility. For some time, of course, there had been active hostility in certain quarters, but this came generally from those who were promoting the interests of some other still more unpopular candidate, such as Calhoun or Tyler, consequently there was little danger from that source. Unless something should occur to cast doubts on

---

[1] Lewis to Crallé, June 10, 1842, *Crallé Papers.*

his orthodoxy or his personal fitness, Van Buren was reasonably certain of the nomination, but unfortunately for him, that something did occur—the unexpected turn in the Texas question. Before the appearance of this firebrand, friends of other aspirants were exerting every effort to weaken his hold on the party and to strengthen that of their favorites. The most active were the supporters of Calhoun and Cass; some were ready to join with the followers of Tyler; and a few, like W. C. Rives,[2] announced that, as Van Buren's nomination seemed assured, they would vote for Henry Clay.

Early in the year, when Van Buren's nomination seemed to be a foregone conclusion, the main topic of discussion in Democratic ranks was the choice for the second place on the ticket. The persons most frequently mentioned were Colonel Richard M. Johnson, of Kentucky, and James K. Polk, of Tennessee. As in Van Buren's case, many were ready to support Colonel Johnson simply because they did not see how the party could drop him gracefully.[3] The Van Burenites favored Johnson, but for this very reason his nomination was vigorously opposed, especially in the South and Southwest. It was felt by many that if Van Buren must be accepted, the Vice-President should be a man more agreeable to the southern wing of the party. For some time the Tennessee Democrats had been urging Polk's claims to this office, and since his second defeat by Jones they were still more determined to procure for him the nomination.

Ardently desiring this office, Polk began as early as the fall of 1843 to ask his friends to use their influence with politicians of other states. In a letter to Donelson he expressed the belief that Van Buren would be made the candidate for President, and if so, "the candidate for the Vice Presidency must come from the West,—and from a slave-holding state." He hoped that the

---

[2] His letter, dated January 1, is printed in *Nat. Intell.*, Jan. 12, 1844.

[3] It was rare to see a person, wrote Cave Johnson, who did not prefer Polk. The main trouble was getting rid of "Old Dick" (Johnson to Polk, Jan. 31, 1844, *Polk Papers*).

press and party leaders would come out early for Van Buren and himself, at least before R. M. Johnson had yielded his "pretensions for the Presidency" and had become his competitor for the second place. Even this early he expressed distrust for the Washington *Globe.*

I do not understand *Blair's* course. . . . I do not think he is inclined to do me justice. Why I know not, unless it be that he has strong attachments for *Col. Johnson,* and looks to his restoration with *Mr. Van Buren.*

The attitude of Ohio and Mississippi, he said in another letter, would go far to settle the question, therefore Donelson and other Tennessee friends should send letters to prominent politicians in those states.[4]

Early in January, 1844, Laughlin and others procured from General Jackson letters to political leaders in various states. These letters were used in an effort to induce state conventions to declare their preference for Polk.[5] A letter signed "Amicus" that appeared in the *Globe* and advocated the nomination of William R. King, of Alabama, gave Cave Johnson and A. V. Brown an opportunity to sound Polk's praises and to urge his nomination. In an article signed "A Tennessee Democrat," they pointed out that King, voluntarily, and Van Buren, under instructions, had voted for the United States Bank, and that it would never do to have two candidates who had endorsed that discredited institution. But, they asked, who does not remember in Jackson's battle against the bank "the unterrified ability displayed by Governor Polk on these trying occasions?" The very fact that Tennessee was a doubtful state was an additional reason for nominating Polk.[6] To a friend in Tennessee Johnson wrote that old-line politicians such as Buchanan, Calhoun, Benton, and Blair were doing their utmost to ruin Polk's prospects, and other

---

4 Polk to Donelson, Oct. 19, Dec. 20, 1843, "Polk-Donelson Letters." The Ohio politicians mentioned were Allen, Tappan, Medary, Dawson, and Medill.

5 Letters of W. H. Polk and Laughlin to Polk (*Polk Papers*).

6 Washington *Globe,* Jan. 15, 1844. Johnson to Polk, Jan. 13, 21, 31, 1844, *Polk Papers.*

letters told Polk that these men feared him as another rival for the Presidency.[7]

In general, conservatives evinced a preference for either King or Colonel Johnson,[8] but the more aggressive element favored Polk. The Mississippi state convention at its Jackson Day (January 8) celebration drank toasts to Polk and nominated him for Vice-President,[9] and in many other states there was growing sentiment in his favor. The attention of the country had recently been called to the state of Tennessee by the introduction in Congress of a bill to reimburse General Jackson for the thousand dollar fine imposed upon him at New Orleans in 1815. William H. Polk moved in the Tennessee legislature to instruct the Senators and request the Representatives from that state to vote for the bill. Although such an action was only to be expected from any Tennessee Democrat, it is not unlikely that Polk had considered the probable effect on his brother's candidacy.[10]

The private correspondence of this early part of 1844 is very interesting in view of the assertion made later that an anti-Van Buren plot had been hatched in Tennessee by the intimate associates of Polk. The letters show conclusively that instead of opposing the ex-President's nomination the leading politicians were trying hard to bring it about. On the other hand, the rank and file of the Democracy of the state cared little for Van Buren and feared that he would be a "dead weight" upon the party. Even Hogan and Heiss, the proprietors of the *Union*, at first declined to place his name at the head of their political column,

---

[7] Levin H. Coe to Polk, Jan. 27, 1844, *ibid.*

[8] In a letter to the editor of the *Globe*, dated January 28, Johnson stated that he had, at various places, been nominated—sometimes for President, sometimes for Vice-President. He would accept either, he said, if ratified by the national convention, but in any event he would support the regular nominees.

[9] Nashville *Union*, Jan. 23, 1844.

[10] When Polk's resolution reached the senate, a Whig member moved that the preamble should be changed to read that the "question is now brought before the American people not with a view to relieve Gen. Jackson . . . but alone for political effect" (Nashville *Union*, Jan. 25, 1844).

although Polk had requested them to do so.[11] Urged by Laughlin
as well as by Polk, the editors finally, though reluctantly, consented. His name appeared for the first time on February 8,
1844, and the editors stated frankly that

in placing Mr. Van Buren's name at the head of our paper, subject to the
action of the National Convention, we assume no new position either in
reference to our views or the preferences of the great body of the democracy in Tennessee.

They would support, they said, the nominee of the convention,
whoever he might be.[12] On March 12, after much urging by Polk,
Laughlin assumed the editorship not only of the *Union* but of
the *Star Spangled Banner,* a weekly campaign journal which
was to be published from the same office.[13] The tone of the *Union*
now became more favorable to Van Buren, and there seemed to
be little doubt that he would be nominated at Baltimore.

Up to the time that Van Buren's Texas letter was published,
there was no indication that influential Tennesseans had any
intention of opposing his nomination. Cave Johnson, who, with
R. J. Walker, was charged later with having instigated the plan
to defeat him at Baltimore, was a hearty supporter of the ex-
President. In a letter written from Washington he told of a
movement in that city to nominate Cass. This movement, he
believed should be vigorously opposed, for "in my opinion *your
only chance* for the position we wish" depends upon the nomination of Van Buren.[14] At a large meeting held at Nashville
on March 15, 1844, to celebrate the anniversary of Jackson's

---

[11] "Tell the General," said Polk in a letter to Donelson, December 20,
1843, "that I had an interview with both Editors of the Union, when I
was at Nashville and both agreed to take decided and bold ground for
Van Buren in their paper. If they do not do so, in their next paper, I
will write to them and urge it upon them. The paper here has done so"
("Polk-Donelson Letters").

[12] Nashville *Union,* Feb. 8. Polk to Heiss, Jan. 21 "Heiss Papers";
Laughlin to Polk, Feb. 4, *Polk Papers.*

[13] Polk's letters to Heiss advising the employment of Laughlin are in
the "Heiss Papers." Various letters of Polk and Laughlin on the subject are in the *Polk Papers.*

[14] Johnson to Polk, March 6, 1844, *Polk Papers.*

birth and the remission of his fine by Congress,[15] efforts were
made to create enthusiasm for both Van Buren and Polk. While
at Nashville Polk answered Johnson's letter and fully concurred
in the views he had expressed. A few days later he wrote again
on the same subject and said that "the movement which you say
is on hand—to profess publicly to support Mr. Van Buren, with
a secret intention to attempt to nominate Genl Cass in the Convention,—can receive no countenance." If there is any movement in Tennessee, said he, to couple his name with that of Cass
to the prejudice of Van Buren, he is not aware of it, and if discovered, he will not permit it.

It is now settled that the preference of a large majority of the party is
for *Mr. Van Buren,* and the whole party should yield to his nomination
and make it unanimous. Such men as *Duff Green,* and the discontented
in our ranks may attempt to produce confusion by resisting the popular
choice of the party, but their movements can receive no countenance or
support from me.[16]

Immediately following the Nashville meeting Laughlin sounded
the trumpet more vigorously than ever for Van Buren and Polk,
and insisted that four-fifths of the Democrats in Congress were
in favor of the ex-President's nomination. Although a friend
of General Cass, Laughlin deplored the agitation in his behalf.
Cass himself, said he, "has frowned upon the design." Those
who had come out for Cass had, in Laughlin's opinion, done so
for the purpose of dividing the party, and most prominent among
them was Duff Green, "a renegade deserter."[17]

On March 20, the day before the appearance of Laughlin's
editorial, Polk had declined an unofficial offer of a place in the
cabinet of John Tyler. Abel P. Upshur, Secretary of State, and
Thomas W. Gilmer, Secretary of the Navy, had been killed in
the *Princeton* disaster of February 28, leaving two vacancies in

---

15 Laughlin submitted a resolution which declared that revenge had
led Judge Hall to impose the fine. Polk seconded the resolution and made
a speech on political questions (*Union,* March 19, 1844).

16 Polk to Johnson, March 18, 1844 ("Polk-Johnson Letters").

17 Nashville *Union,* March 21, 1844.

the cabinet. Calhoun had been selected to succeed Upshur,[18] but John Y. Mason, who had been invited to take Gilmer's place declined, at first, to accept the offer. At this juncture Theophilus Fisk, former editor of the *Old Dominion* and a friend of the President, sent a letter to Polk asking whether he would accept the navy portfolio "without any pledge, shackle, or trammel being asked of you, other than is already guaranteed by your exalted character and standing."[19] Mason, however, changed his mind,[20] and by accepting the appointment left no vacancy to be filled.

Without knowledge of the offer made to Mason, or of his accceptance, Polk had already written to Fisk, stating that he would not accept a place in the cabinet. In a letter to Cave Johnson, which was intended also for the eye of Silas Wright, Polk gave a twofold reason for declining a cabinet position. In the first place, it would seem like withdrawing from the race for Vice-President, and this he had no intention of doing. Again, Tyler's administration was supposed to be hostile to Van Buren; consequently, if he accepted, he would be placed in a false position, for he was heartily in favor of Van Buren. This, in effect, was a notice to the Van Burenites that he was still in the race for Vice-President and that, as he was loyal to their candidate, he expected their support in return. He also called attention to Laughlin's editorial in the *Union* against the attempted movement for Cass. In another passage of the letter he not only declared his own views on the Texas question, but he intimated, also, that he took it for granted that Van Buren would not oppose annexation. Speaking of Calhoun's call to the Department of State, he said:

---

[18] For the circumstances of Calhoun's selection, see Schouler, *Hist. of U. S.*, IV, 455.

[19] Fisk to Polk, March 9, 1844, *Polk Papers*. Fisk said that the idea was his own, but he told Cave Johnson that he was acting by authority of the President (Johnson to Polk, March 10, *ibid.*).

[20] Much to the surprise of both Tyler and Fisk—so said the latter in a letter to Polk, March 13 (*ibid.*).

I think it probable that he will see that it is his interest to co-operate thoroughly with the Democratic party, so heartily for *Mr. Van Buren,* harmonize his friends at the South, and make a great effort upon the Texas and Oregon questions.[21]

At the time that Polk declined to accept a place in Tyler's cabinet, the Texas question was fast approaching its critical stage. Since Polk was soon to become closely identified with this important question, it seems necessary to give a brief summary of its history up to this point and to ascertain, if possible, whether he or his friends had any part in bringing it forward.

The idea of annexing Texas was not new; but since the failure of the first attempt, during Jackson's administration, no party had made annexation an active political issue. That it was made an issue in the campaign of 1844 was due, according to Benton,[22] to the machinations of Calhoun, who hoped by this means to prevent the nomination of Van Buren and the election of Henry Clay. The first move in this direction was made in the winter of 1842–43. At that time a letter, written by Thomas W. Gilmer but inspired by Calhoun, was printed in a Baltimore paper. It advocated the immediate annexation of Texas in order to forestall the designs of Great Britain. The letter, said Benton, was "a clap of thunder in a clear sky," for no one was aware of any such design. Webster left the Department of State in May, 1843, and after the brief term of Legare, was succeeded on June 24 by Abel Upshur, of Virginia. Upshur was a friend of Calhoun and interested in the annexation of Texas. It was probably due to the influence of Upshur and Gilmer that Tyler first became interested in annexation, but before long the President had determined to use it for his own purposes. In his third annual message, which was sent to Congress early in December, 1843,

---

[21] In another letter of the same date which was intended for Brown and Johnson only, Polk made still more explicit the purpose of the first letter, for he pointed out that Wright, if he would, could certainly prevent R. M. Johnson from being nominated (Polk to Johnson, March 21, 1844, "Polk-Johnson Letters").

[22] Benton, *Thirty Years' View,* II, 581 ff.

Tyler alluded to the dangers that might result from continued war between Texas and Mexico, and hinted pointedly at possible annexation.

At this stage of the question Aaron V. Brown, an intimate friend of Polk, became a leading factor in the annexation program. Whether or not he was consciously lending his aid to the Tyler-Calhoun project is not easy to determine. In a conversation with Benton on the first day of the session, Brown spoke of annexation as ''an impending and probable event,'' and he was rebuked by the Senator who said that it was *''on the part of some, an intrigue for the presidency and a plot to dissolve the Union—on the part of others, a Texas scrip and land speculation.''*[23] In a ''confidential'' letter to Polk, Brown alluded to Tyler's message and added: *''But this is not all.* I have reason to suppose it will soon be followed up with some definite and precise proposition—some think a treaty.'' The Whigs, said he, think that Tyler has brought the question up as a firebrand between North and South in order to gain support for himself, and that nothing will come of it; but however this may be, it is Brown's opinion that neither Whigs nor Democrats of the South and West should commit themselves against annexation.[24]

This was not the first time that Brown had shown an interest in the Texas question. In January, 1843, he had sent to Jackson a copy of the *Madisonian* containing Gilmer's letter and had received in reply the famous letter of February 12 in which the General urged the necessity of immediate annexation. Jackson's letter was not made public until a year later, about three months after Tyler had submitted his message on the subject of Texas. The procurement and the publication of Jackson's letter have been declared by Benton to be links in the chain of events which had been forged by Calhoun and his fellow-conspirators for the purpose of making Texas the leading political issue and Calhoun the candidate, although he does not say that Brown was fully

---

[23] *Ibid.*, 583.
[24] Brown to Polk, Dec. 9, 1843, *Polk Papers*.

aware of the part he was playing.[25]   He has intimated, also, that
the letter was purposely dated 1844 instead of 1843; but Brown's
own letter—published at the same time—explained the circumstances under which it had been procured and stated explicitly
that it had been in his possession for a "long time."[26]   However,
Benton's interest in Van Buren's nomination and his opposition
to annexation seem to have led him to associate events which in
reality were not related; on the other hand, Brown's own desire
for Texas is sufficient to explain his soliciting the opinion of
General Jackson on the subject.

If Brown was a conscious participant in any conspiracy to
undermine Van Buren, it is quite evident that his bosom friends,
Polk and Cave Johnson, were not aware of the fact.   Although
Johnson looked with favor on the acquisition of Texas, he was
averse to having it made an issue for campaign purposes.   At
the time that Polk's name was mentioned in connection with
Tyler's cabinet, Johnson stated his opinions very explicitly in a
letter to Polk:

> I fear some secret movements are making here so as to bring up the
> Texas question here prominently before the Convention meets & to make
> it operate if practicable agt Van in the Convention & agt Clay in the
> election—if it can be brought up fairly & properly & with a reasonable
> prospect of getting it I should have no objection, but if it is designed
> merely as a political question to operate in the ensuing canvass then I
> shall deplore it.   An effort no doubt will be made to unite the destinies
> of Oregon & Texas so as to unite the South & West—may you not be
> identified with these movements if in the cabinet? & if unsuccessful what
> follows?[27]

The friends of Calhoun confidently expected that their leader
would profit from the emergence of the Texas question.   Fearing
that "being considered a candidate" would, if left unchallenged,
procure for Van Buren the coveted nomination, they began at
an early date to seek support for their favorite.[28]   Due to their

---

[25] Benton, *Thirty Years' View,* II, 584.

[26] The letters of both Jackson and Brown were published in various
newspapers—among others, the Nashville *Union* of April 2, 1844.

[27] Johnson to Polk, March 10, 1844, *Polk Papers.*

[28] Dixon H. Lewis to Richard Crallé, June 10, 1842, *Crallé Papers.*

efforts the time for holding the national convention was postponed from December, 1843, to a later date, in order that they might have a longer time to educate public opinion; for even before Jackson's Texas letter was written, they were confident that Calhoun would be nominated.[29]

During the summer of 1843 the administration had become convinced that Great Britain was about to interfere in Texan affairs and effect, if possible, the abolition of slavery there. Duff Green was in England gathering information, and his communications were supplemented by reports which came from Texan representatives in London.[30] In December, as we have already noted, Tyler called the attention of Congress to the dangers of foreign interference in Texas, and soon afterwards he began to formulate plans of annexation. The supporters of Calhoun cooperated with the President, and there seemed to be no doubt in their minds that their patron, and not Tyler, would reap the political reward. Their hopes of success mounted high when Calhoun was called to take charge of the Department of State. Like the President they were interested in annexation *per se;* in addition, they fully appreciated its importance as a campaign issue. "It is the greatest question of the *Age*," wrote Dixon H. Lewis, and he rejoiced that Calhoun was in a position "to direct its force & control its fury."[31] Three days after Lewis had made

---

[29] In a letter written from Washington, February 8, 1843, Duff Green told Crallé that although the Van Buren faction wanted an early convention, he hoped that it could be delayed until June. "It has now," said he, "narrowed down to a choice between Calhoun & Van Buren and the demonstrations are becoming more and more decided for Mr. Calhoun so that, in my opinion, the concentration in his favor will become so apparent as public opinion developes that the convention will indeed become obsolete" (Letters of Duff Green, Library of Congress; Benton, *Thirty Years' View,* II, 585).

[30] Smith, *Annexation of Texas,* chap. vi.

[31] "Every thing depends on the Texas question, which is an element of Power so much stronger than Clay, V Buren & their conventions that it unsettles all calculations as to the future course of men & parties. It is the greatest question of the *Age* & I predict will agitate the country more than all the other public questions ever have. Public opinion will boil & effervesce . . . more like a volcano than a cider Barrell—but at

this assertion Jackson's Texas letter appeared in the Richmond *Enquirer*. No doubt it fitted into the Calhoun program, yet it is not at all certain that this was Brown's motive in having the letter published. Surely General Jackson did not write it for any such purpose.[32]

The emergence of the Texas question was not welcomed by Henry Clay. Early in December, 1843, he stated his opinions on the subject in a letter to John J. Crittenden.[33] There were, he said, already a sufficient number of issues without "adding freak ones" of this character, and he did not think it right to allow John Tyler to make capital out of this exciting topic. In his opinion, annexation, either by treaty or by conquest, was entirely out of the question; however, unless Tyler should present some definite project of annexation he did not feel called upon to make public expression of his views. In the following March, when it was rumored that the President was negotiating with Texas, Clay—with his usual faith in his own ability both to shape and to direct political issues—still felt confident that he could stem the tide of Texas agitation.[34]

---

last will settle down with *unanimity* for annexation in the South & West & a large majority in the North. It will in the meantime *unite* the *hitherto divided South*, while it will make Abolition & Treason synonymous & thus destroy it in the North.

"The beauty of the thing is, that Providence rather than Tyler has put Calhoun at the head of this great question, to direct its force & control its fury. It is understood by letters from him that he accepts.

"P. S. It is understood the preliminaries of the Treaty have already been arranged & only awaits the special minister who is daily expected." (Lewis to Crallé, March 19, 1844, Crallé Papers). Alexander H. Stephens believed that "the dissolution of the present Confederacy" lay "near Mr. Calhoun's heart" (Stephens to James Thomas, May 17, 1844, *Rep. Am. Hist. Assn.*, 1911, II, 58).

[32] Benton says that Blair declined to publish the letter in the *Globe* (*Thirty Years' View*, II, 587). Later, however, it was printed in that paper, along with Brown's letter explaining his reasons for publishing it.

[33] Clay to Crittenden, December 5, 1843, *Crittenden Papers*.

[34] Writing from Savannah, he said: "I think I can treat the question in a manner very different from any treatment which I have yet seen of it, and so as to reconcile all our friends, and many others to the views which I entertain. Of one thing you may be certain, that there is no such anxiety for the annexation here at the South as you might have been disposed to imagine" (Clay to Crittendon, March 24, 1844, *Crittenden Papers*).

The time was fast approaching when candidates must take a definite stand either for or against annexation. Despite the desire of some of them to eliminate this topic from the issues of the campaign, every day brought the subject more into prominence. Calhoun's position was already well known, for in his letter accepting the cabinet portfolio he had come out strongly in favor of annexation. Clay would probably be nominated by his party no matter what position he might choose to take with respect to the all absorbing topic. Of greater importance, therefore, was the stand to be taken by Van Buren; for on this would depend, in all probability, his success or failure in the nominating convention.

On March 27, 1844, W. H. Hammet, a member of Congress from Mississippi and an "unpledged delegate to the Baltimore convention," addressed a letter to Van Buren asking for his views on the annexation of Texas. In writing this letter Hammet was evidently coöperating with the most loyal friends of Van Buren, and not, as Benton has intimated, with the supporters of Calhoun.[35] After taking ample time for consideration Van Buren on April 20, drafted his reply and sent it to his most intimate friend, Silas Wright. When it reached Wright on the evening of the 26th, it was read to a number of Van Buren's friends, including Fairfield, King, and Benton. They approved it and decided that it should be published immediately in the *Globe*. This course was decided upon before Hammet had even seen the letter.[36] The ex-President began his letter by asserting his belief that the United States had the constitutional right to annex Texas. He then gave a history of the quesion and of his own attempt to purchase it while Secretary of State under Jackson.

---

[35] Benton, *Thirty Years' View,* II, 587.

[36] Wright to Van Buren, Washington, April 29, 1844, *Van Buren Papers.* "Hammet was frightened," said Wright, "and it was with some difficulty that we induced him to our proposition for publication, before he had read it; but he behaved well and himself and the Major remained at the Globe office until about midnight, to examine the proof."

But, said he, as conditions are now, annexation would in all probability bring on a war with Mexico, and

could we hope to stand perfectly justified in the eyes of mankind for entering into it; more especially if its commencement is to be preceded by the appropriation to our own uses of the territory, the sovereignty of which is in dispute betwen two nations, one of which we are to join in the struggle?

He thought not, for "we have a character among the nations of the earth to maintain." He did not believe that there was danger of foreign interference in Texas or that nothing but immediate action could prevent Texas from being lost to the United States.[37]

On the very day that Van Buren penned his answer to Hammet, Cave Johnson sent him a letter from Washington.[38] He informed the ex-President that within two days the Texas treaty would be sent to the Senate, and, from all appearances, would be the controlling factor in the next Presidential election. For this reason he and other friends hoped that Van Buren would favor annexation, because "they hope such a position will not injure you in the North, whilst it must overwhelm Mr. Clay in the South if he hesitates or equivocates." In order to forestall intrigues to prevent his nomination, Johnson urged him to make his position known at the earliest possible date.[39] Johnson's warning, to be sure, came too late; on the other hand, it seems

---

[37] The letter was published in the Washington *Globe*, April 28, 1844.

[38] Whether Johnson had any knowledge of Hammet's letter to Van Buren, I am unable to say. If he had, Van Buren's long delay in answering probably induced him to write.

[39] "In the event of your being favorable to the treaty, I entreat you to take the earliest opportunity of giving your views—we have intrigues on hand here if practicable, to supersede you in the Baltimore Convention— and this question is one of the means used to arouse some of the Western & S Western members agt you—from a supposition that you are hostile to it—the delay of the Globe in coming out—your delay and the opinion of some of the N. Y. Democrats—all are urged & I fear with some effect among the members." Already, said he, some are expressing fears of Van Buren's "availability" and are talking of other candidates, such as Stewart, Dodge, and Cass. He is gratified to learn that Nicholson, who had headed the Cass movement in Tennessee, now says that Van Buren is the only man who can carry that state. Such, also, is the opinion of Governor Polk (Johnson to Van Buren, April 20, 1844, *Van Buren Papers*).

to show that he was sincerely desirous of Van Buren's nomination until the New Yorker had taken a position which would, in all probability, render his election impossible. The sincerity of Johnson's regret when Van Buren's opposition to annexation became known is expressed in a letter to Polk. "Many of us are in rather low spirits today—his course gives great advantage to the discontents over us and they will make the most they can out of it."[40] Two days later he reported that the excitement over Van Buren's letter was not abating, and that the friends of Texas had called a meeting at the capitol over which R. J. Walker had presided. They wanted another candidate—some were looking to Cass, others to Calhoun.[41]

Clay, who was then on a canvassing tour, reached Wahington in the latter part of April. While there his letter on the Texas question, dated at Raleigh on April 17, was given to the *National Intelligencer* for publication. He was decidedly opposed to annexation, because it would surely result in a war with Mexico. Even if Mexico should agree, he believed that it would be inexpedient to admit Texas into the Union.[42] Knowing that Van Buren, whom he supposed would be his opponent, did not favor annexation, Clay had not the "smallest apprehension" in stating his position.[43]

Inquiries were not limited to candidates for the Presidency. Late in March a nonpartisan, anti-Texas meeting assembled in Cincinnati and a committee of five, including Salmon P. Chase, drafted a letter to Polk asking his views on annexation. When the letter reached Columbia, Polk was on his farm in Mississippi,

---

[40] "A serious & powerful effort," he continued, "will be made to get a new nomination in which I think most of my democratic colleagues will unite, from the little I can learn. The discontents are moving heaven and earth & will never stop until the Convention is over if they do so then." At present, he said, the desertion is toward Cass, but he does not believe that Cass will get the nomination (Johnson to Polk, April 28, 1844, *Polk Papers*).

[41] Johnson to Polk, April 30, 1844, *ibid.*

[42] *Nat. Intell.*, April 27, 1844.

[43] Clay to Crittenden, April 21, 1844, *Crittenden Papers.*

but as soon as he had reached home his reply to the committee was prepared without hesitation. It bore the date of April 23 and advocated unequivocally "immediate re-annexation."[44] Like Jackson in his letter to Brown, Polk emphasized the point that our original title to Texas had been valid beyond question and that the territory had unwisely been ceded to Spain. He conveniently ignored the fact that the cession had been made by those who possessed the constitutional authority to make it. And however unwise such an action may have been, it is difficult tc see the bearing of this lack of wisdom on our subsequent right to re-annex the lost territory. On account of the danger that Texas might become a British colony, Polk maintained that all European countries should be excluded from both Texas and Oregon. "Let Texas be re-annexed," said he,

and the authority and laws of the United States be established and maintained within her limits, as also the Oregon Territory, and let the fixed policy of our government be not to permit Great Britain or any other foreign power to plant a colony or hold dominion over any portion of the people or territory of either.[45]

These remarks on colonization are not without interest, for they are a forerunner of what was later called the "Polk Doctrine."

Polk's letter was written only three days after that of Van Buren and of course without knowledge of its contents. Indeed, as late as May 4, after he had read Clay's anti-Texas letter, he expressed the hope and the belief that Van Buren would "now take ground for annexation."[46] The views which he expressed coincided with those held generally by Democrats in Tennessee. On the very day that Van Buren penned his indictment against annexation, an enthusiastic meeting of Democrats at Nashville

---

44 "I have no hesitation in declaring that I am in favor of the immediate re-annexation of Texas to the territory and government of the United States. I entertain no doubt as to the power or the expediency of the re-annexation."

45 MS, dated Columbia, April 23, 1844, *Polk Papers*. Printed in Washington *Globe*, May 6, 1844.

46 Polk to Johnson, May 4, 1844, "Polk-Johnson Letters."

passed resolutions in favor of it by a unanimous vote.[47]   It is not
surprising, therefore, that Van Buren's letter had a "prostrating
and cooling effect" upon his supporters in that state or that many
who had stuck to him from a sense of duty should now feel relieved from further obligation.[48]   Individuals could express their
sentiments very freely to one another, but Laughlin, who for some
time had been sounding Van Buren's praises, was now in somewhat of a quandary.   As editor of the party organ, he must of
course make some comment.   On May 9, therefore, he pointed
out in an editorial that, while Clay's objections to annexation
were permanent, those of Van Buren were temporary—objections only until certain obstacles had been removed.   Laughlin
himself advocated immediate annexation, regardless of consequences; still, if a majority of Democrats should decide to wait,
he was ready to acquiesce.   This left the way open for continued
support of Van Buren.   Since taking charge of the *Union*,
Laughlin had been bitter in his assaults upon Clay.   The Whig
candidate had perjured himself by challenging Randolph to fight
a duel; he was guilty of Cilly's death, because he had written
the challenge for Graves; but neither crime was surprising in a
man who had "defrauded Gen. Jackson out of the Presidency,
for an office worth $6000 per annum."[49]

Before his treaty with Texas had been consummated, Tyler
seems to have given up hope that he might be nominated by the
Democrats.   His official organ indignantly denied the assertion
made by the *Globe* that he was knocking for admission to the
Baltimore convention; on the contrary, "the friends of the Veto-
Administration intend having a Convention which will represent the Republican party more truly than Mr. Van Buren's

---

[47] Nashville *Union*, April 23, 1844.

[48] "Indeed it has given a pretext for doing that which they have had
in their minds to do—to declare against V. B., and a considerable portion
of them will never be reconciled to him" (Nicholson to Heiss, May 8, 1844,
"Heiss Papers").

[49] Nashville *Union*, March 30, 1844.

Convention, and the nominee will be elected.''⁵⁰   Still, the President was ready to welcome assistance from any quarter, for in May his friend Fisk sounded Cave Johnson concerning Jackson's opinion of his administration, and at the same time Polk was being considered for the War Department or the British mission.⁵¹

Cass was the last of the aspirants to declare himself on the Texas question.   In response to a letter from Hannegan, he, too, came out for immediate annexation.⁵²

On May 1, four days after Clay's Texas letter had appeared in print, the Whig convention assembled at Baltimore.   One day sufficed for nominating the candidates and adopting a platform. Without a dissenting voice, Clay was chosen for the first place, and on the third ballot, Frelinghuysen, of New Jersey, was selected as his running mate.   The platform was drawn to suit the candidate.   It avoided the Texas and bank questions and emphasized tariff, currency, distribution, and usurpation by the Executive.   With one omission—the bank question—Clay took his stand on the traditional Whig policies, and appealed to the people to sustain him.

While the Whigs rallied with enthusiasm to the standard of their chief, harmony within Democratic circles was rendered impossible by the appearance of the ''lone star'' on the political horizon.   The party which had long been distinguished for its effective discipline and its unity of action now appeared to be hopelessly divided on the eve of battle.   Even the great ''chief'' at the Hermitage seemed to be uncertain as to the proper plan of campaign.   His commands were ambiguous, for they resulted from conflicting emotions; he longed to see his old friend Van Buren nominated, but his desire for Texas was still stronger. Although few had a definite idea as to the best means of restoring harmony, as the time for the Baltimore convention approached

---

⁵⁰ *Madisonian*, April 3, 1844.
⁵¹ Johnson to Polk, May 8, 1844, *Polk Papers.*
⁵² His letter was dated at Detroit on May 10.   There is a copy in *Niles' Register*, May 25, 1844.

the conviction that Van Buren could not be elected became very widespread. The Virginia Democratic central committee, by resolution, released the delegates of that state from the obligation to obey their instructions, and delegates of other states announced publicly that they would not vote for Van Buren.[53]

Before the appearance of his Texas letter Van Buren had been accepted generally as the candidate; not because he enjoyed a wide popularity, but because a small minority urgently advocated his nomination and the rest of the party, being more indifferent than hostile, simply acquiesced, since they had no substitute to offer. After the publication of his Texas letter, his downfall was brought about by much the same process that had procured his elevation to party leadership. The few who were violently opposed to his nomination had little difficulty in convincing others, and especially the friends of Texas, that he could not possibly be elected. Those who had supported him from a sense of duty only, now had no hesitancy in transferring their allegiance to another candidate who would be more likely to win. Amos Kendall emphasized this point in a letter written to Van Buren. He told him frankly that he had no good news, and that unless some one else could be nominated at Baltimore the southern delegates would put up a third candidate. Kendall did not believe that the pro-Texas feeling was due to any organized movement, but rather to the "continued ding-dong sung in their ears" by a few of the most interested. Van Buren's letters, he said, had appeared at the worst possible time; the guns were being trained on Clay, and Van Buren appeared just in time to get the shot.[54] Cave Johnson reported the political situation as apparently hopeless. Benton and the New Yorkers seemed to

---

[53] Many such details are given in *Niles' Reg.*, LXVI, 162–163.

[54] Kendall to Van Buren, May 13, 1844, *Van Buren Papers*. Hendrick B. Wright, of Pennsylvania, believed that Van Buren could not be nominated—and if nominated, could not be elected, and Wm. R. King, writing from New York, reported it to be generally admitted that the ex-President could not be elected (Wright to Buchanan, May 13; King to Buchanan, May 14, 1844, *Buchanan Papers*).

be determined not to yield; Calhoun and his supporters were equally uncompromising, while each faction claimed a majority of the convention. "I see no hope," said Johnson, "unless some man can be found disconnected with both these fragments of the democratic party & who will yield to the annexation of Texas."[55] Polk, the man to whom this letter was written, fulfilled these requirements; and before the letter had reached its destination, his *availability* had already been discussed at the Hermitage.

The correspondence which passed between Democratic leaders in Tennessee about the middle of May shows an absence of definite plans for the future. On May 10 Donelson[56] summoned Polk to Nashville to consult with General Jackson and others in the hope that they might find some means of preventing a split in the party over the annexation question. "I feel deeply mortified," said he,

that our wise men should differ so much; and particularly that a measure of such vast consequences should have been kept so long in the dark and precipitated with so much haste.

Donelson was fully aware that Jackson's indorsement of annexation would aid Tyler and Calhoun; and, apparently, although his letter is not very clear, he did not approve making Texas a leading issue.[57] Polk accepted the invitation and reached Nashville on the twelfth. On the following day he and General Armstrong repaired to the Hermitage. They were met on the road by Donelson, who was taking to Nashville for publication in the *Union* Jackson's well-known letter which appeared a few days later under date of May 13th. In it, Jackson insisted that Texas must be annexed.

---

55 Johnson to Polk, May 12, 1844, *Polk Papers.*

56 Gen. Armstrong and other politicians wrote, also.

57 "I am particularly anxious that the ground occupied by the Genl. should be thoroughly understood by you. What he may now say if not modified by disclosures recently made will produce important results. If the Texas question is urged as it doubtless will be by Tyler & Calhoun, and Genl. Jackson gives the weight of his name to sustain their views, making it a leading question in the South, the sooner we know it the better. Come and talk over the matter with the Genl. and our friends generally" (Donelson to Polk, May 10, 1844, *Polk Papers*).

When reporting the interview to Cave Johnson,[58] Polk said that

He [Jackson] speaks most affectionately of *Mr. Van Buren*, but is compelled to separate from him upon this great question, and says both he and *Mr. Benton* have by their letters cut their own throats politically. He has no idea that *Mr. V. B.* can be nominated or if nominated that he can receive any Southern support.

Jackson said that the Baltimore convention must select some other candidate and that he should be from the Southwest; and Polk's letter hinted that the General had suggested that Polk himself ought to be placed at the head of the ticket. Polk asserted that he aspired to the second place only, but that his friends might use his name as they might see fit; in any event the party should unite on some "*one* candidate" and he must be in favor of annexation. "I have stood by *Mr. V. B.*," he continued, "and will stand by him as long as there is hope, but I now despair of his election—even if he be nominated." In another letter written on the following day,[59] Polk was more explicit concerning Jackson's desire to substitute his name for that of Van Buren. The General remarked, said he, that writing the anti-Texas letter was the only vital error over committed by Van Buren; nevertheless, it would be fatal to his election.

He thinks the candidate for the Presidency should be an annexation man and reside in the Southwest, and he openly expresses (what I assure you I had never for a moment contemplated) the opinion that I would be the most available man; taking the Vice-Presidential candidate from the North. This I do not expect to be effected.

Polk thought it was more probable that some northern man would be nominated for first place, and himself for the second. If Van Buren should be withdrawn, his friends would doubtless control both nominations, therefore great pains should be taken to conciliate them. Nothing, said Polk, could prevent Clay's election except the harmonious selection of a candidate at Baltimore. In offering suggestions for bringing about such harmony

---

58 Polk to Johnson, May 13, 1844, "Polk-Johnson Letters."
59 Polk to Johnson, May 14, 1844, *ibid.*

he displayed that shrewedness and attention to detail which made him one of the most astute politicians of his time.[60]   Along with this went another letter to Johnson, marked "Highly Confidential."[61]   Johnson was authorized to show the first letter to Silas Wright, and we are not left in doubt as to the reason.

Mr. Wright's declaration to you, in the conversation which you detail in your letter of the 8th that I was "the only man he thought the Northern Democrats would support if Van Buren was set aside, because I was known to be firm and *true* to the cause," is precisely the opinion which *Genl J.* expressed to me when I saw him two days ago.   The General had previously expressed the same thing to others.

He once more asserted that he had aspired to the second office only and had been loyal to Van Buren; but since the secret attack on the ex-President " 'Fortune is in a frolic,' and . . . there is no telling what may happen."   He recommended General Pillow to Johnson as a shrewd and reliable colleague in carrying out all plans.

In Jackson's letter of May 13 to the Nashville *Union*, in which he commented on Van Buren's Texas letter, the General said his old friend evidently was unaware that conditions had changed since he had been President.   No difference of opinion could change his confidence in Van Buren, but as to Texas, "Let us

---

60 "I have but little hope that union or harmony can be restored among the members, but I have hope that the Delegates *'fresh from the people'*—who are not members of Congress—and have not been so much excited can be brought together.   Let a strong appeal be made to the Delegates as fast as they come in, *to take the matter into their own hands, to control and overrule their leaders at Washington, who have already produced such distraction, and thus save the party.*   The Delegates from a distance can alone do this.   I suggest as a practical plan to bring them to act,—to get one Delegate from each State who may be in attendance to meet in a room at Brown's hotel or somewhere else, and consult together to see if they cannot hit upon a plan to save the party.   If you will quietly and without announcing to the public what you are at, undertake this with energy and prosecute it with vigor, the plan is feasible and I think will succeed.   If the preliminary meeting of a Delegate from each State can agree upon *the* man, then let each one see the other Delegates from his own State, and report at an adjourned meeting the result.   This is the only way to secure efficient action when the Convention meets."   The essential features of this plan were followed, and resulted in success.

61 Polk to Johnson, May 17 [14], 1844, "Polk-Johnson Letters."

take it now and lock the door against future danger."[62] His complimentary remarks about Van Buren were much like an epitaph for a departed friend. When he penned them he felt certain that his former protégé was doomed. In a letter written on the following day he told Benjamin F. Butler that nothing could restore Van Buren except indorsement of annexation, for "you might as well, it appears to me, attempt to turn the current of the Miss[iss]ippi as to turn the democracy from the annexation of Texas to the United States."[63]

Texas must be annexed, and Van Buren must be dropped. So much, at least, was settled; and if Polk could be substituted, so much the better. The *Union* now began to prepare its readers for the change. Laughlin had been chosen as a delegate to the Baltimore convention, and Heiss took charge during his absence. On May 14, Heiss announced that Van Buren's name had been placed at the head of the political column because he was thought to be the choice of the Democracy. It would be left there until some action had been taken by the convention, although the editor disagreed with his weak position on the Texas question. On the 18th, Heiss declared further support of the New Yorker to be hopeless, and by the 23rd he was ready to hazard some "guesses" regarding the nomination. The first was that Van Buren would come out for Texas or withdraw. The second was that one from a suggested list would be selected as the candidate. Heading the list was the name of Governor Polk,[64] but since Laughlin was a member of the pre-convention conference held at Nashville,

---

[62] This letter was dated May 13, and published in the Nashville *Union*, May 16, 1844.

[63] "Clay's letter had prostrated him with the Whiggs in the South & West, and nine tenths of our population had decided in favour of Mr. V. Buren & annexation of Texas—when this, illfated letter made its appearance and fell upon the democracy like a thunderbolt" (Jackson to Butler, May 14, 1844, *Van Buren Papers*. A full copy, also, in *Am. Hist. Rev.*, July, 1906, 833–834). The letter was carried to Butler by Donelson. Both men were delegates to the Baltimore convention.

[64] The others suggested were Calhoun, Cass, Stewart, Tyler, and Buchanan.

the "guess" regarding Polk required no great powers of divination.[65] On May 28, Heiss made another significant statement in the *Union:*

We do not believe Mr. Van Buren will receive one vote from the Tennessee delegation. If he does, that delegate who votes knowingly against the wishes of his constituents, will be marked, hereafter, as a man unworthy of their confidence.

Nearly all the delegates to the Democratic convention gathered in Washington on their way to Baltimore. For what transpired there, we must rely mainly on letters written by Gideon Pillow.[66] Pillow and Laughlin reached Washington on May 21 and began a campaign of interviewing delegates to ascertain their views. Pillow represented Cave Johnson as being rather apathetic and without hope of success. It is true that Johnson was inclined to see the dark side; but he was a shrewd politician and a personal acquaintance of most of the delegates, and it is probable that he exerted fully as much influence as either Pillow or Laughlin.[67]

Pillow reported the party to be hopelessly divided. The insurgents declared that they would not attend the convention unless the two-thirds rule were agreed upon, and that they would not support Van Buren in any event. The Van Burenites were equally insistent on a majority rule.[68] The pro-Texas Democrats

---

[65] On June 4 the *National Intelligencer* quoted the guesses made by Heiss and remarked that the "inference is irresistible" that the arrangement for dropping Van Buren and bringing Polk forward was made in the neighborhood of Nashville.

[66] Pillow was both conceited and unprincipled; still, if allowance be made for his exaggeration of his own importance, his account is probably authentic. His letters to Polk are among the *Polk Papers.* Copies edited by Professor Reeves are accessible in the *Am. Hist. Rev.*, July, 1906, 835ff.

[67] In his letter of May 24, Pillow said: "I saw your letter to C— J— and noted its suggestions." Evidently he refers to the letter to Cave Johnson, May 14, 1844. See above.

[68] In a letter written from Washington to Van Buren, May 26, Wright said that the Texas men were plotting to defeat him by means of the two-thirds rule. New Hampshire men were told, said he, that Woodbury would get the nomination in case Van Buren should be set aside; the Pennsylvanians were told the same with respect to Buchanan, and the Tennesseans with respect to Polk, *Van Buren Papers.*

tried to commit Polk's friends against Van Buren, but all except a few of the Tennessee delegates maintained a discreet silence on this subject. Two of them, Anderson and Jones, were bitterly opposed to the New Yorker and would not coöperate with their colleagues. Even Andrew Johnson was ready to sacrifice Polk in order to get rid of Van Buren. Pillow was satisfied that two-thirds of the delegates favored Polk for Vice-President; many expressed a preference for him as the candidate for President. No agreements were reached before leaving Washington, yet Pillow was quite certain that Van Buren would be forced to withdraw, and, if so, that his friends would never support Cass. On the other hand, he thought it probable that they would be willing to support Polk. If Polk should be brought forward, it must be done by the North, because it would never do for southerners to suggest his name.

The Democratic convention assembled in Baltimore on May 27, 1844. A large majority of the delegates had been instructed to vote for Van Buren by state conventions which had been held before the publication of his anti-Texas letter—in fact, before Texas had been seriously considered as a political issue. But Tyler and Calhoun had precipitated the question, and many who were bitter opponents of both of them were nevertheless in favor of annexation. Because Van Buren had taken his stand against annexation, many held that their instructions were no longer binding, for the conditions under which they had been framed had changed completely, and Van Buren no longer represented the will of the people. In a few cases, as in Virginia, steps were taken to annul the instructions. Some of the delegates from other states openly repudiated their instructions, and others went to Baltimore prepared to vote for Van Buren on the early ballots and then to use their own judgments. Benton, Welles, and other adherents of the ex-President have asserted that there was wholesale intriguing against their favorite. No doubt there was, but the widespread defection which preceded the convention was not wholly due to intrigue.

The convention selected as its chairman Hendrick B. Wright, of Pennsylvania, and as its secretary William F. Ritchie, whose father was editor of the Richmond *Enquirer*. The friends of Van Buren desired a majority nomination, but his opponents succeeded in adopting the two-thirds rule, which had been used on former occasions. The Van Burenites complained that the rule was now adopted for the purpose of defeating their favorite, but, although the charge was true, the majority merely followed the usual practice of Democratic conventions. In asking for a new rule the New Yorkers were requesting a personal favor for their candidate, which, under the circumstances, they had no right to expect. Van Buren himself had not been overscrupulous about accepting a nomination at the hands of Jackson's "made to order" convention. He had small reason to complain because the advantage was now with his opponents. On the first ballot he received a majority of the votes, but not the necessary two-thirds. In succeeding ballots his vote steadily decreased. After the seventh ballot had been taken, J. L. Miller, of Ohio, moved, by resolution, to declare Van Buren the party nominee, on the ground that he had, on the first ballot, carried a majority of the convention. Hickman, of Pennsylvania, caused much laughter by moving that General Jackson be nominated for President by a unanimous vote. Both motions were ruled to be out of order, and the convention adjourned for the day without having selected a candidate.

The evening of May 28, the second day of the convention, was a momentous one for Polk; and Pillow and George Bancroft are in substantial agreement as to what happened, except that each claims first honors in the transactions which took place. In a letter to Polk, in which he chronicled the events of the day, Pillow said: "I have within the last few minutes received a proposition from a leading Delegate of Pennsylvania and of Massachusetts to bring your name before the Convention for President." Pillow explained to them that if done at all this must be done by the North. "There is, I think a strong probability of your name

ultimately coming up for President. I do not think it prudent
to move in *that* matter now. I want the North to bring you
forward as a *Compromise* of all interests."[69] The delegate from
Massachusetts was evidently George Bancroft, for, in a letter to
Polk, Bancroft said that after the convention had adjourned on
the second day "it flashed on my mind, that it would be alone
safe to rally on you."[70] Carrol and Hubbard, of the New Hampshire delegation, heartily agreed, and likewise Governor Morton,
of Massachusetts.

> I then went to your faithful friends Gen. Pillow and Donelson. They
> informed me that if we of N. E. would lead off, they would follow with
> Mississippi and Alabama. . . . Certain of this, I repaired with Gen. Donel-
> son and Pillow to the house where were the delegates of Ohio and New York,
> and I spent the time till midnight in arguing with them.

Medary, of Ohio, was agreeable, and assured Bancroft that Ohio
would go for Polk in preference to Cass. Kemble, of New York,
also agreed to support Polk.

On the morning of the third day, May 29, Tibbatts, of Kentucky, withdrew the name of Richard M. Johnson and, as Pillow
reported to Polk, "we brought your name before the Convention
for the Presidency."[71] On the first ballot of the day, the eighth
of the session, Polk received forty-four votes.[72] As soon as the

---

[69] Pillow to Polk, May 28, 1884 (*Am. Hist. Rev.*, July, 1906, 841).

[70] Bancroft to Polk, July 6, 1844 (Howe, *Life and Letters of George
Bancroft*, I, 253). Years afterward Bancroft wrote a still more detailed
account of his activities during that evening. He stated explicitly that
"Polk owed his nomination by the Democratic Convention to me," and that
"I was the one who of my own mind and choice, first, on the adjournment
of the nominating convention, for the day, resolved to secure the nomination for Polk" (Bancroft to I. G. Harris, *Bancroft Papers*, Lenox Library;
cited by Reeves in *Am. Hist. Rev.*, July, 1906, 841). Perhaps, without
realizing it, Bancroft was inspired by Pillow and Laughlin to suggest
Polk's nomination.

[71] Cave Johnson told Polk that John Kettlewell, of Baltimore, was
"the man who first started your name in the Baltimore Convention"
(Johnson to Polk, Jan. 11, 1845, *Polk Papers*).

[72] In his letter of the 29th to Polk Pillow said 42 votes, but the Baltimore *Sun* reported the vote as follows: Van Buren, 104; Cass, 114; Polk,
44; Buchanan, 2; and Calhoun, 2. Polk received 6 from N. H., 7 from
Mass., 2 from Pa., 1 from Md., 9 from Ala., 6 from La., and the 13 votes
of Tennessee.

result had been announced, Frazer, of Pennsylvania, stated that
he had at first voted for Van Buren because he had been instructed
to do so, and then for Buchanan as the favorite son of his state;
but seeing that neither could be nominated, he had cast his vote
for "James K. Polk, the bosom friend of Gen. Jackson, and a
pure, whole-hogged democrat, the known enemy of banks and
distribution." His remarks were greeted with applause and
several warm friends of Van Buren now announced that for
similar reasons they were ready to unite upon Polk. Governor
Hubbard, of New Hampshire, and General Howard, of Maryland, pleaded for Polk and harmony, and Medary pledged the
vote of Ohio.[73] Roane took the Virginia delegation out for consultation and returned to announce that its vote would be transferred from Cass to Polk.[74] The ninth ballot had not proceeded
far before it became evident that it would be the last. The Polk
list became so large that Butler withdrew the name of Van
Buren, and many who had supported other favorites now transferred their votes to the Tennessean. In this way his vote was
made unanimous, and although South Carolina was not represented officially, Elmore and Pickens were present and pledged
the support of their state to the new candidate. Silas Wright,
of New York, a warm friend of Van Buren, was nominated for
Vice-President; he declined the honor, and George M. Dallas
was chosen in his stead.[75] A series of resolutions was adopted,
one of which declared in favor of "the re-occupation of Oregon
and the re-annexation of Texas at the earliest practicable period."
The committee on resolutions had considered the "one term"
pledge which had been referred to it by the convention, but
reported against such a restriction on the ground that it would

---

[73] Speaking of Bancroft's influence, Laughlin told Polk that "he and
old Morton" were mainly responsible for wheeling the "Yankee States"
into line (Laughlin to Polk, May 31, 1844, *Polk Papers*).

[74] Bancroft to Polk (Howe, *op. cit.*, I, 254).

[75] The above details, unless otherwise noted, have been taken from the
report of the convention published in the Baltimore *Sun*, May 28–30, and
Niles' Register, June 1, 1844.

be inconsistent to take such action after so many had been instructed to support Van Buren for a second term.

When notifying Polk of his nomination, Pillow[76] was inclined to take all the credit for bringing it about. To be sure, he very modestly said that "I had good help in some *true-men* in the North," but that he "got no help" from "our home people." On the other hand, Bancroft has made it clear that Donelson took a leading part in procuring votes for Polk, and it is unlikely that two such veteran politicians as Laughlin and Cave Johnson were entirely inactive. It appears that the knowledge of Jackson's preference for Polk was by no means confined to Tennesseans,[77] and it would be interesting to know in what degree this fact had a bearing on the ultimate choice of the convention.

From the above account it will be seen that Polk's nomination resulted from a combination of influences originally distinct. Seeing no hope of their own election, both Tyler and Calhoun were ready, for two reasons, to lend their support to the new candidate. In the first place, he believed as they did on the Texas question; in the second, so long as the office was beyond their own reach, they would rather see it go to a new man than to one of the competitors who had so roundly abused them. In the long run the Van Burenites were, for similar reasons, constrained to acquiesce in Polk's nomination and to contribute their support to his campaign. The Calhoun faction and the insurgent element led by R. J. Walker were enemies in other respects, but they agreed on annexation and therefore combined successfully to prevent the nomination of Van Buren. There is plenty of evidence that the Van Burenites had no love for Polk,

---

[76] His letter bore the date May 30, but obviously it was written on the 29th (*Am. Hist. Rev.*, July, 1906, 842).

[77] J. B. Jones, writing from Baltimore to his paper, the *Madisonian*, May 29, said: "It is true I hear it whispered about the streets, that the nomination of Mr. Polk was agreed upon at the Hermitage, Mr. B. F. Butler, in behalf of Mr. Van Buren and the *Globe*, concurring" (*Madisonian*, May 30, 1844).

yet their feeling toward him was indifference rather than hostility. Though they were not strong enough to nominate their favorite, they could at least veto the nomination of an objectionable rival like Cass, and, within certain limits, could determine the choice of the candidate. To Polk they had no specific objection; consequently, if all factions would agree to accept him, his nomination would be less objectionable than that of Cass or Buchanan. Therefore they made a virtue of necessity and reluctantly transferred from Van Buren to Polk. They claimed afterwards that they had been responsible for Polk's nomination, and this was true in the sense that they could have prevented it; still, under the circumstances, Polk had small reason to feel under obligation to men who, after all, had acquiesced in his nomination merely as a choice of evils.

Even before the appearance of his anti-Texas letter, Van Burean had little real popularity outside of a small circle of friends. After its publication, his defeat at the polls being inevitable, his nomination would have meant party suicide. This fact should have been obvious to his most ardent supporters, and yet they chose to regard his defeat at Baltimore as the result of a series of political intrigues. They did not, of course, have all the information which is now accessible, consequently the motives of many of their contemporaries were misjudged. Benton's version of Van Buren's downfall has already been noted; still more elaborate and equally erroneous is the version of Gideon Welles.

In a history of the contest which he prepared but never published,[78] Welles, like Benton, attributed the shelving of Van Buren to a many-sided intrigue in which Calhoun, originally, was the chief actor.[79] In a "last desperate struggle for the

[78] MS article, "A Review of the Political History of the United States and Presidential Contests" (*Welles Papers*, Library of Congress).

[79] "If Mr. Calhoun was insatiable in his ambition, he was also fertile in his schemes to promote it. They were often visionary and startling, so much so as to forfeit rather than beget general confidence, yet to those

presidency'' he brought forward the Texas question, and, when
he entered Tyler's cabinet, he believed that the President would
assist him.   His main object, up to this time, according to Welles,
was to make Van Buren's nomination impossible.   But Tyler
appropriated the Texas question and resolved to stand for reëlection; and while many Democrats were ready to espouse annexation, they would not rally to the standard of Calhoun.   In other
words, he had succeeded in weakening Van Buren, but had failed
in the attempt to attract support for himself.   Robert J. Walker,
said Welles, was interested in the annexation of Texas because it
offered an opportunity for land-scrip speculation.   Working
through Mason, Tyler's Secretary of the Navy, Walker had convinced the Richmond politicians that the surest means of defeating the aspirations of Calhoun was the nomination of some other
pro-Texas Democrat.   The preference of the Virginians, said
Welles, was Levi Woodbury, but on arriving at Baltimore they
found that New England would not support him.

Up to this point, with some modification as to Walker's
motives, Welles's account is apparently accurate, but his statements concerning the promotion of Polk's interests are erroneous
in detail and give an unfair impression of the attitude of the
Tennessee politicians.

Although Calhoun had announced before the meeting of the
convention that he would not permit his name to be presented,
Welles believed that he still had hopes of being nominated and
that they had been blasted by the nomination of Polk.   After
asserting that Polk was ''brought forward'' by the friends of
Van Buren who, under the circumstances, would not support any
of the other competitors, Welles then proceeds to tell how the
Tennesseans under the leadership of Cave Johnson and Gideon

---

with whom he was intimate, or who were within the circle of his influence,
there was a charm in his plans that was to the adventurous inviting.
There were always some one or more prominent points in his intrigues
that enlisted ardent supporters, and on these points he concentrated the
energies of an intellect of unusual power, and pursued his object with an
intensity that had no limits.''

Pillow had, for some time before the meeting of the convention, been playing a "deep and subtle game" to procure Polk's nomination. They "concealed their purpose from Genl Jackson who would give no countenance to the movement"[!]; they "fastened themselves on Wright and Benton as friends and partisans of Van Buren, which they were except in the contingency of securing Polk's nomination," betrayed their confidence and secretly intrigued against Van Buren.[80]

Many of the items in Welles's statement may be true enough, but in one of the main clauses the terms are inverted. He contends that the Tennesseans were ready to support Van Buren *unless* they could nominate Polk; whereas, they desired to nominate Polk *because* Van Buren's nomination, or his election at any rate, was no longer possible. Their efforts in Polk's behalf were made not only with Jackson's knowledge, but at his instigation. Under the circumstances, neither he nor they considered these efforts to be a betrayal of Van Buren. Surely Jackson had made it clear to both Van Buren and Butler, as well as to Benton, that he favored the nomination of some pro-Texas candidate. So successful, however, were the Tennessee delegates in their deception, according to Welles, that the friends of Van Buren "had no conception of the duplicity in that quarter" until all was over, and then they were forced to support the party nominee. The "reserve" of Wright and the "indignant resentment" of Benton were caused by the discovery of this "treachery." The New York Democrats worked loyally for the ticket, and "few knew what doubt & repugnance their strongest men entertained for the candidate"[!]

The New Yorkers were chagrined by the defeat of their favorite, and not knowing all the facts, it was natural for them to suspect the motives of those who had profited by their defeat.

---

[80] Welles admits that for two years the Tennesseans had been loyal to Van Buren while others were intriguing against him. He states that New Yorkers desired to associate Polk on the ticket with the ex-President, instead of R. M. Johnson. This is extremely improbable.

It was rumored at Baltimore that Polk's nomination had been agreed upon at the Hermitage, and Whig papers made assertions to this effect.[81] In stating to Polk his reasons for declining the Vice-Presidential nomination, Wright said that the people of New York believed that there had been intrigue against Van Buren in the convention and that votes for Polk could be procured in the state only by asserting that the candidate had had nothing to do with the intrigue.[82] Doubtless Wright shared the belief of his associates; but even if all of the charges against the insurgent element had been true, Van Buren's rejection had been brought about not so much by *intrigue* as by the application of the Democratic doctrine of majority rule. To be sure, he received the votes of a majority of the convention, but the delegates had been selected before his views on Texas had become known; and although there is no means of ascertaining with certainty the desire of Democratic voters as a whole, there is ample reason for believing that a large majority of them did not prefer Van Buren after the publication of his anti-Texas letter. From the first, Calhoun Democrats had been openly hostile, and those led by Walker, whom Welles had called the "chief engine" of the convention, made no attempt to conceal their unalterable opposition to Van Buren. It is not easy to see why their efforts to defeat his nomination should be termed an *intrigue* any more than the efforts of his supporters to procure it. Even "Old Hickory" did not hesitate to say that no anti-Texas man could possibly win, and surely he could not be accused of *plotting* against his old friend and protégé. Naturally Polk's immediate friends did not confide

[81] "There is one circumstance, and only one," said the Nashville *Union* (June 11, 1844) in denying these charges, "which could impress any honest mind with the belief that General Jackson controlled the nomination—that circumstance is this: *the work is so well done, that to an honest mind, it looks reasonable that, it might have been done by old Hickory!*"

[82] Wright to Polk, June 2, 1844, *Polk Papers*. It has been said, continued Wright, that Van Buren was set aside because of his anti-Texas letter. Better leave it so. Had he (Wright), who held the same views, accepted the nomination on an annexation ticket, the people would have concluded that Van Buren had been dropped for some other reason.

their secret hopes to Wright or to Benton, and the realization of these hopes was contingent on the defeat of Van Buren's nomination; but if this amounted to deception, it should be remembered that the ex-President's doom was sealed by the vote of 148 to 118 in favor of the two-thirds rule, and even if the Tennessee delegates had joined with the minority, such action would not have altered the result. Van Buren had always been indifferent when Polk stood in need of assistance, consequently there was no valid reason why the Tennesseans should continue to follow the ex-President in his pursuit of a forlorn hope. On the first seven ballots they voted for Cass, after which they transferred to Polk.

Irrespective of intrigues in his behalf, the selection of Polk as the compromise candidate was quite natural, if not inevitable. Apparently, a majority at least had come to Baltimore prepared to support him for the second place. He was the only aspirant who was not also a candidate for the Presidency, and for that reason, objectionable to the different factions. The Van Burenites would not support any of their hero's rivals, with the possible exception of Colonel Johnson; and the other factions would never consent to make Johnson the Presidential candidate. Some new man must be selected; and of these, who had a better claim than Polk's? As a member of Congress he had done valiant party service, and had proved himself to be a man of ability and discretion. The statements made by Welles[83] that he "was destitute of personal popularity" and especially that he had "no qualities to recommend him" are gross exaggerations. Welles himself had expressed a different opinion in 1844.[84] Even Horace Greely, although he spoke disparagingly of Polk during the campaign, had, in 1839, called him "one of the ablest men and most powerful

---

[83] Welles, *loc. cit.*

[84] In a letter written to Van Buren, Nov. 13, 1844, he asked whether Polk would have sufficient energy and discernment to make the administration his own, and added that "my own belief is, that he will prove himself worthy of being the choice of the democracy, after it could not have its first choice" (*Van Buren Papers*).

speakers in the south west.''[85] General Jackson aptly summarized Polk's qualifications for office when he wrote that

his capacity for business [is] great—and to extraordinary powers of labor, both mental and physical, he unites that tact and judgment which are requisite to the successful direction of such an office as that of Chief Magistrate of a free people.[86]

Joseph Storey was ''thunderstruck'' by the selection made at Baltimore; Governor Letcher exclaimed ''Polk! Great God, what a nomination!'';[87] and the Whig journals predicted an easy victory. But the Democrats, in the public press and in private correspondence, gave abundant evidence of both satisfaction and relief because a party crisis had been averted. Of course, due allowance must be made for partisan zeal, and for a self-seeking desire to stand well with the nominee. No doubt many professed a friendship which they did not feel, and, in the hope of reward, claimed to have been influential in procuring the nomination.[88] Still, he was scarcely less *popular* than any of the other aspirants, and as the campaign proceeded it came to be recognized generally that the convention had chosen the leader who would be most likely to win.

The *Spectator,* which was supposed to voice the sentiments of Calhoun, while expressing surprise that Polk had been selected, nevertheless approved the choice which had been made.[89] Its

---

[85] *Biographical Annual,* 1841, p. 52. When quoting this the Washington *Globe,* July 12, 1844, called attention to the fact that Clay lived in the southwest.

[86] Letter dated June 24. Quoted by Nashville *Union,* Aug. 13, 1844.

[87] Story to McLean, Aug. 16, 1844, *McLean Papers.* Letcher to Buchanan, July 7, 1844, *Buchanan Papers.*

[88] ''If you were here,'' wrote Pillow, ''you would imagine yourself the most popular man in the world, and you would be sure you *never had* an enemy in the convention. You cannot know how much pains they take to give in to me *their adhesion* to you, and to impress me with the *great merit* of their *conduct.*'' ''Never,'' said Benton, ''was such a multitude seen claiming the merit of Polk's nomination, and demanding the reward, for having done what had been done before they heard of it'' (Pillow to Polk, May 30 (29?), 1844, *Polk Papers;* Benton, *Thirty Years' View,* II, 594).

[89] *Spectator,* May 29, 1844.

editor, John Heart, announced his intention to publish a weekly journal, to be called "Young Hickory" in honor of Polk. Tyler was nominated by a convention of his own, but his letter of acceptance intimated that he might cease to be a candidate if Texas should be annexed by treaty or otherwise.[90] Polk entered the canvass, therefore, supported by an apparently united Democracy, and with some prospect of eventual assistance from those who had recently unfurled to the breeze the banner of "Tyler and Texas."

[90] *Nat. Intell.*, May 31, 1844. Several years later he hinted that his main object had been to force the Democrats to stand firmly for Texas (Tyler to Wise, Tyler, *Letters and Times of the Tylers*, II, 317).

CHAPTER XIII

CAMPAIGN OF 1844

"Who is James K. Polk?" Such was the derisive query raised by the Whigs as soon as the result of the Democratic convention had been announced.[1] It was an effective campaign cry. More than argument could have done it attached to Polk the stigma of mediocrity and obscurity, and, to some extent at least, it appears to have influenced the opinion of later generations. But as it turned out this very cry recoiled as a boomerang upon those who hurled it, for this "obscure" person was soon to be known as the vanquisher of their own renowned "Prince Hal."

Justly or unjustly, both in 1844 and since that time, Clay has enjoyed the reputation of being a great man. On the other hand, Polk's opponents have rated him as a man possessed of scarcely second-class ability—a man whom accident alone had placed in an exalted position. Even his friends have usually been rather apologetic—not insisting that he was really a great man, but that he was more able than he has been represented to be by his adversaries.

The Whigs entered the campaign full of confidence in their standard bearer and delighted that the Democratic party had made the "blunder" of passing over a man of ability like Van Buren, and had as the *National Intelligencer* put it, *"let itself down"* to Polk. The Democrats, on the contrary, while they rallied loyally to the ticket, were manifestly full of misgivings because one of the *prominent* men of the party had not been selected to

---

[1] Writing from Columbia, S. C., to Crittenden, Wm. C. Preston said: "The democrats here cry hurra for Polk in the street and come round to ask me who the devil he is" (undated letter in the *Crittenden Papers*, vol. 9).

enter the contest with Clay. Some of the newspapers, while admitting that Polk was not of the first rank, argued that great men and democracy were incompatible.

And yet, what is a great man, and by what standard is he measured? In his long career in the political field, Clay had been an opportunist, and, to a considerable degree, an adventurer. He had mounted one hobby after another in the hope of political advancement. There was little consistency in his record, for the panacea which he advocated on any particular occasion might differ radically in principle from the one offered only a year or two before. Many of the policies championed by Clay were visionary and impracticable, and few of them would now be considered sound. Furthermore, if greatness is to be rated by success, Clay's claim to it was not very well founded; for although he frequently succeeded in upsetting the plans of others, he was seldom successful in inaugurating his own most cherished policies. His greatest strength lay in his power of persuasion, and his greatest achievements were in compromising the divergent views of others and in procuring the adoption of measures after the compromise had been agreed upon.

Polk early adopted the fundamentals of the Jeffersonian creed. A conservative by nature, he was wary of experiments and shaped his course in accordance with the principles of the party which had been founded by his patron. His record, therefore, was consistent, and he could seldom be accused of trimming his sails to catch the varying winds of popular opinion. He was not a creator of issues, but his judgment on those which were presented was far sounder, as a rule, than that of his great opponent. With no pretense to oratory, he was an effective and convincing debater, while his thorough knowledge on public questions was conceded even by his foes. When he was nominated for the Presidency, he could point to a career of almost uniform successes, and as President few have had a more definite program to carry out or have succeeded so well in accomplishing their

250 JAMES K. POLK

purposes. But in spite of all this Clay was conceded a place in the first rank of statesmen, while many, even of Polk's supporters, did not claim for their candidate more than second-rate ability. The *Democratic Review*,[2] although it denounced the methods by which Clay had achieved his fame, did not deny that in the popular mind Clay was rated higher than Polk, so it made the best of the situation by saying that "our opponents are welcome to all their pride in their chief as a 'great man'—we are content with ours as a good one, and great enough for all practical purposes."

At the time that the two men were nominated, it was natural enough that Clay should be heralded as the superior of his rival. It was a period that was dominated by great personalities, and spectacular qualities were regarded as essential attributes of greatness. The influence wielded by Clay, Webster, and Calhoun, resulted more from the eloquence of their delivery than from the soundness of their arguments. Even the tempestuous and generally illogical conduct of President Jackson was easily mistaken for statesmanship.

Polk was not possessed of spectacular qualities, and he never tried to cultivate them. He was by nature secretive, even sly,[3] and the degree of his influence in shaping public policies was known only to his intimate friends. In all of those qualities which are thought to make men *illustrious,* Polk suffered by comparison with his rival; but, as the *Review* pointed out, a Democratic candidate might succeed without possessing them, however essential they might be for the Whig.

In no other campaign has Democracy and Whiggery so definitely contested for victory; in no other campaign have the

---

[2] Article on "First and Second Rate Men," August, 1844.

[3] For example, he made a practice of sending his Nashville correspondence under an extra cover, addressed to General Armstrong, so that his opponents, through the Whig postmaster, might not learn its final destination.

candidates so clearly represented the principles and policies of their respective parties.[4]

Polk was the first "dark horse" ever nominated for President by a political party, but while his name had not been previously associated with that office, it is not true that he was *unknown* or that his nomination was entirely accidental. The Baltimore convention did not simply make a grab in the dark, with the hope that either Providence or Fate would save the party from disaster. The man who, as chairman of the Committee of Ways and Means, had borne the brunt of the war against the Bank was unknown to neither party; a Speaker who was so thoroughly hated that his opponents had wished to deny him the customary vote of thanks could not have been so soon forgotten—least of all by the Whigs. He had never filled any of the great executive offices, but he had been intrusted by his party, during a most critical period, with the two most responsible positions in the lower house of Congress. No faction of his party doubted his ability, but like John Quincy Adams, his personal following was small. For personal reasons, many in the party may have preferred another candidate, but, if a certain newspaper story is to be credited, Clay, at least, recognized that the wisest choice had been made.[5]

---

[4] "The two candidates indeed, with a felicity of adaptation and correspondence, which is no mere accident, may be said in a remarkable manner to represent, respectively, the spirit and character of the two great parties by whom they have been chosen. . . . Mr. Clay is truly the living embodiment and incarnation of his party. Eloquent, showy, versatile, adroit, imperious, . . . the first Whig in America. A second-rate man in point of eloquence, intellectual force, and eminence of rank, would never have answered—could never have been adopted—as the head of such a party. We concede them this credit. They are naturally fond of splendor and strength—large and sweeping action—bold and brilliant energy and enterprise. Such is precisely the character their instinct has ever tended and striven to impress upon the government." Thus abbreviated, this characterization of Clay and his party is by no means an inaccurate description, and it is quite as true that Polk would "have been perfectly satisfactory to us for the presidency, even if he possessed in a far less degree than he has already amply proved, the further addition of the latter qualification [intellectual eminence], for the high office to which he is about to be called" (*Dem. Rev.*, August, 1844).

[5] "When the news of the democratic nomination reached Ashland, young Clay, who was impatiently waiting its announcement at the office,

Apparently the Democrats of all sections received the news of the nominations with genuine satisfaction—only in the Van Buren camp were there signs of resentment and reluctant support. They had not looked with favor on Polk's claim to the Vice-Presidency, and now he had beaten their patron in the race for first place. One of Catron's letters throws some interesting light on the attitude of political leaders toward Polk. It indicates also that, aside from the Texas question, Polk had profited by a desire on the part of the younger Democrats to get rid of the older leaders, by whom they had "been treated as boys." Together with others to be cited presently, this letter seems to make it plain that Polk's desire for a new party organ did not result from any bargain with Calhoun, but from a real distrust of the *Globe,* which of course was the organ of Van Buren.[6]

Polk's nomination was a victory for the annexationists, and it was also a victory for the younger element of the party. All factions were in duty bound to support the ticket, but it was evident from the first that "old fogies" must give way to those

---

hastened with the news to his father, who remained at home. 'Well, my son, who is nominated?' 'Guess, father.' 'Why Matty, of course.' 'No, father; guess again.' 'Cass?' 'No.' 'Buchanan?' 'No.' 'Then who the devil have they nominated?' 'James K. Polk,' said the son. The old man started from his seat, and rushing across the room, with disappointed hopes painted on his countenance, exclaimed, 'Beat again, by G-d' " (N. Y. *Plebeian,* copied in the Washington *Globe,* Oct. 29, 1844).

6 "Mr. Van B.," said Catron, "was out of luck—we again have it. Had the Dem. Con. met a month sooner, we w'd have been ruined in the west & South for ten years. Clay is out fully—many of the undermen are out, on annexation—and we have the strength added of a *rejection* of our V. P. on the precise ground, drawing in all the Calhoun strength—a vast, & controlling power, in the South. Among the leaders, you have many jealousies to quiet; they feared to see you on any ticket as vice, for fear you would set up for chief, after the first success. My position has let me into the deepest recesses of these things. I traversed the city night after night, last winter, encountering and *pledging* myself to the contrary of this opinion: But, sir, I made no converts, as I then believed. Buchanan was for Johnson—Benton for King; the Van B. men for either, sooner than yourself" [Both Calhoun and Tyler friendly to Polk]. "The coarse brutality of the Globe, was loathed last winter, by a large majority of our party." . . . "Your strength lies mainly as I think in this; you are of the present generation—the old leaders are thrown off; to do this has been an ardent wish by nineteen in twenty of our party in the House

who were abreast of the times. Old in years, but young in spirit, Jackson gave his enthusiastic support to both platform and candidates;[7] nevertheless, even his wishes went unheeded in cases where he desired to restore any of the "old guard" to power.

Within a few days after Polk's nomination, his Tennessee friends in Washington began to formulate plans, not only for the campaign, but for his course as President of the United States. The most active—not to say presumptuous—of all was A. V. Brown, who did not hesitate to draft a list of instructions for the guidance of the candidate. First of all Polk was told that he *must,* in his letter of acceptance, commit himself to a one-term policy.[8] The Democratic platform had said nothing on this point, but it was evidently thought necessary to checkmate the Whigs, whose platform had limited their candidate to a single term. Besides, as Brown seems very clearly to intimate, other "deserving Democrats"[9] with high aspirations might be expected to support the campaign with more enthusiasm if they could be assured that the way would be open for them at the end of four

R. for two sessions—but they would not do it, as they believed—not as I believed. They are now gone'' (Catron to Polk, June 8, [1844], *Polk Papers*).

7 ''Although I regret losing Mr. V. B. and the cause, yet I rejoice that the Convention have made choice of those worthy Democrats, Polk and Dallas. They are the strongest and best selection that could have been made'' (Jackson to Gen. Planché, June 14, 1844, *Polk Papers*. Same to W. G. Reeves *et al.*, June 5, 1844, Wash. *Globe*, June 28, 1844). Polk doubted that the Planché (often spelled Plauche) letter was intended for publication, and thought it imprudent in Planché to publish it. He feared the cry of ''dictation'' (Polk to Donelson, July 11, 1844, ''Polk-Donelson Letters'').

8 ''In your acceptance you must some way or other express yourself in favor of the one term system. This is important—I might say all important—you will know exactly *how* it will be highly useful. The thing is right *per se* & under all the circumstances I think you ought not to *hesitate* to do it'' (Brown to Polk, May 30, 1844, *Polk Papers*).

9 Laughlin, although not without some doubt as to the wisdom of such a declaration, thought that ''perhaps all in all it may be best—and will be making assurance doubly sure, and put us on an equality with the Whigs on that question'' (Laughlin to Polk, May 31, 1844, *Polk Papers*).

years. Although Brown's suggestion may have been entirely
superfluous, the one-term pledge found a place in Polk's letter of
acceptance.[10]

The next instruction was for Polk to prepare data on his life
and career for Brown to turn over to Bancroft, Kendall, or some
other person who would incorporate it into a biography.[11] Another thing to be considered, said Brown, was whether the *Globe*
was to be continued as "the Polk organ"; and while he was not
yet certain that it should not be so continued, it is apparent that
the discarding of that paper was already being discussed.[12]

Cave Johnson, as well as Brown and Catron, distrusted the
Globe,[13] but he by no means believed in courting the favor of or
permitting the domination by the southern wing of the party.
On June 1 he wrote to Polk that the party was more united than
at any time since the election of Jackson, but he pointed out that
danger might result from the fact that the South had been zealous
in procuring Polk's nomination. The *Globe,* he said, is noncommittal, and is already expressing doubts of Democratic success—
a new paper of unquestioned loyalty is very much needed. Two
weeks later he wrote that matters are growing worse and must
soon come to a head. "The struggle now is by a few Southern
men to appropriate *you* & the nomination to their exclusive benefit whilst the northern Democrats are determined to yield no such

---

[10] In 1835 Polk had, on the floor of the House, advocated a single term
for all Presidents (*Cong. Globe*, 23 Cong., 2 sess., part 2, 292).

[11] Brown had asked Laughlin to write the biography and it was he in
turn who had suggested Bancroft (Laughlin to Polk, May 31, 1844, *Polk
Papers*).

[12] "Much is said here by *some* as to continuing the Globe as the Polk
organ—this we will manage with sound discretion. The Globe will change
its tone & perhaps take back much that it has said & go in *warmly* if not
heartily—if so—well. But we will not commit ourselves to it *after* the
election."

[13] "Benton & the Globe falls in but not with so good a grace as we
expected" (Johnson to Polk, May 31, 1844, *Polk Papers*). He referred
to an editorial of the 29th in which Blair had said that the nomination of
Polk would at first be received with disappointment by those who had
stood for favorites, but that a little reflection would convince all that it
was for the best.

thing.'' Johnson had called a caucus in the hope of compromising differences, but the northern men became alarmed for fear the Calhoun members would get control; and Johnson decided that the best thing he could do was to prevent *anything* from being done.

I have been to see S. W. Jr. [Silas Wright] hoping to have it controled in some way & ended—he is furious and I think determined to push C[alhoun] and his clique to the wall or finish—in this battle. The object *of both* will be to make us take sides—the Northern know, that you have always been with them, whilst the South think that the question & the position of Genl J[ackson] will take you with them—how both are to be kept I cannot see—already we have much secret talk of upsetting the Globe—turning Benton overboard &c. I was disgusted to day, even Reuben Whitney talked of turning Benton out of the Democratic church. I am sick of this state of things & see no means of avoiding the explosion & most anxious to leave here.[14]

Johnson's fears increased rather than abated, for a few days later he expressed a belief that the combined obstinacy of Benton and the South Carolinians would lead to a southern movement that might imperil not only the Democratic party but the Union itself.[15] It seems very evident that Johnson had entered into no

[14] Johnson to Polk, June 13, 1844, *Polk Papers.*

[15] He has seen, he said, many prominent Democrats and all are pleased with the nominations, but ''the only difficulty I fear arises from the course of T. H. Benton, when connected with the movements of S. C. The latter uses *immediate annexation* for the purpose of uniting the South and killing T. H. B. & will if practicable *identify you* & Genl J. with all their future movements—fears are entertained in the North, that this *may be so*—& if any incident takes place to confirm the suspicion, our cause is jeoparded. I have given every assurance to S. W. Jr. & a few others that you could not be induced to separate yourself from the Northern Democracy—instanced your former course, in the case of White &c &c and also thought it impossible that Genl J. should lend himself to any such purpose. The only danger of the latter taking any step to favor the Southern movement they think will arise, from some letter from him, that will seem to favor the movement without sufficiently weighing the consequences.

''Can not you see him & have a free conversation as to the Southern movement & put him on his guard?'' Johnson fears that there will be a southern convention called to meet at Nashville, and advises that this should be forestalled by an earlier meeting to which Wright and other northern men should be invited. ''I have the most serious apprehensions from the Southern movement not only to our cause but the country. Mason & Dickson's line now divides the Methodist church & will soon

agreement with southern delegates to procure Polk's nomination, and it is equally clear that he had no desire to see the party brought under southern domination. He desired harmony, to be sure, and support from all factions, but harmony that would leave Polk indebted to neither section—free and unhampered in shaping his own course. Polk's replies show that he fully agreed with the views expressed by Johnson. He promptly warned General Jackson and took other steps to forestall a sectional convention; "no countenance must be given to any attempt should it be made."[16] A few days later he asked Donelson to prepare an article on this subject for the Nashville *Union*. "The idea," said he, "of a Southern convention or a sectional meeting at Nashville or elsewhere *must not for a moment be entertained*." He did not believe it to be necessary to allude specifically to disunion sentiments in South Carolina, but

> Let the article strongly enforce the leading idea, that a meeting of the masses from all sections of the Union is what is intended, and let every thing giving it the appearance of a sectional or Southern affair be expressly negatived. This would have the effect of allaying the fears of the North, by satisfying them that we in Tennessee gave no countenance to the suggestion for a Southern Convention upon the Texas or any other subject.[17]

While Johnson was warning Polk against the southern wing of the party, Catron was exhorting him not to listen to those who insisted that the salvation of Democracy depended upon the restoration to office of the old guard that had been ousted by Harrison, "cabinet & all," leaving no place for the rank and file whose money and talents would be responsible for the victory. "You who fought in the very van," said Catron,

---

divide the other churches. This movement will tend to divide political parties by it. The Texas question brings into the contest the fanaticism of the North with increased fervor. Our only safety for the country & our cause depends upon the Southern Democracy maintaining the position we have hitherto occupied—firm & consistent friends of the Northern Democracy—yielding much for conciliation & harmony" (Johnson to Polk, Louisville, June 21, 1844, *Polk Papers*).

[16] Polk to Johnson, June 21 [?], 1844, July 1, 1844, "Polk-Johnson Letters," *Tenn. Hist. Mag.*, Sept., 1915, 245–246).

[17] Polk to Donelson, June 26, 1844, "Polk-Donelson Letters."

and who the worthy old gentlemen thought last winter, had died in the *ditch*, have been brought out alive, not by their consent, nor help, but [by] those who look to chances for themselves. ''Treason & Traitor,'' ''rotten to the core,''—have been the gentle epithets that have greeted every move tending to wrench the power, as a party, from the old clique. Mr. Van Buren thought this public opinion, if Col. Benton let him think at all, which I doubt.[18]

Like Johnson, Catron warned Polk against unnecessarily expressing his views, and, as he had ''a soul to be *saved*,'' he should avoid answering letters of the Sherrod Williams type.[19]

Benton had written a letter in which he had exonerated Polk and Dallas from any part in the ''intrigue which had nullified the choice of the people,''[20] but on June 13 he openly accused A. V. Brown of having ''vicariously'' procured from Jackson the letter in favor of annexing Texas.[21] While General Jackson was charitable enough to attribute Benton's outbursts to insanity, caused by the Princeton disaster,[22] others knew that he was simply expressing what Van Burenites generally were thinking; and, although the appearance of harmony prevailed during the campaign, mutual distrust was manifest in private correspondence,[23] and a break was almost inevitable as soon as the election had been held.

In general, the Democratic press of all sections and factions rallied to the support of the candidates without reservation or

---

[18] Catron to Polk, June 10, [1844], *Polk Papers.*

[19] In 1836 Williams had catechised Van Buren, Harrison, and White as to their opinions on certain campaign isues. See Shepard, *Martin Van Buren*, 264.

[20] Dated June 3. *Nat. Intell.*, July 1, 1844; Benton, *Thirty Years' View*, II, 595.

[21] ''A card,'' printed in the Wash. *Globe*, June 13, 1844.

[22] ''Gen. Jackson was a good deal excited at Benton's course—said 'he shall hear from *me* soon'; and asserts that ever since the explosion of the big gun Benton has not been in his right mind. I think so too'' (J. Geo. Harris to Bancroft, June 25, 1844, *Polk Papers*).

[23] For example, Sacfield Maclin, of Tennessee, wrote from Little Rock, Arkansas, to Polk, on June 14, that ''Colo Benton and the Globe for the last eighteen months have done our party more damage than all the Whig papers in the Union. I have no doubt, and our friends here believe with me, that if Colo Benton thought he could hold his place in the affections of the Democratic party, and go against you, he would do so with all his energy'' (*Polk Papers*).

qualification. Most enthusiastic and influential of all, perhaps, was the Richmond *Enquirer*,[24] but Calhoun's Washington organ was hardly less effusive in its praise.[25]

Cass bore his defeat with better grace than any of the other aspirants. At a ratification meeting held in Detroit he commended the action of the Baltimore convention and promised his support. He spoke of Polk as a man who would follow in the footsteps of Washington, Jefferson, Madison, and Jackson, a statement which caused the Charleston *Courier* to remark that Polk, in order to do this, would have to "walk all sorts of ways."[26] He took an active part in the campaign[27] and spent his energies freely in preaching the Texas gospel in a northern latitude.

Polk's letter accepting the nomination bore the date of June 12, 1844. In it the most significant phrase, aside from approval of the Baltimore platform, was that

I deem the present to be a proper occasion to declare, that if the nomination made by the convention shall be confirmed by the people, I shall enter upon the discharge of the high and solemn duties of the office with the settled purpose of not being a candidate for reëlection.

This self-denying declaration resulted evidently, as we have noted, from an effort to checkmate the Whigs and a desire to

---

[24] "Mr. Polk's nomination has been received at Baltimore, at Washington, and at Richmond, with enthusiasm. It heals all divisions, unites our party with bands of iron. It thwarts every hope the Whigs had indulged of discord and divisions. It blasts the election of Mr. Clay, and saves our country from the sceptre of the dictator. Mr. Polk is true to all our republican principles, and he is the friend of Texas." Quoted by Nashville *Union*, June 11, 1844.

[25] "The great mass of the people wantd a man pure in morals, sound in political principles, *and in favor of the immediate annexation of Texas,* and such they have in James K. Polk. He is a consistent and sound politician, of the Jeffersonian Democratic school; talented, firm and discreet" (Washington *Spectator*, May 29, 1844).

[26] Quoted in *Nat. Intell.*, June 24, 1844.

[27] Geo. N. Sanders to Polk, July 12; Austin E. Wing to Polk, Aug. 2, 1844, *Polk Papers.*

harmonize factional discords in Democratic ranks. ''I said nothing to commit the party upon the *one term* principle,'' he told Cave Johnson, ''but expressed simply my own determination.''[28]

The pro-Texas Democrats may be said to have included three fairly well defined groups. The first was made up of the followers of Calhoun whose interest centered mainly in promoting his advancement. The second comprised those who were not friends of Calhoun, but who were interested primarily in wresting the control of the party from the hands of the older leaders. They saw in the Texas question a possible means of accomplishing this purpose; and, in addition, annexation would enlist southern sympathies and place the party reins in southern hands. Some of them were accused, and perhaps not unjustly, of being influenced by prospective profits from Texas land scrip. The third group was composed of men like Cave Johnson, and apparently Polk, who favored annexation but who, at the same time, did not desire southern domination. They wished above all things to harmonize differences which were threatening to disrupt the party, if not the Union itself. The second group was most active in the nominating convention, and Robert J. Walker, of Mississippi, was its reputed head. Catron and A. V. Brown were close friends of Polk but, unlike Cave Johnson, they had strong leanings toward the southern groups. Walker had long been interested in Texas. During Jackson's administration he had worked hard for the recognition of the new republic. In February, 1844, he had written a long letter in which many reasons were assigned why Texas should be annexed.[29] It was alleged by his opponents that he was influenced by the hope of profit from land speculations, but undoubtedly this personal motive was greatly exaggerated.

---

[28] Polk to Johnson, June 21 [?], 1844, ''Polk-Johnson Letters,'' *Tenn. Hist. Mag.*, Sept., 1915, 245.

[29] For an excellent summary, see Smith, *Annexation of Texas*, 140–144.

The annexation of Texas was not the only question on which the Democrats of 1844 were unable to agree. For a time considerable anxiety was felt for fear that Polk's well-known views on tariff might cost him votes in northern states, particularly in Pennsylvania. The discussion of Polk's views on this subject was precipitated by the so-called Irvin-Hardin correspondence. Shortly after Polk's nomination James Irvin, of Pennsylvania, had addressed a letter to John J. Hardin, of Illinois,[30] asking about the candidate's opinions on tariff. Hardin replied that Polk was a believer in free trade. As soon as Polk read the letters in the papers, he asserted that, although the second letter had been signed by Hardin, it must have been written by Milton Brown, a member of Congress from Tennessee. He asked that the "trick" be exposed.[31]

Walker undertook to instruct the nominee as to the stand he should take on this perplexing subject, and also as to the proper treatment of Democrats who had left the party in 1840. He suggested that Polk should make it known that he would welcome "all Jacksonian Democrats." On the tariff he was to declare for a revenue basis, adjusted in such a manner as to give "incidental aid" and a "reasonable profit" to every branch of domestic industries. He urged especially that the word *aid* should be used instead of *protection*.[32] But before Walker's letter had left Washington, Polk had already announced his views on the tariff in a letter to J. K. Kane, of Philadelphia. When he penned his "Kane letter," Polk had not of course read Walker's suggestions, but their ideas were practically identical and even the phraseology of their letters was very much the same. More straightforward than Walker, however, and less southern in his leanings, Polk did not sugar-coat incidental protection by calling

---

[30] Both men were members of Congress. Their letters, dated May 30, 1844, are printed in *Niles' Reg.*, LXVI, 234.

[31] Polk to Johnson, June 8, 1844, "Polk-Johnson Letters."

[32] Walker to Polk, June 18, 1844, *Polk Papers*.

it an "aid."[33] It was said at the time that Polk in drafting his letter made a definite attempt to face both ways—that his emphasis on incidental protection was for the North, while the substance was for the South. But if the tariff Democrats were in any sense deluded it must have resulted from a meaning which they had read into the letter, for, as Polk had pointed out in the letter itself, his present views were to be found in his own record, the record of his party, and the declarations that had been adopted at the Baltimore convention. In such a statement there was nothing equivocal—nothing to which a protectionist had reason to pin his hopes. "On all great questions," wrote General Jackson in a letter commending Polk, "from the Panama mission to the present day, he has been consistent, orthodox, and true to the standards of old-fashioned Jeffersonian democracy";[34] and the Kane letter promised no departure from such a course. To an intimate friend Polk wrote that his letter had been sent to Kane

with a request that he would show it to *Mr. Dallas* and *Mr. Horn,* ·and if in their judgment, it was absolutely necessary, they were at liberty to publish it, but not otherwise. It was but a re-declaration of the opinions upon which I have acted on that subject; it was carefully prepared and upon its doctrines I am ready to stand.[35]

---

[33] "I am," said Polk, "in favor of a tariff for revenue, such a one as will yield a sufficient amount to the Treasury to defray the expenses of the Government economically administered. In adjusting the details of a revenue tariff, I have heretofore sanctioned such moderate discriminating duties, as would produce the amount of revenue needed, and at the same time afford reasonable incidental protection to our home industries. I am opposed to a tariff for protection *merely*, and not for revenue." [Cites his votes on tariff bills.] "In my judgment, it is the duty of the Government, to extend as far as it may be practicable to do so, by its revenue laws & all other means within its power, fair and just protection to all the great interests of the whole Union, embracing agriculture, commerce and navigation" (Polk to Hon. J. K. Kane, June 19, 1844; copy of original in *Polk Papers;* printed copies in newspapers).

[34] Jackson to M. M. Jones, Utica, N. Y., June 25, 1844, Wash. *Globe,* July 20, 1844.

[35] Polk to Johnson, June 21 [?], 1844, "Polk-Johnson Letters."

Shortly after the adjournment of the Democratic convention the Senate took a vote on Tyler's treaty of annexation. Instead of the two-thirds in its favor which the President had promised the Texan diplomats, more than two-thirds (35 to 16) voted to reject it. Many who were not averse to annexation voted against the treaty, for they resented the manner of its negotiation and despised the renegade President and his Secretary of State. Tyler's friends tried to cast the blame for ill feeling on Calhoun and his Pakenham correspondence, while Calhoun regretted that the question had been brought forward under such a weak administration.[36] In the Senate, Benton now introduced a bill of his own for annexing Texas whenever Mexico should be ready to acquiesce, while McDuffie presented a joint resolution which would require simply a majority vote of both houses of Congress. Both failed, and without taking further action Congress adjourned on June 17, to await the result of the pending campaign.

When, on May 1, Clay was nominated at Baltimore, all signs seemed to augur success for the Whigs. The party was united and the choice of the candidate was unanimous. Tyler's annexation treaty had caused some annoyance to be sure, but by his "masterly" Raleigh letter Clay was thought to have made his own position unassailable. Besides, it did not appear that Texas would be an important issue, for Van Buren, whose nomination by the Democrats seemed a foregone conclusion, had also taken a stand against immediate annexation. Although Van Buren's nomination was fully expected, it was known that many Democrats had set their hearts on procuring Texas, consequently division and weakness appeared to be the inevitable result.

At first it did not seem that Polk's nomination had solved the difficulties which had confronted the Democrats, for despite the professions of harmony it was well known that Benton, Van

---

[36] Schouler, *Hist. of the U. S.*, IV, 470.

Buren, and their followers were dissatisfied with, if not indeed hostile to, their party. Tyler had been nominated on an annexation ticket, barring any accessions from Democrats who with him had deserted to the Whigs in 1840. His official organ even insisted that Polk should decline the nomination in favor of the man who had been responsible for bringing the Texas question forward.[37]

The Democrats had trouble in plenty, but the Whig program was likewise going awry. Van Buren had not been nominated as they had expected, and Clay's Raleigh letter, instead of settling the Texas question, bid fair to cost him many northern votes. In August, 1843, the Liberty party had nominated James G. Birney, of Michigan, on an anti-slavery ticket, and, after the publication of Clay's letter, many who under ordinary circumstances would have voted for him now announced their intention to support the Liberty candidate. Although Clay was a slaveholder and did not oppose the annexation of Texas with the consent of Mexico, still the Whigs had, originally, no reason to believe that the Liberty Party would be more hostile to him than to the Democratic candidate, who was likewise a slaveholder and, in addition, an advocate of immediate annexation. Nevertheless the unexpected happened, for on the stump Birney avowed a preference for Polk, arguing that Clay's superior ability, coupled with his equivocal attitude, made him the more dangerous and objectionable of the two.[38]

The Raleigh letter was denounced even more bitterly in the South, and, as will appear later, it was defection in this quarter which caused the candidate most alarm. No wonder that a leading Whig declared the Texas question to be ''an enigma and

---

[37] ''Mr. Polk is too wise a man to suffer the Blairs and Kendalls to set him up as a mark for the shafts of the Whigs . . . to enter the contest, with Mr. Tyler already in the field, and with the certainty of an overwhelming defeat awaiting him'' (The *Madisonian*, June 1, 1844).

[38] Schouler, *Hist. of the U. S.*, IV, 475; Smith, *Annex. of Tex.*, 306, 308.

a puzzle to the most astute,''[39] for the most ardent advocates of annexation would lose, economically, by its consummation, while the opponents of annexation, for the sake of *principle,* were indirectly aiding Polk.

After Congress had adjourned, all parties were free to devote their energies to the campaign. The Democrats fully realized that the contest would be close, that defection must be prevented, and new recruits gained. Benton and the *Globe* must be whipped into line, and if possible, Tyler must be made to withdraw in favor of Polk. No one was in a better position than Old Hickory to perform this valuable service, and no one was more ready to undertake the difficult task. Jackson was much excited by Benton's heated reply to McDuffie while discussing his own annexation bill, and still more so by the report that his old friend had solicited the coöperation of John Quincy Adams.[40] His irritation was increased because Benton had not been convinced by a letter he had sent him stating that the Union could not be preserved except by annexing Texas and extending the laws of the United States over Oregon. He was certain that Benton had induced Van Buren to declare against annexation. He called Blair's attention to Polk's one-term pledge, and prophesied that Van Buren would succeed Polk if he should take the proper course. ''My dear friend,'' he pleaded with Blair, ''permit not Col. Benton to have controle over your

---

[39] Chas. A. Davis to Crittenden, New York, June 5, 1844, *Crittenden Papers.* It was a curious fact, said Davis, that on two important questions party considerations had made people in the South and West blind to their own interests; they had crushed the bank and thereby driven much needed capital back to the North and East, and were now clamoring for Texas, although the other sections would profit more by its annexation.

[40] Jackson to Blair (*confidential*), June 25, 1844, *Jackson Papers.* ''The last Washington papers give an account of the very irrated reply of Col. Benton to Mr. McDuffie on Benton's annexation Bill in the Senate after which Col. Benton seized J. Q. Adams by the hand & said 'we are both old men, we must now unite & save the constitution'—do my dear Mr. Blair inform me if this can be true—if it is, I want no better proof of his derangement, & it political[ly] prostrates him.''

editorial column, as he will ruin y^r paper. If he will, he must pursue his eratic course, which has, & will political[ly] destroy him if not already done.'' Blair assured Jackson that Benton was zealous in the cause of Polk and Dallas, but that he distrusted Calhoun and opposed his program of Texas with or without the Union. These views were shared by Blair himself. Jackson wrote again to Blair on July 12, criticizing Benton's attitude and urging Blair to attend the ratification meeting to be held at Nashville on the fifteenth of August.[41]

Before Jackson had received his reply from Blair he expressed his opinion of Benton in a letter to Polk.[42] Benton's hatred of Calhoun and his jealousy of the growing popularity of Tyler, said Jackson, had deranged him, but

you will perceive I have estopped Benton or any others from believing that you or I could countenance nullification or disunion. Every letter I get gives us joyfull news—You will get 20 states at least & your one term [pledge] will get you 22.

He told Polk that, while it was quite unnecessary for Cave Johnson to put him on his guard lest he should inadvertently give aid to the nullifiers, still every Democrat should ''put his face against any meeting of *disunion*, or nullification—we must & will have Texas, with & in our *glorious Union*. The Federal Union must be preserved—A. J.''[43]

---

[41] Blair to Jackson, July 7; Jackson to Blair, July 12, 1844; *Jackson Papers*. The ''Texas, with or without the Union,'' program mentioned by Benton was an attempt made in South Carolina, while Tyler's treaty was before the Senate, to call a southern convention and annex Texas to the southern states if it should be rejected by the federal government. See Benton, *Thirty Years' View*, II, 616.

[42] Jackson to Polk, June 29, 1844, *Polk Papers*. ''In my reply to Col. Benton's first letter to me in which he adverted to my toast,—'The Federal Union must be preserved,' amongst other things, I said to him, *The Federal Union must be preserved*, and to do this effectually & permanently—Texas must be reunited to the United States—the laws of the Union extended forthwith over the Oragon, which would place this Federal Union on as permanent basses as the Rocky mountains, and preserve our glorious Union, & our Republican system as long as time lasted.''

[43] *Ibid.*

Johnson was still much concerned for fear that something might be said or done at the Nashville meeting which might be construed as an approval of the South Carolina program of "annexation or a dissolution of the Union." Doubtless he exaggerated both the strength and the determination of the disunion element. So far as the success of the campaign was concerned, much more was to be feared from the attitude of Benton, whose irascible temper could not be held in check. He did not hesitate to discuss, even with Whigs,[44] the "villany" of the Baltimore convention, and no plea for harmony could induce him to abate his attacks on those who had been responsible for reviving the Texas question. To be sure he had, in a public declaration exonerated Polk and Dallas from participation in the "intrigue," but in a speech made at St. Louis he said that the Texas question had been "exploded" only forty days before the Baltimore convention—"just time enough for candidates to be interrogated, and for the novices to amend their answers."[45] Polk was evidently the novice whom he had in mind.

As the campaign progressed Polk came more and more to distrust both Benton and Blair. "Since the nominations," he said in a letter to Donelson,

none can fail to have observed the *coldness* or indifference of the Globe. After *Blair's* professions made confidentially to you, I had expected that he would come zealously into the support of the nominations, and not throw cold water upon them.

After quoting a letter in which Dallas spoke of this hostility, Polk suggested that Donelson and Jackson should urge Blair to alter the tone of his paper.[46]

---

[44] Letcher to Buchanan, July 19, 1844, *Buchanan Papers*.

[45] Speech printed in Wash. *Globe*, Nov. 6, 1844. Yoakum, of Tennessee, in calling Polk's attention to this speech says that he has "no doubt but Col. Benton has injured us 100,000 votes"! (Yoakum to Polk, Nov. 22, 1844, *Polk Papers*).

[46] Polk to Donelson, July 22, 1844, "Polk-Donelson Letters."

Toward the end of June certain overtures made by close
friends of President Tyler gave hope that he might yet withdraw from the race. J. B. Jones, the editor of the *Madisonian,*
approached A. V. Brown and others with a suggestion that
J. George Harris should be brought to Washington to assist in
editing that paper. Harris was an intimate friend of both
Polk and Jackson, and had made the Nashville *Union* an
effective party organ. Harris suggested to Polk that a new
paper might be started with which the *Madisonian* (Tyler) and
the *Spectator* (Calhoun) might soon be merged. A new paper,
in his opinion, would be more likely to succeed because of prejudices against those already in existence. General Armstrong,
like Harris, thought favorably of the plan to merge these papers,
and believed that after the election even the *Globe* might be
joined with the rest. Both Johnson and Brown, however, were
opposed to this plan, and especially to putting Harris in charge
of the *Madisonian.*[47]

Early in July R. J. Walker, who had from the first urged a
friendly attitude toward the deserters of 1840, called on Tyler
in order to ascertain his views. The President told Walker that
he would withdraw at once were it not for the fact that his
friends felt hurt by the abuse heaped upon them by the *Globe*
and other papers. There were, he said, about 150,000 of his
friends who had voted for Whigs in 1840; he would withdraw
and his friends would support Polk and Dallas, provided that
assurance be given that they would be welcomed by the Democratic party as brethren and equals. "Now I think," said
Walker when reporting the conversation to Polk, "that the
importance of this union & co-operation cannot be overrated";
therefore he suggested that Polk and Jackson might write letters
to political friends, speaking kindly of Tyler and his followers.[48]

[47] Harris to Polk, June 27, 29; Johnson to Polk, June 28; Armstrong to
Polk, June 30, 1844, *Polk Papers.*
[48] Walker to Polk, July 10, 1844, *ibid.*

After reading Walker's letter Polk sent it to the Hermitage by Gideon Pillow. In a letter of his own, sent by the same messenger, he told Jackson that, however desirable the object sought by Walker might be, he would not write any letter or make any promises. He would like of course to see a reunion of "all the old Jackson Democrats of '28 & '32," but he would neither write a letter to Tyler nor "make any pledges to any one—except as it regards my public principles, in advance of election." He suggested, however, that if the attacks of the *Globe* were responsible for Tyler's continuing in the race and thereby jeopardizing the result in certain states, something should be done to induce Blair to cease abusing the President. He told Jackson that he was the only one who could influence Blair, but as to the wisdom of exercising such influence Jackson must judge for himself.[49]

Jackson was disgusted with Walker's "want of common sense" in suggesting that he and Polk should write letters in commendation of the President. Such letters, he told Polk, would "damn you & destroy your election," for the Whigs would at once charge "bargain & intrigue."[50] Although not yet ready to ask favors from John Tyler, he was quite willing to remove, if possible, the cause of the President's injured feelings. On that very same day he dispatched a letter to Blair in which he condemned Benton's conduct, urged the importance of annexation, and ordered Blair to "support the cause of Polk & Dallas, & let Tiler alone—leave Calhoun to himself we in the South & West will attend to the Federal Union, it must be preserved."[51] Indeed, on the same day, he authorized Major Lewis to express to the President his (Jackson's) wish for the success of the

[49] Polk to Jackson, July 23, 1844, *Jackson Papers*. See also Polk to Donelson, same date, "Polk-Donelson Letters." In this he doubted the propriety of Jackson's writing a letter for publication; still, he seemed anxious that the general should write a private letter "which might reach the President's eye."

[50] Jackson to Polk, July 26, 1844, *Polk Papers*.

[51] Jackson to Blair, July 26, 1844, *Jackson Papers*.

administration and the assurance that Tyler's friends would be received as brethren into the Democratic fold.[52]

From various quarters pressure was brought to bear upon Tyler, and appeals to his vanity were not wanting. Ritchie, of the Richmond *Enquirer,* who was called the "king of the Democratic press," warmly urged the President to withdraw, while Democratic electors agreed to support Tyler in case it should develop that he was stronger than Polk. The Democratic general committee of New York, on August 6, drafted resolutions lauding the President and asking his support;[53] and on August 1 Jackson sent another letter to Major Lewis in which he argued that Tyler ought to withdraw, for if he did not, it would be said

---

[52] Jackson to Lewis, July 26, 1844 (Tyler, *Letters and Times of the Tylers,* III, 143–146). The letter read in part: "You know I have a great desire that Mr. Tyler should close his term with credit to himself. It is certain he can not now be elected, and he has now a fair field by withdrawing, to add great and lasting popularity to himself by the act, and free himself from the imputation that his exertions to re-annex Texas were to make himself President, and show that his energy in this case was from imperious public duty, to prevent a country so important to the defence, safety and great interest of our whole Union from falling into the hands of England, our most implacable enemy. On Mr. Tyler's withdrawal from the canvass every true American will say, Amen to his patriotism in the case of Texas.

"Several of Mr. Tyler's friends yesterday visited me, and wished me to cause it to be known to him their wishes, as his withdrawal at once would unite all the Democrats into one family without distinction. This would render our victory easy and certain by bringing Mr. Tyler's friends in to the support of Polk and Dallas, received as brethren by them and their friends, all former differences forgotten and cordially united once more in sustaining the Democratic candidate.

". . . It is impossible now that Mr. Tyler should be elected, and if he does not withdraw he will be charged with conniving with the Clay Whigs to defeat the Democratic nominees. *Although this would be untrue,* yet really it would have that affect and would do Mr. Tyler much injury. I told Mr. Tyler's friends I could not write to him on such a subject, but that I had such confidence in his good sense and patriotism, that I was sure he would withdraw in due time, as I believe him to be a good Democrat, and that he would do nothing to promote Clay or injure Democracy. If you think it prudent, you can make these suggestions to Mr. Tyler. I think he would receive them kindly, be his determination what it may. His proper dignified course is a magnanamous withdrawal, with such reasons as his good sense may suggest for the occasion. These hints flow from a real regard for Mr. Tyler and a sincere wish that he may retire with much credit."

[53] Tyler, *Letters and Times of the Tylers,* II, 337–339.

that he had adopted the annexation program merely to obtain a reëlection and that he was remaining in the field in order to defeat Polk. Tyler soon informed Jackson that this letter had determined him to retire,[54] and on August 20 his letter of withdrawal appeared in the *Madisonian*. His present action, he said, had resulted from changed conditions. The people had vindicated him by driving from power those who had tried to crush him; the Democrats had adopted his policies, and he no longer felt compelled to run. On the next day this paper stated that its sole object all the time had been to defeat Henry Clay, and, as the principles of Polk and Tyler were identical, it would henceforth support the Democratic candidates.[55] Two years later Tyler wrote that he had accepted the nomination "for the sole purpose of controlling events . . . . for the public good" and, having accomplished his purpose, he withdrew.[56]

The *Spectator,* also, gave Polk and Dallas its enthusiastic support, and Calhoun predicted that the results would "equal the defeat of 1828."[57] Doubtless he indulged hopes that he, in the event of Polk's election, would be the guiding spirit of the administration.

During the summer considerable anxiety was caused by the fear that British and French influence might induce Houston to agree to some arrangement with Mexico. Major Lewis was authorized by Calhoun to communicate "confidentially" to General Jackson that the State Department was in possession of reliable information that these nations had offered to acknowledge the independence of Texas without any pledge of abolition,

---

[54] Smith, *Annexation of Texas,* 310.

[55] The *Madisonian* (Aug. 24) even supplied an election pun: "Change— It is James *Knox* Polk now, it will be Polk knocks Clay, about election time."

[56] Tyler, *Letters and Times of the Tylers,* II, 341.

[57] Alex. Anderson to Polk, Aug. 22, 1844, *Polk Papers.* "We should have carried North Carolina," said Anderson, "but for the course and speeches of that arch Traitor Benton—so say our letters from North Carolina." Anderson was a strong adherent of Calhoun.

provided that Texas would agree to remain an independent nation. Similar information was given to Polk by Calhoun's friend, Alexander Anderson. Before he had seen these letters, however, Jackson had written to Houston "as strong a letter as he [I] could dictate," exhorting him not to yield to the wishes of foreign nations.[58]

While politicians were emphasizing the foreign menace, the *Democratic Review* was trying to win votes in northern states by maintaining that the area of slavery would be restricted by acquiring Texas, for slaves would be drawn to the new fields, leaving the border states to the Yankees.[59] Some of the slavery advocates, too, believed that such would be the result, and for this reason violently opposed annexation.[60]

There was some defection from their own ranks and there was fear that annexation might be defeated by an act of Texas itself, but the Democrats as a party never wavered from their position in favor of annexation. They had, therefore, the advantage of a consistent program. Clay, on the other hand, in order to retain his hold on both North and South, adopted a shifty course and modified his views from time to time, as the occasion seemed to demand. In his Raleigh letter of April 17 he had definitely opposed immediate annexation, but he soon discovered that such a stand had made him unpopular in the South and West. To retrieve his fortunes in those sections he wrote to Stephen F. Miller, on July 1, his first "Alabama letter." "Personally," said he, "I could have no objection to the annexation of Texas; but certainly I would be unwilling to see the existing Union dissolved or seriously jeoparded for the sake of

---

[58] Lewis to Jackson, July 19, 1844, *Jackson Papers*. Jackson to Polk, July 23, 1844, *Polk Papers*. See also, Polk to Donelson, July 22, 1844, "Polk-Donelson Letters."

[59] *Dem. Rev.*, July, 1844.

[60] Letter of Waddy Thompson to editors of *National Intelligencer*, printed in that paper, July 6, 1844.

[61] Printed in *Nat. Intell.*, Aug. 8, 1844.

acquiring Texas."[61] As this was not strong enough to win votes
in the South, he wrote again on the twenty-seventh that if annexation might be accomplished "without national dishonor, without
war, with the general consent of the States of the Union, and
upon fair and reasonable terms, I should be glad to see it."[62]
Both Democrats and Abolitionists seized upon the last phrase
and widely advertised the fact that "Clay would be glad to see
it." Other letters followed in an attempt to show that he had
not changed his original views, but the more he explained the
more he became the target of denunciation and ridicule. The
papers made much sport of his "six manifestoes," while Jackson
charged that Clay by his letters had made a "perfect devill"
of himself.[63]

Although this was a campaign in which party principles were
clearly defined and important questions involved, nevertheless
the personal element was not wanting. The Whig ignorance even
of Polk's identity was soon replaced by a minute knowledge not
only of his own shortcomings but of those of his ancestors. It
devolved, therefore, upon the candidate's friends in Tennessee
to enlighten the public on his past record and to defend his
reputation against the slanders of his opponents. As soon as
the news of his nomination had reached Nashville a mass meeting
was called to celebrate the event. Speeches were made by prominent Democrats, and A. O. P. Nicholson ridiculed the Whig
cry of "Who is Polk?" Arrangements were made for another
meeting in July to be composed of delegates from all parts of
the state.[64] Biographical materials had already been forwarded
to George Bancroft under the frank of General Jackson. But as
Bancroft, according to Harris, was "somewhat sensitive on the

---

[62] Fourth Alabama letter, in which former letters are quoted (*Nat.
Intell.*, Oct. 1, 1844). The letter of July 27 is printed in *Niles' Reg.*,
LXVI, 439.

[63] Schouler, *Hist. of U. S.*, IV, 477. Smith, *Annex. of Texas*, 309.

[64] Nashville *Union*, June 8, 11, 1844.

point of *authorship*," and declined, it was decided that editorials in the *Union* would do quite as well as a biography.[65]

Some of the Whig papers charged Polk with being a duelist, while others said he was a cringing coward who had feared to fight Wise. The first allegation was refuted in letters written to the *Globe* by Cave Johnson and A. V. Brown, and the second, by the publication of an old letter of Jackson's in which he had expressed approval of Speaker Polk for having treated Wise with contempt.[66] For the purpose of injuring Polk in the North, the Whigs circulated widely the "Roorback" canard the gist of which was that a gang of slaves branded with the initials "J. K. P," had been seen on their way to southern markets.[67]

Polk was most annoyed by the revival of the story that his grandfather, Colonel Ezekiel Polk, had been a Tory during the Revolution. The Washington *Globe* and various northern papers repelled the charge, and the Nashville *Union* printed many letters and affidavits from persons who had certain knowledge that the elder Polk had been a Revolutionary officer; it published, also, a copy of his commission dated June 18, 1775. Under Polk's direction this material was printed in pamphlet form under the title of "A Vindication of Colonel Ezekiel Polk," and General Armstrong was instructed to send copies to prominent Democrats all over the United States.[68] To these Whig campaign stories the Democratic press retorted in kind. Clay's use of profane language was emphasized and he was called a drunkard, a duelist, a gambler, and a perjurer.[69]

---

[65] J. Geo. Harris to Polk, June 25, July 17, 19, 1844, *Polk Papers*. Doubtless Bancroft's sensitiveness on authorship resulted from his experience as campaign biographer of Van Buren.

[66] Wash. *Globe*, June 13, 19, 1844.

[67] See *Niles' Reg.*, LXVII, 73.

[68] *Union*, Sept. 11. Polk to Heiss, Sept. 13; Polk to Armstrong, Sept. 16, 1844, "Heiss Papers," *Tenn. Hist. Mag.*, June, 1916.

[69] The perjury consisted in the alleged violation of his oath of office by challenging John Randolph to fight a duel for words spoken in debate during the campaign. Henly, of Indiana, said on the floor of the House

Naturally Polk was especially desirous of carrying his own state, and his energy and skill as a machine politician are manifested in many ways. Realizing, as usual, the importance of a spirited party press, he induced Heiss to make J. George Harris joint editor with Laughlin of the Nashville *Union.* "The Union," he wrote, "should be made in Tennessee what Medary's Statesman is in Ohio, and what the Union itself was in 1839. It is looked to from all parts of the Union and must be a *great paper* during this canvass." In another letter he urged that "fire and spirit and power should be thrown into it" in order to counteract the Whig falsehoods and misrepresentations.[70]

On July 13 a dinner was given in Polk's home town, Columbia, in honor of delegates to the late nominating convention, Presidential electors, and members of Congress from Tennessee. To Cave Johnson was assigned the duty of inducing prominent Democrats to be present in order to counteract the effect of a Whig rally held at the same place.[71] Early in the campaign arrangements had been made for a great mass meeting to be held at Nashville on the fifteenth of August. Both Polk and Johnson were anxious that the northern states should be well represented at this meeting so that it could not be said that it was a gathering of disunionists. Once more it fell to Johnson to send the invitations and to urge the importance of a large and representative attendance.[72]

On the appointed day the multitudes assembled, and Nashville, according to the *Union,* "was from sunrise to sunset as

---

that "the standard of Henry Clay should consist of his armorial bearings, which ought to be a pistol, a pack of cards, and a brandy-bottle" (Adams, *Memoirs,* XII, 45).

[70] Polk to Heiss, July 31, Aug. 21, 1844; Heiss to Polk, Aug. 3, 1844, *Polk Papers.*

[71] Polk to Johnson, July 1, July 6, 1844, "Polk-Johnson Letters."

[72] Johnson to Polk, June 21, 1844, *Polk Papers.* Polk to Johnson, July 16, 1844, "Polk-Johnson Letters." Among those invited were Wright, Cass, Buchanan, Woodbury, Hubbard of New Hampshire, and Duncan and Medary, of Ohio.

a *Military* Camp."[73]   In the evening the Honorable Thomas F. Marshall, of Kentucky, addressed "thousands" in front of the courthouse on the annexation of Texas.   On the second day, August 16, the throng gathered at Camp Hickory where by noon, "the great grove at the Camp, fifty acres in extent, was as full as it could hold," and there "were two miles of table on which the *Great Dinner* was served."   Speaking followed the dinner, and Cave Johnson, as presiding officer, made the opening address.   We have already noted his solicitude lest a disunion character might be attributed to this meeting, and he now embraced the opportunity

in the presence of this great assembly, to give a direct contradiction to the false charge of disunion, and a wish to dissolve the Union, which had been propagated by the whig press of this and other states, against those concerned in calling and getting up the present meeting.

The number in attendance was so great that speakers addressed crowds simultaneously in various parts of the grove; each speaker, following Johnson's lead, repelled the charge of disunion.   General Case was the principal orator of the day; among the others were Gansevoort Melville;[74] Governor Clay, of Alabama; Colonel Terry, speaker of the house from the same state; and J. B. Bowlin, a member of Congress from Missouri.   Letters were received from leading Democrats of both sections, regretting their inability to be present and expressing hearty coöperation.[75] Among these was Judge Douglas, but within a few days he was in Tennessee stumping the state for Polk and Dallas.[76]

---

[73] Nashville *Union,* Aug. 17, 1844. Also *Niles' Reg.,* LXVII, 3–4. "On every road to the city was to be seen approaching companies, battalions and regiments, mounted and on foot, with their bands of music, their banners and their mottoes, on their way to this great encampment of the sovereign people."

[74] A Tammany Hall leader.

[75] The same number of the *Union* contains copies of letters from Franklin Pierce, Silas Wright, Levi Woodbury, James Buchanan, Stephen A. Douglas, Geo. McDuffie, Robt. J. Walker, R. M. Johnson, *et al.*

[76] Polk to Johnson, Aug. 20, 22, 26, 1844, "Polk-Johnson Letters."

Despite the absence of so many of the party leaders the Democratic meeting was regarded as highly successful, but in glittering pageantry and boisterous enthusiasm it was far excelled by the "Great Whig Convention" which, on August 21, likewise essembled in the city of Nashville and was, to quote Phelan, "the finest of the kind ever held in the Southwest."[77] While the chief feature of the meeting was the display of gorgeous battalions and expensive campaign banners, there were soul-stirring addresses by prominent Whig orators. The great speech of the meeting was made by Sergeant S. Prentiss, of Mississippi, who was regarded by many as the peer of either Webster or Clay. On this occasion Prentiss surpassed even his own brilliant record, for to partisan considerations was added a personal hatred for the Democratic candidate whose casting vote had once deprived him of a seat in the House of Representatives.[78]

The enthusiasm caused by the Whig meeting spurred the Democrats to a still more vigorous effort to win the election in Tennessee. Custom did not permit Polk to mount the platform in his own behalf, but from his home at Columbia he directed the campaign, even to the minutest details. He planned itineraries, assigned speakers, and even arranged for barbecues.[79] Local orators were assisted by prominent politicians from other states. This list included Douglas, of Illinois, Pickens, of South Carolina, Melville, of New York, and Clay, Terry, and McClung, of Alabama. Of local men the most notable were the veteran campaigners, Nicholson, Brown, and Cave Johnson. Johnson was much broken in health, but so highly did Polk value his services that he goaded him to an active part in the campaign.[80]

---

[77] Phelan, *Hist. of Tenn.*, 419.

[78] See above, p. 120.

[79] Various letters of Polk to Johnson, Aug.-Oct., "Polk-Johnson Letters."

[80] *Ibid.* On Oct. 14 he told Johnson that "all our energies are necessary to keep the State safe, as I believe she now is. The least relaxation at the close of the canvass might loose her."

Near the close of the canvass Polk was confident of carrying the state by a "handsome majority," but, instead, he lost it by the small margin of one hundred and thirteen votes.

In southern states the Whigs had little hope of success in opposing the Democratic annexation program, nevertheless strenuous efforts were made to prevent defection from their own ranks because of this annoying issue. The indomitable Prentiss labored to show that Polk was not entitled to profit from the revival of this question,[81] and in a speech at Natchez he referred to Polk as a "blighted burr, that had fallen from the mane of the war-horse of the Hermitage." In an attempt to counteract the work of Prentiss and others, and to win Whig votes in the South, Senator Walker, of Mississippi, wrote a most inflammatory pamphlet entitled "The South in Danger"[82] in which he argued that as Whigs and Abolitionists had joined hands in the North, therefore all parties in the South should unite in the interest of annexation. The pamphlet probably did little good in the South, and many Democrats were fearful that it might do serious damage in the North.[93]

In Ohio the contest bid fair to be close, and, after Clay's repudiation of the utterances of his relative, Cassius M. Clay,[84] leading Democrats had hopes that many Whigs would desert him and vote for Birney.[85] But the result of the state elections made

---

[81] "If ever I join the Mormons," he wrote in August to the editor of the Vicksburg *Whig*, "I shall attach myself to Joe Smith, the founder of the sect, and not to one of his rival disciples, and should I ever turn Locofoco on the question of *the immediate annexation of Texas*, I will support *John Tyler, not James K. Polk*" (*Memoir of S. S. Prentiss*, II, 316).

[82] This pamphlet was issued by the Democratic Association of Washington, D. C., Sept. 25, 1844. Copy in Library of Congress.

[83] For example, William E. Cramer, editor of the Albany *Argus*, informed Polk that New York could never be won on the program outlined by Walker, while Ohio and other states would surely be lost (Cramer to Polk, Oct. 4, 1844, *Polk Papers*).

[84] C. M. Clay had represented Henry Clay as opposed to slavery. The latter in a letter contradicted the former's statements.

[85] Gansevoort Melville to Polk, Oct. 3; Cass to Polk, Oct. 4, 1844, *Polk Papers*. Both wrote from Cleveland and expressed the opinion that the Democrats would carry the state.

it evident that Clay's letter had not produced any defection,[86] while Walker's ill-advised pamphlet added strength to the Whigs.[87] The so-called "Garland forgery" transferred many votes from Birney to Clay, and may possibly have brought victory to Clay in Ohio.[88]

Pennsylvania was normally Democratic, yet there were misgivings lest the strong sentiment in favor of tariff might jeopardize Polk's success in that state. His "Kane letter" had been generally accepted as satisfactory, but the Whigs represented him to be an unqualified free-trader. The *Pennsylvanian* refuted this charge and, on October 15, published extracts from his speeches to prove that he had always favored incidental protection. As noted above, Polk, in his letter to Kane, did not pretend to favor tariff except that which might be necessary for revenue, but by means of construction Pennsylvanians were able to hold voters in line by representing him to be in favor of tariff. "We have succeeded," wrote the oily-tongued Simon Cameron, "in fixing the belief that you 'are as good a tariff man as Clay,' " and he added significantly that no man known to be opposed to protective tariff could possibly carry the state.[89] Polk did not of course take pains to undeceive his supporters in Pennsylvania; on the other hand, he did not, in any of his public utterances, commit himself to tariff for protective purposes. However, Cameron's ruse met with success, and Polk's strength in Pennsylvania greatly exasperated the Whigs.[90]

---

[86] H. C. Williams wrote from Washington that "the letter repudiating C. M. Clay has had no effect in the northern states, while it satisfies the Southern Whigs. The Whig papers will not publish it." Democrats, he said, have to oppose all "fag end" parties, and Greely is now trying to stir up the Irish (Williams to Polk, Oct. 14, 1844, *Polk Papers*).

[87] Armstrong to Polk, Nov. 5, [1844], *Polk Papers*.

[88] See Birney, *James G. Birney and his Times*, 355.

[89] Cameron to Polk, Oct. 18, 1844, *Polk Papers*.

[90] Governor Letcher, of Kentucky, scoffed at the idea of Polk being in favor of tariff, and he tried to persuade Buchanan to refrain from advocating his election. "Polk," said Letcher, "has no more chance to be elected than if he were dead and *buried,* and d—nd, as he will be in due time" (Letcher to Buchanan, Aug. 3, 1844, *Buchanan Papers*).

"Native Americanism" was said to have cost the Democrats votes in Pennsylvania. Catholics, as a rule, affiliated with that party, and the Whigs made political capital out of the fact that Shunk, the Democratic candidate for governor, had been induced to march in a Catholic parade.[91]

It was alleged that the Whigs used money freely in Pennsylvania,[92] and that they were guilty of practicing frauds,[93] but it is unlikely that the Whigs were the sole transgressors in these respects.

New York was regarded as the pivotal state. There thirty-six electoral votes were to be won or lost, and the result seemed to be highly problematical. In this state various extraneous elements helped to complicate the political situation. Both "Native Americans" and Abolitionists commanded a considerable number of votes in the state, but it was by no means certain just how these votes would be cast. At the beginning of the campaign it was feared that the followers of Van Buren might not rally with enthusiasm to the party standard, and besides, there was lack of harmony in Democratic state politics with respect to policies and candidates. In order to carry the state it was necessary to hold the Van Burenites in line, and since the Baltimore convention many of them had been silently nursing their resentment. Governor William C. Bouck wrote that a number of Wright's friends had tried to get up a secret intrigue to procure Polk's defeat, but that Wright had been nominated for governor and his adherents brought into harmony.[94] Van Buren told Jackson that Wright had accepted the nomination reluctantly and not until

---

[91] J. Miller to Polk, Oct. 12; J. M. Porter to Polk, Oct. 12, 1844, *Polk Papers;* also, newspapers.

[92] For examplé, Kane informed Polk that $20,000 had been subscribed at the office of John Sergeant, of Philadelphia. Sergeant's nephew, Wm. B. Reed, had by mistake sent a letter regarding this money to some Democrat (Kane to Polk, Oct. 24, 1844, *Polk Papers*).

[93] Henry Horn, for example, wrote that desponding letters had been sent to his friends with his forged signature attached (Horn to Polk, Oct. 31, 1844, *Polk Papers*).

[94] Bouck to Polk, Sept. 7, 1844, *Polk Papers.*

he had been told that it was the only means of saving New York,[95] but the supporters of Bouck felt that he had been unceremoniously sacrificed to satisfy the ambitions of Wright and his friends.[96] Some of the extreme anti-Texas leaders in New York supported the candidates, but repudiated the annexation plank in the platform.[97] This was the policy of the New York *Evening Post*.

According to William E. Cramer, of the Albany *Argus*, the Democrats in New York "were on a volcano" until Clay repudiated the statements of Cassius M. Clay and changed his position on the Texan question. The Abolitionists, he said, held the balance of power and would poll from fifteen thousand to twenty thousand votes. "Before Mr. C's fatal letter they were hesitating whether they should not vote for him," but "this puts an impassable gulf between them."[98] On the other hand, in predicting victory for Polk and Dallas in New York, Wright reported that "Never have I witnessed an equal degree of enthusiasm among our democracy, not even in the days of Genl Jackson, nor have I, at any time, known greater harmony, activity or confidence."[99] Late in October another letter from Cramer stated that the Whigs were putting forth every effort to form coalitions with "Native Americans," Abolitionists, and Anti-renters, and that they were confident of winning the election. Prospect of success, he said, had brought them much campaign money from manufacturers who desired high tariff.[100]

---

[95] Jackson to Polk, Sept. 26, 1844, *ibid.*

[96] In a letter to Polk, Sept. 11, Marcy stated that Bouck had made a satisfactory governor, and that Wright had been nominated for political reasons; while an anonymous letter, Sept. 14, said that Bouck had been set aside without reason, and that the action might cause Polk to lose the state.

[97] See the signed statement of Bryant and others in *Niles' Reg.*, LXVI, 371.

[98] Cramer to Polk, Sept. 17, 1844, *Polk Papers.*

[99] Wright to Buchanan, Sept. 23, 1844, *Buchanan Papers.*

[100] "The report is that the Bostonians promised $100,000 provided they could receive ample assurance that it would secure New York for Mr. Clay!!" (Cramer to Polk, Oct. 22, 1844, *Polk Papers*).

Still other factors complicated the political situation in New York. The Abolitionists who had formerly voted the Whig ticket were appalled when Birney came out in favor of free trade and opposed to distributing among the states the proceeds derived from the sale of public lands, and it was feared in Tammany circles that his announcement might cause them to vote for Clay.[101] In order to win votes for their national ticket the Whigs withdrew some of their candidates for Congress and the state legislature in favor of the "Native American" candidates.[102] It availed them little, however, for Polk and Dallas carried the state.[103]

It appears that the Democrats, also, withdrew some of their candidates in favor of "Native Americans,"[104] and in the process of rapid naturalization they outrivaled their opponents. "Tammany Hall," wrote Melville, "is a perfect jam from 8 A. M. till after midnight. Naturalization going on among our friends to an immense extent. On Saturday 260—all Democrats—rec'd their papers."[105] Charges of wholesale frauds were made by both parties,[106] but it may be doubted that such frauds materially affected the election results.

The Texas question was of course the paramount issue of the campaign, although it was not, apparently, the chief factor in winning the election for Polk. Many contemporaries believed that Clay's defeat was not caused by the emergence of this question,

---

[101] Melville to Polk, Oct. 26, 1844, *Polk Papers.*

[102] Alex. Jones to Polk, New York City, Oct. 30, Nov. 6, 1844, *ibid.*

[103] Jones told Polk in a letter dated November 21, that some of the Whigs had been so confident of winning that they had bet all of their money, and even their homes. One had lost $38,000; another, $40,000. One Whig's wife lost her mind because of his losses (*Polk Papers*).

[104] John P. Heiss to Polk, Nov. 3, 1844, *Polk Papers.*

[105] Melville to Medary, Nov. 4, 1844, *ibid.*

[106] A correspondent from New London, Conn., informed Polk that in Connecticut, Massachusetts, and Rhode Island "the *lords of the spindle* compelled the degraded operators to vote their will, and thus obtained large majorities for your opponent" (Dr. Charles Douglas to Polk, Nov. 22, 1844, *Polk Papers*). For a useful summary of press opinions on frauds, see Smith, *Annexation of Texas,* 316 ff.

and this belief is held by Justin H. Smith,[107] who has recently made a thorough examination of conflicting opinions and carefully weighed their value. The *Democratic Review* evidently stated the truth when it said on the eve of the election that neither party had won or lost many votes on account of the Texas issue, and that "the issue is between the principles of the two parties more than ever before."[108] If Polk owed his success in the election to the Texas issue, it was due to the fact that it brought him the support of President Tyler and his followers. While we can not be sure that Tyler would have remained in the field if the Democrats had not espoused annexation, certainty that they would continue his Texas program at least furnished him with a plausible excuse for retiring from the canvass.[109]

Polk received 170 electoral votes; Clay only 105. In the North, Polk carried the great states of New York and Pennsylvania, while New Hampshire, also, contributed her six votes. Much to their delight the Whigs carried not only Polk's own state, Tennessee, but even the very precincts of both Jackson and Polk.[110] The Tennessee Democrats were keenly disappointed, of course, because they had failed to win the election in their candidate's own state; but their disappointment soon gave way to rejoicing over the general party victory. On receiving the news that New York had gone Democratic, Jackson sent the letter on to Polk with a marginal note, " 'who is J. K. polk,' will be no more asked by the coons—A. J."[111]

---

[107] Smith, *Annexation of Texas,* 317.

[108] "One Last Word before the Election" (*Dem. Rev.,* Oct., 1844). It thanked heaven that Polk was not a "military chieftain" and had never even killed an Indian; also, that "there is no peculiar eminent 'popularity' attaching to him, of a character personal to himself, and distinct from his simple position as the representative of the general principles and policy of the party whose candidate he is."

[109] See correspondence, including his letter of withdrawal, in Tyler, *Letters and Times of the Tylers,* II, 338 ff.

[110] Nashville *Banner,* Nov. 11, 1844. The *Union* on the 14th retorted that these precincts had been carried by non-resident Whigs who had gone there and voted illegally.

[111] Written on a letter from A. C. Flagg to Jackson, Nov. 7, 1844, *Polk Papers.* The "coons," of course, were the Whigs. The name had been attached to them during the "log-cabin" campaign of 1840.

Polk received the news of his election some hours before it was known to the people of either Columbia or Nashville. The New York mail arrived at Nashville at nine o'clock in the evening, and on the outside of the package the postmaster at Cincinnati had written a note stating that Polk had been elected. This attracted the attention of General Robert Armstrong, postmaster at Nashville and one of Polk's most intimate friends. Without giving out the news, Armstrong sent a messenger to Columbia with a note for Polk. At dawn he read the glad tidings which the note contained, but he said nothing about it to his neighbors and friends. For the next twenty-four hours he went about his work, and calmly received expressions of sympathy on his defeat.[112] Sphinx-like silence was a rôle that Polk dearly loved to play, and an opportunity to do so on this occasion no doubt added much to the gratification caused by the information contained in the note.

When the result of the election at last became known there was great rejoicing in Democratic ranks. On the other hand, desperado admirers of Clay, both in Tennessee and Kentucky, threatened Polk's life, and friends warned him to "take some thought of *where* you go & eat & drink."[113] No violence, however, was attempted, and apprehensions were forgotten in the din of exuberant celebrations. At Nashville Polk was given an elaborate reception. A. O. P. Nicholson made the principal address, and there was general rejoicing because the "Young Hickory" was soon to grasp the helm that had been so firmly guided by the "Old Hickory."[114]

Some of the Democratic factions had little love for Polk, but all could agree with the *Democratic Review* in thanking God for the defeat of Henry Clay. "Had he succeeded," said the *Review,* "it would have stamped him, his ideas and his character upon the future history of our government, with a fatal depth and extent of mischief never perhaps to be again effaced."[115]

[112] Nelson, *Memorials of Sarah Childress Polk*, 76–77.
[113] A. V. Brown to Polk, Nov. 13, 1844. Also Gen. John A. McCalla, Lexington, Ky., Nov. 22, 1844; both in *Polk Papers.*
[114] Nashville *Union,* Nov. 30, 1844. [115] *Dem. Rev.,* Nov., 1844.

CHAPTER XIV

PRESIDENT-ELECT

Various individuals and factions claimed the credit for Polk's nomination and election, and as soon as the result of the balloting had become known their claims to recognition were presented. While in one sense it was true that the successful candidate owed his elevation to a number of discordant elements within the party, in another sense he was under no obligation to any of them. With the exception perhaps of the younger element the several groups within the party had united on Polk, not from choice but necessity, and not until each had found it impossible to procure the nomination of its particular favorite. The circumstances under which he had been nominated—the very fact that he had not been generally considered for the first place—relieved the President-elect from the necessity of making pledges to any one. Although Polk himself fully appreciated this fact and resolved to make the most of it, others did not and the "jockeying for position" at once began.

One of the first to congratulate Polk on his victory was James Buchanan. The Senator from Pennsylvania was usually numbered with the *old* leaders, but his plea, oddly enough, was for the recognition of young men in the distribution of offices. "The old office holders generally," said he, "have had their day & ought to be content. Had Mr. Van Buren been our candidate, worthy as he is, this feeling which everywhere pervaded the Democratic ranks, would have made his defeat as signal as it was in 1840." Even Polk, he added, would have run better in Philadelphia had it not been rumored that he would distribute the patronage among the "old hunkers."[1] Such a letter from Robert

---

[1] Buchanan to Polk, Nov. 4, 1844, *Polk Papers.*

J. Walker would not have been surprising, but Buchanan's solicitude for the younger men was significantly of recent origin.

Tyler's withdrawal from the canvass occasioned speculation as to the recognition which his friends would receive from the Democratic party, and during the campaign Polk received many letters which were designed to pledge him in advance. The candidate discreetly refrained from committing himself, although his supporters may have given assurance that the followers of the President would not be proscribed. Special importance was attached to a letter written by Jackson to Major Lewis[2] in which the General said that Tyler's friends would be received as brethren. Then, too, Walker, as chairman of the national Democratic committee, had made promises to influential adherents of the President. Nevertheless the Tylerites were apparently unwilling to run any risks, and soon after Polk's election they were charged by prominent Democrats with having concocted a scheme whereby they hoped to intrench themselves in office. One part of this scheme, according to H. C. Williams, was to procure the resignation of Whigs so that President Tyler might fill the offices with eleventh-hour Democrats whom it would be embarrassing for Polk to remove.[3] Probably such reports exaggerated the facts, especially as to Whig resignations, but it is certain that the Tyler faction believed themselves to be entitled to a share of Democratic patronage. In plaintive note, John Y. Mason, Tyler's Secretary of the Navy, expressed a willingness to remain in the cabinet. He had, he told Polk, from a sense of duty resigned a judgeship so that he might take charge of the Navy Department, and had felt "very unhappy" since Tyler had become a candidate. Jackson, whom he had consulted, had advised him to remain in the cabinet because Tyler would soon withdraw. He would resign of course on March 3 *unless Polk should*

---

[2] Dated July 6, 1844. See Tyler, *Life and Times of the Tylers*, III, 143 ff.

[3] H. C. Williams, Washington, Nov. 15; Henry Simpson, Philadelphia, Nov. 21, 1844, *Polk Papers*.

desire otherwise, therefore he desired a "frank statement" of Polk's intentions. Mason had been a college mate of Polk and they had since been warm personal friends, but with habitual caution the President-elect replied that he would leave all such matters to be settled after his arrival in Washington.[4]

Directly and indirectly Polk received much unsolicited advice on the subject of patronage, and especially on the selection of his cabinet. Through General Armstrong, H. C. Williams warned him that rival factions were already planning for the succession of their respective favorites, therefore he should discountenance all of them.[5] As usual, Judge Catron was free with his fatherly advice. He had been told by Governor Letcher, of Kentucky, that the Whigs confidently believed Polk to be under pledges to Calhoun; and that because Calhoun's friends and those of Van Buren and Benton could never work in harmony, discord and disaster would beset the new administration. Catron assured Letcher that Polk had made no pledges to any wing of the party, but despite the truth of his statement, the rumors regarding Calhoun continued to circulate. Since Polk had been elected without making promises, Catron's advice was that he should "go to Washington *entirely* unpledged, down to a post office." The cold shoulder, he said, might at first give offense; but no matter, for "you are under no pressure of obligation to your party, other than to administer the government through the agency of men of undoubted strength and worth of character, *from head to foot.*"[6]   John Blair, of

---

[4] Mason to Polk, Nov. 16; Polk to Mason, Dec. 6, 1844, *ibid.*

[5] Williams to Armstrong, Nov. 26, 1844, *ibid.*

[6] Catron to Polk, Nov. 23, 1844, *Polk Papers.* Catron, like others, had his own individual preferences, but he continued to urge Polk to make his own selections. Both Johnson and Brown wrote on December 14 that Catron had suggested Buchanan, Wright, and Cass for the State, Treasury, and War Departments, respectively. "Of one thing I am absolutely certain," wrote Catron to Polk on February 4, "that you must begin as *absolute* master of your will, if this be possible, in framing your cabinet. Strength it must have, and men in it that will work in harmony: This done and you are perfectly safe, regardless of fretting for a brief space. The *old* dare not, as the young will overthrow them—and the young, set up no claim to such assumptions" (*Polk Papers*).

Tennessee, offered a happy solution for sectional discord— patronage in plenty for the North and principles for the South.[7]

Warnings and advice, however well meant, were entirely superfluous, for Polk felt himself to be fully capable of formulating his own plans. He could not prevent gossip and speculation, but he declared emphatically to Cave Johnson that he was "under no pledges or commitments to any of the cliques (if such exist) mentioned by the newspapers." The policy which he had chosen to follow relieved him in a great measure from consulting the wishes of discordant factions, and his success in executing it proved the wisdom of his choice. "My object," he told Cave Johnson,

will be to do my duty to the country, and I do not intend if I can avoid it, that my counsels shall be distracted by the supposed or not conflicting interests of those cliques. Another thing I will say—that I will if I can have a united and harmonious set of cabinet counsellors, who will have the existing administration and the good of the country more at heart than the question who shall succeed me, and that in any event I intend to be *myself* President of the U. S.[8]

No one can follow his career for the next four years without being convinced that he held the executive reins firmly in his own hands.

Selecting a cabinet from men of ability who would subordinate their own personal interests to those of the administration and of the country required an unusual degree of independence. The desired coöperation could not be obtained without the elimination of recognized leaders of factions; and such a course would inevitably subject the administration to attacks from all who had been disappointed.

The claims of the Tylerites might be ignored with impunity, but what to do with Calhoun was a more embarrassing question.

---

[7] "North of Mason & Dickson's line should be *plied* with patronage as principles more congenial to the South must of necessity be established & carried out whatever your personal predelections" may be (Blair to Polk, Dec. 2, 1844, *Polk Papers*).

[8] Polk to Johnson, Dec. 21, 1844, "Polk-Johnson Letters."

Although Calhoun denied emphatically that there had ever been any understanding between Polk and himself,[9] apparently he was not without hope that he would be invited to remain at the helm in the Department of State. Late in November one of his intimate friends, General James Hamilton, sounded Polk on the subject and dwelt on the desirability of having Calhoun continued in charge of the Texas and Oregon questions. For a southern member of the cabinet, said he, the entire South, from the Potomac to Louisiana, would prefer Calhoun.[10]

The difficulties which might result from any attempt to harmonize factions were set forth in a letter from Cave Johnson. He said that it was understood in Washington that Calhoun and other members of Tyler's cabinet desired to remain. It was also the general opinion that should Calhoun be retained Benton and his friends would oppose Polk's administration, while, on the other hand, the southern element would be hostile unless Calhoun should be continued in office. Calhoun, said Johnson, is the choice of southern men for Secretary of State, while many from the North want Silas Wright; and Benton is reported to have declared that should Polk retain any of the Tyler cabinet he would open fire on the "rotten eggs."[11] General Jackson's advice to Polk was the exclusion from his cabinet of "all aspirants to the presidency, or vice"; and the General was so confident that his advice would be followed that he assured Blair that neither Calhoun nor any other aspirant would be appointed. In another letter to Polk, Jackson urged that Calhoun must not be retained, because other members of the cabinet could not get along with him: "England is the place for him there to combat with my Lord Aberdeen, the abolition question." The entire cabinet,

---

[9] "Nothing has ever passed between Mr. Polk and myself, directly or indirectly, on the subject. I neither know his views nor he mine on the subject" (Calhoun to J. A. Stuart, Oct. 21, 1844, *Rep. of Am. Hist.*, 1899, II, 626).

[10] Hamilton to Polk, Nov. 29, 1844, *Polk Papers.*

[11] Johnson to Polk, Dec. 1, 6, 1844, *ibid.*

said he, ought to be composed of new men.[12] Writing late in December, Cave Johnson said that the friends of Benton and Calhoun feared each other's influence with Polk, consequently the breach between the wings of the party was widening. Especially did the northerners fear that Polk would be brought under the influence of Calhoun. In a similar strain A. V. Brown wrote that all elements were working to induce Polk not to retain Calhoun. There was, he said, scarcely less opposition to Cass; while Benton and Wright opposed Buchanan on account of the stand he had taken at Baltimore in favor of the two-thirds rule.[13]

While others were doing their utmost to prevent his retention, Calhoun himself was telling his friends that there was much speculation concerning the cabinet and not a little intriguing in various quarters. He reported himself to be "perfectly passive" and "indifferent." Whether he would remain or not, if invited, would depend on the "probable course of the administration."[14] His supporters, however, were both active and hopeful. Some of them were sanguine enough to believe that Calhoun would be able to build up such a strong party following that Polk would not dare to remove him.[15] Hearing that Gideon Pillow had remarked that Polk's chief difficulty was "how to get rid of Calhoun," even Duff Green felt constrained to warn the President-elect of the dangers which would result from sacrificing Calhoun in order to conciliate Benton and Wright. "I make no pretense of friendship for you," he told Polk very frankly; but as a

[12] Jackson to Polk, Dec. 13, 16, *Polk Papers;* Jackson to Blair, Dec. 14, 1844, *Jackson Papers.*

[13] Johnson to Polk, Dec. 26; Brown to Polk, Dec. 29, 1844, *Polk Papers.*

[14] Calhoun to his son-in-law, Thos. G. Clemson, Dec. 13, 1844, *Rep. Am. Assn.,* 1899, II, 633. Dr. Gwin, who was supposed to be voicing Calhoun's views, suggested to A. V. Brown the following cabinet: Calhoun, Sec. of State; Walker, Sec. of Treasury; Woodbury, Sec. of War; Reed, of Pa., Atty. Gen.; Flagg, P-M Gen.; Mason, Sec. of Navy. Van Buren was suggested as minister to England (Brown to Polk, Jan. 5, 1845, *Polk Papers*).

[15] C. A. Davis, New York, to Crittenden, Dec. 17, 1844, *Crittenden Papers.*

friend of the South, he urged Calhoun's retention.[16] Calhoun himself continued to remain *passive* until February 26, when, in a personal interview, Polk informed him that there was to be an entirely new cabinet and offered to send him as minister to England. On the day following he sent Polk his resignation and assured him that there was neither dissatisfaction nor abatement of kind feelings on his own part.[17]

New England began at an early date to solicit a place in the cabinet. In New Hampshire, Hubbard and Woodbury were mentioned, but her congressional delegation preferred Pierce.[18] Bancroft was suggested as the New England member, but he informed Polk that he would prefer a foreign mission.[19] Maine was especially insistent in her claims for recognition, and Polk received numerous letters from politicians of that state. In several of them Governor Fairfield was suggested as Secretary of the Navy, and Nathan Weston as Attorney General.

The greatest rivalry, however, aside from the solicitation in Calhoun's behalf, was that between New York on the one side, and Pennsylvania and the West on the other. In Pennsylvania Buchanan and Dallas were the recognized heads of two rival factions, each of which was desirous of gaining a strategic position in the new administration. In order to accomplish his purpose, Dallas recommended that Robert J. Walker, of Mississippi, be made Secretary of State.[20] Dallas and Walker were connected by family ties as well as by political sympathies. In addition, Walker had the support of the aggressive forces in the southwestern states. Richard Rush urged the claims of Buchanan.

---

[16] Green to Polk, Jan. 20, 1845, *Polk Papers*. On January 1, Memucan Hunt wrote from Galveston that leading public men in Texas wished Calhoun to be retained and Donelson to be made Secretary of the Treasury.

[17] Calhoun to Polk, Feb. 27, 1845, *Polk Papers*. Same to Clemson, March 11, 1845, *Rep. Am. Hist. Assn.*, 1899, II, 647.

[18] John P. Hale to Pierce, Dec. 3, 1844, *Pierce Papers*.

[19] Lewis Josselyn, of Boston, to J. Geo. Harris, Dec. 4, 1844; Bancroft to Polk, Jan. 1, 1845, *Polk Papers*.

[20] Dallas to Polk, Dec. 15, 1844, *ibid*.

The latter had also received the formal endorsement of the Pennsylvania electoral college, but Dallas informed Polk that this action had been procured by the intrigue of a man who wished to be made collector of the port of Philadelphia. Dallas once more recommended Walker, dwelling on his command of foreign languages and upon the fact that he would be especially acceptable to the Texans.[21]

The rejection of Van Buren at Baltimore made it desirable that the powerful state of New York should be placated if possible. Polk very naturally, therefore, turned his thoughts in that direction, and his offer of the Treasury Department to Silas Wright was the first tender of a cabinet position to any one. Wright promptly declined the offer. The reason, as stated in his letter, was that he had pledged himself to serve as governor, if elected, and should he fail to do so it would be said that his nomination had been a trick to enable him to procure a cabinet position. When expressing regret because Wright had felt constrained to decline, Polk stated that while he had not yet decided upon a person for any of the cabinet positions, he intended to select either the Secretary of State or the Secretary of the Treasury from the state of New York. He asked Wright freely to suggest a man for either position.[22] In his reply Wright recommended Benjamin F. Butler for the State Department and Azariah C. Flagg for the Treasury. Lest Polk might think that he would have accepted the State portfolio, he assured the President-elect that he did not feel qualified to fill that office. Had he been at liberty to fill any such position he would have accepted the Treasury appointment.

In a letter dated January 4, 1845, Polk assured Van Buren that his nomination at Baltimore had been unsought and unexpected. He prevaricated to the degree of stating that: ''Until

21 Rush to Polk, Dec. 27, 1844; Dallas to Polk, Jan. 10, 1845, *ibid.*

22 Polk to Wright, Dec. 7; Wright to Polk, Dec. 20, 1844; Polk to Wright, Jan. 4, 1845, *ibid.*

the moment it was made, it was very far from my thoughts, that any state of circumstances could arise, which could lead to such a result.'' He thanked the ex-President for his ''powerful support'' and requested his advice as to suitable members of the cabinet. Wright, he said, was the only selection he had made without consulting anyone, but as that offer had been declined, he would like to have Van Buren suggest persons for either the State or Treasury Departments.[23] In reply, Van Buren stated that Polk had acted just as he would have done in offering the Treasury portfolio to Wright, and that Wright's refusal to accept was due entirely to the political situation in New York. He knew of no one so well qualified to take charge of foreign affairs as Benjamin F. Butler, and he believed either Flagg or Cambreleng to be suitable for the Treasury Department. A month later he told Polk that Donelson would be a good man to have near him. He had desired to have Donelson in his own cabinet, but had feared that modesty would prevent him from accepting.[24] Jackson believed that Wright's refusal to accept a cabinet position had been due to the fear that Calhoun would be retained. He advised Polk to deliberate well and to make no final decisions until he had reached Washington. He believed Mason and Wilkins to be worthy men, but ''surely you will do well to select an entire cabinett fresh from the people as your own, & leave Mr. Tylers out to be provided for, if thought worthy otherwise.''[25]

Before making another tender of a cabinet office Polk prepared a form of invitation to be used in future cases. Its purpose was to make clear to those who might receive it that a cabinet position was not to be used, during the next four years, as a stepping-stone to the Presidency, and that each member

[23] Polk to Van Buren, Jan. 4, 1845, *Van Buren Papers*. Also, copy in *Polk Papers*.

[24] Van Buren to Polk, Jan. 18, 1845, *Polk Papers* and *Van B. Papers;* Van Buren to Polk, Feb. 21, *Polk Papers*.

[25] Jackson to Polk, Jan. 10, 1845, *Polk Papers*.

must devote his whole time to the duties of his office.[26] Although he was not a military man, Polk possessed at least one attribute of a true soldier. As a private in the ranks of his party he was ever ready to submit without complaint to the judgment of the leaders; and now, as party chieftain, he required from others a similar respect for authority. Jackson, who knew Polk thoroughly, assured Blair that ''He will have no caball about him, his heads of Departments must be a unit. *This is my opinion of the man,* and I think you will, when you know the men be pleased with his selection.''[27]

On January 28, 1845, Polk left his home at Columbia and set out for Washington. The fact that he was going to fill the highest office of his country did not for a moment overcome his habitual caution nor prevent him from giving thoughtful attention to minute details. He had written to Cave Johnson and other friends and asked them to procure rooms for him at Coleman's hotel, but the rates must be reasonable and the bargain made in advance.[28]

When he arrived in Washington in the middle of February the President-elect had not, with the exception of Buchanan, definitely decided upon any member of his cabinet.[29] Early in

---

[26] See *infra,* p. 325.

[27] Jackson to Blair, Jan. 21, 1845, *Jackson Papers.* There were, of course, those who held a radically different opinion. ''Polk,'' wrote Prentiss, ''was elected by a union of factions. He has neither honesty nor capacity to be the president even of his party—he will become at once the tool of those factions'' (Prentiss to Crittenden, Dec. 22, 1844, *Crittenden Papers*). J. K. Paulding, also, considered Polk weak and unable to cope with the situation, ''whether he selects a northern, a southern, or a mixed cabinet.'' ''He is by no means a great man—nor scarcely one of extraordinary mediocrity; and if the truth must be told, I admire Mrs. Polk much more than I do the colonel (Paulding to Van Buren, Jan. 19, 1845, *Van Buren Papers*).

[28] ''You know I have no money to spend unnecessarily,—and to avoid being subjected to an extravagant or enormous charge, it is necessary that a *distinct bargain* shall be made in advance'' (Polk to Johnson, Dec. 21, 1844, ''Polk-Johnson Letters'').

[29] According to Gideon Welles, he had also settled upon Bancroft for the Treasury and Walker for Attorney General, before leaving Tennessee (MS ''Rev. of Pol. Hist. of U. S. and Pres. Contests,'' *Welles Papers*).

the winter, at a meeting held at the Hermitage, Buchanan had been discussed as a possible premier for the cabinet, but then it was believed that his appointment would cause too much jealously on the part of Benton, Calhoun, Cass, and Wright.[30] However, on his arrival in Washington, Polk immediately invited Buchanan to take charge of the State Department, and the tender was promptly accepted.[31]

Having thus provided for Pennsylvania, Polk addressed another letter to Van Buren. When he last wrote, he said, he intended to look to New York for either a Secretary of State or a Secretary of War. Subsequently he had decided to call a citizen of another state to the Department of State, but was still desirous that a citizen of New York should take charge of the Treasury. Such had been his intention when he came to Washington. On his arrival, however, he found that the South had already united on a distinguished individual from that section and that Indiana as well as other western states favored the same person.

I was not satisfied that it was proper to appoint him to that Post—but became convinced—that if I did not—great and extensive dissatisfaction would prevail—unless I could find some individual in some part of the Union who would be unexceptionable to them & also to the North.

Believing that Bancroft would fulfil these conditions, "my present determination therefore is to call him to that [Treasury] Department." He was inclined, he said, to retain Mason in charge of the Navy, and would be glad to have either Butler or Marcy as his Secretary of War.[32] Evidently the distinguished individual mentioned in the letter was Robert J. Walker, of Mississippi. Writing early in January, A. V. Brown told Polk

---

[30] J. P. Brawles to Buchanan, Dec. 20, 1844, *Buchanan Papers*. Brawles was told this by A. V. Brown, who had been present when Polk discussed cabinet appointments with Jackson.

[31] Polk's letter was dated at Washington on Feb. 17 (*Buchanan Papers*) and Buchanan replied on Feb. 18 (*Polk Papers*).

[32] Polk to Van Buren, Feb. 22, 1845, *Van Buren Papers*.

that Joseph A. Wright, Representative from Indiana, had reported that his own section as well as the Northwest wished Walker to be made Secretary of the Treasury so that he might have the appointment of land agents and other western officials. If, said he, Silas Wright should be given the office, he would use it to his own advantage and to the prejudice of Cass. From Cave Johnson, also, came the information that the ''Cass men'' all preferred Walker, and he gave the same reasons for their preference.[33]

Polk did not yield immediately to the importunities of Walker's friends; instead he held to his original plan of making Bancroft Secretary of the Treasury and Walker Attorney General. He even drafted a letter in which he invited Walker to accept the latter position, but probably it was never sent.[34] On February 25, without awaiting a reply from Van Buren, he offered the War portfolio to Benjamin F. Butler. Butler promptly declined because of ''domestic and prudential considerations,'' although he would have made the *sacrifice* if he had been tendered either the State or the Treasury Department.[35]

Van Buren deliberated well before answering Polk's letter of February 22; but on March 1, he drafted a reply and sent it to Washington by his son, Smith Van Buren. In it he said that the ''honest portion'' of the New York Democracy were excited by a rumor that Woodbury was to be made Secretary of the Treasury, and that New York was to be passed over entirely. He did not say, but seemed to assume, that Butler would reconsider his refusal of the War portfolio.[36] Polk appears to have felt

---

33 Brown to Polk, Jan. 9; Johnson to Polk, Jan. 11, 1845, *Polk Papers*.

34 Copy, dated Feb. 19, 1845, *ibid*.

35 Butler to Polk, Feb. 27, 1845, *Polk Papers*. Mrs. Butler wrote to Van Buren that she was responsible for her husband's refusing the War portfolio; that she had promised that if he were offered the State Department she would not object, but this promise did not apply to other departments. Her reason was that she did not like to live in Washington (Mrs. Butler to Van Buren, Feb. 27, 1845, *Van Buren Papers*).

36 Van Buren to Polk, Albany, March 1, 1845, *Polk Papers*.

that Butler's prompt refusal and Van Buren's delay had absolved him from further obligation to that wing of the party, for, on March 1, he informed Van Buren that, as Flagg did not have a *national* reputation, he had decided to make Marcy Secretary of War. He hoped that this appointment would be satisfactory to New York. The rumor that Bancroft was to be made Secretary of the Treasury had "brought down upon me" the delegations from New Hampshire and Maine, and many—on account of the patronage he dispenses—were demanding the appointment of a southern man to that office.[37]

When Smith Van Buren arrived in Washington with the letter from his father he was chagrined to learn that Polk had already appointed Marcy. "Well," he reported to the ex-President,

the letter which you rec'd dated last night from the illustrious cabinet-maker of our day has advised you of the fate of my mission; and unless the excuses & explanations were more skilfully done in writing than in conversation, you will have seen through the flimsy pretexts—the contradictory & evasive & trimming character of the business, at least so far as New York is concerned.

Polk, he said, had declined to receive him for half an hour, in order to give himself and A. V. Brown time to "concoct" an answer. Polk wished that he might have seen Van Buren's letter a day earlier, but the matter had now been decided. "The Treasury arrangement [Walker's appointment] you perceive tells the whole story for New York. The only chance now is that your letter may upset the whole concern, & start anew the business tomorrow." In a letter written on the following day he said that when he read his father's letter to Polk, the latter, instead of feeling crestfallen, had the "impudence" to say that he felt relieved. "I denounced Marcy to him in good round terms" and

---

[37] Polk to Van Buren, March 1, 1845, *Van Buren Papers*. Evidently Marcy had been expecting an offer, for on Feb. 24 he wrote to Dickinson about "my appointment as a member of the cabinet." This must have been speculation, because on the day following (25th) Polk offered the War portfolio to Butler.

said that he was simply an office seeker in whom honest Democrats had no faith. Polk replied that he had never heard these things before and was "thunderstruck," although "Dix has told him the same thing over and over again."[38]

Instead of beginning anew with his cabinet making, Polk dispatched another letter to Van Buren. If he had committed an error, he said, it had been unintentional; and it pained him to think that Van Buren might think he had acted unkindly to him or his friends. He had acted, he said under no outside influence; he had followed his own judgment, and harbored no unkind feeling toward either Van Buren or Wright.[39] Nevertheless, Smith Van Buren had formed quite a different opinion. "The soundest judges here," he wrote, "think P. came here all right—but has been be-deviled since he arrived. To a large extent this is of course evident, but not wholly so."[40]

It is scarcely to be wondered at that Polk should have dissembled during the days just preceding his inauguration. He was beset on every hand by conflicting demands, all of which he was expected to satisfy. That he strove to harmonize factional discord so far as his own self-respect would permit, there is no reason to doubt. He tried to deal fairly with each faction, but to accept the dictation of none. If the Van Burenites suffered disappointment they had only themselves to blame, for Polk had given them more consideration than he had ever received from them. He had tendered cabinet positions to two of their number,

---

[38] Smith Van Buren to his father, March 2, 3, 1845, *Van Buren Papers.* Tilden and O'Sullivan, who bore letters from Butler to Polk, were, on the other hand, thoroughly captivated by the President-elect. The latter reported that Polk seemed like "one of us" and evinced great admiration for both Wright and Van Buren. "He certainly entirely won the hearts of both of us, and has effectually dissipated whatever slight degree of anxiety may have rested in our minds in regard to the Adm'n" (O'Sullivan to Van Buren, Washington, March 1, 1845, *Van Buren Papers*).

[39] Polk to Van Buren, March 3, 1845, *Polk Papers.*

[40] Smith Van Buren to his father, March 4, 1845, *Van Buren Papers.* "Armstrong," said he, "so far as I can observe, is the only honest man about him. He [Armstrong] is sick & very much affected by our affairs. He doubtless sees the approaching storm from Nashville."

and he had kept Van Buren fully informed regarding his plans. He had even told the ex-President of his intention to appoint Marcy unless Butler should accept the place offered to him. Van Buren had delayed in answering his letter, and it was unreasonable to expect Polk to wait indefinitely when inauguration day was already at hand. Surely Polk had the right to make his own choice for the office of Secretary of State, and it was cool effrontery on Butler's part to intimate that the position should have been bestowed upon himself.

Walker's assignment to the Treasury evidently was contrary to Polk's own wishes, yet he felt constrained to make this concession to the western element after his own choice, Bancroft, was found to be unpopular even in New England states. A new adjustment became necessary, therefore Mason was made Attorney General so that Bancroft might be assigned to the Navy. Mason's retention in the cabinet was due to personal friendship, and not to a desire to placate Tyler and his friends. Tyler had, in January, bestowed a diplomatic appointment upon William H. Polk, but the latter declined to accept it in order to free his brother from any obligation to the retiring President.[41] In fact, Tyler was much displeased by the ingratitude of his successor, and, in 1846, wrote that Polk seemed to be "avenging the supposed wrongs to Mr. Van Buren."[42] Marcy's acceptance of the War portfolio[43] completed the cabinet, for Cave Johnson had accepted the appointment as Postmaster General shortly after Polk's arrival in Washington.[44] Although many persons had suggested Donelson as the Tennessee member, Polk evidently preferred Johnson, and Jackson assured Polk that Donelson

---

[41] Cave Johnson to Polk, Jan. 8; J. L. O'Sullivan to Polk, Jan. 20, 1845, *Polk Papers*.

[42] Tyler to Alex. Gardner, July 11, 1846 (Tyler, *Letters and Times of the Tylers*, II, 342).

[43] Welles says that "Gen. [William O.] Butler of Kentucky accompanied the President-elect to the seat of government in expectation of the appointment [War Dept.] then tendered him" (MS "Rev. of Pol. Hist., etc."). I have seen nothing else to indicate that such an offer was made.

[44] Johnson to Polk, Feb. 26, 1845, *Polk Papers*.

would be satisfied with a foreign mission. Jackson had made it clear to Donelson, he said, that he was the one who had suggested a diplomatic appointment in preference to any other.[45] Johnson thoroughly deserved a place in Polk's cabinet, for no one had stood by him so loyally or had rendered more efficient service during his entire political career. Polk was by nature secretive and self-reliant, but to Johnson more than to any other person he disclosed his plans and his aspirations. Johnson had never failed him in the hour of need, and, both in Washington and in Tennessee, had done much to aid his political advancement. As a statesman, Johnson was conservative and rather narrow; but he was a crafty and capable politician, and a recognized leader in the House.

In selecting his cabinet, as in distributing the patronage, Polk had to steer between Scylla and Charybdis. When he tried to be fair to all wings of the party, he was charged with weakness; while independent actions were attributed to vanity and conceit, or characterized as downright treachery to his benefactors. It was freely predicted that leading cabinet members would dominate the President and reduce him to a mere figurehead, yet, from the beginning, Polk was master of the situation.

Scarcely less difficult than the selection of a cabinet was the choice of a party "organ" which would give ungrudging support to the new administration. Historians have indulged in no small amount of conjecture as to Polk's reasons for discarding Blair and the *Globe* despite General Jackson's vigorous protests. His action is usually said to have been the consummation of a preëlection bargain to obtain votes. Sometimes Tyler is made the other party to the contract, sometimes Calhoun; and in an attempt to make out a strong case, some have asserted that Blair's head on a platter had been offered to each of them in return for his political support. Usually their information has been derived

---

[45] Jackson to Polk, Jan. 10, Feb. 15, 1845, *ibid.* On account of Donelson's delicate health, Jackson asked that he might be sent as full minister to Spain, Brazil, or Mexico.

from Benton, and accepted without question. But even von Holst, who had no difficulty in believing the Tyler story, balks at the absurdity of a bargain between Polk and Calhoun.[46] For very good reasons both Tyler and Calhoun despised the editor of the *Globe,* and both supported the nominees of the Democratic party, but such a coincidence does not imply any bargain between them and the Democratic candidates. Calhoun's letter to Stuart concerning the prospective cabinet[47] seems to indicate that he had no knowledge of Polk's plans for the future, and Tyler has specifically and emphatically denied that he and Polk had ever entered into an agreement by which Tyler's withdrawal from the canvass was made contingent on Polk's promise not to make the *Globe* his official organ. As Tyler very aptly remarked, "Blair was already dead," and it only remained for Mr. Polk to chant his requiem.[48]

It is unnecessary to seek some mysterious intrigue or pre-election pact in order to find Polk's motive for establishing a new paper in Washington. The obvious reason for establishing the *Union* was his desire to have an organ at the capital which would give his administration its undivided and loyal support. He had always believed Blair to be hostile or indifferent to his political advancement when he had been a candidate for Speaker, and when he had sought the Vice-Presidential nomination. Both Polk and his friends believed that the *Globe* had supported the nominees of the Baltimore convention with great reluctance and that its editor was now, and would continue to be, under the absolute domination of Senator Benton. This belief is the best of reasons for Polk's refusal to make the *Globe* his official newspaper. Walker and others were hostile to Blair and undoubtedly

---

[46] von Holst, *History of the United States,* III, 7–8.

[47] See above, p. 288, note 9.

[48] Tyler to Ritchie, Jan. 9, 1851; same to John S. Cunningham, May 8, 1856 (Tyler, *Letters and Times of the Tylers,* II, 409 ff., 415). In the second letter, Tyler said that the "conspiracy to supplant the *Globe,* by substituting Mr. Ritchie or anybody else as the editorial mouth-piece of Mr. Polk, is the sheerest invention that ever was conceived of."

desired his elimination. Their feelings may have strengthened Polk's determination to look elsewhere for an editor, but there is no reason for believing that they caused it. Polk's Tennessee friends wrote freely concerning the advisability of establishing a new paper, but in his correspondence there is no letter from Walker on this subject.[49]

Polk's feelings toward Blair are manifested in a letter written to Cave Johnson on January 21, 1844. "Amicus" had published in the *Globe* an article which urged the claims of W. R. King to the Vice-Presidency. In reply, S. H. Laughlin and H. L. Turney prepared an article in Polk's behalf and sent it to Blair for publication. "Blair," said Polk, "surely cannot do me the injustice to exclude it from his columns"; if so, he instructed Johnson to have it published in pamphlet form. After alluding to his nomination by the Mississippi state convention, Polk wondered whether Blair would suppress this news "or stick it in an obscure corner as he did the Tennessee and Arkansas nominations?"[50] Such remarks indicate that he did not, even at that time, regard Blair as his friend.

Immediately after Polk had been nominated at Baltimore, A. V. Brown reported from Washington that "much is said here by *some* as to continuing the Globe as the Polk organ—this we will manage with sound discretion. The Globe will change its *tone* & perhaps take back much that it has said & go in *warmly* if not heartily—if so—well—But we will not commit ourselves to it *after* the election."[51] The last remark might seem to indicate that Blair's fate *after election* had already been determined, but this is disproved by letters written later in the campaign. Cave Johnson, who was hostile to Calhoun and averse to the Tylerites, wrote that the *Globe* was noncommittal and that a new paper was

---

[49] Although Ambler assigns to Walker the chief rôle in the overthrow of Blair, he admits his inability to produce any tangible evidence (Ambler, *Thomas Ritchie*, 252).

[50] Polk to Johnson, Jan. 21, 1844, "Polk-Johnson Letters."

[51] Brown to Polk, May 30, 1844, *Polk Papers.*

needed; but two weeks later, when he had come to believe that
the southerners were trying to "appropriate" Polk, he spoke
with disgust of the "secret talk of upsetting the Globe [and]
turning Benton overboard."[52]   Judge Catron vehemently denounced the *Globe* and declared that its "coarse brutality" was
loathed by a large majority of the party.[53]

Late in June, J. B. Jones, editor of the *Madisonian,* invited
J. George Harris to become joint editor of that paper.   Harris
and General Armstrong looked with favor upon the offer and
believed that all three Washington papers—*Madisonian, Spectator*
and *Globe*—might be merged into one.   However, A. V. Brown,
who had come from Washington recently, did not approve such
an arrangement.[54]   It was not yet a question of an *administration
organ,* for there was no certainty that Polk would be elected, but
many of Polk's friends felt that Blair's support of the ticket was
merely perfunctory and that a more vigorous journal was needed.
This feeling was not caused entirely by what appeared or did not
appear in the columns of the *Globe.*   The campaign leaders believed Blair to be under the thumb of Benton, and the latter was
vociferously denouncing the "intrigue" which had deprived
Van Buren of the nomination and, also, the annexation program.
Despite the need of a reliable party organ there seemed to be no
satisfactory solution of the difficulty, therefore the matter was
dropped until after the election.

The correspondence does not disclose who it was that first
suggested inviting Ritchie to come to Washington, but Brown
rather than Walker seems to have been the prime mover.   In a
letter written to Polk, soon after the election, Brown said that
Walker "entertains the same opinion with us" as to the importance of procuring Blair's half of the *Globe* for Ritchie.   Blair
would not be approached, he said, until Cave Johnson had gone

---

[52] Johnson to Polk, June 1 [1844?, year not given], June 13, 1844, *Polk
Papers.*
[53] Catron to Polk, June 8, [1844], *ibid.*
[54] Harris to Polk, June 27, 29; Armstrong to Polk, June 30, 1844, *ibid.*

to Richmond to sound Ritchie on the subject. "If that dont take—then B & Rives must sink into mere *proprietors,* with *an able & competent* Editor having *absolute* controul of the political character of the paper."[55]   Cave Johnson, also, had become convinced that Blair must go.   Some of the politicians, said he, fear that the *Globe* will be dominated by Benton and they will therefore oppose giving it the public printing; "I see no chance of a reconciliation with them if F. P. Blair is retained."   A few days later he reported that "the Globe is regarded as Benton's organ by the friends of C[alhoun] & will oppose him to the uttermost & will in connection with the Whigs defeat him & therefore B[rown] & myself have been sounding, to learn the prospect of getting Ritchie . . . . T. H. B[enton] has a great dislike to Ritchie & I expect will be greatly provoked, if he learns any such movement."[56]   This letter shows a desire to prevent opposition from the Calhoun faction, but it indicates, also, that there had been no preëlection understanding.   Had there been any such understanding Johnson would have been one of the first to learn of it.

As soon as General Jackson heard of the scheme to supplant the *Globe* he took immediate steps to thwart it.   Assuming that Polk knew nothing about the matter, Jackson warned him that an intrigue was being concocted in Washington which might divide the party and wreck his administration.   Some, he said, wished to substitute the *Madisonian* for the *Globe;* others wanted to make Ritchie editor of the *Globe.*   He urged Polk to discountenance such maneuvers for

the first would blow you sky high & destroy the Republican party— The second would be an insult to the Editor of the Globe & seperate him from you, whose administration he is determined to support— Keep Blairs Globe the administration paper, and William B. Lewis, to ferret out & make known to you all the plotts & intrigues Hatching against your administration and you are safe.

55 Brown to Polk, Dec. 5, 1844, *ibid.*
56 Johnson to Polk, Dec. 6, 12, 1844, *ibid.*

These men had been such a source of strength to Jackson himself that very naturally he desired his friend Polk to have the benefit of their services. But battling for Old Hickory was one thing, and loyal support of the man who had profited by the *intrigue* against Van Buren was quite another. Polk well knew that both men had always been ready to throw obstacles in his way, and he had no reason to believe that their feeling toward him had undergone any change.

Jackson may have been wrong in his belief that Blair and Lewis would labor for the glory of Polk's administration, but another part of his letter showed that he understood Ritchie's weaknesses better than did those who were so anxious to bring him to Washington. ''Ritchie is a good Editor,'' he told Polk, ''but a very unsafe one— He goes off at half bent, & does great injury before he can be set right.''[57] Before many months had elapsed, Polk realized fully the accuracy of the General's statement.

On the following day, Jackson informed Blair of the scheme to merge the *Spectator* and the *Madisonian* into a Polk organ. He attributed this scheme to Calhoun. Believing that his word was still law, he told Blair that ''I am sure polk when he hears of it will feel as indignant at the plott as I do.''[58] In Washington the ''plott'' had already been discovered, and Cave Johnson (on account of his known intimacy with Polk) feared to go to Richmond for the purpose of negotiating with Ritchie. The premature discovery greatly annoyed Johnson, and he complained that ''even old J. Q. A[dams] asked when we were going to Richmond.''[59] Brown, who facetiously called himself ''the President elect ad interim,'' was somewhat disconcerted by Johnson's timidity. He even suspected that his colleague did not desire to

---

[57] Jackson to Polk, Dec. 13, 1844, *ibid.*

[58] Jackson to Blair, Dec. 14, 1844, *Jackson Papers.*

[59] Johnson to Polk, Dec. 14, 1844, *Polk Papers.*

get rid of Blair.[60] General Bayly, of the Virginia delegation, and a personal friend of Ritchie, now undertook to negotiate by letter with the veteran editor of the *Enquirer*. "If my road is blocked there," said Brown, "I shall then go for sinking Blair & Rives into *Proprietors* only & putting the political controul (absolute) into the hands of a new Editor & that man Burke would not be a bad one." Brown believed that Blair would not oppose the change "if he sees that Benton means to be antagonistic to your administration as many of his *Western* friends think likely enough. He shews no *mitigation* of his opposition & nothing but instructions plain & powerful can subdue him."[61] Here again is a statement of the main reason for wanting a new party organ— not pledges to Tyler or to Calhoun, but distrust of Blair and a fear that he would be controlled by Benton, who was considered to be an enemy of the incoming administration. Another indication that Polk had made no bargain with the Tylerites is the sentiment voiced in a letter written by J. B. Jones, editor of the *Madisonian*. The plan contemplated was, in his opinion, the only sensible one, for he believed that discord would surely result from the employment of any of the Washington editors. "When," said he, "Col. Polk shall convince all parties that he is in his own hands—that he will be the *President,* and not a partisan of any aspirant, there will be no door left open for the ingress of factious schemes."[62]

---

[60] "He feared some newspaper squibs at him & *I feared* he was rather indifferent about any matter that was against the Globe Benton & Co but perhaps I was wrong."

[61] Brown to Polk, Dec. 23, 1844, *Polk Papers.*

[62] Party factions can not "object to the [new] paper because its conductor entertains no special partiality for any one of the aspirants to the succession. But if *I* were to conduct the paper it would be said that Mr. Polk had thrown himself into the hands of the Tyler men—if the editor of the Globe, into the hands of Col. Benton—and if the Constitution [successor to the *Spectator*], into the hands of Mr. Calhoun" (Jones to ——, Dec. 23, 1844). Apparently this was written to J. Geo. Harris, for it was inclosed in his letter to Polk, Jan. 4, 1845, *Polk Papers.*

At first Ritchie did not take kindly to the plan which had been arranged for him, and, in a letter to Bayly, he declined the invitation. He was not able, he said, to purchase the *Globe,* and rival Democratic papers would do the party more harm than good.[63] After reading Ritchie's letter, Brown concluded that "If Benton goes right on Texas & Calhoun is not in the Cabinet there would be no insuperable difficulty with the Globe—but you would find it hard to keep in order."[64] Edmund Burke was once more considered, but his former affiliations with Calhoun were urged against his selection.[65] A few days of reflection seem to have convinced Brown that neither Benton nor Blair could be kept in order, for he presented for Polk's consideration an entirely new solution of the difficulty. He offered to purchase Blair's share of the *Globe* and to continue the paper under the firm name of Brown and Rives. Brown was to have exclusive control, and, with Kendall's help, to edit the journal in the interest of the administration.[66] His new scheme, like the others, came to naught, and no arrangement had been made when Polk reached Washington. Apparently the President-elect gave no encouragement to the editor of the *Globe,* for Smith Van Buren reported to his father that "Blair says—'Where am I to go?'"[67]

Polk's own opinions concerning a party journal were expressed in very definite terms before he left Tennessee. In a letter to Cave Johnson, he said:

As to the *press* which may be regarded as the Government organ, one thing is settled in my mind. It must have no connection with, nor be under the influence or control of any clique or portion of the party which is making war upon any other portion of the party—with a view to the succession and

---

[63] His letter, dated Dec. 28, is printed in full in Ambler, *Thomas Ritchie,* 247–249.

[64] Brown to Polk, Jan. 1, 1843 [1845], *Polk Papers.*

[65] Cave Johnson to Polk, Jan. 2, 1844, *ibid.*

[66] Brown to Polk, Jan. 5, 1845, *ibid.* He told Polk that if this plan did not work out he might consent to run for governor of Tennessee, although he would rather "rent a brick yard" than go through that campaign!

[67] March 2, 1845, *Van Buren Papers.*

not with a view to the success of my administration. I think the view you take of it proper and of the proposed arrangement the best that can be made. I hope it may be effected.[68]

Apparently Polk felt that he was regarded as a sort of *chargé d' affaires* who was to keep things running while the great men contended for the prize. He had no intention of playing such a rôle, and his determination to make the administration his own and to have a paper which would promote its interests was both characteristic of the man and an exhibition of sound sense.[69] Even von Holst, who has found little in Polk's career to commend, obsolves him from the charge of subserviency to factional leaders. He says,

Obedience to party commands, was certainly one of the principal articles of his political creed. But if politicians had expected that they were now going to have the mastery, because he was willing to play the part of a manikin, they were greatly mistaken in the man.[70]

As to patronage in general the President-elect maintained a discreet silence. There was much speculation concerning future rewards and punishments, but all had to wait until the new President had canvassed the situation and was ready to act. Although General Jackson made no exception to his rule of attempting to provide for his friends, he did not find Polk as accommodating as Van Buren had been. His solicitation for the welfare of Blair and Lewis has already been noted, and Polk had scarcely been elected before Jackson consulted Amos Kendall in order to ascertain the position which would be most acceptable to the star member of his "kitchen cabinet." Kendall selected the Spanish mission and his wishes were forthwith reported to

---

68 Polk to Johnson, Dec. 21, 1844, "Polk-Johnson Letters." The "proposed arrangement" evidently refers to the attempt to procure Ritchie.

69 A rumor that Laughlin was going to Washington to edit the *Madisonian* caused General Jackson much needless worry. He warned Polk to keep clear of Tyler influence, for, if he did not, he would be in as bad a position as Tyler himself (Jackson to Polk, Feb. 28, 1845, *Polk Papers*).

70 von Holst, *History of the United States*, III, 21–22.

the President-elect. Jackson assured Polk that "there can be no delicacy in recalling Erwin [Washington Irving]—he is only fit to write a Book & scarcely that, and has become a good Whigg."[71]

Congress had already consented to annex Texas before Polk became President of the United States. Nevertheless, since one of the principal planks in the platform on which he had been elected related to this subject, and since he had been an indirect, if not a direct, participant in this important transaction, it is necessary to give a brief outline of the progress of events during the period between the rejection of Tyler's treaty and the passage of the joint resolution of annexation.

Tyler's annexation treaty was rejected by the Senate on June 8, 1844. Calhoun, we are told,[72] disheartened by this action, was ready to abandon all further attempts at annexation. His dejection was so great that Tyler thought of requesting his resignation, but he soon recovered his spirits and his old-time vigor. Since the treaty method had failed, nothing could be done without the coöperation of Congress. During the summer, a rumor to the effect that Tyler was about to convene Congress in extra session caused the Democratic candidate no little anxiety, and he appealed to Jackson as the only man who could dissuade the President from committing such a political error. A month later Jackson assured him that Congress would not be convened, although it is not clear whether Jackson was instrumental in preventing such a course.[73] At any rate no call for an extra session was issued, and no further action could be undertaken until winter; but the death of T. A. Howard, the American *chargé* in Texas, gave Tyler an opportunity to strengthen his position by assigning A. J. Donelson to the vacant post. When notifying

---

[71] Kendall to Jackson, Dec. 2; Jackson to Polk, Dec. 13, 1844, *Polk Papers.*

[72] Tyler, *Letters and Times of the Tylers,* II, 331.

[73] Polk to Donelson, Aug. 27, 1844, "Polk-Donelson Letters." Jackson to Polk, Sept. 26, 1844, *Polk Papers.*

Jackson of Donelson's appointment the President expressed the belief that the selection of "a member of your family . . . . will have a controuling influence with Gen¹ Houstin and incline him . . . . to pause ere he declares against annexation." He declared his determination to proceed with his Texas program, and to protect that country from the threatened aggressions of Mexico. Jackson informed Polk of the President's plans and remarked that "This is the true energetic course."[74]

On December 3, 1844, Tyler submitted to Congress his last annual message. In it he called attention to the threatening Mexican manifestoes that had resulted from the treaty which the United States had negotiated with Texas. Mexico, he said, had no cause for complaint; on the contrary, the measure "should have been regarded by her as highly beneficial." The treaty, said he, had been rejected by the American Senate on the ground that the question had not been submitted to the people, but popular approval had since been expressed at the recent election. Such being the case, he urged Congress to annex Texas by joint resolution.[75] He followed this up with another message on December 18, and along with it submitted a collection of correspondence. He called attention to the abusive character of this correspondence and to the barbarous measures which were threatened by Mexico. Especially did he resent Mexico's criticism of southern states, and he declared with emphasis that annexation was not a sectional question.[76] His statement that "the subject of annexation addresses itself, most fortunately, to every portion of the Union" was, to say the least, an exaggeration; still, since the election had been decided, there were many indications of a change in public opinion, and the question was becoming more *national* every day. Could the subject, when it was presented originally, have been divested of its factional and its sectional

74 Tyler to Jackson, Sept. 17, 1844, *Jackson Papers*. Jackson to Polk, Sept. 26, 1844, *Polk Papers*.
75 Richardson, *Messages*, IV, 341–345.
76 *Ibid.*, 353–356.

concomitants, doubtless there would have been little opposition to annexation. Now that the election was over, those who had really wished to see Texas admitted into the Union no longer had the same incentive to oppose annexation for mere factional reasons. They might still cavil over ways and means, yet the prospect of eventual compromise was perceptibly brightening.[77] There was no certainty, however, that the friends of Texas would be able to effect annexation during the present session, for those who had been defeated at Baltimore still harbored a bitter resentment. Late in December, Calhoun believed that the House would take favorable action, but that annexation would be defeated in the Senate. "The real opposition is from the Benton V. Buren party" who would join with the Whigs against Texas; still he was not without hope that "publick opinion will force them to give up their opposition. Its effects are already apparent."[78] It was at this time that Calhoun was ready to make the "sacrifice" of accepting a place in Polk's cabinet, if the probable course of the administration should appear to be satisfactory.

While Calhoun denounced Benton and Van Buren for their obstructive tactics, others believed that the South Carolinian himself had sounded the knell of the Texas treaty. A long article on "Abolitionists" which· appeared in the January number of the *Democratic Review* held him responsible, in the main, for the widespread hostility to annexation. Although himself in favor of annexation, the writer flayed Calhoun for the position he had assumed regarding the slavery side of the question. In the writer's opinion, the fanatical demands of the Abolitionists and the "gag rule" of Congress were equally to be deplored; but the climax of absurdity had been reached when Calhoun, in his letters to Pakenham and King, had represented the United States as

---

[77] See press comments, Smith, *Annexation of Texas,* 323 ff.

[78] Calhoun to Clemson, Dec. 27; same to Hunter, Dec. 29, 1844, *Rep. Am. Hist. Assn.,* 1899, II, 634–636.

desiring Texas in order to protect slavery. In his effort to nationalize slavery, he had also nationalized abolition. Other critics of Calhoun expressed similar sentiments. Since the opposition had been aimed, for the most part, at the negotiators of the treaty and their methods, acquiescence in annexation was made easier when it became practically certain that Calhoun as well as Tyler would soon depart from the scene of action.

Soon after Congress had convened in December various plans of annexation were offered in each house, some to admit Texas as a state, others to acquire it as a territory. In the House, after several projects had met with serious objections, Milton Brown, one of Polk's Whig antagonists from Tennessee, offered a resolution which, after certain alterations, was eventually adopted by the House. Brown's resolution provided that the territory rightfully belonging to Texas should be admitted as a state. The federal government was to undertake the adjustment of the boundaries of the new state, but was not to assume her debt or take over her public lands. Slavery was prohibted in all territory north of 36° 30′; south of that line the people were to decide the question for themselves.

In the early days of the session, McDuffie once more presented the joint resolution of annexation which had failed to pass in the spring. It voiced the sentiments of the Tyler administration and was, in substance, a restatement of the rejected treaty. As such, it was unacceptable to the Senator from Missouri, and Cave Johnson reported to Polk that "the great battle between Mr. T. H. B. [enton] & Mr. C. [alhoun] has commenced." Apparently the main reason for presenting the resolution in this particular form was the desire to embarrass the Van Burenites by compelling them either to accept a measure which they had denounced or to incur the odium of opposing annexation after they had endorsed the Baltimore platform. Such, at least, was the opinion of Cave Johnson:

The friends of T. H. B.—— Silas Wright, who took general ground before the people for annexation but against the Treaty are to be forced to take that Treaty or appear before the people as hostile to Texas. Mr. C. thinks that he has got the advantage of T. H. B. on this issue & intends to drive him home upon it. The N. Y. democrats will go en-mass ag't the treaty & I have no idea, that the friends of C—— will take any thing but the Treaty.[79]

On the day following the appearance of McDuffie's resolution, Benton met the issue by reintroducing his own bill which had failed at the close of the last session, with a modification for making the territory half slave and half free. Since this bill could not by any possibility get but a few votes, Johnson considered Benton's conduct to be "outrageous." He asked the Senator to coöperate in offering a joint resolution which would assert the determination of the United States to defend Texas against all assaults, leaving the question of annexation to Polk's administration. Benton declined to accept this resolution, and continued to rage against his opponents.[80] Late in December Johnson thought that the hostility between the two factions was increasing; each feared that the other would influence the incoming President.[81] Benton blustered, of course, for, under the circumstances, he could hardly do otherwise. Since the election, however, he must have known that he was championing an unpopular cause. There was also a future ahead, and his course had alienated a large majority of his party—even many of his lifelong friends. In addition, the legislature of Missouri had, by resolution, requested members of Congress from that state to support annexation.[82] This made it clear that his conduct did not meet with approval at home; on the other hand, such a request made it easier for him to modify his attitude on the subject. About the same time a letter from Donelson told him "that his course is injuring his friends and his country, and that I hoped he would

[79] Johnson to Polk, Dec. 12, 1844, *Polk Papers*.

[80] *Idem*, and Johnson to Polk, Dec. 14, *Polk Papers*.

[81] Johnson to Polk, Dec. 26, 1844, *Polk Papers*.

[82] Meigs, *Life of Thomas Hart Benton*, 351.

be willing to modify his position.''[83] No doubt all of these manifestations of displeasure had their influence in determining Benton to retreat, provided he could do so in good order. His avenue of escape was by way of a new bill, and this he introduced on February 5, 1845. No mention was made in the new measure of obtaining the consent of Mexico. It provided for the admission of a state of suitable size and boundaries, said state to be formed out of the territory of the republic; the remainder of Texas was to be a territory of the United States. The measure was to become effective as soon as an agreement had been reached by the governments of the two nations concerned. His plan would delay, but not necessarily defeat, annexation, although defeat is evidently what its author desired. His bill and the House resolution seemed hopelessly irreconcilable until R. J. Walker, a few days later, offered as an amendment a combination of the two methods, and Haywood proposed to leave the choice between them to the President of the United States. To this modification Walker readily agreed.[84] Calhoun, according to a statement made later, believed that Benton's bill would have defeated annexation, and he was scarcely less opposed to the combination measure.[85] He used his ''best efforts'' to defeat both, but was unsuccessful in the second instance. Many counseled delay, but at the evening session of February 27, 1845, the Senate was ready to vote on Walker's combination amendment. Before the vote had been taken, however, Archer, of the Committee on Foreign Relations, offered a substitute bill. This proposed a transfer of the territory of Texas, with the assent of the people thereof, to the United States. The vote on the substitute resulted in a tie, and it looked for a time as if annexation were doomed. Nevertheless, relief was already at hand. When the vote on the Walker

---

[83] Donelson to Calhoun, New Orleans, Dec. 26, 1844, *Rep. Am. Hist. Assn.*, 1899, II, 1012.

[84] Smith, *Annexation of Texas*, 343. Smith gives an exhaustive account of the various proposals offered in each house (*idem,* chap. xvi).

[85] Calhoun to Donelson, May 23, 1845, *Rep. Am. Hist. Assn.*, 1899, II, 658.

amendment was taken in Committee of the Whole, Johnson, a Whig from Louisiana who had voted for the Archer bill, now swung to the Democrats and made the vote twenty-seven to twenty-five. According to Judge Catron, Johnson had difficulty in supporting the joint resolution on constitutional grounds, but, after consulting Catron, finally agreed to do so.[86] As soon as the committee had reported the measure to the Senate, Miller, of New Jersey, offered Benton's original bill as a substitute. Benton said from his seat that he would vote against this substitute, and when asked if he would destroy his own child, he replied, "I'll kill it stone dead." The substitute failed, and Walker's amendment passed the Senate by a vote of twenty-seven to twenty-five, Johnson again aligning himself with the Democrats.[87] The amended resolution was transmitted to the House for approval, and although it met with strenuous opposition there was never any doubt of its passage. This measure was given precedence over other matters; the Speaker, by his rulings, prevented filibustering; and, in Committee of the Whole, the debate was limited to five minutes. Milton Brown, the author of the House resolution, tried to "kill his own child," but the measure as amended by Walker passed by a vote of one hundred thirty-two to seventy-six.[88]

The President-elect had been in Washington since February 13, but whether and to what extent his influence was effective at this time is very difficult to determine. Before Polk had left Tennessee, Cave Johnson assured Calhoun that the incoming President and his friends desired to have Texas annexed during

---

[86] "The amendment offered by Mr. Senator Walker," continued Catron, "was rather sudden; it left the slave line at 36° 30′ N. open. To this Gov. Johnson had most decided objections; it threw Mr. Senator Foster the other way, and endangered the measure." Johnson, said the judge, voted for the measure because he had confidence in Polk, and because he believed that 36° 30′ would be definitely fixed as the northern boundary of slavery (Catron to Buchanan, March 15, 1845, *Buchanan Papers*).

[87] *Cong. Globe,* 28 Cong., 2 sess., 362; Smith, *Annexation of Texas,* 344-345.

[88] *Cong. Globe* (Feb. 28), 28 Cong., 2 sess., 372.

the present session, and Donelson informed Calhoun that both
Jackson and himself hoped for immediate action by the existing
Congress.[89] While at Coleman's hotel awaiting his inauguration
the President-elect, according to his own account,[90] freely expressed the wish that annexation in some form might be effected
before the adjournment of Congress. Should Congress fail to
take definite action, he feared that Texas would be forever lost
to the Union. He did not, he said, have time to examine the
different measures proposed, but thought that any measure would
be better than none. That he desired to have this vexed question
settled before his inauguration, we may very well believe. Indeed, it was said that he offered rewards and threatened punishments for the purpose of influencing votes. Such charges rested
on no tangible evidence and doubtless, for the most part, were
unfounded, although it is quite probable that he may have let it
be known that the disloyal need not look to him for favors.
Always ready to "play the game" himself, he was a firm believer
in party discipline.

Later, a more serious charge was brought against Polk in this
connection—a charge of base deception instead of party discipline. In a letter printed in the New York *Evening Post,* July 28,
1848, Senator Tappan, of Ohio, asserted that, in February, 1845,
Polk had personally assured Senator Haywood that, should the
joint resolution pass, he would choose the Benton alternative and
negotiate under it. In a letter to Tappan, F. P. Blair averred
that he, also, had discussed the matter with Polk, and that the
President-elect had promised to choose the Benton plan of negotiating a treaty with Texas. It was charged, therefore, that at
least five Senators had voted for the joint resolution because they
had been deceived by Polk.[91] Polk denied all recollection of any

---

[89] Johnson to Polk, Dec. 9, 1844, *Polk Papers.* Donelson to Calhoun,
Dec. 26, 1844, *Rep. Am. Hist. Assn.,* 1899, II, 1012.

[90] Polk, *Diary,* IV, 41.

[91] The essential parts of both letters may be found in Benton, *Thirty
Years' View,* II, 636–637.

conversation on the subject with either Blair or Haywood, and
called attention to the fact that no complaint of violated pledges
had been made at the time. In addition, he pointed out that in
August, 1846, Blair had expressed to him a warm approval of
the principal measures of his administration.[92] The members of
Polk's cabinet disclaimed all knowledge of such a pledge, and
even the fine-meshed dragnet of Justin H. Smith has failed to
find any evidence to substantiate the charges made by Tappan
and Blair. On the contrary, Smith offers some valuable suggestions as to why it is highly improbable that the President
elect made pledges to any one.[93] Polk had committed himself to
immediate annexation; and even if he had been as unprincipled
as his enemies alleged, it seems incredible that so crafty a politician should have made so stupid a blunder. Besides, Polk was
a man who seldom disclosed his intentions until he was ready to
act, and, as Cave Johnson said in his letter, it was extremely
unlikely that he would do so to Blair. It is significant, also, that,
as soon as Texas had approved annexation, Polk wrote a letter
to Haywood in which he commented on the wisdom of choosing
the House resolution and expressed the belief that Texas would
have been lost if the Benton alternative had been selected. "It
was not," wrote the President, "until after I entered upon my
duties that I had an opportunity—deliberately to consider the

---

[92] Polk, *Diary*, II, 84.

[93] Smith, *Annexation of Texas*, 347–350. In answer to Polk's request
for a statement on the subject, Cave Johnson (Oct. 6, 1848) said that he
conversed with the President-elect while the joint resolution was before
Congress. Polk said that he hoped one of the alternatives would pass,
but expressed no preference. After the measure had passed, he expressed
no preference until the cabinet had met. Walker (Oct. 6) said that when
the measures were before Congress, Blair came to him and, after saying
that the House resolution could not pass, asked him to vote for the Benton
bill. Walker refused. Blair stated that Texas would prefer Benton's
bill. Walker then said that he would combine the two and let Texas take
her choice. After consulting Benton, Blair said that they would support
the combined resolution, if the choice were left to the President instead
of Texas. Walker agreed, and so it passed. Polk expressed no preference—the cabinet was divided. Bancroft's letter of Oct. 13, Buchanan's
of Nov. 9, Mason's of Nov. 12, and Marcy's of Nov. 20 all stated that
Polk had not expressed any preference. All letters are in the *Polk Papers*.

two propositions—and select between them. I acted upon my own best judgment and the result has proved that I was right."[94] It is inconceivable that he could write thus to a man to whom he had given a pledge to select the Benton method of annexation.

When the provision was added to the joint resolution which gave the choice of alternatives to the President, it was intended of course to give this selection to Polk. Nevertheless, it was suggested during the debate that Tyler and Calhoun might make the selection, but McDuffie, who was a close friend of both men, declared in the Senate that they would not have the "audacity" to do such a thing. When, therefore, the House passed the measure on February 28, it was fully understood that the choice would rest with President Polk. But the resolution gave this choice to the "President of the United States," and for three days more that office was occupied by "Captain" Tyler. Despite McDuffie's assurances Tyler possessed the necessary *audacity,* for he immediately took steps both to make the selection and to carry it into effect. In 1848 he prepared a statement which gives his version of the transaction and explains his reasons for forestalling his successor. As soon as Tyler had approved the resolution, on March 1, Calhoun, the Secretary of State, remarked that the President now had the power to make his selection. Tyler replied that he had no doubt of his power, but that he had some doubt as to the propriety of exercising it. The danger of delay, urged Calhoun, was sufficient to overrule all feelings of delicacy regarding Polk. Next day, at a cabinet meeting, all agreed that Tyler ought to select the House resolution and act at once. He decided to do so and requested Calhoun to call upon Polk, after the meeting, "and explain to him the reasons" for immediate action. Calhoun complied with the request, and reported that "Mr. Polk declined to express any opinion or to make any suggestion in reference to the subject." On the third instructions were dispatched to A. J. Donelson, whom Tyler had recently

---

[94] Polk to Haywood, Aug. 9, 1845, *Polk Papers.*

appointed to be *chargé d'affaires* at the capital of Texas.[95]   When
Polk became President he still had the option of reversing Tyler's
action[96] and recalling the messenger or of acquiescing in the choice
made by his predecessor.   Since he chose the latter alternative
there was little delay in carrying out the mandate of the Baltimore platform.   The progress of annexation under his administration will be considered in another chapter.

---

[95] See statement, Tyler, *Letters and Times of the Tylers*, II, 364–365.
At a later time Tyler was angered by Calhoun's assertion in the Senate
that *he* had selected the House resolution.   "*If he selected*, then Texas is
not legitimately a State of the Union, for Congress gave the power *to the
President* to select, and not to *the Secretary of State.*"   He referred to
Calhoun as "the great 'I am,'" and to Benton as "the most raving
political maniac I ever knew" Tyler to Gardiner, March 11, 1847, *ibid.*,
420).

[96] There was a difference of opinion regarding this.   Walker, and perhaps other members of the cabinet, believed that Polk had no power to
reverse Tyler's action.   See Polk, *Diary*, IV, 44.

CHAPTER XV

ADMINISTRATION AND PATRONAGE

On March 4, 1845, an unusually large "concourse of people" congregated in Washington to witness the inauguration of President Polk. The "arrangements were admirable"[1] and, in true American fashion, men who had bitterly assailed each other in the press and on the platform now joined in doing honor to the new chief executive. Climatic conditions proved to be the only disturbing element. Rain began to descend in torrents as the procession wended its way to the capitol where, according to the picturesque description given by John Quincy Adams, the new executive delivered his inaugural address to "a large assemblage of umbrellas." "At night," said the same writer, "there were two balls: one at Carusi's Hall, at ten dollars a ticket, of all parties; the other of pure Democrats, at five dollars a ticket, at the National Theatre. Mr. Polk attended both, but supped with the true-blue five-dollar Democracy."[2]

Not yet fifty years old, Polk enjoyed the distinction of reaching the highest executive office at an earlier age than any of his predecessors—a fact which he did not fail to note in his inaugural address. This address was in the main a reiteration of Jeffersonian principles and of his own oft-expressed opinions. Strong emphasis was laid on the value of the Union; "no treason to mankind since the organization of society would be equal in atrocity to that of him who would lift his hand to destroy it." On the other hand, he frowned upon the "schemes and agitations" which aimed at the "destruction of domestic institutions

---

[1] *Niles' Reg.*, LXVIII, 1.

[2] Adams, *Memoirs*, XII, 179. He added that "my family and myself received invitations to both, but attended neither."

existing in other sections," and urged the necessity of preserving the compromises of the Constitution.

If the compromises of the Constitution be preserved, if sectional jealousies and heart-burnings be discountenanced, if our laws be just and the Government be practically administered strictly within the limits of power prescribed to it, we may discard all apprehensions for the safety of the Union.

Having thus expressed his disapproval of both abolition and disunion, he again declared himself to be in favor of a tariff for revenue, but not for "protection merely." He congratulated the country on the passage of the joint resolution to annex Texas, and he pronounced our title to Oregon to be "clear and unquestionable." Experience, he said, had disproved the old belief that a federal system could not operate over a large area, and like a true expansionist expressed the opinion that as the system "shall be extended the bonds of our Union, so far from being weakened, will become stronger."

The reference to Texas must have been inserted shortly before the address was delivered, but certain letters written by A. V. Brown indicate that the first draft of the inaugural was written early in December and sent to Washington for criticism and approval by Polk's political friends. The Brown letters are too enigmatical to throw much light on the subject, but as Polk had many times before expressed practically all of the views contained in his address, there was no reason for believing that it was not substantially his own product.[3]

---

[3] On December 14, 1844, Brown wrote from Washington to Polk: "I received yours of the 7th Inst. *our* friend called yesterday & informed me that he would be ready in a few days & I shall loose no time after examination to forward it to you."

On December 23 he wrote: "You must not be impatient—Our friend has been sick a few days—has sent me for examination about *half* to be returned with my comments & then the whole to be finished & polish'd— say all by the first January or sooner. So far it is a happy conception for instance in allusion to the Union.

"'If this be not enough, if that freedom of thought word and action given by his Creator to fallen man & left by human institutions as free as they were given, are not sufficient to lead him into the paths of liberty

Among the rejoicing Democrats none felt more sincere satisfaction in the defeat of Henry Clay or expressed a more ardent wish for the success of the new administration than did the "old hero" at the Hermitage. In a letter written two days after the inauguration he told Polk that

I have the pleasure to congratulate my country on your now being, really, president of the United States, and I put up my prayers to the great Jehova, that he may conduct you thro' your administration with honor to yourself, and benefit to our Glorious Union.

Success could be attained only by "continuing to take principle for your guide, and public good for your end, steering clear of the intrigues & machinations of political clickes."[4] If the General had any misgivings regarding Polk's independence, they must have been removed by the receipt of a letter from Judge Catron—a letter written before his own had reached Washington. "Our friend," wrote the judge, "is very prudent, and *eminently* firm, regardless of consequences. He came here to be—THE

& peace, whither shall he turn? Has the *sword* proved to be a safer and surer instrument of reform than enlightened reason? Does he expect to find among the ruins of this Union a happier abode for our swarming millions, than they now have under its lofty arch & among its beautiful columns? No, my countrymen never, until like the blind Israelite in the Temple of the Philistines, we find ourselves in chains and dispair, shall we be justified in thrusting those pillars from their base; for whenever we do, we shall like him be crushed by their fall.'

"It will be surely ready in time & finished with a polish suitable to the occasion. I shall enclose it to you under an envelope to our friend J. H. Thomas but securely sealed so that he shall [not] be aware of its contents." (Compare the part quoted by Brown with Polk's inaugural. See *Messages*, IV, 376. *Query:* Was Brown quoting from Polk's original draft, or was this paragraph written in Washington and remodeled by Polk?)

On December 26 Brown wrote: "In a few days now I shall hear from our friend K again & be ready to meet your wishes. The Major is here on yesterday we went up to see the President. He is acting very friendly but I shall encourage the idea of his remaining here but a short time or the letter writers will be speculating on the purpose of his visit &c." (*Polk Papers*).

Probably "K" means John Kane, of Philadelphia, but the identity of "our friend" and "the Major" is difficult to conjecture. Major Lewis was not a close friend of either Brown or Polk, and Major Donelson was then in New Orleans.

4 Jackson to Polk, March 6, 1845, *Polk Papers*.

PRESIDENT—which at this date is as undisputed as that you was THE GENL at N. Orleans.''[5]

On March 5 the new President submitted to the Senate his list of cabinet officials. James Buchanan, the Secretary of State, had long been a leader in Pennsylvania politics and for many years a Senator from that state. His selection was a concession to that wing of the party which believed in a moderate protective tariff, and his subsequent opposition to the tariff of 1846 caused the President no little annoyance. He was a man of more than average ability, but he possessed certain traits which made him the source of constant irritation to the President. With a timidity which caused him to quail before responsibility he combined an obstinacy and a petulance which manifested themselves in obstructive tactics and petty insolence. After four years of intimate association Polk concluded that ''Mr. Buchanan is an able man, but is in small matters without judgment and sometimes acts like an old maid.''[6] He was the only member of the cabinet whom the President found it necessary to discipline, and he was the only one whom Polk believed that he could not fully trust. Robert J. Walker, the Secretary of the Treasury, was a man of ability and industry. He was cordially hated by the Whigs and was disliked and distrusted by many Democrats. Originally selected for the office of Attorney General, he was called to the Treasury Department in order to placate the Cass-Dallas element of the party. He was the only member to whom General Jackson offered objections,[7] but Polk had full confidence in both his integrity and his ability. As Secretary of War, William L. Marcy

---

[5] Catron to Jackson, March [1845], *Jackson Papers.*

[6] Polk, *Diary,* IV, 355.

[7] ''*I say to you, in the most confidential manner,* that I regret that you put Mr. R. J. Walker over the Treasury. He has talents, I believe honest, but surrounded by so many broken speculators, and being greatly himself incumbered with debt, that any of the other Departments would have been better, & I fear, you will find my forebodings turn out too true, and added to this, under the rose, he is looking to the vice presidency'' (Jackson to Polk, May 2, 1845, *Polk Papers*).

displayed both ability and tact. He was a leader of that wing of the party in New York which opposed Van Buren, and his appointment greatly imbittered the friends of the ex-President; otherwise his appointment added strength to the administration. George Bancroft, the Secretary of the Navy, had had little experience in practical affairs. His appointment seems to have been a makeshift, and he was soon given a diplomatic position, for which he had originally expressed a preference. His most notable achievement as a cabinet officer was his success in procuring the establishment of the naval academy at Annapolis. John Y. Mason, a college mate of the President, was made Attorney General. He had served as Secretary of the Navy in Tyler's cabinet and was again put in charge of that department when Bancroft was made minister to England. Cave Johnson, the Postmaster General, had for many years been Polk's closest political friend. Although he was not considered to be a brilliant statesman, his good judgment and methodical habits well fitted him for the office assigned to him. He was a democrat *par excellence,* and when a member of Congress he was best known as an enemy of extravagant appropriations. His friends gave him the sobriquet of "watch-dog of the Treasury"; some called him the "scourge of private claimants," and Adams once referred to him as the "retrenchment monsoon."[8]

The appointment of an entirely new[9] cabinet caused general surprise and considerable press comment. None except his intimate friends realized that Polk was a man of unusual determination, and that he was resolved to be President in fact as well as in name. The belief that he would be a mere figurehead— a pliable instrument in the hands of able politicians—had become

---

[8] Adams, *Memoirs,* XI, 223.

[9] Mason, of course, had been a member of Tyler's cabinet, but not in the position assigned to him by Polk. "An entire new Cabinet, at the accession of a new President without a reverse of politics, is a novelty under the present constitution. Rumors of it have been in circulation for some weeks, which I did not believe" (*ibid.,* XII, 180).

so firmly fixed in the public mind that the most convincing evidence to the contrary had little weight. Although it is now well known that Polk dominated his cabinet to a greater degree than most chief executives, so keen an observer as Gideon Welles could at the time write:

> In none of his [Polk's] Cabinet, I am sorry to say, have I any confidence. Yet this cabinet appears to me to have more influence and higher authority than any other I have ever known. The Cabinet is a sort of council of appointments, and the President is chairman of this council, instead of being President of the United States. It is, as I wrote our friend Niles, a sort of joint Stock Company in which the President is, by no means the principal partner. *Yet several of them have been at particular pains to tell me that the President has his own way—does as he has a mind to—makes his own appointments &c.* There is not, however, a man in the cabinet, except Johnson, who does not believe himself the superior of the President in abilities & qualifications as a statesman.[10]

Writing in 1860, Claiborne says that Polk's cabinet was "one of the ablest ever assembled around any executive," but that the President himself "can only be regarded as a man of mediocrity."[11] Both statements are exaggerations. Although each member of the cabinet performed well the duties of his office, none except Buchanan, Walker, and Marcy can be included among statesmen of the first rank. On the other hand, an executive who could formulate important and far-reaching policies, and successfully carry them out despite strenuous opposition, could not have been "a man of mediocrity." To say that the President ranked below the members of his cabinet is only to add praise to his executive ability, for, as a recent writer has well said: "In the Cabinet Council Polk was the unmistakable guide and master."[12] Welles had been correctly informed. Undoubtedly the President had "his own way."

---

10 Welles to Van Buren, April 29, 1845, *Van Buren Papers*. The italics are mine.

11 Claiborne, *Life and Correspondence of John A. Quitman*, I, 229–231.

12 Learned, *Some Aspects of the Cabinet Meeting*, 128.

Polk's control over his cabinet was not the result of accident or of incidental circumstances, for, with his usual forethought, he had planned to be "guide and master." Before leaving his home in Tennessee he prepared the draft of a letter a revised copy of which was sent to each prospective member of his cabinet. After calling attention to the "principles and policy" which he expected to carry out it was made very clear that he desired only such advisers as would "cordially co-operate" in effecting his purposes. Each member would be expected to give his time and ability in promoting the success of the present administration; whenever he should feel that he could no longer do so, he would be expected to retire. Should these restrictions prove acceptable, the person addressed was invited to become a member of the cabinet. The following is a copy of this interesting document:

Sir:

The principles and policy which will be observed and maintained during my administration, are embodied in the Resolutions adopted by the Democratic National Convention of Delegates, assembled at Baltimore in May last, and in my Inaugural address this day delivered to my Fellow Citizens.—

In making up my Cabinet I desire to select gentlemen who agree with me in opinion, and who will cordially co-operate with me in carrying out these principles and policy.

In my official action I will myself take no part,—between gentlemen of the Democratic party, who may become aspirants or candidates—to succeed me in the Presidential office, and shall desire that no member of my Cabinet shall do so. Individual preferences it is not expected or desired to limit or restrain.—It is official interference by the dispensation of public patronage or otherwise that I desire to guard against.—Should any member of my Cabinet become a candidate or an aspirant to the Presidency or Vice Presidency, of the United States,—it will be expected upon the happening of such an event, that he will retire from the Cabinet.—

I disapprove the practice which has sometimes prevailed of Cabinet officers absenting themselves for long periods of time from the seat of Government, and leaving the management of their Departments to Chief Clerks—or less responsible persons.—I expect myself to remain constantly at Washington—unless it may be an occasional necessary absence,—and then for a short time,—It is by conforming to this rule,—that the President and his Cabinet can have any assurances that abuses will be prevented—and that the subordinate executive officers connected with them respectively,—will faithfully perform their duty.—

If Sir: you concur with me in these opinions and views, I shall be pleased to have your assistance as a member of my Cabinet; and now tender you the office of   and invite you to take charge of the Department.—

I shall be pleased to receive your answer at your earliest convenience.

I am with great respect
Your Ob't S'v't.[13]

To every item of the program outlined in this letter the President rigidly adhered. He had "his own way" despite the incredulity of Gideon Welles. Catron's above-quoted remark, and not the opinion expressed by Welles, is a true statement of Polk's position as chief executive. Even Welles at a later date, although he continued to underrate the President's ability, was forced to admit that "he had courage and determination and shrank from no labor or responsibility."[14] Claiborne has called Polk a "political martinet":[15] he was likewise something of an executive martinet, but no member of his cabinet except Buchanan seems to have questioned his right to dictate the administrative policy of the government. Quite frequently the Secretary of State tried to substitute his own policies for those of the President, but invariably he was forced to submit to the will of his superior. On several occasions Polk was on the point of dismissing him from the cabinet for violating his pledge to put aside Presidential aspirations.

On questions of importance the President sought freely the advice of his cabinet, members of Congress and private individuals; very often the advice given led to modifications in matters of detail, but, except in very rare instances, the main essentials of his policies were carried into effect as originally planned by

---

[13] On the back is written: "Rough Draft of Letter. To be revised corrected. Jan. 15, 1845" (*Polk Papers*). The revised copy which was sent to Buchanan is printed in his *Works*, VI, 110.

[14] MS "Review of Pol. Hist. of U. S. etc.," *Welles Papers*.

[15] Claiborne, *op. cit.*, 228.

himself. His habit of considering carefully the problems involved before they were presented for discussion left little of importance for his advisers to suggest. He felt keenly the individual responsibility of his office; it followed, therefore, that his own, and not the opinions of others, should dictate the policies to be pursued.

The President yielded his convictions neither easily nor for petty reasons. Politics influenced him. But he seldom forgot principles even though he had to sacrifice the friendship and influence of men as powerful as Senator Benton of Missouri and to some extent the assistance of Buchanan.[16]

Polk was not indulging in idle flourish when he told prospective cabinet members that he would "remain constantly at Washington," for during his entire term he was absent from the capital not more than six weeks.[17] Being a strict sabbatarian he abstained from Sunday labor except in cases of absolute necessity. The other six days of each week were devoted to unremitting toil, and frequently his labors extended far into the night. Near the middle of his official term he noted in his diary:

It is two years ago this day since I left my residence at Columbia, Tennessee, to enter on my duties as President of the U. S. Since that time I have performed great labour and incurred vast responsibilities. In truth, though I occupy a very high position, I am the hardest working man in this country.

A few weeks later he wrote:

This afternoon I took a ride on horseback. It is the first time I have mounted a horse for over six months. I have an excellent saddle-horse, and have been much in the habit of taking exercise on horseback all my life, but have been so incessantly engaged in the onerous and responsible duties of my office for many months past that I have had no time to take such exercise.[18]

---

[16] Learned, *op. cit.*, 124.

[17] *Ibid.*, 120.

[18] Polk, *Diary*, II, 360, 456. A year and a half later his story is the same: "Since my return early in July, 1847, from my Northern tour, I have not been more than two or three miles from my office, and during the whole period (13 months) my labours, responsibilities, and anxieties have been very great" (*ibid.*, IV, 85–86).

The office of President is never a sinecure, yet why, it may be asked, did Polk find it necessary to expend his energies more lavishly than other chief executives. The answer is that he felt under obligation to make himself familiar with all branches of executive government. He alone must bear the responsibility for efficient administration, consequently he alone must direct the affairs of the various departments. Supervision on so vast a scale meant a sacrifice of time and energy, but he had the satisfaction of believing that he had not sacrificed them in vain. We are not left in doubt regarding his feeling of self-reliance, for on September 23, 1848, he observed:

I have not had my full Cabinet together in council since the adjournment of Congress on the 14th of August last. I have conducted the Government without their aid. Indeed, I have become so familiar with the duties and workings of the Government, not only upon general principles, but in most of its intimate details, that I find but little difficulty in doing this. I have made myself acquainted with the duties of the subordinate officers, and have probably given more attention to details than any of my predecessors. It is only occasi[on]ally that a great measure or a new question arises, upon which I desire the aid and advice of my Cabinet. At each meeting of the Cabinet I learn from each member what is being done in his particular Department, and especially if any question of doubt or difficulty has arisen. I have never called for any written opinions from my Cabinet, preferring to take their opinions, after discussion, in Cabinet & in the presence of each other. In this way harmony of opinion is more likely to exist.[19]

Still another passage from his diary may be cited as indicative of his industry and of solicitude lest some duty might go unperformed:

No President who performs his duty faithfully and conscientiously can have any leisure. If he entrusts the details and small matters to subordinates constant errors will occur. I prefer to supervise the whole operations of the Government myself rather than entrust the public business to subordinates and this makes my duties very great.[20]

Although the excerpts just quoted were written during the last year of his administration, Polk's painstaking supervision

---

[19] Polk, *Diary*, IV, 130–131.
[20] *Ibid.*, 261.

of the "whole operations" of the government began as soon as he had entered upon the duties of his office. His searching examination of all documents presented for his signature and his ability to detect errors caused considerable newspaper comment.[21] His thorough knowledge of affairs enabled him to win a wager from the astute Buchanan in an argument concerning proper diplomatic usage.[22]

The introduction of systematic methods in the handling of department affairs added greatly to the efficiency of the administration. On questions of policy Polk preferred oral discussions to written opinions from his cabinet, but each member was required to report regularly on all matters relating to his department. In a circular dated April 11, 1845, he asked the head of each department to furnish him with a monthly report concerning the work of the various bureaus and clerks under his jurisdiction. The tendency of bureau chiefs to favor large expenditures made it necessary for each cabinet officer to "give vigilant attention" to all estimates, and to pare them down whenever possible.[23] Such reports, supplemented by discussions at regular meetings of the cabinet, enabled the President to understand thoroughly the operations of all departments.

As a rule the cabinet met regularly on Tuesdays and Saturdays of each week, and there were frequent special meetings on other days. Frequency of meeting afforded ample opportunity for the consideration of administrative policies. Apparently the President never attempted to interfere with a free expression of opinions, yet by adroitly directing the discussions he was able to

---

21 For example: "The President is devoted to his official tasks. He signs nothing without the strictest examination, and has frequently, to the confusion of clerks, detected serious errors in the papers sent for his signature" (New York *Evening Post*, May 3, 1845; quoted by the Washington *Union*, May 8).

22 Polk, *Diary*, III, 97–99. The bet was made in a jesting mood and the President declined to accept his basket of champagne. "I record this incident," said he, "for the purpose of showing how necessary it is for me to give my vigilant attention even to the forms & details of my [subordinates'] duties."

23 Polk, *Diary*, I, 48, and *passim*.

"have his own way" without causing offense. That his method of dealing with his cabinet resulted in both harmony and unity of purpose is corroborated by the testimony of Buchanan, the most discordant member. "However various our views might have been and often were upon any particular subject when entering the cabinet council," he wrote, in advising Pierce to follow Polk's example, "after mutual consultation and free discussion we never failed to agree at last, except on a few questions, and on these the world never knew that we had differed." More surprising, perhaps, is his praise of the President for having personally directed diplomatic relations. "Mr. Polk," said he, "was a wise man, and after deliberation he had determined that all important questions with foreign nations should be settled in Washington, under his own immediate supervision."[24] Another proof of the President's ability to gain and to retain the good will of his cabinet is contained in a letter written by Bancroft in 1887 after he had made an exhaustive examination of the *Polk Papers:*

> His character shines out in them just as the man he was, prudent, far-sighted, bold, excelling any democrat of his day in undeviatingly correct exposition of democratic principles; and, in short, as I think, judging of him as I knew him, and judging of him by the results of his administration, one of the very foremost of our public men and one of the very best and most honest and most successful Presidents the country ever had.[25]

In a letter written during the following year Bancroft again sounded the praises of his former chief and gave the reasons for the success of his administration:

> His administration, viewed from the standpoint of results, was perhaps the greatest in our national history, certainly one of the greatest. He succeeded because he insisted on being its centre, and in overruling and guiding all his secretaries to act so as to produce unity and harmony. Those who study his administration will acknowledge how sincere and successful were his efforts, as did those who were contemporary with him.[26]

24 Curtis, *Life of James Buchanan,* II, 72, 76.

25 Bancroft to J. Geo. Harris, Aug. 30, 1887 (Howe, *Life and Letters of George Bancroft,* I, 294).

26 Bancroft to J. G. Wilson, March 8, 1888 (Wilson, *The Presidents of the United States,* 230).

With a deep sense of personal integrity and a desire to avoid everything which might impair his absolute independence, Polk declined to accept presents of more than nominal value. Shortly after his inauguration Thomas Lloyd sent him a valuable saddle-horse, but he promptly gave orders that it should be returned to the donor. Another admirer who sent a consignment of wine and other delicacies for the President's table was instructed to send a bill or to take the articles away. It soon became known that he would accept nothing of greater value than a book or a cane. The same rule applied to presents for Mrs. Polk.[27] The same scrupulous regard for propriety is shown in his refusal to invest in government securities a certain sum of money belonging to his nephew and ward, Marshall T. Polk.[28] His public policies were denounced in unmeasured terms, and his political honesty was frequently impugned, but even his enemies credited him with personal integrity and purity of character. His own personal affairs were characterized by simplicity and frugality. This fact has already been noted in the care with which he guarded against exorbitant charges at the time of his inauguration.[29] On the other hand, his generosity is shown by loans and gifts to friends whenever he believed the recipients to be deserving.[30] The improvident beggar was unceremoniously dismissed, for Polk had no sympathy for the man who believes that the world owes him a living.

One of the first purely political questions which required the new President's attention was the establishment of a newspaper which would serve as the "organ" of the administration. We

---

[27] Letters among *Polk Papers;* also, Nelson, *Memorials of Sarah Childress Polk,* 89.

[28] Polk, *Diary,* III, 15–17.

[29] See above, p. 293, note 28. He was, according to a remark in the *Diary,* his "own barbour" (*Diary,* III, 9).

[30] For example, when the news came that Colonel Yell had fallen in the battle of Buena Vista the President wrote: "His eldest son, and perhaps his only son, is now at College at Georgetown, and as my impression is that Col. Yell died poor, I will in that event educate the boy, and shall take great interest in him" (*Diary,* II, 451–452).

have seen that the subject had already been discussed, but nothing definite had been accomplished when Polk entered upon the duties of his office. The refusal of Ritchie to leave Richmond determined the President to procure, if possible, the services of Donelson, for in no case would he consent to make Blair the administration editor. On March 17 he told Jackson in a "confidential" letter that

> There is at present no paper here which sustains my administration for its own sake. The Globe it is manifest does not look to the success or the glory of my administration so much as it does to the interests and views of certain prominent men of the party who are looking to succeed me in 1848. The arrangement which above all others I prefer would be that, the owners of the Globe would agree to place it in the hands of a new Editor,—still retaining the proprietorship of the paper if they choose. You may rely upon it, that without such an arrangement, the Democratic party who elected me cannot be kept united three months. If *Maj^r Donelson* would take charge of the Editorial Department—all the sections of the party would be at once reunited and satisfied.

Donelson and Ritchie, he said, were the only ones whom he would permit to edit his government organ.[31]

Within the next two weeks the President "had full and free conversation with Mr. Blair and in good feeling frankly told him, that it was impossible for the whole party ever to be united in support of the administration whilst the Globe was regarded as the official organ," and that he must have a new paper. In sending this information to Donelson on March 28 Polk said that within the last forty-eight hours the whole matter had "been brought almost to a head." Ritchie had been in Washington and Blair had agreed to sell the *Globe* and retire, leaving Ritchie and Donelson to take charge as joint editors. Blair had made but one stipulation, that the arrangement should be delayed until he could consult Van Buren and Jackson; "he says positively that if *Genl Jackson* assents, he will at once sell and retire." After repeating the reasons, already given to Jackson, why he

---

could not employ the *Globe* and expressing the hope that the arrangement then pending might be effected, he added that "if it should fail I am still deeply convinced that it will be indispensable to have a new paper and I have so informed *Mr. Blair.*"[32]

After some further negotiation Blair and Rives consented to dispose of the *Globe* and retire. The purchasers were Thomas Ritchie, of the Richmond *Enquirer,* and John P. Heiss, of Tennessee, formerly editor of the Nashville *Union.* A new paper called the Washington *Union* succeeded the *Globe* with Ritchie as its chief editor and Heiss as its business manager. The daily edition of the new "Polk organ" made its début on May 1, 1845, and a semi-weekly followed four days later. Among the noteworthy features of the initial numbers were a eulogy on the late editors of the *Globe,* and the first installment of "Mrs. Caudle's Curtain Lectures," copied from the London *Punch.* The humor of the lectures may have been the more apparent to ingenuous readers.

General Jackson was quite as unsuccessful in his attempt to make Major William B. Lewis the "ferret" of the Polk administration as in his effort to have Blair retained as editor of the "organ." Lewis had for some time held the office of second auditor of the treasury, and, as he was considered to be a still more treacherous politician than Blair, the new President summarily dismissed him. In a letter to Polk, Lewis stated that he had learned from a private source that

you have intimated that my removal from office was rendered necessary, because the position I occupied was dangerous to the Government, in as much as it would enable me to impart information to a foreign power to the disadvantage of my own country.

He hoped that the report was unfounded but desired to know whether Polk had made such a remark. As the President made no reply to this or to other letters on the same subject, Lewis

---

[32] Polk to Donelson, March 28, 1845, "Polk-Donelson Letters."

left for his home in Tennessee and published the correspondence in a Nashville paper.[33] Polk's reasons for declining to make explanations are given in a letter to a friend in Tennessee:

> As to Maj. Lewis I shall of course enter into no controversy with him. What he desires most is to make himself conspicuous by such a controversy. His course since his removal from office proves his unworthiness of which I had full & ample proof before I dismissed him. . . . [Had Jackson known the reasons he would have approved.][34]

The enforced retirement of Blair and the dismissal of Lewis have been given special notice because many have cited them as evidence to convict Polk of ingratitude and disloyalty to General Jackson—the man to whom, it was said, he owed his own political advancement. There is little consistency in some of the criticisms relating to this matter. The man whom the critics denounced for being bold enough to ignore the wishes of "Old Hickory" was, by the same men, said to be weak and temporizing. Such critics commended Jackson for discarding his old friend Van Buren on account of the Texan question; but they condemned Polk for dismissing his own detractors and obstacles to party success because these detractors happened to be friends of the General.[35] Jackson himself, when replying to Lewis's complaints, pointed out that the President had the right to fill offices with men in whom *he,* and not others, had confidence.[36]

Although General Jackson was undoubtedly disappointed because his two most intimate friends had been dismissed, their removal does not seem to have impaired his friendship for the President or his desire for the success of the administration. The last letter which the General ever penned was written to

---

[33] The originals are among the *Polk Papers.* Printed copies may be found in *Niles' Reg.,* LXVIII, 277.

[34] Polk to A. O. P. Nicholson, July 28, 1845, *Polk Papers.* In a letter to Polk, July 19, J. Geo. Harris expressed the belief that both Blair and Lewis had plotted against Polk.

[35] Claiborne, for example, reflects these contrary opinions of Polk. See *Life and Correspondence of John A. Quitman,* I, 228–229.

[36] Jackson to Lewis, April 10, 1845 (*Niles' Reg.,* LXVIII, 277).

Polk on June 6, 1845. It expressed not only personal friendship for the President, but warned him that certain rumored acts of Secretary Walker and land speculators might "blow you & your administration sky high." The letter was characteristic of the writer and exhibited his well-known traits—solicitude for his friend and protégé, a wish to supervise public affairs, and a patriotic desire to serve his country, even though his methods were not always of the best. "Here, my son," he said, as he handed it to Andrew Jackson Jr., "read this letter, I want you to be a witness to the fact that I have warned the government against the disaster with which it is threatened—and have done my duty." The letter was mislaid under some papers and not found until October and it was feared it had been stolen. The high value set upon it by the President, as well as his feeling toward the writer, is stated in a letter in which Polk asked that a search be made to recover it:

> I shall prize the letter as above all price as being the last ever written by the greatest man of the age in which he lived—a man whose confidence and friendship I was so happy as to have enjoyed from my youth to the latest.[37]

On the question of ousting Whigs from office in order to make room for Democrats, Polk's own views accorded with those of his party,[38] and when making appointments, except a few military positions, political orthodoxy was a *sine qua non*. Despite the importunities of Buchanan, he refused to appoint John

---

[37] Jackson to Polk, June 6; J. Geo. Harris to Polk, June 28; Polk to Nicholson, June 28, 1845, *Polk Papers*. Andrew Jackson, Jr., approved what the President had done and when writing, on October 10, to explain how Jackson's last letter had been mislaid said: "*Our old friend Majr Lewis* has completely killed himself here & I expect else where by his imprudent publications—he is now very sick of it, and well he may be" (*Polk Papers*).

[38] In 1846 an officer who had been notified that he would be removed protested that, although he had once been a Federalist, he had been a Democrat for many years. "Although not the only reason for making the change proper," the President observed, "I have no doubt he is a Whig in all his feelings, and that his patronage is bestowed exclusively on members of that party, as far as he thinks he can do so with safety to himself" (*Diary*, II, 113–114).

M. Read to a place on the Supreme Bench, because that distinguished jurist had once been a Federalist. His remarks in this connection on the perdurance of original ideas showed his political sagacity, for Read later deserted the party and became a Republican:

> Mr. Read, I learned, was until within 10 or 12 years ago a leading Federalist, and a Representative of that party in the Legislature. Although he has since that time acted with the Democratic party, I have no confidence in the orthodoxy of his political opinions or constitutional doctrines, and was therefore unwilling to appoint him to a station for life, where he would almost certainly [have] relapsed into his old Federal Doctrines & been latitudinarian in his doctrines. I have never known an instance of a Federalist who had after arriving at the age of 30 professed to change his opinions, who was to be relied on in his constitutional opinions. All of them who have been appointed to the Supreme Court Bench, after having secured a place for life became very soon broadly Federal and latitudinarian in all their decisions involving questions of Constitutional power. Gen'l Jackson had been most unfortunate in his appointments to that Bench in this respect. I resolved to appoint no man who was not an original Democrat & strict constructionist, and who would be less likely to relapse into the Broad Federal doctrines of Judge Marshall & Judge Story.[39]

Even Benton's son-in-law, William Carey Jones, was denied an office because he had once edited a Federalist paper in New Orleans. Like Jackson, Polk seemed to take it for granted that honesty, except in very rare cases, was not to be found among the Whigs, and his naïve remarks about the exceptions which he discovered are very amusing. Senator Mangrum, for example, "though a Whig, is a gentleman, and fair & manly in his opposition to my administration." Senator Crittenden, also, "though differing with me in politics is an honorable gentleman."[40] He does not, however, seem to have found a Whig honorable enough to hold an appointive office. Still, though he declined to place Whigs in appointive offices, he did not, on the other hand, dismiss them for partisan considerations merely. In his diary he

---

[39] Polk, *Diary*, I, 137–138.
[40] *Ibid.*, III, 381, II, 349.

has noted the gratitude of those whom he had retained in office, despite their political opinions:

Many Whigs whom I retained in office were among those who called. Though many removals & new appointments to fill vacancies have been made by me, my administration has not been proscriptive, and the Whigs who were faithful & good officers, whom I have retained in their places, seem to appreciate my liberality towards them and many of them have called to express their gratitude & to take leave of me.[41]

The independence displayed in dropping Blair and Lewis was characteristic of the policy which Polk endeavored to employ in all matters of patronage. He was soon to discover, however, that the dispenser of offices is by no means a free agent, and that "political considerations" must be taken into account.

Although many at the time alleged that the President had made preëlection pledges to the Tyler and Calhoun factions, there is now no reason for doubting Polk's oft-repeated assertions that he was "under no pledges or commitments"[42] to any of the political cliques. Even so, their wishes could not be wholly disregarded with impunity. Hostile elements within the party had united for the purpose of winning the election, and each was ready to claim its share of the "spoils." Having no assured "administration majority" in Congress, the success of his own program must depend upon his ability to enlist the support of several discordant factions. His effort to deal fairly with all of them resulted in general criticism, for each laid claim to all important offices and resented all favors accorded to its rivals. To have allied himself with any one of these factions would have resulted in disaster; the refusal to do so was attributed to timidity and a temporizing disposition.

It has been noted in the preceding chapter that there were three rather well-defined groups within the Democratic party. The first comprised the followers of Van Buren and Benton; the

---

[41] Polk, *Diary*, March 2, 1849, IV, 360.

[42] For example, Polk to Cave Johnson, Dec. 21, 1844, ''Polk-Johnson Letters.''

second, the adherents of Calhoun; and the third, that element
in the South and West which accepted the leadership of Walker
and Cass.[43]   Until the appearance of Van Buren's anti-Texas
letter nothing had occurred to disturb the harmony which long
existed between the Van Burenites and Jackson's followers in
Tennessee, consequently Polk had been identified with the first
group even though his claim to the Vice-Presidency had met with
no cordial response.

Due, no doubt, to this affiliation and to a desire to assuage
the disappointment caused by the dropping of Van Buren by the
Baltimore convention, Polk turned first to New York when making up his list of cabinet appointments.   Wright, as we have
already seen, was invited to take charge of the Treasury Department; and when this invitation was declined, Butler, on the advice
of Van Buren, was tendered the War portfolio.   Rebuffed a
second time, Polk ceased his efforts to placate the Van Burenites,
and appointed their rival, Marcy, to be Secretary of War.   For
the sake of harmony within the party he had done all that any
self-respecting man in his position could have been expected to
do, and if the friends of the ex-President did not receive their
proper share of the "loaves and fishes," the blame rested entirely
upon their own shoulders.   The President's offer, a few months
later, to send Van Buren as minister to England was likewise
declined, and the attitude of the ex-President and his adherents
continued to be one either of sullen reserve or of secret opposition
to the administration.   When Polk reached New York on his northern tour in July, 1847, Van Buren sent him a verbal invitation
to call.   Believing the invitation to be a mere "formal courtesy"
impelled by public opinion, the President promptly declined to
accept it.   "The truth is," is the comment in his diary, "Mr.
Van Buren became offended with me at the beginning of my administration because I chose to exercise my own judgment in the

---

[43] With characteristic pungency J. Q. Adams divided Democracy into
two parts: "Southern Democracy, which is slavery, and Western Democracy, which is knavery" (*Memoirs*, XII, 11).

selection of my own Cabinet, and would not be controlled by him and suffer him to select it for me.'"[44]

Although the President could not consent to retain Calhoun in his cabinet, he was prepared at the outset to deal fairly with that wing of the party. The British mission was offered first to Calhoun himself, and after his refusal, to his friends, Elmore and Pickins. But this faction, like the Van Burenites, declined to accept anything because their chief had not been permitted to control the administration.

The Treasury Department with the patronage incident to the office was assigned to Walker as a clear concession to the South and West. The selection of Greer, a friend of Dallas, for the Supreme Bench was likewise a recognition of the claims of this wing of the party. Apparently Cass did not seek an appointive office, but preferred to remain in the Senate.

When selecting federal officers the President did not, of course, overlook his own personal friends. First of all, Cave Johnson was made Postmaster General, and Donelson, after being considered as possible editor of the *Union,* was, on his return from Texas, sent as minister to Berlin. J. George Harris, whose vitriolic pen and exasperating "buzzard" had made the Nashville *Union* so effective a party journal, was made purser in the navy. The loyal but dissolute Laughlin was appointed to be recorder of the general land office as a reward for his services as editor of the Nashville *Union* and for his support of Polk in the Baltimore convention. The President's old friend and former law

---

[44] Polk, *Diary,* III, 74. Polk had received information from many sources concerning the hostility of the Albany regency. For example, Buchanan, who visited Albany in the fall of 1846, reported that, while Governor Wright himself was friendly, Cambreleng and others avoided him. A month later George Bancroft, who had always been a warm friend of Van Buren, after a similar visit informed Polk that New York politicians were hostile to the administration and that Van Buren evinced no desire to renew friendly relations with the President. Although Bancroft had originally suggested the tender to Van Buren of the British mission, he now advised that no further attempt be made to placate the ex-President (Buchanan to Polk, Sept. 5, 1846; Bancroft to Polk, Oct. 4, 1846, *Polk Papers.* Van Buren's correspondents freely criticized the President, *Van Buren Papers, passim*).

partner, Gideon Pillow, who claimed to be mainly responsible for Polk's nomination at Baltimore, was, when the war broke out, made a brigadier-general of volunteers. Even John O. Bradford, whom a Whig bishop had excommunicated for editing the Nashville *Union,* was now rewarded by a pursership in the navy. Most questionable of all, however, in point of propriety, was the appointment of the President's own brother, William H. Polk, to be *chargé d'affaires* at Naples.

Having pointed out that the President, in an effort to promote harmony, assigned to the several factions some of the most desirable appointive positions, and that friendship rather than merit dictated the selection of certain minor officials, we may now consider his general policy in dealing with the public patronage. The patronage incident to the office of chief executive is a source of great power, and for this reason the popular belief seems to be that it is also a source of great pleasure. The corollary is doubtful in any case and certainly is erroneous when applied to Polk, for his administration had not proceeded far before he came to regard patronage and office-seekers as a veritable nightmare.

Polk was a man of very positive ideas, and one of those ideas was that public office is an opportunity for public service. Although in the finesse of practical politics he was no more scrupulous than his fellows, he never regarded any position held by himself as a sinecure and he believed that offices should not be so regarded by others. The keynote of his policy was foreshadowed in the circular letter, already quoted, that was sent to prospective members of his cabinet. He would aid no aspirant for the Presidential nomination in 1848 and he would not permit his subordinates to use their offices for such a purpose; his and their energies must be devoted to the ''principles and policy'' of the existing administration. Determined to devote his whole time to the public service, he required that cabinet members should do likewise; intrusting of important business to chief clerks was not to be tolerated.

In theory, therefore, the President believed office to be an opportunity for present service and not a reward for acts already performed. And if we except the few instances already noted where appointments were made either for personal reasons or in an effort to promote harmony it may be said that Polk, at the beginning of his administration, sincerely endeavored to carry his theory into practice. The more important appointments received his own personal attention, and, in order that he might conserve his time for affairs of state, the selection of minor officials was turned over to his cabinet.[45] The *Union,* soon after its establishment, repelled in an editorial assertions made by politicians that Polk would have to dispense patronage in accordance with the wishes of the various candidates for the Presidency. On the contrary, said the editor, the President, in making his appointments, will take no thought of whether the person is a Van Buren man, a Calhoun man, a Cass man or a Buchanan man. His thought will be simply: ''Is the man honest and capable?'' Two months later the following editorial appeared:

Mr. Polk has avowed and acted, and will continue to act, upon the settled determination not to permit the course of his administration to interfere with, or influence, the selection of a candidate of the democratic party to succeed him. That important duty he will leave to be performed by the people, unbiased and uninfluenced by his official action. Can any portion of the democracy object to this course?[46]

---

[45] Commenting on this policy, *Niles' Register* said: ''The course adopted by President Polk, on taking hold of the helm of state, in relation to the importunities for office which had grown out of an erroneous course admitted by some of his immediate predecessors, seems to have given satisfaction to every body except those who were in full cry for office. We allude to his having announced semi-officially that personal attendance at the seat of government, and personal importunities for office would operate *against* the applicant;—that the papers designed to urge claims for appointment, must be submitted in the first place to the presiding officer of the department to which the office belonged, and must be by him deliberated upon and presented in due form, together with those of all other applicants for the same office, by the chief of the department to the president, for *his* deliberate judgment—with the whole subject before him.

This announcement occasioned a general *scatterfication.* Washington city immediately lost a large proportion of its transient crowd. It is to be hoped the position will be adhered to in its genuine spirit, and with due decision'' (*Niles' Reg.*, LXVIII, 51, March 29, 1845).

[46] Washington *Union*, May 13, July 14, 1845.

Despite the soundness of the President's position, it was already apparent that not only "any portion" but *every* portion of the party was displeased. A few days before the appearance of the latter editorial he had told Silas Wright that dispensing of patronage was his greatest source of annoyance. Concerning the general policy of the administration, said he, there seems to be no complaint, but much dissatisfaction about offices; "I sincerely wish I had no office to bestow."[47] Could he have seen contemporary private correspondence his wish undoubtedly would have been still more emphatic. For example, old line Democrats complained because room had not been made for them by the ousting of all "Federalists," and because Polk and Walker were too busy to see their fellow-citizens. One of them in reporting to Van Buren this sad state of affairs remarked that one "never had to call twice" to obtain an interview with either Jackson or Van Buren.[48] Enraged because he had not fared so well as certain other Tennesseans, Andrew Johnson pronounced Polk's appointments to be the "most *damnable*" ever made by any President,[49] and this fact he attributed to duplicity and the want of moral courage. Nevertheless, it required greater courage to resist importunities than to gratify them, and dissatisfaction from so many sources is but evidence that an attempt was being made to divorce patronage from factional politics, even though that attempt was destined to prove unsuccessful.

We are not left in doubt concerning the President's own opinions on the subject of patronage, for in making daily entries in his diary he seldom neglected to express his loathing for the

---

[47] Polk to Wright, July 8, 1845, *Polk Papers*.

[48] John P. Sheldon to Van Buren, Oct. 30, 1845, *Van Buren Papers*.

[49] "Take Polk's appointments all and all and they are the most *damnable* set that were ever made by any president since the government was organized, out of Tennessee as well as in it. He has a set of interested *parasites* about him who flatter him till he does not know himself. He seems to be acting on the principle of hanging one old friend for the purpose of making two new ones" (Johnson to ——? [someone in Tennessee], July 22, 1846, *Johnson Papers*).

office-seeker. He had the utmost contempt for those whose "patriotism" consisted solely of a willingness to draw a salary from the government; he regarded them not merely as an incubus but as a serious public menace. The personal boredom caused by listening to their tales became almost intolerable, but Polk was even more exasperated because they prevented him from devoting his time to important governmental affairs.

At the beginning of his administration Polk tried to follow the program announced in the *Union* of making his appointments on the basis of honesty and merit. He attempted also, as we have seen, to conserve his own time by delegating to his cabinet the lesser appointments. But for "practical" reasons he was constrained to modify this salutary program. In the first place his predecessors had made themselves accessible to the public and it was difficult for any President, particularly a Democratic President, suddenly to reverse the precedent. In the second place he had several important measures which could be carried into effect only by the coöperation of Congress, and he soon discovered that such coöperation could not be procured by ignoring the claim of members to their "share" of the patronage. Regardless of his own wishes, therefore, he was forced to give audience to individual office-seekers, and to make many appointments on the recommendation of members of Congress. In order to give a complete history of his patronage tribulations it would be necessary to reproduce his entire diary; some selected passages may serve to illustrate the annoyance experienced not only by Polk but by every chief executive.

Once the horde had been admitted to his presence the President, being a very courteous man, found it difficult to get rid of them. A few months' experience, however, taught him that "the only way to treat them is to be decided & stern." In February, 1846, Washington was infested with an unusually large number of persons "who are so patriotic as to desire to serve their country

by getting into fat offices.'"⁵⁰ On the anniversary of his inauguration he wrote in his diary:

> I am ready to exclaim will the pressure for office never cease! It is
> one year to-day since I entered on the duties of my office, and still the
> pressure for office has not abated. I most sincerely wish that I had no
> offices to bestow. If I had not it would add much to the happiness and
> comfort of my position. As it is, I have no offices to bestow without
> turning out better men than a large majority of those who seek their
> places.⁵¹

The inconvenience of possessing a courteous disposition is illustrated by an entry made on June 4, 1846:

> When there are no vacancies it is exceedingly distressing to be com-
> pelled to hear an office [seeker] for an hour tell his story and set forth his
> merits and claims. It is a great and useless consumption of my time, and
> yet I do not see how I am to avoid it without being rude or insulting,
> which it is not in my nature to be.⁵²

There were times, however, when politeness ceased to be a
virtue, especially after the same individual had called repeatedly
"on the patriotic business of seeking office." After a trying
experience with "old customers," he observed on August 17,
1846:

> I concluded that it was useless to be annoyed by them any longer, and
> I was more than usually stern and summary with them. I said no! this
> morning with a free will and a good grace. The truth is that the persons
> who called to-day, with but few exceptions, were a set of loafers without
> merit. They had been frequently here before, and I find as long as I treat
> them civilly I shall never get clear of them.⁵³

If, as the Whigs would have it, Polk needlessly precipitated
the war with Mexico, he suffered ample punishment in the form
of renewed scramble for office. Congressmen now not only sought
places for their constituents, but many of them desired military
positions for themselves. For the sake of harmony the President

---

⁵⁰ Polk, *Diary*, I, 158 (Jan. 9, 1846); *ibid.*, 255.

⁵¹ *Ibid.*, 261.

⁵² *Ibid.*, 446–447.

⁵³ Polk, *Diary*, II, 85. See also *ibid.*, 105–106.

was ready to suffer much inconvenience, but when it came to a matter of principle he was unyielding. The *Diary* for June 22, 1846, notes that

> The passion for office among members of Congress is very great, if not absolutely disreputable, and greatly embarrasses the operations of the Government. They create offices by their own votes and then seek to fill them themselves. I shall refuse to appoint them, though it be at the almost certain hazard of incurring their displeasure. I shall do so because their appointment would be most corrupting in its tendency. I am aware that by refusing their applications I may reduce my administration to a minority in both Houses of Congress, but if such be the result I shall have the high satisfaction of having discharged my duty in resisting the selfishness of members of Congress, who are willing to abandon their duty to their constituents and provide places for themselves. I will not countenance such selfishness, but will do my duty, and rely on the country for an honest support of my administration.

By December 16, 1846, the unscrupulous methods resorted to by members of Congress in their efforts to procure offices for their clients had become so appalling that Polk began "to distrust the disinterestedness and honesty of all mankind." Complaints and disaffection over petty offices gave him more trouble than did great national policies. "There is," he confided to his diary, "more selfishness and less principle among members of Congress, as well as others, than I had any conception [of] before I became President of the U. S."[54] Every day added new evidence of congressional depravity, and he was "disgusted with the trickery and treachery" exhibited in recommendations for office.[55] The way in which patronage had become a menace to both political parties and to the country is set forth in the entry for January 7, 1847:

> The passion for office and the number of unworthy persons who seek to live on the public is increasing beyond former example, and I now predict that no President of the U. S. of either party will ever again be re-elected. The reason is that the patronage of the Government will destroy the popularity of any President, however well he may administer

54 *Ibid.*, 278–279.
55 *Ibid.*, 296.

the Government. The office seekers have become so numerous that they hold the balance of power between the two great parties of the country. In every appointment which the President makes he disappoints half a dozen or more applicants and their friends, who actuated by selfish and sordid motives, will prefer any other candidate in the next election, while the person appointed attributes the appointment to his own superior merit and does not even feel obliged by it. The number of office seekers has become so large that they probably hold the balance of power between the two great parties in the country, and if disappointed in getting place under one administration they will readily unite themselves with the party and candidate of the opposite politics, so as to increase their chances for place. Another great difficulty in making appointments which the President encounters is that he cannot tell upon what recommendations to rely. Members of Congress and men of high station in the country sign papers of recommendation, either from interested personal motives or without meaning what they say, and thus the President is often imposed on, and induced to make bad appointments. When he does so the whole responsibility falls on himself, while those who have signed papers of recommendation and misled him, take special care never to avow the agency they have had in the matter, or to assume any part of the responsibility. I have had some remarkable instances of this during my administration. One or two of them I think worthy to be recalled as illustrations of many others. In the recess of Congress shortly after the commencement of my administration I made an appointment upon the letter of recommendation of a senator. I sent the nomination to the Senate at the last session & it was rejected, and, as I learned, at the instance of the same Senator who had made the recommendation. A few days afterwards the Senator called to recommend another person for the same office. I said to him, well, you rejected the man I nominated; O yes, he replied, he was without character & wholly unqualified. I then asked him if he knew upon whose recommendation I had appointed him, to which he replied that he did not. I then handed him his own letter & told him that that was the recommendation upon which I had appointed him. He appeared confused and replied, Well, we are obliged to recommend our constituents when they apply to us. The Senator was Mr. Atcheson of Missouri, and the person appointed & rejected was Mr. Hedges as Surveyor of the port of St. Louis.[56]

A week after the above had been written the begging for office had become "not only disgusting, but almost beyond endurance."

[56] *Ibid.*, 313–315. Polk crossed out the last sentence, but undoubtedly Atchison was the Senator in question. Members of Congress frequently signed enthusiastic recommendations for applicants and then sent private letters which requested Polk to pay no heed to the recommendation. The applicant of course blamed Polk when the appointment was not made. See *ibid.*, 278, note.

"I keep my temper," wrote the President, "or rather suppress the indignation which I feel at the sordid and selfish views of the people who continually annoy me about place." The rule which he had adopted under which no member of Congress was to be appointed to office, except diplomatic and high military positions, had already caused twenty disappointed applicants to oppose the measures of the administration; nevertheless he was determined to persist in applying the rule, regardless of consequences. "If God grants me length of days and health," he wrote in desperation, "I will, after the expiration of my term, give a history of the selfish and corrupt considerations which influence the course of public men, as a legacy to posterity. I shall never be profited by it, but those who come after me may be."[57] More than a year later he again expressed his determination to write an exposé of office-seeking,[58] and it is very probable that he would have done so had his death not occurred a few months after his retirement. It would have been an interesting volume, for he possessed both the data and the disposition to do the subject full justice.

The phrenologist who examined Polk in 1839 stated, among other things, that "when he suffers, he suffers most intently." No one who has followed the President's almost daily denunciations of place-hunters will be inclined to deny the truth of this statement. "I was doomed this morning," is the diary entry for February 18, 1847, "to pass through another pressure of importunate office seekers. I am ready to exclaim God deliver me from dispensing the patronage of the Government."[59] His suffering was made the more intense by his efforts to conceal it. His habit

---

[57] Polk, *Diary*, II, 328–330.

[58] Polk, *Diary*, III, 419. "If a kind Providence permits me length of days and health, I will, after I retire from the Presidential office, write the secret and hitherto unknown history of the Government in this respect. It requires great patience & self command to repress the loathing I feel towards a hungry crowd of unworthy office-hunters who often crowd my office."

[59] Polk, *Diary*, II, 382.

of reticence and a desire to preserve his dignity led him, for the most part, to endure the agony in silence; to his diary alone did he communicate his real opinions. "It is enough," he wrote on one occasion, "to exhaust the patience and destroy the good temper of any man on earth, to bear the daily boring which I have to endure. I keep, however, in a good humor as far as it is possible to do so."[60] It was this same passive exterior which led many to believe that he did not have positive opinions on other subjects.

The severest of weather was no deterrent to the procession of the office-seeking "patriots," for "neither ice nor fire" could stop them. Polk "pushed them off and fought them with both hands like a man fighting fire," but "it has all been in vain."[61] He felt the need of "one of Colt's revolving pistols" to enable him to clear the office so that he might attend to his public duties.[62] Most disgusting of all were those who, on hearing a report of an officer's illness, rushed to the President with an application for the sick man's position, "if he should die." Nearly all of them were "mere loafers who are too lazy to work and wish to be supported by the public"—in a word, "the most contemptible race on earth."[63] So far as members of Congress were concerned, Senator Breeze, of Illinois, enjoyed the distinction of being the champion pest. "He has," said the President, "no sooner procured an appointment than he sets to work to procure another," and his recommendations were governed by his political interests and not by the public good.[64]

Although Polk fully realized at the time of his inauguration that he was entering upon four years of incessant toil, he undoubtedly, like all who have not held the office, believed the Presidency to be a position of dignity as well as power. The political intrigues and factional jealousies with which he was beset soon

60 Polk, *Diary*, III, 250.
61 Polk, *Diary*, II, 360–361, 383.
62 Polk, *Diary*, IV, 246.

63 Polk, *Diary*, III, 331, IV, 79.
64 Polk, *Diary*, II, 426.

divested the office of much of its glamour; the political necessity of enduring the importunities of the office-seeking horde made it even contemptible. On this subject we may quote his own words:

> The office of President is generally esteemed a very high dignified position, but really I think the public would not so regard it if they could look in occasionally and observe the kind of people by whom I am often annoyed. I cannot seclude myself but must be accessible to my fellow-citizens, and this gives an opportunity to all classes and descriptions of people to obtrude themselves upon me about matters in which the public has not the slightest interest. There is no class of our population by whom I am annoyed so much, or for whom I entertain a more sovereign contempt, than for the professional office-seekers who have besieged me ever since I have been in the Presidential office.[65]

Scarcely less obnoxious than the office-seeker was the casual visitor who had no business to transact but who nevertheless wasted the President's valuable time. Even though he begrudged the time spent in pointless conversation he realized that a refusal to meet callers would cause adverse criticism and weaken his administration. "I feel," said he, "that I am compelled to yield to it, and to deprive myself of the ordinary rest, in order to attend to the indispensable duties which devolve upon me."[66]

Ceremonious notifications of royal births and deaths added their share of irritation to the busy and democratic President. "I confess," he noted on one occasion, "the practice of announcing officially the birth of Foreign Princes to the President of the United States, has always appeared to me to be supremely ridiculous."[67] When his attention was called by Buchanan to a grave

---

[65] Polk, *Diary*, IV, 160–161 (Oct. 19, 1848).

[66] Polk, *Diary*, II, 280–281.

[67] Polk, *Diary*, I, 237. When not too much absorbed in affairs of state, he sometimes saw the funny side as well. E.g. "These ceremonies seem to be regarded as of Great importance by the Ministers of the Foreign Monarchies, though to me they are amusing & ridiculous" (*ibid.*, II, 215–216). The solemn notification of the death in the royal family of Russia struck him as being so ridiculous that he could "scarcely preserve his gravity." "I simply remarked [to the Russian minister] that such occurrences would take place, and at once entered into familiar conversation" (*ibid.*, 374).

communication from the French Minister of Foreign Affairs relating to a dispute between American and French consuls over
their claims to precedence, Polk related with approval a story
of Jefferson's "pell mell" etiquette, and told Buchanan that "I
was not a man of ceremonies, that he and Mr. Guizot might settle
the dispute between the consuls in any way they pleased."[68]

Although Polk was not, as is generally believed, devoid of all
sense of humor, the austerity of his bearing when President of the
United States very naturally gave rise to this belief. His habitual
gravity was caused in part by ill health, but still more by the
weight of responsibilities. Official cares so filled his mind that
no room was left for amusement. This fact is well illustrated
by an incident which he has noted in his diary. One day a
magician gave an exhibition before a select company at the executive mansion and the President was persuaded by Bancroft and
Mrs. Catron to attend. The rest of the company derived much
enjoyment from the entertainment, but Polk felt that his time
had been unprofitably spent. "I was thinking," he wrote,
"more about the Oregon & other public questions which bear on
my mind that [than] the tricks of the juggler, and perhaps on
that account the majority of the company might think my opinions entitled to but little weight." He could not, like Lincoln,
find relaxation in a homely anecdote or in a chapter from some
humorous writer. Official cares were constantly on his mind and
he had no time for amusements.

The cares of office added much to the gravity of the President's naturally serious disposition. Indeed, he had become, as
Claiborne has said, "grave almost to sadness."[69] While he willingly spent his energies in the public service, he longed for the
day to arrive when he might relinquish the helm of state; it
needed no one-term pledge to prevent him from standing for
reëlection. "I have now," he wrote on his fifty-second birthday,

---

[68] Polk, *Diary*, II, 175.
[69] Claiborne, *Life and Correspondence of John A. Quitman*, I, 228.

"passed through two-thirds of my Presidential term, & most heartily wish the remaining third was over, for I am sincerely desirous to have the enjoyment of retirement in private life."[70]

Polk's success as an executive and as a constructive statesman will, we believe, be made manifest in the chapters which follow. The topics to be considered cover the fields of war, diplomacy, finance, industrial development, and constitutional law. In all of these fields, the President formulated his own policies and, in the main, succeeded in putting them in operation. Soon after his inauguration he announced to George Bancroft that the "four great measures" of his administration would be: reduction of the tariff, establishment of an independent treasury, settlement of the Oregon question, and the acquisition of California.[71] He carried out this program in spite of vigorous opposition. And if we except the coercion of Mexico, upon which there is still a difference of opinion, it is the verdict of history that his policies were both praiseworthy and sound.

---

[70] Polk, *Diary*, III, 210.
[71] Schouler, *History of the United States*, IV, 498.

CHAPTER XVI

COMPLETION OF ANNEXATION

As we have noted in a preceding chapter, the joint resolution adopted by Congress on February 28, 1845, authorized the annexation of Texas by either of two methods. Under the first—the House resolution—Congress consented to admit Texas as a state as soon as the government and people of that republic had agreed to annexation and had conformed to certain requirements specified in the resolution. The second method—the so-called Benton plan—provided:

> That if the President of the United States shall in his judgment and discretion deem it most advisable, instead of proceeding to submit the foregoing resolution to the Republic of Texas, as an overture on the part of the United States for admission, to negotiate with that Republic.

Three days before Polk's inauguration Tyler, as we have seen, approved the joint resolution and selected the first method —the one specified in the House resolution. On March 3 President Tyler dispatched a messenger with instructions to Donelson, the American *chargé d' affaires,* who was residing temporarily in New Orleans.

The action taken by Tyler did not, of course, effect the annexation of the lone-star republic. There was a possibility,[1] at least, that the new President might recall the messenger and select the Benton alternative of negotiating with Texas. Besides, annexation in any case was contingent on the acceptance of the proposed terms by the government and people of the Texan republic.

---

[1] See p. 318 and note 96.

When Calhoun called upon Polk to inform him that Tyler had decided to select the House resolution, the President-elect declined, as we have seen, to express an opinion. And, if we except the seemingly incredible statements made by Tappan and Blair, he did not reveal his opinions concerning the method of annexation up to the time of his inauguration. He says in his diary[2] that his mind was not fully made up as to the choice of method until he met his cabinet on March 10, 1845; he then decided to select the House resolution, or in other words, to acquiesce in the choice made by Tyler. Additional evidence that he arrived at no decision until he had consulted the cabinet is contained in a private letter written to Donelson on the seventh of March. He said:

A despatch was transmitted to you by the late administration on the 3rd Ins. In two or three days another will be forwarded to you on the same subject by a special messenger. But five members of my Cabinet have been confirmed by the Senate; the remaining members I hope will be confirmed at the next meeting of the Senate. I write now to say that I desire you, not to take any definite action in pursuance of the instructions given in the despatch of the 3rd Inst. until after you receive the one which will be forwarded in two or three days, and by which the instructions will probably be modified. I write you this informal note for the reason that *Mr. Buchanan* the Secretary of State has not entered the duties of his office, and because I desire to have the Cabinet complete before definite action is had on my part.[3]

Just what the President meant by saying that Tyler's instructions would probably be modified we can only conjecture. *Possibly* he may have been contemplating a reversal of Tyler's action, although his statement does not seem to warrant such an inference. More likely he was thinking of the reasoning contained in the instructions sent by his predecessor, for this, as we shall see, was criticized in the official dispatch which soon followed.

[2] Polk, *Diary*, IV, 44.

[3] Polk to Donelson, March 7, 1845, "Polk-Donelson Letters." The endorsement on the letter reads: "The President March 7. Recd. from Mr. Pickett on the 19th at New Orleans."

As soon as the decision to proceed under the House resolution had been reached Buchanan, by the President's order, delivered to Almonte, the Mexican minister, an answer to the protest against annexation which that official had addressed to Calhoun. In his letter Almonte characterized annexation as "an act of aggression the most unjust which can be found recorded in the annals of modern history—namely, that of despoiling a friendly nation like Mexico, of a considerable portion of her territory." After asserting that Mexico would exert all of her power in recovering her province of Texas, he concluded by demanding his passports. In reply Buchanan informed Almonte that while President Polk desired to continue friendly relations with Mexico, annexation was "irrevocably decided" so far as the United States was concerned, and that it was too late to raise the question of Texan independence.[4]

On the same day, March 10, Polk sent out another messenger, Governor Archibald Yell, with new instructions for Donelson. The instructions from both Presidents reached the *chargé d' affaires* at New Orleans on March 24, and he set out immediately for Texas.[5]

In the new instructions, Buchanan informed Donelson that Polk did not concur with Tyler in the belief that procedure under the Benton alternative would necessitate the conclusion of a treaty which must be ratified by the Senate, "yet he is sensible that many of the sincere friends of Texas may entertain this opinion." Should this prove to be the case, dissension and delay must be the inevitable result. From all points of view, said Buchanan, the House resolution was to be preferred, therefore he urged Texas to accept it without modification and to trust to sister states for desired adjustments. He desired especially that the public lands of Texas should be transferred to the United

---

[4] Almonte to Calhoun, March 6; Buchanan to Almonte, March 10, 1845 (Buchanan, *Works*, VI, 118–120).

[5] Donelson to Buchanan, March 24, 1845 (*Sen. Ex. Doc. 1*, 29 Cong., 1 sess., 45, 46).

States so that the federal government might extend its laws over the Indian tribes.[6]

Donelson reached Galveston on March 27 only to find that a British vessel had arrived there a short time before and that the British and French ministers had gone to Washington, Texas, to confer with the government of that republic. As it was rumored that these diplomats carried with them the promise of Mexico's recognition of Texan independence and an offer from England of a favorable commercial treaty, Donelson "put off in a hurry after them." When reporting this information to Polk, Yell said that should General Houston espouse the cause of annexation, President Jones would also support it. Yell had conversed with many Texan leaders, including Memucan Hunt. They talked, he said, of getting the people to demand that congress should be called for the purpose of considering annexation.[7]

Not all of the leaders, however, were pleased with the terms of annexation offered by the United States. Donelson did not believe that the people would acquiesce in annexation unless the proposition were presented to them by their own government, and he thought that President Jones was not in favor of the measure. He was not encouraged by the apparent attitude at the capital when he first reached there, but within a month he was able to report that he considered the question as settled, so far as Texas was concerned.[8]

The people proved to be in favor of annexation, and the leaders could not ignore their wishes;[9] nevertheless, the Texan government could not afford to disregard the wishes of General Houston, and he, at first, assumed a hostile attitude. On his arrival, Donelson found the Texan government disposed to offer objections to the American terms of annexation, and he had

---

[6] Buchanan to Donelson, March 10, 1845, *ibid.*, 35–38.

[7] Yell to Polk, Galveston, March 26, 1845, *Polk Papers.*

[8] Donelson to Buchanan, April 1, 3, May 6, 1845 (*Sen. Doc. 1*, 29 Cong., 1 sess., 47, 51, 56).

[9] Smith, *Annexation of Texas*, 434–435.

reason to believe that, in no small degree, this attitude was due to the hostility of Houston. The ex-President was sojourning at some distance from the seat of government. Donelson paid him a visit in the hope that he might overcome his objections to immediate annexation.

In a letter to Donelson, Houston had said that in the House resolution "the terms are dictated and conditions absolute." Believing that Texas should have something to say about the terms of union, he therefore preferred the Benton alternative of negotiation. The proposed method, in his opinion, left too many things uncertain. He opposed, especially, the cession of Texan property to the United States and the ambiguous character of the northwestern boundary.[10] Donelson reminded Houston that the specifications in the House resolution regarding property, debts, and public lands, were substantially those which had been suggested by Houston himself only a few months before, still the ex-President gave no intimation that he would withdraw his opposition.[11]

However sincere Houston's objections may have been, forces were at work which were likely to modify them. Donelson had brought to Houston a letter from General Jackson which praised the work he had already done and assumed that he would aid in its completion.[12] The immediate effect of this letter was not apparent, but Houston, like Benton, always wished to stand well with "the chief." In addition, he could never quite overcome a lingering desire to be once more under the folds of "old Glory." Then, too, the Washington *Globe* and other newspapers intimated that he might be chosen President of the United States in the

---

[10] Houston to Donelson, April 9, 1845 (*Tex. State Hist. Assn. Quar.*, Oct., 1897, 79 ff). Donelson to Buchanan, April 12, 1845 (*Sen. Doc.* I, 29 Cong., 1 sess., 52).

[11] Donelson to Calhoun, April 24, 1845 (*Rep. Am. Hist. Assn.*, 1899, II, 1029). Houston's memorandum of suggestions is given in Jones, *Republic of Texas*, 414–415.

[12] Jackson to Houston, March 12, 1845 (Yoakum, *History of Texas*, II, 441). See also, Duff Green to Calhoun, Dec. 8, 1844 (*Rep. Am. Hist. Assn.*, 1899, II, 1007).

event of annexation.[13] For the present, however, Houston was obdurate, and Donelson returned to the seat of government to continue the struggle with President Jones and his cabinet.

Although Jones was noncommittal and spoke of offers from Mexico, already there were indications that popular pressure would be brought to bear upon the government.[14] Some, it is said, even threatened to lynch Jones if he should attempt to prevent annexation.[15]

On the first of April Donelson transmitted the proposals of his government to Allen, the Texan Secretary of State, and with them a letter explaining why the House resolution had been selected. President Jones complained about the terms offered in the resolution, but on April 15 he issued a proclamation summoning the Texan congress to convene on the sixteenth of June.[16]

As public opinion in favor of annexation rose to a high pitch, Houston's attitude experienced a noticeable change, and early in May he set out for the Hermitage to visit General Jackson. After conversing with him at Galveston, Yell reported to Polk that the ex-President was now friendly and not the least opposed to annexation—that *"he is now safe."* He is, said Yell, the "Power behind the Throne, greater than the Throne itself." Donelson, in Yell's opinion, deserved much credit for the "heroic work" he had been doing; his relationship to the "old hero" had greatly assisted him in dealing with the Texans.[17] Whatever the reason may have been, Houston's conversion to annexation seems to have been complete, and late in May Jackson wrote with enthusiasm that "Texas comes into the union with a united voice, and Genl

13 Smith, *Annexation of Texas*, 439.

14 Letters to Jones from Underwood, Norton, Lubbock, Ashbel Smith, *et al.* (Jones, *Republic of Texas*, 442, 444, 446–449). Jones's endorsements on these letters claim that instead of being opposed to annexation, he was "its chief author." This may be doubted.

15 Smith, *op. cit.*, 441.

16 Donelson to Allen, March 31; same to Buchanan, April 12; Proclamation of April 15, 1845 (*Sen. Doc. 1*, 29 Cong., 1 sess., 48, 52, 54). ·

17 Yell to Polk, May 5, 1845, *Polk Papers.*

Houston, as I know, puts his shoulders to the wheels to roll it in
speedily. I knew British gold could not buy Sam Houston *all*
safe & Donelson will have the honor of this important Deed.''[18]

Houston's conversion did not settle the matter. Another
difficulty now presented itself. The House resolution required
that a convention should be assembled in Texas for the purpose
of framing a new state government, but the Texan constitution
had, of course, made no provision for such proceeding. President Jones could block annexation by declining to exercise extra-
legal authority, and for a time it was feared that he might do
so. On May 5, however, Jones issued another proclamation.
Admitting his want of authority, he nevertheless *recommended*
that delegates be chosen to meet at Austin on July 4 for the
purpose of considering the offer made by the United States.[19]

Allen now pointed out to Donelson that acceptance of the
American proposal of annexation would very likely result in an
invasion from Mexico. He therefore requested that an American
army should be brought to Texas so that it might be ready to
repel such an invasion.[20] Donelson submitted Allen's request
to his government; but Polk and Buchanan had already anticipated the wishes of Texas, and a promise of protection had
been forwarded to Donelson. Buchanan was instructed by the
President to say that as soon as Texas shall have accepted the
American proposal, ''he will then conceive it to be both his
right and his duty to employ the army in defending that State
against the attacks of any foreign power.'' A force of three

---

[18] Jackson to Polk, May 26, 1845, *ibid.* Smith thinks it likely that
Houston was influenced to some extent by the belief that the United
States might seize Texas as it had seized West Florida (Smith, *op. cit.*,
443).

[19] *Sen. Ex. Doc. 1*, 29 Cong., 1 sess., 63–64.

[20] President Jones maintained later that Donelson, by a ''trick,'' had
induced Allen to make the request for troops. This may be a misrepresentation, yet it is interesting to note that Polk and Buchanan made
an offer of troops before they had received Allen's request (Jones,
Republic of Texas, 53, 457–458). As to misrepresentation, see Smith,
Annexation, 445, note 21.

thousand men, he said, would immediately be placed on the border, prepared to enter Texas and to act without a moment's delay.[21]

Shortly after this promise to protect Texas had been sent to Donelson a significant article appeared in the Washington *Union*. It may not, of course, have been inspired by the President; but the coupling of the American claims against Mexico and the desire for California with the question of annexing Texas accords so well with Polk's previously announced policy that one is tempted to assume that Ritchie voiced faithfully the views of the administration. Polk and his cabinet, said the article, are fully capable of handling the Texas and Oregon questions. It is uncertain what course Mexico will pursue, but

Her true interest will be found in peace. Let the great measure of annexation be accomplished, and with it the questions of boundary and of claims. But if she madly rushes on to the alternative of war, who shall pretend to set bounds to the consequences?

We infinitely prefer the friendly settlement of the great question now pending. It will secure the peace and welfare of the Mexican nation. It can now be done, and it should now be accomplished. For who can arrest the torrent that will pour onward to the West? The road to California will open to us. Who will stay the march of our western people? Our northern brethren also are looking towards that inviting region with much more interest than those of the South. They, too, will raise the cry of "Westward, ho!" However strongly many of them may now oppose annexation, yet let California be thrown open to their ambition and the torrent even of their population will roll on westwardly to the Pacific.[22]

The preliminary treaty between Texas and Mexico, which had been arranged by Captain Charles Elliot, the British *chargé*, was signed by the executive officers of the former country on the twenty-ninth of March. Under pretext of making a visit to South Carolina, Elliot had, in April, set out for the Mexican capital.[23] His artifice, for the time being, was successful.

---

[21] Donelson to Buchanan, May 6; Buchanan to Donelson, May 23 (*Sen. Ex. Doc. 1*, 29 Cong., 1 sess., 40, 56, 69, ff.).

[22] *Union*, June 2, 1845.

[23] "I shall go out in the 'Electra,'" Elliot wrote to President Jones on April 5, "*but change ships out of sight of land,* and go down in the

Having sent (May 6) to Buchanan the letter in which he stated that Texas desired military protection, Donelson left for New Orleans—partly to get news of conditions in Mexico, and partly to keep track of Elliot. At New Orleans he heard it rumored that a British fleet was coming to aid Mexico. He notified Buchanan immediately and urged that the United States should take steps to protect Texas. "Of course," said he, "if war should be declared against us, Texas will be its theatre, and the earlier we are in possession of the commanding points on the Rio Grande the sooner we shall be able to bring it to a close."[24]

While at Iberville, Donelson read in a New Orleans paper that Captain Elliot had induced Mexico to recognize the independence of Texas if she would agree to remain a separate nation. He returned immediately to Texas. Before starting, however, he dispatched another letter to Secretary Buchanan in which he prophesied that

Texas will be sure to call the proposal recognizing her independence as nothing but a *ruse* on the part of the British government, by which it is hoped that the people of Texas will be led to reject annexation; and the effect will be, still greater unanimity in favor of the United States, and against all interference on the part of Great Britain in a question *truly* American.

He believed that the United States should be prepared for "an immediate blow upon Mexico" in case that country should declare war, and that "Texas will be as ready as we are to defend the 'star spangled banner,' and denounce British dictation."[25]

On his arrival at Galveston, Donelson learned that Elliot was about to leave for Washington, Texas, for the purpose of submitting to the Texan government the plan of recognition to which Mexico had consented. The two men discussed the plan freely,

'Eurydice.' By this means I shall be reported as gone to 'Charleston' in the 'Electra,' and so hope to arrive unobserved'' (Jones, *Republic of Texas*, 443). The preliminary treaty is printed on pp. 473–475 of the same volume.

24 Donelson to Buchanan, May 11, 1845 (*Sen. Doc. 1*, 29 Cong., 1 sess., 56).

25 Donelson to Buchanan, May 22, 1845 (*ibid.*, 58–59).

and Donelson was disgusted by the hypocrisy displayed in the representation that the overture for an agreement had come from Texas. "Stripped of diplomatic phrase," he wrote, "this recognition is nothing more nor less than a contrivance of Great Britain to defeat the measure of annexation, or involve Mexico in a war with the United States." Since Mexico was reported to be concentrating troops on the Rio Grande "where Texas has, as yet, established no posts," Texas would probably send a force to remove these intruders and Captain Stockton would be ready to coöperate after the acceptance of annexation. In "addition to the suggestions before made on this subject, I would remark that the route for the infantry or artillery in our service which may be thought requisite on the Rio Grande, should be by *water* and not by *land.*" Two days later he wrote again to the Secretary of State. He had just received Buchanan's letter of May 23 which promised protection, but it did not cover the whole ground. If Mexico should invade Texas to the Nueces or farther *before* the convention has had an opportunity to accept the American proposal, "are the United States," he asked, "to stand still and see the country thus invaded, without interposing protection?"[26]

In the same mail with Donelson's dispatches went a letter from Charles A. Wickliffe, Polk's confidential agent in Texas. It informed the President that Captain Elliot was boldly asserting that annexation would be followed immediately by a declaration of war by Mexico. Mexico, said Elliot, would declare war instantly; the United States would blockade the Mexican ports; but Great Britain would not submit to this, and, consequently, there would be war for twenty years. Nevertheless, said the agent, Elliot was fully aware that a majority of the Texans were in favor of annexation. Wickliffe urged that any attempt on the part of Mexico to invade Texas while negotiations for annexation were pending should be repelled with vigor by the United States.[27]

---

[26] Donelson to Buchanan, June 2, 4, 1845, *ibid.*, 64–66.
[27] Wickliffe to Polk, June 4, 1845, *Polk Papers.*

The letter just received from Buchanan authorized Donelson to guarantee protection *after* the American proposal had been accepted, and on June 11, he gave this qualified promise to the Texan Secretary of State. Elliot's bluster thoroughly aroused his indignation, and in his letter to Allen he said that

if Texas cannot be allowed to enjoy the blessings of peace and independence, as one of the sovereign members of the American Union, without asking permission of Mexico or of the monarchies of Europe, the fact is worth volumes of argument in explaining the duty of those who are struggling to maintain a system of government founded on the will and controlled by the authority of the people.[28]

The tone of this letter had a reassuring effect upon the Texans and lessened the hazard of an exercise of independent judgment.

The letters which Donelson and Wickliffe had written on the second and fourth of June procured prompt action on the part of their government. These communications reached Washington on the evening of June 14, and on the following day Polk wrote an interesting and important letter to Donelson. The threatened invasion, said the President,

increases our solicitude concerning the final action by the Congress and Convention of Texas upon our proposition of annexation. In view of the facts disclosed by you, not only as regards the approach of an invading Mexican army—but of the open intermeddling of the British Charge d' affaires with the question of annexation, I have lost no time in causing the most prompt & energetic measures to be adopted here. I am resolved to defend and protect Texas, as far as I possess the power to do so.

This statement makes it clear that Polk did not doubt the genuineness of the British menace, and that he was prepared to meet it at all hazards. He informed Donelson that General Besancon, the bearer of this letter, would be dispatched that night with instructions and that another messenger would be sent at the same time to Fort Jessup, bearing orders for the troops to march at once to the mouth of the Sabine. These

---

[28] Donelson to Allen, June 11, 1845 (*Sen. Ex. Doc. 1*, 29 Cong., 1 sess., 71).

troops were to act as Donelson might direct, under his instructions from the Department of State. The *chargé* was told that the steamer *Spencer* had been ordered to leave New York to report to him at Galveston, and that an additional naval force would be sent immediately to the Gulf of Mexico. Polk urged that the Texan convention should, on the day of meeting, pass a general resolution accepting the offer made by the United States. "The moment they do this," said the President,

I shall regard Texas as a part of the Union; all questions of Constitutional power to defend & protect her by driving an invading Mexican Army out of her Territory will be at an end and our land and naval forces will be under orders to do so.

The convention could then proceed with its deliberations in safety, without fear of Mexican invasion or of "British intrigue" . . . . "The assent of the Convention is all we want." The question of employing the army and navy of the United States to repel a Mexican invasion during the interval between the acceptance of annexation by the Texan congress and the meeting of the convention, Polk left to the discretion of Donelson. He expressed the hope that there might be no necessity for exercising such discretion, nevertheless, should anything occur which was calculated to overawe or interfere with the peaceful deliberations of the convention—

then in my judgment the public necessity for our interposition will be such that we should not stand quietly by & permit an invading foreign enemy to occupy or devastate any portion of Texan Territory. Of course I would maintain the Texan title to the extent which she claims it to be & not permit an invading enemy to occupy a foot of the soil East of the *Rio Grande*.[29]

The troops stationed at Fort Jessup could not, as the letter pointed out, reach Texas in time to afford immediate protection to the convention which would assemble on July 4; nevertheless, as a definite statement of Polk's plans and purposes, this letter

---

[29] Polk to Donelson, June 15, 1845, "Polk-Donelson Letters." Also, a copy in *Polk Papers*.

is extremely interesting. Writing to Donelson on the same day, Buchanan said that Captain Elliot, by obtaining Mexico's consent to annexation, had "deprived that power of the only miserable pretext which it had for a war against the United States."[30]

The troops to be sent from Fort Jessup were commanded by General Zachary Taylor. By a confidential dispatch dated May 28, Marcy had given instructions for the general's guidance, should annexation be accepted by Texas. Taylor sent a messenger to consult with Donelson concerning the necessity of sending troops into Texas and to investigate the resources for their subsistence. Donelson reported to him that all branches of the existing Texan government had assented to annexation, and that the convention would do so on the fourth of July. If any reliance, said he, is to be placed upon the threats made by Mexico and the advice which it may be presumed will be given to her by the British and French governments, "an invasion of Texas may be confidently anticipated"; at all events, the General would be justified in moving to the western frontier in order to give the protection authorized by President Polk. He advised Taylor to transfer the troops from New Orleans directly to Corpus Christi, which is a healthy place and convenient for supplies, "and is the most western point now occupied by Texas." In the same letter Donelson remarked that the "occupation of the country between the Nueces and Rio Grande, you are aware, is a disputed question. Texas holds Corpus Christi; Mexico, Santiago, near the mouth of the Rio Grande."[31]

Von Holst has made much of the phrases just quoted. Isolating them from their context and giving to them an erroneous, or at least an ambiguous, translation, he has used them to substantiate his assertion that Donelson, in this letter which was forwarded by Taylor to Washington, "emphasized the fact that

---

[30] Buchanan to Donelson, June 15, 1845 (Buchanan, *Works,* VI, 174).
[31] Taylor to Adj. Gen., June 18; Donelson to Taylor, June 28, 1845 (*H. Ex. Doc. 60,* 30 Cong., 1 sess., 800, 805).

it was an open question to whom the land between the Nueces and the Rio Grande belonged."[32] His purpose is to show that Polk provoked a war by claiming unjustly a strip of land the ownership of which even his own subordinates had questioned. Whatever may have provoked the war, Donelson's letter conveys no such meaning. As a matter of fact his chief emphasis was placed on the healthful conditions at the places designated and his desire to avoid taking "an offensive attitude in regard to Mexico, without further orders from the government of the United States." Taylor was advised to limit his activities to the defense of Texas unless attacked, in which case he was to drive the Mexicans beyond the Rio Grande. Donelson spoke of *occupation*, not of *ownership;* but even if he had meant the latter, it is clear enough that it was not a "disputed question" so far as he was concerned. The paragraph which contained these phrases was followed by another which said that "the threatened invasion of Texas, however, is founded upon the assumption that Texas has no territory independent of Mexico." Von Holst found it convenient to omit this paragraph, for it did not harmonize with the thesis which he had set out to prove.[33] Donelson's views on the subject had already been expressed very clearly in his letters of May 11 and June 2, above quoted, in which he advised an early occupation of posts on the Rio Grande.

In this same connection, von Holst represents Taylor to have spoken of San Antonio as being situated on the *western boundary* ("redete gar von San Antonio als an der westlichen Grenze gelegen"); whereas the General simply spoke of the immediate occupation of "the western *frontier* (italics mine) of Texas,

---

[32] von Holst, *History of the United States,* German ed., II, 72, Eng. trans., III, 90.

[33] His remark concerning Polk's suppression of facts might well be applied to his own writings: "That his silence about them was deliberately designed is made clearer than day by the false coloring by means of which he manages, without exciting distrust by bold misrepresentations, to give to things which supported his assertion a weight which they did not remotely deserve" (*ibid.,* Eng. trans., III, 89).

from the coast to San Antonio, and ultimately further north.''[34]
On the same page we are told that the Texan Secretary of War
asked Taylor to protect Austin, on the Colorado ''da es an der
Grenze ist,'' which the translators have made to read ''because
it is on the boundary.'' But the Secretary had written that

The town of Austin where the convention will assemble, and the most of the
archives of our government are now deposited, being on the frontier, and
exposed to Indian depredations and Mexican invasion, would require protection, as would also San Antonio de Bexar and Corpus Christi.[35]

In justice to von Holst it may be said that *Grenze* is the German equivalent of *boundary,* and that he may have been ignorant
of the distinction drawn by Americans between the words
boundary and *frontier;* and yet, it seems incredible that he could
have so misunderstood the letters as a whole as not to have known
that the American officials were speaking of a general region,
and were not attempting to fix a boundary line. That von Holst
himself meant *boundary* when he used the term *Grenze* is shown
by the context, and his translators in converting his writings
into English have invariably written *boundary* instead of *frontier,* which had been used in the original documents. Were it
not for the fact that this writer's version of Polk's policy has
influenced both writers and teachers of history, it would hardly
be worth while to dwell on his misuse of official documents.

Donelson's belief that Captain Elliot and his government
were striving to prevent annexation was by no means unfounded.
Great Britain was not willing to extend her interference to the
point of risking a war with the United States, but she was determined to apply every possible pressure that stopped short of
this limit which she had set for her activities.[36] However, the

---

[34] *Ibid.,* Ger. ed., II, 72. Taylor to Adj. Gen., July 8, 1845 (*H. Ex.
Doc. 60,* 30 Cong., 1 sess., 802).

[35] von Holst, *op. cit.,* Ger. ed., II, 72, Eng. trans., III, 90. Cook to
Taylor, June 27, 1845 (*H. Doc. 60,* 30 Cong., 1 sess., 804).

[36] E. D. Adams, *British Interests and Activities in Texas,* chap. ix. It
has been considered unnecessary, in a biography of Polk, to discuss in
detail the acts and the motives of England, France, and Mexico, except
in their bearing on Polk's policy. The part played by England is well
presented in the volume by Professor Adams just cited.

officious meddling of Captain Elliot and the Mexican threats of invasion caused anxiety in Texas, and fear of the latter led the government to solicit the protection of the United States. By instructing Taylor to send dragoons to San Antonio and infantry to Corpus Christi, Donnelson had inspired the people with a feeling of safety, even though Taylor could not reach these points before the meeting of the convention.[37]

The preliminary treaty which Elliot had arranged between Texas and Mexico[38] provided for the suspension of hostilities until the people of Texas had either accepted or rejected the terms of the agreement. Accordingly, on June 4, President Jones issued his proclamaation declaring a truce. The general effect of this proclamation and of the mystery and secrecy employed by Elliot in bringing the two governments together[39] led the people still more to distrust both men, and, consequently, aided the cause of annexation. Donelson handled the question most skilfully and did much to solidify the sentiment in favor of joining the United States. On the other hand, he very sensibly refrained from doing anything which might antagonize the Texan officials who were still trying to maintain a neutral position.[40] Then, too, the apparent insincerity of Mexico added strength to the annexationists. As soon as President Jones had proclaimed a truce, Bankhead, the British minister in Mexico, pressed that government to issue a similar proclamation. Instead of complying, Cuevas, the Minister of Foreign Affairs, made dire threats of war on Texas.[41] Even those in the lone-star republic who were inclined to oppose annexation could no longer contend that Mexico would peacefully concede independence.

---

[37] Allen to Donelson, June 26; Donelson to Allen, June 30, 1845 (*Sen. Ex. Doc. 1*, 29 Cong., 1 sess., 92, 94). Smith, *Annexation of Texas*, 451.

[38] For a copy of this document see Adams, *op. cit.*, 210–211, or Jones, *Republic of Texas*, 473–475.

[39] Elliot was later reproved by the British Foreign Secretary for the secrecy of his proceedings because they ''laid Great Britain open to the charge of intriguing in Texas'' (Aberdeen to Elliot, July 3, 1845; cited by Adams, *op. cit.*, 220).

[40] Smith, *Annexation of Texas*, 452–454.

[41] Adams, *British Interests and Activities in Texas*, 221–222.

On June 16 the Texan congress assembled, and President Jones submitted the American joint resolution; two days later he placed before this body the terms of the conditional recognition of independence which Elliot had negotiated with Mexico. On the congress now devolved the duty of choosing between the two proposals; but as Mexico was already threatening war, there was little probability that any arrangement made with that country would be selected. Without loss of time the congress by a unanimous vote agreed to accept the offer made by the United States, and by a similar vote it rejected the proposed treaty with Mexico.[42]

As the time for the meeting of the popular convention approached, it appeared that there might be greater difficulty in winning the approval of that body. In several respects the terms offered by the United States were unacceptable to the Texans. The American joint resolution had not specified a definite boundary, and there were uncertainties regarding public lands, Indian policy, and other details. Some suggested, also, that before it had entered the Union the republic ought to be divided into several states, in order to increase its political importance.[43] On the other hand, Donelson had been instructed by his government to urge upon Texas the wisdom of accepting the proposed terms without modification, and before the meeting of the convention he had spared no effort in shaping public opinion to sanction such a course. In this connection he pointed out that many of the unsatisfactory matters could be adjusted after annexation, while haggling over terms would result in discord and delay.

---

[42] Donelson to Buchanan, June 23, 1845 (Sen. Ex. Doc. 1, 29 Cong., 1 sess., 83).

[43] Smith, Annexation of Texas, 456–457. General Houston, as we have noted, had had misgivings regarding the boundary question, and although he had left the scene of action Polk deemed it worth while to reassure him on the subject. "You may have no apprehensions," wrote the President, "in regard to your boundary. Texas once a part of the Union & we will maintain all your rights of territory & will not suffer them to be sacrificed" (Polk to Houston (copy), June 6, 1845, Polk Papers).

An interesting account of the part played by Donelson and of the attitude of the Texan officials is given in a letter written to Buchanan from Washington, Texas, by John G. Tod. Tod had evidently just arrived in Texas from Washington (D. C.), and his letter is in the form of a daily journal of events from July 1 to July 11, 1845.[44] Donelson, according to Tod, had no doubt whatever that annexation would be consummated, and he could not understand why officials in Washington were so excited about the question. " 'There has,' said he, 'never been any difficulty about it at all. President Jones has always been open and candid upon this subject and there was no room to apprehend trouble and difficulty if it is not created by the management of the matter in Washington.' "[45] Under date of July 2, Tod recorded that Jones, Allen, and Raymond[46] had called on Donelson. "The President and the latter laughed and joked a good deal about the excitement on the Potomac." After this meeting Tod had a long conversation with Jones and told him that Polk and his cabinet had become suspicious because Ashbel Smith, on his way to England, had passed right by Washington without calling on the President. With a remark that he was not responsible for Smith's acts, Jones proceeded to say that there never had been any doubt of or opposition to annexation. With apparent contradiction, however, Tod reported Jones to have said that "Major Donelson had conducted the affair very ably, and if it had not been for his prudence and good management, the last Congress would have involved the measure with much greater obstacles and probably defeated it." After predicting that there would be no war if the United States would "only keep quiet and cool," Jones said that there were two very

---

[44] *Buchanan Papers.* Tod was a Texas army captain and served as bearer of dispatches. Later, he was employed by Polk as special messenger to carry to President Jones a copy of the joint resolution of Congress which admitted Texas into the Union (Polk, *Diary*, I, 148).

[45] This was written on July 1. Evidently Donelson's opinion of Jones had undergone a change.

[46] Recently the Texan *chargé* at Washington.

unaccountable things connected with annexation: first, that the United States should feel any uneasiness, when the government as well as every man, woman, and child in Texas desired annexation; and second, that Elliot should have entertained any hope that the offer of independence or anything else would prevent Texas from joining the United States. He had, he said, told Elliot that he would lay his offer before the congress and the convention, but that he did not doubt that Texas would be annexed. " 'His object in obtaining the offer which he did from Mexico, was to strengthen the cause of Annexation, and place us on higher grounds with the world. It was truly a great advantage to our cause, that it disarmed Mexico entirely in the estimation of other Nations, and Mexico was fully aware of it.' "[47] Jones's statement that no attempt had been made to deceive Elliot accords with the reports which the British diplomat made to his own government.[48] Houston, also, testified that President Jones had not been guilty of double dealing and denied that European governments had been intriguing in Texas.[49] This denial does not, of course, mean that the ministers of England and France had not done all in their power to prevent annexation; but whether or not their activities amounted to *intrigue* depends upon the definition of the term. "At no time, in no manner," said Ashbel Smith long afterwards,

did the British government attempt to exercise or even hint the remotest wish to exercise any political influence in the affairs of Texas, or to possess any advantage, obtain any facility, enjoy any privilege that was not equally and as fully accorded to every other power in amity with Texas.[50]

On the day preceding that set for the assembling of the convention, some of the delegates, at an informal meeting,

---

[47] Under date of July 9, Tod said that the people of Texas were surprised because articles in American newspapers—even the Washington *Union*—expressed doubts that Texans sincerely desired annexation.

[48] Adams, *British Interests, etc.*, 216.

[49] J. Geo. Harris to Polk, June 12, 1845, *Polk Papers*. Harris had just seen Houston in Nashville.

[50] Smith, *Reminiscences of the Texas Republic*, 38.

drafted an ordinance expressing assent to the American joint resolution. Thus prepared, the convention, which formally organized on July 4, promptly voted to enter the Union, and by another vote agreed to wear crape for a month in memory of General Jackson. On the tenth, Allen, the Secretary of State, notified Elliot of the action taken by both the congress and the convention. When doing so, he pointed out that "these manifestations hardly admit of a doubt that the incorporation of Texas with the Federal Union is destined to an early consummation."[51] By the end of August the convention had finished drafting a constitution for the new state, and the second Monday in October was fixed as the day on which this constitution as well as the question of accepting the American offer of annexation should be submitted to a vote of the people. By November 10 President Jones was able to announce that the people had approved both annexation and the state constitution.[52]

Since both the government and the people of Texas had accepted the American offer, nothing remained to consummate annexation except formal admission into the Union by the Congress of the United States. When, therefore, Congress met in December, 1845, Polk announced that Texas had agreed to annexation and had submitted her new state constitution. Since this had been done, "the public faith of both parties is solemnly pledged to the compact of their union," and "strong reasons exist" why the new state should be admitted without delay.[53]

On December 10 Douglas reported from the House Committee on Territories a joint resolution which declared Texas to be a

---

[51] Allen to Elliot, July 10, 1845 (*Texas Diplomatic Correspondence*, III, 120). No further action was taken by Great Britain or her representatives, and Mexico was made clearly to understand that England would not support her in the event of trouble with the United States (Adams, *op. cit.*, 224–225).

[52] Smith, *Annexation of Texas*, 459–460. As late as September, W. D. Lee presented credentials as *chargé d' affaires* from the government of Texas, but Polk declined to recognize him in that capacity. Instead, he instructed Buchanan to deal with Lee as the agent of a state (Polk, *Diary*, I, 17–20).

[53] Richardson, *Messages*, IV, 386.

member of the Union on an equal footing with the original states. Although this resolution met with vigorous opposition, it was adopted eventually by a majority of nearly two-thirds. It was transmitted to the Senate where it encountered still further opposition, although there was small prospect that the dissenters would succeed in defeating it. Some of the Senators who had originally opposed annexation now agreed with the President that the national faith had been pledged, and the measure was adopted by a vote of thirty-one to fourteen. Within a short time the laws of the Union were extended over the new state, and the Republic of Texas ceased to exist. One important question, however, remained to be answered: What will Mexico do about it?

CHAPTER XVII

PRELUDE TO THE MEXICAN WAR

Under the promises made by President Polk, Texas, after the action taken by her convention on July 4, was entitled to the protection of the American army and navy. The query was raised at the time—and pressed vigorously by the Whigs afterwards—as to what constituted Texas and, consequently, what the United States was bound to protect. The joint resolution of the American Congress which Texas had just accepted had specified no definite boundary, but had consented to annexation "subject to the adjustment by this government of all questions of boundary that may arise with other governments." By an act passed on December 19, 1836, however, the Texan congress had declared the Rio Grande to be her boundary, although her territory as a department of Mexico had extended only to the Nueces; and early in his administration Polk expressed his determination to maintain the claim set up by Texas. Mexico herself made such a position easier by claiming all of Texas and by making no discrimination, at this time at least, between the land lying west of the Nueces and the rest of Texas. As above noted, however, Donelson did not believe that it would be either wise or necessary to provoke a war with Mexico by at once expelling the Mexican settlers on the east bank of the Rio Grande, or by stationing the military forces beyond the actual settlements made by Texas. But at the same time he made it clear that he did not intend by such a policy to abandon the claim to the Rio Grande as the boundary. On July 11, after his instruction to protect Texas had been made obligatory by the

acceptance of annexation by the convention, he again reverted
to the wisdom of such a policy. He told Buchanan that in his
correspondence with Texas he had avoided any discussion of the
boundary between Texas and Mexico, because the joint resolution
had left the question open, and the preliminary treaty of recognition arranged by Elliot had left the question in the same state.
Jones, in his truce proclamation, had in effect agreed to leave
matters as they were—with Texas in possession of part of this
territory, and Mexico in possession of another part. "What
the Executive of Texas," wrote Donelson, "had determined not
to fight for, but to settle by negotiation, to say the least of it,
could as well be left to the United States on the same conditions."
He added, however, that although he had not deemed it expedient
to discuss the boundary question,

> I have been far from advocating that the claim of Texas to the Rio
> Grande ought not to be maintained. This was not the question. It was
> whether, under the circumstances, we should take a position to make war
> for this claim, in the face of an acknowledgment on the part of this gov-
> ernment that it could be settled by negotiation.

In other words, he did not believe that the promise to protect
Texas made it incumbent upon the United States to expel immediately all Mexicans from the territory. What the United
States would decide to do on her own account was of course
another matter. Far from questioning the validity of the claim
to the Rio Grande as the boundary, Donelson, in the same letter,
suggested the grounds upon which this claim might be based.
They were the revolutionary rights of Texas, the agreement made
by Texas with Santa Anna in 1836, rights under the Louisiana
Purchase, and the capacity of Texas to maintain her claim by
force. The last, he said, Mexico herself had admitted but a short
time ago when she agreed to recognize the independence of
Texas.[1]

---

[1] Donelson to Buchanan, July 11, 1845 (*Sen. Doc. 1*, 29 Cong., 1 sess.,
101–103.)

In his letters to Donelson and Houston, Polk had made it clear that he would insist upon the Rio Grande as the boundary of Texas. The method by which he proposed to deal with the boundary question may be deduced from the instructions sent to the military and naval forces of the United States. It was in effect the same as that proposed by Donelson. On June 15, George Bancroft, temporarily in charge of the War Department, informed Taylor that the Texan convention would, in all probability, accept annexation on July 4, and that Texas would then be a part of the United States. Taylor was ordered to move his troops to the western frontier of Texas, with the Rio Grande as his ultimate destination. On July 8, Taylor was informed by Marcy that Mexico had some military posts on the east side of the Rio Grande, and that these were not to be molested "unless an actual state of war should exist." Similar instructions were sent to Commodore Conner on July 11, and in these Bancroft stated still more explicitly the policy of the administration. As soon as the Texan convention had approved annexation, Conner was to protect Texas like any other part of the United States, but it was the President's desire to avoid aggression and bloodshed.

That you may precisely understand what is meant by the aggression you are instructed to avoid, I will add, that while the annexation of Texas extends our boundary to the Del Norte, the President reserves the vindication of our boundary, if possible, to methods of peace.

For this reason, the Mexicans already on the east side of the river were not to be molested while peace continued. Positions were to be selected with regard to the health of the officers and men, and in "such a manner as will be most likely to disincline Mexico to acts of hostility." Should Mexico declare war, Conner was to dislodge all Mexican troops stationed east of the mouth of the Rio Grande, and *"if your force is sufficient,* [you] will take the castle of San Juan d'Ulla, it being the determination of the President to preserve peace, if possible; and, if war comes, to recover peace by adopting the most prompt and energetic measures."[2] A few days later the Washington *Union* said that it would be "difficult to estimate" the importance of Polk's energetic policy in deterring Mexico from hostile movements, and in giving confidence to the Texans.[3] On the other hand, the *National Intelligencer* asserted that Polk had, in order to induce Texas to accept annexation, made promises which exceeded his authority under the joint resolution.[4]

A private letter written by Polk late in July to a friend in Tennessee indicates that the demonstrations, at this time, of the military and naval forces on the Texas frontier were intended purely for defensive purposes. After speaking of the Texan convention and of sending the American forces to protect the new state, he said: "I do not however anticipate that Mexico will be mad enough to declare war. I think she would have done so but for the appearance of a strong naval force in the Gulf and our army moving in the direction of her frontier on land."[5] The fact that Polk saw such beneficial results from sending the troops toward the Mexican border doubtless explains why Marcy, two days later, wrote to Taylor that the President wished him to station a part of his army, at least, west of the Nueces.[6] His

---

[2] Bancroft to Conner, July 11, 1845 (*H. Ex. Doc. 60*, 30 Cong., 1 sess., 232–233. The "methods of peace" which the President wished to employ meant, no doubt, the vigorous pressing of American claims.

[3] "It was most fortunate that President Polk, and our minister, Mr. Donelson, were known in Texas to have held, during their whole lives the most intimate relations with the sage and patriot of the Hermitage, who had manifested so much solicitude for the re-union of Texas with the parent country," and they knew that "Young Hickory" would repel any interference (*Union*, July 14, 1845).

[4] But, it added, "why should any thing else be expected than that the Executive should pay just as little regard to the Joint Resolution as did they who passed it to the Constitution of the United States" (*Nat. Intell.*, July 19, 1845).

[5] Polk to A. O. P. Nicholson, July 28, 1845, *Polk Papers*.

[6] Taylor is still ordered to avoid aggressive measures toward Mexico as long as peace exists. "The Rio Grande is claimed to be the boundary between the two countries, and up to this boundary you are to extend your protection, only excepting any posts on the eastern side thereof, which are in the actual occupancy of Mexican settlements over which

object seems to have been to prevent a hostile act on the part of Mexico by showing her at once that the United States would protect Texas to the Rio Grande at all hazards; but at the same time, he wished to avoid acts that might unnecessarily precipitate a war.

On August 6, Taylor was notified by the Adjutant General that although war might not take place he was authorized to call upon Texas for additional troops. Such troops were to be "received into the service of the United States when actually required in the field to repel invasion, actual or menaced, and not before."[7]

On the day after this order was issued, but apparently without knowledge of it, the *National Intelligencer* expressed a fear that the President was about to make war upon Mexico. It admitted that *necessity* might justify Polk in defending Texas, but

the President is quite indefensible, if, in exceeding the measure of the necessity, he keep not strictly on the defensive and within the *settled limits* of the land, whose proper *population* merely, and not its territorial pretensions, it is now necessary to defend. But it is apparent that Texas claimed, and we fear it is equally apparent that the Executive has granted, the occupation of everything up to the Rio Grande; which occupation is nothing short (as everybody knows) of an invasion of Mexico. It is *offensive war*, and *not* the necessary defense of Texas. And should it prove, as we think it will, that the President has gone this additional length, then the President will be MAKING WAR, in the full sense of the word, on his own authority and beyond all plea of need, and even without any thought of asking legislative leave.[8]

This is a succinct statement of the "disputed territory" argument which was arrayed against the President by the Whigs

---

the Republic of Texas did not exercise jurisdiction at the period of annexation or shortly before that event. It is expected that, in selecting the establishment for your troops, you will approach as near the boundary line, the Rio Grande, as prudence will dictate. With this view, the President desires that your position, for a part of your forces at least, should be west of the river Nueces'' (*H. Ex. Doc. 60*, 30 Cong., 1 sess., 82–83).

[7] *Ibid.*, 83–84.

[8] *Nat. Intell.*, Aug. 7, 1845.

throughout the war period, and which has found its way into many histories and textbooks. The truth of the Whig assertion will be discussed later in this chapter; at this point it is sufficient to note that Americans, not Mexicans, first raised the cry of "disputed territory" as applied to the land lying between the Nueces and the Rio Grande. Mexico, at this time, laid no greater claim to this land than to the rest of Texas. In her eyes, the crossing of the Sabine was an invasion of Mexico and an act of war. To the assertions made by the *National Intelligencer* the *Union* answered that "Texas assumed by law" all territory to the Rio del Norte, including Santa Fé, to which the *National Intelligencer* retorted that their fears as to the President's position were now fully admitted. In reply to the charge made that going to the Rio Grande would be an offensive and not a defensive act, the *Union*, a few days later, cited a letter written by Robert J. Walker which "proves" that Texas as a part of the Louisiana Purchase had extended to the Rio Grande. It cited also a speech made by Walker in the Senate wherein he had quoted the organic law of Texas which essayed to fix the boundary line. Just how Walker's letters and speeches could *prove* anything it is not easy to see, but the *Union* accepted them as proof and from it argued that Polk was bound to enforce the law to the Rio Grande.[9] The President was far more disturbed by the annoyances of dispensing patronage than by the criticisms of the Whigs, and the success of annexation convinced him more than ever of the wisdom of the method that had been selected.[10]

The officials in Washington were rather in the dark regarding the plans and purposes of Mexico, yet on August 23, Marcy informed Taylor that there "is reason to believe" that Mexico is preparing to invade Texas. Upon what this belief was based

---

[9] *Nat. Intell.*, Aug. 9. *Union*, Aug. 11, 1845. For a discussion of the Spanish boundaries of Texas, see Garrison, *Westward Extension*, chap. vii.

[10] Polk to Senator Haywood, Aug. 9, 1845, *Polk Papers*. He expressed the opinion that Texas would have been lost to the Union had the Benton alternative been selected.

the letter does not state, but it was probably based on information given to the Department of State by Baron Gerolt, the Prussian minister at Washington. In a conversation with George Bancroft, Gerolt said that he had received authentic information from Mexico, under date of June 28, to the effect that Mexico was making preparations to invade Texas. Gerolt's informant stated that General Arista with three thousand men, chiefly cavalry, had been ordered to move toward the Del Norte, while Paredes, the commander-in-chief, and General Felisola, were ready to follow with a force of ten thousand men. Gerolt himself believed that the United States must expect protracted guerrilla warfare. Bancroft at once addressed a letter to Buchanan imparting the above information. Buchanan was away at the time, but Mason, who was acting in his stead, showed the letter to the President. Polk accepted the information as reliable. He thought it likely that the Mexicans would cross the Rio Grande, for the American forces already on the ground would be unable to prevent it. He took steps immediately to send additional forces to Texas, and in a letter to Buchanan he urged the Secretary of State to return as soon as possible to take up his duties, and especially, to hasten the settlement of the Oregon question.[11] Taylor was authorized by Marcy to accept volunteers from certain designated states, and, ''should Mexico declare war, or commence hostilities by crossing the Rio Grande with a considerable force,'' he was to lose no time in letting these states know the number of troops needed.[12] This order was followed a week later by another which was more aggressive in tone. Marcy complained of lack of information regarding the activities of

---

[11] Bancroft to Buchanan, Aug. 7; Polk to Buchanan, Aug. 7, 1845 (Buchanan, *Works*, 223–224). Copy of the latter in *Polk Papers*. Buchanan did not share the President's apprehensions caused by Gerolt's information and views. In reply to Polk's letter he stated his belief that the American forces on the Rio Grande should be strengthened, but that the movement of the Mexican troops was mainly a demonstration to insure Herrera's election (Buchanan to Polk, Aug. 11, 1845, *Polk Papers*).

[12] Marcy to Taylor, Aug. 23, 1845 (*H. Ex. Doc. 60*, 30 Cong., 1 sess., 84–85).

Mexico and urged Taylor to write frequently to the War Department. "You have been advised," said Marcy,

that the assembling of a large Mexican army on the borders of Texas, and crossing the Rio Grande with a considerable force, will be regarded by the Executive here as an invasion of the United States, and the commencement of hostilities. An *attempt* to cross that river with such a force will also be considered in the same light.

In case of war, "either declared or made manifest by hostile acts," Taylor's main object was to be the protection of Texas, but in pursuit of this object he was authorized to cross the Rio Grande and take Matamoras and other places.[13] Polk at this time considered the propriety of convening Congress in the event of a declaration of war or an invasion of Texas by Mexico, but Senator Bagby, of Alabama, and perhaps others, advised against such a course.[14] The new order to Taylor was decided upon at a cabinet meeting held on the twenty-ninth of August.[15] It did not, however, result from any sudden panic in administration circles,[16] and Polk has been condemned for holding that even an attempt to cross the river would be an act of war. He has been condemned also for asserting that the crossing of that river by a Mexican army would be "an invasion of the United States."[17] But if it be conceded that Texas extended to the Rio Grande, then the ground taken in the new order was no more aggressive than that taken in the former. It was certainly the duty of the President to defend Texas, and if Texas did extend to the Rio Grande, an attempt to cross the river would indicate the disposition of Mexico to invade the United States quite as well as the actual crossing. Nations do not wait until a hostile fleet is within the three-mile jurisdiction limit before steps are

---

[13] Marcy to Taylor, Aug. 30, 1845, *ibid.*, 88–89.

[14] Polk, *Diary*, I, 12–13.

[15] *Ibid.*, 8–10.

[16] The Adjutant General had written only three days before, August 26, that the country was filled with rumors of movements of Mexican troops, but that they were believed to be exaggerated or untrue (*H. Ex. Doc. 60*, 30 Cong., 1 sess., 87).

[17] E. g., von Holst, *History of the United States* (Eng. ed.), III, 98–103.

taken to repel it. Why should they take greater chances when an invasion by land is threatened?

Whether the land on the east bank of the Rio Grande *was* legally a part of the United States is open to more serious question. From the first, Polk had claimed it to be a part of Texas and consequently of the United States. His right to do so involves points of constitutional law which the writer will not attempt to determine, although some phases of annexation may be recalled in order to indicate the questions upon which such a determination must be based. The joint resolution under which Texas had been annexed did not specify any territorial limits, but left that matter "subject to the adjustment by this government of all questions of boundary that may arise with other governments." The Texan claim to the Rio Grande rested mainly on the agreement made with Santa Anna after his defeat at San Jacinto in which he agreed to withdraw beyond the Rio Grande,[18] and on the act passed by the Texan Congress on December 19, 1836, which had declared that river to be the boundary of the republic. Whatever claim these transactions may have established passed, of course, to the United States. Without attempting to determine the effect of these events on the legal right of Texas to all land east of the Rio Grande, it may be noted that Santa Anna made his agreement under duress and perhaps without authority; and it is by no means certain that Texas could lawfully enlarge her territory by an ordinary legislative enactment. The United States government claimed, also, that Texas as a part of the Louisiana Purchase had extended to the Rio Grande; but, as Abraham Lincoln exclaimed in Congress, "what, under heaven, had that to do with the present boundary between us and Mexico?"[19] All claim to this region had been transferred to Spain by the Florida treaty of 1819. Congress, when passing the joint resolution, had left the boundary for future settlement;

---

[18] This agreement is printed in *Niles' Register,* L, 336.

[19] Lincoln, *Works* (Tandy ed.), I, 322.

and both Texas and Mexico, in the project of a treaty had, in March, 1845, agreed to settle the question by negotiation. By declaring all land east of the Rio Grande to be a part of the United States Polk may, indeed, have exceeded his authority, but it does not follow necessarily from this, so long as Texas asserted ownership, that the President was under no obligation to prevent a hostile army from entering the territory until the question of title could be determined. General Jackson and his loyal adherents had always held that the United States could never be adequately protected until it extended to the Rio Grande, and Polk had promised the Texans to maintain this boundary. Apparently the President attached more importance to these considerations than to an analysis of his constitutional powers.

Various letters written by General Taylor after his arrival in Texas in July, 1845, informed the Adjutant General of rumors that Mexico was preparing to invade Texas. As time passed, however, he came to regard these rumors as groundless, and by September he reported that reliable agents had ascertained that the Mexican government was not mobilizing its forces on the border. Taylor believed that the assembling of the American army along the Nueces had had a deterrent effect upon the Mexicans, but in October he advised a forward movement to the Rio Grande. "It is with great deference," he wrote to the Adjutant General,

that I make any suggestions on topics which may become matter of delicate negotiation; but if our government, in settling the question of boundary, makes the line of the Rio Grande an ultimatum, I cannot doubt that the settlement will be greatly facilitated and hastened by our taking possession at once of one or two points on or quite near that river. Our strength and state of preparation should be displayed in a manner not to be mistaken.

As Mexico had not yet either declared war or committed any overt act of hostility, he did not feel authorized to take this step without further orders from the War Department.[20] In a letter

[20] Taylor to Jones, Oct. 4, 1845 (*H. Ex. Doc. 60,* 30 Cong., 1 sess., 108).

dated October 16 Marcy suggested to Taylor the expediency of putting his army into winter huts, but in this as in other military matters the general was given wide discretion. By the first of November Taylor had received this letter, and on the fifth a letter from Commodore Conner informed him that W. S. Parrott had set out for Washington bearing a message that Mexico was willing to negotiate the questions in dispute between the two countries. Taylor deemed it unnecessary to build winter huts for his troops, but, with negotiations about to begin, he did not believe himself authorized to move to the Rio Grande. He nevertheless urged the occupation of posts on the boundary line at the earliest possible date.[21] Parrott was Polk's confidential agent in Mexico. He had been selected for this position soon after Almonte, the Mexican minister at Washington, had demanded his passports, and, on April 3, 1845, had taken passage on the same steamer that carried Almonte from New York to Mexico. He had at one time practiced dentistry in Mexico, and, later, had engaged in business there. He held a much inflated claim against the Mexican government, but of this Polk was probably not aware.[22] His selection was due no doubt to his knowledge of the Spanish language, for otherwise he was ill fitted for such a mission. Parrott's instructions bore the date of March 28, 1845, and at that time the President seems to have believed an immediate declaration of war by Mexico to be highly probable. On his arrival at Vera Cruz, if he should find that Mexico had actually commenced open hostilities against the United States, Parrott was to return immediately. In that case the administration was determined to "act promptly and vigorously in maintaining the rights and honor of the country." Should hostilities not have begun, the main object of his mission was to ascertain whether Mexico would renew diplomatic relations, and to do everything that could discreetly be done to

[21] Marcy to Taylor, Oct. 16; Conner to Taylor, Oct. 24; Taylor to Jones, Nov. 7, 1845 (*ibid.*, 89, 111, 112).

[22] Reeves, *American Diplomacy under Tyler and Polk*, 268–269.

bring this about. He was to get in touch with the high officials, if possible, and to let them know that, while Texas under no circumstances could be abandoned, the United States was prepared to settle other questions "in a liberal and friendly spirit." He was not to disclose his official character until it had been clearly ascertained that Mexico was ready to renew diplomatic relations, but the nature of his mission was soon discovered by the Mexican government.[23] The "liberal and friendly spirit" included, no doubt, the purchase of Cailfornia and New Mexico, although there seems to be no direct evidence that plans for such a purchase had been definitely formulated at this early date. In his correspondence with Buchanan, however, Parrott emphasized the danger of the seizure of Upper California by Great Britain. He did not believe that Mexico would go to war with the United States on account of Texas, but he nevertheless recommended a chastisement of that country. On August 26, he reported that Herrera and his new cabinet would not go to war, and that there was a desire, even publicly manifested, to receive a "commissioner" from the United States. He believed that an "Envoy possessing suitable qualifications for this Court might with comparative ease settle *over a breakfast* the most important national question."[24] Parrott's dispatch and others sent by John Black, United States consul at Mexico, and by F. M. Dimond, United States consul at Vera Cruz, of similar import, were discussed at a cabinet meeting held on September 16. It should be noted that Parrott used both terms, *commissioner* and *envoy*, for it is possible that this may have misled President Polk as to the desire of the Mexican government. At any rate Polk chose to regard Parrott's statement as assurance that Mexico would receive a "minister," and he determined at once to send an official of that character. It would be interesting to know

---

[23] Buchanan to Parrott, March 28, 1845 (Buchanan *Works,* VI, 132–134); Reeves, *op. cit.,* 269–270.

[24] Parrott to Buchanan, Aug. 26, 1845; quoted by Reeves, *op. cit.,* 271.

whether Polk had really been misled by Parrott's letter or whether he deliberately determined to send a regular minister regardless of the wishes of Mexico, for the nature of the credentials given to the American diplomat was later given by Mexico as the reason for declining to receive him. At the cabinet meeting just mentioned, it was decided that the mission should be offered to John Slidell, of New Orleans. The President recorded in his diary that one great object of the mission would be

to adjust a permanent boundary between Mexico and the U. States, and in doing this the Minister would be instructed to purchase for a pecuniary consideration Upper California and New Mexico. He [the President] said that a better boundary would be the Del Norte from its mouth to the Passo [El Paso], in latitude 32° North, and thence West to the Pacific Ocean, Mexico ceding to the U. S. all the country East and North of these lines.

He believed that such a boundary might be procured for fifteen or twenty millions of dollars, but he was willing to pay as high as forty millions.[25] Here is an explicit statement of Polk's determination to purchase California, if possible. He probably had this method in mind when, shortly after his inauguration, he declared to Bancroft[26] that one of the great measures of his administration would be the acquisition of that country.

News of recent threats of war by the Mexican government, published in the New Orleans papers, led Polk to believe that Parrott had been mistaken, and he decided that it would be inexpedient to send Slidell until the facts could be ascertained. However, he wrote a confidential letter to Slidell asking him to accept the appointment and to be ready to leave for Mexico on a day's notice.[27]

About a month later the President sent for Benton, and sought his advice concerning both Oregon and California, although there had been no intercourse between the two men since the Missouri Senator had so bitterly denounced the rejection

---

[25] Polk, *Diary,* I, 33–35.   [27] Polk, *Diary,* I, 35–36.
[26] See page 351.

of Van Buren by the Baltimore Convention. He told Benton that he thought of reasserting the Monroe doctrine against the planting of any foreign colony on the North American continent. His immediate object was to forestall any contemplated British colony in California. Benton approved such a course, generally, but doubted that the doctrine could be applied to the Frazer River valley in which the British had made discoveries and settlements.[28] Polk's anxiety about California had been increased by a dispatch received from Thomas O. Larkin, American consul at Monterey, California, which bore the date of July 10, 1845.[29] This dispatch stated that the agent of the Hudson's Bay Company had formerly furnished the Californians with arms and money to enable them to expel the Mexicans from that country, but that now Great Britain was instigating a Mexican invasion of California. He stated, also, that England maintained a vice-consul and France a consul in California, although they apparently transacted no commercial business. It was inferred from this that the two governments had designs on that province.

While he awaited developments in Mexico before sending instructions and a commission to Slidell, and influenced probably by the news received from the consul at Monterey, the President caused Buchanan to write a letter to Larkin, under date of October 17, 1845. Larkin was already consul at Monterey, and he was now, in addition, made a confidential agent in California. Polk's desire for California and the method by which he hoped to acquire it are made very clear in this letter. It is made equally clear that whether or not he should be able to acquire it for the United States, he was determined to resist its transfer to either Great Britain or France. "The future destiny" of California, wrote Buchanan, "is a subject of anxious solicitude for the Government and people of the United States." For this

---

[28] *Ibid.*, 70–71.

[29] Mentioned in Buchanan's letter to Larkin, Oct. 17, 1845, *infra*.

reason the President "could not view with indifference the transfer of California to Great Britain or any other Power. The system of colonization by foreign Monarchies on the North American continent must and will be resisted by the United States." Larkin was told that "this Government had no ambitious aspirations to gratify and no desire to extend our federal system over more territory than we already possess, unless by the free and spontaneous wish of the independent people of adjoining territories." After reiterating that the United States would "vigorously interpose" to prevent California from becoming a British or a French colony, Buchanan continued:

> Whilst the President will make no effort and use no influence to induce California to become one of the free and independent States of this Union, yet if the people should desire to unite their destiny with ours, they would be received as brethren, whenever this can be done without affording Mexico just cause of complaint. Their true policy for the present in regard to this question, is to let events take their course, unless an attempt should be made to transfer them without their consent either to Great Britain or France. This they ought to resist by all the means in their power, as ruinous to their best interests and destructive of their freedom and independence.

Larkin was asked to assure the Californians of the friendship of the United States and to ascertain their feelings toward this and other countries. He was instructed further to gather various statistics and to inform his government generally regarding affairs in California.[30] Clearly Polk had hopes that the Texas program might be reënacted in California. Apparently, no conquest of this region was contemplated, unless, perhaps Great Britain or France should attempt to seize or colonize it. He was willing, of course, to purchase both California and New Mexico and thereby settle the whole question both peaceably and speedily. His constitutional authority to declare the so-called "disputed territory" to be a part of the United States has been

---

30 Buchanan to Larkin, Oct. 17, 1845, brought to California by Commodore Stockton (MS in *Larkin Papers*, Bancroft Library, Univ. of Calif.) There is a printed copy in Buchanan, *Works*, VI, 275–278.

seriously questioned; it may be questioned, also, whether his promise to ''receive as brethren'' the Californians was not a stretching of executive powers.

The President appointed Lieutenant Archibald H. Gillespie, of the marine corps, confidential agent and assigned to him the duty of repairing to California to coöperate with Larkin. He was given a copy of the written instructions to Larkin, and was made the bearer of verbal instructions to both Larkin and Fremont. Just what these verbal instructions were no one has been able to ascertain with any degree of certainty. Buchanan's letter to Larkin bore the date October 17, but Gillespie was still in Washington as late as October 30. On that date Polk recorded in his diary that he had just held a confidential conversation with Gillespie concerning his secret mission, and added that ''his secret instructions & the letter to Mr. Larkin,—will explain the object of his mission.''[31] The letter to Larkin tells its own story, but the ''secret instructions'' to Gillespie have been the subject of considerable speculation. The latter will be considered in connection with the operations of Fremont.

The President did not confine his activities with respect to California to the sending of Gillespie with instructions for the consul at Monterey. While Buchanan was preparing these instructions, Bancroft, by the President's order, was inditing secret orders for Commodores Stockton and Sloat. These, too, were given the official date of October 17, 1845.

Commodore John D. Sloat had been for some time in command of the naval forces on the Pacific, and as early as June 24 Bancroft had sent him ''secret and confidential'' orders to seize San Francisco and blockade other ports, if he should ''ascertain with certainty'' that Mexico had declared war against the United States.[32] By the order of October 17 he was told that ''in the event of actual hostilities'' he was to dispose of his entire force

---

[31] Polk, *Diary*, I, 83–84.

[32] *H. Ex. Doc. 60*, 30 Cong., 1 sess., 231.

"so as to carry out most effectually the objects specified in the instructions forwarded to you from the Department in view of such a contingency."[33]

Commodore Robert F. Stockton was given command of the frigate *Congress* which had been equipped at Norfolk for duty in the Pacific. His sealed orders, which were not to be opened until he had passed beyond "the Capes of Virginia," directed him to proceed to the Sandwich Islands, and, eventually, to join the squadron of Commodore Sloat. To Stockton were intrusted the originals of the instructions to Sloat and Larkin, duplicates of which, as we have seen, were sent overland in care of Lieutenant Gillespie.

On November 9, 1845, Parrott reached Washington bearing a note from the Mexican Secretary of Foreign Affairs which expressed the willingness of his government to receive a commissioner from the United States.[34] Three days before Parrott's letter arrived, however, Bancroft had received a dispatch from Commodore Conner which stated that Mexico was willing to negotiate, and the President had directed Buchanan immediately to prepare instructions for Slidell. Slidell's commission was signed on the tenth, and this with his instructions was conveyed to him by Lieutenant Lanier of the navy. Parrott was selected as his secretary of legation.[35]

Slidell's instructions were an elaboration of the plans for territorial expansion which the President had laid before his cabinet on the sixteenth of September.[36] To Larkin had been assigned the task of winning the good will of the Californians, and of letting them know that they would be welcomed into the

---

[33] See Rives, *United States and Mexico*, II, 168.

[34] Polk, *Diary*, I, 93. Polk says that Mexico agreed to receive a *minister*. This, however, is an error, for the Secretary clearly said a "commissioner" . . . "to settle the present dispute" (Peña y Peña to Black, Oct. 15, 1845, in *H. Ex. Doc. 60*, 30 Cong., 1 sess., 16).

[35] Polk, *Diary*, I, 91–94.

[36] See above, p. 385.

Union should they see fit to declare their independence; to Slidell authority was given to adjust the boundary question, and to purchase New Mexico and California, if possible. Taken together these documents indicate the ardent desire of the President to extend the United States to the Pacific, as well as the methods by which he hoped to accomplish his purpose.

The instructions to Slidell first of all reiterated the substance of the Monroe Doctrine and insisted that the United States could not permit the establishment of European colonies in North America. He was instructed to notify Mexico that the United States had waited long and patiently for Mexico to pay the just claims of American citizens, but that "these claims must now speedily be adjusted in a satisfactory manner." It was well known, Buchanan pointed out, that Mexico could not pay in money, but "fortunately" the provision in the joint resolution of annexation relating to the adjustment of boundaries presented a means of satisfying these claims, "in perfect consistency with the interests as well as the honor of both Republics." The means was the assumption of the claims by the government of the United States, and the cession of territory by Mexico as a compensation therefor. With this introduction Buchanan proceeded to discuss boundaries and the lands that might be claimed or purchased. The independence and the annexation of Texas must be considered as settled facts. The United States based her claim to the Rio Grande as the boundary of Texas on the act passed by the Texan Congress on December 19, 1836, and on the fact that that river had been the boundary of the Louisiana Purchase; although Buchanan himself admitted that all rights under the latter had been transferred to Spain in 1819 by the Florida treaty. He did not claim that New Mexico had belonged to Texas or had come with that republic into the possession of the United States. To "obviate the danger of future collisions," however, the American government would, in exchange for it, assume all claims of her citizens against Mexico and pay in addition five millions of dollars. In case Mexico should be unwilling to cede any lands west of the Rio Grande, then the claims would be assumed but the five millions would not be paid. If either of these objects could be attained, Slidell was authorized to conclude a treaty with Mexico.

Reeves, in his *American Diplomacy under Tyler and Polk,* makes the over-confident assertion that

Parrott's mission and Slidell's instructions taken together prove two things: (1) that the Mexican War was *not* the result of the annexation of Texas, and (2) that the reopening of diplomatic relations with Mexico was for the purpose of securing California by purchase.[37]

That one of the motives for seeking to reopen diplomatic relations was the desire to purchase California may be granted at once. But precisely how Parrott's mission and Slidell's instructions *prove* that the acquisition of this region was the main purpose of the administration, or that war did not result from the annexation of Texas the present writer is unable to see. Other evidence, which will be offered presently, indicates that Polk decided to wage war because Mexico had failed to satisfy the American claims; but instead of proving that the Mexican war was waged ''for the fulfillment of Polk's designs upon California,''[38] Slidell's instructions indicate that the President, at the time these instructions were drafted, was ready to release Mexico from further obligation if she would cede only a part of New Mexico. Should he find it impossible to make better terms, Slidell was specifically authorized to conclude a treaty by which the United States would assume all claims if Mexico in return would cede that part of New Mexico lying east of the Rio Grande. Had Slidell been able to conclude such a treaty, Polk would have been deprived of all means of bringing pressure to bear on Mexico, except unprovoked military conquest. To be sure, the President was eager to acquire California. Larkin had been

---

[37] Reeves, 275. He is speaking here of Slidell's original instructions.
[38] *Ibid.*, 288.

instructed to assure the Californians that they would be welcomed into the Union should they see fit to separate from Mexico,
and now Slidell was instructed to purchase that territory, and
was told that "money would be no object when compared with
the value of the acquisition." He was told, also, that his mission
was "one of the most delicate and important which has ever
been confided to a citizen of the United States," nevertheless
there was not the slightest hint that the President had any intention of resorting to force in the event that Mexico should refuse
her consent to the sale. On the contrary, as above noted, Slidell
was to conclude a treaty which would assume all claims even
though Mexico should confine her cession to territory on the east
side of the Rio Grande. It would seem that, at this time, Polk's
plan to acquire California was limited to purchase or to "manifest destiny" of the type that had succeeded so well in Texas.
The outbreak of war was soon followed by the conquest of California, but this fact alone does not prove that the war "was
waged for the purpose of conquest, for the fulfillment of Polk's
designs upon California." Polk may have welcomed the war—
possibly he may have provoked it—but his offer to cancel the
claims for so small a tract of land seems to show that forcible
conquest was not his intention at the time that Slidell was sent
to Mexico.

Slidell was sent to Mexico in the capacity of envoy extraordinary and minister plenipotentiary, not simply as a commissioner to settle disputes incident to the annexation of Texas.
The reception of a minister would have the effect of fully restoring diplomatic relations and of paving the way for the discussion
of all questions concerning which that minister might bear
instructions—unpaid claims, for example. For this reason Mexico declined to receive Slidell. According to a statement made
long afterwards by Bejamin E. Green,[39] secretary of legation

---

[39] The statement is dated Aug. 8, 1889 (Tyler, *Letters and Times of the
Tylers*, III, 176).

at Mexico in 1844, President Polk had been informed, before sending Slidell, that President Herrera would receive a commissioner, and that he was ready to settle all disputes and to cede New Mexico and California to the United States. He was told, on the other hand, according to the same statement, that the Herrera government doubted its ability to sustain itself against the power of Santa Anna if it should receive an ordinary minister as though nothing had happened. If this be true, then Polk must have known that, in all probability, Slidell would not be received, and his sincerity in sending the envoy may be seriously questioned. But it seems incredible that the President would deliberately jeopardize the success of a mission which promised to procure everything he could desire, even California, simply to gratify a whim of sending to Mexico the particular kind of a diplomatic agent which she did not want. Some allowance should be made for the fact that Green's statement was made many years after the event and that he was the son of Duff Green, the champion of Calhoun and the uncompromising opponent of Polk.[40]

On December 2, 1845, before the American envoy had reached his destination, Polk submitted to Congress his first annual message. In it he officially informed that body of the annexation of Texas, despite "British and French interference"; of the severance of diplomatic relations by Mexico; and of Slidell's mission. While expressing a "sincere desire for a peaceful adjustment of all difficulties," the message hinted at drastic measures in the event that negotiations should fail:

---

[40] It is true, of course, that Polk had before him the letter of Peña y Peña, which agreed to receive a commissioner and said nothing about a minister. See p. 389, note 34. It is true, also, that Joel R. Poinsett wrote soon after war was declared that "I took the liberty of remonstrating to one in the confidence of the government that the Mexican govt would not and dared not receive our Minister Plenipotentiary but could and would receive a Commissioner and that any movement of our troops from the Nueces would lead to hostilities. The reply was not to be uneasy. The Mexicans would not cross the Rio Grande to attack our troops & Genl Taylor had orders to remain on this side of the river, that a war with Mexico depended altogether upon the state of our relations with England" (Poinsett to Van Buren, May 26, 1846, *Van Buren Papers*).

The minister appointed has set out on his mission and is probably by this time near the Mexican capital. He has been instructed to bring the negotiation with which he is charged to a conclusion at the earliest practicable period, which it is expected will be in time to enable me to communicate the result to Congress during the present session. Until that result is known I forbear to recommend to Congress such ulterior measures of redress for the wrongs and injuries we have long borne as it would have been proper to make had no such negotiation been instituted.

This passage indicates that, even at this early date, the President believed that the United States had ample ground for war and that he would not hesitate to recommend it if Slidell's mission should end in failure.

Polk's reference to British and French interference in Texan affairs and his allusions to the Monroe Doctrine in connection with the Oregon question were not relished in British official circles. When reporting this fact to the President, McLane wrote that "a favorate scheme of the leading powers of Europe is to compose the Mexican troubles by giving her a settled monarchical form of Government, and supplying the monarch from one of their own families."[41] Doubtless McLane greatly exaggerated the desire for a Mexican monarchy, but his report harmonized so well with the suspicions already held by the administration that his opinions were probably accepted at face value.

Slidell arrived at the Mexican capital on December 6, 1845. His secretary of legation, Parrott, soon followed, accompanied

---

[41] McLane to Polk, Jan. 17, 1846, *Polk Papers*. Before the receipt of the message in England, the British press had spoken in praise of Polk's success in acquiring Texas. For example, the morning *Chronicle* said: "That immense question, the annexation of Texas, which seemed so difficult to solve that it affrighted the boldest men and parties, has been achieved by Mr. Polk in a thrice. The activity of English envoys, the suppleness of the French, the efforts of the most able and most eloquent partisans at home, all pointed at and making against annexation! All obstacles have been overcome. European interference has given color of reason to the act of annexation which it wanted before, since the measure was one which defeated and annulled European intervention. Then the great objection was that it would produce war. Annexation, however desirable, argued the Whigs, is not worth a drop of blood; but lo! it has not cost a drop of blood—the Mexicans are paralyzed.". Quoted by the Washington *Union*, Jan. 2, 1846.

by Gillespie, who was on his way to California as bearer of dispatches to Larkin and Fremont. Black, the American consul at Mexico, had met Slidell at Puebla and informed him that the Mexican government was much perturbed by his early arrival, as he had not been expected until January. President Herrera seems to have feared that the arrival of the American envoy would be used by his enemies to undermine his power. There was foundation for this belief. Broadsides appeared warning the people that Slidell had come to acquire from the Herrera government not only Texas but New Mexico and the Californias, consequently to receive him would be treasonable. Peña y Peña, the Secretary of Foreign Affairs, promptly refused to receive Parrott as secretary of legation, because of his former activities in Mexico; but as to Slidell, he adopted a temporizing policy. His first objection, as already stated, was the early date of the envoy's arrival. After the receipt of Slidell's credentials, the Secretary had a more tangible ground for objection. He pointed out to Black that Mexico had agreed to receive a commissioner to negotiate the Texas dispute, but that Slidell's credentials represented him to be a minister resident. On this ground the Mexican government declined to receive the American diplomat.[42] Slidell did not, however, regard this as a final rejection, for on December 31, Herrera was forced to relinquish the government of Mexico, and on January 2, 1846, General Paredes became President, *ad interim*. It now remained for Slidell to seek recognition from the new government, and he repaired to Jalapa to await developments.

On January 28, 1846, after he had received Slidell's letter of December 17 which reported that the Mexican government had declined to receive him until it had given the matter further consideration, Buchanan wrote again to Slidell, approving his

---

[42] Black to Slidell, Dec. 15; Slidell to Buchanan, Dec. 17; Peña y Peña to Slidell, Dec. 20, 1845 (*H. Ex. Doc. 60*, 30 Cong., 1 sess., 23–27, 28–30, 37).

conduct and giving him further directions. As it was morally certain, said Buchanan, that Paredes would gain control of the government, Slidell was directed to apply again for recognition. The President, he was told, desired to preserve peace, because both inclination and policy dictated this course.

Should the Mexican Government, however, finally refuse to receive you, the cup of forbearance will then have been exhausted. Nothing can remain but to take the redress of the injuries to our citizens and the insults to our Government into our hands. In view of this serious alternative, every honorable effort should be made before a final rupture.

Slidell was therefore to wait a reasonable time for Mexico to decide on his reception, unless he should discover that she was inclined to trifle with "this Government." The length of time and the evidence of trifling were left to the envoy's discretion to determine. It will be noted that the President regarded a refusal to receive Slidell and a failure to pay the claims immediately as ample grounds for taking redress into his own hands— in other words, for making war on Mexico. Protection of Texas from threatened invasion had nothing to do with the question then under discussion. To make still more clear the President's intentions, Slidell was told in another paragraph that in case Mexico should finally decline to receive him he was to demand his passports and return to the United States. "It will then become the duty of the President to submit the whole case to Congress and call upon the nation to assert its just rights and avenge its injured honor." Additional naval forces had been sent to the Mexican coast and "should war become inevitable, the President will be prepared to conduct it with vigor."[43]

While Slidell was seeking an audience in Mexico an agent of Santa Anna (then in exile in Cuba) appeared in Washington and obtained an interview with President Polk. This agent was Colonel Alexander J. Atocha, a Spaniard by birth but a naturalized citizen of the United States. As a friend of Santa Anna he

---

[43] Buchanan, *Works*, VI, 363–365.

had been arrested when that wily ruler's government was overthrown, but on proving his American citizenship he was released and banished. He had called on Polk in June, 1845, for the purpose of urging the United States government to press certain claims which he held against Mexico. He had now returned from a visit to Santa Anna in Havana, prepared to lay before Polk the views of the ex-dictator. In his diary under date of February 13, 1846, Polk stated that Atocha called on that day, and the substance of the conversation was recorded. Atocha represented Santa Anna to be in constant communication with the Mexican leaders.

He said that Santa Anna approved the revolution headed by Paredes and that Santa Anna was in favour of a Treaty with the U. S., and that in adjusting a boundary between the two countries the Del Norte should be the Western Texas line, and the Colorado of the West down through the Bay of San Francisco to the Sea should be the Mexican line on the North, and that Mexico should cede all East and North of these natural boundaries to the U. S. for a pecuniary consideration, and mentioned thirty millions of Dollars as the sum.

This amount, Santa Anna believed, would pay the most pressing debts of Mexico and support the army until conditions had improved.

Col. Atocha said that Santa Anna was surprised that the U. S. Naval force had been withdrawn from Vera Cruz last fall, and that Gen'l Taylor's army was kept at Corpus Christi instead of being stationed on the Del Norte; and that the U. S. would never be able to treat with Mexico, without the presence of an imposing force by land and sea, and this, Col. Atocha added, was his own opinion. Col. Atocha did not say that he was sent by Santa Anna to hold this conversation with me; but I think it probable he was so.

Atocha requested that the conversation should be considered confidential, and said that he had more to communicate.[44]

Polk was evidently much interested in the views expressed by Atocha, and at a regular cabinet meeting held on the following day he related to the members the substance of the

---

[44] Polk, *Diary*, I, 222–225.

conversation. The idea of sending a confidential agent to confer with Santa Anna was mentioned. Walker was inclined to favor such a course, but Buchanan was decidedly opposed to it. The President said that although he did not propose to send such an agent, if one should be sent, C. P. Van Ness, former minister to Spain, would be the best man that could be selected.[45] Atocha called again to see the President on the sixteenth of February. After discussing relations with Mexico for nearly an hour the conversation was adjourned until afternoon when it was continued for more than an hour. Atocha repeated what he had said on February 13. Polk told him that Mexico must satisfy the claims of American citizens and that if her government had any proposition to make, such as he had suggested, the United States would consider it after it had been made. Atocha then pointed out that no government of Mexico would dare to make such an offer and that it ''must appear to be forced to agree to such a proposition.'' It was the opinion of Atocha himself and of Santa Anna that

our [United States] army should be marched at once from Corpus Christi to the Del Norte, and a strong Naval force assembled at Vera Cruz, that Mr. Slidell, the U. S. Minister, should withdraw from Jalappa, and go on board one of our ships of War at Vera Cruz, and in that position should demand the payment of [the] amount due our citizens; that it was well known the Mexican Government was unable to pay in money, and that when they saw a strong force ready to strike on their coasts and border, they would, he had no doubt, feel their danger and agree to the boundary suggested. He said that Paredes, Almonte, & Gen'l Santa Anna were all willing for such an arrangement, but that they dare not make it until it was made apparent to the Archbishop of Mexico & the people generally that it was necessary to save their country from a war with the U. States. He said the last words which Gen'l Santa Anna said to him when he was leaving Havanna a month ago was, ''when you see the President, tell him to take strong measures, and such a Treaty can be made & I will sustain it.''

Atocha said that Mexico owed half a million dollars to the archbishop, and that he could be reconciled by assurance that he would be paid as soon as Mexico had obtained the money from

---

45 *Ibid.*, 226.

the United States. He reported Santa Anna as having said that he could be in Mexico in April or May and would probably "go into power again," but that he and Paredes must have money to sustain themselves. With half a million in hand, they could make the treaty and retain control until the balance had been paid. Arista, he said, was friendly to the United States and in favor of ceding the northern departments to that country —in fact, he was anxious to do so, as he owned a large plantation near Monterey. Atocha intimated an intention to return to Havana and seemed desirous of getting Polk's views to carry to Santa Anna, but the President remained silent. Polk thought him to be a man of talents, but one who could not be trusted; "I therefore heard all he said but communicated nothing to him."[46] We may well believe the President's statement that he listened attentively but offered no hint of his own intentions, for this habit was one of his best known characteristics. Although he believed Atocha to be a person who could not be relied upon, events which followed make it evident that he looked with favor upon the suggestions which had been offered. Some of them were followed, as we shall soon have occasion to note, in the new instructions given to Slidell and in the request made to Congress for money to be used in conducting negotiations.

That Polk was influenced by Atocha's suggestions there can be no doubt, and that his first impulse was to follow these suggestions very closely is made evident by the discussion which took place in the cabinet meeting on the following day, February 17. In giving an account of this meeting Polk says in his diary that, after relating the conversation held with Atocha,

I expressed the opinion that it would be necessary to take strong measures towards Mexico before our difficulties with that Government could be settled; and I proposed that in addition to Mr. Slidell's present instructions, he should be further instructed to demand an early decision of the Mexican Government, whether they would receive him as Minister or not; and, if they received him, whether they would without unnecessary delay pay the

---

46 *Ibid.*, 228–230.

amount due to American claimants; and that if that Government refused to do one or both, that he should leave the country, but instead of returning immediately to the U. States as he had beeen instructed to do, he should go on board one of our Vessels of War at Vera Cruz, and there remain until he had further instructions from his Government.

I stated that in that event I would send a strong message to Congress calling on that body to authorize me to cause another demand to be made by Mr. Slidell, from on board the vessel of war, on the Mexican Government to pay our demands, and if this was refused by Mexico, to confer authority on the Executive to take redress into our hands by aggressive measures.

Walker, Marcy, and Bancroft favored the plan suggested by the President. Johnson was inclined to hold a different opinion, but was willing to acquiesce. Buchanan objected, because—as Polk thought—he was peeved over certain appointments and because he could not control the administration. However, it was decided that Buchanan should prepare new instructions for Slidell, in accordance with the wishes of the President. But within an hour after the meeting had adjourned Buchanan, who was in no amiable mood, sent to the President by messenger a draft of instructions, commencing with "I am directed by President" etc. He requested Polk to make corrections in pencil and return it in time for the mail. Polk was dissatisfied with the draft and replied that he would attend to it on the following day. Buchanan immediately sent the messenger back with a note stating his reasons for dissenting from the decision of the President. On receiving no reply Buchanan sent another note on the same subject, but again he received no response. Polk did not see Buchanan on the following day, but decided, on account of the Secretary's hostility, to postpone instructing Slidell for the present.[47]

The Mexican question was allowed to slumber for about three weeks, and during that time Oregon claimed the attention of both the President and Congress. On March 9 dispatches from

---

[47] *Ibid.*, 233–236, 238. Polk considered the conduct of his Secretary to be decidedly reprehensible, and he closed the entry for the day with the remark: "The draft of the despatch and the two notes, Numbered 1 & 2, I will preserve."

Slidell, for which Polk had been waiting, arrived, and were discussed in cabinet meeting on the day following. The essential features of new instructions to Slidell were agreed upon, and Buchanan was directed to draft them.[48] While the new instructions, which bore the date of March 12, reflected in some degree the suggestions offered by Atocha, their tone was somewhat less bellicose than the declaration made by the President to his cabinet on February 17. The change was probably due to the opposition of Buchanan. Slidell was directed to make a formal demand to be received by the new government. Apparently the administration had slight hopes that Paredes would comply but Buchanan pointed out that the demand should be made in order to satisfy the American people that everything had been done to avoid the necessity of resorting to war. "On your return to the United States, energetic measures against Mexico would at once be recommended by the President, and these might fail to obtain the support of Congress, if it could be asserted that the existing Government had not refused to receive our Minister." Slidell was to make it known to Paredes "in some discreet manner" that the United States was both able and willing to relieve him from pecuniary embarrassment the moment that a treaty had been signed and ratified by Mexico.[49] A rumor was afloat, said Buchanan, of a design of European powers to establish a monarchy in Mexico and to place Prince Henry of Spain on the throne. He thought that these rumors were probably idle speculations, but "should Great Britain and France attempt to place a Spanish or any other European Prince on the throne of Mexico, this would be resisted by all the power of the United States." Whether he should be received or not Slidell was advised to delay his return to the United States, for the Oregon question was rapidly approaching a crisis and his return might influence its settlement by creating public alarm.[50] Nothing

48 *Ibid.*, 282, 287.
49 This is evidently an echo of the suggestion made by Atocha.
50 Buchanan to Slidell, March 12, 1846 (Buchanan, *Works*, VI, 402–406).

was said about Slidell's repairing to a war vessel for the purpose of making another demand, as Atocha had advised and Polk had recommended to the cabinet. Apprehension concerning the Oregon question as well as the opposition of Buchanan may have been responsible for the President's change of mind.

Polk seems to have been confident that Slidell would be received by Paredes. At a cabinet meeting held on March 28, he expressed the belief that Slidell's dispatches indicated his reception to be probable. He apprehended that the greatest obstacle to the conclusion of a boundary treaty, such as Slidell had been instructed to procure, would be the want of authority to make a prompt payment of money at the time of signing it. Paredes was in great need of money to pay his troops and keep them loyal, and Polk was of opinion that if Slidell could be authorized to pay a half million or a million dollars as soon as the treaty had been signed, it "might induce him [Paredes] to make a Treaty, which he would not otherwise venture to make." Some of the cabinet members raised the question of how this money could be obtained from Congress without exposing to the public and to foreign nations the object in voting it. "That object," said the President,

as may be seen from Mr. Slidell's instructions, would be in adjusting a boundary to procure a cession of New Mexico & California, & if possible all North of latitude 32° from the Passo [El Paso] on the Del Norte & West to the Pacific ocean; or if that precise boundary cannot be obtained, then the next best boundary which might be practicable so as at all events to include all the country East of the Del Norte and the Bay of San Francisco. For the boundary desired, see Mr. Slidell's instructions.

The cabinet, except the Secretary of State, agreed. Buchanan thought the plan of asking for an advance appropriation to be impracticable. Polk called attention to the act passed in 1806 to enable Jefferson to purchase the Floridas, and suggested that members of Congress might be consulted informally for the purpose of ascertaining the probability of obtaining the appropriation. He had already broached the subject to Ingersoll, of

Pennsylvania, and Cullom, of Tennessee. After the meeting had adjourned Polk summoned Benton and asked his opinion concerning the feasibility of the plan. Benton concurred in the views of the President and promised his coöperation.[51] On examining the laws Polk found another precedent for his proposed appropriation—the two millions voted in 1803 to enable Jefferson to purchase Louisiana. He conversed with Allen, chairman of the Senate Committee on Foreign Relations, and with Senator Cass. Both approved his plan. On the advice of Allen and Benton the President sent for Calhoun and asked his opinion on the proposed appropriation and on the purpose for which it was to be used. Calhoun was in favor of procuring a boundary which would include California, and said that he had contemplated trying to procure such a boundary when he was Secretary of State. He did not, however, like the boundary suggested by the President. Neither did he approve the plan to ask for an appropriation, for fear it might interfere with the settlement of the Oregon question.[52]

While the President was exerting his influence to obtain from Congress an appropriation to facilitate negotiations, a dispatch arrived, on April 6, from the American consul at Vera Cruz stating that Slidell would probably not be received. The dispatch was read in cabinet meeting next day, and Polk recorded in his diary:

I stated that in the event Mr. Slidell was not accredited, and returned to the U. S., my opinion was that I should make a communication to Congress recommending that Legislative measures be adopted, to take the remedy for the injuries and wrongs we had suffered into our own hands.

On the evening of the seventh dispatches from Slidell arrived, informing the President that he had not been received and that he had demanded his passports.[53]

---

[51] Polk, *Diary*, I, 303, 305–308.

[52] *Ibid.*, 309–313.

[53] *Ibid.*, 319, 322.

On March 12, the day on which Buchanan penned his final instructions to Slidell, the Mexican Minister of Foreign Relations notified the American envoy that he could not be received. He was told that the annexation of Texas had always been and was still regarded by Mexico as a *casus belli*. In spite of this fact she had agreed to receive a commissioner to discuss this question, but the United States had sent instead a minister resident. Should the United States persist in its present course the Mexican government would "call upon all her citizens to fulfill the sacred duty of defending their country," and if war should result, the entire blame would rest upon the United States. As soon as he received this letter Slidell asked for his passports, and they were sent to him by Castillo on the twenty-first of March.[54] He had left, therefore, for the United States before the arrival of Buchanan's instructions of March 12. With one government maintaining that aggressive measures must follow the refusal to receive the American envoy, and the other asserting that an insistence upon his reception must be met by an appeal to arms, it will be seen that Slidell's mission played an important part in bringing about a collision between the two nations. To be sure, Mexico still regarded the annexation of Texas as a *casus belli* and Castillo did not expressly state that she was prepared to acquiesce in its incorporation into the American Union, but at least he still intimated a willingness to negotiate on this limited question.

On receipt of Slidell's dispatch which announced that he had been rejected and had demanded his passports, the President consulted Benton concerning "the steps proper to be taken and especially if the principal Powers of Europe should attempt to force a Foreign Prince on the throne of Mexico." He consulted Houston, of Texas, and Allen, of Ohio, also, and it was agreed that nothing should be done until it had been ascertained that passports had actually been given to Slidell.[55] About a week later

---

[54] Castillo y Lanzas to Slidell, March 12 and March 21; Slidell to Castillo, March 17, 1846 (*H. Ex. Doc. 60*, 30 Cong., 1 sess., 67–72, 79).

[55] Polk, *Diary*, I, 325–327.

(April 18) the President told Calhoun that he "saw no alternative but strong measures towards Mexico." Calhoun deprecated war and expressed the opinion that if the Oregon question could be settled first there would be no difficulty in adjusting the difficulties with Mexico, for he believed that Great Britain desired to prevent a war between the United States and Mexico. Polk, on the contrary, believed that the British minister in Mexico had exerted his influence to prevent Slidell's reception. Calhoun urged against sending a message to Congress on Mexican affairs until the Oregon question had been settled. "I told him," said Polk,

that I would delay a reasonable time, but that whatever the settlement of the Oregon question might be, I would feel it my duty to lay the Mexican question before Congress, with my opinion on the subject, in time for their action at the present Session.[56]

Three days later Polk told his cabinet that "our relations with Mexico could not be permitted to remain *in statu quo*"; that he contemplated asking Congress to adopt strong measures, but thought it prudent to await news from England before taking this step. He did not have long to wait, for on the following day (April 22) a dispatch from McLane was received. McLane was of opinion that Great Britain would take no step on the Oregon question until the Senate had come to some decision on the bill to terminate joint occupation of Oregon. On the twenty-third, the conference committee of the two houses came to an agreement on the bill to give England the required twelve months' notice; and on the twenty-fifth, Polk informed his cabinet that he deemed it to be his duty to make a communication to Congress without delay. "I expressed my opinion," the President recorded,

that we must take redress for the injuries done us into our own hands, that we had attempted to conciliate Mexico in vain, and had forborne until forbearance was no longer either a virtue or patriotic . . . and that we should take a bold and firm course towards Mexico.

---

[56] *Ibid.*, 337–338.

Buchanan, whose opinion was first requested, thought that the President should recommend a declaration of war, while the other members suggested that a message be prepared and submitted to them within the course of a week. After considerable discussion Buchanan was requested to collect materials and prepare the draft of a message for the President's consideration.[57] While Buchanan was preparing "a succinct history" of wrongs on which to base a message to Congress the President once more consulted Benton. The Missouri Senator had not yet made up his mind, but he expressed a decided aversion to a war with Mexico, if it could be avoided. He advised delay until the Oregon question had been either settled or brought to a crisis. "I told him," said Polk, "we had ample cause of War, but that I was anxious to avoid it if it could be done honourably & consistently with the interests of our injured citizens." He would delay, he said, until the arrival of Slidell in Washington, but he could not permit Congress to adjourn without laying the subject before them.[58]

It should be noted that up to this point the President dwelt entirely on the refusal to receive Slidell and the failure to adjust the claims of American citizens. These furnished, in his opinion, ample grounds for war. This fact is significant, for Mexico was in such dire financial straits that she could not pay the claims except by a cession of territory. In other words, the President was ready to wage war to procure a territorial compensation for claims against Mexico. He does not, up to this time, mention any military aggressions on the part of Mexico. But on May 5 Polk received a dispatch from Taylor, dated April 15, stating that he had been ordered by Ampudia to fall back across the Nueces, and the President noted in his diary that "the probabilities are that hostilities might take place soon."[59] On May 8,

---

[57] *Ibid.*, 343, 344, 347, 354.

[58] *Ibid.*, 375–376.

[59] Taylor to Adj. Gen., April 15, 1846 (*H. Ex. Doc. 60*, 30 Cong., 1 sess., 138). Polk, *Diary*, I, 380.

Slidell, who had just returned from Mexico, called on the President and told him that there was only one course left—for the United States to take the redress of its injuries into its own hands. "In this I agreed with him," said Polk, "and told him it was only a matter of time when I would make a communication to Congress on the subject, and that I had made up my mind to do so very soon."[60] The cabinet met on the following day and the President informed them that, although no open act of aggression by the Mexican army had been reported, it was imminent that such would be committed. All agreed that if Taylor's forces should be molested the President ought to recommend a declaration of war. Polk then asked each member whether, in his opinion, a message should be sent to Congress on the following Tuesday,[61] and whether it should recommend a declaration of war. All answered in the affirmative except Bancroft, who, however, favored immediate war should Mexico commit any hostile act. It was agreed that a message should be prepared and considered at the next meeting.[62] On that same evening a dispatch from Taylor arrived, giving an account of the killing of American dragoons on the east bank of the Rio Grande. Polk summoned the cabinet to a special meeting, and it was agreed unanimously that the President should lay the matter before Congress and urge prompt measures to enable the Executive to prosecute the war. At noon on Monday, May 11, the war mesasge was ready and on its way to the capitol. Mexico herself had removed the obstacle which had worried both Bancroft and Buchanan. In addition, she rendered the President a distinct service by enabling him to base his war message on more tangible grounds— grounds which all friends of the administration could endorse with enthusiasm, and those which the opponents, for patriotic reasons, found it difficult to assail. Before the message was sent

---

60 Polk, *Diary*, I, 382.

61 This was on Saturday, May 9.

62 Polk, *Diary*, I, 384–385. Buchanan said that he would feel better if Mexico had committed some hostile act, but as matters stood, there was ample cause for war, so he gave his assent.

to Congress, Benton called, by appointment, and criticized some parts of it. He was, he said, in favor of defending our territory, but was not prepared to make aggressive war on Mexico. Although he had remained silent, he had not favored marching the army from Corpus Christi to the Rio Grande, and he doubted that the territory of the United States extended west of the Nueces river.[63]

The departure of Slidell from Mexico ended all attempt to adjust the international dispute by negotiation. Both nations now agreed on one point at least—that arms alone could settle the controversy. But which nation was the aggressor? Which committed the first overt act of war; and to what extent, if any, was the American occupation of that strip of territory lying between the Nueces and the Rio Grande the real cause of the war? We have already seen that Polk was ready to recommend war because Mexico would not pay the American claims by a cession of territory. Let us now consider the effect of Taylor's march to the Rio Grande upon Mexico's decision to attack the enemy.

As a department of Mexico Texas had extended to the Nueces only; the land lying west of that river belonged to the department of Tamaulipas. Except Santa Anna's agreement of 1836 and the Elliot treaty of 1845, Mexico never recognized the independence of Texas, much less the extension of her boundary. Texas of course claimed everything to the Rio Grande, but throughout her career as a republic the territory between the two rivers remained unoccupied by either country except that Mexico held a few posts on the east bank of the Rio Grande. The legitimate extent and boundaries of Texas, therefore, were not determined when that republic joined the American Union, and the joint resolution of annexation left them as vague as before. "What, then, is Texas?" was the embarrassing question asked by the Whigs, as soon as the administration took steps to protect the new state from invasion. Texas, they said, was bounded by the Nueces, not by the Rio Grande; and they denied the President's

<hr />

[63] *Ibid.*, 386–390.

authority to send an army into the "disputed territory" between the two rivers.[64] The occupation of this territory was later used by Mexico as an excuse for attacking the American army; but at the time that diplomatic relations were severed, the question of boundary was not a definite issue. Almonte demanded his passports and left Washington soon after the joint resolution had passed, without waiting to see what boundary would be claimed. His conduct was approved by his government, and Mexico continued to assert her determination to reconquer Texas—not simply the "disputed territory," but all of it. There was no intimation of an intention on her part to acquiesce in the annexation of Texas until she agreed to receive a commissioner to negotiate that question, and she declined to receive Slidell because his credentials were unacceptable.

Although Polk had, before annexation was completed, announced his intention to claim the Rio Grande as the boundary of Texas, the western frontier was not occupied immediately. On July 30, 1845, Taylor was instructed to station part of his forces west of the Nueces, but it was not until January 13, 1846, that he was ordered to move his army to the east bank of the Rio Grande. On receipt of this order, early in February, Taylor at once made preparations to carry it into effect, and he reported that he did not anticipate that his advance would be resisted. Before leaving Corpus Christi, Taylor prepared and had translated into Spanish an "order" which he caused to be circulated among the inhabitants dwelling along the Rio Grande. This order stated that the advance to the Rio Grande was not a hostile move, and that both the personal and the property rights of the inhabitants on either side of that river would be respected.[65]

---

[64] On September 13, 1845, the *National Intelligencer* said that if the Army of Observation should be sent beyond the Nueces it would not be in Texas and not defending Texas. "Is the *disputed* territory, then, a part of Texas? No. It was not within Texas, as a part of Mexico. It has not been since acquired by arms or treaty."

[65] Taylor to Adj. Gen., Feb. 4 and Feb. 16, 1846 (*H. Ex. Doc. 60*, 30 Cong., 1 sess., 116–117). "Order No. 30," dated March 8, 1846 (*ibid.*, 119–120).

The march of Taylor toward the Rio Grande was undisputed by the Mexicans until he reached the Arroyo Colorado on March 19. Here a party of cavalry was encountered, and their commander warned Taylor that he was under orders to fire on the Americans should they attempt to pass that river. The warning was unheeded by Taylor and the Mexicans retreated without interposing armed resistance, but during the parley one of the officers placed in Taylor's hands a bellicose proclamation which had been issued on March 18 by General Francisco Mejia. This document is of interest, not only as being the first specific challenge to the advance of the American army, but because it draws a sharp distinction between Texas and land lying between the Nueces and Rio Grande. The ''degenerate sons of Washington,'' said Mejia, not satisfied with annexing Texas, were now advancing to take possession of a large part of Tamaulipas. This they had begun ''whilst endeavoring to lull us into security, by opening diplomatic relations.'' ''The limits of Texas,'' he continued, ''are certain and recognized; never have they extended beyond the river Nueces; notwithstanding which, the American army has crossed the line separating Tamaulipas from that department.'' Even though Mexico might acquiesce in the annexation of Texas,

nevertheless the territory of Tamaulipas would still remain beyond the law of annexation, sanctioned by the American Congress; because that law comprises independent Texas, the ground occupied by the rebellious colony, and in no wise includes other departments, in which the Mexican government has uninter[r]uptedly exercised its legitimate authority.

All Mexicans were therefore exhorted to defend their country.[66] While Taylor was on the march from the Arroyo Colorado to Point Isabel he was met by a civil deputation from Matamoras bearing a protest from the prefect of the northern district of Tamaulipas. It stated that Taylor's march was regarded as an invasion of Mexico, and the prefect pointed out that ''nothing has been said officially by the cabinet of the Union to the Mexican

---

[66] *Ibid.*, 125–129.

government, respecting the extension of the limits of Texas to the left bank of the Rio Bravo.'' The citizens of the district, he said, would never consent to separate themselves from Mexico and join the United States.[67] To this protest Taylor paid no heed, but moved on to take a position opposite Matamoras. His batteries bore directly on the public square of that town, and ''their object,'' reported Taylor, ''cannot be mistaken by the enemy.'' A parley was held on the Mexican side of the river by General Worth and General Vega in which Worth demanded an interview with the American consul at Matamoras. The demand was refused, and Worth informed the Mexican commander that he regarded this refusal as a belligerent act. Worth stated also that Taylor would regard the crossing of the Rio Grande by Mexican forces as an act of war.[68] On March 31, General Mejia addressed a note to Taylor stating that all Mexicans looked upon the occupation of the east bank of the Rio Grande as a ''positive declaration of war on the Part of the United States.'' Taylor's march could not be viewed as pacific, ''inasmuch as a question of limits is depending between our respective governments.'' It could not be so viewed, ''because it is not easy to conceive the reason or justice of taking forcible possession of the very territory in dispute, pending the negotiation.''[69] Had such a communication been addressed to President Polk he might have had difficulty in explaining the *peaceful* nature of the advance of the American army, but it was Taylor's duty to obey orders and not to justify his movements. He very wisely declined to assume the rôle of a diplomat.

On April 11, General Ampudia arrived at Matamoras and took command of the Mexican forces. By ''explicit and definite orders of his [my] government,'' he at once summoned Taylor

---

[67] Cardenes to Taylor, March 23, 1846 (*ibid.*, 130–132).

[68] Taylor to Adj. Gen., April 6, 1846; Minutes of the parley held on March 28 (*ibid.*, 133–138).

[69] *Ibid.*, 1204.

to retire beyond the Nueces within twenty-four hours, there to remain until the limits of Texas should be determined by the two governments. "If you insist in remaining upon the soil of the department of Tamaulipas," he was told, "it will clearly result that arms, and arms alone, must decide the question." Taylor replied on the same day that he would remain where he was, "leaving the responsibility with those who rashly commence hostilities." As a result of Ampudia's note, Taylor immediately ordered a blockade of the Rio Grande, which cut off supplies from Matamoras.[70] On April 24, Ampudia was superseded by General Arista, who at once notified Taylor that Mexico could not submit to the indignities heaped upon her by the United States, and that hostilities had commenced. Taylor replied on the following day that he had carefully refrained from committing

any act which could possibly be interpreted into hostility, until the peremptory summons of General Ampudia to vacate my position within twenty-four hours, rendered it necessary to take some action, and I then chose a measure not in itself hostile, but a simple defensive precaution, viz: a blockade of the Rio Bravo.[71]

Although this definition of a blockade may have relieved the conscience of the man who made it, such a bottling-up of the opponent is usually regarded as an act of war. Ampudia protested vigorously and demanded the free use of the river, but Taylor refused to raise the blockade "unless indeed you desire an armistice pending the settlement of the question between the two governments."[72]

The Mexican President likewise considered Taylor's blockade to be an act of war. On April 23, Paredes issued a proclamation directing a "defensive war" to begin. After a recital of the injuries which, since 1836, the United States had inflicted upon the people of Mexico; the sending of Slidell as minister resident

---

[70] Ampudia to Taylor, April 12; Taylor to Ampudia, April 12; Taylor to Adj. Gen., April 15, 1846 (*ibid.*, 138–140).

[71] *Ibid.*, 1204–1206.

[72] Taylor to Ampudia, April 22, 1846 (*ibid.*, 144–147).

at the very moment when the American troops were occupying Mexican territory; and the blockade of the Rio Grande by war vessels: Paredes asserted that

hostilities therefore have been begun by the United States of America, who have undertaken new conquests in the territory lying within the line of the Departments of Tamaulipas and Nueva León while the troops of the United States are threatening Monterey in Upper California.

He had therefore directed the commanding general to "attack the army which is attacking us; to answer with war the enemy who makes war upon us." Like Taylor, Paredes invented a definition to suit his purposes, for he declared the proposed hostilities to be not a war against the government of the United States, but simply a defense of Mexican territory which had been invaded.[73]

Arista, who assumed command of the Mexican forces on the day after Paredes had issued his proclamation, took immediate steps to cross the Rio Grande. General Torrejon, with all of the cavalry and a small body of infantry, was sent across the river above Matamoras, while the main body of infantry and artillery was to cross below Matamoras and cut Taylor off from his base of supplies at Point Isabel.[74] On April 25, Torrejon encountered a scouting party of sixty-three American dragoons, under Captain Thornton. An engagement followed in which sixteen Americans were killed or wounded and the remainder forced to surrender. The prisoners were taken to Matamoras and treated kindly by the Mexicans.[75] The long-threatened war with Mexico

---

[73] "I solemnly announce that I do not decree war against the government of the United States of America, because it belongs to the august Congress of the nation, and not to the Executive, to decide definitely what reparation must be exacted for such injuries. But the defense of Mexican territory which the troops of the United States are invading is an urgent necessity, and my responsibility before the nation would be immense if I did not order the repulse of forces which are acting as enemies; and I have so ordered. From this day defensive war begins, and every point of our territory which may be invaded or attacked shall be defended by force" (*México á través de los Siglos*, IV, 559). Rives, *The United States and Mexico*, II, 141–142.

[74] Rives, *op. cit.*, 143.

[75] Taylor to Adj. Gen., April 26, 1846; Reports of Captains Thornton and Hardee (*ibid.*, 288, 290–292).

was at last a reality. The killing of Thornton's dragoons by the Mexican forces under Torrejon was soon described by President Polk as an unprovoked act of war. In a message sent to Congress on May 11, 1846, the President asserted that

> after reiterated menaces, Mexico has passed the boundary of the United States, has invaded our territory, and shed American blood upon the American soil. She has proclaimed that hostilities have commenced, and that the two nations are now at war.
>
> As war exists, and, notwithstanding all our efforts to avoid it, exists by the act of Mexico herself, we are called upon by every consideration of duty and patriotism to vindicate with decision and honor, the rights, and the interests of our country.

He therefore recommended prompt and energetic measures for bringing the war to a speedy and successful termination.[76]

Whether or not Taylor's advance into the "disputed territory" was the actual cause of Mexico's refusal to renew diplomatic relations and of her determination to resort to arms, it at least served as an excuse for such a course on her part. Although she had from the first claimed the occupation of any part of Texas to be an invasion of Mexico and a *casus belli,* she had, on various occasions, intimated that she might acquiesce in the annexation of Texas and discuss its limits. It was not until Taylor had crossed the Nueces that she actually took steps to attack the American forces. Polk may or may not have acted within his rights in assuming the boundary claimed by Texas, but at least there was some justification in the contention of the Whigs that he precipitated the war by ordering Taylor to the Rio Grande.

---

[76] Richardson, *Messages and Papers of the Presidents,* IV, 442–443.

CHAPTER XVIII

WAR IN NORTHERN MEXICO

President Polk's war message was sent to Congress on May 11, 1846. After a brief debate of two hours the House, by a vote of one hundred and seventy-four to fourteen, passed a bill which authorized the President to prosecute the war that exists "by the act of the Republic of Mexico."[1] Garrett Davis, of Kentucky, denied the truth of the statement just quoted and asserted that: "It is our own President who began this war" by sending General Taylor beyond the Nueces river. In defense of the administration, the Washington *Union* answered this contention by calling attention to the fact that Mexico had always claimed Texas to the Sabine, and that there was no reason for believing that her invading army would stop at the Nueces.[2]

Greater opposition was encountered in the Senate, and for a time the President feared that Benton and Calhoun would join the Whigs and thereby defeat the House bill. However, after a day's debate, the Senate, having added a few amendments, passed the measure by a vote of forty-two to two. Benton voted for the bill and Calhoun, having opposed a declaration of war, declined to vote either way.[3] Some of the members based their objections

---

[1] *Cong. Globe*, 29 Cong., 1 sess., 795. Polk, *Diary*, I, 392.

[2] "No man has yet alleged, so far as we know, that a Mexican invasion of Texas, if permitted by us, *would have stopped at the Nueces;* or would have thought of stopping there. . . . The claim of Mexico is, in terms, that she owns Texas up to the Sabine. She makes not the slightest difference in any one of her state papers between her ownership up to the Nueces and her ownership up to the Sabine. In a great multitude of state papers of old date, and of most recent date, Mexico says that Texas—*all Texas*— is her soil. This claim to *the whole of Texas* is the claim on which she refused negotiation. On this claim, and none other, Almonte threw up his passports. On this claim Mr. Shannon was sent home" (*Union*, May 15, 1846).

[3] *Cong. Globe, loc. cit.*, 804. Polk, *Diary*, I, 394.

on the lack of information as to what had happened on the Rio Grande; others denounced the President for having invaded territory which did not belong to the United States. In general, the Van Burenites of both houses supported the administration with their votes, but in private their criticisms were quite as severe as those of the Whigs. Although Cambreleng was not a member of Congress at the time, a letter which he wrote to the ex-President well expresses the feelings of this faction. The letter is especially interesting, for when Polk occupied the Speaker's chair, Cambreleng was his most loyal supporter. Having pronounced Polk to be worse than John Tyler and invoked divine pardon for having aided in his election, Cambreleng said:

> With regard to Mexico, they make inquiry through a consul—Mexico proposes to receive a Commissioner to treat about Texas if we will withdraw our naval forces—then we send in hot haste, and most secretly, a Minister Plenipotentiary, at a moment too when a revolutionary movement was going on and when it was obvious, that our minister could do nothing whatever but help Paredes to overthrow Herera, which he did very effectively and returned home with his credentials. [Taylor marched across Tamaulipas and blockaded the Mexicans] as if he had instructions [to make war, and Mexico had no choice but to fight].[4]

The bill which decreed war against Mexico was signed by the President on May 13, and General Scott was given command of the army for which it provided, although Polk did not consider him to be ''in all respects suited'' for the position.

At a cabinet meeting held on the same evening the President and his Secretary of State had a sharp disagreement concerning the scope and the objects of the war. Buchanan had brought to the meeting the draft of a dispatch which was to be sent to American ministers at foreign courts. Its purpose was to notify those governments of the declaration of war, and to announce the intentions of the American government. In his draft Buchanan disavowed any intention of dismembering Mexico, and of making conquests. He stated specifically that the war had

---

4 Cambreleng to Van Buren, Washington, May 16, 1846, *Van Buren Papers.*

not been undertaken "with a view to acquire either California or New Mexico or any other portion of Mexican territory." Polk "thought such a declaration to Foreign Governments unnecessary and improper," and believed the causes for war set forth in his message to be entirely adequate. He told his Secretary that while the United States had not gone to war for the purpose of conquest,

yet it was clear that in making peace we would if practicable obtain California and such other portion of the Mexican territory as would be sufficient to indemnify our claimants on Mexico, and to defray the expenses of the war which that power by her long continued wrongs and injuries had forced us to wage. I told him it was well known that the Mexican Government had no other means of indemnifying us.

Buchanan expressed the fear that Lord Aberdeen would demand from McLane, United States minister in London, a statement as to whether his government intended to acquire Mexican territory, especially California. Should a satisfactory answer be withheld, he feared that both England and France would join Mexico in the war against us. Polk replied that the present war did not concern any European power, a demand such as Buchanan had mentioned would be an insult, and "if made I would not answer it, even if the consequence should be a war with all of them." He would give no pledges as to the terms on which he would ultimately make peace with Mexico. Buchanan insisted that if assurances were not given we would surely have war with England, and probably with France, for neither would permit California to be annexed to the United States. "I told him," wrote the President, "that before I would make the pledge which he proposed, I would meet the war which either England or France or all the Powers of Christendom might wage," and that "neither as a citizen nor as President would I permit or tolerate any intermeddling of any European Power on this Continent." Although Buchanan still maintained that unless some pledge were given the Oregon question could not be adjusted and that England would declare war, the President was immovable and said that he would take the responsibility of a war rather than give a pledge which would prevent him from "fairly and honourably" acquiring California. The other members of the cabinet supported this position, and Polk was "much astonished at the views expressed by Mr. Buchanan on the subject." The President himself drafted a paragraph to be substituted for the one which Buchanan had submitted.[5]

Scarcely had the President reduced his Secretary of State to proper subordination when difficulties with his Whig generals presented themselves.[6] He had planned first of all to seize the northern provinces of Mexico and to hold them until the enemy had been forced to make peace. Without hesitation Congress voted the necessary troops and supplies, but the question of selecting suitable commanders to lead the troops to victory caused the President no little anxiety and annoyance. As Scott was the ranking general, Polk tendered him the command and consulted him concerning military arrangements, but he regarded the general as "visionary" and his advice as of no great value.[7]

From the beginning of his administration Polk seems to have looked upon the conquest of Mexico as an easy matter. Like most civilian executives he did not fully appreciate the time required to equip an army for active service. On the other hand, General Scott took both himself and his position very seriously, and was desirous of making his descent upon Mexico as imposing as possible. He was a competent officer, and doubtless his intentions were good, but his vanity and tactless utterances soon involved him in difficulties.

---

[5] Polk, *Diary*, I, 396–399. For the dispatch as finally sent to the American ministers abroad, see Buchanan, *Works*, VI, 484.

[6] Polk was told that not only Scott but General Wool and Adjutant General Jones were using their influence with members of Congress to prevent the passage of a bill to authorize the appointment of two new major generals and four brigadier generals (Polk, *Diary*, I, 418).

[7] "I did not think that so many as 20,000 [the number which Scott had requested for immediate service] volunteers besides the regular army was necessary, but I did not express this opinion, not being willing to take the responsibility of any failure of the campaign by refusing to grant to Gen'l Scott all he asked" (Polk, *Diary*, I, 400–401).

Without consulting the War Department, Scott announced that he probably would not be ready to set out for the seat of war until the first of September. Through the Secretary of War, the President notified him that unless he should proceed to the Rio Grande very soon he would be superseded by another commander.

Polk undoubtedly bore a prejudice against the general from the beginning and may have been too impatient with his delay; on the other hand, Scott's amazing indiscretions soon gave the President no alternative but to deprive him of his command. Not satisfied with telling applicants for military positions that these places had been created "to give Commissions or rather pay to western democrats," he responded to Marcy's notice that the President desired greater promptness, by returning a most insulting and vainglorious letter. Although Polk had verbally tendered Scott the command of the Mexican expedition, the general now complained because he had not received a written order assigning him to the command; he had, nevertheless, been incessantly employed in making preliminary arrangements. "In the midst of these multitudinous and indispensable occupations," wrote the irate general,

I have learned from you that much impatience is already felt, perhaps in high quarters, that I have not already put myself in route for the Rio Grande; and now, with fourteen hours a day of preliminary work remaining on my hands for many days, I find myself compelled to stop that necessary work to guard myself against, perhaps, utter condemnation in the quarters alluded to. I am too old a soldier, and have had too much special experience, not to feel the infinite importance of securing myself against danger, (ill will or pre-condemnation,) in my rear, before advancing upon the public enemy.

He had no fear of the enemy ahead, but unless he could feel confident of support in Washington the selection of another commander was advised. For fear that Marcy and Polk might not have sufficient mental capacity to grasp his meaning, the general added: "My explicit meaning is, that I do not desire to place

myself in the most perilous of all positions—*a fire upon my rear
from Washington, and the fire in front from the Mexicans.*" So
clear was his explanation that both men saw at once the injustice
of placing the gallant and overworked general in such a dangerous predicament. In a very able and dignified—but, at the same
time, withering—letter, Marcy notified Scott that, instead of
leading the Mexican expedition, he was to remain in Washington.[8]
In itself Marcy's letter was galling enough to the pompous general's pride, but, as if to add insult to injury, it was handed to
him just "as he [I] sat down to a hasty plate of soup." In
another letter he made a lame attempt to explain that his allusions to "high quarters" meant members of Congress instead of
the President, but he could not refrain from sneering at Polk's
"magnanimity" in not having him court-martialed.[9] The effrontery exhibited in his letters indicates that the general was still
deluded by the campaign cry, "Who is James K. Polk?" Marcy
enlightened him, for the time being at least. Indeed the President felt himself to be fully competent to discharge the duties
which the Constitution had assigned to the chief executive. To
one of his many volunteer advisers he remarked that: "I hoped
my friends in Congress and elsewhere would suffer me to conduct
the war with Mexico as I thought proper, and not plan the campaign for me."[10]

As already noted, Polk did not anticipate great difficulty in
defeating the Mexican armies. Apparently, he feared most of
all the influence of the Mexican priests. He thought that designing persons in Mexico had led the priests to believe that the

---

[8] After calling attention to the importance of the position to which
Scott had been assigned by the President, Marcy said: "How could you,
under these circumstances, arrest your labors of preparation, and suffer
your energies to be crippled, for the purpose of indulging in illiberal imputations against the man who has just bestowed upon you the highest
mark of his confidence?"

[9] Polk, *Diary*, I, 395, 400, 413–415, 419–421. The correspondence is
printed in *Niles' Reg.*, LXX, 231–233.

[10] Polk, *Diary*, I, 427.

United States had planned to pillage their churches and to overthrow their religion. So long as the priests harbored such fears they would do much to incite the people stubbornly to resist the advance of the American army. Being desirous of weakening the power of the Mexican government by winning the good will of the people, especially in the northern provinces, Polk attached great importance to disabusing the minds of the priests. ''If the Catholic Priests in Mexico,'' he told Benton,

can be satisfied that their churches and religion would be secure the conquests of the Northern Provinces of Mexico will be easy and the probability is that the war would be of short duration; but if a contrary opinion prevails the resistance to our forces will be desperate.

He therefore sought interviews with Bishop Hughes, of New York, and the Bishop of Missouri and asked them to select priests who might accompany the army as chaplains and assure the Mexican clergy that their fear of Americans was groundless. A proclamation in the Spanish language which promised religious freedom and kind treatment was prepared and sent to General Taylor with instructions that it should be distributed among the inhabitants.[11]

In planning the campaign against Mexico the President attached great importance to getting possession of California. As early as May 26 he proposed, and his cabinet unanimously agreed, that an ''expedition be immediately fitted out against Upper California'' if it should be found that the mounted regiments assembled at Independence, Missouri, could reach the Sacramento region before winter. On May 30 he again impressed upon the cabinet the importance of having military possession of California when the time for making peace should have arrived. ''I declared,'' said he, ''my purpose to be to acquire for the U. S. California, New Mexico, and perhaps some others of the Northern

---

11 *Ibid.*, 408–411. For the proclamation see *H. Ex. Doc. 60*, 30 Cong., 1 sess., 284–287. In it the Mexicans were told that their government was in the hands of ''tyrants and usurpers,'' and that the United States was doing the people a real kindness by invading their country.

Provinces of Mexico whenever peace was made." Colonel Stephen W. Kearny, who had already been transferred from Fort Leavenworth to Santa Fé for the purpose of affording protection to American traders, was now selected to lead the expedition to California. By a new commission which accompanied his instructions he was made a brevet brigadier-general. A requisition was sent to the governor of Missouri for one thousand mounted men to supplement the force of dragoons under Kearny's command. It was agreed that Kearny should be authorized to take into his service any American citizens whom he might find in California. He was to be given authority, also, to enlist a few hundred of the Mormons who were now on their way to California, "with a view to conciliate them, attach them to our country, & prevent them from taking part against us." The President directed that arms and provisions should be sent immediately from New York to the Pacific for the use of Kearny's army.[12] About two weeks later he consulted his cabinet on the propriety of sending from New York by sea a regiment of volunteers to join Kearny's forces in California. Benton, whose advice was sought by the President, favored sending such a regiment, but he believed that the men should go as emigrants and be discharged in California at the end of their service.[13] This policy was subsequently adopted.

Although Polk was interested primarily in the acquisition of California and New Mexico he desired to procure, if possible, a much larger area; and the amicable settlement of the Oregon

---

[12] Polk, *Diary*, I, 429, 437–439, 443–444. On June 3, J. C. Little, a Mormon from Petersborough, N. H., called on Polk for the purpose of ascertaining the policy of the government towards this sect. He was told that they would be treated like any other American citizens and that they would be invited to enlist in the army. Polk did not mention the projected expedition under Kearny. Little offered to overtake the Mormons and to muster 500 of them into the United States army; but fearing that they might reach California before Kearny and not wishing that the province should be at the mercy of Mormon soldiers, the President declined the offer. He decided, also, that Kearny should not enlist any of that sect until after they had arrived in California (*ibid.*, 445–446, 449–450).

[13] *Ibid.*, 473, 481.

question by the treaty signed on June 15 made interference by
Great Britain less probable. The extent of territory which he
wished to acquire is stated very definitely in his record of a
cabinet meeting held on June 30, 1846. At this meeting an animated discussion arose between Buchanan and Walker regarding
the objects to be attained as a result of the war. Buchanan expressed himself as being in favor of making the Rio Grande the
boundary up to El Paso, in latitude about 32°; from this point
a line was to be drawn due west to the Pacific ocean. He opposed the acquisition of any land south of 32° because the North
would be unwilling to acquire a tract that was likely to become
slaveholding territory. Walker held very different opinions. He
proposed that the boundary should begin at the mouth of the
Rio Grande, in latitude about 26°, and extend directly westward
to the Pacific. The other members of the cabinet took no part
in the discussion, but Polk agreed with Walker. ''I remarked,''
wrote the President,

that I preferred the 26° to any boundary North of it, but that if it was
found that that boundary could not be obtained I was willing to take 32°,
but that in any event we must obtain Upper California and New Mexico
in any Treaty of Peace we would make.[14]

At this point we may leave the President to develop his program of conquest while we consider a parenthetical episode which
affected his policy of territorial expansion but which was not,
apparently, a part of it.

Long before General Kearny could reach California, John C.
Fremont had, by his indiscretions, come into collision with the
Mexican officials of that province, and the famous ''Bear Flag''
republic had been proclaimed. These events, however interesting
in themselves, call for small space in a biography of Polk, for,
so far as any known evidence exists, they formed no part of the
President's California program and were in no degree inspired
by him. The only possible link which might connect these events

---

[14] *Ibid.*, 495–496.

with the plans of the administration is the "secret instructions" carried by Gillespie, and Fremont had already resisted Mexican authority before the arrival of Gillespie in California. Thomas O. Larkin, American consul at Monterey, who doubtless was cognizant of all instructions brought by Gillespie, continued to use his influence for peace until after the "Bear Flag" insurrection. Another reason for believing that Fremont and his adherents acted without authority from Washington is the fact that the President, in all of his known instructions to naval and military officers, laid special stress on winning over the inhabitants by kind treatment. Fremont adopted the opposite course, and even went out of his way to antagonize them.

During Tyler's administration Fremont had made two expeditions into the western country, and in the summer of 1845 had undertaken a third. Early in 1846 he reached California, and, after making brief stops at Sutter's Fort and San Francisco, he paid a visit to Larkin at Monterey. He explained to the Mexican authorities at Monterey that he was bound for Oregon on a scientific expedition, and his statement was accepted as satisfactory.

Instead of proceeding to Oregon, Fremont, having gone as far north as San José, retraced his steps until he had reached a point not far from Monterey. The excuse for his return southward, long afterward given by Fremont himself,[15] was the desire to find a seaside home for his mother!

His original entry into the province without passports was a violation of Mexican law, and when, contrary to agreement, he returned to the vicinity of Monterey, he was ordered by José Castro, the *comandante general*, to retire from the department. After sending a verbal refusal to obey this order, Fremont repaired to Gavilan Peak, erected a log fort, and hoisted the flag of the United States. Here he was warned by Larkin of the danger of such a proceeding, and, after much vain blustering, he set out for Sutter's Fort, which he reached late in March.

---

[15] Fremont, *Memoirs*, I, 457.

Breaking camp on March 24, Fremont and his party proceeded northward until they had reached Klamath Lake, where
they were overtaken, on May 8, by messengers who announced
that Lieutenant Gillespie was close behind bearing dispatches
from the government of the United States. The dispatches turned
out to be a letter of introduction from Buchanan, a letter from
Senator Benton, and whatever verbal communications Gillespie
may have conveyed. Despite Fremont's assertions that it was
made known to him "that to obtain possession of California was
the chief object of the President," he has admitted that he learned
nothing from Buchanan's letter and that Benton's epistle was
equally harmless except when "read by the light of many conversations and discussions with himself and others at Washington."[16] Concerning the verbal instructions related by Gillespie,
we are told by Fremont himself that they "had for their principal objects to ascertain the disposition of the California people,
to conciliate their feelings in favor of the United States."

As Fremont's subsequent relations with the Californians were
anything but conciliatory, and as he received no communications
from Washington other than those just mentioned, and finally,
as his belligerent attitude toward the California government was
so out of harmony with Polk's general policy of conciliation, we
must conclude that Fremont's later activities were undertaken
without authority from the President.

After Gillespie's arrival at his camp, Fremont returned to
the Sacramento Valley in California. If further evidence were
necessary to prove that the messenger had brought no orders to
precipitate a revolution, it is furnished in letters written by both
men under date of May 24, 1846. To Benton, Fremont wrote

---

[16] "The letter from Senator Benton, while apparently of friendship and
family details, contained passages and suggestions which, read in the light
of many conversations and discussions with himself and others at Washington, clearly indicated to me that I was required by the Government to
find out any foreign schemes in relation to California and so far as might
be in my power, to counteract them" (*ibid.*, 489).

that "I shall now proceed directly homewards, by the Colorado, but I cannot arrive at the frontier until late in September." "He now goes home from here [Peter Lassen's]," said Gillespie when speaking of Fremont in a letter to Larkin of the same date.[17]

While Fremont was encamped at the "Buttes of Sacramento," General Castro at Santa Clara was collecting a body of troops for the purpose of going to Los Angeles to attack Governor Pio Pico, with whom he had had a disagreement. With this object in view he had sent a man named Francisco Arce to Sonoma to purchase mules for his troops. American settlers, having concluded that Castro was planning to attack them, reported the purchase to Fremont. A party led by Ezekiel Merritt set out from Fremont's camp and, on June 10, captured and brought back the mules. On the following day Merritt set out for Sonoma and captured the town on the fourteenth. After a lively debate California was declared an independent republic and the "bear flag" chosen as its emblem. Fremont did not participate personally in these acts, but they were performed with his knowledge and consent.

Captain John B. Montgomery, commander of the United States ship *Portsmouth* in San Francisco Bay, declined to identify himself with the "bear flag" episode. The revolutionists therefore received no assistance from the navy until the arrival of Commodore Sloat, on July 2, at the port of Monterey. While off the Mexican coast Sloat had heard of Taylor's victories and of the blockade of Vera Cruz, and, on June 7, had set out for Monterey. On July 7, Sloat, after five days of hesitation which was due probably to Larkin's desire to win California by conciliatory methods,[18] caused the United States flag to be raised at Monterey. On the following day Montgomery, acting under

---

[17] Letter to Benton, Fremont, *Memoirs*, I, 499. Gillespie to Larkin, *Larkin Papers*, Bancroft Library.

[18] Bancroft, *California*, V, 228, note 6.

orders from Sloat, took possession of the posts on San Francisco Bay. The party at Sonoma now abandoned their "bear flag" republic and hoisted the stars and stripes.

After a circuitous voyage via the Sandwich Islands, Commodore Stockton, on board the *Congress,* reached Monterey on the fourteenth of July. About two weeks later he succeeded Sloat as commander of the Pacific squadron. More arrogant than his predecessor, Stockton rejected peace overtures sent from Governor Pio Pico and General José Castro, then at Los Angeles, and demanded their unconditional surrender. Seeing that resistance was futile, these officials fled to Mexico, and Stockton, with the coöperation of Fremont and Gillespie, took possession of southern California. Having thus completed the "first conquest" of California, Stockton, acting on his own responsibility, undertook to establish a government over the inhabitants.[19]

In antagonizing the Californians and in attempting to establish a civil government Stockton, as we have already noted, acted on his own responsibility, for nothing in instructions which had been received by himself or his predecessor authorized his arbitrary procedure. Instructions prepared by Secretary Bancroft under the direction of the President—some prior and some subsequent to Stockton's arrival in California, but of course not received at the time—expressed very definitely the desires of the administration with respect to California. One addressed to Sloat on June 8, 1846, ordered him to "endeavor to establish the supremacy of the American flag without any strife with the people of California." If California should be inclined to separate from Mexico and establish "a government of its own under the auspices of the American flag," he was to encourage such action, but no authority to make a conquest was given. The United States, said Bancroft, desired to make California a friend and not an enemy, "to hold possession of it, at least during the war; and

---

19 Except where noted, this summary of the first conquest has been drawn principally from Rives, II, chap. 34, and Bancroft, *California,* V.

to hold that possession, if possible, with the consent of the inhabitants.'' On July 12 he stated explicitly why possession was so much desired by the administration. ''The object of the United States,'' Sloat was told,

has reference to ultimate peace with Mexico; and if, at that peace, the basis of the *uti possidetis* shall be established the government expects, through your forces, to be found in actual possession of Upper California.

A month later, August 13, Bancroft stated that ''if the treaty of peace shall be made on the basis of *uti possidetis*, it may leave California to the United States.'' Possession at the date of peace negotiations, and not a revolution as had been effected by Fremont and Stockton, was all that the President had contemplated. To be sure, Bancroft, in his letter of July 12, spoke of the necessity of establishing some sort of civil government under the protection of Sloat, and a copy of Kearny's instructions was inclosed; but he urged that ''in selecting persons to hold office, due respect should be had to the wishes of the people of California, as well as to the actual possessors of authority in that province.''[20] Necessarily the officers in California did not know the contents of these letters, for two of them were written after they had taken possession of California; still, the instructions show clearly that Stockton and Fremont did not, in the course they pursued, correctly divine the wishes of the President.

A discussion of the uprising of the Californians under General Flores, the second conquest by the United States forces, and the establishment of a government by General Kearny, acting under instructions from President Polk, must be postponed while we follow the advance of the main army into Mexico. While the President was making plans for acquiring new territory, and while subordinates without his sanction were making conquests on the Pacific coast, General Taylor was winning battles for his government, and laurels for himself, on the banks of the Rio Grande.

---

[20] Instructions of Bancroft to Sloat, Stockton and Biddle, June 8, July 12 and Aug. 13, 1846 (*H. Ex. Doc. 60*, 30 Cong., 1 sess., 237–241).

The first bloodshed, as we have seen, occurred on April 25 when Captain Thornton's dragoons, after a loss of sixteen men, were surrounded and forced to surrender. As a result Taylor, by authority already vested in him by the President, called upon the governors of Texas and Louisiana for eight regiments of volunteers. Before these could be available, however, he was obliged to meet the invading Mexican army with his small force of regulars. First of all he constructed and garrisoned a fort opposite Matamoras and with his main army returned to his base of supplies at Point Isabel, which was threatened by Arista.

After strengthening the position at Point Isabel, Taylor set out on his return to the fort opposite Matamoras, upon which an attack had been made and the commander, Major Brown, killed. On the way back to this fort, which now took the name of Fort Brown, Taylor, on May 8, met and defeated Arista at Palo Alto. At daybreak on the following morning the Mexican commander retreated to Resaca de la Palma, where Taylor overtook him in the afternoon and won another victory. The Mexican army was completely disorganized, and scattered groups, after a precipitate flight across the Rio Grande, reassembled at Matamoras. This place was abandoned without resistance as soon as Taylor began to cross the river on the eighteenth of May. "The battles of Palo Alto and Resaca de la Palma," wrote General Grant long afterwards, "seemed to us engaged, as pretty important affairs; but we had only a faint conception of their magnitude until they were fought over in the North by the Press and the reports came back to us."[21]

In these battles the Mexican forces outnumbered their adversaries more than two to one, but the American army was better equipped and led by a more capable commander. Fearless and unassuming, Taylor enjoyed the confidence of his soldiers. They were always eager to respond to the call of "Old Rough and Ready." Ever prepared to do his duty, Taylor had no thirst for military glory. In a private letter written on the day after

---

[21] Grant, *Personal Memoirs*, I, 99–100. Grant was then a lieutenant.

his occupation of Matamoras he said that "I heartily wish the war was at an end."[22]

News of Taylor's victories reached Washington on May 23, the day on which Polk read to his cabinet Scott's letter about being fired upon in front and rear. When he received this news the President made no comment in his diary, except to record the fact that the news had arrived, but three days later he sent a message to the Senate nominating Taylor as major-general by brevet.[23] On May 30, just one week after the receipt of Taylor's official dispatch, the new commission was ready and Marcy forwarded it to the general along with an assignment to the chief command. On the same day the President in a letter to Taylor praised the general's "gallant conduct and distinguished services," and stated that the "battles of Palo Alto and Resaca de la Palma rank among our most brilliant victories."[24]

There is no reason for believing that, at the time of Taylor's promotion, Polk harbored other than the most kindly feelings toward the victorious general. The delay in preparing the cordial letter just quoted was due to the pressure of executive business such as planning the California expedition and reducing Scott and Gains[25] to proper subordination. Not knowing the reason why the President's expression of approval had been delayed, Taylor felt slighted, and his distrust of the administration was aroused. "It is strange passing strange," he wrote to his son-in-law, "that I have heard nothing from Washing[ton] since my official report of the battles of the 8th & 9th reached there, which I have seen published in the National Intelligencer & Union." He hinted at politics in high quarters, and mentioned a rumor that members of Congress from the South and West had protested to the President against his being superseded by Scott.

---

[22] Taylor to his son-in-law, Dr. R. C. Wood, May 19, 1846, *Taylor Letters*, 4.

[23] Polk, *Diary*, I, 422, 425, 428. Until this promotion Taylor had been a colonel in actual rank, but brigadier-general by brevet.

[24] *H. Ex. Doc. 60*, 30 Cong., 1 sess., 282–283.

[25] Gains had, without authority, been enlisting troops for the Rio Grande campaign.

He hoped that the report was untrue, for "I consider this command properly his, & I have no wish to prevent his exercising it."[26]

When another week brought no word from Washington Taylor became convinced that the administration was more interested in playing politics than in defeating the Mexicans. Merit and long service, in his opinion, were disregarded at the national capital; "the more one does the more they expect of him, and his services or standing is estimated by political considerations." He was "perfectly disgusted" with the inefficiency in Washington, for small boats and wagons could be brought "from Liverpool" in less time than it had taken the government to supply them. "Was I a prominent or ambitious aspirant for civil distinction or honors," he wrote, "I might very readily suppose there was an intention somewhere among the high functionaries to break me down"; and he feared that such would be the result of the government's policy, "whether from design or not." He regarded as "ridiculous" a report which had just reached camp to the effect that Scott had declined to take command of the army for fear of injuring his Presidential prospects, and that a quarrel with Polk had resulted from his refusal. "They need have no apprehensions," he added, "of being interfered with by me for that high office, which I would decline if proffered & I could reach it without opposition."[27] As late as August 4 he expressed the hope that Scott would be the Whig candidate in 1848, but he put away the crown from his own head with a far less resolute hand.[28]

---

[26] Taylor to R. C. Wood, June 12, 1846, *Taylor Letters*, 9–10. Scott had already notified Taylor that he [Scott] had been assigned to the command, but would not go to Mexico immediately.

[27] Taylor to R. C. Wood, June 21, 1846, *ibid.*, 12–14. When more definite news of Scott's quarrel with the President arrived, Taylor expressed regret, for it would keep him in Mexico "which I by no means desire" (Taylor to R. C. Wood, June 24).

[28] "So far as I am concerned I wish to have nothing to do with that high office; & if I had, this is not the proper time to discuss the subject; let this war at any rate be first brought to a close" (Taylor to R. C. Wood, *ibid.*, 35).

His attitude toward the administration was based on ground-less suspicions, for at this early date there was surely no desire to "break him down." Even the receipt of Marcy's letter which assigned him to the chief command and inclosed his new com-mission did not change his antipathy toward his superiors. The honor of his promotion, in his opinion, was more than overbal-anced by his assignment to command an expedition which "must be a failure owing to the ignorance of some in regard to some matters, & the imbecility of others, for all of which I shall be made the scape goat." He must have received Polk's laudatory letter in the same mail, but of this he made no mention. He pronounced Scott "crazy" because of his letters to Marcy, and he was certain that "Gen'l S. will never hear the last of a fire from his rear, or a hasty plate of soup."[29]

While in this mood, Taylor questioned the good faith of the government in its dealings with Mexico. He was confident that "our ambitious views of conquest & agrandisement at the ex-pense of a weak power will only be restrained & circumscribed by our inability to carry out our view." He did not rate that ability very high, for he predicted that if the Mexicans should hold out for six or eight months "we will be fully as anxious to make peace as they are." Three weeks later he hoped that peace negotiations would soon begin, but he feared that the United States would claim a vast amount of territory as a war indemnity and for "real & pretended roberies committed on our commerce; which will no doubt be double & treble award to certain claimants over & above what they ever lost." No land grabbing act of the British government had been "more outrageous" than Polk's plan to take permanent possession of California.[30]

---

[29] Taylor to R. C. Wood, June 30 and July 7, 1846, *ibid.*, 18–25.

[30] Taylor to R. C. Wood, July 14, Aug. 4, and Aug. 23, 1846, *ibid.*, 28, 37, 49. Undoubtedly Taylor's distrust was increased by letters from Whig friends in the United States. See letters from Scott and Crittenden, in Coleman, *Life of John J. Crittenden*, 256, 278.

Taylor had reason enough to complain of the want of transportation facilities,[31] although the cause was to be sought, not in
any desire to "break him down," but in the lack of preparation
usually experienced at the outbreak of a war, and more especially
in the ignorance of the Washington officials concerning everything in Mexico.

The President and his cabinet knew little of the topography
of the country, or of its seasons, fertility, and accessibility. Even
the geography was something of a mystery. As a result, considerable confusion and frequent misunderstandings were only to
be expected. For the necessary information the executive departments had to depend largely on the reports of General Taylor ;
and the general, fearing that the main object of the administration was to make a "scape goat" of him, did not feel free to offer
advice or to act without explicit orders.

In a letter addressed to Taylor on June 8, 1846, Marcy stated
that nothing had been heard from him since his brief dispatch
announcing the victories of Palo Alto and Resaca de la Palma,
but it was assumed that Matamoras had been occupied. He expressed the hope that Taylor would get possession of all places
on the Rio Grande as far up as Laredo, and that he would be
able to capture Monterey. The measures to be pursued, however,
were left to the general's "own discretion and judgment." The
President very much desired, said Marcy, to have Taylor's "views
and suggestions in relation to the fall campaign." Being desirous
of prosecuting the war with vigor, the President wished to know
whether, in the general's opinion, the present expedition should
be conducted with a view of striking at the City of Mexico, or
of operating in the northern provinces only. "Your views on
this point," said Marcy, "will doubtless have an important influence upon the determination of the government here." Information was requested, also, on overland transportation facilities and

---

[31] "I consider there is an entire break down in the Qr M [quarter
master's] department every where" (Taylor to R. C. Wood, June 21, 1846,
ibid., 13).

on the probability of obtaining adequate provisions, and the general's opinion was asked concerning the number and character of troops to be employed. Four days later Scott impressed upon Taylor the importance of obtaining information regarding movements and designs of the enemy, and authorized him to pay *"employes"* liberally for procuring such information. Kearny's expedition to New Mexico and California, said Scott, would necessarily be independent of Taylor's command, but that of General Wool against the city of Chihuahua would be under Taylor's general directions. The general was authorized to agree to an armistice with a view to peace negotiations, provided he was convinced of the enemy's good faith.[32]

In his reply to these letters, Taylor stated that he had little definite information to impart. He gave, however, his opinions regarding the probabilities of obtaining supplies in the interior. Should the inhabitants prove friendly, he thought that his army might obtain provisions sufficient to enable it to penetrate as far as Saltillo; still, in his opinion, the army under his command should confine its operations to the northern provinces and should not attempt to reach the City of Mexico. He "purposely" abstained "from any reference to movements against Tampico or Vera Cruz." He complained that he was greatly embarrassed by the lack of transportation facilities and closed his letter with the remark that:

> I am waiting with the utmost impatience the arrival of steamboats suited to the navigation of this river to establish a depot at Camargo, and throw the troops gradually forward to that point.[33]

Although General Taylor may have been overcautious in offering suggestions, he seems to have reported all the information in his possession. But officials in Washington, especially Quartermaster General Jesup, were inclined to excuse their own shortcomings by pleading lack of information from Taylor, and the

---

[32] *H. Ex. Doc. 60*, 30 Cong., 1 sess., 323–327.
[33] Taylor to Adj. Gen., July 2, 1846, *ibid.*, 329–332.

President came to feel that the general did not possess the initiative and the vigor necessary for the command which had been intrusted to him. Polk admitted that he had no knowledge of military affairs, but he had ''a strong conviction'' that necessary equipments had been too long delayed. He told the quartermaster general that some of his subordinates had become gentlemen of leisure who ''required to have a coal of fire put on their backs to make them move promptly.'' He feared, also, that Taylor was not the man for the general command:

He is brave but does not seem to have resources or grasp of mind enough to conduct such a campaign. In his communications to the War Department he seems ready to obey orders, but appears to be unwilling to express any opinion or to take any responsibility on himself. Though he is in the country with means of knowledge which cannot be possessed at Washington, he makes no suggestion as to the plan of the campaign, but simply obeys orders and gives no information to aid the administration in directing his movement. He is, I have no doubt, a good subordinate officer, but from all the evidence before me I think him unfit for the chief command. Though this is so, I know of no one whom I can substitute in his place.[34]

These remarks greatly exaggerated Taylor's taciturnity, yet the President was sorely in need of information to aid him in directing the campaign. When in October an expedition to Tampico and Vera Cruz was being considered, so little was known of the character of the coast that Polk found it necessary to send to Rhode Island for F. M. Dimond, former consul at Vera Cruz, ''believing that from him reliable information could be obtained.'' Nearly a month later the quartermaster general just awoke to the fact that: ''Had we foreseen the nature of the Rio Del Norte, and built suitable steamboats several months ago, a million of dollars might have been saved by this time.''[35]

---

[34] Polk, *Diary*, II, 117–119.

[35] *Ibid.*, 180, 196. Jesup to Marcy, Nov. 7, 1846 (*H. Ex. Doc. 60*, 30 Cong., 1 sess., 564). So vigorously had Taylor complained of inefficiency in the quartermaster's department, in a letter dated September 1, that Jesup was sent to New Orleans so that he might personally supervise the equipping of Taylor's army (Corresp. of Taylor, Marcy and Jesup, in same *Doc.*, 557 ff.).

Although the President was lacking in military experience, and although, according to his own testimony, he found it to be ''impossible to give much attention to the details in conducting the war,'' his brain was most fertile when it came to concocting schemes for undermining the control of the Mexican government over its own citizens. Ample proof of this is furnished in a confidential letter sent to Taylor under date of July 9, 1846. The letter was signed by Marcy, but was drafted by Polk, with some assistance from Benton. The President approved Taylor's conciliatory conduct toward the Mexicans and urged him to continue friendly intercourse with the inhabitants. The general was instructed to

take occasions to send officers to the headquarters of the enemy for military purposes, real or ostensible . . . . in which opportunity may be taken to speak of the war itself as only carried on to obtain justice, and that we had much rather procure that by negotiation than by fighting.

Racial and social discords, he was told, made it possible to induce a large portion of the people to wish success to invaders who had no desire to injure them:

In all this field of division—in all these elements of social, political, personal, and local discord—there must be openings to reach the interests, passions, or principles of some of the parties, and thereby to conciliate their good will, and make them co-operate with us in bringing about an honorable and a speedy peace . . . . . Policy and force are to be combined; and the fruits of the former will be prized as highly as those of the latter.

Another paragraph, which was penned by the President alone and which he considered to be the most important, was still more specific in outlining the policy of the administration:

Availing yourself of divisions which you may find among the Mexican people . . . . it will be your policy to encourage the separate departments or States, and especially those which you may invade and occupy, to declare their independence of the central government of Mexico, and either to become our allies, or to assume, as it is understood Yucatan has done, a neutral attitude in the existing war between the United States and Mexico.

After peace had been concluded such departments were to "decide for themselves their own form of government." As to temporary governments Taylor was authorized to follow the course laid down in the instructions to Kearny, a copy of which was inclosed. He was informed that an expedition against Mexico City would probably be sent from Tampico or Vera Cruz, and not from the Rio Grande. Information was requested, and Taylor was instructed to send his answer "directly to the *President of the United States.*"[36] Only two days before this Houston, of Texas, had introduced in the Senate a resolution which extended the thanks of Congress to Taylor for his victories on the Rio Grande, and requested the President to present the general with a gold medal "as a tribute to his good conduct, and generosity, to the vanquished."[37]

As usual, Buchanan was ready with a dash of cold water for the President's scheme of benevolent assimilation of Mexican territory. He was in favor of taking and holding California as far as Monterey but no farther. "He was opposed, too," said the President, "to giving the inhabitants of Tamaulipas or of any of the Provinces South of New Mexico any encouragement to annex themselves to the U. S." Both Walker and Polk preferred to extend the boundary farther south, and the President was sorry to find his Secretary of State "entertaining opinions so contracted & sectional."[38]

About the same time, members of Congress gave the President no little annoyance by introducing resolutions of inquiry concerning the purposes of the war and the manner of conducting it. On June 29 the Senate had passed a resolution, introduced by Johnson, of Maryland, which called on the President for all

---

[36] Marcy to Taylor, July 9, 1846 (*H. Ex. Doc. 60*, 30 Cong., 1 sess., 333–336). Polk, *Diary*, II, 16–17. "I will preserve the original draft for future reference," Polk recorded in his diary, "should it become proper. I do this because it is a document of more than ordinary importance."

[37] *Cong. Globe*, 29 Cong., 1 sess., 1064.

[38] Polk, *Diary*, II, 15–16.

correspondence incident to the raising of volunteer troops. Polk
sent for Johnson, on July 6, and by showing him the correspondence convinced him that it would be unwise to comply, for the
projected conquest of California would be revealed, and this
would "excite the jealousy of England and France, who might
interfere to prevent the accomplishing of our objects."[39] For
the purpose of ascertaining why nothing had been done by Taylor's army since the occupation of Matamoras, Hannegan, on
July 8, introduced a resolution which purposed to ask the President for information concerning all orders sent to the general
since the ninth of May. By his renewal of friendship with Benton
the President had procured an able defender, and the Missouri
Senator was successful in sending this resolution to the table by
asserting that if an officer should furnish the information sought
he would be court-martialed and shot.[40]

In truth, the executive departments had little information to
impart. On August 1, Taylor answered the letter of July 9,
which Benton and Polk had so carefully prepared, by saying that
he had little to add to his dispatch of July second. He still declined to venture an opinion on the practicability of an expedition against Vera Cruz, for the "Department of War must be
much better informed than I am on that point." He told the
President that he would obey his order to seek friendly intercourse with Mexican generals, and to induce the people to declare
their independence, but he stated very frankly that he did not
anticipate much success.[41]

President Polk's subterranean diplomacy was not confined to
an attempt to undermine the loyalty of Mexican generals and
people. Since his conversations with Atocha, he had never quite
abandoned the hope of making use of Santa Anna, and he now
decided to assist the ex-dictator in regaining power in Mexico.

---

   [39] *Ibid.*, 13–14.

   [40] *Cong. Globe*, 29 Cong., 1 sess., 1068.

   [41] Taylor to Polk, Aug. 1, 1846 (*H. Ex. Doc. 60*, 30 Cong., 1 sess.,
336–338).

On May 13, 1846, two days after the President had sent his war message to Congress, Secretary Bancroft instructed Commodore Conner to blockade the Gulf ports of Mexico. At the same time, he inclosed a "private and confidential" order which read: "If Santa Anna endeavors to enter the Mexican ports, you will allow him to pass freely." Atocha, it will be remembered, had told Polk that Santa Anna would probably return to Mexico in April or May, and that he was in favor of ceding territory to the United States. Apparently the President had this conversation in mind when he caused Bancroft to issue the order to Conner.[42]

Early in June Polk decided to send a special messenger to Havana for the purpose of learning the plans of Santa Anna. The messenger selected was Alexander Slidell Mackenzie, a naval officer and a nephew of John Slidell, the minister whom Mexico had rejected. He was furnished with a letter from Buchanan to Campbell, the United States consul at Havana, a copy of Bancroft's confidential order to Conner, and verbal instructions from the President. Mackenzie gave the purport of these instructions when reporting to Buchanan the result of his interview with Santa Anna.[43] He arrived in Havana on July 5 and, by Campbell, was introduced to Santa Anna. From Polk's verbal instructions he had prepared a memorandum, and this he read to the ex-President of Mexico. In substance it stated that the United States had taken up arms to redress its grievances and was determined to prosecute the war with vigor, but that the President was desirous of ending the conflict speedily if an honorable peace could be made. Believing Santa Anna to be able and willing to make such a peace, "the President of the United States would see with pleasure his restoration to power in Mexico." It was made clear that Polk would insist on the Rio Grande as the boundary of Texas and that he must at least have enough of California to

---

[42] *Ibid.*, 744. Polk, *Diary*, I, 229.

[43] Mackenzie to Buchanan, June [July] 7, 1846 (duplicate in *Polk Papers*). This letter is printed in full in Reeves, *Diplomacy under Tyler and Polk*, 299–307.

include the port of San Francisco. For the latter concession he would pay liberally, and his present intention was to demand no indemnity for the expenses of the war. Although, according to Mackenzie's account, Santa Anna aserted that the Nueces was the real boundary of Texas, he finally agreed to make all necessary concessions rather than see Mexico delivered into the hands of a foreign prince or continue under the monarchistic government of Paredes. He even suggested plans under which Taylor could most easily defeat the Mexican armies, and advised the occupation of Tampico. Mackenzie considered these suggestions of such importance that he exceeded his instructions and carried them directly to General Taylor. He had an interview with Taylor late in July,[44] but it is not likely that the general was influenced by Santa Anna's recommendations.

Mackenzie's report of his interview with Santa Anna, according to a note appended by Buchanan, reached Washington on the third of August. The President did not mention the subject in his diary either at the time of sending the messenger or when the report was received. In January, 1848, however, after he and his cabinet had decided not to include this report with other documents submitted in response to a call from the House, the President recorded his version of the mission. In this account Polk stated that he had given Mackenzie no written instructions, and that he had sent "no message" to Santa Anna. In reducing the conversation with the President to writing and in reading it to Santa Anna, the messenger had acted wholly without authority. As to whether Mackenzie's memorandum correctly reported his conversation with Polk, the record in the diary is somewhat ambiguous. "It is fortunate," is the President's comment, "that what he puts into my mouth could do me no injury, if it was genuine & was published; but it would exhibit me in a ridiculous attitude." For this reason, he decided to withhold it from the House.[45]

---

[44] Meade, *Life and Letters,* I, 116.   [45] Polk, *Diary,* III, 290–292.

The President was eager to settle all differences with Mexico by diplomacy instead of war, provided he could obtain the territory he most coveted. Without waiting to learn the results of Mackenzie's mission, he made one more attempt to make a satisfactory treaty with the government of Paredes. On Sunday, July 20, he sent for Benton and read to him a dispatch which had been prepared by Buchanan. It was addressed to the Mexican Minister of Foreign Relations. Benton approved the dispatch and advised that it should be sent. A week later a revised copy was forwarded to Commodore Conner with instructions that it should be delivered to the Mexican government. The document stated that the President was no less anxious to terminate the war than he had been to avoid it in the beginning. To accomplish this purpose he was ready to send an envoy who would be clothed with power to make "a peace just and honorable for both parties." Should Mexico prefer to negotiate in Washington, her envoy would be treated with kindness. "In the present communication," said Buchanan, "it is deemed useless and might prove injurious, to discuss the causes of the existing war."[46]

Having decided to seek a settlement with Mexico through diplomatic channels, Polk revived the plan of asking Congress for money to be used in negotiating a treaty. When discussing with Benton the dispatch just mentioned, the President expressed the belief that he could procure both California and New Mexico if Congress would furnish him with two million dollars which might be paid to Mexico as soon as a treaty had been signed. Benton favored such an appropriation and advised Polk to consult with members of the Committee on Foreign Affairs. The President sent for McDuffie, Cass, and other members of the committee. He cited the appropriation which had enabled Jefferson to purchase Louisiana and urged the expediency of making a similar appropriation now. Archer, the Whig member, agreed to take

---

[46] Buchanan to Min. of For. Rel., July 27, 1846; Buchanan to Conner, same date (*Sen. Ex. Doc. 107*, 29 Cong., 2 sess., 2–3). The former is also in Buchanan, *Works*, VII, 40.

the matter up with Senators of his party. Having thus paved
the way, Polk sent a confidential message to the Senate on August
4, 1846, and along with it, a copy of the dispatch already forwarded to the Mexican Minister of Foreign Relations. Believing
that "the best mode of securing perpetual peace and good neighborhood between the two Republics" would be the acquision of
Mexican territory, he asked for an advance appropriation of two
million dollars as a means of facilitating such an acquisition.[47]
After the Senate had given its approval, the message was transmitted to the House so that a bill might be drafted.

As soon as the message had been read in the House, McKay,
of North Carolina, presented a bill which provided that two
million dollars be appropriated "for the purpose of defraying
any extraordinary expenses which may be incurred in the intercourse between the United States and foreign nations," said
money to be applied under the direction of the President. While
Polk's plans for acquiring California were not, of course, generally known at the time, the Whigs at once charged that the
money was to be used for this purpose, either by direct purchase
or indirectly by bribing Mexican officials. The necessarily indefinite wording of the bill gave ample room for partisan interpretations. White, of New York, was the most uncompromising
critic of the President. He asserted that Polk himself had, in his
war message, furnished abundant evidence that this war had
been "projected, planned, and provoked" long before Congress
had been consulted in the matter. He intimated, also, that the
purpose of the bill was to extend slaveholding territory, and he
challenged any Democrat to propose an amendment which would
exclude slavery from the territory to be acquired. During the
evening session of the same day Wilmot accepted this challenge
by offering his famous "proviso" that slavery should not be
permitted in any teritory to be obtained from Mexico.

---

47 Polk, *Diary*, II, 50–66. Richardson, *Messages*, IV, 456.

The position taken by John Quincy Adams is interesting. A violent opponent of the administration on nearly every occasion, he had supported Polk's claim to 54° 40′ as the Oregon boundary, and he now warmly advocated the appropriation of the two million dollars for which the President had asked. For the sake of clearness, he asked McKay to substitute ''Mexico'' for ''foreign nations,'' but, despite his sympathy with Wilmot's amendment, he was ready to ''vote for the bill in any form.'' He did not believe an anti-slavery amendment to be necessary, for the institution had been abolished by Mexico and would not be reëstablished.[48] Based on the past, this was sound argument, but he could not forsee what the future would bring forth.

The McKay bill, supplemented by the Wilmot amendment, passed the House by a vote of eighty-seven to sixty-four. On the day following, the last of the session, it was considered by the Senate, but Davis, of Massachusetts, prevented a vote on the measure by holding the floor until the session had expired. Whether the Senate would have pased the bill as amended we are, of course, unable to say, but the President believed that it would have struck out Wilmot's ''mischievous & foolish amendment'' and that the House would have concurred. ''What connection slavery had with making peace with Mexico,'' said he, ''it is difficult to conceive.'' In order to preclude all doubt concerning his motives, he confided to his diary an explicit statement of his reasons for requesting the advance appropriation.[49]

---

48 ''There are no slaves in California—slavery is abolished there; and if we were to make peace, and in that peace to acquire California, there could be no law of slavery established there, unless it was made an article of the treaty itself.''

49 ''My object in asking this appropriation has not been fully stated in this diary. It was this. Mexico is indebted to the U. S. in a large sum, which she is unable to pay. There is also a disputed question of boundary. The two countries are now engaged in War. When peace is made the only indemnity which the U. S. can have will be a cession of territory. The U. S. desires to acquire Upper California, New Mexico, and perhaps some territory South of these Provinces. For a suitable cession of territory we are willing to assure the debts to our own citizens & to pay an additional consideration. My information induces the belief that Mexico would be willing to settle the

The disappointment which resulted from the defeat of the appropriation bill was somewhat assuaged by news of the conquest of California which reached Washington on the last day of August. The welcome information and a copy of Sloat's proclamation were brought by a messenger who had just come from Mexico City bearing dispatches for the British minister. The diplomat reported the news to Buchanan immediately, and the President noted in his diary: "This important intelligence comes to us through no other channel."[50] The conquest, however, was of little immediate value, for Polk was soon to learn that Mexico had declined to accept his proffered "honorable peace."

Santa Anna, and not Paredes, dictated the answer to Buchanan's letter of July 27 in which Mexico was invited to open peace negotiations. Relying on Polk's assurances that he would not be molested, Santa Anna left Havana on August 8, 1846, on

---

difficulty in this manner. No Government, however, it is believed, is strong enough to make a treaty ceding territory and long maintain power unless they could receive, at the time of making the treaty, money enough to support the army. Whatever party can keep the army in its support can hold the power. The present Government is without any regular revenue, & without a prompt payment as a part of the consideration would not venture to make a Treaty. Having no doubt that I could effect an adjustment of the pending war if I had the command of $2,000,000, I felt it to be my duty to ask such an appropriation. This I did in the first instance by a confidential communication made to the Senate in Executive Session on the 4th Instant. The Senate on the 6th Inst. passed resolutions approving my views and declaring that it was proper to make the appropriation asked. The Resolution approving my views passed the Senate by a vote of ayes 43 to nays 2, and the Resolution approving the appropriation by yeas 33 to nays 19 (. . .). With a full knowledge of all this Senator Davis had recourse to the desperate resort of speaking against time, to defeat a measure which he had been unable to defeat by his vote. Had the appropriation been passed I am confident I should have made an honorable peace by which we should have acquired California, & such other territory as we desired, before the end of October. Should the war be now protracted, the responsibility will fall more heavily upon the head of Senator Davis than upon any other man, and he will deserve the execrations of the country. I desired when I made the communication to the Senate in Executive Session, to consult that body in secret Session, to the end that the appropriation, if approved, should have been passed quietly and without attracting public attention, or exciting the jealousy of the Powers of Europe; but contrary to my wishes great publicity has been given to it by Congress" (*Dairy*, II, 75–78).

50 *Ibid.*, 108.

board the British ship *Arab,* and eight days later he landed in
Vera Cruz. With him came Almonte, former minister to the
United States, and Rejón and Basadre who had been members of
his cabinet at the time he was forced to leave Mexico. The way
had been prepared for his return by *pronouncement* of the troops,
and General Salas, the commander-in-chief, stood ready to do
the bidding of the returned exile.

On the day of his arrival, August 16, Santa Anna issued an
address which was filled with specious promises and high sounding phrases.[51] If these were to be accepted at face value, the
ex-dictator had returned a sincere patriot and a champion of the
Constitution of 1824, ready to subject himself "entirely to the
decisions of the constitutent assembly, the organ of the sovereign
will of the nation." For a time, Salas continued to act as chief
executive while Santa Anna, the general-in-chief, sojourned at
a country residence. But the late exile selected the cabinet and
controlled the affairs of the nation.

By the last of August internal affairs were adjusted sufficiently to enable the new government to consider the offer made
by the United States. In reply to. Buchanan's note Rejón, the
new Secretary of Foreign Relations, said that the general-in-chief
could not but "fix his attention strongly" on the passage in that
note which suggested the omission of all discussion concerning
the causes of the war. He felt himself unable to negotiate on
such terms; and besides, he was obliged to postpone a definite
answer until the Mexican congress had met on the sixth of December.[52] This aggravating snub was Polk's reward for helping to
reinstate Santa Anna in Mexico. Before many months had passed
he had still greater reasons for regretting that he had listened
to the advice of Atocha.

Rejón's letter reached Washington on September 19 and was
considered by the President as a virtual refusal to negotiate. He

---

[51] A copy in translation, *H. Ex. Doc. 60,* 30 Cong., 1 sess., 777–785.
[52] Rejón to Buchanan, Aug. 31, 1846 (*H. Ex. Doc. 4,* 29 Cong., 2 sess., 43.)

at once decided that the character of the war should be changed so that the Mexican people might be made to feel the consequences of their government's refusal to make peace. The conciliatory policy of paying liberally for supplies was now to be changed for one of forcible seizures. The President directed that the towns in Tamaulipas should be occupied and that a descent should be made upon the coast at Tampico. Contrary to his usual custom of refraining from all labor on the Sabbath, Polk held cabinet meetings on September 20 in order to hasten aggressive movements against the enemy. Colonel Stevenson, who had been put in command of the New York regiment destined for service in California, was reprimanded by the President because his departure had been so long delayed, and Polk "intimated plainly to Col. S. that if further delay occurred he [I] would cause the officers who produced it to be arrested & tried." During the next few days much energy was devoted to war and naval preparations. Major-General Patterson was selected to command the Tampico expedition, and Pillow and Shields were chosen as his assistants. Polk gave personal attention to the quartermaster's department so that there might be no delay. The failure of his diplomatic overtures and the lax conduct of subordinates put the President in a petulant mood. He charged Whig officials with indifference regarding military operations, while General Scott, instead of being an aide to the War Department, was a constant embarrassment. "I will observe his course," wrote the President in his diary, "and if necessary will order him to some other post."[53]

While making preparations for war, Polk still left the way open for negotiations with Mexico. Under his direction, Buchanan, on September 26, prepared and sent a reply to Rejón's note of August 31. He charged the Mexican government with having distorted the meaning of his former letter. He told Rejón that "the President will now await with patience and

[53] Polk, *Diary*, II, 143–151.

with hope the final decision of the Mexican Government.'' He informed the minister, however, that in the meantime the war would be prosecuted vigorously, and there was a veiled threat that Mexico would be required to pay the costs. Buchanan's original draft had stated explicitly that Mexico must indemnify the United States for the expenses of the war, but Polk and Marcy deemed it politic to reserve this blunt demand until negotiations had opened.[54] Commodore Conner was instructed to notify Slidell at New Orleans immediately in the event that the Mexican government should at any time show a disposition to negotiate.[55]

From the middle of May, when he occupied Matamoras, until the first of September, General Taylor spent the time in training and equipping an army for an advance upon Monterey. Due to General Gaines's unauthorized call for volunteers, Taylor was overwhelmed with troops, but the quartermaster had failed to furnish him with adequate supplies or means of transportation. Commenting on the impatience felt by people in the United States, and even by volunteer troops, because the army did not advance into Mexico, Lieutenant Meade said in a letter:

These wise people forget that soldiers cannot march or fight unless they have something to eat, and when in a country totally devoid of resources, they must carry with them the means of sustaining physical nature, and in consequence must have the means of carrying their provisions and other supplies.

He thought that Scott was right in not wishing to go immediately to the Rio Grande, there to idle away his time ''waiting for wagons and pork''; but ''unfortunately, he [Scott] chose to ascribe political reasons to what, I believe, was simply military ignorance on the part of Mr. Polk.''[56]

---

[54] Polk, *Diary*, II, 156–158. Buchanan to Min. of For. Rel., Sept. 26, 1846 (*H. Ex. Doc. 4*, 29 Cong., 2 sess., 44–45).

[55] Buchanan to Conner, Oct. 1, 1846 (*Works*, VII, 90).

[56] Meade, *Life and Letters*, I, 101–111. ''This, with his 'hasty plate of soup,' '' continued Meade, ''has ruined him forever, for it is much better in this country for a man to commit a gross crime than to make himself ridiculous; the former he may get over, the latter, never.''

By the last of August Taylor had collected his invading force at Camargo, and within a few days his army was advancing on Monterey. The march was tedious, and on arriving at that place he found it to be well fortified. The attack upon the city began on September 20, and on the twenty-fourth Ampudia, the Mexican commander, offered to evacuate the city if Taylor would permit the troops to retain their arms and other movable property. Taylor at first demanded "a complete surrender of the town and garrison, the latter as prisoners of war"; but he finally consented to allow the Mexicans to march out with all of their arms and accoutrements. He also agreed to a truce of eight weeks, or until further orders had been received from their respective governments.[57] The period of inactivity was destined to be longer than that agreed upon in the truce, for the President soon determinted to modify his plan of reducing Mexico to submission.

The special messenger whom Taylor had dispatched with a report of the battle of Monterey reached Washington on Sunday, October 11, and the President was much displeased because the general had agreed to the armistice.[58] At a cabinet meeting held on the following day all agreed that the general had committed a "great error." After the meeting, Polk noted in his diary:

But two reasons could have justified the terms granted to the enemy in the capitulation. The first is, if he believed that he could not capture them; & the 2nd. is, that Gen'l Ampudia may have induced him to believe that in consequence of the recent change of rulers in Mexico that Government was disposed to make peace. If the first reason existed Gen'l Taylor has not stated it in his despatches, and we have no information to justify

[57] Taylor's reports (*H. Ex. Doc. 4*, 29 Cong., 2 sess., 83–102). A good account of this battle is given in Rives, *United States and Mexico*, II, chap. 37.

[58] "In agreeing to this armistice Gen'l Taylor violated his express orders & I regret that I cannot approve his course. He had the enemy in his power & should have taken them prisoners, depriving them of their arms, discharge them on their parole of honour, and preserved the advantage which he had obtained by pushing on without delay further into the country, if the force at his command justified it. . . . It was a great mistake in Gen'l Taylor to agree to an armistice. It will only enable the Mexican army to reorganize and recruit so as to make another stand" (*Diary*, II, 181).

the existence of this reason, though it may have existed. If the second reason was the one upon which he acted, then Gen'l Ampudia has over-reached & deceived him . . . . . The Cabinet were united in the opinion that if Gen'l Taylor had captured the Mexican army, deprived them of their arms, and discharged them upon their parole of honour not to bear arms during the war or until they were regularly exchanged, that it would have probably ended the war with Mexico. . . . . It was agreed unanimously that orders should be forthwith sent to Gen'l Taylor to terminate the armistice to which he had agreed, and to prosecute the war with energy and vigor.[59]

Taylor's agreement had, in fact, placed his government in a most awkward position, but the difficulty was due more to the slow means of communication than to bad judgment on the part of the general or the administration. On receipt of Rejón's letter Polk decided immediately, as we have already noted, to strike a blow at both northern Tamaulipas and Tampico, and Marcy,[60] on September 22, notified Taylor of the change in the President's plans. General Patterson was at the same time ordered by the President to invade Tamaulipas. To be sure Taylor had no knowledge of this arrangement when he made the agreement with Ampudia, but his armistice, if permitted to remain in force, would paralyze in a great measure the aggressive movement which had been assigned to Patterson.

The letter in which Marcy instructed Taylor to terminate the armistice was not so drastic as the comments in Polk's diary would lead one to expect. In fact, it contained no phrase that should have given offense to the victorious general. The President, he said, regretted that "it was not deemed advisable to insist upon the terms which you had first proposed," but he added that the "circumstances which dictated doubtless justified the change." After explaining the new plan of campaign and the necessity of beginning operations at once, he instructed Taylor to give the notice necessary for ending the truce.[61]

[59] Polk, *Diary*, II, 183–184.
[60] *H. Ex. Doc. 60*, 30 Cong., 1 sess., 341–343.
[61] Marcy to Taylor, Oct. 13, 1846 (*ibid.*, 355–357).

Although nothing in Marcy's communication could reasonably be construed as a reflection upon Taylor, the ever-suspicious general drew from it evidence of a conspiracy to discredit him and to deprive him of his command. While admitting that Marcy's letter praised him, he detected in it a very cold tone. He believed that the administration was hostile to him simply because his friends had been indiscreet enough to connect his name with the Presidency.[62] In his reply to the War Department, he stated that with his limited force he could not have prevented the escape of the enemy from Monterey, and that his equipment did not warrant the pursuit of Ampudia into a country devoid of supplies. He admitted that he had been influenced, also, by Ampudia's statement that Santa Anna was in favor of making peace, and with a thrust at the President, he added: "It is not unknown to the government that I had the very best reason for believing the statement of General Ampudia to be true."[63] This pointed reference to Polk's part in the reinstatement of Santa Anna must have been read at the White House with anything but pleasure, yet Taylor could not be blamed for believing that the President desired, most of all, a peaceable adjustment with Mexico. All of his instructions had emphasized this point. He was aware of Polk's overtures to Santa Anna and of his recent offer to the Paredes government. Since he had not received Marcy's instructions of September 22 his agreement with Ampudia accorded very well with the policy of his government, so far as he knew it at the time. Still, he had no reason to complain because he had been instructed to end the truce, and the political motives which dictated these instructions existed only in his own very active imagination. The main difficulty, as already stated, was the slow means of communication which made it impossible for either the general or the administration to know the conditions

---

[62] Taylor to Wood, Nov. 10, 1846, *Taylor Letters,* 67.

[63] Taylor to Adj. Gen., Nov. 8, 1846 (*H. Ex. Doc. 60,* 30 Cong., 1 sess., 359–360).

which governed the actions of the other. Even before the armistice had been disapproved, Taylor felt abused because the President had tried to facilitate the advance upon Tamaulipas by sending orders directly to General Patterson,[64] but in this case, also, Polk's action was governed by military rather than political considerations.

Santa Anna's declaration in favor of restoring the constitution of 1824 led President Polk to abandon the hope of inducing the northern provinces of Mexico to declare their independence of the central government. Since the main purpose of Taylor's advance into Nueva León and Coahuila, and that of Wool into Chihuahua, had been to effect this separation, the President decided that both of these expeditions, especially the latter, had now become "comparatively unimportant." Accordingly he suggested at a cabinet meeting that Taylor should be authorized to remain at Monterey, and, if he saw fit, to order Wool to the same place. He suggested, also, that the most effective means of bringing Mexico to terms would be an invasion from Vera Cruz. Marcy embodied these views in a letter to Taylor and his letter was carefully discussed at a special cabinet meeting. In the meantime Marcy's draft had been shown to Scott whereupon the general expressed a desire to command the Vera Cruz expedition, and recommended an army of twenty-five or thirty thousand men. But Polk had not forgotten Scott's indiscreet letters, consequently the request was not granted. After a discussion of more than two hours instructions were agreed upon and delivered to Robert M. McLane who had been selected as special messenger. They covered the points already noted, and the choice between remaining at Monterey or advancing into the interior was left entirely to Taylor's discretion. He was informed that General

---

[64] "I conceive that this mode of regulating details and ordering detachments direct from the Department of War is a violation of the integrity of the chief command in the field, pregnant with the worst of evils, and against which I deem it my duty respectfully but earnestly to protest" (Taylor to Adj. Gen., Oct. 15, 1846, *ibid.*, 354).

Patterson would probably command the Vera Cruz expedition, and he was asked to send about two thousand of his regulars to this commander, if, in his judgment, they could be spared. On the other hand, he was forbidden to send them if, in his opinion, his own position would be endangered.[65]

---

[65] Polk, *Diary*, II, 198–205. Marcy to Taylor, Oct. 22, 1846 (*H. Ex. Doc. 60,* 30 Cong., 1 sess., 363–367).

CHAPTER XIX

CAMPAIGN AGAINST THE CITY OF MEXICO

For some time after instructing Taylor to remain at Monterey the President remained undecided as to what policy he would pursue. He had difficulty in making up his mind whether, after the capture of Vera Cruz, the army should simply hold the territory in possession and wait for Mexico to treat, or whether an advance to Mexico City should be undertaken. Before any decision had been reached, Colonel Richard B. Mason was sent to California via Panama, and instructed to command the troops in that region until the arrival of General Kearny.[1]

Financial as well as military considerations impeded the formation of a definite war policy. Department estimates caused so much apprehension concerning the cost of the war that the number of volunteers asked for by Marcy was cut down from 25,000 to 10,000 men. No decision had been reached as to whether the government should simply preserve the *status quo*, or "prosecute the war into the heart of Mexico." Buchanan advocated the former policy and, apparently, Polk did not wish to decide the question either way until he had consulted the Senator from Missouri. Benton called by appointment on the same evening (November 7) and expressed himself as strongly in favor of taking Vera Cruz and of following this up with a crushing movement against Mexico City. To confine the military operations simply to holding the territory then in possession would, in his opinion, prolong the war and ruin the Democratic party; for "ours were a go-ahead people and . . . . our only policy either

---

[1] This action resulted from Polk's want of confidence in Colonel Stevenson who had been sent round the Horn with the New York volunteers (Polk, *Diary*, II, 209, 215).

to obtain a peace or save ourselves was to press the war boldly.''
He believed that commissioners vested with authority to offer
peace, ''before a battle, during the battle, & after it was over,''
should accompany the army headquarters, and he offered to be
one of the number. Three days later the Senator suggested that
some man of ''talents and resources'' and of military training
ought to be made lieutenant-general, and he modestly offered to
accept the position if it should be created by Congress. After
alluding to his original preference for Van Buren he declared
that he was now ready to give Polk his unqualified support. To
make his declaration more emphatic, he reminded the President
that he [Benton] had quarreled with General Jackson and had
subsequently defended him ''in the gloomy period of the Bank
panic.''[2] The would-be commissioner continued to urge the
necessity of an advance upon the Mexican capital, but the President was reluctant to undertake such an expedition if it could
be avoided. By November 17, however, Polk had decided to
attack Vera Cruz, although he still ''considered it to be an open
question, to be determined according to circumstances hereafter,
whether a column should be sent from Vera Cruz against the
City of Mexico.'' If, by that time, Mexico should decline to make
peace, he would be ''decidedly in favour'' of taking the capital
city.[3]

The selection of a commander for the Vera Cruz expedition
caused the President great anxiety. He would gladly have chosen
Benton; but the Missouri Senator would not accept a rank lower
than that of lieutenant-general, and there was no reason for believing that Congress would create such an office. Polk had lost
faith in Taylor's ability as a commanding officer. He had also
come to regard him as the partisan dupe of Bailie Peyton and
George W. Kendall, ''who were cunning & shrewd men of more
talents than himself, and had controlled him for political purposes.'' ''His constant effort has been to throw the responsibility

---

[2] Polk, *Diary*, II, 221–223, 227–228.   [3] *Ibid.*, 241.

of any disaster which might happen on the administration. In this he had been most ungrateful for the kindness which he has received at my hands.'' These impressions had been derived, in part, from Taylor's dispatches. In addition, Polk's mind had been poisoned by adverse criticisms contained in private letters written to him by his friend and benefactor, General Pillow.[4] Taylor had quite a different story to tell about *responsibility*. He told Crittenden in a letter that:

When it was supposed I was in great peril from which, had I not succeeded in extricating myself, the administration & its friends were prepared to throw the whole responsibility on me—[by saying that he had no authority to take a position on the Rio Grande].[5]

For some time Polk's aversion for Scott precluded all thought of assigning him to the chief command. Scott had, in September, requested that he might be sent to Mexico, and at that time his request was denied.[6] When, however, a majority of the cabinet, at a meeting held on November 17, reluctantly came to the conclusion that Scott ought to be appointed in spite of his faults, Polk consented to ''think further on the subject,'' although ''after his very exceptional letter in May last nothing but stern necessity and sense of public duty could induce me to place him at the head of so important [an] expedition.'' Benton was consulted, and when he, too, advised that, under present circumstances, Scott should be appointed, the President at last felt ''constrained to assign him to this command.'' When notified of his appointment Scott was, according to Polk's account, so grateful ''that he almost shed tears.''[7] If so, his gratitude proved to be ephemeral.

---

4 *Ibid.*, 227, 229, 236, 241. Peyton, it will be recalled, had been one of Polk's most hated political opponents in Tennessee. At this time he was a member of General Worth's staff. Kendall was editor of the New Orleans *Picayune* and accompanied Taylor's army in the capacity of war correspondent.

5 Taylor to Crittenden, Sept. 15, 1846, *Crittenden Papers.*

6 Scott to Marcy, Sept. 12; Marcy to Scott, Sept. 14, 1846 (*H. Ex. Doc. 60*, 30 Cong., 1 sess., 372–373).

7 Polk, *Diary*, II, 241–245.

Meanwhile the President was busily engaged in preparing his annual message to Congress. The original draft was shown to Benton, and the Senator suggested certain alterations.

In his *Thirty Years' View,* Benton stated that the draft contained a ''recommendation to Congress to cease the active prosecution of the war, to occupy the conquered part of the country (. . . .) with troops in forts and stations, and to pass an act establishing a temporary government in the occupied part; and to retain the possession until the peace was made.'' He stated further that he persuaded the President to give up the ''sedentary project.'' Apparently these statements grossly exaggerated the facts, for they agree neither with the President's general war policy, nor with his own description of his original drafts. His diary for December 1 reads:

> I had proposed in my draft to submit to Congress the propriety, *at the same time that the war should be vigorously prosecuted* [italics mine] to establish a line of boundary securing to the U. S. a sufficient territory to afford indemnity for the expenses of the war, and to our citizens who hold pecuniary demands against Mexico. I proposed, also, that a more permanent Government should be provided by Congress over the conquered provinces than the temporary Governments which had been established by our own Military and Naval commanders according to the laws of war. Col. Benton thought these passages should be omitted, and submitted to me in writing the reasons for this opinion.

Whether wise or unwise, these recommendations certainly did not advise a ''sedentary'' policy. The fact that Walker, who wanted all of Mexico, preferred Polk's draft to that of Benton is another indication that the President had no intention of terminating ''the active prosecution of the war.'' Although no suggestion to this effect seems to have been included in Polk's draft, certain modifications were made in order to please the Missouri Senator, for otherwise it was feared that he would oppose, and probably could defeat, everything which the President was about to recommend.[8]

---

[8] Benton, *Thirty Years' View,* II, 693. Polk, *Diary,* II, 258–260.

On December 7, 1846, the twenty-ninth Congress began its second session and, on the next day, received the President's annual message. In it Polk repelled the charge made by some of his opponents that the war with Mexico was unjust and unnecessary. "A more effectual means," said he, "could not have been devised to encourage the enemy and protract the war than to advocate and adhere to their cause, and thus give them 'aid and comfort.' " The intended application of this quotation from the constitutional definition of treason could not be misunderstood, and Polk at once became the object of violent denunciation. In order to disprove the charges that had been made, he gave a history of events leading up to the war, laying emphasis on the fact that Mexico had violated two treaties in which she had agreed to pay American claimants damages awarded to them by a joint commission. The first of these treaties was negotiated in 1839. The second, which postponed the dates of payment, declared upon its face, said the President, that " 'this new arrangement is entered into for the accommodation of Mexico.' " "Notwithstanding this new convention was entered into at the request of Mexico[9] and for the purpose of relieving her from embarrassment, the claimants have only received the interest due on the 30th of April, 1843, and three of the twenty installments."

---

[9] In this connection a letter of Waddy Thompson, who negotiated these treaties, is of interest: "In the unquestionable vindication of the Mexican war by the President I see that much prominence is given to two points both of which I claim exclusive credit of as they were both not only without instructions but in violations of the orders of the state department. By the Treaty of 1839 the Mexican government had the option to pay the awards in cash or in Treasury notes. These latter were worth then not more than 20 cents in the dollar and now are worth even less. But the whole debt could have been paid with less than one fifth of its nominal amount. The brevity of a letter will not allow me to state to you the various means by which I managed to close the eyes of Mexico to the advantages which they possessed. But I did so and on my *own responsibility* made a provisional arrangement subject to the ratification of my government. It was approved with certain alterations. Mr. Webster sent me the draft of a Treaty. The preamble stated that this new arrangement was made at the instance and desire of the American claimants. I took the responsibility of changing this and stated in my despatch accompanying the Treaty that if Mexico failed to comply with the terms of the Treaty it would give us a much stronger justification for inforcing payment than if it had been stated in

The President maintained that the United States had had ample grounds for war long before the Mexican army crossed the Rio Grande. He asserted, also, that hostilities had not been precipitated by Taylor's advance to the western frontier, for "Mexico herself had never placed the war which she has waged upon the ground that our army occupied the intermediate territory between the Nueces and the Rio Grande." After an elaborate argument which proved, to his own satisfaction at least, the Rio Grande to be the rightful boundary of Texas, he said that it would be "difficult to justify the Executive, whose duty it is to see that the laws be faithfully executed if . . . . he had assumed the responsibility of yielding up the territory west of the Nueces."

One passage in the message relating to conquered territories was subsequently attacked in the Senate. Having urged a vigorous prosecution of the war the President went on to say that:

In the Provinces of New Mexico and of the Californias little, if any, further resistance is apprehended from the inhabitants to the temporary governments which have thus, from the necessity of the case and according to the laws of war, been established. It may be proper to provide for the security of these important conquests by making adequate appropriation for the purpose of erecting fortifications and defraying the expenses necessary incident to the maintenance of our possession and authority over them.

---

the Treaty that the change in the Treaty had been made at the instance of the claimants. I see that it is so regarded by the President in his message."

Concerning article six of the treaty of 1843, which Polk had also mentioned, Thompson said: "The sixth clause of the Treaty which provides for a new convention for claims not then adjusted was inserted by me not only without instructions, but it was disapproved by Mr. Webster but nevertheless retained" (Thompson to Buchanan, Dec. 13, 1846, *Buchanan Papers*). In this same letter, Thompson spoke of letters which he and Webster had written to Bocanegra, Mexican Secretary of Foreign Relations, in 1842. These are printed in the appendix of his book, *Recollections of Mexico*. There Thompson agrees that Webster had written his letter before having seen his [Thompson's], but in the letter to Buchanan he accuses Webster of plagiarism: "Mr. Webster stole my reply to Mr. Bocanegra's letter to him and to the diplomatic corps and published it as his own—in a letter to me. He says in his letter to me endorsing his reply to Mr. Bocanegra that he had not received mine when he wrote his. In this he lied. That is the word and no other word will express the idea. He had received it & stole it, and then lied about it. Telling a falsehood to conceal a larceny—a petty larceny if you please—of this I have the proof." But cf. *Recollections*, 284–304.

As will be seen later, some members of Congress interpreted this as a recommendation to provide for permanent possession, before any treaty had been made.

So far as it related to the war, the message concluded with a renewal of the request for an appropriation of two million dollars to be used at the discretion of the President for diplomatic purposes. The reasons which had induced him to ask for that amount at the preceding session, said he, "still exist," and he believed that it would have been granted then if a vote had been taken.[10]

When the message came up for discussion in the Senate, Westcott, of Florida, moved that the part relating to conquered territories, above quoted, be referred to the Committee on Territories. Benton objected, and a discussion ensued as to whether the President's recommendation had contemplated the establishment of permanent governments. Westcott contended that no other meaning could be drawn from it, while Benton insisted that it meant nothing of the kind. No decision was reached, for, on motion made by Crittenden, the question was sent to the table.[11]

In the House, Garrett Davis, of Kentucky, caused a heated debate by introducing a resolution which requested the President to submit for examination all orders to military and naval officers relating to the establishment of civil governments in the conquered provinces. He had in mind, of course, the governments set up in New Mexico and California by General Kearny and Commodore Stockton, and he wished to know whether the acts of those officers had been authorized by the President; if so, he demanded to know "by what imperial or regal authority his majesty undertook to act in the premises." If Polk, said Davis, had authorized the organization of civil governments in foreign provinces, he was guilty of usurpation; and if the Santa Fé region was a part of Texas, as the message seemed to assert, then, the President had no right to set up a government over a portion

---

10 Richardson, *Messages,* IV, 472–495.
11 *Cong. Globe,* 29 Cong., 2 sess., 42–44.

of a sovereign state. Similar arguments were made by Schenck, of Ohio, and by other opponents of the administration. The defense of the President was led by Douglas, although many other Democrats rallied loyally to his support. After a week's debate, the resolution was passed on the fifteenth of December.[12]

The establishment of a government in California by Stockton and Fremont has already been discussed. A brief summary will indicate the objectionable features of Kearny's conquest of New Mexico which led the House to call upon the President for information.

Leaving Fort Leavenworth late June, 1846, in command of a small force made up of United States dragoons and Missouri volunteers, Kearny reached Santa Fé on August 18 and, without resistance, took possession of the capital of New Mexico. Four days later a proclamation was issued in which Kearny announced that he would hold the department "as a part of the United States, and under the name of the 'territory of New Mexico.'" After promising a representative government at an early date, the proclamation added that

The United States hereby absolves all persons residing within the boundaries of New Mexico from any further allegiance to the republic of Mexico, and hereby claims them as citizens of the United States.

Before the end of September he had framed and put into operation an elaborate civil government under the title of the "Organic law for the territory of New Mexico. . . ."[13]

Kearny's authority for thus assuming the rôle of lawgiver was based on the following confidential instructions sent to him by the Secretary of War on June 3, 1846:

Should you conquer and take possession of New Mexico and Upper California, or considerable places in either, you will establish temporary civil governments therein. . . . . You may assure the people of those provinces that it is the wish and design of the United States to provide for them a free government, with the least possible delay, similar to that

---

12 *Ibid.*, 12–33.

13 For the proclamation, "organic law," and other documents, see *H. Ex. Doc. 60*, 30 Cong., 1 sess., 169ff.

which exists in our territories. They will then be called upon to exercise the rights of freemen in electing their own representatives to the territorial legislature. It is foreseen that what relates to the civil government will be a difficult part of your duty, and much must necessarily be left to your own discretion.[14]

The explicit directions given in this letter, supplemented as they were by wide discretionary powers, seem to give ample authority for the action taken by General Kearny. Furthermore, when Polk received the news, on October 2, that Kearny had proclaimed New Mexico to be "a part of the United States," he noted in his diary that "Gen'l Kearny has thus far performed his duty well."[15] Whether, had no objections been raised, he would have given similar approval to the "organic law," we have no means of knowing. This document did not reach Washington until November 23, and, according to their own statements, it was not examined by either Marcy or Polk until after information regarding it had been requested by the House.[16]

Whatever he might have done with respect to Kearny's territorial governments had Congress interposed no objections, Polk now realized that part, at least, of Kearny's work could not be justified. At a cabinet meeting held on December 19, Buchanan expressed the opinion that the House resolution ought not to be answered, but the President decided to transmit the desired documents. In the evening he made the following comment:

> Among them was a document from Brigadier Gen'l Kearney, containing a form of Government over the conquered territory of New Mexico, which among other things declared that territory to be a part of the U. S. and provided for the election of a Delegate to the Congress of the U. S. In these and some other respects he exceeded the power of a military commander over a conquered territory. It was agreed that in my message to Congress I must disapprove this part of the Document, though, without censuring the Gen'l, who had misconceived the extent of his authority, but who had, no doubt, acted from patriotic motives.

---

[14] Marcy to Kearny, June 3, 1846 (*ibid.*, 244).

[15] Polk, *Diary*, II, 169–170.

[16] Marcy's report to the President, Dec. 21, 1846 (*H. Ex. Doc. 60*, 30 Cong., 1 sess., 151). Polk's Message of Dec. 22, 1846. Nothing is said in the *Diary* about this document until the matter had been brought up in the House.

A message to this effect, with an additional statement that "such excess has resulted in no practical injury," was sent to the House a few days later. And yet, not two months before this, the President had expressed satisfaction because Kearny had proclaimed New Mexico to be a part of the United States![17]

While awaiting information respecting territorial governments, the House engaged in an acrimonious debate on the President's annual message and the causes of the war. Polk was assailed for having stated in his message that his opponents had, by their attacks upon the administration, been giving "aid and comfort" to the enemy. In turn, he was charged with having given "aid and comfort" to Santa Anna, the most powerful and unscrupulous of the enemies. Whigs averred that the President had wantonly plunged the country into a war of aggression in order to show the world "who James K. Polk was." Even those who had voted for the declaration of war now asserted that the executive was conducting "an unconstitutional war." Most abusive of all was Gentry, of Tennessee. Polk, he said, was a "petty usurper" who "had come into power without the will of the people of these States, and almost without the wish or knowledge even of his own party"; and his message was "nothing but a low demagogical attempt to deceive the nation—to tell just enough of the truth to cause the people to believe a lie." On the other hand the President was ably defended by his Democratic supporters[18] who maintained, not only that his message had given a true history of relations with Mexico, but that Polk's remark about giving "aid and comfort" to the enemy had been amply vindicated by utterances which were being made on the floor of the House. The receipt of the special message, accompanied by the orders issued to military and naval officers, produced no change in the character of the discussion. The Whigs

---

[17] Polk, *Diary*, II, 170, 281–282. Richardson, *Messages*, IV, 506–507.

[18] In defending the President, Bayly, of Virginia, arraigned the arguments and the attitude of Garret Davis in such scathing terms that a challenge followed. The arrest of Bayly by the municipal authorities prevented a duel (Polk, *Diary*, II, 297).

still continued to fulminate against the "President's war," and to characterize the establishment of civil governments in the conquered provinces as an unwarranted assumption of unconstitutional powers.

The man thus portrayed as a usurper whose imperial ambitions neither Congress nor the Constitution had been able to check believed himself to be hampered by want of adequate authority. Upon his shoulders rested the responsibility of military victory, yet the officers at his disposal were, in his opinion, disloyal to the administration and interested solely in their own political advancement. However erroneous this opinion may have been, there is no reason for doubting that Polk believed both Scott and Taylor to be incompetent and unreliable. Having arrived at the conclusion that Taylor was a "narrow minded, bigotted partisan" who had been "made giddy with the idea of the Presidency," the chief executive felt the need of a commander more in sympathy with the administration. He had selected Scott to lead the attack on Vera Cruz, not because he had great confidence in the general's ability or his loyalty, but for the reason that Scott was the only man in the army "who by his rank could command Taylor."[19] The admixture of war and politics had created a dilemma from which the President saw but one avenue of escape, namely, to follow the advice of Benton, and ask Congress to authorize the appointment of a lieutenant-general.

Before Scott had had time to reach the seat of war Polk began to sound members of Congress for the purpose of ascertaining whether a bill to create such an office could be passed. He even sent for Calhoun and asked his assistance, explaining that Benton would be appointed should Congress see fit to create the position. Calhoun, however, was "decidedly opposed to having such an officer,"[20] and Polk's best friends doubted that Congress could

---

[19] Polk, *Diary*, II, 249, 277.

[20] *Ibid.*, 282. Calhoun believed that the President was governed by political motives—by a desire to deal a blow at Taylor and Scott (Calhoun to Duff Green, April 17, 1847, *Rep. Am. Hist. Assn.*, 1899, II, 727).

be induced to take favorable action. Indeed, the President himself did not believe that the necessary law could be procured, but Benton urged him to make the recommendation, "and if Congress rejected it the responsibility would be theirs." Influenced partly by his own desire to have a Democratic commander and partly by the dread of Benton's opposition, Polk drafted a message on Christmas day in which he asked Congress for authority to appoint a lieutenant-general.[21]

Although a bill for creating the coveted office was tabled by the Senate on January 15, the President by his action succeeded in retaining, for a time at least, the good will of the Missouri Senator. This in itself was of no small importance, for the defection of Calhoun and his coterie of adherents had converted the normal Democratic majority into a minority, and Benton wielded a far greater influence than did Calhoun. On the day that the Senate tabled the bill, Polk noted in his diary:

> With a large nominal majority in both Houses, I am practically in a minority. The several cliques & sections of the Democratic party are manifestly more engaged in managing for their respective favourites in the next Presidential election, than they are in supporting the Government in prosecuting the war, or carrying out any of its great measures. The only corrective is in the hands of the people. I will do my duty to the country and rejoice that with my own voluntary free will & consent I am not to be a candidate. This determination is irrevocable.[22]

He was greatly discouraged because Congress delayed legislation on war measures which he had recommended, among them provision for ten additional regiments of regular troops. "Instead," said he, "of acting upon the great measures of the country, they are spending day after day and week after week in a worse than useless discussion about slavery."[23] His discomfort was increased

---

21 "I found Col. B. fixed upon this point," said the *Diary*. "If I do not propose it, it is manifest from my interview with him that both he and his friends will be greatly dissatisfied" (Polk, *Diary*, II, 275, 286, 293). The message was sent to Congress on December 29.

22 *Ibid.*, 328.

23 *Ibid.*, 334. He referred to the debate on King's slavery restriction resolution introduced in the House on Jan. 4, 1847.

by cabinet opposition to the advance upon the Mexican capital and to the acquisition of any territory except New Mexico and California, although the members believed that other northern provinces should be encouraged to declare their independence. Even Walker, who up to this time had advocated expansion on a large scale, now gave his approval to a restrictive policy. Donelson, also, from his post at Berlin, entered a protest against unrestricted expansion. Since war had come, he believed the Rio Grande boundary to be necessary and Upper California to be desirable; but he was decidedly averse to holding central Mexico. Even California, in his opinion, was not indispensable, for it would eventually become an independent nation any way. He hoped that Polk would not listen to those who desired to incorporate Mexico into the Union.[24]

On January 13, 1847, when the President was downcast because of obstacles which impeded a vigorous prosecution of the war, a harbinger of peace appeared in the person of Colonel Atocha. He came not as an avowed agent of Santa Anna, but as one who professed to have intimate, though unofficial, knowledge of the plans and purposes of his crafty patron. He showed to Benton personal letters received from Santa Anna, Almonte, and Rejón, all of which expressed a desire for peace with the United States. With Atocha's permission, Benton showed the letters to Polk and Buchanan. All agreed that he had been sent by Santa Anna as a confidential agent charged with the duty of ascertaining the terms on which Polk would make peace. When asked about the terms which would be agreeable to Santa Anna, Atocha said that Mexico would consent to the Rio Grande as the boundary of Texas, but "reserving a space of territory between that River & the Nueces as a barrior between the two

---

[24] *Ibid.*, 301. Donelson to Buchanan, Dec. 22, 1846 (rec'd Jan. 27, '47), *Buchanan Papers.* In a letter written two weeks later, he said that Europeans did not like Polk's message and were opposed to his war policy. They feared, he said, that Mexico, when defeated, would desire admission into the Union and would be admitted (Donelson to Buchanan, Jan. 8, 1847, *Buchanan Papers*).

countries.'' He said, also, that Mexico would cede California for a consideration of fifteen or twenty million dollars, but on the subject of New Mexico he seemed to have no authority to speak. He advised that commissioners should meet in Havana and that. pending negotiations, the blockade at Vera Cruz should be raised. As a concession to Mexican pride, he urged that the invitation to negotiate should come from the United States.

For several days the President held consultations with Benton and with members of the cabinet. Although willing to open peace negotiations, he rejected some of the suggestions which had been made by Atocha. New Mexico as well as California must be ceded to the United States, and the proposal to create a neutral zone between the Nueces and the Rio Grande must not be entertained. The blockade of Vera Cruz would not be raised until a treaty had been made, for if it were raised and no treaty resulted, the administration would be subjected to ridicule. At a cabinet meeting held on January 16 Buchanan was directed to prepare a letter to the Mexican Minister of Foreign Relations. In it the Mexican government was invited to appoint peace commissioners who were to meet similar representatives from the United States at either Havana or Jalapa. On seeing the letter, Atocha objected to the passage which said that the war would be prosecuted vigorously until a treaty had been signed. On his suggestion, the President consented to vest the commissioners with authority, ''in their discretion after meeting the Mexican commissioners,'' to raise the blockade and to suspend hostilities. The letter was so modified and delivered to Atocha, and Secretary Walker arranged to have a revenue cutter convey him from New Orleans to Vera Cruz. He was not regarded as an official bearer of dispatches but as ''an individual to whom a sealed letter was entrusted to be delivered.''[25]

---

[25] Polk, *Diary*, II, 323, 325–327, 331–334, 335–336, 339. The letter to the Mexican Minister is printed in Buchanan, *Works*, VII, 198–199, also in *Sen. Ex. Doc. 1*, 30 Cong., 1 sess., 36.

Polk's desire for a diplomatic victory was strengthened by obstacles which seemed to preclude military success. Congress appeared to be more interested in practical politics than in "strengthening the Executive arm," and the President had no faith in either the competency or the loyalty of his commanders in the field. Coincident with Scott's arrival in New Orleans on his way to the seat of war the newspapers of that city published a full account of the administration's plan of campaign. No one except the general could have imparted the information, and the President at once attributed this violation of secrecy to Scott's "inordinate vanity."[26] To cap the climax a New York newspaper published a letter, written by Taylor to Gaines, in which the administration was denounced and its military plans completely exposed.[27] Apparently the "Whig generals" were determined to prevent the Mexican army from being taken by surprise. In his private letters, Taylor said that keeping him "in the dark" seemed to be the "great object" of the administration,[28] and generosity may have led him to protect his Mexican adversaries from similar annoyance!

The President decided that the administration could be vindicated most effectively by the publication of all correspondence which had passed between Taylor and the War Department, and, evidently by his request, a resolution calling for these documents was introduced in the House by Thompson, of Mississippi.[29] Ashmun, of Massachusetts, offered an amendment which solicited information concerning the secret agent who had been sent to confer with Santa Anna at Havana. This amendment and the

---

[26] *Ibid.*, 327–328. "I have no doubt," Polk wrote a few weeks later, "the Mexican Government and Military commanders are as well apprised of the secret instructions which were given to Gen'l Scott when he left Washington as he is himself. His vanity is such that he could not keep the most important secrets of the Government which were given to him" (*ibid.*, 393–394).

[27] *Ibid.*, 393–394.

[28] Taylor to Wood, Jan. 26, 1847, *Taylor Letters*, 82.

[29] Polk, *Diary*, II, 362. *Cong. Globe*, 22 Cong., 2 sess., 296. Taylor was reminded by Marcy (Jan. 27) that his offense had made him liable to dismissal (*H. Ex. Doc. 60*, 30 Cong., 1 sess., 391).

appointment of the returned exile to the position of "lieutenant
general for Mexico" gave an opportunity for a new assault upon
the President, although the speakers were unable to add many
items to the catalog of iniquities which they had been compiling
since the opening of the session.

The Thompson resolution was passed by the House and the
correspondence was published, yet Congress seemed unwilling to
coöperate with the President by enacting the laws which he had
recommended. "I am in the unenviable position," he wrote on
February 5, "of being held responsible for the conduct of the
Mexican War, when I have no support either from Congress or
from the two officers (Scott & Taylor) highest in command in
the field. How long this state of things will continue I cannot
forsee." For this state of affairs he blamed factious members
of his own party who were more interested in the next Presidential election than in the welfare of the country. Said he:

In truth faction rules the hour, while principles & patriotism is forgotten. While the Democratic party are thus distracted and divided and
are playing this foolish and suicidal game, the Federal Party are united
and never fail to unite with the minority of the Democratic party, or any
faction of it who may break off from the body of their party, and thus
postpone and defeat all my measures.[30]

This statement was verified within the next few days when Calhoun and his friends united with Whigs in temporarily blocking
the passage of a bill for raising ten additional regiments of
troops. As a result Polk now regarded Calhoun as the "most
mischievous man in the Senate," and he attributed the South
Carolinian's hostility to the fact that he had not been retained
in the cabinet.[31] Senator Turney, a friend of the President,
charged Calhoun with impeding necessary legislation by depriving his party of a majority in the Senate. He proclaimed this
fact to the people so that they might "place the responsibility
exactly in the proper quarter."[32] However, the rejection of the

---

[30] Polk, *Diary,* II, 368.
[31] *Ibid.,* 371–372.   [32] *Cong. Globe,* 29 Cong., 2 sess., 395.

ten-regiment bill, as reported from the conference committee, proved not to be final; after a reconsideration, it was passed by the Senate on the tenth of February. Congress had already authorized the emission of twenty-three million dollars in treasury notes, for war purposes. The satisfaction which Polk experienced as a result of this new turn of events was counterbalanced by his disgust because members of Congress demanded for their personal friends all offices which had been created by the military bill. "Take the day altogether," he wrote on February 15, "I am sure I have never been so wearied and annoyed in my life."[33]

When the Senate voted, in the first instance, to reject the ten-regiment bill, the Washington *Union* characterized this action as "Another Mexican Victory":

> If Santa Anna, Ampudia, or any other Mexican general could snatch from our soldiers a corresponding victory, we should place them upon the same elevation where their compatriots, friends, and fellow-soldiers in the Senate of the United States now stand.

By a resolution passed on February 13 the editors, Ritchie and Heiss, were denied admission to the floor of the Senate—an action concerning which the President wrote:

> It is a second Duane case, & strikes a blow at the liberty of the press. The foul deed was perpetrated by the votes of the undivided Federal Senators, and Senators Calhoun & Butler of S. C. & Yulee & Wescott of Florida.[34]

On March 3, 1847, the twenty-ninth Congress ended its labors. Although Polk's opponents had filled pages of the *Congressional Globe* in charging him with miscellaneous crimes and misdemeanors, he had nevertheless been provided with men and money so that he might continue his "unholy war" against Mexico. The bill for granting him three million dollars to be used in negotiating a peace was also enacted into law, but not until the "Wilmot proviso," which sought to exclude slavery from all territory to be acquired, had been rejected by both houses.

---

[33] Polk, *Diary*, II, 380.
[34] *Cong. Globe*, 29 Cong., 2 sess., 392, 417. Polk, *Diary*, II, 378.

During the last evening of the session, while the President was at the capitol for the purpose of signing bills, an incident occurred which tested not only his patience but his courage as well. Among the bills which were expected to pass was one authorizing the appointment of two major-generals and three brigadier-generals. His original intention had been to ignore New York, when filling these positions, for he knew that he could not satisfy both Democratic factions in that state—one led by Marcy and the other by Senator Dix, the close friend of Van Buren. However, Marcy insisted that one of the lesser positions should be given to his friend, General Clark, while Dix emphatically opposed the appointment. As a compromise, Polk decided to appoint Enos D. Hopping, who, although affiliated with the Marcy faction, had been recommended for a colonelcy by both wings of the party. Although both Marcy and Senator Dickenson threatened to resign if Clark were not appointed, Polk defied their attempt to "bully" him, and appointed Hopping as soon as the bill had been signed. "I had become perfectly indifferent," was his comment, "whether Mr. Dickinson and Mr. Marcy resigned or not. I knew that neither of them could be sustained in such a course for such a cause."[35]

Among the appointments made and confirmed during the closing hours of the session was that of Benton as major-general. He had solicited the appointment, and had, at the time, attached no conditions to his acceptance, but it soon developed that he had no intention of serving unless the President would assign him to the chief command of the army and invest him with "plenary Diplomatic powers to conclude a Treaty of peace." The cabinet objected to clothing Benton with diplomatic powers, and, besides, Polk himself had planned to send Buchanan as commissioner, should Mexico consent to negotiate. He would gladly have put Benton at the head of the army if he could have done so without recalling the four major-generals already in the field. According

---

[35] Polk, *Diary*, II, 399–405

to his own statement, he would "have no hesitation" so far as Scott and Taylor were concerned, but he thought it would be unjust to recall Butler and Patterson. When informed of the President's decision, Benton declined to accept the appointment.[36]

Polk was ready to go a long way to avoid offending the Missouri Senator, for Benton was the only man in public life for whom he seemed to harbor a feeling of awe.[37] He was influenced still more, however, by his aversion for the Whig generals and by his desire to transfer the chief command to a member of his own party. At the time that Benton was appointed, Polk was especially hostile to General Scott on account of alleged discrimination against Democratic officers.[38]

Since the congressional batteries had ceased their "fire upon his rear," the President could devote more attention to the enemy across the Rio Grande. After consultation with Benton and the cabinet he decided to raise the blockade of the Mexican ports and to substitute a tariff, the proceeds of which were to be used for war purposes. He took steps to hasten the recruiting and equipping of the new regiments which Congress had voted, and to eliminate the "extravagance & stupidity" of the quartermaster's department.[39]

---

[36] *Ibid.*, 406–413.

[37] But there were limits to his concessions. It was about this time that he refused to appoint Benton's son-in-law (Jones) to office, because he "was a short time ago the editor of a Federal paper in New Orleans" (*ibid.*, 455).

[38] He had, said the President, "arbitrarily & without cause" degraded Colonel Harney, of Tennessee. "Gen'l Taylor had acted with the same proscriptive spirit, not only towards Col. Harney, but other gallant Democratic officers." Against the advice of his cabinet, Polk directed that Harney should be restored: "I told the Secretary of War that if he was unwilling to write the letter . . . I would do it myself. . . . I am resolved that Col. Harney shall not be sacrificed to propitiate the personal or political malice of Gen'l Scott" (*ibid.*, 384–386).

[39] "The truth is," he wrote, "that the old army officers have become so in the habit of enjoying their ease, sitting in parlours and on carpeted floors, that most of them have no energy, and are content to jog on in a regular routine without knowing whether they are taking care of the public interest or not" (*ibid.*, 431).

While the President's mind was thus engrossed with details concerning military contracts and pack-mules, Atocha returned to Washington, on March 20, bearing Mexico's reply to his offer to negotiate a peace. "The question of Texas," said the Minister of Foreign Relations, "was a cover to ulterior designs, which now stand disclosed"; nevertheless his government would "accede cheerfully" to the invitation to appoint commissioners, but such appointment would not be made "unless the raising of the blockade of our ports and the complete evacuation of the territory of the Republic by the invading forces shall be previously accepted as a preliminary condition."[40]

For the present this communication put an end to all hope of a peaceable adjustment, for Polk at once declared the conditions to be "wholly inadmissible," leaving no alternative but a "crushing movement" against Mexico. Buchanan interposed objections to an advance upon the Mexican capital, but

> I [Polk] replied that I differed with him in opinion, & that I would not only march to the City of Mexico, but that I would pursue Santa Anna's army wherever it was, and capture or destroy it. I expressed the opinion that if I had a proper commander of the army, who would lay aside the technical rules of war to be found in books, which required a long train of baggage wagons; one who would go light & move rapidly, I had no doubt Santa Anna & his whole army could be destroyed or captured in a short time.

On the same evening rumors reached Washington that Taylor's army was in great danger, consequently the President was still more determined to deal Santa Anna a speedy and crushing blow.[41]

It is necessary at this point to turn aside from the administrative side of the war in order to give a brief sketch of the military operations of Kearny in California, and of Scott in his campaign from Vera Cruz to Mexico City.

---

[40] Monasterio to Buchanan, Feb. 22, 1847 (*Sen. Ex. Doc. 1*, 30 Cong., 1 sess., 37–38). Also, Buchanan, *Works*, VII, 223–224.

[41] Polk, *Diary*, II, 432–434.

On September 25, 1846, having put his "organic law" in operation in New Mexico, Kearny, with a force of three hundred dragoons, set out for California. At Socorro, on October 6, he met the scout, Kit Carson, who was on his way to Washington with dispatches from Stockton and Fremont announcing the conquest of California and the subjugation of its inhabitants.[42] As this news seemed to indicate that no further trouble was to be expected, Kearny sent back two hundred of his dragoons, and retained but one hundred as a personal escort. He forwarded the dispatches by another messenger, and Carson (much against his will) was required to guide the way to California.

Reaching the junction of the Colorado and Gila rivers on November 23, Kearny's army intercepted a messenger bearing mail from California to Sonora, and from the letters examined, Kearny received his first intelligence of the uprising of the Californians under General Flores.[43] On December 2 he reached Warner's rancho, the most eastern settlement in California. Here he was visited by an Englishman named Stokes, who volunteered to carry a letter to Commodore Stockton, at San Diego. On receipt of this letter (December 3) Stockton sent a small force of thirty-nine men, under Captain Gillespie, to coöperate with Kearny. At San Pascual, on December 6, Kearny's army fought a battle with a Mexican force under Captain Andrés Pico. A greater number of Americans than Mexicans were killed, but as Pico retreated, leaving Kearny in possession of the field, it was called a victory.[44] As soon as the troops had recovered sufficiently, Kearny proceeded on his way to the coast. At several

---

[42] Porter, *General Stephen W. Kearny and the Conquest of California,* 11. This interesting pamphlet is a strong defense of Kearny's conduct in California.

[43] Emory, *Notes of a Military Reconnoissance; H. Ex. Doc. 41,* 30 Cong., 1 sess., 96. This document gives a detailed account of Kearny's march from Ft. Leavenworth to San Diego.

[44] Bancroft, *Hist. of California,* V, 341 ff. See also Porter, *op. cit.,* who criticizes Bancroft and defends Kearny.

points Pico harassed his little army; but on the evening of December 10 he was met by a body of marines sent by Stockton, and two days later he reached San Diego in safety.[45]

Kearny's instructions, as we have seen, authorized him to take possession of California and to establish a temporary civil government. All orders relating to that country which were issued by the War Department clearly indicated that the President desired Kearny to have the chief command as soon as he had reached California. Despite this fact Stockton, who had constituted himself "commander-in-chief and governor," declined to surrender the command, even after Kearny had exhibited his instructions, and until the arrival of other land forces, the general was not in a position to assert his rights. He declined to accept a subordinate command under Stockton, yet in the "second conquest" of California, which soon followed his arrival, he loyally coöperated with the commodore.

When Kearny reached San Diego he found the country, except a few of the seaports, in possession of the Flores revolutionists, whose headquarters were at Los Angeles. It had already been planned that Fremont should attack Los Angeles from the north. After consulting with Kearny, Stockton decided to move north from San Diego for the purpose of striking Los Angeles from the south. Having made the necessary preparations the army left San Diego on December 29 under the nominal command of Stockton, although Kearny seems actually to have directed the operations. An engagement occurred on January 8 at San Gabriel River, and another on the following day near Los Angeles. Flores and Pico now abandoned that city; the former fled to Mexico, while the latter moved northward and surrendered to Fremont on favorable terms. Although Stockton and Kearny were displeased with Fremont's assumption of authority in granting these terms to the enemy, they decided to avoid further

---

[45] Emory, *Notes, etc.,* 112–113.

trouble by ratifying the agreement.[46]   The "second conquest" of California was now complete, and no further resistance was offered to the authority of the United States.

Stockton and Fremont, still ignoring General Kearny's authority, proceeded once more to set up a civil government. Kearny returned to San Diego, and soon after repaired to Monterey, where he found Commodore Shubrick, the successor of Stockton. Shubrick promptly recognized Kearny's authority, and the general took steps to organize a civil government. Monterey was made the capital city and on March 1, 1847, Kearny assumed the office of governor. Having put the government in operation, he turned it over to Colonel Richard B. Mason, on May 31, and set out for Washington. By his order, Fremont accompanied him, under separate escort, and at Fort Leavenworth the pathfinder was put under arrest and ordered to report to the adjutant-general in Washington.[47]   Both arrived at the capital city about the middle of September and laid their respective complaints before the Government. President Polk was very favorably impressed with Kearny. He regarded the general as "a good officer & an intelligent gentleman" and one who had "performed valuable and important services in his late expedition to New Mexico & California."[48]

After Kearny had filed charges against Fremont, Polk discussed with the cabinet the propriety of constituting a court of inquiry instead of a court-martial. The latter tribunal was selected. Benton and his son-in-law, William Carey Jones, endeavored to have the scope of investigation broadened so that Fremont might bring counter charges against his opponents, but Polk would grant no favors even though he expected that his refusal would subject him to the wrath of the whole Benton

---

46 Porter, *op. cit.*, 25–29.

47 Bancroft, *Hist. of Cal.*, V, 451–452.   Porter, *op. cit.*, 32–33.

48 Polk, *Diary*, III, 168, 175.

clan.[49] Fremont was convicted and sentenced to dismissal from the army. The President approved the sentence of the court, except on the charge of mutiny, but remitted the penalty and ordered Fremont to report for duty. The pathfinder, however, declined to accept this clemency, and sent in his resignation. As the President had anticipated, approval of the court's verdict caused an immediate break with Benton. All intercourse between the two men ceased as soon as Polk's decision was announced. About a year later a member of the Blair family told Secretary Mason that Benton was about to publish one of Polk's letters which would injure him in the eyes of the public. Unterrified by the threat, the President noted in his diary:

> I told Judge Mason that he had no such letter. I do not know what this means. I am, however, at the defiance of both Blair & Benton. The former has proved himself to be unprincipled and the latter, I fear, is no better. From the day I approved the sentence of the Court martial in Col. Fremont's case, Col. Benton, for no other cause than that I dared to do my duty, has been exceedingly hostile to me. He has not called on me, nor have I spoken to him for more than twelve months. [Also, February 10, 1849.] There is every indication now that he [Benton] will join the Whigs in the support of Gen'l Taylor, at all events until he can get offices for his three sons-in-law. If I had failed to do my duty in Col. Fremont's case, and given an office which he sought for his Whig son-in-law (Jones) he would never have quarreled with me. His course towards me and my administration for more than a year past has been selfish and wholly unprincipled.[50]

It was mainly on Benton's recommendation that Kearny had been selected to lead the expedition to California, yet, after the

---

49 ''I have always been upon good terms with Col. Benton,'' Polk noted in his diary, ''but he is a man of violent passions and I should not be surprised if he became my enemy because all his wishes in reference to his family'' are not gratified. . . . ''I am resolved that Col. Fremont shall be tried as all other officers are tried. I will grant him no favours or privileges which I would not grant to any other officer, even though I should incur his displeasure & that of his friends by refusing to do so'' (*ibid.*, 177, 198, 204). See also page 203 where John Randolph Benton, the Senator's son, threatened Polk for declining to give him an office.

50 Polk, *Diary*, IV, 227, 330. For Benton's account of the court-martial, see his *Thirty Years' View*, II, 715–719.

court-martial, the Senator embraced every opportunity to deal a blow at his former friend. When, in August, 1848, Polk nominated Kearny to be brevet major-general, Benton declared that he would "speak out the balance of the Session, and defeat all public measures before Congress, rather than suffer the vote on Gen'l Kearny's nomination to be taken." In fulfillment of this threat he harangued the Senate for thirteen days with execration of Kearny and laudation of Fremont, at the end of which he announced that he would "break off," although he had not finished a third of what he had intended to say.[51] His effort failed to produce the desired result, for Kearny's appointment was confirmed and he repaired to Mexico for service under Scott.

As already noted, Scott was chosen to supersede Taylor after Congress refused to create the position of lieutenant-general. He received notice of his appointment on November 18, 1846, and within a few days he was on his way to Mexico. From New York he sent an effusive letter to Taylor—praising that general's gallantry and achievements but notifying him that he would be deprived of a large part of his army. He realized that his action would be "infinitely painful" to Taylor, but he relied upon the general's "patriotism to submit to the temporary sacrifice with cheerfulness."[52] According to the plans of operation decided upon in Washington before Scott's departure, Taylor's duties were to be confined to holding the territory already conquered, yet, as will soon appear, Scott greatly misjudged the *cheerfulness* with which Taylor would leave himself exposed to attacks of the enemy.

On November 12, nearly two weeks before Scott had written from New York, Taylor informed the War Department that he

---

[51] "I mean to show," he said, "that this brevet nomination of General Kearny ought to be rejected; that the affair of San Pasqual was a disastrous defeat, through his mismanagement; that his conduct in New Mexico was unfortunate, and in California criminal; and that infamy, not honor, settles upon his name" (Polk, *Diary*, IV, 59. *Cong. Globe*, 30 Cong., 1 sess., App., 977–1040).

[52] Scott to Taylor, Nov. 25, 1846 (*H. Ex. Doc. 60*, 30 Cong., 1 sess., 373).

was about to press forward into the enemy's country. As late as January 7, 1847, he was only "unofficially advised" of Scott's presence in Mexico. By that time he had driven the Mexicans from Saltillo, Parras, and Victoria, while Commodore Perry had captured the port of Tampico.[53]

Although Scott arrived in New Orleans on December 19, it was not until the middle of January that his several communications reached Taylor, and that the victorious general learned that he was to be deprived of a large part of his army. With his usual indiscretion, Scott had not only disclosed his plans to the newspapers while at New Orleans, but when giving orders to his subordinates, he intimated that Taylor was purposely keeping at a distance so that he might avoid the orders of his superior. In a letter written to Scott, Taylor indignantly repelled this insinuation and complained of being left to face an enemy twenty thousand strong with only a thousand regulars and a few volunteers. "I cannot," he wrote,

misunderstand the object of the arrangements indicated in your letters. I feel that I have lost the confidence of the government, or it would not have suffered me to remain, up to this time, ignorant of its intentions, with so vitally affecting interests committed to my charge.

He felt "personally mortified and outraged" by such treatment, yet he promised to obey the orders of his government so long as he remained in Mexico. Soon after this, in a letter to the adjutant-general, he gave vent to his resentment because he had not been notified by special messenger of the government's determination to supersede him. He had been assigned to the command by the President, and had he "chosen to be punctilious," he would have declined to part with his troops without direct orders from the same authority. However, he had decided not to follow this course, and his only regret was that the "President did not think proper . . . to relieve me from a position where I can no longer serve the country with that assurance of confidence and

---

[53] Letters of Taylor to Adj. Gen. (*ibid.*, 374–388).

support so indispensable to success.'' He requested that this letter might be submitted to the President.[54] By this time Taylor was thinking of *serving the country* in another capacity. Nearly two months earlier he had decided to accept the nomination for the Presidency, should it be tendered to him.[55]

Scott's answer to Taylor's letter was conciliatory in tone. He passed over the caustic remarks which it contained by expressing a ''wish to forget them.'' After explaining that conditions had made it necessary to deal directly with Taylor's subordinates without previously consulting him, he asked the general to abandon Saltillo and to make no detachments, except for *reconnoissance* beyond Monterey.[56]

A few days after Scott had sent this letter, and before it had reached its destination, Taylor received word that a reconnoitering party which he had sent out on the road to San Luis Potosí had been captured. He considered this disaster to be a direct result of the ''intrigue'' of Marcy and Scott to discredit him, and he resolved to fight Santa Anna, ''be the consequences what they may.''[57] His determination to hold Saltillo at all hazards was not altered by the receipt of Scott's letter asking him to withdraw to Monterey. It reached him while he was at Agua Nueva, eighteen miles beyond Saltillo, and he notified Scott that he would remain there unless ''positively ordered to fall back by the government at Washington.''[58] In a private letter he alluded to the correspondence with Scott and said that ''he & myself now understand each other perfectly, & there can for the future be none other than official intercourse between us.'' His

---

[54] Taylor to Scott, Jan. 15; Taylor to Adj. Gen., Jan. 27, 1847 (*ibid.*, 863, 1101).

[55] Taylor to Wood, Dec. 10, 1846, *Taylor Letters*, 76.

[56] Scott to Taylor, Jan. 26, 1847 (*H. Ex. Doc. 60*, 30 Cong., 1 sess., 864).

[57] ''We now begin to see the fruits of the arrangements recently made in Washington, by an intrigue of Marcy, Scott & Worth to take from me nearly the whole of the regular forces under my command, while in the immediate front of the enemy if not in their presence'' (Taylor to Wood, Jan. 30, 1847, *Taylor Letters*, 84).

[58] Taylor to Scott, Feb. 7, 1847 (*H. Ex. Doc. 60*, 30 Cong., 1 sess., 1162).

enemies, in his opinion, believed that he would leave Mexico in disgust and that they might use such action to his disadvantage, "but in this I shall disappoint them."[59]

The main Mexican army, commanded by Santa Anna, was stationed at San Luis Potosí. Taylor's perversity in refusing to take Scott's advice about falling back to Monterey left his army in danger of being annihilated by a greatly superior force. However, he took a gambler's chance and won the battle of Buena Vista. He had planned originally to meet the enemy at Agua Nueva, but, on Santa Anna's approach, he fell back to Buena Vista, within seven miles of Saltillo. The battle opened on the afternoon of February 22 and lasted until dark on the following day, when Santa Anna retreated toward San Luis with his thoroughly demoralized army. According to his own report, Taylor's force numbered 4500 men, while Santa Anna commanded 20,000.[60]

Taylor's first reward for defeating the enemy at Buena Vista was the receipt of a reprimand from the President and the Secretary of War. Marcy's letter, dated January 27, rebuked him for having, in his letter to Gaines, criticized the administration and exposed the plans of campaign. Ignoring his own indiscretion which had called forth the rebuke, Taylor was now "satisfied," according to his own statement, that "Scott, Marcy & Co. have been more anxious to break me down" than to defeat Santa Anna. Marcy had supposed him to be powerless since his troops had been taken away, and consequently afraid to defend himself; "but he will find himself somewhat mistaken, & I have no doubt when he gets my reply to his abusive & contemptable letter, he will regret the course he has pursued." Believing Marcy to be "entirely incompetent," he thought that friends of soldiers who had fallen at Buena Vista should hold meetings and memorialize the President to remove him and to recall Scott to Washington.[61]

---

[59] Taylor to Wood, Feb. 9, 1847, *Taylor Letters*, 85, 87.

[60] Taylor to Scott, March 1, 1847 (*H. Ex. Doc. 60*, 30 Cong., 1 sess., 1168).

[61] Taylor to Wood, March 20, 1847, *Taylor Letters*, 90–91.

Two weeks later he received a letter from Marcy[62] which expressed the President's "high appreciation" of his "distinguished services," but this did not in the least remove his distrust of the administration. It will be seen, however, that the distrust on both sides resulted for the most part from misunderstandings due to the slow means of communication.

Although General Scott, as we have seen, arrived at New Orleans on December 19, 1846, it took until the middle of February to assemble troops and make other preparations for his attack upon Vera Cruz. On February 15 he set out from the Brazos de Santiago, and, after stopping at Tampico and Lobos Island, his fleet of transports appeared off the coral island of Vera Cruz harbor on the fifth of March. Not knowing that Santa Anna had gone to attack Taylor, Scott expected that his landing would be vigorously opposed; but instead, he was able to land his troops on the sandy beach in front of the city without resistance from the enemy. For about four days American land batteries and the warships of Commodore Conner kept up a continuous bombardment, and on March 29 the Mexican commander offered to capitulate. Scott took possession of both the city of Vera Cruz and the castle of San Juan de Ulúa.[63]

After the battle of Buena Vista, Santa Anna set out for Mexico City, where he took the oath of office as President and adjusted a revolt of the clerical party.[64] Leaving the government in charge of a substitute President, he left the city on April 2, 1847, and prepared to meet Scott at the pass of Cerro Gordo, about twenty miles east of Jalapa. He occupied a position very difficult to approach, but in the battle of Cerro Gordo, which occurred on the seventeenth and eighteenth, the forces of General Scott won a comparatively easy victory. Within a few days Jalapa and Perote were occupied without resistance, and on the

---

[62] Marcy to Taylor, April 3, 1847 (*H. Ex. Doc. 60*, 30 Cong., 1 sess., 1133).

[63] *Sen. Ex. Doc. 1*, 30 Cong., 1 sess., 216–230.

[64] See Rives, *United States and Mexico*, II, 391 ff.

fifteenth Worth took possession of Puebla. While Scott was at Jalapa, Trist arrived on the scene bearing a commission to negotiate a treaty, but a discussion of the controversy which followed his arrival is reserved for another place.

Late in May Scott left Jalapa and established his headquarters at Puebla. Here he remained for several weeks, impatiently awaiting reinforcements. His time, however, was fully, if not profitably, occupied in quarreling and making friends with Trist, in bombarding the War Department with complaints and denunciations, and in a futile attempt to procure a peace treaty by bribing the Mexican officials.

During the same period Santa Anna was in Mexico City making preparations to defend the capital. By an act passed on April 20, two days after the battle of Cerro Gordo, the Mexican congress had authorized him to "adopt all necessary measures to carry on the war," but had deprived him of the power of making peace except with the consent of the congress.[65] While engaged in his military preparations he received Polk's offer to negotiate a treaty, which Trist had transmitted by the aid of the British minister. The action taken by Santa Anna and his congress will be discussed in the next chapter; it may be said here, however, that nothing resulted at this time from Trist's attempt to negotiate. After he had received for his own use ten thousand dollars from Scott's secret service fund, the Mexican President decided that the time for peace had not yet arrived.

While encamped at Puebla, Scott's army had been augmented by troops which had arrived during the summer. The health of his soldiers was much improved, and they had been made efficient by constant drill. By the seventh of August, nearly four months after the battle of Cerro Gordo, all of the reinforcements had arrived and the army began its march on the City of Mexico. The first engagement occurred at Contreras, where on the nineteenth and twentieth of August Scott's army won a signal victory

---

[65] *Ibid.*, 434.

over its adversaries.[66]   On the following day the Mexicans were again defeated, and this time thoroughly demoralized, in the battle of Churubusco.   It is quite probable that if Scott had chosen to pursue the enemy he could have entered the capital and ended the war.[67]

Scott, however, did not follow up the advantage gained at Churubusco.   Instead, he agreed to an armistice in order to afford an opportunity for Trist to enter into negotiations with commissioners appointed by Santa Anna.   In his report to the Secretary of War he admitted that he might have occupied the capital "with but little additional loss," but Trist and himself had "been admonished by the best friends of peace—intelligent neutrals and some American residents—against precipitation." This admonition and the fear that by "driving away the government" peace would be delayed were the reasons assigned for consenting to an armistice.[68]   The "intelligent neutrals" were members of the British legation, and their opinions seem to have carried more weight than did the wishes of his own government. As will appear in the next chapter, Santa Anna's commissioners declined to accept the terms offered by Trist, and the armistice resulted simply in giving the Mexican army a chance to recuperate.

The commissioners held their last meeting on September 6, and on the same day Scott addressed a note to Santa Anna.   In it he stated that the armistice had been violated and that it would be terminated at noon on the following day, unless by that time he should receive "complete satisfaction" for the offenses which had been committed.   Santa Anna's reply was anything but *satisfactory*, for he not only contradicted Scott's assertions but,

---

[66] In reporting this battle to the Secretary of War, Scott wrote: "I doubt whether a more brilliant or decisive victory . . . is to be found on record" (*Sen. Ex. Doc. 1*, 30 Cong., 1 sess., 308).

[67] Ripley, *War with Mexico*, II, 283.   Ripley served on General Pillow's staff.

[68] *Sen. Ex. Doc. 1*, 30 Cong., 1 sess., 314.

in turn, charged the American commander with violating the principles of civilized warfare.[69] Such an exchange of courtesies meant, of course, that hostilities would be renewed.

Unofficial news of Scott's victories and subsequent armistice reached Washington on the fourteenth of September. As the President had recently decided to force a peace by ordering Scott to prosecute the war relentlessly and to defray his expenses by levying contributions, he was not well pleased when he learned of the truce. He noted in his diary:

> Judging at this distance, I would think he should have improved his victories by pressing the Mexican Government to an immediate decision upon the terms of peace which Mr. Trist was authorized to offer to them, and if they refused these terms I think he should have taken immediate possession of the City, and levied contributions upon it for the support of his army. I fear the armistice was agreed to by the Mexican Commander only to gain time to re-organize his defeated army for further resistance.[70]

On October 4, although he had already heard of the capture of Mexico City, the President decided to recall Trist. "Mexico," he wrote, "must now first sue for peace, & when she does we will hear her propositions."[71] Apparently, he had little hope that the fall of the capital would induce the enemy to make peace, for two days later Marcy, under his instructions, sent to Scott new orders for continuing the war. He was told that reënforcements were on the way. It was hoped that they would enable him to "carry on further aggressive operations; to achieve new conquests; to disperse the remaining army of the enemy in your vicinity, and prevent the organization of another." It was expected that he would conduct operations in the most effective way to "induce the rulers and people of Mexico to desire and consent to such terms of peace as we have a right to ask and expect." One means of effecting this result was the levying of

---

[69] Scott to Santa Anna, Sept. 6; Santa Anna to Scott, Sept. 7, 1847 (*Sen. Ex. Doc. 52*, 30 Cong., 1 sess., 346–348).

[70] Polk, *Diary*, III, 156, 170–172.

[71] *Ibid.*, 185–186.

military contributions.[72] These instructions did not reach Mexico City until the middle of November, and at that time Scott did not feel disposed to follow them.

On September 8, the day following the termination of the armistice, Scott ordered Worth to make an attack on the Molino del Rey (king's mill), which was erroneously reported to be used as a cannon foundry.[73] Worth succeeded in capturing the mill, but not without severe loss. A few days later General Pillow made a "successful, but bloody" attack upon the fortifications at Chapultepec.[74] Scott's army now began its advance on the capital city. Santa Anna offered further resistance at Belén and San Cosmé, but, on the night of September 13, he evacuated the capital and withdrew to Guadalupe Hidalgo.

Although defeated and driven from the capital, Santa Anna was not ready to lay down his arms. Being now thoroughly discredited, there was but one hope of maintaining his authority, namely, by achieving some unexpected military victory. He therefore determined to fall upon the small garrison which Scott had left to hold possession of Puebla. Having issued a decree in which he resigned the Presidency and assigned the duties of this office to Peña y Peña and two associates, he set out for Puebla, where he arrived on the twenty-first of September. His attempt to overwhelm the garrison ended in failure, as did, also, an attempt to capture a force under General Joseph Lane which was on its way from Vera Cruz to Mexico City. While near Huamantla, Santa Anna received an order from Querétaro, dated October 7, which directed him to turn over his command to a subordinate and to appear before a court of inquiry. He complied with the first part of the order, but not with the second.

---

[72] Marcy to Scott, Oct. 6, 1847 (*Sen. Ex. Doc. 52*, 30 Cong., 1 sess., 138–140).

[73] Hitchcock, *Fifty Years in Camp and Field*, 296.

[74] "In later years," was Grant's comment, "if not at the time, the battles of Molino del Rey and Chapultepec have seemed to me to have been wholly unnecessary" (Grant, *Memoirs*, I, 152–154).

After keeping under cover in Mexico until the following spring, he set out for Jamaica, there to await a favorable opportunity to regain his lost power.

The order which came from Querétaro, and which deprived Santa Anna of his command, was dictated by Peña y Peña, who claimed the right to exercise the office of President, not by virtue of Santa Anna's decree, but by the constitution and the laws of the republic. We are not here interested in the validity of this claim. For our present purpose we are interested simply in the fact that Peña's action removed Santa Anna from control and opened the way for a resumption of negotiations. These and earlier negotiations will be discussed in the following chapter.

CHAPTER XX

TREATY OF GUADALUPE HIDALGO

In January, 1847, as we have noted in the preceding chapter, President Polk, in response to overtures made by Atocha, invited the Mexican government to send commissioners to Havana or to Jalapa for the purpose of negotiating a treaty with diplomatic representatives of the United States. In March, Atocha, who had carried the invitation to Mexico, returned to Washington with the reply that Mexico would not consent to appoint commissioners unless the raising of the blockade and the evacuation of Mexican territory "shall be previously accepted as a preliminary condition." Polk at once pronounced such terms to be "wholly inadmissible" and decided to deal a crushing blow at Mexico City.

Before Atocha had set out on his journey to Mexico, and while the personnel of the proposed commission was under discussion, Buchanan expressed a desire to be chosen as one of the number. "I told him," wrote the President, "it struck me favourably, but that if he went he must do so in his character of Secretary of State, & go alone & without being associated with others."[1] When the conditons demanded by Mexico became known there was, of course, no immediate necessity for making an appointment.

The idea of creating a commission which might accompany the army and take advantage of the first opportunity to negotiate a peace appears to have originated in the fertile brain of Senator Benton. He suggested such a commission in December, 1846,

---

[1] "I told him," Polk continued, "that would be due to his position, & that the administration, if he went alone, would be entitled to the whole credit of the arrangement. It seemed to strike him favourably. Indeed I had no doubt he was highly delighted with the idea" (Polk, *Diary,* II, 338).

when the President had under consideration the appointment of Benton to the position of lieutenant-general. His plan provided for three commissioners who were to accompany the main army and who were to be clothed with full diplomatic powers. Polk approved the suggestion and mentioned Slidell as one of the number. To this Benton interposed vigorous objections and, in turn, proposed the names of John J. Crittenden, Silas Wright, and himself. The President was willing to nominate any of the men named, but he did not wish to slight Slidell, who had already performed valuable services in Mexico. Benton would not yield his objections to Slidell's appointment, and the matter was dropped.[2] The Senator's next attempt to procure a diplomatic appointment was his request, during the following March, that the President should make him commander-in-chief of the army and invest him with power to negotiate a treaty.[3]

When, on March 20, 1847, Atocha returned to Washington bearing an unsatisfactory reply to the American offer, the President announced to the cabinet his intention to "lay aside the technical rules of war to be found in books" and to crush Santa Anna at all hazards.[4] His belligerent mood, however, did not preclude a desire for peace at the earliest possible moment.

Nothing occurred which led the President to believe that Mexico might of necessity be ready to accept his peace terms until April 10, when news of the fall of Vera Cruz reached Washington. The effect of this news upon Polk's determination to appoint an ambulatory commissioner and his reasons for selecting Nicholas P. Trist to fill the position are recorded in his own memorandum of a cabinet meeting held on that day:

The subject of· consideration today was the Mexican War. I had several times mentioned to Mr. Buchanan the importance of having a commissioner vested with Plenipotentiary powers, who should attend the headquarters of the army ready to take advantage of circumstances as they might arise to negotiate for peace. I stated to the Cabinet to-day

---

2 *Ibid.*, 262–270. 3 *Ibid.*, 412.

4 *Ibid.*, 432. On this same day the mails brought the news of the battle of Buena Vista.

that such was my opinion, and that I thought it more important since the news of the recent victories, and especially since the information received this morning of the fall of Vera Cruz & the Castle of San juan D'Ulloa. All the members of the Cabinet present concurred in this opinion. The embarrassment in carrying it out consisted in the selection of a suitable commissioner or commissioners who would be satisfactory to the country. This was a great difficulty. Such is the jealousy of the different factions of the Democratic party in reference to the next Presidential Election towards each other that it is impossible to appoint any prominent man or men without giving extensive dissatisfaction to others, and thus jeopardizing the ratification of any Treaty they might make. In this also the Cabinet were agreed. I stated that I preferred that the Secretary of State should be the sole commissioner to negotiate the Treaty, & that I would have no hesitation in deputing him on that special service if the Mexican authorities had agreed to appoint commissioners on their part, but as they had refused to do this he could not attend the head-quarters of the army for an indefinite period of time and with no assurance whether the Mexican authorities would agree to negotiate. Mr. Buchanan expressed his entire concurrence in this view. He said he would be willing to go in person if there was any assurance that negotiations would be speedily opened, but under the circumstances & with our present information he could not, of course, think of going. Mr. Buchanan then suggested that Mr. N. P. Trist, the chief clerk of the Department of State, might be deputed secretly with Plenipotentiary powers to the head-quarters of the army, and that it might be made known that such a person was with the army ready to negotiate. Mr. Trist, he said, was an able man, perfectly familiar with the Spanish character and language, & might go with special as well as defined instructions. The suggestion struck me favourably. After much conversation on the subject it was unanimously agreed by the Cabinet that it would be proper to send Mr. Trist, and that he should take with him a Treaty drawn up by the Secretary of State approved by the Cabinet, which he should be authorized to tender to the Mexican Government, and to conclude [a treaty] with them if they would accept it; but that if they would not accept it, but would agree to appoint commissioners to negotiate, that Mr. Trist should in that event report the fact to his Government, when Mr. Buchanan could go out as the commissioner.

After the entire cabinet had approved such a mission, Trist was sent for and the nature of the mission explained. He accepted the appointment. He and all others cognizant of the President's diplomatic venture were pledged to profound secrecy.[5]

---

[5] *Ibid.*, 465–468. Of the necessity for secrecy Polk wrote: ''To give publicity to such a movement before it was commenced, and to have the federal papers giving their own version of it, and, as their habit is, to have

Although Trist, as we have just noted, was selected on the recommendation of Buchanan, his past career and his qualifications were not entirely unknown to the President. He had studied law under Jefferson, whose granddaughter he had married, and after a brief term of service as clerk in the Treasury Department President Jackson had made him his private secretary. In 1833 he was appointed consul at Havana by Jackson, and, after eight years of service in that capacity, he was recalled by Tyler because he had been charged by Great Britain with having aided the slave trade in Cuba. Similar charges had been made during Van Buren's administration, and even his brother-in-law, Thomas Jefferson Randolph, advised Van Buren to remove him unless they were disproved. "Mr. Trist is disinterested and honorable," said Randolph, "his judgment I have never confided in; whatever his errors may have been they have been doubtless of his judgment, but indiscretions may be carried too far."[6] This characterization seems apposite to his entire career. Bad judgment and inordinate conceit were his besetting sins.

Shortly after Polk's inauguration, Trist began to importune the new President for office and to enlist the influence of the Donelson family in his behalf.[7] Unsuccessful at first, he was, on August 28, 1845, given a commission as chief clerk in the Department of State.[8]

In appointing Trist to conduct the negotiations with Mexico the President, as it turned out, made a most unfortunate selection; yet in passing judgment upon the President's act, the

---

them by every means in their power thwarting the objects of the Government by discouraging the enemy to accede to the measure, would in all probability be to defeat it, hence the necessity of secrecy.'' Trist's appointment was not, of course, ratified by the Senate.

[6] Randolph to Van Buren, Dec. 16, 1839, *Van Buren Papers.*

[7] Trist to Polk, March 14 and April 2, *Trist Papers.* Polk's name does not appear on the latter, but it speaks of ''your Inaugural.'' With customary indiscretion he lectured the President on the meaning of sovereignty.

[8] Buchanan to Trist on that date ''hereby appointing'' him to that position (*Trist Papers*).

special task which was assigned to the commissioner should be taken into consideration. He was given a definite project of a treaty for submission to the Mexican government, with but little discretion to alter its terms. In case Mexico should prove unwilling to accept the essential parts of the project, but nevertheless willing to negotiate, it was Polk's intention to appoint Buchanan or some other qualified person, or persons, to conduct the negotiations. A task so definitely limited did not require a diplomat of the first rank.

Having decided to send Trist to Mexico, Polk directed Buchanan to prepare a project of a treaty and, also, a reply to the Mexican communication which had been brought back by Atocha.

Buchanan's draft of a treaty was submitted and fully discussed at a cabinet meeting held on the thirteenth of April. It fixed the boundary of Texas at the Rio Grande, and provided that New Mexico and both Upper and Lower California should be ceded to the United States. Another article stipulated that the United States should have the right of transit across the isthmus of Tehuantepec. In addition to the assumption of the claims of its citizens against Mexico, the United States was to pay the sum of fifteen million dollars. In the President's opinion, the sum named was too large, but, if necessary, he was willing to go as high as thirty millions. The Secretary of State still opposed increasing the amount. Walker attached greater importance to the free passage across the isthmus than to the cession of both New Mexico and the Californias. If this could be procured he was willing to pay thirty millions, otherwise not. He wished it to be made a *sine qua non*. "To this," said Polk, "I objected & stated that it constituted no part of the object for which we had entered the War"—an indirect admission that he had entered the war to acquire territory. Finally, all agreed to accept the President's terms. Nothing was made a *sine qua non* except the acquisition of Upper California and New Mexico—the Rio

Grande boundary being considered as already settled.[9] The project in its final form provided for cession to the United States
of both Californias and New Mexico, while the United States
agreed to assume the claims and to pay fifteen million dollars; but
Trist's instructions stipulated the modifications which he might
make.

The instructions covered the points agreed upon at the cabinet
meeting of April 13 (see note 9) and, in addition, authorized
Trist to incorporate, if necessary, an article guaranteeing rights
to the inhabitants similar to those stipulated in the treaty by
which Louisiana had been acquired. Should such an article be
included he was to insist upon a provision which would invalidate all recent land grants. Should he fail to make a treaty, he
was authorized to arrange for a peace commission, provided that
"a reasonable prospect shall exist" that Mexican commissioners
would agree to the ultimata already specified by the United
States.

Under the same date (April 15) as the instructions to Trist,
Buchanan prepared a letter to the Mexican Minister of Foreign
Relations. It was a reply to the minister's note of February 22
which Atocha had brought back and in which Santa Anna had
declined to treat unless the blockade were raised and Mexican
territory evacuated. It also informed the Mexican government
of the purpose of Trist's mission. In this letter Buchanan said
that a demand such as Mexico had made was both unprecedented
and unreasonable—that "the war can never end whilst Mexico
refuses even to hear the proposals" which the United States has
always been ready to make. "The President," he continued,

---

[9] Polk, *Diary*, II, 468, 471–475. The maximum amounts to be paid were
to be governed by the cessions procured—$30,000,000 for all desired;
$25,000,000, without passage across the isthmus; $20,000,000 if only Upper
California and New Mexico could be obtained. Trist was to reduce these
amounts, if possible. Polk's views on territorial expansion are expressed
very clearly in his diary entry for January 5, 1847: "New Mexico and
California is all that can ever probably be acquired by Treaty, and indeed
all that I think it important to acquire" (*ibid.*, 308).

"will not again renew the offer to negotiate, at least until he shall have reason to believe that it would be accepted by the Mexican Government."[10]

On April 16, 1847, Trist set out for Mexico bearing his instructions and the project of a treaty and, also, Buchanan's letter to the Mexican minister. Marcy instructed Scott to deliver the last mentioned document to the Mexican commander with a request that it should be laid before the government.[11] The secrecy with which the President tried to envelop the mission[12] was of short duration. On April 21 he was chagrined by discovering in the New York *Herald* a letter which gave a very accurate account of Trist's mission and its purposes.[13] William S. Derrick, a Whig clerk in the State Department, who had assisted in copying the documents, at once became the object of suspicion, but the source of the leakage could not be ascertained.

Arriving at Vera Cruz on May 6, 1847, Trist hastened to tell Buchanan "the results of his [my] reflections" since his departure from Washington as well as his opinions on affairs in Mexico.[14] With characteristic egotism he immediately assumed responsibilities which were never intended for him. A military detachment, selected by himself, was sent on ahead as bearer to General Scott of Buchanan's letter to the Mexican government,

---

[10] Project and instructions, *Sen. Ex. Doc. 52,* 30 Cong., 1 sess., 81–89. Buchanan to Min. of For. Rel., April 15, 1847 (*Sen. Ex. Doc. 1,* 30 Cong., 1 sess., 38–40). All are printed in Buchanan, *Works,* VII, 267–279. Trist's commission and a copy of his authority from Walker to draw on the U. S. treasury for $3,000,000 (both dated April 15) are among Trist's papers.

[11] Marcy to Scott, April 14, 1847 (*Sen. Ex. Doc. 52,* 30 Cong., 1 sess., 118–119).

[12] On the day of Trist's departure Polk wrote in his diary: "Had his mission and the object of it been proclaimed in advance at Washington I have no doubt there are persons in Washington, and among them Editors of the *National Intelligencer,* who would have been ready and willing to have despatched a courrier to Mexico to discourage the Government of that weak and distracted country from entering upon negotiations for peace" (*Diary,* II, 479).

[13] *Ibid.,* 482–483. "I have not been more vexed or excited," noted the President, "since I have been President than at this occurrence."

[14] *Sen. Ex. Doc. 52,* 30 Cong., 1 sess., 153–156.

the confidential instructions from Marcy, as well as a letter from Trist himself. His failure to deliver these documents directly was the main cause of the misunderstanding which followed.

Marcy's letter to Scott[15] explained that Trist had been invested with authority to arrange for a suspension of hostilities, and

> Should he make known to you, in writing, that the contingency has occurred in consequence of which the President is willing that further military operations should cease, you will regard such notice as a direction from the President to suspend them until further orders from the department, unless continued or recommended by the enemy.

In addition, Scott was informed that Trist bore a communication from Buchanan to the Minister of Foreign Relations, and he was instructed to "transmit that despatch to the commander of the Mexican forces, with a request that it may be laid before his government."

The communication which Scott was thus ordered to transmit to the Mexican general had been sealed, but Trist carried a copy which the Washington officials expected him to show to Scott at the time of delivering the original. As already noted, however, Trist did not personally deliver the communication to General Scott. He forwarded it from Vera Cruz, without inclosing a copy; besides, his own letter, which accompanied it, did not explain fully the nature of his mission.

When the documents reached Scott at Jalapa on May 7 other things besides the absence of Trist's copy of Buchanan's letter tended to make the general both suspicious and irritable. While at New Orleans he had learned of the President's attempt to make Benton a lieutenant-general, and, as a result, he regarded Polk as "an enemy more to be dreaded than Santa Anna and all his hosts."[16] Although "very slightly" acquainted in Washington, Trist and Scott had, according to the general's account,

---

[15] Dated April 14 (*ibid.*, 118–119).
[16] Scott, *Autobiography*, II, 400, 403.

developed "feelings of mutual dislike." Indeed, Scott foolishly thought that Trist's "well-known prejudice against him [me] had had much weight in his appointment." Then, too, the general had concluded from a conversation held in Washington that Polk had originally intended to invest him with diplomatic powers—a fact which made him all the more resent Trist's appearance in Mexico.[17]

Nettled by what he considered to be encroachments upon his authority, and without waiting to learn all of the facts, Scott entered into an indiscreet and insolent correspondence with both Trist and Marcy. "I have just received your note of yesterday," he wrote to Trist, "accompanied by communications to me from the Secretary of War, and one (sealed!) from the Department of State to the minister of foreign affairs of the republic of Mexico." After complaining that the army had been weakened by sending the detachment to carry the dispatches from Vera Cruz, and declining to "commit the honor" of his government by having any direct agency in "forwarding the sealed despatch you have sent me from the Secretary of State," the general indignantly continued:

I see that the Secretary of War proposes to degrade me, by requiring that I, the commander of this army, shall defer to you, the chief clerk of the Department of State, the question of continuing or discontinuing hostilities.

I beg to say to him and to you, that here, in the heart of a hostile country, from which, after a few weeks, it would be impossible to withdraw this army without a loss, probably, of half its numbers . . . . this army must take *military* security for its own safety. Hence, the question of an armistice or no armistice is, most peculiarly, a *military* question, appertaining, of necessity, if not of universal right, in the absence of direct instructions, to the commander of the invading forces; consequently,

---

[17] *Ibid.*, 576. There is no reason for believing that Polk ever intended to give Scott such an appointment. The entries in his diary concerning possible commissioners do not mention Scott's name, and from the first, he had a very poor opinion of the General's discretion and judgment. Scott's own account admits that Polk merely left him "half at liberty to believe" that he might be associated with Wright or some other eminent statesman, for "What could have been more natural?"(!)

if you are not clothed with military rank over me, as well as with diplomatic functions, I shall demand, under the peculiar circumstances, that, in your negotiations, if the enemy should entertain your overtures, you refer that question to me, and all the securities belonging to it.[18]

We need not wonder that Trist was provoked by the tone of Scott's letter; still, there was no good reason why he should commit the folly of following the example set by his adversary. A little common sense on his part might, no doubt, have smoothed the ruffled feathers of the irate general. Common sense, however, was a quality of which Trist seldom availed himself. Instead of awaiting a personal interview, at which he might have shown his own instructions and a copy of Buchanan's "sealed" letter, thereby removing the general's misapprehensions, he chose to answer Scott not only in writing but in language still more abusive than that used by the general himself.

A man possessed of Trist's peculiar characteristics very naturally preferred written replies to oral explanations. Quite as vain as Scott himself, proud of his rhetoric and insinuating invective, he was so facile a writer that he could cover folio pages more easily than most persons can write sentences. The fatigue experienced by any one who peruses his tedious and rambling discourses was equaled, apparently, by the pleasure which their author had in penning them. It would have been unreasonable, therefore, to expect him to forego the pleasure of writing, even though a commonplace interview might more effectively have answered the purpose for which he had been sent to Mexico.

While camped at San Juan del Rio, on May 9, he began his reply, and installments were added whenever the army halted on its march to Jalapa. It was finished after that place had been reached and sent to Scott, along with another letter, on the twenty-first of May.

---

[18] Scott to Trist, May 7, 1847 (*Sen. Doc. 52*, 30 Cong., 1 sess., 120–121). A copy of this letter, accompanied by a very crisp note, was sent to Marcy on the same day (*ibid.*, 119).

Some of his remarks were sensible and to the point. When he had sent his brief note from Vera Cruz, he told Scott, he did not anticipate that a correspondence between them would arise, ''or that any communication whatever would be made on your part until I should have the pleasure of congratulating you in person upon the brilliant success which has attended your movements.'' He pointed out, also, that his instructions, which he had intended to show on his arrival, would have made clear to the general that hostilities were to be suspended only after the conclusion of a treaty, and not at the caprice of the chief clerk of the State Department. He reminded Scott that the order to transmit the diplomatic note to the Mexican commander had come directly from the President—an officer who surely had a right to issue it. Commodore Perry, he said, had not caviled at a similar order sent to him—due perhaps to the want of ''discernment'' or to ''his not having equal reason for believing his own personal consequence to be so excessive.''

Having made clear to Scott that the purposes of the government had been misapprehended, Trist might well have rested his case. He chose, however, to show the general that these misapprehensions had resulted from Scott's own density of intellect, jealousy and self-esteem. After stating that there had been no intention to interfere with the general's proper military functions, he continued:

> In a word, sir, the course determined upon by our government, respecting the suspension of hostilities, is what any man of plain, unsophisticated common sense would take for granted that it must be; and it is not what your exuberant fancy and overcultivated imagination would make it.

Marcy's letter, however, was rather ambiguous on this point,[19] whatever might have been taken for granted. In a sarcastic vein Trist accused Scott of being piqued because the President had not selected him to negotiate with Mexico. Admitting that Polk might not have been ''duly sensible'' of Scott's superior

---

[19] See above, p. 494.

qualifications for performing such a service, yet, he did not see that the blame should rest upon the one who had been selected to perform it. In any case, said he, it was the general's duty to obey orders from Washington, whether documents were sealed or unsealed.

This reply to the "tirade against our government," as Trist called Scott's letter, was inclosed in another letter dated May 20, 1847. After informing the general that more important business would "compel me to decline the honor of maintaining a correspondence with you," he ordered Scott to transmit Buchanan's note to its intended destination.[20] Happy in the belief that he had "finished" the "greatest imbecile" that he had ever encountered, Trist thought, apparently, that his fulminations would be approved by the President.[21]

On May 20—the day before he had been *finished* by receiving Trist's letters—Scott wrote from Jalapa an insolent letter to Secretary Marcy. He had, of course, received Marcy's somewhat ambiguous instructions, but he had made no attempt to learn from Trist the real intentions of his government. In it he said:

> Mr. Trist arrived here on the 14th instant. He has not done me the honor to call upon me. Possibly he has thought the compliment of a first visit was due to him! I learn that he is writing a reply to my answer to him dated the 7th instant. . . . It is not probable that I shall find leisure to read his reply, much less to give a rejoinder.

[20] *Sen. Ex. Doc. 52*, 30 Cong., 1 sess., 159– 168.

[21] On May 15, while the letter to Scott was being prepared, he said in a letter to Mrs. Trist: "There is a most extraordinary state of things here between myself & General Scott—decidedly the greatest imbecile (and rendered so by his utter selfishness & egregious vanity) that I ever had any thing to do with. If I don't finish him I will give any body leave to say that all the time I have passed in study has been passed in vain. Show this to Mr. B[uchanan] who can show it to the President." His egotism and his desire for notoriety is still further exhibited in a letter written to Mrs. Trist on May 21. She was instructed to tell Buchanan that he had made his letter to Scott long "in order that he [Scott] should not have a hair's breadth of ground left to support him, and because I knew that this correspondence will make much noise & produce such excitement that what is said in my letter will be read by 100 persons to *one* who would read the same thing better said in editorials of the Union or any other paper. This is my conviction, & this is what supports me through the task. If I have not *demolished* him, then I give up" (*Trist Papers*).

It should be noted that when this was written Scott had received no communication from Trist except a brief announcement of his arrival at Vera Cruz. The fact that Trist subsequently proved himself to be quite as devoid of judgment as was Scott himself can be no excuse for the general's attitude at this time. Besides, no matter what Trist's qualifications may have been, he was, nevertheless, the diplomatic representative of the President, and it was no part of Scott's proper military functions to abuse or to ignore him. As superior in authority to both of them the President had a right to command their services.

In another paragraph, Scott expressed resentment because Polk had thought of investing both Benton and Taylor with diplomatic powers, while the same had been withheld from himself. It was quite natural, perhaps, that he should have felt hurt because of this discrimination, but surely he had no right to *claim* functions not purely military.

His complaint regarding Marcy's instructions was based on more valid grounds, although he had wholly misinterpreted the wishes of the administration. "I understand your letter," he told Marcy, "as not only taking from me . . . . all voice or advice in agreeing to a truce with the enemy, but as an attempt to place me under the military command of Mr. Trist." After quoting a passage from the Secretary's letter, he added: "That is, I am required to respect the judgment of Mr. Trist here on passing events, purely military, as the judgment of the President, who is some two thousand miles off!" There was, he said, one other instance like it in American history—when Bancroft in 1845 instructed Taylor to obey the orders of Donelson—and "I wrote to General Taylor, with the permission of both Mr. Bancroft and yourself, to correct that blunder." He closed by stating that he would cheerfully obey direct orders of the President, but not those of the "chief clerk of the State Department."[22]

---

[22] Scott to Marcy, May 20, 1847 (*Sen. Ex. Doc. 52*, 30 Cong., 1 sess., 124–127).

Scott was neither "finished" nor "demolished" by Trist's rhetorical effusions, which were handed to him as he was about to leave Jalapa. On May 29, having reached Puebla, he acknowledged their receipt and informed their author that he had taken the precaution to have them opened in the presence of staff officers. Said he:

My first impulse was to return the farrago of insolence, conceit and arrogance to the author; but on reflection, I have determined to preserve the letters as a choice specimen of diplomatic literature and manners. The Jacobin convention of France never sent to one of its armies in the field a more amiable and accomplished instrument. If you were armed with an ambulatory guillotine, you would be the personification of Danton, Marat, and St. Just, all in one.

After expressing gratitude to the President for not having degraded him by associating him with Trist on a peace commission, Scott asked the diplomat to make his future communications purely official, for

If you dare to use the style of orders or instructions again, or to indulge yourself in a single discourteous phrase, I shall throw back the communication with the contempt and scorn which you merit at my hands.[23]

While the President was absent from Washington, attending Commencement exercises at the University of North Carolina, Marcy received and answered Scott's note of May 7, in which the general's first letter to Trist (same date) had been inclosed. In a statesman-like manner—and a style in pleasing contrast with the extravagant language employed by the general and the diplomat—the Secretary of War pointed out that Scott's "distressing apprehensions of being degraded" had resulted entirely from his not having waited to ascertain the nature of Trist's mission. He had no doubt that "more reflection and better information" would remove the general's fears. Trist, said Marcy, had been instructed to submit all documents to Scott for

---

[23] Scott to Trist, May 29, 1847 (*ibid.*, 172–173). Original in *Trist Papers*.

examination; and had the general, instead of declining to see Trist, read the documents, he would have seen that nothing unusual had been asked of him.[24]

Apparently, the Washington officials believed that the teapot tempest raging at Jalapa would be quelled by the information contained in Marcy's letter, for Polk made no mention of the incident in his diary until the arrival, on June 12, of Scott's insulting letter of May 20th. This, of course, was written before Scott had received Marcy's letter; but it showed that the general had made no effort to ascertain the facts, although Trist had been at his camp for nearly a week. In another respect this communication was more offensive than the note of May 7, which had been received during the President's absence. That had been addressed to Trist and simply inclosed in a brief note to the Secretary of War; the letter just received was addressed to Marcy himself, and, as noted above, was both impudent and defiant. Little wonder that Polk pronounced it "highly exceptionable in character." He wrote in his diary:

It appears that Gen'l Scott has taken offense because Mr. Trist was sent to his Head Quarters as a Commissioner invested with Diplomatic Powers & full authority to conclude a Treaty of peace. He desired to be invested with this power himself, and although Mr. Trist had been at his camp for six days at the date of his despatch, he states he had not seen him. It is clear from his despatch, as well as one of previous date enclosing a letter from Gen'l Scott to Mr. Trist, that he would not co-operate with Mr. Trist in accomplishing the object of his mission, the conclusion of an honourable peace. His two last despatches are not only insubordinate, but insulting to Mr. Trist and the Government. I gave my views on the subject, in which the Cabinet unanimously concurred. In accordance with them I directed the Secretary of War to prepare a despatch to General Scott rebuking him for his insubordinate course, and repeating the order in a peremptory manner to him to carry the despatch borne to him by Mr. Trist addressed to the Mexican Government to that Government, and requiring an immediate answer, to be returned by the bearer of the despatch, whether he had obeyed or intended to obey the former order of the Secretary of War. He deserves for his conduct in

24 Marcy to Scott, May 31, 1847 (*Sen. Ex. Doc. 52*, 30 Cong., 1 sess., 121–124).

this matter to be removed from the command. I conclude[d], however, to delay acting on his conduct until his answer to the communication which I this day ordered to be addressed to him shall be received. . . . . Gen'l Scott arrogates to himself the right to be the only proper channel through whom the U. S. Government can properly communicate with the Government of Mexico on any subject; which is an assumption wholly unwarrantable & which I will not tolerate. The truth is that I have been compelled from the beginning to conduct the war against Mexico through the agency of two Gen'ls highest in rank who have not only no sympathies with the Government, but are hostile to my administration. Both of them have assumed to control the Government. To this I will not submit & will as certainly remove Gen'l Scott from the chief command, as she [he] shall refuse or delay to obey the order borne to him by Mr. Trist. My doubt is whether I shall delay to remove him until I can hear further from him.[25]

A few days later the President declared that should Scott persist in disobeying orders he would have the general arrested and tried by court-martial. But his caution was stronger than his resentment. He took no step until he had consulted the cabinet, and although fearful that Scott's "arrogance & inordinate vanity" might have jeopardized peace by causing delay, he decided to await further news from Mexico. Marcy and Buchanan were instructed to inform the commander and the diplomat that their conduct had been highly displeasing to the President. Surely he had ample cause for being displeased, for seldom, if ever, has any President had to cope with such folly and such insolence on the part of his agents.

Elated by the thought that he had "finished" General Scott, won the approval of the President, and achieved fame by newspaper commendation, Trist must have been shocked when informed by Buchanan that his *orders* to Scott were both superfluous and unwarranted. He was told that when he had placed the communication to the Mexican government in the hands of Scott his "whole duty respecting it was then performed"; and if the general did not obey orders he was answerable neither to the Department of State nor to the commissioner, but to the

---

[25] Polk, *Diary*, III, 57–59.

military branch of the government. He was directed by the President, said Buchanan, to avoid personal altercations, and to submit to Scott his instructions and the project of a treaty.[26]

Marcy's letter to Scott once more expressed surprise that the general could have so misconceived his instructions. There had, said the Secretary, been no intention to put him under the command of Trist in any particular. The President had ordered him [Scott] to transmit a document to the Mexican commander and

he [Polk] is wholly unable to conceive how you can reconcile with duty and subordination the making of it a topic of remark, I may say of incidental reproof of your common superior, in an official communication to a subordinate officer in another branch of the public service.[27]

While Marcy was writing the above letter another note from Scott was on its way to Washington. Unlike its predecessor this note did not breathe defiance, but with childlike petulance the general asked to be recalled. He inclosed a copy of his rejoinder to Trist's last epistle which, with his usual facility at phrase coining, he called a "flank battery" planted against him amidst critical military operations. "Considering," said he, "the many cruel disappointments and mortifications I have been made to feel since I left Washington, or the total want of support and sympathy on the part of the War Department which I have so long experienced, I beg to be recalled."[28]

The President was absent on a tour of the northeastern states when Scott's letter reached Washington. After his return, this letter as well as a communication from Trist, dated June 3, was considered at a cabinet meeting held on the ninth of June. Polk had good reason for thinking that these dispatches disclosed a "wretched state of things" in Mexico. He writes:

---

26 Buchanan to Trist, June 14, 1847 (*Sen. Ex. Doc. 52*, 30 Cong., 1 sess., 112–113).

27 Marcy to Scott, June 15, 1847 (*ibid.*, 127–129).

28 Scott to Marcy, June 4, 1847 (*ibid.*, 130–131).

Gen'l Scott has written foolish & bitter letters to Mr. Trist & Mr. Trist has written as foolish a letter to him. Between them the orders of the Secretary of War & the Secretary of State have been disregarded; the danger has become imminent that because of the personal controversy between these self important personages, the golden moment for concluding a peace with Mexico may have passed. Gen'l Scott's last despatch to the Secretary of War is full of passion & vanity & is highly insubordinate. In view of the whole case & of the present critical condition of affairs in Mexico, I submitted to the Cabinet for their advice whether they should not both be recalled.

The cabinet agreed in condemning the conduct of both men, but it was not deemed expedient to recall them. Consenting to await further developments, the President directed Buchanan and Marcy to command their respective subordinates to "cease their correspondence and personal controversy and to act in harmony, each in his respective sphere, in obeying the orders, and carrying out the views of the government." He suggested sending some one to act with Trist, and mentioned Pierre Soulé in this connection; but no appointment was made.[29]

On July 14 Colonel Wilson set out for Mexico, bearing the new instructions which had been prepared by the two cabinet officers and revised by the President. In his letter to Trist, Buchanan once more emphasized the fact that so far as the communication to the Mexican government was concerned Trist was simply the bearer of the dispatch for delivery into the hands of General Scott. In all other respects his functions were purely diplomatic, and it was no part of his duty to discipline or supervise the commander-in-chief. Having repeated the President's order to confine his activities to the diplomatic field, Buchanan authorized Trist to make certain modifications in the boundary which had been proposed in the original treaty project.[30]

---

[29] Polk, *Diary*, III, 76–77.

[30] Buchanan to Trist, July 13, 1847 (rec'd by Trist on Sept. 6) (*Sen. Ex. Doc. 52*, 30 Cong., 1 sess., 113–117). Original in *Trist Papers*. In a private letter written to Trist on the same date Buchanan said: "I most deeply regret your quarrel with General Scott. It has been made the text for much Whig abuse & misrepresentation. Still we must bear it as we can. Governor Marcy has written a powerful letter to General Scott by

Marcy's letter to Scott was a very clear-cut and admirable document. With commendable patience he again pointed out that in no way had the government given Scott cause for offense. He assured the general that anything done by Trist, except the mere delivery of the dispatch addressed to the Mexican government, had been wholly unwarranted. In answer to Scott's request to be recalled, Marcy, by the President's order, denied the request and indignantly repelled the charges upon which it had been based.[31]

The new instructions did not reach their destination until September 6, and by that time there was no need of urging co-operation on the part of the commissioner and the commander-in-chief. They had become fast friends; indeed, before the instructions had been drafted they had already taken steps to negotiate a treaty.

On April 20, 1847, soon after the battle of Cerro Gordo, the Mexican congress had passed a law by which Santa Anna had been deprived of the power to negotiate with the United States. Nevertheless, within ten days, overtures were made to General Scott, through the British minister, but nothing resulted from

the messenger which will bear you this. The President's apprehensions are great lest the misunderstandings may defeat or delay the conclusion of a Treaty. Still he is well disposed to do you justice'' (*Trist Papers*). In a letter dated June 3, 1847, Trist had inclosed a communication from an unnamed person regarding a boundary line. The main point of it was that the line should be modified so as to include El Paso within the United States. Trist recommended this alteration. See *Doc. 52*, 168–172.

[31] ''Of 'the many cruel disappointments and mortifications I (you) have been made to feel since I (you) left Washington,' you have omitted to specify a single one, and whether they are real or imaginary is left in great uncertainty. The sending of Mr. Trist to Mexico as a commissioner of peace, and the suspicion you cherished that you had been degraded by his being clothed with military authority to interfere with your rightful command, are probably prominent among these 'cruel disappointments and mortifications.' The exposition which has been made of that case, shows the lamentable extent to which error may prevail in personal matters when prejudice and suspicion pre-occupy the mind. Should your other undisclosed 'cruel disappointments and mortifications' be of a like unsubstantiated character, as it is presumed they are, you may well conclude that they constitute no sufficient motive with the President to grant the indulgence you ask'' (Marcy to Scott, July 12, 1847; *Sen. Ex. Doc. 52, loc. cit.*).

them.[32]   Late in May Santa Anna abandoned Puebla and repaired to Mexico City where he resumed the Presidency and
prepared to defend the capital.   Scott reached Puebla on May
28 where he remained several weeks awaiting reënforcements.
Trist followed Scott to Puebla and established himself at the
headquarters of General Persifer F. Smith, but for some time
there was no intercourse between him and the commander-in-chief.

Scott, as we have seen, had refused to deliver Buchanan's
dispatch to the Mexican government and, on June 6, Trist addressed a note to Charles Bankhead, the British minister at
Mexico City, asking if he would deliver Buchanan's note and
make known verbally to the Mexican government that Trist had
arrived at army headquarters.[33]   Bankhead immediately sent
Edward Thornton, Secretary of Legation, to receive the dispatch
and to consult with both Scott and Trist.   Thornton, who reached
Puebla on June 10, told Trist that Señor Baranda, the Minister
of Foreign Relations, had frequently expressed a desire to discover some way of opening negotiations with the United States,
but that he lacked the courage to avow it openly and had resigned.   The voting of three million dollars for diplomatic purposes by the United States Congress had, said Thornton, made
a bad impression in Mexico, for many believed that the money
was to be used in bribing certain Mexican officials.[34]   Trist inclosed copies of his notes to Bankhead in a letter to Buchanan,
dated June 13, in which he complained because Scott would give
him no information concerning affairs in Mexico.[35]

As soon as Thornton had returned to the capital Bankhead
delivered Buchanan's dispatch (of April 15) to Domingo Ibarra
who had recently succeeded Baranda as Minister of Foreign

---

32 Rives, *United States and Mexico*, II, 432–435.

33 Trist to Bankhead, June 6, 1847 (*Sen. Ex. Doc. 52*, 30 Cong., 1 sess..
181–183).   Copy also in *Trist Papers*.

34 Thornton's report to Bankhead, quoted in Rives, *United States and
Mexico*, II, 440–441.

35 *Sen. Ex. Doc. 52*, 30 Cong., 1 sess., 178–181.

Relations. In a brief note, dated June 22, Ibarra informed Buchanan that the "decision on the affair" would rest with the Mexican congress.[36] Two days later Thornton arrived at Puebla with Ibarra's note, and notified both Scott and Trist that Santa Anna had called a special session of the congress so that it might consider the question of peace negotiations.

Since the Mexican government had thus taken a step in the direction of arranging for peace, the question of meeting possible overtures now presented itself to the American representatives. They were not as yet on speaking terms, and since Trist was the one who had been assigned the duty of conducting negotiations, he was forced to make the first move. Consequently, on June 25, the day after Thornton's return from Puebla, he addressed a note to General Scott. In it he stated that since the information given to himself and to Scott, by Thornton, seemed to indicate that Mexico was inclined to treat, he wished to notify the general that he was ready to negotiate a treaty. He inclosed a copy of his commission.[37] Scott acknowledged the receipt of his note, and "this," wrote Trist to Buchanan, "constituted the commencement of our official intercourse with reference to the duties with which I am charged."[38] It was not, however, the beginning of their friendship.

The next step in the "official intercourse" seems to have been a note written to Trist by General Worth, which stated that Don Emanuel Ibarra, a brother of the Minister of Foreign Relations, lived near by. He was, said Worth, an intelligent man, and in favor of peace. On the same day some one replied, stating that Trist wished to thank Worth for the information, but was too ill

36 Ibarra to Buchanan, June 22, 1847 (*Sen. Ex. Doc. 1*, 30 Cong., 1 sess., 40–41).

37 Trist to Scott, June 25, 1847, *Trist Papers*. This seems to be the only copy of the letter available. Rives (II, 442) says that no copy has been preserved. Trist inclosed a copy of this, as well as one of Scott's reply to it, in his dispatch No. 8, July 7, 1847, but neither the dispatch nor the letters reached the Department of State (see *H. Ex. Doc. 60*, 30 Cong., 1 sess., 830, and note).

38 Trist to Buchanan, July 23, 1847 (*H. Ex. Doc. 60*, as cited above, 831).

to write.[39]   At the same time, Scott sent to Trist a letter written
by Thornton which seems to contain the first suggestion about
bribing Mexican officials.   On July 3, Trist wrote to Thornton
as follows:

> Your note to Mr. Hargous, in which you refer to the impossibility that
> I frankly told you existed to my adopting your suggestion upon a certain
> point, has been sent to me for perusal by Gen'l Scott, who moreover offers
> at once to make every arrangement which may be necessary for imme-
> diately carrying that suggestion into the fullest effect, which circumstances
> may admit.
>
> This being the present state of the case, I shall, of course, be thankful
> for any information pertinent to the subject. If there be any person,
> who, in your opinion, could be safely intrusted with the whole affair, I
> should very gladly put it into his hands.[40]

Evidently the following copy of a letter is the one referred to,
although the date appended is somewhat confusing:

(Copy)

My dear Sir:
   Mr. Trist does not seem to think there is the smallest possibility of
making use of money in Mexico for what I mentioned to you; however
I told him how he might do it *por si acaso*. Should it be in your way,
pray use your influence with Gen'l Scott to allow a *reasonable* time for
taking the note into consideration before advancing.

Yours very truly,

L. Hargous Esq.,
     &c &c &c

   Nemo the name of the writer of the above letter is omitted out of
National delicacy. The writer was at the time on a vist to Mr. Trist, at
Puebla—about June 24, 1847.

Winfield Scott,

Puebla, July 19, 1847.[41]

---

[39] Worth to Trist, July 2, 1847; copy of unsigned letter to Worth of
same date (*Trist Papers*).

[40] Trist (the copy is unsigned, but is in Trist's hand) to Thornton,
July 3, 1847, *Trist Papers*. A pencil note on the margin says that a copy
was "enclosed in my No. 8" to Buchanan. No. 8, as already noted,
did not reach its destination. Louis Hargous was an American merchant
in Mexico City.

[41] On the side margin is written: "(the writer of this was Edw.
Thornton)." Since Trist mentioned what seems to be this note in his
letter of July 3 to Thornton, apparently a copy (the above) was made
for him on the date appended, i.e. on July 19. This is in the *Trist Papers*.

Officially, both Scott and Trist had evinced a disposition to coöperate; but, as yet, there was no indication that a personal reconciliation was near at hand. Nevertheless, a reconciliation came within a few days, and the incident which seems to have effected it was quite as trivial as was the cause of their bitter feelings toward each other. Scott's sensitive nature frequently led him to make dire threats, yet he was an extremely kind-hearted man, even when dealing with his adversaries. The following brief note and the act of kindness mentioned in it, seems to have won Trist's heart completely, and to have been the first step in the amicable adjustment of their differences:

My dear Sir:
Looking over my stores, I find a box of Guava marmalade which, perhaps, the physician may not consider improper to make part of the diet of your sick companion.

Yrs very truly
Winfield Scott,
July 6, 1847.[42]

Genl. P. F. Smith,
&c &c &c

The marmalade seems to have had an immediate effect upon Trist's health and his disposition, for on the following day he told Buchanan in a letter that his health had improved and that

With Gen'l Scott's reply to my letter, I received a message from him evincing so much good feeling that it afforded me the sincerest pleasure to meet it as I did, in a way which should at once preclude all constraint & embarrassment between us.[43]

Indeed, their mutual "good feeling" and admiration soon became so pronounced that they rated each other's judgment higher than that of their respective chiefs in the cabinet, or even the judgment and the authority of the President of the United States.

---

[42] The "sick companion" was Trist, who was staying at Smith's headquarters. On the back of the note Trist wrote: "Brought to my bed side by Genl Smith, and left there with the box of guava, as I lay ill at Puebla."

[43] Trist to Buchanan, July 7, 1847, *Trist Papers*. This is a copy of the dispatch "No. 8" which never reached Washington.

The first fruit of the reconciliation between the two men was the consideration of bribing the Mexican government to consent to peace negotiations. It is evident from the above correspondence that Thornton had discussed the subject with Trist, but whether he or some one else named the definite amount of money asked by the Mexicans is not clear. Trist himself mentioned "specific information obtained from various sources," and Hitchcock wrote that English merchants in Mexico "say a peace can be had for a little money." In another place he said that "our agents in this business are Englishmen."[44] It is probable that Thornton himself gave Trist the information, and that he had received the demand for money from one close to the Mexican President.

On July 15 Trist and Scott held a conference, and on the following day the former addressed a rambling letter to the latter, fully committing himself to the plan of paying a bribe. "We are both convinced," said he, "beyond a shadow of a doubt, *that the only way in which the indefinite protraction of this war can possibly be prevented . . . . is by the secret expenditure of money at the city of Mexico.*" The amounts named as "necessary & sufficient" were ten thousand dollars in advance and one million dollars on the ratification of a treaty. He admitted that nothing of the kind had been contemplated by his government and that he had no authority to take such action, but this fact he deemed it his "duty to disregard." Concurring in Scott's view that a part of the war fund might be used most advantageously in buying peace—the real object of the war—he requested the general[45] to join with him in giving the requisite pledge that the money would be paid. Trist believed that such a pledge would "entirely supersede the necessity for the occupation of the capital."[46]

---

[44] Hitchcock, *Fifty Years in Camp and Field*, 266, 268.

[45] Scott was, of course, more eager than Trist to give the pledge. It had, however, been arranged beforehand that the request should come from Trist, as commissioner. See Hitchcock, *op. cit.*, 267.

[46] Trist to Scott, July 16, 1847, *Trist Papers*, both the original draft and a "fair copy."

Scott was already fully committed to the plan of purchasing a treaty, but in a transaction so irregular he naturally desired the approval of his generals, especially that of General Pillow who was a close personal and political friend of the President. On receipt of Trist's note, therefore, he called together his chief officers—including Pillow, Quitman, Twiggs, Shields, and Cadwalader—in order that he might "post them up" and win their approval. According to Colonel Hitchcock, who was present at the meeting, Pillow "fully and eloquently" supported the scheme after Scott had explained that it was customary to use money when dealing with such people as the Mexicans. Quitman approved the "motives" which had inspired the plan, but was not in favor of paying bribe money. Twiggs "approved the whole scheme." Shields had misgivings, but was willing to leave the whole matter to Trist. Cadwalader expressed no opinion.[47] As a result of the conference Scott "very cheerfully" responded to Trist's letter on the following day. He said:

I fully concur with you, with several of the general officers of this army & with many foreigners of high standing, here & at the capital, who have volunteered their opinions, that the occupation by the U. States' forces of twenty of the principal places in this Republic, in addition to those in our hands, would not, probably, in a year or more, force the Mexican authorities to sue for, or accept a peace on any terms honorable or just to our country—*without the administration, or pledge in advance, of doucers to some of the principal authorities in this miserably governed country.* We have both learned, thro' the most unquestionable channels, that this is invited & expected as an indispensable condition precedent to any negotiation. Indeed the minimums have been specifically indicated:—ten thousand dollars, in hand, to one high functionary, & a million (to be divided, probably among many) on the ratification of a definite treaty of peace.

He had, he said, already sent the ten thousand dollars, and he agreed to unite with Trist, at the proper time, in giving a pledge to pay the million dollars. This amount was to be paid by means of a draft on the War Department under the head of "army

---

[47] Hitchcock, *Fifty Years in Camp and Field*, 266–268. Some of the men concerned later gave a very different version of their respective attitudes.

contingencies,'' and Trist was asked to send a note of explanation to the Secretary of War. Concerning the ethics of the contemplated action, he wrote:

> In regard to the morality of the transaction in question, I have, like
> yourself, not the slightest doubt. We have tempted the integrity of no one.
> The overtures we propose to meet, if corrupt, come from parties previously
> corrupted, & we only profit by that corruption to obtain an end (peace)
> highly advantageous to both the U. States & Mexico. Such transactions
> have always been considered allowable in war.[48]

The Mexican congress, to which Santa Anna had referred
Buchanan's note of April 15, declined to take any part in diplomatic affairs. A committee of that body held that the *Acta de
Reformas* of May 18, 1847, had, by readopting the Constitution
of 1824, rendered inoperative the law of April 20 which had
deprived Santa Anna of his power to conduct negotiations.
Although the congress might easily have solved the difficulty and
prevented ambiguity by specifically repealing the law of April
20, it laid the matter on the table without deciding the question
of the President's authority.[49]

It is probable that Santa Anna never intended to make peace,
and that he made overtures merely for the purpose of procuring
money from the American officials. But in view of the fact that
he had been promised a much larger sum, on the conclusion of
a treaty, it is more likely that his refusal to carry out his understanding with Trist and Scott was due to the attitude of his
congress. At any rate he gave this as an excuse. On July 24
a note from Thornton reached the camp at Puebla. It stated
that while Santa Anna was in favor of peace he could not induce
his congress to repeal the resolutions which had made it treason
for him to negotiate with the United States. The American
army must, said Thornton, advance on the capital, and it will be
met by a flag of truce before Peñon has been reached. ''So,''
wrote Hitchcock, who recorded in his diary the substance of

---

[48] Scott to Trist, July 17, 1847, original, in *Trist Papers*.
[49] See Rives, *United States and Mexico*, II, 444–446.

Thornton's letter, "the idea of peace is all knocked into a cocked hat."[50] As a result, doubtless, of Thornton's advice, Scott, according to a letter written by Hitchcock some months later, prepared a memorandum and sent a copy to Santa Anna. In it the Mexican President was informed that Scott was about to advance upon the capital, and that he would either "defeat the enemy in view of the city," should resistance be offered; or he would halt and give the government an opportunity to make peace.[51] As it turned out, the program outlined in this memorandum was quite closely followed, but apparently the general did not, at the time it was prepared, have much hope of a peaceable adjustment.[52]

Trist and Scott were now fast friends, and each expressed to his chief in the cabinet a desire that the acrimonious letters which both had sent to Washington might be suppressed. Trist now believed that the general's whole conduct had been characterized by the "purest public spirit," while Scott now found the commissioner to be "able, discreet, courteous, and amiable." At this time Scott had not received Marcy's most severe criticism of his conduct, but he resented the rebuke contained in the Secretary's letter of May 31st. Although he had this letter in his possession for nearly three weeks, he told Marcy that the reason "I do not here triumphantly vindicate myself is not from want of will, means, or ability, but *time*."[53] Neither he nor the commissioner mentioned the fact that his time had been occupied in

---

[50] Hitchcock, *Fifty Years in Camp and Field*, 269. He states that "T" wrote the letter, which undoubtedly means Thornton.

[51] *Sen. Ex. Doc. 65*, 30 Cong., 1 sess., 521–532.

[52] Under date of July 30 Hitchcock speaks in his diary of a dinner given by Pillow to the other generals and Trist. He adds: "Everything now shows that the Mexicans intended to carry on the war to the utmost of their ability, and the probability now is that our attempt to enter the capital will be met with most determined opposition" (Hitchcock, *op. cit.*, 269).

[53] Trist to Buchanan, July 23; Scott to Marcy, July 25, 1847 (*H. Ex. Doc. 60*, 30 Cong., 1 sess., 831, 1011–1012). In another insolent passage Scott said: "You will perceive that I am aware (as I have long been) of the dangers which hang over me at home; but I, too, am a citizen of the United States, and well know the obligations imposed under all

trying to purchase a treaty from Santa Anna, and before the news of that questionable transaction reached Washington many interesting events had occurred.

The first division of the American army left Puebla on August 7, 1847, followed on the next day by Trist and Scott, one bearing the olive branch, the other the sword.[54] The latter was first to be used, for, not until the battles of Contreras and Churubusco had been fought was the Mexican President ready for the olive branch. On the evening of August 20, after his defeat at Churubusco, he sought, through the British legation, to arrange for a suspension of hostilities. A deputation from the legation—including Thornton, the secretary, and Mackintosh, the consul-general—met Scott at San Augustin, "ostensibly to ask for a safe-guard for the English Minister and British subjects, but really to prepare the way for peace."[55]

Near midnight of the same day Pacheco, the Mexican Minister of Foreign Relations, called on Bankhead and asked him to use his influence in inducing Scott to save the city from being sacked. The British minister, according to his own account, would not interfere further than to transmit a letter from Pacheco to Trist. It was decided, however, that the letter should be addressed to Buchanan (as a reply to his note of the previous April) instead of Trist. Bankhead himself wrote to Trist, and expressed the hope that peace might be concluded at an early date. Both letters were sent to the commissioner.[56]

The note addressed to Buchanan stated that Santa Anna had continued the fight until the American army had reached the

---

circumstances by an enlightened patriotism." Due to negligence on the part of the messenger, this letter did not reach Washington until December, 1848.

[54] From Ayotla Trist wrote: "It is, indeed, a *noble* army, full of confidence in itself, and full of confidence in its commander. . . . . To appreciate the man, to *know* him at all, one must see him in this sphere." To Buchanan, Aug. 14, 1847 (*Sen. Ex. Doc. 52*, 30 Cong., 1 sess., 187).

[55] Hitchcock, *Fifty Years in Camp and Field*, 280.

[56] Pacheco to Buchanan, Aug. 20, 1847 (*Sen. Ex. Doc. 52*, 30 Cong., 1 sess., 189). Bankhead to Trist, same date, *Trist Papers.* For Bankhead's report to his government, see Rives, II, 496–497.

gates of the capital, and that he had now resolved to hear the proposals which the American commissioner had been instructed to make. In doing so, said Pacheco, the President was acting under the powers conferred upon him by the constitution. This meant, of course, that Santa Anna was ready to ignore the law of April 20, which made it treason for him to negotiate with the United States. This law may, indeed, have been rendered void by the subsequent readoption of the constitution, but since the law in question had not been specifically repealed, some doubt remained as to the legality of any treaty he might make.

On the morning of August 21, while Scott and Trist were on their way from San Angel to Tacubaya, they were met by a "fine carriage" containing General Mara y Villamil, bearer of the letters written by Pacheco and Bankhead to the American officials. Trist read the letters, and a conference was held.[57] The letter addressed to Trist did not expressly ask for an armistice, but apparently Mara verbally made it known that such was the wish of the Mexican President. With more magnanimity than judgment Scott, instead of demanding that the request for a cessation of hostilities should come from the defeated commander, proposed an armistice in a note addressed to Santa Anna. The proposal was accepted, and two days later an armistice was arranged.[58] The agreement made at Puebla probably was Scott's real reason for taking the initiative; the reasons which he gave to the Secretary of War were a desire to leave Mexico "something on which to rest her pride," and the fear that a more drastic course would "scatter the elements of government" and make the negotiation of a treaty impossible.[59]

After some delay commissioners were appointed by Santa Anna, and with them Trist held his first meeting on August 27,

[57] Hitchcock, *op. cit.*, 279.

[58] The correspondence and armistice are printed in *Sen. Ex. Doc. 52*, 30 Cong., 1 sess., 308–312.

[59] Scott to Marcy, Aug. 28, 1847 (*Sen. Ex. Doc. 1*, 30 Cong., 1 sess., 314).

1847.[60]   He soon discovered that the powers of the Mexicans
simply permitted them to receive his propositions for transmission
to Santa Anna.   He told them that he had been authorized to
treat only with commissioners provided with full powers; nevertheless, he delivered to them a statement of the propositions
which he was ready to make.[61]

As soon as the American project had been received, Pacheco
drafted instructions to the commissioners and furnished them
with full powers, but the instructions required them to make such
extravagant demands that the commissioners immediately offered
their resignations.   As a result, Santa Anna, through Pacheco,
authorized the commissioners to make such modifications as the
"circumstances of the country may exact."[62]

The Mexican diplomats met Trist on September 1, and for
two days the questions at issue were discussed.   The terms of
settlement now suggested by the Mexicans were much like those
mentioned by Atocha in the preceding January.   He had spoken
of the Rio Grande as a boundary, with a neutral strip on the
American side; they asked for the Nueces as a boundary, with
all territory between that river and the Rio Grande as neutral

---

[60] The Mexican commissioners were ex-President Herrera, Bernardo
Couto, Ignacio Mara y Villamil, Miguel Atristain, and José Arroyo.

[61] Trist to Buchanan, Aug. 27, 1847 (*Sen. Ex. Doc. 52*, 30 Cong., 1 sess.,
191–192).   On the morning of August 27 an attack made by a Mexican
mob on American supply wagons threatened to prevent negotiations, but
an apology temporarily smoothed over this difficulty.   For details, see
Rives, II, 510–511.

[62] For the instructions (in translation) and the correspondence relating to them, see *Sen. Ex. Doc. 52*, as cited above, 330–335.   By their
instructions the commissioners were to demand: Mexico would relinquish
Texas—not as a result of annexation, but of negotiation.   Its boundary
must be the Nueces, and the United States must pay for the land one
half of the price fixed by Texas laws.   All debt claims against Mexico
must be cancelled, as "an equivalent for entering into negotiation"(!)
and ten leagues on either side of the boundary was to be neutral territory.   Cession of New Mexico and California must be refused, but, as a
last resort, a factory port at San Francisco might be granted to the
United States.   A passage over the Isthmus of Tehuantepec was to be
refused.   Duties on American goods brought into Mexico must be paid.
The United States must restore Mexican forts to the condition in which
they were found.   Lastly, the commissioners were to insist on indemnity
for all damages done by the American army.

ground in which no settlement might be made by either party. He had claimed no authority to discuss a cession of New Mexico; they said that their instructions forbade a cession of this territory. He had stated that Mexico was willing to cede Upper California for a money consideration; they were ready to cede the upper part of this territory, but insisted that Mexico must retain all of Lower California and a land connection with it. They declined to grant a transit across the Isthmus of Tehuantepec. Trist offered to withdraw the claim for Lower California and the transit across the isthmus, if Mexico would cede Upper California and New Mexico for a money payment. He agreed, also, to submit the Nueces boundary question to his government for consideration; they, in turn, agreed to submit to their government the terms which he had proposed.[63] Four days later, and before Trist had taken steps to refer the matter to President Polk, another meeting was held, and the Mexican commissioners presented a counter-project and an explanatory note. The cession of New Mexico was refused, an offer to cede Upper California north of 37° was made, and it was suggested that England should be asked to guarantee the proposed treaty. Trist, of course, declined to accept these terms and, for the time being, negotiations were abandoned. This in itself automatically abrogated the armistice, but General Scott chose to terminate it on the ground that its terms had been violated by the interference of Mexicans with American supply wagons.[64]

At the very moment, almost, when Santa Anna was rejecting the project of a treaty offered by the United States, President Polk was announcing his intention to demand additional territory from Mexico. On September 4 he told his cabinet that, unless the next dispatch from Trist should announce that a treaty had been signed, the commissioner ought to be instructed to

---

[63] Trist to Buchanan, Sept. 4, 1847, and inclosures (*Doc. 52*, as cited above, 195–201).

[64] Commissioners to Trist, Sept. 6, 1847; Trist's reply, Sept. 7; Scott to Santa Anna, Sept. 6 (*ibid.*, 375–380, 214–222, 346).

demand more territory. Three days later he expressed himself as in favor of acquiring Tamaulipas. The question of modifying Trist's instructions was discussed, but when, on the ninth, a rumor reached Washington that the Mexican congress had been called for the purpose of considering the American proposals, Polk noted in his diary: "I sincerely hope that a Treaty of peace may have been concluded and signed."[65]

The mail of September 14 brought the President both encouragement and disappointment. By it he learned of the victories at Contreras and Churubusco, but, also, of the armistice which followed them. The same mail contained Trist's brief dispatch of August 29, in which the government was informed that negotiations had begun. Polk was not pleased with the armistice. He believed that Scott should have demanded an immediate decision on the terms offered by the United States, and in the event of their rejection by Mexico, he should have entered the capital and levied a contribution for the support of his army. "I fear," noted the President, "that the armistice was agreed to by the Mexican Commander only to re-organize his defeated army for further resistance. . . . . I shall wait very anxiously for further information from the army." He waited until October 4, and, as no favorable news arrived, he decided that Trist should be recalled and that Scott should be directed to levy contributions on the enemy.[66]

Letters embodying these views were prepared by Buchanan and Marcy and forwarded to their respective representatives in Mexico. The Mexican counter-project Buchanan pronounced "a most extraordinary document," and the proposal of such terms "a mere mockery." The commissioners must have known,

---

[65] *Diary*, III, 161, 164, 167.

[66] "Mr. Trist is recalled," said he, "because his remaining longer with the army could not, probably, accomplish the objects of his mission, and because his remaining longer might, & probably would, impress the Mexican Government with the belief that the U. S. were so anxious for peace that they would ultimate[ly] conclude one upon the Mexican terms. Mexico must now first sue for peace, & when she does we will hear her propositions" (*ibid.*, 170–172, 185–186).

he said, that the United States would never relinquish New Mexico, Upper California, or the territory between the Nueces and the Rio Grande. The assertion made by the Mexicans that Trist had agreed to refer to his government the surrender of the last mentioned territory was not believed in Washington. If, at the time of receiving Buchanan's letter, a treaty had been signed, Trist was to bring it home with him; otherwise he was to suspend all negotiations and return home "by the first safe opportunity." The letter to Scott instructed him to support his army by contributions levied on the enemy. Any proposals from Mexico to reopen negotiations were to be forwarded by him to the President.[67]

Polk has been criticized for ordering the employment of measures which might destroy all organized government in Mexico, and for demanding that future peace offers must come from the enemy. His reason for adopting this policy, whether valid or not, was his belief that Mexico would never come to terms so long as she held the erroneous opinion that the government at Washington was over-anxious for peace, or too weak to continue hostilities.[68] In a private letter the Secretary of State said that "the spirit of the Country is now thoroughly aroused & the war will be prosecuted with the utmost vigor. This is the character of the American people. They find that peace cannot be made with Mexico upon honorable terms & they are determined to see it out."[69] Owing to the fact that there was, for some time, no communication between Vera Cruz and the interior,

---

[67] Marcy to Scott, Oct. 6, 1847; Buchanan to Trist, same date (*Sen. Ex. Doc. 52*, 30 Cong., 1 sess., 91–93, 138–140). The original of the latter, as well as a duplicate and triplicate are in the *Trist Papers*. Some one (undoubtedly Trist) has underlined in red the part which says that the United States will never surrender Upper California or the land between the rivers Nueces and Rio Grande. The dates of receipt are noted.

[68] In the letter to Trist, just cited, Buchanan said: "They [the Mexicans] must attribute our liberality to fear, or they must take courage from our supposed political divisions. Some such cause is necessary to account for their strange infatuation." For criticism of Polk's change of policy, see Rives, II, 523–525.

[69] Buchanan to Trist, Oct. 7, 1847, *Trist Papers*.

these letters did not reach Trist until November 16 and the same mail contained another dispatch from Buchanan, dated October 25th. When this dispatch was written the Secretary of State had received the letter from Trist which submitted the Mexican proposal regarding a neutral territory between the Nueces and the Rio Grande. The Secretary had, he said, been instructed by the President to say that he "could not for a single moment entertain the question of surrendering a portion of Texas." Surprise and regret were expressed because the commissioner had "gone so far beyond the carefully considered ultimatum" as to refer it to his government. "The President," he added, "has directed me to reiterate your recall." In a private note Buchanan said that he was "extremely sorry" to be obliged to write such a dispatch, but

to propose to consult the Gov't whether they would abandon that portion of the country where Mexico attacked our forces & on our right to which the Whigs have raised such an unfounded clamor, will be a fruitful cause of assault against us in the next Congress. I hope, however, there may never be a necessity for sending this dispatch to either House of Congress.[70]

Notice of his recall and of the adoption of a more drastic military policy were destined to have small influence upon Trist's diplomatic activities, for soon after the dispatches had arrived an opportunity was presented for reopening negotiations. He and General Scott were now boon companions,[71] and while setting a high value on their own combined judgment, each deemed an order from the President and his cabinet to be a nuisance which, in important cases, should be disregarded. If, therefore, the commissioner and the general believed that a treaty ought to be made, why should the President interfere!

---

[70] Buchanan to Trist, Oct. 25, 1847, *Trist Papers.* Rec'd Nov. 16. The official dispatch is printed in *Doc. 52*, as cited above, 94–95.

[71] On October 18 Trist wrote to his wife: "I am General Scott's friend for life. I know him *thoroughly:* he is the soul of honor & probity, and full of the most sterling qualities of heart & head: affectionate, generous, forgiving, and a lover of justice. . . . . Tell *all* my intimate friends of the entire revolution, from the conception I had formed of Gen S. *in my ignorance* of his character, to what I now *know* of him" (*Trist Papers*).

After the interruption of negotiations and the renewal of hostilities Scott's army had won the battles of Molino del Rey and Chapultepec and had captured Mexico City. On September 16 Santa Anna, then at Guadalupe, resigned the Presidency and directed that the office should be held by Peña y Peña, president of the supreme court, until the Mexican congress should otherwise direct. He then set out on an unsuccessful expedition against a small force of Americans stationed at Puebla. Peña assumed the office, not however by virtue of the retiring President's decree, but in accordance with the constitutional provision that the head of the supreme court should succeed to the Presidency in the event of a vacancy. After removing Santa Anna from his military command, the new President succeeded in establishing a government—one of doubtful legality in certain respects—but one which prevented anarchy until the congress could provide another. On November 11 that body selected General Anaya to be President ad interim, and the new executive at once made Peña y Peña his Minister of Foreign Relations.[72]

Nearly a month before he had received notice of his recall Trist had taken steps to renew peace negotiations. On October 20, during the brief administration of President Peña y Peña, he sent a letter, through the British legation, to Luis de la Rosa, the then Minister of Foreign Relations. This letter was dated September 7, 1847, for the reason that it purported to be a reply to the commissioners with whom he had negotiated before the armistice had been terminated.[73] Rosa notified Trist[74] that

---

[72] Technically, Peña was not president of the court—that office being vacant—but as senior member, he acted as president. Hence his right to assume the Presidency was somewhat doubtful. Trist to Buchanan, Jan. 26, 1848 (*Sen. Ex. Doc. 52*, 30 Cong., 1 sess., 281). For other details, see Rives, II, 584–589.

[73] Trist to Buchanan, Oct. 31, 1847 (copy in *Trist Papers*). Printed in part in *Sen. Ex. Doc. 52*, as above cited, 212–213. The part omitted tells of Thornton's endeavor to induce the Mexicans to negotiate. The letter to the commissioners may be found in *Doc. 52*, 214 ff. In a letter dated Oct. 25 Trist told Buchanan that there was a general desire on the part of both Mexicans and foreigners for the annexation of all of Mexico to the United States (copy in *Trist Papers*). This part is omitted from the same letter printed in *Doc. 52*, 205–212.

[74] Rosa to Trist, Oct. 31, 1847 (*Doc. 52*, as above cited, 227–228).

commissioners would be appointed, but this promise was not fulfilled until after Anaya had become President.

On November 22 the new minister, Peña, notified Trist that President Anaya had appointed peace commissioners. Two of the men selected, Bernardo Couto and Miguel Atristain, had been members of the commission which had declined, in September, to accept the American project. The others were Manual Rincon and Gonzago Cuevas. The former declined to serve and his place was not filled. Peña's note was transmitted to Thornton, who accompanied it by a letter of his own. In this, Thornton stated that he had informed Peña of Trist's recall, and that the minister was "thunderstruck" and disappointed. Thornton expressed the hope that Trist might go on with the negotiations, since the Mexican government had been induced to appoint commissioners by the prospect of a speedy peace. Peace could be had now, he said, but delay might jeopardize the prospect of a peaceful settlement.[75] This argument seems eventually to have appealed with great force to Trist's shallow intellect. He did not, however, immediately follow the advice offered, for, two days later, he formally notified Peña of his recall and stated that any communications regarding peace should be handed to General Scott for transmission to Washington.[76]

In thus declining, in the first instance, to proceed with the negotiations after he had received notice of his recall, Trist was not actuated by respect for superior authority; he was influenced solely by the belief that any other course would be futile. On the same day that he formally notified Peña of his recall he told Thornton in a letter that no dread of "the displeasure of those entrusted with the power of dispensing office" would deter him

---

[75] Peña to Trist, Nov. 22, 1847; Thornton to Trist (formal letter of same date) (*Doc. 52*, as above cited, 98–99, 231). Thornton to Trist (confidential), same date, *Trist Papers*. Thornton's confidential letter was written at Peña's urgent request. See Thornton to Palmerston, Nov. 29, 1847, quoted by Rives, II, 595.

[76] Trist to Peña, Nov. 24, 1847 (*Doc. 52*, as above cited, 99–100). Original, recalled by Trist, in *Trist Papers*.

from "disobeying positive & peremptory instructions,"[77] if the President had not deprived him of "all shadow of authority to do anything whatever." However, when Peña y Peña argued that the offer made prior to the receipt of his recall had committed his government, when the British diplomats urged prompt action, and when General Scott "encouraged him, nevertheless, to finish the good work he had begun" and expressed the belief that such action would be "duly ratified at Washington," a man of small mental caliber and excessive vanity, like Trist, could hardly fail to be influenced.[78]

Despite all this pressure he did not decide immediately to disregard his instructions. On November 27 he drafted another dispatch to Buchanan. In it he petulantly resented the President's criticism of his course in offering to refer to Washington the question relating to the boundary of Texas. After pointing out the futility of demanding that Mexican peace proposals must be sent to Washington, he urged that a new commission should be chosen to negotiate with the one already appointed by Mexico. He then expected to leave Mexico in about twelve days.[79] That he had at this time no intention of making a treaty is made clear by a letter written to Mrs. Trist on the following day. "I have," said he, "bid adieu *for ever* to official life. This decision is irrevocable." She was asked to tell Buchanan, with kindest regards, that Trist would not resume his place in the State Department, for he [Buchanan] "will soon

---

[77] But, he added, "not only am I divested entirely of the official character which I lately held, and with it of all shadow of authority to do anything whatever; but I deem it certain, that, in the actual state of things at Washington, the cause of Peace could not fail to be seriously prejudiced, were I to pursue any other course than that of the most absolute & unqualified acquiescence in the Executive will, as announced to me." He will go to Washington, he says, and do what he can for peace: "In a word, the signing of a Treaty of Peace is reserved for another hand than mine" (Trist to Thornton, Nov. 24, 1847 [copy], *Trist Papers*).

[78] Peña to Couto, Nov. 24, 1847, quoted by Rives II, 596. Scott, *Autobiography*, II, 576.

[79] Trist to Buchanan, Nov. 27, 1847 (*Sen. Ex. Doc. 52*, 30 Cong., 1 sess., 228–230). Complete copy in *Trist Papers*.

see the impossibility of this, or my having *anything* to do with Mr. Polk." Apparently the last remark was induced by the belief that the President had been unduly influenced by General Pillow.[80]

We are not left in doubt concerning the date of Trist's decision to reopen negotiations, for, with characteristic egotism, he announced with loud trumpet the very hour on which he decided to play Caesar and cross the Rubicon. In a letter to his wife, he said:

Procure the key to this cipher (. . .) and decipher the following, to be read to him [Buchanan] most secretly. This determination, I came to, this day, at 12 o'clock. It is *altogether* my OWN.

Knowing it to be the very last chance, and impressed with the dreadful consequences to our country which cannot fail to attend the loss of that chance. [Here follows cipher which was interpretd to mean] I will make a treaty, if it can be done, on the basis of the Bravo, by 32°; giving 15 millions besides the 3 millions cash.[81]

In spite, however, of this precision as to the time of making his decision, Trist seems to have told the Mexican commissioners at least a day earlier that he probably would take the responsibility of disobeying his instructions.[82] He had become obsessed

---

[80] Say to Buchanan, he wrote, "that a baser villain, and dirtier scoundrel does not exist out of the Penitentiary, nor in it, than Genl Pillow. This is, not an *opinion*, but a matter of fact, which will be proved to the world." He told Mrs. Trist that he expected to leave for the United States about December 6. Instead, he wrote his famous letter on that date. In a letter written to John A. Dix (copy in *Trist Papers*) on October 31 he had expressed his opinion of Polk's political generals. In it he urged Dix to beware of precipitancy in the confirmation of generals, lest the Senate should become involved in "a deep, damning, irretrievable disgrace—which no earthly power, nor all earthly powers combined, can avert."

[81] Trist to Mrs. Trist, Dec. 4, 1847, *Trist Papers*. In a similar strain he told Edward Thornton that "this letter will occasion you great surprise, but no greater than I should myself have experienced a few hours ago, had a seer, in whose prophetic powers I put faith, foretold to me that I was to write it" (Trist to Thornton, Dec. 4, 1847, *Trist Papers*). This letter with blanks for Thornton's name is printed in *Doc. 52*, as cited above, 266–268. Thornton's reply, dated Dec. 11, is in the *Trist Papers*. He commends Trist's proposed action and feels certain that the United States "will highly applaud your decision." He, too, expressed the belief that peace could be had "*now* or *never*."

[82] Couto to Peña, Dec. 3, 1847, quoted by Rives, II, 597.

with the belief that "if the present opportunity be not seized *at once,* all chance for making a treaty *at all* will be lost for an indefinite period—probably forever" (letter to Thornton, just cited) ; and a desire for fame doubtless helped to reënforce this belief.

Having decided to make a treaty, if possible, Trist informed Buchanan of the fact in a very extraordinary letter, the manuscript of which covered sixty-five large pages. It is not only prolix and extremely tiresome, but, in addition, is one of the most gratuitously insulting documents in our diplomatic annals. He assigned, as reasons for resuming negotiations in spite of his recall, a conviction that his government still desired peace; a belief that a treaty could be made then, but not later; certainty that Mexico would not and could not consent to yield more than his instructions had demanded; and the belief that his recall had been based on "a supposed state of things in this country *entirely the reverse of that which actually exists.*" Had he limited himself to these general statements the letter might not merit severe criticism, whatever might be thought of his assumption of authority. But Trist never knew when he had said enough; his pen rambled on where his brain declined to follow. Consequently, each topic was amplified—but not illuminated—by a seemingly endless profusion of words.

Under the first heading he gave a dissertation on the President's responsibilities, and then proceeded to philosophize upon Polk's mental operations. Having reached the conclusion that the President must still desire peace, he pointed out that the executive indignation mentioned in Buchanan's recent letter was entirely wasted on a weak power like Mexico. Despite his certainty that the President must still desire peace, he hinted very pointedly that Polk wished to convert a defensive war into one of conquest, and for such a wish he should be ashamed of himself. Later in the letter he again recurred to the subject of annexing all of Mexico. He believed ultimate absorption to be desirable;

but a dissolution of the Union would be preferable to the calamity of immediate annexation.[83]

As if disregarding his instructions and questioning Polk's motives were not enough, Trist had the bad taste and the audacity to volunteer opinions which could have no other effect than to wound and to exasperate the President. Well knowing, of course, that the Washington *Union* reflected the President's views, he declared its criticism of Scott's armistice to be "balderdash," "stuff," and "nonsense," which no one outside of Washington, "however low in understanding," would believe. Again, a tactful subordinate would not have told the President that his close friend, General Pillow, was an "intriguer" of "incomprehensible baseness of character." Trist did this. He asserted, also, that because the President had relied on "supposition" and "private representations" from this intriguer, "everything was seen upside down." Having referred to Pillow and Santa Anna as "twin phenomena" in "moral obliquity," he did not hesitate to speak of the former as "an individual who gives himself out as the *maker* of the President (by having procured his nomination at the Baltimore convention), and as the President's *other self*—a pretension which I have reason to believe but too well founded." Even the "justice" done the President in charitably excusing his shortcomings by attributing them to "a blind confidence" in Pillow did not help matters very much. It could not have given Polk extreme pleasure to read that "infallibility of judgment . . . . is not among the attributes of the President of the United States," or to be told that Scott's armistice, instead of being a blunder, had rescued the administration and the Democratic party from a "perilous position."[84] While reading his

---

[83] In this very letter Trist told Buchanan how easily annexation could be accomplished; and, according to Lionel Davidson, agent. of the Rothschilds in Mexico, he had, late in November, been in favor of permanent occupation (Davidson to Thornton, Nov. 23, 1847, *Trist Papers*). And yet he condemned Polk for his supposed desire to acquire the republic.

[84] Trist to Buchanan, Dec. 6, 1847 (*Sen. Ex. Doc. 52*, 30 Cong., 1 sess., 231–266). Complete copy also in *Trist Papers*.

tedious letters one is tempted, at times, to give Trist credit for sincerity—to think that he really believed himself to be performing deeds of heroism; albeit such charity for his motives must be at the expense of his intelligence. On the other hand, certain letters written to his wife show a want of sincerity, and brand him as a man who craved notoriety.

The American diplomat's decision to cut the Gordian knot in order to save both Mexico and his country from impending disaster did not result in an immediate reopening of negotiations. The Mexican officials who had been so anxious for him to remain now pleaded want of authority, and interposed various pretexts for delay. Since the impediments to formal discussions on the part of the diplomats were not removed until the latter part of December, we may turn our attention to Washington for the purpose of ascertaining the views of the administration.

On Ocober 6, as we have seen, the President ordered Trist's recall, not on account of the commissioner's misconduct, but because it was thought that he would be unable to make a treaty. When, however, Polk learned that the commissioner had agreed to consult his government regarding a neutral zone between the two rivers, he remarked that "Mr. Trist has managed the negotiation very bunglingly and with no ability."[85] The recall was repeated in still more emphatic terms.

Having no reason, of course, for believing that Trist would disobey his instructions, Polk gave his attention to the war policy which he purposed to recommend when Congress should have assembled in December. It was necessary that his message should be drafted with extreme care because the control of the House had now passed to his opponents. At a cabinet meeting held on November 9, Buchanan, whose Presidential aspirations had revived, told Polk that his message must advise one of two courses —to designate the part of Mexico which the United States would hold as indemnity, or to occupy all of that country by a greatly

---

[85] Polk, *Diary*, III, 199.

increased miltiary force. He did not recommend either course, but the President thought that he favored the latter. As Buchanan had up to this time wished to confine the acquisition of territory within very narrow limits, Polk believed that the change was due to political considerations. Since there seemed to be some uncertainty as to the policy of the administration, the President read a paragraph which he intended to include in his message.

> My views as thus reduced to writing [said he] were in substance that we would continue the prosecution of the war with an increased force, hold all the country we had conquered or might conquer, and levy contributions upon the enemy to support the war, until a just peace was obtained; that we must have indemnity in territory, and that as a part indemnity the Californias & New Mexico should under no circumstances be restored to Mexico; but that they should henceforth be considered a part of the U. S., & permanent territorial Governments be established over them; and that if Mexico protracted the war, additional territory must be required as further indemnity.[86]

During the next two weeks the President revised what he had written, and, at his request, Buchanan drafted a paragraph which embodied the Secretary's opinions on a proper Mexican policy. Both drafts were presented for discussion at a cabinet meeting held on the twenty-third of November. Avowing a wish to take all of Mexico, Walker preferred Buchanan's draft, for he believed that its construction would make such acquisition possible. "I replied," wrote Polk, "that I was not prepared to go to that extent; and furthermore that I did not desire that anything I said in the message should be so obscure as to give rise to doubt or discussions as to what my true meaning was."[87] This remark indicates that Trist's fears regarding the President's change of policy were wholly unwarranted.

On December 7 Polk submitted to Congress his third annual message. He told of Trist's mission and of his failure to conclude a treaty. The commissioner had, he said, been instructed to demand a cession of territory as indemnity, for in no other way could Mexico satisfy the claims of the United States.

---

[86] *Ibid.*, 216–218.   [87] *Ibid.*, 229.

The doctrine of no territory is the doctrine of no indemnity, and if sanctioned would be a public acknowledgment that our country was wrong and that the war declared by Congress with extraordinary unanimity was unjust and should be abandoned—an admission unfounded in fact and degrading to the national character.

He recited the substance of Trist's instructions and urged the necessity of acquiring New Mexico and the Californias. The war had abrogated the treaties regarding claims, making it necessary for the United States to pay American claimants and to reimburse itself by taking territory. California, he said, should be acquired in order to forestall the attempt by any other nation to infringe upon the Monroe Doctrine. He disagreed with those who advocated the policy of retiring to a fixed line and confining the war to defensive operations. Instead, he recommended the establishment of governments in New Mexico and California, and a vigorous prosecution of the war. Having outlined his policy, he added: "It has never been contemplated by me, as an object of the war, to make a permanent conquest of the Republic of Mexico or to annihilate her separate existence as an independent nation," but a peace "must bring with it indemnity for the past and security for the future."[88]

---

[88] Richardson *Messages*, IV, 533–546. Walker still favored the absorption of all of Mexico. A paragraph in the first draft of his financial report to Congress practically advocated such a policy, but on the President's advice this paragraph was omitted (Polk, *Diary*, III, 241–242). Among the *Trist Papers* is an interesting letter written by a young Mexican to his father. It was written in Washington and bears neither date nor signature, but an accompanying newspaper shows the writer to have been Carlos Landa, and a comparison with events mentioned in Polk's diary shows that the letter was written in December, 1847. Landa visited the Secretary of the Treasury on December 13 and reported that "Walker is entirely in favour of the annexation of the whole of Mexico to the United States; he told me so frankly & also spoke of the manner of governing it during the first years by a suitable form of government which should not be in opposition to the institutions of this country." Regarding Walker as the most important member, he concluded that Polk and the rest of the cabinet likewise desired annexation. He visited Van Buren, Corcoran, Calhoun, and other prominent politicians. He says that Walker was stricken with epilepsy on December 9; Polk in his diary for that day notes that Walker "had been taken suddenly ill & had fallen down in the Treasury building."

The message was vehemently assailed in both houses of Congress. As in the preceding session, the history of the outbreak of the war was discussed in all its details. These recitals shed no new light on the subject, for already nearly every argument had been pressed into service to show that Polk had wantonly usurped authority so that he might rob a sister republic of her territory. On January 3, 1848, by a vote of eighty-five to eighty-one, the House formally declared that the war had been "unnecessarily and unconstitutionally begun by the President of the United States." Among the new Whig members who had the pleasure of adding their votes to the denunciation of the President was Abraham Lincoln. With that consummate skill in debate which was later to expose the sophistry of the "Little Giant," he averred that Polk had falsified the history of our difficulties with Mexico by telling a half truth. The statements in the message reminded him of instances he had known of a lawyer's "struggling for his client's neck in a desperate case, employing every artifice to work round, befog, and cover up with many words some point arising in the case which he dare not admit and yet could not deny."[89]

Resolutions, too, there were in plenty. Dickinson presented one on December 14 which asserted that the "true policy" of the government required the annexation of contiguous territory. In the Senate, on the following day, Calhoun offered a counter resolution to the effect that a conquest of Mexico would be disastrous to the United States, and that "no line of policy in further prosecution of the war should be adopted." On the twenty-second, Lincoln made his début as a legislator by calling upon the President to designate the exact "spot" on which the war had begun, and for proof as to the ownership of that spot.[90]

---

[89] *Cong. Globe*, 30 Cong., 1 sess., 95, 155. The quotation is taken from Lincoln, *Works* (Tandy ed.), 337, which differs slightly from that reported in the *Globe*.

[90] *Cong. Globe, loc. cit.*, 64.

Three days after his message had been sent to Congress the President received a letter from General Pillow which told of the attempt made by Scott and Trist to procure a treaty by the use of bribe money. At a meeting held on December 11 he told the cabinet of the news he had received, and expressed "in the strongest terms" his condemnation of their conduct. Scott's immediate recall was discussed, but it was thought prudent to seek further definite information from Generals Shields and Quitman, who were expected to arrive in Washington within a few days.[91] Although he must have known better,[92] Shields, when consulted, asserted that bribery had not been considered, and that the discussion had related simply to paying part of the money for the territory in advance of the ratification of the treaty. Polk did not accept this version of the matter, and resolved that those implicated in the scheme must be punished, even though his friend Pillow might be one of the number. For the present, however, he was obliged to await further information concerning the "infamous transaction."[93]

Before news of the bribery episode had reached Washington, Polk and his cabinet had discussed the feasibility of promising protection to the peace party in Mexico, if they would form a government and agree to make a treaty. Incensed on account of the bribery scandal and because Scott had arrested Pillow and Worth, the President, against the advice of members of the cabinet, determined to recall both Scott and Trist. The question of their successors had now to be considered. Marcy and Walker felt that Taylor should be put in command of the army, but Polk fixed upon General W. O. Butler. His intention to invest Butler

---

[91] Polk, *Diary*, III, 245–246.

[92] See Hitchcock, *Fifty Years in camp and Field*, 267–268.

[93] Polk, *Diary*, III, 253, 262–3, 340, 383–4. In a letter to Marcy, Scott stated that he had used secret service money simply "to purchase valuable information" (*H. Ex. Doc. 60*, 30 Cong., 1 sess., 1085)—a statement which Polk pronounced "evasive, and leaves the irresistible inference that such a transaction took place and that it will not bear the light" (*Diary*, III, 346). Of course the transaction did take place. See above, pp. 510–512.

with diplomatic powers was opposed by Buchanan, who insisted that the commissioner should be a civilian. A choice was made unnecessary by the arrival of news that Trist had already reopened negotiations.[94] The President's belief that Taylor was wholly out of sympathy with himself and his administration was by no means erroneous. On one point only did the two men agree—they both distrusted and detested General Scott. "Between ourselves," wrote Taylor to his son-in-law on hearing of the victories near Mexico City,

Gen'l Scott would stoop to anything however low & contemptable as any man in the nation, to obtain power or place, & be as arbitrary in using it when in possession; between him, Trist & the powers that be, old Harry may take the hindmost, they are all of a piece.

When, about a month later, a false report of Polk's death reached camp, the hero of Buena Vista remarked: "While I regret to hear of the death of any one, I would as soon have heard of his death if true, as that of any other individual in the whole Union."[95] Perhaps his own brief term in the White House caused him to realize more clearly the perplexities which confront the chief executive of the nation.

On January 4, 1848, Polk was much surprised to read in a letter sent from Vera Cruz by Colonel Wilson that Trist was negotiating with the Mexican commissioners.

Mr. Trist [was his comment] has acknowledged the receipt of his letter of recal[l], and he possesses no diplomatic powers. He is acting, no doubt, upon Gen'l Scott's advice. He has become a perfect tool of Scott. He is, [in] this measure, defying the authority of his Government. . . . He seems to have entered into all Scott's hatred of the administration, and to be lending himself to all Scott's evil purposes. He may, I fear, greatly embarrass the Government.

Next day Mrs. Trist showed to Buchanan the letter of December 4 in which her husband announced, in cipher, that he would make a treaty in accordance with his original instructions.[96]

---

[94] Polk, *Diary*, III, 251, 266, 280–281.
[95] Taylor to Wood, Sept. 27, Nov. 2, 1847, *Taylor Letters*, 136, 148.
[96] Polk, *Diary*, III, 283, 286. For Trist's cipher letter, see above, p. 524.

Before the President had recovered from the amazement caused by Trist's open defiance of authority, his vexation was increased by a call from the House for a copy of Slidell's instructions and for information regarding the return of Santa Anna and Paredes to Mexico. With the concurrence of the cabinet Polk decided to furnish the House with Conner's instructions regarding Santa Anna, but Slidell's instructions and all relating to McKenzie's mission were withheld on the ground that their publication would be prejudicial to public interest.[97]

Truly the new year had brought anything but pleasure to the chief executive. One annoyance succeeded another in such rapid succession that his patience was taxed to the utmost. Three days after he had declined to give the House full information on diplomatic affairs, the mail brought Trist's celebrated sixty-five page letter (of December 6) in which the President was told that the commissioner had decided to save the administration and the party from a "perilous position," and the country from disaster, by making a treaty with Mexico. No wonder that he pronounced this epistle to be the "most extraordinary document" he had ever read.

His despatch is arrogant, impudent, and very insulting to his Government and even personally offensive to the President. He admits he is acting without authority and in violation of the positive order recalling him. It is manifest to me that he has become the tool of Gen'l Scott and his menial instrument, and that the paper was written at Scott's instance and dictation. I have never in my life felt so indignant, and the whole Cabinet expressed themselves as I felt. I told Mr. Buchanan that the paper was so insulting and contemptably base that it require[d] no lengthy answer, but that it did require a short, but stern and decided rebuke, and directed him to prepare such a reply. I directed the Secretary of War to write at once to Maj'r Gen'l Butler, directing him, if Mr. Trist was still with the Head Quarters of the army, to order him off, and to inform the authorities of Mexico that he had no authority to treat. If there was any legal provision for his punishment he ought to be severely handled. He has acted worse than any man in the public employ whom

---

[97] *Ibid.*, 287–291. Richardson, *Messages*, IV, 565–567. For McKenzie's mission, see p. 439.

I have ever known. His despatch proves that he is destitute of honour
or principle, and that he has proved himself to be a very base man. I
was deceived in him. I had little personal knowledge of him, but could
not have believed [it] possible that any man would have acted so basely
as he would have [has] done.[98]

Preparation of letters to Trist and Butler (who had superseded Scott) was delayed for several days while Polk and the
cabinet discussed the propriety of submitting Trist's treaty to
the Senate, if it should turn out that he had already signed one.
Some of the members urged that unless the President had determined to reject such a treaty the suggested notice to the Mexican
government might prove embarrassing. Polk was now unwilling
to restrict his demands to those embodied in Trist's instructions,
and yet he declined to say that he would not accept a treaty made
in accordance with those instructions. Consequently General
Butler was told that if Trist had actually concluded a treaty he
was to send it to Washington, where it would be disposed of as
the President should deem best; if none had been concluded, he
was to inform the Mexican government that the United States
would not recognize a treaty made by the former commissioner.[99]

Polk waited for additional information regarding his insubordinate diplomat. The Mexican mail arrived on February 7,
but contained no dispatches from either Trist or Scott. It
brought, however, a letter from the irrepressible Atocha, and as
usual he was ready to engage in underground diplomacy.
"Atocha is a great scoundrel," was the President's comment,

and his letter contained the infamous suggestion that he should be furnished with money to bribe the Mexican Congress to induce them to ratify
a Treaty of peace, though he does not state whether a Treaty had been
signed by Mr. Trist or not.

---

98 Polk, *Diary*, III, 300–301.

99 *Ibid.*, 313–317. Marcy to Butler, Jan. 26, 1848 (*Sen. Ex. Doc. 52*,
30 Cong., 1 sess., 146). On February 2 the President, in response to a call,
sent to the Senate correspondence relating to Trist's negotiations with the
Mexican commissioners at the time of Scott's armistice (Richardson, *Messages*, IV, 569).

He said that Trist claimed to possess a bribe fund, and Polk thought it likely that the commissioner was base enough to make such an assertion. Silence, in Polk's opinion, indicated a conspiracy on the part of Trist and Scott, and he had little doubt that a treaty would be made: "a few days more will, I trust, develop what they have been doing."[100]

While he awaited developments, troubles nearer home fully occupied the time and taxed the patience of the overworked executive. The hoards of office seekers multiplied. The Whigs, not satisfied with aiding the enemy by "unpatriotic sentiments" and annoying resolutions, were now, in the President's opinion, "insidiously attempting to produce a panic in the money market and thereby, if possible, to break down the Treasury, and thus compel the inglorious withdrawal of our army from Mexico." There were dissensions within the Democratic party among the supporters of rival aspirants for the Presidency, and Polk suspected Buchanan of using his position in the cabinet as a means of injuring General Cass. Members of the party urged the President to cease reiterating his determination not to accept another nomination, for they said that he might be nominated regardless of his own wishes. "To all of them," says the *Diary*, "I have given the same answer, & repeated my sincere desire to retire & my fixed purpose to do so." At this same time he was called upon to perform a duty which was personally disagreeable, and one which would bring additional opposition to his administration. He approved the conviction of Colonel Fremont for disobedience to the orders of General Kearny, and, although the sentence of dismissal was remitted, he fully expected to incur the powerful opposition of Senator Benton.[101] The suspense regarding Trist's activities was broken on February 19 by the arrival of a messenger bearing the treaty of peace. Before discussing

---

[100] Polk, *Diary*, III, 328–330.

[101] *Ibid.*, 319–322, 327. After the approval of the court's decision, Benton, as noted elsewhere, ceased speaking to the President.

its reception, however, we may turn our attention to the negotiations by which it had been concluded.

As noted above, negotiations did not begin as soon as Trist had announced his intention to remain in Mexico. Peña y Peña, the Minister of Foreign Relations, said that the appointment of commissioners must be confirmed by the senate and that the new congress would not meet until January. Both Edward Thornton and Percy W. Doyle, who had recently returned to his post as secretary of the British legation, urged the Mexican government to waive formalities, but, for a time, their arguments produced no effect. Although Trist held informal interviews with the commissioners, not until late in December did Peña consent to take the responsibility of instructing the commissioners to treat with the American diplomat. Even then, in true Mexican fashion, he required them to ask for impossible concessions; and before an agreement had been reached, President Anaya's term of office had expired. As a quorum of the congress had not yet assembled, his successor could not be elected, therefore Peña, as head of the supreme court, again assumed the office of President. Once more, also, Luis de la Rosa was made Minister of Foreign Relations.

Negotiations were resumed, but the new government at first seemed less disposed than the old to make the necessary concessions. The commissioners sat in Mexico City, while the seat of government was at Querétaro, consequently much time was lost in transmitting messages between the two places.

Before the change of government Trist had made it clear that the Rio Grande boundary and the inclusion of San Diego within Upper California would be insisted upon by the United States. He said, also, that his government would not pay Mexico more than fifteen million dollars. On assuming office Rosa objected to the boundary mentioned by Trist, and insisted that the sum to be paid must be at least thirty millions. Doubtless he would have interposed obstacles indefinitely had it not been for threatened uprisings in some of the Mexican states, and had Scott not taken steps to renew military operations. When arguments had failed, Trist threatened to break off negotiations unless a treaty could be signed by the first of February, while Doyle urged both Rosa and the commissioners to avert the calamity of a renewal of hostilities. Such pressure could not be withstood. On January 31 a messenger left Querétaro for Mexico City bearing documents which authorized the commissioners to sign the treaty as agreed upon with Trist. Not until the afternoon of February 2 were all details arranged and copies in both languages completed. In accordance with the wishes of the Mexican commissioners, the treaty was not signed in the capital where the meetings had been held. For affixing the signatures they repaired to the near-by town of Guadalupe Hidalgo, and from that place the treaty took its name.[102]

In the treaty the United States procured the things which had been made ultimata in Trist's instructions. The Rio Grande was recognized as the boundary of Texas; Upper California and New Mexico, but not Lower California, were ceded to the United States. In return, Mexico was to be paid fifteen million dollars; and in addition, the United States agreed to pay all liquidated claims of American citizens against Mexico, and to assume unadjusted claims to the extent of three and a quarter million dollars. Mexico was specifically relieved from the payment of claims not covered by the treaty. The privilege of transit across the Isthmus of Tehauntepec, desired by the American government, was not granted. In a word, Trist contented himself with the minimum which the administration had, in April, 1847, authorized him to accept. As soon as the signatures had been affixed the treaty was borne to Washington by James D. Freanor, a war correspondent of the New Orleans *Delta,* better known

---

[102] For further details concerning the last stage of negotiations, see Rives, *United States and Mexico,* II, 602–613. Some of the Mexican projects in the *Trist Papers* were, according to a note appended by Trist, translated by Thornton and the copies are in his handwriting. Evidently he was familiar with all of the proceedings.

by his pen name, "Mustang." Trist had already asked Scott to disregard his positive orders and to "pledge his word" that he would suspend hostilities.[103]

Freanor arrived in Washington on February 19, 1848, and Buchanan placed the treaty in the President's hands at nine o'clock of the same evening. As Trist had announced his intention to resume negotiations, no surprise was expressed when the document arrived. After a hasty reading of the treaty, Polk confided to his diary:

> Mr. Trist was recalled in October last, but chose to remain in Mexico and continue the negotiations. The terms of the Treaty are within his instructions which he took out in April last, upon the important question of boundary and limits. There are many provisions in it which will require more careful examination than a single reading will afford. Mr. Trist has acted very badly, as I have heretofore noted in this diary, but notwithstanding this, if on further examination the Treaty is one that can be accepted, it should not be rejected on account of his bad conduct.[104]

To this sensible attitude of not permitting personal pique to warp his judgment on matters of state the President steadily adhered. Although Trist's arrogance and unwarranted insolence had greatly exasperated him, the simple fact of negotiating without instructions probably did not worry Polk very much. In April, 1847, while Trist's instructions were being prepared, Buchanan received a letter from Moses Y. Beach, of the New York *Sun*, whom the President had appointed as secret agent in Mexico, and the agent intimated that he might make a treaty. He had not, of course, been clothed with diplomatic powers, yet after reading Beach's letter Polk noted in his diary:

> It is clearly to be inferred from his letter that he will make a Treaty with them if he can. Should he do so, and it is a good one, I will waive his authority to make it, and submit it to the Senate for ratification. It will be a good joke if he should assume the authority and take the whole country by surprise & make a Treaty.[105]

---

[103] Trist to Scott, Jan. 28, 1848, *Trist Papers*.

[104] Polk, *Diary*, III, 345.

[105] Polk, Diary, II, 477. Beach's commission is printed in Buchanan, *Works*, VII, 119.

Probably Trist may have heard the President make similar remarks, and, if so, they may have had some influence on his own conduct in Mexico. However this may have been, Polk, in the present instance, failed to see the humorous side of the transaction.

So important did the President regard an early disposal of the treaty that he waived his scruples against Sunday labor and summoned the cabinet to a special meeting on the evening of the twentieth of February. Of this meeting we have two accounts, one in Polk's diary for the day, another by his nephew and private secretary, J. Knox Walker. After a general discussion Polk asked the opinion of each member concerning the advisability of submitting the document to the Senate for ratification. All agreed that the tenth article relating to land grants in Texas should be stricken out. On the question of accepting the treaty, thus amended, the cabinet was divided—Buchanan and Walker advised a rejection of the whole treaty, while Marcy, Mason, Johnson, and Clifford were in favor of accepting all but the tenth article. After Buchanan's opposition to extensive annexation his present attitude so nettled the President that he asked the pointed question: "Will you take the responsibility of its rejection?" Buchanan's reply, that he would "take all the responsibility which properly pertains to me as Sec'y of State giving such advice," led Polk to believe that the Secretary was playing politics at the expense of his chief. He reminded Buchanan that at the beginning of the war the Secretary had drafted instructions to American ministers at foreign courts which asserted that the government had no intention of taking territory from Mexico—an assertion which the President had required him to omit. He reminded him, also, of his persistent opposition to the acquisition of any land except Upper California and New Mexico—now he objected to the treaty because it did not procure a large enough area. Buchanan admitted this. He told the President that he might go further and mention his (Buchanan's) opposition to Scott's march from Vera Cruz to Mexico City. But, he added, his advice was not taken, and ''I am not now willing to acquire for indemnity what I would then have been very willing to take. The line of the Sierra Madre will give us 'indemnity for the past & security for the future.' '' No agreement was reached at this meeting.[106]

Another meeting was held on the following day, and the President announced that he had decided to submit the treaty to the Senate for ratification, with a recommendation that the tenth article be stricken out. The reasons assigned for this decision are recorded in his diary:

> They were, briefly, that the treaty conformed on the main question of limits & boundary to the instructions given to Mr. Trist in April last; and that though, if the treaty was now to be made, I should demand more territory, perhaps to make the Sierra Madra the line, yet it was doubtful whether this could be ever obtained by the consent of Mexico. I looked, too, to the consequences of its rejection. A majority of one branch of Congress is opposed to my administration; they have falsely charged that the war was brought on and is continued by me with a view to the conquest of Mexico; and if I were now to reject a Treaty made upon my own terms, as authorized in April last, with the unanimous approbation of the Cabinet, the probability is that Congress would not grant either men or money to prosecute the war. Should this be the result, the army now in Mexico would be constantly wasting and diminishing in numbers, and I might at last be compelled to withdraw them, and thus loose the two Provinces of New Mexico & Upper California, which were ceded to the U. S., by this Treaty. Should the opponents of my administration succeed in carrying the next Presidential election, the great probability is that the country would loose all the advantages secured by this Treaty. I adverted to the immense value of Upper California; and concluded by saying that if I were now to reject my own terms, as offered in April last, I did not see how it was possible for my administration to be sustained.[107]

On the next day, February 22, he sent the treaty to the Senate, accompanied by a message which recommended that all except

---

[106] Polk, *Diary*, III, 345–346. Walker's account is in the *Polk Papers*. In a note he says that he prepared it February 22, two days after the meeting. He does not say whether he had been present at the meeting, but comment in Polk's *Diary*, III, 351, indicates that he had been.

[107] Polk, *Diary*, III, 347–348.

the tenth article should be ratified. With it he transmitted copies of the instructions given to both Slidell and Trist, which up to this time had been withheld.[108]

Truly, the President had been placed in an awkward position by his officious diplomat. The war had been unpopular even while Mexico had refused to treat, and Polk had good reasons for believing that he could not hope for means with which to continue it, if he should reject his own terms. During his entire career he had shown excellent judgment as to what was and what was not attainable, and besides, the treaty gave him all that he had set his heart upon. Tamaulipas or part of Sonora might be desirable, if it could be obtained without difficulty; but Polk was not the man to risk losing the objects which he had set out to procure, when the prospect of better terms was by no means certain. Despite all that his opponents might say it seems clear that the President never welcomed a war, and he neglected no opportunity which gave prospect of ending it. He was determined to have Upper California and New Mexico at any cost, for these formed a part of his original program. His interest in further acquisition was never very great. Buchanan's sudden desire for more territory confirmed rather than altered Polk's decision, for he believed that the Secretary was inspired by purely selfish motives.

> He wished [wrote the President] to throw the whole responsibility on me of sending the Treaty to the Senate. If it was received well by the country, being a member of my administration, he would not be injured by it in his Presidential aspirations, for these govern all his opinions & acts lately; but if, on the other hand, it should not be received well, he could say, ''I advised against it.''[109]

Doubtless Polk was justified in attributing to political motives Buchanan's recent change of front on the territorial question. At any rate he had lost faith in the Secretary's loyalty to the

---

[108] Richardson, *Messages*, IV, 573–574.
[109] Polk, *Diary*, III, 350.

administration. He had not concealed his resentment when discussing the treaty, and a few days later he had occasion to speak still more pointedly. Buchanan told him that it was rumored in the streets that he was to be removed from the cabinet because a friend of his named Nugent, a correspondent for the New York *Herald,* had criticized the administration. Polk told him that the rumor was untrue, but that the vile effusions signed by Nugent had been attributed to the Secretary of State. He remarked "in a stern manner" that Buchanan himself must judge of the propriety of having a member of the cabinet holding familiar intercourse with an unprincipled person who "was in daily habit of calumniating" the President. "Their object," said Polk, "seems to be to abuse Gen'l Cass, Mr. Woodbury, and myself, and to praise Mr. Buchanan. The[y] falsely represent that I am intriguing to obtain the nomination for a re-election to the Presidency." He did not doubt that Buchanan had encouraged these attacks, for his own purposes; but he did not wish to act on suspicion alone. "If," said he, "I obtain any reliable proof that Mr. Buchanan has given countenance to Galvienses [Nugent] he shall not remain in the Cabinet. He denies that he has done so, and I am bound to believe him." When informed by Clifford that both Walker and Buchanan had spoken of resigning on account of the controversy over the treaty, he declared that he would follow his own course, regardless of consequences. Although surprised to hear that Walker had made such remarks, he was neither surprised nor perturbed by the hostility of the Secretary of State. "I expressed to Mr. Clifford," says the *Diary,* "an indifference as to the course which Mr. Buchanan might think proper to pursue, but told him there was not the slightest danger of his resigning."[110]

---

[110] *Ibid.,* 353–355, 359. Galvienses was Nugent's pen name. "Mr. Buchanan's real trouble," was another comment in the *Diary,* "is that he cannot use my administration and shape his [its] course according to his own ever varying whims, in order to promote his aspirations to the Presidency. He cares not for the success or glory of my administration further than he can make it subservient to his own political aspirations."

When he had received the treaty and submitted it to the Senate the President no doubt believed that he had received the last of Trist's abusive epistles. If so, he was greatly mistaken. Indeed, Freanor had brought two more along with the treaty, but by an oversight they had not been delivered to Polk until two days after that document had been sent to the Senate. The first bore the date of December 29, and the main point developed was that Polk's annual message had jeopardized peace negotiations by aiding the *puros,* the party which desired to annex all of Mexico to the United States. The particular part of the message criticized was that which suggested that necessity might force the United States to establish a government with which it could make a treaty. By preventing the *moderados,* now in control, from making peace, the *puros* hoped, by continuing hostilities, to force the United States to take all of Mexico, or at least to establish some form of protectorate over it. The second letter, of January 12, 1848, dealt with the difficulty of suspending hostilities, and was still more offensive than the other. At the time of Trist's recall, Polk had required the commander-in-chief to transmit all peace proposals to Washington; at the same time, Scott was instructed to pursue the war with renewed vigor. Such an arrangement, said Trist, prevented any suspension of hostilities while peace proposals were under consideration—except by disobedience of orders—and was "a wanton sporting with the lives of men," a course which, if followed, would cause the whole civilized world to "burst forth with one universal cry of horror."[111]

The arrogant character of these letters completely exhausted the patience of the President, and their author was characterized as "an impudent and unqualified scoundrel." Through Marcy, Polk instructed General Butler to prevent Trist from exercising any official authority in Mexico and to drive him away from the army headquarters. When Marcy hesitated to issue so drastic

---

[111] Trist to Buchanan (*Sen. Ex. Doc. 52,* 30 Cong., 1 sess., 274–280).

an order, the President not only dictated its terms but prepared a note for the files of the War Department to show that Polk himself had assumed the entire responsibility.[112]

Had Polk received at this time another long letter written by Trist, he would, if possible, have been still more exasperated. It bears a date earlier than Freanor's departure for Washington, but apparently it was not sent until later. Besides giving a detailed account of the negotiations, Trist made some really sensible remarks concerning the obligation of the United States to protect its adventurous citizens who had engaged in hazardous enterprises in Mexico. As usual, however, he could not refrain from saying disagreeable things. In his discussion of the boundary he committed the unpardonable sin of asserting that the land between the Nueces and the Rio Grande was as much a part of Tamaulipas (and not of Texas) as the counties of Accomac and Northampton were a part of Virginia.[113] If so, the President was justly entitled to the sobriquet "Polk the mendacious," for his war message had been premised on a falsehood and hostilities had been wantonly provoked.

Private letters written at this time show that Trist derived real pleasure from playing *enfant terrible*. He had developed an inveterate hatred for both Polk and Buchanan, and he seemed to believe that he possessed information which, when disclosed, would make the throne totter. He presumed that the arrival of his treaty had caused a commotion, but it could have been "*nothing* to the *uproar* that is to come."

> Until I shall be ready to speak, [he continued with a solemnity born of conceit], let them remain in the doubt and the hopes, as to my future course, inspired by the falseness & baseness of their own ignoble hearts. Let them go on hoping that I am, or may be made, like themselves; capable of being *bought,* if not to active villany, at least to passive; to silence, if to nothing else.

---

[112] Polk, *Diary,* III, 357–358. Marcy to Butler, Feb. 25, 1848 (*Sen. Ex. Doc. 52,* as above cited, 148–150).

[113] Trist to Buchanan, Jan. 25, 1848 (*Sen. Ex. Doc. 52,* 30 Cong., 1 sess., 290).

These remarks are interesting as coming from one of the two men who alone had been guilty of *buying* others. The disclosures which he expected to cause the "uproar" were Polk's confidential correspondence with Pillow, whom Trist, in his letter, was pleased to call a reptile.

As to whether he was entitled to payment for the extra time put in since his recall, Trist's mind was not quite clear; but he would accept nothing which might depend upon even the "official decision" of the President.

> His official mind is too corrupt or too imbecile. Nothing proceeding from it—in the way of *advantage*, at least—shall touch me. I say the same of every man capable of retaining a seat in his cabinet during the last 3, 4 or 5 months.

The court of inquiry selected to investigate the charges made against Pillow and other accused military officers was, in Trist's opinion, a "pitiable device of the pitiable being in the Presidential chair." When notified by General Butler that he must leave Mexico, Trist once more paid his compliments to the President and denied his authority to order a private citizen out of a foreign country. He was probably right in holding that

> I deem it my duty to deny the lawfulness of any requirement from the President of the United States, pretending to impose upon me the obligation, either to leave the *Republic of Mexico* or to *return to the United States*. I recognize no authority in that functionary competent to create any such obligation. The pretension to create it, & the use of the armed power confided to him, for the purpose of enforcing it, are, to my mind, alike usurpations; usurpations differing but slightly in the shades of enormity.[114]

The President, as we have seen, sent Trist's treaty to the Senate on February 22, but on account of the illness and death of John Quincy Adams its consideration was delayed several days.

---

[114] Trist to Mrs. Trist, March 2, 1848; Trist to Butler, March 17, 1848, *Trist Papers*. In a letter dated March 18 he told Butler that he would not embarrass him by resisting the order. He had, on February 1, written to his wife that he would go to West Chester and keep a boarding school. "For my own part, I will live on bread & water before I ever again hold office of any kind." Also in *Trist Papers*.

Immediately, however, unofficial reports predicted that the treaty would probably be rejected. Cave Johnson shared this belief, and he told the President of a rumor that both Buchanan and Walker had been exerting their influence against ratification. Polk was still more perturbed by another "astounding" rumor— also reported by Johnson—which charged Walker with giving aid to the Presidential candidacy of General Taylor. "If I ascertain this to be true," was the comment in his diary, "it will be inconsistent with the success of my measures for Mr. Walker to remain in my Cabinet. I will require strong proof however before I can believe it to be true."[115]

The Whigs and a small group of Democrats who had been devising means of compelling the President to end the war, now that a treaty had been made, did their utmost to cause its rejection. The prospect for ratification was not encouraging. On February 28 Senator Sevier, chairman of the Committee of Foreign Affairs, reported to Polk that all of the committee except himself had resolved to recommend that the treaty should be rejected and that the President be advised to send to Mexico a new commission, invested with power to make a new treaty. They did not, said Sevier, object to the treaty itself but to the fact that Trist had no authority to make it. The absurd suggestion offered by the committee did not appeal to Polk's practical mind:

> I told him [Sevier] I condemned the insubordination & insolent conduct of Mr. Trist, but that the Treaty itself was the subject for consideration and not his conduct, and that if the provisions of the Treaty were such as could be accepted, it would be worse than idle ceremony to send out a grand commission to re-negotiate the same Treaty. I told him, also, that if the Senate advised me to send out such a commission, I hoped they would advise me also what they would accept. . . . Extremes sometimes meet. . . . They have done so in this instance. Mr. Webster is for *no* territory and Mr. Hannegan is for *all* Mexico, and for opposite reasons both will oppose the Treaty. It is difficult, upon any rational principle, to assign a satisfactory reason for anything Col. Benton may do, especially in his present temper of mind, wholly engrossed as he seems to have been for some months past with the case of his son-in-law, Col. Fremont.

---

[115] Polk, *Diary*, III, 361.

His suspicion that Walker and Buchanan would use their influence against ratification seems to have been removed by their volunteering to urge Senators to vote against the plan for creating a new commission.[116]

While the President was conversing with Sevier, the Senate was passing resolutions which requested him to submit all correspondence that had passed between Trist and the State Department. Without consulting the cabinet, he decided to send it all, despite its exceptionable character. On the next day he was told that the fate of the treaty was extremely doubtful and that about a dozen Democrats would vote against it because of their desire for more territory. Not for this reason, but from personal motives, Polk feared most of all the opposition of Benton:

> He has heretofore maintained that the true boundary of Texas was the Nueces instead of the Rio Grande, & he is apt to think that nothing is done properly that he is not consulted about.[117]

If some Democrats declined to uphold the administration by supporting the treaty, so, also, were certain Whigs unwilling to put ratification on a purely party basis. Polk was especially pleased when on March 1 he was told by the banker, W. W. Corcoran, that Joseph Gales, of the *National Intelligencer,* had refused to prepare an article against ratification, when requested to do so by Whig Senators. For several days after this the fate of the treaty hung in the balance, its chief opponents being Webster and Benton. Polk blamed the insurgent Democrats most of all, for as he said, "if the Democratic party were united in favour of the Treaty, I doubt whether a single Whig would vote against it." Both parties, in his opinion, were interested primarily in the approaching Presidential election, and he did not believe that Whigs would care to incur the odium of casting a strictly party vote.[118]

After much heated discussion and many calls upon the President for information (among other things for "information in

---

[116] *Ibid.,* 363–367.   [117] *Ibid.,* 367.   [118] *Ibid.,* 368–371.

regard to any disposition or overtures on the part of any considerable portion of the Mexican people to be annexed to the U.
States''), the Senate, by a vote of thirty-eight to fourteen, ratified
the treaty on the tenth of March. The tenth article and the secret
article relating to an extension of time for ratification were eliminated as the President had recommended. Other modifications
made by the Senate, on its own account, caused Polk to fear that
Mexico might decline to ratify the treaty. He greatly appreciated the assistance given by Senator Mangum, of the Committee
of Foreign Affrirs, who ''though a Whig, is a gentleman''—
apparently a rare combination, in the President's opinion.[119]

As soon as there was any indication that the treaty would be
ratified, Polk began to cast about for a suitable commissioner
whom he might send to Mexico to urge its acceptance. He fixed
upon Louis McLane, of Maryland, and when he declined to serve,
Senator Sevier, of Arkansas, was appointed. Scarcely, however,
had Sevier's appointment been ratified by the Senate when he
was taken ill and, in order to save time, Attorney-General Clifford was chosen to be his associate. Clifford set out for Mexico
at once, while Sevier's health was sufficiently improved within
the next few days to enable him to follow his colleague.

Ratification of the treaty by the Senate did not entirely relieve
Polk's anxiety, for he feared that his opponents might yet defeat
it by indirect methods. Evidence of a disposition to employ such
methods was seen in a motion, offered in executive session on
March 14, to remove the injunction of secrecy from the Senate
proceedings. Its adoption would expose to the Mexicans the

---

119 *Ibid.*, 369, 377, 381. When the records of the executive session
were finally made public on May 31 it was discovered that several rather
drastic resolutions had been offered. Webster, for example, moved that
all discussion of the treaty be postponed and that the President be
asked to appoint a new commission. Houston held that since Trist had
no authority to negotiate, his treaty was ''utterly void,'' and ought to
be rejected. Both Houston and Jefferson Davis wanted more territory,
while Baldwin, of Connecticut, tried to incorporate into the treaty a
provision for excluding slavery from all territory to be acquired. The
proceedings are printed in *Sen. Ex. Doc. 52*, 30 Cong., 1 sess., 4 ff.

confidential instructions which had been given to Slidell and Trist and, also, the division of opinion in the Senate. They might as a result be induced to reject the modified treaty in the hope of obtaining better terms. No action was taken on this resolution until the last of May, but in the meantime the New York *Herald* began to publish Polk's message which had accompanied Trist's treaty to the Senate and, also, Slidell's instructions and parts of the diplomatic correspondence. As Nugent, the Washington correspondent for that paper, was known to be on intimate terms with Buchanan, the Secretary of State at once became the object of suspicion. Polk was loth to believe that Buchanan could be guilty of such treachery; still, he advised Senators to make a thorough investigation, and he was prepared to dismiss the Secretary if it should be found that he had in any way been connected with giving out the documents. When summoned before a Senate committee, Nugent refused to disclose the name of the person who had furnished him with copies of the documents, but he stated in writing that it was not Buchanan. Polk believed the Secretary of State to be both weak and self-seeking, yet he was very much gratified to have Buchanan "relieved from so injurious an imputation."[120]

Ratification of the treaty by the Senate did not terminate discussion on military affairs. It was not certain, of course, that Mexico would accept the alterations which had been made, consequently the administration forces urged that the pending ten-regiment bill should be enacted into law. Polk's whole war policy was assailed and defended, as before, while opposition members kept annoying the President with requests for additional information. Among other items called for by the Senate was a copy of the letter which, in 1845, Gillespie had carried to Thomas O. Larkin, United States consul at Monterey, California. Our chief interest in this resolution is that when commenting upon it in his diary Polk distinctly implied that Fremont had

---

[120] Polk, *Diary*, III, 396–409.

not been authorized to foment a revolution in California. He transmitted a copy of the letter to the Senate in executive session, so that if it were made public, and trouble should result, the responsibility would rest upon the Senate and not upon himself.[121]

Clifford arrived in Mexico City with the modified treaty on April 11, 1848, Sevier four days later. Under the President's supervision Buchanan had prepared instructions which were to guide them in their discussions with the Mexican officials. Among other things they were to avoid diplomatic notes whenever possible and to hold personal conferences, which would be more conducive to a speedy adjustment of differences of opinion. In a letter to the Minister of Foreign Relations, written at the same time, Buchanan explained in detail the changes which had been made by the Senate. While his letter was very friendly in tone, a pointed reference to the fact that "four votes, taken from the majority, and added to the minority, would have defeated the treaty" was intended to impress upon the Mexican government the futility of asking for better terms.[122]

During the period of more than two months between the signature of the treaty and the arrival of Clifford and Sevier in Mexico the several factions in that country had had time to discuss the question of making peace with the United States, although the details of the treaty were not known to the public. The *puros,* or radicals, being anxious for annexation to the United States, naturally were hostile to ratification. For an entirely different reason the propertied class looked forward with dismay to the withdrawal of the American army, because they feared that adequate protection of their property would be gone. According to his own account, "certain leaders" desired Scott to proclaim himself dictator for six years, with the eventual purpose of joining the United States. The general "ultimately declined"

---

[121] *Ibid.,* 395, 399. Richardson, *Messages,* IV, 578.

[122] Buchanan to Min. of For. Rel., March 18, 1848 (*H. Ex. Doc. 60,* 30 Cong,. 1 sess., 67).

the invitation. One of his reasons was that he had already suggested annexation and "President Polk's Government carefully withheld its wishes from him thereon."[123]

The work of the American commissioners was delayed by the fact that the Mexican congress, which alone could ratify the treaty, had not convened at the time of their arrival. Although the members had been elected in March, not until the first week in May did a quorum assemble in Querétaro. The apparent reluctance of the Mexican government to meet the issue led Polk to believe that ratification "may be regarded as doubtful."[124]

After meeting, however, the congress acted with unusual promptitude. President Peña y Peña in his message, although regretting that the treaty had been modified, nevertheless advised its ratification. In addition, his ministers of war and finance showed by verbal reports that Mexico was too weak to continue hostilities if the treaty should be rejected. On May 19 the chamber of deputies gave its assent and the Minister of Foreign Relations invited Clifford and Sevier to visit Querétaro and present their credentials to the President. They arrived on May 25, just after the senate had ratified the treaty. Ratifications were exchanged on the thirtieth and the commissioners returned to Mexico City and arranged for the fulfillment of the financial obligations of the treaty.[125]

"At 6 o'clock this morning," wrote Clifford on June 12,

the flag of the United States was taken down from the national palace in this city and that of the Mexican republic was hoisted. The customary honors were paid to both, and the ceremony passed off in perfect quiet, although the great square was thronged.[126]

With this formality the two years' war with Mexico had been brought to a successful termination. President Polk had not

---

[123] Scott, *Autobiography*, II, 581–582. Doyle to Palmerston, Feb. 13, 1848, quoted by Rives, II, 643–644.

[124] Polk, *Diary*, III, 447.

[125] Sevier and Clifford to Buchanan, May 25 and 30, 1848 (*H. Ex. Doc. 60*, 30 Cong., 1 sess., 72–73). See also Rives, II, 651–653.

[126] *H. Ex. Doc. 60*, as cited above, 74.

only "conquered a peace," but in all essential details he had effected his program of national expansion. Determined from the beginning to add California and New Mexico to our national domain, he pursued this object with a dogged persistence which neither opposition nor denunciation could weaken. Whatever may be thought of his motives or his methods, to him is due the credit (or censure, if you please) of extending to the Pacific the boundaries of the United States.

The letter in which Sevier and Clifford had announced that the treaty had been ratified by the Mexican congress reached the President on the fifteenth of June. Comment in his diary is limited to a statement that the letter had been received, for he was ill at the time and his mind was occupied with the contemplated purchase of Cuba. His pleasure at being relieved from the burdens of war may be judged by a remark made on the second anniversary of its beginning: "It is two years ago this day since War was declared by Congress against Mexico. They have been two years of unceasing labour and anxiety with me."[127]

On July 4, just as the President had returned from the ceremonies connected with laying the corner stone of the Washington monument, a messenger arrived with the treaty of Guadalupe Hidalgo. He at once directed Buchanan to prepare a proclamation so that it might be signed on "the anniversary of Independence." His private secretaries were set to work at copying a message which had already been prepared, and two days later this and the treaty were submitted to both houses of Congress. Among the documents sent with the treaty was a copy of the instructions given to Slidell in 1845. When the House had asked for these instructions earlier in the session, their request had been denied, but now, as the President noted, "the reasons for withholding them at that time no longer exist."

As a true expansionist the President fully appreciated the importance of his achievements. "The results of the war with

---

[127] Polk, *Diary*, III, 448, 492.

Mexico,'' said his message, ''have given the United States a national character which our country never before enjoyed.'' New Mexico and California ''constitute of themselves a country large enough for a great empire, and their acquisition is second only in importance to that of Louisiana in 1803.'' He saw, on the other hand, that evil as well as good might follow in the wake of the war, and he took advantage of the occasion to warn Congress against unwise legislation. In organizing governments for the new territories, he invoked a spirit of concession and conciliation, so that sectional discords might be avoided and the Union be preserved. The army should be reduced to its ante-bellum footing, for ''our standing army is to be found in the bosom of society.'' A true disciple of Jefferson, he urged that

Upon the restoration of peace we should adopt the policy suited to a state of peace. In doing this the earliest practicable payment of the public debt should be a cardinal principle of action. Profiting by the experiences of the past, we should avoid the errors into which the country was betrayed shortly after the close of the war with Great Britain in 1815. In a few years after that period a broad and latitudinous construction of the powers of the Federal Government unfortunately received but too much countenance. Though the country was burdened with a heavy public debt, large, and in some instances unnecessary and extravagant, expenditures were authorized by Congress. The consequence was that the payment of the debt was postponed for more than twenty years, and even then it was only accomplished by the stern will and unbending policy of President Jackson, who made its payment a leading measure of his Administration.[128]

Some of Polk's friends, including Houston and Davis, of the Senate Committee on Military Affairs, did not share his views concerning a reduction of the army. Not satisfied with his recommendation, the House, also, asked him for additional information. On August 1 he submitted a report from the Secretary of War, and along with it, a message saying that he had ''seen no reason to change the opinion'' expressed in the preceding

---

[128] Richardson, *Messages*, IV, 587–593. The original draft of this message contained a paragraph on the ''misnamed & exploded 'American system,' but by the advice of the cabinet it was omitted (Polk, *Diary*, III, 496).

July. He was "decidedly opposed" to an increase in the army,
and he attributed the anxiety for more adequate defense to self-
seeking military men and extravagant Whigs. Concerning the
latter he said in his diary:

> Some Whig members of Congress favour the measure because it is in
> harmony with their general policy. They favour, as a party, large ex-
> penditures, high tariffs, & Banks, and in addition to this they would be
> pleased to have a large increase of the standing army fastened on the
> country, which they would for political effect charge to be a consequence
> of the Mexican War.[129]

The forebodings of the President regarding the sectional bitterness which might result from attempts to establish governments for the new territories were not without foundation. The
Wilmot Proviso had not been forgotten, and already, indeed, the
debate on the Oregon bill foreshadowed the breakers ahead.
Renewed agitation of the slavery question resulted from the
Mexican war, but was not a part of it; its consideration as a
domestic question is reserved for another chapter.

---

[129] Richardson, *Messages,* IV, 603. Polk, *Diary,* IV, 48.

CHAPTER XXI

OREGON

The treaty of peace which terminated the Revolution fixed the boundary between the United States and Canada east of the Mississippi River. By the purchase of Louisiana with its indefinite boundaries, in 1803, the United States acquired whatever claims France might have to territory lying west of the Mississippi; and by the Florida treaty of 1819 Spain ceded to the United States all her claims to territory lying west of Louisiana and north of the forty-second parallel of north latitude. In general terms, all this was clear enough, but the difficult problem was: What, precisely, are the proper limits of these claims?

The British claim to the Pacific coast region was based mainly on the explorations made by Captain Cook in 1776; the interior of the Oregon region was claimed as a result of the discovery of the Frazer River valley by Alexander MacKenzie in 1793. In 1789, however, the Spaniards, who laid claim to all of this region, sent out from Mexico an exploring expedition. At Nootka Sound they seized two British ships and nearly precipitated a war between the two countries. The matter was adjusted by a convention signed in 1790 which admitted the right of British subjects to establish trading posts for the purpose of carrying on commerce with the natives. The question which came to be disputed later was whether, in this convention, Spain had transferred to England the ownership of the land, or simply the temporary use of it. Russia, also, had laid claim to this region, but by treaties—one with the United States in 1824, and another with England in 1825—had relinquished everything south of 54° 40′ north latitude.

In addition to claims derived from Spain and France, the United States based her title to Oregon upon discoveries and settlements made by her own citizens. In 1792, Captain Robert Gray, of Boston, had explored the Columbia River and named it after his ship; and in 1811, John Jacob Astor had founded the trading post of Astoria. This place had been taken by the British during the War of 1812, but under the terms of the Treaty of Ghent it was restored in 1818.

After 1825, when Russia limited her claims, the Oregon question was reduced to this: Does either Great Britain or the United States have a valid title to all of the territory west of the Rocky Mountains and included between 42°, the northern boundary of California, and 54° 40', the southern boundary of Alaska; if not, how should it be divided? The United States claimed this region by right of discovery—both direct and acquired; on similar grounds Great Britain claimed it, at least as far south as the Columbia River.

Prior to Polk's administration several attempts had been made to establish a definite boundary line between the United States and Canada. In the treaty of 1818 the forty-ninth parallel was agreed upon as the boundary from the Lake of the Woods to the Rocky Mountains. The country west of the mountains was left open to what was commonly called joint occupation; that is, each nation might make use of it without prejudice to the claims of the other. In 1827 "joint occupation" was continued indefinitely, but either nation might terminate the agreement by giving twelve months' notice to the other.

At an early date members of Congress began to take an interest in Oregon. In December, 1820, the House appointed a committee and assigned it the duty of considering the propriety of taking possession of the territory. A month later the committee's report was submitted by Floyd, of Virginia. In substance it recommended that the government should take steps to safeguard the interests of the United States on the Pacific coast.

No action resulted from this recommendation, but two years later after England had (1821) extended her laws over the territory, another committee was appointed to consider the subject. Their report was similar to that made in 1820, but again no action resulted.

A bill to authorize the occupation of the Oregon River valley was introduced in the House in December, 1828. Its most active sponsor, Floyd, of Virginia, urged the necessity of extending over this region the laws of the United States, and of constructing military forts to insure the protection of Americans. Gurley, of Louisiana, proposed an amendment under which lands might be granted to colonists from the United States. Polk opposed both the bill and the amendment on the ground that they would violate the treaty of "joint occupation" with Great Britain. He pointed out that those who participated in the debate had "confined themselves to the expediency of the measure, and have had no reference to the present state of our negotiations in reference to the preliminary question of title to the country." After quoting the terms of the treaty of 1818, he remarked that "The question is not now whether it was wise to make this treaty, but, having made it, what is its spirit and meaning?" Until the treaty has been abrogated, he said, it is the "supreme law of the land," and it can not be abrogated until twelve months' notice has been given. He moved that the Committee of the Whole be discharged from further consideration of the bill and that the subject be referred to the Committee on Territories. He moved further that this committee be instructed to report in favor of extending over the American citizens in that region the jurisdiction of the courts of Michigan Territory, and of providing for the exploration and survey of the Northwest coast. Neither this nor solutions offered by other members were accepted by the House. On January 9, 1829, Polk voted with the majority in rejecting the entire bill.[1]

---

[1] *Reg. of Deb.*, 20 Cong., 2 sess., 125–153. Also, *Abridg. of Deb.*, X, 273–315.

In 1833 the Missionary Board of the Methodist church selected a number of missionaries and sent them forth to found a settlement in Willamette Valley.[2] Two years later President Jackson sent William A. Slacum to investigate conditions in that region, and in December, 1837, Slacum's favorable report was laid before Congress.[3] On February 7, 1838, Linn, of Missouri, introduced in the Senate a bill to organize Oregon as a territory and to establish on the Columbia River both a port of entry and a custom house.[4] As early as December 29, 1829, Linn had offered a resolution which purposed to give the twelve months' notice necessary for terminating the conventions of 1818 and 1827.[5] In both cases Congress declined to take any action, but interest in Oregon continued to increase. Every year added to the number who exhorted Congress to do something for the protection of American citizens in that country. Great Britain, it was urged, had extended her laws throughout Oregon as early as 1821; why should the United States continue to disregard the rights of its citizens?

The arrival in Washington of Lord Ashburton, in April, 1842, gave rise to the hope that the whole vexed question of boundary might be adjusted, for the northwest as well as the northeast boundary was included in the scope of the British diplomat's instructions.[6] But, as Tyler informed Congress in his second annual message, "it became manifest at an early hour in the late negotiations" that any attempt to settle the Oregon question "would lead to a protracted discussion, which might embrace in its failure other more pressing matters."[7]

Eager to succeed where others had failed, Tyler proposed a tripartite treaty whereby he hoped to settle not only the Oregon question, but, also, the diplomatic difficulties with Mexico which

[2] Gray, *History of Oregon*, 106 ff.   [4] *Cong. Globe*, 25 Cong., 2 sess., 168.

[3] *Sen. Doc. 24*, 25 Cong., 2 sess.   [5] *Abridg. of Deb.*, XIV, 18.

[6] Aberdeen to H. S. Fox, Oct. 18, 1842 (*Sen. Doc. 1*, 29 Cong., 1 sess., 139).

[7] Richardson, *Messages*, IV, 196.

had resulted from the revolt of Texas and the non-payment by Mexico of American damage claims. He was willing to let England have Oregon down to the Columbia River if she in turn would induce Mexico to recognize the independence of Texas and to make territorial concessions to the United States. England was to cancel certain claims against Mexico and to induce her to cede to the United States that part of California lying north of the thirty-sixth parallel, and as a compensation for this service the United States was to relinquish her claim to that part of Oregon lying north of the Columbia River. At the time that he formulated this plan, Tyler apparently had little doubt that England would readily agree, or that the combination which he had suggested would reconcile opposing interests in the United States. ''Texas might not stand alone,'' he told Webster, ''nor would the line proposed for Oregon. Texas would reconcile all to the line, while California would reconcile or pacify all to Oregon.''[8] Despite this hopeful language, however, he endeavored, after he had retired from office, to represent this whole matter as a passing fancy to which little importance should be attached. ''I never dreamed,'' he wrote,

of ceding this country [between 49° and the Columbia] unless for the greater equivalent of California which I fancied G. Britain might be able to obtain for us through her influence in Mexico—and this was but a dream of policy which was never embodied.[9]

Nothing, of course, came of Tyler's ingenious scheme for killing so many birds with one stone. Ashburton expressed, unofficially, the belief that Great Britain would not oppose a cession of territory by Mexico to the United States, but that she could take no part in the transaction.[10] While there was never any prospect that Tyler's plan would succeed, had it been

[8] Tyler, *Letters and Times of the Tylers,* II, 260–261. See also Webster to Everett, Jan. 29, 1843 (Curtis, *Life of Webster,* II, 175).

[9] Tyler to his son, Dec. 11, 1845, MS in Library of Congress. Also printed copy in *Tyler, op. cit,.* 447.

[10] Schafer, ''British Attitude toward the Oregon Question,'' *Am. Hist. Rev.,* XVI, no. 2, p. 293.

accepted by the other governments concerned the Mexican war might possibly have been averted. Webster soon left the cabinet and the President turned his attention to the annexation of Texas. The Oregon question remained unsettled and became one of the leading issues of the campaign of 1844.

A bill introduced in the Senate on December 19, 1842, by Linn, of Missouri, gave opportunity for debate on the Oregon question and prepared the way for the approaching Presidential campaign. Among other things the bill provided for the building of forts along the route to Oregon and at the mouth of the Columbia River, and for the granting of land to American settlers. It can hardly be said that the discussion was sectional in character, although westerners were more insistent than others that the government should take some action. Webster attributed the agitation entirely to politics,[11] but it is evident that many were sincerely interested in westward expansion.

The chief opponents of Linn's bill were Senators Calhoun and McDuffie, of South Carolina. The former declared that the passage of the land-grant section would violate the treaty with Great Britain. Besides, he opposed the whole bill on the ground that precipitate action might result in the loss of the entire territory. England, he said, could transfer troops by sea in a very short time, while it would take months for our army to reach Oregon by overland routes. Consequently the sound policy for the United States to pursue was that of ''wise and masterly inactivity.'' McDuffie was averse to the bill, not because he feared that its passage might result in the loss of Oregon, but because he regarded the territory as an incubus which ought to be discarded. He would not give ''a pinch of snuff for the whole territory,'' because it was totally unsuited as a home for civilized beings.[12] Benton and Linn made strong arguments in favor of the bill, and refuted in detail the positions taken by the Senators from

---

[11] Webster to Everett, Jan. 29, 1843, as cited above.

[12] *Cong. Globe*, 27 Cong., 3 sess., 198–200; *idem*, App., 138–141. Benton, *Thirty Years' View*, II, 471–472.

South Carolina. Sevier, of Arkansas, resisted an attempt to strike out the section for granting land to settlers, for he justly regarded this provision to be "the very life and soul of the bill."[13] After passing the Senate by a vote of twenty-four to twenty-two, the bill was sent to the House where it remained to the end of the session without being voted upon.

The importance of the Linn bill can not be measured by its failure to reach a vote in the House, for it elicited a debate in Congress and an agitation in the press which focused the attention of the people on Oregon and made it an important campaign issue. Then, too, its introduction caused British statesmen to give the subject more serious attention. Palmerston went so far as to declare in the House of Commons that should the bill be passed and put in operation "it would be a declaration of war."[14]

Dissatisfied because Webster had not procured, in the Ashburton treaty, all that the United States had claimed on the Maine border, and fearful that Everett, in London, might, under Tyler's directions, compromise the Oregon question, opposition members took steps to prevent such action on the part of the executive. On December 28, 1843, Senator Allen, of Ohio, moved a call upon the President for the instructions given to our minister in London as well as the correspondence that had passed between the two governments. On January 8, 1844, Semple, of Illinois, moved that the President be requested to give the notice necessary for terminating the convention of 1827.[15] It was soon ascertained that no negotiations were in progress in London and consequently Semple's resolution was defeated, but the debate helped to agitate public opinion. Extremists objected to any negotiation whatever on the ground that it would be an admission that Great Britain might have some claim to the territory.

Negotiations were soon renewed, however, but in Washington instead of at the court of Saint James. The man selected

---

13 *Cong. Globe,* 27 Cong., 3 sess., 153.
14 Hansard, *Parliamentary Debates,* LXVII, 1217.
15 *Cong. Globe,* 28 Cong., 1 sess., 77, 116.

by Lord Aberdeen for the American mission was Richard Pakenham (later Sir Richard), and early in 1844 he arrived in Washington. If his official instructions were to be followed there was small prospect of an adjustment, for they required him to insist upon the Columbia River as the southern boundary of Oregon. It is evident, however, that Aberdeen himself did not expect the United States to accept this proposal, and that he was prepared to concede better terms if he could obtain the sanction of Parliament and of public sentiment in England. In a private letter dated March 4, 1844, Pakenham was instructed to

endeavor, without committing yourself or your gov't, to draw from the American negotiator a proposal to make the 49th degree of latitude the boundary, with the proviso that the ports to the south of that parallel to the Columbia inclusive, shall be free ports to G. Britain.[16]

The tone of this letter augured well for the future.

Upshur's tragic death interrupted negotiations before they had fairly begun, and the task of discussing the Oregon boundary with Pakenham devolved upon John C. Calhoun to whom Tyler now intrusted the State Department. According to statements made later, Tyler and Calhoun were reluctant to resume negotiations, consequently the Secretary of State decided that the *"true* policy" was *"to do nothing to excite attention, and leave time to operate."*[17] Nevertheless both Calhoun and Pakenham presented and advocated the claims of their respective governments—including an offer from Great Britain to submit the whole subject to arbitration—but as neither side would yield the essential points, the Oregon question remained unsettled at the close of Tyler's administration.

"Reannexation of Texas" and "reoccupation of Oregon" were twin planks in the platform adopted by the Democratic

---

[16] Quoted by Schafer, "The British Attitude toward the Oregon Question, 1815–1846," *Am. Hist. Rev.*, XVI, 296 (Jan., 1911).

[17] Calhoun to Mason, May 30, 1845 (*Report Am. Hist. Assn.*, 1899, II, 660). Tyler to Calhoun, Oct. 7, 1845 (*ibid.*, 1059).

convention of 1844. Although the former was the main topic of discussion during the campaign, the party was nevertheless committed to the claim that "all of Oregon" was the property of the United States. The candidates accepted the platform without reservation, while the rank and file voiced their approval by lusty shouts of "54° 40' or fight." Did the platform and the campaign cry mean what they said, or were they intended simply to arouse enthusiasm and to win votes for the party? In either case the victorious candidate was placed in an awkward position; to accept less than "all of Oregon" would repudiate the party pledge, while insistence upon the demand made in the platform would almost certainly result in war with Great Britain.

In his inaugural address President Polk bluntly asserted that "our title to the country of the Oregon is 'clear and unquestionable!'" He did not say "all of Oregon," but left it to be inferred that this was what he meant. In addition, he recommended that the laws of the United States should be extended over the people who had established their homes in that distant region. If the propriety of his recommendations may be questioned,[18] the fault lay with the party which had framed the platform rather than with the President who was pledged to carry it out.[19]

The new President's inaugural reached England late in March and his remarks on the American title to Oregon were by no means relished in London. In Parliament and in the press they elicited expressions of surprise and denunciation. Opposition members were especially resentful. On the contrary, Lord Aberdeen was disposed to treat the matter lightly and to regard the address as a declamation rather than an official document.[20]

---

[18] See Benton, *Thirty Years' View*, II, 649, and von Holst, *Hist. of the U. S.*, III, 159.

[19] It is interesting, however, to note that Polk reversed the position which he had taken in 1828. See above, p. 557.

[20] "I wish to observe that this speech is not an address made to Congress—it is a speech made to the public, the Congress not being sitting. Undoubtedly, no speech of such a nature could be made by the President of the United States without drawing towards it the most serious attention. Nevertheless, it does not possess the importance of an official message, forming a part of legislative proceedings."

He believed that a peaceful settlement was still possible; if not, he could only say that "we possess rights which, in our opinion, are clear and unquestionable; and, by the blessing of God, and with your support, those rights we are fully prepared to maintain." In the House of Commons, Sir Robert Peel expressed a desire for an amicable adjustment, but he severely criticized President Polk for referring to "other contingencies than a friendly termination" of pending negotiations.[21] The London *Times* held that the interests of both countries would be served best by a compromise adjustment like that which settled the dispute over the northeast boundary; nevertheless it thought that Americans should be warned that their pretensions, if persisted in, must surely result in war. The editor was not disposed to aggravate "the very serious difficulties with which the indiscreet language of Mr. Polk has already surrounded the Oregon question," still, the extravagant claims of the President could never be admitted.[22]

During April and May the British newspapers discussed the diplomatic situation in all its bearings, and speculated as to what policy Polk really meant to pursue. Only one, the London *Colonial Magazine,* believed that a war with the United States would be "productive of good"; the others cared little about Oregon itself, but they resented the "blustering attitude" of the American President and people. For example, the *Times,* on May 9, said:

As long as we saw in these grotesque exhibitions of national vanity nothing but the expedients of presidential candidates, or the squibs of electioneering rivals, the foreign policy of the United States had nothing very serious or very formidable in its vacant thunders. But the election being over, and the new president installed by the voices of the democratic party for the next four years, foreign nations acquire something more than an indirect interest in his character and position. If President Polk intends to sustain the heroic line in which he passed through his electioneering probation and entered upon his high office, he may rely on having before

21 Hansard, *Parl. Deb.,* LXXIX, 121, 123, 199.
22 London *Times,* April 5, 1845, quoted by *Niles' Reg.,* LXVIII, 114–115.

him a career of no ordinary toil, agitation, and peril. But if he purposes to subside into a positive business-like president, more like the foreman of a thriving business in the city than the champion of an empire, the sooner he descends from the high horse the better; and he would have done well to throw aside the embroidered vestments of the candidate before he delivered the inaugural address of the president. Nobody supposes that in using the very exaggerated and unbecoming language in which Mr. Polk spoke of the American claims to Oregon, he intended deliberately to breathe defiance to the Queen of Great Britain, or to threaten the rights of Her Majesty's subjects with instant violence. He intended simply to flatter a delusion common in all democratic states, but especially amongst the democratic party in the United States, which forces the statesman whom they have chosen to govern their country to gratify their own popular vanity by affecting a temerity and an overbearing recklessness towards foreign nations which, as individuals, neither the president, nor any of his vociferous supporters, can be supposed to feel.

Rulers of democracies, said the London *Standard,* on May 15, are apt to be inclined to war for the purpose of increasing their power and their patronage. To this fact it attributed the claims set forth by President Polk, and therefore it did not believe that the people would support him, except verbally. Americans could not possibly gain anything by precipitating hostilities, "therefore we hold a war to be extremely improbable, if not an absolute impossibility, let Mr. Polk do all that he can." The *Examiner* (April 25) considered Oregon "really valueless to England and to America." It therefore congratulated Lord Aberdeen on his conciliatory attitude, and advocated arbitration or a partition of the territory.[23]

The utterances of British statesmen greatly exasperated the "old hero" of the Hermitage who, in characteristic style, urged the President to combat British pretensions by a vigorous and uncompromising policy:

Weak and debilitated as I am I could not resist endeavoring to wade through the debate in the English parliament—comments on your inaugural as it relates to oragon. This is the rattling of British drums to alarm us, and to give life to their friends in the United States, such as the Hartford convention men—the blue light federalists & abolitionists, and to prevent

23 Extracts from these papers quoted in *Niles' Reg.,* LXVIII, 236–239.

if Britain can, the reannexation of Texas, by shadowing forth war &
rumors of war, to alarm the timid, & give strength to the traitors in our
country against our best interests & growing prosperity. This bold avowal
by peel & Russell of perfect claim to oragon must be met as boldly, by our
denial of their right, and confidence in our own—that we view it too plain
a case, *of right,* on our side to hesitate one moment upon the subject of
extending our laws over it & populating with our people—permit me to
remind you that during the canvass, I gave a thousand pledges for your
cour[a]ge & firmness, both in war & in peace, to carry on the administration
of our government. This subject is intended to try your energy—dash
from your lips the council of the times on this question, base your acts
upon the firm basis, of asking nothing but what is *right* & permitting
nothing that is wrong—war is a blessing compared with national degredation. The bold manner of peels & Russells annunciation of the British
right to oragogon, the time & manner require a firm rebuke by you in
your annual message, and has opened a fair field to compare their claim
to oragon with their right to the Territory claimed by Britain on our north
East boundary, & which we were swindled out of, there being on file in
archives of England the maps on which was laid down our boundary agreeable to the treaty of 1783, which Lord Browman said in eulogy of Lord
Ashburton shewed that England in her claim to that territory *had not* a
leg of right to stand upon—Just so with oragon, & peel & Russell both
well know it—*still, now,* a perfect right to oragon is claimed—make a note
of this, & in your annual message expose England's perfidy to the whole
civilized wor[l]d. To prevent war with England a bold & undaunted
front must be exposed. England with all her Boast dare not go to war.
You will pardon these my friendly suggestions. The Whiggs have held
you forth to England as feeble & inenergetic, & would shrink at the threat
of war—I am sure you will meet this with that energy & promptness that
is due to yourself, & our national character.[24]

As will be seen presently, Polk did not, in the first instance
at least, follow this fatherly advice. But ere the President had
decided to renew the compromise offer which his predecessors
had made, General Jackson had passed to a land where ''peel &
Russell'' no longer disturbed his repose. Even if he had lived
it is highly improbable that his views would have influenced the
President's foreign policy. Polk was ever ready to pay homage
to Jackson on matters of no vital importance. But when the
occasion demanded independent action—as in the discarding of

---

[24] Jackson to Polk, May 2, 1845, *Polk Papers.*

Blair and Lewis—he did not hesitate to follow his own judgment, even at the risk of incurring the General's displeasure.

In the selection of a minister to represent the United States at London Polk was hampered by political considerations. However, his embarrassment was somewhat lessened by the fact that negotiations were already pending in Washington and by the slight probability that they would be transferred to London. Since Calhoun had not been retained in the cabinet, many Democrats thought that he should be given the British mission; even Jackson considered England to be the proper place for him, "there to combat with my Lord Aberdeen the abolition question."[25] But Calhoun made it known that he would not accept the position; so, also, did his friends, Pickens and Elmore, decline the appointment.[26] Having failed in his overtures to the Calhoun wing of the party, the President, through Bancroft, sounded Van Buren on the subject. In reply Van Buren stated his belief that an ex-President should not accept a foreign mission unless there was a crisis to meet. He did not believe a crisis to exist, but if the President thought otherwise, he would, of course, regard it as his duty to go.[27] Levi Woodbury declined the appointment for "domestic reasons," and Louis McLane, of Baltimore, was finally chosen.[28]

About the middle of May, while Bancroft was in correspondence with Van Buren and before any official communications had passed between Buchanan and Pakenham, the recently established Washington *Union* announced what it believed to be Polk's Oregon policy:

Some say we want war—some that we "cannot be kicked into war." Several predict that there will be war. Now, without undertaking to say positively that *there will be war,* or that *there will not be war,* we venture

---

25 Jackson to Polk, Dec. 16, 1844, *ibid.*

26 After declining the mission himself Calhoun spoke favorably of Elmore, but he thought General Hamilton to be best qualified for the position (A. V. Brown (undated) to Polk, *ibid.*).

27 Van Buren to Bancroft, May 12, 1845, *Van Buren Papers.*

28 Correspondence with Woodbury and McLane, *Polk Papers.*

to predict that it is not Mr. Polk's wish to plunge his country into war, and still less to sacrifice her rights and her honor. He will never abandon either; and without meaning to bluster or to brave the British ministers, we undertake to say that this is the general and enthusiastic sentiment of the American nation. The President will carry out the wishes of the people. It will not be his fault if our differences about Oregon should terminate in hostilities; but it will be his fault, and a fault which we are sure he would never encounter, to sacrifice our "clear and unquestionable claims" and our sacred honor to any visionary danger, or to any apprehensions of danger." "Young Hickory," it added, will make good his title.[29]

Although this article purported to give merely the views of the editor, Ritchie, no doubt it had the previous endorsement of the President. Apparently its purpose was to prepare the people for a compromise adjustment of the Oregon question, but, also, to inform the British minister that the administration would not be intimidated by the prospect of a war.

When the Tyler administration declined to accept the terms offered by Great Britain, Pakenham, in a note dated September 12, 1844, asked Calhoun to specify what arrangement he was "prepared to propose for an equitable adjustment of the question." Calhoun did not see fit to comply with this request, and four months after Polk's inauguration no formal reply to Pakenham's note had been made. On July 12, 1845, however, in a communication to the minister, Buchanan set forth the American claims and offered to accept the forty-ninth parallel as a compromise boundary. Whatever Polk's private reasons for thus suddenly reversing the policy announced in his inaugural may have been, his official reasons were set forth in a letter which Buchanan, on the same day, addressed to Louis McLane, the American minister in London. In it he said:

The President, at a very early period of his administration, was called upon to decide whether he would break off or continue this negotiation. Placed in a responsible position, he first inquired whether the national honor required that he should abruptly terminate it by demanding the whole territory in dispute. War before dishonor is a maxim deeply engraven upon the hearts of the American People; and this maxim ever shall regulate

29 *Union* (semiweekly), May 12, 1845.

his conduct towards foreign nations. But it was impossible for him to conceive that there could be dishonor in pursuing the course which had been adopted by Mr. Monroe, his patriot Revolutionary predecessor, more than a quarter of a century ago, and had been either expressly sanctioned or acquiesced in by all succeeding administrations.[30]

In his note to Pakenham, Buchanan gave a comprehensive statement of the American claims to Oregon—both direct and indirect.[31] "The title of the United States," he said, "to that portion of the Oregon territory between the valley of the Columbia and the Russian line in 54° 40′ North Latitude, is recorded in the Florida Treaty," which transferred to the United States all of the claims of Spain. He refuted the claims which Great Britain based on the Nootka Sound convention, for, as he said, no title to land had been acquired by this convention. The valley of the Columbia, said he, belonged to the United States by virtue of the discoveries of Captain Gray, the explorations of Lewis and Clark, and the settlements made by Astor and other American citizens.

"Such being the opinion of the President in regard to the title of the United States," Buchanan told Pakenham, "he would not have consented to yield any portion of the Oregon territory, had he not found himself embarrassed, if not committed, by the acts of his predecessors." But as they had uniformly proceeded upon "the principle of compromise," Polk felt constrained to do likewise. He had therefore instructed Buchanan again to propose that the Oregon country be divided by the forty-ninth parallel from the Rocky Mountains to the Pacific Ocean, with free ports for Great Britain on the portion of Vancouver's Island lying south of that parallel.

---

[30] Buchanan to McLane, July 12, 1845 (Buchanan, *Works*, VI, 190). He emphasized the fact that even General Jackson had been satisfied with joint occupation. But he passed over the other important fact that none of Polk's predecessors had barred themselves from compromise by emphatically claiming title to *all* of the territory.

[31] In a letter written to John G. Palfrey, June 24, 1848, Buchanan said that it was from Greenhow's *Oregon and California* "that my information as to the facts in support of our claim was principally derived" (*Works*, VIII, 106).

The line proposed will carry out the principle of continuity equally for both parties, by extending the limits both of ancient Louisiana and Canada to the Pacific along the same parallel of latitude which divide them east of the Rocky Mountains; and it will secure to each a sufficient number of commodious harbors on the northwest coast of America.[32]

Pakenham replied on the twenty-ninth of July. He controverted every argument which Buchanan had made, and in addition, he endeavored to place the American Secretary of State in a somewhat awkward position. If, said he, Spain had had exclusive title to Oregon down to the Florida treaty of 1819, then Gray as well as Lewis and Clark had been interlopers on Spanish territory and their discoveries could not give the United States a valid title to the Columbia River valley. On what grounds, he asked,

unless it be upon the principle which forms the foundation of the Nootka convention, could the United States have acquired a title to any part of the Oregon territory previously to the treaty of 1819, and independently of its provisions?

The Nootka convention, he continued, was not the "main reliance" of Great Britain in this discussion, but it barred the United States from acquiring "exclusive dominion" from Spain by the Florida treaty. He argued at length to show that the Nootka convention was still in force, and that none of the American explorations had given the United States exclusive title to any part of Oregon. Although he had not referred Buchanan's letter to his own government, Pakenham concluded his reply by declining the offer made by the President, and by expressing the hope that

the American plenipotentiary will be prepared to offer some further proposal for the settlement of the Oregon question more consistent with fairness and equity, and with the reasonable expectations of the British government.[33]

The British minister's categorical rejection of Polk's offer came as a shock to the administration and aroused the fighting

---

[32] Buchanan to Pakenham, July 12, 1845 (Buchanan, *Works,* VI, 194 ff.).

[33] Pakenham to Buchanan, July 29, 1845 (*ibid.,* 212–220).

blood of the President. Regarding Pakenham's note as insolent, Polk decided to withdraw his offer of compromise and to reassert claim to the whole territory. In the belief that the relations with England had become critical in the extreme, he personally dictated the main features of the reply to the British minister. In order to prevent misunderstandings concerning his directions to Buchanan, or discussions in cabinet, he began keeping a diary in which the events of each day were recorded. This daily record is of great historical importance, for it not only gives information nowhere else available, but it displays the motives which inspired the President's policies—at least the motives which he desired posterity to accept as the key to his official acts.[34]

The diary opens on August 26, 1845, and the day's record is concerned principally with cabinet discussion of the Oregon question. As early as August 7, after the Prussian minister had informed Bancroft of a threatened invasion of Texas by Mexico, Polk urged Buchanan, who was on a visit to his home, to return to Washington as soon as possible. "I must confess," he said, after explaining the Mexican situation, "that the developments which are taking place, as well as my daily reflections, make it, in my opinion, more and more important that we should progress without delay in the Oregon negotiation."[35] By August 26, the date of the cabinet meeting just mentioned, the President had become impatient because of Buchanan's delay in drafting a reply to Pakenham's note of July 29. He asked the Secretary when the reply would be ready for consideration by the cabinet; but, without waiting to learn what Buchanan had prepared, he proceeded to tell the cabinet "the settled decision to which his mind had come." In his reply to Pakenham, Buchanan was directed to "assert and enforce our right to the whole of the Oregon territory from 42° to 54° 40′ North Latitude." He was to state that the President had offered to agree

---

[34] For his own version of his reasons for keeping a diary, see *Diary*, II. 100–101.

[35] Polk to Buchanan, Aug. 7, 1845, *Buchanan Papers*.

upon the forty-ninth parallel solely in deference to his predecessors and because of his desire to preserve peace between the
two nations. Since the British minister had, without referring
the matter to his government, rejected the compromise "in
language, to say the least of it, scarcely courteous or respectful"
the offer was now to be withdrawn. "Let the argument of our
title to the whole country be full," said the President, "let the
proposition to compromise at latitude 49° be withdrawn, and
then let the matter rest, unless the British Minister chose to
continue the negotiation."

Buchanan agreed with the President so far as the assertion
of title and the withdrawal of the compromise offer were concerned, but he believed that a paragraph should be added to the
effect that Polk would consider any proposition which Pakenham
might submit. To such an implied invitation for further negotiation the President objected. "Let our proposition be absolutely withdrawn & then let the British Minister take his own
course." With his usual timidity, Buchanan urged that should
Polk's views be carried out, war would result, but the President
replied that "if we do have war it will not be our fault."
Buchanan expressed the opinion that the answer to Pakenham
ought to be postponed until it could be ascertained whether there
would be a war with Mexico, but Polk, after asserting that there
was no connection between the two questions, insisted upon an
immediate reply to Pakenham's note. To his remark that the
United States would do its duty towards both nations and leave
the rest to God and the Country, Buchanan retorted that "God
would not have much to do in justifying us in a war for the
country North of 49°." Secretary Walker concurred in the
President's views, and the other members expressed no opinions.
Undeterred by the opposition of his Secretary of State, Polk
called a special cabinet meeting for the following day and directed
Buchanan to have a draft of his answer to Pakenham ready for
consideration. The draft presented by Buchanan at the special

meeting was considered satisfactory—even admirable—so far as the historical array of facts relating to the title was concerned, but the President ordered changes to be made in the part relating to the withdrawal of the compromise offer. Although the Secretary of State argued that the answer ought to be postponed, Polk ordered him to deliver it as soon as it could be copied. At the close of the discussion the other members of the cabinet gave their hearty support to the policy adopted by the President. Having thus declined to make further overtures to John Bull, Polk, on the following day, directed that orders be sent to General Taylor that in case Mexico should declare war or begin hostilities he was to drive her army across the Rio Grande and invade Mexico.[36]

The note to Pakenham, in its completed form, was an able document. The historical part, prepared by Buchanan, presented the claims of the United States to the whole territory with precision and clearness. The Nootka Sound convention, he asserted, had not procured for Great Britain any territorial rights, and all privileges acquired by that agreement had been cancelled by a subsequent war with Spain. To Pakenham's contention that the admission of Spain's title to Oregon before 1819 would invalidate all claims based by the United States on discovery, Buchanan retorted that "this is a most ingenious method of making two distinct and independent titles held by the same nation worse than one—of arraying them against each other, and thus destroying the validity of both." The United States, said he, now possessed both its own and the Spanish titles; either was better than that of England, and certainly the two, combined, could not be weaker than one.

The compromise offer was officially withdrawn, but Polk's original intention of making no allusion to further negotiations was not carried out. Presumably in deference to the wishes of Buchanan, it was stated that "the President still cherishes the

---

[36] Polk, *Diary*, I, 1–9.

hope that this long-pending controversy may yet be finally adjusted in such manner as not to disturb the peace or interrupt the harmony now so happily subsisting between the two nations.''[37]

In taking such a firm stand the President may have been influenced, to some extent at least, by the knowledge that Pakenham's prompt rejection of the compromise offer had not been authorized by his government. On August 19, Polk had received a private letter from McLane which stated that

The result of all I have learned is that this Government is earnestly desirous of adjusting the Oregon question, & willing to do so upon liberal terms. *Their chief difficulty arises from the opposition & influence of the Hudson's Bay Company.*

His information, he said, had not come directly from Lord Aberdeen, but he felt certain that England would agree to the forty-ninth parallel to the Straits of Fuca, leaving Vancouver's Island to Great Britain.[38] At the same time Robert Armstrong, the American consul at Liverpool and an intimate friend of the President, wrote that it was generally understood that England held a mortgage on California. Great Britain, he urged, must never possess California; Oregon should be made the bone of contention to prevent it.[39]

Several weeks passed during which neither party attempted to break the diplomatic deadlock. At a cabinet meeting held on October 21, however, a dispatch sent by McLane on the third was read and discussed. In an interview with McLane, Lord Aberdeen had expressed regret because Pakenham had rejected the American offer. After condemning Pakenham's act, he intimated

---

[37] Buchanan to Pakenham, Aug. 30, 1845 (Buchanan, *Works*, VI, 231-254). On the same day that Buchanan delivered his official note, Calhoun wrote from his home in South Carolina deploring the possibility of a rupture with England. ''It is beyond the power of man,'' said he, ''to trace the consequences of a war between us and England on the subject of Oregon. All that is certain is, that she can take it & hold it against us, as long as she has the supremacy on the ocean & retains her Eastern dominions. The rest is rapt in mystery'' (Calhoun to Buchanan, Aug. 30, 1845, *ibid.*, 230).

[38] Copy of McLane to Polk, Aug. 4, 1845, *Buchanan Papers*.

[39] Armstrong to Polk, Aug. 4, 1845, *Polk Papers*.

a willingness to agree upon a modified proposition, and asked whether President Polk would negotiate further on the subject. Anticipating that Pakenham had received new instructions by the same mail and would make new overtures, Buchanan asked the President what answer he should make. Polk promptly replied that

all that could be said to him was, that if he had any further proposition to make on his part, it would be received and considered. . . . . No intimation should be given to him of what the views or intentions of the administration were, & [but] leave him to take his own course.

He declared, also, that should Pakenham propose to agree upon the adjustment recently offered by the United States he would not accept the proposal. Should the minister make some other offer, this would either be rejected or submitted to the Senate for its advice. To Buchanan's question whether he might inform the British diplomat that a proposition made by him would be submitted to the Senate, the President answered that such a course "would be improper; the British Minister had no right to know our councils or intentions." Although the Secretary of State prophesied war, Polk was obdurate and refused to modify his views. He told the cabinet that in his first message to Congress he "would maintain all our rights, would reaffirm Mr. Monroe's ground against permitting any European power to plant or establish any new colony on the North American Continent."[40]

The conjecture that Pakenham had received new instructions from Lord Aberdeen seems to have been well founded, for two days after the cabinet meeting he called at the State Department and expressed regret because the American offer had been withdrawn. He suggested that negotiations might be reopened by the signing of a protocol, but as he was not prepared to make a definite offer of terms, Buchanan was not at liberty to accept the proposal. When the conversation was reported to the President,

---

[40] Polk, *Diary*, I, 62–65.

he insisted that "the British Government must move first," and he doubted that any offer would be made which the United States could accept.[41]

Up to this time there had been an estrangement between the President and Senator Benton, as a result of the latter's violent criticism of the course pursued by the Baltimore convention. Due, however, to a common interest in Oregon and, also, to the influence of Buchanan, a reconciliation was effected. With Polk's consent, Buchanan showed Benton the correspondence that had passed between himself and the British minister; he intimated, also, that the Senator would be kindly received if he should feel inclined to call upon the President. Benton approved the action that had been taken and expressed a desire to converse with the President, therefore a meeting was arranged for the twenty-fourth of October. Polk was already preparing his message to Congress, and it is evident that he was anxious to win Benton's support for the policy which he was about to recommend. The Missourian's judgment was not always sound, but he wielded an influence which could not be disregarded.

During the interview the two men agreed upon the following points: that the twelve months' notice for abrogating the convention of 1827 should be given; that the laws of the United States should be extended over Oregon in the same degree that British laws had been extended in 1821; that forts should be built on the route to Oregon; and that the Indian policy of the United States should be extended to the whole region. On some phases, however, Benton was not prepared to go so far as the President; he thought that Great Britain possessed a good title to the Frazer River valley, and he was willing to accept the forty-ninth parallel as a sastisfactory boundary. To Polk's suggestion of reasserting the Monroe Doctrine against all colonization on the North American continent, he replied that while foreign nations should be excluded from California and the Columbia River

---

[41] *Ibid.*, 66–67.

valley, the Frazer River valley was already occupied by the British.[42] From the date of this interview until the court-martial of Fremont the Senator gave his support to the administration. And his support was of no small importance, although his arrogance and dictatorial manner often taxed the patience of the President.

Three days after his conversation with Benton (*i.e.*, October 27), the President received a call from T. W. Ward, Boston agent for the Baring Brothers. After speaking of the absurdity of a war between the two nations and of the unsettled business conditions which had resulted from war rumors, Ward intimated a desire to know whether Polk would persist in claiming title to the whole of Oregon. His visit did not elicit the desired information, for the President told him that "no one but myself & my Cabinet could know what had occurred or what was likely to occur." Two hours later Buchanan sent to the President a diplomatic note which he had just received from the British minister, and as it bore the date of October 25, Polk concluded that it had been held back until Pakenham had learned the result of Ward's interview with the President.[43]

When presenting the note to Buchanan, Pakenham remarked that he would regard it as official or unofficial as he might deem best after he had ascertained the answer which it would receive. A reply was prepared by Buchanan and carefully edited by the President after its contents had been discussed at two cabinet meetings. Against the wishes of the Secretary of State, who desired to leave the way open for further negotiation, Polk directed him not to submit his answer or to reveal its contents unless Pakenham would decide, in advance, to regard his note as official. He was unwilling, he said, to do anything "which would have the appearance of inviting Great Brittain to make another proposition." When told that no answer would be made except to an official communication, Pakenham, after some

---

[42] *Ibid.*, 55, 70–71.   [43] *Ibid.*, 73–75.

anxious hesitation, withdrew the note. During the conversation
he denied that he had rejected the American offer, but had merely
refused to accept it—a distinction which he held to be of great
importance. Copies of the note and the reply which had been
prepared were sent to McLane so that he might know precisely
what had transpired.[44] The President, at this same time, was
holding conversations with Lieutenant Gillespie, preparing him
for his mission to California with secret instructions for Larkin,
the consul at Monterey, and two weeks later Slidell was sent to
negotiate with Mexico.

During the latter half of November Polk was busily engaged
in drafting his first annual message to Congress. He discussed
the proposed recommendations with Ritchie and with several
members of Congress, and all parts of his original draft were
read and considered at cabinet meetings. In general all members of the cabinet, except Buchanan, concurred in the President's views; the Secretary of State dissented from his Oregon
policy and seriously considered leaving the cabinet to accept the
position of Justice of the Supreme Court. He made various
suggestions which were intended to soften the tone of the message,
and when they were not adopted the President noted that ''Mr.
Buchanan seemed to be depressed in spirits, and, as I thought,
greatly concerned lest the controversy about Oregon might lead
to War.''[45] When his own protests had failed he tried to influence the President by saying that many members of Congress
were in favor of accepting parallel forty-nine as the boundary,
but Polk replied that he, too, had conversed with congressmen,
nine-tenths of whom were in favor of ''going the whole length.''
The diary states further that:

Mr. B. expressed the opinion with some earnestness that the country
would not justify a war for the country North of 49°, and that my greatest
danger would be that I would be attacked for holding a warlike tone. I

[44] *Ibid.*, 75–82. Buchanan to McLane, Oct. 28 and Nov. 5, 1845 (Buchanan, *Works*, VI, 285–286, 289).

[45] Polk, *Diary*, I, 102.

told him that my greatest danger was that I would be attacked for having yielded to what had been done by my predecessors and in deference alone, as he knew, to their acts and commitments, [and for having] agreed to offer the compromise of 49°. I told him that if that proposition had been accepted by the Brittish Minister my course would have met with great opposition, and in my opinion would have gone far to overthrow the administration; that, had it been accepted, as we came in on Texas the probability was we would have gone out on Oregon. I told him we had done our duty by offering 49°, and that I did not regret that it had been rejected by the Brittish Minister. . . . . The truth is Mr. Buchanan has from thhe beginning been, as I think, too timid and too fearful of War on the Oregon question, and has been most anxious to settle the question by yielding and making greater concessions than I am willing to make.[46]

The twenty-ninth Congress convened on the first of December, and on the following day Polk submitted his first annual message. While he congratulated Congress on "the continued prosperity" of the country, he nevertheless felt called upon to make many important recommendations. Foreign relations were given first attention, and on the topics of Texas and Oregon the views expressed by the President were uncompromising, if not menacing, in tone.

After giving a brief history of the attempts made by his predecessors to settle the Oregon boundary question, the President informed Congress of the offer which he had made and which Great Britain had rejected. He had become convinced that England would not agree to any adjustment which the United States ought to accept, consequently "the proposition of compromise which had been made and rejected was by my direction subsequently withdrawn and our title to the whole of Oregon Territory asserted, and, as is believed, maintained by irrefragable facts and arguments." Since England by her rejection of the compromise offer had relieved the President from being further influenced by the acts of his predecessors and had left him free to assert the full rights of the United States, two things were recommended: first, notice should be given that the convention

---

[46] *Ibid.*, 107–108.

of "joint occupancy" made in 1827 will be terminated at the end of twelve months; and second, "it will become proper for Congress to determine what legislation they can in the meantime adopt without violating this convention."

While thus fully admitting the right of Congress to determine the degree of protection which might be given to American citizens in Oregon before the termination of joint occupancy, Polk nevertheless freely suggested the laws which he considered to be proper and necessary. "Beyond all question," said he, "the protection of our laws and our jurisdiction, civil and criminal, ought to be immediately extended over our citizens in Oregon." They should be extended to the same extent that England had extended her laws in 1821. Forts should be built along the route to Oregon to facilitate emigration to that region. He doubted that land grants could be made until the convention had expired, but emigrants might rest assured that they would be given land as soon as "joint occupancy" had ended.

So far as Great Britain was concerned, the most objectionable part of the message was that which outlined the policy to be followed by the United States after the convention of 1827 had expired. "At the end of a year's notice," said the President,

should Congress think it proper to make provision for giving that notice, we shall have reached a period when the national rights in Oregon must either be abandoned or firmly maintained. That they can not be abandoned without a sacrifice of both national honor and interest is too clear to admit of doubt.

The claim of Great Britain to the Columbia as a boundary "can never for a moment be entertained by the United States without an abandonment of their just and clear territorial rights, their own self-respect, and the national honor." Evidently with California as well as Oregon in mind, he reasserted the Monroe Doctrine against European colonization on the North American continent.[47]

---

[47] Richardson, *Messages,* IV, 392–399.

According to the account recorded in Polk's diary, Democrats generally—even many of Calhoun's friends—expressed enthusiastic approval of his message.[48] Archer, a Whig member from Virginia, was especially pleased with the part relating to Oregon, and remarked that "he believed he was half a Polkman." "Well!" said Benton, "you have sent us the message," and "I think we can all go it as we understand it," to which Polk replied (alluding to Jackson's famous remark) that the Senator had very high authority for saying "as we understand it." The real meaning of Benton's remark, as further conversation developed, was that England's title to the region drained by Frazer's River was quite as good as that of the United States to the valley of the Columbia.[49]

The President was not moved to modify his uncompromising policy by the opinions expressed by so influential a person as Senator Benton; neither did the continued opposition of Buchanan disturb his equanimity. At a cabinet meeting held on December 9, the Secretary of State, after stating that he anticipated a call from Pakenham, asked the President what reply he ought to make if the British minister should interrogate him on the Oregon question. "Suppose," said he, "Mr. Pakenham inquires whether any further proposition which the British Government might make would be received, what shall I say to him?" Polk replied that Pakenham had no right to ask such a question. The minister, he said, knew the contents of the annual message and of the diplomatic correspondence he had received; let him take his own course without any intimation as to how any future offer would be received. "Mr. B. repeated his anxiety to settle the question at 49° & avoid war. I told him that I did not desire war, but that at all hazards we must maintain our just rights." Pakenham called two days later, and, after expressing an earnest desire for peace, desired to know what the United States proposed

---

[48] Among those mentioned were Cass, McDuffie, Holmes, Seddon, Hunter, and Wilmot.

[49] Polk, *Diary*, I, 116–117.

to do at the end of the year's notice, but Buchanan was, of course, unable to give him a satisfactory reply.[50] In spite of his "high tone," Polk seems to have been rather uneasy because England was reported to be engaged in "warlike preparations," and McLane was instructed to ascertain whether they had been induced by possible hostilities over Oregon.[51]

On December 23 "a grave discussion" took place in the cabinet regarding the probabilities of a war with Great Britain. Buchanan expressed himself as decidedly in favor of vigorous preparations for defense, and in such a policy the President heartily concurred. The Secretaries of War and Navy were directed to communicate the views of the administration to the military and naval committees of Congress and to aid them in drafting suitable bills. Still in fear of war, Buchanan inquired whether, in case Pakenham should offer to compromise on the forty-ninth parallel, leaving Vancouver's Island to England, Polk would submit the offer to the Senate for its advice. "I told him," wrote the President,

if an equivalent, by granting to the U. S. free ports North of 49° on the sea & the Straits of Fuca should also be offered, I would consult confidentially three or four Senators from different parts of the Union, and might submit it to the Senate for their previous advice.

As this was the first intimation, since the withdrawal of the American offer, that Polk might modify his claims, in deference to the Senate, Buchanan regarded the commitment so important that he reduced to writing what the President had said.[52]

Pakenham called at the State Department on December 27, and, after an unsuccessful attempt to induce Buchanan to recall his withdrawal of the American offer, proposed to refer "the whole question of an equitable division of that territory [Oregon] to the arbitration of some friendly sovereign or State." In

---

[50] *Ibid.*, 119–121.

[51] Buchanan to McLane, Dec. 13, 1845 (Buchanan, *Works*, VI, 341–342).

[52] He appended the memorandum: "I took down the foregoing from the lips of the President in the presence of the Cabinet" (Polk, *Diary*, I. 133–136).

anticipation of such an offer Polk and his cabinet had, on that very same day, decided to reject it, if it should be made. Buchanan could not, of course, reject the offer without referring it to the President, but he frankly told the British diplomat that he did not believe it would be accepted. Pakenham regretted that there seemed to be no way of reopening negotiations and intimated that the American government did not desire an amicable settlement. He said, on the other hand, that ''the British government would be glad to get clear of the question on almost any terms; that they did not care if the arbitrator should award the whole territory to us.''[53] This frank remark indicated that England cared little about Oregon—except that she did not wish to be coerced—and the prospects of an amicable adjustment seemed very much brighter.[54]

In his answer to Pakenham, which had been carefully edited by the President, Buchanan explained why the offer of arbitration could not be accepted. The offer to refer to an arbitrator the ''equitable division'' of Oregon, said he, ''assumes the fact that the title of Great Britain to a portion of the territory is valid, and thus takes for granted the very question in dispute''; the President could not admit such an implication, for he believed that England had no claim to any part of the land. Pakenham now asked if the United States would agree to submit to arbitration the question as to whether either nation possessed a valid title to the whole territory, and his query was answered in the negative, because the President did not ''believe the territorial rights of this nation to be a proper subject for arbitration.''[55]

---

[53] Pakenham to Buchanan, Dec. 27, 1845; memorandum of the interview in Buchanan, *Works*, VI, 349–353.

[54] Pakenham's report of his government's attitude agrees with a statement made by Ashbell Smith: ''In the conversation Lord Aberdeen remarked that the British government did not care a pin, comparatively, about Oregon and the Puget sound country; but that the universal conviction in England was that the country to the Columbia river belonged of right to Great Britain and that the United States was attempting to bully England out of it'' (Smith, *Reminiscences of the Texas Republic*, 41).

[55] Buchanan to Pakenham, Jan. 3 and Feb. 4; Pakenham to Buchanan, Jan. 16, 1846 (Buchanan, *Works*, VI, 355, 357, 370).

Polk's unyielding attitude did not necessarily mean that he either expected or desired a rupture with England. Apparently, he believed that he would yet be offered a proposition to which he could agree. When, on January 4, Black, of South Carolina, asked him to use his influence with Congress to induce that body to postpone the date for abrogating the convention of 1827, he declined with the remark that "the only way to treat John Bull was to look him straight in the eye; that he [I] considered a bold & firm course on our part the pacific one."[56] Despite, therefore, the blunt answers to Pakenham, McLane was authorized to let Lord Aberdeen know, "cautiously and informally," that, while the President himself would accept nothing less than the whole of Oregon, he would, should Great Britain offer the forty-ninth parallel as a boundary, refer the proposition to the Senate for its advice. Anything less advantageous to the United States would be rejected by the President without such a reference; "it is manifest, therefore, that the British Government should at once present their ultimatum."[57] A few days before these instructions had been sent Polk had suggested to his cabinet that a settlement might possibly be made on the basis of a mutual reduction of tariffs and the payment to England of a sum of money for the surrender of her Oregon claims. This sum was to enable her to indemnify the Hudson's Bay Company. The subject was postponed for further discussion and seems never to have been seriously considered.[58]

Before he had received the above-mentioned instructions McLane, in a private letter to Buchanan, said that although the Oregon question was becoming more critical every day, yet he believed that the President had it in his power to adjust the matter "upon a basis of a reasonable compromise," should he feel inclined to do so. He believed, also, *"that it may be made to appear* in the end that his [Polk's] mode of conducting the

---

[56] Polk, *Diary,* I, 155.
[57] Buchanan to McLane, Jan. 29, 1846 (Buchanan, *Works,* VI, 366–368).
[58] Polk, *Diary,* I, 191.

negotiation had enabled *him* to do what his predecessors had been unable to accomplish.''[59] The latter suggestion was entirely superfluous, for the President was already endeavoring to create such an impression by his method of conducting the negotiations. His judgment proved to be sounder than that of his critics. His uncompromising attitude did not result in the war which they so confidently predicted, but, eventually, in another and better offer from the British government.

In the meantime Congress was engaged in a spirited debate upon the President's message and the validity of the American title to Oregon. In the Senate, on December 8, Benton presented a memorial from the people of Oregon which stated that they had set up a temporary government and asked its approval by Congress. They requested Congress to create for them a territorial government, or at least to give them civil and military protection.[60] Next day Cass introduced resolutions which instructed the military and naval committees to inquire into the defensive needs of the country.

When first presented, Cass's resolutions elicited no comments, but when, on December 15, he came to urge their adoption the character of his speech caused no little consternation. Negotiations, he said, had failed to settle the dispute, and Great Britain was assuming a menacing attitude; adequate military preparation was the best means of avoiding war. The President, in his opinion, could never recede from the position he had taken, and it was better ''to fight for the first inch of national territory than for the last.'' Allen, the chairman of the Committee on Foreign Affairs, agreed that the best method of averting war was to prepare for it, ''but the only, or rather the most effectual, preparation which could be made in the United States for this state of things, was the preparation of the hearts of the people.'' Webster, Crittenden, and Niles deplored warlike talk, and thought that

---

[59] McLane to Buchanan, Feb. 3, 1846, *Buchanan Papers.*

[60] Unless otherwise stated, the opinions and remarks of congressmen have been derived from the *Congressional Globe* under dates given.

Cass's remarks were most unfortunate. Webster did not believe that Polk expected war, and, in his opinion, the message had been intended as an ultimatum to induce England to make a better offer. Sevier, on the other hand, would not accept this interpretation. There would certainly be war, he said, for the United States could not recede, and Great Britain would not; the only recourse for the United States was to drive the British out of the territory. There was little opposition to the resolutions themselves—the criticism was aimed at the remarks which they called forth—and they passed near the close of the day (December 16) by a unanimous vote.

The Senate having taken the first step in "preparing the hearts of the people" for war, Allen, on the eighteenth, presented a joint resolution which advised the President "to give, forthwith," the necessary notice for terminating the convention of 1827 with Great Britain. On the same day Atchison, of Missouri, moved to instruct the Committee on Territories to inquire into the expediency of organizing a government for Oregon. During the next two weeks Texas rather than Oregon claimed the attention of the Senate, but on December 29 Hannegan, of Indiana, offered a resolution which declared all of Oregon to be "part and parcel" of the United States, and that "there exists no power in this Government to transfer its soil, and the allegiance of its citizens, to the dominion, authority, control, and subjugation of any foreign prince, state, or sovereignty."

The Oregon question was introduced in the House on the second day of the session when Ingersoll read a petition from the citizens of that region asking for a territorial government. It was read and laid on the table, but on December 15 Douglas succeeded in having it referred to the Committee on Territories, of which he was chairman. On the nineteenth, Douglas reported from his committee a bill which provided for the protection of the rights of American citizens until the termination of joint occupation. It was read twice and referred to the Committee of the Whole, there to be made a special order for the first Tuesday in January, and to continue such from day to day until it had been adopted or rejected. Scarcely had the reference been made when Winthrop, of Massachusetts, offered resolutions to the effect that the differences with England were still open to negotiation or arbitration, and that war would be highly discreditable to both nations. Douglas responded immediately with resolutions which asserted that the title to any part of the territory south of 54° 40′ was not open to compromise or arbitration. From the Committee on Military Affairs, Brinkerhoff, on December 31, reported a bill for constructing forts along the route to Oregon; this, also, was referred to the Committee of the Whole.

While the House had been discussing the proposed government for Oregon, its Committee on Foreign Affairs had been trying to agree upon a joint resolution for giving notice to England that the convention of 1827 would be terminated. As the members were unable to agree, Ingersoll, the chairman, on January 5, reported a resolution for the majority of his committee. It directed that the President "forthwith cause notice to be given" that the convention would be abrogated twelve months after the notice had been served. Garrett Davis, of Kentucky, then reported that the minority of the committee—himself and two colleagues—believed that the convention could be abrogated by the treaty-making power only. The House, he said, had nothing to do with it; Congress neither made the convention nor could unmake it, except by a declaration of war. The contention of the minority was well founded, even though the objectors were governed more by partisan feelings than by constitutional scruples. Although the convention of 1827 did not specify by whom the notice should be given, the natural inference was that it meant the treaty-making power.

As soon as the reports had been read, the House proceeded at once to consider the resolution. Giddings, who opened the debate, stated that heretofore he had opposed expansion, but

since the South had succeeded in annexing Texas he now wanted
all of Oregon. The South, he said, was not interested in Oregon,
and he believed that Polk would surrender all north of the forty-
ninth parallel. Rhett repelled the charge that southern men who
opposed giving notice to England were governed by sectional
motives. His own reason for opposing the notice was that John
Quincy Adams favored it; he would be "blackballed" in South
Carolina if he should vote on the same side as the member from
Massachusetts. Cobb, of Georgia (January 9), regretted that
southern men should question the title to all of Oregon; if Congress should fail to back up Polk's message, Great Britain would
be still less inclined to settle the question. In his opinion, it
would be very unfair for Congress to shirk the responsibility by
leaving the discretion to the President. The Washington *Union*
in urging abrogation of the convention pointed out that so long
as joint occupation continued England had no interest in the
settlement of the question, for *"she has now all that she asks
for."*[61]

As the debate proceeded, many arguments—some of them
most unique—were offered in support of the notice and for the
claim to the whole territory. Levin, of Pennsylvania (January
9), based the claim to all of Oregon upon the "genius of American institutions" and the "laws of God"; Kennedy, of Indiana,
upon the "American multiplication table," the operation of which
made it necessary for the people to have more room.[62] Brinkerhoff, of Ohio, was captivated by the convincing logic of Buchanan's defense of the American title as was "the Queen of
Sheba, when gazing on the architectural wonders of Jerusalem."

----

61 *Union*, Jan. 12, 1846. "If we are to govern Oregon peaceably," said
the *Union* on January 16, "we must first get rid of 'joint occupation.'
If we are to govern *any part* of Oregon peaceably, we must first get rid
of 'joint occupation' in that part."

62 "Our people are spreading out with the aid of the American multiplication table. Go to the West and see a young man with his mate of
eighteen; after the lapse of thirty years, visit him again and instead of
two, you will find twenty-two. That is what I call the American multiplication table" (*Cong. Globe*, Jan. 10, 1846).

Sawtelle, of Maine, praised Polk for his firm stand, for he wanted no compromise like the Ashburton treaty; ''we want no more half-English half-American secretaries to barter away any other portion of our territory.'' Douglas would not be satisfied so long as Great Britain held an inch of territory on the northwest coast, and he commended the President for reasserting the Monroe Doctrine. He seems clearly to have believed that Polk would not conclude a treaty of any kind with Great Britain. Had he believed otherwise he would hardly have uttered the remark about to be quoted, for his language would brand the President as unworthy of confidence as soon as the treaty had been signed. After citing the passage in Polk's message which stated that in future no European colony might be planted in North America with the consent of the United States, he asserted that the conclusion of any treaty with England—whether the line esablished were 49° or 54° 40′—would be giving such consent. ''But the President,'' said he,

Has announced distinctly to the world, as our settled policy, that that consent cannot be given. Sir, he who knows the character of the man— he who knows the stern integrity of his political character—he who knows the consistency of his whole political life—he who knows his fidelity to his principles, must know that, during his four years, this ''settled policy'' will not be unsettled by him. Sir, he is not the man to put the distinct declaration forth to the world in the name of his Government of a settled policy, and then to sneak back from it, to violate it, to disgrace himself and his nation during that very presidential term in which he gave the notice. Then, I say, that during these four years, it is a settled, irrevocably settled question, that no treaty fixing a boundary for the northern part of Oregon can be made. Sir, the making of any treaty fixing a boundary, would be a palpable violation of the very principle the President has put forth in his message.[63]

Great difference of opinion existed as to who possessed the power and whose duty it was to notify England that the convention would be abrogated. Could the President alone do so, or must he have the advice and consent of the Senate; could

---

[63] Jan. 27, 1846 (*Cong. Globe,* 29 Cong., 1 sess., 259–260).

Congress alone, or with the approval of the President, serve the notice; if Congress alone lacked power to give the notice, could it direct, or simply advise, the President, to do so? The Whigs, generally, favored leaving the question of serving the notice to the discretion of the President so that he might bear the responsibility, although many of them professed to be certain that notice would be followed by war. On January 7, Hilliard, of Alabama, moved an amendment which empowered the President to give or to withhold notice; Democrats opposed the amendment and declared it to be both partisan and cowardly. "But a few months ago," said Thurman, of Ohio,

Many of them [the Whigs] professed to be unacquainted as to who Mr. Polk was. But so rapid had been their progress, that they had not only found out who he was, but they had ascertained that he was entitled to such confidence that they proposed to confer upon him what they argued was the war-making power.[64]

Andrew Johnson condemned southern men who had accepted the Baltimore platform and supported the candidate and who now refused to sustain the President; Strong, of New York, quoted the London *Examiner* as proof that England hoped to profit by a division in the Democratic party.

Had John Randolph been living at this time he would have beheld another alliance quite as strange as that between "puritan and blackleg,"[65] for the "puritan," Adams, now sided with the Oregon Democrats. He did not, he said, expect to add much to the argument, for in no debate had the subject been "more thoroughly and completely exhausted." He wished to have the convention of 1827 abrogated so that the United States might get *actual possession,* for "that is the only thing we now want, to have a perfect, clear, indisputable, and undoubted right to the

---

[64] When Polk was nominated, said Cathcart, of Indiana, the Whigs cried, "Who is James K. Polk?"; "and yet these immaculate apostles of consistency are willing to vote this tremendous power [the war power] into the hands of this very same James K. Polk!"

[65] On the alliance of Adams and Clay in 1824, see Schouler, *Hist. of the U. S.,* III, 367.

territory of Oregon.'' The government should therefore give notice to England, and occupy the territory. In his *Memoirs,* Adams makes the interesting statement that neither Monroe nor he, when President, really intended to divide the territory with Great Britain:

> This offer was formerly made under the impression that it would not be accepted, but that its effect would be to preserve the peace between the two countries, and postpone the issue of the controversy until the time should come when we should be able to maintain our claims by an appeal, if necessary, to arms.[66]

His independence and his want of sympathy with the attitude of his political associates is manifested in his remarks concerning a conversation held with Representative Moseley, of New York:

> He is a member of the Whig party, the policy of which among the people appears to be concentrating itself upon a system of opposition to the present Administration on the ground of its propensity to war with Great Britain. Dangers of war, and a very contemptuous estimate of the object for which they suppose the President is provoking it, are the only theme upon which they dwell, without sufficiently considering that their terrors and prognostics may furnish to Mr. Polk motives and pretexts for yielding to the pretensions of our adversary, and sacrificing our own just claims to the territory in dispute, of which I think there is much greater danger than of a war for the maintenance of them.[67]

The President's adversaries were unable to agree concerning the most effective method of opposing his Oregon policy. Insurgent Democrats, as a rule, argued against abrogating the British convention because, as they said, war would result. Some of the Whigs offered similar arguments; others, as we have seen, were willing to invest Polk with power to abrogate the convention, and to make him responsible for the consequences. Tooms, of Georgia, Campbell, of New York, Ewing, of Tennessee, as well as others, did not regard the American title to be ''unquestionable'' except to the Columbia River valley; they were ready,

---

[66] Adams, *Memoirs,* XII, 221.
[67] *Ibid.,* 226.

therefore, to agree upon the forty-ninth parallel. King, of Georgia, wished to settle the question by arbitration, while Davis, of Mississippi, like Calhoun, advocated "masterly inactivity." He thought that Polk was in need of being saved from his friends; if the title to Oregon was as "perfect" as the President claimed, it was dishonorable for him and his predecessors to have offered to compromise with Great Britain.

On February 9, 1846, the Committee of the Whole ceased debating and prepared to vote on the bill as reported from the Committee of Foreign Affairs. Numerous amendments were offered,[68] but few modifications were permitted. After much wrangling the House resolved by a vote of one hundred sixty-three to fifty-four that the President "cause notice to be given" to Great Britain that the convention of 1827 would be abrogated at the end of twelve months. A second paragraph explained that such action was not intended to preclude further "negotiations for an amicable settlement." In this form the resolution was sent to the Senate for its approval.

The House resolution reached the Senate on the tenth but instead of giving it immediate consideration, that body continued to debate various joint resolutions which had been proposed by its own members. Among these was one that had been offered by Crittenden, on January 26, and this, with slight modifications, was the one finally adopted as an amendment to the House resolution. Before its adoption, however, the Senate indulged in a prolonged and acrimonious debate.

The question of abrogating the convention of 1827 was discussed from every possible angle, and yet very little new light was contributed by either the friends or the opponents of the administration. Although not a political supporter of the President, Clayton, of Delaware, was willing to trust Polk's judgment

---

[68] For example, as to whether Polk should be requested, required, or left to his discretion, with respect to giving notice to England. Some wanted a long preamble, others, provision for further negotiation (*Cong. Globe*, 29 Cong., 1 sess., 345–350).

in the matter of giving notice. He expressed the belief that war would not result from abrogation of the convention, and quoted the Manchester *Guardian* to show that the British were in favor of such action.[69] Relying with the utmost confidence on Polk's "honesty, integrity, and firmness," Colquitt, of Georgia, was ready to follow the recommendations made in the President's message, for

It has been very properly said that no message that ever emanated from a President of the United States has met with more general approbation on the part of the people than the one to which I now allude. It is able, dignified, and peaceful. All that he has said and all that he has done, and all that he has offered to do, has met a favorable response from the public.

Colquitt did not believe, however, that the American title was so clear as to preclude further negotiation, and he was confident that Polk would not reject a reasonable offer to settle the dispute. In the course of his remarks Colquitt twitted Hannegan, of Indiana, with having been indifferent to the acquisition of Texas. "Both Texas and Oregon," replied Hannegan, "were united in the Baltimore convention. But I dreaded—if Texas went first— I dreaded Punic faith. Yes, Punic faith."[70] Others besides Hannegan accused southern members with having declined, for sectional reasons, to support the President's Oregon policy, but for the most part these accusations seem to have been groundless.

One of the most exhaustive speeches in support of Polk's policy was delivered by John A. Dix, of New York. He did not

---

[69] "With respect to the notice for terminating the joint occupation of Oregon," said the *Guardian,* "we are not sure that President Polk *may not receive it from the English Government before he can possibly be in a condition to give it himself.* But whether given by the one side or the other, we do not conceive that it will add materially, if at all, to the chance of a hostile collision."

[70] "Texas and Oregon," said Hannegan on December 30, 1845, "were born the same instant, nursed and cradled in the same cradle—the Baltimore convention—and they were at the same instant adopted by the democracy throughout the land. There was not a moment's hesitation, until Texas was admitted; but the moment she was admitted, the peculiar friends of Texas turned, and were doing what they could to strangle Oregon!"

agree with Allen's assertion that the time for discussing the title "had gone by," nor with Clayton's contention that "it had not yet arrived." His argument in support of the American claim was so thorough and conclusive that Benton, who followed him, declared that "He [Dix] has left nothing for me to say on the point of title, familiar as I have been with that subject for thirty years."[71] The exhaustive character of Dix's speech may have been sufficient reason for Benton's eschewing the subject of title himself, but a better reason, perhaps, was his own real belief, as he had already informed the President, that England held a valid title to Frazer's River valley. Dix had relieved him from the necessity of dwelling on this subject, and had left him free to employ more general terms in his defense of the administration. Whatever his mental reservations may have been, he supported Polk's Oregon policy with enthusiasm, the first fruit of the recent reconciliation. "I concur with the President," said he, "in what he has done—both in what he has offered—in what he has rejected—and in what he has recommended to Congress to do." In his opinion, the policy pursued had produced a good effect both at home and abroad, had removed misapprehensions, and created a feeling favorable to friendly negotiation. He had no fear of war, for both governments were in good humor and desirous of peace.

To Webster, Polk's Oregon policy was a riddle which baffled solution. He desired to know what the President intended to do, for he did not act like a man who expected a war:

There is nothing in his recommendations to the other House, nor to this, indicative of such an expectation. There is nothing of preparation for defense, indicating that the President expects war. Well, then, he can

---

[71] "He has placed the American title to the Columbia," Benton continued, "and to the coast north of it, on ground from which it can never be removed, and which must put an end to the argument wherever that speech is read. A speech more perfect in its proofs—better sustained by history—more crowded with material pertinent to the issue—more satisfactory to all lovers of truth and justice—more judiciously conceived and victoriously executed, I have never heard delivered."

expect nothing but a continuance of this dispute, or its settlement by negotiation. I am bound to suppose that he expects its settlement by negotiation. What terms of negotiation? What basis of negotiation? What grounds of negotiation? Everything that we hear from the Executive department is "the whole or none"; and yet negotiate! Sir, it is vain to conceal from ourselves, from the country, or from the world, the gross inconsistency of this course of conduct. It is the spirit of that correspondence [Buchanan's] to which my honorable friend has alluded, that the whole of Oregon is ours, and that nothing can be done which admits the existence of a doubt as to our right to the whole, or the possibility of a right existing in another; and yet we are to negotiate! Pray, what is negotiation? Does the Administration expect that, by negotiation, it can persuade the British Government to surrender the whole territory to us? Is that its expectation? It may do that. I cannot say it will not. If that is the expectation of our Government, why then, of course, it will try its hand at it. I wish it success! That is to say, I wish the country could be rid of the dispute. Take the whole of Oregon, if you can get it; but, at all events, settle the question between the two countries fairly and reasonably. But I say I do not understand the position in which the Executive government has placed itself; in favor of negotiation all the time; but all the time refusing to take anything less than the whole! What consideration—what compromise—what basis—what grounds, therefore, for negotiation? If the Government of the United States has made up its mind—I speak of the Executive government—that, so far as it is concerned, it will not treat for anything less than the whole of Oregon, then it should say so, and throw itself on the two houses of Congress and on the country. It should say so.

He promised to support the administration in maintaining the rights of the United States, but insisted upon knowing whether the President intended to negotiate or to make war. In his own opinion, the latter course would be very unwise—the question should be adjusted by a compromise.[72]

---

[72] "The speech of Mr. Webster, Mr. Calhoun, and others in the Senate advocating peace and the Brittish title to a large portion of the country," wrote the President some weeks later, "have made the Brittish Government & people more arrogant in their tone and more grasping in their demands. If war should be the result, these peace gentlemen & advocates of Brittish pretensions over those of their own country will have done more to produce it than any others" (Polk, *Diary*, I, 345). Webster had denounced the war spirit as early as November 7, 1845, in a speech in Fancuil Hall: "The man who shall incautiously, or led on by false ambition or party pride, kindle those fires of war over the globe on this [Oregon] question, must look out for it—must expect himself to be consumed in a burning conflagration of general reproach" (Curtis, *Life of Webster*, II, 258).

Polk told Benton that he had endeavored to write his message "in plain English, & thought no part of it could be misunderstood."[73] Nevertheless, members of Congress seemed to find it ambiguous, and Webster's remarks caused another attempt to fathom its meaning. Colquitt was certain that the President did not mean to insist absolutely on procuring the whole of Oregon. Allen was equally certain that Polk would accept nothing less, since Great Britain had rejected the offer he had made. When asked by Reverdy Johnson, however, whether his assertions had been authorized by the President, Allen had to admit that he possessed no information except that contained in the official message. When making his declaration, Allen knowingly misrepresented the President. In fact Allen himself had, on December 24, 1845, advised Polk, in case England should offer to compromise on the forty-ninth parallel, to submit the offer confidentially to the Senate before acting upon it. Polk "agreed in the propriety of the course he advised," but did not authorize Allen to speak for him.[74] Haywood, a Democrat from North Carolina, although willing to accept 49°, wished to intrust the whole question to Polk, for he would not

do the President so much wrong as to suppose that, if we passed the notice, and thus put into his hand a great moral weapon, that he could be guilty of so miserable a trick as to use it to the dishonor of his country on the one hand, or the reckless provocation of war on the other.[75]

Reverdy Johnson thought that the President was bound to accept the forty-ninth parallel, if offered by England. " 'Who is James K. Polk?' was a question once asked. We all know now who he is, though there are some who do not know what he is." He is President of the United States, said Johnson, and if he had felt bound by the offers made by his predecessors, certainly he could not reject an offer once made by himself. Atchison, of Missouri,

---

[73] Polk, *Diary*, I, 117.

[74] *Ibid.*, 139.

[75] Like Allen, Haywood had not been authorized to speak for the President (*ibid.*, 262).

was unable to see how his colleagues could discern *compromise* in the President's declarations. Polk had accepted the Baltimore platform, and both his inauguaral and his message had claimed all of the territory: "The very moment he gave up any portion of Oregon, every honest man would condemn it."[76]

The debate in the Senate on the question of giving notice to England continued until the middle of April. Many of the Whigs and a few of the Democrats opposed the joint resolution,[77] but Democrats, generally, rallied to its support. The advocates of the resolution still differed in opinion as to the result of abrogating the convention; some argued that such action would lead

[76] W. C. Rives, of Virginia, believed that Polk and his supporters in Congress were simply playing politics: "Surely, such a spectacle was never exhibited before in any country as is now presented in ours. Every conciliatory advance of the British government unceremoniously repelled— the most extreme claims urged on our side—a tone of menace & disdain freely indulged by the chosen champions of the administration in both Houses—everything done which could apparently provoke a *war*—and yet I learn a settled purpose to accept any compromise that can be obtained! The minds of the whole nation kept in constant & painful anxiety & all its business operations deranged, to enable a knot of small politicians to play brag for the retention of public office, & to acquire credit, with a people whom they hope thus to delude, for superior patriotism, spirit & valour! It is impossible to speak with patience, of such low & despicable manoevering, even if it can be carried on without committing the peace of the country. But the game is a most *hazardous* one, & Mr. Polk may yet find he has not the skill to play it out" (Rives to McLean, Feb. 18, 1846, *McLean Papers*). Tooms, of Georgia, likewise charged the President with insincerity: "I do not think a war in the least probable. Mr. Polk never dreamed of any other war than a war upon the Whigs. He is playing a low grog-shop politician's trick, nothing more. He would be as much surprised and astonished and frightened at getting into war with England as if the Devil were to rise up before him at his bidding. . . . His party were already committed to him to 54° 40', they would stand by him, and he expected finally to be forced by the British Whigs and Southern Calhoun men to compromise; but he greatly hoped that he would not be forced even to this alternative until he had 'all Oregon' on every Democratic banner in the Union for his 'second heat.' I have not the least doubt but that he fully calculated that the 'notice' would be rejected by a combination between the Whigs and Calhoun men of this Congress, and then he could have kept it open for a new presidential campaign" (Tooms to G. W. Crawford, Feb. 6, 1846, in *Rep. Am. Hist. Assn.*, 1911, II, 73–74).

[77] "Most of the Whigs in the Senate incline to remain rather quiet, and to follow the lead of Mr. Calhoun. He is at the head of a party of six or seven, and as he professes still to be an administration man, it is best to leave the work in his hands, at least for the present" (Webster to Sears, Jan. 17, 1846, in Webster, *Private Corr.*, II, 215).

to compromise and settlement, others, that the sequel would be occupation of the entire territory. No agreement could be reached as to what the President would do if the resolution should pass, and nothing came from the "Executive Mansion" to aid in solving the mystery. "Was there ever such a case known," exclaimed Mangum, of North Carolina, "as an Executive without an organ of his views and opinions in either House of Congress?"—the *Union* had definitely stated that no one could speak for him; "that no man, beyond his Cabinet, knew his views." It had not been so in Jackson's time, said Mangum, and it would not be so now if Clay, Benton, or Calhoun were at the head of the government. "The present Administration," he continued, was "remarkable chiefly for one thing in the management of this question, and that was, its secretiveness."[78] In answer to Mangum, Cass so far lifted the veil as to disclose that both Polk and Buchanan had given their approval, in advance, to his [Cass's] resolutions which called upon the army and navy departments for information regarding the defensive strength of the country. As to Polk's intentions for the future, however, Cass had nothing to impart. In the opinion of the President himself the debate had

taken a strange direction; that instead of examining and discussing my views as communicated in these documents [message and correspondence], Senators had been guessing and conjecturing what I might do hereafter, and were approving or condemning what they supposed I might or might not do.[79]

---

[78] A few days before, March 30, Barrow, of Louisiana, said: "There never before had been a period when some one in the Senate was not authorized to speak for the Executive, acquainted with his views, and ready to put those right who misconstrued his language or his views."

[79] Polk, *Diary*, I, 285–286. In a letter written a little later Crittenden said: "Bitter dissensions are already manifested among our opponents; they are about equally divided in the Senate. They quarrel about what the President's sentiments and purposes are in relation to Oregon,—each interprets the 'oracle' to suit himself, and each pretends to speak for him, while all are suspicious and jealous of him and of each other. They know that one side or the other is cheated and to be cheated, but they can't yet exactly tell which. In the mean time they curse Polk hypothetically. If he don't settle and make peace at forty-nine or some other parallel of compromise, the one side curses him; and if he yields an inch or stops a

After the Senate had discussed its own resolution for more than two months, Allen who had originally reported it from his committee moved, on April 16, that it be sent to the table and that the Senate proceed to consider the resolution which had been passed by the House on the ninth of February. The motion was carried, and Reverdy Johnson at once offered an amendment to the House resolution. It was almost an exact replica of the Crittenden proposal which, along with other amendments to the Allen resolution, had just been laid on the table. After some discussion, and attempts to alter it, the Johnson amendment was passed by a vote of 30 to 24. The resolution as passed by the House had directed the President to notify England that the convention would be abrogated; as amended by the Senate, Polk was "authorized, at his discretion" to give such notice. After the amendment had been passed, but before the whole resolution, as amended, had reached a vote, Allen bitterly assailed the modification made by the Senate and announced his intention to vote against the measure. The preamble, he said, advised negotiation, while the main clause left the question of notice to the discretion of the President: "they throw the whole subject back to the President, to be managed in future according to his discretion, after having condemned him for a want of discretion in his past management." The measure was passed by a vote of 40 to 14. The effect of attaching this amendment to the House resolution may not, as Allen asserted, have been to array each house against the other, and both against the President; but the affirmative vote on the preamble must have made it clear to Polk that the Senate would ratify a compromise treaty and that, in all probability, it would not coöperate with him in an aggressive Oregon policy. Undoubtedly this action of the Senate had some influence in modifying his diplomatic program.

---

hair's breadth short of fifty-four degrees forty miuntes, the other side damns him without redemption. Was ever a gentleman in such a fix? 'He might almost say like Satan, that 'hell was around him' '' (Crittenden to Letcher, March 9, 1846, in Coleman, *Life of John J. Crittenden*, 235).

On April 18 the House proceeded to consider the joint resolution as amended by the Senate. After adopting an amendment offered by Owen, of Indiana, by which the President was "authorized and requested" to serve notice upon Great Britain, the measure was passed by a vote of 144 to 40. Two days later the House received notice that the Senate had rejected the Owen amendment and had adhered to its own. A conference was then arranged. Slight modifications were made in the Senate preamble, but the main part of the resolution was left unchanged. In the final form the President was "authorized, at his discretion" to give the notice, and, by a vote of 142 to 46, the resolution was passed by the House on the twenty-third of April.[80] The President regretted that action had been so long delayed and that the preamble had been prefixed by the Senate; but "after all," he added philosophically, "Congress by authorizing the notice, have sustained the first great measure of my administration, though not in a form that is altogether satisfactory or one that was preferred."[81] He decided at once to transmit the notice directly to the British government instead of giving it to Pakenham.

---

[80] The Van Buren Democrats supported the administration by their votes, although some of them did so reluctantly. Undoubtedly C. C. Cambreleng voiced the sentiments of many of them when he wrote: "Heaven forgive me for having had any hand in laying the foundation of this blundering administration. Tyler was bad enough but he had this advantage—there was no mock-mystery nor genuine duplicity in his conduct—if he betrayed his friends he was an honest knave, without any hypocritical cant about the sabbath &c &c. But apart from that I am utterly astonished at the little judgment and less integrity which has distinguished the course of this administration. First as it regards England—when some three or four months ago she was making war-like preparations—McLane was instructed to inquire of Aberdeen whether these preparations were intended for us—and now it appears that before that enquiry was made, Bancroft was 'confidentially' recommending ten war steamers—the Bureaus forty war steamers and Marcy fifty thousand volunteers with the knowledge and approbation of the President! . . . How uncandid and dishonorable must the conduct of the President and his prime minister appear in the eyes of all honest men" (Cambreleng to Van Buren, May 16, 1846, *Van Buren Papers*).

[81] Polk, *Diary*, I, 348.

While the resolution for giving notice to England was under discussion attempts were made by both friends and opponents of the measure to induce the President to alter or to supplement the views expressed in his annual message. Opponents of the resolution wished him to commit himself to compromise; its friends, on the contrary, desired additional pledges that he would insist upon the whole of Oregon.

The first to approach him was James A. Black, a South Carolina member of the House and a personal friend of Calhoun. Calhoun was much opposed to the resolution, and his friends had endeavored to effect a compromise with certain western Senators who were its chief advocates. Black visited Polk on January 4, 1846, and told him that he had just held a conversation with Senators Semple, of Illinois, and Atchison, of Missouri. He thought they would agree not to press the notice resolution if the South would unite with the West in supporting the other measures recommended in Polk's message, including that for granting lands to Oregon settlers. He therefore asked the President to induce his western friends to postpone action on the resolution. Polk declined to follow Black's suggestion, for, as he said, his mind had not changed since he had recommended that notice should be given. "I remarked to him," he noted in his diary,

that the only way to treat John Bull was to look him straight in the eye; that I considered a bold & firm course on our part the pacific one; that if Congress faultered or hesitated in their course, John Bull would immediately become arrogant and more grasping in his demands.[82]

The advocates of notice and 54° 40′ were quite as unsuccessful in their efforts to commit the President to a definite future policy. As representatives of a caucus of Senate Democrats, Hannegan and Atchison interviewed Polk on the seventh of March and put the direct question whether he would insist upon 54° 40′, or, if necessary, compromise on 49°. "I answered him [Hannegan]," Polk recorded,

---

[82] *Ibid.,* 154–155.

that I would answer no man what I would do in the future; that for what I might do I would be responsible to God and my country and if I should hereafter do anything which should be disapproved by himself or others, it would be time enough to condemn me. . . . . . I said, I am charged with the Foreign relations of the country, and it was unheard of that the President should declare in advance to any one out of his Cabinet his intentions in reference to them.[83]

Although the President declined, at all times, to commit himself as to his future course, he was careful, on the other hand, to leave the way open for possible concessions. On several occasions he informed both extremists and compromisers that if England should offer the forty-ninth parallel as a boundary he might, before acting, submit the question to the Senate. He was careful, also, to let both factions know that no member of Congress had been authorized to speak for him, and that the policy outlined in his annual message would remain unchanged unless modified by a future official communication.[84]

The want of harmony among Democrats in the Senate was highly displeasing to the President, and the more so because he attributed it to personal ambition rather than to honest difference of opinion. "The truth is," he wrote, on April 22, 1846,

that in all this Oregon discussion in the Senate, too many Democratic Senators have been more concerned about the Presidential election in '48 than they have been about settling Oregon either at 49° or 54° 40'. "Forty-eight" has been with them the Great question, and hence the division in the Democratic party. I cannot but observe the fact, and for the sake of the country I deplore it. I will however do my duty whatever may happen. I will rise above the interested factions in Congress, and appeal confidently to the people for support.[85]

---

[84] *Ibid.*, 262–263 and *passim*.

[83] *Ibid.*, 273.

[85] Polk, *Diary*, I, 345. On March 9 he had observed: "This whole excitement in the Senate has grown out of the aspirations of Senators and their friends for the Presidency. Mr. Allen has such aspirations himself. Mr. Haywood probably prefers Gov. Wright of N. York. Gen'l Cass has aspirations but is more prudent than some others. Mr. Calhoun has aspirations. My fear is that these factions looking to the election of my successor in 1848, will so divide and weaken the Democratic party by their feuds as to defeat my measures and render my administration unsuccessful and useless. Each one of the factions doubtless desire[s] to use the

Although the joint resolution in its final form was not, as we have seen, entirely satisfactory to the President, he accepted it as preferable to no action at all.[86] He had two reasons for desiring some action on the part of Congress, even though details might be unsatisfactory. He suspected that a majority in the Senate would gladly see notice in any form defeated and would therefore effect their purpose if the House would decline to yield. He believed, also, that Great Britain would not make another offer until Congress had taken final action, and evidently he was confident that the serving of notice would induce such an offer. Consequently when the fate of the joint resolution was hanging in the balance, he and members of the cabinet sought interviews with their friends in the House, and apparently it was due to their influence that that body consented to accept the Senate amendment.[87]

While the question was still undecided, no one perused the published correspondence with more care nor followed the debates with more interest than the veteran diplomat, Albert Gallatin. Having negotiated the conventions of "joint occupation," he naturally took an interest in their abrogation, and he now prepared a series of articles in which he considered both the validity of the respective titles and the expediency of abrogating the conventions. He was not in favor of giving immediate notice to Great Britain, for, "in the present state of excitement, an immediate amicable arrangement is almost hopeless." In his opinion,

---

administration for their own advancement, and out of this circumstance has grown the excitement & unfortunate collision in the Senate. They will all be disappointed. I am not a candidate for re-election myself and will lend myself to none of them. I will not be identified with any of them. I will do my duty to the country & if my measures fail the responsibility shall rest where it belongs." He also attributed Buchanan's recent warlike attitude to a desire to supplant Cass in the good graces of the extremists (*ibid.*, 280, 297).

86 While the Senate amendment was before the House, he told Cullom, of Tennessee, that: "I would have preferred a naked notice; that next to that I preferred the House Resolutions; but it being now ascertained by repeated votes in the Senate that neither could be had, I decidedly preferred the Senate form of notice to no notice at all" (*Diary*, I, 341).

87 Polk, *Diary*, I, 334–337.

the first and indispensable step towards an amicable arrangement consists in the investigation, not so much of the superiority of one claim over the other, as of the question whether there be sufficient grounds to sustain the exclusive pretensions of either Governmnet.

This was substantially the policy advocated by Lord Aberdeen.

Unlike J. Q. Adams, Gallatin did not believe that either nation possessed an exclusive title to the Oregon territory; therefore, both might recede from their extreme pretensions "without impairing national honor and dignity." Clear title for the United States must, in his opinion, be based on the claims derived from Spain, and he did not regard the Spanish title as unquestionably complete. He did not, however, accept Pakenham's contention that the claim which the United States based on the Spanish title and that based on settlements made by American citizens were mutually exclusive. Believing that the President, in view of the policy outlined in his message, would be bound to assert title to the whole of Oregon, should the convention be abrogated, he was in favor of withholding the notice and of dividing the territory by negotiation.[88]

On April 13, when it seemed probable that the resolution for giving notice to England would pass, the House, in Committee of the Whole, gave its attention to the bill, which Douglas had reported in December, for extending judicial and military protection to American citizens in Oregon. Among other things this measure proposed to extend to Oregon the jurisdiction of the Iowa supreme court, to build forts, to make grants of land to settlers, and to establish a mail route between Saint Joseph, Missouri, and the mouth of the Columbia River. The debate was not prolonged, and the alignment of advocates and opponents was much the same as it had been when the resolution concerning notice was under discussion. There was difference of opinion among those who favored the bill as to whether jurisdiction should be extended to the whole territory or to the southern

88 Gallatin, *The Oregon Question*, 1–33, *passim*.

part only. Adams once more championed the American title
to the whole of Oregon and, in defense of his consistency, called
attention to the fact that he, in the Florida treaty, had procured
the Spanish claims to that region. When asked if the relinquish-
ment of Texas by the United States had not been "a consideration" in procuring these Spanish claims, he replied emphatically
that "it was no consideration at all"—that the two territories
had in no way been associated in the Florida negotiations.
Douglas, the chief spokesman for the bill, advocated extending
jurisdiction without designating boundary limits as the better
way of procuring the desired effect with the least annoyance to
Great Britain. He desired to have it understood, however, that
he was not in favor of yielding an inch of territory south of
54° 40′, for any administration, present or future, which would
consent to relinquish any portion of Oregon would be guilty of
"perfidy." As already noted, such comments from Douglas
and other ardent supporters of the administration seem to indicate that Polk's most intimate friends did not believe that he
would consent to a compromise. Surely they could not have
intended to brand him in advance as a man about to commit an
act of "perfidy" and "treachery."

After certain amendments had been added, one of which extended the jurisdiction of the Iowa courts to "all that portion
of the territory of the United States which lies west of the Rocky
Mountains," without defining limits, the House, on April 18,
passed the bill and sent it to the Senate for its concurrence.

The Senate Committee on Territories disapproved the House
bill. On May 21 its chairman reported that, since a majority
deemed immediate legislation on the subject to be inexpedient
the committee desired to be discharged from further consideration
of the bill.

During the debate which followed the presentation of this
report Benton expressed his real views on the American title to
Oregon, a subject which he had avoided when discussing the

resolution for giving notice to Great Britain. Oregon, he said, included three main divisions: the islands, Frazer's River valley, and the Columbia River valley. To the last only did the United States possess a clear title. He therefore moved to recommit the House bill to the committee and that it should be instructed to offer the following amendments: (1) to extend the laws of the United States over the territory to the same extent that England had extended hers; (2) the bill to become effective at the termination of the convention; (3) certain provisions for the administration of justice and for fortifications; (4) the boundaries to be settled by treaty, but until this had been done the line of 49° should be regarded as the northern limit of American territory. Cass assailed Benton's arguments and his proposed instructions, and, on Crittenden's suggestion, the latter were withdrawn. Within two weeks further action by Congress was made unnecessary by the conclusion of the Oregon treaty which divided the territory between the two nations.

As the President had anticipated, the passage of the joint resolution for abrogating the convention of 1827 was soon followed by a new overture from the British government. A dispatch from McLane arrived on June 3, 1846, and gave the substance of a proposition which Lord Aberdeen had said would soon be made to the United States by Pakenham. The proposition, as outlined by McLane, was so unsatisfactory that Polk was "certain" that it must be rejected.[89] However, when the subject was brought before the cabinet on the following day, all members present were inclined to think that the project ought to be submitted to the Senate for advice. The most objectionable feature of the British proposal was a stipulation which guaranteed free navigation of the Columbia River to the Hudson's Bay Company. Buchanan suggested that this privilege might

---

[89] "If I reject it absolutely and make no other proposition the probable result will be war. If I submit it to the Senate and they should advise its acceptance I should be bound by their advice yet I should do so reluctantly" (*Diary*, I, 444–445).

be limited to the duration of the company's existing charter, which would expire in 1859.[90]

When the cabinet met again, on June 6, Buchanan laid before it the formal proposition of the British government, which had arrived in the meantime and been delivered to him by Pakenham. It proposed to divide Oregon by the forty-ninth parallel from the Rocky Mountains to the Straits of Fuca, thence through the main channel to the sea. Two reservations were stipulated: first, the Hudson's Bay Company and actual British occupants were to retain title to their lands lying south of 49°, but subject to the jurisdiction of the United States; second, free use of the Columbia was retained for the Hudson's Bay Company and for British subjects when trading with that company. The question was raised as to whether, according to the proposal submitted, the privilege of navigation to be accorded to the Hudson's Bay Company would cease at the expiration of its existing charter in 1859. Without waiting to decide this question, the President asked the cabinet whether he should submit the offer, as received, to the Senate with a request for its advice. Walker, Marcy, Bancroft, and Johnson advised him to submit the offer to the Senate. Buchanan, who had recently assumed a belligerent attitude, said that his opinion would depend upon the character of the message which would accompany the document. "He said the 54° 40′ men were the true friends of the administration and he wished no backing out on the subject." Although nettled by this poniard-thrust about "backing out" the President suppressed his feelings and even prevented Walker from openly resenting the insinuation. He told the cabinet that in case he should decide to submit the British offer to the Senate, he would reiterate the views already expressed in his annual message. Should the Senate advise its acceptance, with or without modifications, he would follow the advice; "but if they declined to express an opinion, or by the constitutional majority to give their advice, I

90 Polk, *Diary*, I, 447–448.

should reject the proposition.'' After hearing this, Buchanan advised that the proposal be submitted to the Senate, but he declined to prepare a message embodying the President's views.[91]

The ill feeling caused by Buchanan's attitude continued for several days. Other members of the cabinet freely criticized his conduct and recalled that he had repeatedly advocated the renewal of the compromise offer. After a conversation on the subject with Marcy and Bancroft, the President wrote:

My impression is that Mr. Buchanan intends now to shun all responsibility for the submission of the Brittish proposition to the Senate, but still he may wish it to be done without his agency, so that if the 54° 40' men complain, he may be able to say that my message submitting it did not receive his sanction. I shall be disappointed if any message which can be drawn will receive his assent. He will choose to dissent and if it is condemned he will escape all responsibility. In his despatches to Mr. McLane I have more than once, & in the presence of the Cabinet, caused paragraphs to be struck out yielding as I thought too much to Great Brittain, and now it is most strange that he should take suddenly, and without the assignment of any reason, the opposite extreme, and talk as he did yesterday of ''backing out from 54° 40'.'' His course is one which I cannot approve. Mr. Marcy and Mr. Bancroft both condemned it in decided terms.[92]

Buchanan called on the following day and expressed doubts concerning the wisdom of submitting to the Senate the correspondence which passed between McLane and himself on the Oregon question. Although he surmised that these doubts had been prompted by the Secretary's fear that his inconsistency might be exposed, Polk permitted him ''to select what portions of the correspondence, if any, should be sent.'' His indulgence was rewarded by renewed insolence, for Buchanan not only refused once more to draft a message for the President, but he had the

---

[91] *Ibid.*, 451–454. Polk attributed Buchanan's change of front to a desire to curry favor with the extremists. ''It was not until within a short time since that he gave indications of a change of position. The first indication I had of it was a remark which fell from him incidentally when speaking of the subject, to the purport that Gen'l Cass had made character by his course in the Senate on the subject. Gen'l C. was a 54° 40' man.''

[92] *Ibid.*, 456.

audacity to remark that "when you have done your message I will then prepare such a one as I think ought to be sent in." At last thoroughly aroused by the insolence of his Secretary, the President indignantly asked:

For what purpose will you prepare a message? You have twice refused, though it is a subject relating to your Department, to give me any aid in preparing my message; do you wish, after I have done, to draw up a paper of your own in order to make an issue with me?

Buchanan at once resumed his normal state of timidity and explained that his remark had been entirely misunderstood. Nevertheless, when Polk submitted his message to the cabinet for discussion, the Secretary of State raised so many objections that some of the passages were eliminated.[93]

On June 10 the President transmitted the British proposal to the Senate and, in an accompanying message, requested advice as to whether it should be accepted. He made it clear that his own opinions, as expressed in his annual message, remained unchanged, and that he would reject the offer unless the Senate by a "constitutional majority" should recommend its acceptance. After two days of deliberation the Senate, by a vote of 38 to 12, advised him to accept the proposal, and on the fifteenth Buchanan and Pakenham signed the treaty which terminated the long-debated Oregon question.[94] As shown by the vote, not many of the extremists were ready to risk a war by rejecting the British overture. Most uncompromising of all was Allen, chairman of the Committee on Foreign Affairs. On the day that the treaty was signed, after a free expression of his feelings, he resigned from the committee.

---

[93] *Ibid.*, 459–462.

[94] Richardson, *Messages*, IV, 449–450. Polk, *Diary*, I, 467, 470. The treaty may be found in Malloy, *Treaties and Conventions*, I, 656. It fixed the boundary at 49°, from the Rocky Mountains to the Straits of Fuca, leaving all of Vancouver's Island to England; the Hudson's Bay Company retained the use of the Columbia River on the same footing as citizens of the United States; that company and British occupants retained title to land already possessed south of 49°

The adjustment of the Oregon question by an extension of the existing boundary between the United States and Canada was eminently fair to both nations. Indeed it was the only sensible solution of the long-standing dispute. The more one examines the respective claims the more apparent it becomes that neither party possessed a "clear and unquestionable" title to the entire territory. Was, therefore, President Polk justified in asserting claim to "all of Oregon," and if so, must be he condemned for accepting less? Neither query can be answered by an unqualified yes or no. Whether wise or unwise, whether designed or controlled by circumstances, Polk's Oregon policy was not so inconsistent as his opponents represented it to be. He offered to divide the territory, and when this offer was declined he steadfastly refused to make another offer of any kind. While he continued to assert that the American title to the whole territory was "clear and unquestionable," at no time did he say that he would decline a compromise, if offered by England. On the contrary, he told both supporters and opponents in Congress that if England should offer 49°, or anything approaching it, he would seek the advice of the Senate before rejecting the proposal. As Webster said in the Senate, Polk did not at any time act like a man who expected war, and the President told Black that he "considered a bold & firm course on our part the pacific one." He stated repeatedly that he did not look for an offer from England until Congress had passed the resolution terminating joint occupation, and, although he did not specifically say so, he inferred that its passage would undoubtedly be followed by an overture from that government. This opinion was well founded—the "bold and firm course" of abrogating the convention proved, indeed, to be the pacific one, for Great Britain very soon afterward made the offer to compromise.[95] Without loss of time, Polk did what he

---

[95] Commenting on the success of Polk's policy, Richard Rush wrote: "For one, I am unshaken in the belief, that it was the President's opening message to the first congress he met on the second of December last, that produced the settlement of the Oregon difficulty. It was like a great

had long promised to do; he submitted the proposal to the Senate, but with a warning that unless that body should advise its acceptance he would reject the offer and adhere to the party platform. It would have been unfair to expect the President to stand alone in demanding the full measure asked by that platform after the debates in Congress and the press had made it plain that neither Congress nor the people would approve his rejection of a reasonable offer. It was not cowardly to ascertain the wishes of the Senate on so important a question, and it would have been criminal to provoke a war for the sake of maintaining a campaign cry, when it was evident that neither Congress nor the people desired it to be maintained.

---

bomb-shell thrown into the British cabinet. It took them by surprise, and first roused them to the unavoidable necessity of a settlement. I thought when it appeared, that it would lead to war—so bold was it, though every word was just; whereas it led to peace'' (Rush to Trist, Sept. 21, 1846, *Trist Papers*).

CHAPTER XXII

SLAVERY AND TERRITORIAL GOVERNMENTS

Although a lawyer by profession, Polk owned slaves and employed them in cultivating his plantation in Mississippi. As a southern man he despised abolitionists, yet at no time during his career does he seem to have taken a deep interest in the slavery question—especially in the extension of the slaveholding area. Like Jackson, he desired to extend the boundaries of the United States and to increase its power and prestige, but neither man was interested in promoting the spread of slavery. In supporting the annexation of Texas and in planning the acquisition of other Mexican territory Polk acted as an expansionist, and not as a slaveholder.

As early as 1826, while a proposed amendment to the Constitution was being debated, remarks made in the House by members from New England led Polk to express his views on the slavery question:

I have regretted exceedingly, sir, that scarcely any subject of general concern can be agitated here, without having this unfortunate subject of slavery, either collaterally, or incidentally, brought into view, and made to mingle in our deliberations. . . . . When this country became free and independent, this species of population was found amongst us. It had been entailed upon us by our ancestors, and was viewed as a common evil; not confined to the locality where it was, but affecting the whole nation. Some of the States which then possessed it have since gotten clear of it: they were a species of property that differed from all other: they were rational; they were human beings.[1]

Fully admitting that the institution was an evil, he did not believe that this fact should affect the solution of great national questions.

---

[1] *Abridg. of Deb.*, IX, 16–17.

As Speaker of the House, Polk was called upon to decide many points in which the slavery question was involved. His task was simplified by the operation of the so-called gag rule under which nearly all petitions and memorials relating to the subject were referred automatically to the "committee of oblivion." As a party man, he rigorously enforced this rule, but in cases which did not clearly fall within its scope he did not seem disposed to support the extreme southern view. For example, when an attempt was made, on February 6, 1837, to prevent John Quincy Adams from presenting abolition petitions submitted by other states than Massachusetts, Speaker Polk decided that "every member had a right to present a petition, come from what quarter it might."[2] This decision ran counter to the well-known southern claim that while, under the Constitution, all citizens possessed the right to petition for a redress of their own grievances, they had no right to concern themselves about the grievances of others.

The Speaker's decision in favor of Adams was not induced by admiration for the ex-President or by approval of his conduct. In a manuscript to be found among his papers[3] Polk complained that Adams, by his petitions, "has consumed so much of the present session of Congress, to the delay of the public business, to the annoyance of the whole House, and the degredation of his own character." After asserting that it was necessary to have a general rule, since the House could not take time to consider each petition, he continued:

Mr. Adams was unwilling to submit to the decision of the majority. On every petition day, he made constant attempts to wreck that decision, to violate the rules, and defy the authority of the House. Upon the plainest propositions he would take appeals from the Speaker's decisions, and consume time in debating the appeal. . . . .

Mr. Adams knew . . . . that it was the duty of the Speaker to observe and execute the *rules* and *orders* adopted by the House for its government. . . . .

---

[2] *Cong. Globe*, 24 Cong., 2 sess., 164.

[3] "Notes on Mr. Adams' letter to the Quincy Patriot," undated, *Polk Papers*.

The Speaker carries out and enforces the decisions of the majority & therefore he represents in his letter that the ''Speaker and the majority of the House'' have undertaken to exercise ''arbitrary authority.'' If Mr. Adams is unwilling to submit to the decisions of the majority of the House, he is unfit to be a member of that body. He seems to have an utter aversion to decisions made by majorities. This principle lies at the foundation of all our institutions. Majorities must govern, and it cannot be helped if a few such refractory spirits as Mr. Adams are unwilling to submit to that Government.

The manuscript is of considerable value, for, as Polk was the presiding officer, his opinions on this important subject cannot be found in official records.

On one occasion during his term as governor of Tennessee, Polk was called upon to repel outside interference with the ''peculiar institution.'' In the summer of 1840 a ''World's Convention'' met in London to consider ways and means of abolishing slavery and the slave trade. Letters were addressed to officials in the United States, and, among others, to Governor Polk. In his last message to the legislature, October 7, 1841, the governor stated that he had received two such letters.

Viewing these communications [said he], as an impertinent and mischievous attempt on the part of foreigners to interfere with one of the domestic institutions of this State, and having received the countenance of a member of the Congress of the United States, under whose official frank one of the packages containing them came to me, I declined entering into a correspondence with a foreign convention, but addressed to the member of Congress alluded to the letter, a copy of which is herewith transmitted to you, accompanied by the communication.[4]

His answer asserted the right of a state to control its own affairs, but it was a vindication of state rights rather than a defense of slavery. In the words of a local editor, he

came boldly and manfully out before the country with a letter containing the sound doctrine of the Constitution of our Union, and rebuked the foreign interference with our State affairs in a spirit as becoming to the patriot and the man as it was honorable to the State over which he presided as Chief Magistrate.[5]

---

[4] *Tenn. Sen. Jour.*, 1841–42, 22–42.

[5] Nashville *Union*, April 15, 1841.

Agitation in favor of annexing Texas to the United States began as soon as that province had declared its independence in 1836. Although its principal supporters were southern men there is little evidence that they were moved by a desire to extend the institution of slavery.[6] When, however, Tyler turned his attention to the annexation of Texas, the question took on a more distinctly southern aspect; and Calhoun, in his correspondence as Secretary of State, brought slavery into prominence by distinctly asserting that the United States desired to annex Texas in order to protect that institution. When commenting on this correspondence, early in 1845, the *Democratic Review* declared that Calhoun, the apostle of state rights, had, in fact, *nationalized* the slavery question:

> What has become of this position [that the national government can not interfere with slavery in the District of Columbia] after a Southern President and a Southern Secretary of State—and that Secretary, John C. Calhoun, of all men living!—have so nationalized, so federalized, the question, as we have lately seen done? When that has been not only acted upon, but avowed, argued, vehemently urged—*that, and that almost exclusivley*—as the ground for a large and momentous measure of national policy![7]

In general, Calhoun's intimate friends were interested in Texas because they were interested in slavery. For example, Dixon H. Lewis deemed annexation to be "the greatest question of the Age" on account of the political power which it would bring to the South. "It will," he wrote, *"unite the hitherto divided South,* while it will make Abolition & Treason synonymous & thus destroy it in the North."[8] This feeling, however, was not shared by the Jackson Democrats.

When his views as a candidate for the Vice-Presidency were solicited, Polk declared himself to be unequivocally in favor of annexing Texas.[9] Neither his public utterances nor his private

---

[6] For a discussion of this whole subject, see Justin H. Smith, *Annexation of Texas.*

[7] *Dem. Rev.,* January, 1845, article on Abolitionists. The whole article is worth reading.

[8] Lewis to Crallé, March 19, 1844, *Crallé Papers.*

[9] Answer to S. P. Chase *et al.,* April 23, 1844, *Polk Papers.* Printed, also, in various newspapers.

letters indicate any interest in extending slavery; on the contrary, the correspondence with his most intimate friends shows a desire to avoid an affiliation with the southern wing of the party. It has been noted elsewhere that Polk's bosom friend, Cave Johnson, tried to induce Van Buren to declare himself in favor of annexation, and that Polk was anxious to coöperate with that wing of the party which was indifferent or hostile to slavery. After Polk's nomination, Johnson warned him repeatedly that the southern faction would try to claim and to control him. When issuing invitations to the Nashville ratification meeting, great care was taken to preclude any attempt to identify the candidate with the South Carolina radicals.[10]

Throughout the campaign of 1844 neither Polk nor his associates urged additional protection for the South, much less for slavery; nevertheless, both of these subjects, to a certain degree, became party issues. Some excitement was created by the appearance of a pamphlet entitled *"The South in Danger."* It was prepared by Robert J. Walker, chairman of the Democratic national committee, and its object was to show that Whigs and Abolitionists had united in the North and that all in the South should join in defeating them. It was published without Polk's knowledge and was deplored by his intimate friends.[11] Despite the fact that the candidate and his chief supporters were interested in territorial expansion rather than in slavery, his opponents undoubtedly believed with John Quincy Adams who, on hearing the result of the election, wrote: "It is the victory of the slavery element in the constitution of the United States."[12]

Having received notice that the Mexican government had agreed to renew diplomatic relations, President Polk, in August, 1846, asked Congress for an appropriation of two million dollars

---

[10] Johnson to Polk, June 21 and June 28, 1844, *Polk Papers*.

[11] W. E. Cramer to Polk, Oct. 4, 1844; Armstrong to Polk, Nov. 5, 1844, *ibid*. The Walker pamphlet was published by the "Democratic Association of Washington, D. C." and bore the date Sept. 25, 1844.

[12] Adams, *Memoirs*, XII, 103.

to be used in conducting negotiations. In making this request the President unwittingly precipitated an "irrepressible conflict" which ceased only with the end of the Civil War.

When he asked for this appropriation Polk had no thought of slavery. He desired to buy Mexican territory and he wished to be able to assure the Mexican government that he could pay an installment of the purchase price as soon as a treaty had been concluded. But when the subject came before the House the slavery question emerged, for Wilmot introduced his well-known "proviso" by which slavery would be excluded from all territory to be acquired by the use of the appropriation. After adopting what the President called Wilmot's "mischievous & foolish amendment," the House passed the bill by a vote of 87 to 64. The amended bill came before the Senate on the last day of the session, and, as Davis, of Massachusetts, obtained the floor and refused to yield it, no vote could be taken. Polk was astonished and chagrined by the unexpected turn of events. He blamed Wilmot for having introduced an irrelevant topic, but he blamed Davis still more for preventing the Senate from acting on the measure. "What connection slavery had with making peace with Mexico," is the remark in his diary, "it is difficult to conceive."[13] While this comment undoubtedly expressed the real attitude of the President, it has nevertheless been charged that his request for the money was "caused by the burning desire to acquire additional slave territory."[14]

On August 5, 1846, the day after the request for the two millions had been sent to the Senate, General Armstrong arrived from London bearing the ratified Oregon treaty. On the same day the President asked Congress to frame a territorial government and to adopt regulations for making land grants to settlers in that region. But the session was nearing its close, and Congress adjourned without having taken action on the subject.

---

[13] Polk, *Diary*, II, 75. He believed that, if permitted, the Senate would have eliminated the proviso and that the House would have acquiesced.

[14] Jay, *Review of the Mexican War*, 184.

When Congress reassembled in December, Polk renewed his request for a two million dollar appropriation. He renewed, also, his recommendation that Oregon should be provided with a territorial government.[15]

On December 23, in response to the latter recommendation, Douglas reported from the Committee on Territories a bill to establish a government in Oregon; it was read twice and referred to the Committee of the Whole. The twelfth section of this bill extended to Oregon both the privileges and the restrictions of the Ordinance of 1787, the most important *restriction,* of course, being the prohibition of slavery.

On the evening of the same day Wilmot called by appointment on the President, and the proviso which he had attached to the appropriation bill at the last session was the topic of conversation. Wilmot told the President that he would not again offer his proviso, but that he would have to vote for slavery restriction if it should be proposed by another member. In his record of this interview Polk thus stated his opinions on the slavery question:

> I told him I did not desire to extend slavery, that I would be satisfied to acquire by treaty from Mexico the Provinces of New Mexico & the Californias, and that in these Provinces slavery could probably never exist, and the great probability was that the question would never arise in the future organization of territorial or State Governments in these territories. I told him that slavery was purely a domestic question, and to restrict the appropriation which had been asked for, so as to require the President to insert it in a Treaty with a Foreign Power, was not only inappropriate and out of place, but if such a Treaty were made it must be opposed by every Senator from a slave-holding State, and as one third of the Senators could reject a Treaty, it could not be ratified, though it might be satisfactory in all other respects.

This argument, of course, overstated the effect of the Wilmot proviso, for no one had asked that it should be incorporated into the treaty. Wilmot answered that in any case he would be satisfied with a simple legislative declaration, and that he would not again take the initiative in asking for this.[16]

---

[15] Richardson, *Messages,* IV, 495, 504.
[16] Polk, *Diary,* II, 288–290.

In spite of Polk's effort to bury the slavery discussion by an agreement with Wilmot, the question of excluding the institution from territories was soon brought before the House. On January 4, 1847, Preston King, of New York, offered a bill to appropriate two million dollars for diplomatic purposes the second section of which was virtually a restatement of the Wilmot proviso. King was not permitted to introduce this bill, and on February 1, when another bill for granting the President three million dollars came up for discussion in the House Wilmot, in spite of the promise made to Polk, moved to amend the bill by adding his anti-slavery proviso.[17] When informed of King's bill Polk noted in his diary:

> The slavvery question is assuming a fearful & most important aspect. The movement of Mr. King to-day, if persevered in, will be attended with terrible consequences to the country, and cannot fail to destroy the Democratic party, if it does not ultimately threaten the Union itself. [At the close of a cabinet meeting held on the following day, he again reverted to the subject.] Slavery has no possible connection with the Mexican War, and with making peace with that country. Should any territory be acquired by a Treaty with Mexico, Congress will have the full power to raise the question of slavery in it upon the organization of a territorial Government in it, or upon its admission as a state of the Union. Its introduction in connection with the Mexican War is not only mischievous but wicked. It is, moreover, practically an abstract question. There is no probability that any territory will ever be acquired from Mexico in which slavery could ever exist.

Buchanan expressed himself as willing to extend the Missouri Compromise line to the Pacific, and in this view all other members of the cabinet agreed. Polk declined to commit himself on this method of dealing with the subject, although urged to do so by both Buchanan and Walker. "Though willing myself," said he, "to assent to the proposition, I was not ready, until I saw further developments, to recommend it to Congress as the policy of the administration." On the same evening he presented the

---

[17] *Cong. Globe,* 29 Cong., 2 sess., 105, 303.

proposition to Benton in order to see if it would meet with his approval, but the Senator declined to give an immediate answer.[18]

While the President was not interested in the extension of slavery, he was, on the other hand, unable to appreciate the fact that there might be such a thing as honest opposition to the spread of that institution. Except as it affected party interests he seemed quite as indifferent toward the subject as Douglas was at a later date when he declared that he did not care whether slavery was "voted down or voted up." Polk attributed all agitation of the subject to the same cause that he attributed everything which thwarted his plans—a desire to promote the interests of candidates for the Presidency. Politicians of both parties and both sections were criticized for their unpatriotic conduct. Commenting on the delay in enacting war measures, he wrote in his diary:

> Even the question of slavery is thrown into Congress and agitated in the midst of a Foreign War for political purposes. It is brought forward at the North by a few ultra Northern members to advance the prospects of their favourite. No sooner is it introduced than a few ultra Southern members are manifestly well satisfied that it has been brought forward, because by seizing upon it they hope to array a Southern party in favour of their favourite candidate for the Presidency. There is no patriotism on either side, it is a most wicked agitation that can end in no good and must produce infinite mischief.[19]

On the day after this was written he told Crittenden that

> I deprecated the agitation of the slavery question in Congress, and though a South-Western man & from a slave-holding State as well as himself, I did not desire to acquire more Southern Territory than that which I had indicated [California and New Mexico], because I did not desire by doing so to give occasion for the agitation of a question which might sever and endanger the Union.[20]

King's appropriation bill, with the section prohibiting slavery in all territory to be acquired, not only raised the issue with respect to anticipated cessions from Mexico, but it affected also

---

[18] Polk, *Diary*, II, 304–309. At a meeting held on January 16 the cabinet again unanimously advised the extension of the 36° 30′ line to the Pacific.

[19] Polk, *Diary*, II, 348.   [20] *Ibid.*, 350.

the Oregon bill. It will be remembered that the twelfth section
of the measure proposed by Douglas extended to Oregon the
Ordinance of 1787. When the bill came up for discussion on
January 14, 1847, Burt, of South Carolina, moved to amend this
section by adding an explanatory statement to the effect that
the restrictions of the Ordinance were extended to Oregon ''inasmuch as the whole of the said territory lies north of 36° 30′ north
latitude.''[21] While willing, apparently, to let slavery be excluded
from Oregon, Burt nevertheless denied categorically the power
of Congress to prohibit slavery in any state or territory. He
argued at some length to prove that neither the Ordinance of
1787 nor the Missouri Compromise was a constitutional law.
This denial of the federal government's power to exclude slavery
from *any* territory was soon echoed by other southern members;
consequently, an attempt was made to eliminate the prohibition
from the Douglas bill or else to defeat it altogether.

The President was embarrassed, and his opponents assisted,
by the hearty support given to his policy of territorial acquisition by southern enthusiasts, both in Congress and in the press.
For example, the *Charleston Patriot* trusted ''that our southern
Representatives will remember that this is a southern war,'' and
the *Charleston Courier* asserted that the war would widen the
field of southern enterprise and power.[22]

In the House, Seddon, of Virginia, declared King's bill to be
grossly unconstitutional. ''It more than violates a single specific
clause of that instrument. It outrages its whole scope and spirit,
and subverts the very basis of its being.'' Bedinger, of the same

---

[21] *Cong. Globe*, 29 Cong., 2 sess., 178.

[22] The former is quoted in Jay, *Review of the Mexican War,* 182. See also
other excerpts from southern papers there given. The latter is thus quoted
by Rathbun of New York: ''Every battle fought in Mexico, and every
dollar spent there, but insures the acquisition of territory which must
widen the field of southern enterprise and power in the future. And the
first result will be to readjust the whole balance of power in the Confederacy *so as to give us control over the operations of the Government in all
time to come.* If the South be but true to themselves, the day of our depression and suffering is *gone, and gone forever''* (*Cong. Globe*, as cited
above, 364).

state, still loved the Union; but he would cease to love his wife (if he had one), "if, like the farfamed Mrs. Caudle, she were forever taunting me with what she chose to regard as a great deformity and annoyance."[23] Should the North persist in its purpose to restrict slavery, he saw no remedy short of a dissolution of the Union. During the debate on the Oregon bill Rhett, also, denied absolutely the power of Congress to exclude slavery from territories, for they belonged to the states and not to the United States.

For that [Oregon] territory [said he], we care but little, since it is not probable that a single planter would ever desire to set his foot within its limits. But the right is important, because it applies to future acquisitions of territory; and by refusing to acknowledge the obligations of the Missouri compromise, you force open the whole question of power.[24]

The question of the control of Congress over slavery in territories came before the Senate by a more indirect route. On January 19, 1847, Sevier reported, from the Committee on Foreign Relations, a bill for granting the President three million dollars with which to conduct negotiations with Mexico. When it came up for discussion on February 1, Berrien, of Georgia, a southern Whig, gave notice of his intention to offer an amendment. His amendment, among other things, declared that "the war with Mexico ought not to be prosecuted by this Government with any view to the dismemberment of that republic, or the acquisition by conquest of any portion of her territory." A few days later Cass offered a substitute which authorized the President to demand indemnity from Mexico. To those who desired an extension of slavery Berrien's amendment was quite as offensive, except in principle, as the Wilmot proviso itself; for no acquisition of territory meant no extension of political power. During the debate, Berrien warned southerners that slavery

---

23 "These northern Mrs. Caudles," he continued, "will not let us rest by night or by day. We get no sleep for them! Their eternal din will drive us to distraction. They interfere with our domestic matters; they enter our very kitchens, and intrude upon our most sacred household affairs!" (*Cong. Globe*, 29 Cong., 2 sess., App., 86). For Seddon's remarks, see *ibid.*, 76.

24 *Ibid.*, 346.

would surely be excluded from all land acquired; therefore both the interest and the safety of the South "demands that we should oppose ourselves to any and every acquisition of territory."

Berrien was not the only southern man who was averse to territorial acquisition. Whigs would naturally oppose any policy advocated by the administration, but there was a still more potent reason why certain Democrats, as well as Whigs, did not favor expansion. This reason was a conviction that slavery would be excluded; and that while their section could not hope to gain any advantage, further agitation of the subject might result in a dissolution of the Union. Why, asked Morehead, of Kentucky, should a policy (of expansion) be followed which would precipitate discord over slavery and probably destroy the institution? In the House, Alexander H. Stephens vigorously opposed the acquisition of territory and gave as one of his reasons his fear of the results of slavery agitation. He had faith in the strength of the Union, but he had "no disposition to test its strengh by running against that rock upon which Mr. Jefferson predicted we should be finally wrecked."

Calhoun joined the Whigs just mentioned in combating the President's expansion policy. He saw even more clearly than they did the approaching "irrepressible conflict." In a lugubrious speech made in the Senate on February 24 he declared that

Every Senator knows that I was opposed to the war; but none knows but myself the depth of that opposition. With my conception of its character and consequences, it was impossible for me to vote for it. . . . On the passage of the act recognizing the war, I said to many of my friends that a deed had been done from which the country would not be able to recover for a long time, if ever; and added, it has dropped a curtain between the present and the future, which to me is impenetrable; and for the first time since I have been in public life, I am unable to see the future. I also added, that it has closed the first volume of our political history under the Constitution, and opened the second, and that no mortal could tell what would be written in it. . . . Since then less than a year has elapsed; but in that short period enough has already been developed to make what was then said look like prophecy.[25]

---

[25] *Cong. Globe*, 29 Cong., 2 sess., 500. Also, Calhoun, *Works*, IV, 371.

The thing which had developed, of course, was the inclination of the North to resist the spread of slavery, and Calhoun fully realized that that section possessed the power if the people should decide to make use of it. His first remedy for the impending disaster was to prevent, if possible, the acquisition of more territory. Later, when he became convinced that this could not be done, he felt constrained to deny that Congress possessed the power to restrict the institution.

Already, indeed, Calhoun had been offered an opportunity for asserting the latter doctrine. On February 15 Douglas had attempted in the House to extend the Missouri Compromise line through the territory to be acquired, as an alternative to excluding slavery from all of it. His amendment for this purpose was rejected by a considerable majority. Four days after this action had been taken, Calhoun announced in the Senate that he was ''against any compromise line.'' He had always, he said, considered the Missouri Compromise to have been a great error, although he had acquiesced in respecting it in order to preserve peace. But since its rejection as a solution of the new territorial question, he was now ready to insist upon the full rights of the South in all territories. An enumeration of these rights he embodied in a series of resolutions which Benton was unkind enough to call a ''string of abstractions.'' In substance the resolutions declared territories to be the property of the several states, consequently Congress did not possess the constitutional power to prevent a citizen of a state from migrating with his slaves to any of the territories.[26]

The real reason why Calhoun and his supporters felt obliged to abandon the historic method of compromise and to deny the power of Congress over slavery in territories is obvious; they were confronted by a condition of affairs which had never before existed. In all land previously acquired slavery was already established, therefore the institution might continue unless

[26] *Cong. Globe, loc. cit.*, 453–455. Calhoun, *Works*, IV, 339–349.

specifically prohibited by Congress. In the proposed acquisition
slavery had been abolished by Mexican law, and, according to
international custom, this law would continue in force until sup-
planted by positive legislation on the subject by the United States.
Now Congress had never specifically authorized slavery anywhere,
and there could be no hope that it would do so in the present
instance. Consequently a new doctrine must be promulgated;
it must deny the power of Congress to exclude slave property
from land which belonged to the *several states*. For the sake of
consistency the doctrine must apply to Oregon as well as to the
proposed Mexican cession.[27] The issue was now squarely joined.
The advocates of the Wilmot proviso claimed full power to exclude slavery from all territories, while Calhoun and his adherents denied *in toto* the existence of such a power. After
Congress had adjourned, Benton told his constituents that at last
extremes had met—Calhoun and the abolitionists had joined
hands in subverting the Union.[28]

Congress adjourned on March 3, 1847, without having provided a government for Oregon. A bill for this purpose had
passed the House on January 16, but on the last day of the session
it was laid on the table by the Senate. Under Polk's direction,

---

[27] The *Baltimore American*, Feb. 17, 1847, pointed out very clearly why
southern members, after applauding the plan suggested by Cass, Buchanan,
and Dickinson for letting the people of the territories decide the question,
turned suddenly to oppose it. ''To leave to the territories themselves the
absolute decision of the existence of slavery upon their soil, might do very
well if slavery had been previously established there, as was the case when
Louisiana was purchased, when Florida was acquired, and when Texas was
annexed. But in the present case it would not do. The old formula must
be changed. The long and fondly cherished doctrine of state sovereignty,
so conveniently inchoate in a territory as the germ of a state—even this
must be abandoned.'' Quoted in *Niles' Reg.*, Feb. 19, 1848, LXXIII, 392.

[28] The Calhoun resolutions, said he, ''go the precise length of the
northern abolitionists, and with the same practical consequence, only in
a reversed form. The abolition creed is, that the admission of slavery in
any part of the Union is a violation of the constitution, and a dissolution
of the Union; the new resolutions declare that the prohibition of slavery
in any territory of the Union is a violation of the constitution and the
rights of the states, and a subversion of the Union! So true it is, that
extremes meet, and that all fanaticism, for or against any *dogma*, terminates at the same point of intolerance and defiance'' (speech at St. Louis
(no date given), quoted in *Niles' Reg.*, June 5, 1847, 223).

Buchanan expressed to the people of Oregon the President's regret because they had been left by Congress without a government. Ignoring the real difficulty, Buchanan stated that the failure of Congress to act had not resulted from indifference to the interests of the territory, but to a pressure of business which did not allow time to perfect the details of the bill![29] Just before adjourning, however, Congress passed the "three million bill" which enabled the President to use this sum in conducting negotiations with Mexico. As we have seen, efforts were made to attach to this bill either the Wilmot proviso or an extension of the Missouri compromise line, but all such restrictions were rejected.

During the session which had just closed Calhoun felt that he had attained a commanding position. "My friends," he wrote, "think I never stood higher, or stronger than I now do"; and he was "now certain that there will be no more Baltimore nominations, or if there should be, the nominee will be assuredly defeated." Through Benton, he said, the administration was trying to build up the old Van Buren party, but their efforts would end in failure.[30] After Congress had adjourned, he went home to begin an active compaign for uniting the South in defense of slavery. He desired, first of all, to prevent the reëlection of Polk, or the election of any of his adherents; if Calhoun himself could not be elected, he was ready to support General Taylor.[31] It is interesting to note that while northern Whigs and "proviso" Democrats were denouncing the President as a slavery extensionist, Calhoun and his supporters were identifying him with Van Buren and other enemies of "southern institutions."

---

[29] Buchanan, *Works*, VII, 258.

[30] Calhoun to Thos. G. Clemson, Jan. 30, 1847, in *Rep. Am. Hist. Assn.*, 1899, II, 717.

[31] "The days of hunkerism is numbered. Mr. Polk is the last of the dynasty. It never can rise again to power. . . . As much as I am opposed to military chieftains for presidents, I shall, thus thinking, be content to see him [Taylor] elected against Mr. Polk, or any one, who contributed to make the war; and, let me add, against the nominee of a convention, either democrat, or Whig" (Calhoun to Clemson, May 6, 1847, *ibid.*, 728).

Early in April the President was informed by his Secretary of the Navy that Calhoun was soliciting signatures for an address to the people on the subject of slavery. "I remarked to Mr. Mason," says the *Diary,*

that Mr. Calhoun had become perfectly desperate in his aspirations to the Presidency, and had seized upon this sectional question as the only means of sustaining himself in his present fallen condition, and that such an agitation of the slavery question was not only unpatriotic and mischievous, but wicked.

He was as little pleased with a story told by Benton to the effect that the supporters of Silas Wright "would be rejoiced at the opportunity to take issue with Mr. Calhoun on such a question."

The truth is, [he continued], there is no patriotism in either faction of the party. Both desire to mount slavery as a hobby, and hope to secure the election of their favourite upon it. They will both fail and ought to. The people of the U. States, I hope, will cast off all such intrigues, and make their own selection for the Presidency, and this if they are wise they will do. I now entertain a worse opinion of Mr. Calhoun than I have ever done before. He is wholly selfish, I am satisfied has no patriotism. A few years ago he was the author of Nullification & threatened to dissolve the Union on account of the tariff. During my administration the reduction of duties which he desired has been obtained, and he can no longer complain. No sooner is this done than he selects slavery upon which to agitate the country, and blindly mounts that topic as a hobby. Gov. Wright's friends in Congress as unpatriotically have shown by their course that they desire to mount the same hobby in the North and hope to be successful by their opposition to slavery. They both forget that the Constitution settles [those] questions which were the subjects of mutual concession between the North and South. I am utterly disgusted at such intriguing men in high place, & hope they will be rebuked by the people.[32]

---

[32] Polk, *Diary,* II, 457–459. Although Polk was wrong in attributing the sectional discord wholly to President-making, it was true that the slavery question was being used on both sides of Mason and Dixon's line to break down party lines and to solidify public opinion either for or against the "peculiar institution." A few months later Holmes, of S. C., wrote: "I wish the Southern Representatives would consent to act together without regard to Whig or Democrat. The Wilmot Proviso is paramount to all Party. We are in great danger. The North is resolved to crush Slavery—are we equally in the South resolved at all hazards to defend it?" (Holmes to Cobb, Aug. 21, 1847, in *Rep. of Am. Hist. Assn.* 1911, II, 88).

What the President desired most of all was to eliminate the slavery question entirely and to have Congress confine its attention to the policies of his administration. However, since the slavery question had emerged, he could not maintain simply a negative attitude with respect to it. He was compelled, against his will, to adopt some positive program for dealing with slavery in the territories. As early as January 5, 1847, the cabinet suggested an extension of the Missouri Compromise line, but at that time Polk declined to commit himself.[33]

About a week after the cabinet had made this suggestion Atocha appeared in Washington and the prospect of an early acquisition of Mexican territory seemed brighter. Since Congress persisted in discussing slavery, some positive plan on the part of the administration seemed desirable. In his diary for January 16 Polk lamented that the session was nearly half over and that Congress, instead of enacting necessary military measures, was engaged in "a worse than useless discussion about slavery." He and the cabinet deprecated this discussion, but "all feared it would be impossible now to arrest it." Although every member of the cabinet advised an extension of the 36° 30′ line through the territory to be acquired, Polk was not ready to commit himself to this solution.[34] In fact, the President does not seem to have decided upon any definite policy during the session, although he intimated to Crittenden that the Missouri Compromise line would be extended;[35] and as Congress voted the three million dollars without attaching the Wilmot restriction, slavery for the time being ceased to be a vital question.

In June, the President decided to made a tour of the northeastern states. Although we have no direct evidence that political considerations induced him to make this decision, it is quite

---

[33] See above, p. 619.

[34] Polk, *Diary*, II, 335.

[35] He told Crittenden that the slavery question in California and New Mexico would not be a practical one ''because there would be but a narrow ribbon of territory South of the Missouri compromise line'' (*Diary*, Jan. 23, II, 350).

probable that he hoped, by making the journey, to retain the support of northern Democrats and to prevent further defections on account of slavery agitation. Among those who accompanied him was Edmund Burke, commissioner of patents and his close personal friend. No doubt Burke voiced the President's views when, on the eve of the journey, he told Franklin Pierce that the signs of the times portended a coalition of the South and West against the North. He attributed this state of affairs to the "foolish course" pursued by the "proviso" Democrats; "it is clear that the Northern and Southern Democracy are now divided, a consummation which the federalists of the North have sought for fifty years to accomplish."[36] Polk did not, during the summer, decide upon any definite policy with respect to slavery in the territories, though his approval (somewhat reluctant, to be sure) of Buchanan's open espousal of an extension of the 36° 30' line indicated that he would not oppose this plan as a solution of the question.[37]

When Congress convened in December, 1847, the President, in his third annual message, informed that body of the failure of Trist's mission. He recommended that California and New Mexico should be retained permanently by the United States and that Congress should at once provide each of these territories with a civil government. In this connection he made no allusion to slavery, but he concluded his message by quoting Washington's admonition regarding the value of union and the calamity of sectional controversies.

> How unimportant [said Polk] are all our differences of opinion upon minor questions of public policy compared with its preservation, and how scrupulously should we avoid all agitating topics which may tend to distract and divide us into contending parties, separated by geographical lines, whereby it may be weakened or endangered.

On December 8, two days after Congress had convened, the Vice-President laid before the Senate a memorial from the Oregon

---

[36] Burke to Pierce, June 21, 1847, *Pierce Papers.*

[37] Polk, *Diary,* III, 142. Buchanan to Berks County Democrats (Buchanan, *Works,* VII, 385).

"Legislative Assembly" praying for the confirmation of their land titles and for the adoption of measures to promote education. This assembly had been created by the people of Oregon, without authority from the United States government. The movement to establish a temporary government began as early as 1843, and one section of the "Organic Laws" prohibited slavery.[38]

On December 14, before any consideration had been given to this memorial, Dickinson, of New York, submitted resolutions which attempted to define the policy of the government for both acquiring and governing territories. They asserted that "true policy" required the United States to strengthen its political and commercial relations on the continent by the acquisition of contiguous territory, and that in all such territories the people should be left free to settle "all questions concerning the domestic policy therein," without any restrictions imposed by the federal government. In other words, Dickinson advocated the "popular sovereignty" program which Douglas later mounted as a hobby in 1854. In his well-known "Nicholson letter" Cass made a bid for the Presidential nomination by casting doubt on the power of Congress over slavery in territories and by espousing the doctrine of "popular sovereignty."[39]

The Dickinson resolutions were followed by others in which individual Senators endeavored to commit the government to what each deemed to be the "true policy" respecting territories. One offered by Calhoun opposed holding Mexico as a province, or incorporating it into the Union. As a substitute for the Dickinson plan, Yulee, of Florida, offered a resolution which declared that territory owned or to be acquired by the United States "is the common property of the Union," and that neither the federal nor the territorial government can prevent any citizen from enjoying full rights therein. Hale, of New Hampshire, offered another substitute which purposed to exclude slavery entirely from lands

---

[38] Gray, *History of Oregon*, chaps. xiii–xiv.

[39] Cass to A. O. P. Nicholson, Dec. 24, 1847. Printed in *Niles' Reg.*, Jan. 8, 1848, LXXIII, 293.

that might be acquired. All of these proposals were defeated, yet they afforded an opportunity for airing divergent views and for illustrating the impossibility of arriving at any practical settlement of the slavery question.

On January 10, 1848, Senator Douglas presented a bill for establishing a territorial government in Oregon, and on February 9 Caleb Smith, of Indiana, reported from the House Committee on Territories a bill for the same purpose. Both measures were referred to committees, and for some time war legislation precluded their consideration.

The Douglas bill did not come before the Senate until May 31, and then Hale moved to amend by adding section twelve of the Senate bill of the last session—the section which extended to Oregon the Ordinance of 1787. Calhoun opposed the inclusion of a slavery restriction, while others like Hannegan and Benton thought such restriction to be unnecessary, since slaves would never be taken to Oregon. Benton was unwilling to have necessary legislation delayed by the introduction of this ''pestiferous question.'' He was especially anxious that military protection should be extended immediately to the people of Oregon. But Hale was obdurate, and insisted upon a positive prohibition of slavery. ''If this Union,'' said he, ''with all its advantages, has no other cement than the blood of human slavery, let it perish!'' When the discussion was resumed on June 5, Foote moved to amend by inserting in section twelve the words: ''provided the same [the slavery restriction] be compatible with the laws and Constitution of the United States.'' In this way he undoubtedly hoped to obtain a ''Dred Scott decision'' at that early date. After Underwood, of Kentucky, had denied the authority of Congress to interfere with local institutions and Baldwin, of Connecticut, had declared that slaves were held solely by state laws and that when a slave left the confines of a slave state—even if accompanied by his master on a temporary sojourn—''his shackles fell off,'' Badger, of North Carolina, offered, as a substitute for

Foote's proposal, a proviso which would exempt the people of Oregon from the operation of the sixth article (the one prohibiting slavery) of the Ordinance of 1787. Foote accepted the modification. After considerable discussion this amendment was withdrawn by the mover on June 23, and Davis, of Mississippi, presented another which asserted that nothing in the bill should be so construed as to prohibit slavery in Oregon while it remained a territory.

After a long delay the House, on March 28, proceeded to consider Caleb Smith's Oregon bill. In a most ingenious speech Gayle, of Alabama, asserted that all laws by which Congress had excluded slavery from territories had been based on precedent merely and had not been authorized by the Constitution. He held that territories were legally states before entering the Union;[40] on the other hand, he denied that their government thereby possessed the power to exclude slavery. In reply, Smart, of Maine, declared that Congress not only had the power but was bound by the will of the majority to prevent slavery from entering all territories.

The President, as we have seen, was reluctant to announce a definite policy regarding slavery in territories, even though the Van Burenites believed this to be the issue nearest his heart.[41] Both he and his cabinet opposed the Wilmot proviso,[42] and, since a negative policy could not be pursued indefinitely, Polk at last decided to advocate an extension of the Missouri Compromise line.

---

[40] "Now, sir, how can a 'new State be admitted into the Union' unless it was a State before admission?"

[41] "The slavery question," wrote John M. Niles, "is evidently first & foremost with the administration; it overrides the Mexican war & any other question. The slave power rules as tyrannically here as it can in Louisiana; that, is made the test & tie of fealty to the administration" (Niles to Van Buren, Dec. 16, 1847, *Van Buren Papers*).

[42] After Clifford had been sent to Mexico the President announced his intention to select some northern man to fill his place. All members expressed an unwillingness to be associated with a Wilmot proviso man (Polk, *Diary*, III, 431).

As already noted, the President desired most of all to eliminate the subject of slavery, but forces beyond his control made
it apparent that this could not be done.   Indeed, since the Treaty
of Guadalupe Hidalgo had been ratified by Mexico, the question
of governments for California and New Mexico had become more
urgent than ever.   Congress persisted in discussing slavery and
there seemed to be no prospect of an agreemnt on the subject.
On May 26 a messenger arrived from Oregon and laid before
the President a memorial from the legislative assembly of that
territory, stating that the Indians were making war on the inhabitants.   Polk transmitted the memorial to Congress along with
a message recommending the immediate creation of a government
for Oregon.   He said nothing about slavery.[43]   But on June 24,
in a conversation with Senator Hannegan concerning ''the dis-
tracting subject of slavery, which is embarrassing the Bill to
establish a Territorial Government in Oregon,'' he advised the
Senator to ''bring forward & press the adoption of the Missouri
compromise line & extend it to the Pacific.''   Hannegan, as well
as the entire cabinet, agreed with Polk that ''the adoption of the
Missouri compromise was the only means of allaying the excitement & settling the question.''   The President sent for other
members of Congress and urged them to support this policy in
order to checkmate the action of the Barnburners:

> The necessity for settling the question is the greater since the con-
> vention of Barnburners, held at Utica, New York, on the 22nd Instant,
> have bolted from the regular Democratic nominations made at the Balti-
> more convention in May last, and have nominated Martin Van Buren for
> President and Henry Dodge of Wisconsin for Vice President distinctly
> upon the ground of the Wilmot Proviso. This is a most dangerous attempt
> to organize Geographical parties upon the slavery question. It is more
> threatening to the Union than anything which has occurred since the
> meeting of the Hartford convention in 1814. Mr. Van Buren's course is
> selfish, unpatriotic, and wholly inexcusable. The effect of this movement of
> the seceding and discontented Democrats of New York will be effectually

---

[43] Polk, *Diary*, III, 463.   Message dated May 29, 1849 (Richardson,
Messages, IV, 584).

co[u]nteracted if the slave question can be settled by adopting the Missouri compromise line as applied to Oregon, New Mexico, & Upper California at the Present Session of Congress. If the question can be thus settled harmony will be restored to the Union and the danger of forming geographical parties be avoided. For these reasons I am using my influence with members of Congress to have it adopted.[44]

He was quite indifferent regarding the extension of slavery, but he was vitally concerned over preserving the Union and insuring the success of his party. He did not believe that sound principles, or what he considered to be such, should be jeopardized by a sudden change in the popular viewpoint. After the Baltimore convention, Cass showed to Polk the first draft of his letter of acceptance, one sentence of which declared that the government should keep pace with public opinion. ''I suggested to him,'' is the comment in the *Diary,* that the assertion

might be misconstrued to mean that constitutional principles might be changed, in order to accommodate themselves to what might seem from time to time to be public opinion, which I thought was an untenable & dangerous doctrine.[45]

A few days after his conversation with Hannegan the President discussed the Oregon bill with Senators Bright, of Indiana, and Foote, of Mississippi. He dictated an amendment which would extend the 36° 30′ line to the Pacific. When Bright introduced the amendment in the Senate, Calhoun again asserted that Congress could not, without violating the Constitution, prevent a slaveholder from carrying his *property* to any territory.[46]

During the first two weeks in July, Polk conversed with various southern members of both houses, nearly all of whom were ready to accept an extension of the 36° 30′ line. Judge Catron wrote from Nashville that the position taken by those who denied the power of Congress over slavery in acquired territory could not be maintained. He was in favor of excluding the institution

---

[44] Polk, *Diary,* III, 501–503.

[45] *Ibid.,* 471–472.

[46] *Ibid.,* 504–505. *Cong. Globe,* 30 Cong., 1 sess., 875–876.

from Oregon and believed that it would be wise, politically, to do so.[47] The pleasure which Polk derived from the support of so many southern men was offset by the acerbity of Alexander H. Stephens. By a resolution introduced on July 10 Stephens called upon the President for information concerning the governments which had been set up in California and New Mexico. In a violent speech he scathingly denounced the President and General Pillow, and characterized the former as ''Polk the mendacious.''[48]

In the Senate, on July 12, after Jefferson Davis had upheld the right of a slaveowner to locate with his ''property'' in any territory, Clayton, of Delaware, moved that the question of slavery in territories be referred to a committee of eight to be selected by ballot—four from the North and four from the South. During the discussion of this proposal Westcott, of Florida, asserted that should the Wilmot proviso be attached to the bill, ''we have a Chief Magistrate at the other end of the avenue who would put his veto on it.'' However true this statement may have been, it must have been based upon pure conjecture, for Polk would hardly have given advance information to a man whom he detested as he did Westcott. The Senate passed the resolution and Clayton was made chairman of the select committee.[49]

Calhoun was made a member of the Clayton committee and, on July 14, Polk expressed to the Senator's friend, Elmore, a hope that he might recede from his extreme position and accept the 36° 30′ line as a compromise. He could not with propriety,

---

[47] ''Were I in Congress, not a moment's hestiation would be felt in voting for the exclusion of slavery from [in?] the Oregon bill; and if this is done, with the sanction of the Democratic party—as it must be in the Senate, the Barnburners may hang their harp on the willows, so far as capital is sought from this slavery question; not that I think so much will come of it as has been supposed, for Mr. V. Buren will have to carry his abolition brethern, who will be very apt to absorb his party, & to incorporate his good self, & Son John.'' Catron ''w'd feel much gratified to see this slavery question adjusted by a compromise on 36° 30′—the true division as I think'' (Catron to Polk, July 12, 1848, *Polk Papers*).

[48] Polk, *Diary*, IV, 14. *Cong. Globe*, 30 Cong., 1 sess., 912.

[49] *Cong. Globe*, 30 Cong., 1 sess., 927–928, 932.

he said, ask Calhoun to call and discuss the subject,[50] so Elmore, two days later, brought the Senator to call upon him. After Polk had expressed a ''decided opinion'' in favor of adjusting the slavery question by an extension of the compromise line, Calhoun said that the Clayton committee had as yet been unable to agree upon a solution. He stated that a suggestion had been made in committee which he was willing to accept: that the existing Oregon laws which prohibited slavery be allowed to operate until changed by the territorial legislature; and that the governments of California and New Mexico be prevented by Congress from legislating on the subject of slavery, leaving the question, should it arise, to be decided by the local judiciary. Polk was willing to accept this adjustment, although he preferred an extension of the compromise line. Calhoun now produced the *loaded dice* by which he hoped to win the game so far as the Mexican cessions were concerned:

> He said that much would depend on me, in appointments to be made of Governor, Secretary, & Judges; that they might be Northern men in Oregon, but that they ought to be Southern men in California & New Mexico, who would maintain the southern views on the subject of slavery. The tone of his conversation on this point seemed to be designed to elicit a pledge from me to this effect. I at once felt the delicacy of my situation & promptly replied that that was a subject upon which I could not speak, that if the laws passed in the form suggested I would do my duty, and jocosely added that my friends, as Gen'l Harrison's Cincinnati Committee in 1844 [1840?] said for him, must have a ''generous confidence'' that I would do so.[51]

Calhoun returned on the following day and reported that the committee had agreed upon the general terms above mentioned, but that the northern members insisted upon a provision which would allow appeals from the territorial courts to the Supreme Court of the United States. He and two other members would

---

50 ''I told him I could not invite Mr. Calhoun to call, 1st, because he was an older man than myself, had been longer in public life, and 2nd, because he might suppose that I desired to exercise some official influence over him.''

51 Polk, *Diary*, IV, 19–21.

not admit this provision, and he now suggested that the whole subject might be postponed until the next session of Congress. Since Polk urged immediate action, the Senator, after another vain attempt to carry his point in committee, finally yielded on the subject of appeal. "There is now some prospect," wrote the President, "that the question may be settled at the present session of Congress, and I sincerely hope it may be." On July 18, Clayton reported a bill which left undisturbed the prohibition in Oregon. The status of slavery was left for the Supreme Court to determine, and until this had been done, the territorial governments were not to legislate on the subject.[52]

When the bill came up for discussion, on July 22, Niles, of Connecticut, asked Clayton whether his bill answered the important question whether Congress had or had not the power to interfere with slavery in territories. He replied that it "neither affirms nor denies the power, and herein consists the compromise." Northern members were unable to discern a compromise in a measure which left slave-owners free to enter California and New Mexico without hindrance, except an improbable decision of a pro-slavery court. The northern press was equally suspicious. Said the New York *Evening Post:*

> Talk as we may of the impartiality of our courts, a judge from the Southern States, allied to the aristocracy of those States, would share their prejudices and decide according to their views. This compromise is, therefore, an ingenious method of giving Mr. Calhoun his own way in the controversy.

And the New York *Tribune:*

> We protest against this juggle. We say it [slavery] has acquired no right to a single foot of the new territory; the South avers the contrary. We press Congress for a decision, and it is refused us. Instead of deciding Congress undertakes to run the matter through so many different crucibles, that slavery will finally be established and that inveterate old rascal, Nobody, be alone responsible for it. . . .
>
> A governor and three Judges are to be the law makers and the law expounders in each Territory—said governor and judges being appointed

[52] *Ibid.,* 21–24. *Cong. Globe,* 30 Cong., 1 sess., 950.

by Polk, and of course chosen from among the most determined, wily and unscrupulous champions of slavery extension. Nobody can pretend to doubt how they will construe the constitution.[53]

The discussion in the Senate continued until the morning of July 27, when, after an all-night session during which numerous amendments were rejected, the measure as submitted by the select committee was passed. On the following day, after a brief debate, the House laid the Senate bill on the table and proceeded to consider its own Oregon government bill.

The President was sorely disappointed by this action on the part of the House. He was especially mortified because the defeat of the bill had been accomplished by the votes of New York Barnburners and Democrats ''who are timid & afriad to risk their popularity at home.'' The result of leaving the slavery question unsettled, to be agitated by ''ambitious aspirants & gamblers,'' would be to produce an organization of parties on geographical lines and to endanger the Union. He did not doubt that the bill would have passed if there had been no Presidential election pending. The Whigs were desirous of preventing any adjustment during the present session,

doubtless in the expectation that in the chapter of accidents growing out of the excitement & agitation which must follow, that they may stand some chance to elect a Whig President. I deplore as a national calamity the want of patriotism which seems to actuate the conduct of the leaders of the Whig party in Congress; a'nd I exceedingly regret that any portion of the Northern Democrats from timidity or other causes have been induced to act with them.[54]

By the eighth of August he had become convinced that Congress would not, at the present session, create governments for New Mexico and California, yet he believed that the Oregon bill, with its clause excluding slavery, might be passed. He asked the cabinet whether, in case this bill should pass, he ought to sign it. Each member responded that, since the whole territory

---

[53] Both quoted in *Niles' Reg.*, LXXIV, 55–56.

[54] Polk, *Diary*, IV, 33–35.

lay north of 36° 30′, he ought to do so. He then asked whether he ought to accompany his approval with a message stating that he had signed the bill because the territory lay north of the Missouri Compromise line. Buchanan feared that such a statement might injure the campaign of General Cass; the others believed that it should be made, either in a message or in the Washington *Union*.[55]

The House passed its own bill on August 2 and sent it to the Senate for approval. The Senate attached certain amendments which the House promptly rejected, and it looked for a time as if no agreement could be reached. Polk was ready to approve slavery restriction for Oregon, but he told the cabinet that he did not wish it to be inferred that he would sanction a restriction south of 36° 30′.[56]

In taking his stand against the application of the Wilmot proviso to all territory it is evident that the President was animated not by a wish to extend slavery but by a desire to preserve the Union. He believed that the Union could be saved by an extension of the compromise line—and, perhaps, in no other way. He had set his heart on having the whole territorial question settled by the adoption of such a policy. The elimination of Oregon would make the adjustment more difficult, consequently he preferred to have the matter setled by a measure that would apply to all three territories. He believed that the South was entitled to the privilege of occupying with its "property" the southern part of the Mexican session; but, personally, he was most interested in allaying sectional discord. He was equally insistent—in defiance of southern pressure—upon prohibiting slavery north of 36° 30′, although he samewhat doubted the

[55] *Ibid.*, 61–62.

[56] "I expressed the opinion that if I approved and signed the Bill in the usual form without assigning my reasons, my opinion in regard to California & New Mexico would not be understood, and that it might be inferred that I had yielded the question in regard to the Territory South as well as North of the Missouri compromise line, which would not be true" (*ibid.*, 67–68).

constitutional power of Congress to apply such a restriction. In this, too, he was moved not by any feeling against the institution, but by the opinion that nothing else would satisfy the North and prevent further agitation. In a word, his attitude toward slavery was one of indifference.

When, on the morning of August 13, Polk learned that the Senate, at the close of all-night session, had passed the House Oregon bill, with its prohibition of slavery, he realized that he must decide the question of affixing or withholding his signature. Although disappointed because the compromise line had not, at the same time, been extended through the Mexican cession, he nevertheless decided to approve the Oregon bill and, in a message, to state his reasons for so doing. Buchanan did not wish Polk to state in the message that he would veto any bill which purposed to exclude slavery south of 36° 30'; Mason, Marcy, and Ritchie advised such an announcement. While the President was drafting his message to the House, Senator Turney, of Tennessee, called and urged him to veto the bill; and Hannegan, although he had voted for the bill, offered to sustain a veto. Calhoun and Burt, of South Carolina, importuned him to veto the measure, but he informed them that he would sign it, "although I would do so reluctantly";

> I told him [Calhoun] that if the question of imposing the restriction was an original one arising for the first time, I would have serious doubts of its constitutionality. I remarked that there might be questions arise effecting [affecting] the very existence of the Union, upon which we ought to yield individual opinions, in deference to what our predecessors had done, and I considered this one of them.

He reminded Calhoun that the Clayton committee of which the Senator was a member had been willing to exclude slavery from Oregon, and that many southern Senators had voted for the Clayton bill. He reminded him also that Burt, who was present, had proposed the amendment in the House for prohibiting slavery in Oregon, on the ground that the territory lay north of the compromise line. Calhoun pleaded for a veto, but

I repeated that I would sign it, and told him that if I were to veto it after all that had occurred, and in the present excited state of Congress & of the public mind, I should do more to inflame that excitement & to array the country into geographical parties and to rend the Union, than any act which had ever been done by any President or any man in the country. He left me fully understanding my opinions & what I would do.[57]

Congress had agreed to adjourn on August 14, the day after Polk had held the above-mentioned conversation with Calhoun. The President rose early and carefully revised his message to the House before the cabinet had assembled for the purpose of accompanying him to the capital. To Buchanan's caustic remark concerning Ritchie's assistance in the preparation of the message Polk retorted indignantly that none of the editor's suggestions had been followed. The Secretary then reiterated his opposition to sending the message.

Shortly after Polk had reached the Vice-President's room at the capitol he was informed that both houses were engaged in a debate against suspending the joint rule under which bills could not be submitted to the President for his signature on the last day of the session. Unless it were suspended not only the Oregon bill but the army appropriation bill would fail. The President communicated to several members his determination to call an extra session on the following day if this session should terminate without passing the appropriation bill. The joint rule was suspended and both bills presented for his approval. As he was about to affix his signature, Calhoun asked him not to assign his reasons in a message, but the request was denied. Nominations to fill the offices created by the Oregon bill were made and confirmed. When the hour for ending the sessoin had arrived the House was so pressed for time that it adjourned in confusion without having read the President's message.[58]

In his message Polk told the House that he had signed the territorial bill, even though New Mexico and California had been

---

[57] Polk, *Diary*, IV, 70–74.
[58] *Ibid.*, 74–77.

left without governments, because Oregon urgently needed legal organization and protection. Turning to the cause of sectional discord, he thus stated the position of the slaveholder:

> In the progress of all governments questions of such transcendent importance occasionally arise as to cast in the shade those of a mere party character. But one such question can now be agitated in this country, and this may endanger our glorious Union, the source of our greatness and all our political blessings. This question is slavery. With the slaveholding States this does not embrace merely the rights of property, however valuable, but it ascends far higher, and involves the domestic peace and security of every family.

After commending the "mutual concession" shown by the framers of the Constitution in dealing with the subject of slavery, as well as the compromise adjustments of the Missouri and Texas questions, he stated that he had not felt at liberty to withhold his approval of the Oregon bill, because all of the territory lay north of 36° 30'. "Had it embraced territories south of that compromise," he continued, "the question presented for my consideration would have been of a far different character, and my action upon it must have corresponded with my convictions." Since the extension of the Missouri Compromise line would leave but a small area in which the people might hold slaves, if they saw fit, "is this a question to be pushed to such extremities by excited partisans on the one side or the other, in regard to our newly acquired distant possessions on the Pacific, as to endanger the Union of thirty glorious States, which constitute our Confederacy?"[59]

Nowhere in his political career did Polk speak so emphatically as a southern man as he did in this message, and yet, as we have just noted, Calhoun tried to dissuade him from sending it to the House. It is unlikely, even at this time, that Polk was desirous of spreading slavery, but he feared that unless some concession were made to the South a dissolution of the Union would

---

[59] Richardson, *Messages*, IV, 606–609.

result. His desire for some immediate and permanent settlement of the slavery controversy was intensified by the defection of the Barnburners and the consequent weakening of the Democratic party. If the vexed question could not be settled during his administration there was, in his opinion, grave danger that no adjustment could be made which the South would accept.

Chagrined because the Van Buren Democrats had coöperated with the Whigs in defeating the California and New Mexico territorial bills, he resolved, as soon as Congress had adjourned, to punish leading Barnburners for inciting insurrection in Democratic ranks. His punitive measures must of necessity be confined to persons actually holding offices, and of these the most objectionable was Benjamin F. Butler, whom he had made United States Attorney for the southern district of New York. At the Barnburner convention, which had recently met at Buffalo to nominate Van Buren, Butler had made a speech in which he had denounced the administration and had practically defied the President to remove him. Polk accepted the challenge and summarily removed Butler from office. He would not have removed the attorney "for his mere opinions upon abstract questions, nor for his free expression of them," but Butler's action in throwing obstacles in the way of successful administration of the government had forfeited his right to an office of honor and profit. In Polk's opinion, Butler was now "one of the worst enemies of the Democratic party and its principles in the Union," and his newspaper organs in New York were more hostile to the administration than any of the Whig papers:

Indeed the whole party of Barn-burners in New York, of which Mr. Butler is a leading & controlling member, are not only abusive of me & my administration, but they seem to challenge and defy me to remove Mr. Butler, in the hope, no doubt, that they may enlist the public sympathy over him as a martyr for opinion's sake. By his removal to-day I have gratified [them], & they may make the most of it.[60]

---

[60] Polk, *Diary*, Sept. 1, 1848, IV, 114–115.

The harrowing question of slavery in the territories could not be disposed of so easily as could obnoxious office holders. As soon as Congress had adjourned, the redoubtable Missouri Senator gave the President new cause of annoyance by writing an officious letter to the people of California. Benton informed the Californians that since Congress had failed to legislate for them they were without a lawful government.[61] Therefore he exhorted them to meet in convention and frame a government under which they could take care of themselves until Congress should act. He sketched the type of government which would suit their purposes and suggested that a governor would be necessary to administer it. The Senate, he said, had voted seven million dollars to pay the people of California for miltiary services, but the bill for this purpose had been killed in the House committee by lies against Colonel Fremont.

Polk was much perturbed by this letter and sought advice from his cabinet as to the best means of counteracting its influence. Without admitting that the governments established in the new territories had "been void from the beginning" he was aware that the military governments had "ceased to exist" and that "the Executive had no authority to organize a civil Government over them." Benton's "extraordinary letter," he told the cabinet, had been sent to California

by Col. Fremont, the son-in-law of the writer, and the inference is plain enough that he means they shall make Col. Fremont the Governor of the Independent Government they shall form. Indeed I think it pretty clear that this was the main object.

He believed that the Secretary of State should inform the Californians, by letter, that the President would urge Congress to

---

[61] "The edicts promulgated by your temporary Governors (Kearny and Mason, each an ignoramus) so far as these edicts went to change the laws of the land, are null and void, and were so from the beginning. . . .

"Having no lawful government, nor lawful officers, you can have none that can have authority over you except by your own consent. Its sanction must be in the will of the majority" (Benton to the People of California, Aug. 27, 1848. Printed in *Niles' Reg.*, LXXIV, 244. Also in *Alta California*, Jan. 11, 1849).

frame a government for them, and that they "need not be deceived by the semi-official and officious proclamation of Senator Benton."[62] A few days later the matter was again brought before the cabinet, and the more the subject was discussed the greater number of legal difficulties did it present. Polk thought it probable that the military government in California was still "a Government *de facto*," yet he was not certain that the President could enforce obedience to it. Toucy, the Attorney General, thought that "the sovereignty of the territory rested in the people, and that they could, in the absence of the action of Congress, govern themselves as they chose." Mason and Walker believed that the sovereignty rested with the people of the United States and that Toucy's view would permit even the establishment of a monarchy. "I stated," wrote Polk,

that it was a subject which from its novelty was surrounded with many difficulties, but I thought instructions could be prepared which would avoid the decision of any abstract, doubtful question.

He instructed Buchanan to tell the people that they had no right, under the Constitution, to abrogate their *de facto* government and form one of their own. These views were embodied in a letter written by the Secretary of State and intrusted to William V. Voorhies, who was about to set out for California in the capacity of postal agent for that territory.[63]

The election of a Whig President made Polk more anxious than ever for an adjustment of the territorial question during his own term of office. His fourth annual message contained an urgent plea for the immediate establishment of civil governments in New Mexico and California. The reasons for the failure to do this at the last session, he said, "are well known and deeply to be regretted," and it would be irrational further to agitate a domestic question which is coeval with the existence of the government itself.

---

[62] Polk, *Diary*, IV, 135–138.

[63] *Ibid.*, 140–143. Buchanan to Voorhies (Buchanan, *Works*, VIII, 211-215).

In the eyes of the world and of posterity how trivial and insignificant will be all our internal divisions and struggles compared with the preservation of this Union of the States in all its vigor and with all its countless blessings! No patriot would foment and excite geographical and sectional divisions. No lover of his country would deliberately calculate the value of the Union.

Although a staunch Union man, the President's conception of the rights of a slaveholder in the territories was quite as southern as that of Calhoun himself. The people of every state, he told Congress, had helped to conduct the war, consequently "it would not be just for any one section to exclude another from all participation in the acquired territory." Whether slavery would enter these territories, even if left to the slaveholding states, was believed, he said, to be rather abstract than practical; but however that might me, "the quesion, involving, as it does a principle of equality of rights of the separate and several States as equal copartners in the Confederacy, should not be disregarded."

His views on the constitutional aspects of the question were quite as southern as those on the political side. The Constitution, he pointed out, had imposed upon Congress no duty to legislate on the subject of slavery in the territories, "while their power to do so is not only seriously questioned, but denied by many of the soundest expounders of that instrument."

Considering the several States and the citizens of the several States as equals and entitled to equal rights under the Constitution, if this were an original question it might well be insisted on that the principle of non-interference is the true doctrine and that Congress could not, in the absence of any express grant of power, interfere with their relative rights.

Since Congress, however, had, when dealing with previously acquired territory, divided the area between slavery and freedom, he was in favor of adjusting the present dispute in a similar manner, but if

Congress shall now reverse the decision by which the Missouri compromise was effected, and shall propose to extend the restriction over the whole territory, south as well as north of the parallel 36° 30', it will cease to be a compromise, and must be regarded as an original question.

After this implied threat to veto any bill for prohibiting slavery south of 36° 30', he expresesd a willingness to accept an extension of the compromise line, the policy of letting the people decide for themselves, or the submission of the whole subject to the decision of the courts.[64]

If the President had entertained hopes that his message would arouse Congress to take action, they seem to have vanished soon after his recommendations had been submitted. In less than a week he expressed to the cabinet a fear that Congress would do nothing and that California would establish an independent government and be lost to the Union. The rapid influx of population would make the demand for civil government imperative, and he believed that "the leading Federalists (alias Whigs) would be glad to avail themselves of the opportunity to give up the country for the purpose of relieving Gen'l Taylor of his embarrassments upon the Wilmot Proviso." This party, he said, had always opposed expansion, and had combated the purchase of Louisiana with as much vigor as they had opposed the present acquisition. Although the prospect seemed discouraging, he urged the members of the cabinet to use their influence with their friends in Congress. "It is," said he, "a question of rising above ordinary considerations. We have a country to serve as well as a party to obey."[65]

Even though the President was ready to go nearly as far as Calhoun in defending "southern rights," apparently his attitude was not prompted by an interest in slavery *per se*. He was willing—even anxious—to admit California immediately as a state, although there was every probability that slavery would be prohibited by its constitution.[66] On December 11, Douglas

---

[64] Richardson, *Messages*, IV, 640–642.

[65] Polk, *Diary*, IV, 231–233.

[66] Indeed, if newspapers may be taken as an index of public opinion, it was certain that slavery would be excluded, for the only two journals in California were emphatic on this point. The *California Star* of March 25, 1848, asserted that ninety-nine hundredths of the population opposed the imposition of "this blight" upon the territory, and the "simple recognition of slavery here" would be a greater misfortune than to remain in

had introduced in the Senate a bill for admitting both territories
as one state, but Polk believed the area to be too large and the
settlements too scattered for a single government. He summoned
Douglas and advised the admission of California as a state, and
the creation of a government for New Mexico by a separate bill.
Douglas approved this policy, but Calhoun, when consulted, refused to commit himself. On that very day, however, the House
by a considerable majority voted its approval of the Wilmot
proviso, some of the Democrats reversing the votes which they
had cast during the preceding session. Polk now saw no hope
of an adjustment except, possibly, the admission of the whole
territory as a state under the bill offered by Douglas.[67]

Not content with approving the Wilmot proviso the House, on
December 21, instructed its committee to bring in a bill for
abolishing the slave trade in the District of Columbia. Southern members were much excited and took immediate steps to
arrange for a caucus. When informed of this fact, Polk declared
slavery agitation to be "a mere political question on which
demagogues & ambitious politicians hope to promote their own
prospect for political promotion." About seventy members, both
Democrats and Whigs, attended the caucus, and, after appointing a committee to prepare an address to be sent to southern
states if the anti-slave-trade bill should be pressed, it adjourned
to meet at a later date.[68]

In another effort to procure some positive action, the President
sent for Senator Butler, of South Carolina, chairman of the
Judiciary Committee to which the Douglas bill had been referred.
He told Butler that no territorial bill which did not include the
Wilmot proviso could pass the House, and that if such a bill

---

the present state of disaster. The *Californian* of October 11 was certain
that the people preferred to remain as they were rather than have "this
blighting curse" put upon them. On December 13 Benton presented in
the Senate a petition from a New Mexico convention which asked Congress
to protect the people there from the introduction of slavery (*Cong. Globe,*
30 Cong., 2 sess., 33).

[67] Polk, *Diary,* IV, 232–235.   [68] *Ibid.,* 248–253.

should pass both houses he would be compelled to veto it. The only way to save California was to admit her as a state; he therefore asked Butler's aid in bringing this about. Like Calhoun, Butler left the President in doubt as to what he would do. Polk then sent for Douglas who, after considerable persuasion, agreed to alter his bill so that California might be admitted and a territorial government be provided for New Mexico.[69]

The adjourned meeting of the southern caucus was scheduled for January 15, 1849, and on the fourteenth Polk held a consultation with several of the southern leaders. They told him that the address to southern states, which Calhoun had prepared, was of such a nature that neither they nor their friends could sign it. The President approved their decision, for he thought that such an address would be mischievous. When nearly all of the Whigs and many of the Democrats who attended the caucus declined to sign Calhoun's address, it was returned to the committee for report at a future meeting. On the following day Calhoun called on the President and said that the South could no longer delay in resisting the aggressions of the North upon its rights. Polk advised the admission of California and spoke with approval of a plan suggested by Douglas for joining to Texas all of the remaining territory south of 36° 30'. When Calhoun opposed every suggestion and declined to offer a solution of his own Polk became convinced that the Senator did not desire an amicable adjustment. "I was firm and decided," said he, "in my conversation with him, intending to let him understand distinctly that I gave no countenance to any movement which tended to violence or the disunion of the States."[70]

The President had come to distrust Calhoun thoroughly and to believe that he compassed a dissolution of the Union. This opinion of the Senator is made very clear in the report of a conversation held with Representative Stanton, of Tennessee, who approved the address to southern states. After urging the

---

[69] *Ibid.*. 253–255, 257.   [70] *Ibid.*, 284–288.

admission of California, Polk told Stanton that meetings and addresses would weaken the South and add to the strength of the northern abolitionists. A gathering of members from any section quietly to discuss a political question was proper, but

> I told him that I could not avoid the suspicion that there were two or three individuals, perhaps not more than *one* (but I named no one [Calhoun?]) who desired to have no set[t]lement of the question, but who preferred a sectional excitement in the South & a dissolution. I set my face against being involved in any such movement. I urged the necessity and importance of going to work in earnest *in Congress,* and not *in caucus,* to settle the question. I told him it was time enough to think of extreme measures when they became inevitable, and that that period had not come. I told him that the people everywhere were devoted to the Union, and that it would be a heavy responsibility if Southern members of Congress should prevent an adjustment of the slavery question by meeting *in caucus* & publishing addresses, instead of meeting *in Congress,* where their constituents had deputed them to act. He seemed surprised at these views. I told him I was a Southern man, and as much attached to Southern rights as any man in Congress, but I was in favor of vindicating and maintaining these rights by constitutional means; and that no such extreme case had arisen as would justify a resort to any other means; that when such a case should arise (if ever) it would be time enough to consider what should be done.[71]

Hopes and fears alternated in the President's mind as daily reports came to him of the debates in Congress on the admission of California. At a cabinet meeting held on January 20 letters received from Commodore Jones, Consul Larkin, and Paymaster Rich were read and discussed. Each reported that, on account of the gold rush, veritable anarchy prevailed and some form of government should be established at once. Polk directed that these letters be published in the *Union* in the hope that they might influence Congress to pass the California bill. He feared, however, that no bill could pass which did not include the Wilmot proviso; and he felt bound to veto any measure which prohibited

---

[71] *Ibid.,* 289–291. Polk was not alone in believing that Calhoun wished to disrupt the Union. "It is thought here," wrote Horace Mann, "by many of the most intelligent men, that Mr. Calhoun is resolved on a dissolution of the Union" (Mann, *Life of Horace Mann,* 273).

slavery south of 36° 30′. He desired the immediate admission of California and thought that no southern man ought to object to its admission, but he feared that southern extremists led by Calhoun and northern extremists led by Hale and Giddings would prevent an amicable settlement of the question. "I stated" to the cabinet, was his comment, "that I put my face alike against southern agitators and Northern fanatics, & should do everything in my power to allay excitement by adjusting the question of slavery & preserving the Union." Once more he exhorted his cabinet advisors to use their influence with members of Congress. His efforts failed to prevent the caucus from adopting Calhoun's address to the southern states, and he apprehended further excitement as a result of this proceeding.[72]

The southern Whigs were not ready for extreme measures. This fact was shown by their support of an address presented by Berrien at the southern caucus as a substitute for the one drawn by Calhoun. On January 22 Tooms told Crittenden that California could never be a "slave country" and that it ought to be admitted as a state. "We have," he wrote, "only the point of honor to serve, and this will serve it and rescue that country from all danger of agitation."[73] Even some of the extreme advocates of the "peculiar institution" had little hope of installing it in the new domain. For example, the Mobile *Tribune* said that nothing could save the territories from becoming free states. If necessary, it was prepared to defend by extreme measures "our abstract right to a participation in them," yet it believed that "the victory would be barren."[74]

In order to facilitate matters and to avoid certain technical difficulties, the Senate referred the California question to a select committee of which Douglas was made chairman. On January 29 he reported a bill by which California was to be

---

[72] Polk, *Diary*, IV, 296–299, 306.

[73] Coleman, *Life of John J. Crittenden*, I, 335.

[74] Quoted in *Niles' Reg.*, LXXV, 75.

admitted as a state and New Mexico given a territorial government. In the evening he called to tell the President that he had
strong hopes of its passage. During the next few days Polk
conversed with various southern members and advised them to
support the bill, for, as he told them, this was the only way to
allay "geographical excitement" on the subject of slavery.[75]
However, northern members attacked certain paragraphs in the
bill which purposed to extend laws of the United States to the
proposed state and territory. They charged that the committee
was attempting to introduce slavery into these communities by
a jugglery of words.

The end of the session was approaching and those who did
not approve the Douglas bill endeavored to prevent debate upon
it by urging the necessity of considering the general appropriation bill. In this they were outgeneraled by Walker, a "dough
face" from Wisconsin, who, after consultation with Foote, of
Mississippi, offered an amendment which joined the territorial
government bill, as a rider, to the appropriation bill. By this
amendment the Constitution of the United States and certain
specified laws were extended to the territories, and the President
was given wide discretion in selecting the laws and regulations
to be enforced.[76] The introduction of the Walker amendment
gave rise to an animated debate on constitutional points, and
Webster and Calhoun took leading parts. It is unnecessary here
to follow this debate, yet it may be said that northern members
considered the amendment to be an instrument for smuggling
slavery into the territories through executive action and judicial
interpretation. Their charges to this effect had more real foundation than those of similar purport already brought against the
Douglas bill. There was a momentary excitement among Democrats due to a rumor that Free Soilers and Whigs had planned
to attach the Wilmot proviso to the Walker amendment and

---

[75] *Cong. Globe,* 30 Cong., 2 sess., 381. Polk, *Diary,* IV, 312–313, 316.
[76] *Cong. Globe,* 30 Cong., 2 sess., 561.

thereby to force the President either to accept the proviso or to veto the entire appropriation bill. When informed of this rumor by Venable, of North Carolina, Polk announced that he would veto an application of the proviso to territory south of 36° 30′, no matter in what form it might be presented to him. In a slightly altered form, the Walker amendment was passed by a bare majority of the Senate on February 26; on the following day, by a vote of 126 to 87, the House passed its own bill by which slavery was excluded from the territories.

Only a few more days of the session remained and nothing short of a miracle seemed likely to break the deadlock of the two houses; and unless some adjustment could be made the government would be left without funds. On March 2 the House rejected the Walker amendment, and on the next day—the last of the session—a conference committee of the two houses reported its inability to agree upon any plan of settlement. The appropriation bill would now be lost unless the Senate should consent to eliminate the Walker amendment. Officially, the session expired at twelve o'clock on March 3, but the Senate indulged in a heated debate—even fist-fights[77]—until daybreak on March 4 without coming to an agreement. Hunter, of Virginia, was ready to let the government go without funds rather than sacrifice southern rights, while Douglas believed a government for California to be more important than either.

Polk had come to the capitol armed with a message with which he intended to veto the Wilmot proviso if it should be attached to the Walker amendment. Late at night he was told that the House had voted to amend the Walker amendment by a provision which declared the laws of Mexico to be in force until altered by Congress. The effect of this provision, as Polk at once saw, would be to sanction the law by which Mexico had abolished slavery. Buchanan, Walker, Marcy, and Toucy advised him to sign the bill if it should be presented in this

[77] Mann, *Life of Horace Mann*, 277.

form. "They drew a distinction, which I did not perceive," wrote the President, "between the amendment in this form and the Wilmot Proviso." Mason, on the contrary, advised him to veto the bill, while Johnson thought that he had no right to take any action, since his term of office had expired. Members of Congress came to the President in excitement and asked him to veto any bill containing the House provision. After telling them that he had already decided to do so he began to alter his veto message so as to meet the new situation. "It was a moment of high responsibility," says the *Diary*, "perhaps the highest of my official term. I felt the weight most sensibly, but resolved to pursue the dictates of my own best judgement and to do my duty." About four o'clock in the morning he retired to his hotel, and two hours later he was aroused by a committee from the two houses of Congress. Having reported that both the Walker amendment and the House provision had been eliminated, the committee presented for his signature a simple appropriation bill and another for extending federal revenue laws over California. He signed these, although he had some doubt that he was still President of the United States; the appropriations were saved, but California and New Mexico were still without governments.[78]

As a believer in territorial expansion, if for no other reason, Polk was sorely disappointed because Congress had not given governments to these territories, for apparently he fully believed that the Whigs would acquiesce in their separation from the United States. He had some reason for this belief, although it is evident that he attached too much importance to statements made by certain members of this party. For example, when he asked Senator Clarke, of Rhode Island, to save California to the Union by supporting the bill for admitting her as a state, the Senator replied with indifference: "Let her go." In the House, Alexander H. Stephens tried to block the payments to Mexico for

---

[78] Polk, *Diary*, IV, 362–369. *Cong. Globe*, 30 Cong., 2 sess., 682–698.

the territories, and when Buchanan remonstrated with him he answered that he was opposed to retaining those lands.[79] Polk was disposed to accept these utterances as indicative of the Whig policy because, as he said, the "Federalists" had always been averse to expansion. As if to cap the climax, Taylor, as the two men rode together in the inaugural procession, stated his belief that Oregon and Califonia were too far distant to become members of the Union and that it would be better for them to form an independent government of their own. Doubtless Polk was not surprised to hear these remarks from the Whig leader, nevertheless he thought that they were "alarming opinions to be entertained by the President of the U. S." and he hoped that they had not been well considered.

Gen'l Taylor is, I have no doubt, a well meaning old man. He is, however, exceedingly ignorant of public affairs, and, I should judge, of very ordinary capacity. He will be in the hands of others, and must rely wholly upon his Cabinet to administer the Government.[80]

Such was his opinion of a successor whom he had never met until a few days before this. He did not foresee that Taylor would develop very decided views on the territorial question and that he would, in effect, adopt Polk's own latest policy of having both California and New Mexico admitted as states.

---

[79] Polk, *Diary*, IV, 294, 300.

[80] *Ibid.*, 375–376. Taylor's attitude toward California was not new. He had opposed the acquisition of this country while he was fighting in Mexico (Taylor to Wood, Aug. 23, 1846, *Taylor Letters*, 49).

CHAPTER XXIII

TARIFF, INTERNAL IMPROVEMENTS, AND THE INDEPENDENT TREASURY

Throughout his political career Polk had been a consistent opponent of protective tariff, and of internal improvements undertaken by the federal government. He believed the so-called "American System" to be decidedly un-American—a breeder of extravagance and a menace to the constitutional rights of the states. Entering Congress at the same time that John Quincy Adams became President, he took a vigorous stand against that administration, particularly against its advocacy of internal improvements. His views on this subject, as well as on others, accorded with those of General Jackson with whom he maintained an intimate correspondence.[1]

In his first annual message, Jackson stated his opinions concerning both tariff and internal improvements. He regretted that nations did not, by common consent, see fit to abolish all trade restrictions; as they did not, he was in favor of adjusting the tariff in a "manner best calculated to avoid serious injury and to harmonize the conflicting interests of our agriculture, our commerce, and our manufactures." He urged that the public debt be extinguished at the earliest possible date and that all revenue not otherwise needed be applied to this purpose. As there seemed likely to be a permanent surplus revenue after the national debt had been paid he was in favor of distributing this among the states, since internal improvements undertaken by

---

[1] In a letter to Polk, Jackson, after expressing friendship for and approval of Polk, stated that "I am sure the general government has no right to make internal improvements within a state, without its consent first had & obtained" (Jackson to Polk, Dec. 4, 1826, *Polk Papers*).

the federal government were considered to be both inexpedient and unconstitutional. All loyal adherents of the President accepted this announcement as the party program.

Polk's utterances in Congress at this time were in full accord with Jackson's message. On December 30, when the House was discussing the expediency of distributing among the states the proceeds from the sale of public lands, he opposed such a distribution as premature, since the public debt had not yet been paid. After it had been paid, he favored distributing the surplus among the states rather than have Congress spend it on public improvements.[2] When discussing the Maysville road bill, which Jackson vetoed later, Polk expressed himself as "opposed altogether to this system of appropriations for sectional purposes." He "conceived these applications to be most pernicious in their tendencies, and unconstitutional in principle." The country, he said, "looked to the present Executive for the adoption of a system of economy and retrenchment," a system entirely out of harmony with the purposes of this bill. During the same session a proposal to allow a drawback on rum made from imported molasses gave him a chance to assert that he was "upon principle opposed to the whole system of the protecting policy called tariff."[3]

Always an advocate of strict economy, Polk, while a member of congress, did not hesitate to apply this rule to small as well as to large expenditures. At the risk of being considered "ungracious" he opposed, in 1831, a resolution for giving thirty cords of wood to the suffering poor of Georgetown. The fact that Congress was the legislature of the District of Columbia did not, in his opinion, entitle it to give the national revenue to the inhabitants. Should it adopt such a practice "the poor of the other sections of the country had nothing to do but to come and sit down here, in this District, and apply to Congress for relief." The resolution was passed, but a year later he succeeded in

<hr>

[2] *Abridg. of Deb.*, X, 594.   [3] *Ibid.*, 677–678, XI, 67.

defeating a semi-philanthropic project to pay forty thousand dollars to certain persons for giving instruction in silk culture. It was absurd, said he, to appropriate public money for such purposes.[4]

In 1832 Polk was made chairman of the Committee of Ways and Means. In this position his most difficult task was the management of Jackson's war on the bank, but he had also to supervise all questions of finance. His attempts to enforce economy very naturally led his opponents to charge him with arbitrary conduct. In 1834 Adams accused him of attempting to force the general appropriation bill through without adequate discussion, while Lincoln, of Massachusetts, charged him with trying to starve the opposition into submission.[5] Criticism did not deter him; he persisted in his opposition to unnecessary appropriations and in many cases was able to carry his point. For example, he advocated, and successfully carried, a reduction in the appropriation for the Cumberland road from $652,00 to $300,000.[6] This was a triumph for economy, and a damper on internal improvements as well.

As early as 1832 Clay became interested in a scheme to distribute among the states the proceeds from the sale of public lands. Successive bills to effect his purpose met with disaster— one by the President's veto—and during the session of 1835-1836 another distribution bill was introduced. It passed the Senate and was brought up in the House on June 7, 1836. A motion made to refer it to the Committee of the Whole for discussion received a vote of 97 to 96. Polk, who was then Speaker of the House, added his vote to the minority and prevented a

---

[4] *Ibid.*, XI, 306–307, 691–693.

[5] "The chairman of the Committee of Ways and Means," said Lincoln on April 25, 1834, "came into this House when we had got only to the 45th line of this bill, with the declaration that he was determined to press this bill through before the House adjourned. We were in consequence kept here eight or nine hours without refreshment, and exhausted by the fruitless efforts of the honorable chairman to accomplish his purpose."

[6] *Cong. Globe*, 23 Cong., 1 sess., 340, 347, 461.

reference to the committee.[7] This particular measure was laid on the table. Another bill was introduced in the House which, instead of giving the surplus to the states, proposed to "deposit" it with them subject to recall. It passed both houses in this form, and while everybody knew that in all probability the money would never be recalled, the modification satisfied Jackson's scruples sufficiently to enable him to affix his signature. The money was to be deposited in four installments, beginning on January 1, 1837.

The panic of 1837 which paralyzed all business activities soon after Van Buren's inauguration transformed the surplus into a deficit and created a demand for legislation to replenish and to safeguard the national treasury. The Whigs very naturally advocated a restoration of the Bank of the United States, but the Democrats, quite as naturally, could not think of rehabilitating the "monster" which they had so recently and so thoroughly crushed. Neither could the latter party rely any longer on "pet banks," for these too had gone down in the general crash.

On May 15 Van Buren issued his proclamation, summoning Congress to meet in extra session on the first Monday in September. It convened on the appointed day and, on the first ballot, Polk was reëlected Speaker over his Whig rival, John Bell. In the message which was submitted on September 5 the President, after calling attention to the financial distress of the nation, recommended legislation designed to separate government finances from all banks and to make the government the custodian of its own funds. The plan which he proposed was known officially as the "independent treasury," but it was more frequently called the "sub-treasury." Despite the vociferation against the continuance of the policy inaugurated by Jackson's "specie circular," the President boldly insisted that government finances

---

[7] This was a power of which a Speaker "rarely, if ever, avails himself," said the *National Intelligencer*, June 9, 1836, in criticizing his act.

should be conducted on a hard money basis. Nearly a month before this message was submitted to Congress, General Jackson learned of the recommendations which Van Buren intended to make, and his approval is thus expresesd in a letter written to Polk:

> I have rec'd lately some very pleasant information from the city—all is harmony and the object of the Executive is, or will be, to separate the Government from all Banks—collect & disburse the revenues by its own agents,—receipts of all public dues in gold & silver coin, leaving the Banks & the commercial community to manage their transactions in their own way.[8]

Polk, like Jackson, approved the sub-treasury plan; on the other hand, it met with opposition even among Democrats in Tennessee.[9] Judge Catron believed that the government should be the custodian of its own money, for, "I care not what private Banks you put it into, it will convert the keepers into Federalists in principle & practice in a few years";[10] but his solution of the financial depression was a large emission of paper money. In the letter just quoted, he stated that a "Treasury circulation must be adopted," and, after reading Van Buren's message, he pronounced the President's recommendations "sound in principle, but hardly possible in practice." The people, said he, are governed by habit and want paper money. They would not be able to understand Van Buren's plan, and the "party will go down with it." A few weeks later he urged Polk to

---

[8] Jackson to Polk, Aug. 6, 1837, *Polk Papers*.

[9] In a letter, August 7, informing Polk of his overwhelming defeat in his race for Congress, W. C. Dunlap stated that every candidate for the state legislature favored some kind of a federal bank. James Walker in a letter to Polk, August 27, stated that should the administration adopt the sub-treasury plan it would find itself in a minority in Tennessee (both letters in *Polk Papers*).

[10] "The treasury," he continued, "dare not pass from the majority, without power passing with it—the Treasury is the arm of power, as much in this Gov't as in any on Earth; the placing it in private hands, is to raise up a rival power in the place of the popular will—of numbers, which will govern in fact, in Congress, & out of it, by sops."

Strike boldly—it is your habit, & the means of your elevation; it is expected of you. Go for 30 or 40 millions, to be circulated fast as may be by the Govt—go for 20ties & over in gradations of tens. Strike out the interest feature—boldly declare that the farmers will hoard the notes bearing 5 per cent.[11]

Polk did not adopt Catron's advice to strike out boldly for paper money. He agreed with Jackson and Van Buren in supporting a hard money policy, although his position as Speaker prevented him from taking an active part in the House debates. At its session of 1837–38 the Tennessee legislature instructed her United States Senators to vote against the sub-treasury bill; and Cave Johnson reported that although he was heartily in favor of the measure, the people did not understand the new financial plan and consequently were opposed to it.[12]

At the extra session of Congress a bill to create an independent treasury was introduced by Silas Wright, a close friend of the President; it passed that body by a small majority, despite the vigorous opposition of both Webster and Clay. In the House it was laid on the table by the combined votes of Whigs and conservatives. Nothing was done to relieve the financial situation except to postpone payment of the fourth installment under the distribution act and to authorize the emission of $10,000,000 in treasury notes to meet the present emergency. Van Buren renewed his recommendation, and at both regular sessions of the twenty-fifth Congress an independent treasury bill was introduced, but each time the plan was rejected. Not even a letter from "Old Hickory" in which he admitted the iniquity of the "pet banks" that he had selected as repositories and commended Van Buren's plan, had weight enough to influence the vote.[13]

With this Congress Polk closed his career as a legislator. He was fully in sympathy with the financial policy of the administration although, as he said in his farewell address, "a sense of

---

[11] Catron to Polk, Sept. 2, Sept. 10, Sept. 27, 1837, *Polk Papers.*

[12] James Walker to Polk, Jan. 25, 1838; Cave Johnson to Polk, March 25, 1838, *Polk Papers.*

[13] Jackson to Moses Dawson, Dec. 17, 1837 (*Niles' Reg.*, LIII, 314–315).

propriety" had precluded him from taking part in the debates. The fact that he had once supported Jackson's state bank policy and now favored a divorce from all banks subjected him to severe criticism from opposition members of the House. Williams, of Tennessee, quoted a speech made by Polk during the session of 1834–35 as the best argument that could be made in favor of employing state banks and against such a fiscal agent as the independent treasury.[14] After Polk had left Congress to become governor of Tennessee the independent treasury bill (but not under that name) passed both houses of the twenty-sixth Congress, only to be repealed by the victorious Whigs at the first session of the Harrison-Tyler administration.

We have noted elsewhere that Polk's "Address to the People" by which he opened his canvass for the governorship of Tennessee dealt principally with national issues. It was an able state paper[15] and, among other things, expressed his views on the "American System" and the independent treasury. One result of protective tariff, he said,

was to take the property of one man and give it to another, without right or consideration. It was to depreciate the value of the productive industry of one section of the Union and transfer it to another—it was to make the rich richer and the poor poorer.

Another result of protection was the accumulation of unnecessary funds in the national treasury, and means had to be devised to get rid of the money without lowering the tariff. "This plan was soon found in an unconstitutional and gigantic system of internal improvements," and these were parceled out among communities where the tariff politicians hoped to get votes.

---

[14] "But all must now be abandoned," said Williams, "for the sub-Treasury scheme, even at the expense of a political somerset. What, Mr. Chairman, is this much-talked-of Sub-Treasury bill? It is simply to substitute individuals in the place of banks as the fiscal agents of the Government. I propose to adopt as my own Mr. Polk's speech, delivered at the session of 1834–5, against this change. It is an excellent argument; I cannot better it; let it speak for itself" (*Cong. Globe* (Feb. 22, 1839), 25 Cong., 3 sess., App., 372).

[15] See page 143 and note.

The assumption and exercise of the power, by Federal authority, to construct works of internal improvement within the States, constituted an essential branch of the system of which Mr. Clay was the reputed father and head, and to which the popular but false name of the ''American System'' was given. It was an essential branch of the falsely called ''American System,'' because it was the great absorbent, the sponge which was to suck in and consume the excessive, unequal, unjust and oppressive exactions upon the people, and especially upon the people of the planting States, levied by a high protective tariff. High, unnecessary and oppressive taxes, levied by a high protective tariff—lavish and wasteful expenditures of the surplus money, by a gigantic system of internal improvement, and high prices of public lands, that emigration to the west might be checked—the laboring poor retained in the manufacturing districts, in a state of dependence on their richer neighbors in whose employment they were, constituted Mr. Clay's far famed and miscalled ''American System.''

The United States Bank, said he, was closely allied to the American System. By use of it ''Federalism'' saw the means, under another party name, to accomplish the ''dangerous purposes'' of Alexander Hamilton—''extending the power and patronage of the General Government, [and] corrupting the sources of Legislation.'' Banks, both federal and state, had ''proved to be faithless fiscal agents,'' and therefore he now advocated the adoption by law of the independent treasury plan.[16]

With the bank controversy of the Tyler administration which followed the repeal of the independent treasury act, Polk had nothing to do. His friend Catron still retained his belief in the virtue of paper money and thought that the Democratic party could regain control if it would take a stand in favor of some sort of a bank—something like the one proposed by Tyler, which would issue paper currency. The party, said he, could not hope to win by simply ''offering nothing,'' and the sub-treasury had always been ''an absurd shadow''; in addition, ''the hard money plan is a theory—& deemed a feeble & exploded theory, by the people.''[17] Uninfluenced by Catron's arguments, Polk held

---

16 Copy in pamphlet form in *Polk Papers.*
17 Catron to Polk, Jan. 2, 1842, *Polk Papers.*

fast to his orthodox opinions. This fact is evidenced by his reply to a series of questions propounded by a group of persons in Memphis during his campaign for governor in 1843. He was in favor, he told them, of a sub-treasury and of metal money, although he did not object to a limited amount of paper currency if issued by state banks. He was in favor, also, of a "moderate tariff," but for revenue purposes only.[18]

The Democratic platform of 1844 said nothing about tariff, except to reaffirm the very general plank in the platform of 1840; nevertheless this subject formed one of the issues of the campaign. The compromise tariff arranged by Clay and Calhoun in 1833 as a settlement of the nullification trouble provided for biennial reductions until 1842, after which it was to remain at a uniform rate of 20 per cent. In 1842, however, just as this rate was about to go into operation, a new act was passed which abandoned the Democratic revenue basis and fixed the rates in accordance with the Whig policy of protection. In addition to protective tariff, the Whigs desired to enact Clay's pet measure of distributing among the states the money derived from the sale of public lands, but Tyler blocked this by insisting upon retaining the so-called safety-valve proviso which had been incorporated into the distribution law passed during the extra session of 1841.[19] It was well known that a revival of the policy of distribution and internal improvements would follow Whig success in 1844, consequently the Democrats, in the Baltimore platform, declared distribution to be both inexpedient and unconstitutional and reaffirmed the declaration of 1840 against internal improvements.

Absence of any new tariff plank in the Democratic platform made it desirable for the candidate, Polk, to declare his views on the subject, and such a declaration was made in the "Kane letter" of June 19, 1844. As noted elsewhere, he expressed his

---

18 Reply dated May 15, 1843. Printed in Nashville *Union,* June 2, 1843.
19 This safety-valve provided that distribution should cease whenever the rate should be raised above 20 per cent.

belief in revenue tariff, sufficient "to defray the expenses of the Government economically administered." In adjusting it, he believed in shaping the revenue laws so as to afford just protection to the interests of the whole Union, "embracing agriculture, manufactures, the mechanic arts, commerce and navigation." In other words, he adhered to the historic doctrines of his party—tariff for revenue, with incidental protection. To be sure, Cameron and others may have tortured this letter into a promise of protective tariff in order to delude Pennsylvanians and other tariff Democrats, but nothing in the Kane letter itself warranted such a construction.

In his inaugural address President Polk reiterated his well-known views on the tariff. After quoting from his "Kane letter" he stated that, when levying duties, revenue should be the object and protection the incident:

To reverse this principle and make *protection* the *object* and *revenue* the *incident* would be to inflict manifest injustice upon all other than protected interests. In levying duties for revenue it is doubtless proper to make such discriminations within the *revenue principle* as will afford incidental protection to our home interests. Within the revenue limit there is a discretion to discriminate; beyond that limit the rightful exercise of the power is not conceded.

Soon after he had taken the oath of office, he announced to George Bancroft "the four great measures" of his administration: first on the list came the reduction of the tariff; and second, the reëstablishment of the independent treasury.[20] Since Congress does not convene until December, his attention was first of all directed to foreign affairs; he did not, however, lose interest in these party measures, even in the midst of foreign complications.

As early as October the President began to draft the part of his annual message relating to the tariff and the "Constitutional Treasury" as he preferred to designate what others called the independent or sub-treasury. His draft when submitted to

---

[20] See Schouler, *History of the United States*, IV, 498.

the cabinet was approved by all except Buchanan. The Secretary of State approved the recommendation to abolish the "minimum principle" and, in general, that of substituting ad valorem for specific duties, but thought that specific duties should be retained on certain articles such as iron, coal, and sugar.[21] Polk agreed to consider Buchanan's suggestions, but eventually he decided not to follow them.

As submitted to Congress on December 2, 1845, the message invited the attention of that body to "the importance of making suitable modifications and reductions" in the existing tariff rates. All duties, he said, should be kept within a "revenue standard," consequently it was necessary to understand distinctly what was meant by that term. By specific illustrations he showed that revenue diminished or ceased after a certain rate had been reached, and the point at which it began to diminish was the maximum limit of the revenue standard. No rate should go beyond this point, and all duties within the revenue standard should be no higher than the expenses of the government should make necessary. Rates need not be uniform, for discrimination within the revenue standard was permissible, but such discrimination must be for the general welfare and not in favor of a particular industry or section.

The tariff of 1842, he told Congress, violated the cardinal principles which he had laid down, because its object had been "protection merely" and not revenue. Its use of "minimums, or assumed and false values" and the imposition of specific duties had benefitted the rich and worked injustice to the poor. Such abuses should be remedied, and

I recommend to Congress the abolition of the minimum principle, or assumed, arbitrary, and false values, and of specific duties, and the substitution in their place of *ad valorem* duties as the fairest and most equitable indirect tax which can be imposed. By the *ad valorem* principle all articles are taxed according to their cost or value, and those which are of inferior quality or of small cost bear only the just proportion of the

---

21 Polk, *Diary*, I, 85.

tax with those which are of superior quality or greater cost. The articles consumed by all are taxed at the same rate. A system of *ad valorem* revenue duties, with proper discriminations and proper guards against frauds in collecting them, it is not doubted will afford ample incidental advantages to the manufacturers and enable them to derive as great profits as can be derived from any other regular business. It is believed that such a system strictly within the revenue standard will place the manufacturing interests on a stable footing and inure to their permanent advantage, while it will as nearly as may be practicable extend to all the great interests of the country the incidental protection which can be afforded by our revenue laws. Such a system, when once firmly established, would be permanent, and not be subject to the constant complaints, agitations, and changes which must ever occur when duties are not laid for revenue, but for the "protection merely" of a favored interest.

Attention was next directed to safe-guarding the government funds after they had been collected. Banks, both national and state, had, in his opinion, proved to be unworthy custodians; besides the framers of the Constitution never intended that the funds of the nation should be turned over to private corporations to be used by them for profit and speculation. Believing that government moneys should be completely separated from banking institutions, he recommended that "provision be made by law for such separation, and that a constitutional treasury be created for the safe-keeping of the public money." The money of the people should be kept in the treasury of the people in the custody of agents directly responsible to the government:

> To say that the people or their Government are incompetent or not to be trusted with the custody of their own money in their own Treasury, provided by themselves, but must rely on the presidents, cashiers, and stockholders of banking corporations, not appointed by them nor responsible to them, would be to concede that they are incapable of self-government.[22]

These two recommendations—for a revenue tariff and for a constitutional treasury—formed the keynote of Polk's domestic policy. He may have been less brilliant than his illustrious opponent, but few will now deny that he held sounder views on

---

[22] Richardson, *Messages*, IV, 406–408.

the industrial and the financial needs of the country. His policy was simple and economically sound; and because, under it, the business of the country was, so far as possible, to be left free to seek its natural channels, little positive legislation was required. Clay, on the other hand, like Hamilton, reveled in thaumaturgy and legerdemain. His system of a government bank, protective duties, and the collection of revenue to be distributed among the states, was highly artificial; and even if they were not unconstitutional, surely Polk was right in saying that they had never been contemplated by the framers of that document.

So far as his own party was concerned the message was well received. Cass told the President that in the part relating to tariff "You have struck out the true doctrine, you have cut the Gordian Knot." His tariff policy was, of course, highly acceptable to southern Democrats, and many of them called to express their approbation. "We Pennsylvanians," Cameron told him, "may scratch a little about the tariff but we will not quarrel about it"; Wilmot, on the other hand, remarked that "the doctrines on the tariff were the true doctrines & he would support them."[23] It was rumored that Secretary Walker had written the paragraphs relating to the tariff, but Polk asserted indignantly that "the tariff part of the message and every other part of it is my own."[24]

Without waiting to see whether the Van Buren independent treasury would prove to be a success or a failure the triumphant Whigs abolished it in 1841, but, much to their discomfiture, Tyler blocked the reëstablishment of the United States bank. After the election of 1844 the Democrats carried through the House a bill to revive the independent treasury, but as it failed in the Senate the whole financial question went over to the Polk administration. The new President, as we have seen, made it one of his leading measures and recommended the establishment

---

[23] Polk, *Diary*, I, 109–110. Cameron, despite his remark, opposed the tariff bill when it came before the Senate.

[24] *Ibid.*, 124.

of a "constitutional treasury" which was simply another name for the independent treasury. In following his advice it can not be said that Congress actually created anything; all that was asked and all that was done was to authorize the executive to collect the government revenues in gold and silver, and to deposit them in the treasury vaults until disbursed in the course of ordinary business transactions. Congress simply made the government the custodian of its own funds instead of having them deposited in banks.[25] When, therefore, on March 30, 1846, Dromgoole, of Virginia, presented the bill which had been prepared by the Committee of Ways and Means, the title merely authorized the building of fireproof vaults for the safekeeping of public money, which vaults were formally declared to be the "Treasury of the United States."[26] The requirement that metal money alone should be received by the government was added later in the form of an amendment.

Caleb Smith, of Indiana, at once opened the attack upon the bill and offered an amendment, the gist of which was to authorize the Secretary of the Treasury to deposit government funds in "any bank or banks which he may deem expedient, and also to receive the Government dues in the paper of specie-paying banks." As this amendment would nullify the main purpose of the proposed law there was, of course, no prospect that it would be adopted. It served, however, to make the issue definite, to align on the one side those who believed in a government treasury and hard money, and on the other, the friends of banks and bank currency.

---

[25] The same may be said of the Van Buren independent treasury.

[26] "*Be it enacted &c.*, That the rooms prepared and provided in the new treasury building at the seat of Government for the use of the Treasurer of the United States . . . and also the fireproof vaults and safes erected in said rooms for the keeping of the public moneys in the possession, and under the immediate control of said Treasurer of the United States; and the said Treasurer of the United States shall keep the public moneys which shall come into his hands in the Treasury of the United States as hereby constituted, until the same shall be drawn therefrom according to law" (*Cong. Globe,* 29 Cong., 1 sess., 574).

Smith's arguments in opposition to the independent treasury were not very convincing. He stated, erroneously, that the Democrats had not made the subject an issue in the recent election; that Polk and other Democrats had once favored state banks; and that the Van Buren measure was a "miserable humbug" which had never really been carried into effect. On the other hand, Grider, of Kentucky, asserted that the sole purpose of introducing the bill was to redeem party pledges, for he was certain that many Democrats did not approve of "reckless financial experiments." J. R. Ingersoll, of Pennsylvania, saw nothing in the measure "to commend it to respect"; besides, everything contained in the bill was already covered by the law of 1789 which had created the Treasury Department. In general the arguments against the bill were so lacking in force— and frequently in pertinence—that Daniel, of North Carolina, had good reason for concluding that the Whigs themselves had "the internal conviction" that much good would result from its passage.

The Democrats had small need for arguments, as they were certain that they could command the requisite number of votes. They maintained with justice that a fiscal agent was superfluous, and that the government was most competent to protect and disburse its own funds. They ridiculed the assertion that the measure was a device to draw all metal money into the coffers of the government, leaving the people with nothing but "rag money." Dromgoole, who made the principal argument for the bill, denied the charge of discriminating against banks, for, as he said, they had no legitimate claim to the use of public money. On April 2, after Dromgoole had added an amendment which required payments to the government to be made in gold and silver, the bill passed the House by an overwhelming majority.[27]

On the following day the bill was received by the Senate and referred to the Committee on Finance. Nothing more was

---

[27] 122 to 66 (*Cong. Globe*, 29 Cong., 1 sess., 595).

heard of it until the twenty-second of April. On that date Webster asked the chairman, Dixon H. Lewis, when it was likely to be reported to the Senate and whether the committee had settled upon any amendments. In response to this inquiry Lewis stated that it was the intention of the committee to give precedence to bills relating to warehousing and mints. This apparent indifference to immediate action on one of the "leading" administration measures did not escape the watchful eye of the President. He sent for Lewis and urged him to give precedence to this and the tariff bill, as postponement might endanger their passage.

> I then told him [said he] that I had great anxiety for the passage of the Constitutional Treasury Bill and the reduction of the Tariff, which I had recommended in my annual message. I told him that I considered them as administration measures and that I intended to urge them upon Congress as such, and that I considered the public good, as well as my own power and the glory of my administration, depended in a great degree upon my success in carrying them through Congress.

Lewis was an ardent supporter of Calhoun, and the President embraced the opportunity to read him a lecture on the way southern men were jeopardizing important measures by petty opposition to the confirmation of northern appointments. Northern Senators, he said, had ratified appointments of southern men, and there was no good reason why southern Senators should not reciprocate. To Lewis's complaint that Colhoun and his friends had been turned out of office, Polk replied that he had made his appointments without reference to any aspirant for the Presidency. Being "the first President who had taken bold ground and fully satisfied the South on the tariff," he thought men from that section ought "to cease their opposition upon these small matters in which no principle was involved, for the sake of enabling me to carry out the great measure which involved principle."[28]

---

[28] Polk, *Diary*, I, 367–371. Polk believed that northern men attached more importance to appointments than southern men did. "I reminded him that Mr. Jefferson's plan was to conciliate the North by the dispensation of his patronage, and to rely on the South to support his principles for the sake of these principles."

Despite the President's anxiety the bill was held by the committee until the eighth of June. Lewis then reported it to the Senate with sundry amendments, the most important of which postponed for six months the operation of the specie clause. After another period of slumber the measure was brought up for consideration, and, after three days of debate, it was passed by a small majority on August 1, the day after the President had signed the tariff bill. The House concurred in the Senate amendments, and the constitutional treasury bill became the law of the land.

As early as January 9, 1846, the erratic McConnell, of Alabama, asked leave to introduce a "bill to repeal the tariff of 1842, with all its iniquities," but not until April 14 did McKay, of North Carolina, chairman of the Committee of Ways and Means, report a revenue bill based on recommendations made by the President and the Secretary of the Treasury. Under it, all duties were to be ad valorem. Commodities were grouped in schedules; those in the first group were to pay 100 per cent, others 75, 30, 25, etc., until the free list was reached. It was by no means a free-trade measure, yet it was attacked as such by the advocates of protection. They seemed to regard the tariff of 1842 as something sacred, something which could not be altered without prostrating industry and ruining the country. "We are in one breath told," exclaimed Biggs, of North Carolina, "that if you do not protect the manufacturers they must be prostrated; and in the next you are informed that by your protection you diminish their profits.[29]

Opponents of the measure denounced the ad valorem principle and charged that it was an invitation to commit fraud in valuation. They ridiculed the claim of the administration that a lower tariff would produce more revenue. "We are called on now," said Senator Evans, of Maine,

---

[29] *Cong. Globe*, 29 Cong., 1 sess., 1022. He quoted from Clay (1833) to the effect that "In general it may be taken as a rule, that the duty upon an article forms a portion of its price."

to reduce the rates of duty, not because too much revenue is raised, but because there is too little, and because more can be obtained by a reduction of the rates. Well, sir, I commend the prudence of those who take this view of the subject. Whether they may be able to demonstrate it in a satisfactory manner, is another matter.[30]

Personal abuse of the President was not wanting. Gentry, from his own state, denounced, in the House, what he termed "the great, damnable, and infamous conspiracy" (Kane letter) by which the people of Pennsylvania had been defrauded out of their votes, and by which the men who had perpetrated it had reached the positions they now occupy: these men were "James K. Polk and James Buchanan."[31]

Seaborn Jones, of Georgia, was selected as chief spokesman for the House Committee of Ways and Means, and indirectly, for the administration. All sections of the Union, he contended, would be benefited by a revenue tariff; for it was based on justice and would insure stability for all lines of industry. "Protection," on the other hand, "operates as a hotbed in bringing forth exotics which the soil and climate would not naturally produce"; and the fostering of special industries was not a legitimate function of government.[32] Of northern Democrats, Wilmot, of Pennsylvania, was one of the most enthusiastic supporters of Polk's tariff policy. He branded the tariff of 1842 as the " 'bill of abominations,' in violation of the genius of our institutions, of the provisions of our Constitution, and fatally subversive of the rights and liberties of the people." He favored a "constitutional tariff" such as the one under consideration, one "which would grant equal protection to all, exclusive privileges to none."[33]

On July 3, after divers amendments had been rejected[34] and an attempt to lay the whole question on the table had been

---

30 *Ibid.*, 1090. 31 *Ibid.*, 1047. 32 *Ibid.*, 990–991. 33 *Ibid.*, 1045.

34 While nearly all of the amendments related to adjustments in rates, a few were grotesque. For example, Schenck, of Ohio, wished to insert Polk's Kane letter in the bill, and Stewart, of Pennsylvania, moved to make the title read: "A bill to reduce the duties on the *luxuries* of the

defeated, the House passed the tariff bill and submitted it to the Senate for approval. On learning the good news, Polk recorded in his diary:

I was much gratified to hear the result, as this was one of the leading and vital measures of my administration. It was in truth vastly the most important domestic measure of my administration, and the vote of the popular branch of Congress, which had fully endorsed my opinions and recommendations on the subject of the tariff, could not be otherwise than highly gratifying.[35]

The House bill was taken up by the Senate on July 6, and after two readings by title, Sevier, of Arkansas, moved that it be made a special order. Evans, of Maine, endeavored to have it referred for consideration to the Committee on Finance, but many Democrats contended that such reference would cause unnecessary delay. During the debate Clayton, of Delaware, in an attempt to outmanoeuver the administration forces, moved certain amendments and instructions which would, if followed, compel the committee to consider the whole bill. He was not successful, however, for Dixon H. Lewis, of Alabama, whose "twenty score of flesh"[36] was a host in itself, promptly reported the measure back from the committee with a request to be excused from its consideration.

As chairman of the Committee on Finance, it devolved upon Lewis to lead the debate in favor of the bill. The belief so widely held, said he, that ad valorem duties would fail to produce sufficient revenue was "one of those axiomatic errors which, upon examination, will be found to be wholly fallacious"; even under the tariff of 1842 such duties had produced more than half of the revenue. Hannegan, Bagby, and many other Senators supported the measure; the main arguments urged in its favor were the abolition of the minimum and specific duties, and the readjustment of rates upon a revenue basis.

rich, and increase them on the *necessaries* of the poor; to bankrupt the treasury; strike down American farmers, mechanics, and workingmen; to make way for the products of foreign agriculture and foreign labor . . . etc.''   [35] Polk, *Diary*, II, 11.

[36] Adams, *Memoirs*, XII, 25. Lewis weighed 430 pounds.

Opponents of the tariff bill consumed more time than did its friends. In replying to Lewis, Webster attacked the policy of relying upon ad valorem duties, and he hoped

to show to the Senate and to the country that this bill, so novel, so dangerous, so vicious in its general principles; so ill considered, so rash, and I must say so intemperate in many of its provisions, cannot but produce in the country the most serious and permanent mischief if it should become a law.[37]

"As a friend of the Administration," Niles, of Connecticut, profoundly regretted the introduction of the bill, and "as a friend of the Administration he would vote against it."[38] Of the Democrats, Cameron, of Pennsylvania, was the most aggressive in combating the measure; but his charge that Pennsylvanians had been deceived by the Kane letter came with bad grace from his lips, for if deception had been employed, Cameron himself had been the chief offender. Benton did not approve all features of the bill, yet he declared himself ready to vote for any measure which would rid the country of the tariff of 1842.

The attitude of two members merits special notice, for the Senate was so evenly divided that the fate of the tariff bill rested in their hands. Like other Democrats, Haywood, of North Carolina, wished the tariff to be reduced, but he maintained that the House bill would effect too radical a change. After several attempts to amend the bill had failed, he broke with his party and resigned his seat in the Senate.[39] Although his act was severely condemned by the party press, the President believed him to be sincere and conscientious.[40]

---

[37] *Cong. Globe*, 29 Cong., 1 sess., 1089.   [38] *Ibid.*, 1117.

[39] The reasons which he assigned for his resignation are given in his "Address to the People of North Carolina" (*Cong. Globe*, 29 Cong., 1 sess., App., 1178 ff.).

[40] Polk, *Diary*, II, 48. He thought that the Senator might be piqued because he had not been given a part in framing the bill, yet "I believe him to be an honest and pure man, but a man of great vanity and possessing a good deal of self esteem. . . . I give not the slightest heed to the painful insinuations which I learn this evening are made by illiberal persons as to the motives & causes which have induced his course."

After Haywood's resignation attention centered on Senator Jarnagin, of Tennessee, for with him rested the power to pass or to defeat the "great domestic measure." Jarnagin was not only a Whig and a believer in protective tariff, but in his home state he had been a bitter personal and political opponent of the President. On the other hand, the legislature of Tennessee had instructed him to vote for the administration tariff bill, and it remained to be seen whether he would follow his instructions. On July 25 the President was much perturbed by a report that Jarnagin had threatened to resign; for "should he do so, and Mr. Haywood's successor reach here in time, the tariff bill will be lost by one vote." Polk sent for Senator Turney, who promised to ascertain the intentions of his colleague. Jarnagin agreed to remain in the Senate and to obey his instructions; but Polk was not wholly relieved from anxiety, for Turney informed him that manufacturing interests were attempting to win votes by the use of bribe money and that even he (Turney) had been offered a bribe.[41]

Jarnagin's position was a most unenviable one. Although he thoroughly disapproved the administration bill, his instructions required him to support it. On July 27 he denounced the measure but declared his intention to vote for it; he did not, however, believe that his instructions precluded him from voting for amendments which did not affect its main purpose—the abolishment of the minimum and specific duties. When, therefore, Clayton moved a reference to the Committee on Finance, with instructions to amend, Jarnagin voted with his party. Polk took this to mean that he would break both his pledges and his instructions. "Jarnegan," he observed in his diary, "holds the fate of the Bill in his hands and there [is] no reliance to be placed upon him," and he regretted the folly of Haywood in resigning at such a critical moment.[42] But the President was mistaken, for Jarnagin yielded the "pound of flesh" even though

---

[41] *Ibid.*, 49–50.   [42] *Ibid.*, 51.

he succeeded in making the operation annoying to his opponents. On July 28 he again announced his intention to vote for the administration tariff, but

I shall, when the question comes on the engrossment of the bill, transfer the whole responsibility, as far as I am concerned, to the keeping of the representative of the whole people, and then we will know whether it be a Democratic measure or not.

He meant of course that on incidental questions he would refrain from voting and compel the Vice-President to save the measure by his casting vote; this done, he would obey his instructions and help to pass the bill. He kept his promise,[43] and the bill was passed by a vote of twenty-eight to twenty-seven after an amendment proposed by Webster for guarding against under-valuation had been adopted. Before the final vote was taken Webster predicted that the measure would be repealed at the next session, for "it is as impossible that the sun should go backward and set in the east, as that the people should suffer the principle contained in this bill to prevail."

Even after the Senate had passed the tariff bill the President was pessimistic. He doubted that the House would concur in the Senate amendment. A report that certain Democrats from New York and Pennsylvania would join the Whigs in opposing the amendment gave him "great uneasiness." They did vote with the Whigs on incidental questions, but, due to fear so the President thought, they joined with their own party on the final vote. Polk's gratification found expression in his diary:

This great measure of reform has been thus successful. It has given rise to an immense struggle between the two great political parties of the country. The capitalists & monopolists have not surrendered the immense advantages which they possessed, and the enormous profits which they derived under the tariff of 1842, until after a fierce and mighty struggle.

---

[43] Writing from his post at Naples to his brother, W. H. Polk said that he had trembled when he read that the fate of the tariff bill depended on "the *doubtful honesty* of Spencer Jarnagin." He had up to this time believed that Jarnagin would sell out even if the price were labeled in plain sight; "his rare honesty in this case, is to me wholly inexplicable!" (W. H. Polk to J. K. Polk, Nov. 6, 1846, *Polk Papers*).

This City has swarmed with them for weeks. They have spared no effort within their power to sway and control Congress, but all has proved to be unavailing and they have been at length vanquished. Their effort will probably now be to raise a panic (such as they have already attempted) by means of their combined wealth, so as to induce a repeal of the act.[44]

The President had reason to be gratified with the passage of this important party measure. It not only dealt a severe blow to Clay's "American System," but it put in operation a tariff policy which Polk had advocated ever since he had been in public life. Much to the disappointment of his critics no industrial calamities resulted from it, and the act was not repealed as Webster had so confidently predicted. Despite the scoffing of Evans, reduction of the tariff rates was followed by an increase in the amount of revenue; it became redundant in 1857 and was still further reduced. While it would be absurd to attribute the prosperity of this decade to the operation of the "tariff of '46," no longer could it be said that an ad valorem revenue tariff would block the wheels of industry.

The reëstablishment of the independent treasury gave additional reason for gratification, and, like the tariff bill, it caused none of the disasters which its opponents had prophesied. With few modifications, the "constitutional treasury" has continued to the present day, and it has done much to extricate national revenue from the field of party politics. With the enactment of these two measures and the settlement of the Oregon question Polk had effected three of the four items of his administrative program. There was no longer need of anxiety for the "glory" of his administration, even though Davis had talked the diplomatic appropriation bill to death.

Having faithfully complied with the recommendations contained in the President's message, Congress believed, apparently, that the law of compensation entitled it to a free hand in "pork barrel" legislation. Despite the heavy drain on the treasury for military purposes, items were recklessly added to the river and

---

[44] Polk, *Diary*, II, 54–55.

harbor bill until it called for appropriations amounting to nearly a million and a half dollars. Clay himself could scarcely have asked for a more cordial endorsement of his internal improvement policy, and especially from a Congress controlled by Democrats.

Polk promptly vetoed this bill, and his message to the House is an able statement of the Jeffersonian doctrine of strict construction. In his opinion, the measure under consideration was both unconstitutional and inexpedient, and parts of it "a disreputable scramble for the public money." "It is not questioned," said he,

that the Federal Government is one of limited powers. Its powers are such, and such only, as are expressly granted in the Constitution or are properly incidental to the expressly granted powers and necessary to their execution.

After quoting Madison's rule for determining the scope of implied power, Polk maintained that:

It is not enough that it may be regarded by Congress as *convenient* or that its exercise would advance the public weal. It must be *necessary and proper* to the execution of the principal expressed power to which it is an incident, and without which such principal power can not be carried into effect. The whole frame of the Federal Constitution proves that the Government which it creates was intended to be one of limited and specified powers. A construction of the Constitution so broad as that by which the power in question is defended tends imperceptibly to a consolidation of power in a Government intended by the framers to be thus limited in its authority.

National appropriations, in his opinion, should be confined to national purposes, and Congress ought to refrain from exercising doubtful powers. He censured in particular the present attempt to include purely local items by a jugglery of words. "To call the mouth of a creek or a shallow inlet on our coast a harbor can not confer the authority to expend the public money in its improvement."[45] Although he did not consult the cabinet on the advisability of vetoing this bill, he believed that Buchanan, Marcy, Bancroft, and perhaps Walker, would, if consulted, have

---

[45] Richardson, *Messages*, IV, 460 ff.

advised him to sign it.[46] He declined, also, to sign a bill for making improvements in the territory of Wisconsin, but his veto message was not submitted until the following December.[47]

In the interest of economy and as a check upon political jobbery the President put his veto on a bill to grant five million dollars in land scrip to persons who claimed damages for French spoliations prior to 1800. In his message he pointed out that this question had often been discussed, yet no former Congress had seen fit to pay these claims, even when there had been a surplus in the treasury. Since the United States had never received anything from France for the injuries done he saw no reason for the assumption that our government had become responsible to the claimants for aggressions committed by a foreign power.[48]

As frequently happens at the halfway point of an administration, the autumn elections showed a decrease in Democratic strength. Doubtless the main cause of defection was the unpopularity of the Mexican War; but the Whigs attributed much of it to abhorrence of the ''free trade'' tariff, although that law had not yet become operative. Among others, Governor Wright, of New York, failed in his canvass for reëlection, and administration candidates were defeated in Pennsylvania. With his usual delight in causing the President discomfort, Buchanan attributed these defeats to the reduction of the tariff. Probably he hoped to get some concessions for his friends in Pennsylvania, but instead, Polk told him that he would, in his next message, recommend that no change whatever be made in the law until it had been given a fair trial. Wright's defeat had, in Polk's opinion, been caused by the treachery of the ''Old Hunkers'' who no longer deserved to be called Democrats; ''this faction shall hereafter receive no favours at my hands if I know it.''[49]

46 Polk, *Diary*, II, 58.   47 Richardson, *Messages*, IV, 610 ff.

48 *Ibid.*, 466 ff.

49 Polk, *Diary*, II, 217–218. In a letter to Henry D. Foster, of Pennsylvania, Nov. 19, 1846, Buchanan said that he had always disapproved

When, early in November, the President began the preparation of his second annual message, the war estimates of Marcy were so large that doubts were expressed in the cabinet as to the ability of the government to meet its financial obligations. In accordance with Democratic tradition, financial ills were readily traced to "the money power," and the difficulty in floating a loan was attributed to the machinations of bankers in Boston and New York who were endeavoring to force a repeal of the independent treasury law. The gloomy Secretary of State doubted that the war could be conducted on a hard money basis; and although he had advocated the independent treasury, he was now satisfied that the government could not finance the war under its operation.[50]

In his message the President dealt with financial questions in very general terms. It was too early, he said, to estimate the revenue to be derived from the new tariff law; but by the simultaneous abandonment of the protective policy by England and the United States, commerce had received a "new impulse," while labor and trade "have been released from the artificial trammels which have so long fettered them." The present tariff law had been framed in accordance with sound principles and consequently ought not to be disturbed. In order to meet the extraordinary expenses of the war a revenue duty might well be placed on certain articles now on the free list, but it should be repealed as soon as the needs of the treasury would permit. Walker, in his report, recommended, for the war period, a special duty of twenty-five per cent on tea and coffee, but like the President, he was averse to making changes in the existing tariff law.[51]

---

the tariff of 1846, and he hoped that a modification "will be effected before the Manufacturers & Coal Dealers can be seriously injured" (Buchanan, *Works*, VII, 117).

[50] Polk, *Diary*, II, 221.

[51] Richardson, *Messages*, IV, 498–502. Walker's Report (*H. Ex. Doc. 7*, 29 Cong., 2 sess.). "All experience," said Walker, "is against the protective policy. . . . It is as unwise and unjust as it is repugnant to equal rights and republican principles, to force, by legislation, any class of the community to buy from or sell to another."

The tariff of 1846 remained the source of revenue for the remainder of the administration, for this Congress and its successor steadfastly refused to vote additional war duties. Nevertheless, Walker was able to say in his annual report of December, 1847, even while renewing his request for duties on tea and coffee, that

> It is now proved that a tariff for revenue not only yields a larger income than the protective system, but also advances more rapidly, in a series of years, the prosperity of the manufacturers, by the augmentation of their foreign and domestic market.

In like manner he could truthfully assert that, instead of paralyzing industry as had been predicted, the independent treasury and hard money had benefited those who had so vigorously opposed them:

> Domestic manufactures require for their permanent and successful operation the basis of specie, checking vibrations and inflations of the paper system. . . . If our manufacturers desire great advantages from the home market, it must be abundantly and permanently supplied with a large specie circulation, which alone can sustain that market for a number of years, and prevent those calamities which follow an inflated paper currency. A home market for our manufacturers, when based upon specie and low duties, is solid, permanent, and augmenting; but when founded upon paper credits, it is inflated one year, only to be depressed the next, or some succeeding year—thus depriving the manufacturer of any well-assured and permanent domestic market.[52]

The Whig Congress was not disposed to aid the administration by voting additional war revenue. On the contrary, the President was certain that attempts were being made to create a panic and paralyze public credit.

> The truth is [he observed] that the Whig party and leading presses, having failed to defeat the Government in the prosecution of the war by the ''aid & comfort,'' they have given to Mexico by their unpatriotic sentiments, are now insidiously attempting to produce a panic in the money market and thereby, if possible, to break down the Treasury, and thus compel the inglorious withdrawal of our army from Mexico.[53]

[52] *H. Ex. Doc. 6*, 30 Cong., 1 sess. When he saw the original draft of this report Polk wrote that ''though in the main sound in its doctrines, I thought some parts of it speculative, and perhaps too highly wrought'' (*Diary*, III, 229).

[53] Polk, *Diary*, III, 322.

While this may have been an exaggerated portrayal of Whig machinations, the intemperate abuse of the President for having "deliberately plotted the war" naturally led him to believe that his opponents would resort to any means of crippling his administration.

If Congress could embarrass the President by declining to follow his recommendations, he was equally determined to thwart its attempt to force his hand on the question of internal improvements. Late in July, 1848, the House passed a civil and diplomatic bill which contained, in the form of a rider, an item for money to improve the Savannah River. Polk well knew that the object was to compel him to abandon the principles of his last veto message, or to incur the odium of defeating the entire appropriation. The Senate later eliminated the obnoxious item, but before this had been done Polk outlined in his diary the course which he intended to pursue:

My mind is made up. I will veto the Bill, if it comes to me with this item in it, whatever may be the consequences. I will do so, if it comes on the last night of the session, and if I am over-ruled by two thirds, & Congress should adjourn without passing the Civil Diplomatic [Bill], I will issue my Proclamation conv[en]ing an extra session of Congress for the next day.

He was much depressed by the "want of patriotism" displayed by Whigs and bolting Democrats, both in the matter of appropriations and in their refusal to create governments for the territories. "Whilst I deplore this state of things, all I can do during the remainder of my term is to adhere undeviatingly to my principles & to perform my whole duty. This I will do at any hazard." The present Congress, in his opinion, was as reckless and extravagant as any he had ever known; the success of its improvement schemes would bankrupt the treasury.[54]

The adjournment of Congress did not relieve the President from the schemes of improvement promoters, for the Secretary of State now presented a project for *external* improvement. He

---

[54] Polk, *Diary*, IV, 35–36, 66.

called Polk's attention to the provision in the treaty recently negotiated with New Granada whereby American citizens had been given the right of passage across the Isthmus of Panama. It was of great importance, he said, that a railroad or canal should be constructed there, and he recommended that engineers should be ordered to make a survey. Without consulting other members of the cabinet the President promptly put a quietus on Buchanan's project. If the government could make the survey, said he, it could also construct the works, and he believed that it did not have the constitutional authority to do either.[55]

Polk's aversion to internal improvements had become almost an obsession, and during the month of October he spent his spare moments in formulating a more thorough exposé of the whole "American System." Originally it was his intention to incorporate his exposé in a veto message, for he fully expected that Congress would pass another internal improvement bill.

> Should another veto become necessary I desire to make it a strong paper, so that if I should be over-ruled, as I may be, by a united Whig vote and a part of the Democratic members, making a vote of two thirds, I may leave my full views on record to be judged of by my countrymen & by posterity. I can add to the strength of my veto message on the same subject of the 15th of December last. If I should not have occasion to use it, it will be left among my papers at my death. I am thoroughly convinced that I am right upon this subject, and therefore I have destowed much labour in preparing a paper which may contribute to convince others that I am so.

His purpose, as he recorded in another place, was to show that the "American System" consisted of several closely allied branches: a federal bank, protective tariff, distribution of the land fund, and internal improvements; that the system had been overthrown in all branches except the last; and if this should be

---

[55] "I told him furthermore that if any improvement Bill should during my time be presented to me, I should certainly veto it, and that if I were to yield my sanction to his proposition it would be argued by my opponents in Congress that while I denied the power to make internal improvements, I was exercising the power, and that too without an act of Congress, to make foreign surveys with a view to make foreign improvements" (*ibid.*, 139–140). How different from the attitude of a later President, who could boast that "I took the canal!"

permitted to survive, all the others would soon be revived.[56] One
may, or may not, agree with his views, yet there can be no doubt
of the President's own belief that, in demolishing this network
of special privilege which had been woven by Hamilton and Clay,
he was performing a most patriotic service. Those who have
charged him—and justly charged him—with being a strong party
man have failed to appreciate his conscientious belief in the
principles of his party. No former President—not even Jefferson himself—had succeeded so well in putting Jeffersonian theories into actual operation. He was grieved by the thought of
retiring without having crushed the last remnant of the system
so elaborately constructed by Hamilton and Clay. He could no
longer hope for reward or distinction from his party, yet he was
quite as willing as he had been in 1834 to ply the oar of the
"galley-slave"[57] in promoting the principles of his party, because
he regarded them as most beneficial to his country. Even if
laborious effort to indite a document so convincing that posterity
must heed it is but an exhibition of personal conceit, still there
can be no doubt that he was impelled by patriotic motives and by
a desire to save his country from what he considered to be a real
and serious menace.

On the advice of his cabinet, Polk decided not to leave the
promulgation of so important a document to the chance passage
of an internal revenue bill. Yielding to their judgment, he made
it a part of his last annual message. The message is well written
and shows a firm grasp of the entire subject. It deserves careful
reading, for it is distinctly the most able indictment of the
"American System" to be found among our public documents.
Although the historical, and perhaps the best, part of the message relating to this subject is too long to be quoted, a few
paragraphs will serve to indicate the conclusions which he had
reached:

---

[56] Polk, *Diary*, IV, 144, 157–158, 167–168.

[57] "Polk worked like a galley-slave to cram down his report" (Adams,
Memoirs, IX, 83).

The several branches of this system were so intimately blended together that in their operation each sustained and strengthened the others. Their joint operation was to add new burthens of taxation and to encourage a largely increased and wasteful expenditure of public money. It was the interest of the bank that the revenue collected and the disbursements made by the Government should be large, because, being the depository of the public money, the larger the amount the greater would be the bank profits by its use. It was the interest of the favored classes, who were enriched by the protective tariff, to have the rates of that protection as high as possible, for the higher those rates the greater would be their advantage. It was the interest of the people of all those sections and localities who expected to be benefited by expenditures for internal improvements that the amount collected should be as large as possible, to the end that the sum disbursed might also be the larger. The States, being the beneficiaries in the distribution of the land money, had an interest in having the rates of tax imposed by the protective tariff large enough to yield a sufficient revenue from that source to meet the wants of the Government without disturbing or taking from them the land fund; so that each of the branches constituting the system had a common interest in maintaining the public debt unpaid and increasing its amount, because this would produce an annual increased drain upon the Treasury to the amount of the interest and render augmented taxes necessary. The operation and necessary effect of the whole system were to encourage large and extravagant expenditures, and thereby to increase the public patronage, and maintain a rich and splendid government at the expense of a taxed and impoverished people.

* * * * * * * * * * * * *

Under the pernicious workings of this combined system of measures the country witnessed alternate seasons of temporary apparent prosperity, of sudden and disastrous commercial revulsions, of unprecedented fluctuations of prices and depression of the great interests of agriculture, navigation, and commerce, of general pecuniary suffering, and of final bankruptcy of thousands. After a severe struggle of more than a quarter of a century, the system was overthrown.

The bank has been succeeded by a practical system of finance, conducted and controlled by the Government. The constitutional currency has been restored, the public credit maintained unimpaired even in a period of a foreign war, and the whole country has become satisfied that banks, national or State, are not necessary as fiscal agents of the Government. Revenue duties have taken the place of the protective tariff. The distribution of the money derived from the sale of the public lands has been abandoned and the corrupting system of internal improvements, it is hoped, has been effectively checked.

It is not doubted that if this whole train of measures, designed to take wealth from the many and bestow it upon the few, were to prevail the effect would be to change the entire character of the Government. One only danger remains. It is the seductions of that branch of the system which consists in internal improvements, holding out, as it does, inducements to the people of particular sections and localities to embark the Government in them without stopping to calculate the inevitable consequences. This branch of the system is so intimately combined and linked with the others that as surely as an effect is produced by an adequate cause, if it be resuscitated and revived and firmly established it requires no sagacity to foresee that it will necessarily and speedily draw after it the reestablishment of a national bank, the revival of a protective tariff, the distribution of the land money, and not only the postponement to the distant future of the payment of the present national debt, but its annual increase.

I entertain the solemn conviction that if the internal-improvement branch of the ''American System'' be not firmly resisted at this time the whole series of measures composing it will be speedily reestablished and the country be thrown back from its present high state of prosperity, which the existing policy has produced, and be destined to witness all the evils, commercial revulsions, depression of prices, and pecuniary embarrassments through which we have passed during the last twenty-five years.[58]

An early payment of the national debt was regarded by Polk to be of such transcending importance that he was loth to relinquish the helm without having made a beginning. With a view to influencing his successor, he told his Secretary of the Treasury that he desired, if possible, to purchase government stock, ''however small the sum might be''; and as soon as the department estimates had been submitted, he directed Walker to purchase half a million dollars' worth.[59]

Like the President's message, Walker's report was an ably written document and a strong vindication of the financial policy of the Polk administration. The predicted disasters had not followed in the wake of the tariff of 1846; instead, Walker had

---

[58] Richardson, *Messages*, IV, 657, 661.

[59] ''I informed him [Walker] that I desired to do this supposing it might exert some influence over the policy of my successor. I deem the speedy payment of the public debt of great national importance. If 1 commence its payment my successor may dislike to take the responsibility of reversing my policy in this respect'' (Polk, *Diary*, IV, 162, 195).

the satisfaction of informing Congress that even the manufacturers did not "desire the restoration of the tariff of 1842." He came out boldly as an advocate of free trade, and although his views were too radical for practical purposes, it would be difficult to find a better statement of the free trade theory. After an elaborate argument to show that nations as a whole, as well as all classes within them, were best served by unhampered trade, he arrived at the following conclusions:

> Whenever the laws of nature are beyond the reach of man, there is perfect order under the direction of Almighty power; but whenever man can disturb these laws, discord and injury are sure to ensue. . . . The laws of political economy are fixed and certain. *Let them alone* is all that is required of man; let all international exchanges of products move as freely in their orbits as the heavenly bodies in their spheres, and their order and harmony will be as perfect, and their results as beneficial, as is every movement under the laws of nature, when undisturbed by the errors and interference of man.[60]

Even though the President declared Walker's report to be "one of his ablest papers," his own remark concerning the Secretary's report of 1847 was applicable to this, also—that it was "in the main sound in its doctrines" but "some parts of it speculative, and perhaps too highly wrought."[61] The two men were in substantial agreement on the fundamentals of economic and financial policy. Polk, however, always directed his attention to the attainable, for he was too conservative by nature to indulge in theoretical discussions.

The specter of improvements—both external and internal—haunted the President to the closing hours of his official term. In January, 1849, he expressed to his cabinet a determination to veto a bill pending in Congress which proposed to pay Aspinwall and others $250,000 annually for twenty years, to enable them to construct a road across the Isthmus of Panama. He opposed the measure first of all on constitutional grounds; in addition,

---

60 Walker, *Annual Report*, Dec., 1848 (*H. Ex. Doc. 7*, 30 Cong., 2 sess.).
61 Polk, *Diary*, III, 299, IV, 224.

he regarded it as "little better than a proposition to plunder the Treasury." On the very last night of his administration he went to the capitol armed with a veto which was to be applied to *any* internal improvement bill. No bill of the kind was presented for his signature, but he regarded the unused veto message as "one of the ablest papers I have ever prepared."[62]

Among the bills signed on the last night of his official term was the one which established the Department of the Interior. "I had serious objections," says the *Diary,* "but they were not of a constitutional character and I signed it with reluctance." He feared that such a department, in its practical operations, would draw power from the states and extend, unduly, the jurisdiction of the national government. Had he been a member of Congress, he would have voted against the measure.[63] Walker, therefore, and not Polk, deserves the credit for this important achievement. It was the child of his fertile brain,[64] and the passage of the bill was due in no small degree to his personal influence.

Those who have been most bitter in their condemnation of Polk's foreign policy have found little to criticize in his internal administration. When he withdrew to private life all industries were in a flourishing condition, and not even the victorious Whigs cared to repeal the "great measures" of his administration. None except Clay was fatuous enough to dream of reviving the obsolete "American System."[65]

---

[62] Polk, *Diary,* IV, 314, 364.

[63] *Ibid.*, 371–372.

[64] Walker had, in his report, urged the creation of such a department, and it was his hand that drafted the bill. See Vinton's statement in *Cong. Globe,* 30 Cong., 2 sess., 514.

[65] See comments on his Ullmann letter in Schurz, *Henry Clay,* II, 299.

CHAPTER XXIV

THE "POLK DOCTRINE" AND MINOR DIPLOMATIC QUESTIONS

In a commencement address delivered before the Yale law school in 1903, Whitelaw Reid attached the name of ''Polk Doctrine'' to President Polk's declarations concerning European interference in American affairs. Although Reid himself condemned the doctrine, yet the very name given to it acknowledges Polk's important contribution to the great American policy of resisting European intermeddling with the affairs of the western hemisphere. Moreover, despite Reid's criticisms and his statement that it originated ''in an intrigue of the slave power,''[1] the Polk Doctrine has been approved and continued by the American people; and Presidents chosen by the party which overthrew slavery, and of which Reid himself was a leading member, have increased rather than diminished the scope of its application.

Polk's first public declaration on the subject appeared in his first annual message of December 2, 1845, and referred to Oregon; but nearly three months before this he had applied the doctrine to the Hawaiian Islands, and certainly not in the interest of slavery. In September, 1845, Anthony Ten Eyck was sent as agent to the islands, and his instructions prepared under the President's order contained the following significant paragraph:

Your mission, under existing circumstances, is one of great importance. The United States have a deep stake in the continued independence of the Hawaiian Islands. They present one of those commanding commercial positions which Great Britain, judging from her past history, would be anxious to annex to her dominions. To promote the prosperity and secure the independence of these Islands, is therefore the clear policy as well as

---

[1] Reid, *The Monroe Doctrine, the Polk Doctrine and the Doctrine of Anarchism*, 7.

the duty of the Government of the United States. We could not view with indifference their transfer to or their dependence upon any European Power.[2]

This is a noteworthy addition the doctrine of Monroe: acquisition of the islands by Great Britain could hardly be regarded as colonization, and the question of suppressing representative government was, of course, not involved. The reason why the transfer could not be viewed with indifference was that it would affect, detrimentally, the commerce of the United States.

It was, however, the Oregon question, and his desire to obtain California, that gave the President the best opportunity to develop his policy of resistance to foreign influence in American affairs. Pakenham's rejection of his offer to fix the Oregon boundary at the forty-ninth parallel made it necessary for him to make recommendations to Congress, and, on October 24, he discussed the subject with Senator Benton. He told Benton that he was strongly inclined to reaffirm Monroe's declaration against permitting foreign colonization, "at least so far as this Continent is concerned." "I remarked," said he,

that Great Britain had her eye on that country [California] and intended to possess it if she could, but that the people of the U. S. would not willingly permit California to pass into the possession of any foreign monarchy, and that in reasserting Mr. Monroe's doctrine, I had California & the fine bay of San Francisco as much in view as Oregon.

The conversation then turned to Cuba and the two men agreed that

as long as Cuba remained in possession of the present Government we would not object, but if a powerful foreign power was about to possess it, we would not permit it. On the same footing we would place California.[3]

There was of course nothing new in Polk's stand on the Cuban question. From the beginning of our national existence Cuba had been regarded as essential to our commercial prosperity, and consequently within the sphere of American influence. His

---

[2] Buchanan to Ten Eyck, Sept. 10, 1845 (Buchanan, *Works*, VI, 255 ff.).
[3] Polk, *Diary*, I, 71.

attitude was the same as Jefferson's,[4] that its possession by Spain might be tolerated, but that it must not pass to a strong maritime power. Although he later attempted to purchase Cuba, Polk was not desirous of acquiring insular possessions, except as a safeguard to American interests. This fact is shown by his refusal, a short time before his conversation with Benton, to purchase from Sweden the island of Saint Bartholomew. In reply to the offer made by the king of Sweden, the President directed Buchanan to state that "the acquisition of distant insular possessions, for Colonial dependencies, has never been deemed desirable or expedient by the United States."[5] In a word, Polk was not an imperialist, albeit he was a most ardent expansionist.

Rumors of British and French designs on California induced Polk to take early steps to prevent their success. Six weeks before Congress had assembled he instructed Buchanan to notify Thomas O. Larkin, American consul at Monterey, that the President could not view with indifference the transfer of California to Great Britain or any other European nation, for "the system of colonization by foreign monarchies on the North American continent must and will be resisted by the United States." The government, he said, did not intend to interfere between Mexico and California, but "it would vigorously interfere to prevent the latter from becoming a British or French Colony."[6] In a communication written during the following month Slidell, also, was given a statement concerning the policy of his government. After speaking of the beneficial results of the Monroe Doctrine, Buchanan said that

The nations on the continent of America have interests peculiar to themselves. Their free forms of Government are altogether different from the monarchical institutions of Europe. The interests and independence of these sister nations require that they should establish and maintain an American system of policy for their own protection and security, entirely

---

[4] See Henry Adams, *History of the United States*, IV, 342–343.

[5] Buchanan to Ellsworth, July 28, 1845 (Buchanan, *Works*, VI, 212).

[6] Buchanan to Larkin, Oct. 17, 1845 (Buchanan, *Works*, VI, 275–276). The original is in the *Larkin Papers*, Bancroft Library.

distinct from that which has so long prevailed in Europe. To tolerate any interference on the part of European sovereigns with controversies in America; to permit them to apply the worn-out dogma of the balance of power to the free States of this continent; and above all, to suffer them to establish new Colonies of their own, intermingled with our free Republics, would be to make, to some extent, a voluntary sacrifice of our independence. These truths ought everywhere, throughout the continent of America, to be impressed on the public mind. . . . . Liberty here must be allowed to work out its natural results; and these will, ere long, astonish the world.[7]

So far, the expression of the President's sentiments had been confined to secret instructions, but his message of December 2, 1845, announced to Congress and to the world the policy which he meant to pursue. He told Congress that certain European nations, in order to check the territorial expansion of the United States, were attempting to extend to America the "balance of power" doctrine which had long been maintained in Europe. But the United States, he said,

can not in silence permit any European interference on the North American continent, and should any such interference be attempted will be ready to resist it at any and all hazards.
. . . . Existing rights of every European nation should be respected, but it is due alike to our safety and our interests that the efficient protection of our laws should be extended over our whole territorial limits, and that it should be distinctly announced to the world as our settled policy that no future European colony or dominion shall with our consent be planted or established on any part of the North American continent.[8]

In this pronouncement Polk professed to be reiterating the Monroe Doctrine, but it differed in two particulars from the declaration of Monroe. In the first place, Polk forbade *any European interference;* and in the second, he spoke only of North America. His statement that "we must maintain the principle that the people of this continent alone have the right to decide their own destiny" evidently applied only in cases where a people desired to join the United States, for his views with respect to Cuba and Hawaii would seem to preclude a transfer of

---

[7] Buchanan to Slidell, Nov. 10, 1845 (Buchanan, *Works,* VI, 295).

[8] Richardson, *Messages,* IV, 398–399.

possessions, even with the consent of the inhabitants. In each case it was the commerce of the United States which he sought to protect, and not the civil rights of the people of those islands. Polk's declaration was, also, much more definite than that of his predecessor; in fact it was a contingent declaration of war.

Some of the London papers were severe in their criticism of the President's message. They perverted it into a declaration of intention to absorb all of North America. "The President advises Congress," said the *Spectator,*

to arm and organize the militia that they may be prepared to receive all communities already settled on the North American continent into the bosom of the Union, and prevent the colonization of any part of the continent by European nations.

Only a part of this statement was true. The *Times* professed to see in the message not merely a bar to future colonization, but "we must infer from the language of the President that existing rights and settlements are held by a questionable tenure."[9] There was, of course, no occasion for this inference, for Polk had stated explicitly that existing rights should be respected.

On January 14, 1846, Senator Allen, chairman of the Committee on Foreign Relations, asked leave to introduce a joint resolution relating to the subject of foreign interference in American affairs. It followed closely the language of the President's declaration, and its object was to reënforce that declaration by giving it the formal approval of Congress. Calhoun objected even to the introduction of the resolution on the ground that a discussion of the subject would stir up enmities and would lead to no possible good. He resented, he said, such outrageous interference as that undertaken by France and England in the affairs of Buenos Ayres, but

the great question presented by this resolution was, whether we should take under our guardianship the whole family of American States, and pledge ourselves to extend to them our protection against all foreign aggression.[10]

---

[9] Quoted by Cass in *Cong. Globe,* 29 Cong., 1 sess., 240.

[10] *Cong. Globe,* 29 Cong., 1 sess., 197.

Allen's motion for leave to present his resolution was sent to the table, but on January 24 the vote was reversed. The main supporters of the resolution were Cass and Allen, the former asserting that the President's declaration would be barren of results "unless adopted by the national legislature." We could not, he said, permit the United States to be "belted round by the fleets, armies, and territories" of England; "Oregon and California, if gained, and Mexico influenced, if not ruled, would complete the circle" of British domination. In opposing the resolution, Calhoun characterized it as "vaporing bravado." He deplored the attempt to lay down general rules, and held that each question should be settled on its merits. For example, the machinations of Great Britain and France in Texas should, if necessary, be resisted by war, for they "would have as much right to induce a member to go out of the Union as to prevent one coming in."[!] The resolution was referred to the Committee on Foreign Relations, from which it never emerged; Polk's declaration, like that of his predecessor, remained a mere dictum of the executive.

Throughout the year 1846 there were persistent rumors of European designs to establish a monarchy in Mexico. As early as January 17 McLane wrote from London that

a favorite scheme of the leading powers of Europe is to compose the Mexican troubles by giving her a settled monarchical form of Government, and supplying the monarch from one of their own families.

There were many protests, he added, against Polk's allusions to the Monroe Doctrine.[11] However groundless such rumors may have been, their recurrence could hardly fail to cause apprehension on the part of the administration.

In March, Buchanan informed Slidell that "we have received information from different quarters, in corroberation of your statement[12] that there may be a design on the part of several

---

[11] McLane to Polk, Jan. 17, 1846, *Polk Papers.*

[12] Slidell had written on February 6 that "for some time past, rumors have been rife of the establishment of a monarchy in the person of a foreign prince" (*H. Ex. Doc. 60*, 30 Cong., 1 sess., 58).

European Powers to establish a monarchy in Mexico.'' It is
supposed, said he, that the clergy would welcome such a change,
and that continued revolution may induce the people to accept
it as a means of security and protection. ''Indeed, rumor has
already indicated the King, in the person of the Spanish Prince
Henry, the son of Francisco de Paula, and the rejected suitor of
Queen Isabella.'' While Buchanan believed these rumors to be
idle speculations, nevertheless Slidell was instructed to use the
utmost vigilance in ascertaining whether such a plot really
existed.

> Should Great Britain and France attempt to place a Spanish or any
> other European Prince upon the throne of Mexico, this would be resisted
> by all the power of the United States. In opposition to such an attempt,
> party distinctions in this country would vanish and the people would be
> nearly unanimous.[13]

Apparently, the President did not believe that foreign nations
would actually attempt to set up a monarchy in Mexico, for his
diary is silent on this subject. Still, he was ever on the alert,
and determined, if necessary, to resist such an attempt. In
December, he denied Donelson's request for a leave of absence
from Berlin, because ''a project has been suggested, of establishing a monarchy in Mexico and placing a foreign Prince upon the
throne.'' Although Prussia, said he, had no special interest in
the matter, she probably would be committed, therefore Donelson should be in Berlin to meet the issue. Whatever the facts
might be,

> Should such a project be attempted, it must be resisted by this Govern-
> ment, at any hazard. This was shadowed forth in a mild manner in my
> late message to Congress.[14]

Rumors of the Mexican monarchy proved to be, as Mark
Twain said of the report of his own death, ''greatly exaggerated'';
but in asserting that he would resist such a project, Polk can not

---

[13] Buchanan to Slidell, March 12, 1846 (Buchanan, *Works*, VI, 404–405).
[14] Polk to Donelson, Dec. 29, 1846, ''Polk-Donelson Letters,'' *Tenn.
Hist. Mag.*, III, No. 1, 72.

be charged with inventing a new doctrine, for this case at least fell clearly within the declaration of Monroe against the activities of the Holy Alliance. It is well known, of course, that at a later date France was compelled by the United States to withdraw her support from the Emperor Maximilian.

None of President Polk's utterances against foreign influence in America has met with so much criticism as his message relating to Yucatan. During the Mexican war this department maintained, as far as possible, a neutral position which necessarily deprived it of the protection of Mexico. In March, 1848, Justo Sierra, Yucatanese commissioner in Washington, applied to Buchanan for military assistance, stating in his application that the white inhabitants were threatened with extermination by the Indians. Buchanan and Walker were in favor of sending them arms and ammunition, and after some hesitation the President consented to authorize Commodore Perry to supply the white inhabitants with ammunition, if he could be assured that it would not find its way to other parts of Mexico.[15]

After several rather unsatisfactory conversations with both Buchanan and Polk, Sierra, on April 25, presented a formal communication from the governor of Yucatan. The governor requested aid against the Indians and stated that the people of the department "were ready to surrender their country & the sovereignty over it to any Government which would protect & save them from extermination." He stated, also, that a similar offer had been made to Great Britain and Spain. Prospect of foreign domination called for prompt action, and Polk informed his cabinet that

we could never agree to see Yucatan pass into the hands of a foreign monarchy to be possessed and colonized by them, and that sooner than this should take place the U. S. should afford the aid & protection asked, but that this could only be done by the authority of Congress.[16]

Without delay, the President began the preparation of a message on the subject of Yucatan. The preliminary draft was

---

[15] Polk, *Diary*, III, 374.   [16] *Ibid.*, 433–434.

shown to the cabinet and to various members of Congress, all of whom approved the sentiments which he had expressed. As submitted to Congress on April 29, 1848, the message, after calling attention to the deplorable conditions in Yucatan, stated that the department had offered to transfer the "dominion and sovereigny of the peninsula" to the United States, and that similar offers had been made to both England and Spain.

> Whilst it is not my purpose, [said he], to recommend the adoption of any measure with a view to the acquisition of the "dominion and sovereignty" over Yucatan, yet according to our established policy, we could not consent to a transfer of this "dominion and sovereignty" either to Spain, Great Britain, or any other European power.[17]

While the president alleged that he was restating the "established policy" announced by Monroe, which "applies with great force to the peninsula of Yucatan," it is obvious that the question under consideration was not covered by either declaration of the Monroe Doctrine. Monroe had spoken of colonization, and of forcible interference with established governments; Polk asserted that we could not consent to a transfer of "dominion and sovereignty," even at the solicitation of the inhabitants. But to show that the Yucatan question did not fall within the purview of the Monroe Doctrine does not prove that Polk should not have announced his own much-criticized doctrine. Monroe dealt with the threatened dangers of his own time; was it presumptuous in Polk to declare, in similar manner, his policy for dealing with new phases of foreign domination? Indirectly, there was a close connection between the Polk Doctrine and that of Monroe. The purpose of the anti-colonization declaration of Monroe was to shut out, for the future, undesirable neighbors; this, also, was the purpose of forbidding the transfer of Yucatan to any European nation. In neither case was any thought given to the wishes of the actual or the prospective inhabitants; the sole consideration was the welfare of the United States. Moreover, Polk's

---

[17] Richardson, *Messages,* IV, 581–582.

announcement regarding Yucatan was quite in line with that of his predecessors with respect to Cuba, and the degree of importance does not affect the principle involved. For example, when Secretary Clay, by order of President Adams, notified France and other powers that we could not consent to the occupation of Cuba and Porto Rico "by any other European power than Spain under any contingency whatever,"[18] he was thinking of the transfer *per se* and of the effect upon the United States, and not of the wishes of the Cubans.

In his message, President Polk made no specific recommendations, but left it "to the wisdom of Congress to adopt such measures as in their judgment may be expedient to prevent Yucatan from becoming a colony of any European power." There was no intimation that he desired to take permanent possession of the territory or that he had any other object in view than to prevent it from falling into the hands of a foreign nation; still, we know from his diary that he was ready to annex the department rather than see it become a possession of Great Britain.[19]

As soon as the message was read in the Senate, Calhoun asserted that the "broad and dangerous principle" announced in it could not possibly be deduced from the Monroe Doctrine. It was, however, referred to the Committee on Foreign Relations, from which, on May 4, Hannegan reported an act to enable the President to "take temporary military occupation of Yucatan." The debate which followed elicited widely divergent opinions, both as to the President's meaning and the expediency of occupying the territory. It is unnecessary to dwell on this discussion, for before it had proceeded far dispatches arrived bearing the news that a treaty had been concluded between Yucatan and the Indians. Calhoun's remarks, however, are worthy of note, on

---

[18] Clay to Brown, Oct. 25, 1825 (*Am. State Pap., For. Rel.*, V, 856).

[19] "Mr. Walker was in favour of its ultimate annexation to the United States, & Mr. Buchanan opposed it. I concurred with Mr. Walker rather than see it fall into the hands of England" (*Diary* (May 6, 1848), III, 444–445).

account of his peculiar interpretation of the Monroe Doctrine. It consisted, he said, of friendly declarations, with "not a word in any one of them in reference to resistance." But Polk, he continued, "seems to hold these declarations as imposing a solemn duty on him as Chief Magistrate to resist on all occasions; and not only to resist, but to judge of the measure of that resistance."[20] As construed by Calhoun, the sole survivor of Monroe's cabinet, the famous "doctrine" became a harmless declamation—a simple statement of our desires, and not a warning to the European alliance. Hannegan, the chief supporter of the bill, disclaimed any desire to annex Yucatan, although, like the President, he was ready to do so if this should prove to be the only means of saving it from British domination. That country, in his opinion, would never neglect an opportunity to strengthen her hold on the Gulf of Mexico: "Cuba was said to be the key, and with Yucatan she would have both lock and key, and control the whole outlet of the vast Mississippi." It was control of the Gulf region, and not the desire to possess additional southern territory, that led the President and his supporters to resist a possible extension of British domination over the department of Yucatan. British activities in Texas had, justly or unjustly, convinced Polk that England was ever ready to deal a blow at the commercial prosperity of the United States.

Discussion of the Yucatan question, and of the alleged attempt of Great Britain to make the Gulf of Mexico a *"mare clausum,"* naturally revived interest in the destinies of Cuba. That island had always been regarded as the key to the Gulf, and administrations of all parties had agreed that its control must never pass to a strong maritime power. As noted above, Clay, under Adams' instructions, had, in 1825, asserted that "we could not consent to the occupation of those islands by any other European power than Spain under any contingency whatever." In similar

---

[20] Printed in full in Calhoun, *Works*, IV, 454 ff.

language Webster, in 1843, informed the United States consul at Havana that his government "never would permit the occupation of that island by British agents or forces upon any pretext whatever," and that the entire naval and military resources of the United States would be employed to prevent it.[21]

At the first session of Congress under the Polk administration resolutions were offered in both houses for the purpose of authorizing the President to purchase Cuba, provided the consent of the inhabitants could be obtained. Nothing resulted from these resolutions, for more pressing questions soon absorbed the attention of both Congress and the executive. But when, in 1847, certain British statesmen urged their government to seize Cuba as security for the interest on Spanish bonds held in England, the American press began to discuss the advisability of purchasing the island. For example, the New York *Sun* came out strongly in favor of annexation. It stated in an editorial that Spain would sell Cuba for $100,000,000, and that the Cubans were so eager to join the United States that they would raise the necessary money if given a week's notice(!)[22] There is no evidence, however, that the President gave serious thought to the subject until the summer of the following year when the importance of acquiring the island was urged upon him by John L. O'Sullivan, editor of the *Democratic Review* and of the New York *News*.

In his diary for May 10, 1848, Polk mentioned a visit from O'Sullivan and Senator Douglas. They had come, apparently at the instance of the former, for the purpose of exhorting the President to take immediate steps to buy the island from Spain. As usual, he declined to give them his own views on the subject, although his decision had already been made. "Though I expressed no opinion to them," is the comment in his diary, "I am decidedly in favour of purchasing Cuba & making it one of

---

[21] Webster to Campbell, Jan. 14, 1843 (Wharton, *Int. Law Digest,* I, 372).

[22] Quoted in *Niles' Reg.,* LXXII, 338 (July 31, 1847).

the States of [the] Union." A few weeks later he wrote that
it was O'Sullivan "who first suggested to me the idea of purchasing Cuba."[23]

Late in the month, when consulting his cabinet on the advisability of making an offer to Spain, Polk emphasized the
danger of the island's falling into the hands of Great Britain.
Walker and Mason were in favor of making an offer, and were
willing to go as high as $100,000,000. Johnson objected to in-
corporating the territory into the Union, while Buchanan feared
that any agitation of the subject might injure the party in the
Presidential election.[24] Two days later Buchanan received an
"important despatch" from the American consul at Havana
which said that on account of impending revolution the creoles
were in favor of annexation. O'Sullivan told the President that
an agent of wealthy Cuban planters had informed him of a
scheme of his employers to overthrow Spanish authority for the
purpose of hastening annexation. O'Sullivan said, also, that a
distinguished American general,[25] now in Mexico, had agreed to
resign his commission at the close of the war and to embark for
Cuba with discharged American troops. But Polk was too cir-
cumspect to indulge in filibustering schemes:

> I at once said to Mr. O'Sullivan that if Cuba was ever obtained by
> the U. S., it must be by amicable purchase, and that as President of the
> U. S. I could give no countenance to such a step, and could not wink at
> such a movement.[26]

When consulted on the subject, Cass expressed himself as
heartily in favor of purchasing Cuba, but Buchanan still maintained that the proposed acquisition was the "gravest & most
important" question that had ever been submitted to the cabinet.
At the next meeting he predicted that war with England and

---

[23] Polk, *Diary*, III, 446, 493. The fact that O'Sullivan was a "Barnburner" and an enthusiastic supporter of Van Buren is evidence that the
project was not prompted by a desire to extend the slaveholding area.

[24] *Ibid.*, 468–469.

[25] Probably Quitman.   [26] Polk, *Diary*, III, 475–477.

France would follow an attempt to acquire the island; but Polk nevertheless decided that R. M. Saunders, our minister at Madrid, should be instructed to buy it if he could. Buchanan petulantly demanded specific instructions as to contents of the dispatch to Saunders. Evidently he was preparing to disclaim responsibility in case the project should turn out to be politically unwise.

In order to forestall filibustering schemes, General Butler was instructed to prevent our troops from taking part in a Cuban expedition, and the American consul at Havana was told that the United States would "preserve national faith with Spain." On Walker's suggestion, it was decided that copies of these instructions should be forwarded to Saunders at Madrid, with directions to communicate them to the Spanish government. Indeed, Saunders was to make it appear that the presentation of this evidence of good will on the part of his government was the main object of his interview with the Spanish minister; he was then to say that the United States would make an offer to purchase the island, if such an offer would be agreeable to Spain. Walker's happy thought caused Buchanan to withdraw his objections, and he announced to that he "would cheerfully prepare the necessary instructions to Mr. Saunders."[27]

The dispatch to Saunders, in which Buchanan had incorporated the President's views, was formally approved at a cabinet meeting held on June 17, 1848. He stated that the United States had no reason to complain so long as Cuba should continue to be a colony of Spain,

But we can never consent that this Island shall become a Colony of any other European power. In the possession of Great Britain or any strong naval power, it might prove ruinous both to our domestic and foreign commerce, and endanger the Union of the States. The highest and first duty of every independent nation is to provide for its own safety; and acting upon this principle we should be compelled to resist the acquisition of Cuba by any maritime State with all the means which Providence has placed at our command.

---

[27] *Ibid.*, 487.

Having thus definitely stated the policy of his government
and the determination to enforce it, the Secretary of State proceeded to show the necessity for such a policy and to give reasons
for believing that American interests were already menaced by
the designs of Great Britain. Incidentally, these reasons had an
important bearing on the President's recent message relating to
Yucatan. Cuba, said Buchanan, is situated between Florida and
Yucatan, and its possession would give England command of
both inlets to the Gulf. In time of war she could effectively
blockade the mouth of the Mississippi and sever the connection
between the Gulf states and those on the Atlantic.

As reasons for believing that England had ambitious designs,
Buchanan cited first

her uniform policy throughout her past history to seize upon every valuable commercial point throughout the world whenever circumstances have
placed this in her power.

Under the mask of protector of the Mosquito Indians, "she is
endeavoring to acquire permanent possession of the entire coast
of the Carribean Sea from Cape Honduras to Escuda de Ver-
agua"—and this, too, in violation of her treaty of 1786 with
Spain. By a similar violation, a simple permission to cut log-
wood and mahogany had led to the establishment of the British
colony at Belise. She had taken forcible possession of the harbor of San Juan de Nicaragua with the evident purpose of obtaining control over all communication between the Atlantic and
Pacific oceans. Inability of Spain to pay the interest on securities held in England had given her a much more plausible pretext for seizing Cuba than she had for assuming the protectorate
of the Mosquito Indians, and the threatening utterances of Lords
Bentinck and Palmerston indicated a disposition to make use of
this pretext. Indeed, the recent dismissal of the British minister
at Madrid had made a rupture between the two nations almost
inevitable; should it come, "no doubt can be entertained that
Great Britain would immediately seize Cuba."

Saunders was then told that, in the opinion of the President, a crisis had arrived which made it desirable for the United States to purchase the island. He was, therefore, to conclude a treaty, if possible, paying as a maximum the sum of $100,000,000. He was instructed to make the offer orally, and not until he had made it plain to the Spanish government that the United States had been moved wholly by a desire to prevent Cuba from passing to another power.[28]

The hope[29] of the President to crown his work of expansion by annexing Cuba to the United States was doomed to disappointment, for the traditional reluctance of Spain to part with her West Indian possessions could not be overcome. After an exasperating delay the Spanish foreign minister replied that it was

more than any minister dare to entertain any such proposition; that he believed such to be the feeling of the country, that sooner than see the island transferred to any power, they would prefer seeing it sunk in the ocean.

After all, this statement amounted to a pledge that Spain would retain Cuba; and so long as the pledge could be maintained, it effected the main purpose which Polk had in view. Fear of British control of the Gulf had prompted his offer, and such control could not be obtained so long as Spain retained possession of the island.

A letter dealing with Central American affairs, similar to the one sent to Saunders, had already been transmitted to Elijah Hise, who had recently been made *chargé d' affaires* at Guatemala. The dissolution of the Central American confederacy, said Buchanan, had encouraged British encroachments on the Mosquito coast, therefore Hise was to promote a revival of the

---

[28] Buchanan to Saunders, June 17, 1848 (Buchanan, *Works*, VIII, 90-102). Polk, *Diary*, III, 493.

[29] A person who represented himself to be a financial agent of the Spanish queen told Dallas that he had been instructed to ascertain whether the United States would be willing to buy the island. Apparently his story was pure fabrication. See Polk, *Diary*, IV, 4–5.

confederacy. The Secretary was not yet prepared to say what course the United States would pursue with respect to the British protectorate over the Mosquito Indians, but

> To suffer any interference on the part of the European Governments with the domestic concerns of the American Republics and to permit them to establish new colonies upon this continent, would be to jeopard their independence and to ruin their interests. These truths ought everywhere throughout this continent to be impressed on the public mind.[30]

Hise concluded a general commercial treaty on the last day of Polk's term of office, but nothing was accomplished in the way of reuniting the Central American states. The Taylor administration adopted a more conciliatory attitude toward England the result of which was the conclusion of the well-known Clayton-Bulwer treaty of 1850.

Early in the Polk administration an event, unimportant in itself, very nearly caused a break in our diplomatic relations with Brazil. On October 31, 1846, Lieutenant Alonzo B. Davis, of the United States ship *Saratoga,* went on shore at Rio Janeiro to apprehend deserters from his vessel. As Davis was about to take them to his ship, the Brazilian police interfered and imprisoned both Davis and the sailors. Henry A. Wise was then minister to Brazil, and, to use his own expression, he played "old Hickory on them" by demanding the immediate release of the prisoners. He wanted, he said, "to make these Spanish & Portugese Mongrells in S. America understand that *the U. States* MUST *be respected.*"[31] All except one of the prisoners were set free, and the affair might have been dropped had not Wise and Commodore Rousseau of the American squadron not wounded the pride of the Brazilian court by further Jacksonian contempt for diplomatic punctilio.

A fortnight after the prisoners had been released, Wise ignored an invitation to the baptismal ceremonies of the Imperial Infanta, and Commodore Rousseau neglected to fire the customary

---

[30] Buchanan to Hise, June 3, 1848 (Buchanan, *Works,* VIII, 78–84).
[31] Wise to J. Y. Mason, Nov. 6, 1846, *Polk Papers.*

salute. A little later, when the Emperor's birthday was being
celebrated, Rousseau neither fired a salute nor hoisted the flag
on his ship, while Wise (not invited this time) made a speech
on shipboard which was anything but complimentary to the
Brazilians. Brazil now requested the recall of both men and
asked for an apology from the United States. The apology was
claimed on the ground of discourtesy to the Emperor and the
more serious charge that Davis had denied the sovereignty of the
empire by resisting the police—conduct which had been approved
and supported by Wise.

When the complaints were presented in Washington by
Lisboa, the Brazilian minister, Polk instructed Buchanan to say
that he would neither apologize nor recall Wise and Rousseau;
recall of the minister would imply dissatisfaction with his conduct, whereas it was highly approved by the President. Buchanan
added, however, that since Wise had, before the trouble had
arisen, asked to be relieved, the President would grant his request; Rousseau, also, would soon be sent to another port. With
this understanding, Buchanan and Lisboa agreed to let the matter
drop; but the Brazilian government recalled Lisboa, demanded
an apology, and declared that a successor to Wise would not be
received until this had been made.

The new demand for an apology was presented by the *chargé
de affaires,* Leal, in the summer of 1847. The only question of
importance was Lieutenant Davis's alleged resistance of the authority of the police in Rio Janeiro, and everything hinged on
whether Davis or the police first had the sailors in custody. The
evidence seemed to show that Davis had apprehended them before
the police arrived on the scene. While it was admitted that the
jurisdiction of any nation is absolute within its own borders, custom permitted naval officers to go on shore to arrest their own
sailors. As this was all that Davis had done, he had, in Polk's
opinion, committed no "infractions of police regulations," consequently Wise was justified in demanding his release from prison.

The threat to reject a new minister was resented as ''dictating terms'' to which Brazil ''could not have expected submission''; but, said Buchanan, ''the President will take no decisive steps'' until he shall have learned that Brazil has actually refused to receive him.[32] This firm but reasonable declaration had the desired effect, and the new minister, David Tod, was received courteously by the Emperor. Wise returned to the United States filled with gratitude for the man whom he had once called a ''petty tyrant'' and whom he had tried to goad into fighting a duel. ''I learn,'' wrote the President, after Wise had called to pay his respects,

that he returns to the U. S. my friend, & his expressions of gratitude to me to-day were as strong & decided as human language could make them, so that I have lived to conquer the hostility of at least one of my political opponents & persecutors. This I have done by performing my duty in a magnanimous and liberal manner.[33]

Zeal of naval officers to protect American rights nearly involved the government in difficulties with another South American state. In January, 1845, Buenos Ayres attempted to invest Montevideo with an absolute blockade; and because this was forcibly violated by French vessels, a United States naval officer, G. J. Pendergrast, demanded exemption for his own vessels. The authorities at Washington, however, held that an offense committed by one nation did not entitle another to disregard belligerent rights, and the officers were instructed to respect the blockade.

Before this question had been adjusted, British and French naval officers announced a blackade of the whole coast of Buenos Ayres and allowed other neutrals only forty-eight hours to withdraw their vessels from the harbors. Pendergrast entered a vigorous protest on the ground that neutrals[34] have no right to

---

[32] The most important letter (written to Leal on Aug. 30, 1847) is printed in Buchanan, *Works*, VII, 388–404. Nearly all of the correspondence relating to this affair may be found in *Sen. Ex. Docs. 29, 35*, 30 Cong., 1 sess.   [33] Polk, *Diary*, III, 192.

[34] England and France had not declared war on Buenos Ayres.

establish a blockade, and that even a belligerent has no right to declare an entire coast to be blockaded. United States vessels were given time to discharge their cargoes and withdraw from the ports, and, since no seizures were made, nothing more serious resulted than caloric speeches in Congress.[35]

On December 12, 1846, Benjamin A. Bidlack, acting without instructions,[36] concluded a commercial treaty with New Granada, one article of which provided for transit across and guaranteed the neutrality of the Isthmus of Panama. Doubtless Bidlack was moved to take this unauthorized step by Buchanan's letter of June 23, 1845, which instructed him to use his influence to prevent New Granada from granting transit concessions to European powers, and which stated that "the United States have strong motives for viewing with interest any project which may be designed to facilitate the intercourse between the Atlantic and the Pacific oceans."[37] Nevertheless, the arrival of the treaty in Washington took the President completely by surprise. At first, Polk doubted that he could approve this "entangling alliance."[38]

In general this document followed the usual form of commercial treaties, and only the thirty-fifth article merits special comment. Among other things, it stipulated that

The Government of New Granada guarantees to the Government of the United States that the right of way or transit across the Isthmus of Panama upon any modes of communication that now exist, or may be hereafter constructed, shall be open and free to the Government and citizens

---

[35] See correspondence, *H. Ex. Doc. 212,* 29 Cong., 1 sess.

[36] While this treaty was on its way to Washington, Buchanan, on January 2, 1847, authorized Bidlack to negotiate a commercial treaty. See Buchanan, *Works,* VII, 183–186.

[37] Buchanan, *Works,* VI, 180–181.

[38] "As a commercial Treaty it was liberal & in all respects satisfactory, but in addition to its commercial provisions it contained an article giving the guaranty of the U. S. for the neutrality of the Isthmus of Panama, and the sovereignty of New Granada over the territory. Serious doubts were entertained whether this stipulation was consistent with our long-settled policy to 'cultivate friendship with all nations, entangling alliances with none'" (Polk, *Diary,* II, 363).

of the United States, [and that] . . . . the United States guarantee, positively and efficaciously to New Granada, by the present stipulation the neutrality of the before-mentioned isthmus, with the view that the free transit from the one to the other sea may not be interrupted or embarrassed in any future time while this treaty exists; and, in consequence, the United States also guarantee, in the same manner, the rights of sovereignty and property which New Granada has and possesses over the territory.

The treaty was to remain in force for twenty years, and then indefinitely, unless terminated by twelve months' notice from either party.[39]

A few days of deliberation overcame Polk's scruples regarding the entangling alliance and convinced him that the transit agreement was too important to be rejected. On February 10 he submitted the treaty to the Senate with a message which stated that "the importance of this concession to the commercial and political interests of the United States can not easily be overrated." He advised ratification because

The treaty does not propose to guarantee a territory to a foreign nation in which the United States will have no common interest with that nation. On the contrary, we are more deeply and directly interested in the subject of this guaranty that New Granada herself or any other country.

Besides, the purpose was commercial, not political, and it was expected that England and France would join in the guaranty. The guaranty of sovereignty was, in his opinoin, indispensable to neutrality and to the protection of property rights; and assurance of New Granada's permanent sovereignty would remove cause for jealousy on the part of maritime powers.[40] Misgivings respecting the thirty-fifth article and pressure of other business caused a postponement of action until the next session of Congress, but in June, 1848, the Senate finally gave its approval. Although the extent of our obligation to insure the "neutrality" and the "sovereignty" of New Granada has been subject to different interpretations, the subsequent history of this treaty is

---

[39] Malloy, *Treaties and Conventions*, I, 302 ff.
[40] Richardson, *Messages*, IV, 511–513.

not within the purview of the present volume.[41]   However, it may
be said in passing that a forced construction of the thirty-fifth
article was utilized by President Roosevelt to prevent Colombia
from suppressing the Panaman insurrection and to facilitate the
process of "taking" the canal zone.

In the last year of his administration President Polk appointed the first diplomatic agent ever sent from the United
States to reside at the capital of Ecuador and diplomatic relations were opened wtih the republic of Bolivia.[42]   In both cases
assurences were given that foreign interference would be resisted, and emphasis was laid on the identity of interests of the
American republics.

One of the last diplomatic events of Polk's official term was
the ratification of a postal convention with Great Britain.   Success in its negotiation was due to the untiring efforts of George
Bancroft, and its importance consisted in removing vexatious
discriminations against United States mails.   Of it the President
said in his diary:

> It places our own steamers and packets upon an equal footing with the
> Brittish and relieves our merchants, naturalized citizens, and others from
> a heavy discriminating charge of postage on letters and other mailable
> matter conveyed in American vessels.   This change has been effected by
> the policy of the administration.   Had it occurred under other circum-
> stances & when so many other great events had not been crowded into a
> single Presidential term, it would have attracted more public attention and
> been regarded as an important achievement.[43]

It was, in deed, an important achievement, for it established
reciprocal privileges and deprived the Cunard steamers of a
virtual monopoly in carrying the mails.[44]

---

[41] See Latané, *Diplomatic Relations of the United States and Spanish
America,* 182–188.

[42] Buchanan to Livingston, May 13, 1848; same to Appleton, June 1,
1848 (Buchanan, *Works,* VIII, 64, 74).

[43] Polk, *Diary,* IV, 271–272.

[44] See Buchanan to Bancroft, July 27, 1847, in which he speaks of the
"conduct of the British Post Office, in charging the same postage on
letters carried on our steamer, the Washington, to Southampton, at the

Polk's remark concerning the postal convention applies equally well to a number of minor diplomatic achievements which were overshadowed by the Mexican and Oregon questions; in a peaceful period they would have attracted more attention and redounded more to the credit of the man who directed our foreign policy. His vigilance in safeguarding American interests prevented foreign nations from gaining additonal influence on this continent. While the original Monroe Doctrine has long ceased to have any practical application, the "Polk Doctrine" has been an active force in our history down to the present day. It has not, indeed, been an unmixed blessing, for it has brought us burdens as well as prestige. But whether we approve or condemn the doctrine, it was Polk who first declared that the United States would not permit any interference, solicited or otherwise, in American affairs, by European monarchies. In general, his doctrine has been indorsed by the people of the United States.

---

expense of the United States, as though they had been carried there by a British steamer, at the expense of the British Government'' (Buchanan, *Works,* VII, 375).

CHAPTER XXV

CLOSE OF CAREER

Despite the one-term pledge included in his letter accepting the Presidential nomination, there were many who believed that Polk would stand for a second term. Some of the Democratic leaders *feared* that he might do so, while certain of his friends *hoped* that he might be induced to accept another nomination. Both fears and hopes were wholly unwarranted, for the President never swerved from his determination to retire at the end of four years. Notwithstanding Claiborne's disparaging remark that "no one but himself dreamed of his re-election,"[1] nothing in contemporary documents indicates that Polk indulged in such dreams; on the contrary, there is abundant evidence to show that he longed to retire from public life.

As early as December, 8145, Senator Benton expressed the belief that certain Tennessee politicians were planning to run Polk for another term. When told of this the President noted in his diary that there was not the slightest foundation for such a belief: "My mind has been made up from the time I accepted the Baltimore nomination, and is still so, to serve but one term and not be a candidate for re-election." In January, 1847, he rejoiced "that with my own voluntary free will & consent I am not to be again a candidate. This determination is irrevocable."[2]

During the course of his administration political leaders frequently suggested to the President that he ought to (sometimes must) run again. On all occasions his answer was the same—that under no circumstances would he again be a candidate.

---

[1] Claiborne, *Life and Correspondence of John A. Quitman*, I, 235.

[2] Polk, *Diary*, I, 142, II, 328.

In 1848, when commenting on Buchanan's scheming for the nomination, the President wrote in his diary:

> The truth is, I have no doubt, though I cannot prove it, that Mr. Buchanan has become apprehensive that in the contest for the nomination between Gen'l Cass, Mr. Woodbury, and himself the Democratic party may ultimately be forced to look to me for re-election. He knows that I have no such views & that I have constantly declared to all who have introduced the subject to me that I would retire at the end of a single term, but notwithstanding this he fears that a state of things might arise in which the party might require me against my will to be placed before the country for re-election.[3]

On May 13, 1848, the second anniversary of the declaration of war against Mexico, the President read to Cave Johnson a letter in which he formally declared that he would not stand for reëlection. It was addressed to Dr. J. M. G. Ramsey, a Tennessee delegate to the Democratic national convention, and was "to be by him presented to the convention if, as has been often suggested to me it might be, my name should be brought before the convention for nomination." Inasmuch as he was determined to retire, he deemed it "proper to relieve the Convention of any embarrassment which the presentation of his [my] name might produce." Subsequently the letter was shown to several of the delegates who had stopped in Washington on their way to Baltimore, and to personal friends. All regretted his determination to retire. Rhett, of South Carolina, and Venable, of North Carolina, went so far as to say that Polk could carry their respective states, but that Cass would be unable to do so. While he could not fail to be gratified with such expressions of approval, the President adhered to his original purpose, and his letter to Ramsey was read to the convention before the balloting had begun.[4]

Not only did the President decline another nomination, but from first to last he had refused to lend his influence to any

---

[3] *Ibid.*, III, 354–355.

[4] Polk, *Diary*, IV, 448–463, *passim*. The letter itself is printed in Jenkins, *Life of James Knox Polk*, 307.

aspirant of his party. Not even in his diary does he express a distinct preference, although there are indications that he probably preferred Cass. He made his appointments and shaped his policies with a view to the success of his own administration. To aspirants and to the public he made it clear that he would affiliate with no faction of the party; he would support the candidate chosen by the representatives of the people, whoever that candidate might be. He even tolerated the Barnburners until they had openly seceded from the party.

The Democratic national convention assembled at Baltimore on May 22, 1848, and its greatest difficulty proved to be the solution of a knotty problem presented by the delegates from New York. Two sets of delegates from this state appeared, and each claimed the right to seats in the convention. On the first day the credentials committee decided tentatively to admit neither faction unless it would agree to abide by the nomination. This decision was regarded as a victory for the Hunkers and as advantageous to Cass, and the Barnburners refused to submit to interrogations. When reporting this to Polk, J. Knox Walker wrote that ''Your true position before the Convention will be presented immediately before any balloting.'' Two days later he reported much bitterness and confusion, and that the convention probably would admit both delegations.[5] This course was adopted eventually, as the convention did not care to assume the responsibility of deciding between the two factions.

The Barnburners, who favored the Wilmot proviso, were dissatisfied and retired from the convention. They met at Utica in June and nominated Van Buren for President. In August, at a convention held in Buffalo, they joined with Whigs and Abolitionists in nominating Van Buren and Charles Francis Adams on a ''Free-soil'' ticket.

The secession of the New York delegation from the Baltimore convention and their subsequent affiliation with old-time enemies

---

[5] Walker to Polk, May 22, 24, 1848, *Polk Papers.*

were regarded by the President as little short of party treason. He lost no time in removing from office B. F. Butler and other active Barnburners. When news of the nominations made at Buffalo reached Washington, he remarked that "Mr. Van Buren is the most fallen man I have ever known."[6]

Party schism and ill health overcame temporarily the iron will of the President, and he yielded to despondency—almost to despair. Schism mean the probable success of the Whigs and the reversal of his cherished policies. Ill health portended an early termination of his earthly career. On November 2, his fifty-third birthday, he confided to his diary:

> It will be 21 years on to-morrow since my father died. My mother is still living. Upon each recurrence of my birthday I am solemnly impressed with the vanity & emptiness of worldly honors and worldly enjoyments and of [the wisdom of] preparing for a future estate. In four months I shall retire from public life forever. I have lived three fourths of the period ordinarily allotted to man on earth. I have been highly honoured by my fellow-men and have filled the highest station on earth, but I will soon go the way of all the earth. I pray God to prepare me to meet the great event.

The news, a week later, that Taylor had probably been elected President called forth another melancholy comment:

> Should this be so, it is deeply to be regretted. Without experience in civil life, he is wholly unqualified for the station, and being elected by the Federal party and the various factions of dissatisfied persons who have from time to time broken off from the Democratic party, he must be in their hands and under their absolute control. Having no opinions or judgment of his own upon any one public subject, foreign or domestic, he will be compelled to rely upon the designing men of the Federal party who will cluster around him, and will be made to reverse, so far as the Executive can reverse, the whole policy of my administration, and substitute the Federal policy in its stead. The country will be the loose [loser] by his election, and on this account it is an event which I should deeply regret.[7]

The defection of the Barnburners, which augured Democratic defeat in November, made the President all the more determined

---

[6] Polk, *Diary*, IV, 36–37, 67.   [7] *Ibid.*, 177, 184–185.

to achieve new victories while his own party remained in power. During the summer of 1848 he busied himself with what proved to be a hopeless attempt to acquire Cuba, and with extending the influence of the United States in South and Central America.

When Congress convened in December, Taylor had been elected and there remained but one short session of Democratic rule. Polk's four great policies[8] had been carried through successfully, but the problem of slavery in the Mexican cession still remained to be solved. Defeat of his party at the polls did not deter the President from urging once more his own solution— the extension of the Missouri Compromise line. His persistency led Collamer, of Vermont, to compare him with the lawyer who, being reprimanded for contending against the opinion of the judge, replied that he "was not rearguing the case, *but damning the decision.*"[9]

Judged by standards of the period which was just closing, the solution offered by the President's message seemed both natural and reasonable. Even so shrewd a politician as Polk did not seem to realize that the days of King Compromise were numbered and that conscience and abstract principles had become the dominating factors in the slavery question. Influential leaders of both North and South were now more interested in constitutional rights than in rquare miles of territory, and the rank and file were rapidly falling into line. To be sure another compromise law was recorded in the statute books in 1850, but Clay's famous omnibus turned out to be Pandora's box in disguise. During the debate on this bill, Calhoun gave warning that disunion would surely result from further agitation against slavery on the part of the North. In reply, Seward announced his "higher law" doctrine which served as a battle-cry in renewed onslaughts upon the "peculiar institution."

---

[8] California, Oregon, Tariff, and the Independent Treasury.
[9] Coleman, *Life of John J. Crittenden,* 328.

Naturally, Polk was chagrined because the slavery question remained unsolved at the close of his administration, and, as we have seen in a preceding chapter, he left Washington harboring the fear that California would become an independent state.[10] Still, he had little cause for discouragement on account of failure in this particular. The most ambitious executive might well be satisfied with the achievements of his administration.

During the course of his official term Polk renewed amicable relations with nearly all of his political antagonists. Bailie Peyton was the first to seek a reconciliation, and in September, 1845, in response to an inquiry, the President said that he "would receive him courteously & respectfully."[11] Peyton was subsequently given a miltiary appointment during the war with Mexico. Wise, as we have seen, was completly won over by the loyal support which the President gave him while he was minister to Brazil. John Bell was the last to seek a renewal of friendly relations, but in January, 1848, he, too, offered the pipe of peace. As the two men had not spoken since the Speakership contest in 1835, the first interview was somewhat embarrassing, especially so on the part of Bell. The President's "manner and conversation," however, "soon put him at his ease."[12] With Clay, the President always maintained cordial personal relations. Clay was a dinner guest at the executive mansion on several occasions, and, according to Foote, he tendered his services to the President in overcoming Whig opposition to the treaty with Mexico.[13]

Polk left office harboring greater resentment for individual Democrats than for members of the opposition party. Blair and Benton had proved themselves to be "unprincipled," and the

---

[10] See above, page 655.   [11] Polk, *Diary,* I, 32.

[12] "I said to him that I was glad to see him, and that so far as I was concerned I was willing to let bye-gones be bye-gones, to let the past be forgotten, and to renew with him our personal intercourse. He said that was his desire, that we were to live neighbors when we retired from public life, and that he desired to be on terms of friendship. I expressed similar desires on my part" (Polk, *Diary,* III, 284–285).

[13] Polk, *Diary, passim.* H. S. Foote, *Casket of Reminiscences,* 22.

"baseness" of Wilmot could not "be adequately described." For the opposition party as a whole, his feelings had undergone no change. As late as February 20, 1849, he recorded that

The Whigs & abolitionists in Congress pursue me with a malignity and a bitterness which can only be accounted for because of their chagrin at the success of Democratic measures during my administration.[14]

Determined to uphold Democratic principles so long as the power rested in his hands, he went to the capitol on the last evening of his official term prepared to veto the Wilmot proviso and any internal improvement bill that might be presented. As we have seen in the preceding pages, he was not called upon to use the veto power, although Congress would in all probability have passed the obnoxious bills if the President's determination to veto them had not become known.

The delight caused by the thought of retirement is recorded by the President on February 13, 1849, the fourth anniversary of his arrival in Washington:

I am heartily rejoiced that my term is so near its close. I will soon cease to be a servant and become a sovereign. As a private citizen I will have no one but myself to serve, and will exercise a part of the sovereign power of the country. I am sure I will be happier in this condition than in the exalted station I now hold.[15]

General Taylor arrived in Washington on February 23, and immediately an annoying question of etiquette presented itself. Buchanan and other members of the cabinet were planning to call upon the President-elect, and one of them consulted Polk concerning the propriety of their doing so. Polk and Taylor had never met; but since their relations during the Mexican war had been mutually distrustful, the President was not at all certain that Taylor would call upon him to pay his respects. He told the members, therefore, that "if my Cabinet called on Gen'l Taylor before he called on me, I should feel that I had been

14 Polk, *Diary*, IV, 227, 343–344.
15 *Ibid.*, 331–332.

deserted by my own political family.'' All except the Secretary of State agreed with the President; Buchanan threatened to disregard Polk's wishes, but did not carry out his threat. Taylor removed the cause for embarrassment by calling at the White House on February 26, after which Polk gave a dinner in his honor and treated him with the utmost cordiality.[16] As they rode to the capitol on inauguration day, Polk found his successor to be well meaning, but ''exceedinglly ignorant of public affairs''; he added to the general's difficulties by *absconding* with the Executive Journal so that poor Taylor did not know what officers he was expected to appoint![17] When reporting to Polk this joke of the season, Cave Johnson said that the new President knew less about public affairs than even his opponents had believed.

On the evening of March 5[18] Polk boarded the steamboat and began his journey homeward. In response to invitations from southern cities, he traveled via Richmond, Charleston, and New Orleans, thence up the Mississippi river. During his whole Presidential term he had suffered much from chronic diarrhoea, and the fatigue of the journey caused its recurrence in an acute form. Medical attention gave temporary relief, and the ex-President reached Nashville much weakened yet apparently on the road to recovery. After a brief rest he was able to visit his mother at Columbia and Mrs. Polk's mother at Murfreesborough.

About a year before he left Washington he disposed of his home in Columbia and purchased the Nashville residence of the late Senator Grundy. It was renamed Polk Place, and under the personal supervision of Mrs. Polk the house was enlarged and refurnished, and the grounds beautified. The President

---

[16] *Ibid.*, 349–359.

[17] ''The old Genl himself says that by some accident or mistake *you* had taken off the *Executive Journal* & therefore he had been dilitory in presenting his nominations—he could not know what offices he had to fill on that acct!'' (Johnson to Polk, Washington, March 17, 1849, *Polk Papers*). Johnson remained in the Post Office Department for a few days after Taylor's inauguration.

[18] As the 4th fell on Sunday, Taylor was not inaugurated until the 5th.

longed for the day to arrive when he might put aside the cares of state and enjoy the quiet of a private citizen, although many of his utterances indicate that he believed the end to be near.

For a time, after his arrival in Nashville, he was more cheerful. The enthusiastic welcome accorded by his neighbors and the interest which he took in supervising the improvements being made at Polk Place restored temporarily his old-time vigor. Whenever he undertook the performance of a task it was his habit to expend his energies freely; and in his present state of health, his storehouse of energy was rapidly exhausted. The labor of arranging the books in his library caused a recurrence of the malady from which he had suffered on his homeward journey, and it was soon apparent that he could not recover.

The Polk family as well as Mrs. Polk were Presbyterians, but the ex-President was not a member of any church. He went regularly with his wife to the church of her choice, although his preference was for the Methodist denomination.[19] A few days before his death his aged mother came from Columbia bringing her own pastor in the hope that her son might accept baptism and unite with the Presbyterian church. But the son recalled a promise once given to Reverend McFerren, of the Methodist church, that, when he was ready to join the church, McFerren should baptize him.[20] Having thus formally embraced Christianity, he felt prepared "to meet the great event."[21] He died on June 15, 1849, in the fifty-fourth year of his age. He was buried in the garden at Polk Place. In 1893 his body, with that of Mrs. Polk, was removed to the grounds of the state capitol. On his tomb is the following epitaph, prepared by A. O. P. Nicholson:

---

[19] "Mrs. Polk being a member of the Presbyterian Church I generally attend that Church with her, though my opinions and predilections are in favor of the Methodist Church" (Polk, *Diary*, I, 86).

[20] Chase, *History of the Polk Administration*, 474–475.

[21] See above, page 716.

By his public policy he defined, established, and extended the boundaries of his country. He planted the laws of the American union on the shores of the Pacific. His influence and his counsels tended to organize the national treasury on the principles of the Constitution, and to apply the rule of freedom to navigation, trade, and industry.

This eulogium by no means exaggerates the national service rendered by President Polk. Indeed, Nicholson might have added that he had made the American continents "safe for democracy" by repelling with vigor all interference by European powers.

Seldom in our history has such an ambitious and so varied a program been carried into effect in the brief space of four years. It was a program conceived, for the most part, by the President himself, and his dogged persistence was an important factor in procuring the legislation necessary for putting it in operation. And yet, as Schouler has truthfully said, when commenting on the ex-President's death:

After this brief-spaced decent tribute Polk's name was seldom publicly mentioned. Over the fruits, sweet and bitter, which his administration had cast so abundantly into the lap of the people, there sprang up very soon sectional quarrel and contention, but the gatherer of those fruits was very soon forgotten.[22]

And, in a great measure, he remained "forgotten" notwithstanding the fact that his tariff policy led to prosperity; that his "constitutional treasury" proved to be successful; that his "Polk Doctrine" has been approved and extended; and that his expansion policy added over five hundred thousand square miles of territory and gave the United States free access to the Pacific.

The acquisition of Louisiana, with its abundant resources and its value as a home for America's surplus population, has commonly been accredited to the statesmanship and farsightedness of Thomas Jefferson. When the centennial of this event was celebrated at St. Louis in 1904, Jefferson's part in the transaction was commemorated by medals struck in his honor. At a

---

[22] Schouler, *History of the United States*, V, 127.

similar exposition held in San Francisco in 1915 to celebrate the opening of the Panama canal, one listened in vain for any mention of the name of the man who had acquired the ground on which the exposition was being held, although days were dedicated officially to many individuals who had contributed little or nothing to the acquisition of the canal or to the prosperity of the Pacific coast. Possibly, many who attended the exposition could not have answered the campaign cry of 1844, "Who is James K. Polk?" And yet, every one who is familair with our history knows that Louisiana was purchased without Jefferson's knowledge or consent, and that a vast empire (including California) on the Pacific coast came into the possession of the United States as the result of a policy conceived by President Polk and consummated despite vigorous opposition, both at home and abroad.

Why, then, has this man's name been enveloped in comparative obscurity? Why has he not received full credit for his achievements? Undoubtedly one reason is that he possessed little personal magnetism, while his uncompromising independence dissatisfied all factions; and, consequently, he had no personal following to sound his praises and perpetuate his memory. The excerpt from Schouler, above quoted, suggests incidentally a more potent reason, although Schouler lays the chief emphasis on the fact that Polk was "soon forgotten." As he says, "there sprang up very soon sectional quarrel and contention," and unquestionably this sectional discord had much to do with attaching odium to the Polk administration and with consigning the President's memory to oblivion.

The introduction of the Wilmot proviso precipitated a real crisis in our history. The debate which it elicited presented new phases of the slavery question and rendered the sectional conflict truly "irrepressible." The determination of the anti-slavery forces to exclude the institution from all territories called forth a counter-determination on the part of the South that the "rights" of the slaveholding states must be guaranteed and protected. Henceforth the slavery question overshadowed all others. Little thought was given to the "sweet fruits" which Polk had gathered. Debates on topics wholly unrelated to slavery inevitably drifted into a discussion of this fatal subject, and all attempts made to solve the problem increased rather than diminished sectional bitterness.

Since the conflict at first[23] concerned the territories acquired from Mexico, Polk's expansion policy was represented to be a conspiracy to extend slavery. But the President was not even given the credit usually accorded to a successful conspirator, for he was alleged to be the mere tool of more capable intriguers. On the other hand, the protagonists of slavery had no gratitude for the man who was charged with being their agent in the plot to extend slavery. His unswerving independence, his refusal to approve the extreme southern program, and his advocacy of an extension of the Missouri Compromise line, made him, in their eyes, a traitor to southern interests. As we have noted elsewhere, Polk's policy of compromise was the policy of a period which had just closed. Total exclusion of slavery from the territories had become the watchword of one of the parties to the all-absorbing contest; unrestricted admission of "slave-property" was demanded by the other. As the advocate of the traditional method of adjusting the slavery question Polk satisfied neither side, and he was charged by each with being weak and temporizing. The achievements of his administration and his valuable services as chief executive were obscured by the focusing of public attention on the slavery question in its new and more acute form. Leaders of more extreme views won the approval of their respective sections. Conservatives like Polk were remembered only to be condemned. In the earlier histories of the Mexican War the writers have derived their information mainly from Whig sources

---

[23] It was not until the introduction of the Nebraska bill in 1854 that territories in the Louisiana Purchase were included in the discussion.

and from distorted accounts written by dissatisfied Democrats like Senator Benton.[24] Very naturally, therefore, Polk has been caricatured as the pliable instrument of the slave power, and little attention has been given to the constructive policies of his administration. More recently, however, much valuable material has been made available, and investigators have approached the subject with minds unprejudiced by the obsolete sectional controversy. They have found—and it is believed that the preceding pages have shown—that Polk was neither a conspirator nor a weakling, but that he was a constructive statesman, an unusually able executive, and a sound patriot. No other President took his task more seriously nor spent his energies more freely for his country; and few, indeed, have done more to increase the power and prestige of the nation.

---

[24] Especially his *Thirty Years' View.*

BIBLIOGRAPHY

PUBLIC DOCUMENTS

Abridgment of the Debates of Congress from 1789 to 1856, edited by Thomas H. Benton. New York, 1857.

American State Papers, Foreign Relations, Vol. V. Washington, 1858.

Congressional Globe. Washington, 1834–1873.

Executive Register of the United States, 1789–1902, compiled by Robert Brent Mosher. Baltimore, 1903.

Hansard's Parliamentary Debates, LXVII, LXXIX. London, 1843, 1845.

House Executive Documents
    212, 29 Congress, 1 sess.
    4, 29 Congress, 2 sess.
    6, 30 Congress, 1 sess.
    41, 30 Congress, 1 sess. (Emory, *Notes of a Military Reconnoissance.*)
    60, 30 Congress, 1 sess.
    7, 30 Congress, 2 sess.

House Reports
    312, 23 Congress, 1 sess.

Register of Debates in Congress. Washington, 1834–1856.

Senate Executive Documents
    1, 29 Congress, 1 sess.
    107, 29 Congress, 2 sess.
    1, 30 Congress, 1 sess.
    29, 30 Congress, 1 sess.
    35, 30 Congress, 1 sess.
    52, 30 Congress, 1 sess.
    65, 30 Congress, 1 sess.

Tennessee
    House Journal, 1839–40.
    House Journal, 1841–42.
    Senate Journal, 1839–40.
    Senate Journal, 1841–42.

Texas

Diplomatic Correspondence of the Republic of Texas, edited by George P. Garrison. 3 vols. *In* American Historical Association, *Annual Report, 1907–1908*. Washington, 1908–1911.

Treaties, Conventions, International Acts, Protocols and Agreements, between the United States of America and Other Powers, 1776–1909, compiled by William M. Malloy. 3 vols. Washington, 1910.

MANUSCRIPTS

BUCHANAN, JAMES. *Papers:* Library of Historical Society of Pennsylvania.
CRALLÉ, RICHARD K. *Papers:* Library of Congress.
CRITTENDEN, JOHN J. *Papers:* Library of Congress.
GREEN, DUFF. *Letters:* Library of Congress.
JACKSON, ANDREW. *Papers:* Library of Congress.
JOHNSON, ANDREW. *Papers:* Library of Congress.
LARKIN, THOMAS O. *Papers:* Bancroft Library, University of California.
MCLEAN, JOHN. *Papers:* Library of Congress.
PIERCE, FRANKLIN. *Papers:* Library of Congress.
POLK, JAMES K. *Papers:* Library of Congress.
POLK, Col. WILLIAM. *Papers:* Library of Congress.
TRIST, NICHOLAS P. *Papers:* Library of Congress.
VAN BUREN, MARTIN. *Papers:* Library of Congress.
WELLES, GIDEON. *Papers:* Library of Congress.

PUBLISHED DIARIES AND CORRESPONDENCE

ADAMS, JOHN QUINCY. *Memoirs of John Quincy Adams, comprising portions of his diary from 1795 to 1848*, edited by Charles Francis Adams. 12 vols. Philadelphia, 1874–1877.

BROWN, AARON V. *Speeches, Congressional and Political, and Other Writings.* Nashville, 1854.

BUCHANAN, JAMES. *The Works of James Buchanan, comprising his speeches, state papers, and private correspondence;* collected and edited by John Bassett Moore. 12 vols. Philadelphia and London, 1908–1911.

CALHOUN, JOHN C. *Correspondence*, edited by J. Franklin Jameson. *In* American Historical Association, *Annual Report, 1899*. Washington, 1900.

CALHOUN, JOHN C. *The Works of John C. Calhoun*, edited by Richard K. Crallé. 6 vols. New York, 1851–1870.

HEISS, JOHN P. ''Papers,'' *Tennessee Historical Magazine*, II, No. 2.

LAUGHLIN, SAMUEL H. ''Diary,'' *Tennessee Historical Magazine*, II, No. 1.

LINCOLN, ABRAHAM. *Complete Works*, compiled by John G. Nicolay and John Hay, edited by Francis D. Tandy. 12 vols. New York, 1905.

POLK, JAMES K. *The Diary of James K. Polk*, edited by Milo Milton Quaife. 4 vols. Chicago, 1910.

''Polk-Donelson Letters,'' *Tennessee Historical Magazine*, III, No. 4. Letters of James K. Polk and A. J. Donelson, edited by St. George L. Sioussat.

''Polk-Johnson Letters,'' *Tennessee Historical Magazine*, I, No. 3. Letters of James K. Polk and Cave Johnson, edited by St. George L. Sioussat.

''Polk-Pillow Letters,'' *American Historical Review*, XI, No. 4. Edited by Jesse Siddall Reeves.

TAYLOR, ZACHARY. *Letters of Zachary Taylor from the Battle-Fields of the Mexican War*, edited by William K. Bixby. Rochester, N. Y., 1908.

NEWSPAPERS

Baltimore
> *Niles' Weekly Register.*
> *Sun.*

Nashville
> *Democratic Statesman.*
> *Daily Republican Banner.* Daily and triweekly.
> *Union.* Semiweekly and triweekly.
> *Whig.*

San Francisco
> *Alta California*

Washington
> *Gazette.*
> *Globe.*
> *Madisonian.*
> *National Intelligencer.*
> *Spectator.*

PERIODICALS

American Historical Magazine. 9 vols. Nashville, 1896–1904. Contains Mary Winder Garrett's ''Pedigree of the Polk Family,'' also letters of Jackson and other statesmen.

Democratic Review. New York, 1838–1859.

ARTICLES IN PERIODICALS

BOURNE, EDWARD G. ''The United States and Mexico, 1847–1848,'' *American Historical Review,* V, No. 3.

SCHAFER, JOSEPH. ''British Attitude toward the Oregon Question, 1815–1846,'' *American Historical Review,* XVI, No. 2.

SIOUSSAT, ST. GEORGE L. ''Some Phases of Tennessee Politics in the Jackson Period,'' *American Historical Review,* XIV, No. 1.

BOOKS AND PAMPHLETS

ADAMS, EPHRAIM DOUGLAS. *British Interests and Activities in Texas, 1838–1846.* Baltimore, 1910.

ADAMS, HENRY. *History of the United States.* New York, 1891–1898.

AMBLER, CHARLES HENRY. *Thomas Ritchie.* Richmond, 1913.

BANCROFT, HUBERT HOWE. *History of California,* Vol. 5. San Francisco, 1886.

BENTON, THOMAS H. *Thirty Years' View.* New York, 1862.

BIRNEY, WILLIAM. *James G. Birney and His Times.* New York, 1890.

CHASE, LUCIEN B. *History of the Polk Administration.* New York, 1850.

CLAIBORNE, J. F. H. *Life and Correspondence of John A. Quitman.* 2 vols. New York, 1860.

COLEMAN, ANN MARY BUTLER. *The Life of John J. Crittenden, with selections from his correspondence and speeches.* 2 vols. Philadelphia, 1873.

CURTIS, GEORGE TICKNOR. *Life of Daniel Webster.* 2 vols. New York, 1870.

CURTIS, GEORGE TICKNOR. *Life of James Buchanan.* 2 vols. New York, 1883.

FOOTE, HENRY S. *Casket of Reminiscences.* Washington, 1874.

FREMONT, JOHN CHARLES. *Memoirs of My Life.* Chicago and New York, 1887.

GALLATIN, ALBERT. *The Oregon Question.* New York, 1846.

GARRISON, GEORGE PIERCE. *Westward Extension.* New York, 1906.

GRANT, U. S. *Personal Memoirs.* 2 vols. New York, 1885–1886.

GRAY, W. H. *A History of Oregon, 1792–1849.* Portland, 1870.

HITCHCOCK, ETHAN ALLEN. *Fifty Years in Camp and Field,* edited by W. A. Croffut. New York and London, 1909.

HOLST, Dr. H. VON. *The Constitutional and Political History of the United States,* translated by Alfred B. Mason and Paul Shorey. 8 vols. Chicago, 1881–1892.

HOLST, Dr. H. VON. *Verfassungsgeschichte der Vereinigten Staaten von Amerika.* 4 vols. Berlin, 1878–1884.

HOWE, M. A. DE WOLFE. *The Life and Letters of George Bancroft.* 2 vols. New York, 1908.

JAY, WILLIAM. *A Review of the Causes and Consequences of the Mexican War.* Philadelphia, 1849.

JENKINS, JOHN S. *The Life of James Knox Polk.* Auburn, 1850.

JONES, ANSON. *Memoranda and official correspondence relating to the Republic of Texas, its history and annexation. Including a brief autobiography of the author.* New York, 1859.

LATANÉ, JOHN H. *Diplomatic Relations of the United States and Spanish America.* Baltimore, 1900.

LEARNED, HENRY BARRETT. *Some Aspects of the Cabinet Meeting.* Washington, 1915.

MANN, MARY TYLER. *Life of Horace Mann.* Boston, 1865.

MEADE, GEORGE GORDON. *The Life and Letters of George Gordon Meade.* 2 vols. New York, 1913.

MEIGS, WILLIAM MONTGOMERY. *The Life of Thomas Hart Benton.* Philadelphia and London, 1904.

NELSON, ANSON and FANNY. *Memorials of Sarah Childress Polk.* New York, 1892.

PARTON, JAMES. *Life of Andrew Jackson.* 3 vols. Boston, 1876.

PHELAN, JAMES. *History of Tennessee.* Boston, 1889.

PORTER, VALENTINE MOTT. *General Stephen W. Kearny and the Conquest of California.* Los Angeles, 1911.

PRENTISS, GEORGE LEWIS. *Memoir of S. S. Prentiss.* New York, 1855.

REEVES, JESSE SIDDALL. *American Diplomacy under Tyler and Polk.* Baltimore, 1907.

REID, WHITELAW. *The Monroe Doctrine, the Polk Doctrine and the Doctrine of Anarchism.* New York, 1903.

RIPLEY, R. S. *The War with Mexico.* 2 vols. New York, 1849.

RIVES, GEORGE LOCKHART. *The United States and Mexico, 1821–1848.* 2 vols. New York, 1913.

SCHOULER, JAMES. *History of the United States.* 6 vols. New York, 1880–1899.

SCHURZ, CARL. *Life of Henry Clay.* 2 vols. Boston and New York, 1887.

SCOTT, NANCY N. *A Memoir of Hugh Lawson White.* Philadelphia, 1856.

SCOTT, WINFIELD. *Memoirs of Lieut.-General Scott, LL.D.* Written by himself. Usually cited as *Autobiography.* 2 vols. New York, 1864.

SHEPARD, EDWARD M. *Martin Van Buren.* Boston and New York, 1889.

SMITH, ASHBEL. *Reminiscences of the Texas Republic.* Galveston, 1876.

SMITH, JUSTIN H. *The Annexation of Texas.* New York, 1911.

SUMNER, WILLIAM GRAHAM. *Andrew Jackson.* Boston, 1888.

TEMPLE, OLIVER P. *Notable Men of Tennessee, from 1833 to 1875. Their Times and Contemporaries.* New York, 1912.

THOMPSON, WADDY. *Recollections of Mexico.* New York and London, 1846.

TYLER, LYON G. *Letters and Times of the Tylers.* 3 vols. Richmond, 1884–1896.

WHARTON, FRANCIS. *A Digest of the International Law of the United States.* 3 vols. Washington, 1887.

WILSON, J. G. *The Presidents of the United States.*

YOAKUM, H. *History of Texas, 1685–1846.* 2 vols. New York, 1856.

INDEX

Pendergrast, G. J., trouble in Buenos Ayres, 708.

Pew, T. J., 85.

Peyton, Bailie, 72–73, 97, 111, 113, 454, 718.

Pickens, F. W., 239, 567.

Pico, Andrés, 473.

Pico, Pio, 427.

Pillow, Gideon, 233; works for Polk's nomination, 235 ff., 240; intrigue, 243, 289; 340, 446, 511; criticizes Taylor, 455; at Chapultepec, 485; denounced by Trist, 526; arrested by Scott, 531; denounced by Stephens, 635.

Pinckney, H. L., 95.

Polk, Ezekiel, his "Toryism," 2, 273.

Polk, Jane Knox, 1, 721.

Polk, James K., ancestry and education, 1–4; lawyer, 5; marriage, 6; personal traits, 4, 7–9, 25, 69, 139, 283; republicanism, 10, 18; in state legislature, 5; enters Congress, 6, 10, 12; and majority rule, 14, 17; on state rights, 18; and Jackson, 19, 21, 30, 39, 65, 81–82, 86–88, 91, 104, 134; opponent of Adams, 19, 20; party man, 20; on Committee on Foreign Affairs, 20; and six militia men, 21; minority report on U. S. Bank, 31 ff.; chairman of Committee on Ways and Means, 37, 38, 41–42; elected Speaker, 90, 93; "unscrupulous partisan," 91; selected to redeem Tennessee, 123–125, 140; and party press, 123, 274; phrenological chart, 139; victim of discord as Speaker, 92 ff.; "Jackson's creature," 92, 102; committee appointments, 93, 101, 116, 127, 136; and slavery petitions, 94, 107, 109, 121; decisions attacked, 96 ff., 110, 122;

decisions praised, 103; 102, 115, 118; decides Mississippi election, 119 ff.; "glorious infamy," 120; last term as Speaker, 125 ff.; scorns "affairs of honor," 129; vote of thanks opposed, 136; farewell to House, 137; "best Speaker," 138; and White, 68 ff., 73, 76, 79, 88, 90; attitude toward Van Buren, 164, 210, 213, 217, 221, 232, 241, 292, 297, 338, 633; and Bell, 50, 63 ff., 68, 70, 75, 85, 91, 96, 123, 659; attitude toward slavery, 191, 464, 612, 614, 618–620, 627 ff., 633, 640, 646; begins gubernatorial campaign, 140; denounced by press, 141 ff., 148; "address to the people" (1839), 142; denounces Hamiltonism and defends Jeffersonism, 143 ff.; political consistency, 145; elected governor, 150; inaugural address as governor, 156; first message as governor, 157; and banks of Tennessee, 169; remedial legislation, 171; denounces Harrison, 183; defeated by Jones, 187; doubts Nicholson's loyalty, 199; no compromise with Bell, 199; runs for governor (1843), 204; favors pledging candidates, 206; defeated, 207; and Vice-Presidency, 161–164, 201, 207, 209, 213 ff., 218, 233; opposed by old line Democrats, 214; nominated for Vice-President by Tennessee, 159, by Mississippi, 315; distrusts Blair, 214, 266; 300; declines place in Tyler's cabinet, 217; Texas letter, 227; availability as candidate, 231; suggested for President by Jackson, 232; nominated at Baltimore, 238–239; reasons for nomination, 240, 245 ff., 251; comments on ability by Jackson, 246; "Who is James K. Polk?," 248; claim to greatness, 249–251; represents younger Democrats, 252, 257; party organ, 252, 266, 299, 331; letter of acceptance, 258;

Y0-AEY-549

Press This	To Do This
Alt+Enter	Display Properties dialog box
Shift+F8	Outdent entire paragraph
Ctrl+Shift+L	Insert a page break
Delete	Clear selected text or object

Keyboard Shortcuts for Reading Documents

You can use the following keyboard combinations while reading documents on Windows and OS/2:

Press This	To Do This
Enter	Read the selected document
Ctrl+E	Edit the selected document
Ctrl+L	Enter and follow a URL to a World Wide Web site
Ctrl+P	Print the selected document
Shift+	Expand all sections
Shift-	Collapse all sections
Esc	Close the active window
Space	Activate a doclink

Keyboard Shortcuts for Viewing Documents

You can use the following keyboard combinations while viewing documents on Windows and OS/2:

Press This	To Do This
Ctrl+A	Select all documents
Ctrl+C	Copy selected documents
Ctrl+F	Find occurrence of a text string
Ctrl+G	Find next occurrence of a text string
Ctrl+L	Enter and follow a URL to a World Wide Web site
Ctrl+P	Open the file Print Dialog box
Ctrl+X	Cut selected documents
Enter	Open the selected document
Space	Select or deselect
Shift+Space, or ↑	Select or deselect multiple documents
F3	Go to next selected document
Shift+F3	Go to previous selected document
F4	Go to next unread document
Shift+F4	Go to previous unread document
F9	Update index of view
Shift+F9	Rebuild the current view
Ctrl+Shift+F9	Rebuild all views in the current database

Using WorkSpace Keys

You can use Workspace keys to perform the following tasks on Windows and OS/2:

Press This	To Do This
F1	Get context-sensitive help
F5	Log off Notes (revoke password login but leave Notes running)
F6	Cycle through open panes
F9	Update the number of unread documents in Notes databases
F10 or Alt	Access the menu bar so you can use arrow keys to choose commands
Alt+F4	Exit Notes
Alt+F5	Restore Notes program window to default size
Alt+F10	Maximize the Notes program window (OS/2 only)
Alt+3	Send a memo
Ctrl+F6	Cycle through open windows
Ctrl+F9	Minimize active window and cascade other active windows
Ctrl+F10	Maximize all open windows
Ctrl+L	Enter and follow a URL to a World Wide Web site
Ctrl+M	Create a new memo
Ctrl+N	Create a new database
Ctrl+O	Open a database (add a database to Workspace)
Ctrl+Break	Cancel a server operation
Ctrl+Shift, ↑, ←, or, → Enter	Move a database icon
Esc	Close a document
Delete	Remove a database icon from your Notes Workspace, or mark document for deletion

Mastering™ Lotus® Notes® 4.6

Third Edition

Kenyon Brown
Kyle Brown
Francois Koutchouk
Kevin Brown
Scot Haberman

SYBEX®

San Francisco • Paris • Düsseldorf • Soest

Associate Publisher: Amy Romanoff
Contracts and Licensing Manager: Kristine Plachy
Acquisitions & Developmental Editor: Maureen Adams
Editors: Kim Wimpsett and Vivian Perry
Project Editor: Raquel Baker
Technical Editor: Matt Riggsby
Book Designer: Kris Warrenburg
Graphic Illustrator: Patrick Dintino
Desktop Publisher: Maureen Forys, Happenstance Type-O-Rama
Production Coordinators: Rebecca Rider and Susan Berge
Indexer: Nancy Guenther
Companion CD: Molly Sharp and Ginger Warner
Cover Designer: Design Site
Cover Photographer: Mark Johann
Cover Photo Art Direction: Ingalls & Associates

Screen reproductions produced with Collage Complete.

Collage Complete is a trademark of Inner Media Inc.

SYBEX is a registered trademark of SYBEX Inc.

Mastering is a trademark of SYBEX Inc.

TRADEMARKS: SYBEX has attempted throughout this book to distinguish proprietary trademarks from descriptive terms by following the capitalization style used by the manufacturer.

Netscape Communications, the Netscape Communications logo, Netscape, and Netscape Navigator are trademarks of Netscape Communications Corporation.
Netscape Communications Corporation has not authorized, sponsored, endorsed, or approved this publication and is not responsible for its content. Netscape and the Netscape Communications Corporate Logos are trademarks and trade names of Netscape Communications Corporation. All other product names and/or logos are trademarks of their respective owners.

The CD Interface music is from GIRA Sound AURIA Music Library ©GIRA Sound 1996.

The author and publisher have made their best efforts to prepare this book, and the content is based upon final release software whenever possible. Portions of the manuscript may be based upon pre-release versions supplied by software manufacturer(s). The author and the publisher make no representation or warranties of any kind with regard to the completeness or accuracy of the contents herein and accept no liability of any kind including but not limited to performance, merchantability, fitness for any particular purpose, or any losses or damages of any kind caused or alleged to be caused directly or indirectly from this book.

Photographs and illustrations used in this book have been downloaded from publicly accessible file archives and are used in this book for news reportage purposes only to demonstrate the variety of graphics resources available via electronic access. Text and images available over the Internet may be subject to copyright and other rights owned by third parties. Online availability of text and images does not imply that they may be reused without the permission of rights holders, although the Copyright Act does permit certain unauthorized reuse as fair use under 17 U.S.C. Section 107.

First edition copyright ©1996 SYBEX Inc.
Copyright ©1998 SYBEX Inc., 1151 Marina Village Parkway, Alameda, CA 94501. World rights reserved. No part of this publication may be stored in a retrieval system, transmitted, or reproduced in any way, including but not limited to photocopy, photograph, magnetic or other record, without the prior agreement and written permission of the publisher.

Library of Congress Card Number: 98-85547
ISBN: 0-7821-2342-2

Manufactured in the United States of America

10 9 8 7 6 5 4 3 2 1

Software License Agreement: Terms and Conditions

The media and/or any online materials accompanying this book that are available now or in the future contain programs and/or text files (the "Software") to be used in connection with the book. SYBEX hereby grants to you a license to use the Software, subject to the terms that follow. Your purchase, acceptance, or use of the Software will constitute your acceptance of such terms.

The Software compilation is the property of SYBEX unless otherwise indicated and is protected by copyright to SYBEX or other copyright owner(s) as indicated in the media files (the "Owner(s)"). You are hereby granted a single-user license to use the Software for your personal, noncommercial use only. You may not reproduce, sell, distribute, publish, circulate, or commercially exploit the Software, or any portion thereof, without the written consent of SYBEX and the specific copyright owner(s) of any component software included on this media.

In the event that the Software or components include specific license requirements or end-user agreements, statements of condition, disclaimers, limitations or warranties ("End-User License"), those End-User Licenses supersede the terms and conditions herein as to that particular Software component. Your purchase, acceptance, or use of the Software will constitute your acceptance of such End-User Licenses.

By purchase, use or acceptance of the Software you further agree to comply with all export laws and regulations of the United States as such laws and regulations may exist from time to time.

Software Support

Components of the supplemental Software and any offers associated with them may be supported by the specific Owner(s) of that material but they are not supported by SYBEX. Information regarding any available support may be obtained from the Owner(s) using the information provided in the appropriate read.me files or listed elsewhere on the media.

Should the manufacturer(s) or other Owner(s) cease to offer support or decline to honor any offer, SYBEX bears no responsibility. This notice concerning support for the Software is provided for your information only. SYBEX is not the agent or principal of the Owner(s), and SYBEX is in no way responsible for providing any support for the Software, nor is it liable or responsible for any support provided, or not provided, by the Owner(s).

Warranty

SYBEX warrants the enclosed media to be free of physical defects for a period of ninety (90) days after purchase. The Software is not available from SYBEX in any other form or media than that enclosed herein or posted to *www.sybex.com*.

If you discover a defect in the media during this warranty period, you may obtain a replacement of identical format at no charge by sending the defective media, postage prepaid, with proof of purchase to:

SYBEX Inc.
Customer Service Department
1151 Marina Village Parkway
Alameda, CA 94501
(510) 523-8233
Fax: (510) 523-2373
e-mail: info@sybex.com
WEB: HTTP://WWW.SYBEX.COM

After the 90-day period, you can obtain replacement media of identical format by sending us the defective disk, proof of purchase, and a check or money order for $10, payable to SYBEX.

Disclaimer

SYBEX makes no warranty or representation, either expressed or implied, with respect to the Software or its contents, quality, performance, merchantability, or fitness for a particular purpose. In no event will SYBEX, its distributors, or dealers be liable to you or any other party for direct, indirect, special, incidental, consequential, or other damages arising out of the use of or inability to use the Software or its contents even if advised of the possibility of such damage. In the event that the Software includes an online update feature, SYBEX further disclaims any obligation to provide this feature for any specific duration other than the initial posting.

The exclusion of implied warranties is not permitted by some states. Therefore, the above exclusion may not apply to you. This warranty provides you with specific legal rights; there may be other rights that you may have that vary from state to state. The pricing of the book with the Software by SYBEX reflects the allocation of risk and limitations on liability contained in this agreement of Terms and Conditions.

Shareware Distribution

This Software may contain various programs that are distributed as shareware. Copyright laws apply to both shareware and ordinary commercial software, and the copyright Owner(s) retains all rights. If you try a shareware program and continue using it, you are expected to register it. Individual programs differ on details of trial periods, registration, and payment. Please observe the requirements stated in appropriate files.

Copy Protection

The Software in whole or in part may or may not be copy-protected or encrypted. However, in all cases, reselling or redistributing these files without authorization is expressly forbidden except as specifically provided for by the Owner(s) therein.

For my wonderful sister and brother-in-law,
Kristen and Scott Tod.
—Kenyon Brown

To my brothers, Kenyon, Kevin, and Keith, who
have opened many doors of opportunity for me.
—Kyle Brown

To Nicole and Gérard, my parents.
Thanks, Athena Perlmutter.
—Francois Koutchouk

To my loving and supportive wife and children,
Robyn, Jordan, and Andrew.
—Kevin Brown

To my wife, Kim, and my daughter, Sydney.
—Scot Haberman

ACKNOWLEDGMENTS

We want to thank the members of the staff at Sybex for their help during the writing of the first edition of this book, especially Neil Edde, Associate Developmental Editor, and Ben Miller, Project Editor. We'd also like to thank Production Coordinators Grey B. Magauran and Michael Tom, and Electronic Publishing Specialists Nathan Johanson and Kate Kaminski. June Waldman did an outstanding job of editing the manuscript, and Todd Headrick gave it a thorough and insightful technical review.

Thanks to members of the Sybex team who pitched in to help with the revision of this book: Developmental Editor Maureen Adams, Project Editor Raquel Baker, Editor Kim Wimpsett, Technical Editor Matt Riggsby, Editorial Assistant Malka Geffen, and Production Coordinators Rebecca Rider and Susan Berge. Also, thanks to Editor Vivian Perry for pulling through with the fastest edits in town. And thanks to Maureen Forys for her very adept desktop publishing.

Finally, Scot Haberman would like to thank his wife, Kim, for supporting and encouraging him to take on this assignment during the latter part of her pregnancy and through the birth of their daughter. He would also like to extend his gratitude to his employer of 12 years, Electronic Data Systems. Through his work experience at EDS, Scot gained the knowledge necessary to undertake this endeavor.

CONTENTS AT A GLANCE

TABLE OF CONTENTS

INTRODUCTION

Mastering *Lotus Notes 4.6* is a comprehensive reference guide for users and application developers alike. The book covers Lotus Notes Releases 4.0, 4.1, 4.5, and 4.6. Regardless of the Notes version you are running, this book can help you use Notes to do your work and to communicate with people inside and outside your company. The book helps users become effective database designers as they take on the job of developing applications to solve business problems and to automate everyday tasks.

Notes is a flexible workflow automation tool that can help any organization, large or small, harness and manage virtually any kind of information. For example, Notes can help you do the following:

- Service customers and requests
- Organize financial information
- Manage sales accounts
- Track product development

What Is Workflow Automation?

Everybody has, at some time or other, probably participated in the popular corporate game of Paper Chase—filling out forms, sending documents, trying to find out if the documents got to the right place, receiving and forwarding documents, filing documents, and throwing away documents in order to reclaim file-drawer space.

The foremost endeavor of Lotus Notes is to *literally* replace paper documents with electronic documents; Notes is not a word processor with which you'll wind up producing paper anyway. Fully replacing a paper document with an electronic version requires not only the means to create the document, but also the means to *move* the document through a business environment as if it were a paper document. This process is the essence of Lotus Notes workflow automation. By re-creating and improving the circuit a document travels, workflow automation brings everyone a little closer to a paperless environment.

What Is Notes?

Lotus Development Corporation, the makers of Notes, refers to Notes as a *document database*, but don't let this terminology mislead you. Notes is not a traditional database. It's more useful to think of Notes as a way of organizing documents and making them accessible to groups of people.

Unlike a traditional database, which requires you to break information into discrete *data fragments* (such as a middle initial or social security number), Lotus Notes uses the *document* as the fundamental unit of information. As you know if you've worked with databases, data doesn't have any meaning outside the context of its database. A document, on the other hand, can stand on its own.

A Notes document can be as long, as complex, and as unstructured as any paper document you already use. Like a word processing document, a Notes document can contain complex formatting, even images. In fact, a Notes document can store anything that you can digitize (a fax, an image, a video, a sound recording, you name it). A Notes document is unlike a word processing document in that many people can read, revise, and respond to a Notes document. It won't be tossed away accidentally or lost in a file cabinet.

The Benefits of Notes

The unique database structure of Notes allows you to keep track of complex, relatively unstructured or semistructured information and to make that information available to groups of users on a network. This database structure keeps your information current and secure. Its applications accommodate the complex flow of information and divisions of responsibility within your group or even within your entire organization.

The efficient flow of information in a group is the most important benefit of Notes. Notes pioneered a new type of application called *groupware*—software that enables a group of people in an organization to use the same information in different ways, depending on each person's specific needs.

What's New in Lotus Notes Release 4.6?

As with Release 4.5, in Release 4.6 Lotus made a slight name change to the Notes product line. The server is still known as Lotus Domino Server 4.6, but the client piece now has two distinct versions. The first new product is called Lotus Notes Desktop, and the second is called Notes Designer for Domino. Most of the major enhancements to the client product are included in the Notes Desktop. The major difference between the two products is that the Lotus Notes Designer for Domino is designed to enable you to quickly develop business applications for the Net. With this new structure, Lotus positions Domino as the leading Web application server, integrating powerful Web server functionality with the proven messaging, collaboration, and application development capabilities of Lotus Notes.

The Domino Release 4.6 server provides services to numerous clients from a broad range of vendors—browsers, alternate mail clients, and Notes clients. The Domino Release 4.6 server still incorporates the ability to "plug and play" the server in a mixed environment. The Domino name emphasizes the fact that Lotus is focusing on the key business opportunity for the next generation of Web products: business community Internet/intranet servers and applications.

Internet Features

Notes 4.6 expands on the program's existing Internet functionality by including a few needed features. These features include:

- **Improved Web browsing:** You can access the Web using Microsoft Internet Explorer without leaving the Notes client. This allows you to maintain all of the Notes services including Web page storage, use agents to better manage information from the Internet, and forward Web pages via mail. All this while retaining your familiar Internet Explorer Web interface.

- **Enhanced Internet Web navigation:** You can explore the Web using the browser of your choice. You can choose between the Notes Personal Web Navigator, Netscape Navigator, Microsoft Internet Explorer, or Notes with integrated Microsoft Internet Explorer.

- **Internet POP3/SMTP mail support:** You can retrieve messages from your Internet service provider (ISP) or any Internet server that supports POP3. This allows you to maintain a universal that can contain both your Notes mail and your Internet mail. You also have the option of placing your Internet mail into a separate local file.

- **Enhanced Personal Web Navigator Internet options:** You can now manage the volume of Web pages stored locally for offline use. An option allows you to purge Web pages from the hard drive if the pages have not been accessed within a certain number of days. You can also import either your Netscape Navigator or Microsoft Internet Explorer bookmarks easily into the Notes Web Navigator.

Contact Management Features

Notes 4.6 has enhanced the Personal Name and Address book to function more fully as a contact manager. Since the Personal Name and Address book is fully integrated with the Notes messaging system, these enhancements make it easier to address memos, schedule meetings, and visit Web pages—all from within the address book. These changes include the following:

- The replacement of the Person document with a new Business Card document. The Person view has been replaced with the Business Card view. This new view allows you to view all of the contact information about an individual.

- A new Categorized view has been added that allows you to categorize your contacts and view your contacts grouped by those categories.

- You can create and address a mail memo, address meeting invitations, or go to a contact's Web site by selecting the contact's document and selecting a button from the Action bar.

- Notes automatically parses the contact's name, street, city, state, and ZIP code when you enter the information. You can also override field names for the contact's phone numbers so the fields can be mapped to the phone numbers appropriate for each contact.

Mail Enhancements

Notes 4.6 adds a few "time saving functions" that help while you are reading your e-mail. These "time saving" options convert mail messages or meeting invitations from your inbox or drafts folder into the following:

- **A new calendar entry:** You can create a new calendar entry that contains the full text of the e-mail.

- **A new task entry:** You can create a new task entry that contains the full text of the e-mail.

- **New memo:** You can create a new memo that contains a full copy of the e-mail or calendar entry.

- **New group:** You can create a new group from the To: and Cc: fields of an e-mail message.

When creating an e-mail message, you can choose to use Notes, Lotus Word Pro, or Microsoft Word as an alternate e-mail editor. This allows you to retain all the functionality of Notes while using an editor you are comfortable with.

Enhanced Programmability

The Notes and Domino application development environment provides tools that make it much easier to create interactive Internet and intranet applications. The Notes Designer for Domino client contains dozens of enhancements in the area of programmability. Among these are:

- **Web templates and samples:** Many of the templates have been enhanced to include support for Web browsers. Also, there are seven new sample databases that can be used as a starting point for applications or as a learning tool.

- **Java support:** The Notes Designer for Domino introduces several enhancements related to Java. They are:

  - **Java applets:** A Java applet is now treated like any other Notes object. You can set a Java applet's properties and pass it parameters.

  - **Run Java applets:** When a Java applet is placed in an application, the applet automatically runs in place, allowing the developer to view and test the applet.

  - **Domino Server Java agents:** You can now use Java to develop server agents.

- **Web design enhancements:** The Notes Designer for Domino has been improved to address the needs of Web developers. A developer can be more productive using the following new options:

  - **Passthru HTML:** HTML can be added or copied to any page by setting the text property to Passthru HTML.

  - **Anchor links:** You can now link to a specific location within a particular Web page.

- **Horizontal rule:** You can add a horizontal rule natively in Notes without having to use HTML.

- **Background images:** You can improve the appeal of your Web page with the use of background images on both forms and documents.

- **Webified Notes objects:** You can place a Notes view, Navigator, Folder pane, or Upload control directly from the Notes menu.

- **Computed text:** You can provide dynamically generated information to a user each time they read the page.

- **Develop for multiple clients:** You can create a single application designed for both client/server Notes clients and Web browsers. The features that support applications for multiple clients include:

  - A single checkbox to hide any design element, depending on which client is accessing the page.

  - The capability to specify different behaviors for design objects depending on the user.

  - The option of previewing pages while in design mode using a Notes client or Web browser.

  - A new Hide-When option found in the Properties box that allows you to selectively hide elements of an application from either Web browsers or Notes clients.

  - On Database Open launch features that are different when the application is accessed using a Notes client rather than a Web browser.

New Portfolio Database

Notes 4.6 adds a new database template called a Portfolio database. This new database allows you to easily group related Notes applications together and makes it easier to find information. Since all the applications can be grouped together, access to them can be available from within a single Navigation pane. This new database allows you to organize your information so that you can concentrate on getting your work done and not on where the work is located.

Domino Server Enhancements

Although this book concentrates primarily on the Notes client software, a few notable enhancements have been made to the server that are worthy of a quick synopsis. These changes and enhancements include:

- A simplified Domino installation process. Now a server can be up and running after completing the four-step, fill-in-the-blanks installation process.

- Native support for the IMAP4, LDAP, SMTP/MIME, and NNTP Internet protocols.

- Enhanced support for the SSL Internet protocol. Domino now supports SSL 3.0, which allows your applications to have the highest level of security.

- Enhancements to Domino templates such as those used by Web mail, Document Library, and NNTP discussions.

- A new Web-based administration capability allows your Domino servers to be administered via a standard Web browser.

How This Book Is Organized

This book is organized in five parts, which make it easy for you to find the information you need quickly.

Part I: Using Lotus Notes 4.6

Part I covers using Notes at work and discusses all the major end-user features. The chapters in this section describe the types of applications in Notes—one-to-one, one-to-many, and many-to-many—and it describes how Notes helps people become more productive in the extended enterprise.

Chapter 1: Putting Notes to Work

This chapter discusses how Release 4.6 enhances the user experience by providing more direct access to Notes functions. It also discusses how Notes behaves within its own environment, with other Lotus applications, and with other platform-specific applications. It covers Notes Release 4.6's increased programmability and the action-oriented paradigm, and it describes Notes' powerful "knowledge management" features. The chapter illustrates how Notes helps users manage sources of information in their daily work. Examples include news feeds, Notes mail, and other e-mail systems.

Chapter 2: What Notes Release 4.6 Is and Isn't

This chapter provides an overview of Notes and a handy reference to the new Notes 4.6 features, with cross-references to chapters that contain more thorough explanations of features.

Chapter 3: Touring the Notes Environment

This chapter describes the enhanced user interface. The three-pane window facilitates navigation through databases; folders organize documents for later use; dynamic, collapsible sections allow users to define expandable sections for easier browsing of large documents; Navigators replace the View/Folder hierarchy in the left panel of the standard three-pane window; Action bars display nonscrolling regions of Notes forms and views; and InfoBoxes enable users to manipulate the properties of Notes objects.

Chapter 4: Accessing a Notes Database

This chapter describes how Notes provides users with easy access to features and direct and powerful manipulation of the environment. It explains how to open a database and add it to the Notes Workspace.

Chapter 5: Viewing the Contents of a Database

This chapter explains the areas in the three-pane window. It also describes Navigators, hotspots, linking, manipulating views, the new folder structure, the action-oriented paradigm, and InfoBoxes.

Chapter 6: Searching a Notes Database

This chapter guides you through the steps of conducting a full text search.

Chapter 7: Creating a Document

This chapter discusses document/text manipulation, object-specific context sensitivity, and database-specific context sensitivity.

Chapter 8: Adding Advanced Features to Documents

This chapter focuses on using standard Actions to work effectively with a database. Standard Actions are inherent in the existing form or view—for example, close, print, open, save, send, edit, and categorize. This chapter shows how certain Actions are bound to a form or view. For example, in a form, users can always close or print the document. In a view, users can always open a document or another view.

Chapter 9: Printing Views and Documents

This chapter explains printing documents and views, as well as setting up pages for printing.

Chapter 10: Importing and Exporting Data

This chapter shows how to import data from other applications and how to export documents and data to other applications. The chapter covers using the Viewer feature, which allows a user to preview attachments.

Chapter 11: Communicating via Notes Mail

This chapter describes the similarities between Notes mail and cc:Mail and explains sending/receiving mail, attaching documents, personalizing a mail account, and using new mail templates.

Chapter 12: Calendaring and Scheduling

This chapter discusses Notes Release 4.6 calendaring and scheduling (C&S). The C&S features enable you to coordinate schedules, record upcoming activities, and view the availability of others in your workgroup—all of which are an integral part of collaboration.

Chapter 13: Working Off-Site with Mobile Notes

This chapter discusses replicating data with the office and using Mobile/dial-up Notes to work off-site.

Part II: Building Notes Applications

Part II describes the steps the developer takes to build a Notes database or application. This section discusses the importance of adding workflow features to

Notes applications. The chapters in this section parallel the features an end user sees when using a form or view from the perspective of the developer.

Chapter 14: Defining the Components of a Notes Application

This chapter describes the basic constructs of Notes and the interaction between components. It covers good user interface design practices, discusses rapid application development (RAD) issues, and explains Release 4 user interface enhancements.

Chapter 15: Incorporating Workflow in a Database

This chapter explains the concept and practice of workflow within a company or department and shows how Release 4.6 enables the developer to incorporate workflow in an application. It covers using a Navigator to walk through a workflow and give users graphical access to Notes data.

Chapter 16: Building Security into a Notes Database

This chapter covers security standards (North American, European, International), taking security measures and making data secure, and encrypting data. It discusses elements to consider in an enterprise-wide security plan and describes new facilities in Release 4.6 that allow administrators to manage security centrally.

Chapter 17: Laying Out a Form

This chapter describes planning the basic design of a form, including subforms and collapsible sections, and utilizing different regions of the form's layout.

Chapter 18: Formulas

This chapter covers using formulas in a form. It discusses defining formulas for different field types and using @functions, variables, constants, and operators.

Chapter 19: Designing Dynamic Forms

This chapter describes the steps of refining the design of a form and ways to achieve direct control over form layout, including pixel-level control of object placement and the ability to define fields visually. It explains how to use named styles, collapsible sections, and hotspots that can sit on top of text, images, or any defined area. Hotspots can launch doclinks, buttons, or pop-ups; run a formula; run an Agent; or run a script. Hotspots can be placed in rich text fields and in Navigators. When combined with the Action bar and Navigators, hotspots provide the user with direct graphical manipulation within the Notes environment.

Chapter 20: Designing Flexible Views with Navigators

This chapter shows you some techniques for creating more readable views for the user: multiple lines per row, word-wrapping within a row, and different colors in alternate rows. Navigators—a new design element of a Notes database—appear in the Navigation pane of the Notes database window and provide graphical access to Notes data within Notes. Developers build Navigators with a new set of graphic design tools.

Chapter 21: Creating Custom Actions

This chapter describes Actions (a workflow-oriented programming element) and the Action bar. The developer creates custom Actions that can take the form of a command, formula, script, or Agent—that is, anything that the developer can put behind a button. This chapter shows how the developer designates which Actions are to be made available to the user for each form or view at any given point (e.g., on creation, when editing, reading, or by a formula). The user sees the Actions in the nonscrolling Action bar or in the File menu.

Chapter 22: Representing Tabular Data and Creating Tables

This chapter describes creating tables and manipulating table data—selecting across cells, applying table properties, and having zero pad around cells.

Chapter 23: Using the Agent Builder to Automate Processes

This chapter describes using the Notes Agent Builder for creating buttons and writing macros to automate tasks within Notes. It covers enhancements to the Notes Macro Editor and explains how to debug applications.

Chapter 24: Basing a Database on a Design Template

This chapter discusses using a Notes design template for developing a new database. It includes the use of a data dictionary, the propagation of schema, and the concept of inheritance; discusses the advantages and disadvantages of using existing third-party Notes templates and databases; and explains how a user can reuse portions of work in multiple applications.

Chapter 25: Indexing a Notes Database

This chapter describes the steps of indexing a database and emphasizes the importance of creating a thorough and logical index to help users find data quickly.

Chapter 26: Rolling Out Notes Applications

This chapter explains providing help to end users, writing Help documents and Policy documents, and using pop-ups and hotspots to display hypertext information. It explains the query-by-form and query-by-example features and reviews tools for rolling out an application, including Lotus Smartcam and Notes-based training.

Chapter 27: Managing Databases

This chapter discusses the role of the developer as database manager, the work of maintaining databases, and ways to reduce occurrences of data corruption. It addresses replication conflicts and how to avoid them, versioning, and a way to manage large attached objects. It explains the role of a designer in the development process and the designer's relationship to the Notes administrator.

Part III: Integrating Notes in the Work Environment

Part III discusses the process of replication—synchronizing multiple copies, or *replicas,* of the same database within a company. This section describes using the new Notes Replicator for maintaining current copies of the same database that are used by people throughout an organization. Part III also discusses using OLE 2.0 and the process of linking and embedding data objects in Notes documents to create "compound" documents. The section describes how to maintain large and complex compound documents by taking advantage of Notes OLE capabilities.

Chapter 28: Replicating Databases

This chapter describes the processes of synchronizing data within a company and connecting with other companies. It includes discussions of the new Release 4.*x* field-level replication, passthru replication, and selective replication.

Chapter 29: Linking and Embedding Objects in Notes

This chapter shows you how to link and embed objects in databases, using data from other applications. The chapter demonstrates NotesFlow, an enhancement to Notes/FX, which supports two-way field-level data exchange. The chapter shows how OLE automation allows the Notes developer to call OLE automation servers from Notes applications, specifically from LotusScripts; and it shows how to use Notes with other applications, such as Microsoft Word for Windows 95, Lotus Word Pro, and Visio 4.

Part IV: Distributing Notes Databases on the World Wide Web

Part IV discusses Notes 4.6 Internet features and capabilities, namely, *Domino* and the *Personal Web Navigator*. Domino is server technology that transforms Lotus Notes into an Internet applications server. Domino enables you to develop a broad range of business applications for the Internet and intranet. The Personal Web Navigator combines the features of a Web browser with the powerful capabilities of Notes. You can also access the Web through a central database called the Server Web Navigator database, which resides on a Notes server. Part IV compares the specific functional differences between the Web and Notes and the relative merits of the two technologies. We explain how to integrate Notes and the Web using Domino. One of Domino's most powerful features is its ability to automatically—and transparently—turn your Notes documents, views, and forms into Hypertext Markup Language (HTML) pages.

Chapter 30: An Internet Primer for Notes Developers

The purpose of this brief chapter is to review the technology behind the Internet, not to teach readers of its intricacies. This chapter is simply a way for readers to focus on the essential elements of the Internet as they pertain to Notes technology.

Chapter 31: Using the Personal Web Navigator

This chapter discusses two tools you can use to navigate the Web and access information: the Personal Web Navigator and the Server Web Navigator. The Personal Web Navigator provides easy access to the Web and allows you to navigate through pages on the Web directly from your Notes workstation. All you need is a direct Internet connection. The Personal Web Navigator combines the features of a Web browser with the powerful capabilities of Notes. You can also access the Web through a central database called the Server Web Navigator database. This database resides on a Notes server. Remote Notes users access this database in the same way as they access other Notes databases.

Chapter 32: Comparing Notes, Domino, and the Web

This chapter examines the specific functional differences between the Web and Notes and the relative merits of the two technologies. Notes 4.6 is both a Web server and a server for Notes clients. This chapter explains how to integrate Notes and the Web using Domino. Domino is server technology that transforms Lotus Notes into an Internet applications server. Domino combines the open networking environment of Internet standards and protocols with the powerful application development facilities of Notes, enabling you to develop a broad range of business applications for the Internet and intranet.

Chapter 33: Using Domino to Publish Notes Databases on the Web

This chapter explains how Domino automatically—and transparently—turns your Notes documents, views, and forms into HTML pages. By marrying the power of collaboration and workflow of Notes to the publishing strength of the Web, you get the best of both worlds. Notes simplifies the management of a Web site because you can use a Notes database to control which documents are published at any point in time and who should have access to them. With Notes you can automatically maintain all the links between HTML pages, including hypertext links, attached files, and associated images, *from within* Notes databases as opposed to having to manually hunt around the Web server's hard drive for broken links.

Part V: Programming with LotusScript 3

Part V introduces using LotusScript and its implications for Notes developers. This section discusses the basics of the LotusScript programming language, including properties and methods. Part V also describes the Notes Integrated Development Environment (IDE) and shows the user how to write, compile, and debug scripts. Finally, the section introduces the Notes Object Classes, the object-oriented extensions to the LotusScript language. The section illustrates how Object Classes give developers a lot of control over design objects in the Notes environment.

Chapter 34: An Introduction to LotusScript

This chapter provides an overview of LotusScript. LotusScript is the object-oriented programming environment for all Lotus applications. The chapter explains the process of writing programs, or *scripts,* for objects. (Users write formulas using the Notes formula language.) The chapter also discusses the strengths and weaknesses of LotusScript and how LotusScript doesn't allow users to combine scripts with formulas or Simple actions.

Chapter 35: Writing Scripts in LotusScript

This chapter explains how to use LotusScript. The chapter shows users how to write scripts, using database examples from the book to illustrate structuring scripts to automate tasks in Notes. The chapter also shows users how to attach scripts and formulas to various objects in Notes depending on need, and explains how the particular object determines what a programmer can use.

Chapter 36: The Notes Class Library

This chapter describes LotusScript's predefined object classes and the properties and methods for the classes. The chapter also explains how Notes oversees the compilation and loading of scripts and automatically includes the Notes class definitions. Finally, the chapter shows how LotusScript supports OLE 2.0 automation and the Integrated Development Environment (IDE).

Appendix: What's on the CD-ROM?

The appendix describes how to use the sample databases, shareware, and demonstration programs on the CD-ROM that accompanies this book. The CD includes Visio Express, a simplified version of Visio, the best-selling business graphics drawing program. Now you can create workflow diagrams to illustrate work processes within an organization, and you can use the diagrams to design Notes applications.

Glossary

The glossary provides brief instructions for using many features or performing specific tasks. It also defines all the important Notes terms that both end users and Notes database designers need to understand.

What's Next?

As Notes continues to evolve as *the* workflow automation platform in the world of client/server systems, we can probably expect significant developments, especially in the areas of intranet technologies and Web publishing tools. Many companies are basing their electronic communications infrastructures on Lotus Notes because of its robust e-mail capabilities and powerful business process automation toolkit. Using Notes as a communication and Web publishing tool is obviously an integral part of distributing and tracking information in organizations throughout the world. As Notes provides new features and enhancements, everyone will benefit from the efforts of Lotus to help people work together more effectively and efficiently.

PART I

Using Lotus Notes 4.6

CHAPTER
ONE

1

Putting Notes to Work

- What Notes is and isn't

- Notes as the hub of a client/server relationship

- Notes as groupware

- Notes as e-mail

- Notes as a document database

- Notes as a Web publisher

- The Power of Notes

Lotus Notes is a flexible tool that can help any organization, large or small, take control of its information. Notes can track product development, organize financial information, or manage sales accounts. You can use Notes to service customers and requests, manage personnel information and employee profiles, and organize schedules and group calendars. The possibilities are virtually limitless.

In this chapter we provide an overview of the basic architecture of Notes Release 4.6 so you can begin to envision how to put Notes to work. We explain what Notes is and isn't, and we describe the benefits of using Notes in general terms. To more vividly illustrate how Notes can help your organization manage, exchange, and share information, we also profile several companies that have adopted Notes.

What Is Lotus Notes?

Lotus Notes is a distributed client/server database application that enables groups of people to organize, track, access, and share information over a network. You might say to yourself, "Big deal. A lot of database applications allow me to do the same thing. Why should I use Notes?" First, Notes architecture—the way Notes structures, manages, and disseminates its data—differs from other distributed database applications in the way it links people together.

The typical client/server application provides ways for people who are connected by a network to access data stored on a central server. However, in most cases, everyone accesses the data in a one-size-fits-all way; all users see the information structured the same way, regardless of their unique needs. By contrast, Notes creates a working environment in which people can access the same database at the same time and then use the information to suit their individual needs, offering more flexibility than the typical database.

Notes also allows you to share information with coworkers by communicating with them through its e-mail system. Like any e-mail system, Notes lets you send mail messages and file attachments to other people over a network. However, the information you can send through Notes mail is different from the information contained in a standard mail memo. For example, the information in a Notes mail message can come directly from a database, which can be accessed by many people at the same time.

NOTE   Because many people can use and exchange a Notes database simultaneously, they can manage, update, and communicate information more effectively and efficiently. When properly implemented, Notes can help organizations increase productivity.

As you can already see, Notes is a multifaceted product. Accordingly, the next few sections examine Notes from several perspectives: Notes as groupware, Notes as e-mail, Notes as a document database, and Notes as a Web browser and publisher. First, however, we'll turn to the client/server relationship because it stands at the center of all aspects of Notes.

The Client/Server Relationship

If you work as part of a group (and most of us do), you are probably already sharing access to documents and files with your colleagues over a network. A network usually stores master copies of documents in a central location, manages each user's access, and keeps track of modifications to shared files. A network can also store printer drivers and other shared resources. This central repository of files on a network is known as a *network file server*, or just as a *server*. The server runs the network's operating system that manages all network activity.

The network file server differs from the *Notes server*. An organization's Notes server is connected to its network as a *database server* or *information server*. The Notes server is the main storage area for Notes databases that many people in an organization share. It provides communication services to workstations and other Notes servers. It runs the programs that maintain databases on all the Notes workstations connected to it. A workstation is also known as a *client* because it runs the Notes client software.

Notes databases are typically stored on a server. All servers work essentially the same way regardless of the operating system or platform. Each user works on a *client* version of Notes, which turns an individual's computer into a Notes workstation. If a Notes server can be considered the central repository of information, the client can be considered the gateway to it. Table 1.1 lists the Lotus Notes client and server platforms available in Release 4.6.

TABLE 1.1: Lotus Notes Release 4.6 Clients and Servers Available

Release 4.6 Clients	Release 4.6 Servers
IBM AIX	NetWare
HP-UX	IBM OS/2
Macintosh 680x0*	Windows 95
Macintosh Power PC*	Windows NT (Intel)
Sun SPARC Solaris	Windows NT (Alpha)
Sun x86 Solaris	IBM OS/390*
Windows NT	IBM OS/400
IBM OS/2	IBM AIX
Windows NT (Intel)	HP-UX
Windows NT (Alpha)	Sun SPARC Solaris
Windows 95	Sun x86 Solaris
Windows 3.1*	

*Indicates platforms that only support up to Lotus Notes 4.5.

Notes as Groupware

Notes falls into a relatively new category of applications known as *groupware*. In contrast to word processing, spreadsheets, and similar computer application programs designed for a single user, Notes was created specifically for groups who want to organize and share information in a document database.

Groupware enables a group of people in an organization to use the same information in various ways that fit their specific and individual needs. It can enhance decision making, and it can encourage the spread of ideas and critical thinking. Using information as a basis for discussion and decision making lies at the heart of Notes. Figure 1.1 shows an example of the kind of information a Notes database can contain.

FIGURE 1.1:

A Notes database can contain a variety of information. This database contains profiles of a company's employees.

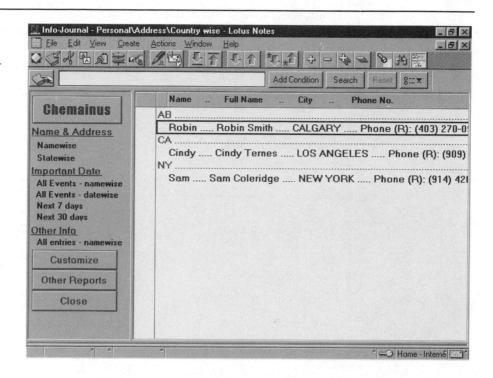

As a more concrete example of how Notes manages information, let's look at how an insurance company uses Notes to keep track of the thousands of home-owner policies it underwrites. Its Notes database contains detailed information on individual policies, including a photograph or floor plan of the property, the location and age of the home, the type of building, the fire-protection class (distance from a water source), the construction costs, and the number of units (for apartment buildings or condominiums).

The company considers many additional factors before it writes a policy or processes a claim, so the database also contains the following information in separate documents:

- Policy quotations from account agents
- Premium evaluations from underwriters
- Construction reports from building inspectors
- Claims from policyholders

The insurance company stores all this information in a variety of formats in one Notes database for use by many of its employees. For example, account agents update policyholder information, underwriters calculate premiums, inspectors write building construction reports, and adjusters track claims.

What sets a Notes database apart from other client/server database applications is the complexity of the information it can store and how it relates each piece of information to others, for example, an inspector's building report and a homeowner's claim. Moreover, Notes gives an organization fine-grained control of who can access this information. Each group in an insurance firm, for example, can view only the information it needs and can add to or change only the information to which it has access privileges:

Type of Information	Who Can View the Information
General information	Group responsible for maintaining information
Policyholder information	Account agents
Premiums	Underwriters
Building construction reports	Inspectors
Claims from policyholders	Adjusters

While Notes enables individuals to access just the information they need, it also allows them to share the information and discuss it among themselves. Through its built-in e-mail (see Chapter 11), Lotus Notes facilitates communication between workers and between groups of workers. In sum, Notes provides all the tools that groups need to manage the information they share.

Notes as E-Mail

Notes features its own sophisticated e-mail system, which is called Notes Mail. (We discuss Notes Mail in detail in Chapter 11.) Notes Mail is similar to other e-mail systems because it allows you to perform routine tasks such as sending mail messages to named recipients, routing mail messages over the Internet and other gateways to their final recipients, and viewing lists of incoming messages. However, Notes Mail is fundamentally different from other e-mail systems because it is integrated with Notes and becomes part of much larger database management workgroup applications.

Traditional e-mail systems send information from one user to another. Lotus refers to the traditional e-mail system as a *send model* system, which places most of its effort on moving messages quickly from user to user. In this type of system, the recipient of a message is responsible for its management.

Lotus calls a system like Notes Mail a *share model* system because it collects information in a central location where users can access it. The system that manages the shared information provides services for managing its collection, including archiving and group access.

NOTE   Notes implements its e-mail system as an integrated messaging component for delivering virtually any document in a Notes database, not just mail messages.

As in traditional e-mail systems, Notes databases are stored on servers that manage the information. Unlike traditional e-mail systems, however, those central servers also focus on document management, structure, categorizing, and the fastest way to move messages.

Notes as a Document Database

Lotus Development Corporation, the maker of Notes, refers to Notes as a document database, but don't let this terminology lead you to think that Notes is just a version of a traditional database. Think of Notes as a way of organizing documents and making them accessible to groups of users, rather than as a database in the traditional sense of the word (Approach, Access, dBASE, Paradox, and so on). Unlike a traditional database, which requires you to break information into discrete data fragments (such as a middle initial or social security number), in Lotus Notes the fundamental unit of information is a *document*. As you know if you've worked with databases, a piece of data doesn't have much meaning outside the context of its database; documents, however, are meaningful by themselves.

A Notes document can be as long, as complex, and as unstructured as any paper document you already use. A Notes document is something like a paper document, except, of course, that you view it onscreen. It won't be tossed away accidentally or lost in a file cabinet because it's always stored on a server. Like a word-processing document, a Notes document can contain complex formatting—even images. In fact, a Notes document can store anything that you can digitize (a fax, an image, a news feed, a video—you name it). In addition, a Notes document can be read, revised, and responded to by many people. The Notes document in Figure 1.2 presents a short description and an example of a graphic element that you can add to documents.

FIGURE 1.2:

This Notes document is from a database that provides a gallery of graphic elements such as lines, boxes, buttons, and icons that you can use to dress up documents.

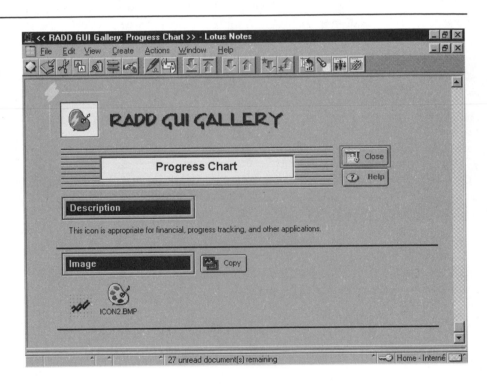

Web-Enabling Your Notes Environment

The Internet is a worldwide network of networks that connects millions of people together in a global work and recreation domain. You might be asking yourself what the Internet has to do with Notes. Well, just about everything! Lotus Notes provides a way for you to organize, share, collaborate with others, and integrate

Internet information in a secure environment. Notes Release 4 seamlessly integrates the riches of the Internet into your work environment.

NOTE   You can use Notes to publish information onto a Web site and to share information pulled from the Internet.

Lotus has made many advances in terms of integrating the standard protocols of the Internet into Notes, developing a common directory service (called NotesNIC), and giving administrators greater flexibility in deploying Notes (such as anonymous access, authenticated passthru servers, and Web-based administration).

With Release 4.6, the Notes client now supports the Internet mail standard (POP3/SMTP). This will allow users to retrieve e-mail messages from any Internet service provider or Internet server that supports the POP3 protocol. Not only can you use Notes for accessing Notes mail, but you can also use Notes Mail for accessing all your Internet mail, as well. This will eliminate the need for multiple mailboxes. For those wishing to keep their Internet mail separate from their Notes mail, you have the ability to pull all your Internet mail into a separate local mail file.

In addition to expanding your reach with greater external connectivity, the Internet offers your organization an inexpensive medium for connecting the Notes servers in your organization to each other or to Notes servers in other companies. Using the Internet as a communications solution can save you and your organization money if you have many point-to-point leased lines for communications to your branch locations or if you make extensive use of dial-up phone lines for transferring large amounts of data. Having a single connection point for each location reduces data communications management time and reduces your connection fees.

Large and medium-sized organizations with experienced and capable IS departments will realize the biggest savings. For small organizations, employing a direct Internet connection may not be a good investment because of the high start-up costs and experience they require. An alternative to setting up a direct Internet connection is to use a Lotus 'Net Service Providers Alliance Partner (NSPAP)—formerly Notes Public Network Provider—such as Interliant, to provide connectivity for mail routing and replication services between multiple Notes servers.

WARNING When connecting your Notes environment to the Internet, security becomes a crucial issue. Before making your actual Internet connection, be sure to check with your Notes administrator about securing your environment.

Using the InterNotes Web Navigator

Lotus integrated Web access into Notes Release 4 with the InterNotes Web Navigator, which enables you to access information on the Web through a database called the Web Navigator. This database resides on a Notes server that's connected to the Internet and is referred to as the *InterNotes server.* Each time you retrieve a page from the Internet, the Web Navigator translates that page into a Notes document and stores it inside the Web Navigator database. The next time you or anyone else wants to read that Web page, it is available for instant access.

Customizing and managing the Web Navigator is easy once you have it up and running. For example, the Web Navigator comes with powerful Agents you can use to purge and refresh the Web pages stored in the Web Navigator database. You can write additional Agents to customize your Web Navigator database by using specially developed LotusScript functions and Notes @functions. As for security features, you get all the security of Notes plus the added feature of being able to control access to specific Web sites.

Publishing Notes Databases on the Web

You can also use Notes as an authoring and document management system for a Web site. Lotus and several other vendors have products that automatically translate Notes databases into collections of Hypertext Markup Language (HTML) documents. These products allow standard Web browsers, such as Navigator or Internet Explorer, to read documents stored in a Notes database.

The Benefits of Notes

The unique database structure of Notes allows you to keep track of complex, relatively unstructured information and to make that information available to groups of users on a network. As a result of this structure, Notes offers you these additional benefits:

- Notes keeps your information current.

- Notes keeps your information secure.

- Notes applications accommodate the complex flows of information and divisions of responsibility within your group or your entire organization.

Notes Keeps Your Information Current

A Notes document gives you a convenient way of reading and modifying information. Over time, many people will make changes to documents. At an insurance agency, for example, homeowners add and cancel policies and premium rates increase (and sometimes decrease). Because they are centralized, easily accessed, and systematically revised through *replication*, Notes documents remain more current and accurate than paper documents. (You'll learn about replication in Chapter 28.)

Keeping documents current is important because many people within the organization use a document database to make decisions. Inaccurate information could hurt an organization and result in bad decisions. Notes gives you and your workgroup the means to keep your organization's information up-to-date.

Notes Keeps Your Information Secure

Notes requires that users who access a Notes database be assigned an *access level* to the database, either as an individual or as a member of a Notes group. For example, an insurance adjuster would have access to claims records that an account agent would not; account agents would have access to their clients' records but not to the records of other agents' clients.

NOTE   Because information is sensitive, Notes enables an organization to build security mechanisms into a database.

An organization needs to protect not only a database's design from unauthorized modification but also the data stored within it. It needs to make sure that only certain people can see certain information. It may also want to control the operations that each user can perform within a particular database. The Notes administrator assigns user-access levels for each database, specifying who can design and manage the database and who can read, modify, and add documents to it. You'll learn more about the different user-access levels and the access control list (ACL) feature in Chapter 4.

Notes Helps Your Group Work Together

The most important benefit of Notes is that it promotes the efficient flow of information in a group. Notes pioneered the concept of *groupware*—software that enables a group of people in an organization to use the same information but in different ways, depending on the specific needs of each user. Figure 1.3 shows an example of a database that contains information contributed by various people.

FIGURE 1.3:

A Notes database can identify the people who contribute information to it, enabling a group to track the data.

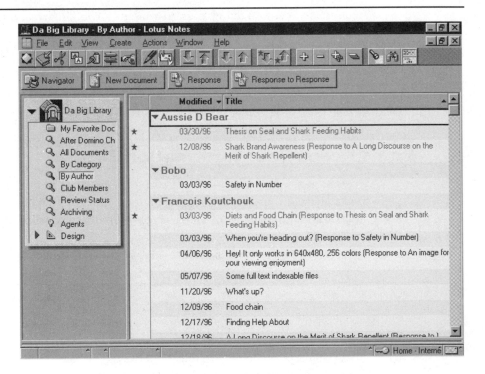

Using Notes to Prepare an Insurance Policy

Let's say a homeowner in earthquake country wants to buy an insurance policy:

- The account agent uses Notes to write the policy quotation. The policy quotation document requires information from several other people.

- An underwriter for California policies uses Notes to write her evaluation report. Before she can give final approval, she needs to verify in the database that the house has been inspected (to make sure it is properly bolted to the foundation and satisfies other building requirements). The underwriter won't give final approval until the inspector determines the house is structurally sound.

- The inspector uses Notes to write his building construction report for the underwriter's review. He adds his information to the original quotation document, indicating that the house passed the inspection.

- The underwriter approves the coverage and sets the premium rate for the policy.

A Group in Action

Of the hundreds of people employed by an insurance company, for example, four groups of people work closely together to process homeowner policies:

- Agents write the proposed policy for the homeowner.

- Underwriters approve the policy and set the premium.

- Inspectors evaluate building structure.

- Adjusters investigate damage and estimate the cost of a claim.

These people probably don't work in the same location; in fact, most agents establish their own offices and work independently. That's the nature of the insurance business. However, a Notes database provides a central storage location for information on all the agency's homeowner policies. By using Notes, everyone involved in the company's homeowner policies is able to evaluate the status of policies, revise them when necessary, change premium rates, and settle claims.

Going with the (Work)Flow

Every organization establishes systems and procedures for people to follow in their work. The way you perform your duties can affect the way other people do their work, and the way you share information with colleagues can help or hinder them.

Workflow is the way a group of people work together to accomplish tasks and achieve the group's goals. By using Notes to organize, access, track, and share information and to automate everyday tasks, your group can devise a more effective workflow.

Improving Workflow: Canyon Corporation

Canyon Corporation of Arizona, a small company of 45 people, designs and markets HealthClub software for the health and fitness club industry. The program tracks memberships and vital member information, schedules and maintains a calendar of events, manages point-of-sale transactions in equipment shops and restaurants, and interfaces with a word processor and desktop publisher. Canyon has installed and customized the program in almost 2,500 health clubs around the country. However, with sales of more than $10 million, the company was concerned that key business information, such as customer feedback, wasn't flowing through the small workforce as efficiently as it could. Efforts were duplicated, and good ideas were ignored.

In particular, the sales department didn't think the product development group was responsive to feedback from clients. Part of the problem was that salespeople were passing along informal suggestions to programmers; that is, they would talk to the programmers if they happened to meet in hallways and during breaks. The vice president of sales would frequently discuss suggestions with the head of product development. But the really useful information that came directly from salespeople in the field—specific suggestions for improving the program's interface and adding new features—wasn't passed along to programmers. In fact, the head of product development didn't want salespeople to share the information with her staff because it "created confusion and uncertainty." Friction between sales and product development grew, developing into an old-fashioned turf war.

A Notes application was the solution. Using a simple feedback form, each salesperson would enter information—suggestions, criticisms, complaints—from clients. Then the product development group could access the information and evaluate the feasibility of making certain changes. Subsequently, the product group developed its own feasibility form to discuss the usefulness and applicability of specific suggestions.

Continued on next page

One of the best suggestions resulted in the development of ClubKit, a much less expensive version of HealthClub. This version is better suited for smaller gyms that don't schedule events and classes, track extensive member information, or generate correspondence and produce newsletters. The new product has almost eliminated the expensive and time-consuming work of customizing the original product. Programmers can now direct their efforts to fine-tuning the company's products and developing new products.

The communication between sales and product development has improved greatly thanks to Notes. Discussions are less confrontational because the groups share product information online over the company's network. By using two simple database documents, one for collecting customer feedback and the other for discussing the feasibility of the feedback, the two groups are working together in a more productive way.

Larry Espinoza, the founder and president of the company, thinks Notes "is a great product. Ultimately we're seeing a savings in product development time, which means we're spending less money. If we can work customer feedback into an application, we're going to produce a better product. Word of mouth is important in the sports club business. Being able to maintain our reputation for providing excellent products makes us successful. If one club likes our product, that's our best advertisement. It helps making a sale at the next club that much easier. More sales is what it's all about."

Resistance to Lotus Notes

Let's face it. No one really welcomes change when *change* means doing a job differently. You've probably had to adapt at one time or another to a change in management. Or you've experienced other changes such as the expansion of a division, a new sales commission rate structure, reductions in departmental budgets, a new supervisor, or a new computer system.

Setting up Notes in an organization means an investment of time, money, network resources, and people. It can also mean a change in the way a group works: decentralized responsibility and greater accountability, at the very least. Not all users will be happy with these changes.

Developing Notes Applications

Out-of-the-box Notes doesn't do much except give you e-mail and a few sample applications. To take advantage of its full power, you need to build applications;

that is, design and construct Notes databases and then create interfaces for the various groups using the databases. Most Notes developers start by analyzing the way an organization conducts its business and uses information. They watch and speak with clients, managers, and staff to discover the different ways in which people share information. They assess the way people use e-mail, scrutinize the kind of data they share or need to share on a network, and ask staff members to articulate what they do with information and how they use it in their jobs. (You'll find a detailed discussion of this topic in Chapter 15.)

Once developers understand how people use information in an organization, they can set about designing an application that matches the way people in that organization share information. Ideally the application should streamline workflow. Using Notes helps to coordinate and optimize the use of information that was once decentralized throughout an organization's employees, departments, and divisions.

TIP   If you are responsible for creating applications, Parts II and III will enable you to do your job proficiently.

What's Next?

As organizations move to network their computers and facilitate communication through e-mail systems, the ways in which people work together change. Lotus Notes helps organizations put information in everyone's hands, keep the information current and secure, and prevent duplication of effort.

The remaining chapters of Part I give you, the Notes user, all the information you need to navigate the Notes environment, use views and forms, print databases, use e-mail, and run Notes from your laptop or home computer using a modem. If you're already developing Notes applications, Part I provides a thorough introduction to the realities confronting your users.

CHAPTER

TWO

2

What Notes Release 4.6 Is and Isn't

■ Comparing programs

■ Designing a Notes database

■ Viewing documents

■ Designing forms

■ Creating documents

■ Replicating databases

■ Comparing Notes releases

You may already be familiar with flat-file and relational database programs. Both types of databases organize information in a rigid file-record–field data structure. Notes, however, is neither of these kinds of databases. Instead of using a rigid structure to organize information, Notes provides a unique document structure for organizing information. The document— the heart of the database—contains fields that hold data. Although this description may sound a bit like a conventional database, Notes gives you more flexibility in the way you enter and view information. The document's design makes the information easy to read and convenient to use.

In this chapter, we build on the conceptual discussion of Notes from Chapter 1 and describe the basic components of a Notes database that distinguish it from a traditional database. We also discuss the significant differences between Notes 3 and Notes Release 4 and briefly describe Release 4's features.

Comparing Notes and Relational Database Programs

Before you begin to learn about the basic components of Notes databases, you should understand how the Notes database architecture differs from relational database architecture. You may be tempted to equate Notes with a relational database because they both use similar terminology such as *form, field,* and *view.* This perception is a mistake; the function of Notes is fundamentally different from the function of a relational database, and you should know when Notes is the right tool for the job and when it isn't.

The architecture of a Notes database is different from that of a relational database in many ways. Notes structures data in *documents*, which are discrete units that store several related pieces of data in *fields*. By contrast, relational databases structure data in *tables* made up of *rows* and *columns*, each row being roughly analogous to a Notes document and each column being roughly analogous to a Notes field. In a relational database, however, a row cannot exist outside the confines of a table where perhaps hundreds or thousands of other rows are also present; you are forced to deal with a row as a member of a larger collection of similar rows rather than as a self-contained structure like a document. Notes is much more flexible in its approach to data interactions when you compare it to the rigid table structure of a relational database.

A Notes database is a workflow-automation application. It uses an organization's computer network to keep the paperwork flowing among a group of people who are involved in the same business process. Each person in the group can access the same data at the same time but use the data for their own purposes. In general, this ability to interpret data in different ways encourages discussion, which eventually facilitates decision making.

NOTE   Communication lies at the heart of a Notes database because it brings a group of people together and acts as a catalyst for change. Notes is an extremely dynamic application.

A relational database is appropriate for transaction-oriented, real-time processes. A record in one table is related to a record in another table based on a common key, thus creating a relationship between the tables. This relationship enables you to perform an operation, or *transaction*, that affects the data in both tables. For example, you could transfer funds from a checking account to a saving account by debiting the checking account and crediting the savings account. One table would store the data for the checking account, and another table would store the data for the savings account. A relational database exists as a single, central repository and confines all database activity to that one collection of data; transactions are reflected without delay.

Notes supports neither the concept of a *transaction* nor an easy way to relate sets of data (documents) to one another; only relational tables afford this opportunity. In addition, Notes employs a *replicated database* architecture, whereby several copies of a database can exist throughout an organization. Consequently, activity in one copy of the database might not be reflected in another copy for hours or days until replication takes place. Under the right circumstances, replication is an extremely powerful facility, but a replicated database architecture is not viable for processes that demand changes be immediately evident to all users. You may say that Notes is a just-in-time database, rather than a real-time database.

TIP   If you need to organize information in one or more rigidly formatted tables for real-time, transaction processing, Notes is not the appropriate application.

TIP   If you want an application that allows you and others in your organization to create relatively free-form documents that can be shared among users, Notes is the application for you.

Now that you know what Notes isn't, let's get a better grip on what it is. The next few sections describe who is responsible for Notes database design, the basic parts of a Notes database, and how to use Notes to disseminate information throughout an organization.

Who Can Design a Notes Database?

Creating Notes databases is usually the job of a specialist. Because of the unique nature of Notes and the complexity involved in workflow automation, the person your organization designates to design and implement its Notes database must have a thorough knowledge of the product. This person may be your organization's Notes administrator, an outside Notes consultant, or a specially trained employee.

NOTE   The Notes administrator manages the databases on the network and makes sure the Notes server is always up and running.

Notes developers assess an organization's information needs, study the "flow" of information from one group to another, and recommend ways to move information through an organization by using Notes. Then developers create forms, views, and other required design objects that attempt to match the way an organization manages the steady stream of information it receives, such as sales leads, customer feedback, or status reports. By designing an application that's convenient for people to use, a developer can ensure that Notes disseminates information efficiently throughout an organization.

TIP   If a database is poorly designed or misconceived, the information it contains won't be of much use.

Notes recognizes that the structure of information should reflect the changing needs of an organization. Therefore, it doesn't restrict a database designer to a particular format. Only the designer's imagination and creativity and the particular needs of an organization limit the variety of formats.

If you are interested in designing Notes databases, Parts II and III of this book will walk you through the process. However, if you're not yet familiar with the issues Notes users face, read all of Part I before you take the plunge.

Viewing Documents in a Database

A *view* is a listing of particular documents in a database. For example, Figure 2.1 shows a view that displays a discussion database by categories.

FIGURE 2.1:

A view is the first element you see when you open a database.

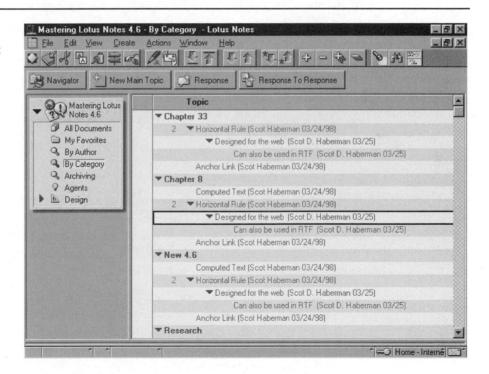

A database can contain many views that organize documents in different ways, depending on the needs of the organization and the groups of people using them. Figure 2.2 shows another view in the same database.

FIGURE 2.2:

A different view in the same database

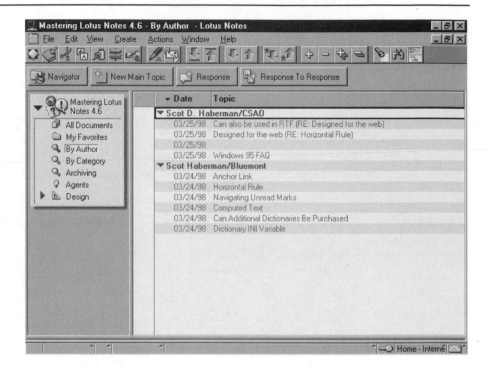

A view is usually the first element you see when you open a database. Like the table of contents you see when you open a book, a view summarizes the documents in a database in a particular way. It structures the information by neatly organizing documents into rows and columns. Each row in a view is a document, and each column is usually a field from a document.

This structure has nothing to do with the actual structure of the documents themselves (and shouldn't be confused with the structure of relational database tables). It's simply a convenient way to display an overview of the documents in a Notes database so you can quickly find a specific document. From a view, you scroll down the list and double-click the document you want to open.

NOTE   Chapter 5 explains how to use views, and Chapter 20 shows you how to create views.

Forms and Documents

A *form* is the basic structure of a document. Figure 2.3 shows an example of a form. You can think of a form as the original blueprint for a document and the documents themselves as what results from the execution of the blueprint, each one identical in structure but different in content—just like a subdivision of tract houses where the floor layouts are exactly the same but the exteriors and furnishings differ. A Notes application may have many different forms from which documents are constructed.

FIGURE 2.3:

The form is the foundation of a Notes document.

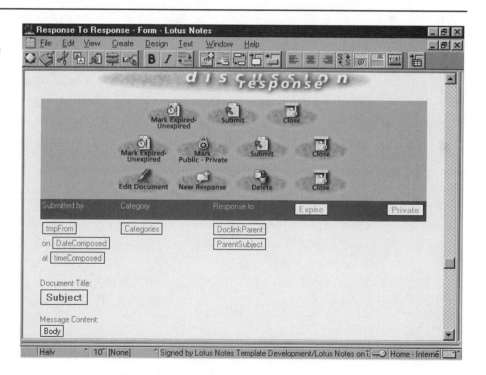

A blank form is the first thing you encounter when you want to create a new document and add it to a database. You create a document by entering data in the empty fields, according to the way the Notes application designer has designed the form and defined the fields. In fact, you can look at a document as nothing more than a copy of a fill-in-the-blank form with a separate field for each item of data. You enter and edit data that constitutes the document's contents directly on the onscreen form, and once you save it, you have a separate document. You can add subsequent documents to the database and modify or remove existing documents.

NOTE   Designers can format onscreen forms in many ways. The designer can add various design attributes such as boldface and italic, change the color of backgrounds and fonts, and choose from a variety of typefaces and point sizes. A designer can modify a form by using familiar formatting tools, just as you can change the appearance of onscreen text in any other Windows application.

The types of information you can enter into a document depend on the types of fields on its form. For example, you can enter text in text fields; numbers in number fields; and text, graphics, and Notes features, such as links and file attachments, in rich text fields. If Notes beeps when you try to enter text into a field, the field is a keyword field; you can press ↵ and select a keyword from the list Notes displays.

When you create or edit a document, Notes puts the document in Edit mode so you can enter information. You enter information in fields, which are enclosed by brackets. When the brackets are red, the field is encryptable.

The Help field is displayed at the bottom of the window when the insertion point is in the field.

A designer can place graphics on a form to enhance its appearance or create tables to display information in a tabular format. The form in Figure 2.4 shows a graphic and table. The designer can add collapsible sections, layout regions, and hotspots (links, automated text and graphics, buttons) to dramatically enhance the look and functionality of a form.

NOTE   Chapter 17 deals with the subject of form design, and Chapter 19 shows you how to enhance the design of a form with several powerful Notes features.

FIGURE 2.4:

This form includes a
layout region.

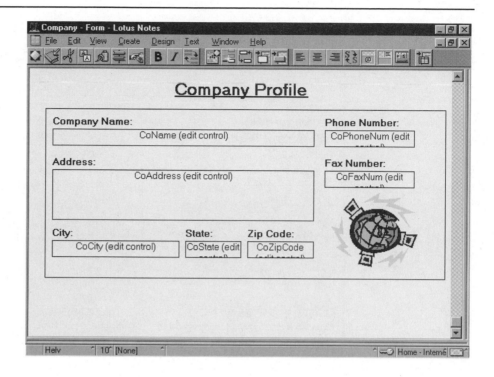

Creating a Document

A *document* is the fundamental unit of information in a Notes database. Figure 2.5 shows an example of a document created from the form shown in Figure 2.4. It's called a document (rather than a record) because it's analogous to a paper document.

Documents can include file attachments from other applications, such as word processors or spreadsheets. This feature is handy when you send e-mail to someone in your group and want to include a file. You can also embed objects in a document—a spreadsheet, for example—and modify it later by using OLE (Object Linking and Embedding; see Chapter 29 for more information).

Notes uses documents to organize information because the format is familiar to people and reflects the way people work. Relationships exist between documents in the same way people discuss topics and issues.

FIGURE 2.5:

A Notes document is analogous to a paper document.

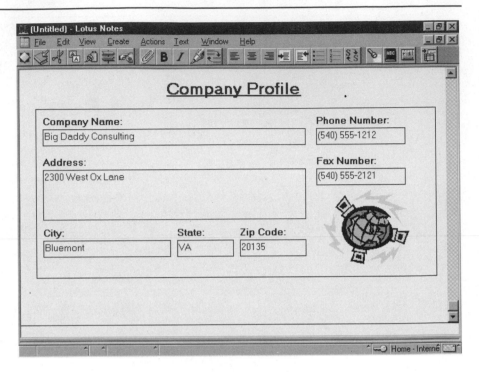

FIGURE 2.5:

A Notes document is analogous to a paper document.

For example, you can relate one document to another in Notes with a response. Suppose you write a memo and send it to three people. The people respond to your memo by sending you their replies. By designating the replies as responses, the recipients of your memo create a chronological hierarchy of information that others can track, and if the database is set up properly, your recipients can also incorporate information from your memo in their responses. In this scenario your memo is the main document, and the three replies are response documents.

Another example of relating one document to another is the way the insurance company in Chapter 1 uses the underwriter evaluation document to "respond" to the policy quotation document. (You'll recall this document summarizes the proposed coverage of the policy and estimates the premium.) The inspector completes a building construction document that "responds" to the underwriter evaluation document. (This document assesses the risk of insuring the building on the basis of its construction.) The information is disseminated over the network and viewed by various people who use the information to make decisions.

NOTE   See Chapter 7 for more information on creating documents.

Exchanging Data through Replication

Replication is a process that distributes several copies, or *replicas*, of a database throughout an organization. It allows users to add, delete, and modify individual replicas, and then synchronizes the replicas so that all replicas reflect the modifications in each replica. Replication is one of the most powerful features in the Notes environment.

Traditionally, a database resides and is maintained in a single, central location within an organization. A database that requires widespread access (beyond the bounds of the location where the database resides) may also require a sophisticated access scheme that involves a wide-area network architecture, as well as the associated expense and expertise.

Notes replication offers a simple mechanism that delivers the database to the users who need to interact with it. Replication enables users to work with a copy of the database that is in close proximity to them, either on a local Notes server or on their workstation hard drive. This arrangement results in better performance and overall usability than systems that access a centrally stored, client/server model database.

Notes uses database replication to distribute and update copies of the same database that may be stored on different servers and workstations. Replication allows users on different networks, in different time zones, or even in different countries to share information. The servers connect to each other at scheduled intervals, and the databases replicate their changes. Over time, replication makes all copies of a database identical. If a user makes changes in a copy of the database, replication ensures that those changes are added to all copies, as long as the replication options are set up to do so. The process takes time and requires specific Notes server resources on a network. Your organization's Notes administrator determines the replication schedule that makes the most sense for the company's system.

NOTE   You'll find a detailed discussion of replication in Chapter 28.

What's New in Notes Release 4

The functionality delivered in Notes Release 4 is a quantum improvement over previous versions. For end users, developers, and Notes administrators, Notes Release 4 provides a new level of power for organizing, sharing, and maintaining information than was previously possible. While the basic look and feel of the previous version remains intact, new features and enhancements to traditional features let you go well beyond what was achievable in the past.

TIP   If you are a Notes veteran, you will be able to leverage your past experience and use it to take Notes functionality to a new level.

End-User Features

The following sections describe the significant features and enhancements that extend the usability of Notes for the end user.

Managing Your Workspace

You can perform the following tasks in the Workspace (the Notes interface that you work in):

- Add or remove Workspace pages
- Keep the Workspace behind other open windows while you work
- Stack database icons for server-based and workstation-based replicas to conserve space within the Workspace
- Compact your Workspace file, freeing space created from deleted database icons
- Display the Workspace in three dimensions

Adding Information to Documents

When you create or edit a document, you can:

- Create a bulleted or numbered list automatically

- Create a table

- Create a collapsed section that readers can expand when they want to read its contents

- Collapse one or more paragraphs into a single line

- Create a link that lets readers switch to another document, view, folder, or database

- Create a button that lets readers perform a Notes action such as sending a mail message or opening a database

- Create a hotspot that lets readers display pop-up text, switch to a linked destination (such as a World Wide Web server), or perform a Notes action

- Create special characters, such as international currency symbols

- Add a picture

TIP

You can also add comments to a document in a distinctive font by using the Permanent Pen.

Formatting Paragraphs

You must be in a rich-text field to change paragraph properties. You can use the Text Properties InfoBox to:

- Format text and change the font, size, style, and color of text

NOTE

4.6 RELEASE   With Notes Release 4.6, 256 text colors are available, up from 16 in Release 4.5.

- Change the Permanent Pen font

- Align paragraphs

- Indent paragraphs

- Create a bulleted list automatically

- Create a numbered list automatically
- Insert page breaks
- Keep paragraphs on one page
- Set margins
- Set line spacing
- Set tabs
- Hide paragraphs
- Format paragraphs with named styles
- Indent paragraphs and set margins and tabs

TIP   You can save paragraph properties you use regularly as a *named style* and then use the style to format paragraphs quickly.

Searching for Information

You can use the search facilities in Notes to:

- Search for text in a document that you are reading
- Find and replace text in a document that you are reading
- Search for text in document titles that appear in a view
- Search for documents that contain specific text or match specific criteria

Creating and Responding to Mail Messages

You can use new Notes mail functionality to:

- Create a new mail message whether or not you are currently using your mail database
- Reply to the sender of a message or to the sender *and* all recipients of the message
- Include the original message in your reply

Help for Notes 3 Users

Notes can show you the new equivalent of any command you may have used in Notes Release 3:

1. Choose Help ➤ Release 3 Menu Finder.

2. In the Release 3 Menu Finder dialog box, select the Release 3.*x* command you want to locate in Release 4. The equivalent command appears in the box (see Figure 2.6).

3. Click Done to close the window.

FIGURE 2.6:

The Release 3 Menu Finder helps you locate the equivalent command in Notes Release 4.

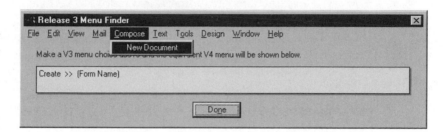

Mobile Notes (Dial-Up) Features

You can use the new Mobile Notes features to:

- Create locations to store communication settings for each place you work with Notes (such as your office or home), and then choose a location from the status bar to use the settings that apply to your current location

- Call a passthru server and access multiple servers through a single phone connection

- Get Help while you travel without sacrificing disk space (Help Lite)

Application Design Features and Enhancements

Release 4 has so many application design features and enhancements that you might find yourself at a loss on how to build your applications.

LotusScript

Use LotusScript, an object-oriented, cross-platform, BASIC-compatible programming language, to create sophisticated, iterative programs and branches within a program and to perform more complicated tasks in Notes than previously possible with @functions alone. LotusScript contains a *class library* that allows you to dynamically access and manipulate named objects—databases, views, documents, fields, agents, embedded objects—in an entirely programmatic fashion (rather than manually through the user interface).

Formulas

You can use @functions (including @DialogBox, @PickList, @Sum, @URLOpen, and @Pi) and @commands, as well as Simple actions, which are predefined tasks that you can incorporate into the design of your database. @commands now execute in the order they appear in a formula, instead of at the end. This change lets you create more flexible formulas.

Forms and Subforms

Design features for forms and subforms allow you to:

- Use form layout regions to move, resize, and display fields, text, and graphics in ways not available within the standard regions of a form

- Create subforms that include any form feature, including layout regions, actions, and fields for use within several forms

- Create forms that do not record users' names when they create or edit a document created with the form, thus protecting the anonymity of the author

- Create forms that do not allow users to print, forward, or copy to the Clipboard documents created with the form, thus deterring the dissemination of confidential documents

- Combine OLE objects and Notes/FX fields on forms to create applications that let users move data easily and transparently between Notes personal productivity tools such as Lotus 123, Lotus Word Pro, Microsoft Word, Visio, and so on

- Create forms and subforms that display a nonscrolling set of Action bar buttons that give users quick access to common or complicated tasks

Views, Folders, and Navigators

Design features for views, folders, and Navigators allow you to:

- Add space between rows and change the color of alternate rows in a view

- Reduce the size of view indexes by using the sort-on-demand feature to combine the utility of multiple views into a single view

- Give users a quick way to change the sort order of columns by clicking the column name

- Create folders that allow users to group frequently accessed or related documents together

- Create views and folders that display a nonscrolling set of Action bar buttons that give users quick access to common or complicated tasks

- Select documents for a view or folder, or define values for columns in a view without using formulas

- Create graphical Navigators that allow users to navigate within a database with ease

- Merge replication conflicts into a single conflict document automatically, rather than creating multiple replication conflict documents

Agents

Create or use Agents that come with Notes to perform a series of automated tasks in a database. Use the Actions that come with Notes or create your own formulas to define actions you want the Agent to perform.

NOTE   Agents replace Release 3 macros; however, you can continue to use macros created with Release 3 in Release 4.

You can set up an Agent to run in one of these ways:

Manually   Runs when users highlight the database icon and choose Actions ➤ <agent name>

As a Hidden Agent   Runs from another Agent or from the Agent list using Actions ➤ Run

On a Schedule in the Background   Runs hourly, daily, weekly, or monthly

When Documents Are New or Modified   Runs only if documents that match the search criteria have been changed since the last time the Agent ran

When Documents Are Mailed to the Database   Runs on any documents that are sent to a user's mail database or a shared mail-in database

When Documents Are Pasted into the Database   Runs only if documents that match the search criteria have been pasted into the database since the last time the Agent ran

Design Templates

Use one of the many redesigned templates that come with Release 4, including:

- Notes mail
- Document Library
- Discussion
- Personal Journal
- Approval Cycle

Database Drivers

Use the ODBC database drivers to access non-Notes databases like Microsoft SQL Server, Oracle, Sybase, Informix, and other industry-standard databases.

Database Management Features and Enhancements

The following sections describe Release 4 database management features and enhancements.

Security

Domino provides robust, proven security at multiple levels. With Release 4, you can now implement these additional security features:

- Increase database security by using local security to encrypt a database on a server or workstation so only the person or server you specify can access it. Local security ensures database security when people are away from their workstations or if they lose their laptops.

- Display a history of changes to the access control list (ACL).

- Enforce an ACL on local database replicas and keep a uniform ACL across replicas so users have the same access to all replicas including their local replica. You can use this feature with Release 4 file format databases only.

- Specify a user type for entries in the ACL. For example, if you specify the Person user type when you add a person named Mark Hunt to the ACL and someone creates a Group user type named Mark Hunt, that group will not have access to the database.

- Specify additional access control options for Agents, folders, views, and LotusScript formulas.

Database Analysis

Using database analysis, you can now collect the following information about one or more databases:

- Replication history

- User reads and writes

- Document creations, edits, or deletions

- Design changes

- Replication additions, updates, and deletions

- Mail messages delivered by the router

Replication

Replication is the process of synchronizing documents from the same databases on different servers. Replication speed has been improved significantly from the following enhancements:

- Maintains a list of documents, design elements, and ACL modifications that have occurred since the last replication

- Replicate only modified fields in a document instead of the entire document to reduce replication time (occurs automatically when replicating Release 4 file format databases)

- Merge replication conflicts into a single conflict document automatically, rather than creating multiple-replication conflict documents

Database Size

Notes 4 made the following enhancements for managing the size of your Notes databases:

- Create databases that can reach a maximum size of 4 gigabytes. In Release 4, ID tables can exceed the 64K limit, which helps expand the maximum allowable size. Notes uses ID tables to store information about the contents of a database, for example, the location of a document in a database.

- Set a database quota that does not allow users to save documents in a database if the database reaches a size you specify. This restriction helps control the amount of hard-disk space a database occupies on a server.

What's New in Notes Release 4.5

Lotus Notes Release 4 provides organizations with a large selection of platforms for configuring their enterprise and groupware systems. With Release 4.5, full client/server capabilities are available for IBM AIX, HP-UX, OS/2, Macintosh, NetWare, Sun Solaris, Windows, Windows 95, and Windows NT systems.

In addition to these new platforms, Release 4.5 includes other new features and enhancements.

Allow Use of Stored Forms

A new option in the Database Properties InfoBox is Allow Use of Storing Forms in This Database, and it protects users from opening a document that may have damaging options set. If you open a document that was created based on a form with the Store form set in the Form Properties InfoBox, you get a warning message. You can also set an option in the Database properties Basics tab to allow you to open documents with stored forms.

Limit for Locally Cached Server-Based Forms

Starting with Release 4.5 you can define a limit for the amount of disk space to be used to store server-based forms locally. The rationale for storing these forms locally is that the server access speed is increased if the form information does not have to be transferred to the local workstation. You can set the limit by opening the Workspace InfoBox and selecting the Information tab. The default setting is 5MB.

Local Full Text Indexing

Local Full Text Indexing is now available on both the Macintosh 68K and Power PC systems. This feature enables you to create a local full text index that you can store on your local hard drives.

Personal Use Exemption Certificate

U.S. citizens can take the North American edition of Lotus Notes overseas as long as they keep careful records of their itinerary. Release 4.5 of Notes includes a certificate that assists you in keeping such legal records.

Web Navigator Features

The following sections describe Release 4.5 Web Navigator features and enhancements.

Adding to a Category View Open any Web page in the database and choose Actions ➤ Add to Category View. Notes displays a dialog box that allows you to add that Web page to the hot lists of topics available from the Home Navigator Sampler icons. (This action is available only to users who have the Webmaster role in the database ACL.)

Creating a View to Display the Retriever of a Web Page You can now save the name of the person who retrieves each Web page into the Web Navigator database. To save the author name, edit the Web Navigator Administration document and choose Yes in the Save Author Information field. The author name will be saved into a field called $Authors. You can then use the @Author function to create a view to display the name of the user (or server) that retrieved the Web page. A variant of the hidden $All view, called $All with Authors, demonstrates this capability.

Launching a URL Automatically from a Document You can design a form that launches a URL automatically whenever a user opens a document created with that form. To design this type of form, add a text field called URL anywhere in the form and then select Auto Launch ➤ URL from the Form Properties Launch tab.

NOTE   This feature will not work with Notes releases earlier than Notes Release 4.1.

Displaying New Web Page Views   When you click any of the Sampler icons on the Home Navigator, a categorized list of Web pages appears. In addition, click any of the Internet search engines in the view to see additional Web pages related to the category you are viewing.

Using the Refresh Agent   The Refresh Agent behavior has been modified to normalize the time and date of the Web pages in the database and on their Internet server. In addition, you can set the following environment variable on the Notes server so that after the Refresh Agent runs, you can see how many pages were actually refreshed:

```
WebDebugRefreshAgent=1
```

Using the Reload and Recommend Buttons   The Reload and Recommend buttons on the Action bar now display icons without text in order to conserve screen space.

Using the @Created Function   You can now use the @Created Function in the Web Navigator database when designing forms, views, and so on.

Using the Personal Web Navigator Template

Notes Release 4.5 comes with an upgraded Web Navigator template called PER-WEB45.NTF. Lotus designed the Web Navigator template to be as customizable as possible because the Internet is a dynamic environment that changes constantly.

When you issue the LOAD WEB console command, Notes checks to see if you have a WEB.NSF database. If not, Notes will create one for you automatically. If you have created your own Web Navigator template, be sure to include the words *WebNavigator* in your template design name so that the Web Navigator can locate the template.

To locate and use a Web Navigator template, Notes first searches your NOTES.INI for the WebTemplateName = x.NTF line:

- If you have specified a Web Navigator template in this line, Notes searches for this template and then verifies that it has the correct design by checking for the words *WebNavigator* in the design name.

- If Notes doesn't find a valid Web Navigator template, Notes then searches for PERWEB45.NTF in your Notes data directory and verifies the design class.

- If Notes doesn't find PERWEB45.NTF in your Notes data directory, Notes searches your Notes data directory for WEB.NTF and verifies the design class.

NOTE   The new Personal Web Navigator Template is designed for Notes Release 4.5 and is not supported on Notes Release 4 servers. Release 4.1 clients will generally be able to use this template, but will not be able to auto-launch the Category documents or Rating documents that make use of the URL Autolaunch Form attribute.

What's New in Notes Release 4.6

The primary focus of the Notes 4.6 client release is aimed at making Notes easier to use. The major enhancements are focused on personal integration and information content management, Internet mail, and the Web. The Notes client is slowly evolving into more of a stand-alone application for managing your messaging, calendaring, Internet, and personal information needs.

Internet Client Features

Notes contains a very powerful interface. Integrating this interface with the Internet is one of the major enhancements of this release.

POP3/SMTP

You now have the ability to send and receive your e-mail from any POP3 mail account on the Internet. This allows the flexibility to use the same Notes mail interface to receive e-mail from an Internet service provider (or POP3 mail server), or a regular Notes mail server, all from the same database. Having to use one mail program for your home or personal mail and the Notes mail interface for your corporate mail has become a thing of the past. With this new feature, you have the option of receiving and storing all your e-mail in one database. For those wanting to keep personal and corporate e-mail separate, you can do that, too.

Internet Explorer Integration

In Notes 4.5, the Personal Web Navigator allowed you to browse and save HTML Web documents in your own personal Notes Web database (Personal Web Navigator). This feature was quite powerful but required using the Notes browser. Release 4.5 would allow you to "call up" a third-party browser (such as Netscape Navigator or Microsoft Internet Explorer) that would only run outside the context Notes. By using the third-party browser, you lost the ability to store the Web pages as documents and browse them offline.

Now that has all changed. With Notes 4.6, you can run Internet Explorer as an ActiveX component. You can now browse with the speed and power of IE all from within the context of your Personal Web Navigator database. This combination retains all the power and flexibility of Notes while using the familiar IE browser interface.

Some other enhancements have also been made to the Personal Web Navigator database. Now you can:

- Forward Web pages via e-mail

- Retrieve and save the Web pages specified by URL for browsing later

- Have the Page Minder agent watch a particular Web page and notify you when the contents change

- Select Web pages to store for offline browsing

- Choose Database Size Options for "housekeeping" the Personal Web Database

Integration with Lotus SmartSuite and Microsoft Office

Using Windows ActiveDoc technology, Notes 4.6 offers superb integration with Lotus SmartSuite or Microsoft Office. Some of the highlights include:

- Lotus Word Pro or Microsoft Word as an alternate e-mail editor

- Inclusion of Document Library templates that allow users to share and route documents using built-in workflow (now you can use familiar business productivity applications and route them for review or approval with Notes built-in workflow)

Portfolios

A new navigational database has been created that allows you to logically group databases by functionality or common theme. For example, each Notes 4.6 user will have a portfolio database called "Favorites," which is created during the installation process. This new database contains icons for your e-mail, calendar, To-Do list, personal address book, personal journal, and personal Web navigator.

This grouping of icons represents a common set of applications that a person needs to access information within Notes.

Contact Management

A few enhancements have been made to the Notes Personal Address Book that allow you to also use it as a fully functional contact management system. The Person document has been replaced by the Business Card document which has been revamped to allow auto-parsing of names, phone numbers, and addresses. A new Business Card view has been added for easier access to "person" information. (This replaces Person in the 4.6 Personal Address Book.) New Action buttons have been added to all the views. By selecting a person from a view, the Write Memo will automatically create a message with the address pre-filled from the selected document. You can also select one or more people and schedule a meeting invitation using the Schedule Meeting action with the invitees pre-filled from the selected documents. You can also go directly to a contact's Web site by selecting the Visit Web Page action (provided that you have typed in a valid Web site address for the contact in the person record).

Some other convenient time savers that have been added to the Notes Mail database for processing information are:

- Converting an e-mail directly into a calendar appointment or meeting invitation
- Converting an e-mail into a To-Do item
- Creating a mailing list (group) using the To and Cc field contents of an e-mail

Printing Calendar Views

With Notes 4.6, you now have the ability to print calendar views exactly as they are displayed. You have the flexibility to print the entire view as is or select a specific date range.

What's Next?

We discuss the nuts and bolts of using and designing databases in subsequent chapters. For now, we put aside our discussion of the conceptual underpinnings of Notes and let you get your feet wet using Notes. In the next chapter, we take you on a tour of the Notes environment.

CHAPTER
THREE

3

Touring the Notes Environment

■ Starting Notes

■ Organizing the Notes Workspace

■ Using the status bar

■ Working with Notes windows

■ Using, customizing, and creating new SmartIcons

Working in Notes is a lot like working in other Windows applications. The graphical user interface provides you with a myriad of tools and features that make getting around Notes easy. In this chapter, you'll learn the basics you need to find your way around in Notes.

Starting Notes

To start Notes, double-click the icon in the Windows NT Program Manager or in the Windows 95 Start menu (Start ➤ Programs ➤ Lotus Applications ➤ Lotus Notes). After a few moments, Notes displays the Notes interface, as shown in Figure 3.1, which is known as the *Workspace*. As you can see, the Workspace displays a set of seven tabbed pages (with the seventh page being the Replicator page) in which you organize your work. (You can create additional Workspace pages and remove pages, but we'll discuss how to modify the Workspace later in this chapter.) The tabbed pages display the databases in any way you choose, allowing you to systematize (and customize) your Workspace just as you would by organizing paper documents in file folders. You can organize the folders to correspond to the way you organize or use information.

Exploring and Organizing the Notes Workspace

The Workspace is an active window that displays many important elements, including:

- Menus
- SmartIcons
- Tabbed pages (which can display database icons)
- The Replicator page
- Any other Notes windows you open
- Status bar

Other elements, such as the control box, window title bar, scroll bars, and mini-mize and maximize buttons, should be familiar to you from using other Windows applications.

FIGURE 3.1:

The Workspace is where you perform and organize your work in Notes.

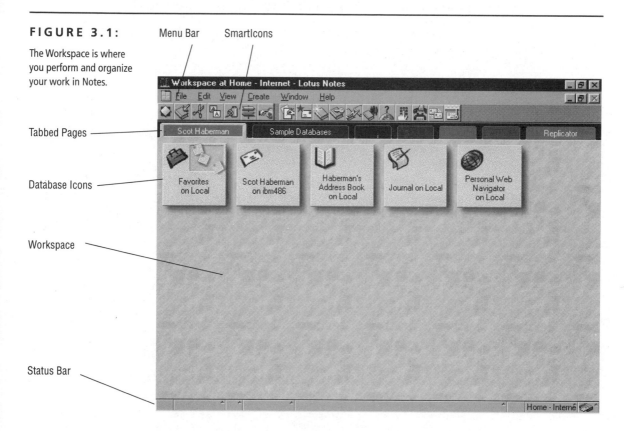

One of the new features for Release 4.6 that can be seen immediately on your Workspace is the Favorites portfolio database, as shown in Figure 3.1. After installing Release 4.6, Notes automatically creates the "Favorites" database icon that contains a group of icons that point to your mail file, calendar, to-do list, address book, jour-nal, and personal Web navigator. A *portfolio database* is a way to group related data-bases so that you can navigate between them from a single navigation pane.

Customizing the Workspace Pages

Each of the tabbed Workspace pages provides you with ways to organize your databases and display information about them. For example, when you start

Notes, the database icons display the names of your databases. Altogether, you can display four types of information on a database icon:

- Title only, which contains minimum information (the default)

- Number of unread mail documents in a database, which you can display by choosing View ➤ Show Unread

- Title of the database and server name, which you can display by choosing View ➤ Show Server Names

- Title, server name, and file name of the database, which you can display by holding down the Shift key while choosing View ➤ Show Server Names

Adding Names to the Workspace Pages

As you use Notes, you will regularly add and remove database icons and also move them from one page to another to organize your work. It's a good idea to group similar databases on a page and give the page a descriptive name.

You add a name to a page by double-clicking on the tab at the top of a page. The Workspace Properties InfoBox appears, as shown in Figure 3.2. Enter an appropriate name in the text box.

FIGURE 3.2:

The Workspace Properties InfoBox lets you add a name and color to each tabbed page.

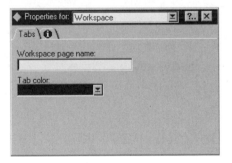

TIP   You can also right-click to display the Workspace Properties menu and then select Workspace Properties to display the dialog box. Alternatively, you can click the Properties SmartIcon, which is the leftmost button in the icon bar.

You can also change a tab's color if you don't care for gray, the default color, or if you want to code the page. Click a color at the bottom of the dialog box to select it. When you've got a color you like, click the Close button (the X in the upper-right corner). The tabbed page will display the name and color that you gave it.

TIP

To display another Workspace page, click the tab of the page you want. You can also press ↑ until the current page's tab is highlighted (changing the page's focus from an icon to a tab) and then press ← or → to reach the page you want.

TIP

The InfoBox can be left open while you work. The changes to your settings are made as soon as you click somewhere else in the box.

Adding and Deleting Workspace Pages

You can add up to 32 Workspace pages (plus the Replicator Workspace page) to help organize your Notes databases. To create a new Workspace page, follow these steps:

1. Click any Workspace tab. (Keep in mind that Notes inserts the new Workspace page to the left of the selected Workspace page.)

2. Select Create ➤ Workspace Page. If you haven't added a Workspace page before, Notes asks if you want to upgrade your desktop file.

3. Click Yes to add the Workspace page and upgrade your desktop file or click No to cancel adding the page.

WARNING

If you add a Workspace page to your desktop file, you can't use the file with previous releases of Notes.

Conversely, you can always remove a Workspace page when you no longer need it or the Workspace appears too crowded. To delete a Workspace page, follow these steps:

1. Click the Workspace page's tab.

2. Choose Edit ➤ Clear or press Delete.

3. Click Yes to confirm the deletion or No to cancel it.

WARNING If you delete a Workspace page that contains database icons, Notes removes the icons from the Workspace.

The Replicator Page

The Replicator Workspace page is always the last page on your Workspace; you *cannot* delete it. The Replicator lets you manage replication of your local databases in one place. In a nutshell, *replication* is the process of making an exact copy, or *replica*, of a database on your workstation and then updating it periodically with a server to make sure you're always working with the most current version of the database. (We discuss replication in detail in Chapters 13 and 28.)

With the Replicator page, you can replicate multiple databases with one or more servers using a single command. When you use the Replicator page, Notes replicates in the background so you can do other work while Notes replicates.

When you use Notes away from the office, you can have the Replicator automatically call each server with which you want to replicate. If you're using a pass-through server or a remote LAN server, you can have the Replicator make a single call and replicate all of your local databases at one time, even if they're on different servers.

The Replicator page also lets you customize replication depending on where you're working. For example, you could set up a local database to receive full documents when you replicate at the office (on a network) and receive shortened documents when you replicate away from the office (using a modem). The Replicator page also provides additional ways to replicate; for example, you can assign high priority to selected databases and replicate only those databases.

Using the Status Bar

The status bar appears along the bottom of your active Notes window, as shown in Figure 3.3. It includes a message area, indicators for network and hard disk activity initiated by Notes, an area that denotes your current location (for example, Office, Internet, Home, Travel), and your access level to the active database.

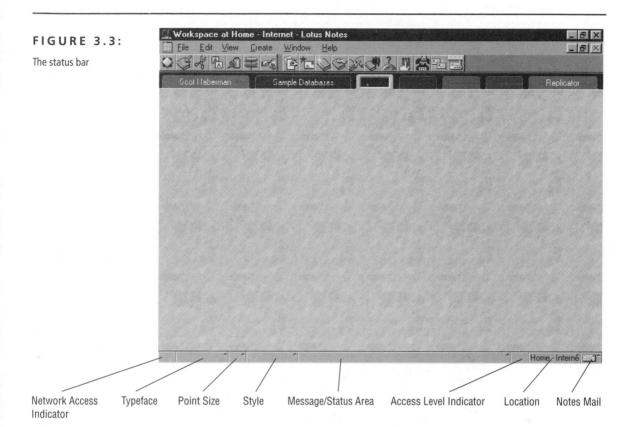

Network Access Indicator   Typeface   Point Size   Style   Message/Status Area   Access Level Indicator   Location   Notes Mail

The status bar is context sensitive, so some of the following options appear only when you're editing a Notes document. The parts of the status bar (from left to right) are described here:

Server Access Indicator   After calling and connecting to a remote server, a modem with flashing lights indicates server activity. For example, you'll see the modem's flashing lights when you connect to a server to open a shared database.

Typeface   Shows the font at the insertion point when you're creating or editing a document. Click this indicator to display a pop-up menu of all available fonts and choose a different font.

Point Size   Shows the text size at the insertion point when you're creating or editing a document. Click this indicator to display a pop-up menu of all available sizes and choose a different size.

Style   Shows the template styles available for the document.

TIP

Additional styles can be defined easily in Notes Release 4.6 to simplify text processing. When you are in Edit mode for a rich text field, open the InfoBox to the styles tab (looks like a price tag). Click the Create Style button and give it a name. Now, that style will inherit the current attributes for the current paragraph where the cursor is located.

Message/Status Area   Shows messages such as "10 documents selected" and "No more unread documents in this database." These messages display brief descriptions of your activities. The status area also displays the meaning of the user access level and setup indicators (at the right of the status bar) when you click those indicators. If you click the status area, a pop-up menu shows the most recent messages that have appeared. Click the pop-up menu again to close it when you are finished reading it.

Access Level Indicator   Shows your database access level for the database that you've selected. Click the icon to display the Groups and Roles dialog box. Your access level for the database appears in the bottom of the dialog box as well as in a message in the status area.

Location   Shows your current location. (See Chapter 13 for additional information on viewing your Location settings.)

Notes Mail   Displays an Inbox when there is mail in your Notes Mail file and an envelope when the Inbox is empty. Click the Inbox or envelope to open the Notes Mail menu. The pop-up menu shows six choices (Create Memo, Scan Unread Mail, Receive Mail, Send Outgoing Mail, Send and Receive Mail, and Open Mail). If your mail file is already open, Notes brings its view window to the front.

Executing Commands in Notes

You can use many keyboard shortcuts—combinations of keys—to execute commands in Notes quickly. Using these shortcuts will make you more efficient—and proficient—when you start designing databases.

Only two Notes tasks actually *require* a mouse: using the ruler (to change tabs and left paragraph margins) and designing a database icon.

Continued on next page

Notes supports Windows standards for choosing menus and commands from the keyboard. For example, to choose the View ➤ Show Ruler command, hold down Alt, press V, and press R. This action is represented as Alt+V, R. You can release the Alt key after you press the V. To choose Text ➤ Alignment ➤ Left, press Alt+T, A, L.

You can also use accelerator keys to choose commands automatically from the keyboard. Simply press the key combination shown to the right of a menu item. For example, to choose Edit ➤ Cut, press Ctrl+X.

Controlling Notes Windows

You can open up to nine active windows at a time in Notes. When you try to exceed that number, Notes responds by telling you to close a window. Each open window consumes memory, and Notes likes memory. You'll experience a slowdown in your computer's performance as you open windows, so don't open any more windows than you really need. To switch from window to window, pull down the Window menu and choose a new window. You can also cycle between all of the open windows by pressing Ctrl+Tab.

Controlling windows means moving, sizing, and closing them, as well as moving among them. You can control all Notes windows by using the mouse or keyboard. You can also move Notes dialog boxes and most messages (alerts and error messages) the same way as you move Notes windows, although you cannot size or scroll dialog boxes and messages. The easiest way to move a window is with the mouse. Just place the mouse pointer on the window's title bar, drag (click and move) the window to the position you want, and release the mouse button.

TIP   You can also use the keyboard to move a window by pressing Ctrl+F7. Use the ↑, ↓, →, or ← to move the window to the position you want and then press ↵.

Sizing a Window

To maximize or minimize all windows with your mouse, do the following:

- To enlarge the window to maximum size, choose Window ➤ Maximize All or click the Maximize button in the upper-right corner of the window.

- To reduce the window to minimum size, choose Window ➤ Minimize All or click the Minimize button in the upper-right corner of the window.

TIP   To maximize a window in Windows 95, click the title bar or the upper-right corner of the window. Alternatively, you can double-click the window's title in the status bar at the bottom of the window. To maximize all windows with the keyboard, press F10, W, X. To minimize all windows, press F10, W, M.

If you use a mouse, you have two additional ways to size the active window: by changing horizontal and vertical dimensions simultaneously and by changing horizontal or vertical dimensions. To change the horizontal and vertical dimensions at the same time, point to the lower-right corner of the window. The pointer changes to a double-headed arrow. Drag the lower-right corner to make the window the size you want.

NOTE   You can't drag a window beyond the boundary of its *parent* window.

To get the same result, point to the size box in the lower-right corner of the window. Drag the size box to make the window the size you want. To change the horizontal or vertical dimension, point to either the horizontal or vertical border of the window. Drag the border to the new position. To restore a window to its previous size, either double-click its title bar or choose Restore from the System menu.

You can also resize the active window from the keyboard. Press Ctrl+F10 to toggle the active window between its current size and its previous size. Press Alt+F5 to make the application window smaller. You can't make it bigger, however, by pressing Alt+F5 again. To restore a window to its previous size, press Alt+F10.

TIP   To display a different open window, press Alt+W and then the number shown next to the window title. You can also pull down the Window menu and select another open window by clicking the name. Alternatively, you can also press Ctrl+Tab to cycle through all of the open Notes windows.

Closing a Window

You can close the active window in a variety of ways. As you work with Notes, you will probably develop a preference for one and forget the others, but for now, here's the whole list:

- Choose File ➤ Close.
- Press Ctrl+W.
- Press Esc.
- Select Close from the control menu, which you access by clicking the bar in the upper-left corner of the window.
- Press Ctrl+F4.

There's another way to close a window. You can change a user preference that enables you to double-click the right mouse button to close any window. (Setting this option should be a cause for celebration for Notes 3.*x* users, who are accustomed to using the right mouse button.) To set this user preference, follow these steps:

1. Choose File ➤ Tools ➤ User Preferences. The User Preferences dialog box appears.

2. Select the Right Double-Click Closes Window option in the Advanced options window at the bottom of the dialog box.

3. Click OK.

You will need to exit and then restart Notes for this user preference to take effect.

Using SmartIcons

A *SmartIcon* is a button that executes a combination of actions when you click it. The SmartIcons bar appears below the menu bar, as shown in Figure 3.4. SmartIcons are context sensitive, which means the set of SmartIcons that's displayed reflects the task you're currently performing. For example, the default set that appears after you start Notes changes when you create a new document. Likewise, the set that appears when you compose a document changes when you select a view.

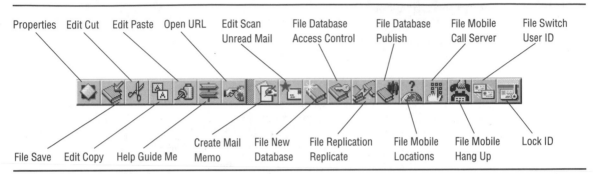

| Properties | Edit Cut | Edit Paste | Open URL | Edit Scan Unread Mail | File Database Access Control | File Database Publish | File Mobile Call Server | File Switch User ID |

| File Save | Edit Copy | Help Guide Me | Create Mail Memo | File New Database | File Replication Replicate | File Mobile Locations | File Mobile Hang Up | Lock ID |

FIGURE 3.4: The set of default SmartIcons

A SmartIcon can perform a simple action, such as choosing a menu command, or a more complex action, such as executing a macro formula. Notes comes with more than 100 predefined SmartIcons, including icons for most Notes menu commands, and a dozen custom SmartIcons to which you can assign your own macros.

For many tasks, clicking on a SmartIcon is quicker than pulling down several menu options or recalling and typing a keyboard shortcut. For example, if you didn't know that Ctrl+S was the keyboard shortcut for the Save command, you could click the SmartIcon that appears second from the left. Using this SmartIcon is much faster than opening the File menu and clicking Save.

You can also find out what any SmartIcon does without activating it. Just place the pointer on an icon; the name of the icon appears in a balloon, as shown in Figure 3.5. If you want to scan all the predefined SmartIcons, choose File ➤ Tools ➤ SmartIcons. The SmartIcons dialog box appears, as shown in Figure 3.6. Scroll down the left list box.

FIGURE 3.5:

Point on a SmartIcon and the description of the icon appears in a balloon.

FIGURE 3.6:

The SmartIcons dialog box

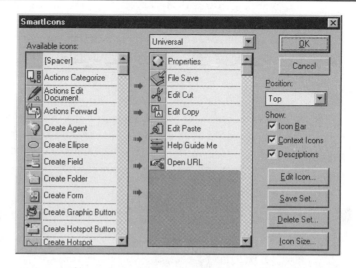

Changing the Position of SmartIcons

Some people don't like having the SmartIcons hanging from the top of the screen. If you're one of these people, choose Tools ➤ SmartIcons. The SmartIcons dialog box appears. Click the arrow on the Position list and choose one of these positions:

Floating   Places SmartIcons in a floating window that you can move, close, and resize. (To move the floating window, drag it by its title bar. To close it, click the small white close box in the upper-left corner.)

Left   Places SmartIcons along the left edge of your Notes window

Top   Places SmartIcons along the top of your Notes window, just under the menu bar (this is the default)

Right   Places SmartIcons along the right edge of your Notes window

Bottom   Places SmartIcons along the bottom of your Notes window

Click OK to confirm your changes (or Cancel to revert to the previous position).

SmartIcons are displayed in the icon bar in two sets. The set on the left is called the Universal Set (which contains seven icons by default). This set is always available in the icon bar. The set on the right is context sensitive and reflects the current task.

Obviously, you can save a lot of time by using the default set of SmartIcons. But if you do specialized work, or if your work leads you to repeatedly use a function that is not in the set of default SmartIcons, you can save even more time by adjusting the SmartIcons to suit your own needs.

NOTE   One of the limitations in Notes is the inability to modify any of the predefined context-sensitive SmartIcon sets. The only icon set you're allowed to modify is the Universal Set. Also, if you decide to create a new SmartIcon set, it will always take the place of the Universal SmartIcons on the icon bar.

Modifying an Existing SmartIcons Set

One of the easiest ways to customize SmartIcons is to modify a pre-existing set. To add SmartIcons to a set, choose File ➤ Tools ➤ SmartIcons to open the SmartIcons dialog box. Then drag the SmartIcons you want (one at a time) from the Available icons list into the scroll box to the right. You're actually dragging a copy, so nothing is removed from your Available icons list.

On the other hand, sometimes you need to use only specific icons to perform particular tasks. Why let icons you don't need clutter the screen? To remove SmartIcons from a set, drag them (one at a time) out of the current set and back to the Available icons list.

To delete a SmartIcons set you no longer use, choose File ➤ Tools ➤ SmartIcons and select Delete Set. The Delete Sets dialog box appears. Select the set you want to delete in the list and then click on OK.

WARNING   Do not delete any of the 16 sets of SmartIcons that comes with Lotus Notes. SmartIcon sets are context sensitive in Notes Release 4.6.

You can also fix SmartIcons when they don't look right on your screen. Ordinarily your operating system displays SmartIcons correctly on any type of monitor supported by Notes. However, some monitors don't communicate their type (EGA, VGA, or SVGA) correctly to the operating system, so you may need to convey the correct information yourself in this dialog box.

To adjust your icons to match your monitor, choose File ➤ Tools ➤ SmartIcons and select Icon Size. To use the Icon Size dialog box, select the option that matches your type of monitor: Small (VGA) or Large (SVGA).

NOTE   The options Small and Large that appear in the dialog box refer to the size of the SmartIcons, not the size of your monitor.

Creating or Editing Formulas for SmartIcons

You can define custom SmartIcons by creating macros—Notes formulas that accomplish specified tasks—in the Edit SmartIcons dialog box or SmartIcons dialog box. You can save yourself a lot of time by defining custom in the SmartIcons for your most-used complex tasks.

To edit or create a formula for SmartIcons, choose Tools ➤ SmartIcons. (See Chapter 18 for information on how to write and edit formulas.) The SmartIcons dialog box appears. Select the icon you want to edit in the Custom Icons list. Click the Edit Icon button, then the Formula button, and edit the formula.

If you want to create a formula, type the formula into the Formula text box. To add an @function, select Add @Func, and then select an @function from the list. (Chapter 18 also covers @functions.) To add a Notes command, select Add Command and then select a command from the list. Click OK (or Cancel, if you don't want to save your formula).

Creating a New SmartIcons Set

Creating new sets of SmartIcons is one of the best things you can do for yourself if you routinely perform certain tasks that always require the use of certain functions. You can define multiple sets of SmartIcons for different purposes, such as one set for reading and writing documents, another for using Notes offsite, and a third for designing databases. Follow these steps to create a set of SmartIcons that you define:

1. Choose File ➤ Tools ➤ SmartIcons.

2. Select the set that's closest to the one you'd like to create. Add and remove SmartIcons until you're satisfied with the new set.

3. Select Save Set. The Save Set of SmartIcons dialog box appears, as shown in Figure 3.7.

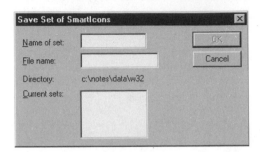

4. Type an appropriate name for the set of SmartIcons, such as DB Design for your set of database-design SmartIcons, into the Name of Set box. You can use any characters supported by your operating system, but the name can't be more than 15 characters. This name appears in the SmartIcons pop-up menu in the status bar.

5. Type a file name into the File Name box. The file name must be in DOS format—that is, up to eight characters (limited to letters, numbers, and underscore), followed by the extension .SMI.

NOTE   If you skip this step, Notes assigns a file name based on what you entered for Name of Set.

6. Click OK (or Cancel if you change your mind about saving this set).

Your new set appears in the right-hand list box in the SmartIcons dialog box with the new set name above the list. The name serves as both file name and menu name. The new set is automatically stored in your Notes data folder in the SmartIcons Sets folder.

TIP   Include the $ sign as the first character in the name of your personal set of SmartIcons. This name convention makes it easy to distinguish your personal set of SmartIcons from the other sets of SmartIcons.

TIP

To create a blank set that's easy to use as a basis for new sets, just remove all the SmartIcons from a set and save the empty set under an appropriate name such as MYSET. Whenever you want to create a new set, select this one from the Set pop-up menu.

What's Next?

As you use Notes, you'll discover the best way to make SmartIcons work for you. They can save you a lot of time as you perform routine tasks. In the next chapter, we discuss the basics of accessing and using a Notes database. Obviously, any Notes database will have some feature that makes it unique. However, all databases have some features in common. The next chapter identifies these common features to help you become comfortable using any database to which you have access.

Accessing a Notes Database

- Understanding your access privileges

- Using the sample databases and templates

- Selecting Workspace pages

- Opening, browsing, and closing databases

- Using database icons on your Workspace

- Compacting Workspaces

Using a Notes database is easy. Before you can use one, however, you need to add the database to your Workspace. If you have access to your organization's databases, you can follow the instructions in this chapter to begin using them. (We suggest that you check with your Notes administrator to make sure you can use the company databases.) If you don't have access to any existing databases, you can use the sample databases and templates on the companion CD.

NOTE Copy the databases from the companion CD to your hard disk and use them as is or modify them to fit your needs.

In this chapter, we explain the basics of accessing a Notes database. You open and close all Notes databases, regardless of their uniqueness, in the same way. You also use the same procedures to organize Notes databases in your Workspace, regardless of the organizational principles you favor.

Knowing Your Access Privileges

If you have the appropriate access level, you can select one or more databases to add to your Workspace. Every Notes database has an Access Control List (ACL) that specifies which users, user groups, and servers can access the database and which tasks they can perform. The database manager sets both ACL elements—access levels and access roles—in the Database Access Control List dialog box. You should check the settings in this dialog box for any database that you want to open.

NOTE You must be on a database's Access Control List to open the database; otherwise, the default access level needs to be set at Reader.

If your name is not listed in the database's ACL, either explicitly or as a member of a group, your access level is set to the default access level, which is usually either No Access, Reader, or Author. The database manager sets the default access level for a Notes database depending on the type of information in the database.

Understanding the Differences in Access Levels

Notes offers seven access levels. The access levels, from highest to lowest, are:

Manager   Can perform almost any operation—reading, writing, or editing—on documents, forms, views, and the database icon. A manager can also record or stop recording user activity, modify the ACL and replication settings, and delete the database (these tasks cannot be performed by any other access level). However, a manager can be prevented from deleting documents. A database always has at least one manager, who may or may not be the person who created the database.

Designer   Can perform the same operations as a manager except for modifying the ACL, user activity, replication, or "other" settings (the settings available when you select Other Settings in the Database Information dialog box), and deleting the database. Designers can also be prevented from deleting documents.

Editor   Can read, write, and edit all documents in a database but cannot modify the design elements (for example, forms or views) or the ACL. Editors can be prevented from deleting documents.

Author   Can read existing documents, create new documents, and edit the documents he or she created. Authors can be prevented from deleting documents or creating documents.

Read   Can read documents but cannot add new documents or edit existing ones.

Depositor   Can add new documents but cannot read existing ones. This level allows users to compose their own documents but not read anyone else's documents. Depositor access is appropriate for mail-in databases, for databases like ballot boxes or suggestion boxes, and for data entry personnel.

No Access   Users who are assigned this level cannot open the database or mail-in documents.

Who Is the Database Manager?

If you use Notes Mail, you can use any of the following methods to discover the names of the database manager(s):

- Select or open the database, and then choose Create ➤ Mail ➤ Special ➤ Memo to Database Manager. In the To: field of the mail memo, you'll see the users and groups assigned manager access. In addition to reading the list, you can send the manager(s) a mail memo if you have suggestions or comments about access to the database.

- Look in the Database Catalog, a Notes database that provides a listing of all the Notes databases available on your server—and sometimes for your entire organization. The Database Catalog should be available on any Notes server in your organization. If you can't find it, ask your Notes administrator.

- Check the Access Control List dialog box by using the People ➤ Servers ➤ Group list box at the top of the dialog box. The default is Show All, but you can also choose Show All Managers or Show All Designers, and so on.

Displaying Your Access Level for a Database

When you click a database icon (to highlight it) on any Workspace page or open a database, the symbol for your access level appears as a key icon at the right end of the Status Bar (actually, it is third from the right); the key icon doesn't appear if the database isn't selected. To see your access level, right-click on the database icon and choose Access Control, or choose File ➤ Database ➤ Access Control.

TIP

A faster way to see your access level is to click a database icon (to highlight it) in your Workspace. Your access level appears in the status area on the status bar. You'll also notice that a key icon appears next to the status area. Click the key icon itself. The Groups and Roles dialog box appears, displaying your access level for the database at the bottom of the dialog box.

The Access Control List dialog box is shown in Figure 4.1. Scroll down the list to see if your name is on the list. If you find your name, highlight it. Your access level appears in the Access pull-down menu in the upper-right corner of the dialog box. Click Cancel to close the box.

FIGURE 4.1:

The Access Control List dialog box, Scot Haberman has Manager access to his Address Book database, which means he can perform almost any operation—reading, writing, or editing—on documents, forms, views, and the database icon.

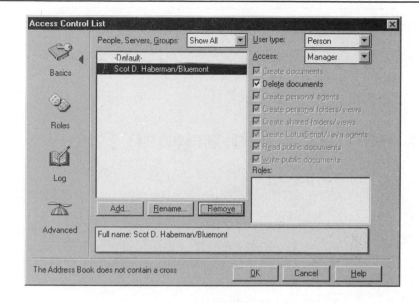

TIP

You'll need to ask your Notes administrator to change your access level if you want to use a database in a way that your current access level does not allow.

Using the Companion CD Databases

As you follow the book's instructions, you may not feel comfortable applying what you learn to your organization's Notes databases. Therefore, we've included Notes databases that you can analyze and modify on the companion CD.

In the next few sections, we're going to take you through the steps of opening and using a database so you can become accustomed to the Notes features found on the Workspace. After you add a database to your Workspace page, you can open the database, select documents, and compose new documents.

If you haven't yet copied the sample databases from the companion CD to your computer (*not* to the Notes server), you should do so now. You'll work with the databases locally; that is, you'll copy and use the databases on your computer—or workstation—only. So make sure you have adequate space on your hard disk.

NOTE   Please read the *What's on the CD?* appendix for descriptions of the sample data-bases, as well as the other applications on the CD. You'll also find installation instructions and suggestions for using the applications.

Selecting a Workspace Page

The pages that appear in your Workspace help you organize the databases you use. Each time you open a new database, you can add it to a particular page that includes other databases with similar traits. For example, one page may display sales-tracking databases, while another page may contain group discussion data-bases. As explained in Chapter 3, you can organize the Workspace to suit your needs. (That's why the Workspace is always referred to as *your* Workspace.) Each of the tabs on the six default Workspace pages can display a unique label name and color that you choose.

TIP   You can change a tab name and its color any time. Right-click the tab and select the Workspace Properties command from the menu or double-click the tab with the left mouse button to display the Workspace Properties InfoBox. Enter a new name, select a new color, and click the Close button. It's very easy to change page tabs when you want to reorganize your Workspace.

Another alternative to organizing your database icons on Workspace pages is through the use of *portfolio databases*. Instead of grouping common databases by Workspace page, you can group common databases within a portfolio database. For example, let's say you have a set of personnel databases on your organiza-tion's server. You also have a replica of these databases on your local machine. Using Workspace pages, you would probably define one Workspace page for the server personnel database copies and another workspace page for the local per-sonnel database copies. An alternative to this approach would be to define one Workspace page for personnel databases. Within this Workspace page, you could define a portfolio database that contains the server copies and another portfolio database that contains the local copies.

We recommend that you name one of the pages *Applications* or *Sample Databases* (or another appropriate name) and then use this new page to organize the databases you copy from the companion CD. From this page you can access the databases and display their icons. At the same time, you may also want to use separate Workspace pages for the databases you create or use in your organization.

Opening a Database

Once you've organized the pages in your Workspace to suit your style, you can open databases to which you have access. After you've added a database to your Workspace, it's very easy to open and use it: just double-click the database's icon. When you open a database for the first time, you need to perform a few special tasks:

1. Switch to the Workspace page where you want to access one of the sample databases or any other database (if you haven't done so already).

2. Click the appropriate tab to display the page. If you don't select a page, Notes will add the database's icon to the page that's currently displayed. When you "add a database," you place a database icon on your Workspace. An icon is a graphical pointer to the actual location of the database on a Notes server or your computer.

3. Choose File ➤ Database ➤ Open to open the database for the first time. The Open Database dialog box appears, as shown in Figure 4.2. (If you've copied the sample databases from the companion CD to your hard disk, you'll need to remember the name of the directory where the database is located.)

FIGURE 4.2:

The Open Database dialog box displays a list of servers that contain database files. The highlighting on Local indicates that someone is working with a copy of a database file locally, that is, on a workstation.

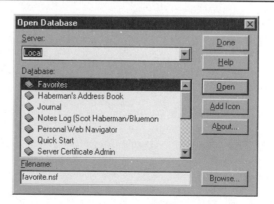

TIP

A faster way to add a database to your Workspace is to right-click the page where you want to add the icon and then select the Open Database command from the menu. The Open Database dialog box appears.

4. Highlight Local (if it isn't already selected) or the name of the Notes server in the Server list and then click the Open button. (You can also double-click Local or the server's name.) The names of the Notes databases will appear along with a list of the subdirectories. For example, our Notes directory includes an APPS subdirectory.

NOTE

If the database file you want to use is stored on a server, make sure you have rights to access that server (separate from the ACL to the database file itself). You'll need to check with your Notes administrator.

5. Double-click the subdirectory where you've copied the database file if you want to open one of the sample databases. The name of the file will appear in the list box (along with the names of other files if you've decompressed them).

6. Highlight the database. You'll notice the file's path name appears in the Filename box at the bottom of the dialog box.

7. Double-click the database's name.

The Open Database dialog box closes and Notes adds the database's icon to the Workspace page. In some cases, when trying to open a database, you may see a message box as shown in Figure 4.3 telling you that the database could not be found.

FIGURE 4.3:

"Database cannot be found" message box

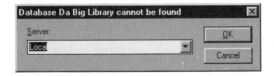

There may be two reasons for this message:

•   The database has been deleted.

•   The database has been renamed or moved.

If the database has been deleted, there is not much you can do but ask your Notes administrator to restore the file. However, if the database has only been moved or renamed, Notes can find the database for you. Just select the server where you think the database is located and click the OK button. Notes will try to locate the file using the Replica ID of the database. Once the database is found, the information for the database icon will be updated to reflect the new location.

Reading a Description of a Database's Contents

The About This Database document is usually the first document you see when you open a database for the first time. Figure 4.4 shows an example of such a document. This document contains information supplied by the database designer, often a description of the database's purpose and contents, how to access its documents, its unique conventions, and so on.

NOTE   The About This Database document may appear the first time you open a database, every time, or only when the contents of the document have changed, depending on how the database is designed.

FIGURE 4.4:

A database's About This Database document provides important information about using the database.

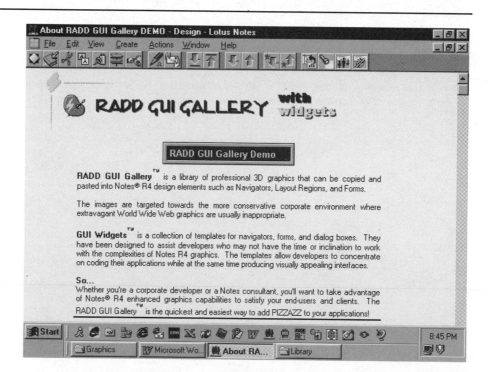

Press Esc to close the document and display the database's default view, as shown in Figure 4.5.

FIGURE 4.5:

A database's default view appears after you open a database.

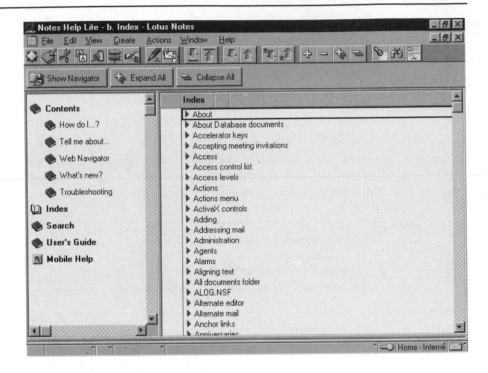

To see the About This Database document at any time, follow these steps:

1. Open the database or select its icon in the Workspace.

2. Choose Help ➤ About This Database.

NOTE   If the database's designer hasn't created an About This Database document, the default view appears instead. Subsequently, you must highlight the database's icon in the Workspace (to select it) or open the database and then choose Help ➤ About This Database to display the document.

Browsing through Databases

Once you learn to open databases, you can browse through the lists of other databases stored on your hard disk (or on your organization's Notes server if you have access). While browsing, you can read a description of the database, its features, and what you can do it with it—before you open it and add its icon to your Workspace.

To start browsing, choose File ➤ Database ➤ Open. Select the Notes server you want to browse and then click the Browse button. A list of databases from the open server appears; subdirectories are listed together following the list of databases. The first database on the list is highlighted, and its file name appears in the Filename box.

To open a subdirectory where other databases may be located, double-click the subdirectory, or click the subdirectory and then click the Select button. The databases from the open subdirectory now appear in the list. You can do one of the following:

- To display information about a database without opening it, click the database. The path name appears in the Filename box. Click the About button. You'll see the document that's displayed the first time you open a database. You can display this information at any time by selecting or opening the database and then choosing Help ➤ About This Database.

- To add a database icon to your Workspace without opening the database, highlight the database and then click the Add Icon button. Notes adds the icon to the page without opening the database.

- To add an icon and open the database in one step, double-click the database; to add an icon and open the database is two steps, highlight the database and click the Open button.

NOTE   One common mistake made by novice Notes users when opening a database is to highlight the database and click the Done button. The Done button does nothing but close the Database Open dialog box.

Closing a Database

To close a view or document, choose File ➤ Close, or press Esc. So for now, press Esc to close the view that's displayed (if a view is displayed) and return to the Workspace page.

Since views and documents are actually active windows, you can press Ctrl+W to close a window and return to the Workspace. You can also click the Close Window icon that appears at the far left of the menu bar. Of the three methods (menu, keyboard, or Esc), pressing Esc is definitely the fastest.

TIP   You can also specify the option of closing the current Notes window by right-clicking twice. Choose File ➤ Tools ➤ User Preferences. Under the Advanced Settings, select the Right Double-Click Closes Window and click OK. You will need to restart Notes for the change to take effect.

Using Database Icons

An icon represents a database you have stored on your workstation or a database that's stored on a server. Icons help to organize databases on your Workspace. You click a database's icon to access the database. An icon also displays the database's title or name, which helps you locate it quickly. The icon may also display a graphic that helps illustrate the database's purpose.

Adding a Database Icon to a Workspace Page

You can add a database icon to a Workspace page without opening the database the first time. In the Open Database dialog box, highlight the database and then click the Add Icon button. The selected database's icon is added to your Workspace, and the dialog box remains open to let you browse some more. Click the Done button when you are finished. Use this method to add multiple databases to your Notes Workspace at the same time. Nothing could be easier.

Moving Database Icons around Your Workspace

To move database icons around on your Workspace, you simply drag the icon around the page. To move the icon to a different page, drag it to the tab at the top of the target page. When an outline box appears around the tab name, release the mouse button.

TIP

You can also drag a database icon and drop it on top of a portfolio database icon. This will add the database icon to the portfolio database.

TIP

You can select several icons to move at the same time by Shift+clicking them and then dragging them as a group. Click an icon (any icon), hold down the Shift key, and click the other icon(s) you want to move. Still holding down the Shift key, point the mouse on any selected icon, press the left mouse button, and drag the icons to the desired location.

You can also move icons around by using the keyboard. Simply select the icon (or group of icons) you want to move; begin the drag operation by pressing Shift+Ctrl and the arrow key that points in the direction you want to move the icon. Once you've pressed an arrow key, you can release the Shift and Ctrl keys.

The Workspace scrolls when you perform an action that would cause icons to move off the screen. Scrolling occurs only if additional Workspace exists in the desired direction; if your computer is set to make a beep sound, it will beep when you can't move icons any further.

TIP

If all the icons on a given Workspace page do not fit on your monitor's screen, you can create additional Workspace pages. Moving between Workspace pages is easier than scrolling around a specific Workspace page. Try to keep 10 to 12 icons on each Workspace page and logically group the Notes databases that you access onto multiple Workspace pages.

Moving an Icon to a Different Page

If you want to move a database icon to a different page, click and drag the icon to the desired page tab until a white box surrounds the tab name. Release the mouse button. The icon will appear on the selected page. Dragging is a handy way to move icons from page to page when you want to reorganize them.

You can also hold down Shift+Ctrl and press the arrow keys to move the icons to the desired location. Press ↵ when the icons are positioned correctly. If you decide not to move the icons, press Esc.

Arranging Icons on a Workspace Page

You can arrange icons into continuous rows starting at the top left of the Workspace page. Make the Workspace window active and select the page on which you want to arrange icons. Choose View ➤ Arrange Icons.

If the icons are already in rows with no spaces between icons, this command has no effect. If you place more icons on a page than fit onscreen, a scroll bar will appear on the right side of the screen.

You can set your Workspace to show all database replicas as stacked icons. Stacked icons take up less room in your Workspace and make it easier to act upon all replicas of a database at once. When you stack icons, the top-left icon appears at the top of the stack. To display icons as replicas, choose View ➤ Stack Replica Icons.

TIP　Stacked icons are a great feature for Notes Release 4.6 mobile users who use laptop computers with small screens.

Removing an Icon from a Page

If you want to remove an icon from a Workspace page (perhaps you accidentally added a database icon to a page twice), click the icon you want to remove and then press Delete. A dialog box asks if you want to remove the selected icon from the Workspace. Click the Yes button. Notes removes the unwanted icon from the page.

WARNING　Don't confuse removing an icon from the Workspace with deleting a database from your computer. *Removing an icon* is simply a housecleaning chore and helps to keep your Workspace pages uncluttered and organized (not to mention dusted and vacuumed). *Deleting a database* permanently erases it from your hard disk.

Compacting the Workspace

If you frequently add and delete icons from your Workspace, there is a house-cleaning chore that needs to be done periodically. All the information about your Workspace is kept in the file DESKTOP.DSK, which is located in your Notes directory. Problems can arise when DESKTOP.DSK file begins to get quite large (I have seen it as large as 300MB), and the file will need to be compacted. You can compact your Workspace using the Workspace Properties InfoBox (discussed in Chapter 3) as shown in Figure 4.6.

FIGURE 4.6:

The Workspace Properties Infobox lets you keep tabs on the size of your DESKTOP.DSK file.

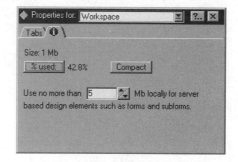

The Workspace Properties Infobox displays the current size of your DESKTOP .DSK file and also what percentage of the file is actually being used by Notes. If the percentage is less than 50 percent, you should compact the Workspace. To compact the Workspace, just click the Compact button. Once completed, your Workspace has been compacted and the excess storage released.

What's Next?

In the next chapter, we discuss viewing the contents of a database. We explain how you access the data that a database contains, as well as how you select specific data.

CHAPTER
FIVE

5

Viewing the Contents
of a Database

■ Using a view

■ Displaying a view

■ Using the three-pane window

■ Identifying the elements of a view

■ Selecting documents in a view

A *view* is a list of documents in a Notes database. Figure 5.1 shows an example of a view. Without a view, you wouldn't be able to access the information in the database. Every view is unique because it is based on the information within the documents.

NOTE All figures in this chapter are based on a Discussion Database that was created using the new Notes 4.6 Discussion Template.

When you start to look for information in a database, a view is the first element you see. A database always has at least one view, but it will probably have several. Each view displays documents in a unique way. These listings are displayed onscreen according to the way the designer defined them.

Using a View

After you get information (documents) into a Notes database, you need to be able to retrieve that information easily. A view allows everyone in an office, department, or division to open documents in a database and pull out the specific data they need. A view displays the information an organization has collected, as shown in Figure 5.1, and it enables individuals or a group of people working together to use the information to do their work and to make decisions based on the data.

Usually you'll use views to access documents, but you can also use views to perform the following tasks:

- Navigate to specific documents

- Find unread documents

- Select documents to act on as a group

- Delete documents

- Find text in any documents in the view

A view's design reflects how different groups of users in an organization need to access the information. For example, account agents for an insurance company need to view policy quotes only; underwriters need to view inspection reports only; adjusters need to view claims only. Any database these individuals work in common with should contain views that reflect their individual needs.

FIGURE 5.1:

A view lists the documents stored in a database

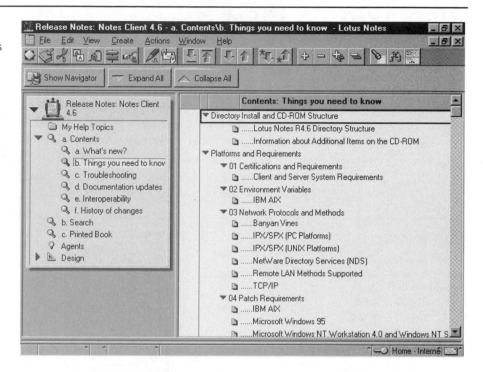

TIP
A view is a unique display of particular documents that summarizes the information in a special format for a specific group of users. Each row in a view refers to a specific document in a database, and each column refers to a field in the document.

The designer of the database creates the views you access. Although a view is the first thing a user sees in a database, a designer creates a view only after creating the forms on which the documents are based. Designers work in that sequence because they must have a good idea of how the information in a database is structured before creating a view. Ideally, the designer creates a view in a way that makes the information in the documents easy to access.

NOTE
When a user opens a Notes database for the first time, the first document that the person sees is the About This Database document for that Notes database. Press the Esc key to display the default view (as defined by the database designer) for the specific Notes database.

Displaying a View

To see a list of views in a database, you must display a view window. Highlight a Notes database by clicking once to select a specific database icon in the Workspace. For example, click a database icon in your Workspace (one of the sample database icons you added to your Workspace will work) and then pull down the View menu. The last section of the menu lists the views for the Notes database, as well as the other components of the database (discussed below), as shown in Figure 5.2. You can click one of these database components to display an expanded view of that component (e.g., Agents, Design). You can also simply double-click a database icon to view the contents of a database in the Notes three-pane window.

FIGURE 5.2:

The View menu displays the folders and views in a database. This example displays three view choices: By Author, By Category, and Archiving.

Using the Three-Pane Window

A faster—and more efficient—way to view the contents of a database is to use the Notes Release 4.6 three-pane window. The three panes in this window are the:

- Navigation pane

- View pane (or Document Navigation/Browsing pane)

- Document pane (or Document Preview pane)

One, two, or all three panes may be visible to you at any time. For example, the default that appears in Figure 5.3 (top) displays two panes. By clicking the View Show/Hide Preview Pane SmartIcon, Notes displays three panes (bottom). The three panes are designed to present information to you. You can easily navigate

FIGURE 5.3:

The two-pane window (top) is the default. The three-pane window (bottom) offers you instant access to data.

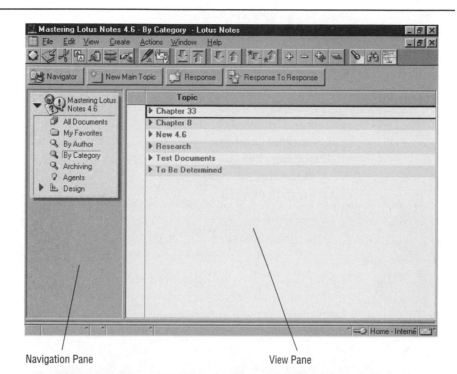

Navigation Pane   View Pane

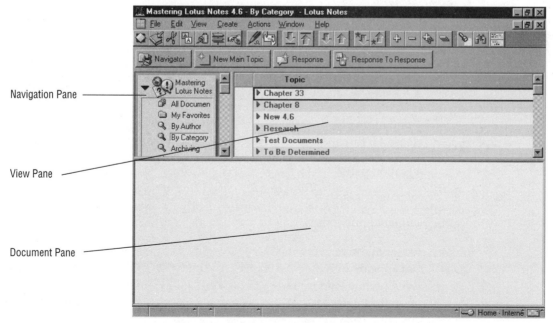

Navigation Pane

View Pane

Document Pane

through information without continually switching among views, view hierarchies, and documents. The value of this presentation is almost instant access to data. You can quickly access features and data because all the data is right in front of you. Nothing is hidden.

The Navigation Pane

The Navigation pane (the pane on the left) displays a hierarchical list of the components of the Notes database. Components include design elements such as forms, views, and Navigators.

TIP   Each component can be viewed collapsed or can be expanded to show its hierarchical structure.

Simply click a view navigator button (the book in this case) to display more of the hierarchy (the book opens). For example, when you click the Index view navigator button (this is a graphical navigator), the view automatically displays its contents in the View pane. Click the button again to collapse or close the view.

The View Pane

When you click one of the buttons in the Navigation pane, the View (or Document Browsing) pane on the right shows the view itself, including categories and documents. As you change the selected view in the Navigation pane, the View pane changes as well. You can double-click a document in the View pane and open it into a separate window called the *Document pane*.

The Document Pane

As we mentioned earlier, the Document pane appears when you click the View Show/Hide Preview Pane SmartIcon on the far right of the SmartIcon bar. You can also display the Document pane by choosing View ➤ Document Preview. For now, click the SmartIcon (it's faster).

You can change the size of the Document pane by grabbing the horizontal and vertical slider bars (or pane separators, which are the fat gray bars between the panes) with your left mouse button. These bars are also sometimes called *splitters*. Simply drag the horizontal splitter (or vertical splitter) up or down (or left or right, respectively) to increase or decrease the size of the Document pane.

You can also change the default preview display of the Document pane by choosing View ➤ Arrange Preview. The Preview dialog box appears, as shown in Figure 5.4. Notes gives you three options for where to locate the Document pane: Bottom Right, Bottom, or Right. Then each time you open the Document pane, the default preview display appears. Notes also gives you the flexibility to change the display to suit an individual document that you want to view.

FIGURE 5.4:

The Preview Pane dialog box allows you to set the default preview display for the Document pane or change the display to suit an individual document, depending on its content.

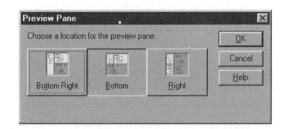

When you click a document in the View pane, the document appears in the Document pane, as shown in Figure 5.5. You can view a document in this pane or in its own window by double-clicking the document in the View pane.

FIGURE 5.5:

Click on a document in the View pane to display it in the Document pane.

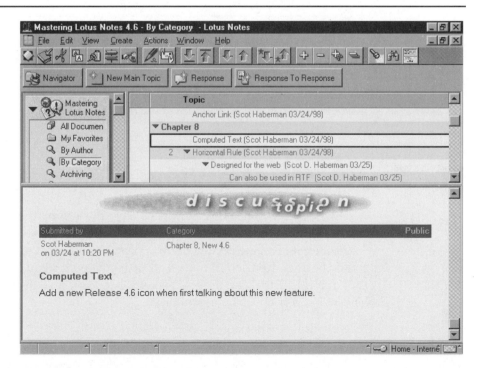

NOTE   The View pane always highlights the document that appears in the Document pane.

TIP   To edit a document, double-click anywhere in the Document pane to change from read mode to edit mode.

As you use the mouse, cursor arrows, SmartIcons, or shortcut keys to move through the view in the View pane, the document in the Document pane changes to reflect your selection. This process allows you to see if the selected document is the one that you want to access.

NOTE   The Document pane is sometimes called the *Document Preview pane*.

TIP   To adjust the size of the Document pane, place the cursor on the pane's splitter, hold down the left mouse button, and drag the splitter up or down until you get the size you want.

To close the view, press Esc. The active document window closes, and you return to the Workspace. Now pull down the View menu again and select the Design view. The view opens, displaying the components of the database. As you can see, the navigation buttons look different. However, they serve a similar purpose; they display the hierarchical structure of the database.

The Elements of a View

A view's design should reflect how people use the information in a database. Therefore, a view can contain different elements, depending on how an organization wants the list of online documents to appear. The information displayed in a view should be organized and formatted attractively, and it should be easy to read. If the user doesn't understand the organization of information in a view, the designer hasn't done a good job of presenting it.

A database can have many views, each of which selects, sorts, or groups the Notes documents in the database in a specialized way. However, the basic structure of a view is the same: Each column corresponds to a field in a document, and each row in the list of documents displays the data in each field. As you can see, the organization of this view enables you to read through the list of documents to find the information you want quickly.

The designer defines the columns in a view by applying various attributes to the view. For example, one attribute might specify that the view's name appear in the title bar, another might designate access levels (who can look at the view), and another might format the appearance of the text in each column.

The designer also identifies which documents are displayed in the view by writing a selection formula. This formula is important because it allows the designer to select specific documents. Not all documents in a Notes database need to be displayed in a particular view. In other words, views can contain subsets of all of the documents in a given Notes database.

Moving through a View

A view can list hundreds or even thousands of documents from the database, so moving through a view to locate a particular document can be time consuming. Here are several shortcuts you can use.

Press	To move
Home	To the left edge
End	To the right edge
Ctrl+Home	To the top
Ctrl+End	To the bottom
↑ or ↓	Up/down one line
← or →	Left/right one character
Page Up/Page Down	Up/down one screen
Tab	To the next unread document
Shift+Tab	To the previous unread document

You can also scroll with a mouse to move to an approximate position within a window. Simply drag the scroll box to the position in the scroll bar corresponding to the desired location in the window. For example, to move halfway through the information, drag the scroll box halfway down the scroll bar.

To move up or down (or left or right) one line (or character) at a time, click the up or down (or left or right) arrows at the ends of the scroll bars.

To move forward or backward one screen at a time, click within the scroll bar above the scroll box to move one screen backward or click below it to move one screen forward.

Working with Views

Although you'll use views mostly to look up information, you're not limited to passively scrolling around a database's views. You can manipulate your views and customize them so that they work for you. The following sections explain some keyboard shortcuts for managing Notes views.

TIP

If you prefer to use the mouse, you can also use SmartIcons for most of the actions described. While you display a view, review the balloon help for the Smart-Icons to familiarize yourself with their respective functions.

Refreshing a View

After you make changes to a document, you will need to *refresh* the view to reflect the changes. If you add documents, delete documents, or revise the data within a document, the changes don't appear automatically. You must refresh the data to recalculate it or confirm the changes that you've made. To refresh a view, press F9 or choose View ➤ Refresh.

NOTE

If a view needs to be refreshed, a refresh icon will display in the upper-left corner of the view. Clicking this refresh icon will refresh the view as well.

NOTE
A view does not always need to be manually refreshed after changes have been made to a document. The designer has four different options for setting the view refresh rate. These options can range from a manual refresh up to an automatic refresh.

Collapsing and Expanding a View

Sometimes you won't want to see all the document titles that are displayed in a view at one time. As a database grows, you'll be able to see only those document titles that can fit in a window. It may be faster for you to see just the main titles in order to locate a particular document. In that case, you can collapse a view. *Collapsing* a view refers to limiting the titles that appear in the view.

Expanding a view refers to displaying all the document titles in a view if it's been collapsed. Expanding a collapsed view allows you to display all the titles at one time.

To expand and collapse document titles in the View pane do the following:

- Press Shift and + (Shift+plus) to expand all document titles.

- Press + (plus) to expand only the document titles under the selected document.

- Press Shift and – (Shift+minus) to collapse all document titles.

- Press – (minus) to collapse only the document titles under the selected document.

NOTE
When expanding or collapsing document titles in combination with the Shift key, use the numeric keypad for the + (plus) and – (minus) keys. Also, make sure the Num Lock is not enabled or pressing the Shift key will be ignored.

TIP
The fastest way to expand or collapse document titles is using the SmartIcon. There are four SmartIcons defined for expanding and collapsing documents. The single + and – icons will expand only the document titles under the selected document. The multi + and – icons will expand and collapse all document titles.

In many views, documents are grouped by category or by hierarchy. In a categorized view, documents are sorted so they appear under the category to which they've been assigned.

In a hierarchical view, you can control the level of documents you want to display in a view at any time—all documents, only documents at a certain level, or only documents within certain categories. You can categorize documents by keyword fields, by date created, date modified, author name, status, and so on. Sometimes you don't want to display all levels because they would clutter the screen, making it difficult to read.

For example, highlight a category and press ↵. This action expands the main category to display a subcategory or document in the view, as shown in Figure 5.6. Press the ↓ and ↵ again. This action expands the next category. Press ↓ and ↵ once again to expand the next category, and so on. You can also click a category (the arrow referred to as a *twistie*) instead of pressing ↓ and ↵. To toggle between expanding and collapsing a category, simply click the arrow or press ↓ and ↵.

FIGURE 5.6:

Highlight a category in a view and press ↵ to expand the category/main document.

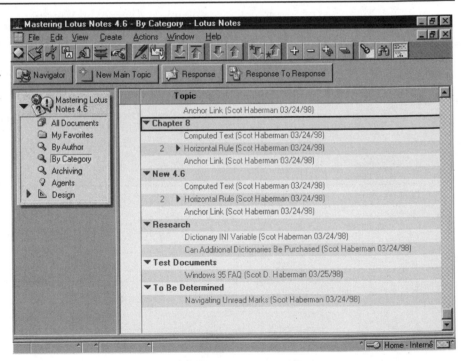

The commands to expand and collapse views are also available from the Notes main menu. They are:

- View ➤ Expand All

- View ➤ Collapse All

- View ➤ Expand/Collapse

Some users prefer to use the menu bar, rather than a multistroke key combination.

TIP

You can also use a view's Quick Search feature to locate a document. You can search a view by typing at least the first part of the name of a category, or, in a view that doesn't use categories, a document. This feature enables you to search the first column of a view for a specific text string. Notes only looks at the first column of the view or the category or document title, not the contents of the actual document. The view window positions itself next to the closest match of a category or a document. Using the Quick Search feature can save you time by navigating through views that contain large numbers of documents.

Another alternative to the Quick Search is using the Find/Replace dialog box. Choose Edit ➤ Find from the menu (or click the flashlight SmartIcon). Type in the text you are looking for, and Notes will try to find a match on any of the document titles in the current view. Like the Quick Search, this method does not search the contents of the document but the text in any of the view columns (not just the first column as in the Quick Search).

Marking and Unmarking Documents in a View

A check mark will appear next to a document when you select it in a view. *Selecting* refers to highlighting a document and then pressing the spacebar or pressing the Delete key to mark the document for deletion. To select a single document, click to the left of its title or press the spacebar. The status area in the status bar displays the number of documents you've selected. To select (mark) multiple documents, drag through the column to the left of their titles, click to the left of each title in turn, or hold the Shift key and press ↑ or ↓.

TIP

If you find a document in one view and want to find it again in a different view, highlight it in the first view, and hold the Ctrl key while you switch to the other view. The document will be highlighted in the second view. If the document isn't included in the second view, you'll hear a system beep.

Notes marks the documents you haven't opened yet with a star (unread mark) in the left margin. Notes removes the star after you open the document.

NOTE

Unread marks are displayed in the left column only if the database designer has selected Unread as an option in the View Properties InfoBox. In some databases, the database designer also makes unread documents appear in colored text in a view.

You can mark documents as Read without opening them, or mark documents that you've already opened as Unread, perhaps to draw your attention to them later. To mark all documents in databases Read or Unread, choose Edit ➤ Unread Marks ➤ Mark All Read (or Mark All Unread) from a view, from within a document, or with one or more databases selected on your Workspace. All documents in the active or selected database(s) are marked Read (or Unread).

You can also mark selected documents in a database as Read or Unread. In a view, select the documents you want to mark Read or Unread. You can select by date or select documents individually. Choose Edit ➤ Unread Marks ➤ Mark Selected Read (or Mark Selected Unread). All selected documents are marked Read or Unread. To deselect the selected documents, choose Edit ➤ Deselect All.

Sorting Documents

Notes Release 4.6 also enables you to perform an on-the-fly sort on documents that you see in a view. If the database's designer has defined a sorting capability for a particular column, you can sort the documents according to the way the designer has intended you to view the information that's displayed under the column. For example, you could display an alphabetical listing of document titles, or you could view documents by authors' last names or by the dates they were created. This feature is handy when you start creating documents and adding them to a view for other people to access. Periodically you might want to sort a column to establish an order to the documents in the view.

A column's sorting capability is indicated by an arrowhead in the column's title header. A column may contain an upward arrowhead (▲), downward arrowhead (▼), or both. Simply click the column header (the header may display a column title, depending on the designer's intent) to see how Notes sorts the documents. When the arrowhead is highlighted, the column has been defined to sort the information in that particular way. Click the column header again and again to toggle through the various sorting attributes (the column behaves like a toggle). When none of the arrowheads are highlighted, the documents are restored to their original order.

NOTE

If you click a column header that does not have any sort arrowheads defined, the column doesn't possess a sort capability.

NOTE

If you happen to see an arrow in the column header, this does not sort the data for the column but actually switches you to another view. This can be a bit confusing for the novice user.

Deleting Documents

When you delete a document from a view, the document is permanently removed from the database. Therefore, you need to be careful when deciding to delete any document. To perform a deletion, you must be assigned the proper access. Obviously, not everyone in an organization can delete database documents willy-nilly. Think of the havoc this would create, since any organization depends on secure data to help it remain successful. Your Notes administrator has taken precautions to limit who can delete documents from a database.

Since your organization's databases are located on a server, you may be working with a copy of the database on your workstation. You may be able to remove documents from the copy you're working with. If you don't know your access level, ask your Notes administrator. To delete selected document(s) from a view, press Delete so that you see a trash can next to each document you want to remove. This does not actually delete the document(s) but only flags the document(s) to be deleted. To actually remove the flagged document(s), refresh the view by pressing F9 and click OK when Notes asks whether you want to delete the documents permanently from the database.

NOTE   In the user preferences, you can set three different options for removing documents marked for deletion. You can choose to have Notes automatically remove the documents marked for deletion when the database is closed, to have Notes prompt you for confirmation to remove the documents marked for deletion when the database is closed, or to manually remove the documents marked for deletion by pressing the F9 key.

Reading Documents

People read documents onscreen primarily to find the data they need. After you open a document, you'll need to spend some time looking for the information you want. Many documents are too large to display their entire contents on one screen, as in Figure 5.7.

FIGURE 5.7:

Sometimes all the information contained in a document can't appear on one screen, which makes the document difficult to read.

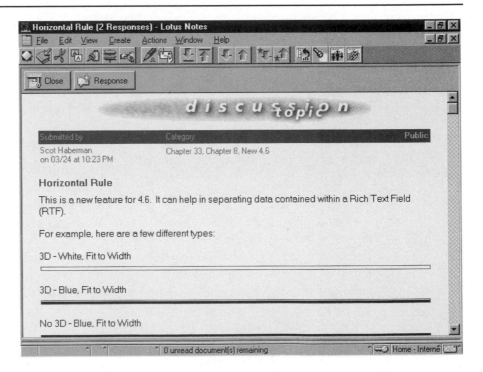

You can scroll within a window horizontally or vertically to display more of it. Simply drag the scroll box to the position in the scroll bar corresponding to the desired location in the window or click the arrows at the ends of the scroll bars.

To see how scrolling works, open a document in a view by selecting it and pressing ↵. To move halfway through the information in the document window, drag the scroll box halfway down the scroll bar. Click the arrows at the ends of the scroll bar to scroll in the direction the arrow indicates. To move forward or backward one screen at a time, click within the scroll bar above the scroll box (to move one screen back) or below it (to move one screen ahead).

If you are using Windows or UNIX, you can hide or display the horizontal scroll bar in a document in the View pane or in the Preview pane. By default, the horizontal scroll bar in Notes Release 4.6 is not displayed. To enable (or display) the horizontal scroll bar, a user needs to select View ➤ Show ➤ Horizontal Scroll Bar from the Notes mail menu. Once the bar has been enabled, a user can use a mouse to navigate left to right in Notes documents whose contents do not fit on the screen horizontally.

Press Esc to close the document and to return to the view. Press Esc again to close the view and display the Workspace.

What's Next?

As you saw in this chapter, a document appears in a view once it's been created. In the next chapter, we take you through the steps of searching a database to find the information you want. The ability to conduct a full text search of a database, especially a large database that contains many documents, can save you lots of time (and headaches) when you want to locate specific documents.

CHAPTER

SIX

6

Searching a Notes Database

- Plain and Full text searches

- Searching a database

- Find and Replace

- Search options

- Search results

- Opening a Web page

Over time, a Notes database can become very large, and inevitably, you're not going to remember all the documents you've composed, edited, or read. You may be able to recall the existence of a document that has an important piece of information, but you may not remember its location (or perhaps not even its name). One of the great strengths of Notes is its ability to search for a particular word or phrase within a document, which enables you to locate the information you need quickly (if it exists). Without the power to search, imagine the amount of time you would spend reading documents and scrolling through views in order find a specific piece of information.

Notes provides two methods for finding text in databases: the plain text search and the full text search. In this chapter, we explain the differences between the two methods.

Using Plain Text and Full Text Searches

You can perform a *plain text search* on a database that resides on a server or workstation running earlier versions of Notes (versions 1.*x* and 2.*x*), or on a database that has not been indexed for a *full text search.*

NOTE   See Chapter 25 for more information on indexing a database.

A plain text search doesn't provide the functionality of a full text search, and it's slower because the database isn't indexed in advance. However, you should use a plain text search when you (or the Notes administrator) want to conserve disk space.

NOTE   A full text index requires 10 to 50 percent of the disk space that the database itself requires.

Performing a Full Text Search

Performing a full text search lets you search for words, phrases, numbers, and data, as well as perform queries using wildcards, logical operators, proximity, and other advanced features. A *query* is a single set of search criteria. It can be a single word or phrase, or it can include the wildcards *and, or*, and other special operators. The results of a full text search can also rank documents by *relevance*, which simply means that Notes will display the document that most closely matches the search criteria you have set. A Notes full text search can also display the results sorted by date, oldest first or newest first.

The Notes Search bar is a convenient way to conduct searches (see Figure 6.1). From within a database, select View ➤ Search Bar. To de-activate, select it again. You can use the Search bar to enter simple or complex queries.

FIGURE 6.1:

You can use the Search bar to build a query.

NOTE

In Notes Release 4 you can search on any attachments (OLE objects displayed as icons or just simple attachments) if you choose the Index Attachments option when you create a full text index. You will need to delete a Notes Release 3.*x* full text index and create a new index if you want to index attachments.

In databases indexed for full text searching, you can expand the Search bar to use advanced search features. You can find out what the full text Search bar buttons do without activating them. Just check the active window's title bar while right-clicking the Search bar button.

TIP

To find out if a database has been indexed for full text searching, highlight the database icon on your Workspace and then right-click and choose Database Properties. The Database Properties InfoBox appears. Select the Full Text tab. If the "Database is not full text indexed" notification appears, the database is not indexed for full text searching. An alternative is to look at the Search bar. If the Create Index button appears, the database is not full text indexed (otherwise the Add Condition button would appear).

Like the ruler, the Search bar can stay at the top of the screen while you perform multiple searches or other unrelated tasks. When you're done searching, you can close the Search bar, but there's no need to do so.

Full Text Search Limitations

A full text index indexes all of the text in all of the documents in the database with the following exceptions:

- Words you exclude when you use a Stop Word file

- Text that is new or has been modified since the database was last indexed

- Text that appears in a view but isn't located in any document (such as column headings)

Because all text is indexed (with the previous exceptions), you can successfully search for text in fields that aren't displayed in the current form and in paragraphs that are hidden using the Hide-When options in the Text Paragraph dialog box.

WARNING   One of the default options when creating a full text index is to use the Stop Word file (DEFAULT.STP). This file determines text to exclude from the full text index (such as *the*, *and*, *or*, and so on). Numbers (0–9) are contained in this exclusion file. If you need to search on numeric values, you will need to ask your Notes administrator to remove this restriction.

A full text search finds all instances of query expressions in all documents located in the current view. If the current view doesn't display all the documents in the database, you may need to query more than one view. To do so just choose another view. The query remains in effect in the Search bar until you change it).

TIP   To find all instances of a query expression in all documents in a database, create and display a view that contains all the documents in the database. For example, many Notes databases provide a view where the documents are sorted by date. These views are useful for full text searching a set of documents for specific documents.

Using Characters

You might wonder what constitutes a "word" in an indexed document. Any text you enter is considered a word. The following characters may also be part of a word:

Character	What It Is
:	colon
\	backslash
.	period

TIP

Ampersands (&) are considered *keywords* in a search. For example, if you searched for AT&T, you would need to enclose the expression between double quotation marks like this: "AT&T".

You can use special characters to search documents for expressions such as *cc:Mail*, *5.95*, and *AT&T*. Also, the @ (at sign) can be used as a prefix or embedded within words. If it's embedded within a word, Notes treats the word as two separate words. For example, Notes interprets the expression *first@last* as the words *first* and *last*.

Matching Numbers

Notes Release 4 supports searches for documents by date created, date modified, and any field that contains a date. You can search date fields with the time/date data type in numerous ways, but you cannot search for dates that include a year earlier than 1932.

NOTE

You can't query time/date or numeric fields added to a form after the database is full text indexed. To do so, you must first delete and then re-create the full text index.

Finding Hidden Text

When a full text search finds hidden (nondisplayed) text, the document containing that text is selected by the search. No text is highlighted, but the status bar displays the following message: "Some highlights are not visible with this form."

Revising Documents

Documents are sometimes revised between index updates. After a document is revised but before it is re-indexed, queries may select this document and return it erroneously in search results. Even if a revised document is appropriately selected, Notes can't always highlight the search terms correctly and you'll receive the following message: "Some highlights are not visible with this form."

Using Computed Fields

Using computed fields in forms can produce unexpected search results. What you see on your computer screen in fields computed for display isn't actually stored in the Notes document; therefore, you cannot index or query computed-for-display data. This data may result in unexpected behavior because you may not know which fields are computed for display and which fields are actually stored in the document.

Using Keyword Fields

Using keyword synonyms prevents indexing of the keyword. However, in the specific case of Query by Form, this restriction doesn't apply. Notes uses keyword synonyms for display and actually stores an alternative value in the document. For example, the database designer can specify a keyword such as *Sunday|1,* where the user can select the synonym *1,* but the actual keyword is *Sunday.*

Performing Multiple Database Searches

You can create queries that span multiple databases within the following limitations:

- You can't execute saved queries and macros for multiple database views.

- You can't print, cut, or copy documents from multiple databases. You must do these operations from one database at a time. For example, to print documents from all the databases in the view, select and print the documents for each view one at a time.

Adding Local Databases to a Local Search Site

A local search site database lets you full text search multiple local databases simultaneously. You must create the search site database before you can add databases to it.

NOTE   See Chapter 25 for instructions on creating the search site database.

To add local databases to a local search site, follow these steps, starting at the Workspace:

1. Select the icon for the first database you want to add to the search site.

2. Choose File ➤ Database ➤ Properties.

3. Click Design and then click Include in Multi Database Indexing.

4. Repeat steps 1–3 for any other databases you want to add to the search site.

5. Select the icon for the search site database.

6. Choose Create ➤ Search Scope Configuration.

7. Do one of the following:

   - To create a search scope document for one database, leave Scope set to Database.

   - To create a search scope document for all the databases in a directory on your computer, click Directory.

NOTE   Don't select either Server or Domain for a local search site database.

8. Leave Server blank.

9. Type the path and file name into the Filename field of the database you want to add to the search site, or type the directory name into the Filename field (containing the list of databases you want to add).

10. Choose a Full Text Index option.

11. Close and save the document in the search site.

12. Repeat steps 6–11 for any other databases you want to add to the search site.

13. Update the full text index for the search site database to include the new database(s).

Searching for Words and Phrases

If a database doesn't have a full text index, you can still find words or phrases using a plain text search. Notes will search for a word or phrase in selected documents in the active view or in the titles of documents in the view. To search multiple views, you must search each view separately.

TIP   If you know a particular view shows all documents in the database, search that view.

When Notes finds a word or phrase in documents in a view, it checks the documents that contain the word or phrase. If you want to use more sophisticated search features, such as wildcard searching, and have Notes visually flag occurrences in the text of documents, the database *must* have an index for full text searching.

To search for a word or phrase, follow these steps:

1.   Double-click the database icon you want to open and search. A view appears.

2.   Choose Edit ➤ Find/Replace. The Find dialog box appears, as shown in Figure 6.2. (To search only selected documents, select those documents in the view before you choose the Find command.)

FIGURE 6.2:

The Find dialog box lets you search for a particular word or phrase.

3.   Enter the word or phrase you want to find in the Find text box.

4.   Select any of the following Match criteria (optional):

   • **Whole word**   Searches only for occurrences of a word with spaces around it. For example, Notes ignores Corp if it occurs within Corporation.

   • **Accent**   Searches for occurrences of the word or phrase that have the accents you typed.

   • **Case**   Searches for occurrences of the word or phrase that have the capitalization you typed.

5.   Select Find Next or Find Previous.

6.   Click the Done button when you're finished.

Using Find and Replace

With Find and Replace, you can find words or phrases in a single document and replace them with other words or phrases. Notes will find and replace a word or phrase in the active document only. You can decide whether to replace each occurrence of the word or phrase as you find it or whether to replace all occurrences at once. To use Find and Replace, follow these steps:

1. Open the document you want to search in Edit mode and choose Edit ➤ Find/Replace. (If you open the document in Read mode, the Find and Replace option will be grayed out or unavailable on the Notes menu bar.) The Find and Replace dialog box appears, as shown in Figure 6.3.

FIGURE 6.3:

The Find and Replace dialog box lets you search for and replace words and phrases in a document.

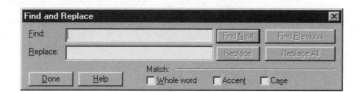

2. Enter the word or phrase you want to find in the Find text box.

3. Enter the word or phrase you want to replace it with in the Replace text box.

4. Select any of the following:

    *   **Whole word**   Searches only for occurrences of a word with spaces around it. For example, Notes ignores Jan if it occurs within Janine.

    *   **Accent**   Searches for occurrences of the word or phrase that have the accents you typed.

    *   **Case**   Searches for occurrences of the word or phrase that have the capitalization you typed.

5. Select any of the following:

    *   **Find Next**   Skips the current occurrence of the word or phrase and finds the next one. When Notes finds an occurrence you don't want to replace, select Find Next. (If there are no occurrences, you see a message saying that your word or phrase was not found. Click OK.)

    *   **Find Previous**   Skips the current occurrence of the word or phrase and finds the previous one.

- **Replace**   Replaces the next or selected occurrence of the word or phrase.

- **Replace All**   Replaces all occurrences of the word or phrase in the document. When you select this option, Notes warns you that your action cannot be undone. Click OK to replace all occurrences or click Cancel to return to the Find and Replace dialog box. When Notes can't find any occurrences in the document, you'll see a message saying that your word or phrase was not found. Click OK.

6.   Click the Done button when you finish searching.

Advanced Full Text Search Techniques

There are several advanced techniques you can use for searching, such as using the Search bar and the Search Builder dialog box. Each is described in the following sections.

Using the Search Bar

The Search bar is a very powerful searching tool that has many options available to help you find specific documents. In some cases, using the full text search may return too many documents so the Search bar may be more practical. Here are a few techniques and keywords to help you in finding your documents, which can be used along with your search text in the Search bar:

?   Can be used to match a single character in any position of a word (*D?g* would find *Dog, Dig,* and *Dug*).

*   Can be used to match zero-to-many characters in any position in a word (*D*g* would find *Dog, Dig, Dug* and *Drag*).

not or **!**   Can be used to imply logical negation (*not cat* would find documents that didn't contain *cat*).

or or **|**   Can be used to imply logical disjunction (*cat or dog* would find all the documents containing either *cat, dog,* or both words).

and or **&**   Can be used to imply logical conjunction (*cat and dog* would find all the documents containing both *cat* and *dog*).

accrue or **,**   Is similar to the *or* operator, although documents score more highly with the more instances of either word they contain (*cat accrue dog* would rate a document with five instances of *cat* more highly than one containing *cat* and *dog* once each).

near, **sentence**, and **paragraph**   Can be used to find documents containing words within a certain proximity of each other. Near has a proximity of eight words, sentence has a proximity of one sentence, and paragraph has a proximity of one paragraph.

Field   Can be used to restrict the search to a specific field (*Field Title contains a* will find all documents that have an *a* in their title field).

NOTE   For numeric and date fields the operators =, >, >=, <, <= are used instead of the contains operator.

---

exactcase   Can be used to restrict a search for the next expression to the specified case (*exactcase dog* will find documents containing *dog* but not *Dog*).

termweight *n*   Can be used to adjust the relevance ranking of the expression that follows, where *n* is 0–100 (*termweight 10 dog or termweight 20 cat* will rank documents containing "cat" higher than documents containing "dog").

Other things to keep in mind when using the Search bar:

- Hyphenated words can also be used to find two-word pairs that are hyphenated, run together as a single word, or separated with a space (*spag-hetti* will find documents containing *spaghetti*, *spag hetti* and *spag-hetti*).

- To search on a search keyword, the query string must be enclosed in quotation marks (to search for documents containing the word *field*, the string **"field"** must be entered in the query string rather than **field**, which Notes would interpret as a keyword).

Using the Search Builder

Another alternative technique for searching documents is using the Add Conditions button that displays the Search Builder dialog box. To open this option, just click the Add Condition button on the Search bar.

The Search Builder allows you to help search for documents using six different conditions.

Words and Phrases   Allows you to specify a list of search words or phrases. You can select the *Any* or *All* keywords to widen or narrow the search. If you need to include more than eight words or phrases, just add another Words and Phrases condition.

By Author   Allows you to search documents by an author who created them. This type of search can locate documents that either contain or do not contain a specific author's name. This technique will not allow you to search for documents created by an Anonymous author.

By Date   Allows you to search documents on the date the document was created or last modified. This option will allow you a lot of flexibility in searching the dates. You can select greater than a date, less than a date, a date range, and many others.

By Field   Allows you to search documents for data that is contained only within a specific field of a document. This type of search can locate documents that either contain or do not contain a specific text word or phrase.

TIP

To search for an empty (blank) field when using the Search By Field condition, select Does Not Contain and place an ***** in the search criteria.

By Form   Allows you to enter your search criteria using an actual form. The database designer has the option of including forms that can be used with this option. To use a form, just select an available form from the Form drop-down list. Once the form is displayed, just type the word or phrase to search for in the appropriate field (you can also use dates in date fields) and click the OK button.

By Form Used   Allows you to search the documents by the name of the form that was used that created or modified the document last. This technique is very similar to searching the Form field in the By Field condition.

Once you have entered all the search conditions using the Search Builder, just press the Search button (or press the ↵ key) and all the matching documents will be displayed.

If you need to change one of the search conditions, just double-click the token in the Search bar that represents the search condition that you would like to edit.

Choosing Search Options

You can specify how to sort the search results, whether to include variants of the word or the thesaurus specified in your search. Open a database and then follow these steps:

1. Choose View ➤ Search Bar.

2. Click the Search Options button in the bar. If you want to search for variants of the query word (the default), select Include Word Variants. For example, if the query word is *print*, documents that contain the words *print*, *prints*, *printed*, and *printing* are selected. To search for the exact word only, deselect Include Word Variants (Stemming). If you want to search using the thesaurus, select Use Thesaurus. This option will find like words to those in your search condition. For example, if the query word is *void*, documents that contain the words *cancel* and *abolish* are selected. For more information on how to change the thesaurus, refer to the note later in this chapter.

3. Select one of the following search result options:

    -   **Sort by Relevance**   Displays only documents in the current view that were selected by the query. Relevance is indicated by the gray-scaled bar to the left of the documents, with darkest gray indicating the most relevant. For example, a document in which the search word appears twice has a higher relevance than a document in which it appears only once. Also, a short document with a single occurrence of the search word is ranked higher than a longer document with a single occurrence.

    -   **Sorted by Oldest First**   Displays only documents in the current view that were selected by the query, sorted by date of last modification, oldest first.

    -   **Sorted by Newest First**   Displays only documents in the current view that were selected by the query, sorted by date of last modification, newest first.

4. Select Maximum Results. The Maximum Results dialog box appears.

5. Enter the maximum number of search results you want to display. When your query is relatively imprecise, you're likely to find many documents. This process can take a while and usually necessitates performing another more targeted search. By restricting the number of search results, you can discover if you need a more targeted query without wasting a lot of time.

6. Click OK.

Interpreting the Results of a Full Text Search

When a user completes a full text search of a particular database, Notes displays a new view of the database. This view contains only the documents that meet the search criteria. These documents are listed in the order of their relevance to the corresponding search criteria. Relevance is based on the number of times your search criteria occurs in each document.

The first documents listed in the view are the ones Notes has found that contain the most occurrences of the search criteria. These documents are probably going to be the most useful to you. The further down the view's list you go, the less likely documents are to be relevant to you because they contain the least number of occurrences of the search criteria.

NOTE   If you find yourself creating the same query over and over on a set of documents, you can create a query and save it for later use. In order for you to be able to save queries for a database, you must have either Designer or Manager access. If you do not have the proper access, talk to your Notes administrator.

WARNING   There is a 126-character limitation when using a Saved Query.

What Is in the Notes Thesaurus?

Using the thesaurus option while searching for documents is a very handy and powerful feature. The two questions that seem to be asked by most users are "What words are contained in the thesaurus?" and "How do I change the thesaurus?" The answer for both questions is that it is not easy. There is not a mechanism within the Notes environment that allows you to do either. Also, the list of words for the thesaurus is not contained in the help file or the printed documentation.

So what do you do? Here is the answer. The procedure that follows is to be used on the Notes Client (although it can be done on the server as well, but you may not have access).

Continued on next page

To view the words contained in the thesaurus, you need to locate the directory where Notes is installed. Under this directory, there should be a VDKHOME\ENGLISH directory. The ENGLISH directory contains a SYNONYM.CTL file, which can be viewed using any text editor. It contains the list of all the words that the thesaurus uses. Following each *list:* keyword is a group of words enclosed in quotation marks. Each list is the grouping of words that Notes uses when the thesaurus is activated.

Changing the thesaurus is a bit more complicated. Edit the SYNONYM.CTL file to contain the word groupings that you would like. Next, run the utility file MKSYD with the following command (assuming Notes to be your executable directory):

**mksyd –f \notes\vdkhome\english\synonym.ctl –syd \notes\vdkhome\
english\vdk10.syd**

The change takes effect immediately (you do not have to restart Notes).

Viewing Search Results

You can view search results in the following ways:

- To display search results sorted by relevance to your query, click the Search Options button (next to the Reset button on the Search bar) and select Sort by Relevance. A gray-scaled bar at the left side of the view indicates relevance; the darker (more intense) the gray next to a document, the more relevant it is. Notes can also display the search results by oldest first or by newest first.

- To display search results as checked documents in a normal view when you are using the plain text search method, choose View ➤ Show ➤ Search Results Only (to deselect it) or select Selected in View in the Search Options dialog box.

TIP You find the selected (checked) documents by clicking the icon for Next Selected Document, scrolling, or pressing F3 (Shift+F3 goes to the previous selected document).

- To show search results in another view, choose the view from the View menu, and then click Search again.

- To find the words that match your query, open any search result document.

Each word that matched your query is enclosed in a red rectangle. To move from one instance of your search word to the next, Press Ctrl plus +. To move to the previous instance, press Ctrl plus –. As you select each search word, its outline turns from red to blue (these colors may vary, depending on the document's background color).

NOTE
If the word that matched your query is found within an embedded or attached file, the text will not be enclosed in a red rectangle.

NOTE
Notes displays the Search bar at the top of the view. The Search bar is a toggle—it stays at the top of the view until you remove it by choosing View ➤ Show Search Bar. All other Notes functions work with or without the Search bar.

TIP
If a database has been indexed for full text search and you want to search only the document *titles* in a view, press Shift while you choose Edit ➤ Find to open the Find dialog box. Select Search within View.

Opening a Web Page from the Search Bar

Starting with Release 4.5, Notes comes with an additional option in the Search bar that allows you to open a Web page from anywhere in Notes.

To open a Web page from the Search bar do the following:

1. Open any database, including the Personal Web Navigator database.

2. Choose View ➤ Search Bar.

3. Click the icon to the left of the Search bar to display the Open URL icon.

4. Enter the URL and click Open.

NOTE
See Chapter 31 for more information on using the Personal Web Navigator database to access the Web.

What's Next?

The ability to search a database can help you find specific information and is an invaluable feature of any Notes database. By searching for particular words, phrases, or numerical data, users can locate specific information quickly (if it exists).

In the next chapter, we take you through the steps of actually creating, or *composing*, a document. A document contains the data that becomes part of a Notes database.

CHAPTER
SEVEN

7

Creating a Document

- Creating new documents

- Editing documents

- Formatting documents

- Changing text properties

- Checking your spelling

When you are ready to create a document to add to a database, you use a form created by the database designer. (We discuss database design and development in detail in Part II.) The user of a database creates new documents by entering information in the predefined fields of a form.

Each database has its own unique forms. For example, a call-tracking database would use a form for logging calls and tracking their resolution. A support-conference database would use a form for sharing information among members of a workgroup. A news database would use a form for entering news from different sources. These are just a few of the many ways forms are used in databases. In this chapter, we show you how to create a document.

Creating a New Document

To create a document for a database, make sure the database is selected by either opening it or clicking its icon in your Workspace. Pull down the Create menu to see the forms you can use to create a document, as shown in Figure 7.1. If a database doesn't provide any forms, you won't see any forms listed on the menu.

FIGURE 7.1:

The Create menu displays the list of the database's forms (if they exist). For example, this database provides three forms: Document (Main Topic), Response, and Response to Response.

For example, the *Mastering Lotus Notes 4.6* database we used to track the development of this book (surprise!) provides three forms from which to create new documents: a Document form, a Response form, and a Response to Response form (this database was created using the Notes 4.6 Discussion–Notes & Web template). You enter information in the documents by either typing or using data created in other applications.

NOTE

Some documents may display the date and time they were created or modified. Notes automatically stores the date and time that a document was created. For example, the Document form contains a Date field, which will display the current system date. Documents created locally (in databases on your hard disk) use your workstation's time. Documents created in databases that are located on servers use the server's time.

To create a new document in a database such as the Mastering Lotus Notes 4.6 database, follow these steps:

1. Choose the appropriate form (in this case, Document) from the Create menu to open the form, which might look similar to the form shown in Figure 7.2.

2. Type text into the fields of the document. You can enter text just as you would with a word processor.

FIGURE 7.2:

A form from the Create menu. This form is named Document.

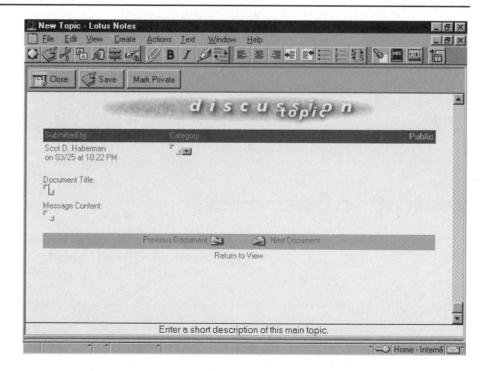

NOTE

Each field in a document is indicated by small angle brackets. When the brackets appear in red (on a color monitor), the field can be *encrypted*. This means you can scramble the information in the particular field so no one can read it except you (or another designated person). See Chapter 16 for more information on encryption and setting system security.

Press Ctrl+S or choose File ➤ Save to save the document, or press Esc if you don't want to save the document. (In some cases, the Database Designer may have provided Action buttons to perform the most common actions such as saving and closing a document.) As a precaution if you have made changes to the document, a dialog box will ask if you want to save your changes (see Figure 7.3). Click the No button. (If you actually *do* want to save the document, click the Yes button. Or click Cancel to return to editing the document.) When you click the No button, the document window closes and you return to either the view or the Workspace.

Be sure to save a document you're writing or editing every few minutes. You don't need to close the document when you save it. When you're finished, save and close the document.

FIGURE 7.3:

A dialog box appears as a precaution.

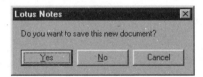

Editing a Document

Editing means adding, deleting, or replacing text as well as specifying text properties. Although a database designer creates and formats the form on which a document is based, you can still change various text properties.

TIP

To put a document in Edit mode, highlight the document in a view or folder and select Actions ➤ Edit Document. If a document is already open in Read mode, double-click anywhere in the document to put it in Edit mode. (Or, you can press the red pencil SmartIcon instead.) When the fields appear, you can make changes to the text. (If you are unable to put a document in Edit mode, it is because you do not have security access to do so.)

Text properties include font, size, special emphasis (like bold and italic), and color. When you specify text properties, keep this in mind: You can format text and paragraphs only in rich text fields. A *rich text* field is a special kind of field that can contain formatted data, graphics, file attachments, OLE objects, and hotspots (which are links to other Notes documents, views, databases, and external objects, such as pages on a Web server). (We discuss the differences between rich text and plain text fields in Chapter 14.) Text menu commands are unavailable when you write or edit any other type of field such as date fields, numeric fields, or keyword lists.

TIP   To determine quickly if you are in a rich text field, look at the Notes status bar. If you can see a typeface, point size, or style on the left side, you are in a rich text field.

Formatting a Document

You can use the default formats that Notes provides or choose your own. Notes gives you an abundance of formatting tools for improving the appearance of your documents. You can format paragraphs by specifying attributes such as margins, tab stops, interline and interparagraph spacing, and alignment (justification). You can format text by choosing different typefaces, font sizes, or text emphases. To format text or paragraphs, your document must be in Edit mode.

To apply a format to selected text, just choose the appropriate command from the Text menu. You can also specify a format without first selecting any text. If you specify a new paragraph format without selecting any text, the current paragraph (the one in which the insertion point is located) is reformatted. However, if you select a new text format without selecting any text, no existing text is reformatted, but subsequent text that you type has the new attributes.

NOTE   You can format text and paragraphs in rich text fields only. Many fields in Notes are plain text. For example, the To field in a Notes mail memo and the Subject field in most discussion documents are plain text fields. The Text Font command is dimmed when your pointer is in a plain text field.

Changing the Text's Appearance

The default text font in Notes is 10-point Helvetica, plain and black, which is displayed in the typeface area on the status bar when you create or edit a document. (A font, such as Helvetica, Geneva, or Times Roman, is a set of characters distinguished by their shapes; a size is a measurement in points of the height of the characters.) Default character spacing is proportional. If you like the appearance of the default text formats, feel free to leave them as they are, but if you want to change text formats, you have several options. The simplest is to select commands from the Text menu. You can also choose Text ➤ Text Properties to bring up the Text Properties InfoBox, as shown in Figure 7.4.

FIGURE 7.4:

The Text Properties InfoBox

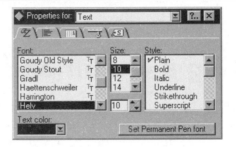

It includes five option folders:

- Fonts
- Alignment and Spacing
- Pagination
- Hiding Paragraph Text
- Style Settings

You can use this InfoBox to review or change any of the attributes associated with each option folder, including text attributes such as font, size, and color; special attributes like bold, underline, and superscript; and styles.

TIP

A faster way to display the Text Properties InfoBox is to position the mouse pointer in a rich text field and then right-click. From the menu that appears, choose the Text Properties option.

The Fonts options folder in the Text Properties InfoBox displays all the fonts, point sizes, predefined styles, and colors that are available to you.

Select the typeface and type size that you want from the Font and Size lists; you may also enter a size into the Size box, or use the up and down arrows to increment or decrement the size setting. The Style list displays various styles you may apply to your text. Using text styles adds variety to the appearance of text. Plain displays text in plain form. Bold displays text using bold emphasis. Italic displays text using italic emphasis. Underline displays text underlined.

The strikethrough attribute displays text with a line through it. A strikethrough is useful to tell a reader that some text has been, or will be, deleted from a document.

Superscript raises the text by half a line and reduces its size. It's a useful way to show registered trademarks (Lotus Notes®) and lets you type exponents (22^{55}). Subscript lowers the text by half a line and reduces its size. It lets you type chemical expressions ($H_2O + CO_2\ H_2CO_5$).

The Text color box allows you to choose different colors for your text. Simply click the color you want.

When you finish selecting attributes from the Text Properties InfoBox, click the Close button.

TIP

The status bar at the bottom of the Notes Workspace provides a quick method of applying fonts and point sizes to selected text or at the insertion point in a rich text field. You will see a font name and point size value displayed in individual *segments* toward the left end of the status bar. By clicking either of these segments, a list of fonts or point sizes will be displayed. Simply choose the font and point size you desire from the lists.

To increase text size to the next available size, press F2 or choose Text ➤ Enlarge Size. To reduce text to the next available size, press Shift+F2 or choose Text ➤ Reduce Size. For example, if text is in 10-point Helvetica, selecting Enlarge changes it to 12 point if that's the next available size.

Notes includes a Permanent Pen feature that allows you to switch quickly to an alternate text style usually for the purpose of adding comments to a document. This feature is useful if you are editing or reviewing someone else's work and wish to distinguish your comments, additions, and modifications from the original text. (As with all formatting options, the Permanent Pen can be employed only in rich text fields.) You "turn on" the Permanent Pen by selecting Text ➤ Permanent Pen or by clicking the Permanent Pen SmartIcon; the default text style is bold red. The Permanent Pen is "modal"; you remain in Permanent Pen mode until you turn it off by repeating either of the two methods above. The Fonts options folder of the Text Properties InfoBox allows you to change the Permanent Pen text style. Select any combination of font, point size, style, and color, and then click the Set Permanent Pen font button found in the lower-right corner of the folder.

TIP   When the Permanent Pen is enabled, you can strike through existing text automatically by selecting the text and pressing Shift+Backspace. Notes will display the text in the Permanent Pen font with the strikethrough attribute.

When you finish selecting attributes, click the Close button.

Formatting Paragraphs

As with text formats, you can either accept the default paragraph formats or change them to suit your needs. To change paragraph attributes such as margins and interline and interparagraph spacing, click the tab for the Alignment and Spacing options folder, shown in Figure 7.5. You can apply the attributes from this folder to paragraphs you've already selected, or you can select attributes at any point and the paragraph that contains the insertion point will take on the attributes you specified.

The default formats are:

- **Alignment**: Left
- **First Line:** Left justified
- **List:** No list
- **Left margin:** $1^1/_2$
- **Spacing:** Interline: Single

Changing Tabs and Margins Using the Ruler

To display the ruler, switch to Edit mode and then choose View ➤ Ruler (or press Ctrl+R). The ruler appears at the top of the document, as shown in Figure 7.6. You can also display the ruler by clicking the SmartIcon that shows a small picture of a ruler.

FIGURE 7.5:

The Alignment and Spacing options folder

FIGURE 7.6:

You can display the ruler when you want to change a document's margins and tabs.

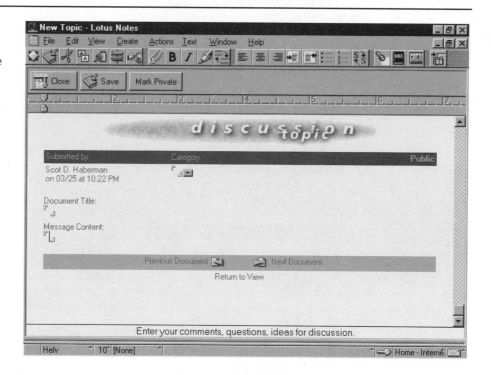

When you open a new document, the position and number of markers on the ruler depend on the settings specified by the database designer in the form used to create the document. If no settings were specified, the default left margin is one inch and the default tab stop is every half an inch. You can override the default margin and tab settings.

TIP   If you would like to change the unit of measure that Notes uses, choose File ➤ User Preferences. Click International, and under Measurements, select Imperial to use inches and Metric to use centimeters.

If you're using a color monitor, black arrows determine the tab stops. Click the ruler wherever you want to insert a tab stop. To remove a tab stop, click the arrow on the ruler.

Indenting and Outdenting Paragraphs Using the Keyboard

When you indent or outdent a paragraph, you are changing its left margin relative to the left margin of the rest of the document. You can use keyboard shortcuts to adjust paragraph indents and outdents in quarter-inch increments; each additional indent or outdent moves the paragraph quarter of an inch in the appropriate direction.

- To indent only the first line in a paragraph, place the insertion point anywhere in the line and then press F7. Subsequent lines in the paragraph wrap to the left margin.

- To indent every line in a paragraph, place the insertion point anywhere in the paragraph, and then press F8.

- To outdent the first line in a paragraph, press Shift+F7 anywhere on that line. All subsequent lines in the paragraph will wrap to the normal left margin. To outdent every line in the paragraph, press Shift+F8 anywhere in the paragraph.

TIP   Use the Text Indent and Text Outdent SmartIcons to change the tab stops for indenting and outdenting paragraph text.

You can also create a hanging indent, often used for bullets or numbered list items. Press Shift+F7 and then press F8. Type the number or bullet, press Tab, and type the text for the item.

TIP   The fastest way to create a bulleted or numbered list in a document is to position the insertion point in a text or rich text field and then click the Text Bullets or Text Numbers SmartIcon. For a bulleted list, you can also position the insertion point in a text or rich text field and then click the right mouse button to display the Text Properties menu. Select the Bullets command.

Setting Alignment (Justifying Text)

Alignment (justification) is the position of text relative to the left or right edges of a window on your screen or of a printed page. For example, this paragraph is left aligned. To set the alignment, select the text or place the insertion point within a paragraph. Choose one of the following alignment buttons:

Left aligns text on the left margin (the default).

Center centers each line of text.

Right aligns text on the right margin.

Full aligns text on both left and right margins.

None turns off word wrap and displays the paragraph as one line.

Setting Pagination Options

Pagination refers to how a document gets broken into multiple pages. A *page break* occurs in a document either automatically because the information exceeds a single printed page or manually because the user inserted it. You may have noticed that when you display a document onscreen, even a very long document, no page breaks are indicated—Notes does not show page breaks by default. (Page breaks are usually not an issue in Notes unless you plan on printing a document.) If you wish to see where page breaks fall in the document, choose View ➤ Show ➤ Page Breaks; since this setting is a toggle, choose the command again to hide page breaks.

TIP

Notes can display symbols that represent hidden characters in a document (such a tabs, paragraph markers, and so on). While in Edit mode, choose View ➤ Show ➤ Hidden Characters.

The Page folder of the Text Properties InfoBox (see Figure 7.7) lets you control where to place page breaks relative to the paragraphs of a rich text field.

To apply a pagination option to a paragraph, position the insertion point in the paragraph, choose Text ➤ Text Properties, and select the Page tab. Check any or all of the pagination options:

Page break before paragraph inserts a page break just prior to the current paragraph.

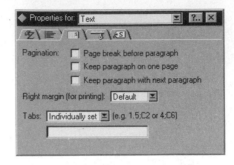

Keep paragraph on one page consolidates a paragraph on a single page in the event that it crosses page boundaries (for example, it starts at the bottom of one page and continues at the top of the next page).

Keep paragraph with next paragraph forces the current paragraph to appear on the same page as the paragraph that follows.

The Page folder also includes options that let you set the right margin (for printing purposes only) and the position of tab stops for the current paragraph.

> **TIP**
>
> The Tabs option is an alternative method of setting tab stops (as opposed to clicking in the Ruler bar) and is particularly handy when you need several, evenly spaced tab stops in a paragraph. For instance, to place tab stops every half inch from the one inch mark to the seven inch mark of the ruler, you simply choose the Evenly spaced Tabs option and enter a value of 0.5 in the box to the right. When you press ↵ or click the check mark icon, the tab stops will automatically appear in their correct positions in the ruler.

Named Styles

Named styles are a tremendous timesaving device when it comes to repeatedly applying the same formats to text and paragraphs. For example, if you wish to format several different blocks of text (in the same rich text field, in different rich text fields of the same document, or in rich text fields in different documents) in exactly the same way, you could use the Text Properties InfoBox to apply the format to each block, selecting the same font, point size, style, and color, as well as alignment and spacing. After the third or fourth time you *will* become exasperated! You can avoid this situation by grouping the format options into a single named style that you can refer to over and over again.

Creating a named style is very simple. The easiest method is to base your named style on an existing piece of text or paragraph that is already formatted to your liking. Position the insertion point in the text or paragraph and then choose Text ➤ Text Properties to display the Text Properties InfoBox. Change any of the formatting options you desire by selecting the appropriate option folder. (Don't close the Text Properties InfoBox yet! You will use the Styles folder to create your named style.) When you are satisfied that you have selected the right combination of format options, do the following:

1. Click the Styles tab from the Text Properties InfoBox.

2. Click the Create Style button.

3. Enter a name for the named style; make the name intuitive for future reference.

4. Check any or all of the following options:

   - **Include font in named style** saves the selected font as part of the named style.

   - **Make style available for all documents** allows you to access the named style from other documents in the database.

   - **Include this style in Cycle Key (F11)** puts the named style into a rotation of named styles that you can access by repeatedly pressing F11, known as the Cycle Key.

5. Click OK to save the named style.

Figures 7.8 and 7.9 show the Styles folder and the Create Named Style dialog box.

FIGURE 7.8:

The Styles folder of the Text Properties InfoBox

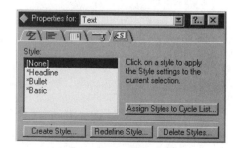

The Create Named Style
dialog box

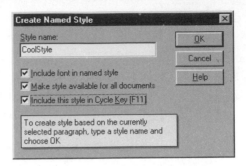

Repeat the procedure above for as many named styles as you wish to create. Notice that you can also redefine and delete existing named styles from the Styles folder.

Using the Spell Checker

The Nots spell cheker looks for mispelled wrds using to dicsionaries: the man dicsionary and the customisable user dicsionary…Okay, now that we have your attention regarding spell checking, the previous sentence should read like this: The Notes spell checker looks for misspelled words using two dictionaries: the main dictionary and the customizable user dictionary. The main dictionary is comprehensive but does not contain proper names or many specialized words. You can add words that are not in the Notes main dictionary to your user dictionary so that the Notes spell checker will not flag them as misspelled words in the future.

In addition to misspellings, the spell checker looks for repeated words, such as *was was*. The spell checker does not check single-character words (such as *a*), text that does not contain letters (such as 75% or 23), or words that contain more than sixty-four characters.

The main dictionary in North America is American English (LOTUSEN1.DIC). If your version of Notes includes more than one language dictionary (for example, if you're using Notes outside North America), you can choose a different dictionary. Language dictionaries have the extension .DIC and are located in your Notes data directory.

NOTE   Your personal user dictionary (USER.DIC) is located in your Notes data directory.

Checking Spelling

It's easy to check the spelling of all text or selected text within a document. Just follow these steps:

1. Make sure the document is in Edit mode.

2. Select the text you want to spell check (not selecting any text will default to spell checking the entire document starting in the first field).

3. Choose Edit ➤ Check Spelling.

4. For each word Notes does not recognize, do one of the following:

   • To change the spelling, enter a different spelling or select a Notes guess and click Replace.

   • To keep the spelling, click Skip (click Skip All to bypass any further occurrences of the unrecognized word).

   • To keep the spelling and add the word to your user dictionary (so Notes recognizes the word the next time), click Define.

5. Click Done when you are through checking your spelling.

TIP   A faster way to check the spelling of a document is to click the Edit Check Spelling SmartIcon.

Adding or Deleting Words from Your User Dictionary

You can customize the user dictionary so that it contains words you want Notes to recognize when it checks spelling.

1. Choose File ➤ Tools ➤ User Preferences. The User Preferences dialog box appears.

2. Click User Dictionary. The User Spell Dictionary dialog box appears.

3. Do one of the following for each change you want to make to the user dictionary:

    • To add a word, enter the word in the text box (below the larger list box) and click Add.

    • To delete a word, select the word from the list and click Delete.

    • To change the spelling of a word, select the word from the list, enter a new spelling in the text box, and click Update.

4. Click OK twice.

Changing the Language You're Using to Check Spelling

If your version of Notes includes more than one language dictionary, you can choose a dictionary more appropriate to the language you are using.

1. Choose File ➤ Tools ➤ User Preferences. The User Preferences dialog box appears.

2. Click International.

3. Click Spelling Dictionary. The Choose Dictionary dialog box appears.

4. Select the language you want.

5. Click OK twice.

NOTE   Additional spell checking dictionaries are available including Medical, Pharmaceutical, Legal, Dental, Geographical, and Technical. For more information, contact Spellex Development at 1-800-442-9673 or visit their Web site at `http://www`
`.spellex.com`. (The additional spelling dictionaries support most Lotus products such as 1-2-3 for Windows, Ami Pro, cc:Mail, Freelance, and Notes.)

What's Next?

Creating a document, in addition to reading a document (and maybe sending a document), is probably the single most important Notes task that you'll perform routinely.

In the next chapter, we discuss ways in which you can dynamically add information to the documents you create, as well as automate tasks you want readers of your documents to perform. You don't have to be a database designer to add "workflow" attributes to your documents. Notes provides several elements, such as Agents, links, and Action buttons, that you can create and add to your documents on the fly. These elements can help other people use your documents in more productive and efficient ways.

Adding Advanced Features to Documents

- Formatting with bulleted and numbered lists

- Adding and formatting tables

- Creating sections

- Adding links

- Using buttons and action hotspots

In the last chapter we talked about the basics of document creation and formatting. We'll use this information as a springboard to our discussion of advanced documents. When we say *advanced*, we mean documents that go above and beyond the ordinary in how they look and act. As a Notes user, you have a large measure of control over how your documents function, provided that the forms you are using allow you to incorporate the advanced features introduced in this chapter. (If they don't, file a complaint with the developer!) Knowing how to exploit the full end-user capabilities of Notes bestows upon you that elusive, hard-won title of "power user."

NOTE You can apply these format controls (discussed in this chapter and the previous chapter) only in a rich text field. If the form (or the database) cannot accept free-form text entry, you might not encounter rich text fields in which you can employ the Notes formatting features.

Advanced Formatting

The information you enter into a field has two components:

- Its content
- Its look, or *format*

Chapter 7 described general format controls such as font, color, point size, style, and alignment. Notes supplies many other formatting options to make your documents more readable and easier to understand.

Using Bulleted and Numbered Lists

Using bullets and numbers are two ways to distinguish or delimit a list of items in a paragraph. (Each bullet or number is a separate paragraph.) If conveying a specific sequence is not important, a bulleted list is usually the better choice; otherwise, use a numbered list. Figure 8.1 displays a document with a bulleted list and a numbered list.

FIGURE 8.1:

A document with a bulleted list and a numbered list

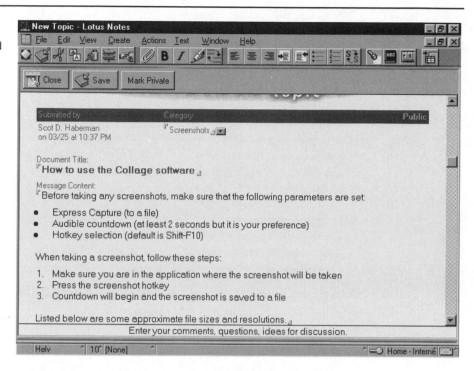

You can use Text menu options, SmartIcons, status bar style options, or the right mouse button (bullets only) to apply bullets and numbers to text either before or after you enter the text. In all cases, the action is a toggle that remains active until you turn it off. Follow these steps:

1. Place the insertion point in the rich text field where the list is to appear.

2. Select one of the following methods to activate a list-formatting option:

   - Choose Text ➤ Bullets or Text ➤ Numbers.

   - Click the SmartIcon corresponding to bullets or numbers.

   - Position the mouse pointer at the insertion point, right-click, and choose Bullets from the pop-up menu. (This applies to bullets only.)

   The chosen list delimiter will appear at the insertion point.

3. Type your text. Press ↵ to create a new list item; a list delimiter will automatically appear on the new line. In the case of numbering, Notes always starts with 1 and increments the number to 2, 3, and so on.

4. Repeat step 2 to turn off the list-formatting option.

You can apply bullets and numbers to existing text simply by highlighting the text where the list delimiter should appear and using one of the methods described in step 2. If you change your mind and want to remove bullets or numbers from an existing list, highlight the list and then choose the bullets or numbers option again.

Adding Tables

Tables allow you to structure information in row/column, or tabular, format. For instance, if you want to display a series of revenue values for the years 1993 to 1998, you can construct a table in which each year appears along a horizontal axis directly above the corresponding revenue value.

TIP   A large table or many tables in a document will tend to slow down operations such as opening a document for reading and editing.

The number of rows and columns in a table, as well as the table layout, is up to you. To create a table, follow these steps:

1. Place the insertion point in the rich text field where the table is to appear.

2. Choose Create ➤ Table or click the Create Table SmartIcon (Figure 8.2) to display the Create Table dialog box (Figure 8.3).

FIGURE 8.2:

The Create Table SmartIcon

FIGURE 8.3:

The Create Table dialog box in which you specify the dimensions of the table in rows and columns

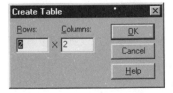

3. Enter the dimensions of the table in rows and columns. If you are not sure of the dimensions you require, take a best guess; you can easily add or remove rows and columns later.

4. Click the OK button. Notes creates the table at the insertion point.

You can enter information in each cell, or you can alter the format and layout of the table. You can apply virtually any format to text within a cell that you can apply to regular text (for example, font, color, point size, alignment, bullets, and numbers).

TIP

Consider entering all the information to appear in the table, including column and row headers, before you modify the format and layout. Since modifying a table's format and layout can be time-consuming, you'll want to make sure that the contents are in place first. Having to reformat a table because you forgot to represent some key information can be an unpleasant task.

Notes supports several ways to control the look of a table, including increasing and decreasing row and column widths, displaying and removing borders from cells, and cell-level text formatting. The Table Properties InfoBox lets you set overall table attributes as well as single- and multiple-cell attributes. Follow these steps to use the Table Properties InfoBox:

1. Place the insertion point in any cell in the table if you are going to modify an overall table property or a property for that cell only, or highlight a selected set of cells to apply changes throughout the range.

NOTE

Notice that if you click anywhere in the table, the Table option appears in the menu bar at the top of the Workspace. If you click elsewhere in the field, the Table option disappears.

---

2. Choose Table ➤ Table Properties to display the Table Properties InfoBox, as shown in Figure 8.4.

TIP

You can access the Table Properties InfoBox by right-clicking anywhere in a table and selecting Table Properties from the pop-up menu. Another option is to click anywhere in the table and then click on the Properties SmartIcon.

FIGURE 8.4:

The Table Properties
InfoBox

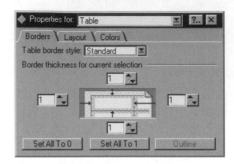

3. Select the style of border to appear for the top, bottom, left, and right borders of the selected cell(s) from the Cell Borders option folder.

    • You can quickly remove all borders or apply a single-line border by clicking the Set All to None or Set All to Single buttons.

    • If you want to apply a border to only the outer sides of a set of selected cells, click the Outline option *before* you choose your border style (the Outline option will be grayed out unless you select more than one cell).

NOTE   You can select from three different border styles for a table. Standard displays the table border as a line. Choose Embossed or Extruded to give the table a 3-D effect.

4. Click the Layout tab.

5. Change the decimal values for each of the options by placing the insertion point in each box and entering a new value. Set the values for the options as follows:

    • **Fit table width to window** indicates that any spacing or width changes made to the table will be automatically adjusted so that the table remains fully within the confines of the Workspace window.

    • **Left Margin** indicates the space between the leftmost edge of the table and the left margin.

    • **Space between rows** indicates how compressed or expanded information appears across the rows of the table (vertically).

    • **Space between columns** indicates how compressed or expanded information appears across the columns of the table (horizontally).

- **Cell width** indicates the width of the current column (the cell width cannot be changed if more than one cell is selected). Also, a column width cannot be changed from within a spanned table cell.

6. Click the Colors tab.

7. Place the insertion point in the cell to which you want to apply a color.

8. Click the Background Color drop-down list to display the color palette.

9. Choose a color. The color is applied automatically to the cell that you selected.

10. Move the insertion point to another cell and select a different (or same) color to apply to the cell. (If you want to change the color of all the cells at the same time, click the Apply to Entire Table button.)

11. If you decide later that you want to make the color of a cell transparent, move the insertion point to the cell and then click the Make Transparent button. Transparency will always let what is behind the table *bleed* through to the table. This is important if the Database Designer allows you to alter the color or background of the document. For example, if you paste a graphic to be used as the background of the form, the graphic will show through the table.

12. Close the Table Properties InfoBox.

13. Press Ctrl+S or Choose File ➤ Save to save the document.

TIP   If you want direct control over column width, deselect the Fit to Window option in the Layout Options folder of the Table Properties InfoBox.

Using the Ruler to Change the Width of Columns

The easiest way to resize columns in a table is with the ruler. The alternative is to use the Layout options tab of the Table Properties InfoBox for each column, but this method is more cumbersome and doesn't give you the "visual control" the ruler provides.

To change column widths via the ruler, do the following:

1. Display the ruler (if it is not already displayed) by choosing View ➤ Ruler or clicking the View Ruler SmartIcon.

2. Place the insertion point in the desired column. You will notice the ruler displays markers indicating the left and right edges of the column, as displayed in Figure 8.5.

3. Position the mouse pointer carefully on an edge marker, and drag the marker to the left or right to increase or decrease the width of the column.

4. Repeat steps 2–3 for as many columns as you want to change.

5. Press Ctrl+S to save the document.

FIGURE 8.5:

The ruler as it appears when the focus (the cursor) appears in a table

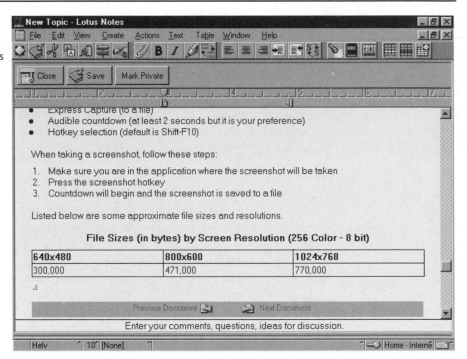

TIP

If you notice that the column edge markers are "snapping back" to a slightly different position than where you positioned them in the ruler, you need to deselect the Fit to Window option in the Layout Options tab of the Table Properties InfoBox.

Inserting and Deleting Table Rows and Columns

After creating your table, you may need to insert or delete certain rows or columns. This can be accomplished easily with Notes. To insert a new row or column, do the following:

1. Place the insertion point in the table.

2. Choose Table ➤ Insert Column to insert a new column to the left of the insertion point (or Insert Row to insert a new row above the insertion point).

TIP
A quick way to append rows to the table is to use the Tab key. Place the insertion point in the last cell of the table and press the Tab key. This will automatically append a new row.

Your new column or row will be inserted into the table. Another option available from the Table menu is the ability to append a column or a row. This option will always append a new column to the right of the table or append a new row to the bottom of the table.

To delete a column or row of the table, do the following:

1. Place the insertion point in the row or column to delete.

2. Choose Table ➤ Delete Column to delete the current column (or Delete Row to delete the current row).

TIP
To delete more than one column or one row, highlight the columns or rows to delete before using the Delete Column or Delete Row menu action.

WARNING
The Undo command is not available when deleting columns or rows from a table. You will get a warning message reminding you that the deletion action cannot be undone. Make sure that what you are deleting is correct, as once it is gone, it is gone for good.

So far, you have seen how to add and delete columns and rows of table data. But what if you need to create rows or columns containing varying numbers of cells?

There are instances when you do not want all the rows in the table to contain the same number of cells. Not a problem. Notes gives you the ability to *merge* cells (termed *spanned cells*) so that any number of cells can be contained in a table.

To merge cells, do the following:

1. Highlight the cells that you want to merge.

2. Choose Table ➤ Merge Cells to combine the selected cells into one cell.

WARNING   After merging cells within a table, you may find that deleting columns and rows is a bit more complicated. If you receive the error message "Cannot delete rows or columns within a spanned cell," you will need to *split* the merged cells in order to complete the deletion process. To do so, choose Split Cell from the Table menu option.

Creating Sections

A section is a formatting option that allows you to group related text, tables, and graphics in a rich text field (assuming that the elements are adjacent to or in very close proximity to one another) for the purpose of displaying and hiding the information as a single entity. Sections are said to be *collapsible* and *expandable*. A document will grow and contract proportionately as users expand and collapse sections while navigating through a document. Figure 8.6 displays three sections in rich text fields—one expanded (File Size Comparison) and two collapsed (Parameters and Steps to Follow).

The most efficient way to create a section is to first enter the text, tables, and graphics that you want to include in the section. Then perform the following steps:

1. Highlight all the items you want to include in the section.

NOTE   The highlight maneuver requires you to position the mouse I-beam either on the line just above the first item (working from top to bottom) or at the beginning of the line that contains the first item. Hold down the left mouse button and sweep the mouse down and/or across to highlight all the desired design items; then release the button.

FIGURE 8.6:

A document's expanded
and a collapsed sections

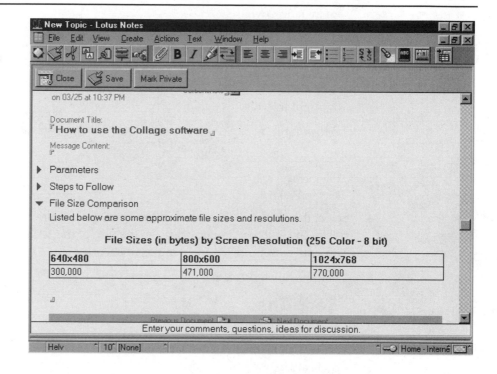

2. Choose Create ➤ Section. Notes immediately collapses all of the highlighted items into a section and displays a triangle controller (▶) in the collapsed position and a default section title. The section title will either correspond to the first line of text in the section or may simply be blank. Click the triangle or section title to expand the section and display the items. The triangle will now be in expanded position (▼).

3. Click the section title so that it is highlighted with a bold underline. Choose Section ➤ Section Properties to display the Section Properties InfoBox, as shown in Figure 8.7. If you click the section title or triangle, the Section option replaces the Text option in the menu bar at the top of the Workspace. If you click elsewhere in the field, the Text option reappears.

TIP

You can access the Section Properties InfoBox by right-clicking the section title and selecting the Section Properties option from the pop-up menu or by clicking the Properties SmartIcon.

FIGURE 8.7:

The Section Properties
InfoBox

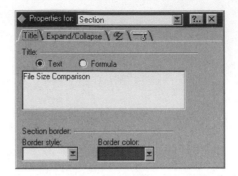

4. Select the Text radio button from the Title option folder and enter a section title in the text box (You can also set the title of the section using a formula. You will learn more about formulas in Chapter 18).

5. Click the Border style list box to display the six choices in the Section border area.

6. Choose a border if you want the section to display one.

7. Click the Border color palette.

8. Select a color.

9. Close the InfoBox, and press Ctrl+S to save the form.

TIP   You may create as many sections in a rich text field as you wish.

Setting Expand and Collapse Options for a Section

When creating sections, you stipulate whether the section should automatically appear as expanded or collapsed (or as the last user left it) in any of the four possible document modes—Preview, Read, Edit, Print. Follow these steps:

1. Click the section title and choose Section ➤ Section Properties to display the Section Properties InfoBox.

2. Click the Expand/Collapse tab. The Expand/Collapse options appear as in Figure 8.8, displaying four modes:

   • Previewed

- Opened for reading
- Opened for editing
- Printed

FIGURE 8.8:

The Expand/Collapse options of the Section Properties InfoBox

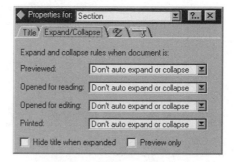

3. For each of the four modes, choose one of the expand and collapse rules:

   - **Don't Auto Expand or Collapse** indicates that the section should appear in the most recent previous state.

   - **Auto Expand Section** forces the section to expand.

   - **Auto Collapse Section** forces the section to collapse.

   Remember that these rules apply to the section relative to the document mode.

4. Click Hide Title When Expanded if you do not want to display the section title when the section is expanded.

TIP

If the Section Title is the same as the first line of text within the section, be sure to select this option. Otherwise, the readers of the document will see two copies of the same text when they expand the section.

---

5. Click Preview if you want the Section feature active only when a document is being previewed. In any of the other modes, the expand/collapse capability will not be available and the section title will not be displayed.

6. Close the InfoBox.

7. Press Ctrl+S to save the form.

TIP

If you select the Auto Collapse Section option for the Printed mode, keep in mind that the data in the section will *never* be printed.

NOTE

The section InfoBox also contains tabs for changing the Font information for the section title. For more information on the Font characteristics, refer back to Chapter 7.

Enhancing the Content of Your Documents

A document is a document is a document.... Not so!

Although many Notes applications do not give you the freedom to change the appearance of documents, you can still add information to documents in ways that enhance their content.

Cross-Referencing Documents with Links

Links provide direct access from a Notes document to one of four possible targets: another document, data within the current or another document, a view, or a database. In the case of document and view links, the linked-to targets don't have to be part of the same database. None of the four possible targets even has to be located on the same server, workstation, or network where the original document is located.

Links are useful when a document depends on information that resides elsewhere in the Notes environment, particularly when the target information is subject to change. Rather than hard-coding the information in your document (which only serves to make your document longer and more cumbersome to navigate) and then updating the document each time the information changes, you can create a link to the information source. If the source changes, no action is required on your part; your document will always reflect the latest state of the source.

TIP

Links make your documents flexible, dynamic, and more compact.

You can implement links when you want one document to refer to another document that's very large, such as a sales account profile. You can also use links when you want one document to refer to another infrequently used document, such as a *Wall Street Journal* article on a company that's featured in a sales account profile.

You must remember that links are hard-wired to a specific database defined by the database's Replica ID number (which is a 16-digit number). If someone deletes the database, you will need to either re-create the link or remove it from the document. Links to views and documents are also hard-wired. Each view or document is defined by a Universal ID (UNID), which is a 32-digit number. If someone deletes either the view or the document, you will need to either re-create the link or remove it from the document.

NOTE   Replica copies of databases can have different names and be stored in different subdirectory locations since Notes uses each database's Replica ID to resolve and find linked documents, views, and databases.

Anchor Links

With the Notes 4.6, you can create *anchor links*. Although this type of link is more common on Web pages, it can also be used in rich text fields within the Notes client. An anchor link is used to "jump" to a specific area of text within a rich text field either within the current document or in another document. The anchor link can only be used within the context of rich text fields.

This type of link can be useful in many different ways, especially for documents with rich text fields that contain large amounts of data. Instead of scrolling through page after page of data, you can set up a table of contents (actually, a table of anchor links) that contains anchor links to various sections of a document. When a user clicks on one of the anchor links in the table of contents, the document is automatically placed at that particular section of the rich text field.

Now that is fine and good if the user is already in that particular document, but what about if the user is in another document and you want to reference a particular section within the contents of the document? This is no problem. Anchor links can be viewed as extensions to document links. When you place an anchor link in the source document, not only will the user be taken directly to the destination document (like a document link), the destination document will scroll and display the text where the anchor link was originally placed.

To create an anchor within the current document, follow these steps:

1. Select or open the document in Edit mode.

2. Place the insertion point where you want the destination of the anchor link within the rich text field data.

3. Choose Edit ➤ Copy as Link ➤ Anchor Link, as shown in Figure 8.9.

4. Type a unique name for the anchor, as shown in Figure 8.10.

FIGURE 8.9:

Menu options for
creating a link

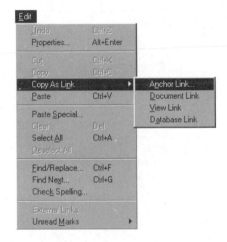

FIGURE 8.10:

Enter a name for the
anchor link.

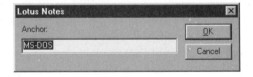

This places the destination anchor in the text as depicted by this icon: This also places a link in the Clipboard.

5. Place the insertion point where you want to locate the anchor link. The anchor link placement can be somewhere in the current document or in some other document (if you are going to place the link in another document, make sure that the document is opened in Edit mode).

6. Choose Edit ➤ Paste or press Ctrl+V. An anchor link icon appears, as shown in Figure 8.11.

FIGURE 8.11:

The anchor link allows you to jump to a specific area within either the current document or another document.

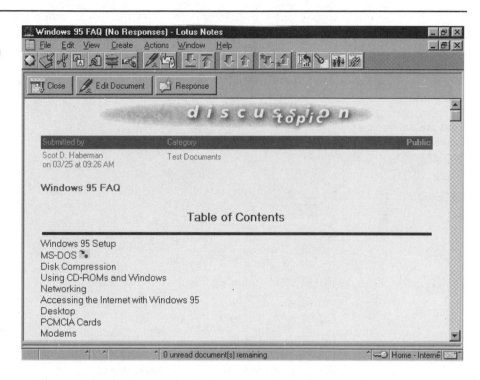

> **TIP**   You must be in a rich text field to create a link.

Now, instead of scrolling through pages of data to get to the section on MS-DOS, all that needs to be done is click on the anchor icon. What could be simpler? You can repeat this process over and over with no limitation on the number of links.

Document, View, and Database Links

The steps required in creating any type of link are quite similar. To create a link to another document, follow these steps:

1. Select or open the *target* document. You can also select the document in a view.

2. Choose Edit ➤ Copy as Link ➤ Document Link. This places the link on the Clipboard.

3. Open the *source* document in Edit mode.

4. Place the insertion point where you want to locate the link.

5. Choose Edit ➤ Paste or press Ctrl+V. A link icon appears, as shown in Figure 8.12.

FIGURE 8.12:

A link enables you to access one document from another. In this case, the link is to a Company Profile document of a competitor.

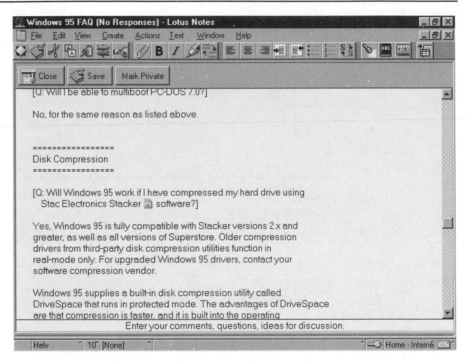

TIP

You follow similar steps to create a link to a view or folder or another database. Choose Edit ➤ Copy as Link ➤ View Link to create a link to a view or choose Edit ➤ Copy as Link ➤ Database Link to create a link to a database. Open the target document and then choose Edit ➤ Paste.

You use the mouse to click a link icon, which opens the related document, view, or database. The link icon will vary depending on whether the target is a document, view, or database.

TIP

Document links and HTML links require only single-click access in Notes Release 4.5 and higher, but double-click in all releases prior to 4.5.

TIP Where should you place a link in a document? You have three basic options: either on a line by itself (with some accompanying text that describes the link), directly within a paragraph where the meaning of the link is obvious, or as a link hotspot.

Notes allows you to modify some of the properties associated with links, for example, the default link description appears when a user opens a document (that contains a link) in Read mode, positions the mouse pointer on the link icon, and holds down the left mouse button.

To change the default description for a link, do the following:

1. Open the link document in Edit mode.

2. Highlight the link using either the mouse or the keyboard (be careful, if you click on the link, you will be taken to the destination of the link).

3. Choose Link ➤ Link Properties to display the Link Properties InfoBox, as shown in Figure 8.13.

FIGURE 8.13:

The Link Properties InfoBox

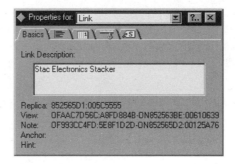

TIP You can access the Link Properties InfoBox by clicking the link icon with the right mouse button and selecting the Link Properties option from the pop-up menu.

4. Delete the current link description that appears in the text box of the Basics option folder and type a new description.

5. Close the Link Properties InfoBox.

6. Press Ctrl+S to save the document.

Link Hotspots

You probably noticed that link icons are not very intuitive for non-Notes users. It is also hard to decide exactly where to place a link icon respective to the data it represents. Link hotspots are an excellent solution to this problem.

Just as the name implies, this option can only be used for links (it does not matter if it is an anchor, document, view, or database link). The purpose of a link hotspot is to associate some object, such as text or a graphic, and the link. Instead of displaying a link icon within your document, you can have text or a picture representing the link.

To create a link hotspot, follow the previous instructions and create either an anchor, database, view, or database link on the Clipboard. Now highlight whatever you want to represent your link and choose Create ➤ Hotspot ➤ Link Hotspot. For more information on link hotspots or hotspot link properties, refer to Link Hotspots in Chapter 19.

URL Links

What is a URL? It stands for Universal Resource Locator, and it is used as the World Wide Web name for a document, file, or other resource. You may be more familiar with the syntax of a URL such as `http://www.lotus.com/` (if you are familiar with using a Web browser, you know that this URL would point your browser to the Lotus Development Corporation Web site). A URL Link is a hotspot that will launch a browser and display the Web site that corresponds to the Web address.

So how can this enhance my document? Anyone reading your document can quickly jump to a Web site, download a file (via FTP), or view a Usenet group with one simple click of the mouse button.

There are actually two types of URL Links in Notes. The first type of URL Link is inherent to Notes. In the User Preferences options, there is an option under the Advanced Options section that will automatically convert a URL into a URL hotspot. For example, if you type `http://www.lotus.com/` into rich text field in a document, Notes will automatically create a URL link out of the address as shown in Figure 8.14. No further intervention is required by you to make this work. The only caveat to this approach is if the Turn URL Links into Hotspots option is not selected, the URL Link will not be activated; hence, nothing will happen when the text is clicked.

FIGURE 8.14:

Notes automatically creates
a URL link from a text URL.

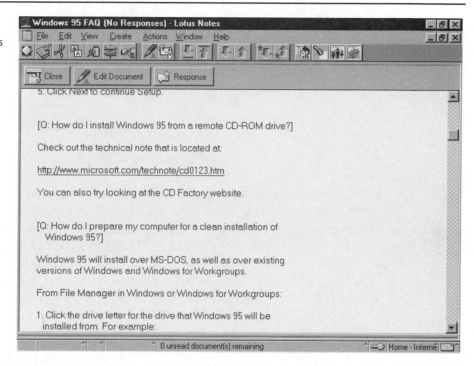

FIGURE 8.14:

Notes automatically creates
a URL link from a text URL.

This brings up the second type of URL link. This approach will work regardless of the settings in the User Preferences dialog box. This type of URL link will allow you to select any text and turn it into a URL link. To create this type of URL link, do the following:

1. Open the document in Edit mode.

2. Highlight whatever you want to act as the link (it must be contained within a rich text field).

3. Choose Create ➤ Hotspot ➤ URL Link.

4. Type in the URL in the URL Link Object Properties InfoBox (you can also set whatever font attributes within this InfoBox as well), as shown in Figure 8.15.

5. Close the InfoBox.

That is all there is to it. Now open the document in Read mode and click on the text you just created as a URL Link. Your browser should activate and take you to the URL address.

FIGURE 8.15:

The URL Link Properties
InfoBox

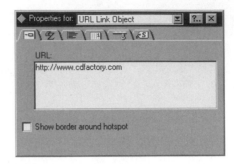

One advantage to creating a URL Link (as opposed to having Notes do it for you) is you can create more meaningful text for the link. For example, suppose you want to have a link to My Great Web Site that has a URL address of `http://www.some` `.site/~internal/5570039/toc/drilldown/mysite.htm`. If you were to display this in the context of your document wherever you want to place link would be quite ugly. Another option would be to type in "My Great Web Site" and create a URL link on that text. Now when someone is reading your document, the text will flow better and allow the user quick access to the Web site, as shown in Figure 8.16.

FIGURE 8.16:

A URL Link placed on a
text string

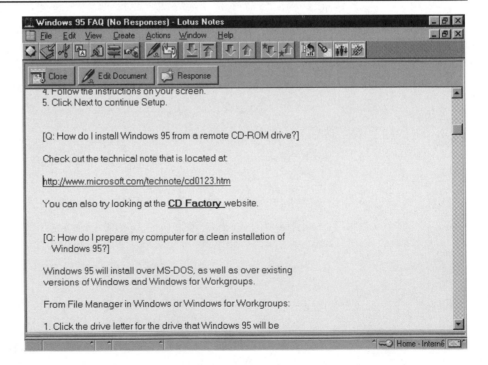

TIP
URL links are not just limited to Web site URLs. You can also include a URL that would download a file using FTP or display various newsgroups.

Horizontal Rules

Although a horizontal rule is usually associated with Web pages, it also makes a nice addition for enhancing the look of any document. A horizontal rule can be used as a graphical separator for data contained within a rich text field, as shown in Figure 8.17.

FIGURE 8.17:

Separating data using
horizontal rules

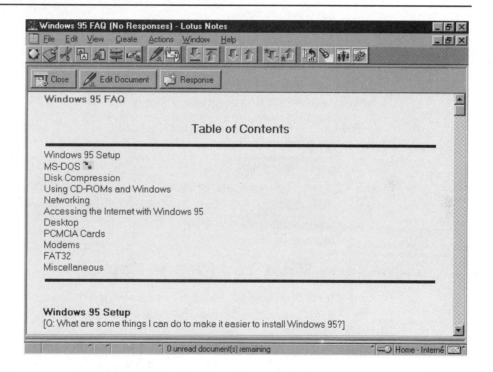

After creating the horizontal rule, you may want to change some of the options so that it blends in with your document. To change the options for the horizontal rule, just do the following:

1. Open the document in Edit mode.

2. Click on the horizontal rule to select it.

3. Choose Horizontal Rule ➤ Horizontal Rule Properties to display the Horizontal Rule Properties InfoBox, as shown in Figure 8.18.

FIGURE 8.18:

The Horizontal Rule Properties InfoBox

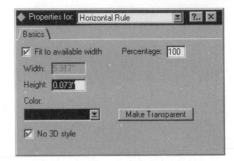

The default width for the horizontal rule is the entire span of the window. You also have the option to have the rule span a percentage of the document window using the Percentage option. If you want to specify the actual width, deselect the Fit to Available Width option and enter the width.

You can also change the height of the horizontal rule. The height can be anywhere from .07 to 3 inches.

The last options allow you to change the color and decide whether you want the 3-D effect. Just select the color you desire from the color palette (or select that the rule should be transparent). The 3-D effect toggles between an ordinary flat line and an embossed one.

Explaining What You Mean—Pop-ups

Have you ever encountered a word or phrase in a document that you didn't know the meaning of? Wouldn't it be nice if the document supplied a definition for that word or phrase on the fly? *Pop-ups* enable you to define or describe words and phrases in your document that might be unfamiliar to users. Pop-ups are particularly useful in applications that use industry-specific (for example, insurance, real estate) or discipline-specific (for example, finance, medicine, Internet) terminology. A pop-up typically appears as text with a border around it. When a user clicks the text, a box that contains the definition or description of the text pops up (see Figure 8.19).

NOTE   You must be in a rich text field to create a pop-up.

FIGURE 8.19:

A pop-up that explains the meaning of the term *Express Capture*

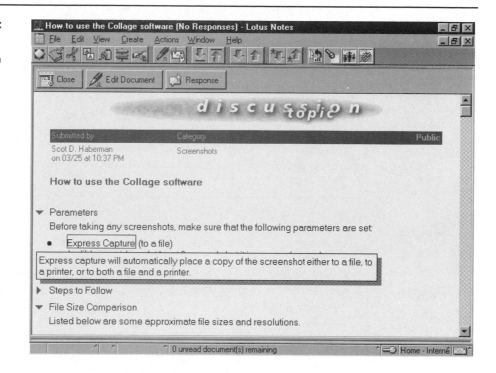

To create a pop-up in your document, do the following:

1. Open your document in Edit mode.

2. Highlight the text that you wish to define or describe.

3. Choose Create ➤ Hotspot ➤ Text Pop-up. The Pop-up Properties InfoBox is automatically displayed, as shown in Figure 8.20.

FIGURE 8.20:

The Hotspot Pop-up Properties InfoBox

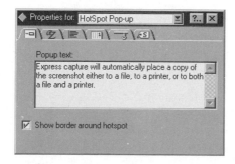

4. Enter the definition or description in the text box.

5. Deselect Show Border Around Hotspot if you do not want a green border to appear around the highlighted text.

TIP

Without a border, users might not know that a pop-up exists, so it is a good idea to leave the border intact. Although green might not be your favorite color, it's a matter of function over form. (Sorry, you can't change the color of the border.) One drawback is that some development shops have strict standards for labels. One alternative is to place a small graphic that contains a ? in it and place the text pop-up on the graphic. It seems to be more intuitive.

TIP

You can create a formula pop-up by choosing Create ➤ Hotspot ➤ Formula Pop-up. A formula pop-up differs from a text pop-up in that the pop-up description is derived through a Notes formula, rather than being a simple text string. Creating formula pop-ups requires some knowledge of the Notes formula language, which is covered in Chapter 18.

If you want to modify a pop-up, do the following:

1. Click any of the text for which the pop-up has been defined.

2. Choose Hotspot ➤ Hotspot Properties to display the Pop-up Properties InfoBox.

3. Click any of the tabs to change the associated options.

Automating Documents with Buttons and Action Hotspots

Notes supports two types of editor objects: buttons, which look like graphical buttons, and Action hotspots, which can be defined by highlighting anything in the editor (text or graphic) and then choosing Create ➤ Hotspot ➤ Action Hotspot. Both of these elements can execute Actions or associated code when a user clicks on them.

Action hotspots are a new feature in Notes Release 4. Earlier versions of Notes can't interpret Action hotspots. If you are using Release 3.x or earlier and try to open a document or form that includes an Action hotspot created in Release 4, Notes will warn you that Action hotspots can't be displayed.

Implementing buttons or Action hotspots clearly requires an understanding of Notes programming, which is discussed in Chapter 18 and in Part V. We are introducing Actions here, however, since you can use them to enhance your documents.

To create a button, follow these steps:

1. Open the document where you want the button to appear.

2. Place the insertion point in the desired location on the document.

3. Choose Create ➤ Hotspot ➤ Button. The Button Properties InfoBox appears, as shown in Figure 8.21.

FIGURE 8.21:

The Button Properties InfoBox and Design pane where the button formula is defined

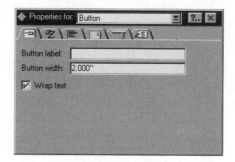

4. Enter the text you want to display on the button in the Button Label field.

5. Change the Button width or use the default width.

6. Deselect the Wrap Text option if you don't want text to wrap around the button.

7. Click the Close button.

8. Enter a formula in the Formula box. The formula defines the action that's performed when you activate the button; it may be a series of Simple actions, a formula, or a LotusScript program.

What's Next?

In the next chapter we discuss printing documents and views in Notes for the times when you need a hard copy of data in a particular database. You'll also discover that reading a printed document is much easier than reading one on a monitor.

CHAPTER

NINE

Printing Views and Documents

- Selecting what you want to print

- Printing views

- Choosing settings for your printer

- Choosing page layout options

- Choosing the paper source

- Inserting page breaks

- Creating headers and footers

Suppose you want to print a view's listing of documents in a database because a piece of paper is easier to refer to than onscreen text. Sometimes you might need hard copies of particular documents because a situation calls for you to refer to the information when you are away from your computer. And sometimes you might just get tired of reading information on your computer's screen.

Whatever your reason, Notes lets you print an open or selected view, part of a view, an open document, or documents you select in a view.

Printing Documents

Printing a document means either printing a selected document from a view or printing the entire contents of an open document. To print a document from a view, follow these steps:

1. Open a view.

2. Highlight the document and then press the spacebar, or position the mouse pointer in the markers column directly to the left of the document and click there to select it. A check mark appears in the markers column to the left of the document title. You can select one or more documents at a time.

TIP   If you only want to print a single document, you do not need to mark it. Just highlight the document and then proceed with printing it.

---

3. Choose File ➤ Print or press Ctrl+P. The File Print dialog box appears, as shown in Figure 9.1.

4. Enter the number of copies you want to print or accept the default number, which is one.

5. Select a Page Range option:

   • **All:** Prints all the pages in the document (the default)

   • **From/To:** Prints the range of pages you specify in the text boxes

FIGURE 9.1:

The File Print dialog box allows you to print a selected document directly from a view.

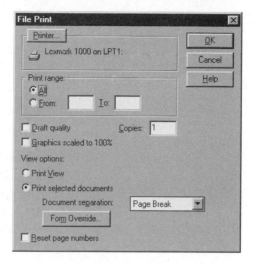

TIP

Leaving the To: box empty will print all remaining pages in the document, starting with the From: page.

---

6. Select the Print Selected Documents option (if it isn't selected).

TIP

Draft quality prints faster on most printers than the regular option, but with reduced print quality.

---

7. Click the Printer button if you need to specify additional printer options, such as the printer's name, paper source, paper size, or paper orientation. The Print Setup dialog box appears.

   • Select a different printer, if necessary.

   • Click the Setup button to make additional changes. The Setup dialog box appears.

   • Choose the options you want to change.

   • Click OK to accept the changes and return to the File Print dialog box.

8. Click OK.

The following options also apply when you print a selected document from a view:

Page Break	Each document starts on a new page.
Extra Line	An extra blank line is inserted between documents, and page numbering is continuous.
No Separation	One document follows another without a separator, and page numbering is continuous.
Form Override	Displays the Print Form Override dialog box, where you can print a document using a form other than the one used to compose the document. This advanced option is used when the database designer has created a form or a set of forms for printing reports, as opposed to reading or editing documents.
Reset Page Numbers	Numbers the first page of each document as page 1 or as specified with Page Setup, and prints the headers and footers on every page. Available only when you select Page Break as the document separator.

You can print an open document in the same manner as you print from a view: display a view, select a document, and press ↵ to open it. With the contents of a document displayed, choose File ➤ Print. As you can see, the File Print dialog box that appears looks different from the File Print dialog box that appears when you want to print a document from a view. (Actually, what you see is just a subset of the options you see when printing a document from a view.) However, the printing procedures are the same as the procedures outlined for printing a document from a view.

Printing Full and Partial Views

Printing a view means either printing all the document titles that you see onscreen when you display a view (a full view) or printing selected document titles in the view (a partial view). To print a full view, follow these steps:

1. Display a view.

2. Choose File ➤ Print. The File Print dialog box appears.

3. Select any, all, or none of the following options: Copies, Page Range, Draft Quality, and Setup. These are the same options for printing an open document described previously.

4. Select Print View. This option prints the entire list of documents in the view (not their contents, just the list as it appears in the view).

5. Click OK.

To print the names of some, but not all, of the documents in the view, follow these steps:

1. Open a view.

2. Highlight a document title and then press the spacebar or position the mouse pointer in the markers column directly to the left of the document and click. A check mark appears in the markers column to the left of the document name. You can mark as many document titles as you want.

3. Choose File ➤ Print. The File Print dialog box appears.

4. Select the Print View option.

5. Click on OK.

Only the names of the documents you selected will appear in the printout.

Choosing Printer Settings

As mentioned earlier, you can specify printer settings, such as how many copies to print, which paper source to use, paper size, and print orientation:

1. Choose File ➤ Print. The File Print dialog box appears.

2. Click the Printer button. The Print Setup dialog box displays a list of the printers available in the overall configuration of your workstation operating system, as shown in Figure 9.2.

FIGURE 9.2:

The Print Setup dialog box

3. Select the printer you want to use. You can use the Setup dialog box to check or change the options for your printer, as shown in Figure 9.3.

4. Click OK to continue or click Cancel if you change your mind.

NOTE   The printers and setup options available to you will vary depending on your operating system (Windows 3.x, Windows 95, and so on).

FIGURE 9.3:

The Setup dialog box allows you to change printer options such as page orientation and paper size.

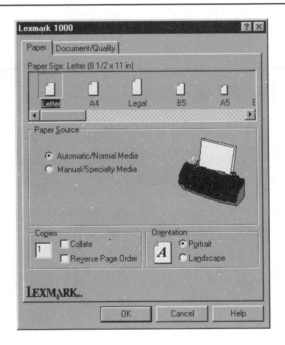

Choosing Page Setup Options

You can specify page layouts for documents and views for the current database. Options include headers and footers, page numbering, margin settings, page cropping, and special page source specifications. To choose page setup options, follow these steps:

1. Choose File ➤ Page Setup. The Page Setup dialog box appears, as shown in Figure 9.4. Options set in this dialog box remain in effect until you change them.

FIGURE 9.4:

The Page Setup dialog box

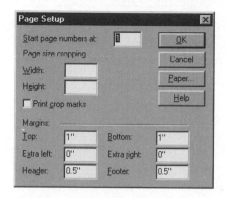

2. Select the page setup options you want.

Start Page
Lets you use a page number other than 1 for the first page. Type the number you want to start with into the text box. Pages are numbered sequentially, starting with the number you specify.

Page Size Cropping
Lets you reduce the size of the printing area of the paper. Type the width and height of the area you want into the text boxes. This area is measured from the upper-left corner. Tell Notes the size of the paper in your printer in the Printer Settings dialog box. See the earlier section "Choosing Printer Settings."

Margins
The margins are the Top, Bottom, Extra Left, and Extra Right edges of the page (which is the printing area, not the paper size). You can also specify where to place the headers and footers. If you specify a page size, Notes calculates the printing area based on the page size and your margin settings.

Print Crop Marks
Prints page boundary indicators that show the edges of the image in the lower-right corner of each page. Crop marks are useful when you are sending documents to your organization's print service.

3. Click OK when you're satisfied with your settings or click Cancel if you change your mind.

NOTE   The printer settings are permanent in Notes until you reset them to something else. Notes does not store the printer settings with a document or a view.

NOTE   You can fine-tune the defined print area by changing the page size settings and adjusting the margins as well as the cropping area. Experiment to find the appropriate settings for your needs.

Selecting the Paper Source

Many printers have more than one paper source built into them. For instance, a printer might have two paper trays, one with standard letter-size paper and the other with high-quality letterhead or legal-size paper. You can specify the paper source you want to use for your document by doing the following:

1. Choose File ➤ Page Setup. The Page Setup dialog box appears.

2. Click the Paper button. The Page Setup–Paper Source dialog box appears, as shown in Figure 9.5.

FIGURE 9.5:

The Page Setup–Paper Source dialog box

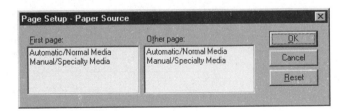

NOTE   Depending on the type of printer you use, the choices of paper source that appear in the Page Setup–Paper Source dialog box will vary.

3. Select one of the options for First Page and for Other Page. Here are the available paper sources for an Epson ActionLaser 1500:

Envelope	Uses envelopes loaded in the printer's standard paper bin.
Lower tray	Uses paper loaded in the printer's optional lower tray.
Envelope manual feed	Pulls an envelope from the printer's standard paper bin. If no envelope is loaded, displays a message and waits for you to insert an envelope in the printer's standard paper bin.
Manual feed	Pulls paper from the printer's standard paper bin. If no paper is loaded, displays a message and waits for you to insert pages in the printer's standard paper bin.
Upper tray	Uses paper loaded in the printer's standard paper bin.

4. Click OK to accept the settings, click Cancel if you change your mind, or select Reset to restore the original settings.

Adding Page Breaks

Your printed document usually looks somewhat different from what you see onscreen. To see where lines will wrap and pages will break in the printed version, you can switch to Preview mode. If you see things you don't like in the preview, you can easily revise the document before you print it.

TIP To enter Preview mode, open the document and choose View ➤ Show ➤ Page Breaks. You should be able to see where the lines wrap, and you can also see the page breaks, which are indicated by a solid line across the screen. To exit Preview mode, choose View ➤ Show ➤ Page Breaks again, or close the document.

To force text onto the next page, try these pagination options found in the Paragraph tab of the Text ➤ Text Properties dialog box: Page Break before Paragraph, Keep Paragraph on One Page, and Keep Paragraph with Next Paragraph. These options are discussed in detail in Chapter 7.

Using Headers and Footers

Perhaps you want a title to appear at the top of every page of a document, and maybe you would like page numbers to appear at the bottom of every page. Notes lets you create custom headers and footers for these purposes.

Headers and *footers* allow you to place text at the top and bottom of each page of a *printed* document; headers and footers do not appear onscreen when you are reading or editing a document. Headers appear inside the top margin area of a document page, and footers inside the bottom margin area. You may specify a global header and footer for all documents that you print in a database, you may specify a unique header and footer for an individual document, or you may combine global and unique headers and footers (whereby a unique header and footer for a document will override the global header and footer for the database).

To create a global header and footer for a database, select the database from the Workspace, choose File ➤ Database ➤ Properties, and click the Printer tab to display the Header and Footer Options folder, as shown in Figure 9.6.

FIGURE 9.6:

The Database InfoBox, with the header and footer options

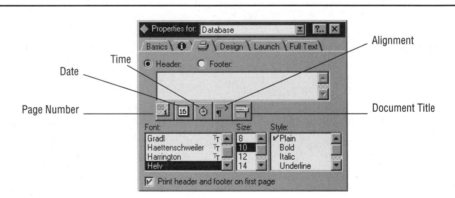

You can set the header and footer options by doing the following:

1. Select the Header or Footer radio button, depending on which one you are specifying. The process for creating headers and footers is identical, so these steps apply to both.

2. Enter text in the scrollable text box below the Header and Footer radio buttons. You may also enter any of the "substitution symbols" defined for

headers and footers or click the corresponding buttons found below the scrollable text box:

- **&P**   Page number
- **&D**   Today's date
- **&T**   Current time
- **|**   Offset text that follows (including substitution symbols) by one-third of a page
- **&W**   Document title

3. Select the font, point size, and style for the header or footer. The format options you choose will apply to the whole header or footer; you cannot format text selectively within a header or footer.

4. Check Print Header and Footer on First Page if you want the header and footer you've created to appear on the first page of the document.

5. Close the Database Properties InfoBox to save the header and footer information.

NOTE   You have to plan your headers and footers so that you don't exceed the space available in the top and bottom margins, either horizontally or vertically. Notes does support multiline headers and footers.

Setting a unique header and footer for a specific document is the same as setting the global header and footer for a database. With the document highlighted in a view or opened for reading or editing, choose File ➤ Document Properties, click the Printer tab, and follow the previous steps.

TIP   If you want to set a unique header and footer for several documents in a view, highlight one of the documents, choose File ➤ Document Properties, click the Printer tab, and enter the header and footer information. Without closing the Document Properties dialog box, select the next document by clicking it in the view. The header and footer options for that document will appear in the dialog box.

WARNING   A third option for setting headers and footers exists at the form level. If both the database and the document print options have the header and footer sections blank, the form may have specified a header and footer that appears automatically. Talk to your Notes administrator if this problem exists.

WARNING   You cannot mix and match the database and document header and footer information. If a document header or footer has any information typed in, both the database header and footer will print on the document. Leaving either the header of footer blank will not default to the contents of the database header or footer. It is a choice of either printing the document header/footer or the database header/footer.

What's Next?

The next chapter explains how to import data from other applications into Notes and how to export data from Notes to other applications. By importing data into Notes, you can increase a database's value because you can integrate information from a variety of outside sources. Furthermore, you won't need to re-create data by manually entering it again. Conversely, exporting data from Notes can aid you in making presentations and writing reports that rely on the information from a database.

Importing and Exporting Data

■ Using the cut, copy, and paste commands

■ Adding files to documents

■ Importing various file formats into documents and views

■ Exporting documents and views to various file formats

■ Supporting import and export formats

Notes supports a wide variety of file formats for importing and exporting data to and from other applications. Importing data into Notes enables you to enhance a database with information from a variety of outside sources without having to enter it manually. Conversely, exporting data from Notes can aid you in making presentations and writing reports that rely on the information from a database.

Table 10.1 lists several ways you can add information to Notes documents from other applications.

TABLE 10.1: Methods for Adding Information to Notes Documents

Method	Goal	Use When	Useful When
Copying part or all of a file	To add data quickly	The source application is available and supports the Clipboard	The data you're copying will not be changing
Attaching a file	To distribute files electronically	Users will work with the file in the source application rather than in Notes	The file is compressed or is a system or executable file
Importing a file	To add large amounts of data in its original format	You want to work with the file in Notes rather than the source application	You want to display data such as tables, styled text, and pictures in their original form and when the data you're importing will not be changing
Linking a file	To add data that updates when the original file changes	The source application is available and supports DDE or OLE linking	You want to display the latest data from the source application in Notes
Embedding part or all of a file	To add data not necessarily associated with a file	The source application is available and supports OLE embedding	You want to use the source application to enter and edit data in Notes
Subscribing to part or all of a file	To add data from Macintosh applications that update when the original file changes	You're using Macintosh System 7.x and the source application is available and supports publishing	You want to display the latest data from the source application in Notes

NOTE   If you want to link, embed, or subscribe to data, but the source application does not support DDE, OLE, or the Macintosh Subscribe command, you can copy, attach, or import data instead. (Chapter 29 discusses using OLE.)

Using Cut, Copy, and Paste Commands

Probably the easiest way to add information to documents is by using the cut-and-paste or copy-and-paste commands, which are standard Windows application features. When you use these features, the data you copy or cut goes to a temporary storage area called the Clipboard. With the Clipboard, you can copy or cut text, pictures, or other data from a Notes document, and paste the data elsewhere in the same document or into another document. You can also copy, cut, and paste selections between Notes and other Windows, OS/2, Macintosh, and UNIX applications that support the Clipboard.

The data that you copy or cut to the Clipboard remains there until you do one of the following:

- Copy or cut new data, which replaces Clipboard data

- Exit Windows or OS/2, or shut down your Macintosh, which removes Clipboard data

To display the contents of the Clipboard, do one of the following:

- If you are using Windows, double-click the Clipboard Viewer icon in the Windows Main program group.

- If you are using Windows 95, choose Start ➤ Programs ➤ Accessories ➤ Clipboard Viewer.

After you open the Clipboard Viewer, you can clear its contents by choosing Edit ➤ Delete.

To copy (or cut) data from another application and paste it into a Notes document, follow these steps:

1. Select the data you want and copy it to the Clipboard.

2. Press Edit ➤ Copy or Ctrl+C. (To cut data, press Edit ➤ Cut or Ctrl+X.)

3. Open the target Notes document. (The Notes document must be in Edit mode.)

4. Click where you want the copied data to appear. If you want to replace existing data with the copied data, highlight the existing data.

5. Choose Edit ➤ Paste or Ctrl +V.

NOTE   Make sure you are in a rich text field when you paste formatted text or graphics into Notes.

TIP   If Edit ➤ Paste produces unexpected results, try using Undo and then Edit ➤ Paste Special to paste the data in a different data format.

TIP   Do not use the Cut/Paste options on graphics when possible. Instead, use File ➤ Import, which will produce better color fidelity, as shown in Figure 10.1.

FIGURE 10.1:

Using Cut/Paste vs. File Import on graphics

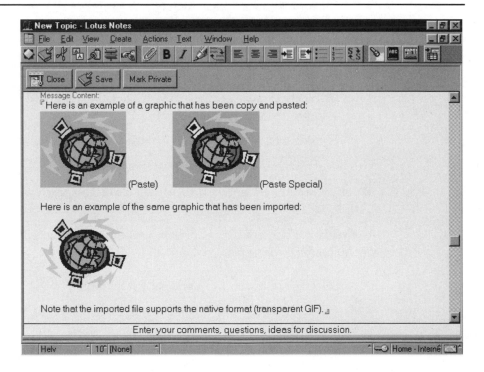

Adding Attachments to Documents

Another way to add information to documents is by using attachments. You can attach virtually any type of file, including binary files, compressed files, executable files, even an entire Notes database file. When you attach a file to a document, you are actually attaching a copy of the file; the original file is not affected.

When you attach a file (and have the file's application installed), Notes displays an icon indicating the file type and name. If you don't have the file's application installed (or if you don't have the application installed properly), Notes displays a generic icon.

You can also view and print attached files directly in Notes. In a view, Notes displays a paper clip to the left of documents that contain file attachments (if the developer sets it up this way).

You can detach and save attached files, and if the application that created the attached file is installed, you can launch the application directly from Notes and display the file.

TIP   You can find out the name of an attached file, the size of the file, and the date and time of the file's last modification. To get information about an attached file, double-click the attachment.

WARNING   Attached files can only be placed within a rich text field.

Attaching a File to a Document

To attach a copy of a file to a Notes document, the document must be in Edit mode. Then follow these steps:

1. Click where you want the file attachment to appear.

2. Choose File ➤ Attach.

3. Do one of the following:

    •   Select the file's drive and directory and then select the file.

    •   Enter the path and name of the file in the Filename box.

4. Deselect Compress to prevent Notes from compressing the file.

5. Click Create. The attachment appears, as shown in Figure 10.2.

FIGURE 10.2:

This attachment is a Word for Windows document.

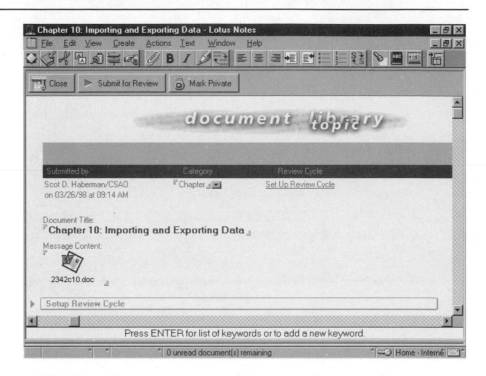

Here are some other ways to attach a file to a Notes document:

- Use the File Attach SmartIcon.

- In Windows, use File Manager.

- In Windows 95, use Windows Explorer. Open the document in Edit mode, drag the file from File Manager or Explorer, and drop it in the document.

Launching an Attached File

If you have the attached file's application installed, you can start the application directly from Notes and read the file.

1. Double-click the file attachment.

2. Click Launch.

WARNING   If you edit and save a launched attachment, Notes does not save the changes you make to the attachment. Instead it saves the changes in a temporary file created in the Temp directory. After you exit the launched application and Notes, Notes deletes the temporary file. If you want to save changes to an attached file, you will first need to detach the file, edit the detached file outside of Notes, save the file, and re-attach the file to the document.

Viewing an Attached File

Notes also provides an attachment viewer, which enables you to see the information in the attachment in Notes. If you are using Windows, you can view an attached file directly in Notes, even if you don't have the application with which the file was created.

To view the data in an attachment, follow these steps:

1. Double-click the file attachment. The Attachment Properties InfoBox appears, as shown in Figure 10.3.

2. Click View.

FIGURE 10.3:

The Attachment Properties InfoBox enables you to view the contents of an attached file even if you don't have the application with which the file was created.

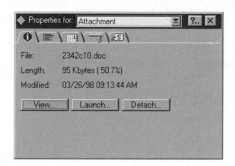

TIP   To close the file when you are through viewing it, press Esc.

Supported Viewers for Notes 4.6

New viewers are added with each release of Notes. Table 10.2 lists the available viewers by platform for Notes 4.6.

TABLE 10.2: Notes 4.6-Supported Viewers by Platform

File Type	Windows*	HP-UX	AIX	Solaris Sparc**
Ami Pro (.SAM)	✓	✓	✓	✓
AmiDraw (.SDW)	✓	✓	✓	✓
MS Word for Windows 6.0 (.DOC)	✓	✓	✓	✓
MS Word for Windows 95 (.DOC)	✓	✓	✓	✓
WordPerfect 5.x	✓	✓	✓	✓
WordPerfect 6.x	✓	✓	✓	✓
Lotus 1-2-3 (.WK3, WK4)	✓	✓	✓	✓
Lotus Freelance (.PRE) [2]	✓	✓	✓	✓
MS Access (.MDB)	✓	✓	✓	✓
MS PowerPoint 4.x, 7.0 (.PPT)	✓	✓	✓	✓
MS Excel (.XLS)	✓	✓	✓	✓
MS Word for Macintosh 4.0,5.0	✓	✓	✓	✓
WordPerfect for Macintosh 2.0, 3.0	✓			
Lotus 1-2-3 for Macintosh	✓	✓	✓	✓
Lotus PIC	✓	✓	✓	✓
PICT and PICT2 Graphics	✓	✓	✓	✓
Windows Metafile Graphics (.WMF)	✓	✓	✓	✓
WordPerfect Graphics (.WPG2)	✓	✓	✓	✓
Lotus 1-2-3 for OS/2 (.WG2)	✓	✓	✓	✓
Bitmap (.BMP)	✓	✓	✓	✓
Computer Graphics Metafile (.CGM)	✓	✓	✓	✓
Executable file (.EXE)	✓			

Continued on next page

TABLE 10.2 CONTINUED: Notes 4.6–Supported Viewers by Platform

File Type	Windows*	HP-UX	AIX	Solaris Sparc**
CompuServe (.GIF)	✓	✓	✓	✓
Macintosh (.PIC)	✓	✓	✓	✓
Rich Text Format (.RTF)	✓	✓	✓	✓
Text file (.TXT)	✓	✓	✓	✓
Zip file (.ZIP)	✓			
JPEG file (.JPEG, .JPG)	✓	✓	✓	✓
TIFF file (.TIF)	✓	✓[1]	✓[1]	✓[1]
Freelance for OS/2 (.PRS) [2]	✓	✓		
Microsoft Office 97	✓			
HTML (.HTM*)	✓			
Lotus SmartSuite 97	✓			
Word Pro 96	✓			
Raster Graphics (PCX)	✓			
Portable Document Format (.PDF)	✓			
CCITT Group 3 Fax	✓			

*   Windows NT for Digital Alpha does not include support for Viewers at this time.

** Solaris Intel Edition does not include support for Viewers at this time.

1   If you attempt to view .TIF files on UNIX platforms, you may experience the following problems: If you are running AIX, you may receive an error message such as: "The chunker could not be initialized." On the Solaris SPARC system, Notes may hang.

2   Freelance views are shown by page name, not page number. Because of this, pages look out of sequence; actually, it is the arrangement of the slides in the original presentation.

If you attempt to view any of the file types that are listed as unsupported in the table, Notes may terminate abruptly.

Other Viewer Notes

- If a user views a file and the format is not supported, but the associated (and Windows registered) application is installed on the PC, Notes will launch the file in the application.

- You cannot print viewers from Notes for the UNIX platform.

- If you view a spreadsheet file, you must resize the height of the window in order to display the button that enables you to view additional pages of the spreadsheet. For example, a spreadsheet document may contain graphics. This button displays a pop-up menu from which you can select other pages in the document.

- There is no viewer for WordPerfect 8. If a user views this file type, a "viewer is not available" message appears, and the file does not appear in the viewer.

- Limitation of the image viewers: Images may be represented as empty boxes in text-type files. The viewers do not support the embedded image format.

- OLE embedded images cannot be launched from the viewer.

- Occasionally, images are too large and may not appear in the viewer window. Select Size and choose Fit to Window or Show Full Screen to display the images.

- Limitation of the spreadsheet viewers: The spreadsheet viewers show only cells that actually contain text and truncate the rest.

- Limitation to the PICT viewer: Users cannot select anything with the mouse in the PICT viewer. Therefore, text cannot be copied or partially printed.

- Limitation of the image viewer: The viewer does not show any PowerPoint autolayout components (tables, organization charts, charts, images).

- Limitation of the word processing viewers: The viewers do not display or print headers, footers, or bullets at this time.

- Limitation of the viewers: The viewers do not support colored text at this time.

- Limitation of the viewers: To print a multipaged document, you must choose each page and print it. The viewers do not print all pages at this time.

Printing an Attached File

If you are using Windows, you can print file attachments directly from Notes.

1. Click the attachment.

2. Choose Attachment ➤ View. (If you want to print only part of the file, highlight the part you want to print.)

3. Choose File ➤ Print. (To print only the highlighted part of the file, click Selection under Print Range.)

4. Choose any (or none) of the following options:

    - To print faster (with reduced print quality), select a lower setting in the Print Quality box.

    - To print more than one copy, enter a number of copies.

    - To sort multiple copies, select Collate Copies.

5. Click OK.

TIP   To specify a different printer, click Setup, select a printer under Specified Printer, and click OK.

Detaching an Attached File

You can save an attached file to disk. If a document has more than one attached file, you can save some or all of the files to disk at once.

1. Do one of the following:

    - To detach one file, double-click the attachment and click Detach.

    - To detach more than one file, select the attachments and choose Attachments ➤ Detach All.

2. Specify the drive and directory in which you want to store the files.

3. Click Detach (or Save on the Macintosh).

NOTE   The option of "detaching" a file from a Notes document is a bit of a misnomer. When a file is detached, the file is not actually removed from the Notes document but a copy of the file is saved to your PC.

Importing Data

Importing means converting non-Notes data into a form that a Notes document or view can use. Importing and exporting map one document or view format onto another, so before you start importing or exporting on a large scale, you may want to read Chapters 17, 18, and 19 on designing Notes forms and views.

You can import word processing, graphics, spreadsheets, and ASCII text files into Notes documents. Similarly, you can import spreadsheets and ASCII text files into Notes views. You cannot import executable files—any file with the .EXE extension—but you can attach .EXE files to Notes documents. For a complete listing of all the file formats that can be imported into Notes, refer to the "Supported Import/Export File Formats" section at the end of this chapter.

In general, to import data into a Notes database, you follow these steps:

1. Open the view or document into which you are importing.

2. Choose File ➤ Import. The Import dialog box appears, as shown in Figure 10.4.

FIGURE 10.4:

The Import dialog box enables you to specify settings for importing many different file formats into Notes.

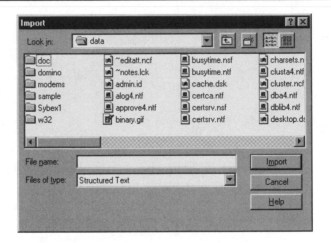

3. Select a file type in the Files of Type drop-down list. For example, you could select a Lotus 1-2-3 worksheet. The items in the list depend on whether you are importing into a view or into a document. If you are importing into a document, the default file type is Structured Text. If you are importing into a view, the default is ASCII Text.

NOTE

Be sure to change the default to match the file you are importing. In particular, be sure *not* to select ASCII Text for non-ASCII files. When you select a file type, Notes displays only those file names that end with the extension corresponding to that file type. For example, when you choose a Lotus 1-2-3 worksheet, Notes displays only files with spreadsheet extensions.

---

4. Select a folder in the Look In field and then open the folder by clicking it.

5. Do one of the following:

    - Select a file from the File Name list box, which displays all files of the file type you selected that are stored in the directory you selected. When you select a file, Notes displays its last modification date and time, as well as its size, at the bottom of the dialog box.

    - To select several files in a row, select a file at one end of the group; then press Shift and select the file at the other end. Both anchor files and all files between them will be selected.

    - To select several files not in a row, select a file and then hold the Ctrl key down while you select additional files. If you know the exact name and location of the file you want, you can skip the steps above and just type the file and path into the File Name text box—for example, type **c:\123w\sample\sales.wk3**.

6. Click on Import to perform the import.

Using Rich Text as an Intermediate File Format

When you import data into Notes from other applications, the data will likely include formatting attributes such as boldface, italics, and different fonts. Notes allows you to retain many formatting attributes because it uses Microsoft Rich Text Format (RTF) as an intermediate file format for importing and exporting files. As we've discussed previously, a Notes document *is* a rich text field that can contain formatted data, graphics, and objects, as well as other rich text fields. This feature enables a Notes database to import (and export) data in rich text format. (See Chapter 14 for more about rich text fields.)

For example, when you import a Lotus Ami Pro file, Notes calls the MasterSoft libraries to translate the file to an RTF file and then imports this RTF file into Notes. Similarly, when you export from Notes to Lotus Ami Pro format, Notes outputs an RTF file and then converts it to the Ami Pro file format.

For importing and exporting, Notes uses the same version of the RTF standard as Microsoft Word for Windows uses. RTF supports tables, fields, annotations, and other features of high-end word processors.

You might wonder what happens to certain features of word processing files that Notes translates using an intermediate RTF file. When importing, Notes fully supports the Windows ANSI, Macintosh, IBM PC, and IBM 850 character sets. When exporting, Notes uses the IBM 850 character set except on UNIX, which Notes uses 8859 ISO Latin 1.

When importing, Notes maps each font to one of the three basic Notes fonts. For documents that support changeable fonts, Notes maps serif fonts to Times Roman, sans serif fonts to Helvetica, and fixed-pitch fonts to Courier. Other fonts default to Helvetica.

Notes fully supports the character attributes of bold, italic, and strikethrough, as well as superscripts and subscripts. Small caps, caps, and shadow attributes are imported as bold text. Outline is imported as italic, and any hidden text is imported as plain text. Notes has only one kind of underline, so continuous, dotted, and word underlining all import as underlined text.

Notes imports font sizes and maps each color to the closest Notes color—black, white, red, green, blue, cyan, magenta, and yellow.

In Notes, paragraph left, first-line indents, and tabs are relative to the left edge of the page, whereas in word processing packages they are relative to the document margins. When Notes imports, it calculates the left margin of a paragraph by adding the document left margin to the paragraph indent. When exporting, Notes checks all paragraphs and sets the document left margin to be equal to the left margin of the leftmost paragraph.

For example, if you import a paragraph with a 0-inch left margin and a .5-inch tab setting, the document under Notes will have a 1-inch left margin and a 1.5-inch tab. To set the right margin when importing and exporting, Notes word-wraps appropriately, depending on the window size. The printer right margin is set to 7.5 inches in the Text Paragraph dialog box.

Notes also imports left, right, full, and center justification. It converts all line spacing into 1, $1^{1}/_{2}$, and 2 lines. Notes imports a section break when the section is also a page break. Otherwise Notes imports a section break as a paragraph break. For special characters, Notes imports a non-breaking space as a normal space and the various kinds of hyphens are imported as dashes.

Notes doesn't import or export headers or footers. Instead, Notes inserts the imported header or footer text into the body of the document at the position where the control code for header or footer exists in the original document.

NOTE   Notes doesn't translate revision marks, style sheets, footnotes, annotations, expanded or compressed text, or bookmarks.

Importing Word Processing Files into Documents

To import a word processing file into a Notes document, follow these steps:

1. Open the target document.

NOTE   If you place the insertion point in a field that isn't rich text, the File ➤ Import command will be dimmed and unavailable.

2. Place the insertion point in a rich text field where you want the imported file to begin.

3. Choose File ➤ Import. The Import dialog box appears. Select the file type (the default is ASCII Text), drive, and folder.

4. Enter the name of the file you are importing.

5. Select Import to start importing.

Importing Graphic Files into Documents

Notes imports (and exports) each picture as a separate entity; also, Notes can't import (or export) a picture that is embedded in a text file, such as a .PIC file in a WordPerfect document. If a file contains more than one picture, Notes imports only the first picture.

To import a graphic file into a Notes document, follow these steps:

1. Highlight the document in a view.

2. Open the document in Edit mode. You can also choose Create ➤ *<Form Name>* to create a new document to hold the imported graphic.

3. Place the insertion point in a rich text field where you want the imported file to begin.

4.   Choose File ➤ Import. Enter the name of the file you want to import, its file type, and its location into the Import dialog box.

5.   Click Import.

Improving the Appearance of Graphics

Imported pictures may look different in Notes than in their source applications because their fonts, colors, text sizes, and overall size are mapped to Notes equivalents. Since you cannot edit imported graphics in Notes—except to resize them—you may want to experiment with the picture in the original application.

You can adjust the shades of colors used to display or print imported pictures with the Color Setup dialog box. Picture colors affect some imported or displayed graphs and pictures, such as those in .PIC files and Freelance Metafiles. When the files contain color information, Windows interprets the colors as defined in the original file. If the files don't contain color information, Notes maps the colors.

Importing Spreadsheet Files into Documents

To bring spreadsheet data into a document, import the worksheet into a Notes rich text field. If you import spreadsheet data into a view, each worksheet row becomes a document, and each column becomes a field whose contents are the original cell contents.

TIP   Import a named range of several rows and columns for test purposes before you import the entire spreadsheet. Although 1-2-3 Release 5 can display multiple spreadsheets at one time, only the entire current spreadsheet or a specified range in the current worksheet is imported. The range name you use to import a range cannot span multiple worksheets.

The default font for spreadsheet imports is Courier. Notes ignores any fonts defined for the field into which you are importing the worksheet. (After you import the worksheet, you can change its fonts to Notes fonts.)

Notes doesn't wrap the lines of an imported spreadsheet. If the spreadsheet has more columns than a Notes window can display, use the horizontal scroll bars to see what's out of view. Notes can handle a maximum text width of 22.75 inches in a document and truncates additional text.

Importing Scanned Images

When importing scanned images, save scanned images in one of the image file formats: JPEG, GIF, PCX or TIFF 5.0 for import into Notes. Then follow the usual import procedure, making sure to choose the correct import filter (for example, JPEG, GIF, PCX Image, or TIFF 5.0 Image) format.

If you are not satisfied with the appearance of your scanned images, try adjusting the dots per inch (dpi) setting or the image size setting in your scanner software, if that's possible. Start with 75 dpi and 100 percent size, increasing the dpi and decreasing the size until you are satisfied with the results. In general, higher dpi settings result in larger images in Notes. Remember that different monitors may display the scanned image differently.

TIP   Choose View ➤ Show ➤ Horizontal Scroll Bar to navigate left-to-right in the Notes Document window.

If you aren't sure how you want to structure the database, use the Worksheet Title Defined option in the Worksheet Import Settings dialog box. It maps the existing worksheet column titles and contents to the fields in a Notes document.

To import a spreadsheet file into a Notes document, follow these steps:

1. Select a document in a view.

2. Open the document in Edit mode.

3. Place the insertion point in a rich text field where you want the imported file to begin.

4. Choose File ➤ Import. The Import dialog box appears.

5. Select the files you want to import on the left and select Lotus 1-2-3 Work-sheet as the file format in the right list box if it isn't already selected.

5. Select Import. Notes displays the 123/Symphony Worksheet Import dialog box, as shown in Figure 10.5.

FIGURE 10.5:

The 123/Symphony Worksheet Import dialog box lets you import an entire worksheet or a named range.

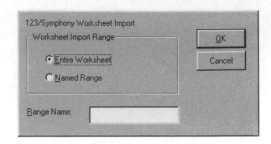

6. Select one of these options:

   • To import the entire worksheet, select Entire Worksheet.

   • To import a named range of data, select Named Range and type the name of the range in the Range Name box.

7. Click OK to perform the import.

Importing Spreadsheet Files into Views

When you import a spreadsheet into a view, each row becomes an individual document and each column becomes a field with the original cell contents as its field contents. To import at the view level, you must create a form and a view that can accommodate the format of the worksheet you are importing.

Notes uses a character translation (CLS) file to translate foreign symbols and characters. This file must be in your Notes program directory to translate symbols and characters.

Notes doesn't wrap lines of an imported worksheet. If a worksheet has more columns than a window can display, use the horizontal scroll bars to see the full width of the worksheet. Notes can handle a maximum text width of 22.75 inches; it truncates additional text.

NOTE   Before importing an entire spreadsheet, consider importing just a named range of several rows and columns for test purposes.

To import a spreadsheet file into a Notes view, follow these steps:

1. Click on the database's icon to select it and switch to the view that will receive the spreadsheet data.

2. Choose File ➤ Import. The Import dialog box appears.

3. Select the files you want to import on the left and select Lotus 1-2-3 Worksheet as the file format in the right list box if it isn't already selected.

4. Select Import. The Worksheet Import Settings dialog box appears, as shown in Figure 10.6.

FIGURE 10.6:

The Worksheet Import Settings dialog box lets you select a database form to use for the imported data. It also lets you define a view and select the labels in the cells in the first row of the worksheet as the column names and fields.

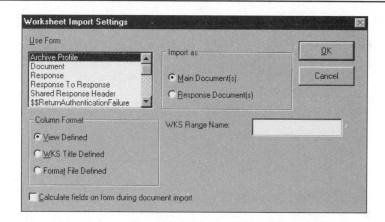

5. Select a form to use for the imported data from the Use Form list. The forms listed are those available in the database you are currently using.

6. Select one of these options under Column Format:

   - **View Defined:** Select this option if the format of the worksheet columns exactly matches the format of the columns in the view. The column names and column widths must be identical.

   - **WKS Title Defined:** Select this option if the cells in the first row of the worksheet file are to be column headers and fields. These cells must be labels. They can be used as the view column names but will not be imported. Field names will be created from the column titles and can be used in the database form.

- **Format File Defined:** Select this option if you are using a Column Format Descriptor File and enter the name of the file in the COL File name text box. Format files provide you with the greatest number of options for controlling how Notes imports information into a database. For more information on COL files, please see the Notes help file.

7. Select one of these options under Import As:

- **Main Document(s):** Select this option in all cases when you want to import the file as a document-type document.

- **Response Document(s):** Imports the file as one or more Response documents.

8. If you are importing a named range from the worksheet file, type the name of the range in the WKS Range Name text box.

9. Click OK to start importing.

TIP

Chapter 20 discusses how to create and modify views. To update the view to show column headings and the data from the import, choose Create ➤ View. When the Create View dialog box appears, select the view you want to modify.

TIP

If you import a multiple-sheet worksheet, Notes imports only the sheet that was open when the file was last closed. Or, if importing a range, Notes imports the range from that sheet.

When the import is complete, the view displays all documents produced by the import.

Importing ASCII Text into Documents and Views

To import an ASCII file into a document, follow these steps:

1. Select a document in a view.

2. Open the document in Edit mode.

3. Place the insertion point in a text field (or rich text field) where you want the imported file to begin.

4. Choose File ➤ Import. The Import dialog box appears.

5. Select the file you want to import.

6. Click Import. A Lotus Notes message box asks if you want to preserve the line breaks in the text, as shown in Figure 10.7.

FIGURE 10.7:

This Lotus Notes message box asks you if you want to preserve the line breaks in the imported ASCII text.

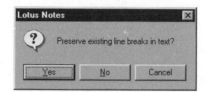

7. Select one of these options:

- **Yes:** To preserve the existing line breaks. This option is useful when the original file contains tables or columns.

- **No:** To make the text wrap at the end of each line when displayed in a window.

8. Click Yes or No to continue the import.

The ASCII file is imported and inserted into the Notes document at the insertion point.

To import an ASCII file into a view, follow these steps:

1. Open the view into which you want to import the file.

2. Choose File ➤ Import. The Import dialog box appears.

3. Select the file(s) you want to import.

4. Select the Tabular Text format if it isn't already selected.

5. Select Import.

6. Select the form into which you want to import the ASCII text file from the Tabular Text Import dialog box, as shown in Figure 10.8.

7. Choose the desired options.

8. Click OK to perform the import.

After the import process, Notes automatically updates the view to show the new documents.

FIGURE 10.8:

The Tabular Text Import
dialog box

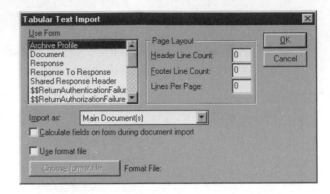

TIP

You can provide greater control on the import of tabular text data into a view by
choosing to use a format file. Format files or files with a .COL extension provide a
great deal of flexibility in specifying file import information.

Exporting Data

Exporting means translating Notes documents or views into a format that other
applications can use. You can also use Export to export a Notes view and then
import it into a Notes document. The details depend on what you are exporting,
but you always use the Export dialog box for exporting documents and views.
For a complete listing of all the file formats that can be exported from Notes,
refer to the "Supported Import/Export File Formats" section at the end of this
chapter.

Exporting a Document to Another Application

In general, to export a document to another application, you follow these steps:

1. Open a view and select or open the document you are exporting.

2. Choose File ➤ Export. The Export dialog box appears, as shown in Figure 10.9.

FIGURE 10.9:

The Export dialog box enables you to choose settings for exporting Notes documents and views to other applications.

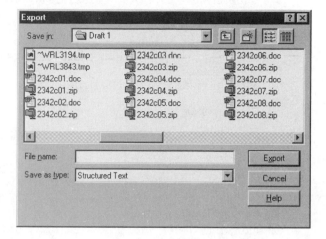

3. Select a file type under Save As Type. The options listed depend on whether you are exporting a view or a document. If you are exporting a document, the default file type is ASCII Text. If you are exporting a view, the default file type is Structured Text.

4. Select a drive in the Save In pull-down menu if necessary.

5. Click to open the folder you want in the Folder box.

6. Type the file name or the complete path and file name into the File Name text box (remember to include the file extension as Notes will not automatically default the file extension to match the export file type).

NOTE   To export to an existing file, select the file name from the list or type its name and path into the text box. Notes asks if you want to overwrite the existing file or append the export material to it.

7. Click Export to perform the export.

Exporting Documents to Word Processing Files

To export a Notes document to a word processing file, follow these steps:

1. Open the document you want to export.

2. Choose File ➤ Export. The Export dialog box opens.

3. Select a file type under Save As Type. The default file type for exporting a document is ASCII Text. You can also choose Microsoft Word RTF, which will retain all the formatting in the document when it's exported.

4. Select a drive in the Save In pull-down menu, if necessary.

5. Click to open the folder you want in the Folder box.

6. Type the file name or the complete path and file name into the File Name text box.

7. Click Export to perform the export.

If you choose to export a Notes document in the default ASCII Text format, the Text File Export dialog box appears, as shown in Figure 10.10. You can set the line length of exported text; the default is 75 characters. Words that extend beyond that length wrap to the next line. To change the line length, type a number. Click OK to export the document using the specified line length.

FIGURE 10.10:

The Text File Export dialog box lets you set the line length of exported text.

Text File Export

Wrap words at [75] characters per line

OK   Cancel

Exporting Document Graphics to Picture Files

To export graphics to picture files, follow these steps:

1. Open the document and select the graphic. If you don't select a graphic, Notes selects the first graphic in the document.

2. Choose File ➤ Export. Notes opens the Export dialog box.

3. Select a file type (CGM or TIFF 5.0 image) from the Save As Type list box.

    • To export the picture into an existing file, select the file from the list of file names. The file name appears in the text box.

- To export the picture into a new file, type the file name into the text box. The file is created in the selected directory.

4. Click Export.

If you are exporting to a new file, the Export dialog box closes and Notes displays a wait cursor until the export is complete. For some file types, if you are exporting into an existing file, Notes opens the Export Warning dialog box where you specify whether you want to replace the existing file or add to it. The dialog boxes close, and Notes displays a wait cursor until the export is complete.

Exporting Views to Spreadsheets

You can export a view to a 1-2-3 spreadsheet file. Each column in the view becomes a column in the worksheet, and each row in the view becomes a row in the worksheet. You can also include the column headings in a view in the first row of the worksheet. To export a view to a 1-2-3 file format, simply follow these steps:

1. Open the view you want to export. The entire view will be exported unless you select specific documents for export.

2. Choose File ➤ Export. Notes opens the Export dialog box.

3. Select Lotus 123 Worksheet as the Save type.

NOTE To export the view into an existing spreadsheet file, select the file from the list of file names. To export the view into a new spreadsheet file, type the file name into the text box. The file is created in the selected directory.

4. Click the Export button. If you are exporting to an existing file, Notes opens the Export Warning dialog box. Specify whether you want to replace the existing file. If you are exporting the view to a new file, the 123 Worksheet Export dialog box appears. Specify which documents you want to export.

5. Click OK.

Exporting Documents and Views to ASCII Text

The process for exporting documents and views to structured ASCII text files is similar to the process for exporting views to spreadsheets. To perform the export, just follow these steps:

1. Select a database in your Workspace.

2. Choose a view and then select the documents you want to export.

3. Open the documents you want to export if you don't want to export the entire view. (A document doesn't have to be in Edit mode.)

4. Choose File ➤ Export. The Export dialog box appears.

5. Specify where to store the exported file.

6. Enter a new file name or select an existing one to which you want to export the view.

7. Select the default ASCII Text as the file type.

8. Click the Export button. If you are exporting the view to a new file, the Export dialog box closes and displays the Text File Export dialog box. (If you are exporting to an existing file, Notes opens the Export Warning dialog box where you specify whether you want to replace the existing file or append it.)

9. Choose the desired options.

10. Click OK. The dialog boxes closes, and Notes completes the export.

Supported Import/Export File Formats

Notes supports a wide variety of import and export formats. It can be somewhat confusing determining which format is used for importing, which formats are supported for views, and so on. Tables 10.3–10.6 summarize all the formats that Notes supports as of Release 4.6. Each table has been broken down by product format type for quicker reference. The file formats may not be supported on all platforms.

TABLE 10.3: Supported File Formats for Spreadsheet Files

File Type	Import Into		Export From		File Extension	File Description
	RTF	View	Doc	View		
Lotus 1-2-3	✓	✓		✓	.WKS, .WK1, .WK3, .WK4	Entire worksheet or named range in Lotus 1-2-3 for DOS 1A or later, 1-2-3 for Windows, or 1-2-3 for Macintosh
Microsoft Excel	✓				.XLS	Microsoft Excel 4.0, 5.0

TIP

To import a Microsoft Excel spreadsheet into a view, save it as a Lotus 1-2-3 spreadsheet.

TABLE 10.4: Supported File Formats for Graphics Files

File Type	Import Into		Export From		File Extension	File Description
	RTF	View	Doc	View		
PCX Image	✓				.PCX	Raster graphic
Lotus PIC	✓				.PIC	Picture created in Lotus 1-2-3 or Symphony
CGM Image	✓		✓		.CGM, .GMF	Picture created in software supporting ANSI Metafile
TIFF 5.0 Image	✓		✓		.TIF	Bitmapped image scanned into software supporting TIFF
Bitmap Image[1]	✓				.BMP	Bitmapped image
GIF Image	✓				.GIF	Graphics Interchange Format image
JPEG Image	✓				.JPG	Joint Photographics Experts Group image

[1] Not UNIX

TABLE 10.5: Supported File Formats for Word Processing Files

File Type	Import Into		Export From		File Extension	File Description
	RTF	View	Doc	View		
Lotus Ami Pro	✓		✓		.SAM	Ami Pro 1.x, 2.x, 3.x
Microsoft RTF	✓		✓		.RTF	Applications that support RTF (such as MS Word)
Microsoft Word	✓		✓		.DOC	Word for Windows 6.0
WordPerfect	✓		✓[1]		.DOC, .WPD, .WPT	WordPerfect 5.x, 6.0, 6.1
Frame Technologies FrameMaker	✓		✓		.MIF	FrameMaker 3.0, 4.0
Interleaf[2] ASCII	✓				.GIF	Interleaf Version 5.0 or later

1 Only versions 5.1, 6.0, 6.1
2 UNIX Only

WARNING When you import a FrameMaker document, Notes replaces all quotation marks (both single and double) with spaces.

TABLE 10.6: Supported File Formats for Text Files

File Type	Import Into		Export From		File Extension	File Description
	RTF	View	Doc	View		
ASCII Text	✓		✓		Any	Unformatted text
Binary with text	✓				Any	Imports text from non-text files
Tabular ASCII text	✓	✓		✓	Any	ASCII text arranged in rows and columns; limit of 1,536 characters per record
Structured ASCII text	✓	✓		✓	Any[1]	ASCII text arranged as fields and field values; limit of 256 bytes per simple text field

1 Except .TAB, .TXT, .PRN, .RPT

What's Next?

In the next chapter, we discuss using Notes Mail, which is a powerful e-mail system that's fully integrated with Notes databases. You can use Notes Mail as you would use any other e-mail system. The major difference between Notes and other e-mail systems is that Notes Mail is a database application that provides unique communication features to support workflow throughout an organization.

Communicating via Notes Mail

- Accessing Notes Mail

- Creating mail messages

- Creating address books for frequent correspondents

- Creating user groups

- Creating distinguishing names

- Sending mail messages

- Receiving, replying to, and forwarding mail

- Using your Notes Mail database

- Managing Notes Mail

- Using Notes Mail tools

- Providing others access to your Notes Mail database

Many people use Notes for its e-mail capabilities alone. Notes Mail enables you to communicate quickly and easily with other electronic mail users. You can send and receive mail memos—from simple, one-line messages to complex, multi-page reports. You can attach files—even an entire Notes database—to a mail memo. You can forward or receive documents from any Notes database. You can even send files created with other Lotus and Microsoft Windows 95 products, such as 1-2-3 and Word, as if they were Notes Mail memos.

4.6 RELEASE

Now Notes supports Internet (POP3/SMTP) mail. You can use the same Notes Mail interface for communicating with other Notes users and anyone with an Internet e-mail address. This gives you the ability to have one universal Inbox for all your mail, whether it comes from a Domino server or some other Internet mail server. You can send and receive personal e-mail from a dial-up connection hosted by an Internet service provider (ISP) with the same client used to check your business e-mail at work.

This new functionality requires a little more setup for a client workstation, but the extra effort is worth it. There are some slight differences in the user interface for a POP3 mail client and some limitations on Notes functionality. These differences are covered in Chapter 13, "Working Off-Site with Mobile Notes," as knowledge of location documents is required.

Every person who uses Notes as part of a companywide system has a *mail database*. Your mail database is like any other Notes database. In most cases, your mail database will be located on your company's Domino server (although you can also have a copy of your mail database that is local on your PC). For the context of this chapter, we will only be referring to your mail database that is located on the Domino server. Chapter 13 will describe how to use a local mail database and the fundamental differences between your server mail database and a local copy.

When Notes 4.6 is installed on your workstation (whether you are upgrading from a previous version of Notes or installing from scratch), you should see two mail-related database icons on your Workspace: the Mail Database icon and the Personal Address Book icon (your last name usually appears in the title of the Personal Address Book). You may also have an Outgoing Mail icon, but this is not automatically installed on your Workspace and will be referred to when discussing how to use Notes as a mobile user. Figure 11.1 shows an example of how the two mail database icons might appear on your Workspace.

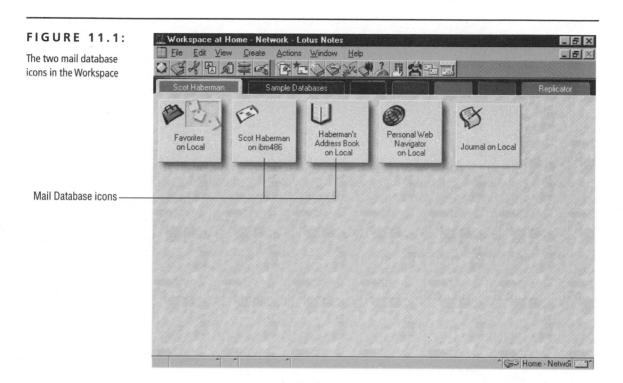

FIGURE 11.1:

The two mail database icons in the Workspace

Mail Database icons

Favorites Portfolio Database

Although not actually part of the Notes Mail system, this new feature in 4.6 incorporates your mail database and Personal Address Book (along with the Journal and Personal Web Navigator) into one database. This allows you to group related Notes applications together and move between these grouped applications from one Navigation pane. Notes automatically creates the Favorites portfolio for you when Notes 4.6 is installed. These groupings of database are not random but are considered the most basic set of what an individual needs to access and manage information. The Favorites portfolio contains an icon for your e-mail, Calendar, To-Do list, Personal Journal, Personal Name and Address book, and Personal Web Navigator. Each icon is located in the Navigation pane and, when expanded (with exception of the Calendar and To-Do list), has the same design layout as if you were to open the actual database.

Continued on next page

Adding database icons is very easy. You can drag a database icon from the Workspace and drop the icon on top of the Favorites database icon. You can also edit the portfolio database list by clicking on the icon located on the Favorites title bar. This will display the Favorites database layout. Using the Action buttons, you can add, remove, and change the sequence of all the databases.

One thing that you may notice is that there is not an entry for the Calendar or the To-Do list. These icons are actually contained within your mail database and are a new feature with Notes 4.6.

With this new database type, you can now group databases into one location. This will allow you to spend more time focusing on accomplishing your goals and less time trying to locate which application database you need to get your work done.

Accessing Notes Mail from the Workspace

You open your mail database as you would open any other Notes database. Simply double-click its icon in the Workspace to open the mail database's view. You can also access your mail from any other open Notes database by clicking the Inbox icon on the far right of the status bar and choosing Open Mail.

NOTE   With Notes 4.6, you will notice that the mail database interface has changed a little. Two additional icons appear in the Navigation pane. The Calendar icon displays all of your appointments, anniversaries, reminders, and so on in a Two Day, One Week, Two Week, or One Month view. The To-Do icon displays a list of "things to do" categorized by status.

With Notes 4.6, you now have the capability to access your Notes Mail database via the Web. Depending on how your system administrator sets up your Notes mail file, you may be able to read and work with Notes mail messages using a Web or HTML browser (such as Microsoft Internet Explorer or Netscape Navigator) in addition to, or instead of, a Notes workstation.

Creating Mail

You can create mail from just about anywhere within the Notes environment. The default mail message form is a *memo*. Notes includes quite a few other predesigned standard mail forms that are accessible from the Create menu (but you can also add your own standard mail forms to this list). Notes also includes some custom mail forms located under the Create ➤ Special menu.

You can create a mail message from scratch depending on where you are working on the Workspace. To build a mail message from scratch, do one of the following:

- If you are using your mail database, click the New Memo button or choose Create and select the type of mail message from one of the predesigned mail forms.

- If you are using a database other than the mail database, choose Create ➤ Mail and select the type of mail message from one of the predesigned forms.

- Click the mail icon located on the far right of the status bar and select either Open Mail, which will open your mail database, or Create Memo, which will create a Memo mail message.

Notes 4.6 has added some new options for creating mail messages that are designed to save you time when creating or responding to e-mail. Now you can:

- Populate the To field of a memo by selecting names from your Personal Address Book:

    - Switch to either the Business Cards or By Category view in your Personal Address Book.

    - Select one or more names to whom you want to send a message.

    - Click on the Write Memo button.

- Create a new copy of an existing message:

    - From your Mail Database, either select or open an existing mail message.

    - Choose Actions ➤ Copy Into ➤ New Memo.

    - Notes will create a new memo, placing both the original subject and the original body of the message in the new message.

- Notes will also place your name in the From field and the originator's name in the To field, and keep all the other addresses as they were from the original message.

- Create a message from an existing calendar entry:

  - From the calendar view in your Mail Database, either select or open an existing calendar entry.

  - Choose Actions ➤ Copy Into ➤ New Memo.

  - Notes will create a new memo, placing the brief description in the subject field.

  - Notes will also place the date, time, and the comments into the body of the mail message.

- Create a message from an existing To-Do (task) entry:

  - From the To-Do view in your mail database, either select or open an existing To-Do entry.

  - Choose Actions ➤ Copy Into ➤ New Memo.

  - Notes will create a new memo, placing the task description in the subject field.

  - Notes will also place the start date, due date, and the additional information in the body of the mail message.

TIP   The fastest way to create a memo is to click the mail icon and then click Create Memo.

Using Predesigned Forms

You can now create mail messages using your favorite word processor, such as Microsoft Word or Lotus Word Pro. When you use a word processor to create a message, Notes will display most of the menu commands of your word processor. The only Notes menu commands that remain are File, Window, and Help. Notes also displays the Action buttons and the toolbar of your word processor.

What happens if you use Microsoft Word to create a mail message and the recipient does not have Word installed? Not a problem. If the recipient has the same word processor installed, the mail message will use the word processor to display the data. If the recipient does not have the word processor installed, the message will be displayed using the Notes editor (because of this fact, the data is actually duplicated within each mail message created using Word or Word Pro).

Using an alternate word processor does have some disadvantages:

- You cannot reply to a message using your word processor.

- You cannot attach files using a word processor.

- If the message is displayed using the Notes editor, some of the formatting may be lost (it may not look the same).

- You cannot use mood stamps.

To set up Notes to use a word processor with Notes Mail, do one of the following:

- Choose File ➤ Tools ➤ User Preferences.

- Click the Mail icon.

- In the Document Memo Editor field, choose the word processor you want or select None to use the regular Notes editor.

- Click OK.

If you opted to use an alternate mail editor, a new option will be displayed under the Create or Create ➤ Mail menu option. For Microsoft Word, it will be the Word Memo option. For Lotus Word Pro, the option will be WordPro Memo. If you decided to use the Notes editor, neither of these options will be displayed.

After you choose Create and select a mail form, Notes displays the appropriate form for you to complete. Using one of the predefined forms can save you the time it takes to create a form, so let's look more closely at the mail forms:

- **Memo:** Figure 11.2 displays the standard Memo form. As you can see, it includes the name of the sender and the current date and time. This form lets you write and send (or just save) a regular e-mail message.

- **Reply:** You can use this form to create a response to an open or selected document and then send it to one or more people. If you try to open a Reply form without first selecting the mail message you want to respond to, Notes beeps and displays a message telling you to select (or open) a document. If the message is a Notes mail recipient, the message will contain a document link back to the earlier mail message. Figure 11.3 displays the Reply form.

FIGURE 11.2:

The standard Memo form shows the name of the sender (in this case, Scot Haberman) and the current date and time.

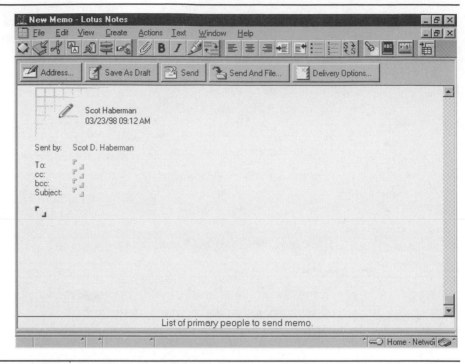

FIGURE 11.3:

The Reply form allows you to respond to a specific e-mail message, which might be a document that someone sent to you.

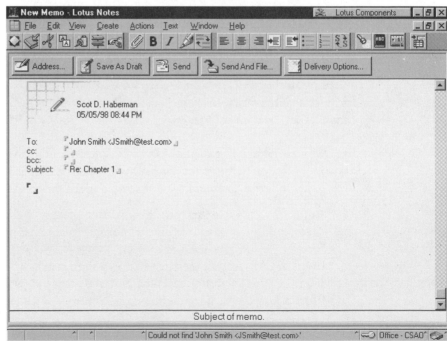

- **Reply with History:** Just like the Reply form, the Reply with History form requires you to select a document to respond to, or you'll get a beep and a message telling you that no document is selected. Once you select a document, you use this form to include the original document that you're responding to in your reply and then send the reply to one or more people.

TIP An alternative to the Reply with History is to use the Action ➤ Copy Into ➤ New Memo. This will retain a copy of the original and all addressees.

- **Task:** You can use this form to create a To-Do item for yourself or assign it (mail it) to someone else. Notes can track tasks that you have to complete and tasks that you assign to other people. Notes updates the status of each task until you complete or discard it. Figure 11.4 displays the Task form.

FIGURE 11.4:

The Task form allows you to create a To-Do item for yourself or assign it to someone else.

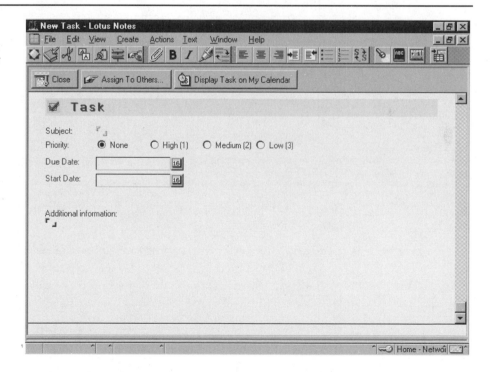

- **Word Memo/WordPro Memo:** This option will only be visible if you have selected an alternate e-mail editor (in our case, we chose Microsoft Word). The mail message is very similar to the standard Memo form with the exception that the actual body of the mail message is created using your alternate editor. When you first create a mail message, you will be prompted to enter the addressing information and the subject of the mail message (this can be changed at any time, so if you are not sure, just leave them blank and click OK). Figure 11.5 displays the Word Memo form.

FIGURE 11.5:

The Word Memo form

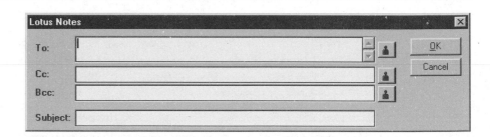

Now let's take a look at some of the important Action buttons that appear in various mail forms:

- **Address:** Displays the Mail Address dialog box where you can fill in the mail address fields by selecting names from any defined Address Book instead of typing them in the To, Cc, and Bcc fields.

- **Save As Draft:** Allows you to save the current form to the Drafts view. Use this action when a message is not completed but you want to save your work.

- **Send:** Clicking the Send button sends the mail memo you are editing to the intended recipients.

- **Send and File:** Performs the same function as the Send button except that you will be prompted to select a folder where you would like a copy of the mail message saved. This should be used in those cases when you want to keep a copy of the mail message you are sending.

- **Delivery Options:** Allows you to select specific options pertaining to your mail message. The options that you can select, as shown in Figure 11.6, are:

  - **Importance:** Informs your recipients that the importance of your mail message is either low, normal, or high.

FIGURE 11.6:

The Delivery Options available when sending mail

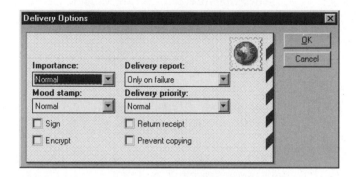

- **Mood Stamp:** Indicates the type of message (via an icon) you are sending such as FYI, Confidential, or Private.

- **Sign:** Allows you to add a digital signature to your mail message so the intended recipient knows you are the person who created the message. This is described in more detail later in the chapter.

- **Encrypt:** Allows you to encrypt your mail messages so no one else can read them (this is described in more detail later in the chapter).

- **Delivery Priority:** Determines when your server sends your message (High sends immediately, Normal sends during next scheduled replication, and Low waits until off-peak hours).

- **Delivery Report:** Tells Notes to inform you when a message is delivered (Only of failure, Confirm delivery, Trace entire path, or None).

- **Return Receipt:** Sends a confirmation message back to you when the recipient reads the mail message.

- **Prevent Copying:** Will not allow the recipient to make any copies of the mail message.

- **Reply to All:** This option is only available from the Reply and Reply with History forms. Selecting this option will deliver a copy of your message to everyone who received the original message.

- **Assign to Others:** This option is only available from the Task form. Allows you to create a task and assign it to someone else. A copy of the task will be sent to the intended recipient(s) and a copy of the task saved in your To-Do list. Once the task is completed by the recipient(s), your To-Do will be updated as well.

- **Display/Remove from Calendar:** This option is only available from the Task form. You can automatically add/remove a task from your calendar.

- **Envelope:** This option is only available from the Word or Word Pro form. Allows you access to the To, Cc, Bcc, and Subject fields.

There are a few other important options that are only available from the Actions menu using the mail forms:

- **Forward:** This command enables you to forward a copy of one or more selected Notes documents to the people you specify. The selected documents become the body of the memo; you can also edit and add to this information. This command is similar to the Copy Into command mentioned earlier.

- **Special Options:** This command has few features that are quite useful under certain situations. When selecting this option, a dialog box will display, as shown in Figure 11.7.

  - **Expiration Date:** You can set an expiration date for the mail message that informs the recipient that your message is not important after that date.

  - **Please Reply By:** You can have Notes automatically insert a "Please reply by" line in your mail message with the date you specify.

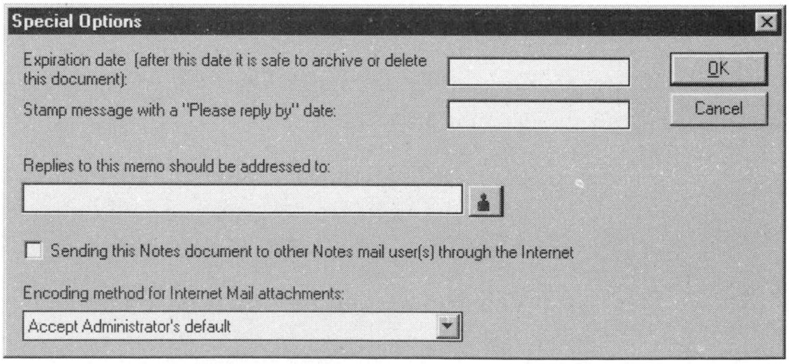

FIGURE 11.7:

The Special Options dialog box

- **Replies Addressed To:** A handy feature that lets you specify a mail recipient where all replies to your message will be sent.

- **Sending a Message through the Internet:** When sending a message through the Internet to another Notes user, you can tell Notes to preserve all the formatting in your message (messages that are sent through the Internet are converted to plain text).

Using the Notes Custom Mail Forms

You can also use the Notes custom mail forms for creating mail memos. These forms are useful in a variety of applications. To create a mail message from one of the Notes custom forms, do one of the following:

- If you are using your mail database, choose Create ➤ Special and select the type of mail message from one of the custom mail forms.

- If you are using a different database, choose Create ➤ Mail ➤ Special and select the type of mail message from one of the custom forms.

Notes provides four special forms for sending mail messages (the Temporary Export Certificate that is also present under the Special menu option is not really a mail form):

- **Memo to Database Manager:** The Memo to Database Manager form puts the names of all of the Database Managers for the active Notes database in the To field. This form lets you create and send a mail message to the manager(s) of the active database.

- **Phone Message:** The Phone Message form is extremely useful for taking phone messages. You just fill in the blanks and send the electronic While You Were Out message to the recipient. To create a phone message memo, follow these steps:

  1. Select the Phone Message memo from the menu.

  2. Enter addressing information in the To, Cc, and Bcc fields.

  3. Type the name of the person who left the message in the Contact field.

  4. (*Optional*) Enter information in the Of, Phone, and Fax fields.

5. Click any applicable options at the bottom of the form.

6. (*Optional*) Type a message in the Message field.

7. (*Optional*) Click Delivery Options and change any delivery options you want.

8. Send the message.

- **Serial Route Memo:** You can send a message sequentially to a list of recipients. Each recipient has the option of adding a comment and sending the message to the next person. To create a serial route memo, follow these steps:

    1. Select the Serial Route Memo from the menu.

    2. List the names of the recipients in the Route To field in the order in which you want them to receive the message. Separate the names with commas.

    3. Complete the rest of the message as you would any other message.

    4. (*Optional*) Click Notify Sender at Each Stop if you want Notes to send you a message each time a recipient receives the message.

    5. Click Send to Next Person.

- **Bookmark:** Notes lets you create a message that includes a link to a document in another database. This link is called a *bookmark*. A bookmark lets the recipient view the linked document while reading your message. To create a bookmark, follow these steps:

    1. Open the database that contains the document to which you want to link.

    2. Select the document.

    3. Select the Bookmark mail message from the menu. Notes creates a new message that includes a link to the document you selected.

    4. Create the rest of the message as you would a normal mail message.

    5. Send the message.

NOTE   The linked document must be in a database to which the recipient has access.

Creating the Message

Whether you are using a predefined form or a custom form, the final step in creating a message—actually writing it—is straightforward. Just type into the blank fields on the screen the same information you would type into the corresponding spaces on a paper memo. To move from one field to the next in any one of the mail forms, press Tab. To move to the previous field, press Shift+Tab.

Most of the fields on the standard mail memo are self-explanatory (refer to Figure 11.2). The following fields appear on this form:

- **To:** The To field allows you to enter the names of the primary recipients. You can type more than one name into this field. By using group names, you can send a single message to numerous individuals under one designation. When sending a message to an individual, you can use *type-ahead addressing*. You can enter just a first name (Jordan) or last name (Andrews); a first and last name (Kristen Tod); or a group name (Sales Dept). Depending on how your location document is configured, the *type-ahead addressing* will search your Personal Address Book, the server's Address Book, or both. Notes will display the results of the type-ahead addressing in the status bar.

- **Cc:** The Cc (carbon copy) field allows you to enter the names of secondary recipients. The same limitations apply to this field as to the To field.

- **Bcc:** You enter the names of secondary recipients in this field, but primary and secondary recipients won't see the Bcc names (*bcc* means blind carbon copy). If you enter more than one name in the Bcc field, Bcc recipients will see only their own name in that field; that is, the names are hidden from other recipients. If you enter a group name, members of the group won't see *any* names belonging to the group, not even their own.

- **Subject:** Enter a brief description of the memo in this field. Filling in the Subject field is a good idea because this field appears in the Subject column in the standard mail view. A specific, accurate Subject column encourages the recipient to open the mail document and read on. A person should be able to figure out the contents of a message from the Subject. If you don't enter a subject, the Subject entry for this document will appear blank in the view; that is, if the view displays a Subject column, no entry will appear in the column for this document.

- **Body:** You type your memo in the Body field, which is the unlabeled field following the Subject field. You can use text and paragraph formatting features by choosing the appropriate commands from the Text menu. You can also add graphics, make doclinks (an icon that represents direct access from one Notes document to another) to other Notes documents, and insert file attachments or OLE data. The red brackets on the screen surround the Body field and indicate that this field will be encrypted if you choose to send this message with encryption turned on.

The From and Date fields appear automatically at the top of the form when you create a new memo.

Addressing Mail

When you write a mail memo, you typically type the names of the recipients into the To, Cc, and Bcc fields. This process is called, sensibly enough, addressing your mail. Notes automatically enters your name and the current date in the memo. However, you must enter the name of at least one recipient in the To field. All the other field entries are optional.

You can also enter names by choosing them directly from a Name & Address book when you select Mail ➤ Address. This step is useful when you're not sure of a name or its spelling or if you prefer to point and click rather than type. You can also use the Name & Address book feature to add correctly spelled user names and group names to the body of a Notes document. (If you don't know what a Name & Address book is, skip ahead to the "Using the Address Books" section.)

To use the address feature:

1. Open one of the mail documents in Edit mode and place the insertion point in a field that will accept names (such as the To field) and then choose Actions ➤ Address or click the Address button on the standard mail form. The Mail Address dialog box appears.

2. Select the Address book you want to search. The options are your Public and Personal Address Books (other address books may also be available depending on your Notes Administrator.

3. Select which types of names you want to see:

    - If you are searching your Personal Address Book, your options are People and Groups (the default) and People and Groups Hierarchical. You will see a listing of all of the people and groups defined in your Personal Address Book. If you highlight a person document and click the Open button, the document will show you the details for the specific person. If you have a Group highlighted and click the Open button, Notes will display the names of members in the highlighted group.

- If you are searching the Public Address Book, the options depend on whether your home server is running Notes Release 4 or an earlier release. The options in the earlier releases are People (the default) and Groups. The options in Release 4 are the same as the ones for your Personal Address Book.

4. Select the name you want (scroll down the list if necessary) or type the first letters in the name.

5. Click the To, Cc, or Bcc button. The name appears in the Addresses list.

TIP   You can also drag-and-drop names to the desired locations (To, Cc, or Bcc).

If you change your mind, you can delete a name from your document with the Remove or Remove All button.

If you want to select more names, you can repeat steps 1 to 5. When you are done, click the OK button to close the mail address dialog box.

You can also add or delete names directly in the To field in the mail memo, but remember to separate the names with commas or by pressing ↵. Before actually sending the message, you can press F9 at any time to see the way Notes interprets the address you've entered so far. It will translate nicknames (or short names) into the explicit e-mail address for the intended recipients.

If Notes does not display the name you want, type the entire name and address.

Using the Address Books

After you have manually entered a long list of recipient addresses a few times, you'll rejoice in using the Notes Address books. These books are special Notes databases that list users, groups, servers, and server connections. Why use these books? Address books help you to locate recipients' addresses quickly, allowing you to send mail to any name in the book without actually typing the addresses yourself. Using the Name & Address books can save you a lot of time.

Notes creates two kinds of Address books for you, personal and public. When you registered as a new user in your company, your name was added to the Public Address Book. During the Notes setup procedure, your Personal Address Book was created. The file name of the public Name & Address book is NAMES.NSF. The file name of your Personal Address Book is usually NAMES.NSF (but it is stored locally on your machine).

Using the Public Address Book

Your name and Notes Mail address must appear in the Public Address Book before you can send and receive mail. You can update your listing if your name or mail address changes and the Notes server administrator for your company provides you with the ability to update your own Person document. To see your listing, open the Address book, choose View ➤ People, and find your document (your name) in the view.

Each Notes domain (and most organizations have only one domain) has only one Public Address Book, although every Notes server in that domain contains a replica of it. What does *domain* mean? If your organization uses only one Notes server, the domain is the group of users with the same Address book. A domain can also be a group of Notes servers with the same Public Address Book.

If your Public Address Book is large, you can omit it from the Workspace. The only reasons to have the Public Address Book on your Workspace are to make use of the Mail Address feature and to get instant notification when you've entered a user's name incorrectly (otherwise you'll receive a Delivery Failure notice at the time of the next scheduled replication when Notes sends your outgoing mail).

However, you can avoid these limitations by copying the People, Groups, and Remote Connection records that you need into your Personal Address Book. Select the documents you want to copy at the view level in the Public Address Book and then paste them into your Personal Address Book. To make sure they arrive safely, be sure to look at the correct view.

You can also use the Public Address Book to look up user groups to whom you want to send mail. Open the Address Book database and then choose View ➤ Groups.

Addressing a Message Using the Quick-Address Method

You can set up Notes to look for names in your Personal Address Book only or in both your Personal Address Book and in the Public Address Book. You can also turn off the quick-address method. (Make these selections in the Recipient name type-ahead field in the Location document in your Personal Address Book.)

Notes helps you address messages by displaying names that contain the letters that you type in the To, Cc, and Bcc fields. Start by typing the first letter or two of the name of a person or group to whom you want to send the message:

- If Notes does not display the name you want, type additional letters in the name.

- If Notes displays the name you want, do one of the following:

  - Press ↵ to accept the name and look for an additional name.

  - Press the down arrow to move to the next field if the list is complete.

Using Your Personal Address Book

The Personal Address Book has had a dramatic makeover. The main function of the Personal Address Book has not been changed. It is still used for private mailing lists for your own use (containing names and addresses of people located on other e-mail systems, such as the Internet, and most commonly accessed users and groups in your domain), location, and connection documents. What has changed is the overall emphasis in using your Personal Address Book as more of a contact management database. The Personal Address Book is fully integrated with the Notes messaging system, making it easier to address memos, schedule meetings, and visit Web pages right from the contact list.

Your Personal Address Book entries only appear in your Personal Address Book. It can contain duplicate entries located in the Public Address Book, but this may cause some confusion when trying to resolve names (discussed later in the chapter). This database usually resides on your workstation (but could also be located on a server). Your Personal Address Book must be located in the data directory specified in your User Preferences (this was originally determined during the installation of Notes). If you have any problems finding or accessing your Personal Address Book, contact your Notes Administrator.

Now on to some of the new features with Notes 4.6.

Business Card Document

For those of you upgrading from a previous version of Notes, this was formerly known as the Person document. Going along with the contact management theme, the Person document has been changed to provide information along the lines of a business card. As shown in Figure 11.8, the document layout has changed dramatically from its former self (those new to 4.6 should compare the layout of the Business Card document to that of the Person document in the Public Address Book). The form allows you to save just about any information that you would want to know about contacts, business associates, and companies. Not only is information easier to store, but the information can now be categorized and displayed using the Business Card view.

FIGURE 11.8:

A portion of the new Business Card document

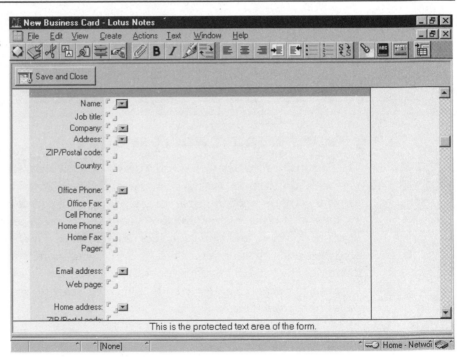

One of the newest features in the Business Card document is the ability to *auto-parse* data. For example, you can type **Mr. Scot D. Haberman** in the Name field, and Notes will automatically parse out the Title, First Name, Middle Name, Last Name, and the Suffix (although you have the option of turning this feature on or off at any time via the Address Book profile). As shown in Figure 11.9, you can also display the dialog box and type each entry in separately.

FIGURE 11.9:

Notes will auto-parse the contact name.

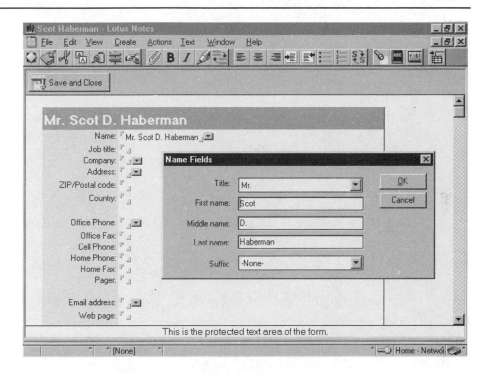

For the Company field, you can type in the company name (or select one from the list), and Notes will automatically fill in the company's address information. The Address field is also able to parse the information or you can type in each entry separately, as shown in Figure 11.10.

One really handy feature is the ability to dynamically override field names. How many people do you know that have many different phone numbers? They might have a business line and extension, fax, cell phone, pager, and the list goes on. With this new feature, you can tailor each individual's phone list to the individual. The default field names feature is quite comprehensive (refer to Figure 11.9 or 11.10). But each individual is different and now you can change the descriptions to fit the individual as shown in Figure 11.11. One person's cell phone field can be another person's pager number field.

FIGURE 11.10:

Notes can also parse the company information or fill it in for you by selecting the company from the list.

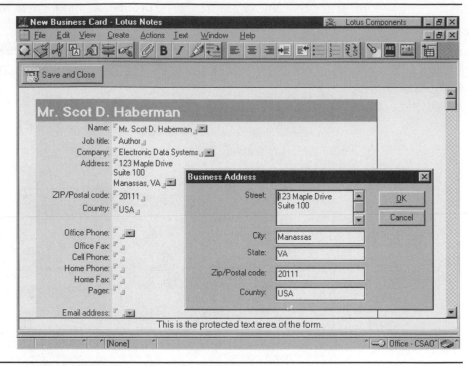

FIGURE 11.11:

Notes give you the ability to dynamically override field names.

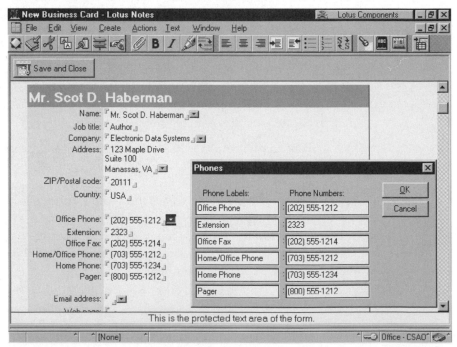

Notes has also made entering e-mail addresses simpler. No longer do you have to remember the awkward syntax of different mail systems. By using the Helper Arrow, Notes will prompt you with a Mail Address Assistant dialog box asking for the type of mail system that the individual is using (see Figure 11.12). You can select from Fax, Internet Mail, cc:Mail, Lotus Notes, Other, and X.400 Mail. Once selected, another Mail Address Assistant dialog box will prompt you for information needed for that particular mail system (this dialog box will vary according to the mail system type selection). Once you complete all the fields, Notes will format the e-mail address in the correct syntax and place the entry in the E-Mail Address field for you.

FIGURE 11.12:

Notes Mail Address Assistant eliminates having to remember the different e-mail syntax.

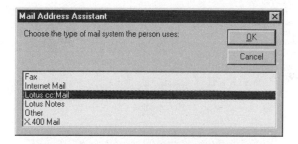

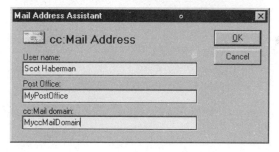

Another added feature is the ability to enter a Web page for an individual. This will allow you to open the Web page directly from within your Personal Address Book. No more having to remember company or contact home pages (how to do this is discussed later on). For example, to jump to a particular company's home page, we would type **http://www.eds.com/** in the Web Page field.

You can also enter a home address for the individual. These fields have the same parsing feature as the business address fields.

Also contained on this form is a Categories field. Now you can group or categorize all of your Business Card documents any way you want.

TIP   To avoid typos in the Categories field, select the categories for each business card from the By Categories view. Just select a document and click on the Categorize Action Button for a dialog box of possible choices. If a category does not exist, just enter a new one.

One last field that is worth mentioning is the Short Name field (commonly referred to as nickname). As mentioned earlier, you can type in a recipient's name when addressing a mail message. Using the Short Name field gives you the ability to assign a different name to an individual when addressing mail. Instead of typing in the full e-mail address or scouring through pages of addresses in the Address Book, you can type in the Short Name and Notes will resolve the actual e-mail address for you. To use this feature, expand the More Info section at the bottom of the Business Card document and enter the individual's Short Name.

Personal Address Book Views

As mentioned before, the theme for this Notes release is information management. With that in mind, there are two views that you will use most often for your contacts, the Business Card view and the By Category view (the Groups view is discussed later in the chapter). Both of these views are similar in looks and functionality. The Business Card view displays the entries sorted by name or by company, while the By Category view displays the entries by, you guessed it, category (see Figure 11.13). The only functional difference between the two views is that the By Category view allows you to categorize selected documents.

Both views display quite a bit of information. Instead of your typical one-line description of a document, these views display the contact information that you are most likely going to need without having to open the document. The more information you type in about an individual, the more information that will be displayed in the view. In helping you use the Personal Address Book as a contact management database, the views display the person's name, full business address, and all the phone number information. No more having to find an individual's document, open the document, and scroll through the data in order to locate an office phone number. Everything that you need is now displayed in the view.

Some other timesaving options have been incorporated into the views. The most common actions are now available as Action buttons. If you want to schedule a meeting, just select all the individuals you want to send an invitation to and

FIGURE 11.13:

The By Category view displays all your contact's information.

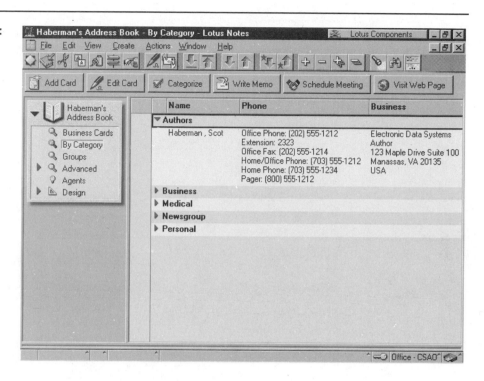

click Schedule Meeting. Notes will automatically place the selected individuals as recipients to the invitation mail message. The same holds true for creating a Memo mail message. Select all the individuals and click Write Memo. Notes will pre-fill the To field with the names of all the selected individuals.

Defining User Groups for a Mailing List

If you often send mail to the same groups of people, you can save time and typing by creating user groups. Once you have defined a group in your Personal Address Book, you can type the group name instead of the individual names in any of the recipient fields of a mail document. A group can include people or other groups from your own domain, a domain other than your own, or from mixed domains.

NOTE Only users with Author access to the Public Address Book can define user groups for everyone in your domain to use. To see a list of these user groups, open the Public Address Book and choose View ➤ Groups.

To define a user group, do the following:

1. Open your Personal Address Book database.

2. Select the Group view.

3. Click the Add Group or Edit Group button. A Group document appears, as shown in Figure 11.14.

FIGURE 11.14:

A Group document

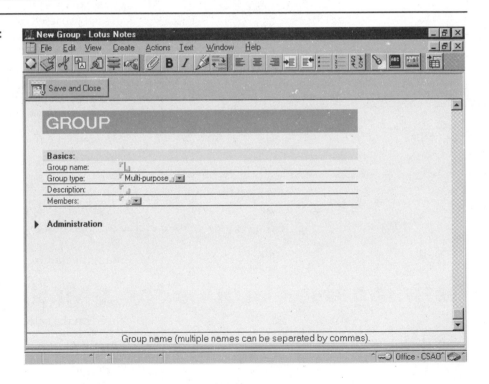

4. Type a name for the group into the Group Name field. For example, if you often send marketing reports to the same group of people, you might name this group MktReport. The group name specified here is the name you will

type into a recipient field of a mail document. (Notice that the Owner field contains your name.)

5. (*Optional*) Type a brief description of the group into the Description field. This description is useful if you define a lot of groups.

6. Type the full name of each person in the group in the Members field or click the icon to use the Address dialog box to add people or group names to the Members list.

7. Choose File ➤ Save—or press Esc—to exit and confirm. Close your Personal Address Book database.

NOTE You can enter names of other user groups as well as names of individuals. Groups can be nested five levels deep, but nesting beyond two levels may be confusing.

TIP If you send mail to a user group that includes yourself, you won't receive the memo unless you choose Save Only or Send and Save a Copy when you send the memo.

 A new timesaving option has been added to Notes 4.6 that allows you to create groups quickly. Now you can create a Group based on the creators and recipients of mail messages, meeting invitations, and tasks.

To define a user group based on an e-mail message, do the following:

1. Open your Mail database.

2. Select one or more documents that contain the names you want to include in the mailing list.

3. Choose Actions ➤ Copy Into ➤ New Group. A group document appears with the Members field already completed based on the selected documents.

4. In the Group Name field, type a name for the Group.

5. (*Optional*) In the Description field, type a brief description of the group.

6. (*Optional*) In the Members field, add or remove names.

7. Save and close the document.

Resolving Name Conflicts

The Ambiguous Names dialog box appears automatically if Notes finds more than one match for the name of a mail recipient specified in the To, Cc, or Bcc fields. When a name conflict occurs *within* your Public or Personal Address book or *between* your Public and Personal Address books, Notes displays all the possible names for you to select from when you choose Actions ➤ Send. For example, if you type **David**, the Notes Ambiguous Names dialog box displays all the *David*s in your Public and Personal Address books so you can select the one you want.

NOTE   When you send mail to someone who is *not* listed in *any* Address book on your mail server, you must type @ followed by the Notes domain name or external domain name (for example, Internet, ccMail) after the recipient's name. For example, to send a message to Kristen Tod who works for ABC Corp. via the InterNet, you need to type the following: **K Tod@ABC Corp.@InterNet**.

TIP   To check for name conflicts across all address books, make sure that the location document specifies Exhaustively Check All Address Books for the Recipient Name Lookup field. The default is to stop after the first match is found.

Using Distinguished Names

Notes can use, and your organization might use, *distinguished names* to differentiate people in the same organization who have exactly the same full name. If your organization began with Notes Release 3, it's probably using distinguished names; if earlier releases were installed, your system may or may not include distinguished names.

Distinguished names include extra information (such as department names) separated by slashes (/). For example, to distinguish three John Smiths working in the same company, each name could include extra information such as

John Smith/Sales/Sirrus

John Smith/Engineering/Sirrus

John Smith/Finance/Sirrus

If your organization uses distinguished names and you know someone's full distinguished name (for example, John Smith/Editor/Sirrus), you can type it directly into the Address field. You must type the full distinguished name including all slashes. You can also mix distinguished and nondistinguished names in the Address field.

If two people have the same full name and you don't know the distinguished name of the person you want to send a message to, Notes can provide the distinguished name. To send the message, enter a non-unique full name in the To field and either choose Actions ➤ Send or press F9. The Ambiguous Names dialog box appears to help you select the correct person. If your company doesn't use distinguished names, the Ambiguous Names dialog box differentiates between people with the same full name by location, for example,

> Marcus Aurelias (Sonoma Street)
>
> Marcus Aurelias (Hayes Valley)
>
> Marcus Aurelias (San Francisco)

To help you find people with non-unique names, you can select one of the following three options:

- **OK:** If the name you want appears in the list, select that name and then select OK to send the message.

- **Skip Name:** This option sends the message to all the other names specified in the field. Select this option if you're sending the message to a group that contains the problem name.

- **Cancel Sending:** This option cancels the message. Select this option if you see an obvious mistake you made in one of the names and want to correct it.

NOTE   Sometimes Notes administrators will put multiple spellings of people's names in the Public Address Book to resolve some of the problems surrounding not knowing how to spell difficult names.

Sending Mail

Once you've composed and addressed your mail message, sending it is a simple matter. You can either click the Send button, choose Actions ➤ Send, Actions ➤ Send and File, or press Esc. If you press Esc, the Close Window dialog box appears, displaying several options, as shown in Figure 11.15.

FIGURE 11.15:

The Close Window
dialog box

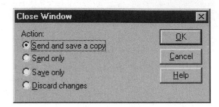

Although sending mail is usually a one-step process, remember you can take advantage of several options to keep your mail messages secure and to ensure that they get to their intended recipients using the Delivery Options button.

Saving Mail

You can save a mail memo and continue to work on it by choosing File ➤ Save, choosing the Save as Draft button, or pressing Ctrl+S while your memo is in progress.

To save a memo-in-progress and go on to other tasks, choose Actions ➤ Save as Draft. Notes saves the draft memo in your mail database. Later when you want to work on the memo, open your mail database and then select the Drafts view. Double-click the particular draft mail document you want to edit, or highlight the document and click the Edit Document button.

Signing Mail

When you send mail, you can "sign" it to assure the recipient that you are the author of the document. Signing a document in Notes attaches a unique electronic signature, derived from your User ID, to that document.

Notes gives you three ways to sign outgoing mail:

- Choose Actions ➤ Delivery Options. Select the Sign option in the Delivery Options dialog box and then click OK.

- Click the Delivery Actions button in the Action bar to display the Delivery Options dialog box.

- To sign all documents by default when you send them, choose File ➤ Tools ➤ User Preferences. Choose the Mail option. Select the Sign Sent Mail option in the User Preferences dialog box and then click OK (see Figure 11.16).

FIGURE 11.16:

You can choose the Sign Sent Mail option in the User Preferences dialog box when you want to sign all mail documents automatically.

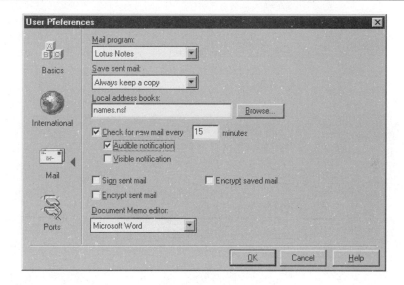

NOTE   You can always deselect signing for any document when you send it.

Encrypting Your Outgoing Mail

You can stop all those prying eyes from reading your incoming or outgoing mail by using the Notes encryption feature. *Encryption* is a technique by which Notes scrambles your outgoing and incoming messages so that only you (or the designated recipients) can read them. When you send mail, you can encrypt it to ensure that nobody except your recipients can read your memos while in transit, when stored in intermediate mail boxes, and on arrival in the recipient's mail file. You can also encrypt all of your saved mail and incoming mail automatically.

When you encrypt a document, Notes scrambles the information using the recipient's public key so that it can be decoded only by the recipient. A *public key* is a 600-character string of apparently random letters and numbers that's assigned to each new Notes user. Your public key is listed at the bottom of your Person record in your organization's Public Address Book. When you tell Notes to encrypt a message to another user, the contents of the message are manipulated mathematically using the recipient's public key to produce a scrambled and indecipherable message.

When you want to send encrypted information or someone wants to send you encrypted information, Notes gets the recipient's public key from the Public Address Book. If the recipient's public key isn't stored in the book for some reason, information can't be encrypted. In that case, you should send your key to the Notes administrator, who will paste it in the Public Address Book.

Transmission and Delivery Problems

Transmission problems and delivery failures fall into two categories: those that occur when you send a message and those that occur when Notes delivers it. In either case, Notes displays a message to help you deal with the problem.

As you learned in the section on Distinguished Names, transmission will fail if you type a name incorrectly or you type a non-unique name. Notes usually displays the error message when you try to send the document. However, recipient names that include explicit domain names (such as Kristen Tod@mecc) are not validated when you send them. Instead, Notes verifies the names when the document reaches the specified domain. If delivery is unsuccessful, you will receive a delivery failure report at that time.

In other situations where Notes can't deliver a mail memo, you receive a delivery failure report containing the recipient's name and the reason for the failure. Once you know what caused the problem, you can resend the document. When you succeed, the delivery failure report is removed from the mail document.

Some of the most common reasons for a delivery failure (and related error messages in the report) are:

- **User Name Not Unique:** Notes found two people with the same name in the Name & Address book. This message appears only when sending mail across domains and usually occurs if you use just a first name (Neil@Editorial) rather than a full name (Neil Edde@Editorial).

- **User Not Listed in Address Book:** The recipient is outside your domain. (If the recipient was in your domain, a message stating that the user name did not exist would appear when you tried to send the document.)

Continued on next page

- **No Route Found to Server X from Server Y:** Notes can't find a route on the network to the recipient's mail server. If the address is correct, report the problem to your Notes administrator.

- **Delivery Time Expired:** Mail delivery was delayed somewhere along the delivery path, usually for longer than twenty-four hours (by default). Report this error message to the Notes administrator.

- **Recipient's Name & Address Book Entry Does Not Specify a Mail File:** The recipient's mail database as specified in the public Name & Address book doesn't exist. You should report this problem to your Notes administrator.

To resend a mail document that was returned with a delivery failure report, open the delivery failure report or select it in a view. Choose Mail ➤ Send or click the Resend button in the Action bar when you are reading the Delivery Failure Report. The Mail Resend dialog box opens. Use this dialog box to resend a mail message that Notes was unable to deliver (and that is now marked DELIVERY FAILURE).

The To text box lists the recipients who didn't receive the original message. Correct or delete their names as necessary. Select Sign or Encrypt if you wish to use these options. Click the Send button. Notes will resend the original message without the delivery failure report.

Notes gives you two methods to encrypt outgoing mail:

- To encrypt a document when you send it, choose Actions ➤ Delivery Options. Select Encrypt and then click OK.

- To encrypt all documents by default when you send them, choose File ➤ Tools ➤ User Preferences. Choose the Mail option. Select Encrypt Sent Mail and then click OK.

NOTE   You can selectively deselect encryption for any document when you send it.

To encrypt and sign every document you send, add **SecureMail=1** to your NOTES.INI file. Exit and restart Notes. Adding SecureMail=1 to NOTES.INI removes the Sign and Encrypt checkboxes from all dialog boxes but automatically encrypts and signs all outgoing mail.

If you want to stop automatic signing and encryption of documents, just remove SecureMail=1 from your NOTES.INI file and then restart Notes.

TIP   If you aren't accustomed to working in files like NOTES.INI, ask your administrator or another knowledgeable person for assistance.

Receiving Mail

When you receive mail, you read your mail messages just like you read any Notes document. You choose a particular view, select a memo, and open and read it. When you select your mail database, eight standard mail folders and views are available to you, along with any private folders and views you may have added. Choose View ➤ Go To. The default folders and views are shown in Figure 11.17. Highlight the Inbox folder and click OK to display a listing of all the mail messages that you've received.

TIP   All mail messages remain in your Inbox folder until you delete them or move them to a different folder.

FIGURE 11.17:

To read any mail messages that you've received, choose the Inbox folder from the Go To dialog box.

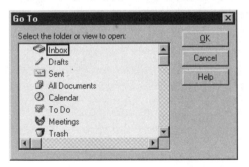

TIP   Here's a faster way to read your mail: Click the mail icon on the far right of the status bar and then choose either Scan Unread Mail or Open Mail.

Adding a Name to Your Personal Address Book

When you receive a mail message from a person whose name is not included in your Personal Address Book, you can easily add the new name while you're reading the message. Simply display the message or select the message in the View pane. Choose Actions ➤ Mail Tools ➤ Add Sender to Address Book. Notes automatically adds the person's name to your Personal Address Book.

TIP   You can select multiple messages in the View pane and then add their senders' names to your Personal Address Book at the same time. After you select the messages, choose Actions ➤ Mail Tools ➤ Add Sender to Address Book.

Replying to Mail

The ability to reply *immediately* to mail you receive is the foremost benefit of Notes Mail. Some people might argue that an "organized" person always performs those tasks that can be completed immediately, leaving the more complex ones for later. The same people might also say that since you send and receive mail through your computer, you don't have any excuse for delaying your replies. Mail is stored on your system, waiting for your responses.

You may decide not to reply right away—or not at all—to a mail memo. However, be forewarned that Notes will notify the sender when you receive the mail and when you open it if the sender asked for a delivery report and a return receipt. Unfortunately, sender notification is another handy feature that Notes Mail provides.

Replying to a mail memo is easy. There are several different options available when replying to a mail message.

If you do not want any excerpts from the original mail message, choose Create ➤ Reply or click the Reply button. A copy of the subject from the original mail message (prepended with RE) will appear in the subject line. Complete the reply memo just as you would any other mail memo and send it as usual.

To include the entire memo in your reply, choose Create ➤ Reply with History or click the Reply with History button. A copy of the subject from the original mail message (prepended with RE) will appear in the subject line. Also, a complete copy of the original mail message will appear in a collapsible section in the body of the new mail message. Add or remove whatever comments you want, complete the reply memo just as you would any other mail memo, and send it as usual.

As stated earlier, a new option has been added that is similar to a reply. The Copy Into option will place an exact copy of the original mail message in the new mail memo (this includes both the subject and body of the memo). In addition, the new memo will be addressed to all of the original intended recipients. To create a copy of the original memo, choose Actions ➤ Copy Into ➤ New Memo. Change whatever information you deem necessary and send it as usual.

TIP Remember that you can also create a new calendar entry or task from any existing mail message using the Actions ➤ Copy Into ➤ New Calendar Entry/New Task menu options.

Forwarding Mail

The Forward command lets you forward a copy of any open or highlighted documents to one or more Notes users. Forwarding a document is just like writing any other mail memo except that Notes automatically inserts the open (or selected) document into the body of the forwarded document (just like the Reply with History except the subject line remains the same and the To field is left blank).

To forward a Notes document, open the document you want to forward or select one or more documents in a view. Choose Actions ➤ Forward (or click the Forward button) and complete the address fields as you would in any mail memo. Edit the body of the document if you wish and then send as usual. If you want to save a copy for yourself, you must add your name to one of the recipient lists (To, Cc, or Bcc).

TIP If you want to combine several short documents in your mail database, select them all in the view, choose Actions ➤ Forward, enter yourself as the To recipient, and save. Notes copies all the documents, one after another, into one new document.

New Mail Notification

You can choose if and when to be notified when you receive new mail. One option is to set Notes to beep and display a notification message when you receive new mail.

To set up new mail notification, choose File ➤ Tools ➤ User Preferences. Select the Mail option to display the Mail Options dialog box. Select the Check for New Mail Every <*Number*> Minutes option and enter a number (of minutes) that Notes should wait before notifying you (the default is 15 minutes). Select Audible Notification, Visible Notification, or both. Click OK.

When these options are enabled, the following actions occur:

- A beep sounds when new Notes Mail arrives.

- The status bar displays the message "New mail has been delivered to you" when you receive new Notes Mail.

- A small envelope icon appears on the far right end of the status bar. You can open your mail file by clicking the envelope and selecting Open Mail.

- If you minimize the Notes window, the Notes icon changes to a small envelope when you receive new mail.

To stop Notes from notifying you when mail arrives, deselect the Check for New Mail Every <Number> Minutes option. Deselection occurs after 30 seconds.

TIP   If you get tired of the generic "beep" for an audible mail notification, you can change it. Just type **NEWMAILTUNE=c:\MyWav\mail.wav** in your NOTES.INI file. Just change the drive, path, and wav file name to whatever wav file you want. Restart Notes and you will be notified with the new sound whenever mail arrives.

Resolving Common Mail View Problems

You may sometimes receive the same memo twice. The reason is usually because you're listed in at least two user groups. When someone sends a message to two of these groups, you receive the memo twice. Unfortunately, Notes doesn't compare the groups to remove duplicate names because groups are used for several purposes other than mail. For example, a member of both the Finance and Executive groups might have her or his mail filtered so that an assistant reads incoming Finance memos but not Executive memos. Removing duplicate names might inadvertently remove this user's name from the wrong list.

Also, the computations needed to remove duplicate names can easily grow beyond the system's capacity. For example, suppose the Finance group contained Accounting and Control subgroups and the Executive group contained Officers and Management. The number of possible combinations to check could grow very fast, affecting system performance.

You may wonder why new mail doesn't always appear when you receive a New Mail message. If you receive a new mail memo while a Mail view is open, you must refresh the view to see any new memos. To do so, simply press F9 (or choose View ➤ Refresh). Any new memos will then appear in the view; also, any memos you had marked for deletion will disappear.

Sending Mail from SmartSuite 97

You can send Notes Mail from within any Lotus product that runs under Windows 95 or Windows NT. You must be running Notes plus at least one of the following products:

- Lotus 1-2-3 for Windows

- Lotus Freelance Graphics for Windows

- Lotus Word Pro

- Lotus Approach

You can install these products in any order, following the instructions that come with each product. You don't have to do anything extra.

TeamMail

TeamMail works with your current electronic mail system to allow you to send and receive mail messages from within Word Pro. Using TeamMail, you can:

- Send a simple text message and distribute it to one or more people.

- Send a message with part of a document or an entire document.

- Route a document from one person to the next.

- Track the progress of a routed message by having a mail message sent to you each time a recipient forwards your document to the next recipient.

- Distribute an entire document to members of a workgroup using TeamReview. This gives you access to the review and comment tools.

- Save a distribution route and use it to quickly send messages to commonly used names and addresses.

To use TeamMail, do the following:

1. Open the file you want to send.

2. Select File ➤ TeamMail and the TeamMail dialog box will be displayed (as shown in Figure 11.18). Select whether you want to send a message or send a message with the file attached. Click the OK button.

3.   If prompted, type in your password and click the OK button.

4.   Select the individuals to route the mail message to, enter a subject, and enter a message as shown in Figure 11.19. If you do not know the recipient's mail address, click the Address button and the Mail Address box will be displayed.

5.   Click the Send button and your mail will be sent.

FIGURE 11.18:

The TeamMail dialog box

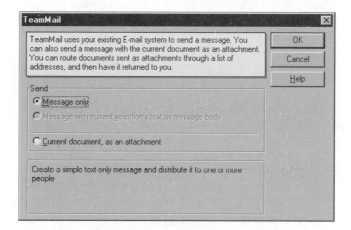

FIGURE 11.19:

The TeamMail Options dialog box

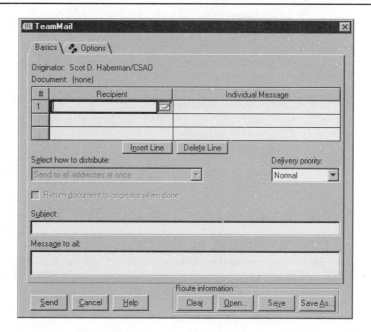

The options in the Send Mail dialog box vary depending on whether you are sending a file attachment with your mail message or just a mail message. If sending an attachment, you can also select to send the file to everyone at once or route the file one at a time (serial route). You can also select if you want the document returned back to you when the route is completed.

TeamReview

TeamReview lets you automate the process of reviewing documents for changes. You can assign which reviewers you want to edit the current document. For example, if several people worked together on a proposal to a client, you can send a copy of the proposal to each person who worked on it.

You can set options for the editing rights for each reviewer, such as whether or not a reviewer can edit in the current version or in a new version.

Then you can select a method for distributing the document to each reviewer, such as saving it to a file or sending it through e-mail. If you send the document via e-mail, you can send it to all reviewers simultaneously or route it to one reviewer at a time. If you send a separate copy of the document to each reviewer, you can use Word Pro's TeamConsolidate function to reconcile each editor's changes into a single document.

Like TeamMail, TeamReview works with your current electronic mail system. To use TeamReview, do the following:

1. Open the file you want to send.

2. Select File ➤ TeamReview, and the TeamReview Assistant dialog box will be displayed positioned on the Who tab (as shown in Figure 11.20). Type in all of the intended recipients for the review. Once completed, click on the Next button.

TIP   For verification on the TeamReview process, always use the E-mail login since this is the most secure.

TIP   If you regularly send documents for review to the same group of people, you can save the information and recall it at any time.

FIGURE 11.20:

The TeamReview Assistant
dialog box

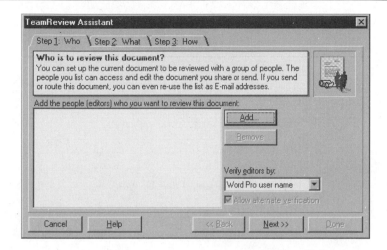

3. The What tab allows you to define the specific options for each reviewer assigned to this document. You can set specific options for all reviewers or by specific reviewers. Once completed, click the Next button.

4. The How tab allows you to specify the method of distribution. The two options that you are concerned about are Sending via E-Mail or Routing via E-Mail. Once completed, click on the Done button.

5. From this point forward, follow the same procedures as defined for Team-Mail (it uses the TeamMail addressing dialog box).

Converting Mail from cc:Mail to Notes and from Notes to cc:Mail

A Notes Mail database can be converted to a cc:Mail mailbox, and vice versa. This conversion is generally performed by your Notes or cc:Mail administrator, but the process may have been set up so that you can perform your own conversion. Add the Mailbox Conversion database to your Workspace and open it. (Ask your Notes administrator where you can find the database.) Then follow these steps:

1. Choose Create ➤ Conversion Request. The Conversion Request document appears. Select one of these options:

    • **cc:Mail to Notes:** Converts your cc:Mail mailbox to a Notes Mail file.

- **Notes to cc:Mail:** Converts your Notes Mail file to a cc:Mail mailbox.

- **Notes Name & Address Book to cc:Mail:** Converts Notes Group lists in your Personal Address Book to cc:Mail private mailing lists. You should do this conversion after you convert your Notes Mail database to cc:Mail.

2. Specify the date and time to start the conversion. Use the same format as the default date and time.

NOTE   Converting mail files during a nonpeak time (such as overnight or on the weekend) is less disruptive than converting during peak hours. Specify the earliest date of mail messages to convert (*optional*). The feature is known as Message Cutoff Date. If no date is entered, all messages are converted.

---

3. Enter your full name as it appears in the Notes Address Book.

4. Enter your cc:Mail password.

5. Press ↵.

6. Select the name of your cc:Mail Post Office.

7. (*Optional*) Choose File ➤ Attachment and attach the Personal Address Book database if you are converting your Notes Personal Address Book to a cc:Mail mailing list.

8. Press Esc to save and exit the document.

9. Open the Conversion Status view of the Mail Conversion database at any time to see whether your mail file is in the Pending, Processed, or Failure category.

Using Notes with cc:Mail and Other VIM-Compliant Mail Systems

You can use Notes and any Windows mail program separately. However, if you want to use the products together (to access your mail program from within Notes and send Notes documents using your mail program), you must use Notes with a VIM-compliant mail system, such as cc:Mail or Microsoft Exchange.

WARNING *VIM* stands for Vendor Independent Messaging. When a product supports VIM, it offers certain mail functions and complies with specific technical standards. Your workgroup can support the use of Notes Mail along with multiple VIM-compliant mail systems, but only one mail product should be present on your workstation at a time. You can install the mail product either before or after you install Notes.

If You Don't Use Notes Mail

Several Notes features aren't available to you when you don't use Notes Mail. For example, the Actions ➤ Address command isn't available. However, your mail product probably has a similar capability.

The Send User ID commands aren't available either. (These commands include mailing encryption keys and requesting certificates by mail.) You can, however, export an encryption key. Choose File ➤ Tools ➤ User ID. The User ID dialog box appears. Select the encryption key that you want to export. Click the Export button. You can get new certificates by delivering a safe copy of your User ID to your certifier. Choose File ➤ Tools ➤ User ID. Select the More Options option. Click the Create Safe Copy button. You can also send and receive Notes encryption keys as cc:Mail attachments.

The Edit ➤ Unread Marks ➤ Scan Unread command is not available for use in your mail file. The Mail options in the User Preferences dialog box—signing and encrypting mail, new mail notification, and mail file location—are not available in the Mail Setup dialog box.

In addition, dial-up mail, including the File ➤ Mobile ➤ Call Server and File ➤ Mobile ➤ Hang Up commands, aren't available in cc:Mail. However, cc:Mail users have a similar remote use capability. Signing a memo isn't available when the Forward command is used. However, you can sign Notes documents sent using the Send command if the mail product supports it.

Notes rich text is converted to rich text format except with cc:Mail, which maintains Notes rich text format very closely. However, tables and DDE links are converted to ASCII text (plain text).

Changing Your Mail System

When Notes was installed on your workstation, you or your Notes administrator had the opportunity to select either Lotus Notes, cc:Mail, Other VIM Mail, or None. However, you can change your mail system at any time. Install your new mail product (skip this step if you're changing from an alternative product to Notes Mail or from any mail product to none). Launch Notes and choose File ➤ Tools ➤ User Preferences. Select the Mail option. From the Mail program pull-down menu, select the mail product you want to use.

Reading and Sending Mail

When you use a VIM-compliant mail system, you'll see the following commands on the Notes Mail menu (some mail systems may not use all commands):

Command	Action
Open	Launches the mail product. Notes remains open.
Forward	Converts the contents of open or selected Notes documents to text or rich text and opens the mail product's standard window or dialog box so you can address and send the text as a mail memo.
Forward as Attachment	Converts the open or selected Notes documents to a database and attaches the database to the message you're sending. You see a dialog box in which you can provide additional information about the attached database (for example, in cc:Mail, you see the Addressing dialog box).
Send	Converts the current or selected Notes document(s) into an encapsulated Notes database and attaches it to a mail memo that you address and send as usual.

Opening Encapsulated Databases Sent to You

Encapsulation is the process Notes uses to store a Notes document in a database attachment when you send a message to cc:Mail or another VIM-compliant mail system. If you are using cc:Mail as your mail system in Notes, the cc:Mail recipient normally receives the message in a Notes database attachment.

If you want the cc:Mail user who is receiving your message to see the message in text format, you can use a special Notes field called MailFormat. Check with your Notes administrator for information on using the MailFormat field.

Notes can encapsulate a database within an attachment. If your mail program supports direct launching of attachments (as cc:Mail does), double-click the attachment icon within the message. The mail product copies the attachment, launches Notes, and opens the encapsulated database. You can also copy the attachment to disk, and at the DOS command line, start Notes and specify the file with the Notes database extension .NSF. For example:

```
NOTES C:\DATA\DOCUMENT.NSF
```

You can create a database just for storing these documents and then copy the documents from encapsulated databases to this new database (or to any other database on your Workspace).

Using Notes Mail from Microsoft Office 97

You can use Notes Mail from within any Microsoft Office 97 program—Word or Excel, for example. During the setup procedure, you create a profile that lets you use the Notes Service Providers for the Messaging Application Programming Interface (MAPI).

You can also use the Windows 95 and Windows NT versions of mail-enabled Microsoft programs and Microsoft Exchange to address and send messages to Notes users, or you can use Exchange to access a Notes Mail database.

Creating a Notes Mail Profile

Before you can access your Notes mail database from Exchange or send a mail message from any of the Microsoft products, you first need to set up your system appropriately by creating a Notes Mail Profile. A profile contains configuration information, such as the location of incoming mail, your Personal Address Book, and other information services that you can use. This profile lets you use the Notes Service Providers for the Messaging Application Programming Interface (MAPI).

To create a Notes Mail Profile, follow these steps:

1. Open the Control Panel and click on the Mail or Mail and Fax icon. This will display the Mail Properties dialog box as shown in Figure 11.21 (you can also right-click the Inbox icon on your desktop and select the Properties menu item). In this example, Windows Messaging has been installed but never used for mail or faxing, so the Mail Properties dialog box is shown by default.

2. Click on the Add button. This will display the Inbox Setup Wizard dialog box as shown in Figure 11.22. Select the Manually Configure Information Services radio button and click the Next button.

3. When prompted, enter a profile name to distinguish that this will use Lotus Notes (a good name would be Lotus Notes Profile) and click the Next button.

4. A Properties dialog box will be displayed with the name of your profile in the title as shown in Figure 11.23. Click the Add button.

FIGURE 11.23:

The Lotus Notes Profile Properties dialog box

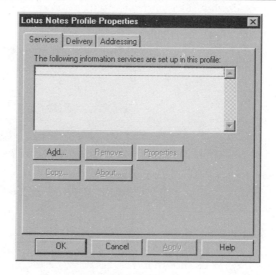

5. The Add Services to Profile dialog box will display. Select Lotus Notes mail as shown in Figure 11.24 and click OK. You should be prompted for your Notes password. Enter your password and click OK.

FIGURE 11.24:

The Add Services to Profile dialog box

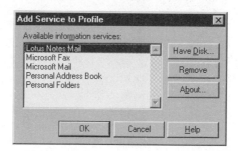

NOTE   If you do not see an option for Lotus Notes Mail on the Inbox Setup Wizard dialog box, you probably installed Notes before Microsoft Exchange and other Microsoft Office applications. To clear up this problem, you need to manually merge the contents of the NOTESPIS.INF file (located in the Windows directory or Notes directory) with the MAPISVC.INF file (located in the Windows system directory).

6. The Lotus Notes Mail service has been added to your profile. Now just a few more things. Select the Delivery tab. The first selection box should have Lotus Notes Message Store selected and the second box should have Lotus Notes Transport selected, as shown in Figure 11.25.

FIGURE 11.25:

The Lotus Notes Profile Properties dialog box Delivery tab

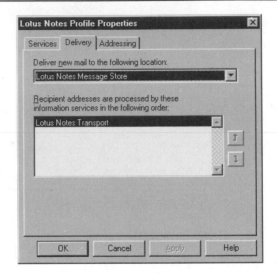

7. Select the Addressing tab. Make sure that your address books have been selected. You can add and remove them with the Add and Remove buttons. If everything is OK, select the OK button and you are finished.

You should have been returned back to the original Mail Properties dialog box, but instead of being empty, it should contain the profile that you just created. Make sure that this new profile is selected as the Default when using Windows Messaging. That is all there is to it. Just click the Close button and you are ready to start using your Notes mail database from Exchange or other Microsoft applications.

Using Mail-Enabled Microsoft Applications in Office 97

After you create the profile for the Notes Service Providers, you can use the mail-enabled features in Microsoft products. To use the mail features, open a document and choose File ➤ Send To ➤ Mail Recipient. This option will open the mail interface. You will notice that the current document is an attachment to the mail message (you do not have to save the document first). Address the mail message and click on the Send button (the moving envelope) as shown in Figure 11.26.

FIGURE 11.26:

The Excel Mail Recipient interface

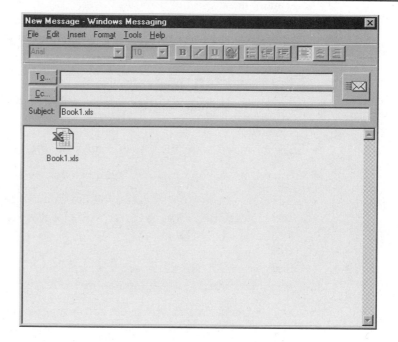

When you address messages, you can choose recipients from any address book. You can address messages to individual recipients, distribution lists, and Notes groups. The Notes Address Book Provider supports prefix matching and ambiguous name resolution.

Using Microsoft Exchange with Notes

If you are using Microsoft Exchange with the Lotus Notes Service Providers, you have access to Notes address books and to your Notes Mail database (this includes all your folders and views). You can create, read, forward, and reply to messages using the same commands you normally use in Exchange. However, you will be accessing the contents of your Notes Mail database.

When you address messages, you can choose recipients from any address book. You can address messages to individual recipients, distribution lists, and Notes groups. The Notes Address Book Provider supports prefix matching and ambiguous name resolution. It also supports an Advanced Search dialog box, which you can access by selecting the Address Book ➤ Tools ➤ Find menu items in Exchange.

You can do the following using Exchange:

- Create rich text messages and then store them and send them using Notes.

- Attach files to messages by using the Exchange commands Insert ➤ File as Text and Insert ➤ File as Attachment.

- Read messages that were encrypted or signed in Notes (but not verify the signatures).

- Create, move, copy, file, delete, read, and edit messages in folders.

- Create, move, copy, rename, and delete folders in your Notes Mail database.

- Access most of your views and folders. You can also access personal folders and views if their designs correspond closely to the default information folder view in Exchange.

To view the size of a message in Exchange, select File ➤ Properties, make a change to one of the properties, and apply the change.

In certain circumstances when you start Exchange, you may notice that the contents of the Inbox do not display your most current memos. Refresh the contents of the Inbox by clicking a different folder. Then click the Inbox to view all memos.

WARNING   Do not change the design of any folder or view in your Notes Mail file by switching the placement of columns. Results of viewing the mail file in Exchange are unknown.

Please observe the following cautions if you use Microsoft Exchange with Notes:

- Select the Lotus Notes Transport provider for Delivery options; without this option, you cannot transfer mail between Notes users and non-Notes users. This selection is made by default during profile setup and should not be removed or changed.

- Select at least one Notes Address Book for Addressing options to check names of recipients.

In addition, you should be aware of the following limitations:

- Exchange does not support an action for undeleting memos filed under the Deleted Items (Trash) folder. To work around this limitation, create a folder in the mail file where you can drag and drop memos should you decide to remove them from the Trash folder. Therefore, if you set the Exchange option Empty the 'Deleted Items' Folder upon Exiting, you should move the sent memo from the Trash folder to the other folder to prevent the memo from being deleted.

- Exchange does not support a folder type similar to Drafts. When you create a draft memo in Exchange by saving it, a copy of the memo gets posted to the Inbox, as well as to Drafts.

- Each time you send messages from Microsoft mail-enabled applications or Exchange, the Notes Service Providers create a temporary file with the generic name *~nmcxxxxx.tmp*. To ensure that temporary files are written to the same place, create a directory off the root of your hard drive called C:\TMP. Later, you can easily locate and delete files of this type to gain space on your hard drive.

Managing Your Mail

Once you save a few dozen mail memos and try to find a specific memo, you will want to manage your mail for easier retrieval. Notes gives you several ways to manage your mail:

- Organize your saved memos by moving them into existing folders.

- Change the subject lines of saved mail memos.

- Limit the size of your mail file.

- Create private folders for your mail messages.

- Sort your mail messages within a folder or view.

- Full text index your mail file on the server or your portable computer.

Organizing Your Mail

Notes Mail comes with several default mail folders and views in which to organize your saved mail memos:

- The **Inbox folder** automatically stores all messages that you receive. Messages remain in the Inbox until you delete them or move them to a different folder.

- The **Drafts folder** automatically stores all messages that you save without sending. You can go back later to these messages, make any changes you want, and then send them. After you send one of these messages, Notes removes it from the Drafts folder. If you save the message when you send it, Notes places it in the Sent folder.

NOTE   If you create stationery, Notes stores the stationery in the Drafts folder. See the "Creating Stationery" section later in this chapter.

- The **Sent view** automatically stores all messages that you save when you send them.

- The **All Documents view** shows all the messages currently in your mail database.

- The **Meetings view** shows a complete list of all your meetings. These documents are not shown using a calendar view. If you want to view your appointments and so on by day, week, or month, use the Calendar icon.

- The **Trash folder** lets you store messages that you want to delete. After placing messages in this folder, you can later delete them or remove them from the trash.

- The **Temporary Export Certificates** store all export certificates that you create. For more information about these types of documents, refer to the Help documentation.

- The **Discussion Threads view** shows messages grouped with their replies and lets you follow an entire conversation.

- The **Archiving view** contains a list of the documents that Notes archived from this database, if any.

TIP   You can create and use as many hierarchical mail folders and views as you want.

Figure 11.27 shows the mail folders and views. Notes displays any unread memos in red text (on a color monitor) and places an asterisk next to them in the left margin of the view.

FIGURE 11.27:

You can organize your mail using the different folders and views that are available when you select your mail database.

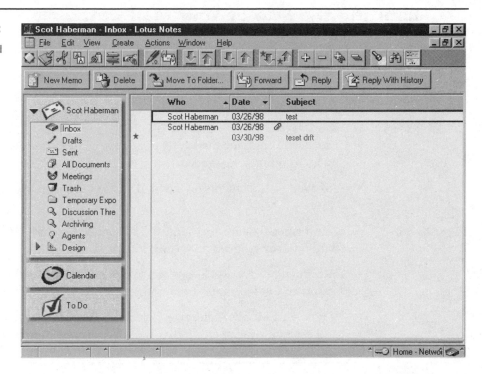

Changing the Subject Line of a Mail Memo

The more specific you make the Subject line, the easier it will be for you to find the memo in the view. To change the Subject line of a mail memo, select the document in the view and press Ctrl+E (or choose Actions ➤ Edit Document) to edit the document. At this point you can enter some meaningful text into the Subject field. For example, change the Subject line:

```
Date: 08/13/98 10:30:23 AM
Subject: Presentation
```

to this:

```
Date: 08/13/98 10:30:23 AM
Subject: Marketing presentation—results of product focus groups
```

Save the memo without sending it by pressing Ctrl+S (or choosing File ➤ Save), and exit from the memo by pressing Esc. Days, weeks, or months later, you'll be able to find this memo fast by glancing at the subject that appears in the view.

Limiting the Size of Your Mail Database

Mail databases tend to grow very big quickly and can take up valuable space on your computer. You might even notice that as your mail database grows—and this rule applies to any database—the system takes longer to open views and documents. Your system starts performing sluggishly. However, you can control the size of your mail database by performing these housekeeping tasks routinely:

- Browse through the mail you've saved at regular intervals and delete those memos you no longer need.

- Save large attachments on the mail server rather than locally on your hard drive.

- Cut memos that are very large or have large attachments from a local database on your system and paste them into a database on the server.

- Export large "goodies"—such as scanned images, graphics, and especially sound and video clips—from your computer to the server.

- If you are a Mobile Notes user, select the Truncate Large Documents option and remove attachments in the Tools Replicate dialog box.

TIP

The key to controlling the size of mail databases is to teach people in organizations that they need to change their paradigms of how they share information. If people are sending many attachments to members of a workgroup, editing these attachments, and then resending them to everyone in the workgroup, they would be better served by a Notes database (a Doc Library) that would allow a group of people to work together on a common project without filling up their mail files.

Creating a Private Folder for Your Saved Mail Messages

You might want to create a special private folder in which to store specific mail messages you want to save. (Remember that the Inbox folder automatically stores all mail messages that you receive.) You can create a private folder in your mail database (any database for that matter) in which you have Reader access. You can base the folder's design on any view already in the database or create the folder from scratch. Select or open your mail database and follow these steps:

1. Choose Create ➤ Folder. The Create Folder dialog box appears, as shown in Figure 11.28.

FIGURE 11.28:

The Create Folder dialog box gives you the option of basing a new folder's design on an existing folder or view, or creating the folder's design from scratch.

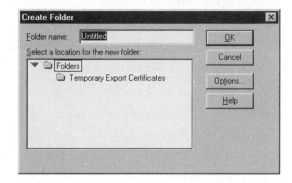

2. Enter a name for the folder in the Folder Name box.

NOTE

To place the folder inside an existing folder, click that folder in the Select a Location for the New Folder list.

---

3. Click the Options button and do one of the following:

    •   To base the design on an existing folder or view, click a folder or view in the Inherit columns from list. When you open up this dialog box, it will default to the Default view for the database, which in this case is All Documents.

    •   To create the folder from scratch, click Blank. Then select the Design now option. (If you don't design the folder now, you won't be able to store any mail documents inside the folder until you do so.)

    •   Select the Design Now checkbox if you want to automatically be placed in the new folder in design mode.

4. Click OK twice. Your new folder appears in the Folders and Views folder (unless you selected another folder to place the new folder inside).

NOTE

You can customize the folder's design. Simply select the folder in your mail database's view. Choose Actions ➤ Folder Options ➤ Design. The Design Folder window opens. Build the folder the way you want and press Ctrl+S to save the folder's design. (See Chapter 19 for more information on building folders.)

Moving Mail Messages into Your Private Folder

You can move the messages you want to save into your private folder to help manage your mail. You can also add the same message to more than one folder.

Moving a Mail Message by Dragging Its Title   Follow these steps to move a mail message by dragging its title:

1. Open the Inbox folder (or another folder) that contains the message.

2. Select the mail message you want to move. You can also select multiple messages if you want to move all of them.

3. Do one of the following:

    •   To add the mail message to a different folder and remove it from the current folder, drag the message to the folder you want.

    •   To add the mail message to a different folder and also leave it in the current folder, hold down the Ctrl key while you drag the message to the folder you want.

TIP
To auto expand collapsed hierarchical folders, simply drag the documents to the triangle icon. The hierarchical folders will expand so that you have access to the second-tier folders.

Moving a Mail Message That You're Reading   Follow these steps to move a mail message that you're currently reading:

1. Open your mail database view.

2. Open the folder that contains the mail message.

3. Double-click the mail message to open it.

4. Click the Move to Folder button. The Move to Folder dialog box appears.

5. Select the folder in which you want to save the message, such as the new folder you created earlier.

TIP
You can create a new folder on the fly. Click the Create a New Folder button in the Move to Folder dialog box. The Create Folder dialog box appears. Enter a name for the folder in the Folder Name box. Select a location for the new folder; otherwise, the new folder will automatically appear at the top level of the Folders hierarchy. Click Options and then choose an existing folder or view on which to base the new folder's design, or choose Blank to create the new folder from scratch. Click OK twice.

---

6.   Do one of the following:

- Click the Move button to move the message from its current folder to the new folder.

- Click the Add button to place the message in the new folder and leave a copy in the original folder.

You can move a message between folders, but you cannot move a message out of a view. Views use selection formulas built into the database design; folders are user-driven organizational tools that allow you to collect documents.

Sorting Mail Messages within a Folder or View

As you receive and save mail messages, you'll want to be able to sort them in some way, either by date, topic, or the name of the sender. The same goes for mail messages that you send and save. You'll want to access saved mail messages quickly. Otherwise, you'll spend a lot of time scrolling through a view to find a message that you want to read.

You can sort a view by clicking a column heading only if the designer (yourself or someone else) has set one or more columns to allow sorting. A small triangle appears on the column heading or any column that allows sorting (an up arrow sorts in ascending order, and a down arrow sorts in descending order). Double triangles allow you to sort the column in both ascending and descending order.

NOTE   See Chapter 20 for more information about setting columns to allow sorting.

Sorting is easy. To sort a view by a particular column, simply click that column's heading. For example, click a Topic column heading to sort mail messages in alphabetical order by topic, or click the Date column heading to sort mail messages in ascending order by date.

Archiving Your Mail

Notes automatically archives (or stores) selected mail messages in the Archiving view in your mail database. If you need to retrieve and read a particular mail message at a later time, you can find it in the archive. Locating an old message (or a series of old messages) can be crucial if you need to track down colleagues' communications about a topic or if you want to follow a thread of discussion about an issue. When you select the Archiving view, Notes displays a list of archived documents based on default settings, such as what documents to archive, when to archive documents, and where to archive the documents.

If you want to change the archive settings, select the Archiving view and follow these steps:

1. Click the Setup Archive button. The Archive Profile document appears.

2. Select the Archive Expired Documents option (if it's not already selected) and enter a number in the After [ ] Days field. The default is five days.

3. Select the Archive Documents That Have No Activity option *only* if you want Notes to archive mail messages on which you no longer need to take any action. Then enter a number in the After [ ] Days field. The default is 365 days.

4. Select Generate an Archive Log each time an archive option occurs *only* if you need a log of archive activity.

TIP

Creating a log is beneficial because it allows you to search your mail file and quickly find documents that are in your mail file or that have been archived.

5. Select the Include Document Links option if you want Notes to include a link to the document in the archive log.

NOTE

The Include Document Links option allows you to locate and access archived messages quickly. (It is similar to a Newsletter summary document.) If you are going to generate an archive log, you should definitely select this option.

6. To specify a location where you want Notes to save the archived mail documents, click on the Specify Archive Location Action button. You can choose to create the archive locally or on a server. If creating on a server, you can also specify which server. You must specify the database full path name in the Path Name field. The default name is mail \a_[name of mail database].nsf. For example, mail\a_kenbro.nsf. Click the OK button to save the Archive Profile Location information.

TIP

Your archive database can become very large very quickly if you archive *every* mail message you receive. Most of us who work in companies that depend on e-mail for communication receive a lot of mail—and most of the mail doesn't demand any action. Perhaps the mail you receive won't need any special action other than reading it and maybe responding to it. Therefore, you might not need to archive all your mail. Be selective in deciding what mail to archive, especially if you're saving the archived mail messages locally on your workstation.

8. Click the Save Profile button if you changed any setting. If you press Esc, a message box appears, asking you if you want to save your changes.

NOTE

The first time you enter the default settings in the Archive Profile document and then save the new settings, Notes must create the archive database for you before it can archive mail documents. When Notes finishes creating the database, the Archive Setup message box appears, notifying you that the Archive database has been created.

TIP

If you have any questions about any of the archive profile fields, click the Instructions Action button for a description of each option.

Archiving Your Mail Messages Manually

You can also archive your mail messages whenever you want. You don't have to wait for Notes to perform the task. Open the folder that contains the message you want to archive and follow these steps:

1. Select the messages you want you archive.

2. Choose Actions ➤ Mail Tools ➤ Archive Selected Documents.

    That's all there is to it.

TIP

You might want to get in the habit of manually archiving messages once a week, say, every Friday afternoon before you leave work. Save this task for when you have several mail documents that you want to archive at the same time. By following a housekeeping routine, you'll be assured that the important mail messages you receive are safe and organized for you to access later.

Encrypting Incoming Mail That You Save

Earlier we discussed encrypting outgoing mail you send to people. You can also encrypt your incoming mail and saved mail. Encrypting your incoming mail increases security, especially for confidential mail messages.

An unwritten e-mail rule states that you should never send or save mail messages that you don't want anyone else to read or that you consider highly confidential. If you have something personal or private to say, you should speak to the person directly. However, because of time zone differences and physical distances, speaking to a person on the telephone or in person isn't always feasible (or possible). Encrypting incoming mail that you choose to save gives you a little added security.

To encrypt saved mail, choose File ➤ Tools ➤ User Preferences. Choose the Mail option. Select the Encrypt Saved Mail option. Click OK. When you enable Encrypt Saved Mail, your saved copy is always encrypted whether you send it to others encrypted. Encrypting saved mail effectively prevents anyone from reading your mail on the server, even the server administrator or others with access to the server.

The Encrypt Incoming Mail option provides additional security for incoming mail from outside your system to your mail server. This option prevents any access to your mail when it reaches your mail server, either by administrative access to your mail database or by unauthorized access to the server.

WARNING   Incoming mail cannot be encrypted when using the following gateways: SSW (SoftSwitch), MHS, and cc:Mail.

To encrypt incoming mail, you must modify your Person document in the Public Address Book:

1. Open the Public Address Book.

2. Choose the People folder to display the People view and then open the Person document that contains your name.

3. Choose Actions ➤ Edit Person. The Edit Person dialog box appears.

4. Type Yes in the Encrypt Incoming Mail field.

5. Press Ctrl+S to save the document.

6. Close the Public Address Book.

The Notes administrator can also set this option for all users. This selection takes precedence over the setting of an individual user.

> **NOTE**
> If you cannot type **Yes** in the Encrypt Incoming Mail field in the Person document, see your Notes administrator.

Using the Notes Mail Tools

The two Notes Mail tools discussed earlier—adding a new name to your Personal Address Book while reading a message and archiving selected mail documents manually—enable you to perform their respective tasks on the fly. Notes also provides four more tools that can automate and streamline routine mail tasks:

- Out of Office
- Choose Letterhead
- Create Stationery
- Delegation Profile

Notifying People Automatically When You Are Out of the Office

You can tell Notes to respond to messages that you receive while you are out of the office. Notes sends a reply saying that you are out of the office and indicates when you will return. In your absence, Notes sends no more than one message to any person who sends mail to you, even if a person sends several messages to you. This feature eliminates the annoyance of repeatedly receiving reply messages that a person is out of the office.

> **NOTE**
> To use the Out of Office feature, you must have access to run Agents (macros) on the server that contains your mail database. If you aren't sure you have adequate access, see your Notes administrator.

To enable the Out of Office feature, select your mail database and follow these steps:

1. Choose Actions ➤ Mail Tools ➤ Out of Office.

2. Enter the dates on which you are leaving and returning in the Out of Office Profile document, shown in Figure 11.29.

FIGURE 11.29:

The Out of Office Profile document enables you to indicate the dates on which you are leaving and returning to the office, as well as to send special "out of the office" messages to people.

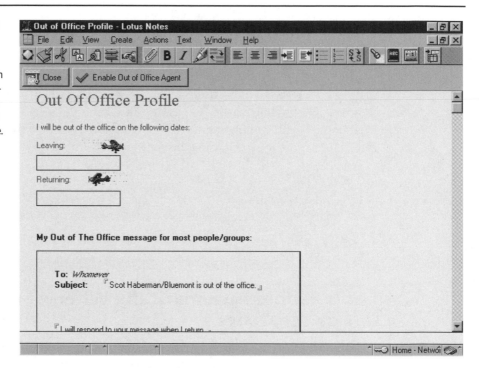

3. Change the subject line in the My Out of the Office Message for Most People/Groups or change the message itself.

4. Enter the names of people to whom you want to send special messages in the People/Groups Who Should Receive a Special Message field. Then enter a subject and message in the My Out of the Office Message for Special People/Groups box. For example, you may want to provide your boss with an emergency phone number.

5. Enter the names of people who should not receive a response while you are out of the office in the People/Groups Who Should Not Receive Any Messages field.

6. Click the Enable Out of Office Agent button.

7. Select your mail server if Notes displays the Choose Server to Run On dialog box.

8. Click OK.

On your return date, Notes sends you a Welcome Back message that includes a list of all the people it sent messages to while you were away. (Notes is so thoughtful.) Notes will continue to send you the Welcome Back message until you disable the Out of Office Agent by choosing Actions ➤ Mail Tools ➤ Out of Office. The Out of Office Profile document appears. Click the I Have Returned to the Office button. That's all there is to it. If you return earlier than you expected, just disable the Out of Office Agent by repeating the same steps.

Choosing a Letterhead Style

Occasionally you may want to change the letterhead style of your memos from the default pencil-and-grid style shown in Figure 11.2. Notes allows you to customize the look of the memos you send:

1. Choose Actions ➤ Mail Tools ➤ Choose Letterhead. The Choose Letterhead list box appears, as shown in Figure 11.30.

FIGURE 11.30:

The Choose Letterhead list box

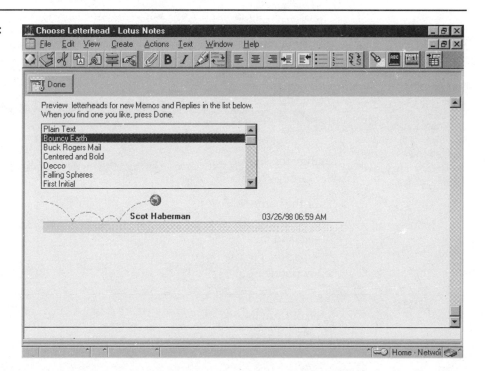

2. Select the name of the letterhead you want to use from the list. If you don't want to use a letterhead, select Plain Text.

3. Click the Done button.

Creating Stationery

Stationery items are templates on which you base messages. You create stationery for messages whose format and recipient list don't change and that you want to use again and again and again. For example, you may want to create custom stationery for different workgroups within your organization, for your department, or for your division.

TIP   If you have to submit a weekly activity report or you use a standard Internet e-mail message style (*sig file*), you can use Stationery to create multiple sig files.

When you create stationery, you can customize a form with text or pictures in the header, footer, and body of the message.

To create stationery, follow these steps:

1. Choose Actions ➤ Mail Tools ➤ Create Stationery.

2. Select Personal Stationery in the Create Stationery dialog box, shown in Figure 11.31.

FIGURE 11.31:

The Create Stationery dialog box gives you the option of choosing Memo or Personal Stationery on which to base a custom mail form.

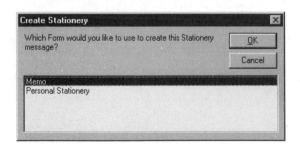

3. Click OK. A blank form appears, as shown in Figure 11.32.

NOTE   If you select Memo, Notes lets you create stationery using the standard memo form that was previously shown in Figure 11.2.

FIGURE 11.32:

When you choose Personal Stationery, you can customize the form with text or pictures.

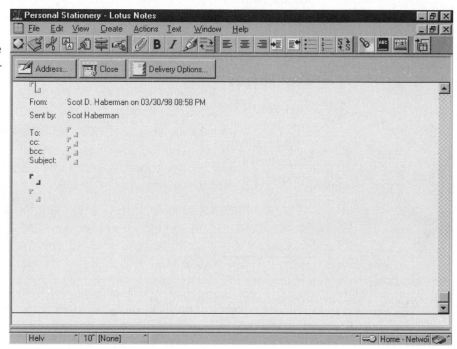

Customizing the Form

Now comes the fun part when you can get really creative. However, since you'll use the custom stationery to send messages at work, you should choose text or pictures carefully. You certainly don't want to offend anyone, nor do you want to appear unprofessional.

To customize the form, follow these steps:

1. Enter text in any format or a picture you want in the first field (above the From field). Treat this area as the header.

2. Fill the recipient information in the address fields and enter information in the Subject field.

3. Type the body of the stationery in the field below the Subject field.

4. Enter text in any format or a picture you want in the last field on the form. Treat this area as the form's footer.

5.   Click the Delivery Options button to change the delivery options.

6.   Click the Close button.

7.   Click Yes when Notes asks if you want to save the stationery.

8.   Enter a name for the stationery in the Save As Stationery dialog box.

9.   Click OK.

Later when you want to create a message using the stationery, open the Drafts folder in your mail database. Highlight the stationery's name and click the Use Stationery button. A new copy of your previously saved Stationery message appears ready to be filled in and sent.

If you want to edit (modify) the stationery, highlight the stationery's name in the Drafts folder and click the Edit Document button. The Edit Document dialog box appears. Select the Edit This Stationery option and then click OK. The stationery appears. Make your changes and then save the stationery.

TIP   You can always rename stationery after you modify the form. Open the Drafts folder, highlight the stationery you want to rename, and click the Rename Stationery button. Type a new name in the Rename Stationery dialog box and then click OK.

TIP   You can create a custom memo on an individual basis by basing the memo on existing stationery. Use this feature only when you need to change the existing default message for a particular recipient. Simply highlight the stationery's name in the Drafts folder and click the Edit Document button. The Edit Document dialog box appears. Choose the Create a New Message from This Stationery option and click OK. Fill in the memo's fields and then send and save the message as you normally would.

Permitting Others to Use Your Mail Database

You can permit other people to open your mail database and read your mail, send messages for you, edit existing messages, and delete messages by identifying specific users in your Delegation Profile. However, be advised that giving users access to your mail database also gives them access to your Notes calendar and to public documents in other databases, if you have any.

To set up the Delegation Profile, follow these steps:

1. Select your mail database.

2. Choose Actions ➤ Mail Tools ➤ Delegation Profile.

3. Do any of the following in the E-Mail Access section of the profile:

    • To let users read your mail, enter their names in the Read My Mail field.

    • To let users read your mail and send mail on your behalf, enter their names in the Read and Send Mail on My Behalf field.

    • To let users read your mail, send new messages, and edit existing messages, enter their names in the Read, Send, and Edit Any Document in My Mail File field.

    • To let users delete messages, enter their names in the Delete Mail field.

4. Click OK.

NOTE   Only users who can send or edit your mail can delete your messages.

Letting Others Manage Your Calendar

You can use your Delegation Profile to give users Read Public Documents and Write Public Documents access to your mail database. This method allows users to read, create, edit, and delete calendar entries (appointments, meeting invitations, meeting responses, events, reminders, and anniversaries), but not to read, create, edit, or delete any other documents in your mail database:

1. Choose Actions ➤ Mail Tools ➤ Delegation Profile.

2. Do one of the following under Calendar Access:

    • To give all users Read Public Documents and Write Public Documents access to your mail database, select Everyone Can Manage My Calendar.

    • To give only selected users or groups Read Public Documents and Write Public Documents access to your mail database, specify the names of the users or groups in the Only the Following People/Groups Can Manage My Calendar field.

3. Click OK.

NOTE   If you give a user Editor access to your mail database (by specifying the user's name in the Read, Send, and Edit Any Document in My Mail file field under E-Mail Access), Notes automatically gives the user Read Public Documents and Write Public Documents access.

Letting Others Read Your Calendar

You can use your Delegation Profile to give users Read Public Documents access to your mail database. This method allows users to read calendar entries (appointments, meeting invitations, meeting responses, events, reminders, and anniversaries), but not to read any other documents in your mail database:

1. Choose Actions ➤ Mail Tools ➤ Delegation Profile.

2. Do one of the following under Calendar Access:

    •   To give all users Read Public Documents access to your mail database, select Everyone Can Read My Calendar.

    •   To give only selected users or groups Read Public Documents access to your mail database, specify the names of the users or groups in the Only the Following People/Groups Can Read My Calendar field.

3. Click OK.

If you give a user Reader, Author, or Editor access to your mail database (by specifying the user's name in any of the fields under E-Mail Access), Notes automatically gives the user Read Public Documents access.

NOTE   Allowing certain groups to read your calendar is very handy when individuals need to know where you are. Just be aware that once you give users this access, they can read all public documents. By default, each calendar entry is public unless you specify that it should be confidential.

What's Next?

In the next chapter, we introduce you to calendaring and scheduling (C&S) and Release 4.6 enhancements to C&S. The C&S features enable you to coordinate schedules, record upcoming activities, and view the availability of others in your workgroup—all of which are an integral part of "collaboration." If you are already familiar with Lotus Organizer (the personal information manager found in the Lotus SmartSuite toolset), calendaring and scheduling in Notes 4.6 will look and feel very similar. In fact, Lotus has simply borrowed the Organizer interface and embedded it within Notes.

CHAPTER
TWELVE

12

Calendaring and Scheduling

- Accessing different calendar views

- Creating a calendar profile

- Creating a calendar entry

- Defining different calendar entry types

- Reserving resources

- Responding to an invitation

The ability to coordinate schedules, record upcoming activities, and view the availability of others in your workgroup is an integral part of collaboration, which is what Notes is all about.

If you are already familiar with Lotus Organizer, the personal information manager found in the Lotus SmartSuite toolset, calendaring and scheduling (C&S) in Notes 4.*x* will look and feel very similar. In fact, Lotus has simply borrowed the Organizer interface and embedded it within Notes.

Calendaring and scheduling is built into each user's mail database and does not require the installation of any additional software. However, Notes does require each user to complete a series of profiles that describe how C&S will behave for them. We'll examine profiles later in the chapter.

Behind the Scenes of Calendaring and Scheduling

The foundation of Notes calendaring and scheduling is the Freetime Manager. This service runs transparently on your Notes server and keeps track of when a time slot is available for a user (in other words, time that has been designated as allowable free time and has not yet been scheduled in someone's calendar). The Freetime Manager maintains a Freetime Schedule in a single, special Freetime Information database (BUSYTIME.NSF) for every user whose mail database is kept on that server. Whenever a user creates an appointment, meeting invitation, event, anniversary entry, or accepts an invitation to a meeting, the Freetime Manager marks that time as "busy" in that person's Freetime Schedule. A person can also define a Freetime range in their Calendar Profile. These time ranges for each day of the week are considered available for meetings with other users. If the user attempts to create another entry during a busy time, the system flags the user. Likewise, when a user wants to check the availability of one or more other users to schedule a meeting, the Freetime Manager checks the Freetime Schedules (kept in the Freetime Information database) of all invitees and reports any conflicts.

Thus, the calendaring and scheduling process has two equally important aspects: the information you see in your personal calendar and the information the Freetime Manager running on the server maintains in its special database.

Familiarizing Yourself with the Calendar

The look and feel of the Notes calendaring system is very intuitive, and you will quickly learn to find the information you need. The first step is to open your mail database from the Workspace by double-clicking its icon. You then click on the Calendar view in the navigational pane (see Figure 12.1).

FIGURE 12.1:

The Calendar view

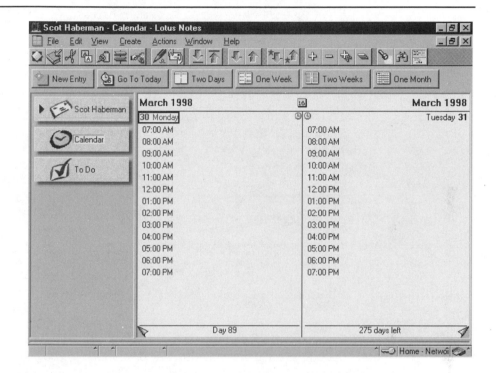

NOTE

If you are upgrading from a version of Notes before Release 4.5, C&S functionality may not be present when you open your mail database. (You won't see a view similar to the one shown in Figure 12.1.) Ask your Notes administrator to replace the design of your mail database with the Release 4.6 mail template.

When you click the Calendar icon, one of several different calendar views is displayed:

- Two Days

- One Week

- Two Weeks

- One Month

Figure 12.2 shows the One Month view.

FIGURE 12.2:

The One Month view of the
Notes calendaring system

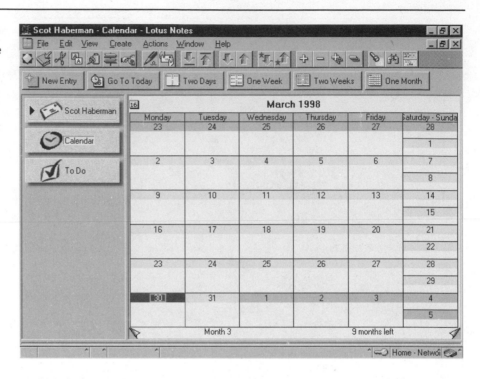

You can use the Action buttons to switch among the calendar views. Simply
click the button that corresponds to the desired view. You can also open a view by
using the View menu at the top of the Workspace. Choose View ➤ Calendar and
then select any of the options that appear in the submenu, as shown in Figure 12.3.

FIGURE 12.3:

Using the View menu
to select a particular
calendar view

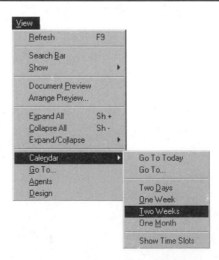

TIP   You can right-click anywhere within a calendar to display a pop-up menu that lets you switch to any of the calendar views.

The appearance of the calendar is really no different from that of a typical appointment book. Calendar entries (discussed later) appear on their respective dates as you create them.

Navigating through the Calendar

Various options enable you to navigate to a particular day, week, or month of the calendar. For all the calendar views, you may click on the curled edges at the bottom corners of the view, known as *dog ears*, to navigate to the following or preceding time period relative to the current view. You can see the dog ears in Figure 12.4.

Clicking the right dog ear of the One Week view moves you to the next week; clicking the left dog ear moves you to the previous week.

You can use the up, down, left, and right arrow keys on your keyboard to navigate within a time period.

FIGURE 12.4:

Click the dog ears (the curled edges at the bottom corners of the calendar) to turn the pages of the calendar.

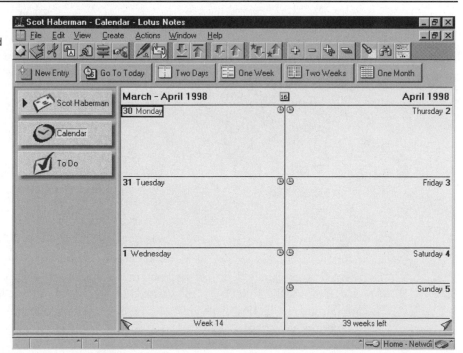

TIP

The Page Up and Page Down keys act identically to the left and right dog ears in the calendar. Page Up moves you to the previous time period; Page Down, to the next time period.

Showing Time Slots

The activities that you enter into your calendar typically, though not always, are associated with a time. In Notes terminology these activities *occupy a time slot*. The calendar page in Figure 12.5 is displayed with time slots.

FIGURE 12.5:

The time slots for March 30, 1998

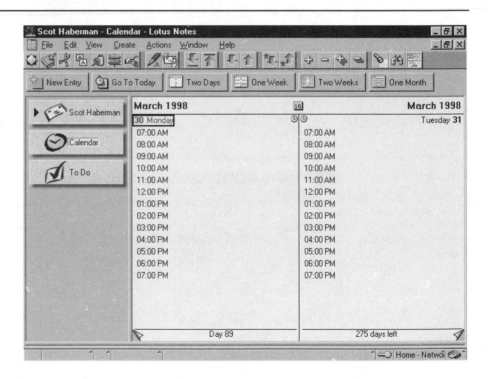

In the Two Days view, the time slots for each day are automatically visible. However, the time slots are not visible in the other views by default; you may display them if you wish. A clock icon appears in the upper-left or upper-right corner of each date for the Two Days, One Week, and Two Weeks views. This icon toggles the appearance of the time slots for that day. Click it once to display the time slots; click it again to hide them.

TIP

If you want to jump to a specific calendar day, instead of using the dog ears, click the calendar icon located at the top of each view (in the middle), and a calendar will display where you can select any day. This is particularly useful when using the Two Day view. You can also choose View ➤ Calendar ➤ Go To from the menu.

For the One Month view, highlight a date and choose View ➤ Calendar ➤ Show Time Slots. As with the clock icon, this option toggles the appearance of the time slots for that day. Select it to display the time slots; select it again to hide the time slots.

TIP

Right-clicking on a particular date displays a pop-up menu of options, including Show Time Slots. Select this option to either display or hide the time slots for that day.

TIP

To jump back to today's entry on the calendar, click the Go To Today Action button, select View ➤ Calendar ➤ Go To Today, or right-click on the calendar and select Go To Today from the pop-up menu.

Notes displays a different icon for each type of calendar entry. For example, as shown in Figure 12.6, "Call about Financial report" is a Task, "Toms Birthday" is an Anniversary, "Team Meeting" is an Appointment, "Accounts Briefing" is a Meeting, "Pick up meat at grocers" is a Reminder, and "Company 10 year party" is an event.

Notes has also enhanced the printing capabilities of the Calendar view. Now you can print the view just like you see it.

If you want to print the calendar entries on the current page of the Calendar view, do the following:

1. If necessary, switch to the Calendar view.

2. Change the display of the Calendar view to Two Day, One Week, Two Week, or One Month.

3. Display the page for the days, weeks, or month that you want to print. For example, if you want to print calendar entries for the month of April, change the display to one month and display the April page.

FIGURE 12.6:

Notes displays different icons for each type of calendar entry.

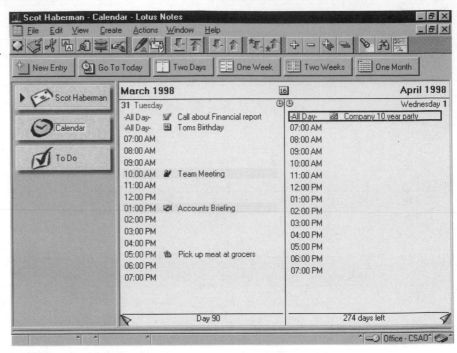

4.   Choose File ➤ Print.

5.   Under View options, select Print View if necessary.

6.   (*Optional*) To print faster (with reduced print quality), select Draft Quality.

7.   (*Optional*) To print more than one copy, specify the number you want in the Copies field.

8.   Click OK.

The Calendar Profile

The first order of business is filling out your Calendar Profile, which is a document that describes how C&S will behave for you (see Figure 12.7). Each Notes user maintains a Calendar Profile.

FIGURE 12.7:

A Calendar Profile for
Scot Haberman

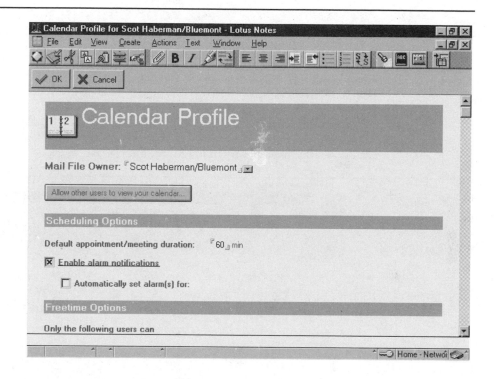

To modify the settings of your Calendar Profile, do the following:

1. Select your mail database from the Workspace or double-click it to open it.

2. Choose Actions ➤ Calendar Tools ➤ Calendar Profile.

3. Select the options in the Calendar Profile document.

4. Save your Calendar Profile by clicking the OK button that appears on the Action bar.

The sections that follow describe the elements of the Calendar Profile.

> **NOTE**
> You must open and save your Calendar Profile at least once. Doing so effectively "activates" your Freetime Schedule so that the Freetime Manager can accurately track your free and busy periods. Failing to activate your Freetime Schedule will prevent others from looking up your free time for meetings.

Allowing Others to View Your Calendar

Notes permits you to open your calendar for viewing either to specific users/groups or to all users in your Notes domain. Going a step further, you can also allow other users/groups to manage your calendar on your behalf. In other words, you can assign a *proxy* who may perform all calendar functions in your name.

You identify the users/groups who can view and manage your calendar through a Delegation Profile (see Figure 12.8). Like a Calendar Profile, a Delegation Profile is a document that all users maintain for themselves.

FIGURE 12.8:

A Delegation Profile lets you assign various levels of access to your calendar.

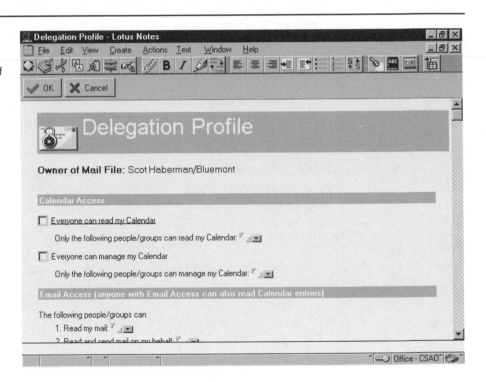

To access and modify your Delegation Profile, perform the following steps:

1. Open your Calendar Profile.

2. Click the button labeled Allow Other Users to View Your Calendar.

3. Select the options you wish under the Calendar Access section by either clicking the checkboxes or displaying the drop-down list boxes to choose specific users/groups:

   • **Everyone can read my Calendar** allows all users to view your calendar.

- **Only the Following People/Groups Can Read My Calendar** lets you selectively assign users the right to view your calendar. This option is not visible if you have chosen the Everyone can read my Calendar option.

- **Everyone Can Manage My Calendar** allows all users to perform calendar tasks for you.

- **Only the Following People/Groups Can Manage my Calendar** lets you selectively assign the right to perform calendar tasks for you. This option is not visible if you have chosen the Everyone Can Manage My Calendar option.

4. Click the OK button to save the Delegation Profile.

TIP   Delegating responsibility for the management of your calendar makes sense if someone else in the organization (an administrative assistant, for example) keeps your appointment book for you. Simply identify that person, assuming he or she is a Notes user, in your Delegation Profile under the Only the Following People/Groups Can Manage My Calendar option.

TIP   You can directly access your Delegation Profile (rather than accessing it through your Calendar Profile) by clicking or opening your mail database from the Workspace and choosing Actions ➤ Mail Tools ➤ Delegation Profile.

Viewing and Managing the Calendar of Another User

If you have been chosen to view or manage someone else's calendar (as specified in that user's Delegation Profile), you will need to periodically open that user's calendar. Follow these steps:

1. Highlight or open your mail database from the Workspace.

2. Choose Actions ➤ Calendar Tools ➤ Open Another Calendar. Notes displays the Open Calendar dialog box.

3. Highlight the name of the individual whose calendar you wish to view or manage from the list of users.

4. Click the OK button. The calendar for the individual you've chosen will open.

If the user has delegated the management of his or her calendar to you, you can create calendar entries just as you normally would create them in your calendar.

Scheduling Options

The Scheduling Options section of the Calendar Profile contains the following options:

- **Default Appointment/Meeting Duration** lets you specify the time duration that will automatically appear in newly created appointment and meeting calendar entries.

- **Enable Alarm Notifications** activates the Alarm options button that appears on the Action bar of a calendar entry. This option allows you to set alarms for your entries so that you are notified of pending appointments, meetings, and so on.

- **Automatically Set Alarm(s) For** appears in the Scheduling Options section only if you have selected the Enable Alarm Notifications option. With this option enabled, Notes automatically notifies you of an upcoming calendar entry and saves you from having to manually set an alarm for each entry you create. You can select the types of calendar entries for which you want Notes to set automatic alarms and specify the amount of advanced notification you want to receive.

The Automatically Set Alarm(s) For options are visible in Figure 12.9 because the Enable Alarm Notifications option has been selected.

Freetime Options

The Freetime Options section of the Calendar Profile contains the following options:

- **Only the Following Users Can Read My Freetime Schedule** specifies who can look up your free time when scheduling meetings. Leaving this field blank gives all Notes users in your organization the ability to access your Freetime Schedule.

- **Allowable Free Times** is the basis of your Freetime Schedule and specifies the ranges of time for each day of the week that are considered available for meetings with other users. All other times are considered unavailable; when users attempt to schedule meetings with you that fall outside the allowable free times you've specified, the Freetime Manager will report that time as busy. (Of course, the same thing will occur if someone attempts to schedule a meeting with you during a time period that an appointment or meeting has already been scheduled.)

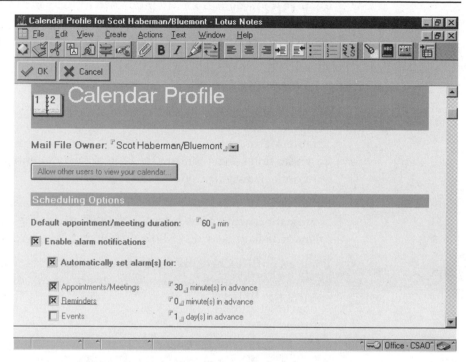

FIGURE 12.9:

Scheduling Options settings

Advanced Calendar Options

At the bottom of the Calendar Profile, you'll find the Advanced Calendar Options that allow you to specify more complex C&S functionality. You can expand this section (it is initially collapsed) by clicking the twistie (the triangle-shaped object) next to the section title.

Autoprocessing Options

The Autoprocessing Options section controls the automatic execution of specific C&S functions:

- **Meetings** indicates that you want Notes to automatically "book" meetings that you are invited to in your calendar and send an acceptance response to the originator. This setting is useful if you have no problems attending every meeting to which you are invited.

- **Remove Invitations from My Inbox After I Respond to Them** causes Notes to automatically discard invitations to meetings you've received after you respond (accept or decline) to them.

Calendar Entry Options

The Calendar Entry Options section of the Calendar Profile contains the following options:

- **Calendar Entry Type** controls the type of calendar entry that is displayed when you create a new entry.

- **Hide New Calendar Entries from Public Viewing** tells Notes to hide all new entries in your calendar from users who have the right to view your calendar. (See the section "Allowing Others to View Your Calendar.")

- **Enable Conflict Checking For** instructs Notes to automatically flag you if an entry (appointment/meeting, anniversary, event) conflicts with another entry in the calendar.

Creating Your Calendar Entries

Notes supports several types of calendar entries:

- Appointments
- Invitations
- Events
- Reminders
- Anniversaries

To create a calendar entry, do the following:

1. Open your mail database by double-clicking it.

2. Select the Calendar icon from the Navigation pane.

3. Use the Action bar to select the calendar view that suits you.

4. Perform any of the following actions to create a calendar entry:

- Choose Create ➤ Calendar Entry. A new calendar entry document will be displayed. The default date of the entry is the date highlighted in the current calendar view. The default time will be the next available time entry based on the current time.

- Move to any of the available calendar views and click the New Entry button on the Action bar. The default date of the entry is the date highlighted in the selected view. The default time will be the next available time entry based on the current time.

- Move to any of the available calendar views and double-click within the cell of a particular date. The date of the entry corresponds to that date. If time slots were displayed within the cell, the time of the entry corresponds to the time you clicked.

The default Calendar entry type setting found in your Calendar Profile controls the type of calendar entry that Notes displays. An appointment entry appears in Figure 12.10.

FIGURE 12.10:

An appointment entry in your calendar

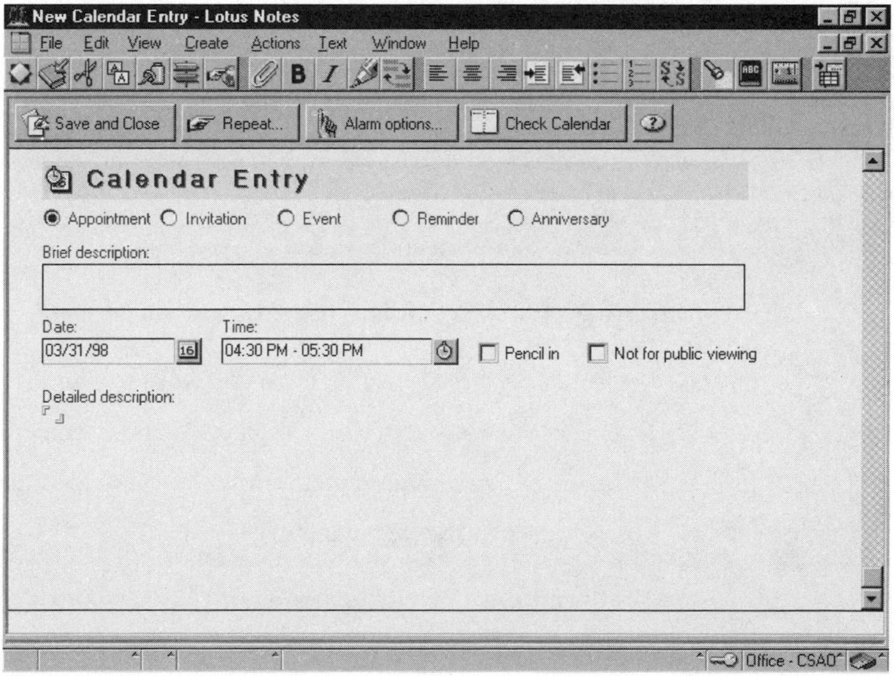

With Notes 4.6, a new timesaving option has been added for creating calendar entries. You now have three additional choices:

- Create a calendar entry from a mail message
- Create a calendar entry from an existing calendar entry
- Create a calendar entry from a task

To create a calendar entry from a mail message, do the following:

1. Select or open the message you want to use.
2. Choose Actions ➤ Copy Into ➤ New Calendar Entry.
3. Change any information you want in the new calendar entry.
4. Save and close the calendar entry.

When you use this option, Notes will perform the following translation of the mail message to the calendar entry:

- Copy the Subject from the mail message to the Brief Description of the calendar entry
- Copy the Body from the mail message to the Detailed Description of the calendar entry
- Place the current date and time in the Date and Time fields of the calendar entry
- Use the default calendar entry type

To create a calendar entry from an existing calendar entry, do the following:

1. Select or open the calendar entry you want to use.
2. Choose Actions ➤ Copy Into ➤ New Calendar Entry.
3. Change any information you want in the new calendar entry.
4. Save and close the calendar entry.

All of the information will be carried over to the new calendar entry.

To create a calendar entry from a task, do the following:

1. Select or open the task entry you want to use.

2. Choose Actions ➤ Copy Into ➤ New Calendar Entry.

3. Change any information you want in the new calendar entry.

4. Save and close the calendar entry.

When you use this option, Notes will perform the following translation of the task to the calendar entry:

- Notes copies the Subject from the task to the Brief Description field of the new calendar entry.

- Notes copies the Additional information from the task to the Detailed Description field of the new calendar entry.

- Notes copies the Start date from the task to the Date field of the new calendar entry. Notes enters the current time in the Time field.

- Notes copies the Start date and Due date from the task to the Body of the new task.

- If you create a meeting invitation from a task, Notes also does the following:

  - Places the name of the originator of the task in the Send Invitations To field of the meeting invitation.

  - Copies the names from the Assign To field of the task to the Send Invitations To field of the meeting invitation.

  - Copies the names from the Cc field of the task to the Optional Invitees field of the meeting invitation.

Calendar Entry Basics

Select the type of entry by clicking one of the radio buttons that appears at the top of the calendar entry form.

An **Appointment**

- Occurs on a specific date

- Occurs at a specific time

- Has a specific duration

The duration is expressed as a set of starting and ending times, for example, 10:00 AM–11:00 AM.

An **Invitation** allows you to call a meeting with one or more people. It specifies:

- A date, time, and duration

- A list of required attendees and optional attendees

- A reservation for a specific room or other resource (for example, overhead projector, flip chart, yacht, corporate jet)

We discuss invitations in detail later in the chapter.

TIP   You can view meetings that you've called or accepted an invitation to from the Meetings view that appears in the Navigation pane of your mail database. This is sorted by the date and time of the meetings.

An **Event** is typically a single occurrence on particular dates and with a particular duration (expressed in days). An example of an event might be a trade show, vacation time, or a holiday.

A **Reminder** is a *tickler* you can set to remind yourself that some action is required at a particular time on a particular date. Reminders do not have a duration associated with them.

An **Anniversary** can be used to record a special upcoming event that has no particular time associated with it.

Common Functionality across Entry Types

Regardless of the type of calendar entry you choose, all or most of them share certain functionality. Therefore, you can apply the following information to the type of calendar entry with which you are dealing:

Descriptions   Notes provides fields in which you enter both brief and detailed descriptions of your calendar entry. A brief description should be less than 100 characters as it appears in the calendar views for that date. A detailed description is a rich text field and can contain formatted text, embedded objects, file attachments, and so on.

Date and Time Controls   You can either enter values directly in the date and time fields of your calendar entry (where applicable) or use the date and time controls that appear next to each field. These controls support a point-and-shoot method of specifying dates and times, which eliminates typing and formatting errors.

For the date control (see Figure 12.11), click the calendar icon next to the date field. You can move from month to month in the mini-calendar by clicking the left or right arrows at the top. Navigate to the desired month and click the correct day; that date is automatically entered in the field.

FIGURE 12.11:

The date control simplifies entering dates.

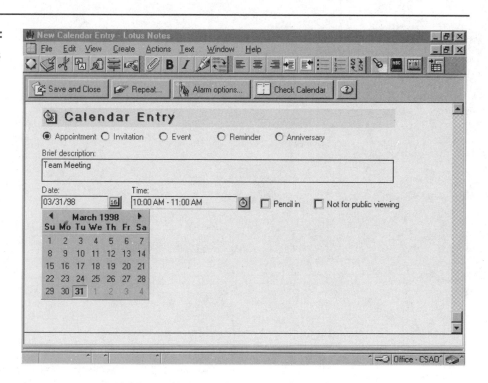

For the time control, click the clock icon next to the time field; a time gauge with a slider lets you select a single time or a time range. To position the slider, drag it up or down. Because appointments and invitations are based on a range of time, you need to grab and drag the top or bottom of the slider to extend or decrease the time range. A duration value appears between the top and bottom of the range. You can even move the entire range up or down by grabbing the duration value and dragging it. Once you've defined the time for your entry, click the check mark in the lower-left corner of the control or press ↵. Notes will enter the time in the field, as shown in Figure 12.12.

FIGURE 12.12:

The time control as it appears for an appointment

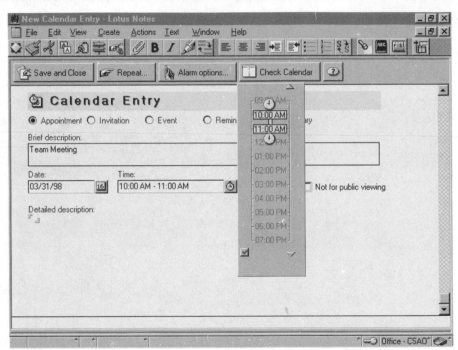

For reminders, only a single time will appear on the gauge:

Pencil In The Pencil In option tells Notes to enter the calendar entry in your calendar but not mark the time as busy in your Freetime Schedule. In effect, this option creates an unconfirmed or tentative entry that does not prevent someone from inviting you to meetings at the same time.

Not for Public Viewing This option makes an entry invisible to other users who have access to your calendar (via your Delegation Profile, discussed earlier in the chapter). This is important if you have elected for others to view your calendar and are entering confidential information.

Using the Action Bar

The buttons that appear on the Action bar of the Calendar Entry form add important functionality to the C&S environment.:

> **Repeat**   Imagine having to manually enter the meeting you attend on the third Thursday of every month from 8:00 to 12:00. Besides having to perform a tedious task, you are likely to forget to put the meeting in your calendar at least once, which could lead to a scheduling mistake.

Luckily, Notes can automatically repeat a calendar entry for you based on rules you specify. The "repeat rules" in Figure 12.13 create an entry in the calendar for the monthly meeting described previously.

FIGURE 12.13:

The Repeat Rules dialog box allows you to specify a repeating calendar entry.

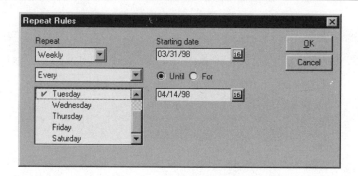

To define the repeat rules, perform the following steps:

1. Click the Repeat button on the Action bar. The Repeat Rules dialog box appears.

2. Click the down arrow to the right of the Repeat field to display a list of intervals (Weekly, Monthly, and so on).

3. Click the interval you desire. The remaining choices in the dialog box will change to fit the interval.

4. Continue through the remaining choices, clicking the down arrow for choices that provide a drop-down list of selections and clicking the calendar icon (which displays a date control) for choices that require a date.

5. Click OK to accept the repeat rules you've specified.

NOTE   If you save and close a calendar entry without specifying repeat rules, you will not be able to go back to the entry later and do so. If you want an entry to repeat, you must specify the repeat rules when it is first created.

TIP   If you've forgotten to specify that a calendar entry should repeat, you can copy and paste the entry from its original date to any other date on your calendar.

WARNING   If you specify a custom ending date, be careful when re-editing the Repeat rules. For some reason, it resets itself back to the default of 2 weeks past the start date.

Alarm Options   It's 1:15 in the afternoon, you've just come back from lunch, and you've completely forgotten the 1:30 meeting you have with the founder of the company. Notes to the rescue! You can use Alarm Options to instruct Notes to automatically notify you of an upcoming calendar event.

To set up alarm options for an entry, perform the following steps:

1. Click the Alarm options button on the Action bar. The Set Alarm dialog box is displayed in Figure 12.14. Notice that the time of the entry appears next to the When label.

FIGURE 12.14:

The Set Alarm dialog box allows you to activate an alarm for a calendar entry.

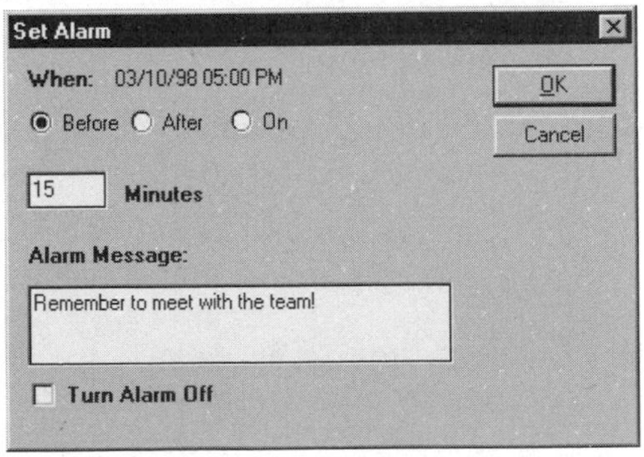

Set Alarm
When: 03/10/98 05:00 PM
◉ Before ○ After ○ On
15   **Minutes**
Alarm Message:
Remember to meet with the team!
☐ **Turn Alarm Off**

TIP   If you have not set Enable Alarm Notifications in your Calendar Profile, Notes may display a dialog box asking if you want to enable alarms.

2. Click the Before, After, or On radio buttons to specify when the alarm should "ring":

    •   **Before** sets the alarm to ring *n* minutes prior to the time of the entry. The number of minutes is specified in the Minutes field.

    •   **After** sets the alarm to ring *n* minutes after the time of the entry. The number of minutes is specified in the Minutes field.

    •   **On** sets the alarm to ring at a specific time. Date and time fields will appear in the dialog box if you choose this option.

3. Do one of the following:

    •   If you selected Before or After, enter a value in the Minutes field.

    •   If you selected On, enter values in the Date and Time fields. Click the calendar and clock icons to use the date and time controls or enter a value manually.

4. Enter the message you want to appear in the notification that is sent to you. The default message is the brief description for the entry.

5. Click Turn Alarm Off if you wish to selectively disable the alarm for this entry.

6. Click OK to accept the alarm options you've chosen. The following message appears at the top of the entry: Alarm enabled: an alarm will occur *xx* minutes before the start time of this entry.

NOTE   Notes allows you to return to the alarm options of an entry at any time in the future and change them if you wish.

If you enable an alarm for an entry, the alarm message appears in a message box on your workstation display at the time specified in the alarm options. Notes also includes a Snooze feature that lets you suspend the alarm for a specific number of minutes. The alarm rings again after the Snooze period expires.

TIP

Remember! Notes must be running for you to receive an alarm notification.

Check Calendar   The Check Calendar button enables you to avoid scheduling conflicts. To use this feature, do the following:

1.   Click the Check Calendar button. Your calendar is displayed.

2.   Switch to any of the other calendars if you wish.

3.   Press Esc to return to the calendar entry.

Moving Your Calendar Entries

If you make a mistake or simply change your mind regarding the date and time of a calendar entry, you don't have to delete the current entry and create a new one. Instead, you can simply drag and drop the current entry to a new location in your calendar.

To move a calendar entry, do the following:

1.   Open the calendar view that is appropriate for the move you wish to make. If you are moving the entry to another day, you might find the One Month view the easiest to work with. If you are moving the entry to another time slot on the same day, you'll probably find the Two Day view the most convenient.

2.   Navigate to the date on which the entry currently resides. (See the discussion earlier in the chapter on navigating through the calendars.)

3.   Drag the target day or time slot and release the mouse button. The entry will appear at that position in the calendar.

Deleting a Calendar Entry

Because calendar entries are simply documents, you can delete them as you would any document. From any of the calendar views, perform the following steps to delete an entry:

1.   Navigate to the date specified for the entry to be deleted.

2.   Highlight the entry by clicking on it.

3. Press Delete. A strike-through line appears on the entry, marking it for deletion.

4. Repeat steps 2–3 for as many entries as you wish to delete.

5. Press F9 to refresh the view. Confirm that you wish to permanently delete the entries you've marked for deletion by responding Yes to the prompt. The entries will be removed from the database.

To "unmark" an entry marked for deletion, do the following:

1. Highlight the entry by clicking it.

2. Press Delete. The strike-through line is removed.

WARNING   Once you've confirmed that entries marked for deletion are to be permanently removed, you cannot "undelete."

A Closer Look at Invitations

Invitations are a powerful feature of Notes C&S and extend your ability to coordinate your activities with other people in your organization.

Besides the basic functions discussed earlier, you can use invitations to resolve scheduling conflicts among the invitees. The Freetime Manager is the key to this feature. Recall that as users schedule appointments, meetings, events, and anniversaries, or accept invitations to meetings, the Freetime Manager marks those times busy in each user's Freetime Schedule. When you construct an invitation and specify a list of people who should attend the meeting, the Freetime Manager can determine if the proposed date and time are workable for all invitees. It performs a search of each invitee's Freetime Schedule, examining the proposed date and time, and reports its findings to you. Based on the results, you can opt to send the invitation as is or enter an alternative date and time and repeat the free-time search.

Specifying a List of Invitees

Notes C&S supports two types of invitees: required and optional. You are free to decide whether someone's attendance is required or optional, and Notes does not force you to use both fields; in fact, all invitees can be required or optional. Bear in mind that the way in which you state the list of invitees affects how Notes handles its free time search. We'll discuss this issue shortly.

In the invitation, do the following to select the names of the users and groups to invite to the meeting:

1. Click the down arrow to the right of the Send Invitations To field. Notes displays the contents of the Name and Address book for your organization.

2. Highlight a user or group from the list that appears in the left window of the dialog box. Click the Add button. The selection will appear in the right window.

3. Repeat step 2 for as many users and groups you wish to add to the list of invitees.

4. Click OK.

The process for selecting optional invitees is identical to that described previously.

Performing a Free-Time Search for All Invitees

Using the services of the Freetime Manager, you can execute a search to determine if the date and time you've stated in the invitation are available for all invitees, both required and optional.

Follow these steps to perform a free-time search:

1. Click the Find Free Time button. The Free Time dialog box appears with a message that states either Scheduled Time is OK for Everyone or Scheduled Time is NOT OK for Everyone. See Figure 12.15.

2. Click the OK button if the scheduled time is available for everyone.

Resolving Scheduling Conflicts Using the Free Time Dialog Box

You can be sure that all invitees will not be available for the proposed date and time for every meeting. When conflicts occur, however, you can use the Free Time dialog box (which appears when you click the Find Free Time button in an invitation) to select an alternative date. Figure 12.16 shows how the Free Time dialog box reports a scheduling conflict.

FIGURE 12.15:

The Free Time dialog box reports that everyone is available at the scheduled time.

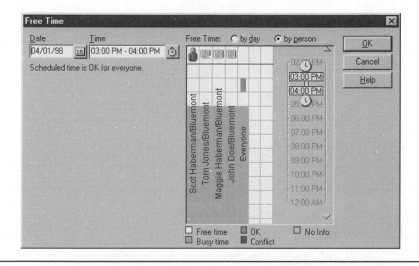

FIGURE 12.16:

The Free Time dialog box reports a scheduling conflict.

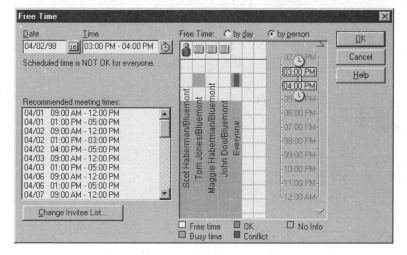

The primary elements of the Free Time dialog box are the following:

- Date and Time fields that allow you to enter an alternate time; these fields work exactly as they do in the calendar entry.

- A window that displays recommended meeting times.

- A free-time grid that depicts the free and busy times of each invitee (including yourself) for the proposed date and time, along with a collective representation of the free time for all invitees labeled Everyone.

The Free-Time Search Algorithm

Notes employs a very specific method for determining alternative meeting times. Notes starts by searching a three-week range surrounding the original meeting date (one week before and two weeks after) and presents any times that are free for all invitees. If it does not find a time suitable for everyone, Notes will search the same three-week range to find time that is available for as many of the invitees as possible, with preference given to the users and groups listed in the Send Invitations To field; that is, the required invitees.

The Free-Time Grid

The free-time grid appears on the right side of the Free Time dialog box. A series of vertical bars from left to right represents each invitee's free time for the day on which the meeting is to take place. Your schedule appears as the first bar in the grid. Each horizontal row of the grid corresponds to the time slot listed at the right side of the grid. A legend directly below the grid describes what each color in the grid means.

To interpret the free-time grid, focus on the bar for one of the invitees. The bar is broken into individual cells, one for each time slot. The color of the cell represents the status of that time slot for the invitee: blue if the time slot has been marked as busy and white if the time slot is free. The last bar of the grid, labeled Everyone, represents the intersection of the free-time schedules of all invitees and is interpreted as follows:

- **Collectively busy (blue):** A time slot is not available for *any* invitee.

- **Collectively free (white):** A time slot is available for *all* invitees.

- **OK (green):** The entire proposed time range is available for all invitees.

- **Conflict (red):** The proposed time range is busy for at least one invitee.

To illustrate the last bullet item, consider the free-time grid in Figure 12.17. Although nearly all of the proposed time range 2:00 PM–3:30 PM is free for the invitees, the time period 3:00 PM–4:00 PM is marked as busy for user Tom Jones/Bluemont. Since the period from 3:00 PM–4:00 PM overlaps the proposed time range, the entire range is considered to be in conflict with Tom's schedule.

FIGURE 12.17:

A free-time grid that reports a scheduling conflict

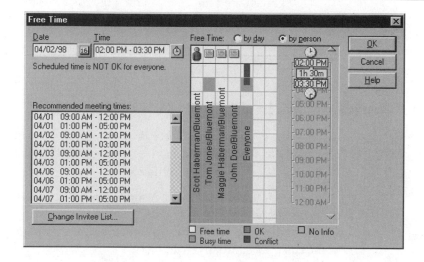

How to Resolve Conflicts

You can use several methods to resolve scheduling conflicts reported in the Free Time dialog box:

- Edit the Date field or Time field; as you do so, Notes will automatically perform a new free-time lookup.

- Choose one of the meeting times that Notes recommends by clicking the selection. (You'll notice that some of the recommended time periods are longer than the original time period you've specified; don't worry, Notes will automatically adjust the time period you choose to match the original time period.)

- Change the list of invitees by clicking the Change Invitee List button and then:

  1. Highlight the name of an invitee in the Invitees box on the right and click the Remove button to eliminate the invitee from the list. Repeat this process for as many invitees as you wish to eliminate. Click the Remove All button to eliminate all the current invitees.

  2. Highlight the name of a user and group in the box on the left and click the Required or Optional buttons to add the user and group to the list of invitees. Repeat this process for as many users and groups as you wish to add. If you wish to examine the membership of a group or look

at detailed information for a user before adding a user or group to the invitee list, highlight the user and group and click the Open button.

3. Click OK to save your choices. Notes will perform a new free-time search and report the results.

Sending an Invitation

Finally, you've found a time that is free for all or most of the invitees and you're now ready to send the invitation. The only detail left is to decide if you want the invitees to respond to your invitation.

If you do not want to receive responses to your invitation, check I Don't Want Responses from the Invitees. This option is appropriate when the absence of individual invitees has no bearing on whether the meeting will be held, for example, in the case of a company meeting.

You are now ready to save the invitation:

1. Click the Save and Close button on the Action bar.

2. Click Yes or No when prompted to send the invitation to the people/resources you've invited. You would typically respond Yes to this question.

The meeting will be entered into your calendar. If you've opted to send invitations, Notes delivers them to the Inbox of each invitee.

NOTE　Notes does not force you to send invitations to the meeting invitees you've specified. You may choose simply to enter the meeting in your calendar and then use some other means of informing the invitees.

Resource Reservations

Many meetings also require specific material resources, such as conference rooms and audio/visual equipment. In fact, the availability of a resource can affect whether a meeting can take place. Notes C&S allows you to reserve resources as part of your meeting invitation. The resources you identify are then included along with any meeting invitees in free-time searches you execute. The Free Time system tracks the free time of a resource exactly as it tracks the free time of an individual.

> **NOTE**   The ability to reserve resources is available only for invitation-type calendar entries, not for meetings, events, reminders, or anniversaries.

When you compose an invitation-type calendar entry, you will see a section at the bottom of the form entitled Reservations. This section is initially collapsed and will need to be expanded by clicking on the twistie (the triangular-shaped object) next to the section title. Figure 12.18 shows you the Reservation section as it looks when expanded.

FIGURE 12.18:

The Reservation section of an invitation-type calendar entry lets you reserve specific resources needed to conduct a meeting.

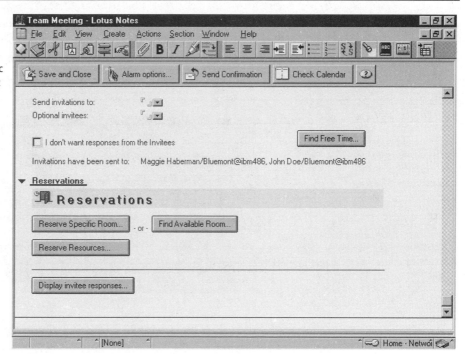

Reserving a Resource

The resources available to you through C&S must be defined in a special database on your Notes server called the Resource Reservations database. The maintenance of this database is usually the responsibility of a selected number of individuals. If you want to reserve a particular resource that has not been defined in the database, ask the Notes administrator to define it for you.

The resources defined in the Resource Reservations database fall into two general categories: rooms and everything else. To reserve a resource, follow these steps:

1. Compose a meeting invitation as described earlier in the chapter, identifying all invitees.

2. Expand the Reservations section at the bottom of the invitation by clicking the twistie.

3. Click the appropriate button to identify a resource to be reserved.

4. Select the resource(s) to be reserved from the list of resources shown in the dialog box that appears. Figure 12.19 shows you an example of the Room dialog box that is displayed when you click the Reserve Specific Room button. (When you click the Reserve Resources button, a Resources dialog box will appear.)

FIGURE 12.19:

The Rooms dialog box shows you the rooms that have been defined in the Resource Reservations database.

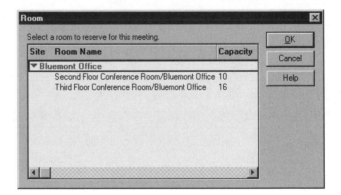

5. Click the OK button in the dialog box to confirm your choices. The selected resources appear next to the corresponding button in the Reservations section.

6. Click the Find Free Time button to identify and resolve scheduling conflicts for invitees and resources. This procedure is described in the section "Resolving Scheduling Conflicts Using the Free Time Dialog Box." The Free Time dialog box in Figure 12.20 includes both invitees and resources.

7. Click the Save and Close button in the Action bar when you are satisfied with the details of the invitation.

FIGURE 12.20:

A Free Time dialog box in which both invitees and resources are displayed

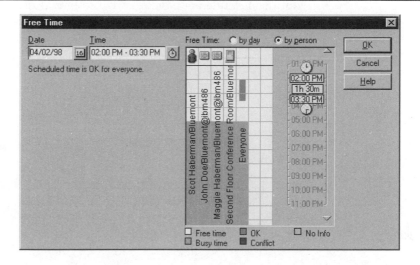

TIP
When selecting non-room resources with the Reserve Resources button, you may indicate multiple resources at once. From the Resources dialog box, click the far left column next to each resource you desire. A check mark will appear in the column indicating the item has been selected. Click the OK button to accept your choices.

Letting Notes Find a Room for You

In many organizations, finding a room in which to hold a meeting is as challenging as finding a time when all the participants are available. However, you can use Notes C&S to do the work for you.

The Find Available Room button in the Reservations section of an invitation automates the process of finding a room with sufficient capacity to hold the number of invitees you've indicated. To use this feature successfully, you should always create your list of invitees first and then click the Find Available Room button.

Responding to Invitations

Lucky you! You've received an invitation to a meeting in your mail Inbox. Now what? Typically you will have the option to respond to it, indicating that you:

- Accept or decline the invitation

- Want to delegate your attendance to someone else
- Want to propose an alternative time or location

Figure 12.21 shows how an invitation appears in the Inbox view of your mail database. (Recall that the meeting chairperson may indicate that he or she does not want to receive responses from the invitees.)

FIGURE 12.21:

An invitation as it appears in the Inbox view of your mail database

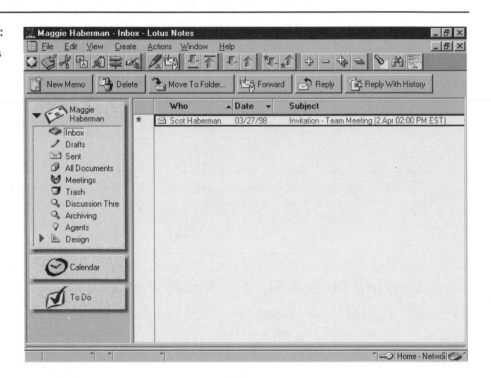

Assuming the meeting chairperson wishes for invitees to respond to the invitation, the invitation will look like the one shown in Figure 12.22. Notice that the invitation provides an Action bar that lets you easily respond to it in different ways.

> **NOTE**
>
> If the meeting chairperson has indicated that he or she does not want invitees to respond to the invitation, the invitation that you receive will not provide any response buttons. Notes refers to this message as a *broadcast* invitation.

FIGURE 12.22:

When you open an invitation that the meeting chairperson wants you to respond to, the form of the invitation includes an Action bar that makes the task of responding easy.

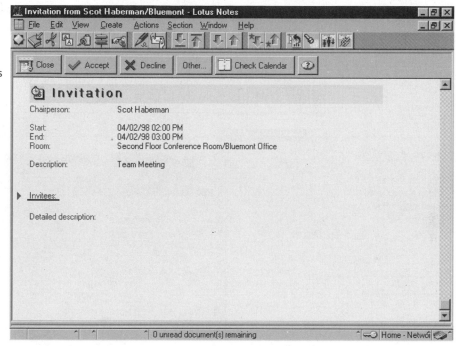

To respond to an invitation, perform the following steps:

1. Open the invitation from your Inbox.

2. Click one of the response buttons found in the Action bar:

    • **Accept** sends a notice to the meeting chairperson confirming your attendance, adds a meeting document to your calendar for the date and time specified in the invitation, and marks that time period busy for you in the Free Time system.

    • **Decline** tells the meeting chairperson that you will not be able to attend.

    • **Other** presents a dialog box from which you can choose Accept, Decline, Delegate, Propose Alternative Time/Location, or Pencil In (see Figure 12.23). The Delegate and Propose Alternative Time/Location responses are discussed below.

NOTE

The Pencil In option displayed when you click the Other button lets you tentatively accept an invitation. Notes sends an acceptance notification to the meeting chairperson and adds a meeting document to your calendar. However, the time period for the meeting is not marked as busy in your free-time schedule. This option allows you to be invited to another meeting scheduled for the same time that may take precedence over the "penciled in" meeting.

FIGURE 12.23:

The Options dialog box lets you specify a response to an invitation other than Accept or Decline.

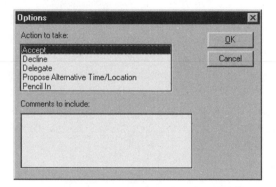

NOTE

Once you've accepted an invitation and the corresponding meeting document has been added to your calendar, you can interact with the meeting document just as you would any other calendar entry (for example, set alarm options, remove it from public viewing, delete it).

Delegating Attendance to Someone Else

Just can't make the meeting? In this situation Notes C&S lets you identify another individual as a "delegate" who will represent you and your ideas at the meeting. Your delegate will receive a "delegated invitation" in his or her Inbox, and the meeting chairperson will be notified. The delegate can then respond to the invitation just as though he or she is an original invitee. (Yes, it is perfectly legal for a delegate to delegate his or her attendance to another person.)

Follow these steps to delegate your attendance to a meeting:

1. Open the invitation from your Inbox.

2. Click the Other button in the Action bar. The Options dialog box is displayed.

3. Select the Delegate option from the list.

4. Enter any comments you wish to add to the response.

5. Click the OK button to close the Options dialog box.

Proposing an Alternative Time or Location for a Meeting

If you really want or need to attend a meeting scheduled at a time that conflicts with another activity or at a location that is inconvenient, you can send a counter-proposal to the meeting chairperson, stating an alternative time and location.

Follow these steps to create a counterproposal:

1. Open the invitation from your Inbox.

2. Click the Other button in the Action bar. A dialog box entitled Options is displayed.

3. Select the Propose Alternative Time/Location option from the list.

4. Enter any comments you wish to add to the response.

5. Click the OK button. A section entitled Proposed Change will now appear in the document. See Figure 12.24.

6. Select an alternative date or time using the controls next to each field.

7. Enter the reason you are requesting the change in the provided field.

8. Click one of the buttons under Proposed Location if you wish to indicate an alternative location.

9. Click the Send Counter Proposal button to submit the change request to the meeting chairperson.

TIP

If you've been dutifully entering information into your calendar, the need to propose alternative times to meeting invitations should be minimal, assuming the meeting chairperson has performed a free-time search of the invitees' schedules prior to sending the invitation. Realize, of course, that certain scheduling conflicts will not be resolvable by the chairperson, and he or she may have to go with a best-case scenario in which most, but not all, invitees are available. Therefore, you may receive an invitation to a meeting at a time you've marked as busy.

FIGURE 12.24:

When you select Propose Alternative Time/Location as your response, the invitation automatically changes form to include a Proposed Change section.

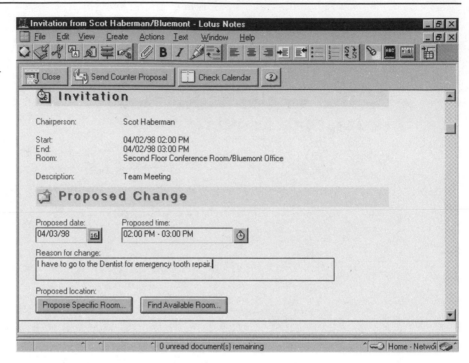

What's Next?

In the next chapter, we discuss Mobile Notes. As a Notes workstation or laptop user, you can connect to a Notes server either through a direct LAN connection or through a remote, dial-up connection using Mobile Notes. The term *Mobile Notes* describes the communications features of Notes Release 4.6, not a standalone product. You'll be able to take advantage of these features whenever you are using Notes on your workstation to connect to a server over a telephone line. If you work off-site or spend time on the road, Mobile Notes can help you keep your Notes database current.

CHAPTER
THIRTEEN

13

Working Off-Site with Mobile Notes

- Setting up your modem for Notes

- Calling your server

- Using database replicas

- Using an outgoing mail database

- Addressing your mail for replication

- Using POP3/SMTP with your Notes mail

- Using TCP/IP to access your Notes server

If you often work outside your office—at home or on the road—and still want access to your organization's databases, you are going to appreciate Mobile Notes. Mobile Notes is a set of Notes features that lets you access Notes via modem when your workstation isn't connected to a local area network (LAN). You can use Mobile Notes on any computer running the Notes workstation software, including desktop computers and many laptops and notebooks. Mobile Notes features and functionality are built directly into the Notes client software.

You can use Mobile Notes to work *locally*, wherever you are, because you can make local replicas (exact copies of shared databases) and then work on these replicas. You can also send and receive Notes mail by working in a local replica of your mail database and then exchanging documents (routing outgoing mail and replicating new mail) with your mail database on the server.

In this chapter you'll learn how to set up a remote Notes connection so you can get all the benefits of working off-site.

Getting Started with Mobile Notes

Before you set up a Mobile workstation, be sure that

- Notes is completely installed on your workstation

- Your workstation has a Notes-compatible modem, as discussed later in this chapter

- You understand Notes locations

Understanding Notes Locations

A *location* is a document in your Personal Name & Address Book that contains communication settings you use when you work with Notes in a specific place. For example, you might use a network port at the office to connect to Notes servers on a LAN and use a remote port while you are traveling to connect to Notes servers over a modem. Figure 13.1 shows the Travel (Modem) Location document.

FIGURE 13.1:

Location documents, such as the Travel (Modem) Location document, contain communication settings you use when you work with Notes in multiple locations.

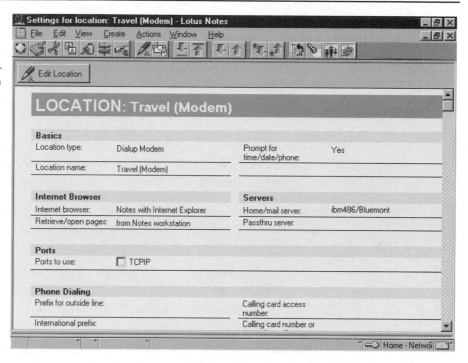

In Location documents, you specify settings such as the ports you want to use (network or remote), the location of your mail file (on a server or local), phone information (such as dialing prefixes), and replication schedules.

When you install Notes, Notes automatically creates these five Location documents in your Personal Name & Address Book:

- Home (Modem)

- Internet

- Island (Disconnected)

- Office (Network)

- Travel (Modem)

These default Location documents will probably meet most of your needs if they're configured properly. You can edit these documents and customize them or create your own. You can even create new Location documents, depending on your communication needs.

NOTE You can access the World Wide Web through Notes from the Lotus InterNotes Web Navigator and Personal Web Navigator databases. For more information on using the Web Navigator databases, see Chapters 31 and 32.

When you use Notes in a specific location, you choose the Location document that contains the settings that apply to where you are working. You could set up your locations in the following ways:

- Set up the Office location to use a network port and your mail file on the server when you are at the office, and set up the Travel location to use a remote port and a local replica of your mail file when you are on the road.

- If your home and office are in different area codes, specify your home's area code in your Home location. Then when you use Home and call a server with a different area code, Notes automatically dials 1 and the server's area code before it dials the server's phone number.

- If you use a calling card only when you make long-distance calls from hotel rooms, you could create a location called Hotel and specify your calling card number. Then when you use Hotel and call a server, Notes automatically uses your calling card number.

TIP You can also set up the Replicator Workspace page in different ways at different locations. This option enables you to tailor your replication settings to your work environments.

Setting Up a Notes Location

Before you can use your modem to send and receive mail or exchange data between databases, you must "prepare" Notes by identifying some important communication settings:

1. Choose File ➤ Mobile ➤ Locations. The Locations view of your Personal Name & Address Book appears.

2. Click the Add Location button to create a new Location document. The Location document appears, as shown in Figure 13.2.

FIGURE 13.2:

You can create a new Location document for any off-site location.

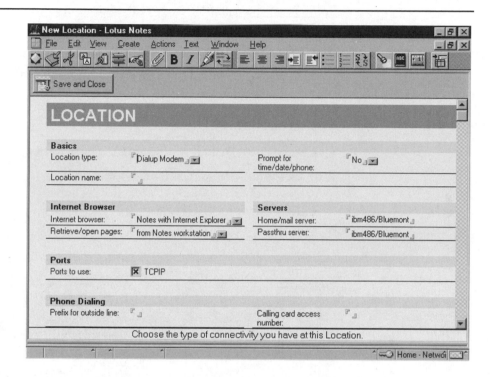

TIP

Follow these same steps to edit an existing Location document; simply change the settings.

---

3. Enter a name for the location in the Location Name field.

4. Select the Dialup Modem option in the Location Type field. (You can also select the Both Dialup and Local Area Network option to set up a location for network and mobile use.)

5. Select a time zone for the location in the Local Time Zone field (located under the Advanced section).

6. Select ports for the location in the Ports to Use field.

7. Specify the telephone dialing prefixes you need to use to call the Notes server.

8. Choose File ➤ Save (Ctrl+S) to save the Location document.

Choosing a Location

You can switch to a location that contains communication settings that apply to your current location.

1. Do one of the following:

   • Choose File ➤ Mobile ➤ Choose Current Location.

   • Click the location indicator on the status bar, as shown in Figure 13.3.

2. Select a location.

3. Click OK.

FIGURE 13.3:

Choose a location from the location indicator list that appears on the Status bar.

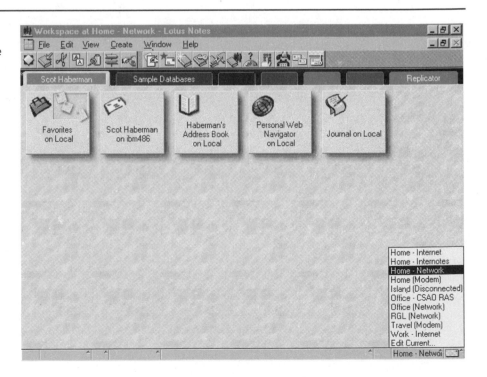

TIP

You can have Notes ask for your current location each time you start Notes. To do so, choose File ➤ Tools ➤ User Preferences, select Prompt for location, and click OK.

Creating a Dialup Modem Server Connection Document

You also need to create a Dialup Modem Server Connection document in your Personal Name & Address Book for each Notes server that you call. You use Dialup Modem Server Connection documents to set up modem connections from your workstation to Notes servers and to schedule calls that take place automatically in the background.

NOTE

If you chose the Mobile Workstation option during Notes setup, Notes has already created a Dialup Modem Server Connection document for your home server. If all the databases you'll use are on that server, you don't need to compose any additional Dialup Modem Server Connection documents.

If you specify your modem settings, mobile settings, and Dialup Modem Server Connection document properly, you can place a call to a server on demand by using the File ➤ Mobile ➤ Call Server or File ➤ Replication ➤ Replicate commands. (The server names that appear are taken from your Dialup Modem Server Connection documents.)

To create a new Dialup Modem Server Connection document, follow the steps below. If you don't quite understand what we're doing here, we'll explain everything over the course of the chapter.

1. Choose File ➤ Mobile ➤ Server Phone Numbers. The Server Connection view of your Personal Name & Address Book opens.

NOTE

Notes ignores parentheses and hyphens, so feel free to use them to make the phone number readable. Use a comma to force a two-second delay, which is useful for separating credit card numbers and digits that access outside phone lines. For example, it is common in the United States to use 9 to access an outside line from a business telephone. If the server has more than one phone number, you can enter each number separated by semicolons.

NOTE

If the first number is busy, your modem will try each number in turn until a connection is established. If you entered a Phone Dialing Prefix in the Location Setup dialog box, enter only the part of the number that follows the prefix. For example, if you entered the area code and exchange as a prefix, enter only the last four digits of the telephone number.

2. Click the Add Connection button. The Server Connection document opens, as shown in Figure 13.4.

3. Select the Dialup Modem option in the Connection Type field.

4. Enter the name of the server you want to access in the Server Name field.

5. Enter the server's country code in the Country Code field.

6. Enter the server's area code in the Area Code field. (Notes dials the server's area code—and if necessary, the country code—only when you call the server from a location with a different area code.)

7. Enter the server's telephone number in the Phone Number field.

FIGURE 13.4:

You create a Server Connection document to connect to a remote server.

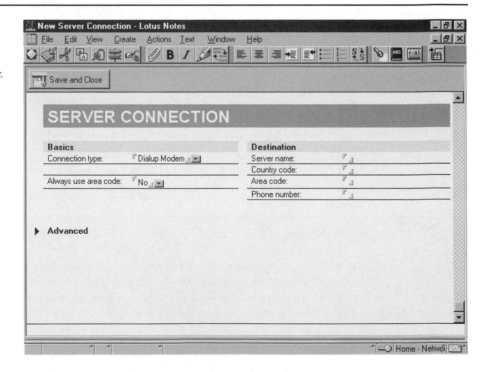

Setting Up Your Modem

You can set up any Notes-compatible modem to use Mobile Notes. However, before you do, we recommend that you refer to your modem's documentation for further advice. Modems that aren't Hayes compatible sometimes have problems running Mobile Notes. To set up your modem, follow these steps:

1. Choose File ➤ Tools ➤ User Preferences. The User Preferences dialog box appears, as shown in Figure 13.5.

FIGURE 13.5:

The User Preferences dialog box enables you to select a communication port and connect your modem to it.

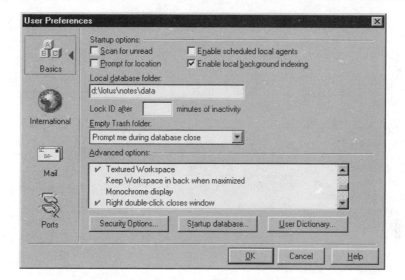

2. Click the Ports option to display the communication ports settings, as shown in Figure 13.6.

3. Select the port your modem is connected to (for example, COM2).

4. Click the Port Enabled option if it is not checked.

5. Click Port options, where *Port* is the name of the port to which your modem is connected (for example, COM2 Options). The Additional Setup dialog box appears, as shown in Figure 13.7. You use this dialog box to select a modem, configure dialing options for it, or monitor your modem's activity during dial-up operations.

FIGURE 13.6:

Choosing the Ports option displays the communication ports settings.

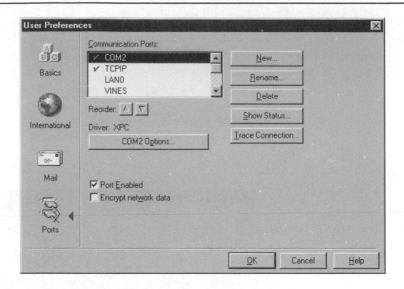

FIGURE 13.7:

The Additional Setup dialog box enables you to select a specific modem and configure dialing options for it.

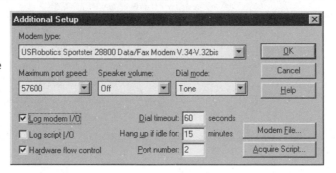

To finish configuring the type of modem you are using, follow these steps:

1. Select a modem command file (.MDM file) for your modem from the Modem type list. In this example, the modem type is USRobotics Sportster 28800 Data/Fax Modem V.34-V.32bis.

2. Set your modem's speaker volume to Off, Low, Medium, or High, depending on your work environment. The default setting is Off, meaning you won't hear the modem. Turn on the Speaker Volume so you can monitor call progress while attempting server connection. This setting is useful to monitor the activity of internal modems that do not have lights.

3. Set your modem's dial mode to Tone or Pulse. Select Pulse if you use a rotary phone or if your modem doesn't support Tone (touch-tone) dialing; otherwise, select Tone (the default).

4. Change the Maximum port speed of data transmission for your modem if you have problems communicating at higher speeds (for example, a noisy phone line). You can always use a lower setting to reduce the speed. Otherwise, Notes determines the maximum data transmission speed from the type of modem you are using. The speed Notes actually uses will be the *lesser* of the maximum speed you select here and the maximum speed specified in the MDM file. For example, if you select 38400Kbps here and the MDM file specifies 19200Kbps as the maximum, you will see a warning similar to the following:

   "The selected Modem command file only allows speeds as high as: 19200"

5. Specify the maximum number of Dial Timeout seconds your workstation tries to establish a connection to a Notes server. When this number is reached, the call "times out" (terminates), and your modem returns to its initial state. You can increase or decrease Dial Timeout to meet specific calling conditions before you try calling the Notes server again.

6. Specify the number of minutes in the Hang Up If Idle For field. This time interval is the maximum time your workstation maintains a connection to a Notes server before it hangs up (terminates the connection). Selecting this option disconnects your workstation from the server when you aren't transmitting or receiving data beyond the specified time. If the Notes administrator has specified a different Hang Up If Idle For time for the server's modem, the shorter time period takes precedence.

NOTE   The Hang Up If Idle For option works only if the value you set is less than the value set for the mail-polling interval in the Mail Setup dialog box.

---

7. Select the Log Modem I/O option to tell Notes to record modem control strings and responses in the workstation's Notes Log. In this way, you can determine or anticipate modem communication problems. You can then review the Phone Calls, Replication Events, and Miscellaneous Events views of the log. You will want to leave the Log modem I/O option selected only while you are initially setting up and testing a modem. After you get your modem working, deselect this option. You should enable the Log Modem I/O option only when you experience problems with your modem.

8. Select the Hardware Flow Control option. This option enables Notes to control hardware flow between the server's modem and your modem. You specify this option when using data compression.

NOTE   If hardware flow control isn't mentioned in your serial card or modem documentation, your hardware probably does not support this option.

---

9. Click the Modem File button to open the Edit Modem Command File dialog box if you want to change your modem command file. Scroll to the settings you want to change and make your changes. Click the Save or Save As button. The Save option saves your changes to the command file, which is stored on your hard disk. The Save As option saves the edited command file to your hard disk under another name that you specify in a standard Save File dialog box and doesn't affect the command file you originally opened.

WARNING   Record your modem's current configuration before editing command or script files, or save edited command and script files under a new name. You should always save any modified script files under a new name and change the MODELS= statement to a unique description that will then appear in the Modem Type list box. (You don't want two modem files with the same description.)

---

10. Click the Close or Done button to close the window. The Close option closes the dialog box. If you haven't selected Save or Save As after making changes, a message asks if you want to save your changes. Select Yes to save your changes, No to close the dialog box and revert to the previous version of the modem command file, or Cancel to return to the dialog box.

11. Click OK to close the Additional Setup dialog box.

12. Click OK to close the User Preferences dialog box.

Calling a Server

After you set up your workstation and modem to use Mobile Notes, you're ready to call a Notes server. You might want to call a server to exchange data between your local database replicas and their corresponding shared databases or to work interactively with databases on the server.

You can use the Call Server dialog box to call a Notes server immediately, or you can set up a schedule for automatic dialing by using the Scheduled Calling part of the Location document.

To call a Notes server, do the following:

1. Choose File ➤ Mobile ➤ Call Server. (Enter your password if one has been set for you.) The Call Server dialog box appears, as shown in Figure 13.8.

FIGURE 13.8:

You select the server you want to call in the Call Server dialog box.

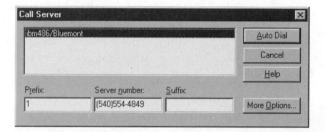

2. Select a server from the Server list. The servers listed here are the ones for which you have Dialup Modem Server Connection documents in your Personal Name & Address Book.

NOTE   The phone number for the server's modem should be displayed in the Server Number box. If it is not displayed correctly, you have not set up any Dialup Modem Server Connection documents yet or you did not enter the phone number correctly.

3. Click the More Options button to specify the maximum number of seconds to wait for a connection to a server before canceling the attempt. The default is 60.

4. Specify the maximum number of minutes your system will stay connected to a server without activity (data transmission). The default is 15.

5. Select Auto Dial or Manual Dial. The Auto Dial option automatically dials the specified telephone number. The Manual Dial option prompts you to pick up the phone and dial the number. Use this option when you require an operator to complete the call, for example, when you are calling from a hotel room that does not support autodial for outside phone lines.

When a connection is made, the dialog box closes and your Workspace reappears.

Making a Database Replica with Mobile Notes

As discussed in earlier chapters, a replica is a copy of a shared database that you store on your local hard disk. It can be displayed in your Workspace just like the source database. When you create a replica, changes to either the original database (source database) or the replica will be reflected in the other.

To update a database replica with information from the source database (and to update the shared database with information that you create locally), you perform replication. You can use a Dialup Modem Server Connection document or call the server directly using the Call Server dialog box.

Before you can use the database exchange feature of Mobile Notes to replicate regularly, you must first call the server where the database is located in order to create a local replica of the shared database you want to use on your workstation. By creating a local database replica, you can use the database without being connected to a Notes server on a LAN or being connected to a modem all the time.

NOTE   You must know the name of the server and the file name of the database you want to replicate before you attempt replication.

Calling the Server

To call the server where the database that you want to replicate is located, follow these steps:

1.   Choose File ➤ Replication ➤ New Replica. The Open Database dialog box appears, as shown in Figure 13.9. If you choose a server that is not accessible across your LAN or WAN, a message box appears asking you if you want Notes to call the server.

2.   Click the Yes button. The Call Server dialog box appears.

3.   Choose the server.

4.   Click the Auto Dial button. Notes initializes the modem and makes the call. The status area in the status bar reports the modem's activity, and a modem icon appears on the far left end of the status bar.

FIGURE 13.9:

FIGURE 13.9:

The Open Database dialog box allows you to select a server in which the database you want to copy (or replicate) is located.

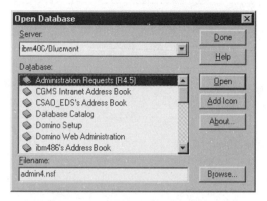

Choosing the Database

After you connect to the server, the Open Database dialog box appears again, this time displaying the databases that are available to you on the remote server. To choose a database to copy as a replica, follow these steps:

1. Choose the database you want to copy as a replica.

2. Click the Select button. The New Replica [*name of database*] dialog box appears, displaying information about the database you selected. The dialog box might look similar to Figure 13.10, depending on the databases available to you.

3. Choose the server on your local workstation in which you want to store the database. (This information is automatically filled in for you if you chose a database in the previous dialog box.) The server should be set to Local to copy the replica to your workstation's Workspace page.

FIGURE 13.10:

The New Replica dialog box enables you to make a replica copy of a database.

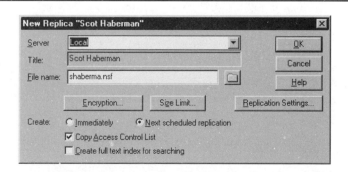

TIP

If you plan to replicate several databases to your local workstation, put them into a subdirectory called \REPLICAS. If you need some extra disk space, you can always delete one of the databases that you have replicated and then re-replicate it later. The is one exception: Always make sure that the local replica copy of your mail file is in a subdirectory of the same name as the subdirectory that your mail file is stored in on your Notes Mail server. By default, the subdirectory is called \MAIL.

4. Select the Create Immediately option to populate the database with documents.

5. Click OK.

Notes copies the replica of the database to your Workspace page.

Using a Database Replica on Your Workstation

Before you can actually use a database replica you copy from a server, you must first initialize it. If you attempt to open the database replica before you initialize it, you get an error message, as shown in Figure 13.11.

FIGURE 13.11:

You must initialize a database replica before you can use it, or you get a message telling you to do so.

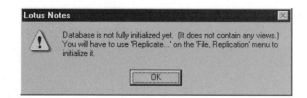

Initializing a Database

To initialize a database replica, follow these steps:

1. Click the database to highlight it on your Workspace page.

2. Choose File ➤ Replication ➤ Replicate. The Replicate [*name of database*] dialog box appears, as shown in Figure 13.12.

3. Choose the server in which the original database you want to copy is stored. Notes fills this box in for you automatically if you selected a database on your Workspace before you chose the command.

FIGURE 13.12:

The Replicate dialog box
allows you to select background replication, which
enables you to continue
working while replication
takes place.

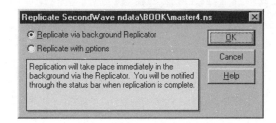

4. Enter the file name, if Notes hasn't filled it in for you.

5. Click the Select button.

Notes calls the server where the original database (not the replica) is located. When the connection is made, Notes begins replicating the local replica on your workstation with the original on the server, copying all the document's database design elements (for example, forms, views, Agents, and so on). Notes automatically hangs up when the replication has finished.

Disconnecting from the Server

When Notes has finished copying the replica to your workstation, you need to disconnect from the server:

1. Choose File ➤ Mobile ➤ Hang Up. The Hang Up dialog box appears, displaying the name of the remote server you are connected to, as shown in Figure 13.13.

2. Click the Hang Up button. Notes breaks the modem's connection to the server. A message such as "COM2: Call has finished" appears in the status message area in the status bar.

FIGURE 13.13:

You end a call to the remote
server by using the Hang Up
dialog box.

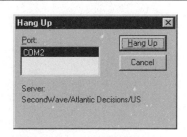

Refining the Replication Process

The next time you replicate, you can select several options to refine the replication settings according to your needs. To limit the number of documents that will be copied to a database replica during the first replication, click the database icon to highlight it and then choose File ➤ Database ➤ Properties. The Database Properties InfoBox appears, as shown in Figure 13.14. Click the Replication Settings button. The Replication Settings dialog box appears, as shown in Figure 13.15. Choose the Other option. Select a Scheduled replication priority level (Low, Medium, or High). The priority level is used for scheduling database replication. The default level is Medium.

FIGURE 13.14:

The Database Properties InfoBox provides options for changing replication settings and viewing a database's replication history.

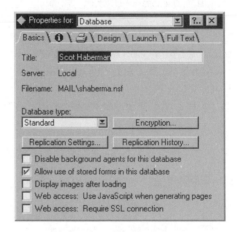

FIGURE 13.15:

The Replication Settings dialog box allows you to change a database's replication settings and to refine the replication process.

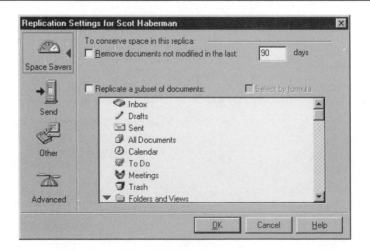

To set how you want Notes to send deletions and handle other changes in a database during replication, choose the Send option and then select any of the following options:

- **Do Not Send Deletions Made in This Replica to Other Replicas:** Prevents deletions to local replicas from being propagated to other replicas of this database. In other words, if you delete documents in the replica database located on your Mobile machine, these deletions won't propagate back to the main server database when you reconnect. Choose this option when you have Author access or higher to a database and need to delete documents to manage space on your Mobile machine, but these documents are still of relevance to the other users of the database.

- **Do Not Send Changes in Database Title & Catalog Info to Other Replicas:** Prevents giving this database the same title, categories, and template names as the original database.

- **Do Not Send Changes in Local Security Property to Other Replicas:** Prevents sending any changes in the access control or security properties of this database to the original.

Click OK to confirm any changes you make.

Replicating a Database on a Regular Basis

After you make a local replica of a database the first time, you can use Mobile Notes to work locally. You share databases on your workstation by calling a Notes server regularly and then exchanging data between your local replicas and the shared databases. In other words, you replicate databases when you want to exchange information between an original and a replica copy of a database.

You can perform a replication using the following method:

1. Click the Database icon to select it. Choose File ➤ Replication ➤ Replicate. Enter your password if you've set one for yourself. The Replicate [*name of database*] dialog box appears.

2. Select the replicate options you want as follows:

   - **Replicate via Background Replicator:** This option is the default. Notes performs data exchange immediately in the background via the Replicator so you can continue using your workstation for other tasks. The status bar tells you when replication is complete. Selecting this option does not perform scheduled tasks; to do so, choose the Replicate with Options option.

- **Replicate with Options:** Allows you to override the Replicator page settings for a one-time replication and select specific tasks to take place during replication. You have to wait as the database replicates before you can continue using your workstation.

3. Click OK.

Notes then calls the server. When a connection is made, the dialog box closes and the Notes Workspace reappears.

Make sure that both the database you are replicating and its counterpart on the server have the appropriate Access rights to share information. If a user has replicated a local database with a server, then that server's name should appear in the local database's ACL with access rights set to either Designer or Editor for the server. When two servers replicate with one another, ensure that the servers' access rights are set properly in each database. Notes administrators often use a group called LocalDomainServers (in which all servers in your company's Notes domain are defined), which is set at Manager rights to ensure that the ACL, design, and all data elements of the databases are replicated seamlessly throughout your organization.

Checking Replication Information

After Notes completes the replication process, the Replicator page displays replication information for the selected database. If you chose the Replicate with Options option, a status box displays the following details about the database documents and mail messages that are affected during database replication:

- **Additions:** Reports the number of new documents that are added (Sent) to the original database or added (Received) to the database replica.

- **Deletions:** Reports the number of documents that are deleted (Sent) from the original database or deleted (Received) from the database replica.

- **Updates:** Reports the number of documents that are changed (Sent) in the original database or changed (Received) in the database replica.

- **Databases Replicated:** Reports the number of databases that are replicated.

- **Databases Initialized:** Reports the number of databases that are initialized.

- **Mail Messages Transferred:** Reports the number of Mail messages transferred from your outgoing mailbox to your mail server.

- **Replication Exception Conditions Logged:** Reports the number of possible error conditions that occurred during replication. Information about these conditions appears in your Notes log file (LOG.NSF).

Using the Replicator Workspace Page

Replicating databases is an easy procedure, especially when you use the Replicator Workspace page, as shown in Figure 13.16.

FIGURE 13.16:

The Replicator Workspace page enables you to replicate databases on a regular basis and watch the progress of each replication.

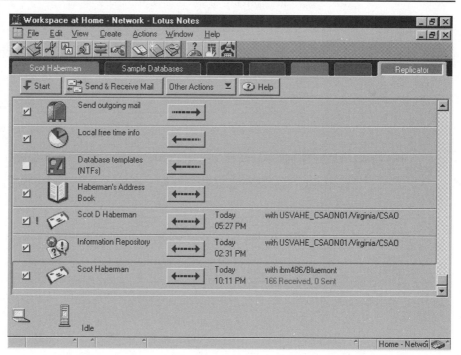

The Replicator Workspace page lets you manage replication of your local databases in one place. With the Replicator page, you can replicate multiple databases with one or more servers with a single command. When you use the Replicator page, Notes replicates in the background so you can do other work while Notes replicates.

When you use Notes away from the office, you can call each server you want to replicate with automatically. If you are using a passthru server or a remote LAN server, you can have Replicator make a single call and replicate all of your local databases at one time, even if they're on different servers.

The Replicator page also lets you customize replication depending on where you're working. For example, you could set up a local database to receive full documents when you replicate at the office (on a network) and receive shortened documents when you replicate away from the office (using a modem). In other words, the Replicator page is "location aware." The Replicator page also provides additional ways to replicate; for example, you can assign high priority to selected databases and replicate only those databases.

TIP   To quickly change database replication settings, right-click a database entry that's displayed on the Replicator page. The Replicator Options menu appears. You can choose from the following commands: Options, Replicate Selected Database, Replication Settings, and Replication History.

Using the Default Replicator Page Settings

The Replicator page is always the last page on your Workspace; you cannot delete it. It automatically contains the following types of settings:

- **Database:** The Replicator page contains a database entry for each local replica you have.

- **Start Replication At:** Use to specify a replication schedule and enable scheduled replication. This entry is always first and cannot be deleted.

- **Send Outgoing Mail:** Use to send all pending messages from your local MAIL.BOX database. This entry cannot be deleted.

- **Database Templates:** Use to refresh the designs of template-based databases. This entry cannot be deleted.

You can also create the following types of entries for mobile locations (such as Home and Travel):

- **Call:** You can use a call entry to connect to a server.

- **Hang up!:** You can use Hang up! to end a connection with a server.

Most types of settings on the Replicator page contain Action buttons that you can use to specify replication options. For example, you can use the arrow button on a database entry to specify the direction you want to replicate in and the server with which you want to replicate.

When you replicate, the status bar at the bottom of the Replicator page displays current replication information, such as call attempt information, the database currently being replicated, and the number of updates that have been replicated.

After replication, the Replicator page displays replication statistics for individual entries such as the server replicated with and the date and time of replication.

Changing Replicator Locations

Notes lets you set up the Replicator page in a different way at each of your locations. Consequently, you don't have to change replication settings every time you work at a different location. For example:

- You could set up a database entry at your Office location so that it sends and receives documents when you are at the office, and you could deselect the same database entry by removing the check mark along the left column at your Travel location so that it never replicates when you are on the road.

- You could replicate all of your local databases on a schedule at your Office location and replicate only your mail on an as-needed basis at your Home location.

- You could arrange database entries in one order at your Travel location and arrange them in a different order at your Home location.

Starting the Replicator

Why do you want to use the Replicator to replicate databases on a regular basis? You save time because Notes runs faster with local databases. You also save money because your telephone calls are shorter when you work locally. It's more convenient and less expensive to move data over telephone lines all at once. Furthermore, you can work whenever and wherever you want, even when a telephone line is unavailable. You already have a replica of a database on your computer.

Calling a Server

To call a Notes server and replicate a database, display the Replicator Workspace page and then follow these steps:

1. Click the database you want to replicate.

2. Choose Actions ➤ Replicate Selected Database. After Notes calls the server and makes a connection, a progress bar at the bottom of the page displays the percentage of the replication and the amount of replication time that remains. Figure 13.17 shows the progress of a replication.

FIGURE 13.17:

A progress bar on the Replicator page shows the status of the current database replication.

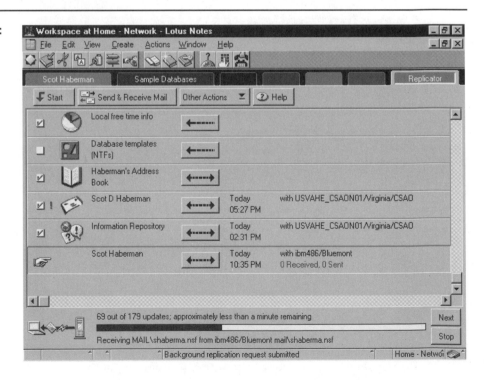

TIP

You can simply click the Start button to replicate all of the databases that you have selected. To stop replication, click the Stop button.

3. Because the replication process automatically takes place in the background (unless you chose another replication option), you can click another Workspace page tab, open another database, and create or edit documents while the replication is occurring.

4. Click the Replicator tab when the replication is finished. The results of the database replication appear, showing you the number of documents that were received and sent. Figure 13.18 shows an example of a completed replication.

5. Click the Workspace page tab where the database is located.

FIGURE 13.18:

When the replication is finished, the Replicator page shows the number of documents that were received and sent.

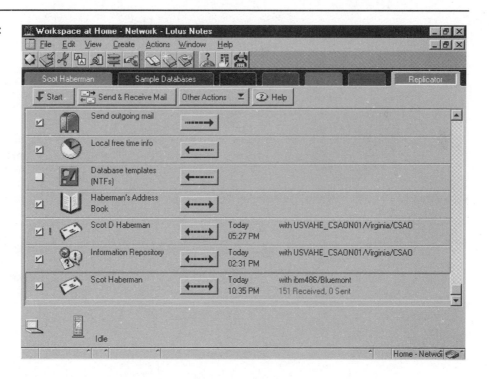

Ending a Connection

Before you continue, make sure you've disconnected from the server. To end a modem connection to a Notes server, follow these steps:

1. Choose File ➤ Mobile ➤ Hang Up. The Hang Up dialog box appears.

2. Select the port you want to disconnect.

3. Click the Hang Up button or click Cancel if you change your mind.

Verifying Replication History

To check when and with which server a database last replicated, follow these steps:

1. Click the database to highlight it (if you haven't already selected it).

2. Choose File ➤ Database ➤ Properties. The Database Properties InfoBox appears, as previously shown in Figure 13.14.

TIP　　　You can also right-click on the database icon to display the Database Properties menu. Choose Database Properties to display the Database Properties InfoBox.

---

3. Click the Replication History button to display the Replication History dialog box, as shown in Figure 13.19. You can show the history information by date or by server name.

4. Select Cancel to close the dialog box.

FIGURE 13.19:

The Replication History dialog box displays a list of dates when you replicated databases.

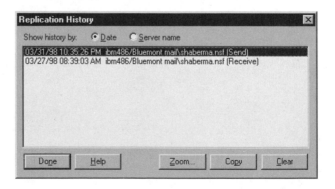

Clearing the History

To delete all history, select the Clear button in the Replication History dialog box. This option is useful if you think your replica doesn't contain all the documents it should or if time/date stamps are out of sync between your replica and others. This option deletes the replication history for all servers that the Notes client or Notes server replicates.

If you clear the history, Notes will no longer have a record of when replication last occurred. The next replication will invoke a *full* search for documents to replicate, not just a normal (incremental) search. Notes will look at the last modified time for all documents in the source database and replicate any changes that the destination database doesn't have. Use full replication *only* if you are sure it's needed; full replications create more network traffic and take longer than incremental replications.

Replicating Mail with Mobile Notes

During setup (if you chose the option for working remotely), Notes created both a local mail replica and your local MAIL.BOX database, which stores your outgoing mail. Notes added the icons to your Workspace, which might look similar to the icons in Figure 13.20, depending on the way your Workspace page appears.

As you can see, Notes doesn't add the icon for the server-based mail file, even when you switch to server-based mail. If you want to switch to server-based mail to work with your mail interactively, you must add the icon manually by connecting to the server and then selecting File ➤ Database ➤ Open for your server.

You can also replicate mail to your server so you can access it locally. To replicate workstation-based Notes mail, display the Replicator Workspace page. Choose Actions ➤ Send and Receive Mail or choose Actions ➤ Send Outgoing Mail. Notes sends outgoing mail from your local outgoing mail database (MAIL.BOX) to the server and then deletes the mail from your local outgoing mail database (MAIL.BOX).

FIGURE 13.20:

Notes automatically created your outgoing mailbox and your mail database during setup.

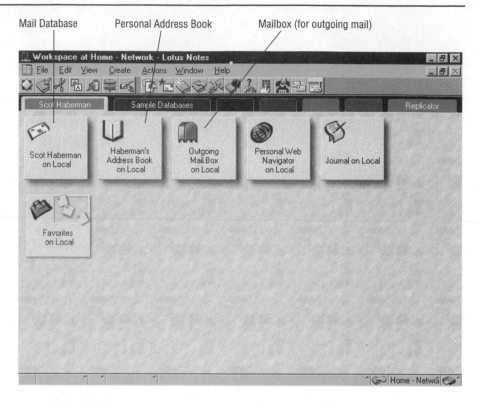

Mail Database   Personal Address Book   Mailbox (for outgoing mail)

Using Your Outgoing Mail Database

Your outgoing mail database (called MAIL.BOX) is a temporary storage area on your workstation for your outgoing memos. It is not used in the same way as your Mail database. Do not try to compose mail from your outgoing mail database. You should use your Notes Mail database instead.

The documents you send are dropped in the MAIL.BOX database and held for pickup. Pickup occurs when:

- You perform replication with your mail server by displaying the Replicator page and then choosing Actions ➤ Send and Receive Mail (or Send Outgoing Mail).

- You close the Workspace and exit Notes.

When you close the Workspace and exit Notes, Notes displays a dialog box telling you that you have outgoing mail pending, as shown in Figure 13.21, and asks if you want to transfer it now. When you click the Yes button, you are prompted to call your mail server. Once the mail is sent, your documents are taken from your local MAIL.BOX database and delivered to the server's mailbox. From there, the server delivers the mail to the intended recipients.

FIGURE 13.21:

When you exit Notes and you have outgoing mail in your mailbox, Notes asks if you want to send it before you exit.

When the data exchange is completed successfully, your MAIL.BOX database is empty.

Addressing Mail for Replication

For your outgoing mail to be delivered properly, the recipients listed in the To field of a document need to be included in your Personal Name & Address Book or the server's Name & Address book.

When workstation-based mail is selected, Notes looks up recipient names in your Personal Name & Address Book first. If the recipient isn't there, it notes the document from your local outgoing mailbox to the server when you connect to the server, assuming the server will look for the recipient in its Name & Address book. If the server can't find the name, it sends a nondelivery report to your mail file on the server to let you know who didn't receive your document. Therefore, you may not be aware that the document was not delivered until the next time you replicate your mail database.

During routine database replications, Notes also transfers mail in and out. When the replication is finished, the Replicator page displays the number of mail messages that you sent and received.

Using POP3/SMTP with Notes Mail

 Notes 4.6 has added a powerful feature to the Notes mail client that allows you to send and receive mail using a POP3/SMTP server. What does this mean to you?

- You no longer need to be connected to a Domino server in order to send and receive Internet mail.

- You now have the ability to access your e-mail account from an ISP using Notes. You no longer have to use another e-mail interface (such as MS Outlook Express) to get your Internet e-mail.

- You now also have the ability to store your personal and business e-mail in one single Notes mail database—or you can keep them in separate databases, but it is your choice.

So what is POP3? Basically POP3 is an e-mail protocol for downloading mail from a mail server. In order to download your mail, your ISP must support this protocol (which most do). So let's talk about the basics of setting up your client so you can access this new functionality.

A New Location Document

The first thing that you will need to do is create a Location document for accessing your mail from an ISP. In this example, you will create a new Location document specifically for accessing the ISP and not your Domino server (we will show this later in the chapter).

To create a new Location document, follow the instructions earlier in the chapter. Once you have a new Location document displayed, make the following changes:

1. Under the Basics section, make the following changes:

    - **Location Type:** Since most ISPs are dial-in, make sure the Location Type is Dialup Modem.

    - **Location Name:** Enter a description that identifies this location document for using the ISP (such as Internet Mail).

2. Under the Internet Browser section, just take the defaults for now. These fields will be explained in more detail in Chapter 31.

3. Under the Servers section, make the following changes:

   - **Home/Mail Server:** Since you are not accessing a Domino server, just blank out this field.

   - **Passthru Server:** Since you are not accessing a Domino server, just blank out this field.

4. Under the Ports section, make this change: Depending on your configuration, you may have many different options. Only select the TCPIP port.

5. Under the Phone Dialing section, just blank out all the fields.

NOTE
One major drawback to using POP3 is the lack of an automatic dialer available from within Notes. In order to dial in to a POP3 mail server, you will need to establish the session outside of Notes.

---

6. Under the Mail section, make the following changes (note that the Mail section contains the information pertaining to only your Notes mail file):

   - **Mail System:** Select the Internet Choice option. This selection will determine the other sections to display in your location document.

   - **Mail File Location:** Select Local for now. We will discuss how to save mail on your server shortly.

   - **Mail File:** Type in where the local copy of your mail file resides. This can be a replica of your mail file from the server or you can create a new local mail file.

   - For the remaining fields, select whatever you prefer.

7. Under the Replication section, keep it Disabled.

8. Under the Internet Mail section, make the following changes (note that the Internet Mail section contains the information pertaining to only your Internet Mail from your ISP):

   - **Send Outgoing Mail:** Select Directly to Internet since this is your only option.

TIP To create mail messages that will be sent via the Internet while offline, save the mail messages as Drafts. Once you are connected, you can open each Draft copy and send it. If you try to send Internet Mail while you are offline, Notes will display an error. Another approach to this problem is to create an additional location document that specifies "No Connection" as the Location Type. All messages will then be stored in the SMTP.BOX database (an icon will be automatically added to your Workspace). Once you are connected again, you can send all your stored messages.

- **Internet Mail Address:** Type an Internet e-mail address (for example, yourname@some.company.com. This is the address that will be placed in the E-Mail From field. When users reply to your e-mail message, this address will be used.

- **Outgoing (SMTP) Internet Mail Server:** This field contains the name of the server to connect to when sending mail directly to the Internet. This will be supplied to you by your ISP.

- **Incoming Internet Mail Server:** This field contains the name of the server to connect to in order to receive your mail from the Internet. This will be supplied to you by your ISP.

- **Internet Username:** This contains your user name assigned by your ISP. This may be required by your ISP.

- **Internet Password:** This is your password for your user name. This may be required by your ISP.

- **Leave On Mail Server:** Most ISPs require that you delete your messages from their servers once you have retrieved them. If this is the case with your ISP, make sure you select No.

- For the remaining fields, just take the defaults.

Once you have completed all these changes, you are ready to access your Internet mail. Save your new Location document and return to your Workspace.

Before you begin accessing your Internet mail, you must first switch to the Location document you just created. The quickest way to accomplish this is to click the location indicator located on the status bar (refer to Figure 13.3). You are now ready to "dial up" or connect to your ISP.

Dial-Up Networking Configuration

Configuring your machine to connect to your ISP can be a complicated task. Most ISPs supply you with installation disks depending on your operating system. This book does not explain how to configure your machine for using dial-up networking. If you have problems in this area, contact your ISP's customer support.

One major drawback in accessing your Internet mail using Notes is the lack of an automatic dialing feature. Hopefully this will be addressed in a future release of Notes. In order to access your Internet mail, you will need to initiate the call yourself outside of Notes. Once connected successfully, your machine will have created a TCP/IP session with your ISP and you continue working in Notes. This same process of connecting to your ISP will be used again when discussing your Personal Web Navigator in Chapter 31.

Once you have connected to your ISP, you are ready to use Notes. Open the Mail database that you selected in your Location document. Select the Inbox folder. The first thing that you will notice is there is not much of a difference between your Internet Mail database and a regular Notes Mail database except for the addition of a Retrieve Mail button (see Figure 13.22).

FIGURE 13.22:

The Inbox folder for a POP3 mail client

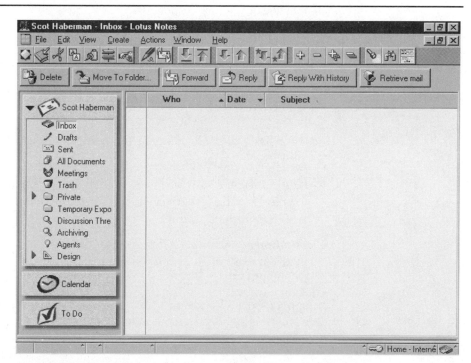

The Retrieve Mail button is used to *fetch* your mail from the POP3 mail server. Clicking this button will activate a background action that polls your POP3 mail server, grabs your Internet Mail, and places it in your Inbox. To see the status of the mail retrieval process, select the Replicator Workspace tab, and Notes will display the current progress.

TIP   You can also "fetch" your mail by switching to the Replicator page and selecting the Send & Receive Mail button. Another shortcut is to click the Inbox icon located on the far right of the status bar and select Receive Mail from the pop-up menu.

Creating and sending e-mail is no different from the process described in Chapter 11. The biggest difference is that mail will be sent immediately to your ISP using the SMTP Internet Server instead of having to route through your Domino server.

Combining an Internet and a Notes Mail Database

You can now use one mail file to access your personal ISP mail and your company Notes mail. You can set up this type of mail file for use on a local Mail database, a server Mail database, or both (your choice).

You can either create a new Location document or modify an existing one. For this example, you will need to create a new Location document that will be used when you are connected to your Domino server. Create a new Location document following the procedures described earlier in the chapter. Once you have a new location document displayed, make the following changes:

1. Under the Basics section, make the following changes:

    - **Location Type:** We know from the previous section that the ISP should be specified as Dial-Up. Since you will also be accessing (or connected) to your Domino server via a LAN, select the Both Dialup and Local Area Network option.

    - **Location Name:** Enter a description that identifies this location document for using the ISP and the Domino server (such as Network and Internet Mail).

2. Under the Internet Browser section, just take the defaults for now. These fields will be explained in more detail in Chapter 31.

3. Under the Servers section, make the following changes:

   - **Home/Mail Server:** Enter the name of your Domino mail server. If you are unsure, look at another Location document that you use to access your server and copy it to this field.

   - **Passthru Server:** Again, if you have one, type it here, if not, leave it blank.

4. Under the Ports section, make the following changes:

   - Depending on your configuration, you may have many different options. Make sure that at least the TCP/IP port is selected. The protocol you use to access your server will determine any other port to select. Refer to an existing Location document you use to access your server.

5. Under the Phone Dialing section, just blank out all the fields.

6. Under the Mail section, make the following changes:

   - **Mail System:** Select the Notes and Internet option.

   - **Mail File Location:** Select the Local option.

Local vs. Server

If you do not select Local for the Mail File Location field, certain Internet Mail fields will not be visible (such as the Incoming Mail Server). The reason for this is Notes assumes that if your mail file resides on the server, all of your mail will be coming through the server. In this example, you want to be able to get your Notes mail and your Internet mail. You will need to fool Notes in order to do this. If you first save your Location document with the Mail File Location as Local, then open it and change it to On Server and save it again, it will work correctly even though not all the Internet Mail options are visible. The values for the Internet Mail fields have already been saved and Notes will find them.

   - **Mail File:** Type in where the server copy of your mail file resides.

   - **Notes Mail Domain:** Enter the name of your Notes domain.

   - For the remaining fields, select whatever you prefer.

7. Under the Replication section, just keep it Disabled.

8. Under the Internet Mail section, make the following changes:

- **Send Outgoing Mail:** Select Directly to Internet. You also have an option to route it through your Domino server (check with your Notes administrator). For this example, you will route all your outgoing Internet mail through your ISP.

- **Internet Mail Address:** Type in an Internet e-mail address (for example, yourname@some.company.com. This is the address that will be placed in the E-Mail From field. When users reply to your e-mail message, this address will be used.

- **Outgoing (SMTP) Internet Mail Server:** This field contains the name of the server to connect to in order to when sending mail directly to the Internet. This will be supplied to you by your ISP.

- **Incoming Internet Mail Server:** This field contains the name of the server to connect to in order to receive your mail from the Internet. This will be supplied to you by your ISP. If this field is not visible on your Location document, refer to the sidebar on "Local vs. Server."

- **Internet Username:** This contains your user name that was assigned by your ISP. This may or may not be required by your ISP. If this field is not visible on your Location document, refer to the sidebar on "Local vs. Server."

- **Internet Password:** This is your password for your user name. This may or may not be required by your ISP. If this field is not visible on your Location document, refer to the sidebar on "Local vs. Server."

- **Leave On Mail Server:** Most ISPs require that you delete your messages from their servers once you have retrieved them. If this is the case with your ISP, make sure you select No.

- For the remaining fields, just take the defaults. If these fields are not visible on your location document, refer to the sidebar on "Local vs. Server."

Once you have completed all these changes, you are ready to access your Notes and Internet mail from a single database. Save your new Location document and return to your Workspace.

Before you begin accessing your Mail database, you must first switch to the location document that you just created. The quickest way to accomplish this is to click the location indicator located on the status bar (refer to Figure 13.3). You are now ready to *dial up*, or connect to, your ISP.

Once you have connected to your ISP, you are ready to use Notes. Open the Mail database that you selected in your Location document. Select the Inbox folder. It should look just like the previous example and contain the Retrieve Mail button.

Using TCP/IP to Access the Notes Server

One major drawback to using a Dialup Server Connection document is long-distance phone calls. If you happen to live in a rural area or are traveling, dialing into your server may start to get expensive. An alternative to this approach is accessing your server via TCP/IP using your ISP account. Many ISPs are now accessible across the United States. Some have toll-free numbers, while others have local numbers in most major cities. If your server is set up properly, you may be able to access your mail and replicate databases without having to incur long-distance phone charges.

If you want to be able to access your server using TCP/IP, you will first need to check with your Notes administrator. Many corporations place their networks behind a corporate firewall. This protects your company's data from being accessed by anyone from the Internet, including you. If this is the case, you cannot use your ISP account to access your server.

If you can access your server using your ISP account, you may need to set up another Location document. To create this type of Location document, talk to your Notes administrator. Just be aware that the option may exist for your situation.

What's Next?

If you work off-site, whether at home or on the road, Mobile Notes can help you to work *locally*, wherever you are, because you can make local replicas (exact copies) of shared databases and then work on these replicas. You can also send and receive Notes mail by working in a local replica of your mail database and then exchanging documents (replicating) with your mail database on the server. With Mobile Notes, you can work in a different location and continue to exchange data with your organization's databases. Updates are literally a telephone call away.

In Part II we show you how to design Notes databases, and we examine all the issues involved in developing workflow-automation applications. In Chapter 14 we explain how all the basic components of a Notes database work together. This information will give you a good foundation for building applications that integrate a database's functionality with ease of use.

PART II

Building Notes Applications

CHAPTER

FOURTEEN

14

Defining the Components of a Notes Application

- ■ Creating an application

- ■ Creating a new database

- ■ Forms and subforms

- ■ Fields

- ■ Static text

- ■ Views, folders, and Navigators

- ■ Creating a document

So far we've been discussing the uses of Notes databases in specific ways, such as creating and viewing documents, searching databases, and sending e-mail. However, the real value of Notes lies in its powerful design features that let you build new applications with ease.

Because most of your work as a designer will be devoted to creating applications from the ground up, you should familiarize yourself with the building blocks, or basic components, of a Notes application.

The order in which the topics in this chapter are presented is meant to approximate a typical application development sequence. Of course, it's your application, so you are the final judge of how to construct it. We give you an overview of the toolbox that Notes places at your disposal for application development. Each section will refer you to a later chapter where you will find an extensive discussion of the particular topic.

The Process of Creating a Notes Application

By now you should be comfortable using a Notes database. If you've been using the sample databases on the companion CD (or one of your own), you've seen the ingenious ways a Notes database can organize and present information. You've also seen how the structure of a Notes database differs from other Windows databases, such as Access, Approach, or FileMaker Pro, that utilize the traditional field-record-file database structure.

As described in Chapter 1, Lotus Notes uses a document database structure, in which information is presented in documents that are accessed by groups. This structure provides you with new ways to work and collaborate with other people on different projects. Up until now we've tried to emphasize in a conceptual way the importance of workflow management and the gains in productivity that can be achieved by using Notes. Now we roll up our sleeves and show you how to do it.

From the Top—the Database

You start creating an application in Notes by creating, or *initializing*, a database. At this point, the database is an empty repository in which the various design elements that make up your application will be stored. The process of creating a new database is simple and is described in detail in Part II. For now, realize that the creation of a database is just a starting point. By itself, a new database doesn't serve any function. It is the introduction of forms, views, Navigators, and other design objects that gives a database its functionality.

To create a new database, follow these steps:

1. Click the Workspace page tab where you want the new database to appear.

2. Choose File ➤ Database ➤ New. The New Database dialog box will appear as shown in Figure 14.1.

TIP   You can also use Ctrl+N to display the New Database dialog box.

FIGURE 14.1:

The New Database dialog box

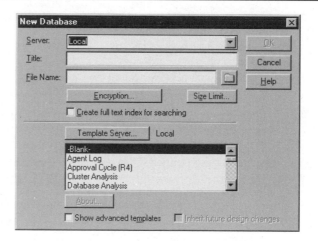

3. Select the server on which to create the new database from the Server drop-down list, or select Local to create the database on your workstation hard drive. If you choose to create the database on a server, it is assumed that you have the authority to do so (as assigned by the Notes system administrator).

The Server drop-down list is determined based on the contents of your Workspace (which is stored in your DESKTOP.DSK file). If you only have icons on your Workspace that refer to Local databases, then the Server drop-down list will only display an option for Local. Once you place a database that resides on a server on your Workspace, that server will show up in the Server drop-down list. You can type a server name in the Server drop-down list, press ↵ and the Servers database list will be displayed (assuming you have access to the server).

> **TIP**
>
> Will you be developing the application on your own or will you be jointly developing the application with others? While Notes is not designed to be a collaborative development environment like Visual Basic 4.0 or Powerbuilder Enterprise version, it is possible to coordinate the development of different parts of an application among a group of developers. In this scenario, it makes sense to create and maintain the database on a server to which everyone involved in the development process has access. If you are the sole developer, you can create and maintain a database on your workstation hard drive and then "promote" the database to a server when it's ready to be rolled out.

> **TIP**
>
> Notes is not a collaborative development environment. It is easy to accidentally overwrite someone's changes. There are now tools on the market that will allow the same check-in/check-out facility for design elements used in many of the traditional enterprise development environments.

4. Assign a title to the database in the Title text box. This title will appear on the database icon itself and, more importantly, in the list of available databases when a user chooses File ➤ Database ➤ Open. Be sure to make the title intuitive enough for users to recognize its function.

5. Assign a file name to the database in the File Name text box. By default, the database will be created in the same context as your Notes client software. You may indicate an alternative location by clicking the folder icon next to the File Name text box.

> **TIP**
>
> If you wish to base the design of your new database on a template, you may select one from the list displayed in the lower portion of the dialog box. (Design templates are discussed in detail in Chapter 24.)

6. Choose any encryption, size limit, or full text indexing options that are appropriate for the new database.

TIP

Placing a size limit on a database is really more an administrative issue than a design issue. You might be faced with disk space constraints on your Notes server that require you to limit the size of a database. Bear in mind, however, that once the size limit is set it cannot be changed, so set a size limit only if you are absolutely sure that the database will never grow larger than *n* gigabytes. You cannot "grow" a database with a size limit to a greater size later on, at least not directly. There are two indirect methods to increase the size of such a database, but both methods require you to create a new instance of the database. You can execute a File ➤ Database ➤ Copy or File ➤ Database ➤ New Replica to create the new instance and then specify a greater size limit.

7. Click OK to create the new database.

Now that you've created a new database, you need to create the forms—the foundation on which every database is built—that people will use to create documents.

Is It a Database or Is It an Application?

The two terms are used interchangeably throughout this book and might lead to some confusion. In a classic client/server architecture, the *database* (which resides on a dedicated server that manages the database) serves as a data repository, and the *application* (which executes at a workstation under the control of a desktop operating system such as Windows or OS/2) is a program through which you interact with the database. Furthermore, these two pieces are distinct, separate entities, each with an associated set of files that reside in different locations.

Notes adheres to this standard architecture with the exception that the design elements of the application—forms, views, Agents, and so on—are actually stored in the database itself along with the data. Therefore, you can think of an application in Notes as the joining of the design elements you've created (and stored in the database) and the Notes client software executing at your workstation. The bottom line is that the idea of database and application are very much bound to one another in the Notes environment.

Introducing Forms

Practically speaking, all Notes documents are derived from forms. This statement alone should convince you of the importance of forms. Simply put, you can't have documents unless you have forms through which to create them. (Advanced readers may argue that it actually is possible, through API programming, to create documents without a form, but API is a very sophisticated topic and well beyond the scope of this book.)

Forms allow users to enter and view information and define the format and layout of documents. Each form can contain fields, static text, graphics, buttons, and other design elements (including subforms, to be discussed shortly). These elements determine how users enter information as well as how that information is processed and displayed. Forms are probably the single most important design element in any Notes application.

When you compose a document, its content is a direct result of the form through which it is created. Information—data—is stored in the fields that you place in the design of the form; the information is then saved as a document and becomes part of a Notes database. When you open a document, you see the data "through" the form. The form dictates the structure of the document and how the data appears onscreen. It's even possible to utilize one form for entering information and another for displaying it! Figure 14.2 is an example of a form that's used in the discussion database.

We'll take you through the details of designing a form in Chapter 17. Generally speaking, though, the process of putting a form together involves the following steps:

- Creating a form
- Defining fields, actions, and hotspots
- Defining properties
- Formatting text
- Writing formulas

When your users begin composing documents, only the forms that you have created will be available to them. These forms will allow users to input and capture information that becomes part of the Notes database.

FIGURE 14.2:

The Main Topic form is used in the discussion database for introducing a topic for discussion.

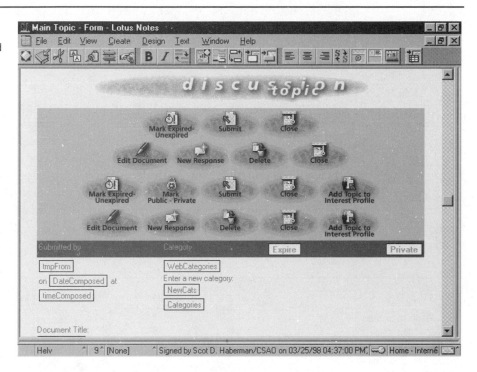

Types of Forms

Each form that you create for any application has a *type* associated with it. The type assignation you give a form dictates how people will use it and is integral in creating workflow applications. For example, the discussion database uses three primary forms: Main Topic, Response, and Response to Response. Each form serves a different purpose. The Main Topic form introduces a topic for discussion or an idea to be shared among a group of users. The Response form allows users to formulate responses to main topics. The Response to Response form allows for responses to be formulated to other responses.

The three forms used in the discussion database coincide with the three types of forms that can exist in any Notes database: Document, Response to Document, and Response to Response.

In the discussion database, the Main Topic form is a Document type, the Response form is a Response to Document type, and the Response to Response form is a Response to Response type. (Don't let the names of the forms in the discussion database confuse you. Their resemblance to the form types listed previously is purely coincidental.)

The connection between the three types of forms can be described as follows: A person uses the Main Topic form to initiate a discussion on a particular topic; Main Topic is the starting point in a workflow process. Upon reading a Main Topic document, another person can subsequently use the Response form to offer feedback, criticism, and so on about the idea under discussion. Many Response documents can result from a single Main Topic. Finally, the Response to Response form lets users continue a dialogue that originated from a Main Topic, creating what is known as a *discussion thread*.

You assign a type to a form through its Properties InfoBox, shown in Figure 14.3.

FIGURE 14.3:

When you design a new form, you assign a type to it by selecting one of the choices in the Form Properties InfoBox.

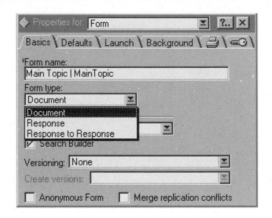

If you don't designate the form as a specific type, it will automatically be assigned the default form type, which is *Document*. You can think of this as the standard form type in Notes. Documents based on a form of type Document are independent of other documents; that is, they are not a response to another document. To create a Response-type document, at least one Document-type document must exist. In other words, a person needs something—in this case, a document—to which to respond.

A Response to Document form is used to create a Response document, which is exactly what the name says it is: a response to a document. Responses can be comments, further thoughts on a topic, or additional information that isn't contained in the original, or main, document; however, these responses will always be associated with the document. Figure 14.4 shows the Response form in the discussion database, which is a Response to Document form.

FIGURE 14.4:

The Response form in the discussion database is an example of a Response to Document form.

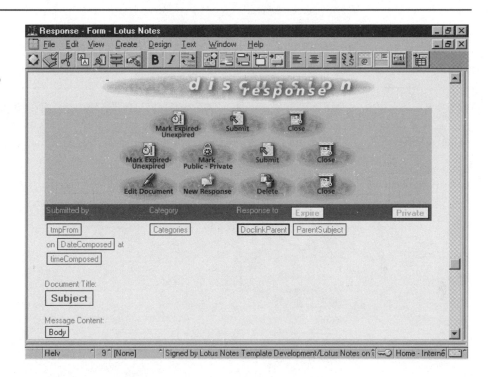

When you design a Response-type form, you will frequently want it to inherit—or use—data from the main document. *Inheritance* enables information in a main document to be transferred into another document. (In this context, we are referring to inheritance between a Document-type document and a Response-type document, although inheritance can occur between documents of any type.) Inheritance can save users the time of having to refer to the main document for key pieces of information that are essential in formulating a proper response or, more significantly, of having to re-enter information that already appears in the main document.

The relationship between the document and the response is created by first highlighting the appropriate document in the view or opening the document before composing the response. If you don't choose a document to respond to, Notes will tell you to select a document before you attempt to compose a document of this type. A view makes it easy for you to locate the documents to which you want to respond.

Response documents create a hierarchy in a view where the response appears below the document and is indented to offset it from its associated parent document. Figure 14.5 shows a response to a document in one of the views in the discussion database.

FIGURE 14.5:

A Response document appears indented below a Main Topic document in a view because it was created using a Response to Document form.

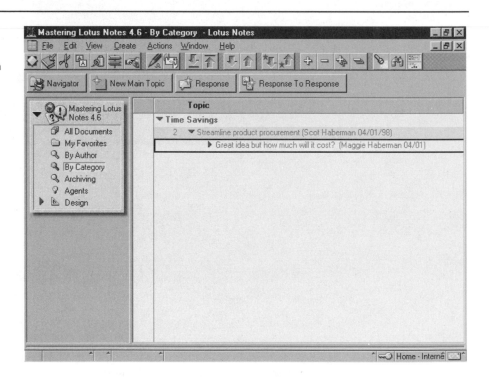

A Response to Response form provides a user with further flexibility when composing documents. Figure 14.6 shows the Response to Response form in the discussion database. Documents based on a Response to Response form can be associated with either a Document-type or any Response-type document. You may notice this form is nearly indistinguishable from the Response form discussed previously. The only real difference is the form type designation and graphic title.

FIGURE 14.6:

The Response to Response form in the discussion database is a type of Response to Response.

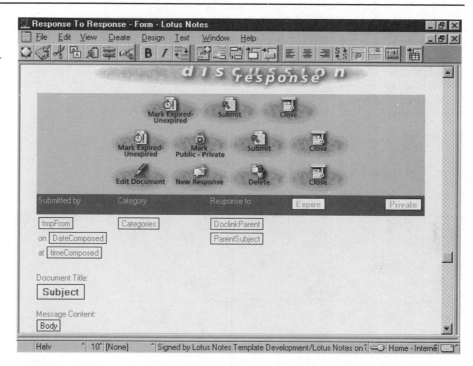

A Response to Response document appears below the document (whether a Document, Response to Document, or another Response to Response) that was highlighted or opened when it was composed and is indented further than its *parent*, the document to which it is responding. Figure 14.7 shows how a Response to Response document appears in one of the discussion database's views.

Forms are a basic component of Notes. Here's a summary of the form types:

Type of Form	Description of Form
Document	The default form type assigned to any main document. This form type is independent of all other documents.
Response to Document	This form type is assigned to a form used to respond to a main document. It is dependent on the main document. It appears indented beneath the main document in a view hierarchy.
Response to Response	This form type is assigned to a form used to respond to either a main document or another response. It appears indented beneath its parent in a view hierarchy.

A Response to Response document appears indented below a Response document in a view because it was created using a Response to Response form.

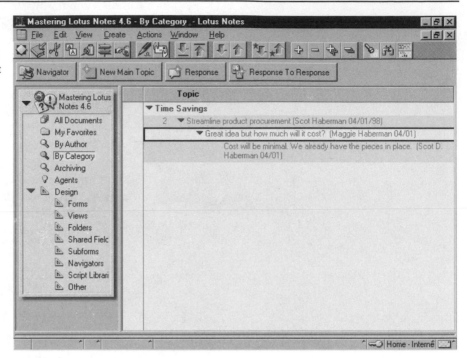

TIP	Before you actually start creating a form, take the time to plan it on paper. Certainly you can create a new form by placing static text, fields, and other items on the form and then moving the items around, but you'll probably leave out something important. You should spend as much time as you need to consider how people will use the form and the information they will want to capture.

You design a new form in Form Design mode. Form Design mode opens with a single design area to which you can add whatever fields, static text, graphics, buttons, and other design objects you want. After you place an item on the form, you can move it around until you're satisfied, or you can delete it.

Subforms

You should maintain a consistent look and feel throughout all the forms in your Notes application to make them easier to use and, from a design standpoint, easier to maintain.

The Notes development environment allows you to implement a reusable "core" functionality across the forms in your application through the use of *subforms*. With subforms you can group several form-related design elements together and then reference the subform as a single element when you are designing other forms. A simple example of this method would be the incorporation of a company logo (a graphic) at the top of all of your forms. Instead of pasting the logo into each individual form as you create it, you could create a subform that includes the logo and then insert that subform at the top of each regular form. Changes made to the logo in the subform are automatically reflected in any other form that uses that subform. A more advanced example would be the inclusion of buttons that allow users to perform routine tasks such as saving, printing, and closing the current document (regardless of its type). Once again, you could define these elements in a subform and insert the subform appropriately in each form. The same subform could easily incorporate both the logo mentioned previously and the task buttons.

Figure 14.8 shows an example of a subform, and Figure 14.9 shows how the subform appears as part of the design of another form.

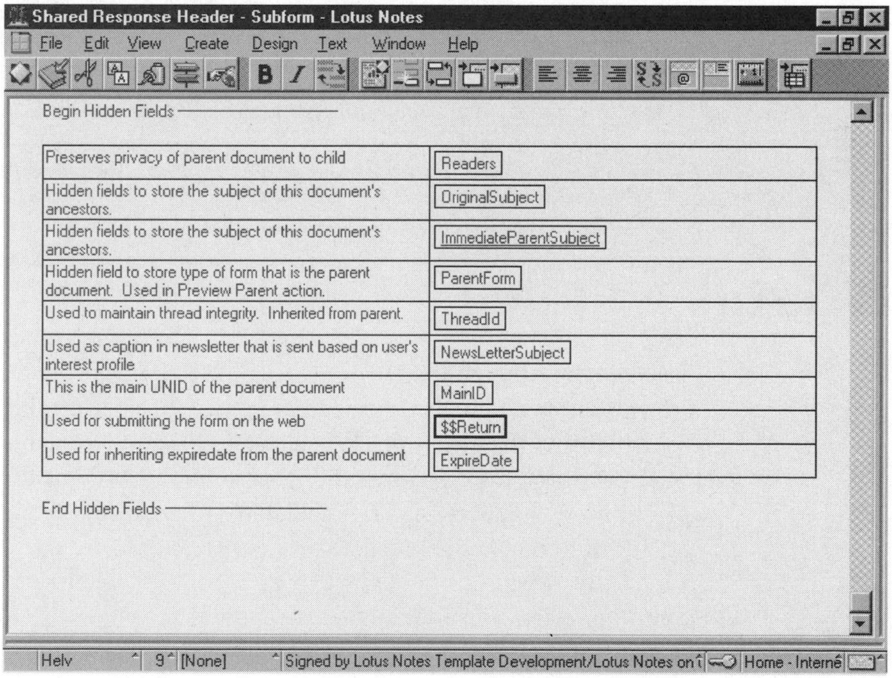

FIGURE 14.8:

A subform in the discussion database groups several hidden fields together. This subform is utilized in both the Response form and the Response to Response form.

FIGURE 14.9:

A subform appears as part of the design of another form.

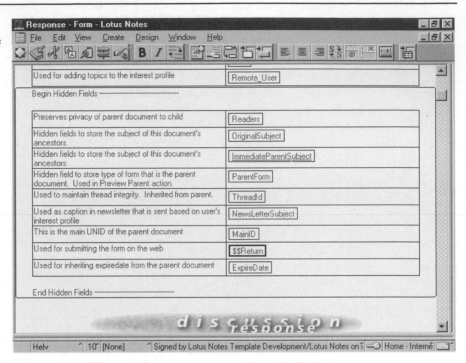

The process of creating a subform is essentially identical to that of creating a form, with some minor exceptions. The specific usage rules for incorporating a subform in a form are discussed in detail in Chapter 17.

What Is a Field?

Fields are the basic containers that store the data users enter in a Notes document. The value that a field can store is a matter of how the application is designed and constructed by the developer. When creating the forms that will be available within the application, the developer defines the fields that will appear in each form and assigns them a data type. A field's data type specifies the type of information that can be entered in it. Textual data and numeric data are the typical types of data you encounter in most Notes applications; however, other types of data can be stored in a field, most notably rich text data.

A rich text field can contain formatted data as well as linked objects, graphics, and file attachments. In other words, a rich text field can hold an assortment of riches. For more information, read the sidebar "The Differences between Plain Text and Rich Text Fields." Regardless of the data type assigned to a field, it can store only a single type of data and no other. Of course, a form can have many fields, each with a different data type. Notes supports the following field data types:

Text	Rich text
Time	Authors
Number	Names
Keywords	Readers

Chapter 17 explains how to use these different field data types in creating a form.

When defining fields in a form, a field's name appears inside the field. Note the Main Topic form that appears in Figure 14.10 and how each field in the form appears with its name. You can use a field's name to refer to that field in formulas, for example, when Response-type documents inherit data from a main document. The Properties InfoBox for a field, shown in Figure 14.11, displays the Field Type area where you designate the specific field type.

FIGURE 14.10:

After you name a field, its name appears inside the field box.

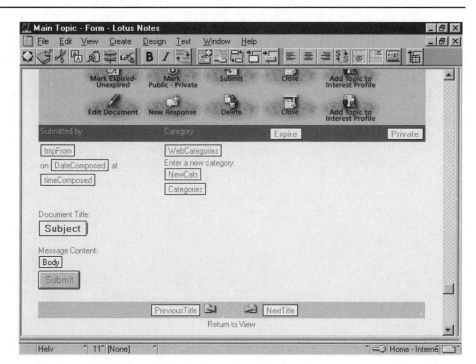

FIGURE 14.11:

The Field Properties InfoBox
for the Subject field

The Differences between Plain Text and Rich Text Fields

Notes allows you to insert two kinds of fields on a form used for entering textual information: plain text and rich text.

A *rich text field* is named as such because a person can enter text and format it. You can enter many kinds of elements in a rich text field. You can also insert tables and attachments. For example, you might want to attach a file to a mail memo.

A *plain text field* is a field that can contain only text with no formats applied to it; you can't change the appearance of the text. You use plain text fields when formatting the appearance of text serves no purpose or when you need to design computations based on string or numerical values contained within.

You'll discover that you can't tell whether an empty field is plain text or rich text simply by looking at it. Furthermore, you can't easily tell the difference when you edit a document that contains information in fields. Sometimes the only way you can tell is to try to change the appearance of the text in some way. If Notes doesn't let you change the appearance, the field is a plain text field.

Another way to distinguish the two is to place the insertion point in the field. If the field is a rich text field, the SmartStatus bar at the bottom of the Workspace will display the font type and point size of the text in the field. If it is a plain text field, then the font and point size options will not be displayed in the SmartStatus bar. Also, if the field is a rich text field, the formatting options of the Text menu, such as Bold, Italic, and Enlarge, will be available; the formatting options are dimmed and unavailable when the field is plain text.

Another aspect of fields, besides the type of data they store, is whether their values are supplied by users of the application or if the application itself generates a value for the field. In Notes terminology, fields are said to be either editable or computed. An *editable* field is one in which a user enters a value. While the application may subsequently take the value and modify it to some degree (a process known as *input translation*), the initial value is user supplied and may be changed by the user in the future. In the case of a *computed* field, the user has no ability to enter a value. Instead, the value of a computed field is calculated by the application and is frequently the result of other values that appear in editable fields. Don't let the term *computed* lead you to believe that the data in question is numeric only. It's possible to calculate a text value in Notes. For instance, the name of the author of a document might be contained in a computed field. The DateComposed field that appears in the Main Topic form in Figure 14.12 is a computed field, as is the From field. The other fields are editable fields.

FIGURE 14.12:

The DateComposed field on the Main Topic form is a computed field. Your computer system's date and time appear automatically in the field.

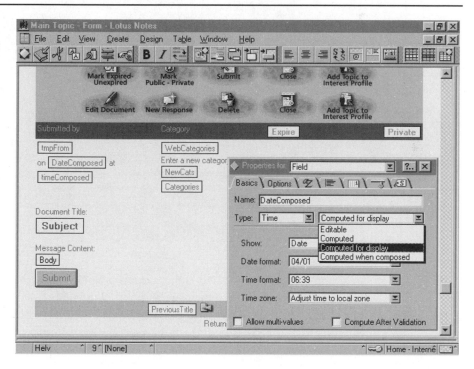

Using Static Text in Forms

Static text is text displayed on a document you create. It's referred to as "static" text because the users of the application cannot change it. Static text can be used as labels for fields or as titles. Fields, on the other hand, are the areas in which users actually enter information or the application performs actions automatically. Figure 14.13 shows examples of static text.

FIGURE 14.13:

Static text identifies fields or acts as a title.

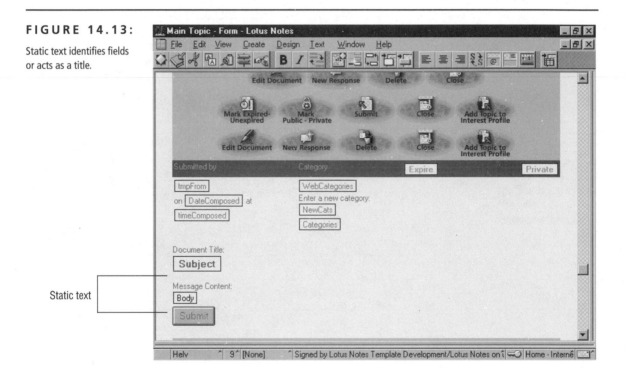

A nice feature of static text is that you can change its appearance. The default font for static text on new forms is 10-point Helvetica. The default text color is black. It's a good idea to display static text in a different color or size than the defaults in order to set it off from the field contents it identifies. You can also make the text appear bold or italic.

You make changes to static text by selecting it and accessing the options on the Text menu or opening the Text Properties InfoBox, shown in Figure 14.14. To change the text attributes without using the menu, use Ctrl+K to display the Text Properties InfoBox.

FIGURE 14.14:

You format text on a form by accessing the Text menu and/or opening the Text Properties InfoBox.

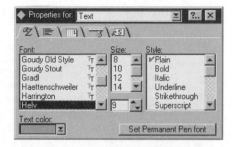

Notes also lets you save combinations of individual style elements as Named Styles to save you the time of having to manually reselect commonly used style combinations. (Named Styles were discussed in detail in Chapter 7.)

We suggest you limit the number of colors and fonts you use to format static text. Try not to mix too many different fonts and point sizes: stick to using no more than two fonts on a form. For labels, keep the size to 10 or 12 points. For titles, use 18 to 24 points. A rule of thumb is to label every editable field with concise, descriptive identifiers so a user doesn't have to guess what to input in a field.

When Do I Create a View?

You create a view after you design a form that people use for composing documents in a database. You can't create a view until you've designed a form and decided what information from the form you want to display in the view. As you've already learned, a *view* is a summary of all the documents, or some subset of the documents, in a database. A view provides an easy way for a person to locate a particular document or collection of documents.

After you select a database, you can access the views that have been created for that database in a variety of ways. In some applications, the available views in a database may be displayed on the View menu, in the Navigation pane, or using a

Navigator. Figure 14.15 shows an example of the By Author view in the discussion database.

FIGURE 14.15:

The By Author view in the discussion database

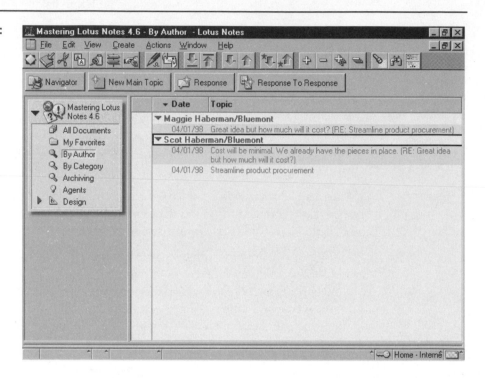

As in any view, each row represents a single document and may be divided into one or more columns. Each column displays the information contained in a field (or from a combination of fields) from the document. A view can include various symbols that indicate further information about the document. Markers in the left column can indicate that you have not yet read a document; similarly, icons in a column can represent a document, folder, person, group, or attachment.

Folders

Folders enable users to manage and organize documents in a database based on individual preferences. Folders look and feel just like views. They display a list of documents with each one represented by a row containing highlight information from the document. Unlike views, what appears in folders is a matter of user choice, rather than preprogrammed selection criteria built into its design.

Consider, for example, a company policies database that contains various views of hundreds of documents describing the procedures that all company personnel must follow. From the perspective of a particular user, only a small subset of the documents are referred to on a regular basis. This subset could vary from user to user. Therefore, a user can isolate in a folder just the handful of procedure documents that have personal significance. The process is analogous to photocopying a few of the pages of a bound manual and placing those pages in a manila folder in your personal filing cabinet. You haven't altered the original manual in any way; you've simply isolated a few items from it for personal reference.

Notes supports both shared folders and private folders. *Shared folders* are created by the application developer and may be utilized by users of the database. *Private folders* may be created by anyone with Reader access to the database (as long as the Access Control List specifies that Readers can create personal folders in the database) or by the application developer on behalf of an individual user or group of users. Because folders are one of the few user-definable design elements, you may choose to leave their creation in the hands of your end users. (Chapter 20 supplies the details on how to create folders.)

Navigators

Another way to access the views of a database is through a Navigation pane. *Navigation panes* are a graphical means of selecting views, and go a long way in making an application more user friendly and intuitive. Rather than a menu selection, Navigation panes contain *Navigators*—graphics objects that, when selected, can perform a Notes task such as displaying a particular view. Navigators can automate many other functions in Notes and give you the ability to build a simple graphical interface for your Notes application. Figure 14.16 shows a Navigation pane (Navigator) in the discussion database.

Developers use a set of built-in graphical design tools to build their Navigators. Chapter 20 covers the details of designing views with Navigators.

FIGURE 14.16:

The Navigation pane in the discussion database gives users graphical access to views and folders. In this example, the Navigation pane allows the user to graphically access the views of the database: All Documents, By Category, By Author, and Archiving.

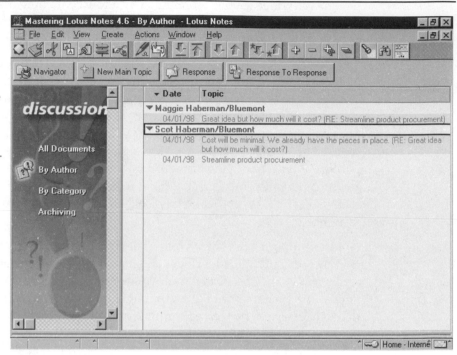

When Can a User Create a Document?

Once you design a form and create a view, users can start creating documents. You'll recall that a *document* is the main unit of storage in a Notes application. It is the finished product that has been derived from a form. In other words, a document contains the information that has been entered into the fields in a form.

Each document in a database corresponds to a particular form you've designed. (Actually, each Notes document contains a hidden field called Form that stores the name of the form used to create the Notes document.) For instance, a person can create three basic kinds of documents in the discussion database. After the database is selected, a user can pull down the Create menu to display the three choices, as shown in Figure 14.17.

The information in a document can be entered manually by an end user, calculated by formulas, or imported from other applications.

FIGURE 14.17:

The discussion database's Create menu displays the three kinds of available documents.

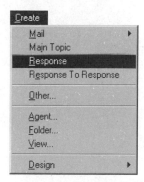

What's Next?

In the next chapter, we discuss the concept of incorporating workflow in a database.

15

Incorporating Workflow in a Database

- Automating workflow with Notes

- Analyzing business process components

- Integrating cross-product workflow with NotesFlow

We have discussed the concept of workflow in various contexts throughout this book. Notes comes with several features expressly designed to enhance workflow automation. In this chapter you'll learn what workflow is, how to evaluate an existing workflow process, and how Notes helps you achieve workflow automation. Try to place the how-to details described in the chapters that follow in the context of a workflow application. Ideally, you will never look at systems development quite the same way again!

Understanding Workflow Fundamentals

Everybody has, at some time or another, probably been a participant in the ever-popular game of Paper Chase—filling out forms, sending documents (and trying to find out if they got to the right place), receiving and forwarding documents, filing documents, and then throwing them away during a spring cleaning frenzy.

One of the major missions of Notes is to *literally* replace paper documents with electronic documents. Notes is not a word processor on which you create and edit documents that you will eventually print.

To fully replace a paper document with an electronic version requires not only the means to create the document but also the mechanism to *move* the electronic document through a business environment in the same way that a paper document would move.

NOTE   Moving documents electronically is the essence of Notes workflow automation.

By re-creating and (ideally) improving on the circuit a document travels, workflow automation brings all of us closer to a paperless environment. To this end, however, you must first understand the current processes of your corporate culture (as they relate to workflow automation) and consider how much reengineering will be necessary to integrate the electronic flow of documents into the environment.

Before you put the first field on the first form of your first workflow application, you should have a clear understanding of the interaction among workers, the documents you plan to "electronicize," security (in regard to sensitive information), time frames (in regard to the delivery of information), and any other issues relevant to workflow.

Evaluating a Business Process

Consider virtually any business process with which you are involved. By *business process* we mean those steps that an organization takes to achieve a particular goal in a business environment; the business process *describes* what is to be done. It can be as mundane as a request for paper clips or as complex as coordinating the purchase, distribution, support, and maintenance of laptop computers for a sales force of 500 people located across the country. (While neither of these examples is ideal for your *first* Notes application, plenty of real-life possibilities fall somewhere in the middle.) The first challenge you face is understanding the business process in its entirety as it currently exists in your organization. Resist any temptation to "hurry up and program"; starting to design and develop an application before you fully comprehend the process only limits your choices later.

TIP   Don't worry about how to change or improve a process until you know what it looks like today.

You begin this journey of discovery by asking the right people the right questions. Sounds simple enough, right? Actually, 50 percent of the battle is in identifying the right people, formulating the right questions, and then getting in front of those people and getting them to answer your questions.

This first phase of the software development life cycle, known as *analysis*, is absolutely crucial to the success of the project. Being a good analyst, however, is a matter of experience; the more you do it, the better you get. If you are new to information systems analysis, the following section can help you get started.

The Right People, the Right Questions

Every business is unique, every business process is unique, and every development project is unique. On the other hand, every business, every business process, and every development project are the same in some respects. Therefore, we will focus on the common aspects of analysis and try to give you a general idea of how to proceed.

Initially, you need to focus on the "big picture," so you should speak with some-one who can give you an overview of the current process. Keep your discussion at a high level and don't try to redesign the process as you go. Remember, you are simply on a fact-finding mission. Asking the following questions will help you draw out the information you need:

- In broad terms, what is the current process? Describe the process in terms of inputs and outputs.

- What works in the current process and what doesn't? Why? (Asking *why* things work or don't work will give you insight into how the customer mea-sures success and failure as it relates to the process.)

- Who performs the actual work? Names of people are less important than functional roles or titles at this phase. (If you can assign a person's name to a role or title, then do so.)

- What are the time frames for completing the various steps of the process?

- Where are the bottlenecks?

- What are your expectations of a new system?

- What is the measure of success?

You will find that any business process is actually a series of *subprocesses*, each of which must be analyzed on its own merits. This step becomes an iteration of the analysis just presented; all of the same rules apply! As you move from the big pic-ture to functional levels in the business, you still must get to the right people and ask the right questions. A subprocess may even contain additional subprocesses, and the cycle continues until the business process is fully described. As you begin to break down the business process into its constituent parts, the questions you ask need to become more and more targeted to the specific subprocess, and the level of detail must increase. Ultimately, you need to know precisely how the organization per-forms each discrete task in its business process.

TIP   Various formal methodologies have been invented that give structure to the process of analysis. Examples of these include data-flow diagramming and entity-relationship modeling. You might consider exploring these or other methodolo-gies to help you analyze a business process.

The Notes Workflow Model

Workflow is the execution of the steps described by a business process. Having stated this, let's clarify a few issues before proceeding. First of all, workflow involves people. (After you have recovered from this earth-shattering revelation, please read on.) While Notes, computers, and computer networks provide the "workflow highway," people still do the driving. Unfortunately, people don't always execute their roles in a workflow sequence in a timely, efficient fashion. Sometimes a person is simply too busy attending to other responsibilities; other times people are not aware that their involvement is required. The consequence, in any case, is that the workflow sequence stalls.

WARNING   Regardless of how well engineered a Notes application may be, you cannot escape the human element that may lead to a breakdown in workflow.

In the context of a Notes environment, adhering to the following principles will maximize your chances of success:

- People have to know how to use Notes.

- People have to know how to use your application.

- People have to understand the business process.

- People have to understand how your application automates the workflow involved in the business process.

- People have to understand their roles in the workflow sequence, the effect of their participation (and nonparticipation), and how that translates into *when and how they use Notes.*

Picture workflow as a circuit. In electronics, a circuit is a path that makes it possible for electrical current to flow from a voltage source to an electronic device and then back to the voltage source. The path returns to its starting point. If a failure occurs in the circuit, electrical current cannot flow. Now, apply what you've just learned in Electronics 101 to a workflow circuit in a business process:

```
Information = Current
Originator = Voltage Source
Recipient = Electronic Device
Notes Network = Circuit
```

By *Notes Network* we mean everything and everyone who participates in accomplishing the workflow automated through your Notes application, including:

- Computer equipment such as workstations and servers

- Networks such as wiring, LAN adapters, and protocols

- Software such as operating systems, Notes, Notes applications

- Users such as originators and recipients

Dividing users into *originators* and *recipients* is not always a simple matter because an originator can also be a recipient and vice versa. A registered letter is an everyday example of this kind of role reversal. People mail registered letters with the understanding that they will receive proof of delivery to the intended recipient; the proof is a receipt with the receiver's signature, which the post office mails back to the originator. As you read in Chapter 11 on Notes Mail, you can request a delivery report to confirm that your message was successfully delivered.

Moving a Document

Having gained an understanding of workflow, the next question is, "How do I move a document?" To answer, you have to understand that moving a document is a relative concept; a document can be:

- Placed at your disposal without you knowing it

- Placed at your disposal with a notification

- Delivered directly to you

NOTE   Notes delivery is a little like the delivery of regular mail. Some pieces of mail arrive unannounced in your mailbox; the burden is on the recipient to make the trek to the mailbox to find out if anything is inside. Other times you get a notification that something is waiting for you at the post office; you know that an item definitely awaits you, but you still have to go and get it. Finally, sometimes a parcel is delivered directly to your office; someone sent you something, and you didn't have to go anywhere to pick it up.

Notes supports two basic methods or models of workflow, known as the *send model* and the *share model* (discussed in Chapter 9). In the *send model*, documents (both data and form) are actively routed to one or more recipients (a user or a database) using Notes Mail. Notifications can be sent to the originator and to those involved in forwarding the document, informing them that the document has reached the next recipient.

At any point along the workflow path, other documents may be automatically "triggered" and routed to additional recipients, creating a sophisticated network of branch paths in the workflow. Applications based on the send model are ideal for situations where workflow is initiated on an ad-hoc, inconsistent basis and participants cannot know with certainty when and if their involvement is needed. This model is also better in situations when a document requires immediate attention or the workflow has an element of urgency.

The share model relies on recipients to routinely check for the existence of a document intended for their viewing in a shared database. This model is common in applications that involve a response-to scheme, where a user composes a Main document, posts the document in the database, and awaits a response (in the form of Response document) from the recipient. The success of an application based on the share model depends on the workflow participants faithfully checking the database for new documents. For this reason, the share model is best suited for applications where workflow is continuous and consistent.

Of course, workflow applications are not restricted to one model or another and may combine the two into a *hybrid model* that uses elements of each. For example, an Agent could automatically notify specific users, via e-mail, to act on particular documents in a shared database. The e-mail message could include links to the documents that require a user's attention. Some of the workflow-related features in Notes include:

- The Notes e-mail engine, which is the basis for moving information through the workflow circuit (discussed in Chapters 1 and 9)

- @Functions, @Commands, and LotusScript functions, which are used specifically in workflow applications

- Form properties and specially reserved fields, which you can incorporate into the designs of your forms to make them "workflow enabled"

As a developer, you are responsible for implementing the appropriate style of workflow into the design of your application. The method or methods you choose should be *application driven*; overengineering or underengineering an application for workflow will simply add unnecessary complications to both the development cycle and end-user usage.

> **TIP**   We suggest that you err on the side of too much workflow, rather than too little, because of the potential difficulty involved in retrofitting workflow functionality to an application that isn't properly designed to support it.

You can avoid most problems altogether if you have a thorough knowledge of the business process you are automating, as well as the Notes tools for accomplishing this task.

Going Beyond Notes

Many times the requirements of a workflow process demand utilizing non-Notes tools in order to achieve the overall business goals; this process is known as *cross-product workflow*. In some cases, Notes is unable to adequately provide a needed function; for example, financial analysis is a function that is better served by a dedicated tool like Lotus 1-2-3. But does a limitation in Notes mean that users will have to deal with the typical awkwardness of switching into and out of several desktop products or the drudgery of having to reenter data already captured in Notes or other data sources? Not at all! By taking advantage of NotesFlow, you can design your Notes application to act as the driver for a coordinated sequence of data exchange between Notes and non-Notes tools.

The Notes tool NotesFlow features the following capabilities:

- **Autolaunching** of other desktop applications when a Notes document is created, edited, or read.

- **Bidirectional data exchange** with non-Notes applications, using an OLE-based technology called Notes/FX 2.0. Data can be automatically passed back and forth between a Notes application and other Notes/FX-enabled applications. For instance, the field values of a Notes document can be transmitted to the cells of a Lotus 1-2-3 spreadsheet, and vice versa.

- **Published actions** that allow you to define an action in Notes and then publish it so that it appears as a menu item in other Notes/FX-enabled applications. This extremely powerful option allows you to smooth the transition between other desktop tools and Notes.

- **Open Database Connection (ODBC)** access to non-Notes databases, such as Oracle, Informix, Sybase, Microsoft SQL Server, dBase, and Paradox,

provides a pathway through which you can integrate external data sources into the flow of your Notes application.

We discuss NotesFlow in detail in Chapter 29.

> **NOTE** With the introduction of Lotus Domino, the idea of "going beyond Notes" takes on a whole new meaning. Web pages can be merged with Notes-based data, Notes documents and databases can be published on the Web, and e-mail messages can be sent to Internet users—all as part of an overall workflow strategy. We discuss Domino at length in Part IV.

What's Next?

A good security scheme can save you a lot of headaches and ease the task of maintaining a database. While you may believe that you have to protect data from malicious activity, inadvertent actions by innocent users is the more frequent cause of data loss. Chapter 16 discusses the various options available for building security into a database and for creating and maintaining secure access to your Notes application.

CHAPTER

SIXTEEN

Building Security into a Notes Database

- Understanding your User ID

- Maintaining User ID security

- Changing your User ID

- Understanding database security

- Choosing security options

- Looking at User ID certificates

- Using certificates

- Restricting database access

- Using encryption keys

Data security is a major issue everywhere. Telecommunications has helped to make information easily accessible through e-mail, online services, and the Internet. However, many people are sending and receiving the information electronically with little monitoring.

Understanding User IDs

A User ID is a file that uniquely identifies a Notes user. Every Notes user—person or server—has a User ID. Your User ID determines your access privileges to Notes servers.

Why You Need a User ID

When you try to open a database on a server, the server looks at your ID to see if you have any *certifiers* in common. If you do, the server allows access; if you don't, the server denies access. This checking process is called *authentication*, and it's the reason you may experience a brief delay when you access a server you haven't used recently.

NOTE Authentication is a bidirectional process; the server authenticates your user ID, and you authenticate the server's ID to ensure a *trusted* communication session.

You also need an ID to sign Notes Mail memos. When you sign a Notes Mail memo and send it, all of your certificates are attached to the memo. The recipient's workstation checks these against its own certificates.

NOTE When setting up users for Web access, the users do not need to be registered. The users do not need a Notes ID or mail file (unless the user will access Web mail). You only need to create a Person document in the Public Address Book and enter information about the user's name, password, and SSL certificate. (SSL certification allows the server to authenticate the client an the client to authenticate the server. It also encrypts the data sent from the client to the server.)

If you receive a signed memo and you don't have a certificate in common with the sender, Notes displays a message saying the authenticity of the memo cannot be assured. If you know you and the sender have a certificate in common, someone may have tampered with the memo en route.

To get information about your User ID, choose File ➤ Tools ➤ User ID. Enter your password if one has been set for the ID file. The User ID dialog box is shown in Figure 16.1.

FIGURE 16.1:

The User ID dialog box displays User ID information.

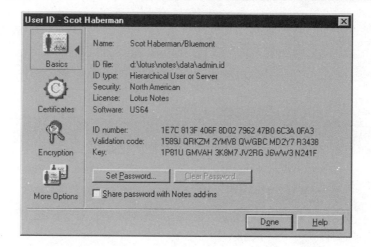

You'll see the following information about your ID:

- File name and location
- Number
- Security (North American or International)
- Type of license (Notes Mail, Notes Desktop, or Notes)
- Name (your user name)

WARNING   Changing the user name removes *all* the certificates from the ID; therefore, after you change the name, you'll need to acquire new certificates before you can use any shared databases.

The Contents of a User ID

The contents of a User ID are either assigned by a certifier when the ID is created or added later. The following information is assigned:

- The name of the ID owner, the Notes license number, and the Notes ID type
- A certificate that allows access to servers that recognize the certifier
- A public key used to encrypt documents sent to the owner
- A private key used to decrypt documents sent to the owner

You or your certifier can add or modify a User ID by doing any of the following:

- Set or change a password to prevent unauthorized access to Notes servers using the ID
- Add certificates to allow access to additional servers
- Change the name of the ID owner

Notes protects your work and the work of other users on shared databases in a variety of other ways:

- User IDs can be protected with passwords.
- Users are granted or denied access to Notes servers through the certificates stored in their User IDs.
- Information can be encrypted so that only specific users can decrypt it.

If you are using Notes with a modem, you can use a secure modem channel by selecting Encrypt Network Data in the Port Setup dialog box.

Keeping Your User ID Secure

Keeping your User ID electronically secure means

- Keeping your ID physically secure
- Protecting it with a password
- Logging off servers when you leave your office

TIP   Notes uses the terms *User ID, ID,* and *ID file* interchangeably.

You can keep your User ID on a floppy disk, your hard disk, or a file server. The most secure option is to keep it on a floppy disk that you store in a safe place when you aren't using it (perhaps in a locked drawer).

TIP   Make a backup copy of your ID file on a floppy disk using your operating system's file copy procedure. Store the backup in a secure place.

If you change your mind about where to keep your ID, you can tell Notes where your ID is located during setup (immediately after installation). You can also change your mind later. If you originally stored your ID on the hard disk, you can later copy it to a floppy disk and delete the file from the hard disk (use Windows to copy and delete the file). When Notes asks for the location of your ID file the next time you access a Notes server, type in its new location, for example, **a:\admin.id**.

When you keep your User ID on a floppy disk, you must insert the disk whenever you access a server, sign mail, or read encrypted mail. Most people just leave the disk in the floppy drive while they use Notes. If you remove the floppy from the drive, you will not be able to access Notes servers.

TIP   You should log off when you leave your workstation to prevent an unauthorized person from using your User ID (posing as you) to access your organization's databases. This precaution is especially important if you work in a cubicle or you don't lock your office when you step out. In the User Preferences dialog box, you can set automatic logoff to occur after any number of minutes that you specify. Otherwise, you can press F5 to log off, thus clearing your password and forcing the next person (who might be you or someone else) to enter a password to gain access to the ID file that will then allow access to a Notes server.

Changing Your User Name

You can change the user name that's associated with your User ID file. You might change your user name for any number of reasons: maybe you just got married (or divorced) and changed your last name, or maybe you'd rather use your nickname.

The process of changing your user name involves several other people and may take a few hours or even a few days. Don't worry, you can continue to use your original ID, switching to the new one once the changeover process is complete.

WARNING   If you are not a Notes Mail user, changing the user name removes *all* the certificates from the ID; after you change your name, you'll need to acquire new certificates before you can use any shared databases.

The way you change your user name depends on whether you use Notes Mail. If you use Notes Mail, you change your user name in this manner:

1. Choose File ➤ Tools ➤ User ID. If Notes prompts you for a password, as shown in Figure 16.2, enter it.

FIGURE 16.2:

The Enter Password dialog box prompts you to enter your password when you want to change your user name and make other modifications to your User ID.

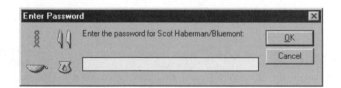

---

2. Click the More Options icon.

3. Click the Request New Name button.

4. Enter the new name in the Change User Name dialog box, shown in Figure 16.3.

FIGURE 16.3:

Enter your new name in the Change User Name dialog box.

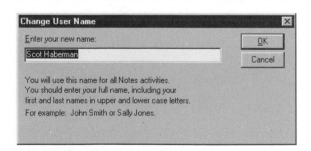

5. Click OK. A message box warns you that changing your name will cause you to lose all of your certificates.

6. Click OK. You new name is automatically sent to your certifier.

7. Choose File ➤ Tools ➤ User ID when you receive the new ID.

8. Select the More Options option.

9. Click the Merge a Copy button to merge new certificates into your ID file.

TIP   When requesting a name change, you can merge your new ID from within your Mail database by selecting Actions ➤ Accept Certificate.

Keeping a "Safe" Backup Copy of Your User ID

Losing your certificates usually means that you inadvertently changed your User ID name. (Alert your Notes administrator.) To see if you indeed changed your User ID name, open the User ID dialog box. Your User ID name appears at the top of the dialog box. Has your name changed? If so, you will have problems accessing databases stored on the server. Consequently, you won't be able to replicate with a server to update the databases on your workstation. When you attempt to replicate, you'll receive a replication error message that the server isn't responding. (This message really means the server doesn't recognize your User ID.)

As a precaution, you should always make a backup, or "safe" copy, of your User ID file and store it either on a diskette or in a different folder on your computer. To restore your certificates, erase the old User ID file from your Notes data folder (or wherever you store your User ID) and paste the safe copy of the User ID file in the folder. Open the User ID dialog box to see if the correct name appears. If you're still experiencing problems, contact your Notes administrator (again).

If you don't use Notes Mail and you want to change your user name, follow these steps:

1. Back up your ID and switch to the backup copy.

NOTE   Using this method causes you to lose any certificates that you have in the newly named ID file until you get it back.

2. Choose File ➤ Tools ➤ User ID.

3. Click the More Options icon.

4. Click the Change Name button.

5. Enter your new user name in the Change User Name dialog box, and click OK.

6. Click the Create Safe Copy button to save a copy of the newly named ID onto a floppy disk and then deliver the disk to a certifier to be stamped with certificates.

NOTE   You have the option of choosing File ➤ Tools ➤ Switch ID to use your old ID until you get the new one.

---

7. Switch to this ID again, and choose File ➤ Tools ➤ User ID when you receive the ID back.

8. Select the More Options option, and then click the Merge a Copy button to merge new certificates into this ID file.

NOTE   Your Notes administrator will update your Person document and Group documents in the Public Name & Address Book to reflect your name change.

You, your Notes administrator, and various database managers may need to change the ACL for any databases where your name is listed individually, including your Notes Mail database. If you and the administrator don't have the necessary access to change the ACL, contact the database managers.

Setting a Password for an ID File

You can use a password to prevent other users from accessing shared Notes databases with your user ID. Once you set a password, Notes always prompts you to enter it when you access a Notes server for the first time after starting Notes. For security reasons, when you enter your password in the text box, the entry is not displayed onscreen.

Passwords can consist of any combination of keyboard characters. The first character of the password must be an alphanumeric character. Your password should have at least the minimum number of characters required (the default is eight but is set by your Notes administrator); the maximum number is 63.

TIP

To determine the minimum length your Notes administrator has set for your ID, contact your Notes administrator.

You can clear your password or change an existing password at any time. However, if your Notes administrator required a password to be used when your ID was created, you won't be able to clear it.

To set your password, follow these steps:

1. Choose File ➤ Tools ➤ User ID. Click the Set Password button. If your ID file is already password protected, you'll see the Enter Password dialog box and then you'll see the Set Password dialog box, as shown in Figure 16.4.

FIGURE 16.4:

Enter a new password for your User ID in the Set Password dialog box.

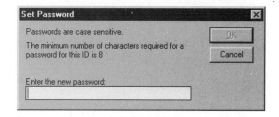

Set Password

Passwords are case sensitive.

The minimum number of characters required for a password for this ID is 8

Enter the new password:

OK

Cancel

2. Enter the current password.

NOTE

If you are setting a new password for the first time, only the Set Password dialog box appears.

3. Enter a new password.
4. Click OK.
5. Confirm the password by typing it again exactly as you did the first time.
6. Click OK again.

TIP

If you are really concerned about security, you can assign more than one password to an ID file. Notes allows you to set up to eight passwords for an ID.

Notes passwords are case sensitive. For example, Notes considers *MysteryTour* and *mysterytour* to be different passwords. Notes won't accept a password unless it matches the original exactly.

NOTE

You may notice that when you type in a password, Xs are displayed each time you type a character. Each X does not map to a character but rather Notes randomly displays a number of Xs for each character. This is just another security precaution to prevent someone from determining how many characters you are actually typing.

Securing Databases

We cannot overemphasize the importance of securing databases you use regularly. A breach in security that results in a loss of data can cripple an organization. Therefore, building security into your Notes databases is one of the most important aspects in the development process. People who use your databases can also take routine security measures that can safeguard data.

Switching to a Different User ID

You can share a workstation with other Notes users (who have different User IDs) by using the File ➤ Tools ➤ Switch ID command to tell Notes that one of you is leaving and the other is beginning Notes. All users can keep their IDs on floppy disks or on the workstation's hard disk. Be sure to password protect the IDs. After you use the command to select the ID you want to use, Notes prompts you for a password if that ID file is password protected.

NOTE

When two or more people use Notes on the same PC or Macintosh workstation, each user installs Notes separately, storing the Notes *program* files in the same directory but storing *data* files in his or her own data directory. Each user then has his or her own copy of the DESKTOP.DSK file and sees a different set of database icons in the Notes Workspace. In Windows, each user must also have his or her own copy of the NOTES.INI file; other copies, such as the one usually stored in the Windows directory, must be removed.

After switching to a different ID, a user changes to his or her personal data directory in the User Setup dialog box.

Locking Your ID File

As we've said, password protection forces you to enter your current password each time you want to access databases on a server, locally-encrypted databases, or encrypted mail, or perform other activities that require your ID file.

During the password entry procedure, you can set Notes to automatically lock (prevent access to your Notes ID files) after the number of minutes of inactivity that you specify. This security precaution is useful if you tend to forget to log off when you leave your desk.

To lock your ID file, follow these steps:

1. Enter your password in the Enter Password dialog box.

2. Close File ➤ Tools ➤ User Preferences. If you want Notes to automatically lock your ID after a certain number of minutes of inactivity, specify that number in the Lock ID after [X] Minutes of Inactivity option, as shown in Figure 16.5.

3. Click OK.

FIGURE 16.5:

You can set Notes to lock your user ID automatically after a specific number of minutes of inactivity.

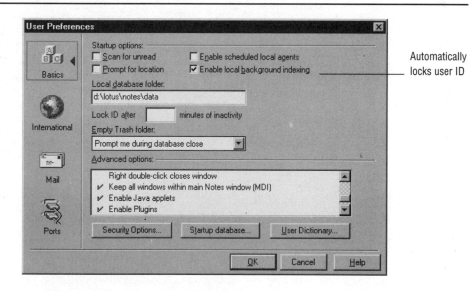

Automatically locks user ID

Setting Security Options

You can protect your workstation by controlling access to it by people who execute Notes scripts or formulas—for example, through forms, documents, or mail messages—on your workstation. You can specify different types of execution access for different people or organizational certifiers. For example, you may give all types of execution access to your Notes administrator, but allow no execution access to unsigned scripts or formulas. Follow these steps:

1. Choose File ➤ Tools ➤ User Preferences. The User Preferences dialog box appears.

2. Click the Security Options button. The Workstation Security: Execution Control List appears as shown in Figure 16.6.

FIGURE 16.6:

The Workstation Security: Execution Control List

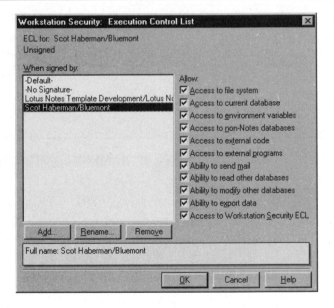

3. To add an item to the When Signed By list, click Add, enter the name of the person or organizational certifier—for example, **/Whatsit**—and click OK.

4. To edit an item in the When Signed By list, select the item, click Rename, edit the item or enter a new item, and click OK.

5. Select the person or organizational certifier whose access you want to specify.

6. Choose the types of access you want this person or organizational certifier to have from the Execution Control List (ECL) options (refer to Figure 16.6).

7. Click OK.

NOTE   Your Notes administrator may predefine all execution control access settings for your organization, making the settings in this dialog box unavailable.

Changing Your Password

You can change the password that controls access to databases on Notes servers from your Workspace. Choose File ➤ Tools ➤ User ID. Enter your current password in the Enter Password dialog box and then click OK.

NOTE   If your Notes administrator required a password to be used when your ID was created, you won't be able to clear it.

You can set a password, change an existing password, or clear a password at any time. To set or change your password:

1. Choose File ➤ Tools ➤ User ID.

2. Enter your password in the text box.

3. Click Set Password.

4. If you are changing an existing password, type this password in the text box and click OK.

NOTE   If you did not previously have a password, skip this step.

5. Enter a new password in the text box.

6. Click OK.

7. Confirm the password by typing it again, exactly as you did the first time.

8. Click OK.

To clear your password:

1. Choose File ➤ Tools ➤ User ID.

2. Click Clear Password.

3. Enter your password in the text box.

4. Click OK.

Examining Your User ID Certificates

A *certificate* is an electronic stamp attached to your User ID by a Notes certifier. (The certifier is usually the Notes administrator.) Certificates grant you access to one or more Notes servers.

When you originally registered as a Notes user, your User ID should have included the certificates required to access the servers you need for your job. As you make wider use of Notes, your job changes, or your organization adds servers, you may need access to other servers. If you are denied access to them because you are not certified, ask the proper Notes administrator (or certifier) for the certificate you need.

You can see information about the certificates attached to your User ID. The information provided about your certificates includes:

- The names of each certificate on your ID

- The date and time each one was created

- The date and time each expires

- The ID number and name of the certifier

To review the certificates that you already have, choose File ➤ Tools ➤ User ID. If your ID file is password protected, you must enter your password in the Enter Password dialog box. Choose the Certificates option. The Certificates dialog box, shown in Figure 16.7, lists your current certificates. Select the certificate for which you want information.

The Certificates dialog box lists the names of the certificate on your ID.

WARNING   You can delete a certificate by selecting it and clicking Delete. However, do not do this unless instructed to by your Notes administrator.

Sending and Receiving Certificates

You may send your ID file to a certifier and receive it back for several reasons. You generally send an ID file to obtain new certificates, but you may also send an ID file to request cross certificates, to request a new user name, or to get a new public key. To get more certificates when you and your certifier both use Notes Mail, follow these steps:

1. Get the name of the certifier from your Notes administrator (if it's not the same person).

NOTE   The certifier's name might be a person or an organizational unit, for example, Administration.

2.   Choose File ➤ Tools ➤ User ID.

3.   Click the Certificates icon.

4.   Click the Request Certificate button.

5.   Enter the name of your certifier in the To box (or select the address using the Address button). The Mail Certificate Request dialog box, shown in Figure 16.8, allows you to create and send a "safe" copy of your ID file—minus the private key and current certificates.

FIGURE 16.8:

The Mail Certificate Request dialog box enables you to create and send a "safe" copy of your User ID file to the certifier.

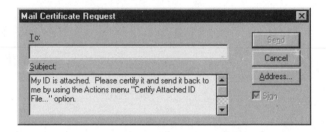

6.   Once the certifier sends it back to you (it will be in a Notes Mail memo), open the memo and choose Actions ➤ Accept Certificates.

If neither you nor your certifier uses Notes Mail (or if neither of you is authorized to access the other's server), follow these steps:

1.   Get the name of the certifier from your Notes administrator.

2.   Choose File ➤ Tools ➤ User ID.

3.   Click the More Options icon.

4.   Click the Create Safe Copy button. The Enter Safe Copy ID File Name dialog box, shown in Figure 16.9, is where you create a safe copy of your ID file on a floppy disk.

5.   Physically take (or mail) the disk to the certifier, who adds a new certificate to your ID file. (You have to physically obtain a safe copy that's been certified by the administrator.)

6.   Insert the certified ID file into your floppy disk drive.

7.   Choose File ➤ Tools ➤ User ID.

FIGURE 16.9:

The Enter Safe Copy ID File Name dialog box allows you to create and save the safe copy of the ID to a floppy disk.

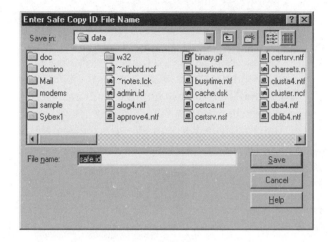

8. Click the More Options icon.

9. Click the Merge a Copy button. The Choose User ID to Merge into Current ID dialog box appears, as shown in Figure 16.10. Enter the path and file name of the safe copy of the ID.

FIGURE 16.10:

You enter the path and file name of the safe copy of the ID in the Choose User ID to Merge into Current ID dialog box.

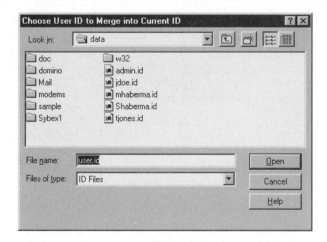

10. Click Open. The Merge Certificates dialog box appears.

11. Click OK in order to merge the new certificate into your User ID or select Cancel if you change your mind.

Protecting Access to Databases

As we discussed in Chapter 4, Notes allows you to set user access privileges for databases. Each Notes database contains an access control list that appears in the Access Control List dialog box, as shown in Figure 16.11. The ACL details who can open the database (access level) and what someone can do to its information (access role). If users have appropriate access level, they can access the particular database. If not, access is denied. The database manager sets both ACL elements, access levels and access roles. To assign access levels and access roles in the ACL, choose File ➤ Database ➤ Access Control. (Users with Designer access to a Notes database cannot change the Access Control List.)

FIGURE 16.11:

The Access Control List dialog box details who can open the database and what a user can do to its information.

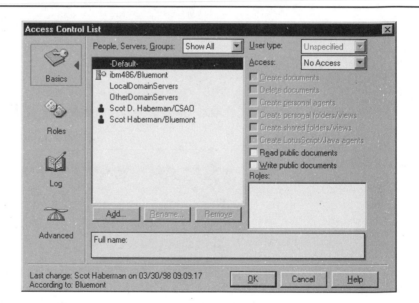

TIP   A quicker way to access a database's ACL is to right-click on the database icon and select Access Control from the pop-up menu.

The database manager may ask you for information from this dialog box if you are having difficulty accessing a database.

Ways to Update the Access Control List

You can update the ACL by:

- Adding a name
- Assigning access levels
- Assigning user types
- Renaming entries
- Removing entries
- Creating access roles
- Enforcing a consistent ACL for all replicas
- Using an agent to update the ACL
- Monitoring changes to the ACL

Identifying Your Level of Access to a Database

You can learn what level of access you have to a database at any time. You can also see whether you are listed in any groups or have any roles for a database.

1. Display the Workspace.

2. Select or open the database.

3. Click the key icon in the status bar.

NOTE   Notes displays the key icon while the database is closed, but when you open the database, the icon changes to indicate your level of access.

Notes displays your level of access for the particular database.

Encrypting Documents

Notes provides document security by allowing you to encrypt fields in documents. *Encryption* means encoding or scrambling data so that only people who have the secret encryption keys can read your documents. (We discussed encrypting Notes Mail memos in Chapter 11.)

Encrypting a document means applying a secret encryption key to one or more fields and then sending the key to users of your choice. Users who don't have this key can still read any unencrypted fields in an encrypted document.

You cannot encrypt a document unless the application developer defines one or more of its form's fields as encryptable. If you have a color monitor and you are composing a document, you can recognize encryptable fields by their red field brackets. To encrypt an encryptable field, use an existing encryption key of your own or create a new one.

All encryptable fields in a document will be encrypted using the keys you select.

WARNING   Any user who has *at least one key in common* with a document can read *all* the encrypted fields in that document. If you give out a key to one field, you are providing access to all other fields you want to keep secret.

As the database designer, you may want to encrypt all documents created with a specific form. You can do so by adding encryption keys to the form or by adding keywords that refer to encryption keys. Add encryption keys when you want to decide which keys to use with a form. Add keywords that *refer to* encryption keys when you want users to choose their own keys from a set that you provide.

You must send the appropriate encryption keys to any user who needs to read the encrypted documents. Just follow these steps:

1. Choose File ➤ Tools ➤ User ID.

2. Enter your password, if one has been set, in the Enter Password dialog box.

3. Choose the Encryption option. Select one or more encryption keys from the list if they exist.

4. Click the Mail button. The Mail Address Encryption Key dialog box appears. Enter the names of users to whom you want to send the keys. Notes will ask you whether you want to let the recipients send the key to other users. If you select Yes, the recipients can distribute the key; otherwise, they can only use it themselves. Your decision depends on the nature of the documents encrypted with this key and on your relationship with the recipients.

Using Encryption Keys

You can select encryption keys to apply to an open document or a form. You also must select an encryption key to remove it from a document. If you add an encryption key to a form, all documents composed with that form are automatically encrypted with the selected key.

To select the encryption key, follow these steps:

1. Choose Edit ➤ Properties while a document is open or choose File ➤ Document Properties while a form is open. The Document Properties InfoBox appears, displaying the Encryption folder tab (the folder tab that displays the key).

2. Click the Encryption Keys tab to display document encryption information, as shown in Figure 16.12. It displays the following settings and options:

    -   **Who Can Read This Document:** Lists the users who can access and read the documents.

    -   **Secret Encryption Keys:** Allows you to apply a secret encryption key to one or more document fields that only users you select can read (as long as you remember to send them the key). A user may have access to a document but cannot read specific fields within the document. However, any user who has any secret key or keys to a document can read all the encrypted fields in that document. Be careful not to give out a key to one field and forget that you are providing access to some other field that you want to keep secret.

FIGURE 16.12:

The Encryption Keys tab enables you to manage the keys in your User ID and the keys applied to the current document.

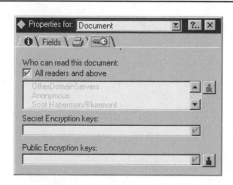

- **Public Encryption Keys:** To encrypt mail, Notes creates a unique public and private key for each user. If someone sends you encrypted mail, Notes uses your public key to encrypt the message, making it unreadable to any user except you. When it delivers the message to your mail database, Notes uses your private key to decrypt (decode) the message for you.

3. Click the Close button.

To add a new encryption key, follow these steps:

1. Choose File ➤ Tools ➤ User ID.

2. Click the Encryption icon.

3. Click the New button. The Add Encryption Key dialog box appears, as shown in Figure 16.13.

FIGURE 16.13:

You can add an encryption key to a document to prevent unauthorized users from accessing information.

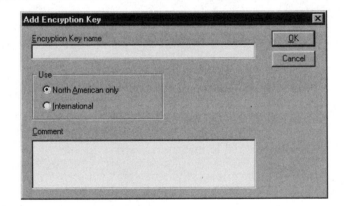

4. Enter an encryption key name. You can also add an optional comment that describes the key.

5. Click OK.

6. Click the Done button.

WARNING   An encryption key doesn't take up much space, so don't delete it unless you are absolutely sure that you won't need it.

TIP   It's a good idea to include a comment for each encryption key you create so that you'll always know the name of the database, the form, and the fields that the encryption key can use to decrypt information.

You can also select encryption keys to apply to documents in a view or remove a current encryption key from a document.

To select encryption keys to apply to documents in a view, follow these steps:

1.   Double-click a database icon on your Workspace to open a view.

2.   Select the documents in the view.

3.   Choose Edit ➤ Properties while a view is open. Click the Encryption Key folder tab.

4.   Select an individual key from the Encryption Keys field.

5.   Repeat step 4 for each document as needed.

6.   Click the Close button.

Since you'll be sharing valuable documents with other people in your workgroup, you'll need to give them the encryption keys you've used. They must have the keys stored on their workstations, or they won't be able to access the documents.

As a precaution, you can specify a password for an encryption key when you export it. (Although you can export an encryption key without password protection, doing so undermines the security obtained by using an encryption key and sharing it with a limited number of users.) Follow these steps:

1.   Enter a password into the Password box.

2.   Enter the same password into the Confirmation box.

3.   Click OK. The Specify File for the Exported Key dialog box appears.

4.   Enter the file name and the name of the directory to which you want to export the file.

5.   Click OK again to perform the export.

The status bar will display the message that the key encryption [*name of key*] has been successfully exported. From now on, people in your workgroup can access the information contained in the documents.

Encrypting Incoming Mail

You can prevent any unauthorized access to your mail—either by administrative access to your mail database or by unauthorized access to the server—when it reaches your mail server. Only you can read your encrypted incoming mail. The administrator can set a default for all incoming mail to be encrypted by using

```
MailEncryptIncoming=1
```

in the NOTES.INI file that's located on the server, or users can elect to encrypt their incoming mail by setting the option in the Person entry on the server's Name & Address book.

Encrypting Outgoing Mail

As discussed in Chapter 11, you can also encrypt outgoing mail to ensure that nobody except your recipients can read your memos while in transit, when stored in intermediate mail boxes, and on arrival in the recipient's mail file. When you encrypt a document, Notes scrambles the information using the recipient's public key so that only the recipient can decode it. You set this option by selecting the Encrypt option in the Delivery Options dialog box. Choose Actions ➤ Delivery Options (or click the Delivery options button when it's displayed in the Action bar when you are composing a new mail memo) and click the Encrypt checkbox. Then click the Send button to send the mail message.

Encrypting Saved Mail

You can encrypt saved copies of your mail memos whether or not you send them to others encrypted. Encrypting saved mail prevents anyone from reading your mail on the server or on your local workstation—even the server administrator or others with access to the server—without your Notes ID.

To encrypt mail, Notes uses the public and private keys stored in each user's Notes ID file. Your public key is also available to other users in the Public Name & Address Book on every Notes server in your company (or Notes domain) for each user. If someone sends you encrypted mail (by selecting Encrypt in the Mail Send dialog box), Notes uses your public key to encrypt the message, making it unreadable to any user except you. When it delivers the message, Notes uses your private key to decrypt (decode) the message for you.

NOTE   We discuss using your private key and your public key to communicate via Notes Mail in Chapter 11.

Since your public key must be available to anyone wanting to send you encrypted mail, the Notes administrator must put your public key in the Public Name & Address Book when you first register as a Notes user. However, to maintain security, your *private* key is stored in your User ID, where only you can access it. This means that any user who has access to your public key can *send* you encrypted mail, but *only you* can decrypt that mail. If your public key is ever lost or corrupted in the Name & Address book, here's how to send a new copy to your Notes administrator using the Mail Public Key dialog box:

1. Choose File ➤ Tools ➤ User ID.
2. Select the More Options icon.
3. Click the Mail Public Key button.
4. Fill in the To, Cc, and Subject text boxes. (You must enter a recipient in the To text box; entering information in the other text boxes is optional.)
5. Select the Sign and Encrypt options if you desire.
6. Click the Send button to mail your public key to the designated recipient.

What's Next?

Building security into your Notes databases is one of the most important aspects in the development process. A breach in security that results in a loss of data can cripple an organization.

In the next chapter, we discuss the basics of laying out a form. Forms are the most important design objects you create with Notes. Users will interact with the forms you create more than they will interact with any other component of a Notes database. Forms are the basis for documents that users will create and add to a Notes database. Users also need forms to read any data that's stored in a database. Therefore, the design of a form—its look, feel, and function—plays a major role in the day-to-day usage of the database.

A well-designed form makes life easier for your users. A poorly designed form can cause much confusion and frustration.

C H A P T E R

S E V E N T E E N

17

Laying Out a Form

■ Defining Notes forms

■ Considering form design

■ Creating a new form

■ Defining the properties of a form

■ Testing form functionality

■ Breaking down a form into parts

■ Displaying a title in the form's Window Bar

■ Taking advantage of Notes' graphics capabilities

■ Working with the About This Database and Using This Database documents

Forms are the most important design objects you create with Notes. Users will interact with the forms you create more than with any other component of a Notes database. Forms become the basis for documents that users will compose and add to a Notes database, and users need forms to read any data that's stored in the documents in the database. Therefore, the design of a form—its look, feel, and function—plays a major role in the day-to-day usage of the database. A well-designed form makes life easier for your users. A poorly designed form causes confusion and frustration.

This chapter shows you how to begin designing a form. It assumes you have created a new database either on your local hard drive or on a Notes server. (Refer to Chapter 14 for instructions on how to create a new database. You will need special authority from the system administrator to create databases on a server.) If your database resides on a Notes server, you must have either Designer or Manager access to it. This chapter covers the following topics:

- Understanding Notes forms
- Designing a form
- Creating a form
- Breaking a form into manageable parts

We will take you through the steps of creating the rudimentary look and feel of a form and describe how to control the properties of a form, add fields and subforms, and apply security. We will also introduce basic formulas (as they apply to form design). Chapter 18 is dedicated to a discussion of formulas; as you encounter formulas in this chapter, you may find it useful to flip back and forth between the two chapters. After you are familiar with the main elements of a form, you will learn how to design dynamic forms in Chapter 19.

Understanding Notes Forms

You can begin to understand the importance of forms by considering the meaning of the word *form* itself: A form is something that adds shape and structure to raw materials. Without form, most raw material lacks shape or structure and is probably not too useful.

The same is true of Notes databases and forms. At a rudimentary level, a Notes database is a container for raw data—someone puts information in, and someone takes information out. The data that resides in a database—text, numbers, dates—has no inherent structure, at least not at the user-interface level. (Of course, the raw data has structure at the machine level, but this structure is not our concern.) The role of the application developer is to give structure to the raw data (i.e., give it form) from the dual perspective of the user adding the data to the database (putting information into the container) and of the user reading the data from the database (taking information out of the container).

TIP   The form provides the filter through which we input data and subsequently view it.

The Separation of Form and Data

One of the most difficult concepts for a new Notes developer to grasp is that Notes stores design objects, such as forms and views, separately from the data that they are responsible for creating and presenting. (We discuss occasional exceptions to this rule, as it relates to forms and documents, later in the chapter.) You know by now that a document is the result of data entered through a form. However, when you save a document and close it, Notes puts the document in a "drawer" separate from the form that was used to create it. The document, as it is stored internally in the database, is literally just a collection of field values *without form*. Later, when you call up the document for reading or editing, Notes pulls the document from one drawer and the form used to create it from another (where all of the design objects reside) and "reunites" the two so that the document can be properly visualized on the screen.

Notes knows which form to couple with the document through a special field named *Form*, whose value is the name of the form that was used to create it. If, for some reason, the form is not available (deleted or renamed), Notes will attempt to present the document through the application's default form, discussed later in the chapter.

The single greatest implication of the separation of form and data rule is that changes made to the design of a form later on cannot possibly affect the integrity of a document created through the form, since the document is a totally autonomous entity. When the document is called up for reading or editing, its content will simply be presented in a new way.

In addition, Notes allows you to present the same document in a variety of ways by coupling it with different forms in different circumstances. (This task is accomplished by reassigning the value of the Form field or by utilizing a design feature in Notes called *form formulas*; we don't cover these advanced design techniques in detail, but as you gain experience in creating Notes applications, keep them in mind.)

The simplest Notes application consists of a single database with a single form (and a single view). Such a simple setup may be sufficient for some uses; however, it's more likely that your applications will require multiple forms and that each form will capture a unique set of related data.

> **NOTE**   A good example of a simple database is your Personal Journal database. It contains only three forms and one view.

Typically, your general user community uses certain forms for data entry and viewing, while specific users (perhaps just you) use certain forms for maintaining information, which another form incorporates for lookup purposes.

What Is a Form?

The term *form* means many things. It can be as structured and static as the infamous 1040 Internal Revenue Service tax form (see Figure 17.1), or it can be as sophisticated as a succession of "intelligent" online screens that walk you through the process of subscribing to an Internet service provider. Notes forms can cover that entire spectrum.

In the early days of consumer software, vendors created programs that provided electronic versions of the IRS forms. These programs eliminated common arithmetic errors and made the forms printable at home. The real success of such products has been in automating the process of filling out the forms rather than in simplifying or improving their design.

Newer versions of tax programs walk you through an interview and offer unsolicited recommendations—not just validations. In addition to finishing your taxes in record time, you may also learn something about tax strategies. The value of the exercise is much greater because the whole process focuses on the goal of managing your taxes, rather than filling out a paper form.

Most forms in existence at your company—expense reports, travel requests, employee change record requests, and/or commuter pass requests—can be "automated" in a similar manner.

With Notes forms, you can attempt to automate an existing paper form or take on the challenge of trying to improve its overall functionality. How to reengineer the process behind a form is beyond the scope of this chapter. However, you should not ignore the opportunity to improve the way people will use the form.

FIGURE 17.1:

The 1040 form causes millions of people to lose sleep and a few hairs as April 15 approaches.

Your Tax Return Quick Reference

Got a question about what to put on a line? Turn to the page shown in the circle.

Form **1040** Department of the Treasury—Internal Revenue Service
U.S. Individual Income Tax Return **1995** (99) IRS Use Only—Do not write or staple in this space.

For the year Jan. 1–Dec. 31, 1995, or other tax year beginning ____, 1995, ending ____, 19 ____ | OMB No. 1545-0074

Label (11)
(See instructions on page 11.)
Use the IRS label. Otherwise, please print or type.

Your first name and initial	Last name	Your social security number (11)
If a joint return, spouse's first name and initial	Last name	Spouse's social security number (11)
Home address (number and street). If you have a P.O. box, see page 11.	Apt. no.	**For Privacy Act and Paperwork Reduction Act Notice, see page 7.**
City, town or post office, state, and ZIP code. If you have a foreign address, see page 11.		

Presidential Election Campaign (See page 11.) (11)
Do you want $3 to go to this fund? . . . . | Yes | No | **Note:** *Checking "Yes" will not change your tax or reduce your refund.*
If a joint return, does your spouse want $3 to go to this fund? . . . . .

Filing Status
(See page 11.)
Check only one box. (11)

1 ☐ Single
2 ☐ Married filing joint return (even if only one had income)
3 ☐ Married filing separate return. Enter spouse's social security no. above and full name here. ▶ _____
4 ☐ Head of household (with qualifying person). (See page 12.) If the qualifying person is a child but not your dependent, enter this child's name here. ▶ _____
5 ☐ Qualifying widow(er) with dependent child (year spouse died ▶ 19 ____). (See page 12.)

Exemptions (12)
(See page 12.)

6a ☐ **Yourself.** If your parent (or someone else) can claim you as a dependent on his or her tax return, **do not** check box 6a. But be sure to check the box on line 33b on page 2
b ☐ **Spouse** . . . .

c **Dependents:**
| (1) First name | Last name | (2) Dependent's social security number. If born in 1995, see page 13. | (3) Dependent's relationship to you | (4) No. of months lived in your home in 1995 |

If more than six dependents, see page 13. (12)

d If your child didn't live with you but is claimed as your dependent under a pre-1985 agreement, check here ▶ ☐
e Total number of exemptions claimed . . . .

No. of boxes checked on 6a and 6b ____
No. of your children on 6c who:
• lived with you ____
• didn't live with you due to divorce or separation (see page 14) (14) ____
Dependents on 6c not entered above ____
Add numbers entered on lines above ▶ ☐

Income (33)

Attach Copy B of your Forms W-2, W-2G, and 1099-R here.

If you did not get a W-2, see page 14.

Enclose, but do not attach, your payment and payment voucher. See page 33.

7 Wages, salaries, tips, etc. Attach Form(s) W-2 | 7 | (14)
8a **Taxable interest income** (see page 15). Attach Schedule B if over $400 | 8a | (15)
b Tax-exempt interest (see page 15). DON'T include on line 8a | 8b | (15)
9 Dividend income. Attach Schedule B if over $400 | (B-1) | 9 | (15)
10 Taxable refunds, credits, or offsets of state and local income taxes (see page 15) | 10 | (15)
11 Alimony received | 11 | (16)
12 Business income or (loss). Attach Schedule C or C-EZ . . . . . | 12 | (16)
13 Capital gain or (loss). If required, attach Schedule D (see page 16) | 13 | (16)
14 Other gains or (losses). Attach Form 4797 . . . . . | 14 | (16)
15a Total IRA distributions | 15a | (16) | b Taxable amount (see page 16) | 15b | (16)
16a Total pensions and annuities | 16a | (16) | b Taxable amount (see page 16) | 16b | (16)
17 Rental real estate, royalties, partnerships, S corporations, trusts, etc. Attach Schedule E | 17 |
18 Farm income or (loss). Attach Schedule F . . . . . | 18 |
19 Unemployment compensation (see page 17) . . . . . | 19 | (17)
20a Social security benefits | 20a | (18) | b Taxable amount (see page 18) | 20b | (18)
21 Other income. List type and amount—see page 18 .... | 21 | (18)
22 Add the amounts in the far right column for lines 7 through 21. This is your **total income** ▶ | 22 |

Adjustments to Income

23a Your IRA deduction (see page 19). . . . . . | 23a | (19)
b Spouse's IRA deduction (see page 19) . . . | 23b | (19)
24 Moving expenses. Attach Form 3903 or 3903-F . . . | 24 | (21)
25 One-half of self-employment tax . . . . . . | 25 | (21)
26 Self-employed health insurance deduction (see page 21) | 26 | (21)
27 Keogh & self-employed SEP plans. If SEP, check ▶ ☐ | 27 | (21)
28 Penalty on early withdrawal of savings . . . . | 28 | (21)
29 Alimony paid. Recipient's SSN ▶ | 29 | (21)
30 Add lines 23a through 29. These are your **total adjustments** . . . . ▶ | 30 | (22)

Adjusted Gross Income

31 Subtract line 30 from line 22. This is your **adjusted gross income.** If less than $26,673 and a child lived with you (less than $9,230 if a child didn't live with you), see "Earned Income Credit" on page 27 ▶ | 31 | (22)

Form **1040** (1995)

– 2 –

Form Design Considerations

A form's layout should reflect not only the purpose of collecting information but also the relationship between the user and the process. Will people use the form willingly? Do you want to encourage terse data entry or textual profusion? Are users proficient with Lotus Notes? Graphical environments? Computers?

Less Is More

Part I explained the new design elements that a Notes form can incorporate. However, the great improvements in Release 4 also provide more traps for designers. You can focus too much on the cosmetics of the form and not enough on its functionality. Ironically, the limitations of Release 3 worked to a developer's advantage when designing forms. A form couldn't be too long and couldn't contain too many images or tables; the limitations tended to keep the form focused and specific. Don't get bogged down in bells and whistles! Images and tables are notorious culprits for bringing the performance of a form to its knees! Also, take it as fact that as you add fields to a form, you slow down performance. As with everything, practice moderation—and don't shy away from using multiple forms to break up the information you want to capture (discussed later in the chapter).

TIP

Don't spend too much time up front looking for images and icons to add to your Notes forms—you can always add them later.

The problem with discussing form design is that the aesthetics are highly subjective. That being the case, we will avoid some aspects of the topic. Whether the form background is blue or yellow, the font is Helvetica or Times Roman, or the point size is 10 or 12 is ultimately up to the designer (taking user preferences into account, of course). What we will discuss is the actual creation of a form along with some general design guidelines related to the usability of your forms. We'll leave the pretty details to you.

When you are designing a form, you need to keep in mind that a form is a vehicle for both *data input* and *data presentation* and that it must handle both functions satisfactorily. Notes provides the tools to help the designer identify the look and modify the functionality of the form so that it is appropriate for use in the following cases:

- Data Input

  - **Initial document creation:** The user chooses the form from the Create menu, bringing up a brand new instance of the form.

  - **Document editing:** The user opens a document in Edit mode.

- Data Presentation

  - **Document preview:** The user double-clicks a database icon in the Workspace and displays the database's views with the Preview pane active (i.e., the documents appear as the user scrolls through the items in the view).

  - **Document reading:** The user double-clicks a document in a view to open and read it.

  - **Document printing:** The user chooses a document and prints it.

In all cases, the underlying form of a document dictates the structure, and thus the efficiency, of the particular interaction. As a designer, you have control over these functions.

Visualizing Your Form Ahead of Time

Notes allows you to create a form from scratch and to add design objects as needed. And nothing stops you from using this ad hoc method once you start to develop your own Notes databases. If you will be the main beneficiary of the application (or you happen to be a tyrant), you can prototype your whole effort and roll it out without consulting anyone and without any up-front planning.

More likely, you are the developer and the main beneficiary of the application is a community of users. Let them in! Given the rapid pace with which you can prototype and develop Notes databases, you can easily fall into the trap of "cowboy programming."

TIP   Save yourself the effort of having to redesign your forms by collaborating with the end users in the development stage. Chapter 15 discusses the basics of good systems analysis.

We recommend that you invest the time to "sketch out" the form before you begin to create it. Some of the best forms we have seen were actually designed on the back of a napkin because:

- The number and size of the text and drawings that you can comfortably scribble on the napkin are coincidentally close to the number of design elements you want to fit on a regular notebook screen.

- Similarly, you can use other napkins to represent other forms. Rotating the napkins on the table should give a good overview of the flow from a user's perspective.

- If your waiter becomes impatient with your pile of crumpled napkins, you need to think through the process some more.

Notes puts at your disposal many tools that help break the form into more manageable parts, as we will see shortly.

NOTE   LotusScript (see Part V of the book) provides still more opportunity to break down the form. It allows a designer to read and write values in documents that are not currently displayed on the screen. This feature frees you from Release 3 restraints that often forced you to lay out a form based on technical limitations rather than logical groupings.

Creating a Form

You have two basic options when creating a new form:

- You can create the form from scratch.

- You can create the form by copying its design from another form.

If you want to base your form on an existing form, you can turn to Chapter 24 for a full discussion of creating forms from preexisting templates. In this chapter, however, we assume that you are creating a form from scratch. Before you begin, you need to select an existing database that will include the form or create a new database. To select an existing database, simply click its icon in your Workspace.

With your hand-drawn layouts spread out on an open surface (the floor if your desk is as cluttered as ours), you are now ready to pick your design elements.

To create a form from scratch, follow these steps:

1. Click the database in which the form will be created. If you haven't already created a database, refer to Chapter 14 for details on how to do so.

2. Choose Create ➤ Design ➤ Form. The Design Form window appears as shown in Figure 17.2.

We now have a few general tasks at hand:

- To define the list of general characteristics that describe the overall behavior of the form, called the *form properties*. These properties will apply to documents based on that form.

- To create the actual substance of the form, including labels and other static text, fields, buttons, and other *design objects*. We will focus on more advanced form design possibilities in Chapter 19.

- To break up the design into *manageable parts*, such as subforms.

For now, let's proceed and set the key properties of our new form.

FIGURE 17.2:

You begin designing a form by opening the Design Form window.

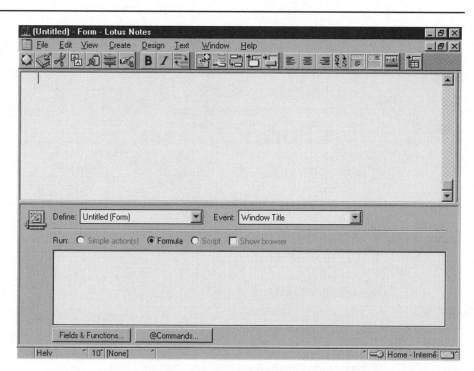

Defining a Form's Properties

The characteristics or properties associated with a form give it identity and establish its important overall qualities. A property can be as simple as the form's name, or it can be more sophisticated. For example, a property can specify whether one document can pass information to another document based on this form (a process known as *inheritance*).

Certain properties are mandatory, and you must provide a value for them. (Sometimes Notes provides a default value for you.) You can ignore other properties entirely, since only more obscure implementations require them.

To define the form's properties, follow these steps:

1. Choose Design ➤ Form Properties, or right-click anywhere in an unused area of the form itself and choose Form Properties from the pop-up menu. Figure 17.3 shows the Form Properties InfoBox.

2. Assign a name to the form (required) by typing it in the Form name text box (for this example, you are going to define a Job Offer form).

3. Make sure that Document appears in the Form type list box.

4. Press Ctrl+S to save what you've done so far.

FIGURE 17.3:

The Form Properties InfoBox lets you a specify a form's attributes.

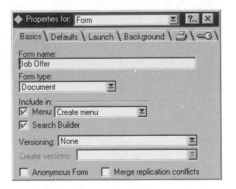

Naming a Form

A requirement of any form is that it have a name. If you attempt to save a new form without assigning a name to it, Notes will prompt you for one. Form names usually, though not always, appear on the Create menu. As such, the name of a form should clearly reflect its function.

Identifying the Form's Type

All forms have a type associated with them. A form's type establishes where a document based on the form will reside in the Notes document hierarchy. You'll recall from Chapter 14 that the basis of many Notes applications is a discussion style of interaction among users in a workgroup—a user initiates a discussion of some topic, and other users respond with a series of responses. There are then responses to those responses.

> **TIP**
>
> You can incorporate this discussion style of back-and-forth interaction in any Notes application that requires group participation in order to produce a final result.

To accommodate this interaction, Notes gives you the ability to classify forms based on where they fit in the hierarchy, as shown in Figure 17.4. For instance, a particular form is designed for discussion initiation, another for response formulation, and still another for response-to-response formulation.

FIGURE 17.4:

This diagram shows the hierarchy of document types.

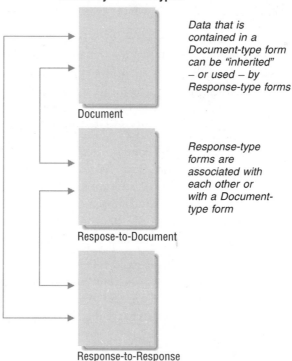

Hierarchy of Form Types

Data that is contained in a Document-type form can be "inherited" – or used – by Response-type forms

Document

Response-type forms are associated with each other or with a Document-type form

Respose-to-Document

Response-to-Response

Typically, data passes from documents higher in the hierarchy to documents lower in the chain, maintaining a consistent thread in the documents throughout the discussion's life cycle. The three supported form types are as follows:

- **Document** is the default form type for all new forms. Notes documents based on this form type are considered Main, or lead, documents in that they do not respond to another document. They occupy the topmost position in the document hierarchy.

- **Response** is, by definition, composed in response to a Main document. A link is established between Main and Response documents that persists as long as the documents remain in the database. In a view, Response documents typically appear beneath the Main document to which they are related, and are indented several spaces.

- **Response to Response** is, as the name implies, composed in response to a Response document, a Main document, or another Response-to-Response document. Like Response documents, Response-to-Response documents appear indented and beneath the documents to which they are related.

Limiting Access to Forms and Documents

When the Form Properties InfoBox was open, you may have noticed the Key tab (the rightmost tab of the five property tabs). Clicking this tab displays Read access and Create access options, which enable you to limit access to reading documents and using forms to create documents. As a security precaution, you may want to identify individuals who can read documents created with a particular form as well as individuals who can create documents with the form.

A workgroup may want its members to be able to use only specific documents and forms. Therefore, it can set read and compose access. Similarly, individuals within the group may also want to limit access to particular documents and forms among themselves. For example, the manager of a project development team may want to limit the access to status reports to individual team leaders who are responsible for overseeing specific components of the project.

You can set a form's Read access, Create access, or both when you create the form. You can also set one now and the other later. If you should change your mind, you can remove access limitations and allow all users to access documents and forms. If you want to limit access later, follow these instructions:

1. Double-click the database's icon to open the database.

2. Choose Design ➤ Forms from the Navigation pane.

3. Double-click the form's name to open it. The Design Form window opens.

4. Choose Design ➤ Form Properties, or right-click anywhere in the form itself and choose Form Properties from the pop-up menu that appears. The Form Properties InfoBox appears.

5. Click the Key tab to display the Read access and Create access options.

NOTE Notes provides a flexible way to set access and to remove access limitations because the needs of people using the documents and forms in a database will change over time.

Setting Access Levels and Roles

We discuss access levels and roles in Chapter 4 and other security precautions in Chapter 16. However, setting access levels for a particular database is very different from limiting Read and Compose access to specific documents and forms. The former limits access to a particular database on a server, thus providing an effective means of security. The latter provides security for limiting access to documents and forms in a database. Consequently, a person may be allowed to access a database but read only specific documents or compose documents only with a specific form.

WARNING Don't forget to include yourself in the list of authorized readers and creators of documents during the testing period of the application. Otherwise, you may be unable to create and access your own test documents.

Controlling the Default Attributes

Beyond the basics we have already defined, we need to set other attributes for the Job Offer form. To do so, click the second tab (Defaults) of the Form Properties InfoBox, as shown in Figure 17.5. By default, none of the options are selected.

Let's review the options.

FIGURE 17.5:

You can alter the fundamental behavior of the form by setting its default properties.

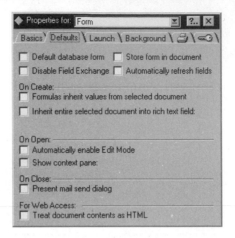

Default Database Form

Select this option if the form is the primary form for the database or the most commonly used form. Notes uses the default form in the event that a form with which a document was created no longer exists. When that document is accessed in the future, Notes will attempt to present the document using the default form.

> **TIP** You should always specify a default form in the database.

Store Form in Document

In workflow applications where documents are routed to a user or to another database via Notes mail, you will need to ensure that the recipient can successfully display the document. Because the form with which the document was created does not typically exist outside the database where it was designed, the form must accompany the document on its journey if the document is sent to a user (technically, to his or her mail database) or to any other database. This option has two major drawbacks:

- **It's a space hog!** The document grows substantially because it now includes the form used to create it.

- **The form of the document is frozen.** Since the form is now "hard coded" into the document, the document will not reflect changes to the design of the form. If, for instance, the form contained a bug that was subsequently fixed, documents (created before the bug fix) that store the form will remain in their "bugged" state.

An alternative to sending a document with a form stored inside is to send a standard mail memo with a document link that lets the recipient open the original document in the source database, assuming the recipient has adequate access privileges.

Automatically Refresh Fields

In some situations you need a form to recalculate the values in a document as a user enters data in a field, rather than force the user to perform a manual refresh (press F9) of the document. (This behavior resembles a spreadsheet application that automatically computes certain cell values based upon data entered in other cells.) This option allows fields within the form to derive their values automatically from values entered in fields above.

TIP Because Notes recomputes a document from left to right and top to bottom, values that appear in fields "higher" in the document can be used to derive values in fields "lower" in the document. (A loan approval form, for example, could automatically calculate numeric values as someone fills in the form.)

However, this option does have a few drawbacks that you should be aware of when evaluating its overall usefulness:

- The performance of larger forms will be negatively affected, since *every* field is recomputed each time a user navigates from one field to another. On slower machines, pressing the Tab key to move to the next field will create an unsightly "screen wobble," and keyboard response time will be noticeably slower for fast typists.

- Validation (discussed later) occurs every time you enter a value in a field.

TIP You can use LotusScript to automatically refresh *specific* fields in a form as opposed to relying on the Automatically Refresh Fields option, which refreshes *every* field. Refer to Part V for a discussion of LotusScript.

Disable Field Exchange

This option disables a feature in Notes called *Field Exchange* (or commonly referred to as Notes/FX), an OLE-based technology that allows the bidirectional transfer of field values with other field-exchange-capable applications, such as Lotus 1-2-3 for Windows. Field exchange is discussed in Chapter 29.

On Create Options

The On Create options control a very important function in Notes known as *inheritance*. Inheritance causes two possible actions to occur:

- **A formula inherits values from a selected document:** A document can automatically adopt specific values from another document. First, however, you must program fields in the form to inherit the values of fields in the selected document (the document currently highlighted at the view level or opened for reading or editing). When a document is created using the form, the values appear in their respective fields. For example, if you select the Account Profile document in a sales tracking application, you can create a new Contact document using a form (we'll call it the Contact form) that inherits the company name and address of the account as they appear in the Account Profile.

- **A rich text field inherits an entire selected document:** This process inserts the selected document (in its entirety) or a document link that points to the selected document into a rich text field of the new document. (You must define a rich text field in the design of the form.) For example, a Review document could assess the information collected in a Loan document; a document link to the Loan document, or the entire Loan document, could appear in the Review document so that all pertinent information is readily available.

TIP
A document link to a selected document takes up much less space than the full contents of the document. Additionally, you are not storing the same information in two places when you use document links. If the linked document changes, the latest and greatest version will always appear to the user when he or she clicks the document link icon.

A user can suppress inheritance by pressing the Ctrl key while choosing a form from the Create menu.

On Open Options

The On Open options affect the behavior of a document when it is opened.

- **Automatically Enable Edit Mode:** Automatically places a document in Edit mode whenever it is opened. You would use this option with versioning or in situations where the only access to a document is for editing purposes.

- **Show Context Pane:** Shows either a split-screen view of the parent document or of the first document link in the document.

On Close Options

Only one On Close option is available, but don't be surprised to see more in the future. This option controls the behavior of a document when it is closed.

- **Present Mail Send Dialog:** This option turns a form into a virtual customized mail memo. When you close a document with this form property activated, Notes will present the same dialog box you see when trying to send standard mail from your mail database. You typically use this option in conjunction with the Store Form in Document option discussed above so that the document can be properly displayed when it arrives at its destination (a user's mail database or any other database).

For Web Access

The For Web Access option affects how Domino treats the contents of a document when rendered for the Web.

- **Treat Documents as HTML:** This option tells Domino to convert all the data on the document, the form, and the subforms to HTML.

Defining the Form's Design Elements

So you thought we'd never get to the fun part of forms design? Don't despair, we are just about to create a Job Offer form in record time—we've already laid out the form properly (get out those napkins) and set all the attributes that would get in the way of our untamed creativity. The page is still blank, so let's proceed! The Job Offer form will be very simple. The completed form is already on the companion

CD-ROM (located in the directory Employ under the file name JOB.NSF). Feel free to either follow along, cut and paste, or ignore your keyboard altogether and read along.

Adding Labels

You'll recall from our earlier discussions that the two basic elements of a form are labels and fields. A *label* is a piece of static text that indicates the type of information a nearby field contains, as a result of either input or automatic calculation. Creating labels on a form is not a mysterious event. Just position the cursor and start typing. That's it! The static text you add to a form will appear on documents composed with the form.

NOTE　No formal relationship exists between a label and a field.

We place labels near fields in a form to convey to users the kind of data we expect them to input. The only trick is to come up with meaningful labels. For instance, the human resources department, the most likely sponsor for our Jobs application, might insist on calling a job title a *position* or calling a personnel representative an *HRC* (for human resources counselor, or something like that). The wording should be concise and obvious to the thickest candidate applying for a job at your company; as a designer, your responsibility is to facilitate the gathering of information, not to do a skills assessment. Follow these steps to enter your first labels:

1. Type **Job Title**: on the second line.

2. Type **Hiring Department**: on the fourth line.

3. Press the Tab key a few times to open up some white space after the Hiring Department: label.

4. Type **Hiring Manager**: on the same line.

5. Type **Job Description**: on the sixth line.

6. Type **Job Requirements**: on the eighth line.

7. Type **Preferred Qualifications**: on the tenth line.

Next, let's make a few cosmetic improvements to the labels:

1. Highlight all of the labels and choose Text ➤ Text Properties to bring up the Text Properties InfoBox.

2. Select a nice, *readable* font such as Arial (if it's available on your system) from the font list.

TIP

When selecting a font, don't choose something so exotic that it will not be available on a majority (or better yet, all) of the workstations used to access your application. Also, make sure to only choose basic fonts such as Courier or Helvetica if your Notes community includes Macintosh or UNIX users.

---

3. Pick dark blue from the Text color list.

4. Select Bold from the Style list. The form should look similar to Figure 17.6.

We are now ready to add fields to the form.

FIGURE 17.6:

The basic Job Offer form

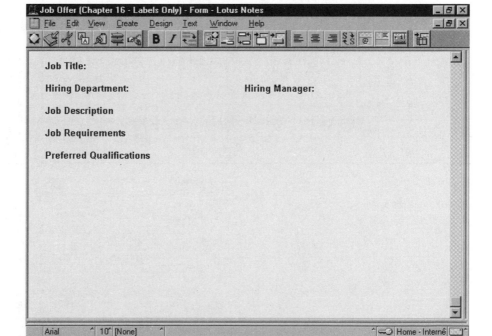

Defining Fields

Placing fields on a form is somewhat more involved than creating labels. Nevertheless, fields are the design elements that give meaning to the form. You can think of a *field* as a container for a single piece of data—a string of text, a number, a date and time, an embedded object, etc. Your forms will include several of these containers into which users will place specific types of data.

NOTE

In many of the field definitions described below, you are instructed to enter formulas. Since formulas aren't officially discussed until Chapter 18, we are asking you to simply go through the motions for now. As you work through Chapter 18, refer to the formulas you've entered here.

TIP

You should have a complete list of the fields you intend to place on the form sketched out on a piece a paper—before you start creating them.

To add a field to a form, follow these steps:

1. Position the cursor at the location where you want to place the field—typically to the right of a label that indicates what goes into the field. If necessary, open up some white space between the label and the field by using the spacebar or Tab key. For instance, insert one space to the right of the Job Title label and leave the insertion point at that position.

2. Choose Create ➤ Field. Notes places a new field called Untitled on the form, and the Field Properties InfoBox appears, as shown in Figure 17.7.

FIGURE 17.7:

The Field Properties InfoBox lets you define each field on a form.

3. Type **Title** in the Name text box. The name must be only one word with no spaces, but you can create the effect of multiple words by using lowercase and uppercase letters, as in OfficialJobTitle, or by using an underscore, as in Official_Job_Title.

WARNING   A field name must begin with a letter and can contain letters, numbers, and the symbols "_" and "$". A field name is limited to 32 characters.

4. Click the Options tab and enter a brief description in the Help description text box, such as "Enter the official title of the job being offered." This field description (known as *field help*) will appear on the status bar at the bottom of the screen when a user positions the cursor in the field.

WARNING   The help description for a field will only be displayed when the document is placed in Edit mode. The user must also select the Show Help option from the menu (choose View ➤ Show ➤ Field Help).

TIP   Don't overlook using help descriptions in editable fields. They are a very efficient means of explaining the purpose of a field, in a way that is more informative than the label you include to identify the field.

Naming Conventions for Fields

Many schools of thought exist on how to properly name the fields in a form. We tend to lean to the informal but consistent side. If your background is in programming in other languages, you may be used to naming fields (you call them "variables") based on their data type. In the following example, *Title* is a string, *Salary* an integer, and *PostDate* a variant, since it contains a date/time value.

strTitle

intSalary

varPostDate

Continued on next page

We have seen Notes developers call the same fields by their object type. In the following example, *Title* is of the Notes data type Text, *Salary* is of the type Number, and *PostDate* is of the type Time.

txtTitle

numSalary

timPostDate

Our preference is to avoid systematically enforcing specific naming rules. Instead, you should "type" your fields only when the possibility for ambiguity exists. Most people would assume that *Title* is text, *Salary* a number, and *PostDate* a time. However, a field named *Locations* is less obvious in that it could contain either a single text value, such as "Headquarters," or multiple values, such as "Atlanta : San Francisco : Paris : San Diego." Whoever follows you as the developer of the application (which might very well be yourself a few months down the road—when you've had plenty of time to forget how you've designed the application) will not need to dig too deeply to remember that the result of lstLocations needs to be processed as a list rather than as a single string.

Naming the field (aside from the typing issue) is entirely up to you. Our recommendation is to ask if the name makes sense to the next person who has to look at the design of this application. *Sal* is somewhat less obvious than *Salary*. The same holds true for *Manager1*, *Manager2* versus *HiringManager, ReviewManager*. Whatever you decide to do, don't skimp on letters. In most cases you won't have to retype that word because Notes provides handy ways to pick the field from a list in its formula and LotusScript dialog boxes.

Designating a Field's Data Type

Notes fields support eight unique data types:

- Text
- Time
- Number
- Keywords
- Rich Text
- Authors
- Names
- Readers

When you assign a data type to a field, you are telling Notes how to interpret the data stored (or just displayed) in the field. If the type of data that appears in the field does not agree with what Notes expects (e.g., letters entered into a number field), you will have to correct the offending data before you can save the document. Let's examine the types of data supported in the Notes environment.

Text

The text data type indicates that the field will contain alphanumeric characters (letters and numbers), punctuation symbols, and spaces. The contents of a text field cannot be formatted, except by you, the developer. Furthermore, the contents of a text field cannot be directly involved in a mathematical calculation. Even if a text field contains only numbers, Notes does not view the contents as numeric data, but rather as "text." You would have to convert the contents to a number to use it in a calculation. Text fields can contain up to 15KB of data.

TIP

> Though it may sound strange, you should probably classify fields that will contain numeric data as text unless you need to perform mathematical calculations on the data or require that the data have a specific numeric format (such as a percentage or currency). The reason is that you often use standard text and numbers together in string concatenations and various other string manipulation formulas. As a result, you wind up having to convert numbers to text anyway (see the @TEXT function, discussed in Chapter 18). Classifying numeric data as text simply eliminates that step.

Time

The time data type allows you to capture and display time and date information in a variety of formats, including:

- 06/01/96
- 06/01
- 06/96
- 06/01/96 12:30:01 P.M.
- 06/01 12:30 P.M.
- 12:30:01 P.M.

- 12:30 P.M.

- 12:30 Today

- Yesterday

Notes supports both 12-hour and 24-hour formats. Dates may range from 1/1/0001 to 12/31/9999.

TIP   Notes is Year 2000 compliant. For input and display purposes, Notes will drop the century unless the century is not the current century. For example, if the user enters "3/3/98," Notes will store the date as 3/3/1998 even though it will always be displayed without the century. Notes infers the century based on the current date for the two-digit years 50 to 99. The two-digit years from 00 to 49 are treated as twenty-first century. If the user enters "3/3/2098", the date will always be displayed with the century until the year 2000. Once the year 2000 is upon us, all the 1900 dates will display the century.

Number

The number data type indicates that the field will contain numeric data, including the mathematical symbols +, –, ., (plus, minus, decimal), E, and e. The format characters % and $ are also permitted. Number fields are typically involved in mathematical calculations and/or format conversion operations. Notes accepts numbers from 2.225E-308 to 1.798E308 with fourteen-digit accuracy.

Keywords

Keywords fields allow you to establish a predetermined list of *text* values for that field. That is, users simply choose a predefined value from a list rather than manually entering a value. Keywords fields help eliminate invalid input (as may be the case in free-form editable fields) and can streamline the task of data input. Keywords fields come in three varieties:

- **Dialog list:** Presents a list of choices in a dialog box. The user displays the list by clicking the "helper button" (a down arrow) and then selects one or more of the items. The user can also select items without displaying the list, either by typing the first letter of one of the keywords or by pressing the spacebar repeatedly to cycle through the list of items.

- **Checkbox:** Presents a list of choices in checkbox format. A user can check one or more items.

- **Radio button:** Presents a list of choices in radio button format. A user may choose *only* one of the items.

TIP You should make liberal use of keywords fields in your forms wherever they are appropriate. Keywords improve the accuracy of input and make the input process faster (once users get the hang of them).

Rich Text

The rich text data type includes all the functionality of the text data type and accepts format attributes, such as boldface and italic, and supporting graphical data—pictures, bitmaps, graphs—various fonts and point sizes, links, file attachments, and OLE objects. For example, you can cut and paste a range of spreadsheet cells or embed an entire spreadsheet into a rich text field in a document. (The rich text data type, however, doesn't permit computations on strings or numbers.)

WARNING You can't display the contents of a rich text field in a column on a view. Keep this in mind when designing a form.

Authors

Author Names fields are used to identify a list of users, groups, and access roles that can edit a specific document.

An Author Names field *refines* only Edit access to a document. Users indicated (either directly, or as part of a group or access role) in an Author Names field must have Author access in the ACL of the database. Users with Reader access or lower cannot gain edit rights to a document through an Author Names field. The contents of an Author Names field do not affect users with Editor access or greater.

Names

You use the Names data type for fields that will capture and display user and server names. A Names field automatically converts Notes hierarchical names to an abbreviated form. For example, CN=Kyle Brown/O=Sirrus Consulting becomes Kyle Brown/Sirrus Consulting.

Readers

Reader Names fields identify a list of users, groups, and access roles that can read a specific document.

A Reader Names field *refines* only Read access to a document. Users indicated (either directly, or as part of a group or access role) in a Reader Names field must have Reader access in the ACL of the database. Users with access lower than Reader (or no access at all) cannot gain read rights to a document through a Reader Names field. Users listed in an Author Names field in the same document are automatically granted Read access.

Reader Names fields differ from Author Names fields in that they affect all users, regardless of their ACL rights to the database. For instance, a user with Editor access will not be able to read a document that contains a Reader Names field in which they are not listed.

TIP　　If you are going to implement a Reader Names field in a form, be sure that the value of the field defaults to or computes to *some* value (the name of the user who created the document, for instance). Otherwise you run the risk of creating orphaned documents that sit in your database but can't be seen! If the database is to be replicated to another server, you must include the server name in the Reader Names list of a document to allow the server to access it.

Designating How Data Is Put into a Field

The data type defines *what* will go into the field. Equally important is the issue of *how* the information will actually get there. You may assume that the user is responsible for supplying all the information to be captured in a document, but that is not the case at all. The value of a field may be the result of an automatic calculation over which the user has no direct control (although they will very likely have some indirect control). You can think of this type of field as a "read only" field. This field simply *shows* the user some information that the person may not directly alter, as opposed to a read/write field where the user provides a value. In Notes terminology, the former is a *computed* field and the latter is an *editable* field. Whether a field is editable or a field's value is computed depends on the precise function of the field as an element in the overall design of the form.

TIP

A field is either editable or computed, never both.

Creating Editable Fields

When we defined our first new field, you may have noticed that its default field type was *editable.* This type is appropriate for fields where you want the user to supply a value. Notes allows you to establish an initial, or default, value in an editable field to ensure that a value appears in the field when a document is first created.

NOTE

It's a subtle point, but you should realize that although a default value appears in a field of a newly composed document, the field will not actually assume that value until you save the document. Before saving, the value acts as a placeholder that can be changed to something else.

A user-supplied value in an editable field may have some action taken upon it, including a variety of transformations (e.g., a text value might be converted to all uppercase characters) and/or a validation to ensure that the supplied value satisfies specific criteria (e.g., a numeric value is checked to see if it falls within an acceptable range of values). The editable field type is available with all data types. For now leave the Job Title type as text and editable. Follow these steps to add the other fields to the Job Offer form:

1. Place the insertion point to the right of the Hiring Department label, insert one space, and choose Create ➤ Field.

2. Type **Department** for the Name. Leave the type as text and editable.

3. Repeat steps 1 and 2, this time creating a field named Manager to the right of the Hiring Manager label.

4. In the Options tab, under Security options, enable encryption for the Manager field, as shown in Figure 17.8. We do not want to reveal the name of the hiring manager to outside candidates.

FIGURE 17.8:

Use the Options properties for a field to encrypt or sign a field.

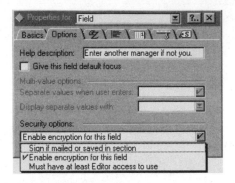

5. In the Design pane at the bottom of your screen, enter the following formula in the formula box for the Default Value event of the Manager field:

    `@Name([CN]; @UserName)`

    This formula will insert the name of the person creating the document as the default value for Hiring Manager. The assumption is that hiring managers will most likely create their own Job Offer documents. Since the field is editable, the value can be changed if necessary.

NOTE   If the Design pane is not currently visible, display it by choosing View ➤ Design Pane. Repeat this procedure to close the Design pane if you wish.

6. Repeat steps 1 and 2 above, creating rich text/editable fields named Description, Requirements, and Qualifications on the form. The form should now look similar to Figure 17.9.

7. Change the font for all the fields. Turn off the bold attributes of the rich text fields but keep the others bold. A good plan is to apply one color to the fields the user has access to and another color to fields that are computed.

Creating a Keywords Field

Let's add another keywords type field on the first line and name it Status. Select the method of construction for the keywords list. You have several options:

- **Enter Choices (One per Line)** allows you to type words in the text box underneath the option. By hard coding a list, you will have to modify the field definition any time you need to change the list.

FIGURE 17.9:

The Job Offer form with fields defined

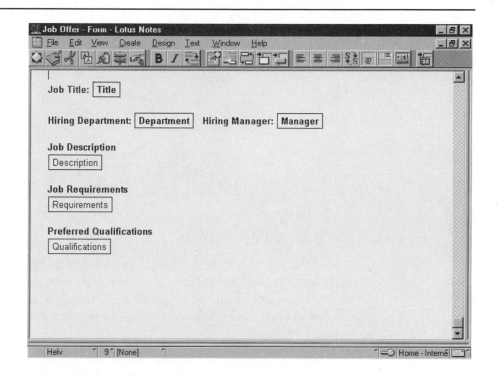

- **Use Formula for Choices** allows you to execute an @Db or @Picklist function to pull the list of values from a column in a view. This method is convenient if the list of choices is extremely dynamic or if you want to maintain the list of choices outside the design of the form. Chapter 18 describes @Db and @Picklist.

- **Use Address Dialog for Choices** brings up the same dialog box you use to pick destinations for an e-mail memo. This feature is useful for selecting the names of people who should receive the document.

- **Use Access Control List for Choices** brings up the same dialog box you use to set the security for the database, as discussed in Chapter 16.

- **Use View Dialog for Choices** is exactly the same as the @Picklist function we described earlier.

For now, choose Enter Choices (One per Line), as shown in Figure 17.10. Be sure that Allow Values Not in List and Allow Multi-values are not selected. (After all, the job is available or it isn't.) For more about keywords, see the sidebar *Externalizing Your Keywords* in the following section.

FIGURE 17.10:

Set the method of construction for the keywords list in the Field Properties InfoBox.

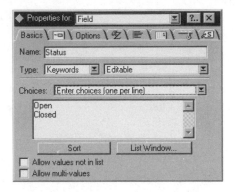

Creating Computed Fields

A computed field derives its value from some form of calculation as set forth by a formula associated with the field. The user cannot directly alter the value. Often, however, the value of a computed field is based on the value of an editable field (or perhaps several editable fields), which gives the user a degree of control over the computed value.

For example, a user inputs a value into an editable field, which is then used as part of a formula for a computed field. When in Edit mode, a user will not be able to position the cursor in a computed field. Notes actually defines three types of computed fields:

- Computed

- Computed for display

- Computed when composed

Each type of computed field is appropriate in certain circumstances. In all cases, the value of the field is the result of a formula, not the result of user input. Notes will not let you save the form until you have specified the formula.

Computed

A *computed* field type may be used in conjunction with any data type (except for the rich text, which is treated essentially as compute-when-composed). Notes stores the value in the document where views and Agents can reference it. Each time a document with computed fields is opened, refreshed, or saved, Notes recomputes the values in its computed fields.

TIP   A computed field is appropriate for fields whose values will change over time. Typically, the formula associated with a computed field refers to other editable fields in the document. The value of the computed field changes as the values in the editable fields change.

Externalizing Your Keywords

We suggest using formula keywords in which you build the list of keyword choices through a lookup process, instead of hard coding the keywords in the field itself. The process requires a little bit of extra work. Here is the overall design:

1. Create a Definition form, which is available only to administrators/developers of the database. The form needs to contain at least two text/editable fields, Category and Detail. Make sure the Detail field definition does not allow multi-values. Once the form is finished, create your keywords documents. The idea is to create one keywords document for every keyword you want to support. The value of the Category field ties related keywords together, that is, keywords documents that share a common value in their Category field will appear together in a keywords list. For instance, you could have two keywords documents with Category set to Status, and each with a different value for Detail, such as Open and Closed. The administrator adds new categories and new details as needed.

2. Create a Hidden view (covered in Chapter 20) whose selection formula selects only documents created with the Definition form. This view, typically called Keywords Lookup, sorts and categorizes by the Category field in the first column of the view.

3. Any time you need to access a list of keywords, simply insert the following formula in your keywords field, replacing <KEY> with the proper Category value, for instance, Status:

```
@Dblookup(""; ""; "Keywords Lookup"; "<KEY>"; 2)
```

Clearly, this method slows down development a bit, but it allows nondevelopers to maintain keyword lists, getting you out of the loop for minor changes like replacing the keyword Open with Available.

A form can contain a computed field whose value is based on the value of another field (either editable or computed) in the *same form*. The formula for the computed field is simply the name of the other field. Whatever value appears in the other field passes to the computed field. This field type is particularly useful when you want to link an input (editable) field to a presentation (computed) field and the input value is displayed elsewhere in the document with special formatting characteristics.

Computed for Display

A *computed for display* field type may be used in conjunction with any data type except rich text. Unlike a computed field, the value is *not* stored in the document. Rather, the value exists only when the document is opened (or displayed) and is discarded when the document is closed. The computed for display field type is appropriate for computed fields that will never be referenced outside the document, such as in views and Agents.

If you think of a field in terms of its scope, a computed for display field's value is not usable beyond the document level—for instance, in a view. The value of the field is recomputed when the document is opened or refreshed. As a performance mechanism, computed for display fields can streamline the speed of your database (because the value is discarded when the document is closed, disk access is not necessary to store the value) and its size (no value stored, no disk space required).

Follow these steps to add a field that will appear only in Read mode and won't be stored in the form:

1. Insert a line on top of the form by pressing ↵.

2. Select Create ➤ Field and call it Title_Display.

3. Center the field and make its font larger and bolder.

4. Select Computed for Display as a type.

5. Type **Title** in the formula box for the Value event (in the Design pane).

6. Click the Hide-When tab in the Field Properties InfoBox (the tab that looks like a window shade—second tab from the right). Click the Hide-When options Printed, Previewed for Editing, and Opened for Editing, as shown in Figure 17.11. The field will pick up its value from the Title field below and show it only when the document is read.

FIGURE 17.11:

You can control when a field is visible using the Hide-When options of the Field Properties InfoBox.

Computed When Composed

A *computed when composed* field type may be used in conjunction with any data type except rich text. It is similar to a computed field except that the value is calculated only once—when a document is created. From that point forward, the value is static and will not change. Like the computed field type, the value is stored in the document and may be referenced in views and Agents.

TIP   A computed when composed field is appropriate in instances where you simply wish to hard code a value for a field at composition time and leave it intact.

We have such an instance where we want to "stamp" the Job Offer form with the date it was first posted—the date it was composed. Follow these steps to affix a time stamp to our Job Offer form:

1. Click to the right of the Status field. Press the Tab key two times and type **Posted:**.

2. Select Create ➤ Field and type the name **PostDate**.

3. Set its Type to Time and Computed when composed.

4. Set the format of the time/date field, as shown in Figure 17.12. Choose to show only the date.

5. Type **@Today** in the formula box for the Value event (in the Design pane).

FIGURE 17.12:

Set the format for a time field to show the portion of a time/date you wish to display.

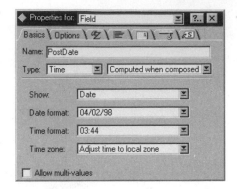

Whenever the form is created, today's date will be computed and stored permanently in the PostDate field. It will not recompute in the future, which would have reset the date to the current editing date of the document.

Shared Fields

Shared fields are like regular fields except that they are not defined within the context of a form. In other words, shared fields are autonomous design objects that you can insert into the design of a form. After you define a shared field, you can reuse it in as many forms as you wish. For instance, you can define a shared field named LastName as a text/editable field and then insert it into one or more forms in your application; if the definition of LastName changes later, all forms that contain the field will automatically reflect the change.

We don't make use of shared fields in our Job Offer form, but we'll explain how to create one so that you can try it on your own:

1.   Select the database from the Workspace in which the shared field is to be defined.

2.   Choose Create ➤ Design ➤ Shared Field. The Field Properties InfoBox is automatically displayed on top of a maximized Design pane, as shown in Figure 17.13.

3.   Enter the properties of the shared field *exactly* as you would a regular field, including name and type.

4.   Press the Esc key to save the shared field.

FIGURE 17.13:

The Shared Field Design window

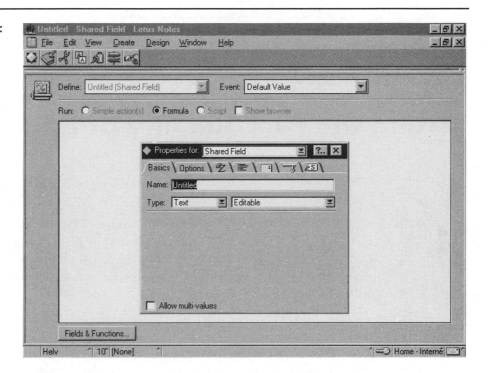

To incorporate the shared field in the design of a form, do the following:

1. Open the form in Design mode.

2. Position the insertion point where the shared field should appear.

3. Choose Create ➤ Insert Shared Field.

4. Select the shared field from the list of fields available, either by highlighting the field name and clicking OK or by double-clicking the field name.

You will notice that shared fields appear with a thick border around them, which distinguishes them from regular fields, and that they appear in the same Navigation pane as forms, views, and other design objects.

NOTE   Deleting a shared field from the design of a form does not delete the definition of the field but only that instance of the field in that form.

TIP   You can also create a shared field from an existing field from a form. To do this, select the field that you want to convert to a shared field. Choose Design ➤ Share This Field. The field will now have a thick border around it.

Testing the Functionality of a Form

Notes Release 4 supports two ways to test the functionality of a form: a casual check, through the new Test Form feature, and a full check by performing a standard Create.

With Notes 4.6, a new feature has been added that allows the developer to test a form using a Web browser. This feature is only available if the Notes Designer has been installed on the workstation. With Notes 4.6, the Notes client has been divided into two separate applications. One is called Notes Desktop and the other is called Notes Designer for Domino.

Notes Desktop gives the end user the majority of the functionality available in the Notes Designer for Domino with the exception of some Web development tools. The ability to view databases, forms, and so on via a Web browser locally is one of those features that is not available. Refer to Chapter 33 for more details about enabling your applications for the Web.

Testing a Form Using Test Form

Using the Test Form function is the method of choice when you are in the midst of designing a form. It will give you a good idea of how the form will look and behave. Plus, it's rewarding to see your work in progress. Try it often before finishing the form.

To test our form, follow these steps:

1. Choose Design ➤ Preview in Notes.

2. Respond with Yes when Notes asks you to save the form. (Better to save often than to swear at your computer later.) The form appears as if it were called from the Create menu, as shown in Figure 17.14.

3. Press the Esc key to return to Form Design mode.

If everything looks good and otherwise seems to work appropriately, congratulate yourself and move on to the full test.

You can test the functionality of a form with the Test Form feature.

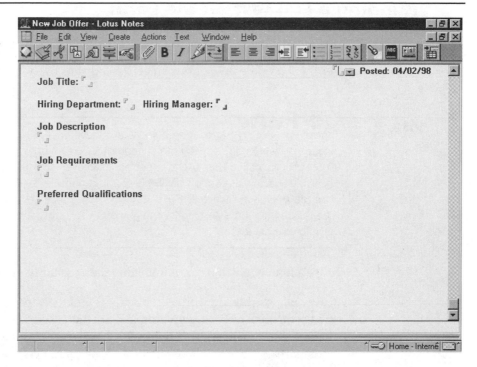

An Intelligent Approach to Form Design

If you anticipate designing several forms with similar functionality (either generally or as it relates to the implementation of a specific feature you intend to incorporate in each of the forms), you should consider concentrating on one of the forms only, making it the prototype. Use the prototype to work out the logic of any complex formulas and/or calculations in a controlled manner and then propagate that logic to the other forms. You'll find working on a prototype is easier than designing multiple forms in parallel and trying to maintain logic changes across them all.

After you work with Notes for a while, you'll usually discover more than one way to implement a particular feature in your application. Chances are pretty good that you'll change your mind on how to accomplish the implementation of a complicated feature (even if it's a subtle change) at least once. With one form serving as a prototype, you can confine your changes to that form, rather than attempting to synchronize changes across several forms.

Running a Full Test on the Form

Unfortunately, there is no great way to guarantee that you haven't left a bug here and there on your form. The only thing you can be sure of is that your users will uncover them at some point. You can get a head start by "impersonating" an end user.

NOTE   Since your security rights to a database as a developer are greater than those needed by your end users, you should request (or create on your own) a separate Notes User ID that you can use to impersonate an average user. Place the ID file in the same directory as your official ID file so you can quickly switch back and forth. (Use File ➤ Tools ➤ Switch ID.) This "test user" should be granted what you consider to be the typical ACL rights and any other security access an end user will have to your database.

Here are a few suggestions for minimizing the possibility of bugs in your forms:

- Cover all possible keyword combinations and lookups. When the form asks the user to pick or type keywords that are then used to process information, make sure that you walk through every possible error path. In other words, enter garbage or errors in the fields and see if your code is strong enough to handle it. We call that the "brainless" test.

- Save the documents from your test and make sure that you can view them properly in all the views. (We'll talk about views in the next chapter.)

- Test all form Actions. (We'll talk about Actions in Chapter 21.)

- Print the form and make sure it still looks good.

- Forward the form to yourself via e-mail to see if it is readable.

Breaking a Form into Manageable Parts

Now that you have created a basic form, adding new forms to your own application should be a simple matter. First, however, you need to be familiar with a number of techniques that let you construct forms that are more modular and easier to maintain and use. You'll appreciate these features, particularly if your forms are becoming very complicated or large, or if you notice that you are using similar logic and functionality across many forms. The three primary Notes features that support modularity are:

- Subforms
- Collapsible sections
- Layout regions

These features let you split an otherwise monolithic form into smaller parts. We'll talk about subforms in this chapter and cover collapsible sections and layout regions in Chapter 19.

Subforms

One of the key design decisions you need to make is whether you should break up the functionality of a form into two or more forms. *Subforms* are forms that you can include within the design of regular forms; in other words, a subform is a single, reusable design object that you handle just as you would a *shared field*. As you modify the design of a subform, all the forms that include it will automatically reflect the changes. For instance, you can add a standard routing slip to all the forms that need to go through an approval process.

NOTE   In the following discussion of subforms, you will create a button and a corresponding formula. (Formulas and buttons are officially discussed in Chapters 18 and 19.) You can refer back to this material as necessary.

We recommend that you use subforms when you expect to reuse a specific design—without changes—in multiple forms in the database. Designing a subform typically requires additional planning to ensure that its functionality is common and generic.

Follow these general steps to create a subform:

1. Select one of the databases you copied from the companion CD to your Workspace.

2. Choose Create ➤ Design ➤ Subform. The Subform window appears, as shown in Figure 17.15.

3. Choose Design ➤ Subform Properties. The Subform Properties InfoBox appears, as shown in Figure 17.16.

FIGURE 17.15:

The Subform window

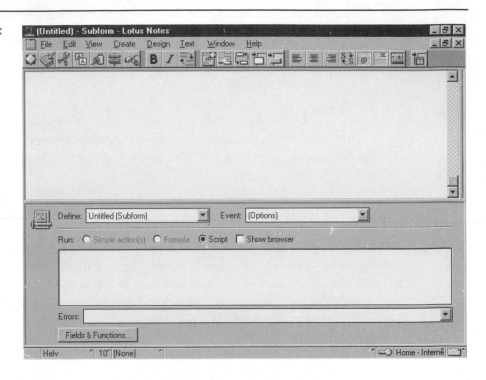

FIGURE 17.16:

The Subform Properties
InfoBox

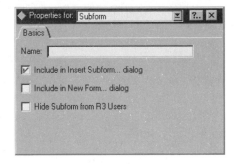

4. Enter a name for the subform in the Name field. For example, type **Welcome**.

5. Select the option(s) you want.

6. Press Ctrl+S to save the subform.

TIP   Everything in a subform looks and feels like a regular form.

At this point, we need to get a little bit ahead of ourselves and add a few design elements to make the subform usable. (You will learn about design objects such as buttons in much more detail in the following chapters.)

For once, please follow us blindly, we'll drive slowly (now, that's a first!), as we add a button:

1. Choose Create ➤ Hotspot ➤ Button. A blank button appears in the subform and the Button Properties InfoBox is automatically displayed.

2. Enter a name in the Button label field. For example, type **Welcome**.

3. Click the Close button. The label appears on the button, as shown in Figure 17.17.

4. Type the following formula in the formula box inside the Design pane at the bottom of the screen:

   ```
   @Prompt([OK]; "Greetings"; "Hello World")
   ```

5. Press the Esc key to save and close the subform.

FIGURE 17.17:

The Welcome button of the Welcome subform

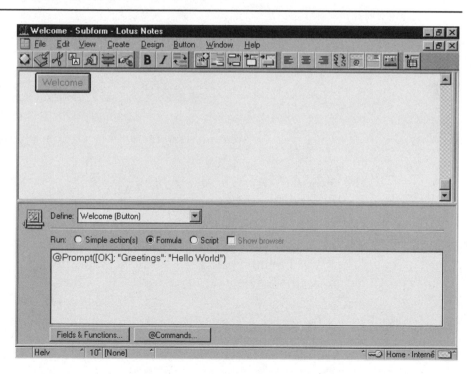

Inserting Subforms

The main difference between a subform and a regular form is that you can insert subforms into other forms (but not into other subforms). A subform will behave and appear to the end user as if it were an integral part of the form.

To insert a subform follow these steps:

1. Open an existing form in Design mode. The Form Design window appears, displaying the elements of the form.

2. Position the insertion point in the form where you want to insert the subform.

3. Select Create ➤ Insert Subform. The Insert Subform dialog box appears, listing the names of the subforms you've created. The list should look similar to the one shown in Figure 17.18.

4. Select your Welcome subform from the list.

FIGURE 17.18:

The Insert Subform dialog box lists the subforms you've created.

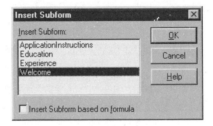

5. Click OK. The Welcome subform (with its Welcome button) appears in the form.

6. Press Ctrl+S to save your work.

You may have noticed the Insert Subform Based on Formula option in the Insert Subform dialog box. This option lets you establish a computed subform, whereby a formula dictates *which* subform to display and *when* to display it. For instance, you could choose to reveal the Welcome subform only if the user does not appear in your Public Address book.

Creating a Title for a Form's Window Bar

As the final touch to our first form, we'll program the form to display a title in a window bar at the top of the Workspace to help users identify the form's name as they create new documents. The title can also display useful information, such as the date and time, or a name or subject that is significant to the database. To create a title to appear in the window's title bar, follow these steps:

1. Click on any open area (i.e., wherever there is white space) of the Job Offer form.

2. Select Window Title from the Event drop-down list.

3. Enter the following formula in the formula box of the Design pane:

   `@If(@IsNewDoc; "New Job Offer"; Title+",posted:"+@Text (PostDate))`

4. Click the green check mark to confirm the formula. The pane should look similar to Figure 17.19.

FIGURE 17.19:

Enter a window title to show the context of the form to the user.

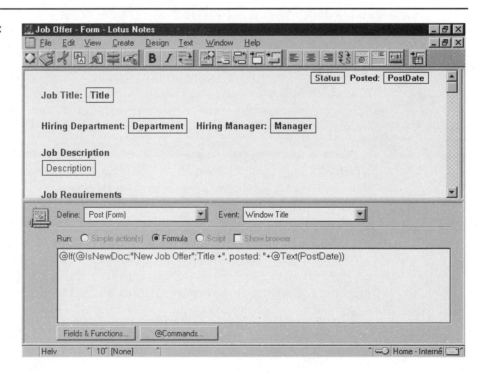

Each time a user creates a document using the Job Offer form, the title New Job Offer will appear in the window bar. When the user opens a view and selects a document to read or edit later, the window bar will display the value of the Title field followed by the word Posted: and the value of the PostDate field, as in "Notes Developer, Posted: 06/01/96."

Using Notes' Graphics Capabilities

Up to now, we haven't discussed using graphics in a database in detail. Graphics certainly enhance the appearance of documents, and they can help to communicate their intent. For example, you'll notice that all database icons in the Workspace display graphics that strive to capture their purpose. These graphics have been created in Notes. As a database designer, you'll need to learn to create and insert graphics in forms, in addition to creating graphics for icons.

Creating Bitmap Graphics with Notes

Graphics purists who like to create original artwork for forms can take advantage of the Notes Design Icon Editor to design *bitmap graphics*. If you don't use or have access to another Windows drawing program, the Notes Icon command works in a pinch (although it does have limitations). Unfortunately, you can use this method only for a database that doesn't display a graphic on its icon. The secret is to create the graphic(s) before you create the bitmap you want to display on the database icon.

When you create a new database or open an existing database, Notes adds the icon to the Workspace. Subsequently, selecting the icon enables you to access the database quickly. After you open an existing database, such as the Jobs database that's included on the companion CD-ROM, the icon that appears in the Workspace displays a bitmap graphic. When you create a new database, however, only the title you gave the database and the default bitmapped graphic (the three figures) appear on the icon. The area above the title is empty. Our advice is not to create the bitmap graphic you want to appear on the icon yet. Instead, create the graphics you want to include on the database's form(s) first.

What happens if you don't follow this sequence? To illustrate the problems that you'll encounter, select the Jobs database by double-clicking the icon in the Workspace and then follow these steps:

1.   Choose Design ➤ Other in the Navigation pane.

2. Select Icon in the Document pane. The Design Icon Editor appears, as shown in Figure 17.20. (Notice the bitmap graphic that appears on the icon.)

3. Click the Copy button to copy the graphic to the Clipboard.

WARNING   Make a copy of the graphic before you go on to the next step!

---

4. Click the Clear button. The graphic disappears from the screen. If you click the Undo button, the graphic reappears.

NOTE   If you selected the Undo button in the previous step, choose the Clear button again to clear the dialog box.

---

5. Click OK to accept the change. The dialog box closes.

FIGURE 17.20:

The Design Icon Editor displays the bitmapped graphic that appears on the selected database's icon.

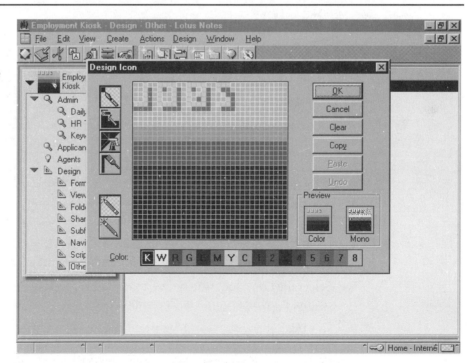

6. Press Esc to return to the Workspace. You'll notice that the icon's graphic has been erased. Don't panic! You copied the graphic to the Clipboard.

7. Open the Design Icon Editor again (with the icon still selected).

8. Select Paste. The graphic reappears.

9. Click OK to confirm. Once again, the database icon displays the graphic.

Always create an icon's graphic *after* you've created the other graphics you want to use in a database. Otherwise, you'll delete the graphic from the icon, and you won't be able to store a permanent copy of it on the Clipboard. Any other graphic you create and then copy to the Clipboard will *replace* the graphic you stored previously on the Clipboard.

Don't expect to create a graphic, copy it to the Clipboard, paste it in forms, return to the Design Icon dialog box, and then retrieve the graphic for the database icon. It will be long gone!

Creating Graphics for Forms

You create a graphic in Notes by painting individual pixels, just as you would in any other drawing program that enables you to create bitmap graphics. (Each one of the squares on the grid in the dialog box represents a *pixel*, which stands for "picture element.")

To create a new graphic that you want to use in a form, follow these steps:

1. Open the Design Icon Editor.

2. Select the Drawing tool (the icon with the highlighted pencil tip).

3. Select the Paintbrush tool, which enables you to fill one pixel at a time. (This tool gives you more flexibility than the other tools for adding detail to the graphic.)

4. Point to the pixel you want to change and then click the mouse button to add color, which you select at the bottom of the dialog box.

5. Select the Erase tool (the one with the highlighted eraser) and click a pixel to restore it to the original background color.

6. Use the Roller, Spray, and Snap-to-Line tools to fill large areas of the grid. You'll need to experiment in order to discover which tool suits your needs. (Remember: If you make a mistake, you can always click the Undo button to undo your last action.)

7. Click Copy to store the graphic on the Clipboard when you are happy with the design and size. (Warning: Do this before performing the next step.)

8. Click the Clear button to erase the graphic, or it will appear on the database icon.

TIP   If you change your mind, click the Undo or Cancel buttons.

---

9. Click OK to confirm and to close the dialog box.

10. Open the form where you want to use the graphic, position the graphic in the desired location, and select Paste from the Edit menu (or press Ctrl+V). The graphic will appear.

If you want to modify the graphic later, select it and then choose Copy from the Edit menu (or press Ctrl+C). Open the Design Icon dialog box. Click Paste. Make the desired changes to the graphic and then copy it to the Clipboard. Return to the form and paste the graphic. (If the old graphic hasn't been removed, select and delete it first.)

Creating the Graphic for the Database's Icon

As we mentioned above, each database icon in your Workspace will display a graphic that identifies it. Therefore, the graphic that appears on a database's icon should reflect the application's purpose. The name of the database should also communicate its function.

You can design the icon's graphic by using the Notes Design Icon Editor. Although the design icon tools aren't very sophisticated, they allow you to create simple bitmap graphics. You paint individual pixels, just as you would in any other drawing program that enables you to create bitmap graphics. To create the graphic, follow these steps:

1. Open the Design Icon Editor.

2. Click the Drawing tool (the highlighted pencil tip icon).

3. Click the Paintbrush tool, which enables you to fill one pixel at a time. (This tool gives you more flexibility than the other tools for adding detail to the graphic.)

4. Click the pixel you want to change to add color, which you select at the bottom of the dialog box.

5. Select the Erase tool (the one with the highlighted eraser) and click a pixel to restore it to the original background color.

6. Use the Roller, Spray, and Snap-to-Line tools to fill large areas of the grid. You'll need to experiment with each one in order to discover which one suits your needs. (Remember: If you make a mistake, you can always click the Undo button to undo your last action.)

7. Click OK to save the graphic when you are satisfied with its design and size. The Design Icon Editor closes, and the graphic will appear on the database's icon in the Workspace.

TIP   A graphic doesn't need to be very complex to convey a message.

Inserting a Database Icon's Graphic on a Form

You can also insert the graphic that appears on a database icon on a form so that it appears on all the documents that users create with the form. Inserting a graphic in this way is an easy and convenient method of adding graphics to forms without much fuss. To insert a graphic on a form, follow these steps:

1. Double-click any database icon to display its view.

2. Open the Design Icon Editor to display the graphic you created for the icon.

3. Click the Copy button to copy the graphic to the Clipboard. (If you press Ctrl+C, Notes will beep to let you know that you can't use this keyboard shortcut.)

4. Click the Cancel button to close the Design Icon Editor.

5. Choose Design ➤ Forms in the Navigation pane.

6. Double-click a form to open it in the Design pane.

7. Press Ctrl+V to paste the graphic on the form. The graphic appears.

8. Click the graphic to select it.

9. Click the Center Justified icon to center the graphic.

10.   Press Ctrl+S to save the form.

11.   Press Esc to close the form Design pane.

As we discussed previously, you can Insert Graphic objects anywhere on a form because a form is actually a large rich text field that can contain text and graphics.

When you click the graphic to select it, a marquee will appear around it with a resizing handle in the lower-right corner. The graphic might also appear darkened (highlighted). You can drag the handle to increase or decrease the size of the graphic. This action is similar to the way you might modify the appearance of a graphic you've created in another application. If you've never used a drawing application to create a graphic, all you're doing is changing its size to fit the form. It's no big deal.

If the graphic appears marqueed but isn't highlighted and you open the Edit menu, you'll notice that the Cut and Copy commands aren't available (they appear dimmed). However, the Paste command is available, and the graphic appears selected with the marquee. What's going on? You must make sure the graphic is highlighted in order to cut or copy it.

TIP

After you select a graphic, open the Edit menu and see if the Cut and Copy commands are available. If they appear dimmed, the graphic hasn't been selected correctly. You need to make sure that a marquee surrounds the graphic and that it appears darkened.

With the graphic still selected, open the Edit menu. You'll see a Resize Picture command under the Insert command. When you choose the command, the current width and height of the graphic will appear at the bottom of your screen. This information is handy when you resize the graphic. As you drag the handle, the width and height will change accordingly.

NOTE

If you are using a third-party drawing or graphics tool, draw your graphic and save the file as a BMP, CGM, GIF, JPEG, PCX, or TIF. Then use the File ➤ Import command from the Notes menu to import your graphic. Sometimes the Paste command doesn't display the graphic the way you expected.

Creating the About This Database and Using This Database Documents

As the designer of a database, you have the option of including two help documents with the application. One is called the "About Database" document, and the other is called the "Using Database" document. Together, these documents describe a database and explain how to use it. Although you don't *have* to create these documents, every database should include them.

When a user is unfamiliar with a database, they can read the documents to learn more about it. In many situations, these documents are the only assistance users will receive. Therefore, as the database's designer, you have a responsibility to explain the functionality of a database as thoroughly as you can. If users don't understand your database, they won't use it. If they don't use the database, it serves no purpose.

Writing the About This Database Document

When a user opens a database for the first time, the About This Database document appears. Since this document is a user's introduction to the database, it should include a thorough description of the database's purpose and features, in addition to any other pertinent information. A user can subsequently display the About This Database document by choosing Help ➤ About This Database.

The About This Database document is also useful for displaying information about a database when a user browses through the list of databases in the Open Database dialog box (File ➤ Database ➤ Open). A user can highlight a database in the list box and click the About button to read about the database before deciding to open it. To create the About This Database document, follow these steps:

1. Double-click the database's icon to select it.

2. Choose Design ➤ Other in the Navigation pane.

3. Select the "About Database" Document. The document opens in Edit mode.

4. Write a description of the database.

5. Press Ctrl+S to save the document.

6. Press Esc to close the window and return to the Workspace.

Writing the Using This Database Document

The Using This Database document should explain how to use the database and include a description of its forms and views. It should also include explanations of macros. For example, the Using This Database document for the Jobs database explains how the employment kiosk works. The document describes the process of installing the database and provides release notes.

A user can display the Using This Database document by choosing Help ➤ Using This Database. To create the Using This Database document, follow these steps:

1. Double-click the database's icon to select it.

2. Choose Design ➤ Other.

3. Select the "Using Database" Document. The document opens in Edit mode.

4. Write a description of the database.

5. Press Ctrl+S to save the document.

6. Press Esc to close the window and return to the Workspace.

What's Next?

In the next chapter, we discuss the essentials of the Notes formula language. The formula language is a powerful, yet easy-to-use, tool that is indispensable in automating your applications. Formulas are used in practically every facet of most Notes applications. Put simply, you won't get too far as a developer without a thorough knowledge of formulas. So get to it!

CHAPTER

EIGHTEEN

18

Formulas

- Understanding and creating formulas

- Understanding the rules of formula syntax

- Exploring the uses of Notes @functions

- Using different types of @functions

- Introducing @commands for programming Notes applications

Formulas play a significant role in virtually all Notes applications and are indispensable in bringing functionality, user friendliness, and automation to your databases. Formulas enable you to customize or create new applications easily. Using Chapter 17 as a foundation for a discussion of formulas, we will now describe how to incorporate formulas in the design of your database and will cover the following topics:

- Formula language

- Formula syntax

- @Functions

Understanding the Formula Language

Unless you are using a database template as is (see Chapter 23 for more on using templates), avoiding formulas altogether is virtually impossible. Formulas (and scripts, to be discussed later) are the active ingredients in Notes; a thorough understanding of them is vital if you wish to be a successful Notes application developer. You need to use formulas whenever you have to "compute" the value of a Notes design object, including editable and computed fields of forms, Actions, buttons, columns of a view or folder, and Agents.

The Notes formula language resembles the Lotus 1-2-3 macro language and also borrows concepts from the BASIC programming language. The good news is that you don't need a degree in computer science or even any experience in programming to start creating simple formulas. In fact, it is socially acceptable to have a real business job and become competent in writing Notes applications that contain formulas!

If you are a trained programmer (nonprogrammer types may leave the room for a moment), you will quickly notice the absence of many elements found in most high-level programming languages, such as flow control, type declarations, and data structures. If you are new to programming, you'll find formulas relatively painless, so don't be put off by terms like *syntax*, *arguments*, or *evaluate*.

Of course, we can't possibly cover all the possibilities for creating and using formulas in one chapter. Our modest goal is to give you a firm foundation in the basics of formulas, including some practical, everyday uses. You should be able to apply the principles you learn here to developing more sophisticated formulas. This discussion will focus on answering the following questions:

- What is a formula?

- Where are formulas found?

- How does a formula work?

- When is a formula evaluated (and what happens then)?

What Is a Formula?

Before we go any further, let's define the term *formula*. This task turns out to be a little tougher than you might think because a formula has several important aspects. For the moment we'll propose a definition in terms of what a formula *does*: A *formula* is something that performs an action, which in turn yields a result.

If you find this definition a little too vague, sit tight; we will refine our definition as we go along. (Given the diversity of circumstances where formulas can be applied, it's an appropriate start!) For example, consider the following events that might occur in a Notes application:

- A lowercase word is converted to uppercase.

- A number is multiplied by another to produce a new value.

- A value is checked to see if it is a valid time/date.

In each of the preceding examples, we see an *action*—conversion, multiplication, validation—which produces some kind of *result*—an uppercase word, a numeric value, TRUE or FALSE. In Notes, we can implement formulas to handle each of these events. However, formulas do not stand by themselves; they must always be associated with some design object—a field, a column, a button, and so on. A formula is "activated" only through these design objects.

Next, let's describe a formula in terms of what it looks like and how it works. To the eye, a formula is one or more expressions, each made up of specific parts that we can classify very precisely. An *expression* is an operation stated in some kind of symbolic form. (We will expand upon this concept in great detail very shortly.) A formula may be very simple or very complex, depending on the needs of the application. Some formulas consist of a single expression, while others consist of multiple expressions. In any event, a formula really amounts to a set of instructions to be carried out relative to the design object where the formula is found. The general structure of a formula in Notes is:

```
Expression 1;
Expression 2;
    .
    .
    .
Expression n
```

In a formula with multiple expressions, each is separated from the next by a semicolon. You may include as many expressions as necessary in your formulas, although longer formulas will take more time to evaluate and, of course, to debug.

TIP

Formulas may be sprinkled with statements that start with the word REM. REM stands for remark and allows you to insert comments about the formula so that other developers (or yourself) can understand what the formula is supposed to achieve.

How Does a Formula Work?

Each month most of us sit down and dutifully balance our checkbooks after receiving a statement from the bank. A statement shows the ending balance from your last statement, deposits, withdrawals, various charges for the current period, and, finally, the new balance. The back of the statement instructs you to plug specific dollar values into a preformatted calculation (typically a series of lines, boxes, and arithmetic operators) that eventually gives you your account balance (which, for us, *always* agrees with the balance in our checkbooks). We bring up this depressing topic to illustrate a classic formula that most of us can relate to, albeit a formula in which we do most of the work. The point is that when we insert the proper numbers and proceed through the calculation step-by-step, we get a result at the end. Notes formulas are really no different except that they do the work for us.

TIP

Think of a formula in Notes as a mechanism that automates a series of steps.

Using Environment Variables

Variables are valid only within a single formula. In other words, they "expire" immediately after the formula completes its execution, unless you write down its value within the field of a document. If you need to use a value between multiple Notes applications or over a period of time, you need to create an *environment variable*.

An environment variable is, in fact, an entry in the Notes configuration file called NOTES.INI. This file is typically located in your Windows directory and includes many entries required for Notes to function properly on your machine. An environment variable is a special entry that starts with the $ character, for instance

```
$SupportCallCounter=143
$ProfileCompany=Atlantic Decisions
```

To retrieve the value of the SupportCallCounter in a formula, you need to use the @Environment("SupportCallCounter") @function. To create or reset the value of the ProfileCompany environment variable, you need to use the @SetEnvironment("ProfileCompany";"Atlantic Decisions") @function. Note that the variable starts with the $ character when written in the NOTES.INI but is actually used without it in @functions.

Try to use unique names for environment variables to avoid overwriting a variable used by another Notes application. When you are not using an environment variable, we recommend that you set it to nothing, using the @SetEnvironment("SupportCallCounter";"").

Variables

We're still missing an ingredient in our definition of a formula, though. In that a formula is only framework for producing a result (just like the calculation on the back of a bank statement), clearly that formula needs to act upon something; otherwise, it is essentially useless. So now we can refine our definition to include the stipulation that a formula acts upon values provided to it, what we will loosely call *input*, in order to produce a result. In other words, a formula must have something to work on for it to be meaningful. The most common "something" that you find in Notes formulas is the variable. (The concept of the "variable" is consistent across virtually all programming languages.) A *variable* is simply a term in an expression that represents a value. In the expression $A + B$, the terms A and B are variables that represent values to be added together. As the word *variable* implies, the represented values can change over time. In Notes, *fields* are the most obvious example of variables—a field in a document is representative of a value that may change at any time. In the formula

```
CheckingAccount * 1.05
```

CheckingAccount is the name of a field (defined in the design of a form) whose value is to be multiplied by 1.05 (not that it would matter given the pitiful amount of money left in ours). If you've ever used an electronic spreadsheet like Lotus 1-2-3, you are probably familiar with cell formulas such as

```
+B6 - B5
```

that subtract the value that appears in cell B5 from the value that appears in cell B6 to produce a value that appears in the cell in which this formula was entered. The concept of using cell names to represent the values in those cells in a formula is the same as using Notes field names in Notes formulas.

Temporary Fields

In many cases you will want to declare *temporary fields* in your formulas. A temporary field exists only while the formula is being evaluated; then it is discarded. (In programming terms, a temporary field is like a local variable in a function; its scope is confined to that function only.) Temporary fields are useful when you want to store the value of an operation momentarily or if you simply want to make your formulas more readable. Compare the readability of the following formula:

```
@If((CheckingAccount * 1.05) > 100; "This month we eat"; "A good time for a diet")
```

with this formula:

```
BalancePlusInterest := CheckingAccount * 1.05;
@If(BalancePlusInterest > 100; "This month we eat"; "A good time for a diet")
```

In the second formula, the temporary field BalancePlusInterest is assigned a value that is then referenced in the @If formula, making it easier to read. While the difference in readability between the two examples above might not be earth shattering, temporary variables are very effective in simplifying complex formulas.

TIP   If you use temporary variables in your formulas, give the variables names that will be meaningful to someone else reading the formula and keep the name as short as possible to avoid typos. (Remember, you're going to be referencing the variable name elsewhere in the formula.) Cryptic names such as *x* or *y* will not convey the meaning of the temporary variable.

Constants

A *constant* is simply a hard-coded value that appears in a formula, as opposed to a value that is represented by a variable. Many formulas you create will use a combination of variables and constants. A constant is treated as a literal value and is taken exactly as it appears. Notes supports three types of constants:

- Text strings
- Numbers
- Time/date values

A *text string* is any set of characters enclosed in quotation marks (""). For example

```
"(" + AreaCode + ") " + Exchange + "-" + TelNumber
```

combines a series of text constants (those items in quotation marks) with text values that are represented by the field names AreaCode, Exchange, and TelNumber to produce a formatted phone number such as

```
368-2837
```

Two special characters, " and \, require extra attention if you wish to display them in a text string. You must immediately precede these symbols with a backslash (\), which is sometimes referred to as an *escape character*. For example, the string

```
"\"Hello world\""
```

produces "Hello world" with the quotation marks included, and

```
"\\Hello world\\"
```

produces \Hello world\.

The \ symbol is also used in cascaded form names and view names. For instance, the selection formula

```
SELECT Form = "Main Forms\Main Topic"
```

will produce an error because Notes will interpret the \ as an escape character and remove it from the text string, resulting in "Main Forms" as the directory entry. To correct this error, enter the selection formula as

```
SELECT Form = "Main Forms\\Main Topic"
```

TIP
Remember to always use the double-slash convention in formulas that involve hierarchical form names, view names, and Agent names. Certain formulas may also require the use of DOS-type directory paths, for example, C:\NOTES\MYDB.NSF. In this case you must use the double-slash convention as well, for example, C:\\NOTES\\MYDB.NSF, or Notes will not interpret the path correctly.

Numbers are any numeric values made of the numerals 0 through 9 and the symbols ., −, + , E, and e. In the expression

```
CheckingAccount * 1.05
```

1.05 is a numeric constant.

Time/date values are any characters that represent a valid time/date and are enclosed in square brackets ([ ]). Notes determines the validity of a date value based on how the date separator is configured for the workstation operating system (in Windows 3.*x* you configure this option through the International applet of the Control Panel, and in Windows 95 through the Regional Settings applet of the Control Panel). If the separator is set to a slash (/), the constant [11/01/94] is valid whereas [11-01-94] is not. This formula example:

```
@Adjust([02/13/97]; 0; 0; 16; 0; 0; 0)
```

yields a time/date value that is sixteen days beyond 02/13/97.

Where Are Formulas Found?

Formulas can be found virtually everywhere design objects are found:

- In forms
- In fields
- In hotspots (buttons, pop-ups)
- In Actions
- In view/folder columns
- In view selection formulas
- In selective replication formulas
- In Navigators
- In Agents

Fields typically provide newcomers to Notes development with their first exposure to formulas. A *field formula* is a formula that is built into the definition of a field. Fields do not always have formulas associated with them, but they frequently do. A field formula produces a value that is stored in the field (except in the case of a computed-for-display field, in which the value is displayed but not stored in the field). Depending on the type of field, the input to the field formula will come from different sources:

Field Type	Source of Input
Editable	Values entered by the user
Computed, Computed for Display	Values entered or computed in other fields
Computed when Composed	Values inherited from fields in another document

Figure 18.1 shows an Input Translation formula for the FName field.

FIGURE 18.1:

The Input Translation formula for the FName field

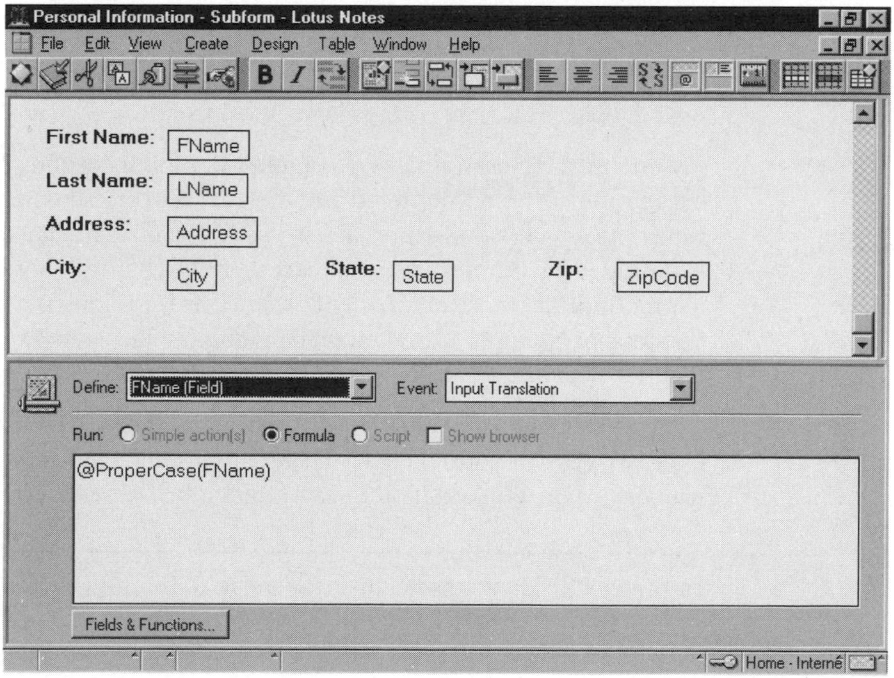

In this case, if a user were to enter the value "kim," the formula would convert that value to "Kim."

When Is a Formula Evaluated (and What Happens Then)?

Technically, we say that a formula in Notes is *evaluated*, which is a fancy way of saying that Notes executes each expression in the formula in a precise order and produces a final result. Just staring at a database icon in the Notes Workspace isn't enough to get formulas to do what they do. (An exception to this rule might be background Agents that execute at periodic intervals.) In most cases, a user needs to perform some action to trigger the evaluation of a formula. Some typical actions (or *events*) include:

- Opening a document or view
- Saving a document
- Clicking a button (in the Action bar or in the document)
- Pressing the F9 key to recalculate a document or view

When these events occur, Notes evaluates the formulas associated with the design objects affected by the event.

Generally, Notes evaluates a formula from top to bottom; Notes executes each expression as it is encountered and then moves on to the next expression. Many times the result of one expression is used in a subsequent expression (recall the example of a temporary variable earlier in the chapter). In some instances an expression can be executed out of order. This technique is a remnant from earlier versions of Notes; it caused much pain and suffering among Notes developers in its time. Thankfully, Notes Release 4.*x* addresses this quirk, much to our delight.

Notes demands that most formulas contain a main expression, which is an expression in the formula that will generate some kind of resulting value: text, numeric, date, Boolean (that means either TRUE or FALSE), success or failure.

TIP When choosing whether to use a formula or LotusScript code, keep in mind that the execution speed of formulas is faster than that of LotusScript code.

---

60 Seconds on Events. . .

Every action a user performs in a Notes application is classified as an *event*. Opening and closing a document, clicking a button, pressing the F9 key, moving the insertion point into and out of a field—all of these activities are considered events. Many other events occur in Notes; some of them are behind the scenes and not under the direct control of the user.

Writing formulas and scripts that react to specific events, like those mentioned above, is known as *event-driven programming*. (Not all of the events that occur in a Notes application can be "reacted to.")

Events are always related to the design object with which they are involved. The behavior of an object relative to an event will vary from object to object; some objects will "respect" an event, while others will ignore it entirely. A single object, like a field, may respect several different events, and each of these events can have a unique program associated with it. This behavior is expressed either as a formula or as a script, but never as both.

Sometimes you can choose to use either a formula or script, and other times you are forced to use one or the other. In cases where you are allowed to choose, the complexity of the operation will dictate your choice. For a relatively simple operation, formulas are best; for more complex operations or in situations where formulas don't provide the functionality you're looking for, use LotusScript.

For instance, if the formula for a field named Status is simply

```
temp1 := "Open";
```

which assigns a value of Open to a temporary variable called temp1, Notes will display the formula error message "No main or selection expression in formula." This formula, as it stands, does nothing to produce a meaningful result—unlike CheckingAccount * 1.05, which added 5 percent interest to our pitiful balance. In other words, the statement does not return anything to the underlying design object, the field named Status.

Design objects that store or display information, such as fields or view columns, will expect something meaningful back from their formulas. The correct syntax might therefore be

```
temp1 := @If(Signed = "Yes"; "Closed"; "Open");
@Return(temp1)
```

which says that if the Signed field contains the value "Yes," we set the value of the temporary variable temp1 to "Closed"; otherwise, we set it to "Open." We then return the value to the Status field where it is displayed or stored, or both. A shorter version of the same operation returns the results to the Status field directly without the use of a temporary variable:

```
@If(Signed = "Yes"; "Closed"; "Open");
```

How Do I Define a Formula?

By this point you are probably wondering, "When are they going to show us how to create a formula?" If you are comfortable with the concept of formulas and the events that trigger them, you're ready to work with the genuine article. (If you are still scratching your head, continue on anyway. With luck, the "learning by doing" rule will work its magic.) For now, we will stick with field formulas as a vehicle to illustrate the actual creation of a formula.

> **TIP**
>
> Regardless of the design object, the process of creating a formula is largely the same. Throughout the remaining chapters of the book, we'll be discussing more advanced design objects; you simply need to apply what you learn here about formulas to those objects.

Figure 18.2 shows an example of a subform in Design mode. The screen is split between the actual form (in the upper half) and the Design pane (in the lower half). You enter a formula for the current design object through the Design pane.

You choose an object by either clicking it in the form or selecting it from the drop-down list next to the Define label in the Design pane, as shown in Figure 18.3.

You may have noticed that the Personal Information subform, along with the names of the fields it contains, appears in the list of available objects in the Design pane. The explanation is very simple—forms (and subforms) are themselves objects that react to specific events! We'll table our discussion of this perplexing functionality for now and return to it when we discuss dynamic forms in the next chapter.

Focusing on just the FName field in the subform, we have to decide upon the event that will trigger the formula. The drop-down list in Figure 18.4 displays the events that are available for this object. Remember that this list will vary for different object types.

FIGURE 18.2:

The Personal Information subform in Design mode

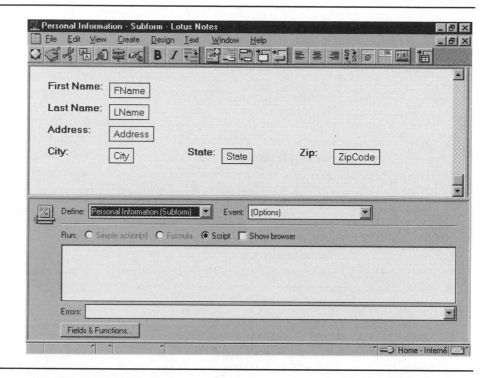

FIGURE 18.3:

The list of objects in the subform for which formulas and scripts can be defined

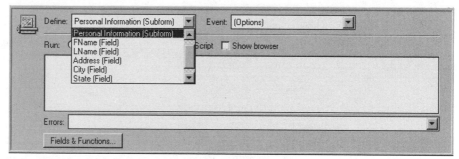

FIGURE 18.4:

The list of available events for the FName field

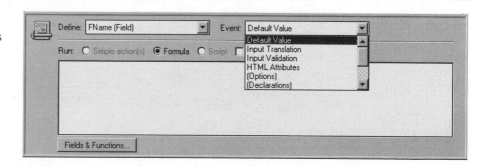

Choosing the Input Translation event, we will enter the formula @Propercase (FName) in the scrollable text box of the Design pane, shown in Figure 18.5, and then click the button that instructs Notes to run a syntax check on the formula. (We discuss formula syntax in the next section.) If we've improperly formatted our formula, Notes will display an error message; otherwise, we are free to define other formulas for the same object or move on to other objects.

Notice that with the Input Translation event chosen, the program options Simple action(s), Script, and Show browser (which is directly related to the Script option) in the Design pane are dimmed and unavailable. This screen tells us that only formulas are permitted for this event. If you were to select other events for FName, you would see the program options dim and undim appropriately.

TIP	The basic formula to validate the input of a field is @If(Field = Value;@Failure ("Warning message");@Success) where you replace the word Value with whatever string, number, or date the Field should not be equal to.

FIGURE 18.5:

A formula for the Input Translation event of the FName field

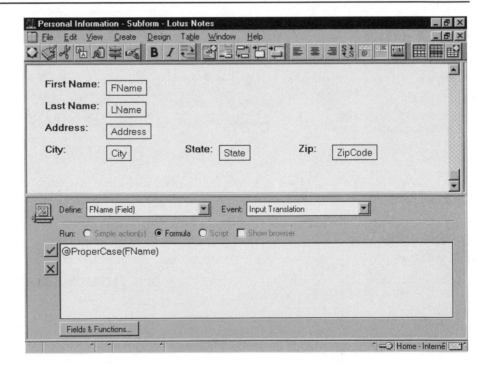

The other option you see in the Design pane is the Fields & Functions button. (If it is legal to use @Commands with the current design object, you will also see an @Commands button next to the Fields & Functions button. @Commands are discussed later in the chapter.) The Fields & Functions button helps you construct your formulas in an automated fashion. When you click this button, the dialog box shown in Figure 18.6 appears.

FIGURE 18.6:

The Fields and Functions dialog box

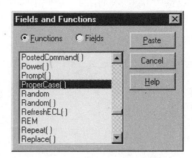

As you pick and choose from the list of @functions and field names, your choices are inserted into the formula in the text box. Don't mistake this process for a "formula builder," which does everything for you; you will typically need to modify the formula to some extent.

Understanding Formula Syntax

Syntax describes the grammar of a formula. Notes formulas have a very specific syntax to which programmers must adhere. Most errors that occur in formulas are syntax related, so pay close attention to how you format a formula.

The Structure of a Formula

Recall that the general structure of a formula is

```
Expression 1;
Expression 2;
.
.
.
Expression n
```

and that a formula may be made up of a single expression or multiple expressions separated by a semicolon. We will now proceed to break down an expression and look at its various elements.

Variables and Constants

Earlier in the chapter we talked at length about the use of variables (field names, temporary variables) and constants (text, numeric, time/date) in Notes formulas. Let's revisit them in the context of proper syntax.

In the case of variables, you must make sure that the data type of the variable matches what is expected in the expression. If a field named *Status* has a value of "Open" and you attempt to use the field in the expression

```
Status * 5
```

Notes will display the error message "Incorrect data type for operator or @Function: Number expected" because multiplying a text string and a number together is illegal (and illogical). Similarly, if a field named *CheckingAccount* has a value of 100 and you attempt to use the field in the expression

```
@Uppercase(CheckingAccount)
```

Notes will display the error message "Incorrect data type for operator or @Function: Text expected" because the function @Uppercase expects a text value as an argument.

Obviously, field names must be spelled correctly in order for a formula to yield a correct result. Misspelling a field name may also produce a syntax error because Notes will treat the misspelled name as a variable representing a *null value* (""), which will cause problems in numeric and time/date expressions. A field name may appear in a formula in uppercase, lowercase, or mixed case, regardless of how it is expressed in the field definition.

TIP   To ensure the correct spelling of field names, use the Fields & Functions button rather than manually typing in the field names.

Like variables, the data type of constants must match the expectations of the expression in which they appear. The other syntax-related "gotcha" that you find with constants is improper formatting: a missing double-quote in a text string, an improperly punctuated numeric value, or a time/date value with incorrect separators.

Operators

In broad terms, an operator is a symbol that lets you express an action you want Notes to carry out relative to a single value or multiple values. The result of the action is a new value. If you are not accustomed to using operators beyond the "big four"

    +, -, *, /

you might not recognize the action that is occurring.

Notes supports a large number of operators that we will classify into six categories: assignment, list, unary, arithmetic, text, comparison, and logical. Table 18.1 lists them in *order of precedence*, which dictates the order in which Notes performs an operation when a statement has multiple operators.

TABLE 18.1: Notes Operators Listed in Order of Precedence

Operator	Operation
:=	Assignment[1]
:	List operator
+	Positive
-	Negative
*	Multiplication
**	Permuted multiplication
/	Division
*/	Permuted division
+	Addition, string concatenation
*+	Permuted addition
-	Subtraction
*-	Permuted subtraction
=	Equal
*=	Permuted equal

Continued on next page

TABLE 18.1 CONTINUED: Notes Operators Listed in Order of Precedence

Operator	Operation
<>	Not equal
!=	Not equal
=!	Not equal
><	Not equal
*<>	Permuted not equal
<	Less than
*<	Permuted less than
>	Greater than
*>	Permuted greater than
<=	Less than or equal
*<=	Permuted less than or equal
>=	Greater than or equal
*>=	Permuted greater than or equal
!	Logical NOT
&	Logical AND
|	Logical OR

[1]Precedence is not applicable

While virtually everyone is familiar with some of the operators listed in the table, some might be new to you. Let's examine those that are less obvious.

Assignment   The assignment operator := assigns a value to a variable. Don't attempt to use the standard equal sign = for assigning values—it will not work. In our experience, the confusion between the use of := and = is the biggest hurdle to getting started with Notes formulas.

```
DogLegs := 4;
```

assigns the number 4 to the variable called DogLegs. := means that you are trying to tell a variable to remember that number. The following does the same, except that Notes will first evaluate whatever is to the right of the := and then return the value to the variable on the left. Four (4) would be a good guess.

```
DogLegs := 2 + 2;
```

On the other hand, the following formula is incorrect:

```
DogLegs = 2 + 2;
```

= means that you are asking Notes to compare the current value of DogLegs to the result of the operation, 2 + 2. This statement presents two problems. First, while we suspect that a dog has four legs, Notes has no idea unless you assign a value to the variable DogLegs. Second, once Notes compares it, assuming that DogLegs has a value, it doesn't know what to do with the value. Notes wants to return either TRUE or FALSE, but can't communicate this desire to anything, so it displays the error message "No main or selection expression in formula."

The following code segment illustrates the difference between comparison and assignment.

```
DogLegs := 4;
@If(DogLegs = 2 + 2; "Good Dog"; "Bad Dog")
```

The first statement assigns the value of 4 as a standard number of legs for a dog. The second statement adds 2 + 2. We then ask Notes to compare the result of the addition to the value of DogLegs. Notes determines that the values are equal (the result of comparison is TRUE) and returns the first value of the @If statement, "Good Dog" (trust us for now, we'll talk about @functions later).

NOTE   When using the assignment operator, the variable assumes the type of the value on the right side.

TIP   If you are still confused about the difference between an assignment and a comparison, a good question to ask is, "Am I *telling* Notes or *asking* Notes what the result of an operation is?"

List   The list concatenation operator : expresses a list of values. While you might typically work with single values in Notes, other operators (described later) and several @functions are expressly designed to handle lists of values. For example, the statement

```
@Elements("New York" : "Boston" : "San Francisco")
```

returns the value 3 (the number of values in the list).

TIP

All the values in a list must be of the same type.

TIP

Since the List Concatenation operator has the highest precedence, list elements that are expressions must be in parentheses.

NOTE

You can assign *multiple* values to a Notes field. This statement is true for fields where you have selected Allow Multivalues in the Properties InfoBox, as well as in the keyword field that, by definition, may have multiple values. Any field assigned multiple values is technically a *list* unto itself and can be used like any "manually" concatenated list (as in the example above).

Unary The unary operators + and – specify the sign of a numeric value.

Arithmetic The arithmetic operators *, /, +, and – let you combine two or more numeric values.

Text The text operator + allows you to combine two or more text values. For example

```
LName + ", " + Fname
```

results in

```
"Haberman, Scot"
```

Comparison The comparison operators =, <>, !=, ><, <, >, <=, and >= compare values of the same type and produce either a TRUE or FALSE result.

Logical The logical operators ! (NOT), & (AND), and | (OR) let you create complex conditions that determine whether some further action will be taken. Since they are used in conjunction with comparison operations, the result of a logical operation is also TRUE or FALSE (Boolean).

To illustrate the use of logical operators, let's take two variables, Months and Days, and assign Months the value 12 and Days the value 24. The individual comparison operations

```
@If(Months > 10; ...
@If(Days < 31; ...
```

both yield a TRUE value. If we want to create a complex condition using the individual comparison operations above, we have to introduce a logical operator, as in the following example:

```
@If(Months > 10 & Days < 20; ...
   TRUE   FALSE
```

In this expression we're testing for two independent conditions. Since the logical operator in this case is &(AND), *both* conditions must be TRUE for the expression to be TRUE. The conditions on either side of the logical operator are evaluated on their own to yield a TRUE or FALSE value, and then those values are combined with the logical operator to yield a TRUE or FALSE value for the expression as a whole. This expression yields a FALSE value because although Months is greater than 10 (a TRUE value), Days is not less than 20 (another FALSE value). However, the expression

```
@If(Months > 10 | Days < 20 ...
   TRUE    FALSE
```

also yields a TRUE value because our test condition—using the logical operator "|" (OR)—requires only that *either* Months is greater than 10 (a TRUE value) *or* Days is less than 20 (a FALSE value).

In the expression

```
@If(!(Months = 12) ...
   !TRUE (FALSE)
```

we see the use of the logical operator ! (NOT) in conjunction with a comparison operation. We know that Months *does* equal 12, and so the Boolean value of the comparison is TRUE. But the effect of NOTing any Boolean value is the *opposite* value, in this case FALSE, and so the whole comparison operation yields a FALSE value. This example illustrates the effect of the NOT operator, but we don't actually recommend constructing a comparison in this way. A more streamlined method would be

```
@If(Months != 12; ...
```

which translates into *if Months not equal to 12 then ...*, and immediately produces a FALSE value.

Changing the Order of Precedence To alter the order of precedence, you have to place parentheses around the operations that you want to perform first. Consider the following two statements, one in which "natural" precedence exists and the other in which "forced" precedence exists.

```
Days := 1 + 2 * 2 + 1
Days := (1 + 2) * (2 + 1)
```

In the first statement, the multiplication operation 2 * 2 is performed first and results in a value of 4. The addition operations are then performed in the order in which they appear, the result being the value of 6 assigned to Days. In the second statement, the addition operations that appear in parentheses, (1 + 2) and (2 + 1), are performed in order, followed by the multiplication operation; the result is the value of 9 assigned to Days.

TIP We recommend using as many parentheses as possible because they make your formulas a lot more readable and don't cost a penny.

What Does "Permuted" Mean, Anyway?

The table of operators contains several instances of permuted operators, which look vaguely familiar to the standard arithmetic operators except that they have an "*" in front of them. Notes is somewhat unique in its ability to support lists and multivalue fields.

A multivalue field is simply a field that has more than one value, which might sound odd but is extremely powerful when put to proper use. For instance, you might use a keyword field named *whichProducts* that displays a checkbox-style list of products your company offers in a form that records sales prospect information. You can simply check those products the prospect is interested in and store the list in a single, multivalue field. Notes includes many @functions specifically designed for use with lists.

Notes also supports several operations, which you can perform on pairs of lists, categorized as *pairwise* and *permuted*. Consider the two numeric lists 1 : 2 and 3 : 4. What would you expect to happen when we add the two lists together, as in

```
1 : 2 + 3 : 4
```

Continued on next page

The result is the list 4 : 6. Pairwise addition between the elements in the first list and the parallel elements in the second list gives us this result. The permuted version of this operation would be stated as

```
1 : 2 *+ 3 : 4
```

with the result being the list 4 : 5 : 5 : 6. In this case, every element in the first list is added to every element in the second list. Nearly all of the operators available in Notes have a permuted equivalent, prefaced with the tell-tale *.

Using @Functions

Technically speaking, @functions are prepackaged formulas that exist inside other formulas. Notes includes hundreds of @functions that perform a variety of actions integral to most Notes applications. As a formula itself, each @function returns a result of some type.

You will find a comprehensive list of @functions, including required syntax, descriptions, and examples in your Notes documentation. You can also choose Help ➤ Help Topics, click on Printed Books in the list of available views, click on Programmer's Guide, and click on Chapter 7 Formulas: @Functions Reference to expand the collapsed category and display a complete list of @functions. Double-click any of the @functions to see a description of syntax, return value, and usage. Take some time to explore all of the @functions that are available and think of ways to use them in your Notes applications.

Understanding @Function Syntax

@Functions come in two basic varieties: those that require arguments and those that do not. An *argument* is a parameter or value that the @function requires to perform its action and generate a result. Very often Notes field names (which represent a value) are used as arguments in @functions. You may also use @functions as arguments to other @functions. The general syntax of an @function that uses arguments is as follows:

```
@<functionname>(argument1;argument2;...;argumentn)
```

The argument list of an @function must be enclosed in parentheses (), and each argument must be separated from its neighbor by a semicolon (;). The number of arguments will vary according to @function—some require only one while others require several. The position of arguments is not arbitrary—every argument has its place—and the data type of an argument must be consistent with the explicit syntax of the @function. For example, if an @function specifies that argument1 must be a text string, supplying any other type of value for that argument (e.g., a number) will result in an error. An @function may be used as an argument to another @function, as long as the @function-as-argument yields a result that matches the data type required of the argument. For @functions that do not require arguments, use the @function name by itself without parentheses.

The *Many* Uses of the Semicolon

Using the semicolon character as a separator for arguments in @functions is very confusing, since the semicolon is also used to separate expressions in a multi-expression formula. If you do not have the proper number of arguments for an @function (and, therefore, the proper number of semicolons), Notes will get confused when it encounters the semicolon at the end of the expression. The same is true if you are missing a closing parenthesis in a multi-argument @function or when enclosing an @function inside another @function. If you are getting syntax errors in your formulas, be sure that you have the correct number of arguments, parentheses, and semicolons.

Identifying Types of @Functions

We'll briefly illustrate the main categories of @functions that are used commonly in Notes. Many @functions support more than one possible syntax, so refer to your Notes documentation for a complete description.

String @Functions

Because Notes is heavily text oriented, you will probably use these functions more than any others. The string @functions are used in operations related to text strings. The @Text function converts a value to text using the syntax

```
@Text(value)
```

For example, the formula **"Project started on " @Text(StartDate)**, where *StartDate* is a time/date value, results in "Project started on 1/1/96."

The @Trim function removes all redundant spaces, including leading and trailing spaces, from a text string using the syntax

```
@Trim(string)
```

For example, the formula **@Trim("Mastering Lotus Notes 4.X")** results in "Mastering Lotus Notes 4.X."

The @Middle function returns a substring from the middle of a string using one of a number of possible syntaxes, including

```
@Middle(string; startString; endString)
```

For example, the formula **@Middle("Flavor: Coconut Ice-cream"; "Flavor:"; "Ice-cream")** will return the word in the middle of "Flavor: " and "Ice-cream," which is the string "Coconut."

The @Matches function lets you test whether a string corresponds to a particular pattern using the syntax

```
@Matches(string; pattern)
```

The pattern-matching capabilities of @Matches is quite extensive and makes use of several wildcard characters. For example, the expression **@Matches(@Lowercase(State); *mont*)** will yield a Boolean value of TRUE if the value of *State* is either Montana or Vermont.

Mathematical @Functions

The mathematical @functions are used in operations related to numeric values. The @Round function rounds a value to the nearest whole number using the syntax

```
@Round(number)
```

For example, the formula **@Round(99.5)** results in 100.

The @Sum function adds a series of numbers together using the syntax

```
@Sum(numbers)
```

For example, the formula **@Sum(10; 11; 12)** results in 33. Notes Release 4 supports several trigonometric functions and an @Pi function.

Time/Date @Functions

The time/date @functions are used in operations related to time/date values. The @Created function returns the time/date when a document was created using the syntax

```
@Created
```

For example, the formula **@Created** results in 5/1/96 8:45:00 if the document was create on May 1, 1996, at 8:45 in the morning.

The @Today function returns today's date using the syntax

```
@Today
```

For example, the formula **@Today** results in 4/19/97 if today is April 19, 1997.

The @Adjust function lets you calculate a time/date value based on another time/date value using the syntax

```
@Adjust(dateToAdjust ; years ; months ; days ; hours ; minutes ; seconds)
```

For example, the formula **@Adjust(@Today;1;2;9;0;0;0)** results in 09/02/97 if today is June 23, 1996 (06/23/96). The year value is adjusted by 1 to 1997; the month value is adjusted by 2 to August, but because the day value is adjusted by 9, Notes is smart enough to roll the month value over to September (09), and the day value becomes the second day (02) of the month. You can adjust a date backward instead of forward by using the minus (–) sign before the adjustment arguments, as in **@Adjust (@Today; –1; –1; –1; 0; 0; 0)**, which results in 05/22/95.

Logical @Functions

The logical @functions are used in operations that are related to conditional statements, typically involving the @If function (described below). The @If function is used to test for a particular condition whose TRUE or FALSE value will specifically determine some further action. The function uses the syntax

```
@If(condition1;action1;condition2;action2;...;else_action)
```

For example, the formula

```
@If(Revenues < 1000; "Poor"; Revenues < 10000; "Better"; "Right on!")
```

returns one of the three text strings, namely Poor, Better, or Right on!, based on the value of the field or variable called Revenues. This formula can be placed in a computed text field that a view uses to categorize documents.

Since @If is such a prominent @function in most Notes applications, let's discuss it in detail. The purpose of any @If statement is to test for a condition and then take action if the condition is met. A condition is said to be "met" if it yields a TRUE value. For this to be the case, the condition must be one of the following:

- A comparison operation

- A logical @function that yields a Boolean value (TRUE or FALSE)

- Any of the above, or combination of the above, used in conjunction with the logical operators ! (NOT), & (AND), and | (OR)

NOTE

You may have up to ninety-nine different conditions/action pairs in an @If state-ment. (Why you'd want to have ninety-nine conditions is beyond our understand-ing, but it looks good on somebody's checklist.) If you truly need to test for several conditions, writing a LotusScript program may be a better solution.

In the event that none of the conditions are met, Notes executes the *else_action*, which serves as a "when all else fails" event. If you don't want any specific *else_action* to occur, place "" (NULL) in the *else_action* position. Translating an @If statement into a phrase, we have

```
"If condition1 is met then perform action1, else if condition2 is met
then perform action2...else if none of the conditions are met perform
else_action"
```

As soon as one of the conditions in the @If statement is met, the corresponding action is performed and no further evaluation of any remaining condition/action pairs occurs; the evaluation of the @If statement ends then and there.

An @If statement may be nested in another @If statement as the resulting action of a particular condition. Of course, all the same rules of syntax apply to the nested @If statement. With nested @If statements, you can create very complex (and, if you're not careful, confusing) logic in a formula. We prefer to break down a large nested @If statement into multiple @If statements.

Lookup @Functions

The lookup @functions are used to retrieve data from views, folders, and documents (either in the current database or another database). We talk about views and folders in Chapter 20, so for now you just need to know that @DbColumn, @DbLookup, and @PickList retrieve the contents of a specified column or field in a view, folder, or document. Moreover, @DbColumn and @DbLookup tend to return lists of values, which you can use as a list of choices in keyword fields, whereas @PickList returns a single value. As we talk about how to enhance the functionality of forms in the next chapter, we'll be making good use of this type of function.

The syntax of the @DbColumn function is

```
@DbColumn(class: "NoCache"; server: database; view; columnNumber)
```

For example, the formula **@DbColumn(""; ""; "Outstanding Problems"; 1)** returns the entire contents of the first column of the Outstanding Problems view in the current database as a list of values.

The syntax of the @DbLookup function is

```
@DbLookup(class : "NoCache"; server : database; view; key; fieldName or
➥ columnNumber)
```

For example, the formula **@DbLookup(""; ""; "Outstanding Problems"; "Urgent"; "ProblemNumber")** searches for all documents in the Outstanding Problems view of the current database where the word *Urgent* (our lookup key) appears in the first sorted column of the view and returns the contents of the ProblemNumber field in each document as a list of values. For both the @DbColumn and @DbLookup functions, the NoCache keyword instructs Notes to not cache (store) the results of the lookup in server memory and to perform a fresh lookup each time. This step ensures that each lookup retrieves the latest information in a view. (The application will pay a penalty in performance because noncached lookups take longer to execute.)

TIP

Omitting the NoCache keyword keeps the results of the lookup in server memory so that subsequent lookups are substantially faster. However, if new documents have been added to the view in the meantime, they will not be reflected in the subsequent lookups.

The syntax for the @PickList function is

```
@PickList([Custom]; server : database; view; title; prompt; columnNumber)
```

For example, the formula **@PickList([Custom]; "": ""; "Outstanding Problems" ; "Please select one of the current problems:" ; 1)** instructs Notes to open a dialog box in which the contents of the Outstanding Problems view of the current database is displayed, along with a prompt asking the user to select one of the current problems. (We know that views show us a collection of documents in row/column format.) The user chooses a document from the view, and the formula returns the value of the first column of that row.

TIP

@Dbcolumn and @Dclookup are limited in that they can return only a little less than 64KB of data, while @Picklist can accommodate large lists of values (> 64KB).

@Commands

The special @functions called @commands let you program your Notes application to automate a sequence of menu selections or keystrokes. Unlike most of the other @functions, @commands do not yield a result in the traditional sense, but have a success or failure associated with them. The syntax follows.

```
@Command([command]; parameter; ...)
```

For example, the statement **@Command([FileCloseWindow])** closes whatever document or view is currently open. This command is equivalent to manually choosing File ➤ Close or pressing the Esc key.

NOTE   You can also choose Help ➤ Help Topics, click Printed Books in the list of available views, click Programmer's Guide, and then click Chapter 8 Formulas: @Commands Reference to expand the collapsed category and display a complete list of @commands. Double-click any of the @commands to see a description of syntax and usage.

In a change from Release 3, @commands are now evaluated in the sequence in which they appear in a formula. Previously, @commands were always evaluated last, regardless of where they appeared, much to the frustration of Notes developers.

@Commands are very powerful and dramatically enhance the functionality of buttons (Chapter 19), Actions (Chapter 21), and Agents (Chapter 23).

@Command Compatibility between Release 3 and Release 4.x

If your Release 4.x application needs to be backwards compatible for use by Release 3 users, it must use the @PostedCommand instead of the @Command. For example, the formula

```
@Command([FileOpenDatabase]; "DEV" : "PROBLEMS.NSF");
rs := @Prompt([YesNo]; "Problem Report"; "Do you have a
problem?");
@If(rs = @True; @Command([Compose]; ""; "ProblemForm");
@Command([FileCloseWindow])
```

Continued on next page

will work as advertised in Release 4, performing the following actions:

- Opens the database PROBLEMS.NSF on the server DEV
- Asks the user if they have a problem
- Creates a problem report document based on the form ProblemForm if the user has a problem; otherwise closes the current window

The formula above would not execute correctly on a Release 3 workstation because @commands are evaluated last in Release 3, no matter where they appear in a formula. The **@Command([FileOpenDatabase])** will execute *last* even though it appears as the first expression in the formula! To achieve Release 3 compatibility, the code would need to be rewritten as follows:

```
rs := @Prompt([YesNo]; "Problem Report"; "Do you have a problem?");
@If(rs = @False; @Return(""); "")
@PostedCommand([FileOpenDatabase]; "DEV" : "PROBLEMS.NSF");
@PostedCommand([Compose]; ""; "ProblemForm");
```

@PostedCommand is the Release 4 equivalent of the Release 3 @Command.

What's Next?

In the next chapter, on designing dynamic forms, we will expand our discussion of form design, showing you how to add life to your forms by implementing collapsible sections, layout regions, graphic buttons, and hotspots. We will apply many of the concepts introduced in this chapter, placing formulas in a context that you can easily grasp.

CHAPTER

NINETEEN

19

Designing Dynamic Forms

- ■ Adding sections to a form

- ■ Collapsing and expanding a section to hide or display its contents

- ■ Adding a layout region to a form

- ■ Using fields within a layout region

- ■ Adding a graphic background and graphic buttons to a form

- ■ Using hotspots to associate Notes formulas or LotusScript to static text and images in a form

- ■ Using computed text, horizontal rules, and Java applets

Whhat do we mean when we say "designing dynamic forms?" We will demonstrate the answer by adding functionality and better usability to the basic form we designed in Chapter 17. In short, we'll make the basic form more dynamic and responsive to the needs of the user. We'll achieve this lofty goal by incorporating the following design features:

- Sections
- Layout regions
- Hotspots

Sections

By now you should be familiar with how to add fields and static text to the design of a form. Beyond the consideration of what information your form will capture, you should also be thinking of how your form will capture the information. Where will you place fields and static text in the form? In what sequence will fields appear in the form? What overall progression will the user follow when entering information in a document based on the form?

Forms designers have a natural tendency to place related fields and static text together. For instance, the fields and static text used to capture a company's name, address, and phone number will usually be placed in very close proximity to one another. The result is a "visual grouping" that suggests a relationship among the items. You can go a step further by formally grouping these related items in a *section*. Sections enable you to keep related pieces of information together in a way that allows them to be viewed or hidden as a group, as well as to be secured as a group for the purpose of permitting or denying "editor access" to the fields. The Server document in the public Name & Address book shown in Figure 19.1 makes extensive use of sections in a document.

Notes supports two types of sections, *standard* and *controlled access;* the difference is that the latter allows you to specify the users and groups that can access the section.

FIGURE 19.1:

A Server document in the public Name & Address book

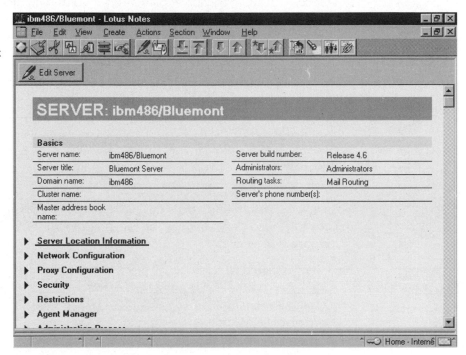

The most efficient way to create a section is to first define the fields, static text, and other design objects that you want to include in the section. Then perform the following steps to create a Standard section:

1. Highlight all of the design objects (fields, static text, etc.) to be included in the section by positioning the mouse I-beam either on the line just above the first design object (working from top to bottom) or at the beginning of the line that contains the first design object. Highlight all the desired design objects.

NOTE   Technically, you need to highlight only the *lines* in which design objects appear. For example, if you were to sweep the mouse downward to a point at the beginning of a line, all of the design objects that appear on that line would be included in the section even though they were not formally highlighted.

---

2. Choose Create ➤ Section ➤ Standard. Notes immediately collapses all of the design objects into a section and displays a triangle controller (twistie) in the collapsed position (▶) and the default section title. The section title will either correspond to the first static text label in the section or be blank. Click the triangle or section title to expand the section and display the design objects. The twistie will now be in expanded position (▼).

NOTE

Notice that if you click the section title or triangle, the Section option replaces the Text option in the menu bar. If you click elsewhere in the form, the Text option reappears. Notes is displaying its context sensitivity.

---

3. Click the section title so that it is underlined in bold. Choose Section ➤ Section Properties to display the Section Properties InfoBox, as shown in Figure 19.2.

FIGURE 19.2:

The Section Properties InfoBox for a Standard section

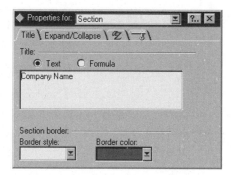

TIP

You can access the Section Properties InfoBox by right-clicking the section title and selecting the Section Properties option from the pop-up menu.

---

4. Select the Text radio button from the Title option folder and enter a section title in the text box.

5. Close the InfoBox.

6. Press Ctrl+S to save the form.

We'll cover the other section properties shortly. For now, we have a fully functioning section in our form. You may create as many sections in a form as you wish.

Collapsing and Expanding Sections

So much information to capture and so little space available in a single screen. Although forcing a user to scroll to areas of a document below the boundaries of a single screen is not the end of the world, you can provide more streamlined navigation by taking advantage of a built-in feature of sections called *collapsing and expanding*. Sections let users expand or collapse the fields, static text, and other design objects that make up the section. When expanded, the items in the section are available for use. When collapsed, the items are hidden from view, and the area of the form that they would normally occupy is condensed to a single line that displays the section title and triangle. Figure 19.3 shows sections as they appear (to a user) in an expanded and a collapsed state.

FIGURE 19.3:

Sections of a document in an expanded and a collapsed state

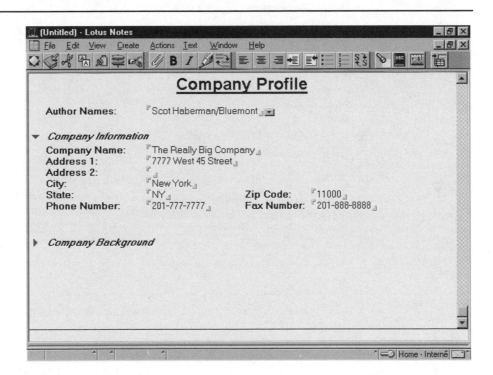

TIP	Collapsed sections are no substitute for reducing the number of fields you want to display in a form. Even with sections, a form can still be painful to use!

When designing sections, you stipulate rules that dictate whether the section should be automatically expanded or collapsed (or displayed as it was left by the last user to access the document) in any of the four possible document modes—Previewed, Opened for Reading, Opened for Editing, or Printed. With a Standard section, follow these steps:

1. Click the section title and choose Section ➤ Section Properties to display the Section Properties InfoBox.

2. Click the Expand/Collapse tab.

3. For the four modes available choose one of the expand and collapse rules:

   - **Don't Auto Expand or Collapse** indicates that the section should appear in the state it was last left in.

   - **Auto Expand Section** forces the section to always be expanded.

   - **Auto Collapse Section** forces the section to always be collapsed.

Remember that these rules will be applied to the section relative to the document mode.

4. Click Hide Title When Expanded if you do not want the section title to be displayed when the section is expanded.

5. Click Preview if you want the "sectioning" feature active only when a document is being previewed. In any of the other modes, the expand/collapse capability will not be available, and the section title will not be displayed.

6. Close the InfoBox.

7. Press Ctrl+S to save the form.

TIP   We do not recommend including *required fields* in sections that are collapsed by default.

Controlling Access to a Section

The utility of sections goes beyond the purely visual. When design objects are grouped within a section, access to those objects can be controlled. As a simple illustration, consider a proposal form designed to allow multiple people to work in a collaborative manner as a proposal team. Most business proposals are made up of multiple sections (did we say *sections*?) such as an executive summary, a body, and financials. With one user acting as the proposal manager and Controlled Access sections built into the design of the form, a specific user (or multiple users) can be designated as section editor for each of the sections. Section editors may edit and modify only their assigned section(s) and no other, even though other sections are visible.

NOTE   Section editors must have Author rights or greater to the database.

Areas of the document that do not fall under a Controlled Access section will be globally accessible.

NOTE   Controlled Access sections behave just like Standard sections except that Controlled Access sections let you decide which users or group of users can edit a particular section of a document.

To create a Controlled Access section, follow steps 1 and 2 for creating a Standard section (at the beginning of the chapter), substituting Create ➤ Section ➤ Controlled Access in step 2. Notes immediately displays the Section Properties InfoBox. From this point, perform the following steps:

1. Enter an appropriate section title in the Title text box or leave the title blank.

2. Enter a section field name. The name you choose should reflect the nature of the section. For instance, if the section is meant to capture background information for a company, you might name it CoBackground, as in Figure 19.4.

FIGURE 19.4:

The Title option folder of the Section Properties InfoBox for a Controlled Access section

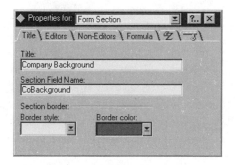

NOTE
Why do Controlled Access sections require a field name while Standard sections do not? The reason is that a Controlled Access section (also called a *Form section*) is a recognized field type in Notes, just like a Text or Keyword field, and so it must be assigned a name. As a "section field," the section will take on a value, which is the list of users and groups assigned as section editors.

3. Click the Editors tab and select the expand and collapse rules for each of the four modes. These rules will apply only to designated editors of this section.

4. Click the Non-Editors tab and select the expand and collapse rules for each of the four modes. These rules will apply to users who are not designated editors of this section. (Remember, non-editors can read the information in the section, but they cannot edit or modify it.)

5. Click the Formula tab. From the Type list, select a field type and enter an Access Formula, if appropriate. In the case of Computed, Computed when Composed, and Computed for Display Types, you must enter an Access Formula. (See the next section for more about Access Formulas.)

6. Press Ctrl+S to save the form.

Access Formulas

Access Formulas are used to set the list of section editors in a programmatic fashion. The result of an Access Formula has to be a concatenated list of user and group names. Your formula may simply be a hard-coded list, as shown in Figure 19.5. As with all formulas, you can also use field names and @functions to calculate a list. For instance, for greater flexibility than a hard-coded list, you can use an @dbcolumn that retrieves a list of users or groups from a view, as covered in Chapter 20. Note that if the type of the formula is Computed when Composed, the list of authorized users will be determined only once (when the document is first created), and it cannot be changed afterwards.

By selecting the type called Editable, as opposed to Computed, you can delegate the responsibility for setting section editors to the users themselves. With the proper database-level and document-level access rights, users can select section editors directly in the document. A user with Editor or greater access to the database, or a user with Author access to the database and Author Names access to the document, can specify section editors in any Controlled Access sections of the document.

FIGURE 19.5:

The Formula options folder for a Controlled Access section. This example shows a hard-coded list of two people with their names separated by a colon.

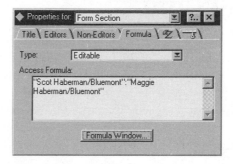

WARNING   If a user has rights to edit a document, then he or she can define the section editors in *any* Controlled Access sections. The implication is that users can add themselves to a list of section editors that they do not currently appear in, effectively giving themselves rights to the section. This is absolutely correct! Controlled Access sections can prevent only *accidental* changes to a section a user shouldn't be making changes in.

With a document opened for editing, a user can double-click a section title or anywhere in a section (static text, fields, etc.) to bring up the Edit Section dialog box, as shown in Figure 19.6.

FIGURE 19.6:

The Edit Section dialog box used to select section editors

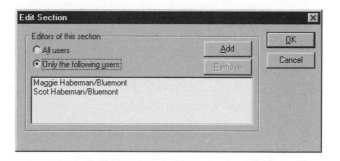

User and group names can be added to the list box (assuming Only the Following Users has been selected) from either the public or private Name & Address books.

Layout Regions

A layout region groups a form's objects in a special design frame that improves the appearance of the user interface. The documents in Figures 19.7 and 19.8 are based on two different forms. Although both forms have the same basic functionality, one incorporates a layout region and the other does not. Layout regions allow you to specify data input boxes (or fields with their boundaries defined on the screen) and 3-D effects, whereas standard field definitions only use the dual brackets at the upper-left and lower-right corners of the field input boxes.

Both of these documents capture the same information, but the one with the layout region goes about it with a little more pizzazz.

To create a layout region in a form, follow these steps:

1. Position the insertion point in the form at the location where the new layout region should appear.

2. Choose Create ➤ Layout Region ➤ New Layout Region. Notes places an empty rectangular box on your screen.

3. Click the layout region to select it, and choose Design ➤ Layout Properties. The Properties box for the layout will appear.

4. Select the Snap to Grid and Show Grid Options because they facilitate the horizontal and vertical alignment of fields, images, and text on the layout.

5. Choose Create ➤ Field. A field object named Untitled appears within the layout region.

Let's pause here a moment and discuss what has occurred. First of all, you have to think of a layout region as a "unique universe" within a form; different laws apply within a layout region than apply in other parts of a form when it comes to the look and feel of typical design objects, including:

- Bounded fields, which can be sized and can have borders and scroll bars

> **WARNING**   Bounded fields have a fixed size. The layout region fields will not automatically shrink and grow like non-layout region fields.

- Pixel-level control of object placement
- Graphic backgrounds
- Graphic buttons

FIGURE 19.7:

A document without a
layout region

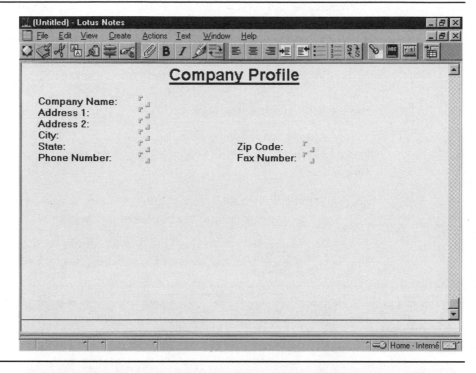

FIGURE 19.8:

A document with a layout
region

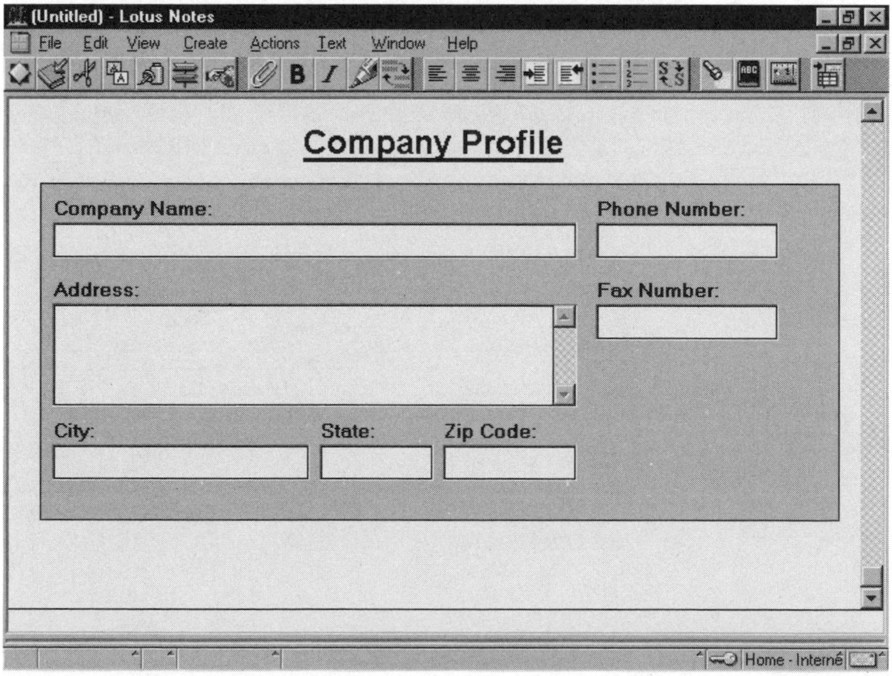

Within a layout region a field appears as a bounded area that can be sized to any dimension you wish, unlike fields outside a layout region that have no sizing capability whatsoever. The significance of bounded areas is evident when a user creates or edits a document where fields have been defined within a layout region. Instead of the fields being demarcated with corner brackets, the fields appear as text boxes. Properties can be set for the fields (and the layout region), which give them a three-dimensional look.

While in Design mode you can "size the field" (in reality, you are sizing the text box in which the field value will be entered and/or displayed) by doing the following:

6. Click the field in the layout region. A series of black boxes, known as *handles*, appears around the border of the field, as shown in Figure 19.9.

7. Use the mouse to pull one of the handles either vertically, horizontally, or diagonally—depending on which handle you grabbed.

FIGURE 19.9:

A field within a layout region with handles displayed

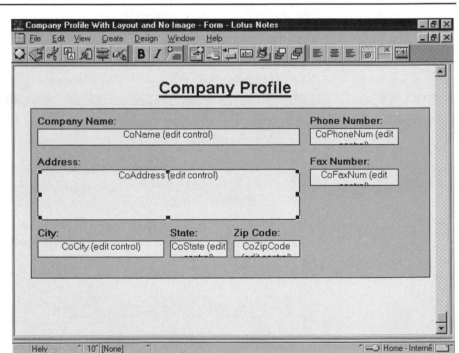

Layout regions also give you pixel-level control of object placement, which means that you have very precise control over where objects appear. Outside of a layout region, objects must be placed in a fairly rigid system of lines and tab markers. To move a field to a different location within the layout region, do the following:

8. Place the mouse pointer within the field object.

9. Click and hold down the left mouse button and drag the field object to the desired location. Notice that the granularity of the movement is extremely fine.

TIP   The granularity of movement can be altered from as small as 0.02" up to 1.00". You can also display the grid, which will show up as dots across the layout region.

Next, let's examine placing static text within a layout region. You may have noticed that you are unable to simply place the insertion point in the layout region and start typing. Static text within a layout region is treated very much like fields. To insert static text, do the following:

10. Click the layout region to select it.

11. Choose Create ➤ Layout Region ➤ Text. A static text label appears as (Untitled).

12. Double-click the label to display the Control Properties InfoBox, as shown in Figure 19.10.

13. Replace (Untitled) with the correct label.

FIGURE 19.10:

The Control Properties InfoBox

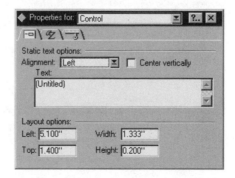

14. Use the method described in step 8 to move the label to the desired location, or you can use the Control Properties InfoBox to set the location down to the 1/1000 of an inch.

15. Press Ctrl+S to save the form.

Special Considerations for Fields in a Layout Region

Fields are fields, whether they are defined inside or outside of a layout region. (Fields are discussed in detail in Chapter 17.) At this time, all of the field types except rich text are supported within layout regions. The only distinguishing feature of fields within a layout region is *how* they appear. Notes gives you a lot more flexibility in this department, and layout fields have some properties that do not apply to nonlayout fields. Likewise, you will see that many of the properties available for nonlayout fields do not apply for layout fields.

To manipulate a field defined within a layout region, do the following:

1. Click the field to select it.

2. Choose Design ➤ Field Properties to open the Field Properties InfoBox. Specify the field name and type (as discussed in Chapter 17).

TIP   To display the Properties InfoBox for any object in a layout region, double-click the object.

---

3. Click the Interface tab (second tab from the left) to display the interface options for the field. If the field type is anything other than keyword, you will see the following options:

   - **Multiline** specifies that the value entered in the field can span multiple lines. Depending on the dimensions of the field, a multiline value may or may not be entirely visible.

   - **Scroll bar** makes a scroll bar available on the right edge of the field. This bar is helpful when the value of the field (usually a text string) goes beyond the boundaries of the field. Without a scroll bar, a user must use the up/down and Page Up/Page Down keys.

   - **Border** specifies that a solid-line border will appear around the field. This gives the field a three-dimensional appearance within the layout region.

4. Press Ctrl+S to save the form.

WARNING Be aware that layout regions cannot be translated by the Domino server and displayed on the Web. If you plan on allowing Web access for your database, you should not use layout regions in your form or you should create one form for the client and one form for the Web.

NOTE If the field is defined as a keyword field, you will have two options for the field definition, combobox and listbox, which are not available for keyword fields that are not defined within a layout region.

WARNING If you define a keyword field in a layout region, you will not have the option of allowing values that are not in the list that is available for keyword fields not defined in a layout region.

Creating a Graphic Background

A graphic image (or images) can serve as a background within a layout region. Background graphics help to define (and enhance) the layout area. Unfortunately, you cannot import an image directly into a layout region in Notes. Using a graphics application like Microsoft Paint (in Windows 95), you must access the graphic image and then place it on the Clipboard. Having done that, you can paste the image into your layout region. With an image as a background, you can overlay other layout features such as fields, static text, and graphic buttons. Follow these steps to create a graphic background (we'll use the built-in graphics applications that come with Windows for this example; you can use any package you desire):

1. Launch Microsoft Paint (choose Start ➤ Programs ➤ Accessories ➤ Paint). The application opens.

2. Choose File ➤ Open.

3. Select the WINLOGO.BMP file (or another file) that's located in your Windows directory.

4. Choose Edit ➤ Select All to select the image.

5. Press Ctrl+C (or Choose Edit ➤ Copy) to copy the image to the Clipboard.

6. Return to Notes.

7. Click the layout region to select it. Choose Create ➤ Layout Region ➤ Graphic. The image you copied to the Clipboard is placed inside the layout region. From here, you may drag the image to the desired location.

NOTE   You can have more than one graphic as a background for a given layout region.

---

8. Choose Design ➤ Bring to Front or Design ➤ Send to Back to manipulate the foreground/background orientation of any of the layout objects.

TIP   You can change the tabbing order of fields within a layout region. The default tabbing order is the order in which you place the fields in the layout region. If you need to change the tabbing order, select each field in the order that you would like the tabbing order, and choose Design ➤ Bring to Front.

---

9. Press Ctrl+S to save the form.

TIP   We highly recommend that you purchase a library of images on CD-ROM if you plan on using graphics extensively.

Figure 19.11 shows a layout region with a graphic background.

Creating a Graphic Button

Carefully developed graphic buttons help to simplify a user's interaction with the form. To add a graphic button to a layout region, you follow the same basic routine used to add a graphic image. Once again, you cannot simply import an image directly into a layout region; you have to go outside of Notes to get the image. The following steps demonstrate how to create a graphic button:

1. Launch Microsoft Paint (choose Start ➤ Programs ➤ Accessories ➤ Paint). The application opens.

2. Choose File ➤ Open.

3. Select a .BMP that's located in your Windows directory. Be sure to select an area of the image that is only about the size of a postage stamp. In Windows graphics applications, use the Select tool (the one with a dotted rectangle on it) for this purpose.

FIGURE 19.11:

A graphic background in a layout region

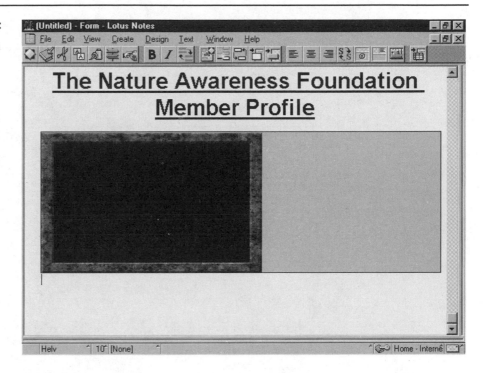

4. Press Ctrl+C (or Choose Edit ➤ Copy) to copy the image to the Clipboard.

5. Close the application and return to Notes.

6. Click the layout region to select it.

7. Choose Create ➤ Layout Region ➤ Graphic Button. The image you copied to the Clipboard is placed inside the layout region. Drag the image to the desired location.

8. Enter the following formula in the design panel at the bottom of the screen, as shown in Figure 19.12.

```
answer := @Prompt([YesNo]; "Thank you for Clicking!"; "Do you want
➥to quit?");
@If(answer = @True; @Command([FileCloseWindow]); "")
```

TIP Notes requires that you put a formula in the design panel at the bottom of the screen before you save the form. (See Chapter 17 for details on formulas.)

9. Press Ctrl+S to save the form.

FIGURE 19.12:

A formula for a graphic button

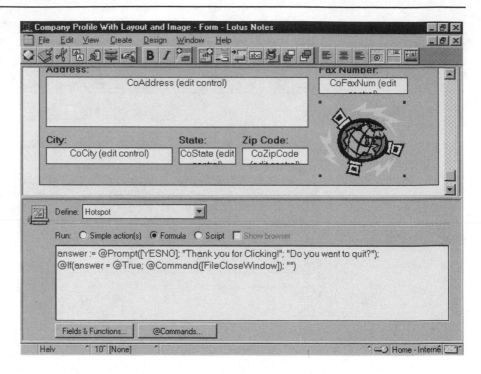

To test the functionality of the graphic button, choose Design ➤ Test Form. With the test version of the form displayed, click the button and be sure to say "You're welcome!" Click Yes in the Thank You for Clicking! prompt box to return to Form Design mode.

This Must Be the Place—Hotspots

As the name implies, hotspots are areas within a form that react when they are touched. The areas in this case can be either static text or graphics that you want to automate. An example might be a piece of static text ("ROI"), which when clicked displays a text box that describes its meaning to the user ("ROI is an acronym for Return On Investment. ROI is calculated by…"). Another example could be a graphic image that launches an Agent when clicked. Notes supports several types of hotspots:

- Text popups
- Formula pop-ups

- Link hotspots

- Button hotspots

- Action hotspots

- URL links

In all cases, a hotspot *does something*; the specific behavior of a hotspot will depend on its type. (In the discussion of layout regions, you may have noticed that Notes actually called your graphic button a hotspot. Graphic buttons are considered hotspots.)

NOTE   Those with experience in developing Notes Release 3 applications will find that hotspots are the Release 4 version of doclinks, pop-ups, and buttons. The names have remained largely the same, and the functionality of hotspots is *at least* equivalent to their Release 3 counterparts. In some cases a more powerful formula language and the introduction of LotusScript and Agents greatly enhance hotspot functionality.

Pop-ups

Let's start with a simple hotspot example, a text pop-up. A pop-up is a piece of static text (typically) or a graphic image that, when clicked, displays a text box with information. (A common situation where pop-ups are very useful is when a user is faced with unfamiliar terminology. In effect, you can put a definition behind an unfamiliar word or phrase.) The information that appears in the text box can either be a hard-coded text string (a *text pop-up*) or be derived from a formula (a *formula pop-up*). Formula pop-ups let you dynamically define the text string that will appear in the Pop-up window while a user is using the Notes application. In the steps below, we will create a text pop-up:

1. Open your form in Design mode.

2. Highlight the text or graphic image where the pop-up is to be established.

3. Choose Create ➤ Hotspot ➤ Text Pop-up. The Hotspot Pop-up Properties InfoBox appears as shown in Figure 19.13.

The Hotspot Pop-up Properties InfoBox for a text pop-up

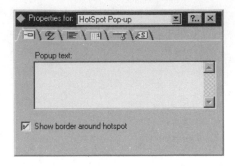

4. Enter the information you would like to appear when a user clicks the text or graphic image.

5. Deselect Show Border Around Hotspot if you do not want a standard green border to appear around the text or graphic image as a pop-up indicator.

TIP   Without a border present, users might not know that a pop-up exists, so it is a good idea to leave the border intact. While green might not be your favorite color, it's a matter of function over form. (No, you can't change the color of the border.)

---

6. Press Ctrl+S to save the form.

You can the test the functionality of the pop-up hotspot by choosing Design ➤ Test Form. With the test version of the form displayed, click the text or graphic image. A shaded text box appears as shown in Figure 19.14. Press Esc to return to Form Design mode.

Link Hotspots

Link hotspots let you tie a piece of static text or an image in a form to a specific document, view, or database in Notes. When clicked, the link will display the linked-to item. (In the case of a database link, the database is opened to either the default view or the last view that was opened.) Links are useful when you need frequent access to information outside the current document. Linked-to documents and views may reside in the current database or in any other database in the Notes network. Databases, by definition, reside outside the current database.

FIGURE 19.14:

A text pop-up in action

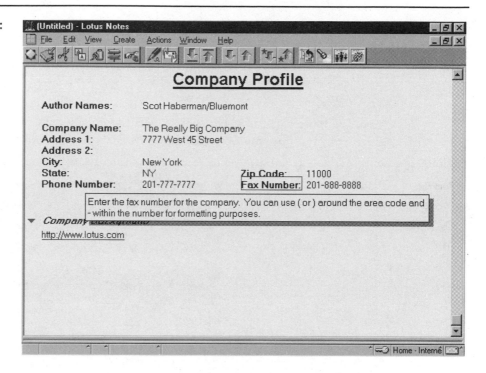

NOTE   If the original linked-to item is not available or no longer exists, Notes will attempt to find a replica of the item either locally or on the Notes network. If all attempts fail, Notes will display an error message indicating that the linked-to item cannot be found.

To create a Link hotspot, follow these steps:

1. Access the linked-to item:

    • For a document link, highlight the document in a view or open the document for reading or editing.

    • For a view link, open the view.

    • For a database link, click the database in the Workspace to select it.

2. Choose Edit ➤ Copy as Link and then select Document Link, View Link, or Database Link from the submenu.

3. Open your form in Design mode.

4. Highlight the text or image where the pop-up is to be established.

5. Choose Create ➤ Hotspot ➤ Link Hotspot. A link will be created between the highlighted text or image and the target item, and a green border will appear around the hotspot.

6. Choose Hotspot ➤ Hotspot Properties to display the Hotspot Link Properties InfoBox, as shown in Figure 19.15.

FIGURE 19.15:

The Hotspot Link Properties InfoBox

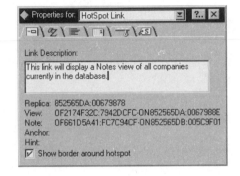

7. Enter a link description in the text box or leave the default description in place. The link description will appear in the Notes status bar when the cursor is placed over the hotspot.

8. Deselect Show Border Around Hotspot if you do not want a standard green border to appear around the text or graphic image as a pop-up indicator.

9. Press Ctrl+S to save the form.

You can test the functionality of the Link hotspot by choosing Design ➤ Test Form. With the test version of the form displayed, place the mouse pointer over the hotspot and the Notes status bar will display the link description. Click the hotspot to display the linked-to item. Press the Esc key to return to Form Design mode.

Action Hotspots and Button Hotspots

Action hotspots and button hotspots are mentioned together because they behave and are defined by Notes practically identically. Clicking either type of hotspot invokes a Simple action, formula, or LotusScript that can perform a very rudimentary task, a very complex task, or anything in between. Both objects also respect the same LotusScript events. (Refer to Chapter 18 for a basic discussion of events or to Part V for a detailed discussion.) The difference between an action hotspot and a button hotspot is largely cosmetic. Like the other types of hotspots, actions are associated with a piece of static text or a graphic image, while buttons are completely unique objects that have an appearance all their own—in fact, they look like buttons.

NOTE   Release 3 developers will remember buttons very well because they were the only design object that provided programmable, point-and-shoot functionality in a form. With Release 4, there are now action hotspots, button hotspots, graphic buttons in layout regions, and the Action bar, along with rectangular or polygon hotspots on Navigators.

Figure 19.16 shows an action hotspot and a button hotspot.

FIGURE 19.16:

An action hotspot and a button hotspot

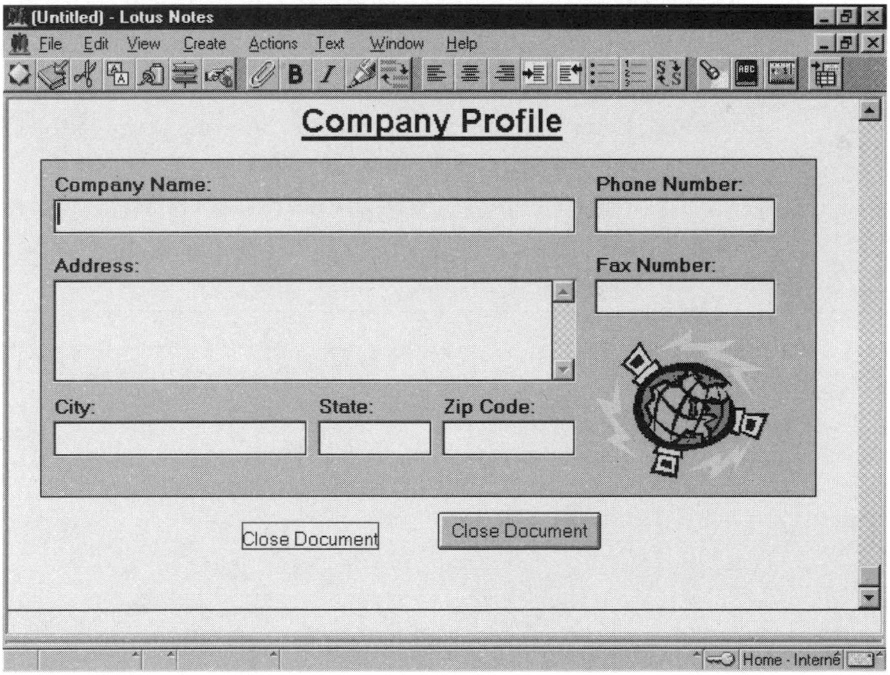

To create an action hotspot, follow these steps:

1. Open your form in Design mode.

2. Highlight the text or image where the action is to be established.

TIP

Use graphic images, rather than text, for action hotspots. Design your own button graphic and lay text descriptions on top of it before pasting it into Notes.

---

3. Choose Create ➤ Hotspot ➤ Action Hotspot. The Hotspot Button Properties InfoBox appears as shown in Figure 19.17. (In case you're wondering, Button is not a typographical error. We mentioned at the outset that in this context actions and buttons are virtually identical!)

4. Deselect Show Border Around Hotspot if you do not want a standard green border to appear around the text or graphic image as a pop-up indicator. You shouldn't need a green border if your graphic image is enticing and self-explanatory.

5. Close the InfoBox or drag it to a location where it does not obscure the Design pane in the lower portion of the window. If the Design pane is not displayed, choose View ➤ Design Pane.

6. Enter a Simple action(s), a formula, or a script in the Design pane to execute when a user clicks the action hotspot. For instance:

   `@Prompt([Ok];"Hotspot Button Demo;"Thank you for that click!")`

7. Press Ctrl+S to save the form.

FIGURE 19.17:

The Hotspot Button Properties InfoBox for an action hotspot

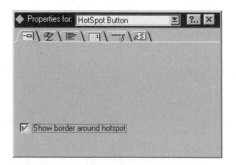

To create a button hotspot, follow these steps:

1. Open your form in Design mode.

2. Place the insertion point at the location where you want the button to appear.

3. Choose Create ➤ Hotspot ➤ Button. The Button Properties InfoBox appears as shown in Figure 19.18.

FIGURE 19.18:

The Button Properties InfoBox for a button hotspot

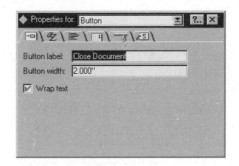

4. Enter a button label to appear on the button or leave it blank. If you are entering a label, enter a button width that will accommodate the length of the label. Notes will always shrink the button to fit the label, even if you specify a greater width.

NOTE

If the label length is greater than the width of the button, the label will word-wrap, causing the button to expand vertically. Deselect Wrap Text to prevent the label from word-wrapping.

TIP

If you want to force a button to a certain width, enter spaces before and after the button label in the Button Properties InfoBox. The number of spaces on either side of the actual text should be proportional so that the label does not appear off-center.

5. Close the InfoBox or drag it to a location where it does not obscure the Design pane in the lower portion of the window. If the Design pane is not displayed, choose View ➤ Design Pane.

6. In the Design pane, enter a Simple action(s), a formula, or a script to execute when a user clicks the button hotspot.

7. Press Ctrl+S to save the form.

You can the test the functionality of the action hotspots and button hotspots by choosing Design ➤ Test Form. With the test version of the form displayed, click the hotspot to execute the programmed task. Press Esc to return to Form Design mode.

URL Links

The URL link was described very thoroughly back in Chapter 8. It is basically a hotspot, but instead of executing a formula or LotusScript, the link jumps to a specific Web page. As an information management product, Notes is designed to take advantage of the Web, which is becoming more and more prominent as an information resource. This type of hotspot is not used only for Web applications. The Web browser and Notes are becoming tightly integrated, as will be shown in Chapter 31. URL links are just another tool available to help you enhance your applications. For details on how to create a URL link, refer back to Chapter 8.

New Form Tools

Before closing out the discussion of designing dynamic forms, there are some new tools in Notes 4.6 that should be mentioned: computed text, horizontal rules, and Java applets. All of these new design elements have been created to make Web design much easier for the developer. As this section will show, they may have their place in Notes client applications as well.

Computed Text

The computed text design element does exactly what its name says: it computes text. This may cause you to ask, "So what? I can do that with a computed field." That's true. Using a computed for display field will accomplish the same end result. We're mentioning it here because it can be used to dynamically place data on your form. As you become more involved in designing Web applications, the primary function of computed text will become apparent.

To create a computed text element, follow these steps:

1. Open your form in Design mode.

2. Place the insertion point at the location where you want the text to appear.

3. Choose Create ➤ Computed Text. The Hotspot Popup Properties InfoBox will appear.

4. In the Design pane, type in the formula that you want the computed field to evaluate.

5. Press Ctrl+S to save the form.

Here is a quick example. In Figure 19.19, a Computed Text field has been placed at the bottom of the form to give each user a greeting based on the time of day. The formula for the computed text is

```
@If(@Hour(@Today)<7;"You should be in bed ";@Hour(@Today)<12;"Good
➥ Morning ";@Hour(@Today)<6;"Good Afternoon ";"Good Evening ") +
➥ @Left(@Name([CN];@UserName);" ") + "."
```

FIGURE 19.19:

You can give your users a personalized greeting.

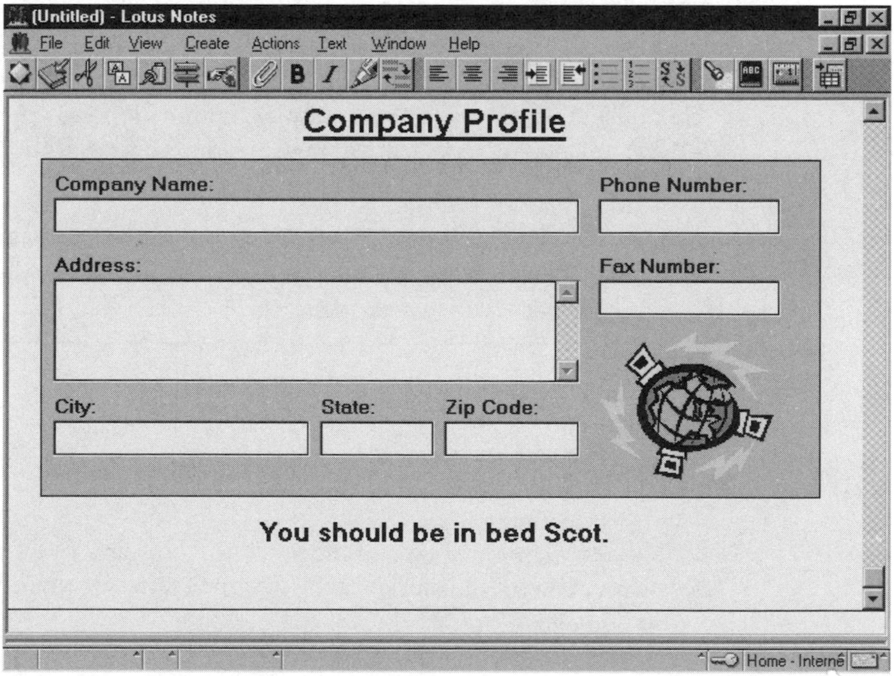

Horizontal Rules

The horizontal rule element follows the same pattern as computed text. It's primarily for Web use, but it can be handy for creating some nice effects on your Notes client forms as well.

The horizontal rule is a line that can be of varying thickness, color, and length. To create this element on your form, follow these steps:

1. Open your form in Design mode.

2. Place the insertion point where you want the line to appear.

3. Choose Create ➤ Horizontal Rule. The Horizontal Rule Properties InfoBox will appear.

4. In the InfoBox, select the size, color, 3-D effect, etc., that you would like.

5. Press Ctrl+S to save the form.

Java Applets

Notes 4.6 lets you store and execute Java applets from within forms. With this feature Web developers can create a richer, more interactive experience for users by using Java applets in the forms that are presented to both browser and Notes client users. The storage of Java applets within Domino application databases allows developers to take advantage of Domino's replication technology to keep their Java applets synchronized in multiple locations.

WARNING The Store Form in Document option is not supported for Java applets that use serialization or externalization parameters.

What's Next?

In Chapter 20 you will explore the process of building Notes views, and you will learn about one of the most exciting design features of Notes Release 4: Navigators.

Using dynamic forms to get information into a Notes database is only half the battle. Of equal importance is getting information out; and logical, well-designed views make this task simple for users.

Navigators enable the designer to provide a graphical interface to an application, something that was previously possible only through the use of external tools like ViP for Lotus Notes (from Revelation Technologies) or Lotus Notes HiTest Tools for Microsoft Visual Basic.

CHAPTER

TWENTY

20

Designing Flexible Views with Navigators

■ Getting information from a database

■ Learning about view basics

■ Working with column formulas

■ Creating a new view and producing a response hierarchy

■ Creating and using form formulas

■ Changing and saving a view

■ Using a view as a lookup table

■ Applying the Calendar view

■ Creating and working with folders

■ Understanding and creating Navigators

Through our discussion of creating a form (and the subsequent composition of documents), we've explained how to get information into a Notes database. However, getting data in is really only half the battle. Of equal importance is the user's ability to get data out of a database in a way that is easy, efficient, and sensible. At this point, views become a very important part of the Notes picture.

A view serves as a table of contents for a Notes database, displaying a list of stored documents and providing users with the means to read, edit, and delete those documents. A database may have several views, with each one displaying the contents (though not necessarily the entire contents) of the database in a different way. For example, one view might list *all* the documents in the database, while another view lists only a subset of documents in the database based on specific selection criteria.

Navigators further enhance the concept of views by providing a graphical interface for jumping between views. Well-designed Navigators provide an intuitive layout to guide your users through the multiple facets of the information contained in the application. In this chapter, we take you through the steps of creating a view with Navigators. We discuss the following topics:

- Getting information out of your database

- Understanding view basics

- Using column formulas

- Creating a new view

- Producing a response hierarchy

- Using form formulas

- Editing and saving a view

- Using views as lookup tables

- Understanding and creating folders

Getting Information Out of Your Database

Imagine pouring information into the database, yet having no way of accessing that information later, or having to rely on a method of access that doesn't allow you to find and retrieve the information you need. Using the database would be like using a dictionary with no index entries at the top of each page—you could eventually find the word you were looking for, but it would certainly take a long time. A Notes database is not meant to be a black hole where information goes in, never to be seen again. Therefore, a view serves as a table of contents for a database; it displays a list of stored documents and provides users with the means to read, edit, and/or delete those documents.

A database may have several views, with each one displaying the contents (though not necessarily the entire contents) of the database in a different way. For example, one view might list all the documents in the database, while another view lists only a subset of documents based on specific selection criteria. For example, a view could display only those documents that were composed after a certain date.

To gain a better understanding of the problems we face in getting information out of our database, let's step back a moment and consider a few factors that play a role in this process:

- We've designed a series of forms so that end users can populate our database with documents. The result is that we have documents of all types in the database. For instance, in the Employment Kiosk (Jobs) sample database (included on the CD), we created two fundamentally different forms—the Job Offer and the Job Application.

- The forms are made up of fields (or "containers," as you recall from the previous chapter) that allow us to capture specific types of data, and each field has been assigned a name. For instance, the Job Offer has a field called Title, and the Job Application has a field called LastName.

- The overall content of a given document depends on the form with which it was composed. We can safely say that documents composed with the same form are generally alike—even though the specific information may differ, these documents share common fields.

- It's often the case that multiple documents share common values for specific fields. For instance, the Job Application documents capture address information. It's a pretty safe bet that several documents will have the same value for the State field. We should be able to use this information to group those documents together. The same holds true for all the job offers outstanding for a each department.

- Some documents are designated as responses to other documents—this relationship should somehow be made evident to the end user who is viewing the contents of the database.

You should take into account all of the above features when deciding how to show the contents of a Notes database through a view. First, however, let's consider exactly what we mean by "show the contents." How does a view work?

Understanding View Basics

A view presents a user with the documents in a database by extracting specific field values from each document and displaying those values in a horizontal format, or *row*, in a view window. Each row refers to a particular document. Technically, the rows of a view are not the documents themselves but rather are mini-representations of the documents. By selectively pulling field values from the documents, assembling those field values in row format (again, one row for each document), and presenting the rows in a window known as a *view*, users have the means to do the following:

- Identify documents

- Open those documents for subsequent reading and/or editing

- Delete documents from the database

For identification purposes the field values for each row should give users a clue as to what document the row represents. It's essential, therefore, that there be some uniqueness in the field values so users can quickly differentiate one document from another in the view. Let's use the Document form from the Da Big Library database to illustrate this concept. Figure 20.1 shows how the field values in a document correspond with the field values in a row from a view.

How does a view accomplish this feat? First of all, you must understand the core structure of a view. We know that a view has rows and that those rows represent documents. To really get a handle on things, however, we need to break down the structure of a row and understand how it is assembled. Let's examine a single row and the values that appear in it, as shown in Figure 20.2.

FIGURE 20.1:

The field values in the Document form correspond to the values that are displayed in the columns of the Da Big Library by Category view. You'll notice that both the document and the view display the category and the author.

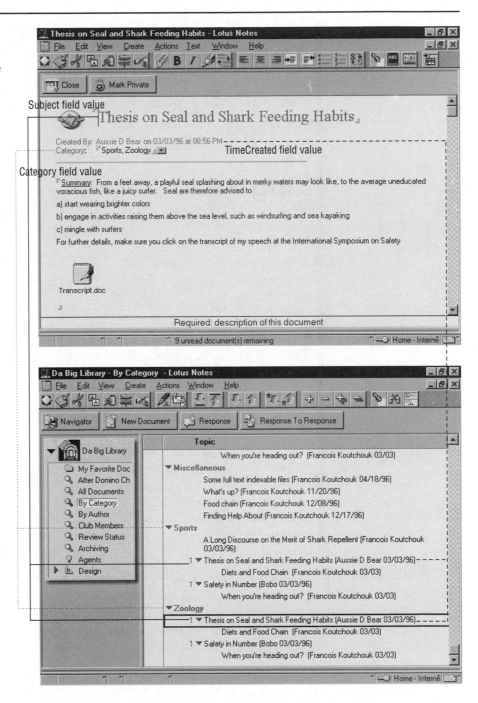

FIGURE 20.2:

A view is a tabular summary of a collection of documents in a Notes database where each row is used to display a given document.

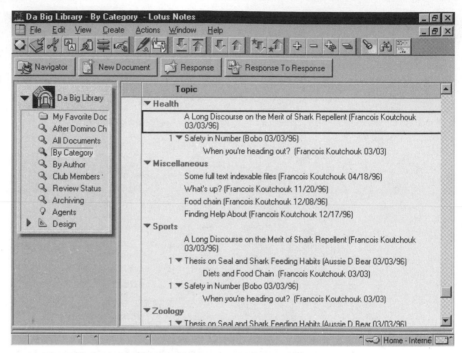

A View Is Definitely Not a Spreadsheet

Although a view looks deceptively like a 1-2-3 for Windows or an Excel spreadsheet, it is definitely not a spreadsheet. There are some vague similarities—column labels with values aligned underneath, some rudimentary totaling capability—but don't look for anything near the power of a full-featured spreadsheet package. In fact, you cannot directly edit any of the data displayed in the view because the individual data items are not independent "cells" as they are in a spreadsheet. To change the information in the view, you must open the individual documents and make any changes there or run an Agent that directly changes the values.

The row is actually made of a series of independent segments that each contain a value. Figure 20.3 shows the parts of a row.

If you extend this idea of identical segmentation to all the rows of the view, the result is a series of vertical partitions, or *columns*. Figure 20.4 shows the columns in a view.

FIGURE 20.3:

The information displayed in a row is actually divided into separate columns. Segment lines appear while the view is in Edit mode. Each column displays a unique value that usually corresponds to a field value in a document.

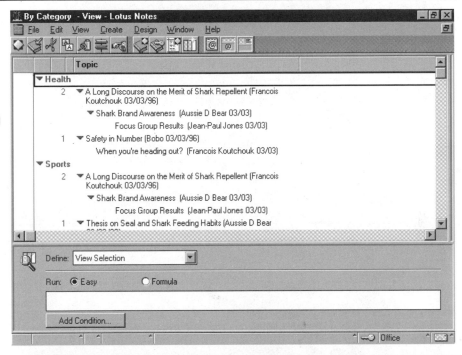

FIGURE 20.4:

If a view displayed partition lines between columns, you would see that the information in each row corresponds to a particular column.

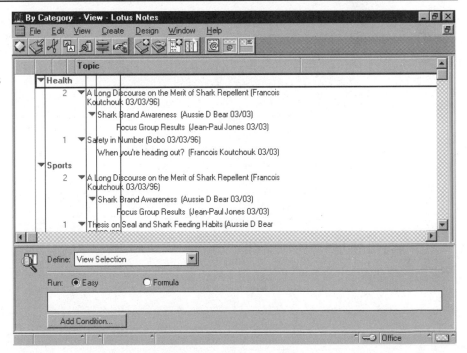

Using Column Formulas

By creating and "programming" each column of the view, you determine which field values will be presented, where the field values will appear in the row, and how they will be displayed (i.e., point size, font, number of lines, etc.). Specifically, the *column formula* dictates the values that appear in that column for each document.

Typically, a column formula makes reference to a field name (or combination of field names), the field being a component of the design of a form. The value of the field(s) being referenced will appear in the column of the view for the documents that have a value specified for the field(s).

TIP

The value of a field in a form has a direct connection to a formula you write for a column. The column formula returns a value that is displayed in the view's column.

For example, in the case of the Document form, you (or the designer) decide to display the value of the Subject, Author, and TimeCreated fields in a view, as shown in Figure 20.5.

When a user accesses a view, the view behaves simply as it has been told to; namely, the view retrieves the information from each document as specified in the column formulas. In a sense, a view is a program that executes a series of commands (the column formulas) and then displays the results, very much like a stored query in other database environments.

NOTE

A view is also called an *index,* and you can read more about how to fine-tune an index to optimize performance and disk space in Chapter 25.

Now, let's look at how you actually create, program, and access a view.

FIGURE 20.5:

The value of the Categories field in the Document form is returned by the column formula, which, in turn, displays the value in the Cat column of the By Category view.

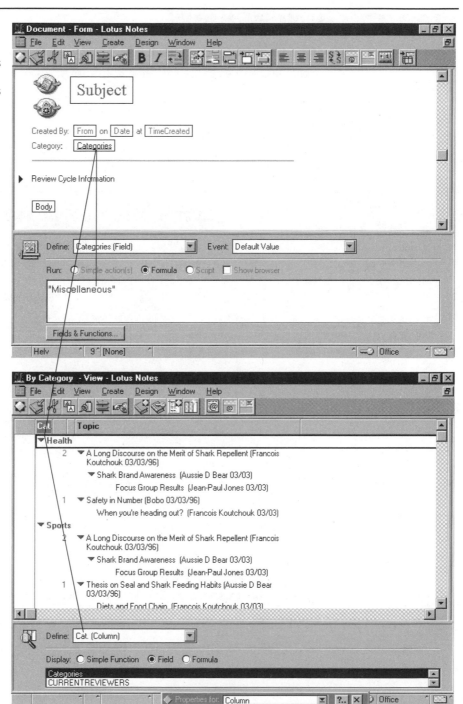

Creating a New View

Let's create a Job Offer view for the Jobs database. The columns in the view correspond to the field values in the Directory Entry form. To create the view, follow these steps:

1. Select the Jobs database in the Workspace.

2. Choose Create ➤ Views. The Create View dialog box appears, as shown in Figure 20.6.

FIGURE 20.6:

The Create View dialog box lets you create a new view for a selected database.

You do not have to create a view from the ground up if you only want a slightly different version of an existing view. As you'll see, many views are simple variations of each other; that is, you may have to make only a few changes in the columns, attributes, or formulas. To base the design of a new view on an existing one, follow these steps:

1. Click the Options button in the Create View dialog box. The list of folders and views that exist in the database will appear, as shown in Figure 20.7.

2. Click any existing view to inherit its entire design.

3. Click Cancel—we actually want to create the view from scratch!

FIGURE 20.7:

The Options dialog box for Create View allows you to base the design of a new view on an existing one.

At this point we have a brand new empty view, a blank canvas. Before we start creating columns, we need to set the key attributes for this view, also called its *properties*.

Defining the Key Attributes

You'll notice that the current name of the view is Untitled. Associated with each view is a set of attributes (or properties) that assign certain general characteristics to the view. One of the attributes is the view's name. To define view attributes, follow these steps:

1. Overwrite the name Untitled with the new name Job Offers.

2. Click Shared, as shown in Figure 20.6, so that we can share this view with everybody authorized to access the database.

NOTE When you click the Shared checkbox, the Personal on First Use checkbox will display. Leave this blank for now. We will discuss it later in the chapter.

3. Click OK to create the view.

Name

Every view must be assigned a name. This name appears in the View menu and should, therefore, reflect the nature of the view to the user. The length of a view name cannot exceed 64 characters (double the size of Release 3) unless you are using synonyms or cascaded names, to be described later. Make the name as descriptive as possible (so that end users know what they'll see if they elect to display the view) while maintaining a consistent naming convention. The name Job Offers is a good example of a descriptive name.

You can give more than one name to a view. These additional aliases, which are called *synonyms*, are typically used to give you, the application developer, a shorthand method of referring to the view in formulas. For this reason, synonyms are usually shorter than the formal view name. Like the view name, synonyms cannot exceed 64 characters in length.

NOTE   You may assign as many synonyms as you need in the alias field, separating them with the vertical bar character (|). Multiple synonyms are common when an application is passed around to multiple developers over a period of time.

Get into the habit of assigning synonyms to view names. For instance, later on, we will be assigning the synonym JO to our Job Offers view. Assuming you keep the length of synonyms down to just a few characters (and you should), you'll find them much easier to use within @functions that require view names as arguments—you simply substitute the synonym for the full-blown view name. Later, if you (or the new owner of the database) decide to change the view name, be sure to maintain the same synonym. That way all formulas that reference the view name via the synonym will continue to function correctly. On the other hand, if you use view names themselves in formulas, you will have to edit each formula manually any time you change the view name—a very tedious task indeed.

Another feature of the view name is the ability to group several views under a common heading in the View menu. This effect, known as *cascading*, keeps the View menu more manageable by creating a two-tiered selection scheme. Rather than choosing a view name directly from the View menu, the user chooses a heading that displays a submenu of actual view names, such as the one shown in Figure 20.8.

You are allowed to cascade as many levels as you wish using the backslash (\) character as the separator between levels. The entire view name can only be up to 64 characters long. Make sure that the headings portion of the view name is identical for all views that you wish to group under a common heading. The headings are case sensitive and also recognize leading and trailing spaces.

FIGURE 20.8:

A View menu can display a submenu of view names by cascading the names under a common heading. Three views in this figure, Daily Log, HR Team, and Keywords, are grouped under the heading Admin.

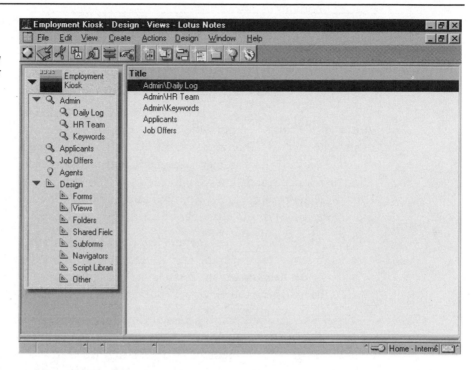

TIP

If you want to number your views to ensure that they appear in a specific order in the Navigation view, always start them with a space and then the number (for views 1–9). With any view over 9, eliminate the space. This will ensure that the views will stay in numerical sequence.

Type

Each view has an associated *type* that determines whether a view is available to the general public or to an individual user. The type of a view is either shared or personal. A third type (Shared, Personal on First Use) is a hybrid that can be used in special circumstances.

Shared Views   As its name implies, a shared view is designed to allow more than one person access to the view and makes sense only in the context of a server-based database (as opposed to a local database).

TIP

The collection of shared views associated with a database should represent those views that are useful to a majority of the end users. It's important that you gather input from the end users as to what views they want to see before you begin the actual design process. Above all, you want useful, sensible views.

Personal Views   A personal view is accessible to—and relevant to—only the user who created it. For instance, the HR manager of a small satellite office may need to see only the documents related to that specific site. However, as an application developer, you do not want to get into a situation of creating new shared views to satisfy every whim and fancy of your user population. Therefore, users with Reader access to the database can create their own personal views of the database.

As a design element, a personal view can be stored in the database on the server or stored locally in the user's DESKTOP.DSK file. If the manager of the database turns on the Create Personal Folders/views checkbox (located in the ACL settings), personal views will be stored in the database.

From a visual standpoint, personal views appear in the Views and Folders list below shared views (they are also displayed in a different color). In the Design Views dialog box, personal views are distinguished from shared views by the placement of square brackets around their names, as shown in Figure 20.9. They are further distinguishable by their gray rather than yellow icon—but you need good eyesight or lots of patience to figure that one out.

TIP

A personal view will not give a user access to documents that he/she does not already have, so you don't have to worry about your users circumventing security.

Shared, Personal on First Use   Perhaps users do not have the necessary expertise to create their own private views, or you wish to create a view that will display the contents of the database differently relative to the user accessing the view. The Shared, Personal on First Use type lets you create a shared view that becomes personal to a user the first time they access it. Prior to first access (and relative to each user), a Shared, Personal on First Use view name appears as a standard shared view in the View menu and is actually in a "shared state." After the first access by any user, the view name will appear as a personal view in the View list, as described previously. It will no longer appear in the list of shared views. Notes has made a copy of that view for the "Personal" use of anybody accessing it for the first time.

FIGURE 20.9:

A personal view is sur-rounded by square brackets in the design and appears last in the list of Views and Folders.

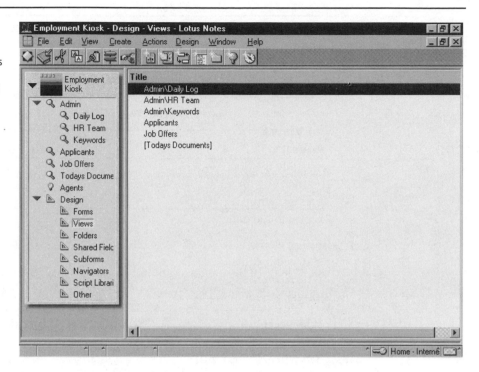

Once the shared view becomes personal, a user is completely free to modify the view. Again, the name of the (now personal) view is surrounded by square brackets in the Design Views dialog box. As the database designer, the obvious question is, "How do I restrict access to a Shared, Personal on First Use view to only the users for whom it was designed?" This task is accomplished by modifying the Read Access list for the Shared, Private on First Use view to include only the target users.

Shared, Personal on First Use views are very powerful in that they allow you to programmatically create views that best fit the specific requirements of a variety of users. These advanced design techniques are beyond the scope of this chapter.

Until it is used for the first time, a Shared, Personal on First Use view is stored in the database. But once it becomes personal, it can be stored with the database on the server or locally in the user's DESKTOP .DSK file. If the manager of the database turns on the Create Personal Folders/Views option, these views will be stored in the database unless the designer of the view selects the Store in Desktop option.

WARNING   If the manager of the database does not allow the storage of personal views in the database, views are stored locally, not on the server. This means that if you further modify a Shared, Personal on First Use view, the user will need to remove or rename their Personal view. Use this type of view only when the requirements are not expected to change too frequently. Or make sure the Create Personal Folders/Views option is turned on for the database.

TIP   Using a personal view, you can select documents based on the function @Username (shared views cannot).

Condition

Which documents in the database should a view include (and, therefore, exclude)? Remember that you can design many views for a database, each presenting the contents of the database differently. Moreover, a given view may present only a subset of documents in the database. This arrangement is critical in light of the fact that a typical database will consist of documents composed with a variety of forms, each with unique fields. With such a database, a view that displayed all the documents in the database would look rather messy (for reasons that will be made clearer later).

We said earlier in this chapter that the columns of a view and the formula associated with each column dictate which field values will be displayed there for each document. It should be self-evident that you need to maintain consistency between the fields referenced in the column formulas of a view and the fields of a *particular* form (or related forms, such as a main form and its associated response forms). Consider the following scenario.

Imagine a database that contains only two documents. Each document was composed using a different form. The design of the forms is such that they do not have any fields in common; that is, the documents consist of unrelated data. In order to build a view that will display the contents of such a database in a meaningful way, and knowing what we do about the structure of a view, the columns would require formulas that reference field names that appear in the design of *different* forms. The result is that a particular column will reference a field that exists in only one of the two documents. (This solution is acceptable in certain situations but not in this example.)

To ensure that a view will include only documents that meet specific criteria (and are relevant to the column formulas of the view), we have to make use of a design element known as a *condition* or *View Selection* (formerly called a selection formula in Notes Release 3). When applied to a view, a condition simply narrows the scope of the view to include only a subset of documents in the database, excluding all others. A condition expresses the criteria that a document must meet in order to be included in the view.

Each view will, by default, display all the documents available in the database. If you have multiple types of documents, for example, Job Offers and Job Applications, you need to separate the documents into multiple views. The *condition attribute* allows you to easily restrict the list of documents to specified criteria, as shown in Figure 20.10.

FIGURE 20.10:

Use the Search Builder to define the condition attribute of a view.

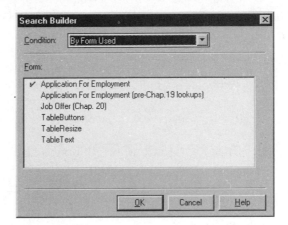

The concept of *search criteria*, by the way, is identical to what you need to define the scope of action of an Agent, as you'll see in Chapter 23. So, for the time being, we'll cover only the main conditions:

- **By Form** allows you to fill up the fields as if you were using the real form. Whatever documents contain the same information in their fields will be displayed in the view. This method is quite convenient if you do not know the name of the fields or want to build a very specific view. For instance, you could type *Engineering* in the Hiring Department field of the form called Job Offer.

- **By Field** allows you to base the selection process on a single comparison to a specified field. If you know that the field for the Hiring Department is called Department, you would select it and indicate as a condition that it should contain the word *Engineering*. The result would be the same as the example described in the By Form condition. More sophisticated conditions can be set for date and number fields.

- **By Date** allows you to pick only the documents created or modified, as compared to a date condition you set, for example, between certain dates, after a specified date, and so on. You could use this condition to see all the new Job Applications that came in this week, or to see all Job Offers that have been out for over three months.

- **By Form Used** is the quickest way to restrict the documents displayed to a certain type. Many Notes databases support a one-to-one or one-to-many relationship between forms and views. For instance, a Rolodex view in a sales database will show only the documents composed using the Contact or Ship To forms. In our current database, a Job Offers view should select only the documents created with our Job Offer form as well as future Comment forms used during interviews.

Follow these steps to add a condition to the Job Offer form:

1. Click the Add Condition button to display the Search Builder.

2. Select By Form Used in the Condition selection list.

3. Choose Job Offer from the list of forms. A tick mark will appear next to it.

4. Click OK to close the Search Builder. Note that the selection condition appears in the grayed out format of a Simple Action in the Create View dialog box, as shown in Figure 20.11.

   Because we want to display only the Open position, let's add another condition.

5. Click the Add Condition button to display the Search Builder.

6. Choose the By Field condition. Select "Does not contain" and type the word **Closed.** The view will not display offers that are closed.

7. Click OK to complete the creation of the view.

FIGURE 20.11:

The Add Condition button places Simple Action look-alike formulas in the Create View dialog box.

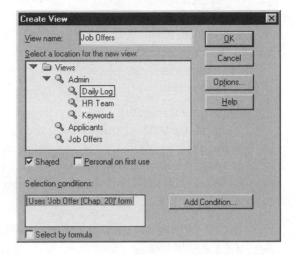

TIP

You can refine the selection condition by clicking the Add Condition button multiple times. By default, the conditions will be listed next to each other with an AND logical parameter. You can change AND to OR by simply overwriting it. We recommend using this method to assemble complex conditions, rather than using the formula language.

You have now set all the main attributes of the view. You could live happily ever after, but please bear with us before jumping into column creation (the fun part). Setting the optional properties may save you a lot of work.

TIP

To aid you in understanding the formula language, build a View Selection using the Search Builder. Once your selection is complete, click the Formula radio button located in the Design pane. This will show you the same view selection but it will be translated into the formula language.

Setting Additional View Properties

Unlike Notes Release 3, Release 4 provides a rich set of options to manage the way users experience views. In Chapter 17, we explained why you should sketch out your application before starting development work. In contrast to forms, Notes views tend to come last because their design depends on the data contained within the forms. In other words, it's OK to plan the views later in the process. But the design of a view is as important as the design of a form because the best laid out forms are rather useless if users cannot find documents. The old adage "Information has no value until it's shared" comes to mind.

Among many things, the additional view properties let you control the look and feel of the view. "Feel" means how the view will behave when opened. "Look" means how it will appear, including its fonts and colors. Other options include security and indexing (the latter is covered in Chapter 25).

The Look

The look of any view is up to the designer. Without further ado, as opposed to showing you what you are supposed to do, let us illustrate what not to do with Figure 20.12 as our guide.

FIGURE 20.12:

Use the View Options to turn a view into a perfectly ugly representation of documents.

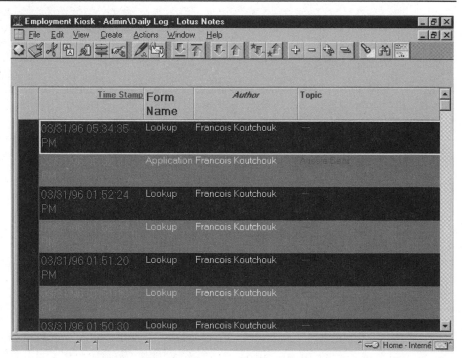

Unfortunately, the black and white print of the book fails to bring out the truly outrageous color combination. Follow these steps if you have the courage:

1. Open the Jobs database from the companion disk.

2. Open the view Admin\Daily Log in Design mode.

3. Stand back a little and press the F9 key to refresh the view.

4. Bring up the View Properties panel.

5. Click the third tab, the colorful S as shown in Figure 20.13.

FIGURE 20.13:

You can set the look of the view through the optional attributes in the View Properties box.

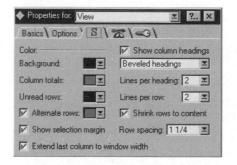

Let's examine some of the poorly chosen options in terms of look (the feel is fine), including the background and alternate colors.

Background Color   In Figure 20.13, we set the background to black, usually a bad idea since it tends to contrast so much with the usual white background of most word processors and spreadsheets. A black background also forces you to use harder-to-read bright colors to display any text. In general, you should pick a neutral, light color (we have heard the term *pastel* used) for your background while maintaining a consistent color schema throughout the application, just as you did with the forms. If the view contains documents displayed with a light green background, it's not a bad idea to make the view background green, too. We recommend using a white background when in doubt.

Alternate Row Color   This feature of Release 4 allows you to place a different background in one row out of two. Try to choose a light color, for instance, light green or light blue. The dark gray of our example adds nothing except another color to the screen. Use this option any time you'll have multiple-line rows or rows that tend to contain a lot of information.

Row Spacing Height   The spacing can be set from single-space to double-space in increments of one-quarter space. Use this feature when the font pitch is very small to start with or when multiple lines are displayed per row. In our example, the setting of $1\frac{1}{4}$ adds nothing but an opportunity to see more background colors. The trade-off with this feature is between displaying too many documents at a glance or forcing users to press the Page Down key.

Show Column Heading   In certain situations, the view is self-evident without the use of a heading. We would even argue that most well-designed simple views should be clear enough without looking at the heading. Our example does not need a heading, since it contains only a date, a form name, an author, and a topic.

Heading Height   You can set heading height from one to five lines to display multiline column titles. Our example is set to two lines for no apparent reason, since none of the headings need to wrap. This option is particularly useful in views where you need to write more than a few words of text to explain the meaning of a column or how to use the entire view. In that case, we recommend the use of a smaller font pitch for the column title, as we'll illustrate later in this chapter.

Show Selection Margin   The selection margin is to the left of the view columns and is used to display small symbols about the documents. For instance, a tick mark will appear next to a document once it is selected, and a little trash can will show next to documents marked for deletion. In our example, there is no point displaying the selection margin because the view is most likely going to be used for read-only purposes, as are most log views. Eliminating this column provides more horizontal space for the other columns.

Unread Rows   Change the color to tell users whether they have read particular documents in a database. Each unread document is indicated by an Unread mark in the selection margin at the left of the view; read documents have no such marker. Notes maintains independent Unread marks for every user (on the server) so that what shows up as unread to one user does not necessarily show up as unread to another. Once a user opens and closes an unread document, the Unread mark will be removed for that user. It's a good idea to implement Unread marks for active databases where new documents are frequently being added and timely viewing of new documents is critical. We recommend that you use the color red to identify unread rows.

Lines per Row   This Release 4 feature allows you to display the lengthy contents of a field over multiple lines. In other words, the row will expand to allow the text to wrap. Without this option, you would have to either truncate the text or force the user to scroll horizontally to see all the contents of a column. Use this feature in combination with the Shrink Row to Contents option to make sure that no row stands with empty space (use the row spacing height option to leave space between rows). You can set the number of lines per row to a maximum of nine lines.

We recommend that you avoid putting too much information in one row because:

- The view is intended to summarize documents, not list them in full.

- At-a-glance browsing becomes slower and more difficult.

- Notebook users would have to scroll down the view.

- You only need enough information to convince users that the document contains what they are looking for.

The Feel

Now that you know what not to do with the look, let's examine the options at your disposal to dramatically improve the way your users will interact with the view. All these options are located under the Options tab of the Properties box, as shown in Figure 20.14.

FIGURE 20.14:

Use the View Properties box
to change the feel of a view.

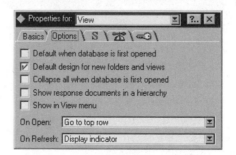

Default View   One view in each database is usually designated as the default view. When the database is first opened, this view is automatically displayed, giving the new user a first look at the contents of the database. From then on, the last view a user accessed will be the first view they see when they open that same database again (although it is possible to open another view by setting the database launch option to invoke a Navigator). As a rule of thumb, the view that is accessed most frequently typically becomes the default view, although a database is not required to have a default view at all. In the list of views in the Design Views dialog box, the default view (if any) is prefaced with an asterisk character (*).

TIP

Always specify a default view for a database. Certain commands will fail if a default view is not selected (such as the AppendDocLink() and FTSearch() Lotus-Script commands).

Show Response Document in a Hierarchy   At the outset of this chapter, we noted that you can show a response hierarchy, if one exists, in a view. Usually, you express a response hierarchy by indenting response documents, as shown in Figure 20.15.

FIGURE 20.15:

Three document types are displayed in this view: a Main document, a Response, and a Response to Response. With the Show response documents in a hierarchy option selected, the response documents appear indented under the main document to indicate their relationship.

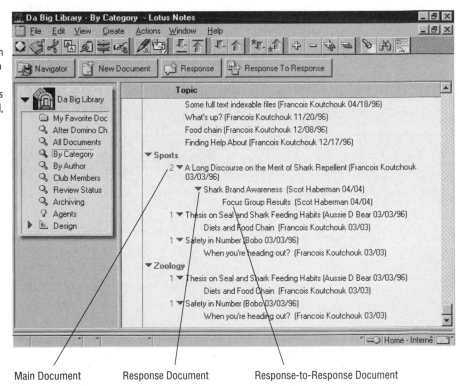

Main Document   Response Document   Response-to-Response Document

Notice, for instance, the horizontal alignment of "Shark Brand Awareness." Rather than being perfectly aligned with the Topic column title, it appears offset to the right relative to the document directly above it. This indented format indicates that the document is a response to the document "A Long Discourse on the Merit of Shark Repellent." (We explain the conventions for indenting shortly.) You may, however, choose not to show a response hierarchy (like the one above) in a particular view. By not selecting Show Documents in a Response Hierarchy (and with the appropriate column definitions), you can force response documents to appear aligned with their corresponding main documents.

Default Design for New Folders and Views   You may recall at the outset of this chapter that we had the option of creating the view by inheriting its design from an existing view or folder, but we opted to start from scratch. If any view had been marked with this option, we would not have had this choice: our new view would have automatically inherited that design.

In most cases, default inheritance is a minor nuisance for the database designer because when creating a new view (as previously shown in Figure 20.6), they would have to do the extra steps of clicking the Options button (as previously shown in Figure 20.7) and choosing the blank template.

However, we recommend using this option if the application is meant to allow users to create their own folders or private views. We will talk about folders shortly, but suffice it to say that this option will strongly suggest a design based on the default view. We say *strongly suggest* because most users will not know to click the Options button of the Create View or Create Folder dialog box.

Collapse All When Database Is First Opened   Choose this option to specify whether categories in the view will be either fully expanded or fully collapsed when the view is opened. You may recall that a field can be used to categorize documents in a view. Fields placed in columns marked as categorized provide the hierarchical functionality of a view. In other words, the view displays the documents using *categories*.

When categories are fully expanded, all documents within each category are displayed in the view. When categories are fully collapsed, only the categories themselves appear in the view and users will have to manually expand the categories by choosing menu selections under the View menu or pressing the + key on the numeric keypad.

Show in View Menu   There is no catch here! If you select this option, the view is available on the menu; otherwise, you will need to use the list in the left-hand column or a Navigator (covered later on in this chapter). If the majority of your users prefer to use the keyboard instead of a mouse, use this option. Otherwise, keep the menu free from any unnecessary clutter.

On Open   The Today's Log view of the Jobs database (also called the Ugly View) is set to go to the top on open because we have sorted the documents in descending order, showing the newest item as the first document. It therefore makes sense to position the user on the first document of the view. Alternatively, you can place the user on the last document of the view. By default, Notes will open the view at the last document opened by the user. We recommend this option whenever the activity in a database view revolves around threads rather than sequential activity.

On Refresh   If documents are added or modified by other users while the view is opened, you will not see the changes unless you press F9 (refresh the view) or the Display Indicator. In other words, the view is *not* live. Note that every time you close and reopen a view, you always pick up the latest changes. If a view has many documents, depending on the index setting on the server (see Chapter 25), the refresh process can take a bit of time.

Release 4 allows you to force the indexing changes to first show for the documents on top or at the bottom of the view. The purpose of this option is to reduce the amount of time a user would have to wait before the changes that are most relevant appear. Since the latest information is always at the top of our log view, we want to make sure that the top of the view is refreshed first.

Read Access

You can restrict who can use a specific view through the Read Access settings of the view. Choose this option to make sure that only the people named in the read access list can read documents displayed in a view. (This list is a subset of the people who have access to the database.) To view the list of people with access to a view, follow these steps:

1. Open the Job Offers view in the Jobs database in Design mode.
2. Bring up the Properties box.
3. Click the Key tab (the last one), as shown in Figure 20.16.
4. Deselect All Readers and Above.

FIGURE 20.16:

Use the Read Access option to restrict who can open a view.

5. Select who should be able to use this view from the list of authorized readers (based on the Access Control List of the database).

WARNING   View restrictions give the illusion of protecting documents from prying eyes, but users may still be able to create their own private views or folders displaying these very documents. View restrictions are no substitute for proper database ACL settings; read access restrictions in the forms, which apply read access control to the documents created with those forms; and the use of field-level encryption.

If not set properly, view restrictions may also create replication problems that are difficult to trace. You must include all the servers that will need to hold a copy of the database (even those not directly accessed by users) in the list of authorized readers—otherwise, the documents will not replicate.

---

6. Reselect All Readers and Above, since the Job Offers are accessible to all users.

Index Options

The index options are found under the fourth tab, the one with a propeller hat.

Index options define the rules by which the database index will be updated. (We discuss creating and updating a full text index in Chapter 25.) Every view is in fact an index that enables Notes to locate documents within a view. Every time documents are added, modified, deleted, or recategorized, the index must be updated to reflect the change. (With large databases, indexing can consume substantial Notes server resources, which is why you have control over the On Refresh option.) You can determine how often the index is updated and how long it is saved. These choices make trade-offs between performance and disk space usage and are fully explained in the discussion on indexing a database in Chapter 25.

TIP   Also located on this tab is the Unread Marks option. If this option is set to None, the user will not get unread marks and so the color chosen for your unread-rows color will not appear.

 The For Web Access: Treat View Contents as HTML option is new in version 4.6. This option is used when creating a specialty view for a Web application. By default, Domino will automatically translate a view using the default row and column settings. If you want to override these default settings, you can select this option and add your own HTML formatting attributes. If you decide to use this option, it is your responsibility to format all the column entries and document linking for the view. If you embed a view within a form that has the option For Web Access: Treat Document Contents as HTML activated, you must select the view option For Web Access: Treat View Contents as HTML.

Defining the Optional Properties

To finish the design of the properties of our view, follow these steps:

1. Open the Job Offers view in the Jobs database in Design mode.

2. Bring up the Properties box.

3. Enter an alias called JO in the Basics tab.

4. Make sure you type a comment—for example, "Lists all the outstanding postings"—to keep the designer who succeeds you happy.

5. Click the second tab for Options.

6. Mark the view as the default when the database is first opened.

7. Mark Show Responses in a Hierarchy.

8. Keep the default On Open as "Go to last opened document" and On Refresh as "Display Indicator."

9. Click the third tab.

10. Click Alternate rows and pick a light yellow.

11. Select 2 Lines per Row and Shrink Rows to Content.

12. Select File ➤ Save to preserve your changes.

Defining the Columns in a View

The vertical partitions, or *columns*, in a view give the view its structure and meaning. When designing a new view, you'll notice that you're presented with an undefined column at the far left. This is known as the *default Document Number column*. We are going to delete the column because we don't need to display a number next to each document in the view. However, before we do so, let's look at the column's properties, as shown in Figure 20.17. Follow these steps:

1. Open the Job Offers view from the Jobs database (if it isn't already opened) and bring up the Properties box.

2. Click the first column marked with the pound character (#).

3. Define the tabs of the column as follows:

Basics Tab	Title: # Simple Function: # in view (e.g., 2.1.2) Width: 10 Multi-value separator: None
Sorting Tab	Sorting: None Totals: None
Appearance Tab	Font: Helv, 10, Plain Text Color: Black Justification: Left
Numbers Tab	Number: General
Date/Time	Time: mm/dd/yy hh:mm:ss
Title Tab	Title: Helv, 8, Bold

As you can see, you can use the default definitions for most of the items. The defaults will save you a lot of time when you have several columns to define.

For the Job Offers view, you are going to define columns that correspond to the Department, Title, and Date Posted fields in the Job Offer form.

Use the Column Properties box to set the Attributes of a column. In the Formula pane, you can easily select a Simple Function.

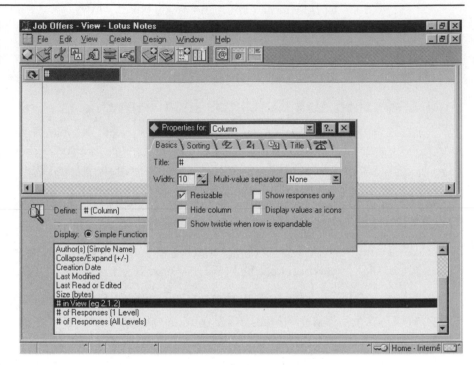

Setting the Basic Column Properties

Notes provides a wide variety of properties to let you control the appearance and the use of a column within a view. All are optional except the column definition. As we noted in talking about the View properties, the look and feel of each column is entirely up to you.

TIP   Double-click a column heading (the box at the top of the column) to display the Properties box for the column.

Creating a Column Definition   Without a definition, the column serves no purpose. A column can contain either a Simple Function, a field, or a formula.

To define each column, follow these steps:

1. Click the # column to select it.

2. Click the Field radio button in the Formula pane. A warning message will appear, as shown in Figure 20.18.

FIGURE 20.18:

When changing the definition of a column from a Simple Function, field, or formula, Notes warns you that you will lose all existing data.

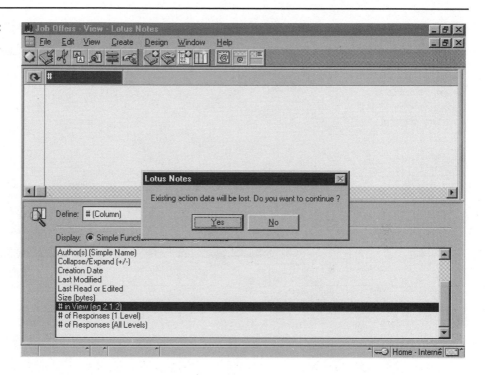

3. Click Yes. A complete list of all the fields available in your database will appear (including hidden fields, which are those that may not be visible in any form unless it is placed in Design mode).

4. Select Department, as shown in Figure 20.19, which is a field from the Job Offer form.

5. Double-click the second column.

6. Click the Field radio button and choose Title as a field.

7. Double-click the third column.

8. Scroll down the list and select Creation Date, which is a Simple Function. Notes will automatically extract the date the document was composed.

TIP

We recommend performing calculations in the document and storing the results in a hidden field, which is displayed in the view. The fewer calculated columns in the view, the better its performance! Remember that a view is similar to an index and the fewer calculations that need to be performed in the index, the faster the view documents will be displayed.

FIGURE 20.19:

The Field Column Definition list lets you pick a field from all the forms. The Properties box lets you enter a title, set the width of the field, and select other basic options.

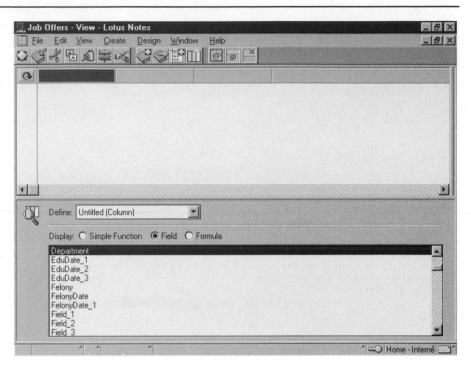

You are now ready to reindex the view to see the results of your work. Note the little blue arrow icon at the top of the first column. It means that the view needs to be refreshed to display its latest contents. Click the icon to admire your first attempt at building a view.

Creating a Column Definition Using Formulas

A column formula usually allows you to enter more complex search criteria or to represent data beyond the contents of the fields or simple functions. For instance, you may need to combine independent fields of a form into a string, such as one that will show (John F. Kennedy) if MiddleName contains "Fitzgerald."

```
"("+FirstName + " "+ @Left(MiddleName;1) +". " + LastName+")"
```

Continued on next page

Other uses of formulas include the computation of a number based on fields contained in a document, such as earnings per share, or the difference between two dates, such as the date the document was created and the date it was closed.

Advanced uses include @functions that will evaluate parts of the documents, for instance counting the number of response documents or adding up the total size of the attachments.

Note: All of the rules of writing Notes formulas apply to writing column formulas. (See Chapter 18 for a discussion of writing formulas and macros.)

Clearly the view needs help, both in terms of appearance and functionality. Let's examine the options available to you.

Setting the Column Title   For each column you can include a title, which is simply a text label that appears at the top of a view column. The column title should indicate what information the column contains. Be sure that the width of the column (discussed below) is large enough to display the column title fully. Follow these steps to enter a title:

1.   Double-click the first column and then click the Basics tab.

2.   Type **Dept.** in the Title text box.

3.   Type **Posted on** as a title for the third column.

The second column does not need a title—if it's not clear to the applicant that the second column deals with job titles, you probably don't want that person on your payroll. More seriously, the concept is to minimize the amount of text the user has to read.

Setting the Column Width   The width of a column, though not a critical element, plays a role in how the column appears to the user. A column should be wide enough to display the full column title and the values displayed through the column formula. (Information will be truncated if it's wider than the column.) Follow these steps to specify the width of the column:

1.   Double-click the first column and then click the Basics tab.

2.   Set the width of the Dept. column to 5.

Notebook users (or users of 640×480 displays) can see only a total width of approximately 54 characters. You can squeeze more characters than that by reducing the font, but we suggest being conservative when allocating widths to columns.

Setting Other Basics Options The other options under Basics also influence the look and feel of a column.

Re-sizable: This option (a.k.a. "sliding pane columns") allows users to modify the default width of the view by pulling on the margin of the column. This technique is not *necessary* if the column of the view is of a fixed width and you are displaying all the columns in their entirety in a 640×480 display. It is not *desirable* if the shrinking could hide information that is otherwise essential, such as decimal points of an important financial value.

Show Twistie When Row Is Expandable: Use this option only in combination with the Categorize option of a column, covered in the next section (when we make Department a category). The twistie places a symbol (that looks very similar to the section expand/collapse symbol used in the Navigation pane for listing the available views and folders) next to the value of the field to tell the user that documents match this category.

Multi-value Separator: If a column formula specifies a multi-value field, such as checkbox-style keyword field, you can designate the character—space, semicolon, comma, or new line—for separating the individual values in the column. In other words, if a Department field contains the values Sales, Engineering, you chose the comma (,) as a separator.

Hide Column: You may occasionally wish to include in a view a column whose values are hidden to the eye. This situation usually occurs when you want to sort documents in the view based on the value of a field, yet you don't want to display the value sort key (or to sort in a specific order other than alphabetical, such as Urgent, Very Important, Normal).

TIP Since the column is hidden, the setting of the column title or column width does not matter. You can see the actual values in the hidden column only when you're in View Design mode.

Display as Icons: Notes allows you to include icons in a view window to give users more information about the items they are viewing. (Perhaps a title alone isn't obvious enough.) For example, an icon that looks like a paper clip can represent an attachment, and another icon that looks like a dog-eared sheet of paper can represent a document.

Notes contains more than 150 predefined icons: document, folder, person, group, and so forth. When you define the icon column, you'll need to enter a number from 1 to 170 in the Formula box.

Obviously, displaying the same icon throughout a column is of limited interest. The number should be the result of a formula. For instance, if a form contains a field for approval and it contains the value OK, use icon 82 (thumb up). Otherwise, use icon 83 (thumb down) to indicate that the form is not approved.

TIP

Icons are very useful to convey a lot of information in a small amount of space. Take advantage of them but don't overuse them!

NOTE

You can add new view icons or change the existing ones. The icons are located under the Notes data in the Domino\Icons directory. The naming convention for the icons is VWICNXXX.GIF where the xxx is a zero-filled number. An example of the icon file name for the thumbs up would be VWICN082.GIF. Be aware that the icons for server-based databases reside on the server and those for local databases are on the user's machine.

To complete the Basics settings of our Job Offer form, follow these steps:

1.   Select the Re-sizable option for the Position column.

2.   Select the Twistie option for the Dept. column.

Setting the Sorting Order

The sorting options that appear when you click the Sorting (second) tab of the Column Properties box are shown in Figure 20.20. You can use these options to define the order in which documents in the view will be displayed.

Sorting   Sorting establishes that the documents of a view will be sorted according to the value of the fields contained within that column. Ascending or Descending determines the order in which the documents will be sorted.

Standard versus Categorized   Categories are a simple yet effective way of making long listings of documents easier to read. Essentially, categories allow you to organize documents in a view into logical groupings based on a common field value.

FIGURE 20.20:

Click the Sorting tab to set the sort order.

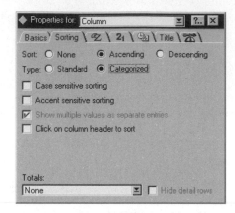

For example, the Job Offers view of the database might contain several documents in which the value of the Department field in the Job Offer documents is Engineering. We can take advantage of this fact by grouping together all Job Offer documents with Engineering in the Department field. The common value, Engineering, is shared by a subset of Job Offer documents in the database. This value relates the documents to each other. Therefore, we can express this relationship in the view. In this case, we can identify *Department* as a category that we'll use to organize documents in the view.

Follow these steps to categorize the Job Offers view by department.

1. Double-click the Dept. column to bring up the Properties box.

2. Click the Sorting tab.

3. Select Ascending to sort the column.

4. Select Categorized as a Type.

Your view should now look similar to Figure 20.20.

NOTE When you use categorized columns, the text that is displayed in the column is not affected by the width (it only effects how much of the column title is displayed). The width does affect where the next column begins to display its text. For example, if you were to make the width of the Department column 1, the title for Department would only show the "D" but the actual text would still display normally. In many views where a categorized column is used, it is common to not have a column title (it should be obvious) and to set the width to "1". This provides more room to display data from the other columns.

You are not limited to a single category in a view. Multiple categories make sense where documents share additional common field values. The idea is to produce subcategories within categories for a more highly organized view. The physical placement of a category column determines whether it's inside or outside another category—a category to the left envelops categories to its right.

As with any good thing, you can overuse categories, so ask yourself, "Does the common value represent a useful category and will it enhance the view?" Too many categories can make a view *less* readable and more cumbersome if users are continually having to expand categories to get to the desired document(s) or collapse upper-level categories in order to fit the view contents in a single window.

Setting Totals   You can use this option to define the method for calculation and display of numeric totals in a column. You can calculate totals for columns displaying numeric fields, for columns containing formulas that return a numeric result, and for columns that use @Number to successfully convert a text-like digit to a number (such as "3" to 3). The following options are available:

> **None:** Does no totaling.

> **Total:** Calculates a grand total for all main documents in the view and displays this total at the bottom of the view.

> **Average per Document:** Calculates an overall average for the view. Notes totals the main documents and then divides that value by the number of documents. For example, if there are four documents in the database and their total is 10, the average per document is 2.5.

> **Average per Subcategory:** Calculates an average for each subcategory. Within each subcategory, the documents are summed; that value is divided by the number of documents in that subcategory.

> **Percent of Parent Category:** Calculates a total for all main documents in the view; for each category, Notes displays the percentage of the overall view's total represented by that category.

> **Percent of All Documents:** Calculates a total for all main documents in the view; for each document, Notes displays the percentage of the category's total represented by that document. For each category, Notes displays the percentage of the overall view's total represented by that category.

The Hide Detail Rows option suppresses the display of subtotals for each category and subcategory. We've found the Totals option useful in summary or reporting views.

NOTE Totals perform calculations only for main documents; they do not work with response documents. Because column totals recalculate each time you open the view, they may affect database and overall server performance.

Manual Sorting   Release 4 allows you to click on a column header to change the sort order of the view. This option is quite convenient to reduce the proliferation of views that display the same data sorted in different ways. To turn on manual sorting, select a column header to sort, as shown in Figure 20.21. Thereafter, users of this view will be able to manually sort by any column by clicking it. For example, manual sorting would allow a user to reverse the sorting order of a date from descending to ascending, in order to display the latest documents last in the view.

FIGURE 20.21:

The Manual Sorting column option allows a user to click a column header to sort on the fly. The sort order can be ascending, descending, or both.

WARNING   There is a catch with the Click to Sort option: it doesn't support categorized columns. If the first column is a category and you mark the second column for manual sorting, the contents of the first column will disappear when the column is clicked. You can click the column again to restore it to its original state.

Manual sorting of noncategorized views allows the user to produce a variety of sort orders. The concept of clicking the column title to sort the contents of a table is quite common in many applications, in particular mail packages. Try to implement this functionality whenever someone might have a reason to sort by the criteria defined in a column—it takes only one extra character in the column title.

Setting the Column Format

When you click the third tab of the Column Properties box, symbolized by a couple of letters, the font options appear, as shown in Figure 20.22. (We showed you how to change fonts, attributes, and colors in our discussion of formatting text in Chapter 7.) Using different fonts, point sizes, attributes, and colors in a view enhances its appearance and helps the user to differentiate among items.

FIGURE 20.22:

Click the Format tab of the Properties box to set the look of a column.

Justification lets you set the column alignment to left, right, or center. Left aligns all values in the column along the left edge of the column. Choose this option to display text and time/date values. Right aligns all values in the column along the right edge of the column. Generally, you use this option to display numbers; however, if you use this option, you should use a numeric format that displays a standard number of decimal places to ensure that the decimal points in the various numbers line up. Center aligns all values at the center of the column. Select this option to display icons and small values that you want to emphasize.

To enhance the look of our view, follow these steps:

1. Double-click the Dept. column to bring up the Properties box.

2. Click the Format tab.

3. Make the column blue and bold.

4. Adjust the formatting of the other columns to your satisfaction.

5. Press Ctrl+S to save the view.

Setting the Number Format

When you click the fourth tab of the Column Properties box, symbolized by several numbers, the number options appear, as shown in Figure 20.23. You'll use the number format option only when a field uses a number data type or when the formula returns a numeric value. If you want to display a number in a column, choose an appropriate format.

FIGURE 20.23:

Click the Number tab of the Properties box to set the format of a column of number fields.

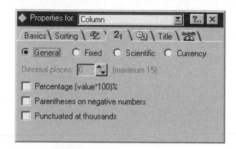

Setting the Time Format

A small clock and a page of a calendar symbolize the fifth tab of the Column Properties box. (These symbols may appear as small spots on your screen.) Click the tab to set the time/date options, as shown in Figure 20.24. You'll use the time format option only when a field uses the time data type or when the formula returns a time/date value. If you want to display a time/date value in a column, choose an appropriate format.

FIGURE 20.24:

Click the Time/Date tab of the Properties box to set the time/date look of a column of Time/Date fields.

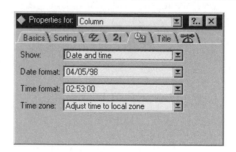

Since the time of the posting of a job offer is generally not important, modify the third column to show only the date by following these steps:

1. Double-click the Posted On column to bring up the Properties box.

2. Click the Time/Date tab.

3. In the Show list box, select the Date Only option.

4. Press Ctrl+S to save the view.

Setting the Title Format

Release 4 introduced the ability to control the font, pitch, and size of the title of a column. This feature is available through the sixth tab of the Column Properties box. It works exactly the same way as the options you used to change the look of a column (third tab) and includes a quick way to apply these style changes to all the titles of the other columns.

We recommend that you avoid mixing multiple-column styles within a view. As you saw in Figure 20.12, multiple-column styles tend to crowd the screen without adding anything relevant for the user. If you feel the urge to change the format of the titles, try to maintain some sort of consistency among all the views or at least between the column and its title.

Advanced Topics

The For Web Access: Show Values in This Column as Links option for viewing columns is new. When a view is generated for the Web by Domino, the default document link is always the first viewable column in a view. This may be fine for most views, but in certain situations, it doesn't make much sense. Selecting this option for a view column will override the default action. You can select one or more columns as the columns for document linking.

TIP

If you don't want document linking to be enabled for any columns, you'll need to make that clear. First, select any view column and select the For Web Access: Show Values in This Column as Links option. Save the view. Now go back to the same column and deselect the option (the same option you just enabled). Save the view again. Now none of the columns will be document link enabled.

Producing a Response Hierarchy

When one document is composed as a response to another, it is helpful to users to be able to see the relationship at a glance. We can accomplish this by arranging a view so that the correspondence between a response document (the main document) and a responded-to document is obvious. By introducing an indenting scheme in the view, where response documents are positioned directly under their corresponding main documents *and* offset to the right, we can show users the response hierarchy quickly and easily. While this scheme may sound easy to implement, it's actually a little tricky.

As you define a column, one of the options that you might select in the Basics tab is Show Responses Only. By activating this option as part of a column definition, you are saying that only response documents will qualify for inclusion in that column in terms of displaying a value. Rows that represent nonresponse documents will not display a value for that column, even if they satisfy the column formula. So what we've done through the Show Responses Only option is to limit the scope of the column to include values only from those documents of type Response or Response to Response.

> **NOTE**   A view may have one column, and only one column, designated as a Responses Only column.

The placement of the Responses Only column is the next item of business and causes most of the confusion. Consider a plain-vanilla view (with no Responses Only columns). The values that are displayed in the view, based on the column definitions, are vertically aligned with the column itself.

For example, you expect the values in the column at the far left of the view to be the values for that column—a typical "what you see is what you get" result. This sounds simplistic and, in fact, it is. However, the familiar WYSIWYG rule does not apply to a Responses Only column. This anomaly stems from the fact (and you should keep this in mind throughout this discussion) that we are trying to produce a hierarchical look in the view where Response documents appear underneath and offset relative to their corresponding main documents.

Let's look at the view by category in the Da Big Library database from the companion disk. It contains a Responses Only column in column 4, as shown in Figure 20.25.

> **TIP**   Columns can appear to the left and right of the Responses Only column, but the other columns cannot display values for Response documents.

FIGURE 20.25:

The Responses Only column appears to the left of the Topic column. The information in the Responses Only column will appear indented under the document in the Topic column.

Responses Only column

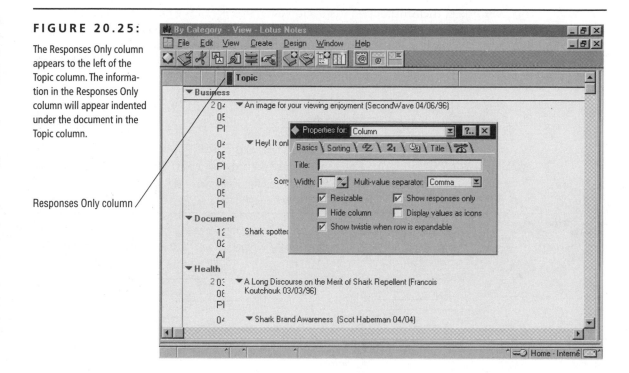

You'll notice that the placement of the Responses Only column is to the left of the Topic column, yet the value that's produced by this column appears indented beneath the main document. Several things are going on here.

- Notes has automatically matched the Response document with its main document.

- The Response document has been automatically indented in the view.

Where you place the Responses Only column in the design of the view, either to the left or right of other columns, affects what other values may be displayed for Response documents based on other columns. We know that the Responses Only column itself will yield a value for Response documents, but what about the other columns of the view—will they yield a value for Response documents as well?

The answer is—maybe. You might expect that Response documents, which satisfy the column formulas of other columns, would produce values for those columns in their respective rows. However, this is not the case. When considering the placement of a Responses Only column, two rules will affect the outcome.

- Columns to the left of the Responses Only column will yield a value for both Main and Response documents.

- Columns to the right of the Responses Only column will yield a value for Main documents only.

However counterintuitive this might seem, it's simply the way Notes views work. You can think of a Responses Only column as a barrier that prevents any column to its right from displaying values for Response documents.

TIP   Even with a column width of 1, the values in the Responses Only column will be fully displayed—yes, another Responses Only anomaly! Also, there is no need to include a column title—given a column width of 1, you would not be able to add a title.

Using Form Formulas

We've characterized a form as a "filter" through which data is entered and displayed. What constitutes a document, in a strict sense, is really an unstructured collection of data (field values) that is maintained separately from the form through which it was created. Consequently, we can display and edit a document through a form other than the one with which the document was originally composed.

When you open a document, what is actually happening? Basically, Notes plugs in the field values of the document (currently in an unstructured state) into the fields of a particular form, creating a structured interface to the data, which is then displayed on the screen. Notes knows which form to couple with the "raw" field values through the value of either the internal fields FORM or $TITLE, or through an alternative method known as *form formulas*.

A form formula is an optional component of a view that specifies the form(s) through which documents in the view will be displayed. If no form formula exists for the view, documents are displayed with either the form indicated by their FORM field (usually the form with which they were composed), the form indicated by their $TITLE field (the form stored with the document), or the default form for the database.

Understanding Form Design

The key to facilitating this type of "hot swap" from form to form is in the design of the forms themselves. If the field values of a document are to be filtered through a series of forms, there must be some consistency in the field definitions across the forms. For example, consider a document composed through Form A. As part of the design of Form A, we've defined several fields, including one named LastName. After composing a document using Form A, we decide to display the document (more accurately, the specific field values in the document) through an alternate Form B.

If the value of the LastName field is one of those fields we wish to display, we must define an identical field LastName in Form B as well. By no means do you have to define *all* the same fields across the two forms that we're discussing in this example. The power of form formulas is that you can selectively "reveal" field values established through one form in another. You are also free to add fields to the design of Form B that do not appear in Form A.

Creating a Form Formula

As we stated above, form formulas are an optional component of a view and are created as part of the view design. In a typical implementation of form formulas, you first design the alternate form (discussed above) and then design a new view that includes a form formula based on the alternate form. An example of a very simple form formula is one that expresses the name of a form in quotation marks, such as `"FormB"`.

To create a form formula, follow these steps:

1. Open a view in Design mode, for instance, the Job Offers from the Jobs database.

2. Click the propeller hat tab to bring up the advanced options.

3. Click the Formula Window button, as shown in Figure 20.26.

4. Enter a form formula in the text box, for instance:

    `FormB`

5. Click OK to accept the formula.

FIGURE 20.26:

Enter a formula in the
Design Form Formula dia-
log box to substitute one
form for another.

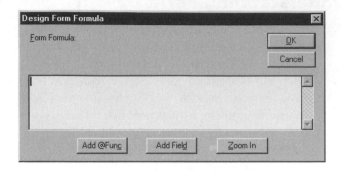

Form Formulas and Selection Formulas

Earlier in the chapter, we discussed the use of selection formulas in order to restrict which documents will appear in a view based on some criteria. If the selection formula utilizes the value of the FORM field to determine inclusion in the view, you must account for this when implementing form formulas. For instance, if you've composed a document using Form A and want to display that document in a view whose form formula is `FormB`, the selection formula for the view would be:

```
SELECT Form = "FormA"
```

This ensures that documents composed with Form A will appear in the view, though they will be *displayed* using Form B.

Some Rules Regarding Form Formulas

You should be aware of a few rules for using form formulas:

- If you modify a form formula, you must reinitialize the view after saving it in order for the modification to take affect. *Reinitialization* is accomplished either by switching to another view and then switching back, or by closing the database and reopening it. This action is not the same as pressing F9 or clicking the reindex icon.

- Documents in which a form is stored are not affected by form formulas—they will always display using the stored form.

- If you open and *modify* a document from a view with a form formula, the value of the internal FORM field for that document will be set to the form expressed in the form formula. This modification has implications in views in which the selection formula is based on the value of FORM.

Editing and Saving a View

The next time you want to edit a database's view, select the database's icon in the Workspace. Then choose View ➤ Design. The list of design objects will appear. Select Views from the Navigation pane, and then select the view you want to edit by double-clicking the view's name. The view window will open.

When you want to edit a column, either double-click the column heading or click the column heading to select it and then right-click to bring up a context-sensitive menu that allows you to edit the properties. You can also select Design ➤ Column Properties from the menu. Make the desired changes and then click the green tick mark, where necessary, to accept the changes. When switching between options in the Properties box, your changes take effect immediately. When you return to the view window, press F9 to refresh the view (or click the refresh icon [the blue arrow] in the heading of the first column) to see if the changes you made have taken effect.

Although you may have clicked the green tick mark in different dialog boxes to accept changes you made to different elements in a view, you still need to save the view before closing it and returning to the Workspace or another open window. When you want to save the changes you made to a view, press Ctrl+S. If you press Esc before you save the changes, a message box will ask if you want to save your changes. Click Yes. You'll return to the Workspace or another window that may be open.

Using Views as Lookup Tables

The usefulness of a view doesn't end at simply being a "table of contents" to the database. A view can also serve as a lookup table that can be integrated into the design of a form.

Consider a typical keywords field in a form. The allowable keywords are usually text items that you specify in the Design Keyword Format dialog box. However, you can automatically build a list of allowable keywords by specifying a formula that returns the contents of a column from one of your views.

Now that you've created the new Job Offers view that displays the Job Offer documents that hiring managers compose, the view can function as a source of choices for the positions available in each department in the Job Application form.

Currently, the Position Applied For field in the form is simply an editable field that users have to fill in manually. However, by redefining the field type as a keyword field (all the departments and job titles could be listed as keywords), a user could choose a department and open position from that list.

Clearly, you do not want to type (and retype) all these lists in the keyword field itself. As a rule, hard coding lists of values forces the database designer to change the form every time a value is added or removed. What we are looking for is a more flexible, dynamic approach to updating the list of departments and job titles in the keywords field. This situation is where using a "lookup" of the contents of a view comes into play.

We are going to add a field allowing applicants to pick from a list of departments and then to select one or more jobs they wish to apply for. Follow these steps to enhance the form:

1. Select the Jobs database and bring up the Application for Employment form in Design mode.

2. Create a field called Department (in the section called Employment Desired) and locate it before the PosApplied field.

3. Make it a keyword field whose selection is by formula. Type the following formula in the text box:

   ```
   @dbcolumn("";"";"JO";1)
   ```

   This formula will look up the list of all departments from the Job Offers view using the first column. In other words, it will dynamically present the list of all the departments that have job openings.

4. Double-click the PosApplied field, change the Data type from Text to Keywords, and select Use Formula for Choices.

5. Select Allow Multi-values and Allow Values Not on the List.

The Properties box now allows you to type a formula in its text box, as shown in Figure 20.27. If you need more space to type (after all these years riveted in front of a computer monitor our eyes are not what they used to be), click the Formula window.

The Properties box for a keyword field allows you to enter a formula to dynamically retrieve a list of keywords from existing documents elsewhere in the database.

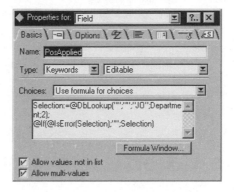

6. Type the following statements:

    ```
    Selection:=@dblookup("";"";"JO";Department;2);
    @If(@IsError(Selection);"";Selection)
    ```

    The first statement retrieves the list of jobs available for the department specified in the previous field. The second line indicates that nothing should be displayed in the keyword list if no department was selected.

7. Press Ctrl+S to save the changes you've made to the form.

Notice that the Use Formula for Choices option has been selected; this option is essential if the allowable keywords will be derived from a formula. By using the @DbColumn function, you instruct Notes to return the contents of column 1 from the Job Offers view, which is the Department column. Now, any time the Job Offers view changes—such as when an entry is added or removed—the list of keywords that is displayed through the Department and Title field in a Job Application document will automatically reflect the change!

This functionality is essential to master. You could also have used this technique to maintain the list indicating the type of salary (Day, Week, Month, Year in the field called SalPeriod) in an administrative view. Many sophisticated Notes applications maintain their list of parameters outside the forms, sometimes even in separate Notes databases that people call "data dictionaries" or "lookup libraries." Of course, it takes longer to write all these @dbcolumn and @dblookup formulas, but in the long run, database maintenance will be easier for users who don't have much knowledge of Notes application development.

TIP

When using data tables located in a separate Notes database, you must coordinate with your Notes administrator to make sure that the external data table databases have replicated wherever your application is distributed, including notebooks. Otherwise your keyword lists will not work. Given this logistical issue, most people tend to place the data tables within their applications but in hidden views. If notebooks use selective replication, make sure you include the data tables in the formula.

Using the Calendar View

The calendar is a view in your Notes mail database that you can use to manage your time and to schedule meetings. You can add appointments, meetings, reminders, events, and anniversaries to the Calendar view. You can also display tasks in the Calendar view.

NOTE

Remember that in version 4.6, the Calendar view is displayed by clicking the Calendar icon.

You can display the Calendar view in four different formats:

- Two days
- One week
- Two weeks
- One month

In Figure 20.28, for example, the Calendar view is displayed in one-week format.

Note that time slots appear on Thursday, April 2. When you display the time slots on a date, Notes displays each time period for which you have scheduled an appointment or meeting as a shaded blue area. If two appointments or meetings overlap, Notes displays a red bar to the left of the conflicting entries.

FIGURE 20.28:

The Calendar view gives you the option of displaying your calendar in two-day, one-week, two-week, or one-month format.

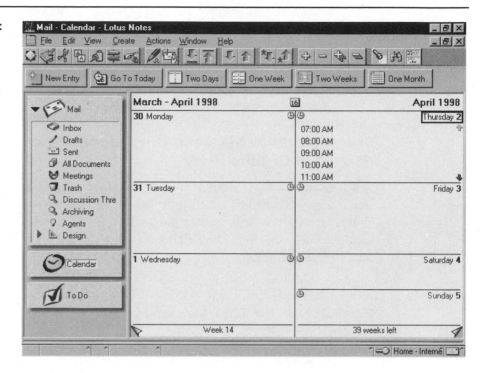

Displaying a View in a Calendar Format

You can display the documents in any view as a calendar instead of as a table or outline. For example, a calendar view can display a date, a meeting or appointment time, a duration, and optional text describing the entry. To display a view as a calendar, the first column must be a Time/Date field.

1. Select the database and choose View ➤ Design.

2. Click Design ➤ Views in the Navigation pane.

3. Double-click the view.

4. Create the first column based on a field with a time/date value. Specify that the view sort according to this column.

5. Create the second column based on a field with a number value that specifies the duration, in minutes, of a calendar entry.

6. Create a view selection formula that selects all documents containing the time/date field.

7. Choose Design ➤ View properties.

8. Select Calendar as the style.

9. Close and save the view.

The Difference between the Calendar View and the Standard Outline View

A Calendar view style is similar to the standard Outline view except that the Calendar view is limited to sorting only on a Time/Date field, which must be the first column in the view. You use the LotusScript IsCalendar property to indicate whether each view in the current database is a Calendar view or a standard Outline view. For example:

```
Dim session As New NotesSession
Dim db As NotesDatabase
Set db = session.CurrentDatabase
Forall view In db.Views
   If view.IsCalendar Then
      Messagebox "Calendar view",, view.Name
   Else
      Messagebox "Standard outline view",, view.Name
   End If
End Forall
```

If Notes returns a True value, the view is a Calendar view. If False, the view is a standard Outline view.

NOTE   See Chapter 34 for a thorough discussion of using LotusScript in designing Notes database views.

The basic features of the calendar view style are:

• Two Day, Week, Two Week, and Month displays, selectable by the end-user

• Point-and-click navigation between days, weeks, and months

• Ability to create new calendar entries and edit existing entries

• Ability to print calendar entries on the current page

- Ability to print a list of calendar entries (this only prints the titles of each entry)

- Ability to print the contents of one or more calendar entries

For example, the Castro Cheesery, a delicatessen and specialty foods store with five locations, maintains a calendar for coffee bean deliveries. For each delivery, a document describes the date, time, and description. A Calendar view displays the delivery documents in one-week, two-week, or one-month format.

NOTE Notes 4.6 offers enhanced the calendar printing capabilities. One option is to print the calendar entries on the current page. This is similar to WYSIWYG. The view that you see is exactly what will be printed. Another option is to print a list of calendar entries. This is accomplished by selecting a date range in the File Print dialog box. Just select the date range and all the entries within the range will be printed. This option will only print the date, time, title of the entry, and an icon identifying the entry type. The last option is to select entries to print. To select an entry, press the Shift key and then click one or more entries (if you do not hold the Shift key, you cannot select documents). Each selected entry document will be printed.

Ways to Display the Calendar

You can navigate and change the display of the Calendar view by

- Turning to a different calendar page

- Displaying the calendar in two-day, one-week, two-week, or one-month format

- Displaying or hiding time slots on a date on the calendar

TIP You can also display a chronological list of your calendar entries. To do so, switch to the Meetings view.

Turning to a Different Calendar Page

To turn backward or forward one page in the Calendar view, do one of the following:

- Click the dog-ear in the bottom left or right corner of the calendar.

- Press Page Up or Page Down.

To turn to a specific date, do one of the following:

- Click the date icon at the top of the calendar and specify the date you want to turn to.
- Choose View ➤ Calendar ➤ Go To, specify the date you want to turn to, and click OK.

To turn to the current date, click Go to Today.

Displaying the Calendar in Two-Day, One-Week, Two-Week, or One-Month Format

To display the Calendar view in two-day, one-week, two-week, or one-month format, click Two Days, One Week, Two Weeks, or One Month, respectively.

TIP   When you display the calendar in two-day, one-week, or two-week format, you can also display or hide time slots on a date by clicking the clock icon in the top-left or right corner of the date.

Displaying or Hiding Time Slots on a Date on the Calendar

To display or hide time slots on a date on the calendar, do the following:

1. Click the date.
2. Choose View ➤ Calendar ➤ Show Time Slots.

You can also choose a calendar display format from the View ➤ Calendar menu.

Understanding and Creating Folders

This may be the shortest section of the entire book! In a nutshell, a folder is just like a view—except it doesn't have a selection criteria. Folders can be of the type Shared, Personal, or Shared, Personal on First Use. The Search Builder works the same way as it does in a view. Formatting is identical. You create folders and define columns the same way. So what's the difference between a folder and a view?

- You can drag a document from a view or folder into a folder, but not into a view. If you are looking for a "most salient point" (to quote Steve Jobs), that's it.

- Instead of creating categories to sort your documents, create personal folders. We find them useful when dealing with very large databases, such as our mail file or a knowledge base.

- Notes represents folders with, you guessed it, a small icon that looks like a folder. The views appear as a magnifying glass—or a frying pan to some.

- The word *folder* has a lot more curb appeal than the word *view*.

Congratulations! You have officially mastered the concept of a folder.

Understanding Navigators

As you saw in Chapters 14 and 15 (which cover the design elements of Notes and the ability to build a workflow), Navigators play an important role within Notes, but they are more than a pretty face to simplify switching from one view to another. In fact, Navigators give you the ability to design a custom user interface for your Notes database without using other development tools such as Visual Basic. Combined with Actions (a special Notes object covered in the next chapter), Navigators give you complete control over how a user interacts with a database. You can manipulate the flow of the application, deciding what users can do and see from the moment they first click the database icon to the moment they close the application. To say that we are excited about Navigators would be an understatement!

TIP   Think of Navigators in terms of blank pages that can contain geometrical shapes and images that can be clicked, invoking whatever action (note the lowercase) you can dream up. You can create as many Navigators as you wish and connect them so that one Navigator can call another.

In most cases, a full-page Navigator will lead to other Navigators; the last one in the chain will most likely display a view in the right pane of the window.

In Chapter 17, we discussed the importance of laying out a form ahead of time. The same holds true for Navigators. Figure 20.29 shows a sketch of a series of Navigators and their interactions with the application.

Notes has two major types of Navigators: those that open in their own windows (i.e., full screen) and those that open in a pane, next to a view you select.

FIGURE 20.29:

Lay out the flow of your Navigators on paper before starting development.

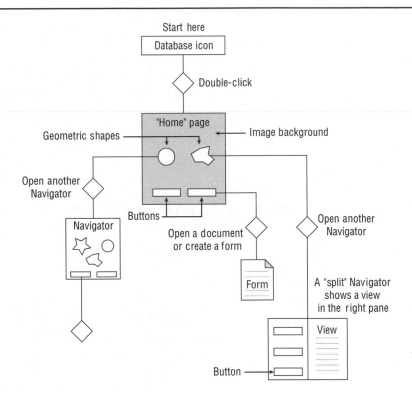

Full-Screen Navigators

A full-screen Navigator is displayed over the entire window, without any other pane opened. These Navigators can be used to greet users of a database with a home page, to use the Web terminology. This top-level Navigator should be clear and appealing—it is the entry point to the whole database and you want to entice people to go on! For instance, from this Navigator, users should be able to click and

- Access "families" of views

- Access help, disclaimers, greetings, warnings, or instruction documents
- Create the most important documents, if they do not require any other information contained within the documents of the database (e.g., a generic request for more information)

NOTE   The Hide-When functionality described in the previous chapters on forms is unfortunately not available in Navigators. You cannot change the display of a Navigator or its elements based on the membership of a user to a given group. Similarly, you cannot make the display of a Navigator context sensitive, for example, based on the documents contained in the database.

Split-Screen Navigators

This type of Navigator, the most common, replaces the hierarchical listing of views and folders in the left pane, as shown in Figure 20.30.

FIGURE 20.30:

A split-screen Navigator replaces the listing of views and folders with a graphical interface.

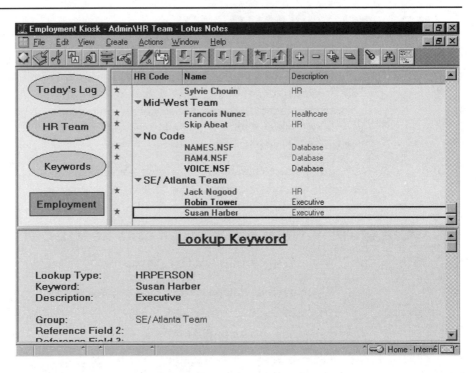

Note that you can place any image of geometrical shape in the left pane, as many as will fit within a screen. Keep in mind though, that some of your users may have 640×480 displays (such as notebook users), so don't place essential functionality too far down the Navigator. Split-screen Navigators provide you with a very intuitive way to guide users through what they could perceive as a maze of views. While it is worthwhile spending time creating sophisticated graphic buttons, keep in mind that simple ovals, such as those shown in Figure 20.30, suffice to dramatically improve the flow of the application.

TIP	
	Keep a consistent color scheme as a background for Navigators and their objects. For instance, if the background of the Administration rectangle that leads to the Administration Navigator is yellow, make sure that the rectangle or the background of the Administration Navigator is also yellow. This color coding provides a not-so-subtle, but effective, subliminal message.

Creating a Navigator

The good news is that you won't have to write much code. The bad news is that you need to have a very clear sense of the flow of the application and know your artistic limitations. If your views tend to look like the example in Figure 20.12, stick to simple rectangles and basic colors. If you cannot sketch out how most people will interact with your database, you may create more confusion and frustration with Navigators than without.

We are going to create two Navigators within our Jobs database: first a homepage with a few tricks and then a split-view Navigator.

Creating a New Navigator and Setting Its Properties

Follow these steps to create a new Navigator:

1. Open the Jobs database from the companion disk.

2. Choose Create ➤ Design ➤ Navigator. The Navigator Design window will appear, as shown in Figure 20.31.

3. Choose Design ➤ Navigator Properties to display the Properties box, as shown in Figure 20.32. Type **Home** in the Name text box.

FIGURE 20.31:

The Navigator Design window allows you to place Navigator objects on a blank page.

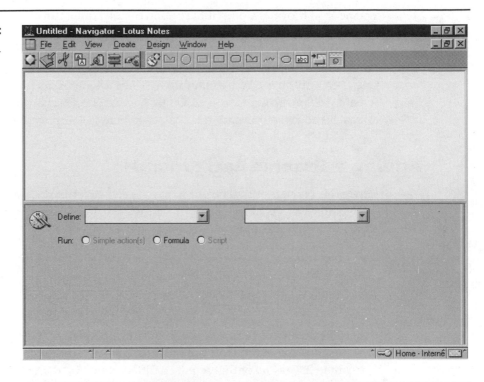

FIGURE 20.32:

Set the name and the initial view of a Navigator in the Navigator Properties box.

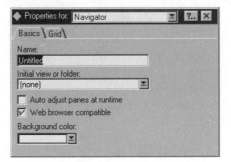

4. The option to set the Initial view or folder is used only in split-screen Navigators. But we want to create a full-screen Navigator first, so leave it at (none).

5. The Auto Adjust Panes at Runtime option means that Notes will display the views or folders wherever there is empty space to the right of the Navigator. This option is most useful with split-screen Navigators. Leave it unchecked.

We are now ready to start adding some objects to the Navigator.

The Web Browser Compatible option on the Navigator Properties Basics tab is new in Notes 4.6. If you are going to use a Navigator on a Web page, you must select this property. With this setting selected, Domino can translate the Navigator into an HTM image map. All the objects on the Navigator (except for polygons) will behave the same way on the Web as they do in Notes. Using a Navigator is an easy way to create Web image maps. You no longer have to specify coordinates for "clickable" areas, because the translation to the image map is completed for you.

Adding a Graphic Background

Since this Navigator will be our home page, we want to add an image or some nice pattern as a background to the entire Navigator. There are a few issues to consider when choosing the image for the background:

- Notes doesn't know how to resize an image to fit the screen. This means that while it may look OK on a notebook with a 640×480 size screen, it will be too small for the higher resolutions of desktop screens. You should use an image that will fill up the entire screen of the highest resolution available at your site.

- The quality of the background image depends on the number of colors the users are able to display on their machines. Avoid images that require more than 256 colors or that require a different palette than the default Lotus Notes palette. Older computers may be able to display only sixteen colors.

- Color images are large and take disk space. This means that every replica copy of the database will include those Navigator images. And worst of all, the dial-up notebook users will need to pull down the image over a slow modem line—a frustrating experience if they are accessing the Notes server online.

For your convenience, we have included a 256-color, 640×480 image on the companion disk. To proceed to create a graphic background, follow these steps:

1. Open the Da Big Library database from the companion disk.

2. Open the For Your Viewing Enjoyment document in the All Document view.

3. Double-click the attached file. The Attachment property box will appear.

4. Click View to launch the attachment viewer add-in program.

5. Choose Edit ➤ Select All and then Edit ➤ Copy. The image will be placed in the Clipboard. Select File ➤ Close to terminate the viewer.

6. Click the Close Action button and choose File ➤ Close to close the Library database.

7. Switch to the Design Navigator window and choose Create ➤ Graphic Background. The Navigator will display your image, as shown in Figure 20.33.

8. Choose File ➤ Save to save your work.

FIGURE 20.33:

You can use an image as a graphic background to a Navigator.

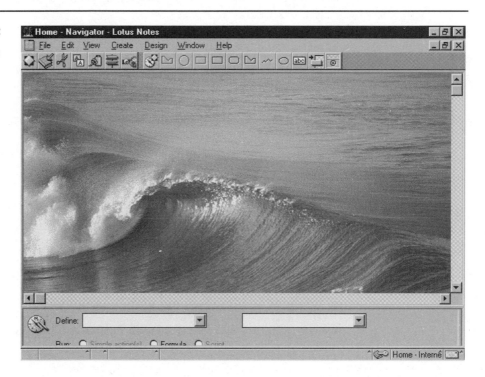

Now that we placed a background to our "canvas," we are ready to add some objects to the Navigator.

Adding Hotspots to a Navigator

Hotspots are areas of the Navigator that are highlighted automatically when you drag your mouse over them. A hotspot is a transparent polygon (that's a shape with as many corners as you wish, for those of us who dozed off during math class) or a circle (new to Notes 4.6) that you can draw on top of any graphical background.

For instance, you could display a map of Europe and manually draw a polygon around the borders of each country. A Notes Action hides behind each polygon.

Note that you can use five hotspot types:

- Polygon hotspots
- Rectangular hotspots—the answer to the question, "What is a polygon with only four corners?"
- Circular hotspots
- Button hotspots, prepackaged hotspots that are not transparent
- Graphic button hotspots

NOTE   Polygon objects display on the Web, but clicking them has no effect.

Follow these steps to add hotspots to your homepage:

1. Open the Home Navigator from the Jobs database if it isn't already on your screen.

2. Select the first red icon labeled Create Hotspot Polygon in the bubble help (displayed whenever you leave your mouse cursor over the SmartIcon for a few instants).

3. Click anywhere on the edge of the foam in the wave and repeat your clicks until you've drawn a line all around it. Then double-click to close the sides of your polygon.

4. Continue defining areas as shown in Figure 20.34—especially if you are a surfer or are still amused by polygonal hotspots.

5. Choose Create ➤ Button. Place it anywhere on the screen, as also shown in Figure 20.34.

TIP   If you want truly good-looking buttons, create them using a separate paint program, place them in the Clipboard, and choose Create ➤ Graphic Button.

Once you lay out the hotspots on a graphical background, you need to set their properties—otherwise, no action will take place when users highlight or click them!

FIGURE 20.34:

Use hotspots to mark areas of a graphical background in a Navigator.

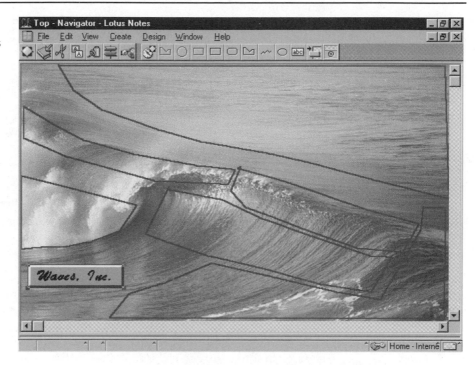

FIGURE 20.34:

Use hotspots to mark areas of a graphical background in a Navigator.

Setting the Properties of Hotspots

You need to set the behavior of the hotspot when a user moves a mouse over it or clicks on it.

Follow these steps to bring life to your hotspots:

1. Double-click the button in the Home Navigator to bring up the Properties box.

2. In the Basics page, name the button Go and write a caption such as the name of our fictitious company, Waves, Inc.

3. In the second tab, Fonts, pick a large pitch, such as 18, and bold.

4. In the third tab, Look, pick a new face for the button, such as light blue. Increase the bevel width to make the button truly stand out. Keep the outline color as black.

5. In the last tab, shown in Figure 20.35, select Highlight When Touched; do not select Highlight When Clicked. Set the outline color to red.

FIGURE 20.35:

The Properties box for Navigator hotspots lets you indicate how the hotspots will look when users select or click on them.

Repeat these steps for the other hotspots you have defined on top of your graphic background. You are now ready to assign some actions to the hotspot.

Setting the Action for a Hotspot

As with most objects in Notes, you need to assign either a Simple action, an @function formula, or LotusScript to hotspots. We are going to connect the button we just created to another Navigator (already in the Jobs database from the companion disk) using a Simple action and then show you the use of formulas with a hotspot.

> **NOTE**   The Simple Actions available from a Navigator are Open Another Navigator, Open a View, Alias a Folder, Open a Link, or Open a URL.

The Jobs database contains another Navigator called HR, a split-screen Navigator used to control the flow of the essential elements of the database. We could have made the HR Navigator the homepage, but we wanted a little more sizzle, given that this application is essentially meant to entice people to apply for a job at our company, Waves, Inc. After all, not everybody is interested swimming with the sharks.

If it isn't already on your screen, bring up the Home Navigator in Design mode and then follow these steps to assign actions to the hotspots:

1.   Select the button and display the Formula pane.

2. Select Open Another Navigator as an Action and choose HR from the list of available choices.

TIP   The last icon in the SmartIcon bar (assuming you are using the default SmartIcon settings) toggles the Formula pane on and off.

---

3. Click any visible polygon hotspot, select Formula as a Run Option in the Formula pane and type the following line, as shown in Figure 20.36:

```
@Prompt([Ok];"Tranquility...";"A good place to hang out awaiting
➡ the next wave.")
```

This will prompt users with your message whenever they click the area you defined.

FIGURE 20.36:

Enter an action for a hotspot using the Formula pane in the Navigator Design window.

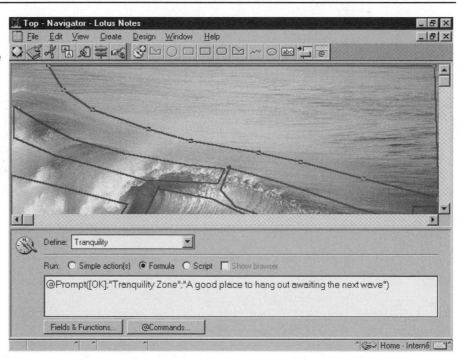

You are now ready to see if the Navigator is performing as expected.

Testing the Navigator

Notes Release 4 allows you to quickly test your design work without actually saving it. You can check that everything functions as planned without having to make multiple backups of your work. You may recall using this feature while creating forms.

To test your new Home Navigator, simply choose Design ➤ Test Navigator. Your hotspots will highlight when you move your mouse on top of them.

NOTE   Clicking the Navigator objects will not actually execute any formula or Simple action. Instead, a dialog box will tell you what Notes would do if it weren't in Test mode, for instance, "Switches to Navigator HR" or "Runs a Formula."

If everything works as predicted, save your Navigator by choosing File ➤ Save.

You have just completed your first Navigator using hotspots and a graphical background. Equally important, but more common, is a split-screen Navigator that graphically eases the switching of views.

Creating a Split-Screen Navigator

The concept is essentially the same as the full-screen Navigator, with one exception: Auto Adjust Panes at Runtime is not selected when using a split-screen Navigator. That way, whatever view is displayed will show in a pane to the right of the Navigator.

You can create a simple split-screen Navigator by following these steps (note that we are skipping over the detailed steps already covered above):

1. Choose Create ➤ Design ➤ Navigator in the Jobs database.

2. Call it **Administration** in the Properties box and set the initial view or folder to Admin\Daily Log.

3. Select Auto Adjust Panes at Runtime.

4. Place three ovals in the leftmost part of the screen, as shown in Figure 20.37, by choosing Create ➤ Ellipse.

5. Name the ellipses, respectively, Today's Log, HR Team, and Keywords.

FIGURE 20.37:

You can add geometrical shapes to a Navigator to facilitate navigating between views.

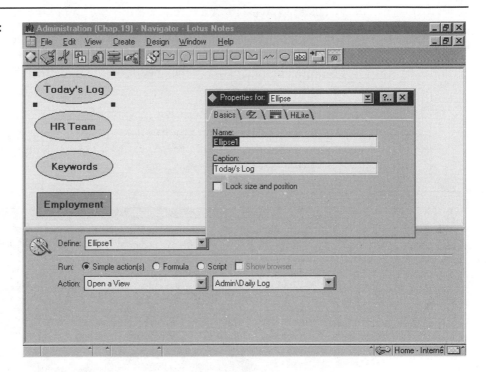

6. Place a rectangle at the bottom of the column of ellipses, as shown in Figure 20.37, and name it Employment.

7. Change the color of the ellipses to yellow and the color of the rectangle to light blue. These colors are consistent with the HR Navigator.

8. Select each ellipse in turn and in the Formula pane set a Simple action to open a view for the respective matching view names, as shown in Figure 20.37.

9. Set the Simple action of the rectangle to open the HR Navigator.

You now have a fully functional split-screen Navigator, or at least you may think you do. There is only one way to tell—choose Design ➤ Test Navigator and click the Ellipses and Rectangle. If everything looks right, save the Navigator by choosing File ➤ Save. That testing is, however, rather rudimentary. For a full test, you need to actually run the Navigator in full production mode by following these steps:

1. Select View ➤ Show ➤ Home (the Navigator you completed, or use Top, which came with the application on the companion disk).

2. Click the Waves, Inc. button. It should take you to the HR Navigator. Note the list of Jobs in the right pane.

3. Click the Administration button. It should take you to the Administration Navigator you created or the one that came with the Jobs database, as shown in Figure 20.38.

If everything is working properly, you've just mastered the art of creating Navigators. There is one more thing to do—if your Navigators are working right. You need to force your database to open in your Home Navigator, rather than in the standard list of views and forms.

FIGURE 20.38:

The split-screen Navigator shows a graphical alternative to the list of views and forms in the left pane, showing the view in the right pane.

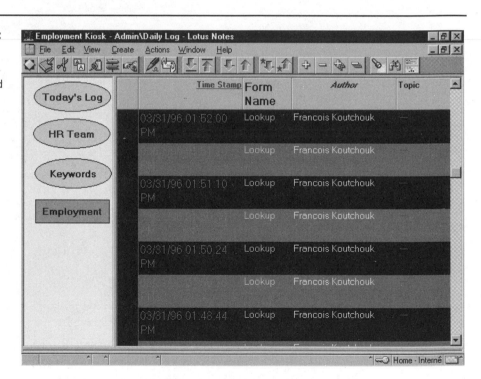

Launching a Navigator Automatically

In Release 4, you can control what will be displayed when you open a database. Figure 20.39 shows the Launch tab with your choices:

Restore as Last Viewed by User: Restore the same view the user last opened, displaying the standard views and folders in the left pane. This is the default mode.

The Database Properties dialog box allows you to launch an event automatically when opening the database.

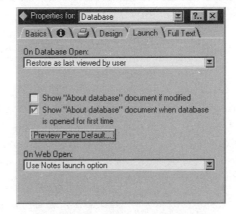

Open "About Database" Document: You can use this option as an alternative to creating a Home Navigator. However, the graphical tools available to you are much more limited. For more information on the About document, please see Chapter 26 on rolling out Notes applications to users.

Open Designated Navigator: The most common way to open a database is to link the opening of the database event to a specified Navigator. It allows you to place a split-screen Navigator in the full screen. The space normally occupied by the view will be filled with whatever background color you selected for the Navigator.

Open Designated Navigator in Its Own Window: The use of this method is a little counterintuitive. All the Navigators chained to the specified Navigator will also open full screen, regardless of their design properties. The view will show the views and folders list in the left pane. When closing a view, Notes will return you to the last Navigator that called the view, still full screen.

Launch 1st Attachment in "About Database": Whatever file you attach to the About document will be launched automatically. For example a word-processing file could bring up a form used to register the user into the system. A utility could be used to invoke code that looks up the hardware setting of the machine.

Launch 1st Doclink in "About Database": You can place a doclink in the About Document that opens a Notes document automatically.

WARNING You cannot place an OLE object in the About document. Be careful when attaching an executable, since it will run automatically without authorization and could contain potentially undesirable effects—or even a virus.

 Notes 4.6 has added a couple of new options to the Database Properties Launch tab. The first is the ability to set the Preview pane for the database. As mentioned in Chapter 3, you can preview the contents of a document in the Preview pane. With the Preview Pane property, you can set whether the Preview pane will display on the bottom right, the bottom, or the right. This can alter where the Navigator and View pane will display.

The second new option, On Web Open, is essentially the same as the On Database Open except you can control what is displayed when the database is opened from the Web. Your choices are:

Use Notes Launch Option: Defaults to the same option specified for the On Database Open.

Open "About Database" Document: Uses the About This Database as the opening page.

Open Designated Navigator: Uses a specified Navigator as the opening page.

Launch First Doclink in "About Database": Uses the first document link in "About Database" as the opening page.

Launch Designated Doclink: This is something of a misnomer since you can paste a document, view, or database link. This link can be from any database on the server as the opening page. Use Edit ➤ Copy as Link ➤ Document Link/View Link/Database Link to copy the link to the Clipboard, select Launch Designated Doclink from the On Web Open list, then click Paste Doclink.

Launch First Document in View: Use the first document in a designated view as the opening page.

To complete this section on Navigators, go to the Workspace and follow these steps:

1. Select the icon of the Jobs database that came on the companion disk.

2. Right-click to display the Database Properties dialog box.

3. Click the Launch tab to display the Launch properties for the database.

4. Select Open Designated Navigator on Database Open.

5. Pick the Navigator called Top or Home, if you feel your Navigator is complete.

6. Close all windows and reopen the Jobs database. It will open with the Waves, Inc. homepage.

Using Navigators is necessary to take full advantage of the functionality of Notes Release 4. We hope you agree that creating Navigators is relatively simple and highly rewarding in terms of the simplification they add to the use of a database.

What's Next?

A well-thought-out set of Navigators dramatically improves the flow of a database and leverages the work done in views. Elegant Navigators add a professional touch to applications at a very limited cost in terms of development. Navigators also reduce the amount of training you will need to provide when you roll out your applications (the topic of Chapter 26).

You may have noticed that we did not use Navigator objects to launch complex processes, or even to compose a form. Although we had the capability to run any formula or even to execute LotusScript, we restricted our Navigators to things like displaying a simple Prompt dialog box or switching between Navigators and views. Although there is no technical reason not to place a lot of functionality behind the Navigators, we prefer to let Navigators "navigate" through the application and to have Actions "act" on the information. If this sounds all too suspicious, move on to the next chapter where you'll learn how Actions work. Then you can decide for yourself how much functionality to incorporate in your Navigators.

CHAPTER

TWENTY-ONE

21

Creating Custom Actions

■ Understanding the role of Actions

■ Using Actions to represent possible tasks

■ Setting Action properties

■ Creating an Action

■ Programming a custom Action

■ Putting drop-down lists on the Action bar

Actions are workflow-oriented programming elements that provide an easy way to associate intelligent buttons with a form or a view. Conceptually, Actions are very similar to buttons that you place within a form, but they allow you to convey the flow of your application more clearly by virtue of their prominent presence within the Notes desktop.

Actions fall into the same category as Navigators, which we reviewed in the previous chapter; they are nice to have, but not essential. In other words, you don't have to use Actions to access important Notes functionality, but if you ignore Actions, you miss quite an opportunity to enhance your database with very little effort. Because Actions are essentially graphical design elements (as opposed to core design elements, such as columns or fields), there is no hard and fast rule on when to use them. The purpose of this chapter is to help you understand Actions and to illustrate their use.

We are going to cover the following topics:

- Understanding Actions
- Creating and setting the properties of Actions
- Programming custom Actions

Understanding Actions

Actions reside on an icon bar underneath the Lotus SmartIcon bar, as shown in Figure 21.1. Both icon bars contain small buttons that you can click to invoke predefined functionality. Both are context sensitive, and both are programmable.

The term *Action* is confusing in itself—but not as much as the role of Actions compared to similar Notes design elements such as SmartIcons, Agents, and regular buttons placed on views and forms.

FIGURE 21.1:

The Action bar is below the SmartIcon bar.

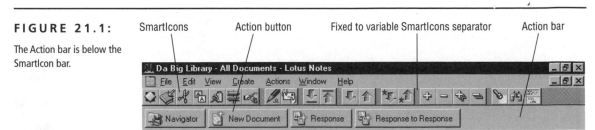

SmartIcons   Action button   Fixed to variable SmartIcons separator   Action bar

Defining the Term Action

The most confusing part about Actions is the use of the word itself. Notes uses the term in several areas of the product for different purposes. You may recall from the chapters on forms and views that it is possible to invoke some Notes functionality using formulas, LotusScript, or Simple actions. Unfortunately, those *actions* have nothing to do with the *Actions* we are talking about in this chapter. To further confuse you, it is possible to assign Simple actions to an Action. If you have particularly sharp eyes, you may notice the subtle difference as you read:

- (Simple) actions are in lowercase.

- Actions are in uppercase.

As we have seen in previous chapters, and will see in much more detail in Chapter 23, Simple actions embed common programming tasks that you would otherwise have to write using @function formulas or LotusScript. With a few clicks, Simple actions can walk you through programming the modification of a field or the selection of certain documents.

Actions, the topic of this chapter, are specific design elements serving a well-defined purpose in your database.

The Difference between Agents and Actions

Agents (covered in Chapter 23) are mostly used to run a process on a Notes server. In other words, an Agent is a design element containing Notes code (for instance a formula) that runs in the background—either on a predefined schedule or whenever a certain event occurs in a specified database. An Agent can, for example, notify you via e-mail any time your boss adds a document to a meeting minutes database. An Agent can also automatically move expired or closed contract documents to an archive database.

In contrast, Actions require your intervention to run. They cannot run any code without somebody clicking on them, and the code will always run on the local machine—never on the server. Technically, Actions can run the same code as Agents because they (Actions) also support the three modes of Notes programming: Simple actions, formulas, and LotusScript. However, in addition to appearing as menu commands, Actions can appear as buttons on top of forms or views in an area called the Action bar.

To muddy the waters just a little, there is such a thing as an Agent that runs from the menu, just like an Action, that you can manually invoke and execute on your local machine. Moreover, such an Agent will be listed as a command underneath the Action menu option, thinly separated from the "real" Actions, but separated nonetheless, by a fine dividing line. And, if that isn't confusing enough, you can call an Agent from an Action with the function:

```
@Command([ToolsRunMacro];"myAgent")
```

Table 21.1 tells you when to use an Agent and when to use an Action.

TABLE 21.1: So When Do You Use an Action Instead of an Agent?

Use an Agent	Use an Action
When you want to run an automated process on the server that is either time driven or event driven	When you need a button to simplify the launching of an Agent
When a large number of documents will be affected by your process and you do not want users to have to wait	To assist a user with the major steps of an application
For infrequent processes, in particular administrative tasks	In any other situation

The Difference between SmartIcons and Actions

The origin of SmartIcons was to provide one-click or keystroke access to complex tasks, as opposed to forcing the user to make selections from a series of cascading menus. The icons often symbolize functions that would otherwise be difficult to find in the menus or would require multiple steps. For instance, to attach a file to a Notes rich text field, all you need to do is click the intuitive Paperclip icon.

In Notes Release 4, the list of icons displayed on the SmartIcon bar is *Notes context sensitive.* The bar has two parts: the left side that stays constant throughout your Notes session and the right side (separated by a space) that varies according to what you are doing in Notes. This context-sensitive behavior is true regardless of the Notes database that you are using.

Think of Actions in a similar way except that Actions are *database context sensitive.* In other words, the list of icons that is displayed on the bar will vary from database to database, and even better, from form to form or view to view within a database. The good news is that you have complete control over the number of Actions and their functionality. And most important, Actions replicate with the database—in contrast to SmartIcons, which are not easy to distribute.

Taking Advantage of SmartIcons

The Notes SmartIcons are preprogrammed (or custom) keyboard shortcuts. SmartIcons were originally created by Lotus to create a consistent interface throughout its products (1-2-3, Freelance Graphics, Approach, Word Pro, and Notes).

Users fortunate enough to remember the meaning of a vast array of tiny icons found them invaluable in speeding up their daily routines. Others simply turned them off. To turn off the entire Icon bar in Release 4, choose File ➤ Tools ➤ SmartIcons and deselect the Icon Bar checkbox. You can also deselect the Context Icons and Bubble Help (descriptions) from this dialog box as well.

Even though the SmartIcons could be positioned in a "floating" window, most people elected to keep them attached to the top or bottom of their screen. That's because floating icons always seemed to get in the way in the Notes desktop. A fixed SmartIcons bar, however, limited the number of icons that could be displayed at any time. Consequently, only a finite set of icons could be displayed, and users had to manually rotate among sets of SmartIcons depending on what they were doing.

Release 4 keeps the space restriction on fixed SmartIcon bars but introduces context-sensitive icons. The set of context-sensitive icons automatically changes when you are editing a document versus designing a form. That flexibility ought to convince many menu-only users to convert to SmartIcons. Unfortunately, there is no programmatic way to force the SmartIcon bar on a user who has turned it off. (The @Command([SmartIconsFloating]) does bring up the SmartIcons but accepts no parameter and won't work if the user has clicked off the floating bar.)

One overwhelming problem with custom SmartIcons is that they are truly personal tools. If you wish to introduce a SmartIcon to multiple users, you need to physically install it on each machine. Each custom SmartIcon (developed with formulas) requires two files, a 22-by-22-pixel .BMP image file (if you are not using the macro buttons provided by Notes) and a .MAC file containing its formula. Those files must be placed in the appropriate Notes data subdirectory (\w32 in NT, \OS2 in OS/2, etc.). Clearly, the distribution of custom SmartIcons is a logistical nightmare.

We have seen the successful use of custom SmartIcons in situations where an installer physically accessed each desktop, for instance, in a medical environment where physicians typically do not have a high level of computer experience. In this type of setting, you can tie SmartIcons into existing work habits for such things as dialing telephone numbers or connecting to electronic schedules.

Custom SmartIcons also exist in situations where IS centrally upgrades all corporate users. Other successful users of custom SmartIcons include groups of advanced Notes users who share them in an informal way by passing around diskettes. The most common type of custom SmartIcons invokes another application that inserts an object into a rich text field, for instance, invoking Visio to create a drawing of a network topology.

The Purpose of Actions

We said that Actions are basically buttons located on a bar below the SmartIcons that derive their functionality from the design of individual views and forms. In other words, it is possible to assign functionality otherwise embedded within the design of a view or a form into the Action bar. So when should you use Actions instead of plain buttons? The technical answer is wherever you feel like it! In reality, Navigator button hotspots, form buttons, and Actions all have their specific best uses.

Differences between Form Buttons and Actions

You may recall from the discussion of designing dynamic forms in Chapter 19 that it is possible to create buttons within a form that invoke whatever process you need. Those buttons contain as much Notes code as you wish, either as Simple actions, formulas, or LotusScripts.

Form buttons are *inline*, that is, within the form itself, permanently positioned wherever you place them. If the form expands to multiple screens, you would need to scroll through the form to display and use its buttons. This requirement is not a problem if the purpose of the button relates only to a few fields surrounding it (e.g., a button that allows the editor of a document to add a variable number of days to a field containing the deadline). But it is a problem if the use of the button applies to the entire document (e.g., a button that mails a document after verifying that all the appropriate data has been entered).

Buttons should be used in the following situations:

- The scope of their functionality is restricted to an area of the form rather than the entire form.

- They provide nonessential functionality to the document. *Essential* refers to the importance of the feature for the proper functioning of the form, not the number of users needing it.

Actions, therefore, should be used in the following situations:

- The form does not fit on one page of a 640 × 480 screen.

- The functionality is important enough to warrant using space on the screen.

- The impact of using the action relates to the entire form. This does not mean that its impact is on all the fields—just that the document is considered in its entirety.

Differences between Navigator Button Hotspots and Actions

You may recall from the discussion of Navigators in Chapter 20 that it is possible to add a button to a Navigator. In fact, you can add many other objects that contain Notes code to a Navigator—such as, Simple actions, formulas, or LotusScripts. Unfortunately, the line between Navigator hotspots and Actions is much more subjective than the line between Actions and forms.

Use Navigator hotspots in the following situations:

- The application indicates a navigational need (e.g., asking a question and then switching to another Navigator or view).

- The result of clicking on the hotspot is a one-time only task (e.g., registering users the first time they use the database).

- The Navigator is used in its own window (i.e., without a view displayed in the right pane).

Consequently, Actions should be used in a view in the following situations:

- The functionality is important enough to warrant using space on the screen. At the risk of being boring: Don't clutter your screen!

- The impact of using the Action relates to the entire view. This does not mean that its impact is on all the documents—just that the view is considered in its entirety.

- The Action is not valid to all the views referenced by the Navigator.

- The limited available space on the Action bar still allows the use of an icon or a description that will make the purpose of the Action clear to most users.

Using Actions

In general, we recommend that you use Actions for the following purposes:

- To combine multiple steps into one simple click. In other words, if a form always requires the same sequence of actions, combine them in one Action that walks the user through the entire process.

Continued on next page

For instance, in a stock portfolio application you may need to (1) refresh the data from a live source of quotes, (2) rebuild the computed values in the appropriate analysis Notes documents, (3) export a summary to the accounting database, and (4) send alarms and other notifications via e-mail to the managers.

- To display the essential steps or processes available or required by a view or form.

For instance, if the choices available to a manager reviewing a document are Approve, Ask for More Information, or Deny, then create three Actions. Similarly, you can use Actions to display the list of possible forms a user can compose from a view.

Now that you have a good idea of where and when to use Actions, it is time to build your first Action.

Setting the Properties of Actions

Action building is similar to building most Notes design elements. You begin by setting the properties, and then define the code.

You can build two types of Actions: those using a System Command and those that you fully define yourself. The main difference is that—you guessed it—you cannot change the code of the definition of the System Command actions. But their properties are identical.

Setting the Properties for Actions

Since Actions are associated with a specific view or form, you need to define them by placing a view or form in Design mode. Follow these steps to define the properties of a System Command Action:

1. Open the Jobs database from the companion disk.

2. Open the Job Offers view in Design mode.

3. Display the available Actions, shown in Figure 21.2, by selecting View ➤ Action Pane (you can also click the vertical separator bar and slide it over or double-click the vertical separator bar to display the Action Pane). Note that all System Command Actions start with a star (*) and that it is not possible to modify their code in the Design pane.

FIGURE 21.2:

The Action pane displays the available Actions in a view. The Design pane shows what code will run.

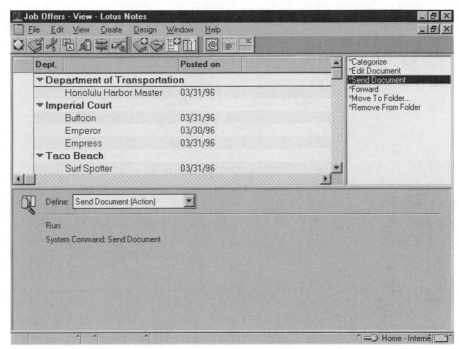

TIP

You can't delete the System Command Actions but you can disable them so that they are not available to the users of the application.

TIP

System Command Actions will not be displayed on the Web. To overcome this, create your own Action Button that mimics the System Command Action.

4. Display the Properties box (shown in Figure 21.3) for the Forward (mail) Action by selecting Design ➤ Action Properties (you can also double-click the Action).

5. Change the title from _Forward to _Send Copy. The underscore character (_) is an accelerator key that allows the user to type the letter *S* in the Actions menu to invoke the Action.

6. Pick a button icon from those shown in Figure 21.4. Try to select a button that indicates that you are sending this document via e-mail; in this case, the second button in the top row is appropriate.

FIGURE 21.3:

You can define the attributes of Actions in the Properties box.

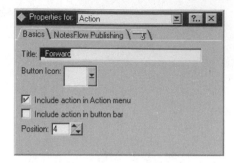

FIGURE 21.4:

Notes provides 156 icons for your Actions.

NOTE   You cannot modify or add icons to the list provided by Notes.

7. Include the Action in both the menu and the button bar and place it in the first position. Try to position the Actions in either their order of importance or the order in which the user should invoke them.

8. Save the view by pressing Ctrl+S.

9. Switch to the Job Offers view. It will automatically display a bar below the SmartIcons and the new Action button, as shown in Figure 21.5.

The Action button is now fully functional. When pressed, it will create a new mail memo that includes the entire contents of whichever Job Offer you were positioned on.

FIGURE 21.5:

The Action bar is displayed automatically with a new Action.

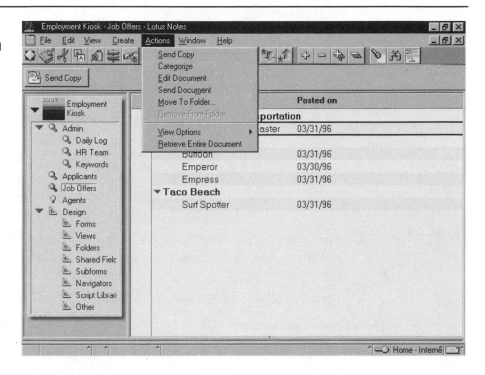

You may want to disable other System Command Actions available by default in all views, in particular Send Document and Categorize. Send Document will not work on this view because the Job Offer does not contain a Send To field. Similarly, Categorize will return a rather cryptic error because there is neither a category field in the forms nor a column sort that uses a category field in the view. To disable System Command Actions, simply deselect the checkbox options.

Setting the Properties for the Action Bar

You noticed that the Action bar appeared automatically when you tested the view with the new Send Copy Action. The bar's default background color is Background, and a thin line separates it from the Navigator pane and the View pane.

If you feel strongly about color coordination, or otherwise wish to customize the Action bar's appearance, follow these steps:

1. Open the Job Offers view from the Jobs database in Design mode.

2. Choose View ➤ Action Pane.

3. Choose Design ➤ Action Bar Properties. The Properties box will appear as shown in Figure 21.6.

FIGURE 21.6:

You can change the presentation of the Action bar through the Properties box.

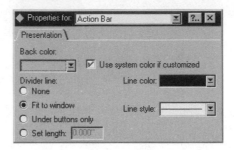

4. Pick a background color. Notes kindly names the color as you select it, avoiding artistic faux pas such as calling something pink when, in fact, it is apple blossom or flamingo.

5. Choose a color for the line, pick a larger width, and place it Under Buttons Only.

6. Save the view.

When you reenter the database, the new Action—with its perfectly trendy Action bar (grape on apple blossom)—shows up on top of the full-screen Navigator. The Navigator did not select a default view because the Job Offers view is the default view. In other words, the choice was made for you without your asking. This is another case where the distinction between an unwanted feature and a bug tends to blur.

NOTE   If you select an alternate color but leave the Use System Color If Customized option checked, your selected color will not display but will default to the system color.

Setting the Hide-When Property for Actions

You may recall from Chapter 19 that the Hide-When function allows you to tailor the display of a design element to its use and that you can hide the object if it is being read or edited. You should take advantage of these simple Hide-When options with Actions (see Figure 21.7). For instance, an Action that places a document in Edit mode should not be visible when the document is already in Edit mode.

FIGURE 21.7:

Use the Hide-When property of an Action to control when it will be displayed.

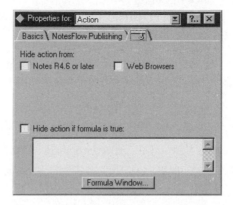

If the condition of the display of an Action is more complex than the read or edit condition, you need to extend its use with @function formulas. Granted, the Hide-When functionality is never trivial because it requires a formula that returns a value of True, but by now you should feel comfortable with writing basic Notes formulas. (Refer to Chapter 18 to brush up on formulas.)

At this point, we want to force the Send Copy button to appear only when we are in the Job Offers view, not in the default view that opens automatically when a user double-clicks the icon of the Jobs database.

To disable the display of the Send Copy Action, follow these steps:

1. Open the Job Offers view from the Jobs database in Design mode.

2. Display the Action pane and select the Send Copy Action.

3. Bring up the Properties box and click the Hide tab.

4. Select Hide Action If the @Function Formula is True and type the following formula:

```
!@Contains(@ViewTitle;"Offers")
```

The @ViewTitle function returns the text of the title of the view being displayed. The @Contains function checks to see if it contains the word *Offers*. If it does, it returns the value of True.

Remember that the Action is hidden if the formula returns a value of True. The exclamation mark (!) is the Boolean NOT operator that returns the reverse of whatever is to its right.

The statement will return a value of False if the view title contains the word *Offers* and will *not* hide the Action button.

5. Save the view. To avoid any confusion, you need to close the miscellaneous windows opened in the Jobs database and reopen that same view from the icon.

The Hide-When functionality, while a little counterintuitive to use, enables you to control the display of the Action buttons.

If all the functionality you needed was available in the list of System Command Actions that come with a view or a form, you have completed your task. But in most cases, you will need to develop a custom Action that contains Notes code.

4.6 RELEASE

Notes 4.6 has integrated additional Web functionality in many of the Notes options. One new option in most Hide-When selection tabs is the ability to hide a selection if the user is viewing through the Notes client or the Web. The Hide Action From: option allows the developer to hide the Action button from either the Notes client or the Web browser using the Notes 4.6 or Later or Web Browsers option.

Instantiation and Hide-When Formulas

To understand how the Hide-When formula works, you need to think in terms of *instantiation*, a technical term used in the object-oriented world. Understanding this concept will help you debug Notes applications.

Think in terms of a cookie cutter. Suppose you have a mold (the cookie cutter) in the shape of a star and a batch of cookie dough. When you press the cutter on the dough, you "instantiate" a cookie. The shape and thickness of the cookie is determined forever by the cutter.

What we do with Notes design elements is, in most instances, to create cookie cutters. How they work depends on the context and the order in which they run.

If the dough is runny, the cookie won't look anything like a star. If the dough is too hard, the cutter won't work (in that case, forget instantiation and bake bar cookies).

Just like a cookie cutter, the Notes design element is aware only of the conditions that are valid at the time it is instantiated, not after it has been instantiated. An Action is instantiated when the view is called to the screen. Before the view is displayed, the Hide-When formulas execute for the Actions, deciding which should show. Consequently, the formulas must refer to things that exist at that time, that is, the attributes of the view, such as the view title. The view Actions cannot base their Hide-When formulas on fields in the documents of the view because the view has not displayed its documents yet! In contrast, the Hide-When formula of a form Action can be based on the value of fields contained within a document.

When trying to debug Hide-When problems, ask the question, "What does this design element know about its environment at the time it is instantiated?"

Programming Custom Actions

The most common use of Actions in a view is to display a list of forms that can be created, as shown in Figure 21.1 at the beginning of this chapter. View Actions are certainly not limited to this role, and they can include complex functionality that calls an Agent or operates on a group of documents displayed in a view. But more complex Actions typically appear in forms.

Now we are ready to add two buttons to the Job Offer form. One button allows an applicant to create a Job Application form, and another button sends a request for more information from the applicant to the manager of the position. The first Action is rather basic; the second requires a formula.

Creating a Simple Action Action

You've read this right, there is such a thing as a Simple action Action. Simple actions streamline the task of creating an Action, just as they simplify the creation of other design objects in forms and views.

In this case, we want to allow someone who is reviewing a Job Offer to send an e-mail request for more information to the position manager. To implement a More Info button, follow these steps:

1. Open the Job Offer form from the Jobs database in Design mode.

2. Select View ➤ Action Pane.

3. Choose Create ➤ Action. The Design pane and the Properties box will appear, as shown in Figure 21.8.

4. Change the title from (Untitled) to Ask for More Info and click the green tick mark to save it.

TIP   The parenthesis around the title hides the Action from being displayed even though the Include in Action Bar and Include in Action menu options may be selected. Similarly, you can use parentheses for form and view names. This convention is a carry-over from Notes Release 3.*x*, since Release 4.*x* has checkboxes to control whether a form, view, or Action appears as a menu choice.

---

5. Set its position to the second location. Pick the icon of your choice, such as the flashlight at the end of row two.

FIGURE 21.8:

FIGURE 21.8:

The Design pane and the Properties box appear after you've created a new Action.

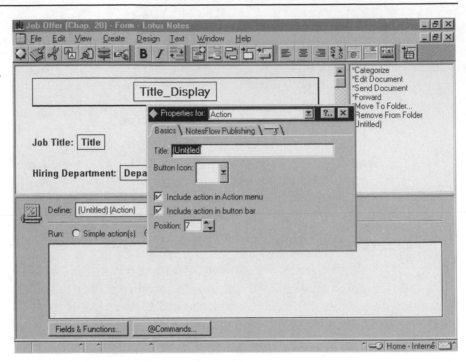

6. Click the Simple action(s) radio button in the Design pane and then the Add Action button. This button does not actually add another Action button, it adds an action for the Action. The Add Action builder appears, as shown in Figure 21.9.

7. Select Send Mail Message as an Action. The Add Action dialog box will change to reflect the new set of options, as shown in Figure 21.10.

8. Enter or select a name in the To field. Ideally, your recruiters should receive these inquiries. For the time being, select your name from the list.

9. Type **Applicant seeking more info** in the Subject field.

10. Select Include Link to Document—this option allows the recipient of this message to know what position the applicant is referring to. You could also select the option to include a copy of the document.

FIGURE 21.9:

The Add Action dialog box

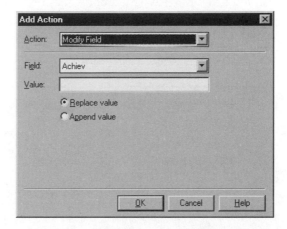

FIGURE 21.10:

The Add Action dialog box changes to reflect the new set of options.

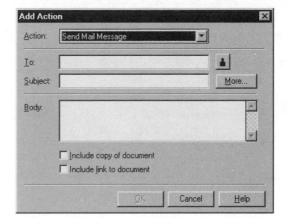

TIP

Whether to include a link or a copy depends on where you are sending the e-mail. If the recipient has access over the network to the database containing the job openings, include the doclink. That way the e-mail will be smaller in size than one that contains a copy of the document. Also, the e-mail with the link will point to the latest revision of the job opening, whereas the e-mail with a copy will have the version that was current at the time the e-mail was sent.

11. Click OK to save the Action and then choose File ➤ Close. (Make sure you save the form.)

12. Open a Job in the Job Offers view. Your Ask for More Info button will appear, as shown in Figure 21.11.

FIGURE 21.11:

A form Action button appears on top of a document.

Ask for More Info button

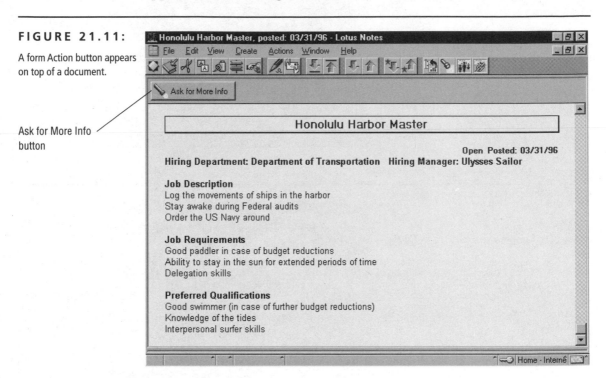

13. Click the Action. If the mail address you specified in step 8 is legitimate, it will send a message, as indicated by the Lotus Notes Status bar message "Mail submitted for delivery (1 Person/Group)."

As you can see, adding Actions is very easy thanks to the simple Simple actions. But the functionality is limited—for instance, we might like to collect some additional information about the Job Offer or perhaps tell the user that the request was submitted. To enhance the functionality of Simple actions, you need to use the @function formula language.

TIP
An Action is explicitly tied to a specific view or form. You can copy and paste Actions between views and forms, but don't do so until you are convinced that the Action works as desired. Otherwise, you would have to change its code in all the places where you copied it. If you have many Actions that are common to multiple forms, you can also create a subform that contains only Action buttons. By including the subform in the actual form, all the Action buttons will be included as well. This will allow you to maintain all the Action buttons in one central location.

Creating a Formula Action

Not all simple tasks are covered in the Simple actions. Sometimes you need to write a formula. For example, to create an Action button that composes a new form, follow these steps:

1. Open the Job Offer form from the Jobs database in Design mode.

2. Select View ➤ Action Pane.

3. Choose Create ➤ Action. The Design pane and the Properties box will appear.

4. Change the title from (Untitled) to Apply! and click the green tick mark to save it.

5. Set its position to the second location. Pick an icon of your choice, such as the pen on a paper in row 3, column 6.

6. Close or move the Properties box out of the way to display the entire Design pane.

TIP
The Properties box seems to be constantly in the way, sitting on top of an area of the screen you need. Instead of closing and reopening it all the time, or minimizing and maximizing it, try to drag it on top of the Status bar. To restore the box, all you need to do is drag it back up!

7. Click Formula in the Design pane. Click the @Commands button. The familiar Paste @Command dialog box appears as shown in Figure 21.12.

8. Select the Compose @Command and click the Paste button.

FIGURE 21.12:

Use the Paste @Command dialog box to select a function for the formula of the Action.

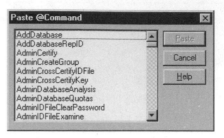

TIP

Most of the dialog boxes in Notes are "keystroke" aware. Instead of scrolling through pages of @Commands, you can type a "c" from the keyboard and the dialog box will automatically scroll to the first @Command that starts with a "c."

---

9. Use the Design pane to modify the formula (as shown in Figure 21.13):

   `@Command([Compose];"Application")`

FIGURE 21.13:

Use the Design pane to enter a formula for an Action. Note the "hiding" spot for the Properties box at the bottom of the screen.

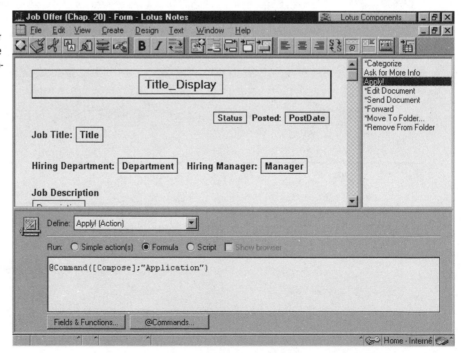

10. Save the form, close it, switch to the Job Offers view, and open any document. The new Action will be displayed.

As you can see, it is very easy to add a custom Action to a form. Given the limited amount of space available on the toolbar, you may need to restrict the length of the title and consider whether you need both the title and the icon. Along the same lines, make sure that the essential Actions show up first.

Adding Drop-Down Lists to the Action Bar

Actions simplify the interface of your database because they place the most commonly used tasks on a set of buttons located in the Action bar.

NOTE Actions relate to things the user does, whereas the Navigator navigates around the database.

Given that an Action should have a meaningful label and may optionally include an icon, you are often limited to fewer than eight Actions when designing for 640 × 480 screens. You do not have the option of changing the font size of the labels, and the Action bar is not scrollable either vertically or horizontally. A maximum display of eight Actions on the Action bar may turn out to be a serious limitation.

WARNING The Action bar will only allow one line of Action buttons. If your Action buttons are too wide for the screen, they will scroll off to the right where the user cannot see them.

When Actions are used with views, one workaround is to move the overflow of Action code into Navigator hotspots. When Actions are used with forms, the workaround is to create buttons within your form—just as you may have done in Release 3.

Our recommendation is to avoid both of these workarounds and instead to *cascade* the Actions. For instance, instead of having three Actions called Refer to Assistant, Refer to Boss, and Refer to Support that take a lot of real estate on the Action bar, you could create one Action called Refer that prompts you for the three options: Boss, Assistant, or Support.

Cascading the actions is an elegant way to reduce the clutter on the Action bar while keeping the integrity of the interface. To illustrate a cascading Action, let's build an Action that launches some familiar Windows utilities:

1. Open the Jobs Application database from the companion disk and bring up the Job Offers view in Design mode.

2. Create an Action. Name it Utilities.

3. Type the following code in the formula field:

```
choice:=@Prompt([OKCANCELLIST];"Utilities";"Please select an
accessory";"";"Calculator":"Calendar":"WordPad":"Solitaire");
```

NOTE   The statement in step 3 displays a prompt asking the user to choose between Windows utilities, namely, the calculator, the calendar, Wordpad, or the most widely used Windows application at the office, Solitaire. The variable called choice returns the item picked by the user. The following statement inspects the variable and executes the corresponding Windows program (assuming that it is in the path):

```
@If(choice="Calculator";@Command([Execute];"calc.exe");choice=
"Calendar";@Command([Execute];"calendar.exe");choice="WordPad";@
Command([Execute];"wordpad.exe");@Command([Execute];"sol.exe"))
```

---

4. Save the view.

The Utilities Action, shown in Figure 21.14, can be extended to invoke whatever program you wish to launch from within Notes.

FIGURE 21.14:

A cascading Action button allows you to provide more functionality than would fit on the Action bar.

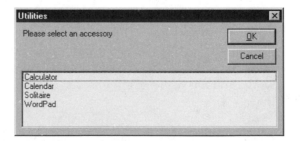

TIP
Cascading Actions enable you to extend the Action bar by grouping tasks behind one button that requires a second selection. Note that we do not recommend more than one level of cascading, that is, more than one prompt after pressing on the button.

What's Next?

Actions, when combined with Navigators, can completely guide a novice (or an experienced!) user through a database. Because Actions allow the designer to determine the flow of the database, we recommend that you allocate enough time in your development process to think through the use of Actions.

In the following chapters, you will expand your knowledge of Notes application development by learning about advanced techniques, such as tables, Agents, and templates. If your learning track is more focused on workflow, make sure you read Chapter 23, "Using the Agent Builder to Automate Processes."

CHAPTER

TWENTY-TWO

22

Representing Tabular Data and Creating Tables

- ■ Representing tabular data in a single document and multiple documents

- ■ Creating tables

- ■ Setting the properties for a table

- ■ Formatting a table

- ■ Creating variable-size tables

- ■ Creating an automatic variable-size table

At the risk of stating the obvious, a spreadsheet is basically a large table. So is your wall calendar or your monthly bank statement. Many of the printouts loitering around your office are, in fact, tabular reports, sometimes decorated with paragraphs of text. Tables placed in a form enable you to present a great deal of information in a concise and logical way.

In our experience, many users and developers get confused when they try to implement tabular information in Notes. The confusion comes from the fact that one of the design objects in Notes forms is named *table*—but Notes also supports many other ways to achieve tabular functionality without using the *table* object.

Notes provides multiple ways to enter and display tabular data. Using a combination of separate documents properly organized in a view, or single documents containing layouts or Notes table objects, you can assemble information in a concise way.

This chapter is meant to help you design Notes databases that can represent and manipulate the kind of data that you normally think of as tabular. You'll learn about the major benefits and pitfalls associated with creating tables and tabular data. You'll also learn how to lay out forms that contain tables and how to make the best use of the new table features in Release 4. The chapter covers the following topics:

- Choosing design elements to represent tabular data
- Creating a Notes table
- Creating a variable-size table

Choosing Design Elements to Represent Tabular Data

People tend to approach the concept of tables from the perspective of their work environment. Someone who works with relational databases may associate the word *table* with a printed report, focusing on heading, subheading, detail section, page totals, and so on. A financial person is likely to arrange data into neatly intersecting rows and columns. Project managers will have a bias for putting a list of collapsing tasks and subtasks in the first column and using additional columns for assignee, deadline, description, and prior dependencies. You need a bit of all three approaches to represent tabular data in Notes effectively.

Notes offers you three ways to design tables:

- You can use multiple documents that represent one or more Notes views.

- You can use a single Notes document that contains details of all the information in a database.

- You can use a single main Notes document that gathers data from many documents.

Using Multiple Documents and Views

Notes lets you display tabular data using multiple documents that represent one or more views in a database. To illustrate what we mean, open any database's view by double-clicking its icon in your Workspace. You can also follow these steps to open your Notes Log database:

1. Choose File ➤ Database ➤ Open. The Open Database dialog box appears.

2. Select the server where your Notes Log database is stored.

3. Double-click the Notes Log database (LOG.NSF) to add the icon to your Workspace.

TIP

You can also click the Notes Log database to highlight it and then click the Open button.

NOTE

If the server denies you access to the file, either ask your Notes administrator for Reader access or pick any other database.

---

4. Select Replication Events (or a view that's provided by the database you choose) in the Navigator pane. The right pane should display something similar to Figure 22.1.

FIGURE 22.1:

This view shows tabular data in columns using categories and details and includes totals and subtotals.

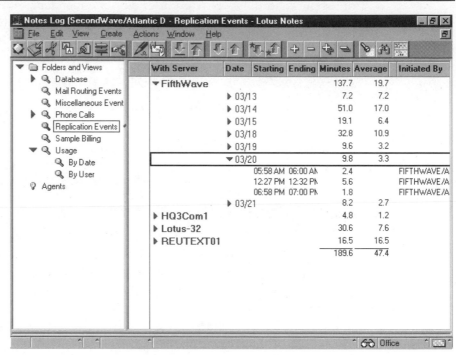

In this example, the view picks only the values of the originating server, the time, and the duration of the call, using the latter value for calculations. No one "document" contains all the values for all the replications that occurred during the week. What you are looking at is a live table that can be printed as is or exported to a spreadsheet, a structured text file, or tabular text. We'll examine the tabular option, mostly because it uses the term *tabular*.

To prove our point that Figure 22.1 is really a table, follow these steps. If you couldn't open the Notes log file, proceed with whatever file you picked; the file you use won't make any difference to this example:

1. Display the database's view.

2. Choose File ➤ Export. The Export dialog box appears, as shown in Figure 22.2.

3. Select a directory where you want to save the data, such as c:\temp.

4. Type a name, such as **untable.txt**, in the File name field.

FIGURE 22.2:

The Export dialog box allows you to select Tabular Text as the format for exporting Notes data.

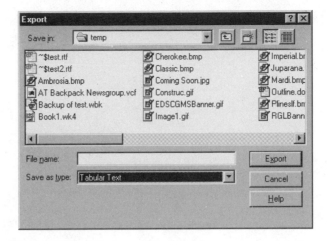

5.   Select Tabular Text in the Save as Type list box.

6.   Click the Export button. The Tabular Text Export dialog box appears, as shown in Figure 22.3.

FIGURE 22.3:

The Tabular Text Export dialog box gives you the option of choosing the documents and the view titles that you want to appear as exported text.

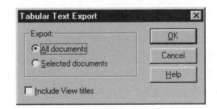

7.   Choose the All Documents option.

8.   Select the Include View Titles option.

9.   Click OK.

Notes proceeds with the export.

Let's now observe what a view looks like in tabular format. From the File Manager or the Windows 95 Explorer, double-click the C:\ TEMP\UNTABLE.TXT file. The Windows Notepad should start automatically and will display the text file, as shown in Figure 22.4.

FIGURE 22.4:

A view exported to tabular format is ready for further processing by other tools.

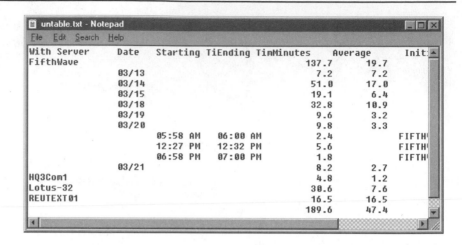

Clearly, each "row" of information is not necessarily a document—only the detail rows contain data. If the data you sketched out on a piece of paper before starting your development effort looks like the file in Figure 22.4, you can implement the design as multiple documents. A good illustration of this type of environment is a call service center where each call for software support is an individual document and the views summarize the information for managers in a variety of ways.

Although we cannot give you hard and fast rules for when to assemble your information within a single Notes document and when to break it up into multiple documents, we will offer some guidelines. You can treat multiple documents as a single entity for the following reasons:

- **They have a beginning and an end.** For example, the Notes Log entry describes events that occurred during a replication session.

- **They have a lot of internal information that is not relevant elsewhere in the database.** Only a small subset, or aggregate, of the Notes Log database is used for other purposes, such as for keeping track of a replication's duration.

- **They do not derive their information from other sources.** The document is "whole," although it may pick up information from another database. For example, the Notes Log picks up the caller's telephone number from another database. The document does not need to list all the prior calls from that person; it represents the entire event of the call.

Using a Single Document

Here are a few guidelines for when to use a single document, although nothing is cast in concrete:

- **The detailed information has no intrinsic value.** Consider, for example, a resume. The list of achievements and responsibilities for a job is relevant only to the prospective employer within the context of the resume.

- **The document contains a great deal of detailed information.** Breaking up such a document would create large, unwieldy views that display multiple levels of categories. For example, a view could list all the individual parts of a printer as opposed to grouping the parts into documents. Power Supply could be a document that groups the power cord (the plug differs from country to country), the transformer (110 volts or 220 volts), and legal disclaimer ("Don't operate in your bathtub"). A second document, Peripherals, could group the options, such as fax module, envelope feeder, and so on. Another good example of a highly detailed document is an employee's expense report. Such a document could list all of the itemized expenses for one individual in an organization. The database could display a view that summarizes the expense reports for each individual and workgroup in an organization in addition to totals for each department and division.

- **The document should look like a table.** Users frequently ask for this type of document. Maybe they see their business world as one big table (twenty years of pouring over mainframe COBOL-generated outputs can do that to you!) Or maybe they just like things to line up in rows and columns. A clean user interface has a certain linear harmony. Users like data to line up *neatly* in a Notes form.

Using Multiple Documents in a View Combined with a Single Document

The decision to use multiple documents to represent tabular data as opposed to putting everything in a single document is not an either/or decision. It is always possible to assemble information contained in multiple separate documents into a single document.

You can use the following methods to pull information from multiple documents:

1. **Look up values from a view** when composing a new document or displaying an existing document.

2.   **Run background Agents** that collect information from one or more Notes documents and reinsert the data into new or existing documents.

3.   **Launch foreground Agents** from the Action bar to analyze a given set of documents and display the results in a pop-up dialog box on the screen.

Looking Up Values

In Chapter 20 you read that Notes has the ability to return information from a view based on certain criteria. For instance, using the name of a training course as a criterion, you can look up the names of the employees who are enrolled in the course. The @Dblookup function can return a list of names that you can place in a student roster. We mentioned previously that the challenge in using a list for tabular purposes is that you may have difficulty using each element of the list separately. For example, maintaining additional information about the students in a list, such as their other courses, would be difficult.

TIP

When you need a list, we recommend that you consider using a lookup to a view to assemble the list on the fly.

Using Agents

You will soon learn (in Chapter 23) that you can schedule Agents to work automatically. This functionality can be used to populate the table of a main document with the contents of either its Response documents or completely unrelated documents. For instance, at the end of the week, the Product Plan Summary Agent could collect the status and one-line comment on each feature document that was broken off into separate documents. Typically, you will need to write such Agents in LotusScript.

A tell-tale sign that you may have gone too far in breaking data into multiple documents is the need to have to run very complex background Agents to keep the main or parent document up-to-date.

Tabular Design Tools

Regardless of why you need tabular data within your Notes form, Notes gives you three basic design tools:

• Text formatting (tabs, margins) to set alignments

- Layout design objects
- Notes tables

Using Alignments to Fake a Table

If you open any document in the log file, as shown in Figure 22.5, you'll see that it contains much more information than was displayed in the view.

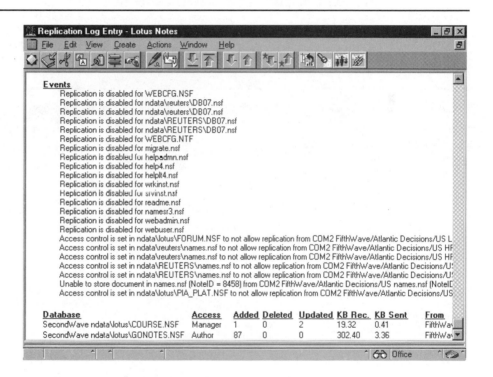

If you scroll through the document, you'll notice the Events and Database areas looking very much like a table. If you pay close attention to the design of the form (trust us on this!), you will not find a table object in the entire form—not even for the Database area. Instead, the designer elegantly formatted the information to line up properly under the text headings, such as Accessed, Added, or Deleted.

TIP

You can, with a bit of fancy footwork, align things to give the impression that you are displaying a table without actually having to create a Notes table.

If you are fortunate enough to have access to a large log file, read a handful of documents like the one displayed in Figure 22.5, paying close attention to the Database area. Eventually, you'll notice that things don't always line up neatly in that area, perhaps because the path name in the first column is so long that it extends into the space of the second column. Once one column is longer than predicted, all the columns to its right become misaligned.

Using Layouts to Create Columns

Suppose you have two fields that you wish to display side by side. If you lay them out next to each other, you can set the text to wrap only once, as illustrated in Figure 22.6.

FIGURE 22.6:

You'll notice that data in the Responsibilities field pushes the data in the Achievements field out of alignment when tables or layouts aren't used.

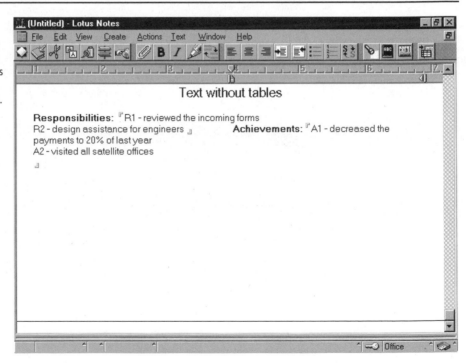

To force the text to wrap in fixed-width columns, you need to use the new Release 4 design object called layout, already covered in Chapter 17. Layouts allow you to position and move a label, image, button, or field anywhere you want within the layout.

NOTE As you may recall, Notes forms do not support the concept of parallel columns that you find in word processors.

Follow these steps to look at the layout used to create a table:

1. Open the Jobs database from the CD-ROM.

2. Open the form called TableText in Design mode.

3. Bring up the Field Properties InfoBox for the field called Resp_2 in the layout region, as shown in Figure 22.7.

FIGURE 22.7:

In the Field Properties InfoBox, add a scroll bar to a layout region to display more information than fits in the specified width and height of the field.

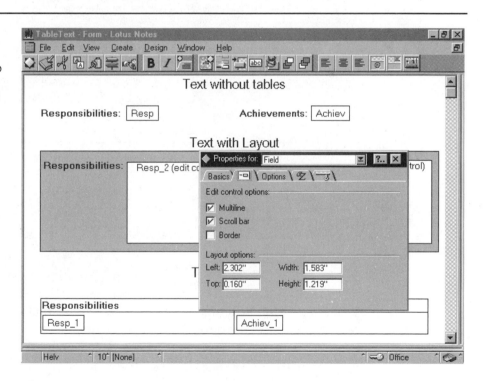

4. Select the Multiline option to allow the user to enter text that will automatically wrap. Select the Scroll bar option if you suspect text will regularly expand beyond the height of the field you defined. Optionally, you can show the border.

The border creates a three-dimensional effect, as you can see in the contrast between the Resp_2 and Achiev_2 fields in Figure 22.8. Layouts enable you to place the fields side by side. (You can examine the forms used in Figure 22.8 in more detail in the Jobs example database located on your CD-ROM.)

FIGURE 22.8:

By placing fields side by side, you can control the horizontal and vertical positioning of multiple fields to simulate a table.

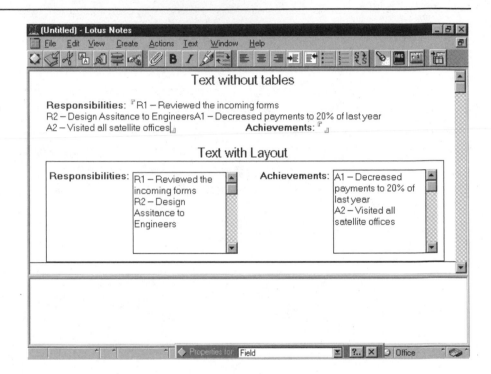

Layouts are a convenient way to achieve precise control over the exact position of fields, labels, images, and buttons in a form. However, the task of manually aligning more than a few fields, on the layout region, even with the snap-to-grid option, is tedious. Several of our developers had to be tranquilized after trying to use layouts on a tiny notebook screen with a pesky keyboard mouse pointer. What you may need in many situations is a "real" Notes table.

TIP

So far, you've seen several ways to create the illusion of a table without actually using a table. Using some formatting features, such as tabs and margins, is more obvious than using Agents. We recommend that you examine your options carefully before you begin to create a Notes table.

If you have a field in a layout region, printing will only print what you see and not what may be hidden (you need to use the scroll bar to see it).

Using a Notes Table

A Notes table allows you to organize a series of fields in cells in a particular way. A *cell* is the intersection of a row and a column. A Notes cell looks like a cell that you'd find in a spreadsheet. Each Notes cell can contain one or more fields or other objects. In addition to data, cells can contain buttons or labels.

Since each column of a table includes its own ruler, in one step you can set the fields or buttons contained in all the cells of the column to any attribute. This shortcut is handy if you want to line up a logo at the far left of the screen and a set of buttons at the far right of the screen, as shown in Figure 22.9.

TIP

In general, we recommend using Notes table objects versus layouts. Layouts are time consuming and should be reserved for forms where you need high-quality graphics and precise control over the look and feel.

FIGURE 22.9:

You can use real tables to align fields and buttons vertically. The text wraps on to two lines, and the buttons align flush right in the last column.

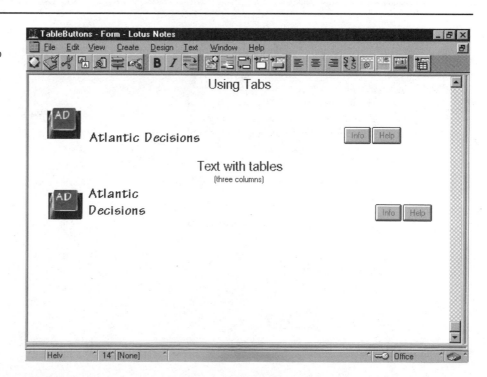

WARNING Layout regions do not translate to the Web when using Domino to publish databases and documents.

The Report Syndrome

Forms are not the right tool for delivering pretty reports. Also, Notes views are not intended to solve all of the problems of creating sophisticated printed reports. Views are meant to sort, categorize, and present information in a meaningful manner. It's relatively easy to create new views to suit the needs of specific groups of users of the application. And it's even easier if you teach the users how to create their own private views or shared folders.

In reality, Notes views will not meet everyone's requirements. As you saw in Chapter 19, the Notes formatting options are fairly limited. Notes views are meant to be traversed and analyzed visually, with basic counts and percentage calculations. If you need more sophisticated reporting features, you will need to purchase add-on products such as Lotus Reporter or Lotus Approach. And if you need more advanced computations, you may need to export subsets of the data to relational databases, a relatively easy task using off-the-shelf third-party products.

The Blender Bender Syndrome

The blender bender syndrome manifests itself when you try to display a lot of unrelated information within a single form or try to include everything, plus the kitchen sink, just because one particular field appears to be related to another. A good example is trying to include a list of all the features of a product within a single product plan document. This type of design is a bad idea because it becomes difficult to spawn additional threads or activity on each feature. For example, each feature may lead to multiple comments, task assignments, and status reports. The point is, you may need to track each feature separately from the main product.

Similarly, sometimes different types of information have different archival considerations. For example, you will need to keep the main Company Profile document in a sales database, but every quarter you may choose to archive all associated activity documents that are "closed" and more than twelve months old. We have found that thinking about how long each piece of information needs to remain in a database is a fairly effective way to separate information into Main documents and Response documents. Ask yourself, "What information will I need forever, what will I archive, and when will I archive it?"

Creating a Table

Because we usually find that the best way to deal with tabular data is through the use of Notes tables, we will now examine this design element in detail. This example reconstructs a subform that exists in the JOBS.NSF database on your CD-ROM. We are going to create a table to list a candidate's academic degrees in a section of the job application form.

To create the table, follow these steps:

1. Open the Jobs database located on your Workspace in Design mode. If the Navigator is on your screen, simply choose View ➤ Design.

2. Choose Create ➤ Design ➤ Subform. A blank form will appear. We are creating a subform because we may want to recycle this table in other forms in the future.

3. Choose Create ➤ Table. The Create Table dialog box will appear, as shown in Figure 22.10.

4. Type **4** for the number of rows and type **6** for the number of columns.

5. Click OK. The table appears on the form, using the entire width of your window.

FIGURE 22.10:

The Create Table dialog box allows you to specify the number of rows and columns in a table.

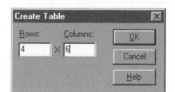

We now have a complete table—or rather a completely useless table, since it does not contain any fields or text labels. In other words, this table defines only the lines of a grid, not the cells. We need to set its properties, format it, and then add fields in each cell where we want to put data.

Setting Table Properties

To set the properties for the table, follow these steps:

1. Right-click and choose Table Properties from the menu to display the Table Properties InfoBox, as shown in Figure 22.11.

FIGURE 22.11:

You specify layout settings for a table in the Table Properties InfoBox.

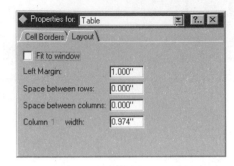

2. Click the Layout Tab and turn off Fit to Window, as we want to control precisely the space occupied by each column.

3. Click in the table and in row 1, columns 2, 3, 4, 5, and 6, respectively, type **Degree, Major, Institution, Date, Grade**. In column 1, rows 2, 3, and 4, respectively, type **1, 2, 3**.

4. Click in row 1, column 2, and drag your mouse all the way to the end of the column to select the cells in that row. This selection technique was introduced in Release 4.

TIP

If you prefer to use the keyboard, hold the Shift and Ctrl keys and then press the right arrow a few times until the whole row is highlighted.

---

5. Click the Bold and Center icons on the SmartIcon bar. Your table now looks like Figure 22.12. You can add any attribute that you desire to these fields.

As you can see, all the cells in the table are the same height and width. Fortunately, Notes Release 4 provides new tools to tweak groups of cells to meet your needs, as you'll see in the following section on formatting.

Formatting Tables

As you enter labels and insert fields, you will increase the height of the cells. At this point, you can format the table to suit your purposes. You may want to change the width of the columns or the height of the rows, change the fonts and alignments, or insert graphics.

FIGURE 22.12:

Borders and labels enhance the appearance of this table.

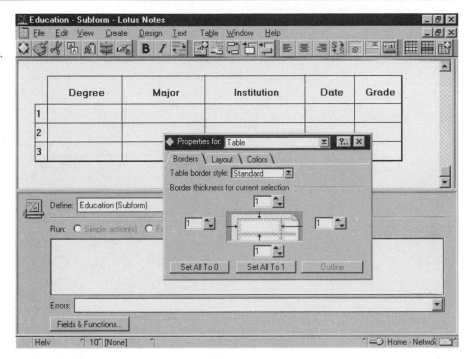

To format a table, do the following:

1. Press Ctrl+R or click the Ruler icon in the SmartIcon bar to display the ruler.

2. Click in the column you want to resize.

3. Drag the vertical bars to resize the column, as shown in Figure 22.13.

4. Click in the cells and set the cell borders to look like Figure 22.12. (The Table Properties InfoBox is still displayed.) When Notes notices that you've run out of space to stretch a column, it won't let you increase the width.

TIP

Neglecting to mention how to set the height of a row was not an oversight on our part. You have to play tricks by inserting a one-space character and setting its font size high enough to force the row to expand. You must then copy and paste this character to all the cells of the row to maintain the alignment of the labels or fields.

FIGURE 22.13:

You can resize columns and add borders to achieve some special effects.

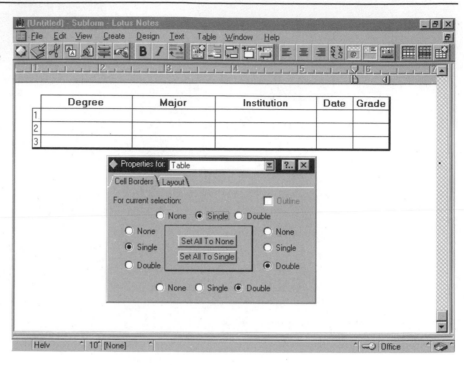

To add a little pizzazz to a form, you can also paste a tiny icon in the cell at row 1, column 1. Since our column is already very narrow, we won't add an icon to this example.

Limitations of Tables in Release 4

Notes tables are rather uninteresting in terms of their user interface appeal. While you can insert graphics in a cell, you cannot overlay them with a field or a label. Layouts are not permitted inside a cell. Users cannot resize or reorder columns.

Similarly, Notes does not provide programmatic access to tables (i.e., their design functionality is not exposed in LotusScript, so you have no way to resize a column or access the value at the intersection of a specified row and column).

If you require additional capabilities, you can embed an OLE (Object Linking and Embedding) Spreadsheet object (e.g., Lotus 1-2-3 or Microsoft Excel) inside of a Notes form (or Notes document).

Finally, we want to insert a little padding between the rows of the table in order to separate the academic degrees clearly, as some entries are likely to spread over multiple lines of a cell. To change from a default of zero pad, follow these steps:

1. Position the insertion point anywhere in the table.

2. Display the Tables Properties InfoBox.

3. Click the Layout tab.

4. Change the default of zero to 0.050 inches in the Space between the rows text box. This padding adds a little room above and below the text fields of each row.

Now that the form looks exactly the way we want it to, we are ready to start placing fields within its cells.

Defining the Fields

Now that you've entered and formatted the static text, you can create and position the fields for the labels in the table. To add the fields in the table, follow these steps:

1. Place the insertion point in the cell of row 2, column 2.

2. Choose Create ➤ Field.

3. Bring up the Field Properties InfoBox and select the Basics tab.

4. Type **Degree**.

5. Set the Font (third tab) to Helv 9 points if some of your end users will be using a low-resolution 640x480 display (most notebooks). Nine points is more difficult to read, but screen real estate is expensive when using tables.

6. Copy and paste the field three times to automatically set the field names to Degree_1, Degree_2, Degree_3 for the rows labeled 1, 2, and 3.

7. Delete the original Degree field.

8. Repeat this process for the other columns in order to create a table similar to the one that appears in Figure 22.14. Note that you should select the Time type for each Data column field and select the Data format for the fields to accept input of the month and year only. Again, you need to save space.

FIGURE 22.14:

Inserting fields in a table and then setting the values they can display helps to save space.

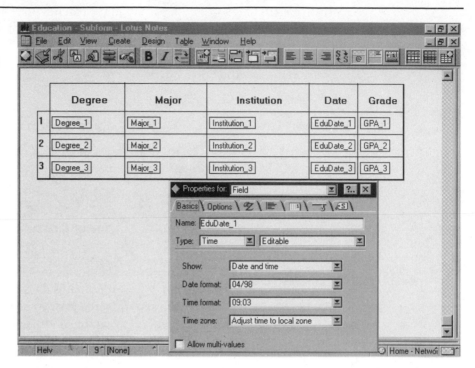

We now have a fully functional table. One of the most common requirements of your users is to have the table grow and shrink as needed. In Release 3 this feature would have required major development on your part. Our strategy was to first try to commit the sponsor to a limited number of rows and columns, and if that failed, cringe all the way back to our computer. In Release 3 many decisions to split tabular data between multiple forms were made simply because variable-size tables were very difficult to implement.

Creating a Variable-Size Table

Unfortunately, tables in Notes forms cannot be resized without Designer access. In other words, a user cannot shrink or increase the size of the table while using it. This limitation is a major drawback when the number of items listed in the form may vary according to the situation, for example, a table for meeting minutes or a list of features for a new product. Three basic approaches will provide the functionality you need to produce a variable-size table:

- Use computed subforms to pull in a table of the right size.

- Use Hide-When formulas to display only the portions of a table that actually contain data.

- Use Hide-When formulas and LotusScript to dynamically resize the table.

The third approach is the most desirable but requires adding just a little bit of LotusScript code. (Don't worry, it's very simple and you don't have to master the last section of this book to proceed.)

Creating a Variable-Size Table Using Computed Subforms

If you are fortunate enough to know in advance the precise number of rows the table should contain, you can use computed subforms to select the appropriate table. This method works well when the table contains data collected after the fact, for example, the minutes of a meeting. Here's how to use a computed subform (assume that the number of items for the table is either two, five, or ten):

1. Create three subforms, each containing a table of the size indicated by its name, and call them Table2, Table5, and Table10. (Refer to Chapter 17 if you are not familiar with laying out subforms.)

2. Insert a field (e.g., resp) in the main (parent) form that is computed automatically when the form is composed. The field should ask the user how many items will go in the table.

3. Insert a subform in the main form by choosing Create ➤ Insert Subform.

4. Select the Insert Subform based on a formula option.

5. Type a formula that will select the appropriate form in the Formula dialog box.

```
@if(resp="2";"Table2";resp="5";"Table5";"Table10")
```

When users compose a new form, they are prompted for the number of items they wish to enter. The main drawback of this method is that the subform is inserted (or *instantiated*) only at the time it is displayed, either in Read mode or in Edit mode. This restriction means that resizing is not possible while the document is being used. You could add a button that would change the value of resp, but you would need to force the user to save the document and then reopen it.

NOTE The key advantage of this approach is simplicity. You create and maintain various forms separately from the main form and decide which table to display at the time you need to present the form.

Release 3 Variable-Size Tables

If you still have to maintain Notes Release 3 applications, you can use two approaches for a variable-size table. We are not going to describe them in detail; we'll just outline their respective functionality.

- **Create multiple forms, each containing a table of a different size.** Add a button on the form to grow and shrink the table. When pressed, the button saves the form, resets the value of the Form field to the appropriate number of rows and columns, and then reopens the document. For example, when using a form with five rows (called FiveRows), pressing a Grow button invokes a formula that resets the value of the Form field to TenRows. When the document is reopened, it will use the form called TenRows.

- **Make extensive use of lists.** The table contains only two rows, one for the titles and one for the data. Users separate multiple values by pressing ↵. Thus in a course roster document, the table could contain the names of all employees signed up for the class, with their respective office numbers and managers' names in separate fields, neatly lined up with tabs to simulate columns. If the authors of the document play along, everything will line up properly and your table will appear to have multiple rows of data. Unfortunately, things get hairy when you need to provide the functionality of removing a row of data from the middle of the table, for instance, to remove a student who has dropped out of a course.

Using Hide-When to Show Portions of a Large Table

In Chapter 19 we explained that the Hide-When feature is one of the most powerful design features of Release 4. Tables take advantage of Hide-When by not displaying the lines of a column or row if all the cells it contains compute as being hidden. For example, if you have a three-row table with a line around all cells, but you've marked the fields in the last row as hidden, Notes displays a two-row table when the document is in Read mode.

To take advantage of Hide-When in tables, the first step is to create a table as large as the maximum number of expected rows in the final application. Users may tell you, for instance, that the maximum number of items jotted down after a meeting is twenty or that no product contains more than ten major features or that classes are restricted to forty students because the biggest room in the building seats forty.

TIP

If you are creating a Notes table to handle more than forty rows of information, you may want to rethink your design and consider using Response documents to capture the information and a view to summarize the documents.

Follow these steps to create a Hide-When field formula to control how much of the form is visible:

1. Open the Jobs database from the companion CD-ROM.

2. Open the TableResize form in Design mode.

3. Select the Mgr_6 field.

4. Display the Field Properties InfoBox.

5. Select the Hide-When tab (second from the right), as shown in Figure 22.15.

FIGURE 22.15:

To hide rows in a table, you can force the table to appear as if it is shrinking. The table will automatically decrease in size when rows are empty.

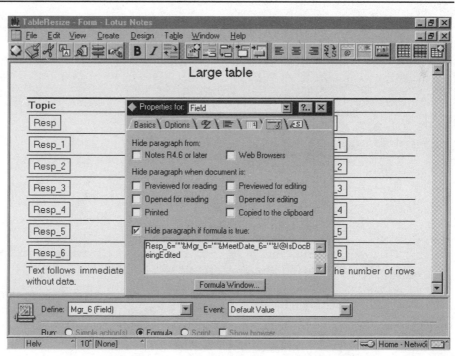

The formula in the Hide Paragraph If Formula is True option window reads

```
Resp_6="" & Mgr_6="" & MeetDate_6="" & !@IsDocBeingEdited
```

This formula means that Notes will hide the entire last row of the table if the document is in Read mode (the "!" in the formula represents the logical operator NOT) and if all of its fields are empty.

The main drawback of this method is that it does not allow users to "grow" the table. You need to decide on its largest size up front. And the users of the document will see all the empty rows, whether or not they need them.

Using LotusScript to Resize a Table Automatically

If you are willing to go to the next level of complexity, you can create the illusion that the table is growing as needed—although not beyond its original maximum size. This technique requires a little bit of LotusScript code, so read the following section if you are comfortable with the power programming tools available in Notes Release 4.

You can give the editor of a Notes form the illusion that a form is growing by modifying the table in two ways:

- Modify the Hide-When formula to force Notes to figure out if a row contains text

- Force a refresh of a field every time the user moves on to another field

Modifying the Hide-When Formula To modify the Hide-When formula, follow these steps:

1. Open the Jobs database from your companion disk.

2. Open the Experience subform in Design mode. We are using a subform because we want to include it in the Job Application main form.

3. Select the Mgr_6 field.

4. Inspect the Hide-When formula by displaying the subform's Field Properties InfoBox. The formula reads

    ```
    @If(@IsDocBeingEdited;Resp_5="" & Mgr_5="" & MeetDate_5=""
    &Resp_6=""& Mgr_6="" & MeetDate_6="";Resp_6="" & Mgr_6=""
    &MeetDate_6="")
    ```

This formula means that if the document is being edited, we want to hide the fields if no values appear in the entire row above (row 5) and no values appear in the current row. In Read mode (the third part of the @if function), we need to check that none of the three fields has a value to mark the Mgr_6 field as hidden. (Remember that the field will be hidden whenever the formula returns a value of True.)

Using LotusScript to Refresh the Hide-When Formulas To refresh a form's fields automatically, you could use the Refresh Fields Automatically property in the Default tab of the Form Properties InfoBox. However, this approach is often undesirable because it forces all the fields to be validated—something we may not want to do until the user completes the form. Auto refresh also tends to slow down data entry in large forms dramatically—not to mention causing the screen to "jitter" occasionally. A better solution is to use just a few lines of LotusScript. Follow these steps to accomplish a refresh:

1. Open the Jobs database from your companion disk.

2. Open the Experience subform in Design mode.

3. Select the Mgr_5 field.

4. Drag the bottom panel to display the code window. The Define drop-down list should display Mgr_5(Field).

5. Select the Exiting event because we want to force a refresh whenever the user tabs or clicks outside of the field. (Instead of forcing a refresh for every field on the form, the refresh is performed only when the user exits out of the Mgr_5 field.)

6. Write the following line of code:

    ```
    Call Resize
    ```

TIP Because this code will be invoked for all the fields (except the last row), we want to place it in one central area for easy maintenance (and to reduce typing). LotusScript calls these reusable portions of code subroutines or procedures. See Part V for much more information on LotusScript.

---

7. Select (Globals) Experience in the Define drop-down list. Select Resize as an event.

8.   Make sure the following code is displayed:

```
Sub Resize
'the current front-end user
Dim ws as New NotesUIWorkspace
'the current document
Dim doc as NotesUIDocument
'select the current document
Set doc=ws.currentdocument
'refresh all the hide-when formulas
Call doc.REFRESHHIDEFORMULAS
End Sub
```

That's it! As you can see when testing the Experience section in the completed Application for Employment form in the Jobs database, anytime you enter a value in any of the fields of a row, a new row automatically appears. Similarly, as you delete the values in the fields in a row, the table automatically shrinks.

NOTE   Another way to provide refresh functionality is by placing the Resize LotusScript call only in the last column or by placing buttons on the forms that allow bulk resizing. You can also enhance the form by moving the rows to automatically fill an empty row in the middle of the table.

What's Next?

Now that we have completed our tour of the core design elements of a database—forms, Navigators, views, Actions, and tables—we are ready to move on to the last step in database design: creating Agents to automate processes.

CHAPTER
TWENTY-THREE

23

Using the Agent Builder to Automate Processes

- Using Agents

- Understanding personal and shared Agents

- Disabling background Agents completely

- Determining whether the server allows Agents

- Controlling the performance impact of Agents

- Defining the Agent parameters

- Using the Agent Builder

- Using the Search Builder

- Using Simple actions to define Agents

Agents are self-contained mini-programs that you can implement and use in a variety of ways. The power of Agents (called "macros" in Notes Release 3.*x*) lies in their ability to automate a series of operations. A smart applications developer will "recruit" an Agent to perform routine tasks on a database.

Agents come in many shapes and sizes. An Agent can come in the form of an option in the Actions menu, a button on a form, a button on the Action bar, a hotspot on a Navigator, or a custom SmartIcon. Other types of Agents can be automatically triggered at specific times or as the result of particular events. This chapter covers the following topics:

- Understanding Agents
- Understanding the differences between personal and shared Agents
- Understanding Agent security
- Viewing Agents in a database
- Creating Agents

In this chapter, you will write an Agent that notifies a group of users via e-mail when certain individuals create or modify information in a database. You will also learn how to write a formula Agent to do maintenance work on your documents.

Understanding Agents

The types of operations an Agent can perform are endless and depend on the context in which the Agent is run.

- **View-level Agents:** Perform a "batch" update of several documents in a database based on a specific selection criteria. The Agent can be tied to an Action button or a Navigator. For instance, an Agent could mark as obsolete all the documents for a canceled project.

- **Document-level Agents:** Appear in the form of a button or a hotspot in the form and can make the process of data entry more user friendly by automating certain tasks. For example, a button could connect to an external relational database and retrieve a report for the company specified in the document.

- **Custom SmartIcon Agents:** Perform a series of tasks associated with a particular database or the Workspace as a whole. For instance, the manager of an employee records database could automatically synchronize it with the latest updates from a central corporate human resources information system that keeps track of personnel changes.

TIP

Attaching Agent functionality to custom SmartIcons should only be used to customize your personal Notes client. The Notes Release 4 Action bar should be used to deliver Agent functionality to Notes Release 4 users, since the Action bar is a design element that is replicated to all copies of a Notes database. SmartIcon Agents would have to be manually distributed and updated if they were used by more than one user.

- **Background Server Task Agents:** Perform a routine operation on a database based on a specific time schedule or when documents are modified or added. For instance, it can look for topics in the new documents on behalf of individual users and send them notifications via e-mail. An Agent could look at the attributes of a document and automatically move it to an archive database. This type of Agent is the most powerful because it does not require your intervention to work.

All of the previous types of agents still apply, but now you can also use Java to develop an Agent. Although this does not replace Simple Agents, Formula Agents, or LotusScript Agents, it allows organizations that already have an investment in Java to make the most of their Java resources. A backend class has been created for Java that is very similar to the backend classes for LotusScript. You have about the same amount of control over your Notes data as you would using LotusScript, with the advantage of also having the native power of Java. You cannot access any of the front-end or UI pieces of Notes using a Java Agent.

NOTE

You cannot compile or write the Java code for an agent in the Notes environment. You need to write and compile the Java program outside Notes and then attach the program to the Notes Agent.

Understanding the Difference between Personal and Shared Agents

Notes has two types of Agents: personal and shared. Personal Agents in Release 4 can perform a wide range of tasks formerly reserved for complex C server APIs or very tricky macro programming in Notes Release 3. Personal Agents will roam a database tirelessly, looking around on your sole behalf for the information you tell them to look for and performing chores that you define, such as forwarding notifications or modifying other data fields. Shared Agents are even more powerful. They enable you to define Simple actions. Simple actions can be useful to all users of the database; for instance, Simple actions allow all users to place a Newsletter summary of high-priority questions into their personal folders.

Notes personal Agents are poor spies: even when running on the server, their authority is no more and no less than that of their owner. When spawned onto a server, your Notes Agent cannot read documents you wouldn't otherwise be able to read from your workstation. And it certainly cannot write or modify documents that you do not have Editor access to.

The major drawbacks of personal Agents are that they take up server disk space and (more importantly) eat up processing time. While it is difficult to assess the impact of an Agent, thousands of them will slow things down considerably. For that reason, a database designer can restrict the number of users of a database who can create their own personal Agents.

To restrict a user whose access is less than Designer from creating personal Agents, follow these steps:

1. Select the icon of the Jobs database from your companion disk.

2. Select File ➤ Database ➤ Access Control List (ACL), as shown in Figure 23.1.

3. Deselect the Agent creation options so the checkboxes are empty.

NOTE   For now leave these settings on. Note that LotusScript/Java Agents are listed separately from regular personal Agents. We'll come back to that distinction later in this chapter.

FIGURE 23.1:

Use the ACL to restrict the ability of users to create personal Agents in the database.

TIP

The need for personal Agents may reflect the need for additional design work. If many personal Agents are used for a similar purpose, you may want to create a new design element to perform that task.

TIP

You can learn a lot by observing the behavior of personal Agents. The tasks they perform can serve as a list of user enhancements for the next release of the application. We recommend that you not systematically disable personal Agents, but instead keep a close eye on them in the initial rollout of an application.

If many personal Agents function in the same way, it is desirable to create a shared Agent that provides similar functionality to all users of the database. For instance, if multiple personal Agents are searching for similar terms in the pool of job candidates, such as "Cobol," "Pascal," or "Fortran," you should consider creating a shared Agent. Such an Agent would need to be more versatile than each individual personal Agent and would be best developed in consultation with the human resources professional recruiters at your company. You could then further enhance the shared Agent to include links to resumes otherwise stored in an external database in its e-mail responses.

You may also have situations in which you do not want any background Agent to run on the database. To disable Agents, follow these steps:

1. Select the Jobs database icon from the companion disk.

2. Bring up the Properties box for the database.

3. Turn off the Disable Background Agents for This Database option at the bottom of the screen of the first tab, as shown in Figure 23.2.

FIGURE 23.2:

You can disable background Agents for the entire database in the Properties dialog box.

NOTE For now, though, leave the background Agents option on—assuming that you have at least Designer access to the database.

Understanding Server Agent Security

The word *Agent* invokes images of LeCarre and Checkpoint Charlie. Several workflow products even associate them with the icon of a person wearing a trench coat and dark sunglasses. None of us would want such characters sleuthing around our corporate data, and certainly not around our personal e-mail files. Fortunately, Notes provides several ways to manage the scope and strength of Agents.

Although as a designer you have the ability to set shared and private Agent security for each database, these rights will not override the server settings set by the manager of the server's Name & Address book—the administrator who has the final responsibility for the performance and security of all the databases.

To avoid being at the "mercy" of databases that would spawn countless rogue Agents, the server administrator can completely turn off the ability to run any Agent on the server. To learn if your server supports background Agents, follow these steps (this sequence assumes that you have access to a Release 4 server):

1. Open the Name & Address book on your server. If the icon is not on your Workspace, select File ➤ Database ➤ Open. Then select your server and open the file called NAMES.NSF.

NOTE   To determine if your server is running Release 4, look at the list of available views in the left pane of the window. If you see Locations as a category of views, chances are that the server is a Release 4 server. But it could be a Release 3 server holding a Release 4 Name & Address book. To be 100 percent sure, talk to the server administrator.

---

2. Switch to the Server view category and then to the Server view.

3. Locate the entry for your server and open it.

4. Find the Agent Manager section and expand it. Your screen should look similar to Figure 23.3.

Who Can Run Agents on a Server?

At the heart of server Agent security is the Agent Restriction table. The table, like most other Notes security settings, is based on the membership to groups defined in the Notes Name & Address book. In other words, the Agent Restriction table functions as a mini Access Control List specifically set for Agents. This table determines whether your Agents will or will not execute on the server based on two criteria: the type of Agents you are trying to run and your membership in a group.

In Notes Release 4, three options determine who can run Agents:

*   **Run Personal Agents:** If the field is empty, anybody can run personal Agents. Security is set at the database level, as we saw in Chapter 16.

FIGURE 23.3:

The Notes Administrator controls when and who can run Agents on a server.

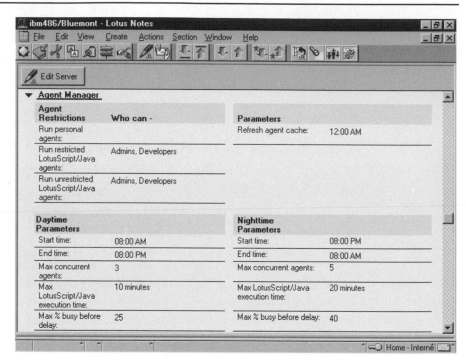

FIGURE 23.3:

The Notes Administrator controls when and who can run Agents on a server.

- **Run-Restricted LotusScript/Java Agents:** By default, nobody can run LotusScript/Java Agents. In our example, only members of the Admins and Developers groups are authorized to do so. We will cover the distinction between regular Agents and LotusScript/Java Agents later on in this chapter. In a nutshell, because LotusScript and Java are more powerful programming languages, its Agents have the ability to perform many more functions than regular Agents and therefore warrant extra security.

- **Run-Unrestricted LotusScript/Java Agents:** By default, again, nobody can run unrestricted Agents. Unrestricted Agents have access to the file system of the server, and therefore only people fully trusted by the server administrator should be authorized to run them. In our example, only members of the Admins and Developers groups can perform such operations.

These options are essential to the proper functioning of Agents. If you are not a member of the groups listed, you will be able to create Agents, but they simply won't run.

How Agents Will Run on a Server

Notes servers also determine how an Agent will run on them.

These important settings are part of the Daytime/Nighttime parameters table of the server entry in the Name & Address book. Remember that Agents consume resources on the server, and as fewer resources are available on the server, it will respond more slowly to requests from users. Notes separates the usage of the server into two periods: daytime and nighttime. Daytime is when you wish to maximize the server response time because most users will be connected to the server. Nighttime is when you should run Agents that will slow down the server.

> **TIP**
>
> We recommend that you define the daytime and nighttime periods to reflect the typical work day for each server and that you run background Agents during the defined "nighttime" period of the server.

The restrictions imposed on Agents are as follows:

- **Max Concurrent Agents:** The number of Agents that will run at the same time on the server. For example, in Figure 23.3, three Agents can run concurrently during the day and five at night. If the Agents in your database don't seem to work, check this parameter—it's often the culprit. The setting of this parameter depends on the configuration of your server. Unfortunately, there is no hard and fast rule, as both the complexity of the Agents and the type of hardware of the server will determine the correct setting.

> **TIP**
>
> The default is one in the daytime and two for nighttime. The maximum setting is ten.

- **Max % Busy before Delay:** This important parameter controls how much processing time the overall Agent Manager can take. The *Agent Manager* is the task on the server that runs all the Agents. In other words, the Agent Manager dispatches all other Agents. This task, like others such as the Mail Router, Database Replicator, Indexer, or the Catalog, competes for resources on the server. If you expect your scripts to be complex and resource hungry, you may need to set the concurrent number low in order to stay within the limits of Max busy.

TIP

We recommend not letting the Agents that run together during the daytime consume more than 25 percent of your processing power. When they exceed that limit, the Agents will be delayed. If your Agents run sluggishly or not at all, check this parameter.

- **Max LotusScript/Java Execution Time:** This setting protects the Agent Manager from rogue programs. Just as you can protect a server from gigantic documents that hog the connection between two servers during replication (a setting called "max replication time"), you can protect the server from being taken hostage by a poorly written LotusScript or Java program. As you will see in the last part of the book, LotusScript provides the ability to loop and loop forever. Once a script has exceeded its allocated time slot, as defined by the max LotusScript execution time, it will be rudely terminated without warning. The Agent log file will, however, record that event (to view the Agent log, select the Agent in the View pane and choose Agent ➤ Log).

TIP

Break down large Agents into multiple Agents so that you have a "master Agent" and several Agents that are called into action by the master Agent. When writing large LotusScript Agents, try to group all the data changes together and commit them fully at once, as opposed to frequently saving portions. For example, assemble all the fields of a new document and then create it, rather than creating a new document with a few fields at a time and then modifying as you go along.

If you expect your most complex script to run for a very long time, you need to ask yourself, "Will these documents be corrupted if the script is interrupted midcourse?" Remember to test your complex scripts using Actions ➤ Test and generously estimate the completion time to see if you fall within the limits defined in the Name & Address book.

Before creating Agents, you need to check that the server Agent management setting will support them. Similarly, before blaming your own programming for Agents that don't seem to perform properly or on time, you should check whether the server is too busy to handle the processing load. Debugging the execution of background Agents requires a careful analysis of the Agent log file. Note that only the most recently run Agent will be recorded.

Viewing Agents in a Database

Before creating an Agent, you need to examine what other Agents are already available (in order to avoid duplication or even conflicting behavior). Notes enables you to view at a glance all the Agents in a database. To see the attributes of the Agents running in the Big Library from the companion disk, follow these steps:

1. Select the Big Library database from your companion disk.

2. Open it in Design mode.

3. Click the Agents in the left pane, symbolized by a turned on light bulb. You'll see the Agents listed in the right pane as shown in Figure 23.4. If none is available, the light is still on but nobody is home.

FIGURE 23.4:

List of Agents for Da Big Library database

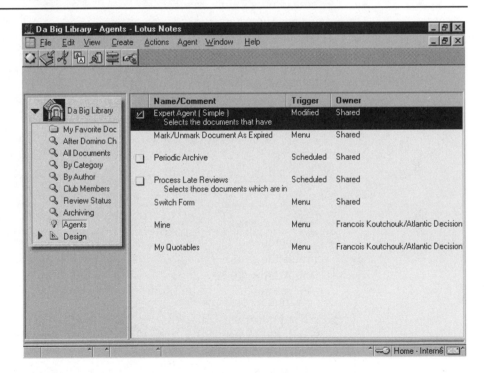

NOTE

It may appear counterintuitive not to see the Agents listed under the Design category in the left pane. In fact, you do not need to have designer privileges to create Agents, but you do need to have reader access to the database. If the Create Personal Agents checkbox is selected in the ACL, then your personal Agents are stored in the database; if it is not selected then your Agents are stored in your Notes Desktop file (DESKTOP.DSK).

Before proceeding with the creation of an Agent, we need to review the attributes and functions of an Agent, as these settings dramatically impact the development of an Agent.

Understanding the Properties of an Agent

The list of Agents displays the main characteristics of an Agent in a four-column table, as shown in Figure 23.4.

- The **Status** of an Agent is indicated in the first column, although it is not labeled as such. If the first column does not contain a symbol, the Agent is launched manually by an end user. Mark/UnMark Document as Expired falls into that category. If the corresponding checkbox is empty, then this is a scheduled Agent that has been turned off (disabled). Process Late Reviews, as shown in Figure 23.4, is such an Agent. After you turn it on, it will be marked, indicating that it will run at the specified trigger interval.

- **Name/Comment** may be the only indication of the purpose of an Agent provided to the prospective user of the Agent. The second line provides additional comments (more is visible under Options once you open the Agent in Design mode).

- **Trigger** indicates how the Agent will wake up. The options are Menu, Hidden, Scheduled, New Mail, Modified, or Pasted.

- **Owner** indicates whether the Agent is meant for all users (shared) or a specific individual (personal). You can see that five shared Agents and two personal Agents are defined in Figure 23.4.

NOTE

If your Agents need to select documents based on any condition based on data contained within a document or a set of documents, the database will need to be full text indexed. (See Chapter 25 for a full explanation of how to set up your database with a full text index.)

Understanding the Three Criteria of an Agent

All design activity with Agents occurs in only one window, called the Agent Builder, which simplifies things considerably. To see the Agent Builder, as shown in Figure 23.5, double-click the My Quotables Agent.

FIGURE 23.5:

Use the Agent Builder window to create or modify Agents and to set their criteria, such as when, which, and what.

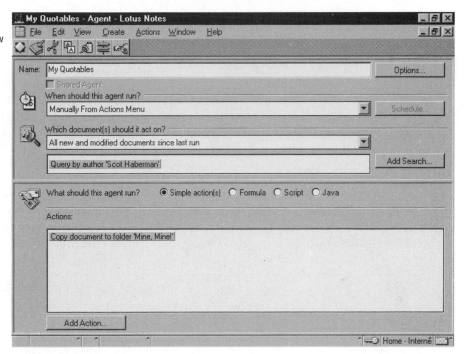

When designing Agents, you need to define three major criteria: when, where, and what. The Agent Builder groups the available options for you. We strongly recommend that prior to opening the Agent Builder, you jot down (on a low-tech piece of paper) the answers to the following questions:

- **When should this Agent run?** Invokes the Agent manually, automatically on a schedule, or whenever a change occurs, such as new mail being delivered or a document being added to the database.

- **Where should this Agent act?** Selects which documents the Agent should act on, such as all the documents, those meeting criteria you define, or those matching a sophisticated full text search condition.

- **What should this Agent do?** Defines an action for the Agent using four levels of programming, including Simple actions, @function formulas, LotusScript, or Java.

At this point, we know that Notes security is set properly and we have a good idea of the behavior of an Agent. Now we are ready to create our first Agent.

Creating an Agent

In Notes Release 3, Agents were called macros and were often only accessible to more advanced Notes programmers willing to wrestle with the @function formula language. In addition to the formula language, Release 4 introduces Simple actions, and Release 4.6 introduces Java.

Think of Simple actions as elements that will simplify your life by empowering users to do things they otherwise would ask you to code for them within the Notes application. As you'll see, the simplicity of Simple actions is their strength as an Agent development tool. Release 4 Agents now also satisfy advanced programmers by supporting LotusScript and Java.

NOTE   When upgrading applications to Release 4, all macros will automatically be transformed into Agents with @function formulas. You may choose to recode them using either Simple actions or LotusScript, at a later time.

The next section will cover the four types of Agents, namely Simple actions, formulas, LotusScript, and Java. Suppose you are interested in keeping track of the occasional contributions to a discussion database by a person in your company who usually intervenes when highly sophisticated issues come up. Unfortunately, many other people contribute comments of dubious relevance or arguable quality. If there is a lot of traffic in the database, the unread flag will not help you to sort out the relevant information from all the noise. What you need is an Agent that notifies you whenever an individual or a group of people creates a new document.

Follow these steps to create an Agent that you will call Expert Agent:

1. Open the Big Library database from the companion disk.

2. Select Create ➤ Agent. The Agent Builder window will appear, as in Figure 23.5.

3. Type **Expert Agent** in the Name field.

4. Mark this Agent as a Shared Agent because we are going to share it with other members of our group.

WARNING   Once you save an Agent as either personal or shared, you cannot change that designation.

You are now ready to set the three criteria of the Agent, starting with the settings to trigger it.

Setting the Trigger (When Condition)

Several options can trigger an Agent depending on the behavior we wish to produce. As we have seen, Agents may run manually, that is, when you pull the trigger. But the more interesting Agents run automatically when a certain condition is met, which is either a recurring time-based event or document-level event. A review of the types of When conditions follows.

Manually from Actions Menu   The Agent is totally inactive until somebody calls it by selecting it from the Actions menu. This type of Agent is very similar to an Action button in a view.

Manually from Agent List   The main purpose of this option is to hide the Agent from the view of users. This option is the correct way to list Agents that call other Agents. If you are working without a net (in other words, asking to lose your job) directly on a production database, this option will protect other users from inadvertently invoking this Agent—the only way to call it is by selecting Agents ➤ Run while the specific Agent is selected in the Agents view. Similarly, Agents that you no longer need can be reset to this condition until you decide to purge them for good from the application. These Agents must contain code to first switch to the appropriate view to be tested. Agents you tie to an Action button, a Navigator, or even a hotspot in a document should be defined with this type.

On Schedule Hourly, Daily, Weekly, Monthly   The shortest frequency available for running an Agent is every 30 minutes (this is an option within the selection for running every hour). This limitation avoids excessive resource utilization by Agents on servers. If your application calls for more frequent looping, you will need to write a server-based API or create custom code in LotusScript or Visual Basic running on the Notes clients that need very frequent polling. Regardless of which frequency you are using (every 30 minutes, hour, two hours, four hours, or eight hours), you have the option of setting a start/stop time and a start date/end date. You also have the option of disabling it on weekends. Notes defines the weekend as Saturday and Sunday, so don't waste your time asking your boss for Fridays off. Figure 23.6 shows the Schedule dialog box for Agents. You need to specify which server the Agent should be run on. (Skip ahead to Figure 23.12 for a view of one of the Schedule dialog boxes.)

FIGURE 23.6:

When you schedule Agents, you can specify a start/stop time and a start/end date, as well as which server the Agent should be running on.

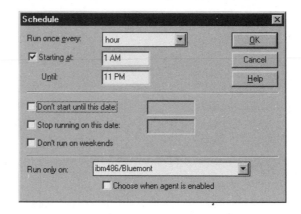

TIP

We recommend that you run the Agent at "off times" and no more frequently than necessary out of consideration for your fellow users—Agents take resources off the server. Similarly, don't set an Agent to run forever—it's very easy to re-extend its use because expired Agents are not automatically erased from the list of Agents. Our advice is to keep a low profile to avoid a crackdown on Agents from the Notes system administrator.

WARNING

The list of servers you can send an Agent to run on does not list the servers that have a replica copy of the database. It's just the list of available servers, based on other Notes criteria not related to the existence of that database on the server. If you select a server that does not have the database, the Agent is guaranteed to do absolutely nothing. Similarly, you must make sure that the database ACL of the server running the Agent allows changes to propagate to the replica copies on other servers and verify that the server allows Agents to run.

Performance Impact of Background Document—Triggered Agents

The Documents Have Been Created or Modified option can create a lot of overhead in a very busy database. Make sure that you further refine the selection criteria using the Search Builder described below.

Unfortunately, the database must be full text indexed for adding search criteria. The trade-off for the administrator of a database with many daily updates is either to allow Agents to run too frequently (processing resources) or to full text index the database (storage resources). We recommend the full text index option (see also Chapter 25 on indexing) and requiring Notes developers, and users who are allowed to create Agents, to specify narrow search criteria.

Determine the time-critical nature of the information in the database and whether an hourly update (or even every other hour) is acceptable. Do you really need to have an Agent run every time a document is added to the database, or can it be set to run once per hour on all of the new documents that have been created or modified during the past hour?

On Schedule Never   This setting serves no purpose in Release 4, unless you are upgrading a Release 3 database. If you are going to forget anything in this chapter, this is a good candidate.

If New Mail Has Arrived, If Documents Have Been Created or Modified, If Documents Have Been Pasted   These document-level options, generated automatically by the Notes server on which the Agent is running, are in fact powerful shortcuts to realize very common combinations of when/what. With Notes Release 4 you have granular control over which event a specific Agent will launch. You can easily set up a "watchdog" that wakes up every time a document changes or is added to the database. As you can see in the Agent Builder, the Where option is automatically selected to match this option.

Here's how to get the Agent we are creating to run automatically on the server: In the When dialog box, select If Documents Have Been Created or Modified.

Now that we have decided when the Agent will wake up, we need to define the scope of its work. The two conditions, *when* and *where,* are often correlated.

Setting the Scope (Where Condition)

The Where condition determines which documents will be processed by the Agent. You need to set it properly, particularly if the Agent will write or modify any information. Let us rephrase this: Accidentally erasing or deleting data with an Agent is a career-limiting move.

The Where condition depends on the When condition, as shown in Table 23.1:

TABLE 23.1: The When Condition Triggers the Where Condition

When (trigger)	Where (selection)
Time based	All documents
	New and modified since last run of this Agent
Document level	Automatically selected, either the pasted, mailed-in, modified, or newly created documents
Manual	All documents in the database
	All documents in the view
	New and modified since last run of this Agent
	All unread documents in the view
	Selected documents in the view
	Run once

The All Documents option in the time-based trigger is new to Release 4 and avoids the ugly and painful workarounds that were necessary in Release 3.

The Run Once option allows you to run the Agent against the opened document or a single document selected at the view level. Run once is very similar to a hotspot button or an Action at the form or view level in that it allows you to insert @Commands.

The When option we set in our example—If Documents Have Been Created or Modified—automatically set the Where option to Newly Modified Documents.

We need to refine our Agent to tell it to worry only about documents created by a few specified people. The Where condition is refined by using the Search Builder.

Using the Search Builder

Click the Add Search button. The Search Builder window will appear, as shown in Figure 23.7.

FIGURE 23.7:

The Search Builder allows you to select the precise documents that match your criteria.

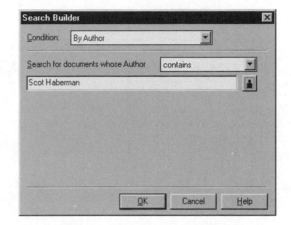

The conditions available in the Search Builder should meet most of your needs without requiring any programming. Let's explore the richness of these conditions. You can follow along by toggling the values in the Condition drop-down list.

Searching by Field   There are several options depending on type of field: date, number, or text.

- **If the field is text**, you specify whether it should contain or not contain a string you type. Make sure you do not enter a typo.

- **If the field is a number**, you can choose equal, not equal, greater than, less than, and inclusive or exclusive of a range. If you need more sophisticated arithmetic, you will need to use the Formula functionality of the Agent Builder.

- **If the field is a date**, you have a wide range of choices, including before or after a date and in the last or next number of days. Make sure you enter dates according to the Notes format, which may vary from country to country.

Searching by Date   The scope applies to the entire document, not just a field within the document containing a date. You can choose either the date the document was created or the date of its last modification.

Searching by Form   Searching by form is a very intuitive way to define a search criteria. The window presents a list of forms you can use in the database to create new documents. After you select a form, the Search Builder will display the form with all its fields. The formulas and keyword lists don't work in the fields, but you can type in values. For instance, you can type the word *Health* in the category field.

How to Discover the Names of Fields

You can figure out the names of the fields using the following technique:

1.   Open a document.

2.   Display the Properties dialog box for the document.

3.   Click the Fields tab.

The list of fields is in the left side of the Properties dialog box on a white background, and the value of the fields is on the right side, as shown in Figure 23.8. The fields are sorted in alphabetical order. As you click on the fields, the right-hand side will display their name, type, and most importantly, their value.

Given enough time and patience, you should be able to match the field names to the contents listed on the document on your screen.

FIGURE 23.8:

The Document Properties dialog box displays the list of fields and their values.

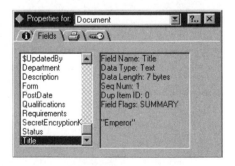

The major drawback of the Searching by Form method is that it forces you to be less specific than the others—you can specify only a value that the field should contain, not ranges, exclusions, and other pertinent parameters. On the other hand, Searching by Form is quite convenient if you know precisely what values various fields should contain. For instance, if you have a technical document that contains multiple category fields, you could place the words *Engineering, Software,* and *Notes* in the three fields to obtain an accurate list of documents relevant to Notes within your entire organization.

You may have to use this method if you do not have access to the meaning of the fields: certain developers unfortunately give fields names that nontechnical users would never guess, for example, listCatLev1, listCatLev1_1, or listCatLev1_2. Depending on their mood, or the time of night they were designing the form, you may see some very bizarre naming, such as Smeh, BlurgMa47, or DoogleSnopper_1032a.

Searching by Form Used   You can select multiple forms, such as Response and Response-to-Response documents only. This setting is a simple way to make global selections of documents and to act on them as a block, perhaps for the purpose of logically splitting a database. For instance, if a sales database contains account profiles, sales leads, and contact information, you could select all the contacts to automatically update a large corporate Rolodex database.

Searching by Folder   Works the same way as the Forms Used condition. You select all the documents that happen to reside in the folder at the time the Agent runs. The Folders option includes all the views of the database as well as your personal folders. In our previous example, you could have built a view containing only Contacts documents using the selection formula for the view. (See Chapter 20 on designing views for more information.)

Searching by Words and Phrases   You have up to eight fields for entering phrases or single words. This option is very useful for searching within the contents of the rich text fields. The syntax is identical to a full text search (see Chapter 25). You can actually chain multiple searches together, so that you can search for more than eight words or phrases.

Searching by Author   The form must have a field of the type Authors in order for this setting to work. You can base the criteria on "contains" or "does not contain." Use this option when the most likely condition to distinguish documents is the author. Note that this option may be confusing in certain databases when the "author" may be defined as the latest editor of the document.

Creating a Where Condition

In our example, we are interested only in documents originating from a certain list of persons. To define the Where condition for our Agent, start in the Agent Builder and follow these instructions:

1. Click the Condition drop-down list in the Search Condition dialog box.

2. Select the criteria By Author and "contains" and then click the person icon to bring up the Names window, as shown in Figure 23.9.

FIGURE 23.9:

In the Names window you can select names and groups directly from the Notes Name and Address book to be used as conditions in the Search Builder.

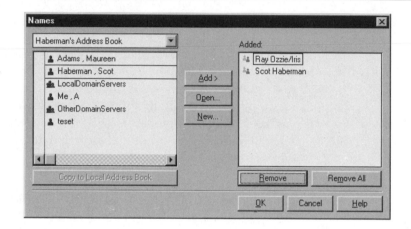

TIP

The Where documents search condition may be based on specific forms, folders, or fields. As much as possible, you should create your Agents at the end of the development cycle.

---

3. Add a few names from your Name & Address book and click OK.

TIP

You can add conditions to the search query for the Where condition simply by repeatedly clicking the Add Search button. Notes will automatically put an AND between the clauses. You can type over the word AND to replace it with an OR.

TIP

If you wish to redisplay the Search Builder in the Where search criteria text box, simply double-click the gray Search token in the search window. Similarly, although you can type directly in the text window, we recommend that you use the Search Builder to avoid introducing typos or syntax errors.

TIP   You can use the full text search capabilities to determine which documents you want your Agent to process. Cut the search token out of the full text search window and then paste it into the search window on the Agent Builder screen.

We are now ready to tell the Agent what to do when the experts we specified have created or modified a document.

Setting the Actions (What Condition)

So far our Agent was told when to run and which documents it should operate against. Now it is time to program our Agent to take an action (not be confused with the Action button actions that were covered in Chapter 21). There are three ways to program an Agent for action.

- The first and easiest way is to invoke a Simple action, described in detail in Chapter 21.

- Database designers may prefer the @function formula language to set up more complex conditions.

- Advanced programmers may write the action using LotusScript or Java.

Even if you consider yourself an advanced programmer, there is plenty of merit in using the Simple actions method. Given the potential damage a rogue LotusScript Agent or Java Agent could cause, you are taking fewer chances with Simple actions. And if you take chances and lose, you may have no choice but to use Simple actions or formulas if the Notes administrator or the database manager shuts you off (see the beginning of this chapter on security restrictions).

We would rather be surfing than writing Script, Java, or formula code, so we strongly recommend that you master the Simple actions and use LotusScript and Java in Agents only as a way to avoid writing Notes API code or doing the dishes.

Simple Action Agents

Simple actions are prepackaged Notes tasks that enable you to "program" tasks without having to understand the intricacies of a programming language. When using Simple actions, Notes walks you through the steps required to achieve a certain task. Simple action Agents are similar to the wizards seen in other programs except that this Notes wizardry actually does the work. (Other wizards just tell you what to do.)

Table 23.2 summarizes the types of Simple action Agents.

T A B L E   2 3 . 2 : Types of Simple Action Agents

Action	Requires	Comments/Frequent Use
Copy to Database Delete from Database	Server and database name for the copy	Background administrative tasks such as archiving or cleanups.
Copy to Folder Move to Folder Remove from Folder	Name of the folder	Automatically file or remove documents into private or shared folders.
Mark Document Read		Toggle the unread mark of a document. Use to systematically ignore things.
Mark Document Unread		Toggle the read mark of a document back to unread—as if you hadn't read it already. Use if you loaned your ID to somebody else or your cat walked across the keyboard randomly opening documents.
Modify Field	Name of the field	Replace or Append text, shows number of date value you specify. Substitute values globally, change the status of documents, etc.
Modify Fields by Form	Name of the form	Same as above except you write the value directly in the form. Great if you can't remember the name of the field.
Reply to Sender	Document is a mail message	Use in e-mail files to send an automatic reply, for instance, while you are on vacation. Note the Reply Only Once per Person option to avoid reminding the same colleague that you are on vacation when she is not.
Run Agent	Name of another Agent	Use daisy chain Agents.
Send Newsletter Summary		Automatically sends via e-mail a viewlike summary of documents—with doclinks back to the documents—from a database you or the recipients don't read frequently. Very powerful!
@Function Formula	Knowing the formula language	Identical to the Formula option Formula except that the formula is "hidden" behind a grayed-out text tab.

Continued on next page

TABLE 23.2 CONTINUED: Types of Simple Action Agents

Action	Requires	Comments/Frequent Use
Send Mail Message		Used for all kinds of notifications and sorting tasks. You can even use a formula to compute the recipients' addresses or the subject of the mail message. Very powerful.
Send Document		Tricky to use because the document must contain prepopulated SendTo and other mail fields.

Creating the What Condition

To continue with our example, we want to notify our group via e-mail whenever the experts write something in the database. Start in the Agent Builder and follow these steps to enter a What condition for our Agent:

1. Select Simple actions in the Run radio buttons of the "What should this Agent do?" section of the Agent Builder window, as shown earlier in Figure 23.5.

2. Click the Add Action button at the bottom of the Agent Definition window to display the Add Action dialog box.

3. Select Send Mail Message, since we want to automatically notify our group that the experts added new information to the database. The Edit Action dialog box will appear, as shown in Figure 23.10.

4. Click the Person icon on the To: line and select a few people or a group.

FIGURE 23.10:

Sending an automatic e-mail notification. Specify the recipients, the subject, and whether you wish to include a link or a copy of the original document.

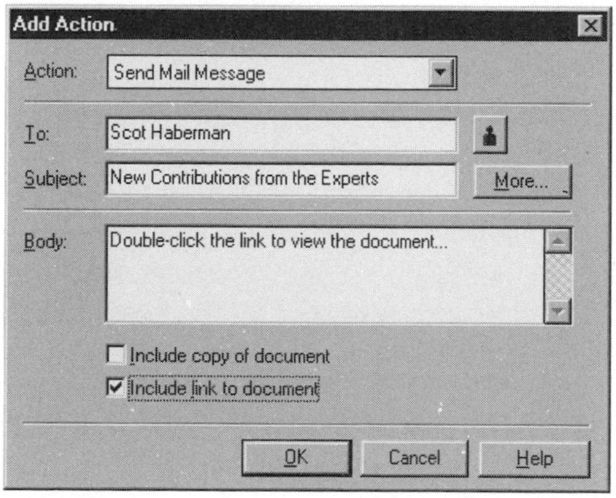

5.   Type a subject, for instance "New Contribution from the Experts." Note the More button that allows you to assign a *cc* or *bcc* on the distribution list.

6.   In the Body field, type **Double-click the following hypertext link to access the document**.

7.   Make sure you select Include Link to Document. If the recipients of the notification use laptops or do not have physical access to the database, you can include a copy of the document. As a rule, we tend to always include the link.

8.   Click OK.

TIP

Links use very little resources and provide an opportunity and incentive for readers to participate directly in the original repository of the information.

You have now defined the three essential criteria of an Agent—the When, Where, and What conditions. The Agent is complete and ready for immediate use.

Enabling Your Agent

Before setting your Agent loose on innocent documents, we strongly recommend that you use the new Release 4 feature that allows you to test an Agent without actually mailing anything or changing any data. If you are a corporate standard type of person, make sure to require this step in all Agents before they are rolled out in production mode. Let's test our Agent by selecting Actions ➤ Test. Carefully review the information in the text window, shown in Figure 23.11:

•   Were the right number of documents selected?

•   Was an e-mail sent?

•   How many documents were modified?

NOTE

Unfortunately, you cannot print the results of the Test Run Agent Log from Notes. Given that it reports the proper functioning, a date stamp for the test, and the length of its execution, it would be valuable to keep a printed copy in your drawer for further reference or to prove that you took the required precautions. You will have to use a low-tech method to print the entire screen: use either the Print Screen key or a shareware utility that takes a snapshot of your screen.

FIGURE 23.11:

The Test Run Agent Log allows you to observe what an Agent would do without actually modifying any data.

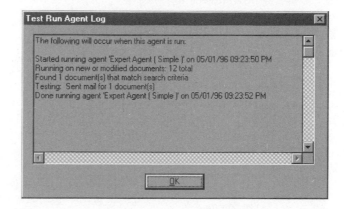

We strongly advise you to read this report carefully. If you have spent a long night developing this Agent, wait until your head clears up the next day before you test and review the output of the test *line by line*.

If everything looks fine, you are now ready to release the Agent on the production database. But you still need to make sure that your Agent can run in a live setting by following these two steps:

1. Click the Expert Agent in the first column of the Agent view or select Actions ➤ Enable.

NOTE   If you were scrutinizing the screen during our description of the When section, you may have noticed the Choose When Agent Is Enabled option (see Figure 23.12). This option asks the user to select a server every time he or she turns on that Agent. This option is particularly useful for manually triggered Agents distributed through replication since the target server will vary with the user.

2. Turn on your Expert Agent Agent. That's it! Your Agent will collect information for your team automatically at the frequency you specified on the server you designated (as soon as the Agent replicates to that server).

You have now completed your Agent. Step back and wait for information to be delivered to your fingertips—or at least to your mail file.

FIGURE 23.12:

To set a schedule for an agent, indicate the start and end date and whether you want to prompt for an execution server every time the Agent is enabled.

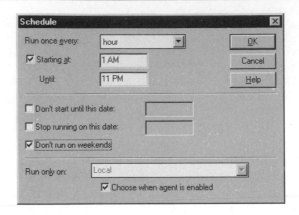

Formula Agents

You just completed the first of three ways to program an action Agent—by creating a Simple action Agent. You could just sit back and relax, unless, of course, the functionality we described in the Simple action Agent did not meet your requirements.

Although we strongly recommend that you attempt to write a formula only after exhausting all combinations of When, Where, and What settings using Simple Actions, a little extra work can produce big results.

Formulas can be used to either refine the Where or the What condition (not the When).

Refining the Where Condition

In certain situations the selection methods provided through the Notes Agent Builder interface are not sufficient to define your Where criteria. Some of the most common cases are as follows:

- **The contents of a field used in the search cannot be evaluated using the conditions provided.** In a text field, you may not be able to use either the contains/does not contain comparison operators—for example, the relationship is the existence of a pattern (@Matches) or belonging to a list (@IsMember).

- **A number field evaluation requires some arithmetic**, such as a conversion to another currency at today's rate or taking the @Power of an exponent.

- **A date field requires matching based on multiple conditions** that need to be computed, such as the sum of the elapsed time between two periods.

- **The value the field is compared to cannot be determined directly at design time** (i.e., it is obtained at the time the Agent runs)—for example, it may be necessary to derive it from another field @Left (AnotherField;1) or retrieve it from the environment (@Today or @Environment).

NOTE   You cannot select documents based on a selection that is defined in a relationship external to the document (parent or children). In addition, none of the functions related to the organization of the documents in the view (@DocChildren, @AllDescendants, etc.) will work in Agents.

Refining the What Condition

Given the wide variety of tasks that can be accomplished using the formula language, the list of possible situations that require the use of formulas instead of a combination of Simple actions is rather large. Some of the most common situations follow.

- **Obtain data from the user** when certain values may not be known at design time. You may need to ask the user for a choice or a value (@Prompt), or you may need to derive the values from the environment or other fields.

- **Perform lookups** when the Agent needs to obtain a list of values from existing documents or through a lookup to an external data source.

- **Perform conditional modifications**, such as setting values in multiple fields in a certain order or based on decisions paths depending on the data contained in the document processed.

- **Perform list operations** (similar to the Where condition) that require the Agent to compare or operate on lists that are likely to require formulas.

TIP   Except for Run Once Agents, you cannot use the @Command functions in Agents. If you need this type of functionality, you will need to write your actions in LotusScript.

Creating a Formula Agent

Let's say we want to write an Agent that will insert the name of the manager for all the documents a user happened to select at the view level, for example, the name of the hiring manager in the job posting form we developed in Chapter 17. Why would the name of the hiring manager be missing? Who knows... maybe the developer of the form forgot to insert a validation formula requiring a value in the field. Or maybe some other rogue Agent decided to "eat" that field. Regardless of the reason, this Agent would fall in the category of a "maintenance" Agent, since it is likely to be used infrequently. In our example, it may be executed only when the database manager realizes that some documents are missing essential information.

You can write this type of Agent using Simple actions, but you may find that it is faster to write this process using the formula language.

Follow these steps to use the formula language to create a manual Agent:

1. Open the Jobs database from the companion disk.

2. Choose Create Agent to bring up the Agent Builder.

3. Type **Reset the Hiring Manager** in the Name field.

4. Leave the Shared Agent option unselected—we are assuming that you, as a database manager, will be the only person using this Agent.

5. Keep the default When condition—to run the Agent Manually from Action Menu.

6. Select All Documents in View in the Where condition.

7. Select Formula in the What condition.

8. Type the following code:

    ```
    daBoss := @Prompt([OKCANCELEDIT]; "Assign Hiring Manager.";
    "Please enter the name of the Hiring Manager for the " +
    Title + " position";"Jim Senior Sr.");
    SELECT Manager = "";
    FIELD Manager := daBoss;
    ```

9. Keep the default Modify Documents option at the bottom of the screen. The Agent Builder should look similar to Figure 23.13.

FIGURE 23.13:

Use the Agent Builder to create a formula Agent.

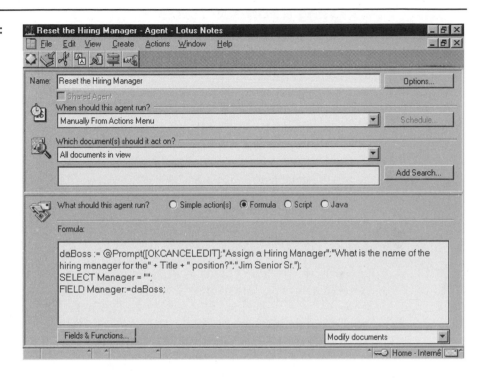

The formula asks the name of the manager for whatever title the Agent is currently working on. It suggests "Jim Senior Sr." as a default manager name. This prompt will repeat for every document selected, substituting the title values appropriately.

It then proceeds to select all the documents in the view for which the Manager field does not contain a value (""). If you had not specified a SELECT statement in your formula, Notes would have automatically appended the following line of code:

```
SELECT @All;
```

forcing the Agent to execute on all the documents in the selected view, even those that already have a manager.

Finally, the formula forces the value collected in the prompt to be assigned to the Manager field.

That's it! All you need to do is test your Agent in the Job Offers view of the database the same way you tested the Simple action Agent. You may question whether it is faster to write a formula than to create a Simple action in this example. We'd say it's about even, with one caveat: You are taking more risks and may have to do some tedious debugging when you write a formula instead of using Simple actions.

NOTE   We cannot give you a hard and fast rule on when you should write an Agent with Simple actions instead of with a formula. Assuming that you do not require functionality uniquely available in formulas, as described above, Simple actions tend to be easier to develop because they are less likely to require difficult debugging and tend to walk you through the steps. But formulas, when coded properly, tend to take less time to write.

Risks of Formula Agents

In our Reset the Hiring Manager Agent described above, the value of Manager is immediately overwritten with whatever the user types. You can see the great potential for losing data with Agents if you are not careful. The risk was limited in our example because only the documents that did not have a Manager value were affected. But many Agents are actually background Agents, acting automatically, without any intervention from the user.

For instance, suppose the Agent did not prompt for a new value using the @Prompt function, but instead performed an automatic lookup from another database.

```
daBoss := @DbLookup(""):"NoCache";"IVORY-TWR":"CORP\\TOTEM.NSF";
➦ "Direct Reports";Department;"Manager")
```

If the @dblookup function fails to retrieve the name of the Manager for the Department for whatever reason, it returns an error to the variable called daBoss.

If you do not have a SELECT statement to limit the damage to the document that meets a certain Where condition, you will swiftly and elegantly blast away all the values for the Manager field in all the documents of the view of the current database. Ditto if you make a typo such as

```
FIELD Manager := dasBoss;
```

Don't feel bad—after many years we still make that kind of error from time to time. The longer the code of the formula, the later in the night, the more frequently we err. Sometimes even twice in a row. The Actions ➤ Test option does not detect an error—after all, the Agent *did* replace the values in the appropriate documents.

WARNING Never test Agents that modify data in a production database. Use design templates and make copies of the data from the production database (see Chapter 24 for more details). The test process is time consuming for an apparently innocuous Agent but well worth it. Trust us on that one.

Limitations of Formula Agents

Formula Agents face the following restrictions:

- Execute only within a single Notes database. They can read but cannot write to other databases and cannot jump between databases. You may even have difficulty modifying the fields of documents in a view different from the one where the Agent is currently running.

- No access to external information, such as spreadsheets and files on your disk and very limited interactions with relational databases.

- No debugger. You can use the Actions ➤Test log for a preview but need to work on a copy of the data to truly test the functionality. You cannot step through the code line by line to figure out where things went wrong.

If you run into these limitations when using the @function formula language, you have no choice (or have the perfect excuse, depending on your preferences) but to use a LotusScript Agent.

LotusScript Agents

LotusScript Agents are as close as you are going to get to independent programs running in Notes (other than Java). Their only restriction is that they must be "attached" to a Notes database (but they can work across multiple databases). Here are some benefits of LotusScript Agents:

- Read and write to external files and applications through the file system, OLE automation, or LotusScript:Data Object (covered in Chapter 29).

- Read and write entire documents or single fields in any view of any database.

- Line-by-line debugger to step through the call.

- Plus all the benefits of developing in LotusScript as described in Part V of this book, such as looping, functions, and call to external programs.

- Minus all the hazards of developing in LotusScript as described in Part V of this book, such as infinite loops and wrong assignments in functions.

NOTE   Remember that your Agent must have sufficient security privileges to execute on the server, as we saw at the very beginning of this chapter. There are two flavors of LotusScript Agents: restricted and unrestricted. The distinction lies in the ability of the script to access resources outside of Notes on the machine running the script, for example, writing a file to the disk or modifying the operating system time/date.

Scripts can have code that runs either when the Agent initializes or terminates. Typically, the bulk of the program will be placed in subroutines or functions. To examine a LotusScript Agent, follow these steps:

1. Open Da Big Library database from the companion disk (the same one we have been using throughout this chapter).

2. Open the Process Late Reviews template Agent.

3. Click the Events drop-down list in the Actions panel.

This Agent contains two subroutines, SendReminder and MoveToNextReviewer. Further description is beyond the scope of this chapter, but you may want to peruse its code once you've completed the chapters on LotusScript in Part V.

Java Agents

Java Agents are very similar to LotusScript agents. Lotus has supplied a Notes Object Interface class for Java that allows the developer the same access to backend classes as a LotusScript program. These classes have been given similar names to the LotusScript methods and properties to ensure a smooth learning curve to Java. The same rules that apply to LotusScript Agents apply to Java Agents.

Some of the benefits of writing Java Agents rather than LotusScript Agents are:

- If you know Java, you do not have to learn LotusScript.

- You have access to more programming functionality (such as URL programming).

- In addition, you get all the same benefits as LotusScript.

Some of the drawbacks to a Java Agent are:

- No access to any of the Notes user interface objects.

- You must write and compile outside of the Notes environment.

- It is more complicated to debug.

NOTE   Since Java programming is an advanced subject, it is beyond the scope of this book. *Mastering Java 1.1* (also from Sybex) covers this information in much greater detail.

What's Next?

Agents are accessible to all levels of Notes users, from the casual user to the advanced developer. Agents can automate most repetitive tasks and should be the last element you complete in an application. Within a few minutes, assuming that the proper security settings are in place, any Notes user can create a process that will intelligently collect information on their behalf and send mail conditionally. Most administrators will find that they can perform routine maintenance automatically, freeing them to perform more important Notes system tasks.

In the following chapter, you will learn how to base a database on a design template. We will cover all the aspects of distributing and maintaining the design of an application apart from its production database.

Basing a Database on a Design Template

- Understanding templates

- Creating a new database from a template

- Creating a template

- Placing a template in the catalog

- Inheriting design changes from an existing database

- Manually refreshing the design of a database

A template is a prefabricated frame from which a new application may be initiated. It contains skeletal design elements such as forms, subforms, views, folders, shared fields, script libraries, Actions, Agents, and Navigators, as well as the icon, About, and Using documents.

You can use a template to create a new database that is ready to accept documents or to refine the design of an existing database. In this chapter, we cover the following topics:

- Deciding whether to use a design template
- Initiating a database from a template
- Using templates to save design time

Deciding Whether to Use a Design Template

In Notes, instead of building a database from the ground up, you can modify an existing template. A template enables you to assemble your database from preexisting pieces—forms, fields, views, Agents, etc.—and to customize it or add design elements as you need them.

In a way, a template is a lot like a prefabricated house. Just as you can save time and money by building a prefab house instead of building one from the ground up, so you can save time and effort (and of course, money) by using a template.

If you can find a template that resembles the application, then use it! The trick is to discover if a template does indeed fit. Determining the usefulness of a template requires a fair amount of investigation on your part and is based largely on visual evidence. Further investigation requires an inspection of the code sprinkled around the design elements.

"Used Template" Check List

Think of templates in terms of used cars. You can save money if you buy one, but you need to do your homework. Templates don't include a warranty, but you can recycle work that cost somebody else months of development time.

As you proceed through your template investigation, put yourself in the shoes of an end user of the application. Is it easy to use? Is it intuitive? If you can't figure it out, chances are, users won't either. Think about how you might modify the design of the database for the purposes of your specific application and how much work that would entail. As a general rule, consider the repercussions a specific change would have throughout the application.

The Value of Templates

A template can serve as a powerful learning tool. If you've ever seen a Notes application in action and a particular feature really caught your eye, you may have asked yourself, "How does that great application work?" As politically and diplomatically as possible, request a template of the database! Since it will contain only design elements and no documents, there is no possibility that you might inadvertently receive actual data.

Of course, many businesses may be skittish about revealing how they record and maintain data within Notes (for competitive reasons). So don't be surprised if your request is denied. However, if you are lucky enough to get your hands on a well-designed, interesting, and useful template, it's time to put on your engineer's (actually, reverse engineer's) hat and pry the design apart.

Lotus supplies about 35 templates with Release 4 (the exact number depends on the version) and gives users permission to modify them for their own purposes. Another excellent source of Notes templates is the Lotus Web site at www.lotus.com. The Web site provides online discussions where subscribers post templates and sample code.

Lotus also sponsors an annual database design contest and presents awards to the best application developers at the LotusSphere conference. Winning this award is a great way to become known as one of the premier Notes application developers in the world.

Discovering how a particular form, view, or macro operates by stepping backward through the structure and design of the finished product is a fantastic (and the quickest) means of sharpening your programming skills and adding tricks to your Notes programming repertoire.

We strongly recommend that you spend some time taking apart the databases provided on the companion disk.

Changing Views

It is usually easy to modify views. Don't worry about the labels of the columns or the overall format, but do check that the contents are somehow displayed in a logical way. See if the fields you may want to categorize on are available in one of the columns. Adding views is a bit more complex, but armed with the information in Chapter 20, you should be able to create new views rather easily.

Do the views generally represent the requirements of the different groups of users that need access to the database? For instance, creating a new view categorizing documents by month is easy, but adding a view that categorizes by group and status of the document (such as approved or rejected) may be more complex.

Changing Navigators

The difficulty level of changing Navigators ranges from complex to simple. The flow implied in the use of a Navigator is difficult to change, as it may create an avalanche of subsidiary changes. If the changes are mostly cosmetic, however, you should find the task easy and highly rewarding—overwrite a few graphics, change some keywords, and your database will look like a brand new one.

> **NOTE** Actions, documents, forms, and views do not depend on Navigators. Therefore, the risk of changing or deleting a Navigator because of a change to another design element is relatively limited.

Changing Forms

Forms are usually tougher to modify than other design elements. Even figuring out how a form works may take some time; if the original designer made full use of subforms or computed subforms, you'll have to follow a trail of forms calling each other. Chapter 19 talks extensively about the different design objects available in forms.

Again, don't worry about the labels, sections, and other formatting issues. Adding fields is easy if they are not "essential," that is, if they are not used for categorizing or structuring the information. On the other hand, adding a level of categorization may lead to extensive changes throughout the lookups in the views.

> **NOTE** Adding a fax number field to an address or a region field to a customer form is easy.

> **NOTE** Removing a department field used to compute the Hide-When values of other fields is hard.

Changing Subforms

Subforms also tend to be tougher to modify than other design elements. On one hand, widespread use of subforms may simplify the task of modifying the database to fit your needs—instead of having to modify many individual forms, you can focus on one portion of a form. For instance, you can change a subform used for a table without worrying too much about repercussions elsewhere in the database. But there is no tool in Notes that allows you to see all the dependencies on a field.

WARNING   You need to take great care—even more so than in forms—when deleting or renaming the fields of a subform.

Changing Actions

It is usually simple to add, modify, or remove an Action. The main reason is that, as we saw in Chapter 21, Actions depend on existing Notes fields, views, and forms to function, but the dependency does not extend both ways. In other words, the containers of data (the forms) cannot have dependencies on Actions.

Before creating a new Action, check first to see if the special Action buttons (those beyond menu shortcuts) meet your needs.

Modifying Agents

In general, modifying agents is a pretty complex undertaking. If you are lucky, the template designer wrote a description somewhere (perhaps in the Using document or even the Comment field of the Agents) that highlights the functionality of the Agents and—even better—documents the code. Pay close attention to Agents written with formulas, LotusScript, and Java (as described in Chapter 23).

In general, the existence of many Agents in a database suggests the potential for substantial maintenance requirements in the future. On the other hand, the presence of many Agents could indicate that the database is well integrated with other Notes databases and external sources of data. Our advice is to poke around Agents carefully to make sure they are not pieces of patchwork hiding more fundamental design problems. As you learn how things work, you can add your own comments (internal documentation) to LotusScript, Java, or @function formula Agents.

Changing Code

Modifying somebody else's code is never easy, regardless of the programming language. Make a random pass through the formulas for computed fields, view form formulas, column formulas, etc. Is the code commented? Perform the "diagonal reading" test: Can you scan the code without paying attention to every quote and parenthesis and still figure out what it does? Reread Chapter 18 for more about using formulas.

Also check for "hard wiring," which is the existence of constants directly in the code. For instance, make sure that long lists of keywords are parameterized using table lookups (see Chapter 20), as opposed to being written in full in the field. Similarly, check that the code does not contain too many constants. The following program lines show readable code with clearly marked constants:

```
"--constants --";
Company := "Waves";
LegalStatus := "Incorporated";
" -----------------";
...
" --- Change action based on legal entity";
StatusResult:=@if(Variable=LegalStatus;FieldA;FieldB);
...
" --- create output message ";
Greetings := "The " + Company + "has the following status: " +
➥ StatusResult;
...
```

Note that the Company and LegalStatus constants are placed at the top of the formula and clearly labeled so that you can modify the code by changing only these lines. A less maintainable version of the same code would have been:

```
Greetings:="The Waves has the following status: " + @if(Variable=
➥"Incorporated";FieldA;FieldB)
```

TIP

Formulas are generally difficult to read because of the poor editor provided with Lotus Notes. However, the Cambridge Software Group sells a rather inexpensive alternative editor called, not surprisingly, Formula Editor that allows you to see the code in a structured way (with appropriate indents and formatting for each line). Your nervous system will be grateful if you install this utility.

LotusScript versus Formulas

In Notes Release 4, LotusScript and formulas can sometimes be used interchangeably. If you are not comfortable with LotusScript (even after reading the final part of this book), stay away from a template that contains a lot of LotusScript code. If you are comfortable with it, given its strong internal structure and debugging tools, you may be better off modifying LotusScript than modifying long Notes formulas.

Accept or Reject the Template

To continue with the used car analogy, take the template for a spin, open the hood (pretend you know what's going on), kick the tires, and check the paint for rust spots. After you've used the template a bit, checked the design, reviewed the flow, and looked at the cosmetics, you may be left with nothing but a cup of bad coffee and your own judgment call. The more templates you look at, the more Notes development you do, the better you will get at analyzing the usefulness of existing templates/databases. Remember that there is always a middle ground between rejecting a template on the basis that it was "not invented here" and accepting any lemon that comes your way.

Notes 4.6 Templates

Notes 4.6 has greatly improved some of the existing master templates from Notes 4.5 and has added quite a few new ones. These templates are installed on your computer when you install the Notes software. Table 24.1 lists some of the more notable templates that are available with Notes 4.6 and/or Notes Designer, their file names (.NTF), designer template names, and a brief description of each. Note that some of the templates are designed for use with Notes 4.6 and are not backward compatible. You can use any of these templates, or others located on your computer, as a starting point for any application.

TABLE 24.1: Modified or New Notes 4.6 Master Templates

Database Title	File Name	Template Name	Description
Discussion–Notes & Web (R4.6)	DISCSW46.NTF	StdR46Disc	Electronic conference room that has the same features as the Discussion (R4) with the addition of multiple Navigators, alternate view templates, and hotspot actions for Web users.

Continued on next page

TABLE 24.1 CONTINUED: Modified or New Notes 4.6 Master Templates

Database Title	File Name	Template Name	Description
Doc Library–Notes & Web (R4.6)	DOCLIBW4.6.NTF	StdR46WebDocLib	Document storage that features review workflow (serial only) and archiving and hotspots for Web users.
Frameset (R4.6)	FRAMEW46.NTF	StdR46WebFrames	Customizable HTML frame layouts for creating frame-style Web sites and home pages.
Mail (R4.6)	MAIL46.NTF	StdR46Mail	Notes mail template which has the same features as the Mail (R4) with the addition of POP3/SMTP support, document memo, and document handling improvements.
Mail–Combined (R4.6)	MAILC46.NTF	StdR46ComboMail	The best of both worlds—allows access from either the Notes client or the Web by combining the features in the Mail (R4.6) and Mail–Web Only (R4.6).
Mail–Web Only (R4.6)	MAILW46.NTF	StdR46WebMail	Same as Mail (R4.6) but for Web users only.
Microsoft Office Library (R4.6)	DOCLBM46.NTF	StdR46DocLibMS	Special document library dedicated to the MS application suite. It automatically launches, stores, and supports review cycles of documents created with the suite products.
Personal Web Navigator (R4.6)	PERWEB46.NTF	StdR46Personal-WebNavigator	Access to the Internet. Save pages for browsing while offline.
Portfolio (R4.6)	PRTFLO46.NTF	StdR46Portfolio	Grouping of common application databases within one navigation database.
Web Pages (R4.6)	PAGESW46.NTF	StdR46WebPages	Quick Web site creation that features automatically linked pages, basic server entry setup, and custom page naming.

Initiating a Database from a Template

Let's say that after exploring a particular template you come to the conclusion that its design suits your purposes. The next step is to actually create the new database, indicating that it will inherit its design from the template of choice. Follow these steps:

1. Choose File ➤ Database ➤ New. The New Database dialog box appears, as shown in Figure 24.1.

FIGURE 24.1:

The New Database dialog box allows you to specify a database name, title, and location and to pick a template.

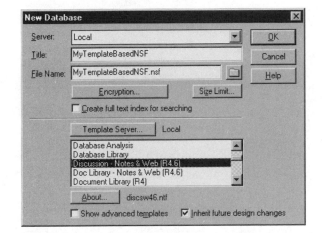

You'll notice the list of templates at the bottom of the dialog box. The default selection is Blank, which means that your new database will not take its design from a template at all and will be developed from scratch.

2. Select the template from which you will initiate your new database. If the template resides on another server, click the Server drop-down list. If you want to know more about the template, click the About button (see Figure 24.2) to display the About document for the Notes template. The About document should provide sufficient information for you to decide if this template will meet your application need (if the designer of the template read this book!). For now, use Local and select Discussion.

NOTE   By default, Inherit Future Design Changes is selected. This means that whenever somebody modifies the discussion template, your database will benefit from those changes. We will review the impact of this decision later in the chapter. For now, keep it on.

You can see the purpose and use of a template before using it with the About option.

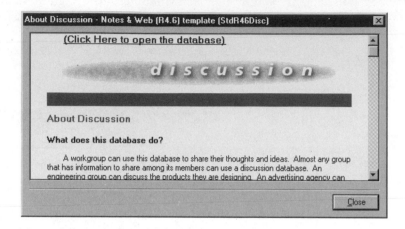

3. Give the template a title. Note that the file name is created automatically. The folder icon allows you to choose a directory other than your default Notes data directory.

4. Click Encryption. This feature allows you to protect a database stored on your local drive (see Figure 24.3). Select Medium Encryption.

FIGURE 24.3:

Choose the database encryption option to protect a database from unauthorized access by somebody who has physical access to the machine that holds it.

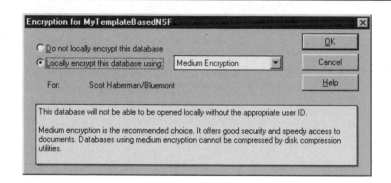

5. Click Size Limit. This feature allows you to assign a maximum size to the database (see Figure 24.4). Choose from 1, 2, 3, or 4 gigabytes.

6. Click the OK button to create the database. If you selected Create Full Text Index for Searching, Notes will ask you if you want to index the database manually.

FIGURE 24.4:

Set a maximum size for new databases using the Size Limit dialog box.

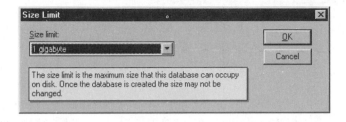

WARNING   The only way to set the size limit higher is to create a New Copy or New Replica Copy of a database. Better to choose 4 gigabytes now than to have to do extra work later.

Protecting a Database with Local Encryption

In Release 3, free, physical access to a Notes database meant complete access to the documents it contained except for the fields specifically protected by a Notes "encryption key." This meant that a Notes administrator with physical access to the servers could read any and all of the unencrypted data it contained. Of more concern was the problem of unattended or stolen notebook computers containing strategic technical or corporate information. Although encryption always takes some toll on performance, our recommendation is to use it on every notebook in your organization that carries proprietary information and on all particularly sensitive databases located on servers or desktop machines. Low encryption won't fool a smart hacker for too long but does protect your data from nonprogramming prying eyes—like those of competitors or curious colleagues. High encryption, on the other hand, requires dedicated top-notch programming resources to compromise your data; use it to protect your strategic data. Medium encryption is a nice compromise for highly confidential data. *Keep the following trade-off in mind: higher security degrades performance.*

You now have a database—built from a template—that will automatically inherit changes whenever the template is modified. If the database is not physically located on a server, you will need to update it manually. Your Notes e-mail file is an example of such a database.

Recycling Templates

If you are really lucky, a database initiated from a template may require no modification. If you conclude that the template fits your needs, or at least comes close, you may then use it as is or as a platform from which to build a more full-featured application.

Practically speaking, however, it's highly likely that you'll have to make some modifications to tailor the database to the precise requirements of your application. If the design includes many items that you don't find useful, removing them is a fairly simple matter. But don't reinvent the wheel if you don't have to. At this point, pay more attention to how the database operates than to why the template operates as it does.

There is no rule against building a database from multiple templates. The process would be similar to building a house from prefabricated elements from several styles. For instance, you may say, "I want the master bedroom of prefab style #1 and the kitchen of prefab style #2." While this type of mix-and-match construction might be impossible—or just plain ugly—in terms of building a house, it is quite easy in terms of building a Notes application.

NOTE   Many third parties develop Notes templates. Licensing such applications may be more economical than in-house development. Some developers make the design available to you—and others insist that you use their services for any post-purchase customization. Access to the source code (the design), even at a premium price, may be an extremely valuable teaching tool for your programmers.

Two basic methods enable you to borrow specific design elements from a template. Regardless of which method you use, you'll incorporate the standard cut-and-paste features of the operating system with specific Notes features that allow you to build your database by using the design elements from other databases.

Using the Strip-Down Method

This method assumes that you have initiated your application from a template that had all (or most) of the design features you wanted, plus some you didn't. Your major task is to strip out the design elements you don't need. When cutting things out, cut them to the Clipboard and try out the application frequently to make sure you didn't remove something vital to its functioning. Our recommendation is that, at the risk of proceeding too cautiously, you cut features one at the time. A few things can go wrong when "weeding out" a Notes database:

- A discarded view is needed for a table lookup by a keyword field in a form.
- A discarded field in a form is used by another form or field for a computation, or worse, for validation.
- A discarded Shared field is used by other forms.
- A discarded subform is used in multiple forms.
- A hidden field or Agent is inadvertently discarded.

We tend to err on the "sloppy but safe" side—hiding active views, forms, and fields, rather than removing them altogether. Once we know the final application well enough to test it thoroughly, we then proceed to remove hidden views, forms, and fields that serve no obvious purpose.

TIP

If you are designing many applications, create a local database where you can save all your old design objects (e.g., views, forms, subforms, Navigators). Our Junkyard database is a poorly organized but large repository of bits and pieces that always seem to come in handy—a bit like a box of spare nuts and bolts rusting in the garage. You never know when you are going to need that "Is it a leap year?" button.

Using the Build-Up Method

This method assumes that a template contains only a few design elements that you want to use for your database. In the build-up method, you cut and paste design elements between template(s) and your new database. When piecing an application together from design elements found in different templates, add the templates to a single Workspace page (the same one as your new database). Open one template at a time, displaying the design elements in the left panel. Tile the template along with the target new database and cut and paste between them. This procedure is a lot easier to do if your computer supports resolutions beyond 640×480.

TIP

You could even employ both methods in a hybrid fashion—initiate the database from a template, strip out unwanted design objects, and cut and paste design objects from other templates.

Taking Advantage of Templates

How do you make modifications to the design of a template without disrupting usage of that database? Answer: Link the database to a design template.

A *design template* is like a standard template in all respects except that its design actually controls the design of other databases through a process called "inheritance." This powerful concept is a bit tricky, but it won't attract the tax collector.

> **NOTE**   Inheritance can be invoked manually by the Notes developer or can run automatically on the server. In automatic mode, the server periodically reloads design changes into the databases that you marked as based on a template. Your e-mail database is an example of a database whose design is updated automatically on the server.

> **WARNING**   Be careful if you are testing changes using a template that is linked to a production database. If the server automatically reloads design changes into a database, you may have changes propagated to a production server by mistake.

For instance, if you add a sales call report form to the Account Management design template through inheritance, every person on the entire sales force worldwide will see this new option in his or her local database. (The same result would have occurred if you had modified the Account Management database itself.) Reloading designs from a template versus directly modifying the production database has several advantages:

- You don't have to work with a live production database. Instead you make your changes offline on the template, test it thoroughly, and then apply it. It's a bit like simulating a face-lift on a computer before going to surgery.

- Templates can replicate like databases (see Chapter 28 for details on replication). Through a process called selective replication, it is possible to control which portions of a design will propagate to various servers. Selective replication may be particularly important if your application runs in multiple languages, because it allows you to maintain alternate forms depending on the destination server.

- Once the application has gone live, designers may not have access to the contents of the database. For instance, the developers of investment banking applications may not be authorized to access information about the accounts. Although you can restrict access through the ACL, isolating documents from the design through a template is easier.

- If you are developing templates for commercial purposes or for sites that are not connected to your Notes network, the only way to send your design changes may be through templates that you mail to them. Templates are much smaller than the databases because they don't contain data.

Creating a Design Template

Creating a design template entails the following basic steps:

- Extract the design of your application to a separate (new) template.
- Design the template as a design template.

> **TIP**
>
> Make sure you have created a meaningful About document before creating a design template. Other developers will greatly appreciate that courtesy when browsing for new templates or trying to figure out how and when to use it. Plus, you get to put your name in the credits.

Extracting the Design from a Database

Extracting a design means you take the design elements of your application, but not the documents, and create a template from them. To accomplish this task, perform the following steps in the Notes Workspace:

1. Select one of the applications from the companion disk.

2. Choose File ➤ Database ➤ New Copy. The Database Copy dialog box appears, as shown in Figure 24.5.

3. Fill in the title. We strongly recommend that you use the word *template* in the title. What's obvious today is likely to be obscure two years down the road. Trust us on that one.

4. Add the file extension .NTF if you want to make the template available for new databases. (Note the *T* instead of *S*; it's not a typo.) That's all it takes for Notes to present this file as a template, as shown in Figure 24.6.

FIGURE 24.5:

The Copy Database dialog box lets you select a database and create a new design template from it.

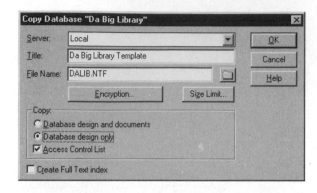

FIGURE 24.6:

The list of templates available includes the .NTF file we just created.

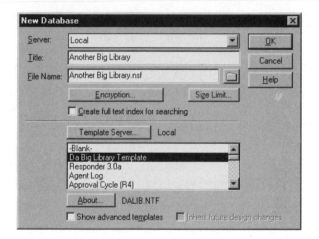

5. Pick a server. If you wish the template to become available on the list of server templates or intend to use automatic inheritance, place it on the server. However, unless your template is finished or you need to share it with other developers, we do not recommend placing it on the server (you should select Local as a server). You can always copy it there later.

> **NOTE**   In this case, the Notes New Database dialog box is somewhat confusing because you need to select Local as a server, although Local is clearly not a server.

6. Click OK to add the template to your desktop. We recommend that you create a Workspace page dedicated to your templates and move the icon to that page.

Designating a Template as a Design Template

The next step is to designate the design as a template. This step is very important and the choices you make may have important repercussions.

1. Select the icon that was just added to your desktop (or that you just moved if you are following our steps!)

2. Bring up the Properties box and choose the Design tab, as shown in Figure 24.7.

FIGURE 24.7:

You can set the design properties of a design template with its Properties dialog box.

3. Click the Database Is a Template option. In the template name, either use your corporate naming convention or make sure that you indicate the main characteristics of this template. If your template is meant mostly for system administrators, select List as Advanced Template in the Database dialog box.

4. Click Catalog if you want to list the template in the catalog. This listing is important to "advertise" your template to other developers in your company. (You can also send them an e-mail and brag about it.) Try to categorize the template so that potential users are most likely to find it. It is possible to enter multiple values for the category field. We prefer to place design templates next to regular databases. For instance, if you categorize Notes databases that hold attachments and reference documents as *Library* in the catalog, it would make sense to also categorize a template providing similar functionality as *Library*. That way, users may be inclined to look at a new application if their existing applications do not quite meet their expectations.

NOTE When naming a template, try to answer the following questions:

- Is it corporate-wide or restricted to a certain department?

- What version of Notes is it written in?

- What is its basic functionality?

Examples of good template names are CorpR46Docs and SalesR46Reports. Application templates usually encompass standard applications such as tracking, libraries, and correspondence. Advanced templates include system functions such as Name & Address books, Mail Router, and Log files.

You have now extracted the design of your application to a design template. You don't have to wait for your database design to be completed to do so—as a matter of fact, we recommend that you take this step at the time your application goes into beta testing. (See Chapter 26, on rolling out Notes applications, for details on the proper management of a development cycle.)

How to Find Design Templates

You won't be able to find your .NTF (Notes Template File) file using the File ➤ Database ➤ Open functionality until you declare it a design template.

Similarly, Notes Release 4 is smart enough to identify Notes Design Templates in the Open Database dialog box, making them much easier to locate, as shown in Figure 24.8—but only if you did not name the template with an .NTF extension.

.NTF templates must be located in the root directory of the Notes data directory on a Notes server or a Notes client to become available during design activities such as File ➤ Database ➤ Replace Design.

NOTE Remember that a lot of potentially proprietary work goes into a Notes template; you may decide whether to lock your own design away from prying eyes. The Lock Design option makes it impossible for anybody to reverse-engineer the database. You invoke this option by replacing the design of a database with a template while selecting the Hide formulas option and LotusScript. When sending demonstrations or replicating with colleagues and business partners, use this option if you need to protect your design.

FIGURE 24.8:

Notes displays design templates in the Open Database dialog box using a different icon. Notice the Da Big Library template.

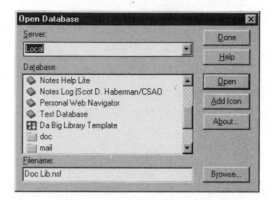

Linking an Application to a Design Template

After you establish a design template, you must link the application to its design template. The method you choose reflects the different strategies of inheritance.

- If the database does not already exist, create a brand new database using the template (see Figure 24.6). Note the Inherit Future Design Changes option at the very bottom of the dialog box. Accept the default (on), and that's all you need to do!

- If the database already exists, select it on your Workspace. Bring up the Properties box and choose the Design tab. Mark the database to Inherit Design from Template, as shown in Figure 24.9.

FIGURE 24.9:

Link the application to a design template with the Properties dialog box.

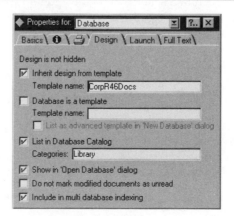

Cautions and Warnings for Template Users

Notes does not provide a lookup list of available design templates nor does it describe the template name you type. Much confusion can be created by inheriting from the wrong template or not inheriting at all.

Notes issues warnings when trying to inherit from multiple templates with identical names, but a busy system administrator can overlook the warnings.

When creating multiple copies of a template during a long development project, make sure you rename the template name—not just the file name. Similarly, avoid renaming production templates because applications in the far corners of your network may rely on that name alone.

You have now tied your application, for better or for worse, to a design template in a fully referenced fashion. Any changes made to the design elements of the template will propagate to the application on a scheduled basis, when forced, or both.

Synchronizing Changes between a Design Template and an Application

If an application and linked-to design template reside on the same server, the process of synchronizing changes between the template and the application can be handled on an automated, scheduled basis. By default, a Notes server will apply changes made to the design template to all fully referencing applications at 1 A.M., as indicated in the NOTES.INI file that is located in the Windows or Notes executable directory of your server:

```
ServerTasksAt1=Catalog,Design
```

The synchronizing routine can run more often or at a different time. For instance, adding an additional line to the NOTES.INI file, such as

```
ServerTasksAt4=Design
```

forces the Design server process to run at 4 A.M.

How to Juggle Replication and Design Templates

If you replicate the design template and it obtains changes from another server, you may want to complete replication before the design task executes on the server. Otherwise, your design will always be behind the last replication that occurred.

If both the design template and the database replicate between multiple sites, set the ACL to disallow the replication of the design between the databases—you want to pick up changes through the templates and then let the design task apply them to the database automatically on each server.

In other words, the database replication picks up the documents, the database template picks up the design changes, and the server's design task applies the design changes to the database.

Our recommendation, however, is to avoid the replication of design templates and let a full replication occur between the databases, including design changes—unless you maintain multiple versions of the template (usually used for applications that support multiple languages) through selective replication. In other words, use the design process to update the design on a copy of the database that will then be used to replicate the changes to all of the other databases.

Using the Refresh Template Method

If the template and the application are not on the same server or if one is local and the other is on the server, you can also force the synchronization manually. Follow these steps to force inheritance:

1. Select your database by pointing and clicking its icon in the Workspace.

2. Choose File ➤ Database ➤ Refresh Design.

3. Select Local when you are prompted to choose a server (or choose the server where the template is located). Notes displays the warning message shown in Figure 24.10.

4. Click OK. Notes will search throughout its directory and subdirectories for design templates. If it finds a match, it will automatically refresh your design.

FIGURE 24.10:

Notes displays a warning
when refreshing a design.

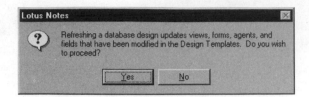

NOTE   Design elements that may have been added to the database after the last inheritance will not be deleted. New forms, public folders, or Agents will continue to exist in the database. If you deleted a design element that originally came from a template, it will come back—a blessing if you accidentally removed it; a curse if you wanted to permanently get rid of it.

NOTE   To use the Refresh Design command, the template does not have to reside in the Notes root data directory. You can place the templates wherever you wish. Templates only need to be placed in the Notes root data directory if you want to be able to select a template from a template list.

Using the Replace Template Method

The other method to force synchronization manually is to replace the design of a database.

1. Select your database by pointing and clicking its icon in the Workspace.

2. Choose File ➤ Database ➤ Replace Design.

3. Choose from a list of template (.NTF) files, as shown in Figure 24.11.

4. Decide if you want to inherit changes in the future (the option is enabled only if the template is a design template) and if you want to Hide Formulas and LotusScript.

TIP   The last option is useful if you do not want other people to modify code that may be overwritten by inheritance or you simply want to protect your code from the curious eyes of managers of the target database.

FIGURE 24.11:

Replacing a database design

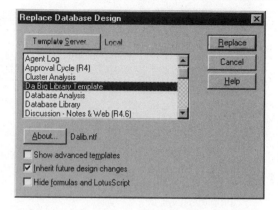

After displaying a warning, Notes will propagate the changes you made to the selected application.

Selectively Disabling Refresh/Replace Inheritance

One of the most frustrating aspects of templates in the early stages of your development experience will be the reappearance of design elements you thought you had removed. The more forms, views, and other design elements you have collected from other templates, the more likely this situation is to occur. Sometimes old elements mysteriously reappear because the server reloaded the design from an old, lost relative of the design template you based some of your new design on during an automatic synchronization. That is because individual design elements (forms, views, shared fields, etc.) also define whether they should inherit their functionality from the copy of the form in a specific design template. To ensure that all inheritance is turned off for each design element, do the following:

1. Select the "offending" view, form, subform, shared field, Agent, or Navigator from the list of design elements.

2. Choose Design ➤ Design Properties.

3. Click the Design tab. The Design Document Properties box will appear, as shown in Figure 24.12. Select Do Not Allow Design Refresh/Replace to Modify or remove the element by typing its name in the Inherit from the Design Template box.

FIGURE 24.12:

Selectively enable or disable
the inheritance of a design
object through the Design
Document Properties box.

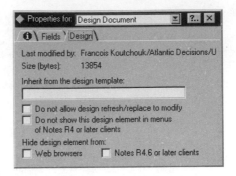

What's Next?

Basing a database on an existing design template can save you the time it takes to create a new database, especially if the template contains elements you want to use. If you don't like some of the elements, you can choose only those you want.

In the next chapter, we start the process of finalizing a Notes application by indexing it. Your application is just about ready to become a real product, and you need to begin the task of managing your new Notes database.

CHAPTER

TWENTY-FIVE

25

Indexing a Notes Database

- Understanding indexes

- Controlling the size of views

- Reducing the resource utilization of a plain text index on a server

- Estimating the size of a full text index

- Creating a new full text index

- Reducing the size of a full text index

- Searching multiple databases

- Managing full text indexes

As you learned in Chapter 6, one of the greatest strengths of Notes is its searching capability. This chapter explains how to create the *plain text indexes* and the *full text indexes* that control the way you can search for, or access, the information contained in Notes documents. We show you how to make the best use of the search engine while optimizing the use of system resources.

In this chapter we cover the following topics:

- Understanding the role of indexes
- Making the best use of the search engine without compromising system resources
- Creating and managing a full text index

You can create a full text index to search for information in multiple databases simultaneously. You can set up a multiple-database full text index on a server that others can use or on a workstation for your personal use.

You can also use the Search bar to enter URLs for Web sites. See Chapter 6 for more information.

Understanding the Role of Indexes

A view is essentially a list of documents that is displayed in response to the user's request (refer to Chapter 19 for more on views). The unique appeal of Notes views compared to database reports lies in the programmatic control that you have over the display of the information. You can categorize elements of the view, show icons, and compute values and terms based on the contents of the documents—without showing the documents themselves.

Chapter 6 showed the strength of full text searching of a Notes database. We tend to refer to full text searches as the "brute force" approach to finding information because they ignore the structure of the data to retrieve it and search every word contained within the documents. Unfortunately, all this functionality is expensive in terms of the system resources required on the server.

Plain Text Indexes

A plain text index contains the elements required to select and display the documents you want to collect and show to the user. A Notes view is a plain text index of the fields defined in the columns of a view. When we created views in Chapter 19, Notes transparently created many indexes.

Each view requires space in the Notes database and CPU cycles to keep it up-to-date or indexed. The more complex the view (in terms of formulas), the more resources it consumes.

Notes offers several parameters for controlling the impact of the views on server performance—and for helping users interact with your application. Let's examine the options.

1. Click a database icon to highlight and select it.

2. Choose View ➤ Design. The database's view(s) opens in Design mode.

3. Click Views in the Design category in the Navigation pane to display all the designs for the database's views.

4. Double-click one of the designs to open the View Design window.

5. Click the right mouse button to display the View Properties menu.

6. Click View Properties to display the View Properties dialog box.

7. Click the propeller hat tab (second tab from the right) to display the View Index Properties options, as shown in Figure 25.1.

You can control three major aspects of the index through the View Index Properties dialog box.

- **Refresh Index:** This option allows you to control the frequency of processing (CPU, memory, disk access). Our advice is to use the default setting unless you expect the database to grow very large (tens of thousands of documents) or very complex (dozens of complex views).

  - **Auto, After First Use:** The default option updates the views as soon as one document is modified. *First use* means that the index will not be rebuilt until the first user opens the view. In other words, the early riser may pay the price of a long night of replications that has collected a lot of new documents.

FIGURE 25.1:

The View Index Properties dialog box displays options for controlling an index.

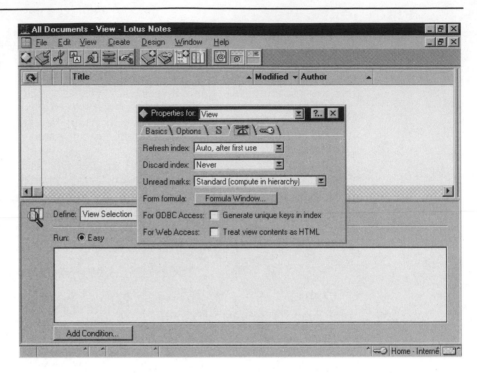

- **Automatic:** The views are always updated on the server.

- **Manual:** This mode requires the user to press F9 (Refresh) to obtain the newest list of documents. This option makes sense if documents are rarely added to the view or if you want to control the refresh from your application.

- **Auto, at Most Every:** This option allows you to specify a time interval in hours. It is the most convenient way to control the indexing of a large database on a server.

- **Discard Index:** This option allows you to control the disk space occupied by your views. The trade-off is simple: save disk space but lose performance, since the view may need to be rebuilt on the fly. There are three options:

  - **Never:** The default—the Notes server never tosses out the index for that view. The index exists for as long as the view exists in the database design.

- **After Each Use:** The only time we would use this option is for views that are accessed so infrequently that the users don't mind waiting extra time, for example, views opened once a quarter.

- **If Inactive For:** The inactivity period is measured in days. After that period, the server will automatically purge the index. This function is used to regain space from outdated views. If, as a database designer, you expect users to lose interest in certain views after a period of time, set this option.

- **Unique Keys in Index (for ODBC Access):** ODBC is a standard that defines the interface to relational databases such as Informix, dBase, or Oracle. ODBC gives Notes the ability to access and be accessed by such databases. This option should be left off unless you are expecting external SQL front ends to access a database.

Full Text Indexes

A full text index is made up of special index files of a database's text and allows Notes to process queries within seconds. These separate index files enable Notes to conduct a complex search of a specific database. When Notes creates the index files, it catalogs all the data in the documents in a selected database on the basis of options you have set. (We describe the options in the following section.) The structure of the index files provides users with a sophisticated way of locating documents in a database.

Full text indexes are particularly useful when the database contains many documents with large rich text or plain text fields, such as policies and procedures manuals or technical documentation.

Creating a Full Text Index

As you learned in Chapter 6, you can search Notes databases through its full text search engine. The engine (based on software from Verity) runs automatically on the Notes server and creates a separate directory (e.g., MYAPP.FT) where it places a set of files for a given Notes database (e.g., MYAPP.NSF) that is full text indexed. The engine processes all the text in the documents during a search and, in Notes Release 4 can optionally search through certain file attachments.

Estimating the Size of an Index

To estimate the size of an index in megabytes, estimate the amount of text in all your documents by subtracting all bitmapped graphics and other elements (such as buttons and links) from each document—anywhere from 25 percent to 33 percent of the total. If you use the Word Breaks Only option, estimate your index to be about 50 percent of that total, or 75 percent if you are using the Word, Sentence, and Paragraph option.

For instance, if the size of your database is 10MB after it's been compacted and it contains an even mix of materials, plan on a 25 percent or 2.5MB overhead. Use 33 percent to be on the safe side and maybe 50 percent for "denser" databases that contain policies and procedures documents or legal briefs.

Indexing a Database

To create a full text index, follow these steps:

1. Select a database from the companion disk and make sure you have copied it to the Notes server or your workstation. (If you run the database locally, you can follow these steps, but you will get additional messages from Notes.)

2. Right-click to display the Database Properties dialog box.

3. Click the Full Text tab to display the index options, as shown in Figure 25.2.

FIGURE 25.2:

The Database Properties dialog box enables you to set options for creating a full text index for a Notes database.

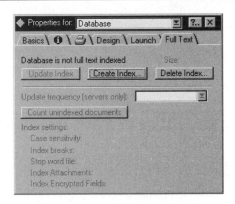

4. Click the Create Index button. The Full Text Create Index dialog box appears, as shown in Figure 25.3.

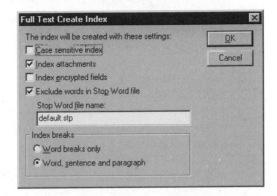

FIGURE 25.3:

The Full Text Create Index dialog box allows you to set the main parameters of the index.

You must now make decisions that affect not only the resources that the Notes server (or your workstation) requires to host the database's index but also the index's functionality to users.

Choosing the Settings for an Index

Choose the settings for the index from the following options:

Case-sensitive Index: Notes will distinguish between lotus (the flower) and Lotus (the company) when the user searches. This setting is convenient for highly specialized databases using well-known acronyms. For instance, "DDE" will not retrieve documents that contain the term *addendum*. Selecting this option will increase the size of the index by about 5–10 percent.

Index Attachments: The text in OLE embedded objects and other attachments will be included in the index. Your index will grow proportionally. This option is often necessary, as users will get frustrated if they cannot find their documents. (The fine technical distinction between attached documents versus native Notes documents is lost to most novice users.)

NOTE   Notes will not index a document (including its attachments) that contains more than 100,000 words. You may not have to worry about size unless your Notes document is larger than 100 single-spaced pages. Notes administrators can edit the file VDKHOME\STYLE\STYLE.PLC on the server to change this default.

Index Encrypted Fields: Omit these fields unless you want to include their contents in the index—and compromise security.

WARNING

A sure way to lose your job is to full text index encrypted fields. This setting bypasses all security measures by making the information visible to the search engine, thus acting as a "curious proxy" on the behalf of users who are otherwise unauthorized to read the information contained in the protected fields. For example, suppose an encrypted field contained information about John Smith's presidential campaign. Users with read access would be able to search for "Smith" and then for "presidential campaign." Notes would find the document—although not the specific field. The field *is* encrypted after all—but not to the full text engine searching through the documents.

Exclude Words in the Stop Word File: Common words such as *the, because, about,* and *however* are excluded from the index. Select this option to save space (10 percent or so depending on the frequency of the stop words, usually related to the style of the documents) without compromising functionality. The stop word file is called DEFAULT.STP. It is a text file, and you can customize it as needed. You can, for instance, create a LEGALEZE.STP file to which you add common legal terms such as *notwithstanding* or *herein*.

WARNING

The default DEFAULT.STP stop word file will exclude the numbers 0–9 for text fields.

NOTE

You can create your own stop word file for a database. If a full text index is local, you can edit the contents of DEFAULT.STP to suit your needs using a text editor. Each word to be excluded must be on its own line followed by a carriage return. You can also create additional Stop Word files and customize them for specific local databases. For example, if you have a local database that discusses medical topics, you can create a Stop Word file specifically for it that includes words like medicine, doctor, and so on that appear so frequently in documents that they're not useful in searches. If you create an additional Stop Word file, you must do so before you create the index that uses it. Once you create the Stop Word file, you can select it when you create the index. The file name must be eight characters or less and use the extension .STP, for example MEDICAL.STP. The Stop Word file must be located in the program directory.

Index Breaks: This option is very important. You can either accept the default (Word breaks only) or select Word, Sentence, and Paragraph. The latter allows you to take full advantage of the Verity proximity search engine. You may recall that the results of full text searches are ranked by relevance. By allowing the index to remember the constructs of the sentences and paragraphs, you will be able to refine your search by the use of terms such as *near* and *within*—for example, "Notes" near "IBM." Deciding whether to use this option is a tough call because it has such an impact on the size of the index. We suggest the following criteria for determining when to choose the Word, Sentence, and Paragraph option:

- The database is rather unstructured (few categories or views).

- It contains a lot of documents (thousands).

- Documents are very similar (e.g., they are mostly computer press articles).

- The users are familiar with sophisticated full text search techniques (e.g., attorneys or market research specialists).

If the database is local (stored on your workstation), the next message box states that the database must be indexed manually and asks if you want to index the database. If the database is located on a server, the next message indicates that the request to full text index the database has been sent to the server.

Completing the Index

A percentage bar appears, indicating the number of documents to be indexed. When the indexing is complete, a message box displays the number of documents added/updated, the number of documents deleted, and the size of the index, as shown in Figure 25.4.

FIGURE 25.4:

When Notes completes the indexing of a database, it displays the number of documents added/updated, the number of documents deleted, and the size of the index.

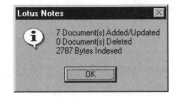

Lotus Notes

7 Document(s) Added/Updated
0 Document(s) Deleted
2787 Bytes Indexed

OK

The Full Text tab now displays the results of the index procedure, including the Index settings, as shown in Figure 25.5.

FIGURE 25.5:

Notes displays the results of creating a full text index for a database in the Full Text tab of the Database Properties dialog box. You can also see the date and time the index was last updated and the current size of the full text index.

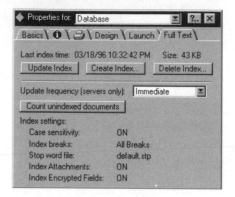

After a few minutes (or more if your database is very large), the full text index Search bar will become available to all the users on the server.

NOTE The new full text index may not be available for several minutes while the server is creating the index. The duration of the delay depends on the level of activity on the server and the overall size of the database.

Index Limitations

You need to be aware of several index limitations so that you won't accidentally omit information.

What Is Not Indexed

As we noted in Chapter 6, an index does not consider every single word in a document, although most rich text attachments, such as Visio drawings, HTML files, Word or WordPro documents, and Acrobat files, are indexed. The following elements are among the index exclusions:

- Text contained within images, such as TIFF or GIF files

- Field names, column headings, and other values set in the design

- Fields of the Keyword type that use synonyms (only the synonym, typically an abbreviation, is stored—for example, Sunday | 1)

- Pop-ups within a document and messages that appear only when using the form

- Computed values, in particular those in the fields of the Computed for Display type.

A good way to figure out what will be indexed is to look at what is actually written in the database. To examine the contents, follow these steps:

1. Open a document in any Notes database from the companion disk.

2. Bring up the Properties dialog box.

3. Click the Fields tab.

4. Examine the contents of each field, as shown in Figure 25.6.

FIGURE 25.6:

The Notes Document Properties dialog box shows the contents of a field that will be processed by the full text index engine.

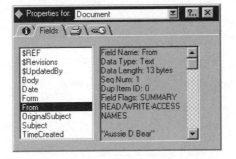

> **NOTE** The full text index will work against all the views. This means that even the views or folders created after the full text index is created are full text indexed.

Document Size Limitations

When creating an index in a Windows environment, the default size limitation for individual documents is approximately 100,000 words on all platforms. You can increase the limit by changing the following variable in NOTES.INI on the server, the workstation, or both:

```
ft_max_instances=<max # of words>
```

For example, the expression

```
ft_max_instances=200000
```

would increase the document size to 200,000 words.

The full text index uses an amount of memory equal to about ten times the setting of ft_max_instances. On Windows 95, changing the setting to 200,000 uses about 2MB of memory to index documents. If your workstation or server runs low on memory as a result of specifying too high a setting, performance will be adversely affected.

When Full Text Index Is Not Finding All the Documents

There may be occasions where one or more documents are not being included in the full text index. When an error is found with a document while trying to create or update a full text index, Notes writes the error to a file, omits the document from the index, and continues processing the remaining records. To check for a possible document error, look for a file called SYSINFO.LOG located in the .FT directory for the database. If a document was encountered that Notes could not process, this file will list the problem.

Recommendations

We recommend that you use the indexing options conservatively as they impact global server performance. But you need to balance global performance against the need to optimize the response time of the Notes desktops, in particular for databases used routinely and frequently. In those databases, set the view-indexing options for maximum performance.

Although disk space is always at a premium on servers, we highly recommend that you full text index all the databases that contain any important textual information. When using Release 3, many companies were reluctant to enable this functionality. With the explosive growth of the Web, however, users are getting accustomed to searching large domains of information, as the popularity of Yahoo! and other search index services on the Internet shows. Also, some of the most powerful Agent capabilities (or Actions) in Notes Release 4 rely on the existence of a full text index.

NOTE   If you want to choose different options for a full text index after you have created the index, you should delete the index and then create a new one choosing the new options. For example, if you initially created an index with the Case Sensitive Index option selected, but you no longer want the index to be case sensitive, delete the original index and create a new one that is not case sensitive.

NOTE   It's not necessary to delete and re-create a full text index if you're only changing its update frequency.

Setting Up Multiple-Database Searching

To set up a search site database to enable users to search for information across multiple databases, you do the following:

- Enable databases for multiple-database searching
- Create a search site database
- Configure a search scope
- Create a multiple-database full text index
- Notify users of the search site database

Enabling a Database for Multiple-Database Searching

Enabling a database for multiple-database searching allows the database to be included in the search scope of a search site database. You must have Manager or Designer access to a database to enable multiple-database searching.

1. Choose File ➤ Database ➤ Properties to display the Properties dialog box.

2. Click the Design tab.

3. Select Include in Multi Database Indexing.

Creating a Search Site Database

After enabling databases for multiple-database searching, create a search site database. Do not choose the Create Full Text Index for Searching option as you create the search site database. Create the full text index after you configure a search scope. Follow these steps:

1. Choose File ➤ Database ➤ New.

2. Select the server on which to store the database.

3. Enter a title for the database, for example, **Marketing Search Site**.

4. Enter a file name for the database, for example, **MKTGSRCH.NSF**.

5. Select the Search Site template (SRCHSITE.NTF).

6. Click OK. The Search form launches by default.

7. Click File ➤ Close to close the Search form.

8. Disable automatic launching of the Search form. Choose File ➤ Database ➤ Properties. Click Launch and in the On Database Open box, select a different option—for example, Restore As Last Viewed by User.

9. Choose File ➤ Database ➤ Access Control and set the -Default- access to No Access to prevent users from using the database while you configure it.

Configuring a Search Scope for a Search Site Database

After you create the search site database, configure a search scope:

1. Select the search site database you created.

2. Define a search scope. Choose Create ➤ Search Scope Configuration. Select a scope and an indexing option for the scope; then close and save the configuration document. The Search Scope Configurations views display the new document. Create additional configuration documents as necessary.

3. Switch to the server console and type the following command to display in the search site database a database entry for each database included in the search scope:

```
Load updall SEARCHSITE arguments
```

SEARCHSITE is the file name of the search site database and *arguments* are these optional arguments: -A -B.

4. Select the search site database, choose View ➤ Go To, choose one of the database views, and click OK to see the databases you've included in the scope.

5. (Optional) If you want to change the view used to display the information users see in a list of search results for a specific database, open a database entry and select a different view in the Search Results Should Use box. The default database view is used otherwise.

6. (Optional) If you want to refine the search scope, do one or more of the following, and then repeat steps 3 through 5.

- In one of the database views, open a database entry and select a different indexing option for a specific database.
- Repeat step 2 to create additional Search Scope Configuration documents.

Creating a Multiple-Database Full Text Index

After you configure a search scope, you create a multiple-database full text index for the search site database. You must have at least Designer access to the database. Follow these steps:

1. Choose File ➤ Tools ➤ Server Administration and click Database Tools.
2. In the Server box, select the server that stores the search site database.
3. In the Databases box, select the search site database.
4. In the Tool box, select Full Text Index.
5. You can optionally select Case Sensitive Index and/or Exclude Words in Stop Word File.
6. Below Index breaks, select Word Breaks Only or Word, Sentence, and Paragraph.
7. Click Create.

Notifying Users of a Search Site Database

After you create a multiple-database index for a search site database, notify users:

1. Change the -Default- access to Reader. If you disabled automatic launching of the Search form, enable it again.
2. Choose File ➤ Database ➤ Properties, click Launch, and in the On Database Open box, select Launch 1st Doclink in the About Database.
3. Send an e-mail or otherwise notify users of the new search site database.

Managing a Full Text Index

Because most databases change over time (documents are added, deleted, and modified), their indexes need to be updated periodically and perhaps even deleted.

Updating a Full Text Index

Server-based databases can be set up to update automatically. Release 4 also supports the automatic updating of local databases. To do so, follow these steps:

1. Select a database that is local to your machine.

2. Choose File ➤ Tools ➤ User Preferences. The User Preferences dialog box appears.

3. Select Enable Local Background Indexing.

4. Restart Notes.

From now on, any time you add documents (by hand or through replication) to your local database, the full text index will be updated automatically.

If you did not enable the automatic update, you can force a manual update by following these steps:

1. Right-click the database's icon. The Database Properties menu appears.

2. Choose Database Properties. The Database Properties dialog box appears.

3. Select the Full Text tab.

4. Click the Update Index button.

Notes proceeds with updating the database. If the server or workstation runs out of disk space during index creation, the index is unusable. When this happens, click the Delete Index button to remove the unusable index. Retrieve or add disk space (if you can), and then re-create the index by clicking the Create Index button.

Errors that occur during index creation or updating are indicated in the server's log.

Deleting the Full Text Index

Do not delete individual index files from the index directories in which they are stored. If you delete the DATABASEFILENAME.FT directory using Windows 95, the index will no longer function.

If you do delete an individual index file (either by mistake or to reclaim server disk space), you can re-create the index any time by clicking the Create Index button that appears in the Full Text tab of the Database Properties dialog box. If the index is set to update automatically, you don't need to take any action because the index will be re-created at the next scheduled update time.

In order to delete a database's index, the index must be stored locally on your workstation. (If the database is located on a server, you can delete the full text index only if you have proper security rights.) To delete the index, follow these steps:

1. Right-click the database's icon. The Database Properties menu appears.

2. Choose Database Properties. The Database Properties dialog box appears.

3. Select the Full Text tab.

4. Click the Delete Index button. A message box asks if you're sure that you want to delete the full text index for the database, as shown in Figure 25.7.

FIGURE 25.7:

As a precaution, Notes verifies that you do want to delete a database's index.

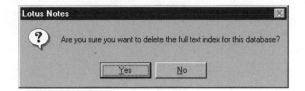

Lotus Notes

Are you sure you want to delete the full text index for this database?

Yes   No

5. Click the Yes button.

Notes proceeds to delete the index. Remember that you won't be able to conduct a full text search of the database unless the database is full text indexed.

NOTE To move a database and the associated full text index, click on the Delete Index button that appears on the Full Text tab in the Database Properties dialog box, and then create a new one.

What's Next?

Although creating a full text index for a database can help users search for specific information, proper indexing is not the last step in developing a Notes application. In the next chapter, we recommend some things you can do to ensure a successful rollout of an application to end users.

Rolling Out Notes Applications

- ■ Understanding how to manage application development

- ■ Using implementation milestones

- ■ Providing help within the database

- ■ Creating an effective About This Database document

- ■ Using the Notes catalog and library

- ■ Publishing a database to the library

- ■ Implementing end-user training on a new database

You may have heard the expression "Information has no value until it's shared." Likewise, any Notes database that you design is only an exercise in style unless you make it available—or roll it out—to users. In this chapter, we discuss the notion of "database productization," which we define as the final steps in the process of turning a Notes application into a production-grade product.

We cover some of the issues you'll need to address before people begin using your database on a full-time basis, such as

- Managing application development
- Providing help
- Providing training

This chapter explains the basics of project management, how to include online help with an application, and how to distribute your application.

Managing Application Development

The purpose of this section is not to cover the details of managing application software development. Plenty of other books are available on that topic. Our point here is that Notes is, in terms of control and procedures, no different from other application development platforms. Consequently, when you develop Notes applications, you also have to worry about the entire roll-out process.

TIP   We cannot overemphasize the importance of managing the development of a Notes application through its many stages. By doing so, you stand a better chance of completing the project on time—and winning points with your boss.

By now, you have probably realized that adding or modifying the features of a Notes application is very easy. You may even be convinced, as we are, that Notes is the fastest business application development tool around. Unfortunately, your users may be convinced of the same thing! Knowing that it is so easy to add a view here or a field there, or to change the color of a Navigator or the background of a layout, they may continuously ask you to enhance the database. And you may be tempted to do so on a rare day when you have nothing better to do.

Eventually, however, endless changes to an application will wear the patience of both the developer and the end users. You could just say no or lock yourself in your office until the requests for changes stop. In fact, what you need is a plan. We are not talking about a foot-high specifications manual—we keep those around to start the barbecue. All you need is a simple document with the milestones for the project and a commitment from all parties to stick to it.

Implementation Milestones

No matter how limited the scope of your application may be, you need to implement the following milestones:

- **Functional freeze:** The point where the functionality described in the specification is met. When you reach this point in development, no change will be made to the workflow or the overall architecture of the application.

- **Feature freeze:** The critical point where no additional new features can be added; they belong to the next release of the application (version 1.1). The concept of *feature* is measured not only in terms of programming for the developer (adding a feature may take only a few minutes), but also in terms of user training, documentation, and testing. Our advice is to call anything that is not a bug or an obvious flaw in the design a "feature."

- **Code freeze:** The point where the developer stops *all* activity on the application. Not a line of code should change; it's the "gold" build.

If you are not regularly involved in software development projects, don't panic! What we are suggesting is a simple methodology to apply some sense of discipline to the process and avoid disappointment likely to occur when deliverables do not meet expectations in either functionality or timetable. In the next section, we review the processes necessary to implement each milestone.

Milestone Processes

For each one of these milestones, you need to implement the following processes:

- **Review cycles:** A subset group of end users reviews the application. *Functional freeze* ("prototype") calls for a period of time during which users compare the adequacy of the application to their specified requirements. *Feature freeze* ("beta") calls for testing the application to see if all the forms, views, and Navigators are working properly. The more closely the sample of testers represents the actual end users, the more likely the review cycles will bring out the drawbacks or failings of your application. Note that depending on the complexity and scope of the application, you may have more than one cycle between the milestones (for instance, several beta releases).

- **Signoff:** At the risk of sounding unnecessarily bureaucratic, nothing beats a formal signoff at the end of each review cycle. If the requester of the application is a group of users, the signoff should come simply from its nominated sponsor, or otherwise from all members of the team. It can be as simple as an e-mail or as complex as a vote at a meeting. A milestone signoff document can list the items that still need to be remedied before a final signoff document (all milestones and deliverables have been achieved) will be granted.

- **Development cycle:** Whenever signoffs are completed—or the milestones are delivered but rejected by the sponsors—application development should enter a new cycle. For instance, instead of fixing a few bugs in a beta and then releasing it, development should fix all the bugs as well as all reported or known problems and then formally resubmit the application for further testing.

Notes Release 4 provides you with the ability to develop mission critical applications that can impact thousands of users in your organization. However, we have repeatedly seen projects that went over budget or didn't meet deadlines. Why? Because all the parties involved in a project were lured into the Notes design trap: the flexibility Notes offers as a database development environment.

NOTE One fundamental advantage that Release 3 has over Release 4 is that Release 3 supports a relatively limited set of tools and features to use in an application. By comparison, Release 4 provides too many new tools and features. These goodies make it hard to end the application development cycle in order to roll out an application.

Providing Help

A well-designed application may be obvious to its primary intended users, but less so for occasional users. What makes sense to seasoned employees may be less apparent to new hires and transfers. In many instances, printed documentation does not accompany a Notes application. However, this lack of paper needn't be a problem. Notes provides the following tools to create comprehensive online help:

- The About This Database document
- The Using This Database document
- Field help, pop-ups, and hotspots
- The database icon and title
- Notes catalog database
- Notes library database(s)

About This Database

The About This Database document (About...) is basically a special Notes document that users can display for a selected database. In Release 4 you can force the About document to appear according to the following scenarios. (See Figure 26.1.)

- The first time the database is opened by the user after adding it to their desktop
- Every time the user opens the database
- Every time the About document is modified

FIGURE 26.1:

You can force display of the About This Database document every time it changes.

NOTE   If the user opens the document directly from the library (using the Browse or Open actions), the About document will not appear.

Just as a Web home page is important to convey the purpose and attract the interest of a visitor, the About… document should provide enough information to explain the following:

- Its title, which is not always obvious!

TIP   You may copy the Abstract from the library (see below).

- Who should use the application
- The benefits of the application
- The level of confidentiality of the data
- How to contact the manager
- Who has access to the various parts of the database
- Other databases that provide similar or complementary information

Unfortunately, the About document does not provide layout regions to insert fancy images—but you should at least paste a copy of the database icon.

Try to keep the document short—a few pages at most. In Release 4, you can insert Sections to group the different parts of the About document. We also recommend that you use Action hotspots and text pop-ups to explain specific terms in the document, for instance, an acronym unknown to visitors from another department, or additional contact information for the database manager.

Link hotspots are convenient for building hypertext links to other related Notes documents or databases. Action hotspots or buttons can also be used in conjunction with LotusScript to provide a sign-up mechanism to the database. Figure 26.2 shows an example of a thorough About This Database document. Note the Join button. The first time users access the database, they have the opportunity to fill in a registration form, enter their interests, or store their demographics in a profile form.

FIGURE 26.2:

The About This Database document contains the essential information about the database.

TIP

Although we do not believe in setting standards for the sake of setting standards, the About This Database document is one area where the enforcement of a corporate policy makes sense.

The policy should specify how developers should write an About document and what functionality the document should contain. Companies that are effective at enforcing this policy turn the database catalog into a great resource for documenting their important business processes. All too often companies do not invest enough time in defining application development standards, especially when it comes to creating basic documentation.

Using This Database

The Using This Database document (Using...) serves a different purpose than the About document. The About document explains the mechanisms of the application;

the Using document is a how-to guide. Most Notes developers dread creating a Using document—but don't skimp: doing it well will save you a lot of phone calls after the application is rolled out (RTFM). Ask your IS support engineers for an explanation of the acronym.

A good Using document should contain at least the following elements:

- **Description of the roles:** Who are the intended editors, authors, and readers of the database? If the application is using the Notes Role feature, list the roles and indicate who is a member or how to become a member.

- **Responsibilities and security:** Explain clearly how the different roles are expected to participate in the database, set the tone and state the security parameters (for instance: all information contained herein is Company Confidential). List the encryption keys in use and indicate who holds them.

- **Description of the workflow:** If the database encompasses more than a few steps of a process, include a flowchart, such as a Visio drawing (it speaks volumes). Don't overdo it; simply point out the different stages of a document and the approval steps.

- **List the views:** Name and explain the purpose of all the views accessible to users with reader privilege. A few sentences should suffice to indicate the uniqueness of the view and explain when a reader may want to use one view over the others.

- **List the forms:** Name and explain the purpose of all the forms accessible to users with read and compose access. If the forms change when in Preview mode, make sure to explain why—there is nothing more confusing to users than "missing fields." Point out the technique used for required fields (for instance, the little symbol you place near them), color coding (a yellow background for response forms, a green for background information documents). Don't list every single section and field: a well-designed form should be self-explanatory (see below); just outline the overall approach and the areas of particular importance.

- **List the Agents:** Walk the administrator or user through the scheduling of the Agents to ensure that they will work properly. The user should be aware of background Agents or other processing that takes place.

- **Action buttons:** You don't need to describe the Action buttons or other design elements that are self-evident. The point again is not to bore users with extensive documentation but to provide enough information for them to help themselves and to invite them to explore new features of the database.

- **Administrator's notes:** Create a special section, using the Hide-When feature, that explains how to maintain the application, including external lookups, specific server installation guidelines, training requirements, and other relevant information for somebody to take over responsibility for the database.

- **Developer's notes:** Create a special section, using the Hide-When feature, that explains the "gotchas" of the application. Feel free to skip this section if you are confident that you can develop an application without limitations, known bugs, hard-wired data elements, quirks, and other "improvements postponed until further notice."

Using Hide-When...

The Hide-When feature, as we saw in Chapter 19, allows you to control when to display a specific design object (such as text, a field, or an entire section) to the user. In its most basic form, Hide-When allows you to selectively display the design object if it is used for reading, editing, or printing mode. For instance, a text string "Country" placed in front of a field of the same name will appear only in Edit mode because the value of the country field itself is sufficient in Read mode.

A more advanced use of the Hide-When functionality involves @function formulas. Formulas allow you to set conditions beyond the status of the document (read, edit, print, and preview). You can use any formula that returns a value of True or False. For instance, you can hide a section of text in the About This Database document if the user name is not a member of a Name & Address book group. Or you can hide certain information in a document based on the value of a field within that document.

Field Help, Pop-ups, and Hotspots

You may have noticed that many of the Windows applications you purchase (such as Visual Basic or Quicken) create a help file during their installation process. This standard Windows file allows you to press the F1 key at any time and obtain context-sensitive help. It also typically contains a table of contents and a searchable index.

In contrast, Notes provides all its help in a 35MB Notes database called Notes Help (i.e., HELP4.NSF) or Notes Help Lite (an 8MB database called HELPLT4.NSF, if you are using a portable computer). Unfortunately, you cannot insert your own application help screen within the Notes help file that ships with the product. In other words, if you develop a sales tracking system, you cannot place ad hoc help directly in the Notes help file; instead, you must create your own separate database. Since Notes does not provide the ability to tie an external online .HLP help file to its design objects, you will need to use native Notes tools to provide similar functionality. Those tools include textual comments, field help, hotspots, and pop-ups.

Textual Comments

On one hand, you want to minimize the number of fields and lines of text in a form to reduce the clutter. On the other, you can—and should—insert comments in the form whenever you suspect the user might "freeze" and not understand what to do next. This situation occurs more frequently with users who are not familiar with Lotus Notes or graphical user interfaces. You can use a smaller font than the field and field label and perhaps even a different color to write the comment. You can also use the paragraph Hide-When feature to have the textual comments appear while a user is creating a new document or editing an existing document (but not appear when he or she is reading or printing a document).

Field Help

When editing the form, place a short (one-line) help message in all the fields that require data input except the most obvious ones. Open any form in your sample databases in Design mode. Select a field and right-click to bring up the Properties dialog box. In the Options tab, enter a short explanation in the Help description text box, as shown in Figure 26.3.

FIGURE 26.3:

Use field help to provide a one-line explanation on the Edit mode Status bar.

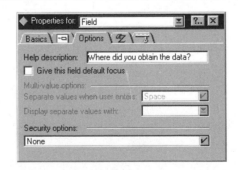

We prefer to enter a question to stimulate the user. For instance, if the field label was Source and the choices were Quarterly Report or Grapevine, Magazine, or

Consultant, and you were expecting the user to select an item to describe the source of the information, you might write: "Where did the data come from?" Remember, though, prompts and field help are no substitute for descriptive field labels where space permits.

Hotspots and Pop-ups

A pop-up is an area of text bordered by a green line (see Figure 26.4). If your users have attended a short seminar on how to use Notes, you can be sure that they will have learned that clicking and holding down the mouse button on a hotspot displays additional information.

FIGURE 26.4:

Click a word with a green border to display a pop-up.

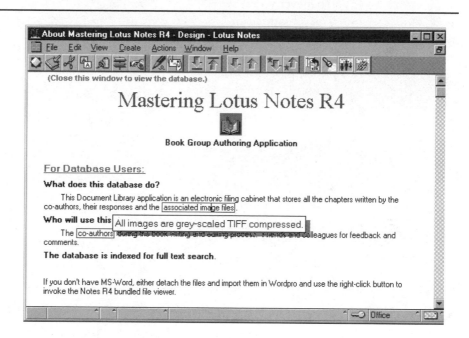

TIP

Hotspots can also be used while you are entering text in a rich text field, and they can be a great way to put in side comments or snide remarks.

You should use text pop-ups in Edit mode forms to explain abbreviations, choices, and even the relevance of certain fields. In our field help example, the pop-up for the word *Source* could be "The application uses sources to categorize information by degree of certainty and relevance."

NOTE Pop-ups are available only for text, not for fields. Also, you cannot have pop-ups in layout regions.

You can create your own secret messages (or "Easter eggs"—a computer term for hidden messages) by placing a pop-up behind even just one letter—simply deselect the Show Border around Hotspot option in the Pop-up Properties box. Follow these steps:

1. Select one of your example databases by double-clicking its icon in the Workspace. The database's view appears.

2. Click Design in the Navigator pane.

3. Click Forms. A list of the database's forms appears in the Document pane.

4. Open a form by double-clicking its name. The form opens in Design mode.

5. Highlight a word. (You might need to double-click the text area first in order to change to Edit mode. Then highlight the word.)

6. Choose Create ➤ Hotspots ➤ Text Pop-up. The Hotspot Pop-up Properties dialog box appears.

7. Type a message in the Pop-up text box, as shown in Figure 26.5. The message will appear when a user clicks the word.

8. Click the Close button.

9. Choose File ➤ Save, or press Esc and then click Yes to save your changes.

FIGURE 26.5:

Type the text for the pop-up in the Hotspot Pop-up Properties dialog box.

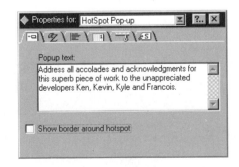

Formula pop-ups behave the same as hotspot buttons and Action hotspots—they give you the ability to invoke a Notes formula when the user clicks on the area. Use Action hotspots if you need to insert LotusScript code. We recommend using LotusScript and formula pop-ups in moderation, because they tend to be difficult to find and modify when the application needs to be changed substantially. It can also be rather unnerving for a user who expects some informational text to appear to click on an area of text and instead invoke unexpected functionality.

Pop-ups also support links to documents, views, and databases. The easiest way to implement an external online help system is to create a document database that contains all your help documents and link them individually to the different hotspots of your form.

The Database Icon

In the heyday of software development, no development project would start without first designing a brand new T-shirt. In the days of tighter budgets, Notes developers have had to satisfy their artistic urges by designing icons. Although icons are clearly not a priority in the early stages of a project, they should not be relegated to "nice to have" feature status.

If your company is new to Notes, icons are important. All third-party and network applications have cool icons—and you don't want to look like an amateur.

If your company has had Notes for several years, chances are that your application icon will compete for Workspace attention with dozens of other icons.

The icon should be a meaningful symbol that all intended users can understand regardless of their cultural background. Avoid writing words or using pictures of items not available everywhere. Figure 26.6 displays several icons.

FIGURE 26.6:

Guess which icon will not be understood in Russia.

Mailbox
Toolkit
Employment
Library

The Notes Catalog and Library

It is not uncommon for organizations to have hundreds of Notes applications replicated through dozens of servers. If your new application is intended for a group beyond your department, you need to advertise it. Both the catalog and the library contain listings of the Notes databases. They can be set to automatically propagate throughout the Notes domain, guaranteeing that all users have access to them. Think of the catalog and the library as the "yellow pages" of Notes databases. The catalog is a special database (called CATALOG.NSF and located in the root of the data directory of Notes) that is updated automatically every night by a process running on the server (not surprisingly called Catalog).

> **TIP**
> We recommend that you create a replica of the catalog stored on your servers—the database may end up being quite large, but you'll thank us the day you need to hunt for a long-lost database.

The library (Figure 26.7), introduced in Release 4, is more user friendly than the catalog in that it shows a short abstract for each database at the view level. Unlike the catalog, you can create a multitude of libraries, for instance, an Executive or an Engineering library. Using access control, you can restrict access to a library. You may want to restrict access to a library to avoid revealing the list of confidential applications it may contain (e.g., Merger Litigation or Bug List). Whereas all databases are automatically added to the catalog (unless the designer specifically turned off that option for a database in its Design Properties), a database must be manually published to one or more libraries (File ➤ Database ➤ Publish).

The Add Icon button is useful for adding a database to your Workspace without opening it.

> **NOTE**
> You cannot select multiple titles in the library and click the Add Icon action.

The Browse button allows you to visit the database without adding it to your desktop. By double-clicking an individual title, you will see a long description of the database and technical information otherwise available in the catalog, such as Replica ID and Manager(s), as shown in Figure 26.8.

FIGURE 26.7:

A Notes library provides an index of all the published databases. You can create as many libraries as you wish.

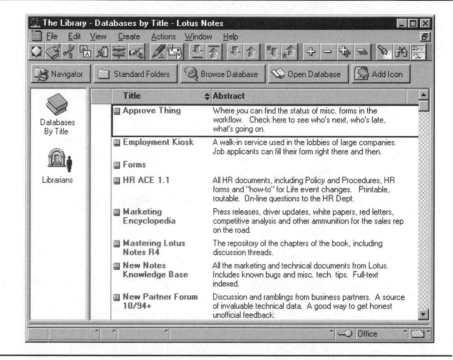

FIGURE 26.8:

The library title document displays the essential information about a database.

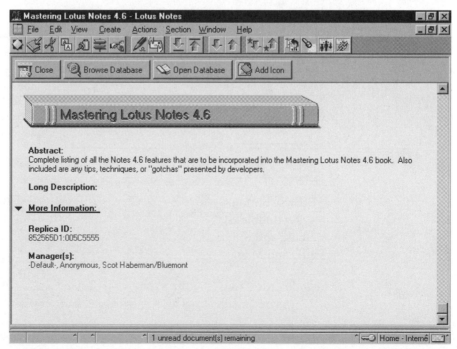

To add your database to the library, you need to publish it, as shown in Figure 26.9.

FIGURE 26.9:

Choose the library where you want to publish your database.

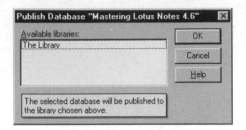

To publish your database, follow these steps:

1. Select your database on the Workspace.

2. Choose File ➤ Database ➤ Publish.

3. Select the library in which you want to advertise this database.

If your database has not already been published, you will have to compose a new library title document. We highly recommend that you spend time creating a short abstract—short enough to be entirely visible at the view level (no more than five lines).

TIP   Create a library local to your machine. Then publish all the icons on your desktop to this library, writing a short abstract meaningful to you. In the event your DESKTOP .DSK file (the file that describes the contents of your Workspace) becomes corrupted, you could use this library to rebuild it.

NOTE   The library does not provide a copy of the About document—but the catalog does. Similarly, the catalog does not contain a copy of the Abstract and the Long Description. You may want to copy the Abstract and the Long Descriptions from the About document and paste them in the library document. You can use the Cut and Paste commands to move information from the About document into the library document.

The catalog (CATALOG.NSF) is also a list of databases. Administrators use the catalog to find out if a database replicates to all the appropriate servers. The Catalog view (Figure 26.10) is also useful for identifying all the replicas of a database when you are troubleshooting template inheritance problems.

FIGURE 26.10:

The Catalog view shows the location and title of databases.

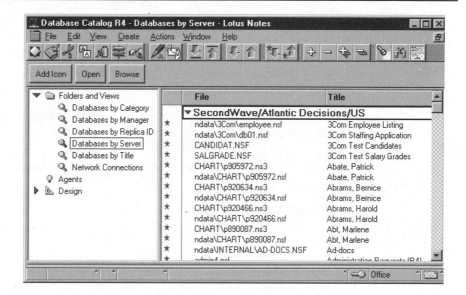

FIGURE 26.10:

The Catalog view shows the location and title of databases.

To add your database to the catalog, select the database icon on your Workspace, right-click, and choose Database Properties to display the Properties dialog box. Click the Design tab and then check the List in Database Catalog option, as shown in Figure 26.11. We recommend that you also enter one or more descriptions, such as Marketing: Sales or Documents: Reference, in the Categories text box.

FIGURE 26.11:

You can add a database to a catalog by selecting the List in Database Catalog option.

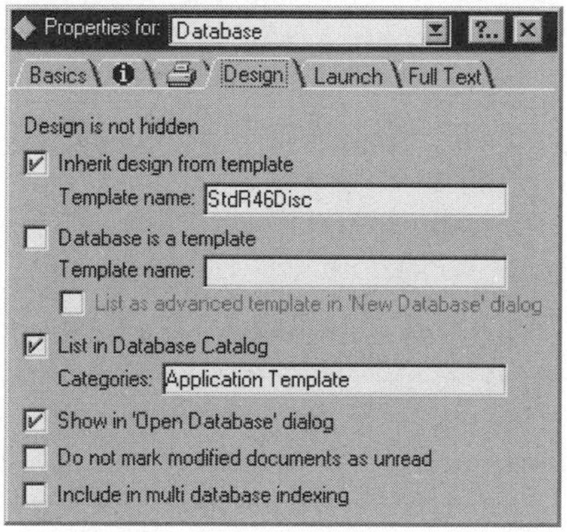

Providing Training

Once you have fully documented your application (you have, haven't you?), inserted online help, managed the project in phases, and published the application to the library and catalog, pat yourself on the back if you have any strength left. You may actually be finished! But if your application includes specific technical knowledge or a workflow that differs from the current routines of the users, you should consider formal training.

There are several ways to train your users, depending on the resources available for your project.

- Train the sponsor and his or her team to become trainers. Hands-on practice is required.

- Develop a courseware ("Getting Started") narrative version of your Using document and ship it to team leaders at the sites where the application will be used.

- Travel around to train the trainers. Local experts become your front line of support. Don't laugh; this approach may be cost effective compared to a deluge of support calls from inexperienced users.

- Create a ScreenCam movie of the application that walks users through the features of a real application at their own pace. We find that ScreenCams are highly effective training tools for novice and expert users alike.

NOTE   ScreenCam is a Lotus application that records your screen as if somebody is standing behind your shoulder with a video camera. If you want to do a voice-over commentary, you will need to run a multimedia PC with a microphone. The result is a software "video tape." Users run ScreenCam movies using a free ScreenCam viewer utility. (They need speakers on their machines if the movie has sound, though.)

TIP   We highly recommend that you break down your ScreenCam script into as many "scenes" as possible. Make sure you also write your script in advance. Try to keep ScreenCam movies to less than two minutes; users prefer to watch several shorts, rather than a long, boring feature film.

What's Next?

Now that you have learned the basics of project management and established a comprehensive program to train your end users, you are ready to move on to the next step. Database management covers the maintenance work you will need to do once your application gains an increasing number of users.

CHAPTER
TWENTY-SEVEN

27

Managing Databases

■ Using backups to protect a database

■ Using replication to propagate information

■ Resolving database replication conflicts

■ Avoiding replication conflicts

■ Keeping the space used by the database under control

■ Setting a quota to multiple databases at the same time

In the previous chapters, you learned how to design databases and how to take the necessary steps to ensure a successful rollout. Your Notes application is ready for use throughout your department or perhaps throughout your world-wide organization, right?

Wrong. Your job is not over.

Even if you have the good fortune of having Notes administrators you can rely on, you are still responsible for the integrity of the application's contents and its access by the users. The administrators may have promised to "protect and serve" your Notes data—but just like your favorite highway patrol officer, they don't write the rules.

You own the contents.

In many organizations, the Notes administrators do not take over the responsibilities of the Notes database manager and the designer or sponsor often ends up as the Notes manager. This chapter presents a set of skills to help you manage a Notes database over an extended period of time and includes the following topics:

- Appropriate uses of replication and tape backups

- Resolving replication conflicts

- Versioning

- Managing disk space

Appropriate Uses of Replication and Tape Backups

Replication propagates a Notes database to multiple servers. At the end of the replication process between two servers (or a client and a server), two copies of the database exist. (In Chapter 28 we describe the process of replicating databases in much more detail.)

When you make a backup, you also end up with two copies of the Notes database: one on the disk and one generally on a tape.

Although the end result appears the same—you double the number of copies—replication and backup are not the same at all in terms of the protection they provide to your data. This distinction is essential and very often misunderstood by Notes database managers.

As a database manager, you have full responsibility for the integrity of the data users entrust you with when they create their Notes documents or when they expect to access important information. Proper use of replication and backups is essential to protect Notes databases. Read on unless you enjoy taking calls from irate or confused users.

Backing Up Notes Databases on Tapes

If your company owns a Novell NetWare file server or an Oracle database, you probably already have a backup plan. Typically, at the end of every day, an incremental backup of the data is written to a tape, and at the end of every week, a full copy of the entire disk is saved to a separate tape. Sophisticated installations rotate the tapes frequently and keep copies off-site, just in case the sky happens to fall on the roof of your building. Larger companies should include Notes servers in the list of machines they back up regularly.

Since Notes databases can be very large, you need to make sure that you have sufficiently large tape drives to accommodate the databases. You will also consume many tapes because the Notes databases will most likely change every day—unless you've turned off the indexing of the views, as discussed in Chapter 25. Regardless of your backup schedule, your company should allocate a generous budget for the purchase of blank tapes and a large tape backup system.

TIP   Your backup tapes will need to be at least as large as the largest database after compression, if such an option is available with your backup software, and probably even as large as the entire directory containing all of these databases. At the very least, however, you should be able to back up the contents of your largest hard drive on a single tape.

If you are smart enough to follow a strict backup routine, the backup tape will allow you to reload an older version of a Notes database when it is destroyed by viruses, erratic hard disk drives, rogue APIs, or fat-fingered administrators. Anything modified since the last backup is, of course, gone forever. And remember that a backup plan is important, but developing a recovery plan and practicing it is just as important.

Limitations of Notes Backups

The software doing the backup uses the file system, such as Windows NT NTFS, OS/2 HPFS, or Windows 95 FAT. Since each Notes database is a file and only Notes knows what is inside that file, the level of granularity of the backup is the file. In other words, Notes databases look like monolithic files to backup systems; they are not capable of selectively backing up a view or a set of documents.

NOTE   You may recall from Chapter 14 that with Release 4, the size of Notes databases may grow to 4GB, so even after compacting, they use a lot of disk space. Compression programs, such as PKZIP, can reduce the size of files by 30 to 95 percent.

Check that you have large enough backup tapes. Check that you have purchased enough blank tapes to hold your Notes databases over the length of the backup cycles (i.e., if you recycle your tapes every two weeks, you need as many blank tapes as you will fill up over two weeks of backing up data). If you have gigabytes upon gigabytes worth of databases, make sure that you have enough time during the night to back up all the data you need—if you don't, you need to make sure that you've purchased additional tape backup systems.

Granted, all this equipment can be expensive and is not terribly exciting compared to writing Notes applications. But what's the point of creating great applications if nobody can trust your ability to keep the data around long enough to be useful?

Backing Up Using Replication

If you read those glossy Lotus marketing brochures or glance at the trade rags before placing them at the bottom of the litter box, you probably understand that Notes replication is a powerful way to distribute information without doing much work. It's easy to multiply the instances of a Notes database and keep them synchronized.

Destroy any Notes database on any Notes server and you can easily reload from another replica copy of that database on another Notes server. There is no single point of failure. Perfect. Who needs backups, anyhow. Right?

Wrong. Read on. There are a few black clouds in the sky.

Understanding Selective Replication

Selective replication (see Chapter 28) allows you to propagate a subset of the documents to another database, for example, only the sales leads relevant to a regional sales office. If the California office falls into the ocean (a common fear among locals), you can recover the documents from corporate headquarters in Missouri. That approach assumes that headquarters acts as a "hub" and collects all the documents from all regional offices. In fact, you need to make sure that your hub does not exclude certain types of documents, such as discussion threads, to save on resources.

Understanding Data Replication

In contrast to tape backups, Notes Release 4 replicates changes down to the field level (it used to be at the document level in Release 3).

WARNING   Minor changes will propagate automatically throughout all the servers...including corrupted documents...and deletions.

In other words, thanks to a rogue Notes server agent, a bad Notes API, a mere bit flipped by a defective hard drive, or a Notes user with Editor rights, one Notes document (or a large number of documents) may disappear or become unusable on one server—and depending on your replication schedule, on all other instances of that database on other servers. At that point, no recovery of the data is possible because all the copies now have the bad data.

Tape backups are your best defense!

Resolving Replication Conflicts

Distributed use comes at a price. By now, you know that laptop users may have a replica copy of your database, and so do users on a network in a remote office. If two people edit the same document at the same time, you have a replication conflict. Conflicts occur whenever a user edits a document before the changes made by another user reach the replica copy of the database they are both using. For instance, a sales rep updates the main contact of an Account Profile on her laptop while someone in the shipping department updates the ZIP code in the same Account Profile document.

Save Conflicts vs. Replication Conflicts

There are two very different and very distinct types of conflicts that can happen in Notes, the save conflict and the replication conflict. Just to make sure you understand the difference (they can be quite confusing), we'll spell out the terms:

- **Save Conflicts:** When more than one user opens the same document to edit at the same time on the same server, a save conflict occurs. Notes designates the document that has been saved first as the main document. When another user tries to save the same document, Notes prompts the user to save it as a save conflict document. If the user does, Notes displays it as a response to the main document with a diamond symbol in the left margin.

- **Replication Conflicts:** When more than one user opens the same document to edit in different replicas between replications, a replication conflict may occur (note the "may occur," which is explained later). At the next replication, Notes designates the document that has been saved the most frequently as the main document. If each has been edited and saved the same number of times, Notes designates the document that has been saved most recently as the main document. Notes displays the other documents as a response to the main document, with a diamond symbol in the left margin.

- **Replication Deletes:** If a document is edited and saved one time in one replica and deleted in another replica, the deleted document takes precedence. However, if a document is edited and saved more than one time or if a document is edited and saved after the deleted document, the edited document takes precedence.

- **Replication Note:** The designer of the database can specify that Notes merge replication conflicts into a single document (if possible). In this case, if two users edit the same document but different fields on separate replicas, Notes saves the edits to each field into one document. However, if two users edit the same document and the same fields on separate replicas, Notes saves one document as the main and the other as a response following the rules specified above.

The good news is that Notes does not lose any information—it simply creates a *replica conflict*. A replica conflict appears as a document in the view with a black diamond in the margin, as shown in Figure 27.1. Since Notes cannot decide by itself which document it should keep, it keeps both in the database and patiently waits for a human brain (yours, to be precise) to decide.

FIGURE 27.1:

The black diamond in the margin identifies replication conflict documents.

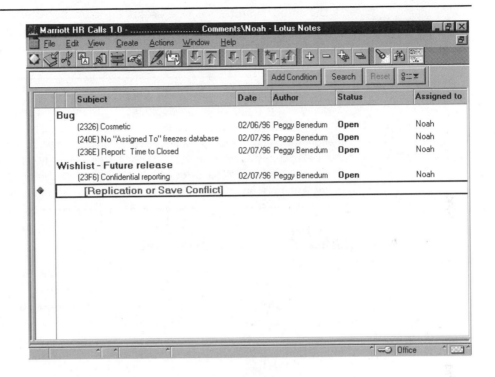

Avoiding Conflicts

In our experience, the issue of replication conflicts is more often academic than real. Way back in the days of Notes Release 1, experts warned about the impracticality of a distributed offline database without a "locking" mechanism. Even in large installations, this characteristic turned out to be less of a problem than predicted, mostly because a Notes database designer can take many protective measures to avoid conflicts.

Reducing the Number of Editors

To avoid replication conflicts, the easiest strategy is to make sure that just a few people have the ability to edit the same document. If there is a need to obtain feedback on a given document, use response documents to collect feedback. For instance, all the members of a marketing group could comment on a product plan by creating response documents under the product plan document. Once all members have expressed their opinions, or a specified period of time has passed, the author would revise the original document. Alternatively, a member of the team may be assigned the task of compiling the comments and incorporating them into the plan.

TIP

Don't try to use Notes to do things word processors do well, such as revision marking and merging of multiple versions. Try to think less in terms of the final published document and more in terms of the process to collect the relevant information, the role of the participants, and the steps required to get the job done. If classical co-authoring is really what you need, take a look at Lotus Word Pro group features integrated with Lotus Notes. Word Pro allows you to simultaneously track multiple authors, and it date/time stamps their individual revisions.

Breaking Down the Document

Remember that replication is done at the field level in Release 4. A conflict will arise any time the same fields of the same documents are edited at the same time. Try to break the document into multiple fields; for example, separate a general Body field into Executive Summary, Body, and Supporting Material. By separating the data into multiple fields, you reduce the chances of two people simultaneously modifying the same field!

Similarly, you can break down a document by using multiple forms (see Chapter 17). Instead of a lengthy document that contains many different sections, create separate Notes forms that inherit the fields in common. For instance, in a sales tracking database, you can break down an Account document into Summary Profile, Rolodex Card, and Sales History. You can then use the view to group the forms logically. In our example the view category is the name of the account, and the three document types are listed underneath. You may also need to place buttons on the forms to facilitate navigation among them. In our example you could jump to the Rolodex from either of the other forms.

Accelerating Replication

Frequently replication reduces the opportunity for conflict. We recommend that you accelerate the replication schedule between sites that tend to make frequent changes to the same documents. With Release 4, replication at field level is fast, requires little overhead, and consumes fewer server resources. The only drawback to frequent replication is the potential cost of communication.

Designing for Sequential Access

Whenever multiple users in different sites need to update information, group the roles by site—if possible. Suppose that advertising is done by an outside company, your PR group is located at headquarters, and the trade show folks are traveling continuously with their laptops. To put together our product launch plan, we would create roles for the advertising team, the public relations team, and the trade show reviewers. We would then establish the workflow for sequential routing as opposed to parallel processing.

Centralizing External Interfaces

If a Notes database automatically picks up updates to its documents from an external source, for instance, the latest stock prices retrieved via OLE from a spreadsheet, make sure these changes occur only on *one* server. The version of the database located on that server would then propagate to all other servers. If the process that updates the database from an external source were to run accidentally on multiple servers, you would end up with many replication conflicts. You may want to run this type of task on the hub, once all of the changes have been collected from the other servers. Where and when to run server-based APIs is beyond the scope of this book, but as a general rule, it's a good idea to locate these tasks on the server where the most "writes" occur.

Merging Replication Conflicts Automatically

This option enables Release 4 to use its field-replication functionality to merge the changes into one document automatically—assuming that the changes were made to separate fields in the document. To turn on this feature, follow these steps:

1. Open one of the forms on the companion disk.

2. Bring up the Properties dialog box.

3. Select the Merge replication conflicts option in the Basics tab, as shown in Figure 27.2.

If two people update the same field, Notes will display two copies of the document, one marked with a black diamond.

FIGURE 27.2:

Select Merge Replication Conflicts to integrate changes into a document automatically.

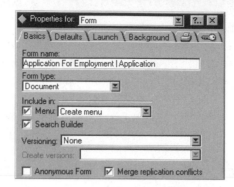

Using Versioning

This last strategy is so important that we devote a whole section to it later in this chapter.

Removing Conflicts

Notes picks the most recently saved document as the winner—no questions asked. There is one exception to that rule: If one of the documents has been edited and saved more often than the others, the more frequently edited document is the winner (contrary to common belief). This rule makes a lot of sense. Take for instance a laptop that hasn't communicated with the network in a long time, one belonging to a traveler in the West African plains or at certain chains of American hotels. When reconnecting, you wouldn't want to instantly relegate the "active" document of the home office to the less-than-desirable status of "replication conflict." This is particularly important if the traveler has deleted the document while others were working on it.

To sort out a replication conflict situation, you have a few options:

- **Delete** the loser (the document with a black diamond in the margin), no questions asked.

- **Merge the contents** (a painful experience), by following these steps:

    1. Open the winning document.

    2. Open the loser.

3. Figure out what changed: Look through both documents carefully—Notes doesn't leave any indications.

4. Cut and paste the relevant information from the loser into the parent.

5. Save the parent.

6. Delete the conflict document.

- **Promote the loser** by following these steps:

    1. Open the loser.

    2. Save it. It will show as a normal document at the view level.

TIP   Don't cut a main document after promoting a replication conflict document if it has children (response documents). A Notes document has only one parent at a time. If it loses its parent, the document becomes an orphan, never to be seen again in the database (at least not without some advanced design work).

---

3. If any response documents are associated with the parent, follow this procedure:

    - Cut all the response documents associated with the parent document.

WARNING   Make sure that the view you are using contains all the children of a parent document.

- Select the newly promoted document.

- Paste the children documents you just cut so they appear under the new parent document.

4. Cut the formally winning document.

5. Refresh the view to verify the changes (press F9).

Removing conflicts is a time-consuming, manual process that the manager of the database must undertake periodically. If you have to follow the steps described above too often, you probably should read on to discover one of the best ways to avoid conflicts: versioning.

Unsupported Document Comparison Utility

There is an unsupported feature for Win32 clients that allows you to compare two documents and see the differences. This process eliminates the guesswork in figuring out what data was changed between replication conflicts. To use this feature, do the following:

1. Add the following line in your NOTES.INI:

    ```
    AddInMenus=c:\notes\nntediff.dll
        * (if c:\notes is your Notes program directory)
    ```

2. Restart your Notes client.

3. In a view, select two documents.

4. In the Actions menu, select Difference of 2 Documents. A window will appear where you can compare the two documents field by field as shown in Figure 27.3.

This is a handy utility but Lotus does not guarantee that it will be available in future releases of Lotus Notes.

FIGURE 27.3:

Comparing the differences of two documents by field

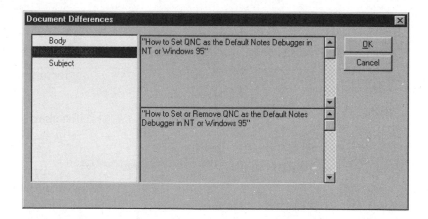

Versioning

Versioning allows multiple users to edit the same document—one at a time. This functionality is quite common in traditional document management systems.

Setting Up Versioning

To set up versioning for a Notes form, follow these steps:

1. Open a form from one of the databases on the companion disk.

2. Bring up the Properties box.

3. Select the Form object.

4. Select Versioning in the Basics tab, as shown in Figure 27.4.

FIGURE 27.4:

Select Versioning for
the form.

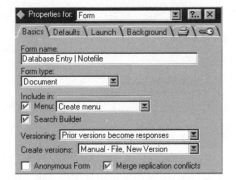

You have several options from which to select:

- **None:** There is only one instance of the document. Each modification is saved in the document.

- **New Versions Become Responses:** As users make changes to the contents, their version of the original document will appear indented underneath the original. Use this option when the author of the original document needs to retain control or when the edits need to be approved before becoming an integral part of the document. This mode also works well for parallel reviews. Typically the original author will incorporate the changes manually.

- **Prior Versions Become Responses:** As users make changes, the last change shows up as the main documents and older versions are indented underneath as responses. Use this option when all editors have equal right to the contents or when the latest change is relevant to all users immediately. This mode works best with a sequential review process and provides a historical thread of the document.

- **New Versions Become Siblings:** As users make changes, all documents are equal underneath; they do not appear indented. This option combines the two previous modes, reflecting the fact that all editors are equal. It has the disadvantage of making it more difficult for users outside the editing group to figure out which document is the most relevant.

Two modes are available to indicate how the document will be saved after a modification:

- **Automatic–File, Save:** The behavior you selected in the versioning settings will occur automatically, any time you save the document.

- **Manual–File, New Version:** In addition to the traditional File Save option, File Save as New Version also appears on the menu. If you save as usual, no versioning occurs. Otherwise, the rules defined under versioning will prevail. Use this mode only if your users are comfortable with the concept of versioning in Notes.

Versioning will provide you with a historical trail of all the revisions of a document. One side effect may be that old versions stick around the database longer than you wish. You may want to consider writing an Agent (see Chapter 23) that automatically archives or purges outdated versions of the documents, for instance, every six months or anytime the status of the document marks it as "final."

Managing Space

Notes databases, like good vacuums, have the unique ability to suck up all available space on your disk. Users may add an increasingly large number of documents, sometimes with very large images of file attachments. Replication starts taking longer and longer, and locating documents becomes very difficult. As performance decreases, so does usage.

Without proper management, the success of a database can become the source of its demise. What you need is proper space management.

We will show you a few techniques to keep your databases under control, including compacting, archiving, and monitoring usage. These tools should enable you to breathe new and lasting life into your application.

The overall strategy is to first assess how much space your databases are taking and whether you need to compact your data. If compacting does not relieve your space crunch, you will need to archive.

Assessing Space Usage and Compacting

When documents are deleted, Notes tries its best to recover space. But what you often end up with is a lot of void—and we are not referring to the value of contents left. The dialog box shown in Figure 27.5 will help you decide whether you need to regain lost space by compacting.

FIGURE 27.5:

Check the percentage used of a database to decide if it needs to be compacted.

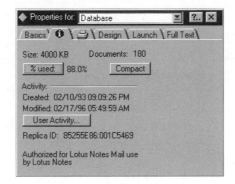

To check if a database needs to be compacted:

1. Select the icon of one of your example databases from the companion disk.

2. Bring up the Properties box.

3. Click the Information tab (the second one from the left).

4. Click the % Used button.

5. Press on the Compact button if the number is below 80 or 85 percent.

TIP   A good rule to follow is to compact if the database is > 20MB and the space used is below 90 percent or if the database is < 20MB and the space used is below 80 percent.

If you are using a local copy of a Notes database, the process will start immediately; otherwise, a request will be sent to your server, and compacting will run as a background process on the Notes server. The duration of the process on the server depends on the performance of its hardware on the amount of space that needs to be reclaimed.

NOTE

You need twice the amount of space of the database you want to compact because Notes needs to make a temporary copy. If you do not have enough space on the disk, compacting will not occur—you will need to provide additional space first.

Note that it is not worth your time to compact small databases (the space regained is negligible). The easiest way to identify which databases need compacting is to look at the Databases by Size view in the Notes Log database (LOG.NSF) on your Notes server, as shown in Figure 27.6.

FIGURE 27.6:

The Log file on the server lists the databases sorted by size and includes percentage used.

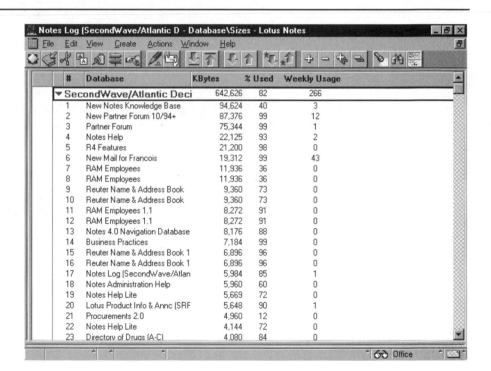

#	Database	KBytes	% Used	Weekly Usage
▼	**SecondWave/Atlantic Deci**	642,626	82	266
1	New Notes Knowledge Base	94,624	40	3
2	New Partner Forum 10/94+	87,376	99	12
3	Partner Forum	75,344	99	1
4	Notes Help	22,125	93	2
5	R4 Features	21,200	98	0
6	New Mail for Francois	19,312	99	43
7	RAM Employees	11,936	36	0
8	RAM Employees	11,936	36	0
9	Reuter Name & Address Book	9,360	73	0
10	Reuter Name & Address Book	9,360	73	0
11	RAM Employees 1.1	8,272	91	0
12	RAM Employees 1.1	8,272	91	0
13	Notes 4.0 Navigation Database	8,176	88	0
14	Business Practices	7,184	99	0
15	Reuter Name & Address Book 1	6,896	96	0
16	Reuter Name & Address Book 1	6,896	96	0
17	Notes Log (SecondWave/Atlan	5,984	85	1
18	Notes Administration Help	5,960	60	0
19	Notes Help Lite	5,669	72	0
20	Lotus Product Info & Annc (SRF	5,648	90	1
21	Procurements 2.0	4,960	12	0
22	Notes Help Lite	4,144	72	0
23	Directory of Drugs (A-C)	4,080	84	0

Archiving

Left to our own whims, most of us will let documents pile up until the database becomes unusable. We won't reveal the size of our personal Notes mail file, growing mostly without pruning since 1988, but we can tell you the market price of new hard drives. If others had to access or replicate the database, its size would quickly stop being a joke.

Archiving means that only the current and relevant documents remain in the active database. Older documents migrate to a single central location, perhaps even to offline devices such as backup tapes. When the archive is still online, you can take a few steps to make sure that it is still usable:

- **Remove unnecessary design elements:** Each view consumes space and resources. You probably really need only a few views, such as by date, by author, or by title. The same holds true for fields in the form. Just make sure the design changes do not replicate back to the active database.

- **Remove full text indexing:** Unless it is really necessary, this is a space-eating luxury. See Chapter 25 for the space impact of full text indexing.

- **Provide read-only access:** Only the person or process moving documents to the archive should have write access.

- **Index manually or periodically:** Indexing reduces server resource requirements. If data is written to the archive in a batch mode (for instance, at the end of each quarter), run the index at that time.

Notes provides several ways to move information to an archive, depending on the frequency and the complexity of the archival rule.

- **Manual process:** Only one person, the database manager, should have this responsibility. Define a view that assembles nothing but the documents that need to be archived, for instance All Closed Contracts. Then cut out these documents from the Notes view (All Closed Contacts) and paste them into a view in the archive database.

NOTE   The archive database should be based on the same Notes database design as the production database.

- **Automatic Agent:** Release 4 provides you with Agents to simplify that task. In a nutshell, a server agent will move all the documents of a view meeting a certain criteria to the archive database.

- **API:** If you have many documents to move rapidly or you need to combine them with external information, you may need to write a program in C or C++, for example, if you are trying to archive all the closed customer inquiries and combine them with their bank account balances.

- **Mail-in:** You can create a mail-in entry for the archive database located at a remote site and use an Agent to send a copy of the documents to archive. The appeal of this solution (used frequently in Release 3) is that remote offices can send archival documents to a central administrative server. There is also no possibility of corruption between the two databases, since the archive communicates only by accepting incoming mail.

NOTE

Many of the Notes 4.6 templates provide a mechanism for archiving documents. If you base your databases on one of these templates, you're all set. If not, you can always "borrow" the forms, views, agents, etc., and implement archiving in any database of your choosing.

Monitoring Usage

If you are interested in knowing the actual usage of your database, you need to turn on the Database Activity monitoring flag:

1. Open the Jobs database from the companion disk.

2. Bring up the Properties box.

3. Click on User Activity in the information tab.

4. Select the Record Activity option.

If the option was already selected, you may see a table breaking down the number of uses, reads, and writes by day, week, month, and since the database was first created, as shown in Figure 27.7.

FIGURE 27.7:

The database usage table shows how often users accessed the database.

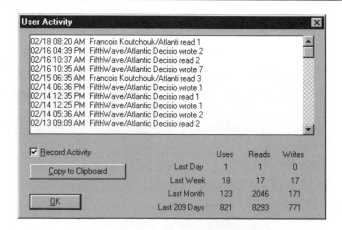

Using Server Administration to Manage Multiple Databases

It would be rather tedious to have to monitor every single database individually. Fortunately, Notes supplies a tool for global management of the space occupied by your databases. Follow these steps to assign a quota to databases:

1. Choose File ➤ Tools ➤ Server Administration. The Administration panel appears.

2. Pick a server (one to which you have access or Local) and click the Database icon. The Tools to Manage Notes Databases dialog box appears.

3. Click the Tool drop-down list and select the Quotas tool. The Database Quotas options screen appears, as shown in Figure 27.8.

FIGURE 27.8:

The Database Quotas options screen allows you to assign a maximum size to one or more databases at the same time and send an alarm once a threshold has been reached.

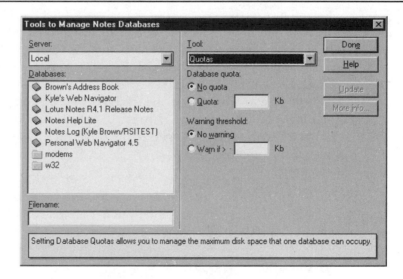

4. Select one or more databases that you want to run the Quotas tool against.

5. Enter a quota, such as 1500KB, and set a threshold size, such as 1200KB, that will send a warning to the server administrator.

6. Click the More Info button. The Database Quota Information dialog box appears, as shown in Figure 27.9.

7. Click the Done button to close the dialog box. Complete the process by clicking the Done button again.

FIGURE 27.9:

The Database Quota Information dialog box displays size information about each database that you've selected.

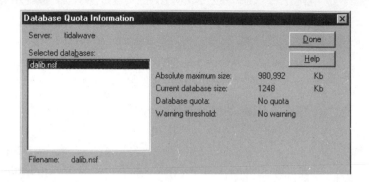

Keeping It Alive

Over the years, we've observed that a Notes database, like most products, tends to have a life cycle of its own. Initially, a small group of core users frantically use it. Then a larger group starts contributing a lot of information. Later on, a wide group of people will read information more than they contribute. If left alone, the database will start its progressive decline; readers will outnumber active participants. The end is near when the wealth of information prevents users from easily finding what is truly relevant to them. Death arrives when the original core users, often the sponsors or managers of the application, lose interest and move their attention to another database.

Allowing a database to live out its life naturally has many merits. But in many cases too many development efforts are wasted and too much knowledge is lost if a database disappears prematurely. A few simple techniques will prolong the life of your database.

Automatic Install

If usage is rather low, perhaps your users cannot find the database—even though you published it and placed it in the catalog (see Chapter 25). Sometimes the only approach is to actually send users (or potential users) an e-mail with a hotlink, or better yet—a button that places the database on their Workspace.

To create an e-mail with a database link and send an e-mail message to potential users, follow these steps:

1. Select the icon of a database on your Workspace.

2. Choose Edit ➤ Copy as Link ➤ Database Link.

3. Create an e-mail memo.

4. Paste the link.

TIP

You could have created a link directly to a specified view within that database by first opening the database in the intended view and then Choosing Edit ➤ Copy As Link ➤ View Link.

You can easily send an e-mail message containing a button that automatically adds a database to the recipient's desktop and opens the database in response to a simple click. Follow these steps:

1. Select one of the database icons from the companion disk.

2. Bring up the Properties box.

3. Click the Information tab and carefully write down the Replica ID that is on the last line, as shown in Figure 27.10. You need to write down the number as is.

FIGURE 27.10:

Remember to enter a database's Replica ID in the formula exactly as the ID appears on screen—or you will encounter link conflicts when you attempt to mail the database to users.

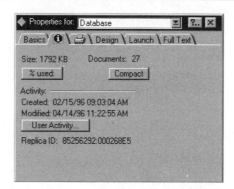

4. Click the mail icon at the very bottom right corner of your screen.

5. Select Create Memo.

6. Select Create ➤ Hotspot ➤ Button in the Body field.

7. Type **INSTALL!** in the button label text field in the Properties box.

8. Select Formula in the Code panel.

9. Type

```
@Command( [FileOpenDatabase]; "12345678:12345678"; ""; ""; ""; "" )
```

10. Replace the number between quotes by the Replica ID.

11. Add contents to your message to advertise and explain the purpose of the database. You may also want to paste in a copy of the database icon.

12. Mail it!

When your users receive the message, they will only need to click the INSTALL! button to add the database icon to their Workspace and open your database.

Notifying Users of Changes

If usage seems to be dropping, you may need to take measures such as archiving (described above) or indexing (described in Chapter 25). Or you may need to redesign the application either to allow users to locate relevant documents faster or to facilitate the process of contributing information.

TIP
One of the keys to keeping a database alive is to define a "business process owner" or forum moderator who makes sure that the information in the database and its design of elements meet the specific needs of the user.

Avoid sending e-mail to notify current users of changes to a database. Instead use the Release 4 feature that forces the display of the About Document if it has been changed.

While the specific description of the functionality of the application belongs in the Using document, significant changes should be posted in the About document. (See Chapter 26 for more about About.) If you are a Web user, think of your About document as if it were your home page. You should design your message to be brief and attract the attention of the user who would otherwise press Esc without blinking. A red box, a slick icon, or any other "marketing" trick may come in handy. You can set up the database to display the About document whenever it is modified. To automatically display the About document to a user when the database is first opened, do the following:

1. Select a database icon from the companion disk.

2. Bring up the Properties box.

3. Select Launch tab for the Database object.

4. Click Show "About Database" Document if Modified.

What's Next?

You have finally mastered the essential elements of turning your Notes application into a product: database management, indexing (Chapter 25), rolling out (Chapter 26), and security (Chapter 16).

In the next part of the book, "Integrating Notes in the Work Environment," you will face the challenge of integrating Notes into a larger work environment. We'll consider large corporate Notes networks, diverse desktop applications, disparate mail systems, relational databases, and the Internet.

PART III

Integrating Notes in the Work Environment

Replicating Databases

- Understanding database replication

- Creating a new replica of a database

- Updating replicas

- Using the Notes Replicator

- Reviewing the replication history of a database

- Using the Notes Log database

One of the most distinctive and impressive features in Lotus Notes is a process known as *database replication*. Basically, replication is a procedure that updates and distributes copies of the same Notes database, (i.e., *replicas*) that are stored on different servers. A replica is a copy of a shared database that you store either on a server or on your workstation (desktop-style or laptop computer). You can work on the replica in your Notes Workspace as if you were working on the server database.

Replicated architecture is based on the philosophy of a decentralized database that resides in many places at once, making it easily accessible to all end users within an enterprise. Contrast this concept to the traditional centralized database scheme in which an information store resides in a single location in an organization, requiring a more sophisticated access method for remote end users. We will examine the pros and cons associated with both architectures in this chapter. We also explain how to

- Create a new database replica

- Update a replica

- Perform selective replications

- Track replication events

- Handle replication conflicts

Replication is a powerful tool because the process enables copies of the same database on different networks, in different locations, or even in different time zones, to reflect changes and become identical over time. The servers connect to each other at scheduled intervals, and the databases replicate changes to documents, access control lists, and the design objects like forms and views. The power of Notes is that it not only synchronizes the data during replication but also synchronizes all of the changes to the design objects as well, thereby automating the software distribution of Notes applications between Notes servers and between all Notes workstations.

NOTE   Since this book is geared toward end users (and developers), rather than administrators, we confine our discussion to replication as it applies to the end user.

How Does Replication Work?

Replication makes all copies of a database essentially identical *over time*, which means they don't become exact copies instantly. The process is an ongoing one. If a user makes changes in one copy of a database, replication ensures that those changes are added to all copies, as long as the appropriate replication options are set. However, since many people can be using copies of the same database and updating the individual copies daily, making all of them identical at the same time is unlikely.

Suppose two copies of an insurance policy database exist—one on a claims adjuster's laptop computer and the other on a Notes server at company headquarters, which is used by her assistant. Yesterday the copies were identical, but today the claims adjuster went out on the road to investigate a house that was damaged by fire and an office building with burst water pipes. She subsequently wrote her reports and added them to the replica of the database on her laptop computer. In the meantime, her assistant responded to telephone calls from the distraught policy holders and recorded the status of the calls in the replica copy of the database on the company's Notes server at headquarters.

The two copies of the database are now "out of sync" because changes have been made to them separately. Both copies must now be resynchronized and made identical again through replication. Notes can handle this task automatically when the claims adjuster returns to her office or replicates remotely via modem. She replicates the copy of the database on her laptop computer with the copy on the Notes server at headquarters. She sends the changes she made to her local copy to the server copy, and her local copy receives the changes made to the server copy (by her assistant or anyone else at headquarters). The exchange is completed, and the two copies are now back in synch with one another!

Replication takes time and requires specific Notes server resources. If you are developing a database for a multiserver environment and you want to have the database replicated, work with the Notes administrator to determine the replication schedule that makes the most sense for the system topology.

You can set up replication between servers or between a workstation and a server for Mobile (dial-up) Notes users, which we discussed in Chapter 10. The methods are similar.

NOTE Defining replication settings for a database requires Manager access; however, Designer access is sufficient to define the selective replication formula.

Handling Frequent Document Updates

Notes handles periodic database updates with two types of replication: server-to-server replication and workstation-to-server replication. *Server-to-server replication* occurs during scheduled server replication or when the Notes administrator manually forces replication. Server-to-server replication is necessary when a database is to be distributed to Notes servers throughout an organization, making access convenient to the end users who will use, add, and modify the information in the database. Workgroups access the database replica that is nearest to them, typically via a LAN-based connection. Servers communicate changes made to replicas stored on them over LAN, WAN, or dial-up connections to other servers and across the Internet.

Workstation-to-server replication is handy if you use Notes remotely (over a dial-up connection) as well as on a LAN workstation. You can create a complete or partial database replica on your laptop or remote computer (at home, for instance) and work with it as a local database; later, you transmit your updates by replicating with a server-based copy, simultaneously receiving updates made to the server copy by other users of the database. Your mail database is a good example of using workstation-to-server replication. Placing a replica copy of your mail file on your laptop or remote computer allows you to create and respond to mail messages without being connected to the server. Once all your messages are complete, you just replicate with the server; your messages are sent and any new messages are received.

Replication for a local database on a workstation occurs when you perform a data exchange using the File ➤ Replication ➤ Replicate command or use the Replicator Workspace page (discussed later).

Scheduling Regular Replication

Replication is typically scheduled every few hours (or sometimes every hour) of a work day for Notes databases with time-sensitive information. This short cycle can be crucial for organizations whose databases are accessed and modified by many people. For databases that aren't modified as often or where the information isn't critical, replication can occur once a day or even less frequently. When a database is replicated over telephone lines between distant sites, replication might be scheduled once or twice a week and during the evening hours when phone rates are lower.

NOTE   Your organization's Notes administrator is the person responsible for setting up and scheduling replication of databases between your company's Notes servers. If you work off-site or on the road and you dial up Notes, you should find out from the Notes administrator when is the best time to replicate.

Monitoring Database Replication

If you are a user of off-site, dial-up Notes, replication keeps your local replica copies of databases current with databases on the server. However, the process isn't fool-proof and isn't without its problems, especially when you are using telephone lines. You should always monitor the process once databases begin replicating to make sure they continue to replicate as you want them to. The message area on the Status bar at the bottom of your Workspace displays all activity during the replication process. If a problem or conflict should occur, such as the sudden interruption of a telephone call that results in stopping replication, Notes will notify you.

NOTE   When you work off-site, scheduling server calls shortly before you begin working and when you are done inputting new documents for the day is a good plan. This routine assures that you get the most up-to-date information from servers at the beginning of the day and send your updated information to servers at the end of the day. If you are really busy, you may replicate four or five times to ensure that your changes are available in the server's replica copies of the databases. (Remember from Chapter 11 that the process of replication can run in the background, allowing you to continue working on other tasks on your remote machine.)

Creating a Replica of a Database on a Workstation

Before you can use the database exchange feature of dial-up Notes, you must create local replicas of the shared databases you want to use. Creating local database replicas lets you use Notes databases without being connected to a Notes server via a LAN or over telephone lines.

You can create a partial (selective replica) or full replica of any shared database to which you have at least Reader access. (Reader access allows you to "pull" information from a shared database, but not update it. You'll need Author access or greater to *send* and *receive* updates.) A partial replica contains a subset of the documents in the source database, based on selection criteria you specify in the Selective Replication dialog box. A full replica contains all the documents that exist in the source database at the time the replica is made. (Partial and full replication are subject to any form of document-level security that may have been implemented, such as by Reader Name and by Author Name fields.)

You will usually replicate several databases to your laptop computer so that you can have access to the information while you are on the road. Traveling Notes users usually replicate a copy of their Notes Mail database, along with several other Notes databases depending on their job responsibilities. For example, a sales person would replicate a sales contacts database and a sales forecasting database; a person in product development would replicate a project status database and a product brainstorming database; a member of the legal department would probably replicate a litigation tracking database and a newsfeed database.

NOTE You must know the name of the server and the file name of the database you want to replicate before you attempt to replicate a database.

To create a new replica of a database, follow these steps:

1. Choose File ➤ Replication ➤ New Replica. The Choose Database dialog box appears.

2. Choose the server that contains the desired database from the Server drop-down list. Notes will display a message asking if you want to call the server.

3. Click the Yes button.

4. Enter a password to access the server, if prompted.

5. Click OK. The Call Server dialog box appears.

6. Click the Auto Dial button. Notes calls the server. (The status of the call and the subsequent connection appear in the Status bar area.)

7. Highlight the database you wish to replicate from the list of databases that appears in the Choose Database dialog box, as shown in Figure 28.1, or enter the file name of the database in the Filename text box at the bottom of the dialog box.

The Choose Database
dialog box lets you select
the "source" database
you wish to replicate.

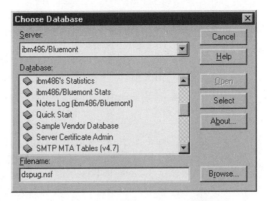

TIP

If the database to be replicated does not reside in the Notes data directory of the
server, it will not appear in the list of databases.

8. Click the Select button to display the New Replica dialog box, shown in
   Figure 28.2.

The New Replica dialog box

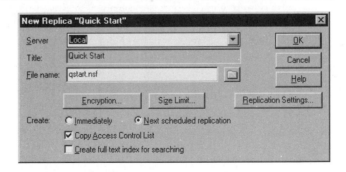

TIP

If you've been working with a shared database (located on a Notes server) and
wish to make a local replica copy of it to your laptop later on, you can avoid the
Choose Database dialog box. Assuming that the shared database icon appears in
your Notes Workspace, simply click the database from your Workspace before
choosing File ➤ Replication ➤ Replicate. Notes will know that you wish to replicate the selected database.

9. Choose the server where your new replica will be stored. For the purpose of workstation-to-server replication, choose Local to store the new replica on your workstation hard drive.

10. Type a name in the Filename text box or accept the default file name as shown (which is the same name as the source database). If you enter a new file name, Notes adds the .NSF extension if you leave it off.

TIP

Unless you have a compelling reason to change the default file name (it conflicts with an existing file, for instance), leave it as is. Although replicas of the same database do not have to have the same file name, maintaining a consistent name makes administration and troubleshooting easier.

11. Accept the default, Copy Access Control List option, or select the Create a Full Index for Searching option, which immediately indexes the replica and lets you perform text searches. (Searching a database is discussed in Chapter 6.)

TIP

When making a local replica copy of a Notes database, selecting the Copy Access Control List option will keep the ACL access rights intact. If you deselect this option, you will be given Manager access rights to the replica copy. The Notes administrator can also select an option for the database that will enforce a consistent ACL across all replicas of the database. If this option is in effect, you will only be given the access rights you currently have for the database residing on the server.

12. Select one of the options next to the Create label:

    • Immediately fills the replica with documents and design objects as soon as you select OK.

    • Next Scheduled Replication option fills the replica with documents and design objects at the first scheduled or forced replication. The replica is called a *replica stub* because it contains no documents or design objects; it's essentially a placeholder for information to follow. The file name of the database appears on the database icon.

NOTE Creating a replica stub is a good idea when you want to postpone filling the replica because of time constraints or expense. A typical example involving workstation-to-server replication is a dial-up user who wishes to replicate a large database back to his or her workstation, but does not want to incur the expense of doing so during the time of "peak" telephone rates. The user can create a replica stub and then schedule an automatic replication during the night, at which time the replica is filled in with all of the data (documents) and design objects (forms, views, Agents, etc.).

13. Click OK to create the new replica. The Status bar at the bottom of the Replicator page indicates the progress of the replication.

When you replicate your mail file to your laptop computer, store it in a subdirectory under the Notes data directory with the same name as the subdirectory for the Mail files on your corporate Notes server. For example, create a subdirectory called /Replicas under the Notes Data directory. As you create local replica copies of Notes databases (except for your mail database), store the replica copies in the /Replicas subdirectory. If you ever run low on hard disk space, simply replicate all of the changes that you made to your local copies to your Notes server and then delete one or more of the local replica copies. You can always replicate the databases again, fully or partially, when you return to the office. However, if you are a mobile Notes user, consider the time you will need to re-replicate all the data before you haphazardly decide to blow something away.

Updating a Replica

Now that you have created a replica copy of a database on your workstation, you can update it at regular intervals if you have access to the server (and to the database on the server). To update the replica copy, follow these steps:

1. Click the database's icon in your Workspace to select it, or you can open it by double-clicking the icon.

2. Choose File ➤ Replication ➤ Replicate. The Replicate dialog box appears, as shown in Figure 28.3.

TIP You can initiate replication by clicking the database with the right mouse button and selecting the Replicate option from the pop-up menu, or you can choose Replicate from the Stackable ("hinky minky") icon or twistie.

FIGURE 28.3:

The Replicate dialog box lets you set replication options for replicating a selected database.

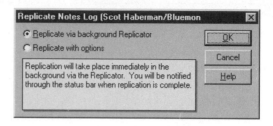

3. Select Replicate with options.

4. Click OK. Typically, you would choose the server on which the source database you originally replicated resides and both the Send Documents to Server and Receive Document from Server options for a bidirectional exchange of information.

5. Select one of the following options from the drop-down list at the bottom of the dialog box:

   • **Receive Full Documents** indicates that you do not wish to restrict the amount of information your replica will receive.

   • **Receive Summary and 40KB of Rich Text** indicates that you wish to receive only basic document information, such as author and subject, as well as the first 40KB of available rich text in each document.

   • **Receive Summary Only** indicates that you wish to receive only basic document information, such as author and subject.

6. Click OK to begin replication. When replication has completed, the Replication Statistics dialog box will be displayed, as shown in Figure 28.4.

FIGURE 28.4:

The Replication Statistics dialog box appears after the replication process is completed.

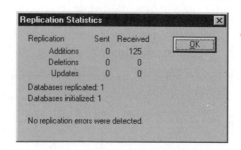

Restoring Truncated Documents

You can shorten the documents that a replica receives and then retrieve the rest of the documents later. Notes can shorten, or *truncate*, documents by removing all but a document summary and the first 40KB of rich text.

1. Click the replica.

2. Choose File ➤ Replication ➤ Settings.

3. Select the Receive Summary and 40KB of Rich Text Only option.

4. Click OK.

> **NOTE** Summaries include basic document information such as author and subject.

To receive the rest of a document after it has been shortened, open the document and choose Actions ➤ Retrieve Entire Document.

To receive the rest of more than one shortened document in a view, select the documents, choose Actions ➤ Retrieve Entire Document. Select the Get Documents Now via Background option and click OK. If Notes can retrieve the document(s) from more than one server, it prompts you to choose the server.

> **TIP** The length of time for replicating a database depends on the number of changes that have been made. Sometimes the procedure can take quite a while. So a word to the wise: If you need to replicate long distance, do it in the evening when telephone rates are lower. (Also, read on to find out how you can restrict the number of changes that are replicated.)

Using the Replicator

Notes provides an easy, alternative method for replicating databases: the Replicator. Choose the Replicator by clicking the last tab in the Notes Workspace. Rather than displaying a series of menu options, the Replicator presents a graphical interface for initiating, modifying, and scheduling workstation-to-server replication.

Using the Replicator can be as easy as pointing and clicking or may be more involved if you wish to customize your overall replication strategy. Figure 28.5 shows an example of a Replicator Workspace page.

FIGURE 28.5:

The Replicator
Workspace page

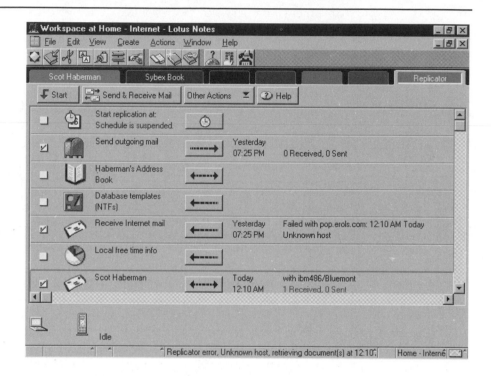

The advantage of using the Replicator is that it allows you to replicate several databases located on one or more servers with a single command. The alternative is to replicate each database individually, which can be tedious and requires your attention from start to finish. With the Replicator, you initiate the replication process once and then walk away or continue working while Notes replicates in the background. You can also schedule replication to occur between your laptop and the Notes server several times per day or when a certain number of outgoing mail messages are pending.

How the Replicator Works

The Replicator page consists of a number of "entries." Whenever you create a local replica of a database (as we did above), Notes automatically places an entry for the database in the Replicator page. Other types of entries also appear in the Replicator page, such as Start Replication At and Send Outgoing Mail. If your current location type is designated as Travel (Modem), you will also see Call Server and Hang Up! entries.

Each entry represents a task for Notes to perform. For instance, a database entry instructs Notes to replicate that database using options associated with the entry. An entry is activated by clicking the white checkbox located at the far left of the entry and is deactivated by clicking the box again. When you activate the appropriate entries, set the options associated with each entry (some entries don't have any options), and click the Start button, the Replicator executes each entry in the order it appears. You can change the sequence of certain entries (database entries, for instance) by dragging and dropping them to the desired position.

Putting the Replicator to Use

Using the Replicator to perform ad hoc and scheduled replication is easier and less time consuming than using the conventional menu options. Since Notes does most of the work, you probably don't have to do much more than click the mouse a few times.

To make use of the Replicator, do the following:

1. Click the Replicator tab in the Notes Workspace.

2. Click the white checkbox for each entry you wish to activate (if not already activated).

TIP   If your current location type is Dial-up Modem, be sure to activate the Call Server and Hang Up! entries.

---

3. Set the options for each entry appropriately. For example, click the arrow button for a database entry to specify the replication options (previously described in the "Updating a Replica" section).

4. Click the Start button. The Replicator executes in the background, freeing you to continue with your work.

Scheduling Replication

A replication schedule lets you replicate local databases on a regular basis automatically. You specify replication schedules in Location documents in your Personal Address Book. You can specify different replication schedules for different places that you work. For example, you can specify a replication schedule for your Office location only or specify different replication schedules for your Office and Home locations.

> **NOTE**
>
> Notes administrators can also specify replication schedules for server-to-server replication. For more information, see Notes Administration Help.

When you start Notes, Notes checks to see if scheduled replication is enabled for the current location. If it is, Notes performs replication in the background based on the current location's schedule. For example, suppose you have scheduled replication for 8:00 A.M. to 6:00 P.M. Monday through Friday with a 360-minute repeat interval. If you start Notes at 9:00 A.M. on Tuesday, Notes immediately attempts to replicate and then attempts to replicate again 360 minutes later. If a scheduled replication attempt fails, Notes tries to replicate again each minute until the attempt is successful.

Modifying a Location Document

As we discussed in Chapter 13, a *location* is a document in your Personal Address Book that contains communication settings you use when you work with Notes in a particular place.

When you install Notes, Notes automatically creates five Location documents in your Personal Address Book: Home (Modem), Internet, Island (Disconnected), Office (Network), and Travel (Modem). You can edit these documents and customize them or create your own. When you use Notes in a different location, you choose the Location document that contains the settings that apply to your current location.

You could also set up the Replicator Workspace page in different ways at different locations. Notes allows you to use unique replication settings that correspond to your various work locations.

Specifying a Replication Schedule for a Location

You can specify a replication schedule for a location. When the location is current, you can use the Replicator Workspace page to select databases and replicate according to the schedule.

1. Choose File ➤ Mobile ➤ Locations.

2. Select a location, such as Travel (Modem), and click Edit Location. The Edit Location document appears, as shown in Figure 28.6.

3. Do the following under Replication:

   - In the Schedule field, select Enabled.

   - In the Replicate Daily Between field, specify start and end times that define the period of the day during which you want replication to occur.

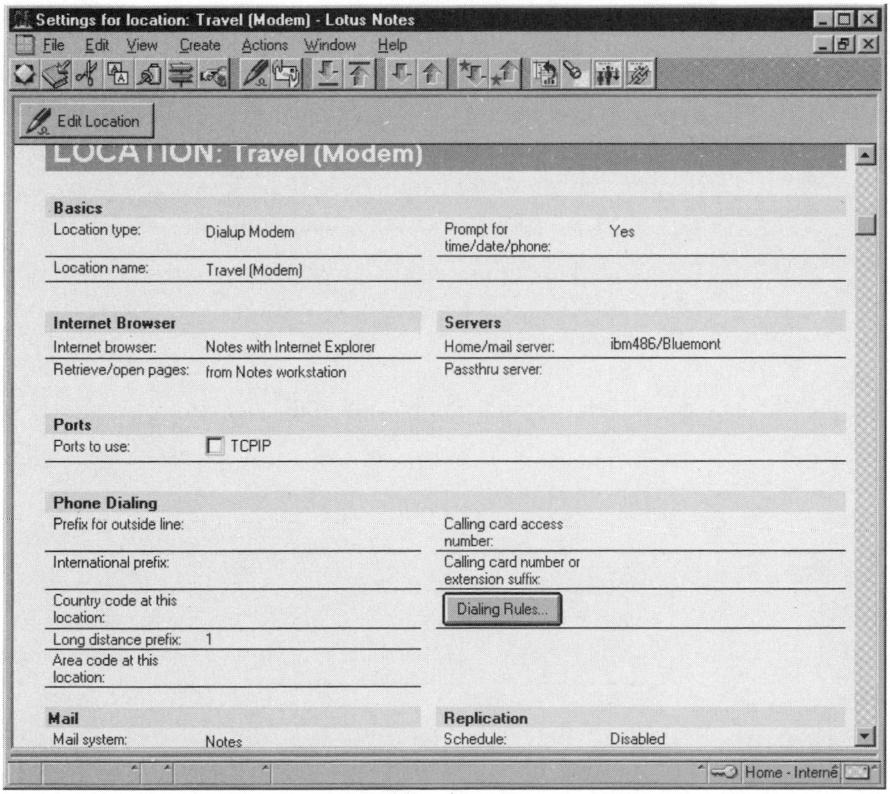

FIGURE 28.6:

You can edit a Location document, such as the Travel (Modem) Location document, to set a schedule for replicating databases.

- In the Repeat Every field, specify the number of minutes you want to elapse between replication sessions.

- In the Days of Week field, specify the days on which you want replication to occur.

4. Choose File ➤ Save to save the Location document.

TIP You can specify a replication schedule for the current location by clicking the Replicator tab and then clicking the Start Replication at Entry Action button.

Replicating Selective Information

At times you may wish to replicate only a subset of the documents in a shared database to a workstation replica. For example, this approach would be suitable if space on your workstation is limited and you want your replica copy to receive only certain types of information from the source database. Another situation where partial replication makes sense is when only certain information is relevant or of interest to you; any additional information is simply "clutter" and serves no purpose. By replicating only part of the source database, you can save the time and expense of long remote replication times.

You need to define selective replication for the current database only. To specify which documents a replica should receive when replicating a particular database, follow these steps:

1. Click the local database icon to select it.

2. Choose File ➤ Replication ➤ Settings. The Replication Settings dialog box appears.

TIP You can also display the Replication Settings dialog box by clicking the database with the right mouse button and selecting the Replication Settings option in the pop-up menu.

---

3. Click the Replicate a Subset of Documents option. Notes displays a list of folders and views that have been defined by the application developer as part of the database design.

4. Select one or more of the folders and views if the subset of documents you wish to replicate is completely isolated in specific folders and views of the database. Only the documents that appear there will be subject to replication. This method is not appropriate if the folders and views you select contain other, irrelevant documents.

5. Click the Select by Formula option if the subset of documents you wish to replicate is not fully contained in specific folders and views of the database, that is, the documents are "scattered" and can be identified only through a formula.

6. Write a formula to select which documents will replicate from the source database to the workstation replica in the Selection Formula box (see Figure 28.7). The default formula SELECT @All selects all documents from the source. Notes adds the word SELECT to all selection formulas when they are saved, so you don't have to type it.

FIGURE 28.7:

The Replications Settings dialog box allows you to enter a selection formula in the formula text box, which enables you to replicate only certain types of information from the source database based on a special formula.

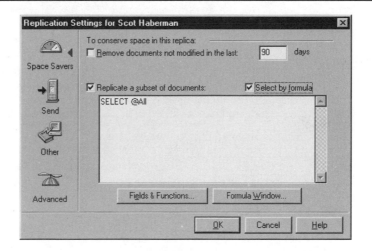

Replication Settings for Scot Haberman

To conserve space in this replica:
☐ Remove documents not modified in the last: `90` days

☑ Replicate a subset of documents: ☑ Select by formula

    SELECT @All

Space Savers
Send
Other
Advanced

Fields & Functions...   Formula Window...

OK   Cancel   Help

TIP   Selection formulas for replication are the same as selection formulas for views.

- Click the Fields & Functions button to display a list of available @functions and field names that you can paste into the formula box.

- Click the Formula Window button to enlarge the editing area when you're writing a formula.

Figure 28.8 shows an example of a selection formula that pulls only specific documents from a replica of a mail database.

FIGURE 28.8:

This selection formula, which would be useful in a replica of a mail database, does not replicate documents whose From field is Scot Haberman.

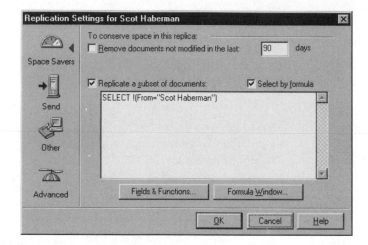

7. Click OK to save the replication criteria. This information will be saved with the database and will not appear in other replicas of the database unless the managers have chosen to replicate replication formulas.

WARNING   The @IsResponseDoc function will replicate *all* Response documents, even those whose main (parent) documents are not selected by the formula. However, the Release 4 function @AllChildren replicates only the Response documents of the parent documents that were selected by the replication formula. These orphaned Response documents will not show up in any hierarchical views. This function behaves differently when used in view selection formulas.

Handling Replication Conflicts

Database replicas aren't identical at all times. As we have mentioned, servers connect to other servers, and workstations connect to servers, to update their replicas on a scheduled or manually driven (forced) basis. If two users edit the same original document in different replicas between data exchanges (resulting in two unlike versions of the same document), a *replication conflict* develops when the replicas exchange modifications later.

Notes handles the situation by maintaining a revision history of each document. During replication, Notes updates the revision history and detects the concurrent updates. At this point, Notes designates the document that has been edited and saved the most frequently as the main (original) document, or the "winner." The other revised document is considered a Response document, or "loser." (In case of a tie, the document saved most recently wins.) A view marks the Response document with a diamond-shaped symbol in the left column and displays it below the main document. The losers are considered "conflicting" documents and are labeled [Replication or Save Conflict]. Users can see immediately that a conflict has occurred and must be resolved.

Resolution of a replication conflict involves manually merging the changes made to one of the documents into the other. Which document you choose as the ultimate "winner" usually depends on the extent of the changes in each document; if you will obviously need less time to add the updates to one document than to the other, take the shortest route. In the event that the same information has been updated in both documents, you'll have to coordinate with the other user in order to resolve the conflict.

Depending on which document will emerge as the ultimate winner, complete one of the following procedures.

To resolve the conflict in favor of the main document:

1. Update the main document with the changes made to the Response document. You can simply flip back and forth between the two documents and either retype the information or copy and paste information to and from the Clipboard using Edit ➤ Copy and Edit ➤ Paste.

2. Choose File ➤ Save to save your changes to the main document.

3. Highlight the Response document in the view and press the Delete key. A trash can icon appears in the left column next to the Response document.

4. Press F9 to refresh the view and remove the Response document from the database.

To resolve the conflict in favor of the Response document:

1. Update the Response document with the changes made to the main document as described in step 1 above.

2. Choose File ➤ Save to save your changes to the Response document.

NOTE   Even if you are not going to include changes made to the main document in the Response document, you must open and save the Response document in order to promote it to a main document.

3.   Highlight the original main document in the view and press Delete. A trash can icon appears in the left column next to the document.

4.   Press F9 to refresh the view and remove the original main document from the database.

If a document is edited in one replica and deleted in another, the deletion takes precedence. The database designer can exclude conflicting documents from a view by adding the following code to the view's selection formula (see Chapter 20 for more information):

```
& !@IsAvailable($Conflict)
```

Because replication occurs at the field level, rather than at the document level, two users can edit the same document in different replicas and not produce a replication conflict. If the users have modified different fields in the document, Notes can merge the changes into a single document. This technique is possible only if the database designer has enabled the Merge replication conflicts property for the form on which the documents are based.

Keeping Track of Previous Replications

One of the most useful features of replication is how Notes tracks each replication event for each database. By tracking the events, Notes creates a replication history of a database. Notes uses the history to determine which documents to replicate the next time it replicates with the same server or workstation. This information can be useful for reviewing replication events and troubleshooting problems. To review the replication history of a database, follow these steps:

1.   Click the database's icon to select it.

2.   Choose File ➤ Database ➤ Properties. The Database Properties InfoBox appears.

3.   Click the Replication History button to see all previous replications (since the history was last cleared) in the Replication History dialog box, as shown

in Figure 28.9. The replication history reflects the date and time of the last replication, the server or workstation with which the database replicated, and whether documents were sent or received or both.

The Replication History
dialog box

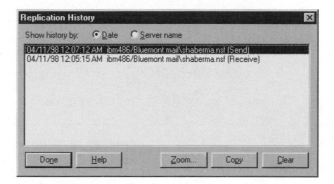

> **TIP**
>
> When you experience replication problems, you can manually clear a database's history and start over with a clean slate. Just click the Clear button in the Replication History dialog box. This action forces Notes to replicate all the documents that have changed since the database was created, not just those documents that have been modified since the last replication.

4. Click one of the Show History By options to display information sorted either by date (newest first) or by server name.

5. Click Cancel to close the dialog box.

Notes will update the replication history of a database only if the replication has been successful. If the replication fails, no history will be recorded. During the next replication, Notes will pick up where it left off and restart the replication process on the documents that were not replicated during the previous session.

Notes includes or excludes a document from the next replication by comparing the date of the last replication with the date when each document was last modified. If a document contains changes that occurred since the last replication, Notes includes the document in the next replication. If the document hasn't been modified since the last replication, Notes excludes it from the next replication. Notes doesn't take any more time than it needs to complete replication, thus making the replication of large databases that contain hundreds of documents an efficient process.

To see a document's last modification date, follow these steps:

1. Select a database.

2. Open a view.

3. Select or open a document.

4. Choose File ➤ Document Properties. The Document Properties InfoBox, shown in Figure 28.10, displays the date of the last modification, as well as other pertinent field and database information.

5. Close the Document Properties InfoBox.

FIGURE 28.10:

The Document Properties InfoBox displays the date of the last modification, as well as other pertinent field and database information.

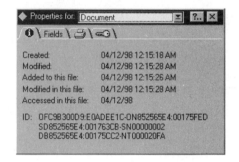

You can find additional replication information in the Notes Log database that's located in your Workspace. Select the database and choose the Replication Events view (see Figure 28.11) from the View menu from the Navigation pane. When you expand one of the dates and double-click one of the replication events in the view, a Replication Log Entry document appears, as shown in Figure 28.12. The document reveals how many documents in a particular database were added, deleted, and updated on both sides of the replication. The Events field displays additional information or problems that may have occurred.

What's Next?

In the next chapter, we discuss a powerful technology called object linking and embedding, or OLE. You can use OLE to integrate other desktop applications and information in your database in unique and interesting ways and extend the power of your Notes applications. OLE allows users within the Notes environment to use tools that provide functionality not found in Notes itself.

FIGURE 28.11:

The Replication Events view lets you choose a server and see the number of database replications that have taken place on the server.

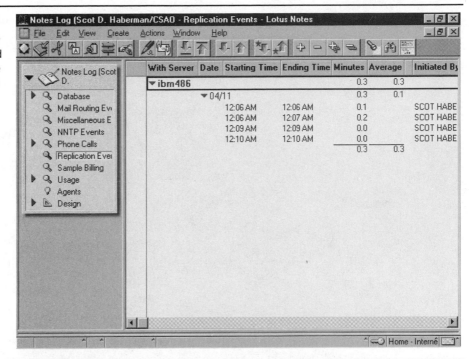

FIGURE 28.12:

The Replication Log Entry reveals how many documents in a particular database were added, deleted, and updated on both sides of the replication.

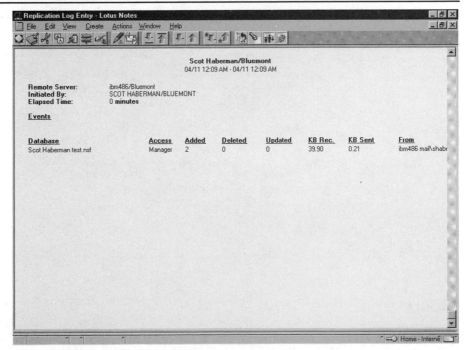

Linking and Embedding Objects in Notes

■ Linking data to a document

■ Embedding data into a document

■ Embedding a blank object into a document

■ Indexing and searching linked or embedded text

■ Placing an object in the design of a form

■ Controlling the automatic launching of objects in documents

■ Using Notes/FX

By taking advantage of a key Windows feature—Object Linking and Embedding (OLE)—you can give your database applications the additional power of using information created with other Windows software. OLE allows you to insert objects—files, parts of files, or links to files—into Notes documents that have been created in other Windows applications. A linked or embedded object resembles any other element displayed in a Notes document—with one significant difference. The object maintains certain connections with the original document or application in which it was created. In this chapter, we'll discuss several topics related to linking and embedding objects, including:

- The differences between linking and embedding
- How to insert objects in documents
- When and how to use linking
- How to edit embedded or linked objects
- When and how to use embedding
- Notes/FX

Linking and Embedding Objects

Okay, the world doesn't revolve around Notes. You probably use a number of different desktop tools, each designed to perform a particular task, such as creating proposals, spreadsheets, schedules, and presentations. But what do you do when you want to integrate information you've created outside of Notes within the Notes environment?

If you're a fan of Windows applications, you're familiar with the copy and paste commands that true Windows applications provide. You can select data (such as a portion of a word processing document, the cells of a spreadsheet, or a graphical image) from one application, copy the data to the Windows Clipboard, and paste it elsewhere in the same application or in another application. The Clipboard enables you to transfer static data from one application to another. But no awareness or connection exists between the two applications sharing the data in this way. If you need to update the data, you'll have to use the copy-and-paste routine to transfer the data again.

Once you "paste" data, you must deal with it in terms of the "receiving application," not in terms of the "originating application." If you were to highlight a range of cells in a Lotus 1-2-3 spreadsheet, copy the range to the Clipboard, and then paste the range to a Lotus Word Pro document, the range would appear as a table of elements, rather than as a range of cells (i.e., in native 1-2-3 format). You would manipulate the data as elements in a table, not as cells in a spreadsheet. Microsoft Corporation, the creator of Windows, addressed the problem of performing manual updates by creating technologies that automate the process in several different ways. These technologies are known as Dynamic Data Exchange (DDE) and a newer, more powerful extension of DDE called Object Linking and Embedding (OLE).

What Is Linking?

As we mentioned above, when you choose the Edit ➤ Paste command, Notes inserts the data that you've copied to (and which is subsequently stored by) the Windows Clipboard in the receiving application's data file where you want it to appear. You can continue pasting the same data until you copy new data to the Clipboard; when you paste new data to the Clipboard, the new replaces the old. If you exit Windows entirely, you lose the data on the Clipboard forever; Windows does not save it for future sessions.

Use the Paste Special command on the Edit menu (Edit ➤ Paste Special) when you want to incorporate *dynamic* data into a Notes document. Instead of treating the data in a *static* fashion, that is, pasting it in a document and then updating it manually if need be, Paste Special allows you to create a connection between a Notes document and an external data set. The command appears dimmed and unavailable unless you put data from an application that supports DDE and OLE in the Clipboard.

When Paste Special is available, Notes (acting as an OLE client application) allows you to establish a *link* to data maintained in another Windows application, known as the OLE server application. Creating this link establishes a persistent relationship between the server application's data and the document.

Let's say you want a particular field in a document to contain data that's been created in another Windows application. You want the document to reflect the latest state of the external data, so you create a link. When the data in the server application changes, Notes displays the change in the field's contents the next time you open the document.

When you create a link in a Notes document, you are inserting a pointer to information in an external file. Since the link points to the original data, the Notes document automatically reflects any changes made to the linked file. You can think of a link as a pipeline between the Notes document and the source file, which can be anything from a word processing document to a presentation file (e.g., Lotus Freelance or Microsoft Powerpoint). For example, suppose you want to include the latest sales figures from a 1-2-3 spreadsheet in a financial research document that resides in a Notes database. Instead of frequently pasting, importing, or retyping the sales figures to keep them up-to-date, you can create a link to the source 1-2-3 file in your financial research document in Notes. The Notes database will reflect every change that you or any other user makes to the 1-2-3 file.

You must adhere to a few rules to ensure successful linking. First, since the data set is an external file, you need proper access to it. Access is not an issue when the file resides on your local hard drive. However, if the file resides on a file server, you must address various complications of file server access, including log on, directory security, and directory mapping. (These issues are entirely a function of your network environment and the file server operating system that is in use.)

Recall, as well, that when you update a linked or embedded object from within Notes, you deal with the data in terms of the server application (1-2-3, Word Pro, etc.); therefore, you must have access to the server application. The application has to be installed either on your local hard drive or on a file server whose security permits you access to the application. Users whose only need is to read the information do not need access to the original file or to the server application as long as the data is fully visible in the Notes document. (An object is "rendered" in the client application either as it appears natively in the server application or simply as an icon that you must double-click to launch the server application and present the data in its native format. For the data to be directly readable, the link must not be rendered as an icon in the Notes document.)

Finally, if the linked file is moved or deleted from the directory in which it resides, you will have to re-create the link.

What Is Embedding?

Embedding allows you to insert information from a server application file into a Notes document so that you create a true "compound" document made up of data from several different sources. A compound Notes document, by definition, means that the document utilizes data from different sources, which may come from another database or another Windows application.

You might think that embedding sounds exactly like creating a link to an external data file in a Notes document. A very significant difference exists between linking and embedding. Whereas a linked object's data is external to the client application, an embedded object's data is stored within the client application. In the context of Notes, the data represented by an embedded object in a Notes document is stored in the Notes database, not as an external file that can be maintained outside of Notes. Many of the stipulations that apply to linked objects, primarily having to do with access to the source data file, simply vanish.

Let's say you, as a database's designer, paste a graphic that you created in Visio 4.0 into a form, but you later want to modify the graphic. You're going to have to switch out of Notes, open Visio, edit the graphic, copy it to the Clipboard, exit Visio, switch back to Notes again, delete the old version of the graphic, and paste the new version. What a bother! Unfortunately, the only physical change you can make to an object that you insert in a form (and documents for that matter) in this way is sizing it. You're limited to selecting the object and then dragging the object's handles to increase or decrease its size.

However, if you embed the object in a document, you simply double-click the object to launch the server application where you created it. You don't exit Notes. With the server application open, you can edit the object, save the changes, and then return to Notes and the document that contains the object. The object will reflect the changes you made to it in the server application. Although the data is physically attached to the document, Notes relinquishes control over that part of the document to the OLE server application. Once the object is embedded in the Notes document, it's no longer associated with the original file. Consequently, changes made to one are *not* automatically reflected in the other, as would be the case if the object were linked to the original file.

NOTE   When you embed an object in an OLE client application (such as Notes), the entire file is embedded, not just the selected portion that is copied to the Clipboard. For instance, if you select a 10x10 range of cells in a Lotus 1-2-3 for Windows spreadsheet that is 2MB in size and then embed it in a Notes document, the whole spreadsheet is embedded (even though you only see the 10x10 range of cells). The entire spreadsheet is stored in the Notes database.

TIP

The current implementation of OLE, version 2.0, has no ability to detect that a particular object has already been embedded in an OLE client application. Therefore, if you embed an object in a Notes document and then embed the same object in another Notes document (or elsewhere in the same Notes document, for that matter), the object is stored twice in the database.

You use embedding when others with whom you want to share the information may not have access to the original source file, for example, when you cannot store the data on a file server where everyone can access it or when the data may be moved or deleted. As an embedded object, the data is stored within the Notes database itself, and access to it is a matter of a user's ability to access the document where it resides.

Embedding versus Linking

Embedded objects are much more robust than linked objects and are typically more useful in networking environments, such as Notes, that implement workflow automation applications. Notes databases, particularly in large organizations, are more often than not designed as compound applications so they can utilize other Windows applications to furnish data in documents. These Windows applications must be stored on a central file server that the Notes server can access. In this way, embedded data can be shared more easily with Notes users in other locations. (Remember that an organization might support more than one worksite and maintain several Notes servers.) However, keep in mind that an embedded object uses more disk space in the Notes database than a linked object. The size of an embedded object, such as a graphic, can be large.

Using Object Linking and Embedding in Notes Databases

OLE is the next step beyond DDE in sharing data between Notes databases and other Windows applications and in creating compound documents. OLE is a superset of DDE functionality that includes improved linking as well as object embedding.

OLE works in Notes like this: Two copies of the data are maintained in a Notes document (the client application). One copy appears in a graphical format that is used only to visually represent the embedded object. When a user selects this object in the document, Notes launches the server application (e.g., Lotus 1-2-3) and transfers to it the second copy of the data, which appears in the original server format. The user can then utilize the server application to modify the data in its original form. When the user is finished in the server application, the updated data is immediately available as an updated object in the Notes document.

You can embed existing files or parts of files, or you can create a new, "empty" OLE object while your Notes document is open. Once an object has been embedded, changes to the original file or to the embedded object have no effect on each other because the object is a copy of the original and is no longer associated with it. Activating an object launches the application that was used to create it so you or other Notes users can edit the data.

If you want the users of a database to see a document from an OLE server application when they enter or read information, you can design a database form as an OLE "seamless" object. When users enter or read information in such a form, they see a document from the OLE server application instead of a Notes document. For example, in an expense report database, you might want users to compose a 1-2-3 spreadsheet instead of a Notes text-based document.

NOTE   A good example of this "seamless" object is contained in either the Lotus SmartSuite 96 Library or Microsoft Office Library templates that are supplied by Lotus.

You shouldn't use OLE when you want to include a link in one Notes document to another. You should create a Notes Document Link (or doclink) to allow readers to jump directly to the document or use the Clipboard for copying and pasting data. If readers need to *edit* the data and don't have the server application, they should use the Import command or the Clipboard. When the server application doesn't support OLE, you should use file attachments, the Import command, or the Clipboard.

Linking Data

If you are creating a new file using an OLE server application and you want to create a *link* to it in Notes, you must save the file before you attempt to create the link. To link data into a document, follow these steps:

1. Select the data you want to link to, such as a range of spreadsheet cells or some text from a word processor, and copy it to the Clipboard using Edit ➤ Copy.

2. Open the Notes document and place the insertion point in a rich text field where you want the object to appear.

3. Choose Edit ➤ Paste Special. The Paste Special dialog box appears, as shown in Figure 29.1.

FIGURE 29.1:

The Paste Special dialog box

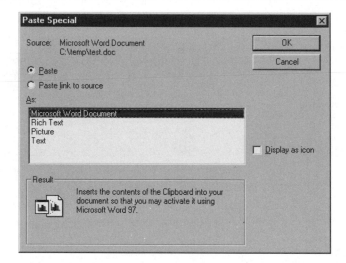

4. Select the Paste Link to Source option.

5. Select the name of the server application from the As: list.

NOTE   You may choose any format you wish from the As: list, but you should stick with the server application format unless you have a particular reason for not doing so.

6. Click OK to insert a copy of the source data in Picture format in the Notes document. This object will act as a pointer to the original file if you wish to edit it later.

7. Press Ctrl+S to save the pasted information in the Notes document.

Whenever you access a document that contains a link to an external object, Notes will ask you whether to refresh the link so that your document reflects the latest state of the external object, as shown in Figure 29.2.

FIGURE 29.2:

For documents that contain links to external objects, Notes prompts you to refresh the links whenever you access the documents.

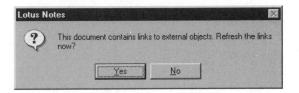

TIP

To perform a simple paste (without linking or embedding) using the default format, use Edit ➤ Paste, rather than Edit ➤ Paste Special.

Modifying OLE Links

You can activate OLE links to update or edit the data, switch between automatic and manual updating, change the link parameters, or break a link. To edit a link in a document, follow these steps:

1. Open the document in Edit mode.

2. Choose Edit ➤ External Links.

3. Select the link(s) you want to use from the External Links dialog box, shown in Figure 29.3. You can activate only one link at a time; if you select more than one link, the Open Source and Edit Link options remain unavailable.

FIGURE 29.3:

The External Links dialog box lets you select the link(s) you want to use. You can activate only one link at a time.

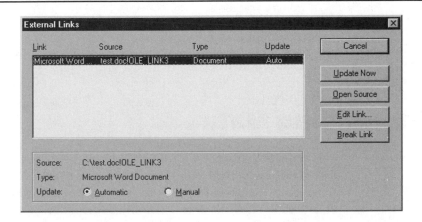

4.   Select any of the following options:

- **Update Now**: Refreshes the data for all selected links.

- **Open Source**: Launches the server application so that the linked data may be edited.

- **Edit Link**: Opens the file browser for the version of Windows you're using and lets you select an alternative file to link to.

- **Break Link**: Permanently breaks the connection to the external data file. Notes converts the object to a simple graphic in Picture format. You will no longer be able to use the object's server application to modify the data.

5.   Click OK or Cancel if you change your mind.

As we said before, a link is actually a pointer to an external file. If for some reason the external file cannot be accessed (for example, the file was deleted), you will receive the message shown in Figure 29.4 and the linked data in your document will be grayed-out.

FIGURE 29.4:

The link to the external file could not be located.

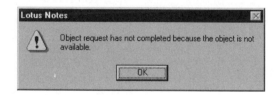

If you receive this message, you will need to reestablish the link. This is one of the problems that can plague you when using external file links. Something as simple as a file being renamed can render a link invalid.

Embedding Data

You have a choice of several methods for embedding data in a rich text field of a document. In contrast to linking, if you want to *embed* an object in Notes, you do not have to save the file in the OLE server application before embedding it. To embed data into a document, use any of the following methods.

Method 1: Using Copy and Paste

1. Select the data you want to embed, such as a range of spreadsheet cells or some text from a word processor, and copy it to the Clipboard using Edit ➤ Copy.

2. Open the Notes document and place the insertion point in a rich text field where you want the object to appear.

3. Choose Edit ➤ Paste Special.

4. Select the Paste option.

5. Select the name of the server application from the As: list.

6. Click the OK button, which embeds a copy of the source data into the Notes document that can be edited later using the server application.

NOTE   If you choose any format from the As: list other than the server application's native format, the selected data will be inserted in the document, but it will not be an embedded object. The distinction is that embedding lets you launch the server application and work with the data in its native environment.

---

7. Press Ctrl+S to save the pasted information in the Notes document.

Method 2: Using Menu Commands

1. Open the Notes document and place the insertion point in a rich text field where you want the object to appear.

2. Choose Create ➤ Object.

3. Select the Create an Object from a File option in the Create Object dialog box, as shown in Figure 29.5.

4. Click the Browse button and navigate to the file that you want to embed as an object in the current document.

5. Click OK. The OLE object is embedded in the Notes document in the default format, Picture.

6. Press Ctrl+S to save your work.

FIGURE 29.5:

Use the Create Object dialog box to embed a file as an object in a document.

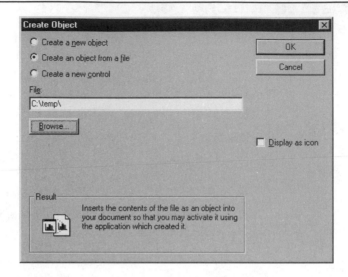

Method 3: Using Drag and Drop

1. Open the Notes document in Edit mode. Be sure that the Notes window is *not* maximized.

2. Switch to the Windows Explorer and navigate to the file that you wish to embed. Position the Notes window and the browser window so that they are side by side.

3. Place the mouse pointer on the file to be embedded, click and hold down the left mouse button, and drag the file to a rich text field in your Notes document. Release the mouse button to drop the file into the field.

4. Press Ctrl+S to save your work.

NOTE   Remember! When you embed an object, any connection with the source file is broken. The embedded object will not reflect later changes made to the source file.

NOTE   If you are using Windows 95 or NT 4.*x*, you can drag and drop files via the status bar. Drag the file to the status bar and hold it over the Notes application button. After a few seconds, the Notes application will be displayed and you can drop the file into the field.

Creating a Blank Object

At times, you may wish to simply embed a "blank object" that can be modified later in a Notes document. (Or you may embed a blank object into the design of the form itself. Then each document that is created with the form automatically has an instance of the embedded object in it. We'll discuss this situation in more detail later in the chapter.) Before you begin, open the Notes document and place the insertion point in a rich text field where you want the object to appear. Then follow the steps below to create a blank OLE object:

1. Choose Create ➤ Object.

2. Select the Create a New Object option, as shown in Figure 29.6.

3. Select an Object type from the list box that contains all of the registered OLE servers.

4. Click OK. Notes launches the application you selected, which creates a blank work document that becomes your active window.

5. Create your object data in the OLE server application. You can even insert other objects into this object if the OLE server application can also act as an OLE client.

6. Click anywhere outside the object or press Esc to return focus to the Notes document.

7. Press Ctrl+S to save your work.

FIGURE 29.6:

The Create Object dialog box lets you select an object type. Every OLE server application registered in your database appears in the Object type box.

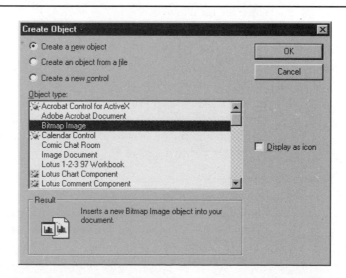

The OLE object is now embedded in your Notes document in the default format, Picture.

NOTE When clicking on an embedded object in your Notes document, the menu titles in the menu bar at the top of the Workspace change to include an object-specific menu option. For instance, if you embedded a Microsoft Excel spreadsheet, the menu option Worksheet appears.

Creating a Custom Object

You can also add an OLE custom object to your form. All of the object types that have an "star" next to them are OLE custom controls. An OLE custom control is a small, self-contained software module with its own data. Lotus Components are examples of these types of controls. To add a custom control to your form, follow these steps:

1. Choose Create ➤ Object.

2. Select the Create a New Control option.

3. Select the type of control from the list box that contains all of the registered OLE custom controls.

4. Click OK. Notes embeds the custom control and makes it active.

5. Add your data to the custom control.

6. Click anywhere outside the object or press Esc to return focus to the Notes document.

7. Press Ctrl+S to save your work.

When a custom control is active, the menu is a combination of the Notes menu and the custom control.

NOTE If your custom control is not listed in the Object type listbox, the Create a New Control option will allow you to add new controls using the Add Control button.

Problems with Embedding

If you have trouble with an embedded object, first check the following:

- Make sure the server application is available. It must be installed on your hard disk or be available to you on a networked file server.

- Make sure the location of the server application executables hasn't changed.

Selecting the Data Format for an Object

The OLE object is now embedded in your Notes document in the default format, Picture. To select a different display format, follow these steps:

1. Click the object in the Notes document.

2. Select Display As from the object-specific menu (in this case Document) that appears in the menu bar at the top of the Workspace, as shown in the example in Figure 29.7.

3. Specify a format type for the object.

4. Click OK.

FIGURE 29.7:

The Display As dialog box lets you specify a format type for the object.

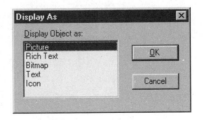

Performing a Full Text Search of OLE Information

Notes can index and search for text within linked or embedded information under the following conditions:

- The data type is in either text or rich text format.

2 • The object is rendered in its native format in the Notes document.

3 • The Index Attachment option was selected when the database was first full text indexed using the Full Text options folder of the Database Properties InfoBox. (Choose Database ➤ Properties and click the Full Text tab to index a database. See Chapter 6 for a discussion of creating text indexes.)

Placing Objects in the Design of a Form

If you are responsible for developing Notes applications, you may choose to *link* or *embed* an object directly into a form. Whenever a user creates a document based on the form, the linked and/or embedded object(s) will automatically appear. This method is useful in cases where you anticipate that users will frequently (if not always) require the functionality that the object provides. For instance, if you know that a particular Notes document requires some kind of sophisticated financial calculations, you could embed a spreadsheet object (either a blank object or one that already incorporates the necessary structure and formulas) into the form itself. This design saves the user from having to insert the object manually into a rich text field (as described in the sections above).

To build an object into the design of a form, do the following:

1. Open the form in Design mode.

2. Place the insertion point where you wish to place the object.

3. Use any of the methods for linking or embedding objects detailed in the sections above. The difference is that you are inserting the object into the form rather than into a specific rich text field as you would if you were an end user. (You can think of the form as a big rich text field.)

4. Press Ctrl+S to save the form.

With Notes 4.6, some new properties have been added for OLE objects and custom objects that are placed directly onto forms.

Some of the properties that are now available for OLE 2 objects, as shown in Figure 29.8, are:

• **Size Object to Window:** You can now set an option that will fill the entire Notes window when the object is launched. (If the document contains information other than the object, you cannot see that information while the object is expanded.)

- **Update Object from Document:** Now a user can make changes to the data within an object and save those changes with the document. In layman's terms, you can set this property so that all changes to the data within the object will be reflected on the form. If you do not set this property, the object will always look the same to the user.

FIGURE 29.8:

OLE 2 form properties

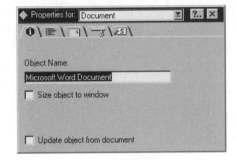

Some of the properties that are now available for custom controls, as shown in Figure 29.9, are:

- **Size Object to Window:** When a user creates a document or opens an existing document in edit mode, the custom control automatically expands to fill the entire Notes window. If the document contains information other than the custom control, the user cannot see that information while the custom control is expanded.

- **Size Object below Field:** When a user creates a document or opens an existing document in edit mode, the custom control automatically expands to fill the area of the Notes window below the layout region. Some of the limitations are:

  - If the document does not contain a layout region, the custom control expands to fill the entire Notes window.

  - If the document contains information below the layout region, the user cannot see that information while the custom control is expanded.

  - If the document contains two or more layout regions, the custom control expands below the first layout region. The user cannot see the other layout regions.

- **Run Object when Reading Document:** When a user opens a document, the object automatically launches in read mode. In this mode, the user can make changes to the object but cannot save the changes. The document has to be in edit mode to save the changes. However, the user can print the changes.

- **Update Object from Document:** Has the same functionality as the OLE 2 objects except that it applies to custom controls.

FIGURE 29.9:

Custom control form properties

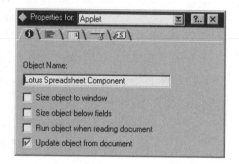

Controlling the Automatic Launching of Objects

Another aspect to designing forms that handle OLE objects (as well as file attachments and document links) is the ability to automatically launch (or "auto launch") an object under specific conditions. For example, you can set a form up to launch the first OLE object that Notes encounters in a document (i.e., the object's server application is automatically started and the object data presented) whenever a user edits the document. Another possibility is to have Notes automatically create a new object in a rich text field when a document is created. In all cases, you can also control the behavior of the Notes document once an object is launched. For example, you can choose to hide the Notes document entirely and display only the object's server application window, providing a smooth transition from the Notes view level (where the document is opened) to the object's environment.

To control the auto launch properties of a form for objects either embedded in the design of the form or inserted into rich text fields by users, do the following:

1. Open the form in Design mode.

2. Choose Design ➤ Form Properties and click the Launch tab to display the Launch properties.

3. Click the down arrow of the Auto Launch list box to display the available options and select -First OLE Object-. Several additional options will appear in the Launch Options folder, as shown in Figure 29.10.

FIGURE 29.10:

The Launch properties of a form

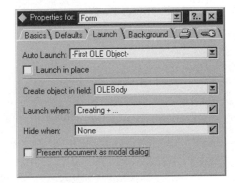

4. Pick the appropriate options for the type of functionality you wish to achieve:

- **Launch in Place**: Specifies that the object will be launched entirely within the Notes document, rather than having Notes placed in the background and the object in the foreground. The result is an almost seamless transition to the object's server application.

- **Launch When**: Specifies the conditions in which the object will be launched. You may choose any combination of Creating, Editing, and Reading a document. (If you selected Launch in place, the Reading option will not be available.)

- **Hide When**: Controls what happens, from a visual perspective, to the Notes document when the object is launched. When focus shifts to the object, the Notes document can remain visible, or you may choose a combination of the Hide When options, which will cause the Notes document to become effectively invisible. (If you've selected Launch in Place, the Hide When option will not be available.)

5. Press Ctrl+S to save the form.

To force the automatic creation of an object in a rich text field of the form, do the following:

1. Open the form in Design mode.

2. Choose Design ➤ Form Properties and click the Launch tab to display the Launch properties.

3. Click the down arrow of the Auto Launch list box to display the available options and select one of the registered OLE object types from the list, as shown in Figure 29.11.

4. Click the down arrow of the Create Object in Field option and choose either -First Rich Text Field- or the name of one of the rich text fields in the form in which the new object will be inserted.

5. Click the down arrow of the Launch When option and choose any combination of Creating, Editing, and Reading to specify when to create the new object.

6. Press Ctrl+S to save the form.

FIGURE 29.11:

Choose the type of object to be automatically created in a rich text field of the form from the list of registered OLE object types.

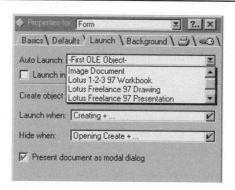

Using Notes as an "Object Container"

A typical work environment uses many different desktop tools—word processors, spreadsheets, personal information managers, etc. A given user may produce tens or even hundreds of data files. But when you want to organize all of that data so that it's easily accessible and retrievable, what options do you have? Because Notes is fully OLE-compliant, you can use Notes as a repository for non-Notes data. By linking and embedding objects in documents or directly within forms and then making smart use of the auto launch features that are part of Notes form design, you can create an environment in which users can access non-Notes tools and data completely from within the Notes interface. This Notes-driven architecture gives users a consistent look and feel whether they work specifically with Notes or with any other OLE-compliant application.

Notes/FX

We've seen that, with object linking and embedding, you can integrate data from external, non-Notes applications into Notes documents in a way that maintains the native format of the data. But the object remains an autonomous element that is distinct from the document in which it resides. No "awareness" exists between an embedded data set and the data captured elsewhere in the document; the data sets cannot "feed" off of one another.

Lotus has developed a technology—called *Notes/FX* (*FX* stands for "Field Exchange")—to address this issue. Notes/FX is an extension of OLE that makes it possible to exchange data automatically between a Notes application and other Notes/FX-enabled applications. These applications are OLE server applications, just as in a standard OLE implementation in a Notes document or form. The difference is that Notes/FX-enabled applications can also exchange their data with fields in a Notes form. For instance, the field values of a Notes document can be transmitted to the cells of a Lotus 1-2-3 spreadsheet, and vice versa. Either application can initiate the exchange.

> **NOTE**
>
> The Notes/FX capability is incorporated into Lotus Components, a technology that lets you extend the functionality of your Notes applications through a series of small, task-focused software modules that you embed in Notes forms. Lotus Components includes modules for charting, comments, file viewing, drawing and diagramming, spreadsheets, and project scheduling.

Notes/FX is one of a suite of tools in Lotus's NotesFlow architecture. The idea behind NotesFlow is to allow the developer to design a Notes application to act as the driver for a coordinated sequence of data exchange between Notes and non-Notes tools.

In addition to Notes/FX, NotesFlow also features the following capabilities:

- **Auto Launching** of other desktop applications when a Notes document is created, edited, or read. (This topic is discussed earlier in the chapter.)

- **Published Actions** that allow you to define an action in Notes and then publish it so that it appears as a menu item in other Notes/FX-enabled applications. This extremely powerful option supports the smooth transition between other desktop tools and Notes.

- **Open Database Connection (ODBC)** access to non-Notes databases such as Oracle, Informix, Sybase, Microsoft SQL Server, dBase, and Paradox. ODBC provides a pathway through which you can integrate external data sources into the flow of your Notes application.

Using Notes/FX

Exchanging data between Notes documents and another application requires that the application be Notes/FX-capable. Lotus 1-2-3 for Windows is an example of a Notes/FX-capable application. (Notes/FX capability is found in Lotus's SmartSuite tool set, as well as in third-party applications like Visio 4.0 from Visio Corporation.) You also have to make sure that Notes/FX is enabled within the forms that will be used to exchange data. To enable Notes/FX in a form, do the following:

1. Open the form in Design mode.

2. Choose Design ➤ Form Properties to display the Form Properties InfoBox.

3. Click the Defaults tab to view the default options for the form, as shown in Figure 29.12.

4. Deselect Disable Field Exchange if it is currently selected.

5. Close the InfoBox.

FIGURE 29.12:

Deselect the default option Disable Field Exchange to enable Notes/FX for the current form.

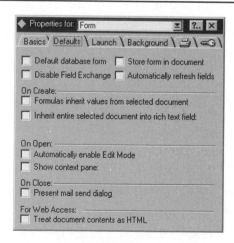

Precisely how you implement Notes/FX will depend on the OLE server application. (You will have to consult the documentation for the OLE server.) From the Notes perspective, you need to perform the following general tasks:

1. Embed the object that contains the data you want to exchange in your Notes form. This process was described in a previous section of this chapter.

2. Create one field in the form for each corresponding field in the server application to be exchanged. The names of the Notes fields must match the field names in the server application.

3. Save the form and close it.

What's Next?

Part IV, "Distributing Notes Databases on the World Wide Web," discusses new Notes 4.5 Internet features and capabilities, namely, *Domino* and the *Personal Web Navigator*. Domino is server technology that transforms Lotus Notes into an Internet applications server. Domino combines the open networking environment of Internet standards and protocols with the powerful application development facilities of Notes, enabling you to develop a broad range of business applications for the Internet and intranet.

The Personal Web Navigator provides easy access to the Web and allows you to navigate through pages on the Web directly from your Notes workstation. All you need is a direct Internet connection. The Personal Web Navigator combines the features of a Web browser with the powerful capabilities of Notes, creating an easy way for you to access and explore the Web. You can also access the Web through a central database called the Server Web Navigator database. This database resides on a Notes server. Remote Notes users access this database in the same way as they access other Notes databases.

In Part IV, we compare the specific functional differences between the Web and Notes and the relative merits of the two technologies. We also explain how to integrate Notes and the Web using Domino. One of Domino's most powerful features is its ability to automatically—and transparently—turn your Notes documents, views, and forms into HTML pages. By marrying the power of collaboration and workflow of Notes to the publishing strength of the Web, you get the best of both worlds. Notes simplifies the management of a Web site because you can use a Notes database to control which documents are published at any point in time and who should have access to them. With Notes you can automatically maintain all the links between HTML pages, including hypertext links, attached files, and associated images, *from within* Notes databases as opposed to having to manually hunt around the Web server's hard drive for broken links.

PART IV

Distributing Notes Databases on the World Wide Web

An Internet Primer for Notes Developers

- Reviewing the technology behind the Internet

- Defining File Transfer Protocol, Net news, and Internet mail

- Understanding the three major components of the Web

- Using Uniform Resource Locators (URLs)

- Marking up documents with HTML

The purpose of this brief chapter is to review the technology behind the Internet, not to teach its intricacies. As you probably noticed when you went to the bookstore to buy this book, the shelves are packed with Internet primers and technical treatises. This chapter is simply a way for readers to focus on the essential elements of the Internet as they pertain to Notes technology—which is the theme of the following chapters.

The term *Internet* has many meanings. Some people consider it the greatest technological achievement since the Wright brothers' plane; others think of it as a marketing breakthrough that will topple the Microsoft empire. Instead of turning to Hollywood, Wall Street, or Madison Avenue for answers, we are going to attempt to explain this near-mystical term by breaking it into manageable components.

Major Components of the Internet

We start with a review of the following technologies and protocols that make up the Net:

- The network
- File Transfer Protocol (FTP)
- Net newsgroups and bulletin boards
- E-mail
- The Web

The Network

The Internet, technically speaking, refers to a gigantic worldwide network of machines running the TCP/IP (Transport Control Protocol/ Internet Protocol) protocol.

NOTE   TCP/IP is a way to move packets of data between multiple computers that are connected to each other. Each computer uses a unique, centrally assigned address.

The U.S. military designed, financed, and built this network (originally called the ARPAnet) to be particularly resilient to mundane disruptions such as nuclear attacks and electronic warfare.

What the military origin of the Internet means to the business (and casual) user is that the Internet has no single point of failure and no real owner. Its actual topology and bandwidth are a mystery to most users (and many system administrators!) who know only the name and access number of the vendor (also known as the Internet service provider or ISP) they pay to enter the network. For dial-up users, setting up an Internet connection may be as simple as configuring Warp Connect or Windows 95 or loading one of the many promotional diskettes that come in the mail from companies such as America Online, Prodigy, and CompuServe.

NOTE   Regardless of the Internet service provider you choose, this simple rule often applies: The more you pay, the faster your connection.

Simple access may start with an off-the-shelf 28.8Kbps modem (although 56Kbps is becoming the norm). Small-workgroup access requires at least ISDN (also called digital telephone access at 128Kbps), its supporting hardware, and much cooperation from your local phone company. Larger groups will require dedicated leased lines (Frame Relay, T1, or T3) with special communications equipment. If you allow the Internet network to call you, as opposed to your calling it, you may also need network routers, firewalls to filter out potential intruders, and increased network administrative resources.

NOTE   Notes clients can access servers over the Internet, and Notes servers can replicate with each other over the Internet without any modification.

So far we managed to avoid using the corny superhighway analogy. Sure, both the Internet and the highway system are large networks. Similarly, you pay to ride on both, and you pay more to move faster. The government financed both networks, and both are in various states of disrepair and congestion. Pushing the analogy much further leads to political statements, which is probably why it is so overused!

File Transfer Protocol (FTP)

FTP is a way to manipulate files remotely between machines that do not necessarily run the same operating system. One machine is the FTP server; another is the

FTP client. Armed with adequate security rights and an FTP client, you can navigate through directories on another machine and copy, delete, rename, and append files and directories, as illustrated in Figure 30.1.

FIGURE 30.1:

You can navigate through a remote directory and copy files using an FTP client.

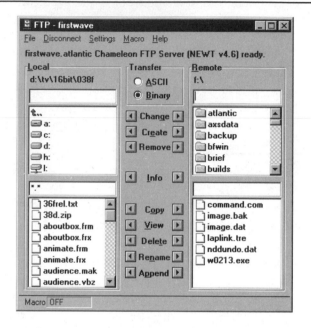

Some servers on the Internet, called FTP servers, are dedicated to the storage of large numbers of files. For example, software companies often place their latest drivers and bug fixes on FTP servers. Once you know the Uniform Resource Locator (URL) address of these servers (see the section "The World Wide Web" for an explanation of the term *URL*), you can use an FTP client to download whatever file you have access to. Sometimes, before giving you access to the directories and files, the FTP server asks you to log on under the name "anonymous" with the password set to your e-mail address. Otherwise, you need a real account on the FTP server, with a user name and password given to you in advance.

The current trend is to integrate FTP functionality into Web servers and Web browsers. In some sites you can simply click an image or a link within a Web page to start a download. Regardless of how it is implemented, FTP remains a powerful way to expose directories of files to other users in a standard way over the Internet without having to worry about the platform. FTP servers and FTP clients exist for most operating systems—from mainframes to plain-vanilla Windows machines.

A Notes Domino server allows a user with a browser to download files attached to Notes documents as easily as if they were stored on an FTP server.

TIP
You can use a Notes database to manage the distribution of patches and drivers. Standard security features allow you to create accounts and restrict access. Lotus Domino may be the easiest way to roll out an FTP server!

Net Newsgroups and Bulletin Boards

Thousands of newsgroups reside on the Net, and they cover topics beyond most people's imagination, interest, or patience. The predefined metacategories include science (sci), business (biz), computers (comp), alternate and very alternate viewpoints (alt), and unclassifiable (misc).

Newsgroups are basically bulletin boards, and as such, are based on a simple hierarchical structure of threads upon threads of messages and their responses. The contents, or *postings*, may be moderated by a designated administrator who controls how long messages stay in the system, deletes irrelevant threads of conversation, or even edits the contents of the messages. Messages are text only and contain, among other things, a title, a date, and the name (or nickname) of the author, as shown in Figure 30.2.

The ease of use of these newsgroup services depends primarily on the quality of your Net news reader. Readers range from free utilities to full-fledged applications that come with Internet connectivity products, such as Netmanage Chameleon 4.5 or IBM OS/2 Warp Connect. Some news readers can download new postings automatically from a list of preferred newsgroups, allowing you to read and respond to new information without having to be connected to the Internet. Good news readers also expand and collapse threads of postings (responses to responses) in a manner similar to Notes categorized views, as explained in Chapter 20.

TIP
By now, you know that a Notes database can provide a very rich environment for discussions, including threads of responses and categories. Lotus Domino does not require a Net news reader to deliver this functionality.

FIGURE 30.2:

A news reader shows the list of newsgroups in the left pane, the threads of postings on the right pane, and an individual posting in the bottom pane.

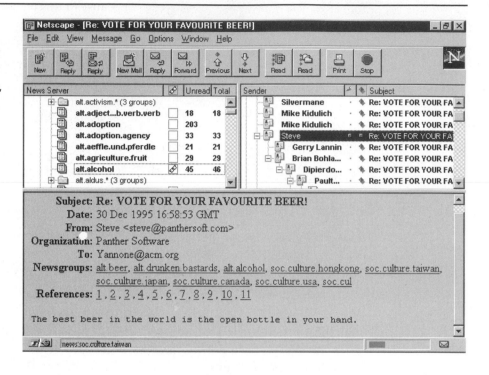

The ability to run the Network News Transport Protocol (NNTP) is now part of Domino. Previously, this option was only available by purchasing the Domino add-on called InterNotes News. NNTP allows the Notes Administrator to configure a Domino server to also become a NNTP server allowing users to participate in private discussions or public USENET newsgroups using the Notes client, a standard NNTP news reader, or a Web browser.

Internet E-Mail

Internet e-mail is based on the Simple Mail Transfer Protocol (SMTP), a standard message format that provides for bi-directional message transfer with other SMTP networks by passing simple text messages through the Message Transfer Agents (MTA). An MTA is a machine that stores and forwards a message to another MTA, just as your corner post office sends mail to other post offices. SMTP represents the contents of a message in plain text and defines the behavior of MTAs. To continue with the post office analogy, when you address an envelope, the name always goes on the first line; the street address follows on a separate line; and the city, state or province, and zip code go on the last line. Because of this universally accepted practice, post offices around the world know how to handle a piece of mail coming from any other post office.

In the last few years, the Multipurpose Independent Mail Extensions (MIME) public standard has defined an extensible way to create multimedia messages (containing, for instance, images, rich text, or file attachments) without changing the infrastructure defined by SMTP. As you'll see later, MIME and HTML have many similarities in that the application displaying the message decides how to represent it. For instance, MIME indicates that a message contains an image, but the mail reader application is free to show the image either in the text of the message or in a separate window.

NOTE   Many Web browsers include a basic SMTP mail client that allows you to read and write Internet mail messages.

The Lotus Notes SMTP/MIME MTA is now included as a component of the Notes Messaging Services family of products. Configuration and management are made easy since the MTA is integrated into a Domino environment. Notes networks can be integrated with SMTP networks in a variety of different topologies by the installation of SMTP MTAs on one or more Notes servers. Customers can even use SMTP to send Notes messages between Notes servers with no loss of form or content when companies desire an SMTP backbone.

Also included as part of Domino is the ability to set up your server as a Lightweight Directory Access Protocol (LDAP) server. The Domino LDAP server allows other LDAP-aware clients to access specific fields in the Person and Group documents in your Public Address Book such as e-mail addresses, telephone, fax numbers, etc. Think of LDAP as directory assistance for LDAP clients.

The World Wide Web

For the most part, when people talk about the Internet, they are referring to the World Wide Web (WWW). Web sites provide access to documents that are transported over the Internet network. The novelty is that all documents are accessible throughout the network by a simple convention called the URL (Uniform Resource Locator). If you know the exact spelling of a URL—and where to type it in your Web browser—you will be able to read a document that resides in your local library or in a research center in Africa. (We talk about Web browsers later in the HTML section.)

Advanced Uses of the Internet

Other uses of the Internet include CB-like services (IRCs) that allow users to "enter" electronic rooms belonging to a third-party machine, type messages, and exchange files. Chat and telephone applications are available for users with high bandwidth or an affinity for conversation that sounds like Mad Max with a slur. More exotic uses, such as video-on-demand, virtual radio stations, and electronic games, are beyond the scope of this introduction.

Now included with Domino is iChat. This software allows the Notes Administrator to set up a *chat room* that is integrated with the Public Address Book. Now users can communicate with each other in real time. The chat room is configurable by the developer so it can meet your ever-changing needs.

A URL has three parts: the identifier, the server address, and the document location. For example:

```
http://info.cern.ch/hypertext/WWW/Protocols/ HTTP/HTTP2.html
```

The first part, `http://`, is a standard way to identify a Web server. `HTTPS://` refers to a Web server supporting the Secure Sockets Layer. You identify an FTP server as `ftp://` and a Web page located on your local hard drive as `file://`.

The second part, `info.cern.ch`, is the address of the Web server; the `.ch` indicates that the server is located in Switzerland (as in Chwitzerland); `.au` indicates that a server is in Australia, and `.ca` identifies a Canadian server. Table 30.1 identifies the types of servers that are based in the United States.

TABLE 30.1: Server Types in the United States

Type	Organization	Example	Site
.com	Commercial	lotus.com	Lotus Development
.org	Nonprofit	cil.org	Opendoc Consortium
.gov	Government	ustreas.gov	U.S. Treasury (the IRS)
.mil	Military	navy.mil	U.S. Navy
.edu	Education	berkeley.edu	UC Berkeley
.net	Network	community.net	Community network

Traditionally (but not always), the servers are named www, for instance, www
.lotus.com or www.berkeley.edu.

The third part of the address, /hypertext/WWW/Protocols/HTTP/ HTTP2.html,
is the file name and full path of the Web page called HTTP2.html.

The beauty of a URL is that it can take you to a specific document anywhere in
the world regardless of your current location.

To help you understand how a URL leads to a transparent network of documents,
the rest of this chapter focuses on the specific components of the Web: Hypertext
Markup Language (HTML), Hypertext Transfer Protocol (HTTP), and Common
Gateway Interface (CGI).

Understanding HTML

Practically speaking, an HTML document is a physical file, usually with an .htm or
.html extension, that describes the formatting of a document on a Web server. HTML
is also called a markup language because special characters surround the contents
and indicate how they should be displayed or what should be done with them. If this
sounds a little confusing, bear with us while we show you a few examples.

Basic HTML Functionality

A title in the header text of a Web page is marked as

```
<head>
<title>Fantastic Marketing Demos</title>
</head>
```

The syntax is rather simple and describes the format of the header. *Descriptors*,
called "marks" or "tags," always appear in the following format:

```
<tag>
```

NOTE   The less than (<) and greater than (>) special characters around the descriptor
word delimit the tag.

In the preceding example, head and title are descriptors. Think of them as attributes. The slash character indicates the end of the descriptor. In other words, a
descriptor is good until the next occurrence of that attribute preceded by a slash.

Text or descriptors that follow a descriptor are under the control of that attribute. To figure out what the text will look like, you need to drill down the nested levels of attributes. In the preceding example, the title `Fantastic Marketing Demos` is itself a header.

Any "standard" version of HTML (1.0, 2.0, or 3.2) contains a finite list of agreed-upon marks. The concept of marking formats is not new—most word processing files mix and match formatting with content. Some readers may have fond memories of the formatting codes that made Wordstar famous in the early '80s.

> **NOTE**   The most current version of HTML is 4.0. It has been recommended by the World Wide Web Consortium and is expected to become the standard.

The unique feature of HTML is the standardization of the format. It is not proprietary, does not belong to any company, and evolves based on committees and Request For Comments (RFCs), rather than on marketing muscle. Companies (or ambitious individuals) are free to develop royalty-free programs, called HTML browsers, that can read HTML files over the Internet.

Figures 30.3 and 30.4 show the same HTML document as it appears in two browsers. Notice how the title, "Blaster Board: Power through the Surf," appears in each browser.

FIGURE 30.3:

The Netmanage Websurfer HTML browser displays an HTML document.

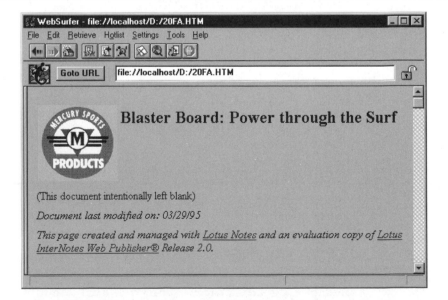

FIGURE 30.4:

The Netscape HTML browser displays the same HTML document shown in Figure 30.3.

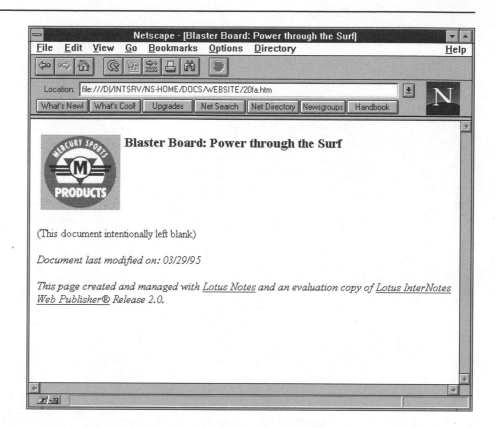

The browser may decide that all headers should be in Helvetica font, 24 pitch, with two spaces above and below to identify them as titles. But the developers of the browser could have chosen to represent headers as Courier 12 bold and included a background with tie-dyed colors. One thing that is common to all HTML files is that the entire content, including the marks, is always in plain, readable ASCII text. (This convention contrasts with a 1-2-3 file or an MS-Word file.) In other words, you can type any HTML file at the prompt of your operating system to read it. You will see the actual text of the file plus many extraneous characters for the marks. The following is a printout of the HTML file displayed in Figures 30.3 and 30.4.

```
<!-- Lotus InterNotes Web Publisher 2 -->
<HTML>
<HEAD>
<TITLE> Blaster Board: Power through the Surf</TITLE>
</HEAD>
<BODY>
```

```
<H2></H2>
<P>
<P>
<TABLE>
<TR valign=top>
<TD>
<P><IMG src="gifs\15e0.gif"></TD>
<TD>
<P>
<H3><B>Blaster Board: Power through the Surf</B></H3></TR>
</TABLE>

<P>
<P>(This document intentionally left blank)
<P>
<P><I>Document last modified on: </I><I>03/29/95</I>
<P><I>This page created and managed with <A
HREF=http://www.lotus.com/home/notes.htm>Lotus Notes</A> and an
➥ evaluation copy of <A HREF=http://www.internotes .lotus.com> Lotus
➥ InterNotes Web Publisher&reg;</A> Release 2.0.</I>

</BODY>
</HTML>
```

The printout should give you a good idea of how to create an HTML file that includes a title, different fonts, an image, a table, and a hypertext link.

The fact that an HTML file is in plain text is important because plain text can be transported between most operating systems and through all e-mail systems without modification.

TIP Most software packages such as SmartSuite 97 and Office 97 can read, create, and display HTML files. Unless you need to create very specialized Web pages, most off-the-shelf suite products will produce good quality HTML code.

Advanced HTML Syntax

HTML files act as containers for other items such as images or sound (that's the multimedia of the Web) or small programs. Audio or picture files reside in their own files—apart from the HTML file—and are referenced through pointers. For instance, the home page of a company usually contains a picture of the logo. The logo, perhaps a .GIF file, is stored as 15e0.gif in a separate directory. Within the home.html file, you will see a pointer, such as

```
<IMG src="15e0.gif">
```

In this system your browser first retrieves the HTML contents of the URL and then automatically but separately retrieves associated images and other objects. If you're connecting to the Net with analog modems, you may have observed slowly refreshing images—and shortly thereafter discovered the use of the Esc key. The same holds true for sound files, video clips, and, more interestingly, pointers to other HTML files. The following mark defines a pointer to another Web site:

```
<A HREF=http://www.lotus.com/home/notes.htm>Lotus Notes</A>
```

HTML will underline the text before the </A> tag. When a user clicks the underlined words Lotus Notes, the browser automatically connects to the www.lotus.com server and then displays the notes.htm HTML document stored in the /home subdirectory.

The newest, most exciting feature of HTML is the ability to include small programs that the browser invokes either automatically or when you take an action, such as clicking on a button, entering text in a data entry field, or moving from one page to another. HTML currently supports several types of programs, the most common being JavaScript, ActiveX, and Java.

Java and ActiveX are full-fledged applets sometimes called plug-ins, Java beans, or ActiveX controls. They're what software vendors used to call *add-ins*—that is, programs that run within a browser. Applets are called within the <APPLET ...> </APPLET> tags. For instance, you can write the following code to invoke a Java applet that brews five cups extra strong:

```
<APPLET CODE="brews.class" WIDTH=100 HEIGHT=50>
<PARAM NAME="intparm" VALUE="5">
<PARAM NAME="strparm" VALUE="extrastrong">
</APPLET>
```

Brews.class is the Java program. More code is required, particularly for the driver to the coffee machine, but you should get the idea.

With Notes 4.6, you can now place Java applets directly on a form or within a rich text field. Java applets are widely used for Web applications; you can also include them in Notes applications (just make sure that the Enable Java Applets option is selected in the User Preferences).

JavaScript is a scripting language, just like LotusScript. The code is literally embedded within the HTML page and executed by the browser. HTML invokes the scripting programs by using the tag <SCRIPT LANGUAGE="*JavaScript*">, where *JavaScript* stands for the language used. Note that different browsers support different languages—and sometimes provide different support for a given language. The following listing is a VBScript program:

```
<HTML>
<HEAD><TITLE>Net Juice</TITLE>
<SCRIPT LANGUAGE="VBS">
<!---
Sub ClickMe_OnClick
cups=InputBox("Please enter the number of cups.",1)
strength=Document.NetJ.Jolt.Value
MsgBox "Brewing " + cups + " cups " + strength + "."
End Sub
-->
</SCRIPT>
</HEAD>
<H3>Brew Choices for Today</H3><HR>
<FORM NAME="NetJ">
How strong do you want your coffee?
<INPUT NAME="Jolt" TYPE="TEXT" SIZE="15">
<INPUT NAME="ClickMe" TYPE="BUTTON" VALUE="ClickMe">
</FORM>
</BODY>
</HTML>
```

To use this code, follow these steps:

1. Type it into Notepad or any text editor.

2. Save the file as a text file, using the extension .htm, for example, vbs1.htm.

3. Open the file with your Web browser. If you are using Netscape 3.*x* or a version of the Microsoft Internet Explorer below 3.0, the page will appear but the button won't do anything. If you are using Internet Explorer 3.*x*, the button will work as shown in Figure 30.5.

To prevent the text of the script from appearing in browsers that do not support the language, a <!-- --> follows the <SCRIPT LANGUAGE="VBS" > tag in the header. The script refers to a field in the form with the Document.NetJ.Jolt syntax, which is very similar to LotusScript. Other elements of the syntax are either pure HTML or pure Visual Basic.

FIGURE 30.5:

Internet Explorer 3.0 executes VBScript code embedded within an HTML page.

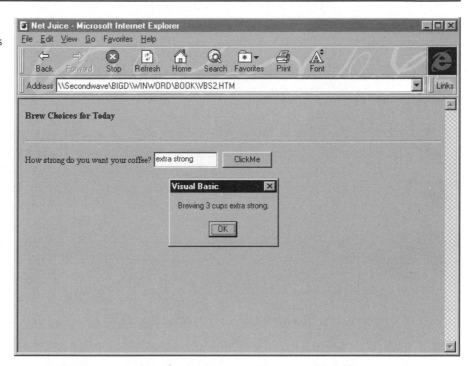

An option has been created for Notes 4.6 databases that allows the developer to include multiple buttons on a form and use additional @Commands. To enable this functionality, select the Web Access: Use JavaScript when Generating Pages option on the Database Properties Default tab.

NOTE   To use this option, the user's browser must support JavaScript, and the Domino Web Server must be running Release 4.6.

Using this new option will result in Web documents and Navigators displaying more quickly. You can design forms with multiple buttons, but Domino will not automatically create the Submit button (you will need to code it yourself).

Hypertext Transfer Protocol (HTTP)

HTTP is what runs on the receiving end of your request—the World Wide Web server. As a protocol, HTTP defines how to connect and how to respond to a request. In the example, `http://www.lotus.com/home/notes.htm`, the server `www.lotus.com` first establishes a connection to your browser, then "gets" the request for the file home/notes.htm, looks for it, and returns the contents to your browser. If other files, such as images, are associated with the file you requested, the server will send them sequentially. Consequently, you usually see part of the document before the icons and other pictures appear on your screen.

HTTP servers are rather simple, and like HTML, the technology does not belong to any vendor. Multiple companies are free to develop their own HTTP servers, competing on performance, ease of installation, availability of maintenance utilities, and of course, price. HTTP servers are available on many platforms where Notes Release 4 servers run, such as Windows NT, Sun Solaris, IBM AIX, HP-UX, NetWare NLM, Windows 95, or OS/2. The Domino Notes server includes an HTTP server that can deliver Notes databases as well as any HTML file. Lotus Domino translates Notes documents on the fly so that Web users cannot distinguish between pages created and maintained in Notes databases and pages created by other means.

Common Gateway Interface (CGI)

CGI is a way to extend the limited functionality of HTTP. Part of the HTML protocol supports the definition of forms. All Web forms contain a Submit button to pass data from the browser to the server. That data can also contain the name of a program that the HTTP server should run. CGI is a gateway program developed specifically to process the information collected in an HTML form. For example, a product information HTML form will return the e-mail address of the sender (e.g., `Bob@nowhere.com`), the name of the product for which the sender wishes to receive more information (e.g., `Whatabout`), and the name of the CGI program to invoke upon clicking the Submit button.

```
http://www.elsewhere.com/cgi-bin/ prod-info?email=Bob@nowhere.com+
➡product=WhatAbout
```

HTTP will invoke the program by passing it as a command to the operating system with parameters.

```
prod-info email=nowhere.com product=whatabout
```

No relationship exists between HTTP or HTML and the CGI program. The CGI is a piece of code (a shell script in UNIX; an .EXE file in Windows NT) that is invoked when you type the command at the operating system prompt.

Typically, the program will return an HTML file at a predefined location with the results of the request, for example, a short message acknowledging receipt of the product information request. CGI programs are frequently used as gateways to relational databases, allowing HTML forms to issue SQL queries to relational databases. The return result may be an HTML page that displays a table of records, perhaps the stock inventory of matching parts for a given product.

CGI programs are also called *scripts* because they are often written in a language called Perl. Perl is an interpreted language available on most operating systems. JavaScript and other script languages are starting to become available on servers. Netscape LiveWire, for instance, allows you to write and test a script on a browser and then move the code to the server, thereby reducing the overhead for the workstation pulling the Web pages.

What's Next?

Our goal in this chapter has been to demystify the Internet by examining its individual technical components. The Web includes URLs that provide a method to address documents worldwide, HTML to define a format for all documents, and HTTP as a protocol to negotiate the client/server relationship between Web browsers and servers. You should now realize that Notes can easily use the Internet. Both the Internet and Notes support bulletin board services (newsgroups for the Internet and discussion databases for Notes), file transfers (FTP for the Internet and attachments for Notes), e-mail (SMTP mail for the Internet and Notes mail), and document services (HTML files for the Internet and Notes documents).

In the next chapter we discuss the personal Web Navigator. In subsequent chapters we consider the respective merits of Notes and the Web and explain how to leverage both technologies with Lotus Domino. We will also discuss how you can use the Domino server to develop and maintain a Web site—and the technical advantages of using Domino rather than non-Notes options.

CHAPTER

THIRTY-ONE

31

Using the Personal Web Navigator

- ■ Setting up the Personal Web Navigator

- ■ Opening a default Web page each time you open the Personal Web Navigator database

- ■ Opening a Web page when you already know its URL

- ■ Customizing the Personal Web Navigator

- ■ Opening, saving, and forwarding Web pages

- ■ Searching the Web with an Internet search engine

- ■ Searching indexed Web pages

- ■ Enabling Web Ahead

The Personal Web Navigator (or simply Web Navigator) provides access to information on the Web and allows you to navigate through pages on the Web directly from your Notes environment. The Web Navigator is much more than a Web browser, however. It combines the features of a Web browser with the powerful capabilities of Notes, creating a comfortable way for you to access and explore the Web.

In this chapter we show you how to access Web pages through your workstation. We discuss the following topics in detail:

- Setting up the Personal Web Navigator

- Viewing Web pages in a database

- Opening pages

- Searching the Web

Before we go on, we need to make a distinction between the Personal Web Navigator that you can set up on your workstation and the Server Web Navigator that may be available on your organization's Notes server. You can access the Web through your Personal Web Navigator. All you need is a direct Internet connection.

You can also access the Web through a central database called the Server Web Navigator database. This database resides on a Notes server connected to the Internet. Local and remote Notes users access this database in the same way they access other Notes databases.

With the Server Web Navigator, only one computer needs to be connected to the Internet in order to give multiple Notes clients like yourself access to the Web. If an organization wants to provide several places where users can access the Web, you can set up multiple Notes servers with the Server Web Navigator, each with its own separate database.

As you read on, you'll learn how to customize your Personal Web Navigator and retrieve the Web pages that you need to access regularly.

How the Web Navigator Works

Each time you retrieve a page off the Internet, the Web Navigator can translate it into a Notes document and store it inside the database. (Whenever you retrieve a page off the Internet, Notes displays a spinning globe and status bar messages.) Opening a page that is already inside the database is much faster than retrieving it from the Internet. After a Web page is loaded into the database, as shown in Figure 31.1, you won't need to retrieve it from the Internet the next time you request it.

FIGURE 31.1:

You can retrieve a Web page, such as the Web page from IBM, and load it into a Notes database.

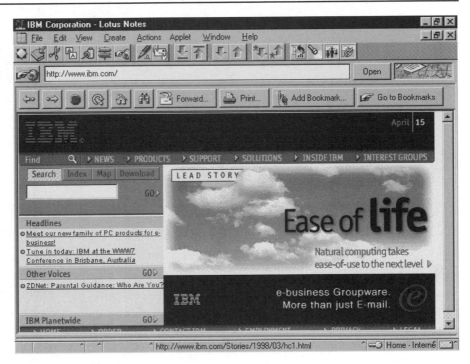

Once the page is in the database, you can view it, copy it into a private folder, cut and paste it into another Notes document, mail it to another Notes user, and so on. All the capabilities of Notes are available for you to use with the pages inside the Web Navigator database.

TIP

The Web Navigator database is designed for you to read existing pages. If you want to create your own Web page, you can use Lotus Domino or the Notes Web Publisher to translate Notes documents into Web pages.

Understanding Web Pages and URLs

As we discussed in Chapter 30, the Web connects millions of pages of information stored on Internet servers located all over the world. To access and display these Web pages, you use Web browser software. Almost all Web pages contain hot links (or HTML links) that you click to jump from one page to another. As you click these hot links, you may jump from one Internet server to another and from one part of the world to another.

Internet servers contain various types of information. The native Web server is a Hypertext Transfer Protocol (HTTP) server. However, Web browsers can also access other types of Internet servers, such as File Transfer Protocol (FTP) servers and Gopher servers. By using a Web browser, you gain instant access to information stored on a variety of Internet servers all over the world.

Web pages are identified by a unique address, known as a Uniform Resource Locator (URL). For example, the URL for the Lotus home page is http://www .lotus.com/home.nsf.

The first part of the URL (http) specifies the network protocol used to access the page. The second part of the URL (www.lotus.com) is the Internet server name. (You may see some URLs that contain numbers for the server address instead of the name; Web browsers can handle both formats.) The third part of the URL (home.nsf) is the name of the database that contains the home page.

When Web pages are created, they almost always contain URL links to other Web pages. Users click these URL links to display the target Web pages. The Web Navigator supports the following URL links:

- **HTTP:** Hypertext Transfer Protocol allows you to display HTML documents.

- **FTP:** File Transfer Protocol enables you to search for and download files on FTP servers.

- **Gopher:** This menu system allows you to search for and download files on Gopher servers.

- **Mailto:** This link opens into an e-mail system (Notes mail in this case) and enables you to send e-mail to the person specified in the link.

The URL links inside the Web Navigator database appear as blue, underlined text or graphic regions. If a Web page contains a URL link that the Web Navigator does not support, the Web Navigator displays the URL as plain text. If you want to change the color of the URL links inside the database, you can modify the color by editing the Web Navigator Administration form.

WARNING   Before you can start opening Web pages through the Web Navigator database (other than pages that are already stored in the database), you need to set up Notes so that it can locate the Web Navigator database. If you have upgraded to Notes 4.6, this should have already been done for you during the install.

Setting Up the Web Navigator for Your Own Personal Use

Notes 4.6 offers a new type of Personal Web Navigator. You use the same Personal Web Navigator database as before but make the change in your location document to use Notes integrated with Internet Explorer. Now you can use the power of Notes while keeping the features of Internet Explorer—all from within the Notes environment. The Personal Web Navigator has been completely redesigned to use Internet Explorer whenever a URL address is encountered.

You can set up a Personal Web Navigator database on your local Notes workstation so that all Web pages can be retrieved and stored in that local database.

NOTE   The Personal Web Navigator relies on network connections to the Internet; therefore, you need to ensure that your Notes environment is working properly before you configure and use the Web Navigator. Test your TCP/IP network connection to verify that your personal computer can use TCP/IP to make successful connections to the Internet outside of your Notes environment. If you have a direct Internet connection, you can test your connection by using a Ping utility, which sends network packets to a remote computer and asks that computer to return network packets. If your network connection and your Notes environment are working properly, but you are still having problems setting up and administering the Web Navigator, contact your Notes administrator.

To set up the Personal Web Navigator, follow these steps:

1. Verify that you meet all the system requirements to run the Personal Web Navigator. If you're not sure, ask your Notes administrator.

2.   Edit or create a new Location document in your Personal Address Book:

   • Select the type of browser you would like to use to view Web pages. Your choices are Notes (we would advise against this option since it cannot support many of the Web features), Notes with Internet Explorer (our choice), Netscape Navigator, Microsoft Internet Explorer, or Other (you will need to specify the location of the browser).

   • If you chose either Notes or Notes with Internet Explorer, you will need to select how to retrieve/open Web pages. If you elected Notes as your browser, you have the choices "from Internotes server," "from Notes Workstation," or "no retrieval." If you elected Notes with Internet Explorer, you will only have the latter two choices. If you elected either of the remaining browsers, you will not be able to use the Personal Web Navigator and the Retrieve/Open Web pages option will not be present. Choose the From Notes Workstation option in the Retrieve/Open Pages field. This option specifies that the Notes workstation will perform retrievals and that Web pages may be stored in the Personal Web Navigator database.

   • If you connect to the Internet through a proxy, enter the name or IP address of the proxy in the Web proxy field (in the Basics section). Ask your administrator if you are unsure about what kind of Internet connection you have. This option will only be available if you connect via a LAN connection.

TIP   Another very useful but sometimes confusing option is Update Cache Field in the Advanced section of the Location document. There are three choices that can adversely effect the information that gets displayed in the browser. Whenever you access a Web page, the browser may store (or cache) the Web page for faster access. For instance, if you happen to visit a Web page over and over, the Web page may be displayed from cache instead of actually being retrieved from the Web server. If you want always to get the most up-to-date Web page, set this option to Every Time. If you only want to get the most up-to-date Web page for the current browser session, set this option to Once per Session. If you really do not care if the page is up-to-date, set this option to Never. No matter which option you select, you always have the option of pressing the Refresh button in your browser to get the most current version of a Web page.

3.   Save your Location document, and name the Location document if necessary (for example, Local Surfing).

4. Click the Close button.

5. Choose your new location by clicking the location indicator on the status bar.

6. Choose File ➤ Open URL from your Notes Workspace and enter a URL for a Web page in the Open URL dialog box, as shown in Figure 31.2; for example, `http://www.ibm.com/`.

Notes automatically creates your Personal Web Navigator database and opens the Web page that you specified.

FIGURE 31.2:

Open a Web page by entering its URL in the Open URL dialog box.

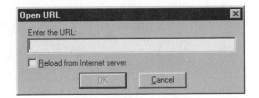

Using the Personal Web Navigator

You can use the Personal Web Navigator database as you would use any Notes database. If the Web page fills the entire window when you open the database, a default home page has been specified (see the next section). What actually happened is that your Personal Web Navigator database opened and then immediately launched the browser. Click on the Window menu option and you should see an entry for your Personal Web Navigator and a second entry for the Web page you are currently viewing, as shown in Figure 31.3.

Select the Personal Web Navigator entry and you will see that the database comes with several folders and views so you can manage and find Web pages inside the database.

Using Action Bar Buttons

When you open the Personal Web Navigator, you will see Action Bar buttons at the top of the window that you can use to browse the Web, share information with others (including sharing by way of the Server Web Navigator database), print Web pages, search for information using Internet search engines, find information already in your Personal Web Navigator database, and so on.

FIGURE 31.3:

The Personal Web Navigator and Browser entries for the Window menu option

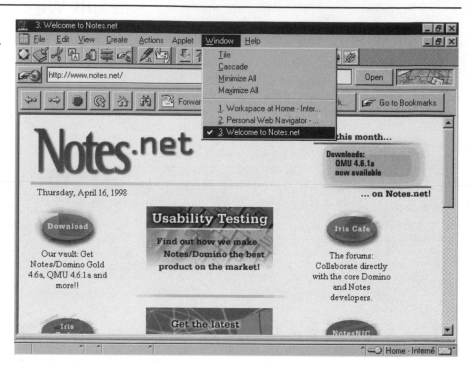

Opening Web Pages with the Personal Web Navigator

You can open Web pages with the Personal Web Navigator database in these ways:

- Open to a default Web page

- Open a page by its URL

- Open the latest version of a page

- Open a page that has Java applets

Opening the Database to a Default Web Page

To open a default Web page each time you open the Personal Web Navigator database:

1. Open the Personal Web Navigator database.

2. Choose Actions ➤ Internet Options. The Internet Options document appears, as shown in Figure 31.4.

FIGURE 31.4:

You can set your default Web page by entering its URL in the Internet Options document.

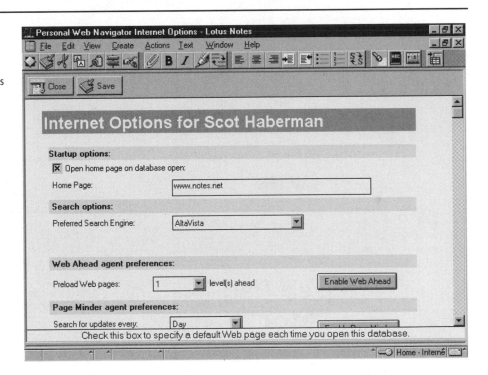

3. Check the Open Home Page on Database Open option in the Startup options section.

4. In the Home Page field, type in the URL for the Web page you want to open each time you open the Web Navigator database.

5. Exit and save your changes.

TIP

You can set a Notes startup option to open a specific database when you start Notes. You can choose the Personal Web Navigator as your default startup database by choosing File ➤ Tools ➤ User Preferences, clicking the Startup database button, and choosing the Personal Web Navigator database. If you set your Personal Web Navigator to open to a default Web page, Notes opens to that page each time you start Notes.

Opening a Page by Its URL

To open a Web page if you already know its URL, you can enter the URL in the Open URL dialog box:

1. Display the Open URL dialog box in one of the following ways:

   • From the File menu, choose Open URL.

   • From the Notes Workspace, click the Open URL icon in the SmartIcons set.

2. Enter the URL and click OK.

TIP

The default URL protocol the Web Navigator uses is http://. If you enter www.ibm.com, the Web Navigator assumes that the complete URL is http://www.ibm.com/.

Opening the Latest Version of a Web Page

Web page authors often update and redesign their pages. To make sure you are viewing the current version of a Web page, you can retrieve the newest version of the page from the Internet even if that page has already been retrieved and stored in the database. You can force Notes to retrieve a new page as you open each page. If you open the page by specifying its URL in the Open URL dialog box, click the Reload from Internet Server checkbox. If you open a page from one of the database views, click the Reload button at the top of the page. Set Notes to automatically check whether the page has changed on its Internet server.

TIP

Remember, you can also set the Update Cache option in your Location document (described earlier in the chapter).

> **NOTE** Some Web pages contain internal expiration dates. Notes deletes these pages when they have expired.

Opening a Page That Has Java Applets

Notes provides support for running Java applets through the Web Navigator on Windows NT, Windows 95, and some UNIX platforms. To view Java applets within the Web Navigator:

1. Choose File ➤ Tools ➤ User Preferences and go to the Advanced Options section.

2. Check the Enable Java Applets preference.

3. (Optional) If your Internet connection is through a proxy server, you need to enter the proxy name in the Web Proxy field in your Location document so that applets can run on your workstation.

4. (Optional) Change the Java applet security settings in the Location document.

Creating Action Bar Buttons for the Web Navigator

Actions allow you to perform certain tasks within Notes databases. Users run Actions from either the Actions menu or the buttons located on the Action bar. The Web Navigator template includes several Action Bar buttons to perform tasks such as sharing a Web page, printing a Web page, or deleting a Web page. You can create your own Action Bar buttons as well.

For example, you could create an Action Bar button that opens a newsgroup directly from the Web Navigator database. (Note that to perform this action, you need to be running USENET news software.)

To create a newsgroup Action Bar button:

1. Select the Web Navigator template and choose View ➤ Show ➤ Design.

2. Click Design ➤ Forms.

3. Double-click the form in which you want to create a button. (To create a button that will appear on each Web page within the database, choose HTMLForm.)

4. Select Create ➤ Action.

5. Type a title for the button in the Action Properties InfoBox and choose a button icon.

6. Select the position where the button will appear.

7. Click the Design pane and choose Formula. Type a formula in the Edit window, such as

   `@Command([FileOpenDatabase];YourNewsServer: "recnews.nsf")`

NOTE   Replace *YourNewsServer* with the name of your InterNotes News server and replace RECNEWS.NSF with the name of the newsgroup database you want to open.

---

8. Close the form and click Yes to save it.

Creating Agents

Notes uses *Agents* to automate tasks you would otherwise have to perform manually. You can create and use Agents for simple tasks, such as filing documents and sending mail, or for complex tasks, such as manipulating field values and bringing in data from other applications. The Web Navigator comes with a Purge Agent and a Refresh Agent to help you manage the documents in your database. You set up and control both of these Agents from the Web Navigator Administration document.

You can also create your own Agents to automate routine tasks.

NOTE   You cannot use the @URLOpen or @URLGetHeader function to create an Agent that runs manually from the menu.

Creating New Database Views

The Web Navigator template comes with multiple views to help you browse and organize Web pages within the database. However, you can create additional views based on the type of information you want to see. The following fields are built into the Web Navigator template. Use these fields, in addition to any fields you create, to add customized views to the Web Navigator template.

- **HTTPContent_Type:** Describes the type of Web page; for example, text/HTTP, FTP, Gopher, and so on

- **HTTPURL or URL:** Contains the actual URL string; for example, `http://www.ibm.com/home.html`

- **Title:** Contains the title of the page taken directly from the HTML header

- **LastRefreshed:** Contains either the Notes creation date of the page or the last-retrieved date (if the URL is reloaded)

- **HTTPExpires:** Pulls the expiration date from the HTTP header if that date has been specified on the Web page

- **HTTPHeaders:** Pulls the HTTP header information from the Web page

- **HTTPLast_Modified:** Pulls the last modified date from the HTTP header if that date has been specified on the Web page

WARNING You cannot use the @Created function in the Web Navigator template because it returns incorrect data; use the Time_Date field instead.

Other Ways to Open Web Pages

You do not have to be in the Web Navigator database to open a Web page. You can open pages from anywhere within Notes because the Web Navigator has been fully integrated with Notes. You can open Web pages in various ways, depending on where you are working in Notes: the Home Navigator, the View Navigator, other Notes databases, the Notes Workspace, or the Quick Search dialog box.

Opening a Page by Its URL

As you become more familiar with the Web, you will also learn to locate Web pages by their URLs. If you know the URL of a Web page, you can enter it directly in the Open URL dialog box. To open a Web page if you know its URL:

1. Open the Open URL dialog box in one of the following ways:

    - From the Home Navigator, click the Open URL icon.

    - From a Web page, click the Open button.

    - From the Actions menu, choose Open URL.

    - From the Notes Workspace, click the Open URL icon in the SmartIcons set (if you have added it already).

2. Enter the URL.

3. Click OK.

When you open a page by its URL, you can force the Web Navigator to retrieve the page from its Internet server (regardless of whether the page is in the database) by selecting the Reload from Internet Server checkbox. This option is useful when you know that the page has changed recently and the page stored in the database is outdated.

Opening a Page from Other Notes Databases

You do not have to be in the Web Navigator database to open a Web page; you can open a Web page from any Notes document that contains a URL link. A URL link is a hotspot that Notes creates out of URL text found in any rich text field. When you click a URL link, Notes automatically opens the Web page in the Web Navigator database and displays it for you.

This technique is especially helpful when you want to send your coworkers a mail message that contains pointers to Web pages. To send a mail message with pointers, create a mail message and type the URL of the Web page (such as http://www.lotus.com) in the body of the message. When your coworkers open the message, Notes creates a URL link out of the URL text. Then, when they click the URL link, Notes automatically opens the Web page through the Web Navigator database.

WARNING   By default, Notes displays URLs in the Web Navigator database as hotspots. To enable Notes to convert URL text into hotspots in other databases, make sure the Make Internet URLs into Hotspots option is checked in your user preferences by choosing File ➤ Tools ➤ User Preferences.

Opening a Page from the Quick Search Dialog Box

You can open a Web page from the Quick Search dialog box from any Notes database. To open a page this way:

1. Open a Notes database and click any document in the View pane.

2. Start typing the URL you want to open; for example, `http://www.lotus` `.com`. As you type, Notes displays a Quick Search dialog box in which you can continue typing the URL.

3. Finish typing the URL and click OK to open the Web page.

Retrieving the Latest Version of a Web Page

Web page authors often update and redesign their pages. If you want to make sure you are viewing the latest version of a Web page, you can force the Web Navigator to retrieve the page from the Internet even if it is already in the database. Depending on how you open the page, you can do one of the following:

1. If you open a page by specifying its URL in the Open URL dialog box, click the Reload from Internet Server checkbox.

2. If you open a page from one of the database views, click Reload at the Top of the Page.

Browsing a Page from a Portfolio

Once you have your Personal Web Navigator database set up, you can also browse Web pages from within your Favorites portfolio database:

1. Open your Favorites portfolio.

2. Click the Personal Web Navigator button from the Navigation pane.

3. Select the Web page to browse.

Browsing a Page from Your Personal Address Book

You can also browse Web pages of people who have a Person document in your Personal Address Book. Notes will retrieve the Web page listed in the Web page field listed in the Person document. To see this in action:

1. Open your Personal Address Book.

2. Switch to the Business Card or By Category view.

3. Select the name of the person whose Web site you want to visit.

4. Click the Visit Web Site button and you'll see the Web site you've requested.

Displaying Images

To display images after the page has loaded in the Personal Web Navigator:

1. Select the Personal Web Navigator and choose File ➤ Database ➤ Properties.

2. Click the Basics tab and verify that Display Images After Loading is checked.

3. (Optional) If the Display Images After Loading option is checked, you can specify whether you want to display images automatically or only when you click them after the page is loaded:

    *   Edit your current Location document.

    *   Go to the Load images field in the Advanced section. Choose Always to display images automatically after the page is loaded. Choose On Request to display images one-by-one as you click them.

4. Exit and save your changes.

NOTE   While the Display Images After Loading option is checked, Notes stores all the objects on each newly retrieved page as separate documents in the database. You can view these documents in the House Cleaning view.

Searching the Web

You can use the Web Navigator database to look for specific information on the Web. You can search pages that are already in the database, as well as search for pages on the Internet.

You can search for information on the Web in several ways:

- With Internet search engines
- On categories and titles in the view
- On text within pages in the database
- On indexed Web pages

Searching with Internet Search Engines

You can use any of the powerful search engines available on the Internet to locate information. If you haven't already specified your favorite Internet search engine in the Search options section of the Internet Options document (as shown previously in Figure 31.4):

- Go to the Search options section and select one of the predefined search engines or enter the URL of any other search engine you want to use.
- Exit and save your changes.

When you click the Search button, the Web Navigator retrieves the Web page for the Internet search engine (see Figure 31.5) you specified. Depending on the Web page for the search engine, enter the search criteria and click the particular button on the Web page to start your search.

Searching on Categories and Titles in the Database

You can search the categories or titles in your database to find pages that match the word you specify:

1. Choose the All Documents view.
2. Start typing the word you want to find; for example, **Lotus**. Notes displays a Quick Search dialog box in which you can continue typing your word.
3. Click OK to find the first document that matches the search criteria.

FIGURE 31.5:

You can specify the search engine you want to use to conduct a search of the Web.

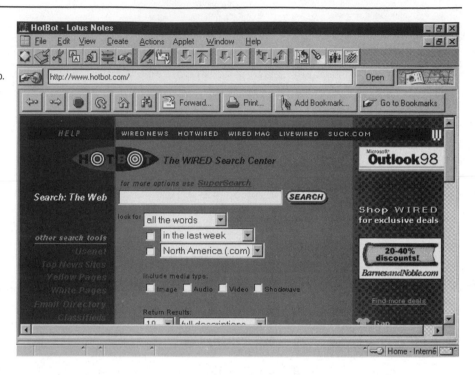

TIP

You can also use the Find and Replace dialog box to search for titles. Click the Document Title column, click the Find button in the Action bar, type your search word, and click Find Next. Notes highlights the first instance of the text, whether it is a category or a document title.

Searching Text within Pages in the Database

To find information within pages in the database:

1. Open the database and choose File ➤ Database ➤ Properties.

2. Select the Full Text tab in the InfoBox and then choose Create Index.

3. Specify any settings you want in the Full Text Create Index dialog box and then click OK. Notes creates an index of the database.

4. Choose View ➤ Search Bar if the Search bar is not visible. Be sure the search icon to the left of the Search bar is visible instead of the Open URL icon.

5. Type in the text to search for.

6. Click Search.

Notes displays the found pages in the View and highlights the text you specified within the pages.

Searching Indexed Web Pages

Some Web pages are indexed and allow you to perform searches on their contents. When you open a Web page that has been indexed, you can use the Search button in the Action bar to search the contents of that Web page. (Note that this Search button also opens an Internet search engine when you are not on an indexed Web page.) Typically, the indexed Web page provides some text to inform you that the page is indexed and searchable.

The following steps describe how to search the Pathway Services indexed Web page (which points you to government information on the Internet):

1. Open the Personal Web Navigator database.

2. Choose File ➤ Open URL.

3. Type the following URL in the Open URL dialog box:

    http://www.access.gpo.gov/su_docs/aces/aces760.html

4. Click Search.

5. Type your search text in the Search Internet Server dialog box.

6. Click OK to display the search results from that Web page.

Canceling the Retrieval of a Web Page

As you are retrieving Web pages off the Internet using the Personal Web Navigator, you may decide to cancel the retrieval before it finishes. To cancel the retrieval of a Web page, click the graphical stop sign button on the Action button bar.

Saving and Forwarding Web Pages

As you browse the Web, you may come across pages that you want to save for later or forward to other users. You can save pages:

- In your Bookmarks folder

- In any folder in the database

When you save or forward pages, all the URL links remain on the page as active links.

Saving a Page in Your Bookmarks Folder

The Personal Web Navigator database contains a Bookmarks folder where you can save your favorite Web pages. To save pages in this folder:

1. Open the page you want to save.

2. Add the page to the private folder called Bookmarks in one of these ways:

    - From a Web page: Click the Add Bookmark button or choose Actions ➤ Add Bookmark. In the Add Bookmark dialog box, select the Bookmarks folder and click Add.

    - From the View pane: Drag and drop the page onto the Bookmarks folder icon in the Navigation pane.

3. Open a page you have saved in your Bookmarks folder by clicking Bookmarks in the Navigation pane and then double-clicking the page.

NOTE   You can also organize Web pages in different folders within your Bookmarks folder. To create new folders, choose Create ➤ Folder. In the Create Folder dialog box, click Shared and then type the name of the new folder. Click the Bookmarks folder to indicate that your new folder should be inside the Bookmarks folder. Click OK.

Saving a Page in Any Folder

You can save pages in folders other than your Bookmarks folder. To create another folder and save a page in that folder:

1. Open the database and choose Create ➤ Folder.

2. Enter the name of the folder, select a location, and click OK.

3. Go to the View pane and select the page you want to save.

4. Drag and drop the page onto the newly created folder icon in the Navigation pane.

Sharing Web Pages with Coworkers

You might come across a Web page that you want to share with colleagues. To make the page available to others, follow these steps:

1. (Optional) If you haven't already specified a database in the Internet Options document with which to share your Web pages:

   - Go to the Collaboration Options section and specify the database and Notes server with a WEB.NSF database where you want to share your Web pages.

   - Exit and save your changes.

2. Click the Share button.

3. Select one of the sharing choices:

   - Copy Page to Shared Web Navigator Database: Copies the Web page into the Server Web Navigator database

   - Create Rating in Shared Web Navigator Database: Allows you to rate the Web page and save the Rating document in the Server Web Navigator database

4. Click OK.

Forwarding a URL

To forward a URL to someone:

1. Select or open the Web page you want to forward.

2. Click the Share button.

3. Select the Forward Only the URL option and enter the name of the recipient in the Send URL To: text box. (Click the Address Book button to display the Names dialog box where you can look up names in a choice of Address Books.)

4. Click OK to forward the URL.

Forwarding Web Pages

You can forward a Web page to anyone you specify, just as you might forward an e-mail message to someone. To forward a Web page:

1. Select or open the Web page you want to forward.

2. Click the Forward button.

3. Address the mail message and send it to the desired users.

NOTE   When you forward a Web page to someone, only the body of the Web page gets forwarded—no other fields are forwarded.

Viewing the HTML Source of a Web Page

You can view the HTML source of any Web page retrieved and stored in the Personal Web Navigator. To set an option to save the HTML source of all Web pages, follow these steps:

1. Edit your Internet Options document.

2. Check the Save HTML in Note? checkbox in the Presentation preferences section.

To view the HTML source of a Web page:

1. Select the Web page in the database.

2. Choose File ➤ Document Properties.

3. Click the Fields tab.

4. Click the HTMLSource field in the left column to display the HTML source in the right column.

Using the Server Web Navigator

When you first open the Server Web Navigator database, you will see the Home Navigator, as shown in Figure 31.6. This Navigator has been designed to help you browse the Web.

FIGURE 31.6:

The Home Navigator lets you browse the Web with ease.

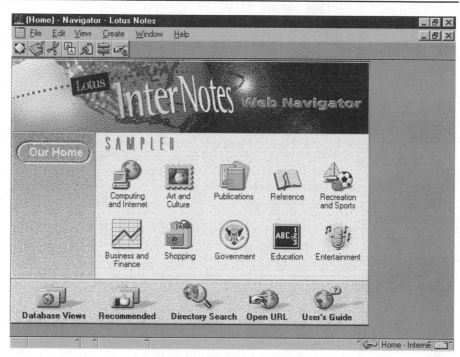

Customizing the Server Web Navigator Template

You can use the Server Web Navigator template to create different Web Navigator databases. The template is programmable and customizable, and you can fine-tune it in several ways.

WARNING   Be sure to customize the template (WEB.NTF) instead of the database (WEB.NSF), to prevent your changes from being accidentally overwritten.

You can use the Notes programming language as well as LotusScript to customize the template. Several @functions and LotusScript methods have been specifically designed for use in the Web Navigator database.

NOTE   See Part V for a discussion of using LotusScript to program Notes databases.

The @functions specific to the Web Navigator are:

- **@URLGetHeader**: Returns specific HTTP header information from URLs
- **@URLHistory**: Navigates, saves, and reloads a URL history list
- **@URLOpen**: Retrieves a Web page specified by its URL

The LotusScript methods specific to the Web Navigator are:

- **OpenURLDb method**: Returns a pointer to the location of the Web Navigator database specified by the Notes client
- **GetDocumentByURL method**: Sets a Notes document equal to a specific URL document
- **GetURLHeaderInfo method**: Returns specific HTTP header information from a URL

WARNING   You cannot change the Web Navigator file name (WEB.NSF) or the names of forms, views, Navigators, or Agents within the template (other than any new design items you may create). These changes will adversely affect the operation of the Notes Server Web Navigator. You should always keep a backup copy of the Web Navigator template (WEB.NTF) in case you need to revert to a clean copy. When you back up the template, be sure to copy both the design and the documents so you will have a copy of the Administration document.

Modifying the Existing Home Navigator

The Home Navigator is a bitmap with links to specific URLs attached to it. You can modify the hotspots in the bitmap to point to different URLs, open different views, or go to a particular form within the database. To change the hotspots:

1. Open the Web Navigator template and open the All Documents view.

2. Choose View ➤ Show ➤ Folders.

3. Click Design ➤ Navigators and double-click the (Home) Navigator. (If you do not see Design, choose View ➤ Show Design.)

4. Click the hotspot that you want to change. (For example, you may want to replace the Our Home bitmap with your company's graphic and a URL link to your company's home page.)

5. Go to the Design pane and specify the action that you want to execute when the user clicks the hotspot.

6. Press Esc and click Yes to save your changes.

Creating a New Home Navigator

To create a new Home Navigator, follow these steps:

1. Create a bitmap using your favorite drawing program.

2. Open the Web Navigator template and choose Create ➤ Design ➤ Navigator to create a new Navigator.

3. Choose Edit ➤ Paste to paste it in the Design window.

4. Choose Create ➤ Hotspot Rectangle or Create ➤ Hotspot Polygon and draw a box around the part of the bitmap where you want to attach a link.

5. Specify the properties for the hotspot in the InfoBox.

6. Go to the Design pane and specify the action that you want to execute when the user clicks the hotspot.

7. Press Esc and click Yes to save it. Enter a name for the Navigator and click OK to close the window.

8. Delete the old Home Navigator and rename the new one as Home.

9. Make the new Navigator the default upon database open by specifying its name in the Database Properties InfoBox under the Launch tab.

Launching Folders Instead of Navigators

To display traditional folders instead of Navigators when opening the Web Navigator database, change the setting in the Database Properties InfoBox under the Launch tab to the Restore as Last Viewed by User option. Then open a window with the traditional Folders view (by opening the Views Navigator and choosing View ➤ Show ➤ Folders) and close all other windows in the Web Navigator before exiting the Web Navigator. The next time you open the Web Navigator, it will launch your last open view (the traditional folders view) instead of the Home Navigator.

Using Local Replicas of the Server Web Navigator Database

You can create a local replica of the Server Web Navigator database and open pages from it. This technique is handy when you want to read Web pages while you are on the road. If you create a local replica and replicate the database just before you disconnect your computer, you will have a local cache of the latest Web pages inside your database.

To use a local replica of the Web Navigator database, you need to create a new location so Notes can find and open pages inside the database. Keep in mind that when you change to your new location, you will be able to open pages inside the database, but you will not be able to retrieve new pages from the Internet.

Opening a Page from a Local Replica of the Database

You may want to create a local replica of the Server Web Navigator database and open pages from there. To open pages from a local replica:

1. Create a local replica of the Web Navigator database.

    - Be sure to name the file WEB.NSF.

    - Be sure WEB.NSF is in your Notes data directory.

2. Set up Notes to open pages from the local replica.

    - In your Personal Address Book, create a location document that you will use for opening pages from a local replica.

    - In the Location name field, type a name for the location, such as **Local Web.**

    - In the Location type field, choose the No Connection option.

3. Save your changes and change to your new location.

You cannot retrieve new pages from the Internet if you are using a local replica, but you can open pages already in the database. If you have added the Open URL icon to your SmartIcons set, you can use that icon to open pages that already exist in the database.

Recommending Web Pages

Millions of Web pages are available today. With that number increasing daily, knowing where to look for the information you need is becoming more and more difficult. Often, the best way to learn about valuable Web pages is from someone else. You can use the Server Web Navigator both to recommend Web pages to others and to see the pages that they have recommended.

Creating a Web Page Recommendation

To create a recommendation, follow these steps:

1. Open the page you want to recommend.

2. Click Recommend (the thumbs-up icon).

3. Fill out the dialog box:

   - Click the button to indicate your rating for the page.

   - Select a category for your recommendation.

   - Enter any additional comments about the page.

4. Click OK.

The Web Navigator saves your recommendation in the database.

Viewing Recommended Web Pages

You can view all the recommended pages along with their ratings directly from one of the Recommended views. Then you can open any of the recommended Web pages by double-clicking it in the view. To view the recommended pages:

1. Open the Home Navigator.

2. Click the Recommended icon at the bottom of the Navigator.

3. Click one of the following buttons in the Recommended Navigator:

   - By Category displays recommendations by the categories the reviewer chose in the Recommendation dialog box.

- By Reviewer displays recommendations by the name of the reviewer.

- Top Ten displays the ten pages with the highest cumulative ratings.

4. Open the Web page associated with the ratings by double-clicking the recommendation in the view.

Using Web Ahead: Automatically Following Links on Web Pages

Web pages usually contain URLs that point to other Web pages. You can run a background Agent called Web Ahead that retrieves all the Web pages specified by the URLs on a particular Web page and saves those in your database for you to read later. You can set Web Ahead to retrieve the URLs several levels down from the page you specify.

WARNING   Web Ahead runs only while your Notes workstation is running.

Enabling Web Ahead

To enable Web Ahead (which you do just one time):

1. Choose File ➤ Tools ➤ User Preferences and select the Enable Scheduled Local Agents option.

2. Open the Internet Options document in the Personal Web Navigator database.

3. Click the Enable Web Ahead button next to the Agent.

4. Choose Local in the Choose Server to Run On dialog box and click OK. (This dialog box appears only if you have not yet enabled the Agent in this database.)

WARNING   Web Ahead allows you to retrieve four levels of pages ahead of the current Web page. Start with one or two levels; otherwise, your hard disk will fill up quickly.

Running Web Ahead

To run Web Ahead on a Web page:

1. Choose Actions ➤ Internet Options.

2. Specify the number of levels of pages you want the Agent to retrieve in the Web Ahead Agent preferences section.

3. Exit and save your changes.

4. Select any Web page and drag it into the Web Ahead folder. (By default, Web Ahead runs every hour on any new documents that have been placed in the Web Ahead folder.)

Web Ahead runs immediately.

Using Page Minder: Keeping Track of Changes to Web Pages

Page Minder is a background Agent that monitors a particular Web page and notifies you when the contents of that page change.

NOTE   Page Minder runs only while your Notes workstation is running.

Enabling and Configuring Page Minder

To enable Page Minder (which you do just one time):

1. Choose File ➤ Tools ➤ User Preferences and select the Enable Scheduled Local Agents option.

2. Choose Actions ➤ Internet Options to open the Internet Options document in the Personal Web Navigator database.

3. Fill out these fields in the Page Minder Agent preferences section:

    *   **Search for Updates Every:** Choose how often you want the agent to check to see if the page contents have changed. You can choose Hour, 4 Hours, Day, or Week.

- **When Updates are Found:** Specify how you want Page Minder to notify you of a change. Choose the Send Me a Summary option to send a message notifying you that the page has changed. Choose the Send Me the Actual Page option to send the newly updated Web page.

- **Send To:** Specify the name of the person to alert when the page content changes.

4. Exit and save your changes.

5. Click the Enable Page Minder button next to the Agent.

6. In the Choose Server to Run On dialog box, choose Local and click OK. (This dialog box appears only if you have not yet enabled the Agent in this database.)

To run Page Minder on a Web page, select any Web page and drag it into the Page Minder folder. Page Minder runs based on the times you selected in the Internet Options document.

NOTE   You can run both Web Ahead and Page Minder on pages from authenticated servers where you are required to supply a username and password before you can gain access to the page. Similarly, you can run the Agents through an authenticated proxy server where you have to supply a username and password to gain access to the Internet. As long as you have successfully retrieved the page during your current Notes session, Notes stores your username and password in a field on the Web page and pulls it from there when it runs the Agent. For security purposes, if you run either Web Ahead or Page Minder on authenticated servers or through authenticated proxy servers, you should encrypt your database so that the field is not visible to others.

What's Next?

The Web Navigator combines the features of a Web browser with the powerful capabilities of Notes. Once the page is in the database, you can view it, copy it into a private folder, cut and paste it into another Notes document, or mail it to another Notes user. All the capabilities of Notes are available for you to use with the pages inside the Web Navigator database. In the next chapter, we discuss Notes, the Web, and the advantages of using Notes as the primary means of browsing the Web.

CHAPTER
THIRTY-TWO

Comparing Notes, Domino, and the Web

- Securing data

- Evaluating security systems

- Understanding the differences between Notes views and Web views

- Distinguishing between Notes forms and Web forms

- Developing applications rapidly

- Comparing the Notes API and Java

This chapter examines the specific functional differences between the Web and Notes and the relative merits of the two technologies. The Web versus Notes contest is an incorrect way to approach the question because Notes 4.6 is both a Web server and a server for Notes clients. Figure 32.1 depicts the unique and overlapping components of Notes and the Web.

FIGURE 32.1:

The components of a Notes and Web system

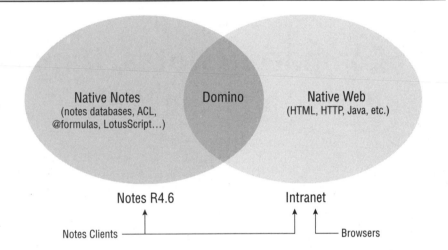

Various terms describe the technologies represented in Figure 32.1—depending on whose marketing message you are listening to. We propose the following terminology to simplify this chapter:

- **Notes Release 4.6** includes everything that came with Release 4, the @formula and LotusScript programming languages, administrative and security features, the server, the Notes client, and all the Notes applications ever written by corporate developers and consultants.

- **Intranet** includes all the elements we talked about in Chapter 30, such as HTML, HTTP, JavaScript, and browsers. An intranet site is generally a Web server holding several Web applications meant to be used within the walls of a company rather than accessed by outsiders over the Internet.

Before Notes Release 4 you had to decide whether to use intranet technology or Notes. Then Lotus introduced a gateway with InterNotes Web Publisher, which allows you to exchange Notes information with Web servers using HTML files. If you ever used InterNotes Web Publisher you probably realized that it was an appropriate, yet stop-gap, solution.

With the rapid growth of the Web, Lotus/IBM took the plunge in Notes Release 4.5, releasing Domino with much fanfare. Domino presented a way to bridge Notes and the Web and subsequently to turn Notes into a major player in the Web market. Notes 4.6 took this one step further by incorporating more Web features such as SMTP, LDAP, NNTP, IMAP, and SSL 3.0. The picture breaks down into three subcomponents:

- **"Native" Notes** means everything Notes can do, but that is not available through Domino to browsers. In other words, to take advantage of native Notes, you need a Notes client.

- **"Native" Web** means everything that you can do without Domino. Netscape Commerce servers, Java Development Kits, JavaStations, and everything you read about intranets fall into this category. You can access these components using either a browser or a Notes client.

- **Domino** is the Lotus product that delivers intranet functionality using Notes technology. Domino delivers the strength of Notes database views, forms, and documents to browsers while respecting security. Domino also delivers native Web HTML pages and can run CGI programs like any other Web server. You will learn how to develop applications with Domino in Chapter 33.

To add to the confusion, Lotus image consultants and spin doctors (the fancy term for people deliberately trying to confuse you) decided to call the whole Notes server "Domino Server, Powered by Notes." If the spin doctors have already gotten to you, all we ask is that you please keep our Figure 32.1 in mind at least for the rest of this chapter.

Now that you know what we mean by the terms *Notes Release 4.6, intranet, native Notes, Domino,* and *native Web*, we can compare these technologies.

When you are starting an application from scratch, you first need to decide whether to use Notes Release 4.6 or an intranet. Even if the answer turns out that you need a bit of both (i.e., Domino), you still need to decide which component(s) to build first and how to prioritize features based on the respective merits of each technology. If you choose to do an intranet, you still need to decide whether to use a Domino or a native Web approach. This chapter explains how to integrate Notes and the Web using Domino. This information will help you make the three-way native Notes, Domino, or native Web decisions by exploring the following topics:

- Security

- Data access and maintenance

- Views

- Forms

- CGI (Common Gateway Interface) and Rapid Application Development

Security

The most important aspects of security are authentication, encryption, and implementation. (You may want to review Chapter 16 before continuing with this section.) Recall that *authentication* allows a server to verify that you are who you claim to be. Authentication is, in computers as elsewhere, based on trust and always relies on the concept of an "authority in common." *Encryption* is the process that prevents unauthorized users from reading information not intended for them. *Implementation* deals with the way security features are actually used.

In addition to these three aspects of security, we also discuss client security, data access, and maintenance issues. Client security deals with the infamous problem of viruses and potentially dangerous programs, and data access considers the need to control who sees what information. Maintenance reflects the key issue of the availability of tools to maintain data security from an administrative perspective.

Authentication

Authentication is the most important component of any security system because you cannot establish trust without it. To illustrate the concept of trust, consider the underlying assumptions of a successful dialog with your credit card company. Say you are calling American Express about a late payment.

1. You trust the number you called belongs to American Express rather than to a swindler.

    - You assume that the magazines that advertise this phone number verified that it belongs to Amex.

- You assume that the telephone company protects your call from being detoured.

2. You connect to a human being—after a game of press this number, press that number—and you trust that the agent on the phone works for Amex.

   After all, you are giving your credit card number to a stranger whose name you probably won't remember—you assume you aren't talking to the late-night cleaning crew.

3. You identify yourself to the agent by providing two pieces of information, one of which is likely to be your social security number (SSN).

   - When you signed up, Amex verified your SSN with one of the nation-wide credit-reporting organizations and perhaps some internal data-base of deadbeats. The trusted authority in common to you and Amex is the Social Security Administration.

   - You need to provide a second piece of information to make sure that no one is impersonating you. Amex asks you for some other information that in theory only you or its database would know, for instance, how many other cards are issued under your name, your mother's maiden name, or something about your last transaction or payment.

4. As you begin to explain your predicament to the Amex agent, both of you trust the phone company to prevent anyone else from listening in and to maintain the connection until the conversation ends.

5. You trust Amex not to let unauthorized users look at your records.

This example illustrates that a benign telephone conversation with your bank involves a great deal of implied trust—much more than most people are willing to grant to an electronic conversation between the same parties. The same level of trust needs to be established when a client and a server engage in a conversation. For example:

1. Trust that your machine is connected and stays connected to the intended server, without somebody tampering with the data. Chapter 30 showed that packets of data bounce around many unknown servers.

2. Trust a third party, called a *certifier*, that the server you are connected to also trusts. This certifier is an authority respected by both you and the server.

3. Trust that the server remembers your machine from the last time you communicated with it, in other words, that the server won't confuse you with another machine pretending to be you.

4. Trust that nobody is listening to your conversation or will be able to use or replay that conversation for their benefit.

5. Trust that the records used for identification are secure. It's 3:00 A.M. in cyberspace; do you know where your social security number is?

Public and Private Keys

Security in Notes clients and browsers is based on a private/public key combination. Your ID is split into two unique chunks—one that sits on the server, called the *public key*, and one that resides on your local machine, called the *private key*. Your ID is a file (sometimes named *user.id* or *mine.key*), and often a password protects it from unauthorized use. An administrator creates the public and private keys when he or she sets up your account. Although the underlying algorithm is very complex, the key mechanism is rather simple: a (complex) formula compares the public and private keys and yields a match or no-match answer. Intranet servers using secure HTTP (see Chapter 30 for a definition of HTTP and other Internet terms) use the `https://` prefix to indicate that the URL is taking advantage of the Secure Socket Layer (SSL), a protocol based on keys.

Certificate Authorities

A trusted authority in common (the certifier) stamped both your file and the server. When you connect to a server, you and the server must have a trusted authority in common—equivalent to the Social Security Administration. This certificate may be your own internal entity (e.g., `/Corporate/Acme`) or be delivered by an external commercial entity.

Here is a partial listing of commercial and public certificates:

- United States Postal Service CA

- Verisign/RSA Commercial CA

- MCI Mail CA

- AT&T Directory Services

- GTE CyberTrust Root CA

- Canada Post Corporation CA

Similarly, the server must believe that you wouldn't be foolish enough to misplace both your user.id file and its password (this would be the equivalent of keeping your cash card PIN number in your pocketbook).

Sending an Encrypted Message

Suppose you wish to send an encrypted message to Francois, one of the authors of this book. To post an encrypted document that only Francois could read, you would need to retrieve and use his public key. For that, he would need to post his public key in a directory accessible to you and other readers. Since you and Francois probably have not communicated in the past, you cannot be sure that the entry in the directory is from Francois, not from an impersonator. That's where authentication plays a role. If you trust the person maintaining the directory, you trust that he or she verified the integrity and validity of Francois's public key. When you encrypt the message to Francois using his public key, only Francois will be able to decrypt the message using the private key stored in his Notes ID file.

NOTE   Secure intranet sites provide identification. Typically, you apply for clearance by connecting to a public section of the server and filling out a form. You receive an e-mail response that includes your password. That process is different from native Notes in that a Web server can catch an impersonator only when the completed form is being processed.

Domino maintains a list of users in the Notes Name & Address book, but security is based on a password/name match rather than on the certified public key concept of native Notes. Although Domino SSL allows the issuance of keys, the bottom line is that today the authentication of a browser is inferior to the authentication of a Notes client.

Encryption

Encryption schemes scramble data so that eavesdroppers cannot easily decipher data communicated between two parties. Encryption is particularly useful when sending e-mail or posting a document that is private and/or confidential. Encryption also protects data in transit from tampering.

Once two parties are authenticated, both the client and the server can encrypt data transmitted between them. In all cases, encryption requires making a section of the authorized user's key public.

Native Notes manages public keys for all users of the Notes corporate network through its Name & Address book. Intranet servers do not provide a corresponding central repository of keys—mostly because doing so would require its integration with mail directory services that Web servers do not provide. Domino does not provide any additional encryption facilities to a native Web solution.

Implementation

Authentication and encryption schemes on the Web and in Notes are essentially similar. Although Notes provides better security, both are appropriate for most applications. We believe, however, that the real difference rests in the setup and administration of the security components.

Notes clients can find in their Mail database a utility that creates a temporary export certificate. The form is shown in Figure 32.2. If you are concerned about international travel and exports, read the fine print.

Security and U.S. Export Regulations

U.S. software export regulations limit the strength of the encryption available for use outside North America.

It's tough enough for the National Security Agency (NSA) to locate regular radio and electronic exchanges between individuals outside the United States who may be potential threats to national security. Imagine how many more acres of computers the NSA would require to decrypt messages on the fly—and the tougher the encryption, the more acres of computing power it needs.

Consequently, Notes and most browsers are available in two versions: one is for export, and one is for use in North America. Both are secure enough for commercial transactions, but the North American version contains a higher grade of encryption than the NSA is willing to deal with. Notes Release 4.6 allows a U.S. resident to use a North American version of Notes on a notebook computer for short travel periods, but not to export the software.

Security is built on trust, as you saw in the telephone example, and trust is built on experience, as opposed to intuition (extrapolate the concept to your life at your own risk). Technology itself is therefore less important than its proper implementation. A poorly set up Notes Release 4.6 security system may provide an illusion of security, but may, in fact, be less effective than a simple, well-monitored native Web password-based schema. But a native Notes security system installed by the book by properly trained system administrators is superior to an intranet site—for technical and nontechnical reasons.

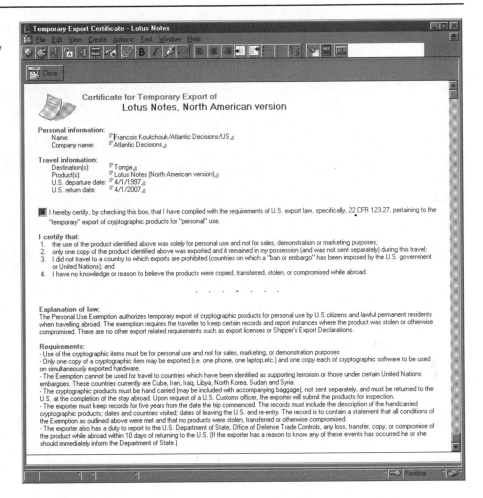

FIGURE 32.2:

You can create a temporary export certificate directly from the Notes mail file.

The more a security system is challenged, the more likely it is to show its problems. People have tried to break into Notes since it's been around, yet it is still considered secure. But the "challenge" is less from breaking and entering by brilliant university hackers with too much time on their hands than it is from inadvertent access by legitimate corporate users exposing flaws in the setup and maintenance of the system.

A Domino-based security system, although less sophisticated than a native Notes system, is superior to it. By default, Notes sets up each user with a private/public key and a password, as shown in Figure 32.3, and requires authentication for each server. Each application created from a template can inherit corporate security—without burdening the developer with the responsibility of authentication and encryption.

FIGURE 32.3:

When registering a new user, Notes allows you to require a password to protect the user.id.

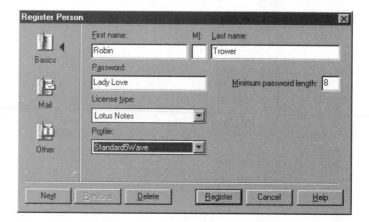

Table 32.1 summarizes the security trade-offs between native Notes, Domino, and native Web.

TABLE 32.1:   Security Trade-Offs between Native Notes, Domino, and Native Web

	Native Notes	**Domino**	**Native Web**
Authenticate User	Public/private key ID + certifier	N&A book person entry with password	Name and password file
Authenticate Server	Public/private key ID + certifier	SSL public/private key	SSL public/private key
Encryption	Database, mail, document, field, network	SSL network only	SSL network only
Data Access	Notes to ACL to server, database, view, form, document, section, field	ACL to database, view, form, document, field	Read/write to document and form set manually

Client Security

The other important aspect of security relates to how a client protects itself from bad data coming in from a server. Don't forget that properly authenticated servers and safely encrypted data could still be dangerous data. Given the vast number of documents carried by a Notes Release 4.6 or an intranet server, some of them are bound to be suspicious.

You may recall from Chapter 30 that HTML pages can contain executable code in the form of Java applets, ActiveX controls, or JavaScript. Similarly, native Notes documents can contain executable code in the form of LotusScript or embedded ActiveX objects. Any time you download code to your local machine and run it, you risk picking up a program full of bugs.

NOTE   A virus is a rogue computer program, conceived with the intention of creating havoc. A bug is an unintentional feature of most programs that also creates havoc, but with the blessing of the vendor's marketing department.

Notes protects its clients through an Execution Control List that decides what type of executable program to run based on the authentication of its author against a list stored on the client's workstation. Figure 32.4 shows the Execution Control List as well as a setting to enable Java applications.

FIGURE 32.4:

The Execution Control List allows you to restrict the activity of code downloaded to your machine based on its author.

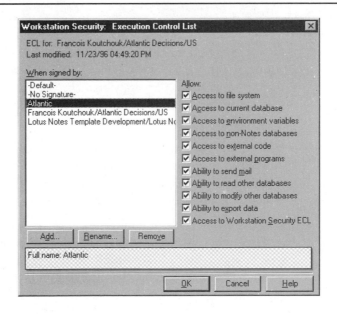

Challenges to Security in Notes Release 3

In Notes Release 3, a user could gain additional access by creating a group containing his or her name. For instance, you could create a group called Lou Gerstner and insert one name, Francois Koutchouk, into it. This ruse would provide Francois and Lou with equal access to Lou's data. Most system administrators know about this scheme and disable the right to create groups in the public Names & Address book.

In Release 3, physical access to a Notes server or the server's ID created a dangerous situation by allowing users to access many Notes databases. Lotus fixed this problem in Release 4 by introducing a distinction in the ACL (access control list) of databases between a server and a person.

In Release 3, disabling server access to a stolen ID was very difficult. For instance, you had to specifically exclude Ken Brown from the list of users authorized to access the server and then had to re-create an ID for Ken with a different name (Kenyon Brown perhaps). The change of name creates all sorts of inconveniences—from changing group memberships to changing e-mail addresses. Beginning with Release 4, Notes allows you to enforce a matching of the public key so that only a user known to the server's Name & Address book can access it—without requiring a change of the name.

Java, a compiled language, cannot access your file system or the network when executing. Sun spent a lot of time and publicly sought challenges to Java to ensure that Java applications run safely on all browsers. The work seems to have paid off, but given the lack of track record of the code, many browsers have implemented a setting that allows a user to turn off the automatic execution of Java applets.

Similarly, HTML code is very restricted as to what it can do and how it interacts with the browser. It can download files from a site but cannot access local files or modify data outside the context of the browser. Figure 32.5 shows how a browser can restrict the type of executable code allowed on your machine.

A native Notes client and most newer browsers display a pop-up dialog box any time they suspect something dangerous is about to happen on your machine. We recommend that you read those warnings carefully and stop for a second to assess whether the source of the information is trustworthy. You are probably safe when accessing `https://www.ibm.com/~/PositionStatement.htm` and less so when reading `http://www.BingoJokers.com/~/cool.htm`. As in most security situations, your best defense is common sense.

FIGURE 32.5:

You can disable the downloading of files and the execution of scripts or programs in most browsers.

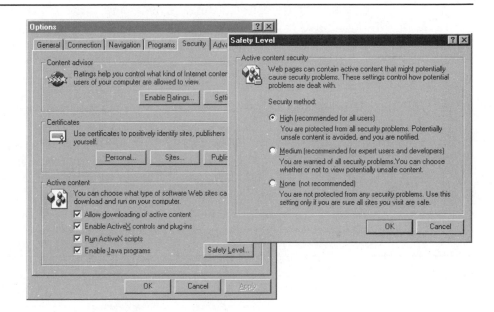

Data Access and Maintenance

Once the parties are properly authenticated and certain that no one is eavesdropping on their conversation, servers and clients are ready to exchange real data. As indicated in Table 32.1, data access differs according to the tool you use.

- Notes Release 4.6 controls access at all its object levels: server, database, view, form, document, section, and even field. Notes uses a central directory (called the Name & Address book) to maintain lists of users and groups. Based on this secure directory and authenticated users, Notes defines Access Control Lists and Editor or Reader roles for its various objects. Please review Chapter 16 for additional information on Notes security.

- This multilevel access control contrasts with native Web, where access granularity is restricted to the document level. You have access to the site, or you don't. Once in the site, security is based on either the right to read a document or the right to compose and submit a form. In addition, you cannot break HTML documents into fields with selective access. If such functionality is desired, HTML documents must be assembled on the fly using a CGI program add-on (a rather challenging task, as seen in Chapter 30).

- One of the greatest advantages of Domino is the ability to use native Notes security to protect your site. As Table 32.1 shows, you can use Domino to restrict access based on a database, view, form, document, or field. Note the absence of server or section security.

Multilevel access control affects the construction of documents and the maintenance of databases. In Notes Release 4.6, you simply create a database that fits the needs of all your users—all their roles and functions—and then you restrict access to given views, forms, or fields. In other words, design elements—not the data"control access. For instance, a recruiting database may contain summary views of applicants' backgrounds visible only to the HR department. Candidate interview evaluation documents may be accessible only to line managers, and field information about criminal background on a candidate application may be visible only to the hiring manager, as shown in Figure 32.6.

FIGURE 32.6:

A controlled-access section determines who may read certain information in Notes Release 4.6.

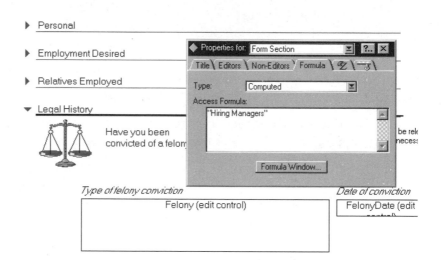

On a native Web site, you would need as many instances of a document as there are possible roles for its access (or a lot of CGI or LiveWire code). For instance, you need two job postings: one with the salary range and one without. Then you need to separate the documents according to the desired access level for different users. In essence, the recruiting application is a hierarchical tree with multiple branches—like a directory. In this example, you need a branch or subdirectory to store Equal Employment Opportunity (EEO) documents for the HR department.

(EEO information includes highly confidential data such as ethnic origin and disabilities.) You would then grant read access using your operating system's read/write privileges.

The key difference between a native Web site and a Domino site is how they maintain such an application. In Notes Release 4.6, the multiple designers of various applications—not the administrator of the server—control security using the ACL, as shown in Figure 32.7. Once again, design elements, not the physical locations of files, control access. Without better tools, Webmasters without Domino have quite an administrative burden on their hands.

FIGURE 32.7:

The Notes ACL manager distributes the responsibility of granting access to information among the owners of the data and the Notes administrator managing the membership in the user groups.

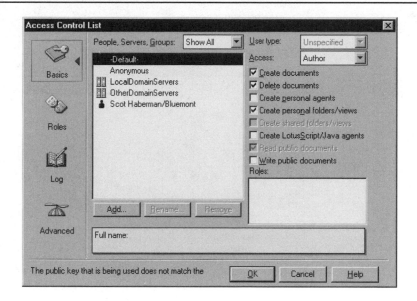

Views

Notes Release 4.6 views, as shown in Chapter 20, are "live" reports of existing records presented in various ways depending on the purpose of the view. Views are similar to outlines. Notes represents each individual view as a hierarchical dynamic collection of documents, as shown in Figure 32.8. As documents are modified, added, or deleted, the view will compute and show different categories, counts, or textual information. Notes views are logical collections of context-sensitive information.

The Notes Release 4.6 view is a design element that selects the appropriate documents to display in the view based on the built-in selection formula. (Each column can also have a formula based on the contents of the fields.) The indexes of the views are automatically computed and maintained on the server. The key here is that Notes Release 4.6 views are independent design elements.

FIGURE 32.8:

Notes Release 4.6 represents each view as a hierarchical dynamic collection of documents.

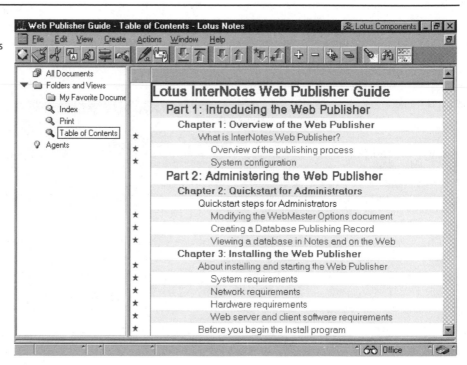

In contrast, a native Web "view" is an HTML document that was assembled from a predefined list of documents. Just as a Notes designer needs to create a different view for each purpose, a Web designer needs to create a unique HTML document for each perspective on the list of documents. For example, if you need a view that displays product names and a view that displays part numbers, you need two Notes views or two HTML documents. Figure 32.9 shows a native Web site that uses Java-Script to display an outline view that looks like a Notes view. Note, however, that expert-level JavaScript coding was required and remains necessary to manage the categories.

A Web view is not dynamic. If you change any component of the list (e.g., add a product in the line or even edit a part number), you need to re-create the HTML document manually or through a JavaScript code change. HTML is essentially static, which works if the underlying information is also mostly static, for example, a policies and procedures manual. If the application calls for many views on the same data, the native Web designer would have to modify all the relevant documents to correspond to the modified data. A native Web view lacks internal logic; it cannot, for instance, display the requisitions opened over 30 days or exceeding $75,000 and flag those that fall under the new cost-control measures without the developer writing some JavaScript.

FIGURE 32.9:

A Native Web site requires quite a bit of JavaScript code to display an outline, functioning like a Notes view. It's not exactly "live" either, requiring code changes as main categories are added.

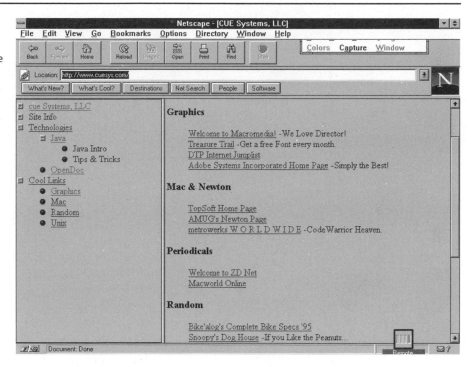

Another key component of Domino is the ability to use the Notes views "as is" to manage the display of document lists to browsers, as shown in Figure 32.10. That feature alone distinguishes Domino from native Web solutions.

NOTE

In a collaborative environment, native Notes users have the unique ability to create their own views (folders) and share these perspectives with other users. They can also browse through the views to obtain the information they need without opening the underlying documents because the view may select and compute the "meta" information about these documents.

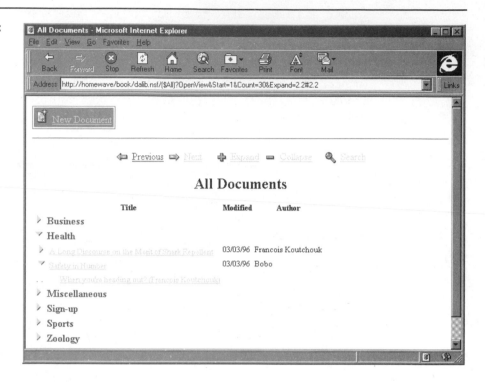

FIGURE 32.10:

You can display a "live" Notes view with Domino without writing any code.

Forms

As you already know (from Chapter 17), Notes forms serve two purposes: They display and collect information. (The latter purpose is more commonly associated with the term *form*.) In both modes, as with views, Notes forms are dynamic entities; forms are design elements that are separate from the document. Forms serve as "masks" to present underlying documents either in Read or Compose mode.

A native Web page is a physical entity, a file stored on a native Web server. You cannot display a unique version of the document that is tailored to a specific person. For instance, you cannot use one HTML document to show a job applicant's EEO information to an HR representative and not show that information to a hiring manager. In other words, you cannot display multiple versions of the same HTML document to different people and expect them to interpret the data in ways that are relevant to them.

NOTE To implement context-sensitive or user-sensitive documents on the Web, you would need multiple copies of the document sitting in multiple subdirectories. In contrast, in native Notes a form formula can select an alternative form.

As you saw in Chapter 30, an HTML page mixes data and tags to render a document. Similarly, an HTML form associates special tags to form objects such as buttons, drop-down lists, and text entry fields. The fields that the user fills in are plain text without any underlying code. Like its Notes relative, a native Web form allows a value entered in a field to be validated or translated by placing code behind the fields (for instance when the user moves to another field). Native Web uses JavaScript code, native Notes @formulas, or LotusScript. One of the limitations of Domino at this point is that it can validate data in the fields only when the entire form is submitted back to the server, while in native Notes each field can be validated as a user enters the information.

Creating Interactive Web Forms

Once you've published all your policy and procedures manuals and copies of every piece of literature produced by your prolific marketers, you will undoubtedly recognize the need to create interactive forms. By now you realize that Notes excels wherever the forms are complex and require a sophisticated workflow. If you want to publish simpler interactive applications, such as discussions, a document repository, a status report system, or benefit enrollments, you will need to start programming. Your options, in the spirit of this chapter, are to

- Go native Web
- Go Domino
- Rewrite your resume

Programming with Native Web Tools

You can create complex forms in a native Web solution three ways. You can write JavaScript code that runs on the client, move the code to the server in the form of CGI or LiveWire code, or mix the methods. LiveWire is basically JavaScript that runs on a Netscape server. If your users are running the Microsoft Internet Explorer, you can write VBScript. We talked about the scripting language in Chapter 30. If you are familiar with Visual Basic or LotusScript, you will master native Web tools quickly. JavaScript is slightly more difficult than LotusScript because it requires you to follow a basic object-programming discipline while referencing the various elements of an HTML form.

Programming with Domino

Domino does not allow you to run LotusScript on the browser. Processing needs to occur after the HTML form has been submitted back to the Domino server. At this point you can invoke a LotusScript Agent (invoked when a document is pasted in the database). As you'll learn in Part V, LotusScript easily supports OLE2 automation, relational database access, and file input/output—tasks that are very difficult, if not impossible, to do in JavaScript (mostly for security reasons).

Using Both Domino and Native Web Tools

You don't have to make an either/or decision, native Web forms or Domino! As we explained in Chapter 30, because JavaScript is simply text typed within HTML tags, you can include it in your Domino applications. Chapter 33 will show you how to associate HTML code within Notes documents. We discuss the respective merits of the languages later in this chapter.

Using External Programs

At times you may need to process file formats not supported natively by your browser, for instance, Acrobat files or live video feeds. An HTML form can use "helper" applications to reference different types of file formats that users will access. These helper applications use a standard "application/x type" format to identify the application and the type of file users can access from the HTML document.

NOTE Many plug-ins are available, either free or for a small charge.

As explained in Chapter 30, you must use an external program, called an *applet*, to achieve functionality that is not available natively in HTML. For instance, a browser cannot annotate a document (i.e., place yellow sticky notes on it). However, third-party Java applets implement this functionality. Java applets are very powerful because they are full-fledged, compiled applications.

Rapid Application Development

These days the winner is often the programmer who gets his or her application out the door the fastest—balancing in (or out) technical elegance, ease of maintenance, scalability, and performance. You need to look at the ease of use of the programming language, that is, the amount of code required to write a program. If you are a project manager, a few basic rules apply: smaller code, fewer bugs; simple code, fewer bugs; well-known programming language, cheaper coding. The next sections review the various programming languages at your disposal, including @formulas, LotusScript, CGI, JavaScript/VBScript, ActiveX, and Java.

CGI

You can program a Web server to process an HTML form submitted by a browser using a Common Gateway Interface (CGI) program that will execute on the HTTP server. If you are using UNIX, you can write these programs as shell scripts or Perl; if you are running Windows NT, you can write Perl or develop them in C and compile them as .EXE executable files. In contrast to Notes Release 4.6 where code is sprinkled throughout the various design elements (views, forms, fields, Agents, etc.), all the logic that ties HTML documents or forms and their interaction with the server must be contained within separate CGI programs. *Separate* is the key word.

A CGI parses the data only after it has been returned to the server. In other words, the logic runs only after the input has been completed. Data is passed as name/value pairs. The HTML form itself identifies the program that will need to run on the server to process the pairs:

```
cgi-bin/zbrains?field1=value1&field2=value2&field3=value3
```

The HTTP server invokes the zbrains CGI program, passing it the pairs (field1, value1), (field2, value2), and (field3, value3). Without going into considerable detail, transforming all possible interactions between a user and an application as name/value pairs is difficult, particularly when the requests are logically complex or include many keywords.

NOTE   Each CGI is a self-standing program, without any knowledge of the process or the thread of activities of a user during a session. The only input to a CGI program is a one-shot string of name/value pairs, and its only output back to the browser is an HTML file.

CGI programs suffer from several drawbacks:

- The code always executes on the server—simple form validation requires server processing.

- Each time a user presses the Submit button on a form, a new instance of the CGI program starts on the server.

- In many applications, we've found that breaking down the input of a process in name/value pairs may be difficult to express, particularly if conditions exist between the fields of a form.

- The Web administrator must maintain a potentially large number of individual CGI programs.

- A CGI program has no state with the browser. In other words, the server does not remember the last thing the user submitted. Implementing transactions that require an interaction with the browser over several HTML forms is quite difficult.

The HTTP server needs serious horsepower to handle intensive CGI activity. Many vendors are working on improvements to CGI, including proprietary APIs that understand the concept of states (i.e., maintaining a session with the user) and multithreading (i.e., not invoking a new instance of the program for every Submit). Microsoft IIS API or Netscape NSAPI are examples of improved CGI implementations.

The equivalent of CGI in Domino is a Notes Agent that is invoked when a new document is submitted to the Notes database. (Chapter 23 explains how to create an Agent and set its properties to run if documents have been created or modified.) This Agent parses the values of the fields in the new Notes document created by the HTML form and can execute whatever LotusScript code you need, from the simple sending of an e-mail notification to a complex lookup against a relational database using LotusScript Data Objects (LS:DO).

Internet Languages

The Internet supports two categories of languages, the "applets" created with Java or ActiveX tools and "scripts" developed in JavaScript or VBScript. This section reviews the pros and cons of applets versus scripts and compares each approach to the LotusScript and Notes macro languages.

Applets: Java and ActiveX

Java is a compiled language, which means that you write the code, compile it, and then test it in your browser. It will run in any browser that supports Java (most do, these days). The unique aspect of Java is that the compiled code is platform independent; that is, it will work on a Mac, a UNIX box, or an NT machine. The browser that translates the platform-independent compiled Java code into instructions that the CPU understands does all the work. Needless to say, performance is less than optimal, as anybody who has tried to run Windows under Solaris for the Sparc or MacOS will tell you. Sun is building a processor chip that will process Java instructions directly. Many software vendors are busily working on optimizing Java compiled code.

Java, a C++ derivative (and like the Notes HiTest C++ API, not for the faint of heart), is gaining in mind and market share. The purpose of Java is to deliver programs, called *applets, plug-ins,* or *Java Beans* that can run on the client, unlike CGI programs that can run only on the server. Such functionality can be compared to Lotus Components and other OLE2 applications running on a Notes client.

Using Java requires a serious understanding of object-oriented programming—not necessarily an impossible task. However, if you've never written a line of C, C++, or Pascal, you're in for a long ride. A lot of hype says that Java is "the programming language for idiots." (We are quoting a famous journalist best left unnamed.) We believe that Java is a language for professional developers, rather than a tool for casual developers. As such it contrasts with the native Notes tools or the scripting languages (described below) that are accessible to anybody in an organization with a desire to build basic applications.

ActiveX applications are written using C++ or Visual Basic and are platform dependent—that is, they run only on Windows 32-bit operating systems (e.g., Windows 95 and Windows NT). Such specificity permits optimization: in theory, an ActiveX application will run faster than a comparable Java applet in Windows. In practice, the comparison is more difficult. *ActiveX* is essentially another name for what used to be called *OCX objects*. If you've created OCX objects with Visual C++, you will have no difficulty creating ActiveX applications. Otherwise, forget the *rapid* in Rapid Application Development unless you have a professional development team standing by.

Scripting Languages

JavaScript and VBScript are interpreted languages; that is, the lines of the program are read and executed one by one. As explained in Chapter 30, the scripts live within the HTML page, between special tags (<SCRIPT ... > </SCRIPT>). In other words, all you need is a text editor, such as Notepad in Windows, to write scripts. In Notes, you simply insert the program wherever you insert HTML code in a Notes form or document, as explained in Chapter 33. There is no compiler; you simply read the HTML page in a browser, and the code will execute, assuming that it is bug free.

The script language differs from LotusScript in the following ways:

- LotusScript does not run in browsers or in Domino.

- VBScript and JavaScript, at this time, do not have a debugger or even a way to step through the code. This deficiency may sound familiar if you've written code using the Notes @formula language.

- JavaScript requires a certain level of understanding of object-oriented programming, more so than LotusScript requires.

- Writing in VBScript is trivial for experienced Visual Basic programmers—the syntax is almost identical.

Your choice of language depends on what you are trying to accomplish. Lengthy, complex client processing clearly requires applets (for instance, an Acrobat file viewer). Complex, end-user driven applications can be developed in a script (for instance, an online ordering system). Here are a few questions to ask when you have to make an applet-versus-script decision:

- Do you have Java or C++ programmers at hand? Although Java is smaller than raw C++, scripting languages are much simpler to use, requiring less structure and discipline.

- What platforms do you need to support?

- How much interaction with the HTML page is required? At the time we are writing this book, the ability for an applet to directly interact with an HTML page or the browser is very limited. For instance, an applet won't know that a user clicked on the Submit button of an HTML form.

- Do you need network access, data access, or image manipulation? If so, you will need an applet.

Both ActiveX and VBScript allow you to use OLE automation to set properties and methods of OLE controls—even Java applets.

You Don't Need to Choose

Native Notes is an object repository that provides context sensitivity; that is, the inherent workflow processes in a database define the dynamics of documents, which cause data to trigger actions and events. The true value of Notes lies in its ability to facilitate the process of assembling the elements for each interactive document over the course of a database's life span.

How much of that functionality you need determines where you start and what tools you should use. We've shown that Domino is the way to go if you need to build an intranet rapidly, but choosing between an intranet and a native Notes solution on day one is not so clear-cut. You need to consider what functionality is simply not available on a Web site and the difficulty of porting an existing Notes application to the Web.

Notes 4.6 has the following advantages over intranets:

- Allows users to customize the look of forms and documents. Developing and customizing applications is within the reach of the end user.

- Integrates logic in form/smart forms using a simple macro language (@formulas).

- Provides granular access to data down to section and field level.

- Provides a highly secure environment.

- Provides tools for faster prototyping, application development, and ongoing database maintenance.

- Offers sophisticated workflow features that go beyond simple routing.

- Integrates a one tool/one vendor solution instead of multiple tools from many vendors. With Notes 4.6, you get an HTTP server, administration and logging services, a full-text search engine, document link management, and database integration from one vendor.

Although the browser is a universal client, it needs to mature to provide the full functionality required to deliver sophisticated applications—and we don't believe that Java is the answer, because it is beyond the reach of most end users or even part-time programmers within a department. The Web scripting languages have great potential, and we may eventually see a merger with the Notes programming languages.

From a Rapid Application Development perspective, there aren't too many reasons not to use Domino to develop and deliver applications.

Considerations When Porting a Native Notes Application to Domino

When evaluating commercial native Notes applications or reviewing in-house projects, you have to decide if you want to port the application or rewrite from scratch. *Porting* means that you remove or modify all aspects of the Notes application so that it works in Domino—in other words, take out the native Notes constructs. *Writing from scratch* means that you re-create the application with the design elements available in Domino. Here are a few pointers based on our experience with both techniques; unfortunately, we can't give you any fixed rules:

- Where is the value? If the application embeds a lot of expert knowledge (e.g., semiconductor manufacturing processes, ISO 9000), rewriting may produce a better product.

- The more native Notes code is written to run on the Notes server (rather than the Notes client), the easier the port. For instance, an Agent that accesses a relational database every time a new document is submitted will port easily.

- LotusScript code invoked on the Notes client won't port easily—but the skills to write such code should transfer smoothly to other scripting languages such as JavaScript and VBScript.

- Applications requiring high security benefit from a port.

- When time-to-market is the critical factor, trimming large applications may be more difficult than starting from scratch.

- Privilege business groupware application development experience (such as an understanding of issues and the approaches to solving them) over raw technical skills: The issues are the same; only the platform changes. In other words, the team responsible for producing a well-written, well-accepted native Notes application is very likely to write a similar well-written, well-accepted Domino application, whether it starts from scratch or ports from an existing Notes application.

Regardless of which method you are using, we recommend that you start by writing or porting the components that present the least technical challenge for two reasons:

- Technology, including Domino technology, is moving so fast that Lotus or a third party might create a utility to solve your problem by the time you need it solved.

- With intranets, you must deliver to your users (or to management) a functional application very rapidly, even if it embeds only a portion of your original application.

What's Next?

In this chapter you learned about the key differences between Notes and the Web in terms of security and application design. As usual, you should understand the requirements of your users before starting development. List them on a piece of paper and see how many features seem to fall into the Notes area of qualification. Prioritize the features (low, medium, high) and assign a development cost according to the tool (low, medium, high).

In the next chapter you will learn how to use Domino, map Notes forms to Web forms, display views, and use other techniques to maintain your Web site through Notes. If you develop the application and content in Domino, you can use it both with a native Notes client and through a browser.

CHAPTER

THIRTY-THREE

33

Using Domino to Publish Notes Databases on the Web

- Using Lotus Domino

- Viewing a published Notes database

- Granting access to databases and providing authentication

- Controlling which documents are published

- Customizing the look of published documents

- Including links in published documents

- Making a database searchable through the Web

- Using the Domino command language

Domino might be the quickest shortcut between the hype and reality of the Web. In a nutshell, it automatically—and transparently—turns your Notes documents, views, and forms into Hypertext Markup Language (HTML) pages. By marrying the power of collaboration and workflow of Notes to the publishing strength of the Web, you get the best of both worlds.

As explained in previous chapters, Notes provides an easy way to build a custom application that handles the traditional life cycle of documents, namely, authoring, revising, approving, and updating within a distributed group. In other words, Notes coordinates the process of publishing documents without forcing the Webmaster to transfer individual files by hand, call people on the phone, and otherwise do a lot of manual labor.

One of the big changes in Notes 4.6 is the differentiation of the Notes client from the Notes development environment. The Notes client for an end user is now referred to as the Notes Desktop. The Notes development environment is now referred to as the Notes Designer for Domino. The most notable difference between the two is that the Notes Designer contains sample Web databases, additional templates, and the ability to locally preview your development efforts through a browser.

Notes simplifies the management of a Web site because you can use a Notes database to control which documents are published at any point in time and who should have access to them. With Notes you can automatically maintain all the links between HTML pages, including hypertext links, attached files, and associated images, *from within* Notes databases as opposed to having to manually hunt around the Web server's hard drive for broken links.

In Chapter 30 we compared Notes to the Web. The question is not whether you need Notes *or* the Web to share information, but rather why you wouldn't use Domino as a tool to manage a Web site. If you are a Webmaster, Domino will make your life easier by providing the tools you need to delegate publishing responsibilities to the owners of the information. But if you are the kind of Webmaster who likes to be in the midst of things you have no control over, enjoys taking the heat for broken links and unauthorized or outdated documents, and looks forward to user complaints and a flood of requests, Domino is not for you.

In this chapter we cover the following topics:

- Understanding Domino

- Publishing an existing Notes database

- Customizing a Notes database for the Web

Understanding Domino

This section explains how Domino works, including its architecture and how data moves around. Our goal is to dispel some of the myths surrounding Domino Web technology. Then we show you how the various Notes design elements map to HTML components. (If you are not familiar with the basic concepts of the Internet, we strongly recommend that you review Chapters 30 and 32.)

Putting Notes and the Web Together

Domino includes one program, called HTTP, that moves data from Notes documents to browsers. To activate the HTTP server, type **load http** from the server console. You could also add the task in the notes.ini ServerTasks variable to start http automatically. In contrast to the previous version of Notes publishing (called InterNotes), publishing in Notes Release 4.6 is completely automatic and happens on the fly as users request information.

Setting up Security

You can either set up Domino on all your Notes servers or put it in just one system that replicates with the others. If you choose to use only one machine and the Web server is directly accessible from the Internet (i.e., the Wild Web World), make sure you place Domino behind a firewall or take measures to protect the Notes database files.

As you may recall from reading the back of the Lotus Notes box (if you are lucky enough to own the real stuff rather than some paper license), a Notes server is accessible over TCP/IP and also over various other network protocols such as Novell IPX/SPX and NetBIOS. You may wish to set up a dual protocol Domino server that contains one adapter running TCP/IP to communicate with the Web server and one adapter running your other protocol (e.g., IPX/SPX or NetBIOS). This kind of dual network server completely isolates your corporate network from the TCP/IP network that may be connected to the Internet.

A variation on this theme is possible even though your internal network may also be running TCP/IP. Use two adapters inside the same computer to achieve the same degree of isolation. Just make sure you configure the adapters so that TCP/IP packets from the adapter connected to the Internet cannot "jump over" the other adapter.

To further enhance security, use selective replication (see Chapter 28) between Notes servers.

TIP   The dual-adapter configuration combined with selective replication may be the cheapest and most effective firewall you can build.

Configuring Domino

Domino 4.6 includes a new simplified installation process, which makes setting up and configuring the Domino server a lot easier. Most of Domino's configuration settings are located in the server document of the Public Name and Address database. Since 4.6 includes support for many new Internet standards and protocols, explaining each is beyond the scope of this book. This chapter will briefly discuss some of the more prominent server settings. Below is a list of the new features found in Domino 4.6:

- A separate administrative client

- Administration from a browser

- SSL 3.0 support

- Synchronization of NT and Notes users and groups

- Native support of all key Internet messaging standards/protocols: SMTP/MIME, HTTP, HTML, POP3, LDAP, and IMAP

- An updated HTTP server that is faster and supports both HTTP 1.1 and SSL 3.0

Configuring the Server

As explained in Chapter 32, Domino supports the Secure Sockets Layer (SSL) that allows authenticated and encrypted communications between browsers and the Notes server using the https:// syntax. Web client/server communications are based on port numbers that the browsers and the servers agree upon. By default, Notes will use port 80 for plain text traffic and port 443 for SSL, as shown in Figure 33.1.

The Notes server entry in the Name & Address book is where you enable the TCP/IP and SSL ports. You can choose either one or both. If you choose to communicate with SSL, you need to create SSL keys (a topic beyond the scope of this book, but fortunately very easy to do if you read the instructions in the Domino SSL Administration database provided with every Domino server). These settings are located in the Internet Port and Security Configuration section.

The HTTP Server section allows you to decide what happens when a browser presents itself to the server (called Home URL in Figure 33.1). The default setting is /?Open, which means that all the databases present on your server will appear as a list of choices on the browser, as shown in Figure 33.2.

FIGURE 33.1:

The Notes server entry in the Name & Address book allows you to configure many of the Domino settings, including security.

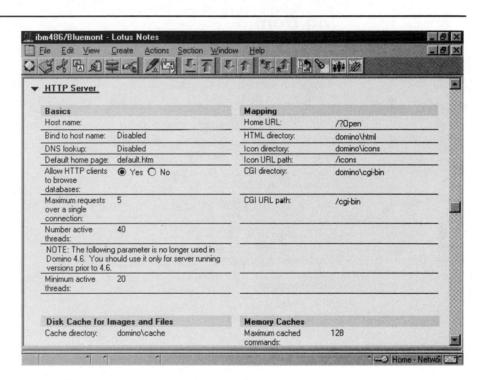

/?Open is a Domino-only command that translates into File ➤ Database ➤ Open, as if you had selected those options on the menu of the Notes client. If you had entered

```
/catalog.nsf/Databases+by+Title/?OpenView
```

the browser would have automatically opened the Notes database catalog in the Database by Title view. We'll return to the command syntax later in this chapter. For now, just remember that you can point the incoming browser to any Notes database, view, form, or document located on the server; any URL accessible from the Domino server; or any HTML file.

By default, the Domino server will display the entire list of databases available on its data directory.

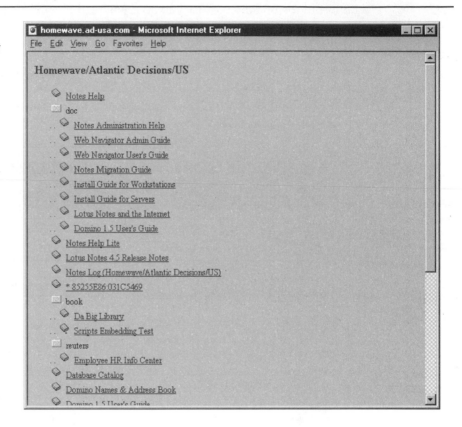

A Domino administrator should be familiar with plenty of other Domino server settings, such as the path to CGI programs and icons, as well as all kinds of things to tune performance and logging. The good news is that for the purpose of this chapter the default settings work perfectly well!

Configuring Users

If your server does not contain any confidential information, you can either set the -Default- group or a group called Anonymous in the ACL of your databases to a level of Reader or above. This strategy is fine for public databases such as a product catalog, but you may need to enforce security for most other databases. The Notes ACL defines the level of access for users accessing the Domino server with a browser (e.g., Netscape Navigator, Microsoft Internet Explorer, Lotus Notes Web Navigator). Because browser users do not have Notes IDs, they will need accounts on the Domino server. This process, called Registration, requires you to create a Notes Person document for each authorized user in the Notes Name & Address book of the server, as shown in Figure 33.3.

FIGURE 33.3:

You need to register every user allowed to access databases that are not public by default.

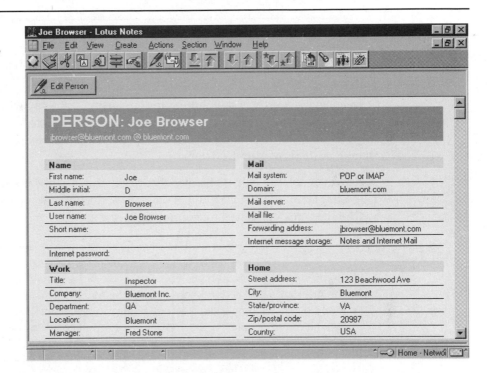

The Password field is set by the Notes administrator and is stored in an encrypted format in the Person document in the Name & Address book. To illustrate this functionality, Lotus provides on its Domino Web site (accessible through www.lotus .com) a downloadable template that allows you to register users online and allow those users to change their passwords.

Configuring Databases

Although you can use the ACL of databases in combination with the person documents to set access to an entire database, you cannot use this technique to control which documents Web users should be allowed to read or edit. To control the views that a user should have reader or editor access to, you need to use Notes roles or an option in the security settings of a form, called Available to Public Access Users.

WARNING
The @Username function does not work in view selection or view column formulas. You can, however, find out if the user is on a browser or on a Notes client by testing for @ClientType="Web".

You can restrict access to specific documents just as you would in native Notes, by using the form's read access list, a reader names field, or the new Available to Public Access Users option.

Field-level security is standard Notes fare, using options covered earlier on in this book, such as User Must Have at Least Editor Access to Use and the ability to add author fields to expand the list of authorized editors without granting a user overall editor access to the database.

However, the full extent of Notes security features is not available over the Web (see Chapter 32). The encryption of databases, documents, and fields does not work. The same holds true for controlled access sections.

TIP
The database ACL provides an option for additional security when providing access to browsers. Select the database icon, choose File ➤ Database ➤ Access Control. In the ACL dialog box, click Advanced. Select the Maximum Internet browser access level from the drop-down list. This option may be redundant with the regular ACL settings, but it will protect you from inadvertently opening up access to browsers while testing different ACL or group settings for your Notes clients.

How Notes Databases Become Web Applications

Beyond the hype of Domino, you need to understand what will happen to your Notes databases once you publish them to the Web. This section covers the mapping of Notes design elements to HTML, reviews which features of your Notes application will work, provides a few tips on when to decide to completely rewrite your existing Notes application, and finally describes the structure of the Domino command language.

Mapping Notes Elements to HTML

Domino publishes databases as a set of HTML (version 3+) documents. The logical breakdown of the various Notes design elements appears in Table 33.1.

TABLE 33.1: Mapping of Design Elements

Notes Design Element	Web Element
About This Database document	HTML page
View	HTML page; multiple linked pages if too long to fit on one page
Document	HTML page
Embedded HTML code ("Passthru")	HTML code
Doclink, Link Hotspot, etc.	Hypertext link
Table	Table
Bitmap images	GIF files
Attachments	Downloadable files
Full text	Search bar

A few design elements in Lotus Notes will not translate into Web page elements. Table 33.2 highlights some of these incompatibilities. For a complete list, refer to the Notes Help database.

TABLE 33.2: Notes/HTML Incompatibilities

Notes Design Element	Comment
Collapsible categories, column icons	Supported.
Alignment settings	For a list of labels/fields, create two columns, right align the first, left align the second.
Most fonts	Changed to preset mappings.
Table borders, width	Shrink/grow to fit text in the cells.

Continued on next page

TABLE 33.2: Notes/HTML Incompatibilities

Notes Design Element	Comment
Rich text colors, others	Only bold and italic attributes remain.
Sections	Supported (except controlled access).
Layout regions	Not supported—use tables instead.
Actions	Support limited to navigating views; creating forms; or opening databases, views, or forms.
Form events	LotusScript code does not work at all, anywhere in a Notes database except in server-based Agents (Web open or Web save Agents).
Field, column formulas	Formulas that interact with the user interface will not work.
Buttons	Can display multiple buttons if the Use JavaScript option is enabled for the database. Otherwise, the first button in a form will work as a substitute for the Web form Submit button.
Table borders	If the top-left cell has a border, the entire table will contain a border, otherwise there is no border. This is a limitation with HTML.

Understanding What Works on the Web

Tables 33.1 and 33.2 contain a lot of information. To understand what will and won't work when publishing your Notes databases on the Web, you need to understand that an HTML page is essentially a static element. Once the page is displayed on the browser, it's completely "out of sight" of the Domino server. This concept is a little hard for many users (it was for us the first few times around) to understand, so we'll try to explain it in several ways. Keep these points in mind:

- One conduit for passing data back to the server is the Submit button. That Submit button will return field/value pairs to the server for further processing. In other words, once the Notes form is displayed as a Web form on the browser, no Notes formula or LotusScript code will run until the data is returned to the Notes server. The server is not aware of any piece of data you type into your Web form until you submit the entire form. (Another conduit for passing data back to the server is server Agents. This is a complicated topic that is not covered in this book.)

- Once you've submitted the form, the Notes server will be able to trigger an Agent based on the fact that a new document was created in the database. Whatever LotusScript code was meant to run on the client will not execute, but input translation and input validation formulas will—as long as they do not have functions or commands that interact with the user interface.

- One of the best ways to understand what will or will not work is to think in terms of the user interface. Code that will paint something on your screen generally won't work unless it is a navigation to another *existing* Notes element. For instance, you can jump from one document to another, or between a form and a view.

If this explanation is still confusing, simply remember that code needs to occur on the Notes server in the form of an Agent or a set of input translation/input validation formulas in order to run. If you need to have code running on the Web browser, you need to write JavaScript, VBScript, or Java, as described in Chapter 32.

Deciding When to Rewrite a Notes Application

With so many changes required, you may wonder when you should rewrite your application from scratch versus modifying it for use on the Web. We can suggest a few rules of thumb, sometimes contradictory, but at least they are a starting point for further thinking:

- When the core value of the application is the expert knowledge it embeds (e.g., ISO 9000, semiconductor manufacturing), a rewrite provides an opportunity for a better product.

- The less workflow, the easier the port (e.g., electronic catalogs, scheduling).

- The more code running on the Notes server versus the client, the easier the port (e.g., RDBMS synchronization, intelligent Agents).

- LotusScript code is not easy to port, but if you know LotusScript you can quickly learn how to write JavaScript or VBScript code.

- Applications requiring high security benefit from a port.

- When time-to-market is the essence, trimming large applications may be more difficult than starting from scratch.

Understanding the Domino Command Language

While configuring the Domino server, you had a glimpse of the Domino browser syntax in the form of a /?Open command as a default value of the URL home page of the Domino server. The overall structure of a Domino command is

```
Name of the Element / Name of the Element / ... / ? Action & Arguments
```

The name of the element is taken from the list of Notes design elements and includes things like databases, views, and forms. The order of the elements must follow the Notes design structure, that is, a database before a view.

The actions are selected from a list, a subset of which is shown in Table 33.3. The arguments depend on the action and typically further refine its behavior.

TABLE 33.3: Examples of Domino Commands

Element	Action	Example
Database	Opendatabase	`http://www.eg.com/dalib.nsf/ ?Opendatabase`
Navigator	OpenNavigator	`~/dalib.nsf/Main+Navigator/ ?OpenNavigator`
View	OpenView	`~/dalib.nsf/By+Category/ ?OpenView`
Form	OpenForm	`~/dalib.nsf/Document/?OpenForm`
Search	SearchView	`~/dalib.nsf/By+Category/ $searchform?SearchView`

When you navigate with your browser in a Notes database, you will notice that Notes issues these commands on the Address (or URL) field of your browser. In addition to the commands listed in Table 33.3, other commands are also available, for example, ?Create, ?Delete, and ?Edit. The arguments depend on the command used; for example, &ExpandView applies to the ?OpenView command only. None of this syntax should concern you too much if you're going to publish Notes databases "as is." But you will need to understand this syntax if you expect to customize your Domino applications, a topic we touch on later in this chapter.

Now that you know what to expect from a Notes database accessed from a browser, you are ready to put these concepts to work. This section moves from the simple rendition of the Big Library database used elsewhere in this book to a more advanced customization that optimizes its use from a browser. In the process, we introduce tips and techniques that may save you a lot of time.

Testing the First Notes Database with a Web Browser

You need the items on this shopping list to continue:

- One fully functional Domino server, properly configured and running as described earlier in this chapter.

- One current browser, such as Microsoft Explorer 4.0 or Netscape Navigator 4.0, available from www.microsoft.com or www.netscape.com, respectively, for the modest price of a phone call through your ISP. Version 2.*x*-vintage browsers will do, but since Domino publishes in HTML 3.2, you could be missing out on some cool features. Alternatively, you could use the Notes Web Navigator that comes with the Notes Release 4.6 client.

- One Notes Release 4.6 client.

- One copy of some image manipulation tool, such as Paint Shop Pro 4 or NT4 Paint.

- One copy of the Da Big Library database (from the companion CD-ROM) properly loaded somewhere on your Domino server. Make sure that it is configured to allow you to access it, as specified earlier in this chapter.

Follow these steps to view the Big Library through a Web browser:

1. Start your Web browser.

2. Type the address of your Domino server including the subdirectory for the database (such as http://homewave.ad-usa.com). If your server is using the default configuration, the entire list of available databases will be displayed, as shown earlier in Figure 33.2.

3. Open the Big Library database. The Main Navigator will appear as shown in Figure 33.4.

The first thing you'll notice when comparing the Web to the Notes rendition shown in Figure 33.5 (in addition to the missing view in the right pane) is that the text of the Navigator images has disappeared.

You will need to perform the following tasks:

1. Create a Navigator just for Domino, opening in its own window, in which the image is a full-page graphic background.

2. Provide a way to return to that Navigator from a view (since in this example, the view won't show on the same page as the Navigator).

FIGURE 33.4:

The Main Navigator is used as the home page of the database if you specified it as the element to automatically launch on a database open.

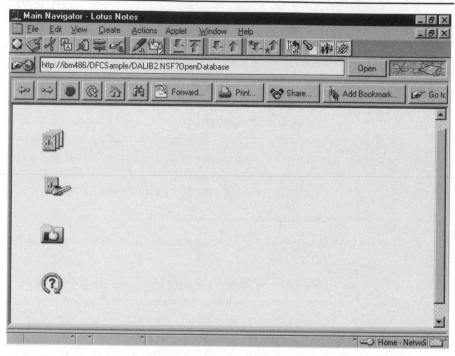

FIGURE 33.5:

In Notes, a Navigator can be opened in a left pane, with the view on the right.

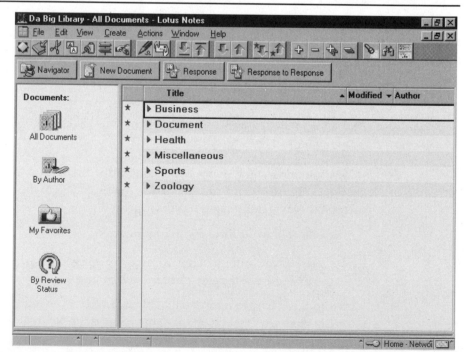

Wave your mouse above the second icon from the top. The message Shortcut to By+Author?Openview may appear in your status line. This message is a reminder that Domino controls the interface through its command language. Click the icon. The view should look very similar to Figure 33.6.

FIGURE 33.6:

Notes Domino views include collapsible categories, action items, and a second toolbar to navigate through the document displayed in the view.

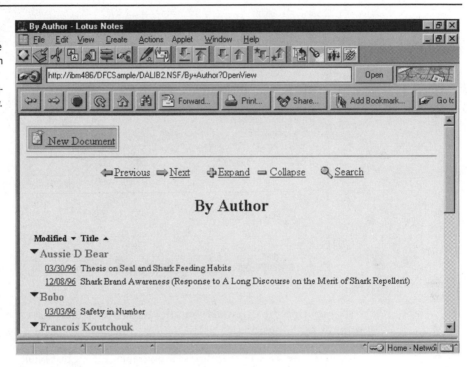

A few things are missing, including the Responses action items and Navigator action button, and the Title column is a little off-center. If you were curious enough to visit the bottom of the page on your browser, you may have noticed that the toolbar is repeated at the bottom. Domino automatically inserts this toolbar of basic navigation tools. The Previous and Next buttons appear because Domino automatically breaks down long views into multiple linked pages. Expand and Collapse operate on the entire view. (We'll come back to the Search button shortly.)

Here are a few more elements to add to our shopping list:

3.   A background color to the view.

4.   A way for the user to return to the homepage.

For now, let's continue exploring the Da Big Library database as Domino published it. The very first document in the view should look similar to Figure 33.7. The original Notes document appears in Figure 33.8.

FIGURE 33.7:

The Web browser displays a
Notes document published
by Domino.

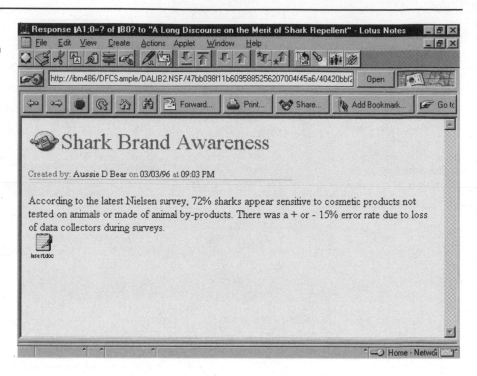

Comparing the original Notes document to its HTML rendition, we notice the
following changes:

- The fonts and colors are somewhat different but basically respect the theme.

- The action buttons are gone.

The good news is that the file attachment remained available inline, as indicated by the icon in the document, and that everything looks identical to the same
document displayed in the Notes client. Here are a few more chores to add to the
to-do shopping list:

5. Figure out a way to return to the parent document from this response
   document.

6. Find a way to place the document in Edit mode.

Let's do one more test of the published Notes database by composing a new
document in the database. Simply back out of your browser to return to the By
Author view shown in Figure 33.6. Now click the New Document button. A Web
form similar to the form in Figure 33.9 appears.

FIGURE 33.8:

The Notes Release 4.6 client displaying the same document as Figure 33.7

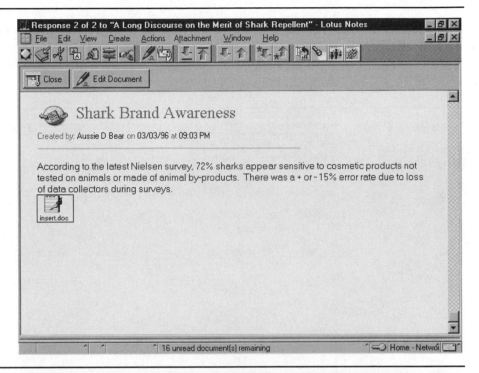

FIGURE 33.9:

You can use a Notes form as a Web form with very few modifications. Domino automatically inserts the Submit button.

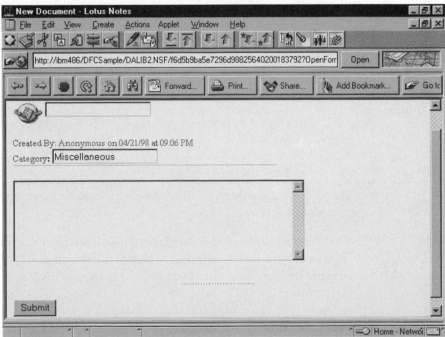

Comparing the Notes form in Figure 33.10 to its Web rendition, you can see that the fields remained in the same spot and that Domino added a Submit button at the bottom of the screen, as expected. The action buttons have also gone away. If you enter some data and press the Submit button, you will get a message similar to the one shown in Figure 33.11.

FIGURE 33.10:

The Notes form used in Figure 33.9

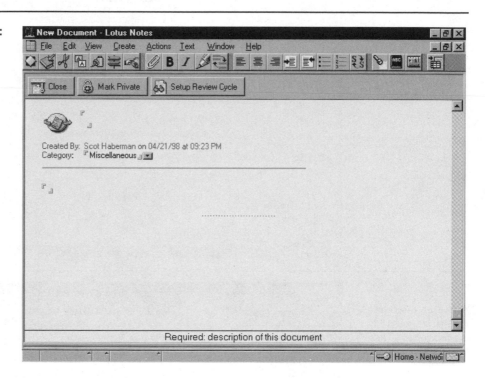

All in all, the form is still usable. Here are two final entries for the list of things to do:

7. Add a way to insert a file attachment.

8. Return something a little more pleasant to the user submitting a new document.

When publishing an as-is Notes database, Domino renders all documents, views, attachments, and images in their original form, within the HTML mapping and Domino limitations outlined earlier in this chapter. Domino also creates an easy way for users to navigate between views via Navigators and within a view by expanding its categories and breaking the view into multiple pages.

FIGURE 33.11:

Domino returns a standard response when submitting a Web form back to the Notes database.

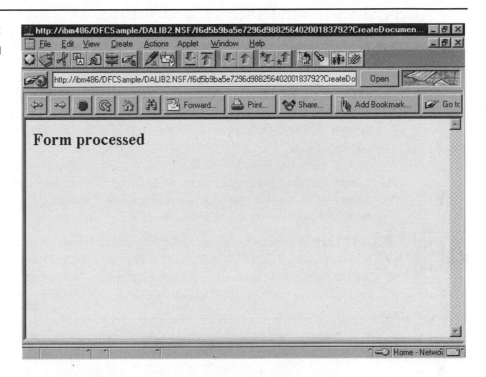

At this point you could call it a day and move on to the next database you need to publish. But you would be missing an opportunity to greatly enhance your Web site with just a little extra customization work. Besides, during this first test, we made a list of eight items that needed fixing.

Customizing Web Publishing

The more time you spend tweaking your Notes database, the more its appearance will improve on a Web browser. In other words, the quality of the output is linearly proportional to your efforts, a rare phenomenon in computing, where the results are often conversely proportional to the pain incurred. We are going to improve the look and feel of the Da Big Library in three steps:

1. Fix the default Main Navigator.

2. Implement the eight changes we identified during the first test of the database.

3. Add nice-to-have touches such as scripts and a few other tricks.

Creating a Navigator for Domino

The problems with the Main Navigator of the Da Big Library are (1) it assumes we are using panes to display the Navigator in one part of the screen and the view in another, and (2) it uses text boxes to label the icons. Unfortunately, these problems are not easy to solve. In most cases you need to make heavy use of a drawing or paint program to lay out your Navigator the way you want it. That's where your artistic skills may shine and ours pale. The first thing to remember is that you need to fill the screen. The existing Main Navigator serves its purpose of pointing users around the database. We'll spare you the gruesome details of capturing screen images, clipping portions of them, and adding other images using Microsoft Paint—none of which has anything to do with Domino or Notes. Figure 33.12 shows our best effort at creating a new Navigator for Domino.

You can specify different launch options for a Notes client and the Web browser when opening a database in Notes 4.6. For the previous example, you can keep the original client Navigator and have it open for Notes clients. The new Domino Navigator can then be specified as the Navigator for Web access.

FIGURE 33.12:

A full-screen Navigator to use with Domino

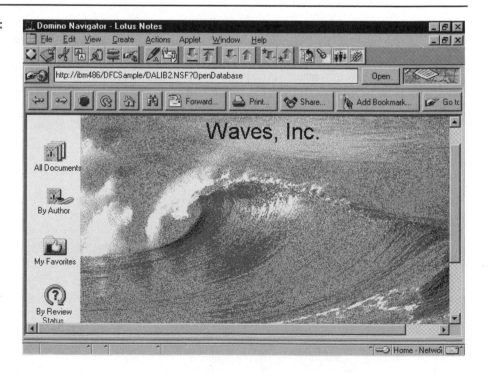

Follow these steps to set the new Navigator:

1. Select the icon of the Da Big Library database.

2. Choose File ➤ Database ➤ Properties. The Property box will appear.

3. Click the Launch tab.

4. Select Open Designated Navigator in the On Web Open field.

5. Select Domino Navigator as a Navigator.

The main Navigator will now serve as the "home page" of the Da Big Library. You can test your efforts by reopening the Big Library database with your browser. (You may need to use the Refresh/Reload button in your browser.)

If you've clicked on any icon, such as All Documents, you will pull the standard view as shown previously in this chapter (refer to Figure 33.6). We need to make this view a little prettier and, more important, we need to add a way to return to the application home page without having to click the Back button of the browser.

Notes 4.6 includes a few new elements for form design aimed specifically at the Web developer. You can now embed a Navigator, view, folder pane, or file upload control directly on any form. You no longer need to use the cryptic $$ fields for displaying these types of items. This not only simplifies Web development but also allows for more creativity.

To add a button to return from a view to a Navigator or to modify the background color of a view, you need to add HTML code within Notes. Fortunately, this task is rather simple. A small modification to a Notes form will serve as an example.

You can add your own HTML code directly within the text of a Notes document, within the design of a form, or within the design of a view—basically anywhere you can type a Notes formula. Domino reads the HTML code and passes it as-is to the Web browser, which displays the resulting code properly. The technique is very simple.

1. Type the HTML tag within square brackets:

    ```
    [<html code>]
    ```

TIP   With Notes 4.6, there is a new font option called Pass-Thru HTML. This is the same as using the square brackets for passing HTML text. Also, most form objects now have a new event called HTML Attributes that is designed for placing HTML text about the specific object.

---

2.   To hide the HTML code from Notes clients, do one of the following:

- Select the Hide Paragraph from Notes R46 users.

- Use the Hide-When property of the text to hide it from readers of the document or editors of the form.

- Use the following form formula in the view to limit the form to Web purposes:

```
@ClientType="Web"
```

The formula tests if the user is accessing via a browser.

Adding HTML Code to Customize a Notes Form

Suppose you wish to create an alternative form that displays only selected fields from the documents in the Big Library. Follow these steps:

1.   Open the Da Big Library database.

2.   Select the Document form and make a copy using the Edit ➤ Copy and Edit ➤ Paste commands. Notes will call the new form Copy of Document. Edit your newly created form.

3.   Go to the line above the line that starts with the static text Created By:. Type [**<HR>**] before the words *Created by*.

NOTE   The [<HR>] HTML tag indicates that you want to represent a horizontal line.

TIP   In Notes 4.6, a new menu option under the Create option allows you to insert a horizontal rule (line) directly on the form. This can be viewed by either a Notes client or a browser.

---

4.   Remove everything except the first icon and the Subject, From, Date, Time-Created, and Body fields, as shown in Figure 33.13.

5.   Choose Design ➤ Form Properties and call it DocPublish. Deselect the options to make it not appear on the menu or the Search Builder on the Basics tab.

FIGURE 33.13:

You can create an alternative Notes form to display documents accessed over the Web.

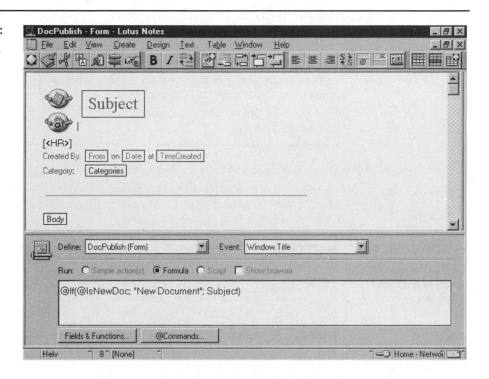

TIP

Make sure not to set the Store the Form in the Document property for forms used with Domino-published documents.

---

6. Close and save the form.

7. Edit the (*All) view. Choose Design ➤ View Properties.

8. Click the Advanced tab (the one with the propeller hat) and then click the Formula window button.

9. Type the following code into the Design Form Formula dialog box:

```
@if(@ClientType="Web"& !@IsResponseDoc;"DocPublish";Form)
```

This code means that if a Web browser accesses the document, it should be displayed with the DocPublish form; otherwise, the document should be displayed with the form that was used to create it. We add the !@IsResponseDoc condition to make sure that response documents are represented using their original form

(Response or Response to Response) regardless of whether they are retrieved over the Web using a browser or from Notes.

TIP

To hide embedded HTML code from Notes clients, enter a formula such as @If(@ClientType="Web";0;1) in the Hide-When property. You can also use the new Notes 4.6 option that allows you to hide elements from either Notes clients or Web browsers.

---

10. Close and save the view and test the form formula with your Web browser by opening any document in the All Documents view. The document should look like the document shown in Figure 33.14.

FIGURE 33.14:

Include HTML code within a Notes form to customize its Web look.

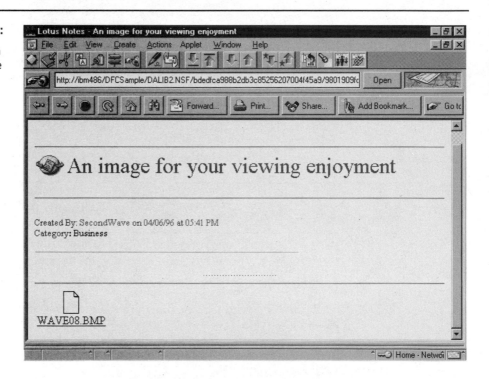

By combining form formulas to display an alternative form to Web users, you have the additional benefit of adding field-level security. For instance, you can choose not to publish the fields that contain the phone numbers of employees.

TIP

> Web browsers tend to cache the pages read since the last time you launched them. You need either to reload each document manually after you republish it (most browsers have a button to refresh or reload a page) or to temporarily disable page caching in the network configuration of your browser.

Adding HTML tags within a form allows you to customize the look and feel of both Notes forms and individual documents. You could even design Notes documents that contain no Notes elements—only HTML code!

Adding HTML Code to Customize a Notes View

You've already customized the (*All) view to display documents using a form we started to modify for browsers. You can do the same with a view. Follow these steps to add a color background to the ($All) view in the Big Library database:

1. Open the ($All) view whose form formula you just modified.

2. Double-click the first column.

3. Type the following HTML code in the Title text box:

   ```
   [<body bgcolor="#FFD0C0">]
   ```

4. Close the view and save it. If you refresh the display of the view in your browser, its background will appear in a lovely shade of pink (or is it salmon?). Of course, all this work produces exactly the same result as simply changing the background color in the design of the view itself using View ➤ Properties, but the point here is to show the range of options available to customize a view. It is nice that Notes does not force you to have to learn the codes for all the background colors.

4.6 RELEASE

Notes 4.6 has added a new option to views that tells Domino to treat the contents of the view as HTML. This allows you the flexibility to create a very powerful view that can display whatever you want in just about any format you want. What you give up is the automatic creation of document links to the documents displayed in the view.

TIP

> When placing code in a column title, use a narrow categorized column and insert a few spaces in front of the HTML tag so that the text of the code doesn't show in the view when viewed by a Notes client.

Similarly, you could add a little "new" image next to the document modified in the last six months by simply inserting a column whose formula value is

```
@if(@Now>@Adjust(@Modified;0;6;0;0;0;0);"";"[<img src=/icons/
new.gif no border>]")
```

assuming that you have a NEW.GIF in your icons directory under the Domino directory on your server.

Now, let's add a button on the toolbar of the view to provide a quick (and obvious) way to return to the application's home page:

1. Open the ($All) view.

2. Choose Create Action and type **Home** in the Title text box.

3. Click the option to include this action in the button bar.

4. Click Formula in the code pane at the bottom of the screen and type the following code:

   ```
   blurb:="?OpenDatabase"; @URLOpen(blurb)
   ```

5. Save the view and reopen the database with your browser. The Home button will appear as shown in Figure 33.15.

If you click the Home button, you will return to the home page of this database, the Domino Navigator. In essence you are telling the Notes server to follow a URL that opens its own database—by default because there is no `http://`....

TIP
As before, if you don't want to use any of the Notes images for your Action buttons, you can simply refer to an external one using the `[<img src=...>]` HTML.

Inserting Links

If you've been browsing around the Da Big Library database, you must have realized that navigating between documents is not a one-step process. Once you open a response, for instance, you have to click the Back button of your browser to return to the view, point your mouse at the parent document, and then open it. If you've used the default Discussion database template in Notes, you know that you can insert a doclink in a response.

For a browser, you can insert two types of links into your document: Notes links that will be automatically published as hypertext links and HTML links written as code within Notes.

FIGURE 33.15:

You can create Action buttons in views to call HTML code, including Domino commands.

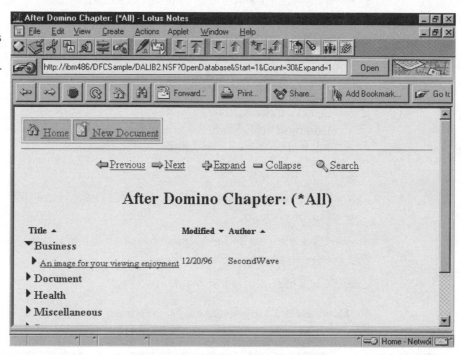

Notes Links

Think of Notes links as the equivalent of Web links except that the location of the link is irrelevant. Notes can find an alternative replica copy of the database containing another instance of the object. In other words, Notes will follow the link through its internal ID (a unique number given to Notes documents and design elements), not a physical path or a file name. Therefore, you can move documents and databases around without breaking the links. Notes Release 4.6 can create a link to a document, a view, or a database.

NOTE   With Notes 4.6, you can also create an anchor link.

Follow these steps to insert three types of links that will be accessible through Web browsers:

1.   Open the About This Database document of the Da Big Library in Design mode.

2.   Open the By Authors view and select any document.

3. Choose Edit ➤ Copy as Link ➤ Document Link.

4. Switch to the About This Database document, type a few words, such as **Click here for help on using the database**, and choose Edit ➤ Paste.

5. Create a view link for the By Author view and paste it after some text in the About This Database document.

6. Select a database on your workspace and choose Edit ➤ Copy as Link ➤ Database Link. Paste the link in the About Database document. The document should look very similar to Figure 33.16.

7. Save the About document.

8. Use your browser to open the Finding Help About document in the Miscellaneous category.

9. Click the icon in the document to open the About document. It should look very similar to Figure 33.17.

10. Click the links to test them.

Database links are an easy way to connect multiple Notes databases.

FIGURE 33.16:

Insert document, view, and database doclinks in Notes forms or documents to create HTML hypertext links that are strictly maintained within the Notes database. You can also insert hard-coded URLs as links.

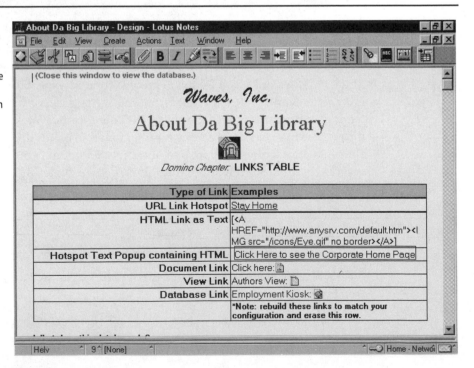

FIGURE 33.17:

Domino allows you to maintain links between documents and views using native Notes doclinks, rather than hard-coded URLs.

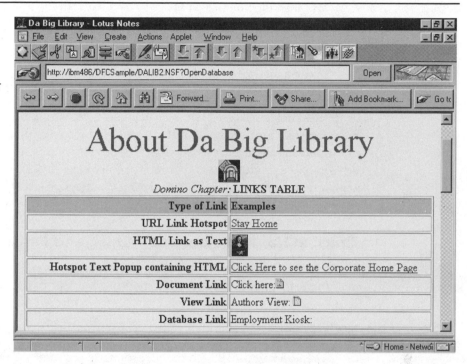

HTML Links in Pop-ups

You can write HTML links directly into the text of a Notes form or document. If you know the name of the HTML file, including its URL, you can place the code directly in the text. For example:

```
[<A HREF="MyHaven.htm"><IMG src="/icons/toBetsy.gif"></A><BR>]
```

TIP   When typing URL addresses of files stored on a UNIX system, such as a Solaris server, remember that the file names are case sensitive. `<img src="/icons/toBetsy.gif">` is not the same as "`<img src= "/icons/tobetsy.gif">`". If you are constantly switching among systems, keep that rule in mind. Best of all, if you have a choice, establish a naming convention and stick to it.

You also have the option of placing the HTML code within a pop-up. The main advantage to the pop-up method is that you are free to type whatever text you want and then include the HTML code as the text of the pop-up. You could include a link to a home page by typing a URL, as shown in the following line:

```
[http://www.lotus.com/]
```

Note that you do not need brackets (<>) because a pop-up is not an HTML tag.

The features of Notes links alone may justify the use of Domino in certain types of applications, such as marketing catalogs, in which tracing the constantly changing information is difficult. For instance, a product description may contain links to a technical specification sheet that points to last-minute updates for the latest version of the product. Several groups of employees (sales, engineering, support) are likely to manage this information, and it will move among servers, databases, and views. Notes doclinks assist in keeping the hypertext pointers consistent.

Links to Navigate between Child and Parent Documents

The easiest way to allow users to jump back to the parent document is to add a field in the response document that inherits the value of the parent document ID. To do so, follow these steps:

1. Open the Response form of the Da Big Library database in Design mode.

2. Create a computed field in the response document; name the field Link.

3. Switch to Properties and make Link a text field, computed when composed.

4. Type the following formula in the Formula pane:

```
@InheritedDocumentUniqueID
```

5. Save the form.

To test the proper functioning of the linking:

1. Open with your browser any existing Notes document.

2. Click the Respond button to compose a response.

3. Submit it. An unfriendly form will remind you that everything worked fine. Furiously hit the Back button of your browser to get back to the view. (We'll fix all that very soon!)

4. Refresh the view.

As expected, your document will appear as a response underneath the parent document. If you open the response document, a doclink appears, allowing you to return quickly to the parent document. If you like this feature, repeat the steps for the Response-to-Response form.

Adding Action Buttons to Notes Forms

You may recall that when a Notes form becomes a Web form, it essentially becomes completely static. In fact, the only button that remains as part of the Web form is the Submit button that passes all the values of the fields back to the Domino server so that it can create the document (but remember that with Notes 4.6 you can override this functionality and add as many buttons as you would like to a form).

We've seen how you can add a button to a view to navigate to other views or to create documents. The same holds true with a Web form: certain Action buttons will appear on a Web client. This functionality is restricted, however, to a few @Command functions, including Compose and Edit, unless you select the Web Access: Use JavaScript When Generating Web Pages option on the database properties InfoBox (the Basics tab).

The functionality we want is the ability to edit a document. Please follow these steps:

1. Open the DocPublish form from the Big Library in Design mode.

2. Choose Create Action.

3. Type **Edit as a Title** in the properties box.

4. Select Hide During Edits from the Hide-When properties.

5. Save the document.

6. Use your browser to open any main document in the view. The Edit button will appear.

7. Click Edit to place the Notes document into a Web form, as shown in Figure 33.18.

NOTE Don't worry about a security breach—if you are not authorized to edit a document, you won't be able to save it.

NOTE If you've used Web servers other than Domino, this simple feature should impress you!

FIGURE 33.18:

You can use a browser to
edit a document stored on
a Domino server.

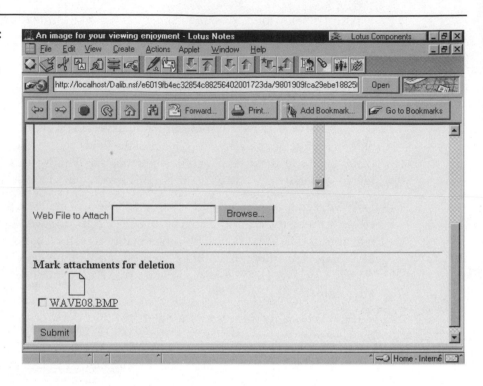

Manipulating File Attachments

You can view files attached to documents by simply clicking them to launch the appropriate application, as defined in your browser settings. You may have also noticed that Notes automatically inserts an area above the Submit button to remove files attached to the document (refer to Figure 33.18). Files marked for deletion will be removed from the document when you press the Submit button.

Follow these steps to allow a user to insert an attachment into a form:

1. Open the DocPublish form of the Da Big Library in Edit mode.

2. Type a line below the body field to prompt the user to enter the file name, for instance, **File Name to Attach:**. This text will serve as a label.

3. Select the text you've just typed and bring up the Properties box in the Hide-When tab.

4. Click the option to hide the paragraph when the document is being read.

5. Select the Hide Paragraph If Formula Is True option and type the following formula to avoid displaying the text to non-Web users:

   ```
   @ClientType="Notes"
   ```

6. Leave the text you just typed still selected and choose Create ➤ Hotspot ➤ Action Hotspot. The Hotspot button property box and the code pane will appear.

7. Type the following formula in the code pane:

   ```
   @Command([EditInsertFileAttachment])
   ```

8. Save the form.

Now that you have completed the form, you are ready to test it using your Web browser. When you display the form in Edit mode, a dialog box appears under the Body field area, as shown in Figure 33.19.

FIGURE 33.19:

You can use a Web browser to attach files to a Notes document placed in Edit mode.

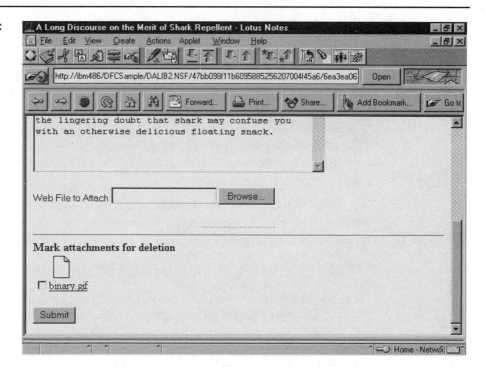

With Notes 4.6, a new Web option is available that allows you to insert a File Upload element wherever you want on the form. This is easier to use than the @Command function. Remember also that any element on a form can be hidden from a Notes client or Web browser using the new checkboxes located on the same tab as the Hide-When formulas.

TIP   Whenever you develop a Domino application, we recommend that you test it on the most popular browsers or put some comments in your forms to tell your Web users which browser works with this file.

The use of a Hotspot Action is a bit counterintuitive in that it becomes a text entry field on the Web, but otherwise it is all you need to provide support for file attachments. This functionality can serve as a foundation for more complex applications, such as replacements to FTP sites or full-fledged document management systems.

Providing Full Text Search Capability to Your Notes Databases

If Domino is not managing your Web site, you will need to purchase and maintain a separate full text indexing and search engine. Chapter 25 explained how to create a full text index of a Notes database and outlined the pros and cons of this type of index. We strongly recommend that you create a full text index for all the databases you intend to publish through the Web. Sure, it will eat up disk space, but with the cost nearing $100 per gigabyte, the gain is well worth the investment.

The good news is that a full text index to your database is all you need to provide searching capabilities to your users. As you may have noticed, every view contains a default Search icon. When you click the Search icon, the familiar Notes search form shown in Figure 33.20 appears.

You can enter search queries as if you were using the Notes Search bar; you can include conditions, such as AND or OR, and use variants of the words by default. As shown in Figure 33.20, you can sort the results by relevance or by date (ascending or descending) from the Options button. The results of the search will appear as a list of document titles, as shown in Figure 33.21.

FIGURE 33.20:

Searching on the Web requires only that the Notes database(s) be full text indexed on the Domino server. The Search button appears in all the published views.

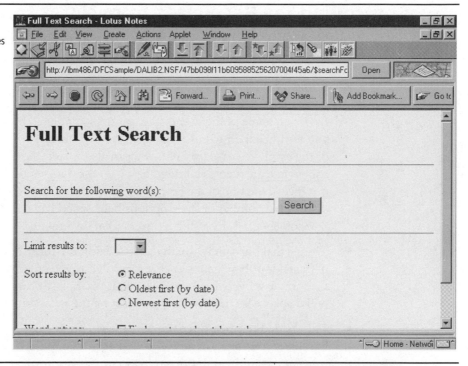

FIGURE 33.21:

A search against a Domino server results in a list of documents sorted either by relevance or by date.

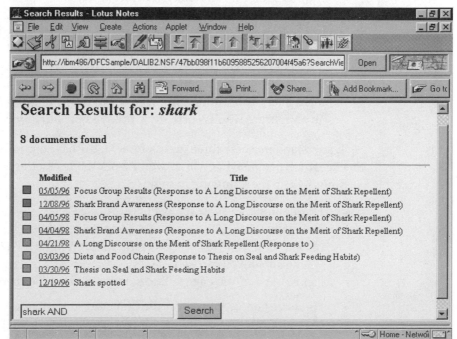

Controlling the Responses from Notes to the Web

In a Notes client, you have many tools at your disposal to control interaction with the user. We can divide these tools into three categories:

- **Things that happen before the user gets control.** As an application designer, you can decide which fields, sections, or Action buttons to display based on the logon name of the user or the last step completed by a user. For instance, if you are not a member of a manager group, you don't see the Approve button or the employee's salary field. You can also design the application to execute code while the form is loading, based on the data residing on the form. For instance, if the title of the employee in the document is Supervisor, you can display the number of stock options held or send an e-mail to notify security that somebody is accessing a confidential document.

- **Things that happen while the user is using the form.** You can take advantage of the Hide-When feature that recomputes as you enter values in the fields of the form. For instance, if you select that you have a criminal record, the system will display a section (politely) requesting the types and dates of conviction.

- **Things that happen once the user closes the form.** Code can run either on the server (through a When Modified agent) or on the client. On a client, input translations and validations may occur and appropriate messages will be generated back to the client. For instance, if you enter California as a state but 30319 as a ZIP code, the system will stop saving the form and request a 9*xxxx* ZIP code. Once the data of your form is accepted, Notes can execute any code that will create a user interface change, such as jumping to another view or displaying another form on the screen. For instance, after completing the Job Application form, you could post a Request for Transfer form to any applicant who is currently employed in your company.

Understanding these three types of interactions is very important when you are trying to determine what will or won't work while reacting to a Web form in Domino. Keep the following in mind:

- The second item is the easiest to control—you have no control over a Web form once Domino has pushed it out to the browser. If you are old enough to remember 3270/batch processing or VT100/VMS, you'll know what we are talking about. You can issue various @Commands (such as the RefreshHidden-Fields) but the Web page will be submitted to the Web server for processing.

- You have good control over the first item, as you've seen previously in this chapter. Almost everything will work, including testing for the name or role of a user or hiding fields/sections based on data values. Notes controls the show until it needs to ship the Notes form as an HTML page. When in doubt, ask yourself whether Notes knows everything it needs to "print" the form the way it wants the user to interact with it. Once the form is printed, it can't add or look up anything like new keywords. You can also use a WebQuery-Open agent that allows you the flexibility of controlling content of the Web page as well.

- The third item works along the same lines as the first two. The server returns an entire document, as a block, and you have to decide what to do with it. Translation and validation formulas will run and return a message to the user. But nothing else will run unless a server Agent invokes the code. When in doubt, assume that Notes knows nothing until the document is returned in its entirety, errors and all. You can use the WebQuerySave agent that can be run whenever a page is saved to the server.

Armed with this knowledge, you should not waste as much time as we did trying to create interactions where batch processing was required. The next section covers the two main types of responses: validation checking and responses to a submit.

Adding Notes Formulas to Web Forms

If you don't have a validation formula, a user could enter nothing in the form and submit it—not something you want to encourage—because this action will write an empty document in the database. Remember that formulas execute only in Notes—not on the Web. Therefore, you need to stop the saving event before it occurs with an @failure @function. You then need to notify the user that the data he or she entered is incorrect.

Follow these steps to force an entry in the Categories field:

1. Open the DocPublish form of the Da Big Library database.

2. Select the Categories field; in the Formula pane, select the Input Validation event.

3. Type the following code:

```
daURL:="/book/dalib.nsf?OpenDatabase"; @if(Categories="";@Failure
➡("<h3>You did not enter a category. We need that!. </h3><br><hr>
➡<a href="+daURL+">GET ME OUTTA HERE!</a>");@success)
```

The HTML code includes a few simple tags, such a header level 3 <h3>, a line break <br>, a reference to a GIF file (a copy of which is included in the About document) <img src>, and a horizontal line <hr>. The interesting part, however, is in the <a href>, which opens the database, as indicated in the daURL variable.

4. Save the form.

5. Use your browser to enter the database and create a new document. Make sure that there is no value in the category. Press the Submit button. A message similar to the one in Figure 33.22 appears.

6. If the database is located at /book/dalib.nsf, clicking on the GET ME OUTTA HERE link will return you to the (*All) view.

FIGURE 33.22:

You can customize you validation formulas to return Web pages.

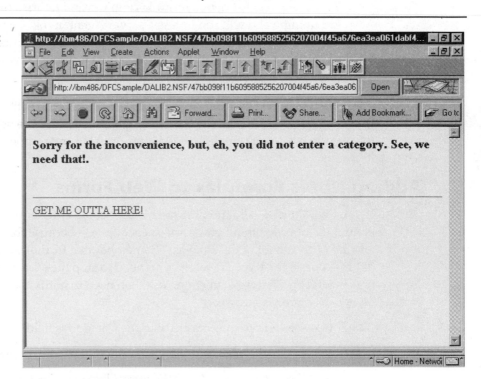

Creating a Response Formula

Assuming that the form passes validation, the next step is to return the user to the view, as opposed to simply returning a drab Form Processed message.

We recommended writing a generic subform that you can use to customize the response of all your forms. Follow these steps:

1. Open the Big Library database in Design mode.

2. Choose Create ➤ Design ➤ Subform.

3. Choose Create ➤ Field. Call it $$Return.

4. Make the field a Computed for Display field and type the following formula in the Formula pane:

    ```
    dbName:=@Text(@Subset(@Dbname;-1)); view:="By+Author"; daURL:="
    ➡[/"+DbName+"/"+View+"?OpenView]" daURL
    ```

    - The first statement selects the current database for the return link.

    - The second statement is where you indicate the name of the default view. Note the + sign to mark the space in the Notes view name.

    - The third statement constructs a legitimate Domino command URL.

5. Close and Save the subform as SubReturn.

6. Open the DocPublish form in Design mode and scroll to the bottom of the form.

7. Choose Create ➤ Insert Subform. The Insert Subform dialog box appears with a list of choices.

8. Select SubReturn and click OK. The subform will be added at the bottom of the DocPublish form.

9. Close and save the DocPublish form.

10. Use your browser to compose a form and submit it. You should return directly to the By Author view.

TIP By default, Web forms use a Submit button that appears at the bottom of the page, but you can replace it with a button of your own design. Simply create a Hotspot button and a label and place them anywhere on the form. Don't bother inserting a formula because the button will always function as a Web Submit button. Note also that Domino displays only the first button appearing on the Notes form and ignores all other buttons.

What's Next?

Throughout the book we've mentioned the power of LotusScript and the potential it offers developers. In the next chapter, we'll lay the groundwork that will help you make the most of this important Notes feature: programming in LotusScript.

PART V

Programming with LotusScript 3

CHAPTER

THIRTY-FOUR

34

An Introduction to LotusScript

- Capitalizing on the potential of LotusScript

- Understanding the difference between scripts and formulas

- Using scripts instead of formulas

- Writing a script

- Understanding the effects of object-oriented programming in LotusScript

- Defining the terms: class, properties, methods, containment, and events

Of all the new features introduced in Notes Release 4, the integration of the LotusScript language is probably the most significant from a developer's perspective.

However, learning how to write effective programs in LotusScript is not a trivial task. Our aim in this chapter is to lay a foundation from which you can progress to more sophisticated programming. By extensive use of examples, we will show you what LotusScript programs (called subprograms or just "subs") look like, how they are structured, and exactly what's going on inside of them. Our focus will be on popular uses of LotusScript. (LotusScript is a very rich language, and we can't possibly hope to cover it all.) This chapter:

- Describes the LotusScript programming language
- Explains the differences between scripts and formulas
- Describes objects and objected-oriented programming
- Describes the role of events

We deal with the topics introduced here in more detail in the chapters that follow, so don't worry if the meaning of what we're saying is not immediately clear. Proceed through the material methodically, and before you know it, you'll be a LotusScript programmer.

What Is LotusScript?

LotusScript is a cross-platform, BASIC-compatible, object-oriented programming language and development environment. As a structured programming language, LotusScript provides functionality that was previously unachievable (or at least, maximally difficult) within Notes. You can now do the following:

- Create true structured programs (rather than unstructured formulas) for executing tasks in Notes.
- Incorporate *iteration* and *flow control* in programs to achieve precise direction over program execution.
- Manipulate databases, documents, fields, and other design elements in many interesting and exciting ways.

LotusScript gives you a very high degree of control over Notes applications through object-oriented extensions called *classes*, which you use in LotusScript programs. Figure 34.1 shows an example of a LotusScript program.

FIGURE 34.1:

An example of a LotusScript program

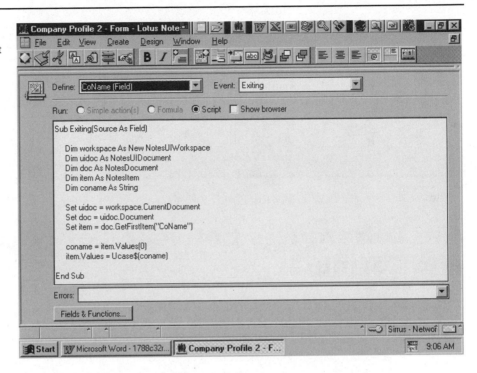

The use of classes reveals the structure of a Notes application, and lets you manipulate the application on a basic programmatic level. While this design adds complexity to your development efforts, the reward is more responsive, full-featured, and cleaner applications. If you're a battle-tested Release 3 developer, you've experienced the gyrations that it forced you to execute in order to implement applications; when we say *cleaner applications*, we mean applications that don't require the seemingly inevitable kludges of the past!

NOTE   Apart from LotusScript, the only way you can access the underlying structure of Notes is through the Notes Application Programming Interface (API), which requires very sophisticated programming in C or C++, or through various third-party tools. Since these options offer little or no integration with the Notes client software, you almost have to re-create a Notes user interface from scratch. However, because LotusScript is embedded directly into Notes, you never have to leave the confines of the Notes environment.

LotusScript Is Everywhere

LotusScript is available in most Lotus products and some third-party products, as well. It is embedded in the majority of the applications in SmartSuite 97 for Windows 95, NT, and OS/2. LotusScript is also available in the newly released Lotus Components, which are functional building blocks, or "applets," (e.g., Chart engine, Cell engine, Drawing engine, Project Manager) that you can integrate into your Notes applications. Once you know how to use LotusScript, you can actually do some incredible cross-product integration.

The Differences between LotusScript and Formulas

One of the first questions that might occur to you (particularly if you've been developing Notes Release 3 applications and are a seasoned veteran of formulas) is, "When should I use LotusScript and when should I use formulas?" In some cases you don't have a choice because certain design objects support the use of only one or the other for certain events. (Recall from Chapter 18 that an *event* is some kind of occurrence in Notes that triggers an Action. Clicking a button is an example of an event.)

For example, you must use a formula to program the Input Translation event of an editable field—end of story. (*Input Translation* is an event that occurs when a document is saved or refreshed. In editable fields for which the Input Translation event has been defined, the contents of the fields are transformed in some way, for example, a text value is converted to uppercase.) However, the Exiting event of that same field will accept only LotusScript. (The Exiting event occurs when the insertion point is moved from the field to some other location.) This discrepancy becomes an issue when the design object supports either LotusScript or a formula for a given event.

When to Use a Formula

Suppose you have created an Action to appear as a button in the Action bar. Clicking the button can launch either a LotusScript program or a formula. Which one should you use? We suggest that formulas should be the rule, LotusScript the exception. To put this recommendation in simpler terms: If a formula can reasonably handle the functionality that you wish to implement, then use a formula. (Also, don't forget about the Simple actions that are available with many design objects, which can be used in place of formulas. You'll recall from earlier chapters that a Simple action is a predefined operation that Notes lets you choose with a few clicks of the mouse button.) Our intention is not to prejudice you against LotusScript (on the contrary, we love it!) but to give you a basic guideline to help you in your decision. If you are a novice Notes developer with little or no programming experience, your initial applications will typically not require the power of LotusScript.

When to Use a Script

On the other hand, if you are an experienced Notes developer and/or programmer, you'll really appreciate the control that LotusScript gives you over the Notes environment. You will probably want to jump right to writing scripts. The key is to strike a balance between formula and script usage; don't lock yourself into a formula-centric perspective (a possible pitfall if you've been using formulas for a long time) or a script-centric perspective (a possible pitfall if you are one of those programmer types). The combination of formulas and scripts affords you a tremendous amount of flexibility in how you develop your applications, so take advantage of it.

TIP   A formula will execute much faster than a similar script program.

A Few Additional Guidelines

The best way to approach the question of when to use scripts or formulas in your application is to place them in some kind of context to which you can compare your particular situation. In all cases, the deciding factor is the complexity of the functionality you're attempting. Ask yourself the following questions as part of your decision-making process.

Can a Simple Formula Perform the Same Operation as a LotusScript Program?

The following script closes the current open document when a user clicks the Close Document button, as shown in Figure 34.2.

```
Sub Click(Source As Button)
    Dim workspace As New NotesUIWorkspace
```

```
        Dim uidoc As NotesUIDocument
        Set uidoc = workspace.CurrentDocument
        Call uidoc.Close
   End Sub
```

The following formula achieves the same result:

```
@Command([FileCloseWindow])
```

Don't create complexity where it's not needed!

FIGURE 34.2:

The Close Document button of a form: a script and a formula can both accomplish the task of closing the current document, but using a formula is easier.

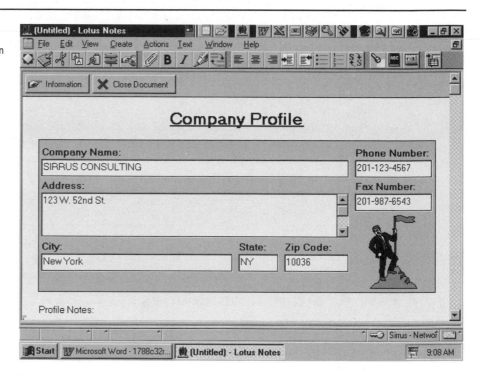

Is the Operation I Want to Perform Confined to the Design Object?

The question we're trying to answer here is whether the operation involves only the design object itself (or other immediately accessible objects), or does the scope of the operation involve going beyond the current context to other objects. If the answer to this question is that the operation involves only the design object, then a formula will probably suffice; otherwise, use LotusScript.

An example might be a button that calculates a value from several values entered into fields of the current document and then places that value in a field in the same document. The scope of the operation is completely confined to the current document, so a formula would probably do the trick. If the calculated value depended not only on values in the current document but also on values in other documents, or if the value was to be written to a field in another document, then a script would be a better choice.

How Do I Write a Script?

Scripts are written using the Integrated Development Environment, or IDE. *Integrated* is the operative word; the IDE lets you write, compile, and debug your scripts without ever leaving the Notes environment. The following components comprise the IDE:

- The Design pane
- The Debug window
- The Utility pane

Figure 34.3 shows the Design pane in which you enter and edit your scripts.

FIGURE 34.3:

You use the Design pane to write, compile, and debug scripts.

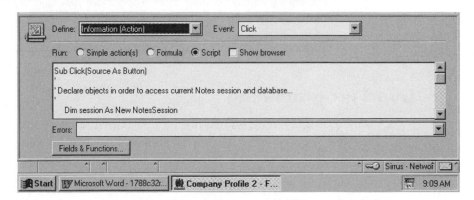

Programming 101

Before we dive into writing scripts, we want to discuss the concept of programming. What is *programming*? The term does not have a succinct definition. So many different tools provide so many different approaches to programming that the process defies an easy description.

While you might not have realized it, you've been programming all along if you've proceeded through this book and developed a Notes application. Notes is a programming methodology, but it is very different from the classic high-level, structured languages such as BASIC, COBOL, and C. Nevertheless, the end result is still *the application* that embodies whatever functionality you've designed into it.

With LotusScript, you have to depart from the largely "visual programming" you've performed with Notes thus far. If you're an old pro at the Notes formula language, you'll find that LotusScript is a radically different way of building automation into your applications. (Experience using the Notes formula language is quite valuable because it helps you figure out the *logic* of a process; it also forces you to become proficient in the ever-popular art of debugging.)

Coding is the term we use to describe the process of writing a program because it really captures the essence of the activity: Using a specific code (language), with all of its rules of syntax and structure, we describe a series of instructions to be carried out in a precise order. If we deviate from "legal code," the system we are using (in this case, Notes) will not be able to interpret the program and errors will occur.

NOTE Because LotusScript is a high-level language, the code we use to describe what is to be done is a fairly natural extension of our everyday language. Granted, LotusScript implements many shortcuts to keep programs concise, but you should still find this language easy to understand.

Good Programming

Good programming is not a mystery. Although individual programmers may choose to code a particular process in various ways, all well-constructed programs share some characteristics.

For our purposes, we'll consider the following characteristics as elements of good programming practices:

- Consistent structure (spacing, indentation) and naming conventions (case, symbols)

- Clear, concise comments that describe what is occurring in the program

- Explicit variable declaration (to be discussed later)
- Modular, reusable code

With any kind of programming language, such as LotusScript, unstructured, inconsistent, and undocumented code is difficult to maintain. Remember that someone else may have to modify your code in the future; the small amount of extra time you spend to make your programs readable and easy to follow will save work. (If that's not enough to motivate you to practice good programming methods, just consider the possibility that *you* may be the person who has to modify your code after six or seven months.)

Object-Oriented Programming

LotusScript provides extensions that allow you to access and manipulate a variety of Notes structures, or *objects*. These extensions are called classes. A *class* is a LotusScript programming construct that lets you record and retrieve information for an object and take action relative to an object. In the Notes environment, databases, documents, views, and Agents are examples of objects. Each object is derived from a class, which dictates an object's characteristics and the operations that can be performed in relation to it.

Before Release 4, classes and objects were largely masked to the developer. While some rudimentary capability was provided for creating and destroying objects through formulas (databases and documents), no serious means existed within Notes for performing complex operations on objects. You could, for instance, create a new database on the fly in Release 3, but you couldn't automatically assign access control rights to it. That version of Notes forced you to take mouse in hand and manually make the assignments. With Release 4 and LotusScript, you can create a database and build its ACL in a completely programmatic way.

An application can now reach out for information across a Notes network. For example, while a user edits a document in one database, he or she can open another database, search its contents for a document about a particular topic, and bring that information into the original document in a way that is completely transparent.

What Are Objects and What Do They Do?

The mysterious world of objects and object-oriented programming! Before proceeding to bigger and better things, you should fully grasp the concept of classes and objects in a general sense.

Without getting into gruesome detail, objects are the outward representation of a class. All right, before your eyes start to glaze over, let's put this in a context that you can easily understand by relating classes and objects in the programming world to objects and classes in the real world.

Classes and Objects—A Simple Analogy

"Automobile" represents a category or *class* of object that we encounter almost every day. As a class, Automobile does not represent a specific car; it is a general description for a particular means of conveyance. As it turns out, Automobile comprises a collection of constituent classes of objects. Generally speaking, we can identify the *components* of Automobile, each with its own form and function, as follows:

- Body
- Interior
- Tires
- Engine
- Transmission
- Brakes

Automobile is just the assemblage of a series of parts. Each part represents a class of object and may be broken down into its own constituent parts. A class of object, therefore, may embody or *contain* other classes of objects.

NOTE   The Automobile class in our example is itself part of a larger class that we can call Mode of Transportation.

Another aspect to our description of the Automobile class is the characteristics or *properties* of this class of object. We can say that Automobile has the following properties associated with it:

- Make
- Model
- Year

Finally, we need to identify operations or *methods* that are associated with the Automobile class. These operations describe the actions that are linked to the particular class:

- Designed

- Manufactured

- Purchased

- Driven

- Junked

Our description of a class, then, encompasses three areas:

- Components, or classes contained within the class

- Characteristics called *properties*

- Operations called *methods*

Moving beyond generalities, we can cite an actual example of the class Automobile, such as Chevrolet Corvette; *Corvette* is an instance, or *object*, of the Automobile class and, therefore, embodies the components, properties, and methods of Automobile.

TIP   Think of *class* as the generic description of an *object* and think of object as a tangible representation of a class.

Classes and Objects in Notes

In Notes, Database (formally called NotesDatabase) is an example of a class of object. Like Automobile, it doesn't represent a specific database, but is a general description that encompasses its components, properties, and methods. For components, we can specify:

- Documents

- Views

- Agents

- Access Control List (ACL)

For properties, we can specify:

- File name
- Title
- Date created
- Size

and for methods, we can specify:

- Create
- Open
- Search
- Remove

This listing is not an exhaustive description of the Database class. Notes defines many more properties and methods than are listed here.

When you create a database, you're establishing a Database class object, just as a Corvette is an instance of the Automobile class. With most of the classes of objects supported in Notes, you can access the properties and methods associated with a class through the Notes graphical interface, and, more relevant to our discussion here, through LotusScript programming. (In the case of a database, you can choose File ➤ Database ➤ Properties to view and manipulate its properties.)

The point is that objects and object-oriented programming give you control over the Notes environment in ways that formulas cannot. The following code represents a very simple example using objects in LotusScript, as illustrated by Figure 34.4.

In this example the code is associated with the Click event of a button that appears in a form:

```
Sub Click(Source As Button)
'
' This script retrieves information about the current Notes
' session
'
```

```
' Declare object reference variables...
'
    Dim session As New NotesSession
    Dim db As NotesDatabase
    Set db = session.CurrentDatabase
'
' Display message box with information about the
' current session...
'
    Messagebox "Running " & session.NotesVersion _
    & Chr(10) & "User is " & session.CommonUserName _
    & Chr(10) & "Current database is " & db.Title,,"Current Session
    ➥ Information"
End Sub
```

FIGURE 34.4:

A form with an Information button that provides details about the current Notes session

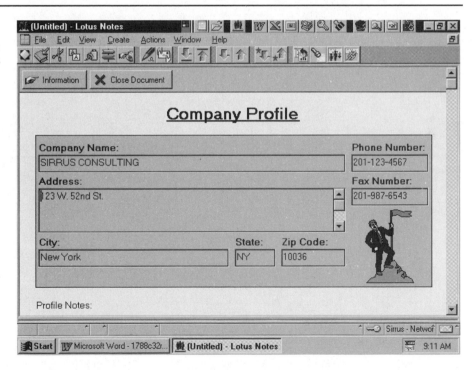

Clicking the button invokes a dialog box that displays information about the current Notes session, as shown in Figure 34.5.

FIGURE 34.5:

The result of clicking the
Information button

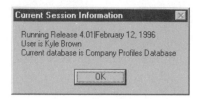

The Tale of Classes

Most programming languages support several built-in data types, such as integer, double, or string; each data type represents a class of value that can be handled in the language. When your program needs to deal with a specific type of data, you declare *variables* and "type" them accordingly. For example, you might declare a variable called CurrentBalance as type double because your program needs to handle double-precision values (which are typical of dollar amounts).

The C++ programming language introduced a new mechanism, called a *class*. Classes enable you to define your own data types. For example, you can define a class called BankAccount and then declare an *object* of type BankAccount; an *object* is an *instance* of a class just like a variable is an instance of built-in data type. The definition of our class includes all of the attributes of a bank account, including the name, address, and telephone number of the owner; the account number; the type of account; and the current balance. The other critical aspect of the definition of our class is the possible actions involving the bank account, such as how money is debited, credited, or transferred. In other words, the class definition includes not only what is to be stored in an object of this type, but also the *behavior* or *operations* associated with the object.

This type of programming is called *object-oriented programming* because you define the objects as you use classes. What does this have to do with Notes and LotusScript? Everything! First, Notes is an object-based environment; databases, views, forms, fields, Agents, buttons, layout regions, document links, and every other design element are objects based on predefined classes that are built into Notes. We've referred to these as design objects throughout the book. Being able to create these objects without writing a single line of code is a tribute to the Notes graphical interface, which completely shields you from the complexity of classes and objects you would normally face using a programming language like C++. Nevertheless, the largely visual programming environment of Notes can't always give you the level of functionality you need in certain applications. Therefore, the Notes implementation of LotusScript makes many of the predefined classes available at a structured programming language level. The ability to go beyond the predefined classes and construct entirely new classes, and therefore new objects, is the feature that ultimately makes LotusScript object oriented.

Containment

One of the more abstract, although critical, concepts in object-oriented programming is the notion of *containment*. Containment amounts to a box within a box within a box...; in other words, Notes must access certain structures before it can access other structures.

In our Automobile analogy, we stated that the Automobile class encompasses other classes of objects, such as Engine. Let's say that the engine of a car requires repair. (*Repair* is a method associated with Engine.) To gain access to the engine, you must raise the hood, which is part of the car's body. So we say that Engine is a class of object that is contained by Body; before you can access one, you must access the other. The essence of containment is a progression that you have to respect in order to get at the thing you want to get to.

In Notes, for example, if you want to write a script that accesses a field in an open document, you first must access the document itself, which means that you have to access the Workspace in which the document is opened. The field is contained by a document, which is contained within the Notes Workspace. As we navigate upward through the hierarchy, each succeeding structure is a *container class* of the class that preceded it. (The previous example is a slight simplification of the concept, but we hope you get the idea.) Once you get the hang of it, containment will be something that you automatically account for in your LotusScript code. For now, keep the concept in mind as we proceed through examples of LotusScript in which objects are referenced.

Events and Event-Driven Programming

In Chapter 18 we introduced the concept of *events* and *event-driven programming*. We'll pick up the discussion again, this time in the context of LotusScript because scripts (as well as formulas) are intimately bound to events. In fact, scripts are meaningless without events.

You'll recall from the discussion in Chapter 18 that everything that happens in Notes, from the perspective of the end user, is a reaction to some event. A database opens because its icon was double-clicked from the Workspace; an Agent runs because a predefined time interval has expired; a new document is created because a form is selected from the Create menu. As an application developer you tie scripts to those events in which a specific reaction is required.

The events that an object "respects" vary from object to object. For instance, in considering the typical events that surround a field in a document, we can build an "event list" that includes:

- Navigated to (entered)

- Navigated from (exited)

- Translated

- Validated

(Notes defines other events for fields that aren't important to our discussion here.) The point we're making is that certain objects have certain events associated with them, which may be controlled by a program. Notes does not force you to create a script relative to an event; you decide which events to develop scripts for. As we mentioned previously, certain events for design objects can be responded to only with formulas, others with LotusScript, and still others with either formulas or LotusScript.

What's Next?

So far, we've only scratched the surface of what programming with LotusScript is all about. Next, we'll describe how to use the Notes Integrated Development Environment (IDE) for building, compiling, and debugging scripts. We'll also take a closer look at the LotusScript language, including variables and constants, iteration and flow control, and a variety of built-in functions and statements that you can incorporate into your programs.

CHAPTER
THIRTY-FIVE

35

Writing Scripts in LotusScript

- Understanding the Integrated Development Environment

- Structuring your scripts

- Declaring variables in LotusScript

- Using arrays and lists

- Declaring and using constants

- Using flow control and iteration

- Working with functions and statements in LotusScript

- Using the IDE debugger

- Working with script libraries

As a high-level, structured, object-oriented programming language, Lotus-Script contains many elements. In this chapter we show how to construct a script, explain the more salient features of LotusScript, and suggest some practical, everyday uses for scripts. This chapter discusses:

- Working in the Integrated Development Environment (IDE)
- Using the Design pane
- Structuring scripts
- Using Elements of the LotusScript language
- Debugging scripts

This chapter is a primer to the LotusScript environment. More advanced information is available in the documentation that accompanies Notes and in the Help database.

The Integrated Development Environment

To help you develop and debug your scripts more easily, Notes includes an Integrated Development Environment, or IDE. The rationale behind the IDE is to make the task of programming look and feel the same throughout all Lotus products. In the context of Notes, both scripts and formulas are created through the IDE.

The components of the IDE are:

- The Design pane
- The debug window
- The Utility pane

While you are in Form Design mode, the only component of the IDE that is visible is the Design pane. The debug window and its associated Utility pane are visible only when you have "turned on" script debugging and are testing a form by using Design ➤ Test Form or by accessing a document based on the form. We'll talk about debugging in more detail later in this chapter. Figures 35.1 and 35.2 show the Design pane and debug window/Utility pane components of the Notes IDE.

FIGURE 35.1:

The Design pane component of the IDE in Notes

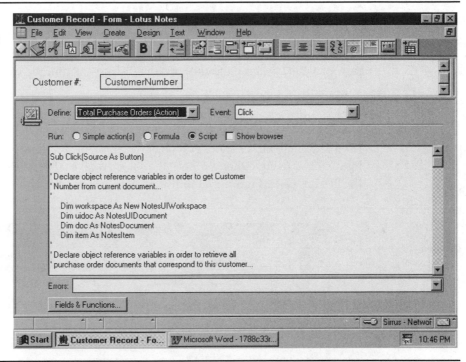

FIGURE 35.2:

The debug window and utility pane components of the IDE in Notes

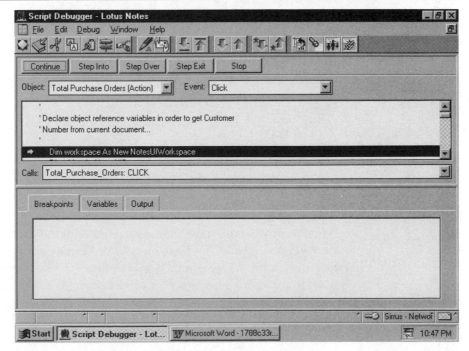

Entering a Script in the Design Pane

To create a script for a design object, you first have to select the design object and then choose the event that you wish to program for that design object. For this purpose, the Design pane contains the Define box and the Event box.

The Define box lists all objects that are available to you in the current context. For example, if you are in Form Design mode, the list will contain all the scriptable design objects in the form, including fields, Actions, buttons, and the form itself. You may either choose an object from the list or simply click on the object in the form; using either method, the selected object becomes the current object in the Design pane. Figure 35.3 shows an example of a list of objects related to a form.

FIGURE 35.3:

An example of objects that appear in the Define box while a form is being designed

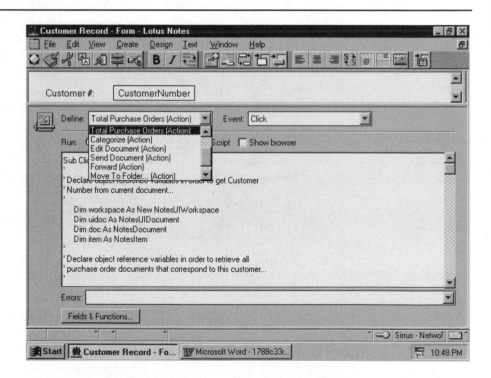

The Events box lists all the events associated with the current object. This list will vary depending on the type of object. (You'll notice that certain events, like *Initialize* and *Terminate*, are common to all objects.) Choose the event for which you want to construct the script. Figure 35.4 shows the events that are associated with a field in a form.

FIGURE 35.4:

The list of events that appears in the Event box for a field

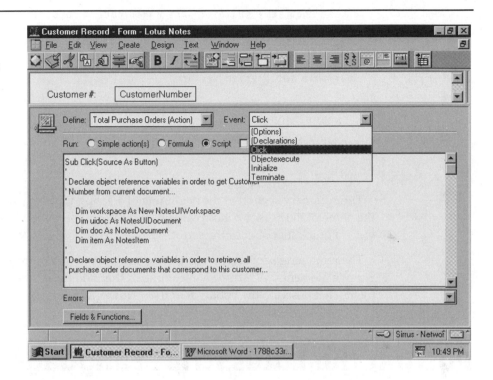

Once you've decided upon the object and event, you're ready to write your script. (We'll return to the topic of debugging scripts later in the chapter.)

How to Structure Your Scripts

You should try to establish a consistent, intelligent structure for the scripts you create. Doing so makes your scripts more readable and easier to maintain, for your own sake as well as for others who may need to modify your scripts in the future. The extra minutes you devote to this effort will make your life much easier later!

There's no *absolutely right* method for structuring scripts. However, we've found that the following structure works well:

```
Sub <name of sub>
'
' Description: <short description of script>
' Author: <name of script creator>
```

```
' Last Modified: <date of last modification to script>
' Modified By: <name of person who last modified script>
' Description of Changes: <short summary of changes to script>
'

<variable declaration section>

<initial Set commands for assigning objects>

<body of script>

End Sub
```

The summary section at the beginning of a script, which includes a description, the name of the person who created it, and information about modifications, provides a quick snapshot of the script.

The remaining sections in our sample structure above represent actual Lotus-Script statements. We strongly recommend that you make liberal use of comments that describe the behavior of the script within each section.

Putting the LotusScript Language to Work

With the preliminaries out of the way, we are ready to put the LotusScript language to work. The next few sections discuss some key elements of LotusScript and should be more than enough to get you on your feet. The best way to learn how to write scripts is to simply start writing (with a little coaching). You'll find that working with form design objects, specifically fields and buttons, is the easiest platform from which to launch your "scripting career." Once you get the hang of writing scripts in the context of form design, you can add Navigators and Agents.

In the previous chapter we stated that Notes (forget LotusScript for the moment) is a visual programming environment. When you examine the similarities between the graphical design elements of Notes (fields in a form, for instance) and the various language elements of a high-level programming language like LotusScript (variables, for instance), you will begin to see how Notes application development is really just an abstraction of traditional programming methods.

Variables

Variables are part of virtually every LotusScript program. You establish or *declare* variables to temporarily hold values that you need to use in your script. As the term *variable* implies, the value it represents can change at any time. The following block of code shows an example of variable declaration and usage:

```
Dim currentDir As String

currentDir = CurDir$()
MessageBox currentDir
...
```

You declare variables using the Dim statement and assign a data type to them using the As <data type> clause. The variable *currentdir* is declared as type String and assigned the value returned by the CurDir$ function in LotusScript. The MessageBox statement displays the value of *currentdir* in a dialog box. The value assigned to a variable must match the data type of the variable; otherwise, errors will occur.

In Chapter 18 we talked about variables in the context of Notes formulas and saw that fields in a document are actually variables themselves; each field holds a value, yet the value can be changed either directly by a user or through an automatic calculation. For example, in the following Notes formula, LastName is a reference to a text field defined within a form.

```
@UpperCase(LastName)
```

The @UpperCase function will be applied to whatever the value of LastName happens to be at the time this formula is evaluated.

Practically speaking, variables in a script behave in a way that is almost identical to fields in forms and formulas. Like fields, variables hold a value and have a data type associated with them; the data type dictates what kind of information they can hold. (Because field values are typically saved to disk, the way a field "holds" its value differs from the way a variable holds its value. The value of a variable in a script is maintained *in memory* only while the script is executing, after which it is discarded.) Table 35.1 shows the scalar data types for variables that are recognized by LotusScript.

TABLE 35.1: Scalar Data Types for Variables

Data Type	Value Can Be	Similar Data Type in Notes
Integer	Any integer from −32,768 to 32,767	Numeric
Long	Any integer from −2,147,483,648 to 2,147,483,647	Numeric
Single	Any single-precision, floating point number from −3.402823E+38 to 3.402823E+38	Numeric
Double	Any double-precision, floating point number from −1.7976931348623158E+308 to 1.7976931348623158E+308	Numeric
Currency	Any fixed-point integer scaled to four decimal places from −922,337,203,685,477.5807 to 922,337,203,685,477.5807	Numeric
String	Any combination of legal characters from 0 to 32KB in size (64KB)	Text

You may have noticed that the LotusScript data types do not look like any of the field data types in Notes, although there are similarities between the two. LotusScript also supports the data structures shown in Table 35.2 (so called because they are able to hold multiple values at once).

TABLE 35.2: Data Structures Supported by LotusScript

Data Type	Value Can Be	Similar Data Type in Notes
Array	Any set of values, possibly of different data types (up to 64KB)	Multivalue field
List	Any set of values of the same data type	Multivalue field

We still need to mention one other data type—the *Variant*. A variable of type Variant can hold any of the types of values listed above, as well as other data types, namely, date/time values and Boolean (True/False) values.

NOTE   A variable will default to type Variant if you declare it without explicitly stating its type with an As <data type> clause in the Dim statement.

To assign a date/time value to a variable of type Variant, you can use one of the built-in LotusScript functions that return a date/time value, as shown in the following example:

```
Dim todaysDate, yesterdaysDate As Variant
todaysDate = Today
yesterdaysDate = todaysDate - 1
...
```

Arrays and Lists

Turning our attention back to forms and fields for a moment, Notes supports fields that can hold more than one value at a time, known as *multivalue fields*. The individual values, or *elements*, held by a multivalue field must all be the same type (text, numeric, etc.). LotusScript provides similar functionality by letting you declare *arrays* and *lists,* which can also hold several values at once. You utilize arrays and lists when you want to capture a set of related values for access later in the script.

Arrays

An *array* resembles a multivalue field insofar as it can hold multiple values. However, an array can be much more complex in terms of how elements within it are organized and much more functional in that it allows easy access to individual elements. An array has a characteristic associated with it called *dimension*. The simplest type of array is a one-dimensional array; the elements are essentially held as a list of linked items. (Multivalue fields are basically one-dimensional arrays.) The following example shows how to declare a one-dimensional array:

```
Dim myArray(1 to 10) As String
```

The result is *myArray*, which can hold a maximum of ten elements, all of type String. The number 1 represents the *lower boundary* of the array, and the number 10 represents the *upper boundary* of the array. You could then put values into the array as follows:

```
myArray(1) = "This"
myArray(2) = "LotusScript"
myArray(3) = "stuff"
myArray(4) = "is"
myArray(5) = "much"
myArray(6) = "easier"
myArray(7) = "than"
myArray(8) = "I"
```

```
myArray(9) = "ever"
myArray(10) = "thought"
```

You refer to a position in an array through its "index," or *subscript*. The subscripts 1, 2, 3,... above dictate the position at which the text strings are stored in the array. Likewise, you access individual elements in an array by their subscripts, as shown in the following example:

```
Print myArray(2)
```

This statement prints the string "LotusScript" to the status bar at the bottom of the screen. A *multidimensional array* allows you to create fairly complex structures for storing related values. For example, with a two-dimensional array you can construct a list of lists, with a three-dimensional array a list of list of lists, and so on, up to eight dimensions. (We've never seen an eight-dimensional array, nor do we know of a situation in which you'd need one, but LotusScript lets you create one just in case the need arises!)

The following statement declares a two-dimensional array:

```
Dim myArray(1 to 12, 1 to 31) As String
```

The result creates an array *myArray* with a dimension of 12 by 31. We might use such an array to capture information relating to each day of the year. Populating a multidimensional array is not much harder than populating a single-dimension array except that you must account for extra dimension(s). For example:

```
myArray(1,1) = "New Years Day"
myArray(7,4) = "Fourth of July"
myArray(12,25) = "Christmas"
```

As with all arrays, you make reference to a position in the array using subscripts. Once you move beyond a single-dimension array, you have to include additional subscripts to pinpoint an element's position.

TIP   Think of a two-dimensional array as a table with rows and columns. The position of each element simply becomes the intersection of its row and column numbers.

Lists

A *list* is a simple set of related values of the same data type. It behaves like a one-dimensional array except the method of referencing elements in a list uses *tags*, rather than subscripts. A list tag is a String value that labels an element in a list, making the process of accessing elements more intuitive than with numeric subscripts. For instance, you could declare a list as follows:

```
Dim myList List as String
```

Lists do not have dimension associated with them because they are always effectively one dimensional. Also, lists are not assigned an upper boundary that restricts them to *n* number of elements. (We draw the comparison to arrays to make the concept of a list easier to understand. Technically, lists are not arrays, so we must be careful about taking the comparison too far.) To put values into a list, you'd do the following:

```
myList("First Name") = "Jackie"
myList("Last Name") = "Beck"
<continue adding elements to the list>
...
```

Constants

Constants are names you assign to key *static* values that you reference within a script or across several scripts. Declaring and using constants gives your scripts a cleaner, more readable appearance. In addition, constants make your scripts easier to maintain by letting you change recurring values quickly. For example, the following block of code has multiple references to a value that represents a "fringe benefits multiplier" (1.3), which is applied to an employee's yearly salary:

```
emp1totalcost = emp1salary * 1.3
emp2totalcost = emp2salary * 1.3
    .
    .
    .
```

The effect is to add 30 percent to an employee's salary to account for the cost of fringe benefits (medical insurance, 401K plan, etc.). But what if management decides to calculate fringe benefits at 35 percent? In modifying your script to reflect the new percentage, you'd have to change 1.3 to 1.35 in *every* place where the value occurs. If you happen to overlook an occurrence or accidentally enter an incorrect value, your script will produce erroneous results. However, if you initially wrote the script as follows, this task would be trivial:

```
Const FRINGE = 1.3
emp1totalcost = emp1salary * FRINGE
```

```
emp2totalcost = emp2salary * FRINGE
.
.
.
```

The Const statement establishes a constant named FRINGE, whose value is fixed (i.e., held constant) at 1.3. Wherever the constant appears in the script, the value 1.3 is substituted. If the percentage needs to be changed to 35 percent in the future, you simply change the value of the constant FRINGE to 1.35.

You should make use of constants whenever your scripts contain static values that are subject to change and/or referenced frequently.

> **TIP**   A Const statement may appear anywhere in a script, but for the sake of consistency, you should declare constants at the beginning of the script.

Flow Control and Iteration

A Notes formula executes its operations from top to bottom, in a process called *top-down execution,* without exception. Script execution generally proceeds in the same way, although you have many options at your disposal for altering this progression, a concept known as *flow control.* (We'll explain why you might want to use flow control very shortly.) Unlike scripts, the formula language has very few mechanisms for controlling the flow of operations, namely, the following functions:

- @If: Allows for conditional execution of an operation

- @Return: Halts the evaluation of a formula

True flow control means the ability to precisely dictate the progression of the operations in your programs, and LotusScript provides several methods for accomplishing flow control:

- **Iteration:** A sequence of statements is executed a predetermined number of times or until a particular condition is satisfied.

- **Branching:** The top-down execution of a script is interrupted and routed to another point in the script. Execution may return to and continue at the location where the interruption ("branch point") occurred.

- **Termination:** A script, or an iterative process within a script, is prematurely terminated before reaching its "natural" end.

Using Iteration

Iteration, or looping, is extremely useful when you need to repeat a sequence of statements either a predetermined number of times or until a specific condition is satisfied. In this discussion, we'll focus on two of the iteration mechanisms found in LotusScript: the For and Do statements.

The For Statement

The following code sample calculates a total for an order amount value that appears in several purchase order documents. (The full script appears in the next chapter.)

```
...
' Cycle through all documents in current collection, get value
' of POAMOUNT field, build total purchase order value...
'
pototal = 0
For x = 1 To collection.Count
  Set doc = collection.GetNthDocument(x)
  Set item = doc.GetFirstItem("POAMOUNT")
  poamount = item.Values(0)
  pototal = pototal + poamount
Next x
...
```

The For statement executes a block of statements a particular number of times. The program initializes the variable x, called *counter*, to the value 1 and then compares x to the value of *collection.Count*. If the value of x does not exceed the value of *collection.Count*, the block of statements that follows is executed. When the Next statement, called the "terminator," is encountered, the value of x is incremented by 1 and execution returns to the For statement above. Once again, the value of x (this time, one greater than its previous value) is compared to the value of *collection.Count*, and the whole process begins again. When the value of x is incremented beyond the value of *collection.Count*, execution jumps from the For statement to the MessageBox statement below. Notice, as well, that x is used as an index for the GetNth Document method.

You may initialize a counter variable to any value you wish:

```
For x = 100 To 200
...
Next x
```

You may alter the step value by which a counter is incremented. In the following example, the Step keyword increments the value of *x* by two for each iteration:

```
For x = 1 To 1000 Step 2
...
Next x
```

A variation of the For statement lets you *decrement* the counter, as opposed to incrementing it; decrementing has the effect of a countdown:

```
For x = 1000 To 1 Step -1
...
Next x
```

The Do Statement

The Do statement executes a block of statements *while* a condition remains True or *until* a condition becomes True. The Do statement has several variations that alter how a loop is evaluated.

NOTE   Recall that in the For statement the comparison of a counter to an ending value occurred at the beginning of the loop. If the value of the counter exceeds the ending value at the outset, execution immediately jumps to the statement beyond the terminator and the block of statements within the loop never gets executed.

With the Do statement, you can place the comparison operation either at the beginning of the loop or at the end of loop, or you can forgo the comparison altogether. The form you use depends on whether you want the block of statements within the loop to be executed *at least once*, in which case you'd put the comparison operation at the end.

The following examples express a Do loop in two different ways:

```
x = 0
Do While x < 500
  x = x + 1
Loop

x = 0
Do Until x > 500
  x = x + 1
Loop
```

Both examples initialize a variable x to the value 0 and then compare x to an end value, 500. Although the difference may seem subtle, using the While keyword versus the Until keyword changes the entire logic of the loop. The While form says, "Keep looping as long as the condition remains true," whereas the Until form says, "Keep looping until the condition becomes true." The terminator for the Do loop is the Loop statement.

As mentioned, you can place the comparison operation at the end of a Do loop to ensure that at least one iteration of the block of statements is executed:

```
x = 0
Do
 x = x + 1
Loop While x < 500

x = 0
Do
 x = x + 1
Loop Until x > 500
```

The Politics of GoSub and GoTo

Some programming "purists" frown on the use of GoSub and GoTo (or variations of the two). The traditional opinion about these mechanisms is that they lend themselves to creating unstructured, undisciplined coding because they allow for ad hoc branching and do not support parameter passing. Abuse of GoSub and GoTo can produce code that is very untidy and difficult to maintain. While we won't go as far as saying, "Thou shalt not use GoSub or GoTo," we strongly recommend that you carefully consider creating a separate *sub* in cases where you want to partition a sub block of code from your main program. You can then invoke the sub using the CALL statement.

Branching

Branching is a programming technique in which the normal top-down execution of a script is interrupted by execution "jumping" to another point in the script. The LotusScript statements GoTo and GoSub, along with variations of the two statements, let you redirect execution to a labeled statement elsewhere in the script.

LotusScript Functions and Statements

You recall that the Notes formula language has an extensive set of prepackaged formulas called @functions and @commands, which let you perform a variety of actions on data in your Notes database. The LotusScript language has an equally extensive set of elements known as *functions* and *statements*.

Functions

LotusScript functions are very similar to Notes formula @functions; in fact, you will discover that many LotusScript functions and formula @functions are identical in both name and behavior.

A function performs an operation that *returns a value*. For this reason, functions are often found to the right of the "=" (the assignment operator in LotusScript) as part of a variable assignment operation. For example, the following statement uses the Trim$ function to remove leading and trailing spaces from the value stored by the variable *FirstName* and assigns the result to the variable *trim_fname*:

```
trim_fname = Trim$(FirstName)
```

Functions can also be employed as arguments to other functions (or statements, discussed below). In the following statement, the value returned by the Date$ function is used as the first argument to the Right$ function:

```
Right$(Date$,2)
```

If Date$ returned 07/04/96, the Right$ function would return the two rightmost characters, 96.

The value returned by a function has a specific data type associated with it: String, Integer, Variant, etc. When using functions to assign values to variables or as arguments, the data type returned by the function must match what each context expects. For example, don't attempt to assign a value to a variable of type String using a function that returns a value of type Integer!

Statements

The LotusScript language uses statements to execute an action; these statements are akin to @commands in the Notes formula language. Whereas functions return a value, statements do not. When a statement is executed, the task indicated by the statement is performed and execution then continues. The following statement displays a value to the user in a dialog box:

```
Messagebox "Total Purchase Orders from starting date = " _
& Format(pototal, "Currency"),,"Total Purchase Orders"
```

Many of the keywords we've discussed, such as Dim and Const, and the flow control and iteration mechanisms For and Do are examples of statements.

NOTE At times a LotusScript statement can double as a function. MessageBox, for example, has both a statement and a function form. In the case of the latter, MessageBox can be used to return a response to a prompt, such as Yes or No.

Debugging Your Scripts

Unless you're very good or very lucky, the scripts you write will occasionally contain errors. Many of the errors that newcomers to LotusScript encounter are *syntax related*, meaning that a particular instruction was not formatted correctly. As you write scripts using the IDE, the Errors text box at the bottom of the Design pane reports syntax errors to you immediately. Figure 35.5 shows an example of a syntax error.

To understand how Notes catches errors in scripts, you have to become familiar with the process that translates a script into a low-level, executable format, known as *compilation*.

NOTE Even if you've never programmed before, you've probably heard the term compiler. A compiler is a programming tool that converts a program written in a high-level language to machine code, which is a very low-level (binary) representation of your program. Compilation makes the program executable within the microprocessor/operating system environment in which the program is intended to run.

Compilation in Notes is a two-phase process. As you enter a script line by line in the Design pane, Notes performs a partial compilation on each line in order to discover syntax errors. If it finds an error, an error message appears in the Errors text box, along with the line number of the offending instruction. When you save

FIGURE 35.5:

The Errors text box of the IDE Design pane reports syntax errors.

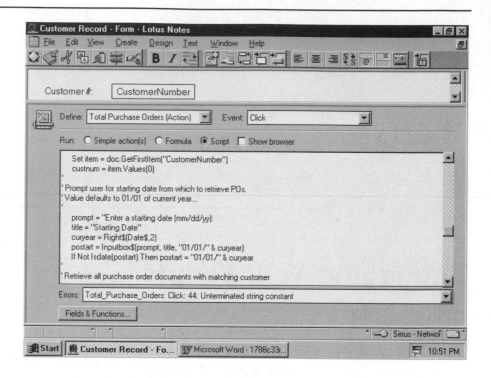

the script, Notes performs a full compilation on the script and reports any other *compile-time* errors that exist. A typical compile-time error occurs when you attempt to assign a variable of one data type a value of another data type (e.g., a numeric value to a String variable). This assignment would produce a "type mismatch" error in the Errors text box, along with the line number where the error was detected.

Unfortunately, not all errors can be detected at compile time. *Run-time* errors are encountered when the script is actually executed as part of the normal function of the application and are reported at that time. Notes will display a dialog box that indicates what the error is, as shown in Figure 35.6.

Using the Debugger

Your script isn't doing what you think it should be doing? You're getting run-time errors, and you can't figure out why? You've been staring at your script for thirty minutes, and you can't figure out what's wrong with it? It's time to use the IDE debugger.

FIGURE 35.6:

A Notes application reports a run-time error.

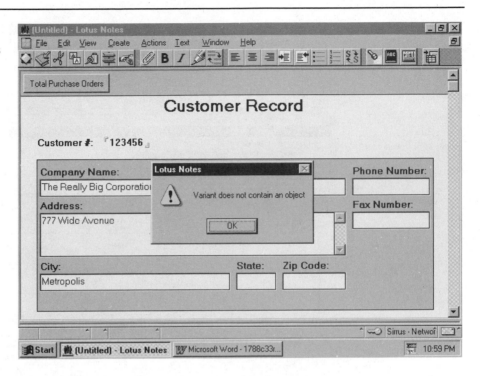

NOTE   Only scripts can be debugged using the IDE debugger. The debugger does not support *formulas*.

The IDE debugger lets you step through your script, executing one line at a time, or a series of lines up to a designated breakpoint. Using the debugger lets you isolate the problem. As you step through the script, you can examine and even set the value of variables that you've declared. To enable the debugger, choose File ➤ Tools ➤ Debug LotusScript. A check mark next to the option indicates that the debugger is activated. The debug window will now appear for each script that is executed in your application, as shown in Figure 35.7. To deactivate debugging, choose File ➤ Tools ➤ Debug LotusScript again, making sure that the check mark no longer appears next to the option.

FIGURE 35.7:

A script as it appears in the debug mode

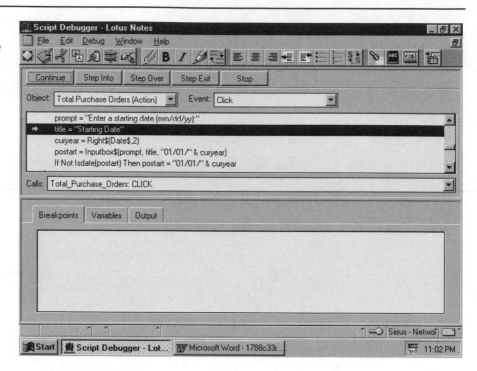

NOTE

The debug window will appear *once* for each script executed within the current context. For example, if you open a document that contains a button for which a script has been written and then click the button, the debug window will appear, allowing you to step through the script. Once you've completed debugging the script, the debug window will close. Clicking the button again, *with the same document still open*, will not result in the debug window being opened a second time. The script has already been debugged once within the current context, the open document. You must close the document and then reopen it if you want to debug the same script again.

Single-Stepping through a Script

The easiest way to debug a script using the debugger is the single-step method:

1. Click the Step Into button; the line in the script with the yellow pointer to its left is executed. The pointer moves to the next statement.

2. Repeat to execute each succeeding statement.

Using Breakpoints

It might not always be necessary to single-step through an entire script. If you have an idea where the problem lies, you can set a breakpoint in your script. With a breakpoint in place, the debugger will execute all statements prior to the breakpoint without interruption. When execution hits the breakpoint, it halts. At this point you can examine variable values, single-step through the remainder of the script, or do both. To implement breakpoints, do the following:

1. Scroll through the script in the Script Debugger window to find the line where you wish to place the breakpoint.

2. Double-click the line. A stop sign symbol appears to the left of the line, as shown in Figure 35.8.

FIGURE 35.8:

A breakpoint appears as a stop sign symbol.

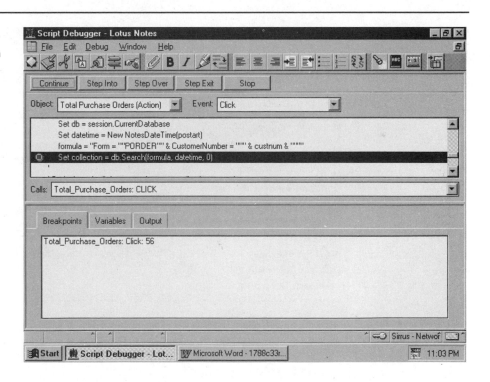

3. Click the Continue button. The script will execute without interruption until the statement just prior to the breakpoint.

To disable or clear a breakpoint:

1. Scroll through the script to find the breakpoint.

2. Double-click the line. A yellow slash appears through the stop sign symbol, disabling the breakpoint.

3. Double-click the line again. The stop sign symbol disappears, clearing the breakpoint.

Examining and Setting the Value of Variables as You Debug

The Utility pane in the bottom portion of the debug window contains three tabs that you can use to display different information about your script. The Variables tab lets you examine and set the value of variables used in the script as you step through it, as shown in Figure 35.9.

FIGURE 35.9:

The Variables tab of the Utility pane shows the current value of variables in your script and also lets you set their values.

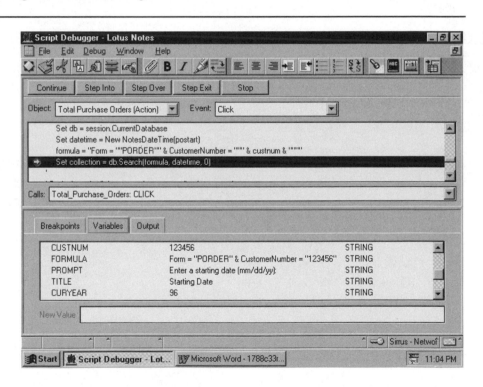

Click the Variables tab to display the current value of variables in the script. If you want to assign a value to a variable, select it from the list and enter a value in the New Value box at the bottom of the Utility pane.

Using Script Libraries

Notes allows you to create and maintain script libraries. A script library contains (Option), (Declaration), Initialize, Terminate, and User scripts. To create a script library, choose Create ➤ Design ➤ Script Library. To access a script library, choose View ➤ Design, click Script Libraries under Design, and double-click the name of the library.

The script library appears as a Design pane. To name the library, choose Edit ➤ Properties. To write code in a script, select the script in the Event box.

To write a new script, enter a statement such as Function or Sub in an existing script. The editor automatically creates a new script and transfers your code there.

To incorporate a script library into a scriptable object, enter a Use statement in the (Options) script for the object. For example, to make the Market2 script library available to a form's script, enter the following statement in the (Declarations) script for the form:

```
Use "Market2"
```

The name is case insensitive and should not contain spaces. Specify the name as a character literal (previous example) or named constant (following example):

```
Const m2 = "Market2" Use m2
```

The code in the (Options), (Declarations), Initialize, and Terminate scripts of the library becomes available as though it were in the current object's corresponding scripts. User scripts in the library become available as though they were in the current object.

The scope of a script library is the current database. All scripts in a database can avail themselves of the code in a library in that database. However, the library is lost to scripts outside the database. For example, if a button in a document uses a script library and you mail the document to or paste it in another database that does not have the same script library, the script fails. If a script attempts to use a library not in the current database, you see the following error message: "Error loading USE or USELSX module."

What's Next?

Hold on to your seats. The final chapter of this book explains how to use *Notes classes*, the object-oriented extensions that come with Notes. More so than any other element of LotusScript, classes let you add incredible functionality to your Notes applications.

CHAPTER

THIRTY-SIX

The Notes Class Library

- Exploring a class library case study

- Working with object references and object reference variables

- Understanding properties and methods

- Working with and retrieving the value of an item from a current document

- Going beyond the current document

- Retrieving a subset of database documents

- Completing the execution of the script

The Notes class library is a collection of object-oriented extensions to the Lotus-Script language. These extensions are called *classes* and give you, as the database designer, ultimate control over virtually all the design objects in the Notes environment. These extensions expose much of the underlying structure of Notes so that it can be accessed and manipulated programmatically at a low level.

Databases, views, documents, fields, Agents, embedded objects, and other objects that make up your application are now under your direct control. While these riches add complexity to your development efforts, the reward is more responsive, full-featured, and "cleaner" applications. When we say cleaner applications, we mean applications that don't require the seemingly inevitable kludges that you probably experienced in the past! (If you're a battle-tested Lotus Notes Release 3 developer, you've experienced the gyrations that this version forces you to execute in order to get your applications to work.)

In this chapter we discuss what we consider to be the "essential" classes that are available in the library. (The library also contains several other classes, but we'll leave you to explore them on your own.) To illustrate how to use these classes, we will concentrate on a single script that incorporates all the classes we wish to present. This script will show you how to:

- Declare object reference variables
- Set object references
- Use properties and methods

We also discuss how Notes distinguishes classes from each another. Generally speaking, Notes divides classes into two groups: *front-end* classes, which provide access to whatever a user is currently working on, and *back-end* classes, which provide access to background objects.

The Case Study

Rather than employ several unrelated scripts to demonstrate the use of Notes classes, we decided to focus on a single script (albeit, a fairly complex one to the novice developer), working through it bit by bit, from beginning to end. This method provides a cohesive structure for showing the interrelationships among the different classes.

To set the stage, the Notes database in question is designed to track purchase orders received by customers. For each customer, a single Customer Record document is created. As a customer orders products, a Purchase Order document is created for each order. A purchase order may encompass several different items. The sum total of all of the items plus any applicable taxes, shipping, and handling costs constitute the total amount of the purchase order. A given customer can have an unlimited number of purchase orders in the database.

```
The script below is associated with the Click event of an Action that
appears in the Action Bar of the Customer Record form. Its purpose is
to seek out all purchase orders related to the current customer and
display a total dollar amount. Sub Click(Source As Button)
'
' Declare object reference variables in order to get Customer
' Number from current document...
'
    Dim workspace As New NotesUIWorkspace
    Dim uidoc As NotesUIDocument
    Dim doc As NotesDocument
    Dim item As NotesItem

' Declare object reference variables in order to retrieve all
' purchase order documents that correspond to this customer...
'
    Dim session As New NotesSession
    Dim db As NotesDatabase
    Dim collection As NotesDocumentCollection
    Dim dateTime As NotesDateTime

' Declare scalar variables that will be used in this script
' to store the customer name, purchase order amounts, and
' total...
'
    Dim custnum As String
    Dim formula As String
    Dim prompt As String
    Dim title As String
    Dim curyear As String
    Dim postart As String
    Dim poamount As Currency
    Dim pototal As Currency
    Dim x As Integer
'
```

```
' Get value of CustomerNumber field from the customer record
' currently open in the Workspace...
'

    Set uidoc = workspace.CurrentDocument
    Set doc = uidoc.Document
    Set item = doc.GetFirstItem("CustomerNumber")
    custnum = item.Values(0)
'

' Prompt user for starting date from which to retrieve POs.
' Value defaults to 01/01 of current year...
'

    prompt = "Enter a starting date (mm/dd/yy):"
    title = "Starting Date"
    curyear = Right$(Date$,2)
    postart = Inputbox$(prompt, title, "01/01/" & curyear)
    If Not Isdate(postart) Then postart = "01/01/" & curyear
'

' Retrieve all purchase order documents with matching customer
' number...
'

    Set db = session.CurrentDatabase
    Set datetime = New NotesDateTime(postart)
    formula = "Form = ""PORDER"" & CustomerNumber = """ &_
    custnum & """"
    Set collection = db.Search(formula, datetime, 0)
'

' Cycle through all documents in current collection, get value
' of POAMOUNT field, build total purchase order value...
'

    pototal = 0
    For x = 1 To collection.Count
    Set doc = collection.GetNthDocument(x)
    Set item = doc.GetFirstItem("POAmount")
    poamount = item.Values(0)
    pototal = pototal + poamount
    Next x
'

' Display total in dialog box...
'

    Messagebox "Total Purchase Orders from starting date = " _
    & Format(pototal, "Currency"),,"Total Purchase Orders"

End Sub
```

This script performs the following tasks:

- Retrieves the value of the field in the currently displayed document (the customer record) that contains the customer's customer number, which is a unique identifier for each customer and serves as a key for unifying the customer record and all other documents related to the customer (purchase orders, letters, etc.)

- Prompts the user for a starting date from which to retrieve purchase orders; only purchase orders from this date forward will be retrieved

- Searches the database for purchase order documents that contain a matching customer number and stores them in a temporary structure

- Cycles through each purchase order and finds the total dollar amount of the order

- Derives a cumulative total for the dollar amount of all the purchase orders and displays the total in a dialog box

Declaring Object Reference Variables

These declarations are all examples of an *object reference variable*:

```
Dim workspace As New NotesUIWorkspace
Dim uidoc As NotesUIDocument
Dim doc As NotesDocument
Dim item as NotesItem
...
```

An object reference variable, like a regular variable, is assigned a data type; however, the data type is the name of a class (NotesUIWorkspace, NotesUIDocument, etc.), rather than a built-in data type (Integer, String, etc.). Establishing object reference variables is an essential step in preparing to access existing objects or to create new objects in the Notes environment. When an object reference variable is declared, the variable adopts the properties and methods contained in the definition of the class. For example, the declaration

```
Dim workspace As New NotesUIWorkspace
```

establishes an object reference variable *workspace* of data type NotesUI Workspace. The *workspace variable* now takes on the behavior of the NotesUIWorkspace class, including its properties:

- CurrentDocument

and its methods:

- ComposeDocument
- DialogBox
- EditDocument
- OpenDatabase
- ViewRefresh

TIP

Plese see Notes Help for more information on classes.

NOTE

As Lotus continues to integrate LotusScript into its suite of desktop applications, (Approach, Word Pro, 1-2-3, Freelance, and Lotus Components), each product will come with its own library of class definitions. These product-specific classes allow you to access objects that are unique to the application; for instance, the LotusScript implementation in Lotus 1-2-3 for Windows provides classes for accessing objects inherent to the spreadsheet environment.

Setting Object References

Ultimately, an object reference variable must be assigned an object reference. To establish actual objects, you use the Set command, as shown in the following example:

```
...
Set uidoc = workspace.CurrentDocument
```

```
Set doc = uidoc.Document
Set item = doc.GetFirstItem("CustomerNumber")
...
```

The declaration of the object reference variable by itself does not establish an actual *object*, that is, a tangible instance of the object class.

Using Properties and Methods

Within the definition of every class in the Notes class library is a list of possible *properties* associated with it. A property is a characteristic that has been defined for the class of object. In the case of the NotesUIWorkspace class, which is used to represent the Notes Workspace window as a whole, a possible characteristic is the presence of an open document. To account for this possibility, a Current-Document property has been defined.

```
Set uidoc = workspace.CurrentDocument
```

Just as a class definition contains a list of possible properties, it also contains a list of possible methods. A *method* is an operation or action that can occur relative to the class of object. If you consider a document, for instance, you can easily recognize a number of operations that you might perform on it. The definition of the NotesDocument class describes the operations that are supported for documents. The GetFirstItem method used in the statement below allows you to retrieve the value of a field in a document.

```
Set item = doc.GetFirstItem("CustomerNumber")
```

Both properties and methods are referenced using a "dot notation." The general syntax is

```
<object reference variable name>.<property or method>
```

Methods must always be used in conjunction with a specific number of *arguments*, which convey needed values to the method—for example, CustomerNumber in the GetFirstItem method above. Arguments must be enclosed in parentheses and must match the data type demanded by the method.

Properties do not have arguments associated with them because they are used only to get or to set the value of an object's property.

Working with the Current Document

A Notes database stores documents. (If this statement is a revelation to you, you're at the wrong end of the book!) To an end user working within Notes applications, documents are "exposed" either through a form that presents a document as a configuration of fields, labels, and other design elements or through views that present a collection of documents in row/column format. In both cases, these mechanisms provide an outward representation of the basic unit of storage in Notes, the document, to the end user.

In the Notes class library, a critical distinction is drawn between the representation of a document (i.e., the document currently displayed on the screen) and a document as it is stored on the hard drive. The former falls under the Notes-UIDocument class (*UI* stands for "user interface") and the latter under the Notes-Document class.

> **NOTE**
>
> Classes are divided into two groups, *front-end classes* that provide access to what a user is currently working on and *back-end classes* that provide access to objects as they are stored in the database. The NotesUIDocument class is front-end class, and the NotesDocument is back-end class.

The NotesUIDocument class enables you to manipulate the document currently open on the screen by acting as a gateway to the *true document* (as it is stored in the database). From this point, the NotesDocument class takes over, providing access to the properties and methods associated with a document. The following code shows the sequence of commands that provides the foundation for accessing and manipulating the current document:

```
Set uidoc = workspace.CurrentDocument
Set doc = uidoc.Document
```

The object reference variable *uidoc* represents the document that is currently opened in the Workspace, i.e., the front-end representation of the document. The object reference variable *doc* is then set so that the back-end representation of the document, its stored state, can be accessed and manipulated.

Retrieving the Value of an Item from the Current Document

Having established a link to the document back end, the items stored in the document now become accessible. (See the sidebar "Items versus Fields.") The statement

```
Set item = doc.GetFirstItem("CustomerNumber")
```

uses the GetFirstItem method of the NotesDocument class to assign the object reference variable *item* to an item object, CustomerNumber—that is, to the object that CustomerNumber represents. (*Item* is not assigned the *value* of Customer-Number.) The value of an item is just one of many properties associated with it. To get the actual value of an item, we can use the Values property of the Notes-Item class. In the following example, *custnum* is a simple scalar variable that must match the data type returned by the Values property (i.e., the data type of the stored item).

```
custnum = item.Values(0)
```

Because the data type of the CustomerNumber field is text, we declare custnum to be of a compatible data type in LotusScript, in this case String.

Items versus Fields

Technically speaking, a document stores *items* rather than *fields;* the Notes class library reflects this distinction by including the NotesItem class. The distinction is that an item is simply a piece of data in a document, whereas a field is essentially an input and presentation device used to enter and display an item. Using the term *field*, instead of *item*, is an accepted convention when referring to the values stored in a document. As long as you understand the distinction, don't worry about it.

As an object class unto itself, a field has properties and methods associated with it. However, the Notes class library does not make this type of object available to you; that is, you won't find a NotesField class defined in the library. You may manipulate a field only while in Form Design mode through the Properties InfoBox. (If you've been paying attention, the term *Properties* should not have escaped you; yes, these are the same *properties* that we've been referring to in this chapter, only you access them through a visual interface, the InfoBox, rather than programmatically through LotusScript!)

Reaching Beyond the Current Document

Now we'll turn our attention to the world outside the currently displayed document. Because we want to total all purchase orders for the current customer, we need to lay a foundation for retrieving this information. The major differentiating factor between this process and the previous tasks is that the "target data" (the purchase order amounts) is not represented in the current Workspace; it's essentially behind the scenes.

The steps for accessing information *elsewhere* are identical in concept to what we did to access information in the current document. The following declarations establish the object reference variables necessary to retrieve the purchase order documents associated with the current customer record:

```
Dim session As New NotesSession
Dim db As NotesDatabase
Dim collection As NotesDocumentCollection
Dim dateTime As NotesDateTime
```

In a way that is very similar to how the NotesUIWorkspace class provides access to whatever is currently on the screen, the NotesSession class acts as a gateway to virtually everything else in the Notes environment. Our interest is specifically the database in which the purchase order documents reside, which may or may not be the database we're currently accessing. Therefore, we establish the variable *db* of type NotesDatabase.

To temporarily store the documents that we'll be retrieving, we need to declare an object reference to the NotesDocumentCollection class, the variable *collection*. The NotesDateTime class is required in order to pass a date/time value from a LotusScript program to Notes.

NOTE   The date/time formats of LotusScript and Notes are not the same. For instance, if you attempt to use a LotusScript date/time value in conjunction with a Notes object, Notes will not be able to interpret the value correctly. The NotesDateTime class provides a means of translating between LotusScript and Notes date/time formats.

Retrieving a Subset of Documents from a Database

We're now ready to retrieve the purchase orders for the current customer. First, we must state in which database the purchase order documents reside. In our application, we keep the purchase orders in the same database as the customer records, although doing so is not a requirement. We use the CurrentDatabase property of the NotesSession class to assign an object reference to the variable *db*.

```
Set db = session.CurrentDatabase
```

The variable *datetime* is set to the date/time value that the user enters as the starting date from which to retrieve purchase orders. We have to use the Notes-DateTime class to translate the LotusScript date/time value (stored in the variable *postart*) to a format that is compatible with Notes, as in

```
Set datetime = New NotesDateTime(postart)
```

We can now search the database using the Search method of the NotesDatabase class, returning the resulting documents to our *collection* variable. The Search method requires three arguments:

- A search formula that defines the criteria a document must meet to be included in the set of documents returned.

- A cut-off date that confines the search to documents created or modified since the cut-off date.

- An integer that specifies the maximum number of documents to return. A value of 0 indicates that all documents that meet the search criteria should be returned.

The String variable *formula* is assigned the value of the search formula we'll use. The assignment utilizes the *custnum* variable, which was the value of the CustomerNumber item in the current customer record. *Custnum* is then used as an argument to the Search method.

```
formula = "Form = ""PORDER"" & CustomerNumber = """ & _
custnum & """"
Set collection = db.Search(formula, datetime, 0)
```

The search criteria that we need to supply the Search method are stated in the *formula* variable as a series of conditions that a document must meet to be included in the resulting collection. These conditions are:

- The value of the Form field must be "PORDER," which indicates that the document is a purchase order.

- The value of the CustomerNumber field must match the value script variable *custnum*, which contains the value of the customer number in the current customer record.

The Grand Finale

Assuming that our search has yielded a set of purchase orders that correspond to the current customer record, we can now cycle through the set, retrieve the purchase order amount from each one, and derive a total dollar amount for all purchase orders.

```
pototal = 0
For x = 1 to collection.Count
  Set doc = collection.GetNthDocument(x)
  Set item = doc.GetFirstItem("POAmount")
  poamount = item.Values(0)
  pototal = pototal + poamount
Next x
```

A For...Next loop (described in the previous chapter) is the appropriate iteration mechanism for getting the purchase order amount from each document in the current collection.

The Count property of the NotesDocumentCollection class returns the total number of documents in the collection (i.e., that matched the search criteria we specified) and establishes an upper boundary in the For statement. The GetNthDocument method of the NotesDocument Collection class retrieves an individual document from the collection based on an index value in the collection, the "counter" variable *x*.

Just as we did with the CustomerNumber item of the current customer record, we retrieve an item from the current purchase order document, POAmount, using the GetFirstItem method of the NotesDocument class. We then assign the value to the Currency variable *poamount*. With each iteration the Currency variable, *pototal* is recalculated as the sum of its previous value plus the current value of *poamount*.

Finally, the following MessageBox statement displays the total amount of all purchase orders for the current customer:

```
MessageBox "Total Purchase Orders from starting date = " _
& Format(pototal, "Currency")
```

The Format function causes the value of *pototal* to be expressed as a dollar amount.

This step completes the execution of the script. If purchase orders exist in the database for the customer whose record is currently displayed on the screen, a grand total will be calculated and presented. If no purchase orders exist, the total will simply be $0.00.

What's Next?

LotusScript represents the common programming language across the entire family of Lotus desktop products—1-2-3, Word Pro, Approach, Freelance Graphics, and Lotus Components—as well as third-party development tools such as Notes ViP from Revelation Technologies. The idea is simple: Provide a unified programming environment that lets developers and users leverage their efforts and knowledge across a wide range of applications.

LotusScript will continue to evolve as new LotusScript classes emerge. With Notes 4.6, new classes have been added, such as NotesRegistration and NotesRichTextStyle. Some new methods and properties have also been added or modified for existing classes. Lotus Components technology includes classes for accessing and manipulating a series of applets that can be integrated into the design of Notes applications. These applets provide features and functionality not inherent to Notes—spreadsheets, project scheduling, drawing/diagramming, and more—and the new LotusScript classes that accompany them will give you a high degree of control over their operation.

Stay tuned for more!

APPENDIX

What's on the CD-ROM?

The first thing that we want to say about the CD-ROM that's packaged with this book is that its use is entirely optional. The only reference we make to the CD-ROM in the book is to suggest that you copy the sample databases from the CD to your workstation in order to work through some of the tutorials. We like to think of the CD as a little bonus for people who own CD-ROM drives. But we also like to think that the book has merit on its own, even if you never use the disc.

Many of you might not have access to CD-ROM drives in the office, and there's no reason to feel left out if you never use the CD. If you use Mobile Notes off-site and your laptop computer has a CD-ROM drive installed in it, take advantage of the applications. This appendix describes all the applications that are included on the CD by category:

- Database applications

- Graphics programs

- Demonstration programs

- Utility program

The pages that follow contain portions of the actual README files for many of the shareware programs on the disc. Each README file is printed pretty much as is—that is, neither we nor the publisher altered the material significantly, although we did condense the information for space considerations. You'll be reading exactly what each shareware author has to say about his or her own product.

Disclaimer

Use the programs on this CD-ROM at your own risk. All liability for damages, whether direct or consequential, is explicitly disclaimed by the individual program authors, Sybex, and the authors of this book. All warranties expressed and implied arising out of the use or purchase of the individual programs are disclaimed by the program authors, Sybex, and the authors of this book.

Except for those rights that are associated with the individual program names, all rights associated with other names that are mentioned in the program descriptions and in the program files are held by their respective companies. Other than the individual program names, all names and trademarks mentioned herein belong to their respective owners.

Using the CD-ROM

The CD that accompanies this book contains commercial, shareware, and demo applications. Each application is located in its own folder. To view the contents of the CD, follow these steps:

1. Insert the CD into your CD-ROM drive.

2. Double-click My Computer.

3. Double-click the icon for your CD-ROM drive. You should see files and folders.

4. Double-click the CLICKME.EXE file to open and launch the CD interface.

   You can install the applications from the CLICKME.EXE file, or you can install each application directly from the installation file in its folder. If you don't have the book handy while you're exploring the CD, you can double-click the README file to review the installation information on the screen, or to print it.

About Shareware and Demos

The programs on the CD are mostly try-before-you-buy shareware. That is, you can explore any program, without payment or commitment, to see if it's suitable for your needs. If you find a program you like, you can purchase the complete version of the program simply by registering the copy you have. Registration instructions are available within each shareware program's menus or help system.

   If you are new to the shareware game, we'll explain some things you need to know. Shareware generally is distributed via online networks, such as CompuServe, and the Internet. The idea behind shareware is to allow you to try out a product before you pay a registration fee. If you use a shareware program for a while and like it, you must register the program with its author. That part costs money, of course. But in return, you usually get a complete version of the product and information on updates; in some cases, you also may receive a printed manual.

   In addition, you'll be supporting the entire shareware industry. Many talented programmers and digital artists are producing excellent products, but they don't have the resources required to flood the international market with shrink-wrapped products. Instead, they publish their products as shareware.

Every product on the CD—shareware, a demo, a database, freeware, whatever—is offered as is, with no warranty of any kind. The best attitude to carry into the shareware industry is "we're all in this together." The programmers and artists have the talent to create these great products, but they need your feedback, tolerance, and support to grow their products into ever-better and more reliable versions.

So, enjoy—and please be tolerant of bugs and any other problems that you may encounter. Shareware authors don't have the resources to perform large-scale beta testing. In a sense, *you* are the beta tester when you take a shareware program for a spin. If you find a bug, report it to the author of the program; he or she probably will correct the problem in the next release of the product.

Summary List of Programs on the CD-ROM

The following table provides a quick alphabetical listing of programs on the CD.

Name	Folder on CD	Category
Da Big Library	\Library	Database
Employment Kiosk	\Employ	Database
Paint Shop Pro 5	\Paintshp	Graphics
PAVONE Espresso-	\Pavone	Demonstration
PAVONE Group-flow Movies	\Pavone	Demonstration
NotesWare EIS	\Pavone	Demonstration
RADD GUI Gallery	\Gallery	Database
Screen Thief for Windows	\Scrnthf	Graphics
Visio Express 4.0	\Visio	Graphics
WinBiff 3.6a	\Winbiff	Utility
US Zip Code Database	\Zipcodes	Database

Database Applications

Name	Folder on CD
Da Big Library	\Library
Employment Kiosk	\Employ
RADD GUI Gallery	\Gallery
US Zip Code Database	\Zipcodes

Installing the Databases

To install a database on your system, follow these steps:

1. Copy a database file from the CD-ROM to the default data directory on your workstation.

2. Choose File ➤ Database ➤ Open. The Open Database dialog box appears.

3. Locate and highlight a database to select it.

4. Click the Open button to add the database's icon to your Workspace.

NOTE   You can also refer to Chapter 4, "Accessing a Notes Database," for more detailed instructions on installing databases on your system.

We suggest that you open the About This Database and Using This Database documents for each database application. These documents contain information about the respective database and provide additional instructions for using the database.

Da Big Library

The Da Big Library database is a document library application, which allows you to capture and track information about documents. This type of application is like an electronic filing cabinet that stores reference documents and enables members of a workgroup to access information easily.

What Does This Database Do?

The database might contain anything from environmental impact statements for a group of engineers to financial statements for a group of loan officers. The design of this Document Library template is very flexible.

Who Will Use This Database?

Anyone who wishes to create a record of a document or review available documents may use this database.

Setting Access Control

Access level should be Author for all users of this database to prevent unauthorized editing of documents within the database. The Author fields within the forms govern who will be able to edit/review particular documents. Errors will occur if someone with Editor access, who is not an authorized reviewer of that document, attempts to review a particular document.

Using the Database

To add a document to this database, select Create ➤ Document. You can enter document information in several ways: by typing it, by scanning in hard copy, or by importing or attaching an electronic file.

To respond to a document, highlight that document in a view and then select Create ➤ Response.

To respond to a response, highlight the response you wish to respond to and then select Create ➤ Response to Response.

Setting up a Document Review Cycle

As the author of a document, you have the option of setting up a document review cycle for that document, which you use to route a document to a series of recipients. Simply click the Setup Review Cycle Action button and fill in the necessary information. Enter only Person names as reviewers. Group names are not supported.

You can choose from several review styles:

Serial Review   Documents are routed for review one at a time in sequence to the reviewers chosen by the author.

- All edits are made within the same document, but an unedited copy of the original document is also saved.

Serial Review (Keep All Revisions)   Documents are routed for review one at a time in sequence to the reviewers chosen by the author.

- Edits are made within a copy of the original, which also includes all comments from previous reviewers.

- All old versions become response documents (as well as a copy of the original).

Document Reservations   Requests for document review are routed in parallel (that is, all at the same time). When one reviewer opens the document, a "file locking" occurs at the server that warns any other user who happens to edit the document simultaneously that a review is in progress.

- Review comments or edits are made in a copy of the original document.

- As with the others, a clean copy of the original is always kept.

Response Review   Requests for document review are also routed in parallel (but don't allow file locking).

- Review comments or edits are saved as response documents to the original document.

- As with the others, a clean copy of the original is always kept.

Archiving Documents

You archive documents when you want to move expired documents from the current database to an archive database. This process removes certain documents from the current database and stores them in a different database. Archiving keeps the library up-to-date. Most of the archiving activities take place from the Archiving view. You must switch to this view in order to initiate archiving on a library database.

To set up archiving on any library database, switch to the Archiving view and click the Action called Setup Archive. The Archive Profile appears. This document contains criteria that the user specifies for archiving topics in a library (e.g., inactive after x days or expired after x days). The archive database is automatically created when the Profile is saved. The archival database file name is also specified in the Archive Profile; the title of the archive will be the title of the database followed by (Archived). After the archive criteria have been specified in the Archive Profile, other Agents run on the database to move the document(s).

Mark/Unmark Document as Expired   Marks a topic as *expired*. If the Archive Profile specifies that expired topics should be archived, the documents marked with this Agent would fall into that criterion. If a document is already marked as expired, this Agent tells the user what the expire date was and will ask if the user wants to reinstate it.

Periodic Archive   Reviews the Archive Profile and moves documents that meet the archive criteria into the archive database. This Agent is run automatically on the server; the schedule is set by the database manager/designer.

Disclaimer

Use Da Big Library database included on this CD-ROM at your own risk. All liability for damages, whether direct or consequential, is explicitly disclaimed by the database authors, Sybex, and the authors of this book.

Da Big Library database included on this CD-ROM is copyright the authors. All rights reserved.

Employment Kiosk

Throughout *Mastering Lotus Notes Release 4.6*, we refer to documents and design elements included in this database. This database is not a "finished" Notes application. It contains elements in varying states of completion, depending on what is required in each chapter.

Think of this database as a large "sandbox" that allows you to try its elements without any risk. If you delete anything, simply copy it back from the original version on the companion CD. When things work right, copy and paste them into other applications.

The default access to the database is No Access. If you will be adding this database to a server, add yourself as manager and change the groups to reflect the needs of your organization.

Some of the functionality (such as the Ask for More Info Action button in Chapter 21) will work better if you create a group called Recruiters in your Personal Name & Address book. Include yourself, and anybody else you wish to bother with junk mail while you are testing this database, in the list of members.

If you are modifying this application to roll it out within your organization, you need to set up Read access restrictions at least for the view called Applicants and Document Creation access to the Admin views.

Web-Enabling the Database

After reviewing the chapters on InterNotes, you may want to consider posting the job offers to the Web. Web-enabling the Application for Employment form is a bit more difficult because several features, such as the "growing table" and the layouts, need to be recoded manually for the Web form to still work. As an intermediate step, you could mail-enable the database and accept incoming Internet mail messages with attachments.

Imaging

You may want to add resume scanning and OCR features. The new Lotus Notes Document Imaging for Notes 4 works well and integrates easily in Notes. You can call the @command [*Insert object name*] function with a few well-placed buttons/Actions.

Application Gotchas

You may occasionally see some inconsistent displays of the Application for Employment form, such as shadowing or overlaps. We are not sure why, but several people have reported similar problems when using multiple layouts and multiple sections within the same form.

The Application for Employment form is a little hefty because we included everything but the kitchen sink to demonstrate the functionality of Notes forms. It may take a few seconds to load on certain machines. To speed up the form, remove the sections you don't really need and the images in the layouts that you can live without.

The Job Offer form uses an encryption key. Some of the fields in the example documents, such as hiring manager, may not be visible. You should modify the form and create your own key.

Disclaimer

Use the Employment Kiosk database included on this CD-ROM at your own risk. All liability for damages, whether direct or consequential, is explicitly disclaimed by the database authors, Sybex, and the authors of this book.

The Employment Kiosk database included on this CD-ROM is copyright the authors. All rights reserved.

RADD GUI Gallery

RADD GUI Gallery is a library of professional 3-D graphics that can be copied and pasted into Notes Release 4 design elements such as Navigators, layout regions, and forms.

The images are targeted toward the more conservative corporate environment where extravagant World Wide Web graphics are usually inappropriate.

GUI Widgets is a collection of templates for Navigators, forms, and dialog boxes. They have been designed to assist developers who may not have the time or inclination to work with the complexities of Notes Release 4 graphics. The templates allow developers to concentrate on coding their applications and still produce visually appealing interfaces.

Whether you're a corporate developer or a Notes consultant, you'll want to take advantage of Notes Release 4 enhanced graphics capabilities to satisfy your end users and clients. The RADD GUI Gallery is the quickest and easiest way to add pizzazz to your applications!

This demo package contains a representative sample of the over 100 images in the RADD GUI Gallery. It also contains a sample of the GUI Widgets to be found in the full product. To order the full product, choose Create ➤ Order Information from the Notes menu bar.

Using an Image

To use an image, simply click the Copy button next to the Image label on an Entry document. The image is now on the Clipboard and can be pasted into your application or into Windows Paintbrush to modify it as you wish.

Entering Your Own Images

To enter your own image, simply select Create ➤ 1. Entry from the Notes menu bar and complete the form that appears. The Copy button will copy everything in the Image field. Therefore, you should include only a single image in the field.

Keeping Track of Favorite or Most Used Items

To keep a collection of your favorite or most used images, simply drag and drop any entry from a view to the Favorites folder on the Main Navigator. To remove entries from the Favorites folder, highlight the entries in the folder and select Actions ➤ Remove from Folder.

Contact Information

Workgroup Productivity Corporation
Attn: Product Division
3075 Highland Parkway, Suite 150
Downer's Grove, IL 60515
Telephone: (800) 380-3806 or (708) 953-8888 outside the United States

Disclaimer

Use the RADD GUI Gallery database included on this CD-ROM at your own risk. All liability for damages, whether direct or consequential, is explicitly disclaimed by the database authors, Sybex, and the authors of this book.

The RADD GUI Gallery database included on this CD-ROM is copyright the authors. All rights reserved.

US Zip Code Database

This database contains ZIP codes, city names, and state names for all ZIP codes in the United States as of 1994. You can use the database to look up a city and state when the ZIP code is known by creating a lookup test after the ZIP code data has been imported. Using a lookup speeds up data entry and improves accuracy at the same time.

If you register the database, you will receive the most current data (the database is updated quarterly). The registered database also includes county names and place names.

Using the Database

To access the ZIP Code Database for Notes, follow these steps:

1. Choose View ➤ ZIP Codes to open the ZIP Codes view of the ZIPCODES.NSF database.

2. Choose File ➤ Import.

3. Select Tabular Text in the List Files of Type list box.

4. Locate and select the ZIP.TXT file (which should be stored in the Zipcodes directory).

5. Click the Import button.

6. Choose the ZIP Code form.

7. Select the Use Format File option.

8. Click the Choose Format File button.

9. Locate and select the file ZIP.COL (which should be stored in the Zipcodes directory).

10. Click OK.

11. Click OK again.

The import process can take up to two hours, so be prepared to wait.

Creating a Lookup Test

You need to create a lookup test to try out the ZIP Code lookup function.

1. Choose Create ➤ Lookup Test.

2. Enter a ZIP code.

3. Press the Lookup button on the form to look up and display the city and state.

The data in this demonstration version is from 1994. The registered version of the US ZIP Code Database contains current data and includes county as well as place names.

Adding a Formula

The formula for the lookup button can be found on the Lookup Test form. Simply copy it to the button in your database and change the server name. You will have a ZIP code lookup capability in your own program. Data entry will be more accurate and faster.

Contact Information

To order, simply compose an order form and send it in or contact the author directly via one of the methods listed below:

US ZIP Code Database for Lotus Notes
HELP Software
P.O. Box 1423
Raymore, MO 64083
Telephone: (816) 331-5809
E-mail: BDBenson@helpsoft.com

Disclaimer

Use the US Zip Code Database included on this CD-ROM at your own risk. All liability for damages, whether direct or consequential, is explicitly disclaimed by the database authors, Sybex, and the authors of this book.

The US Zip Code Database included on this CD-ROM is copyright the authors. All rights reserved.

Graphics Programs

Name	Folder on CD
Paint Shop Pro 5	\Paintshp
Screen Thief for Windows 1.01	\Scrnthf
Visio Express 4.0	\Visio

Paint Shop Pro 5

Paint Shop Pro is a complete Windows graphics program for image creation, viewing, and manipulation. As a general-purpose graphics tool, it's an impressive alternative to the Windows 95 Paint program.

Program features include painting with eight brushes, photo retouching, image enhancement and editing, color enhancement, image browsing, batch conversion, and scanner support. The program includes twenty standard filters and twelve deformations. The program supports plug-in filters and more than thirty file formats.

Installing Paint Shop Pro

Before you can use Paint Shop Pro, you have to run the Paint Shop Pro setup program from Windows. You cannot just copy the files from the CD to your hard disk. Follow these steps:

1. Insert the CD in your CD-ROM drive.

2. Choose Run from the Start menu.

3. Type **d:\paintshp\setup** in the Open box; d is the letter assigned to your CD-ROM drive.

4. Click OK and follow the instructions on the screen.

If you want to install the Paint Shop Pro program files on a different drive or directory, type in the new designation. Paint Shop Pro Setup will place the files into the directory of your choice. The setup program will notify you when the installation is complete.

Using Paint Shop Pro

To run the program, click Start ➤ Programs ➤ Paint Shop Pro ➤ Paint Shop Pro 5.

Contact Information

JASC, Inc.
PO Box 44997
Eden Prairie, MN 55343-0997 USA
Telephone: (800) 622-2793 or (612) 930-9171 outside of the United States
Fax: (612) 930-9172
CompuServe: GO JASC
World Wide Web: http://www.jasc.com

Disclaimer

Use Paint Shop Pro at your own risk. All liability for damages, whether direct or consequential, is explicitly disclaimed by the Paint Shop Pro author, Sybex, and the authors of this book. All warranties expressed and implied arising out of the use or purchase of Paint Shop Pro are disclaimed by the Paint Shop Pro author, Sybex, and the authors of this book.

Except for those associated with the name Paint Shop Pro, all rights associated with names mentioned in this program and in the accompanying Windows help file, are held by their respective companies. Other than the name Paint Shop Pro, all names and trademarks mentioned herein belong to their respective owners.

Screen Thief for Windows 1.01

Screen Thief for Windows 1.01 is the ultimate screen capture system for Windows. Program features include:

- Up to eight user-defined capture configurations, each with hotkey invocation
- Capture from desktop, active window, active application, defined area, and Clipboard
- Send capture to disk, printer, or Clipboard; zoom in/out; crop images
- Auto color reduction
- Page preview
- BMP, RLE, GIF, PCX, and TIFF file formats

Installing Screen Thief

To install Screen Thief for Windows, follow these steps:

1. Insert the CD in your CD-ROM drive.

2. Choose Run from the Start menu.

3. Type **d:\scrnthf\setup** in the Open box; d is the letter assigned to your CD-ROM drive.

4. Click OK and follow the instructions on the screen.

Running Screen Thief for Windows

To run Screen Thief for Windows, click Start ➤ Programs ➤ Screen Thief for Windows ➤ Screen Thief. We suggest that you open the STWIN.HLP help file first and get to know the program. If you have the shareware test-drive version, you must read through the first topics regarding the shareware concept and the limits on the use for this version. You should run Screen Thief for Windows only if you agree to abide by these restrictions.

Contact Information

Nildram Software
82 Akeman Street
Tring
Herts
HP23 6AF
United Kingdom
Telephone: +44 (0) 1442 891331
Fax: +44 (0) 1442 890303
BBS: +44 (0) 1442 891109
E-mail: sales@nildram.com

Disclaimer

Use Screen Thief at your own risk. All liability for damages, whether direct or consequential, is explicitly disclaimed by the Screen Thief author, Sybex, and the authors of this book. All warranties expressed and implied arising out of the use or purchase of Screen Thief are disclaimed by the Screen Thief author, Sybex, and the authors of this book.

Except for those associated with the name Screen Thief, all rights associated with names mentioned in this program and in the accompanying Windows help file are held by their respective companies. Other than the name Screen Thief, all names and trademarks mentioned herein belong to their respective owners.

Visio Express 4.0

Visio Express is a simplified version of Visio, a business graphics drawing program. Visio enables you to create diagrams, flowcharts, project timelines, workflow processes, and other business drawings by using task-specific stencils that include hundreds of SmartShapes.

Visio fully supports OLE 2.0 technology, which makes it convenient for you to add diagrams and schematics to documents that you create in Lotus Notes. Visio allows you to embed Visio objects in Notes documents and then exchange and update information between the two applications.

We include three bonus Visio drawing files that you can embed in Notes documents:

- ANTHRQTY.VSD

- FLOW1.VSD

- NETWORK2.VSD

The files are located in the Visio folder on the CD. The files provide three work-flow diagrams that you can customize for your own needs.

Installing Visio in Windows 95

To install Visio in Windows 95, follow these steps:

1. Insert the CD in your CD-ROM drive.

2. Choose Run from the Start menu.

3. Type **d:\visio\setup** in the Open box; d is the letter assigned to your CD-ROM drive.

4. Click OK and follow the instructions on the screen.

Installing Visio in Windows NT

To install Visio in Windows NT, follow these steps:

1. Insert the CD in your CD-ROM drive.

2. Choose Run from the File menu in the Windows Program Manager.

3. Type **d:\visio\setup** in the Command Line box; d is the letter assigned to your CD-ROM drive.

4. Click OK and follow the instructions on the screen.

After you install Visio, copy the bonus Visio files to the same folder.

Using Visio with Notes

To include a Visio drawing in Lotus Notes, embed it as an object in a Notes database. For example, to embed one of the workflow diagrams in a document, simply follow these steps:

1. Start Visio.

2. Open one of the workflow diagrams.

3. Choose Edit ➤ Copy Drawing.

4. Launch Notes.

5. Double-click a database icon in your Workspace. The database's view appears.

6. Open a document.

7. Double-click the document to change to Edit mode.

8. Insert the cursor in a rich text field.

9. Choose Edit ➤ Paste. The drawing appears in the document.

In addition, when you have a Visio drawing embedded in Lotus Notes, you can use Notes/FX, which allows Visio and Lotus Notes to pass data back and forth (see Chapter 29). You can write information from a Visio shape, custom formula, or the Properties InfoBox to a Lotus Notes field.

For example, you can combine Lotus Notes and Visio to keep track of a company's processes, such as writing and prototyping specifications. To make this feature as easy to use as possible, in Lotus Notes you embed a Visio diagram for each process. Then you create a table that shows just the titles of the processes (which is data you wrote from Visio to Lotus Notes). Anyone who needs to see the process can click the flowchart's title to see the embedded Visio diagram. To edit it, the user can double-click the embedded Visio diagram to start Visio.

You can also read data from a Lotus Notes field and display it in Visio. For example, in a timeline, you can have a Lotus Notes date field automatically update the Visio timeline.

Disclaimer

Use Visio Express at your own risk. All liability for damages, whether direct or consequential, is explicitly disclaimed by the Visio Express author, Sybex, and the authors of this book. All warranties expressed and implied arising out of the use or purchase of Visio Express are disclaimed by the Visio Express author, Sybex, and the authors of this book.

Except for those associated with the name Visio Express, all rights associated with names mentioned in this program and in the accompanying Windows Help File, VISIO.HL, are held by their respective companies. Other than the name Visio Express, all names and trademarks mentioned herein belong to their respective owners.

Demonstration Programs

Name	Folder on CD
PAVONE Espresso	\Espres
PAVONE Groupflow Movies	\Grflow
NotesWare EIS	\EIS

PAVONE Espresso

PAVONE Espresso demonstrates a process-oriented information management system. It enables automation of important business processes by tracking and routing documents within an organization; and includes graphical modeling of workflow, to do lists sorted by person or task, and automatic condition routing.

Installing the Demonstration Program

To install the demonstration program, follow these steps:

1. Insert the CD in your CD-ROM drive.

2. Choose Run from the Start menu.

3. Type **d:\pavone\setup** in the Open box; d is the letter assigned to your CD-ROM drive.

4. Click OK and follow the instructions on the screen.

For more detailed instructions and information, see the appropriate files for this program on the companion CD-ROM.

Running the Demonstration

Click the Screencam icon to start the demonstration. Use the Lotus Screencam buttons to stop, restart, or quit the program.

Contact Information

PAVONE Informationssysteme GmbH,
Elsener Str. 95,
D-33102 Paderborn,
Germany
Telephone: (+49) 5251 3102-0
Fax: (+49) 5251 3102-99
E-mail: Info@pavone.de

Please direct all inquiries to:
www.pavone.de or www.notesware.com

Disclaimer

PAVONE Espresso is a product of PAVONE Informationssysteme Gmbtt.

PAVONE Groupflow Movies

The PAVONE Groupflow Movies demonstrate a workflow management system that is based on Lotus Notes. The demonstration consists of a graphical editor, which models workflow processes; a configurable runtime system; and a workflow simulator.

Installing the Demonstration Program

To install the demonstration program, follow these steps:

1. Insert the CD in your CD-ROM drive.

2. Choose Run from the Start menu.

3. Type **d:\pavone\setup** in the Open box; d is the letter assigned to your CD-ROM drive.

4. Click OK and follow the instructions on the screen.

For more detailed instructions and information, see the appropriate files for this program on the companion CD-ROM.

Running the Demonstration

Click the Screencam icon to start the demonstration. Use the Lotus Screencam buttons to stop, restart, or quit the program.

Contact Information

PAVONE Informationssysteme GmbH,
Elsener Str. 95,
D-33102 Paderborn,
Germany
Telephone: (+49) 5251 3102-0
Fax: (+49) 5251 3102-99
E-mail: Info@pavone.de

Please direct all inquiries to:
www.pavone.de or www.notesware.com

NotesWare EIS

NotesWare Enterprise System (EIS) facilitates analysis of information using a simple point and click interface. It allows users to see reports in greater detail.

Installing the Demonstration Program

To install the demonstration program, follow these steps:

1. Insert the CD in your CD-ROM drive.

2. Choose Run from the Start menu.

3. Type **d:\pavone\setup** in the Open box; d is the letter assigned to your CD-ROM drive.

4. Click OK and follow the instructions on the screen.

For more detailed instructions and information, see the appropriate files for this program on the companion CD-ROM.

Running the Demonstration

Click the Screencam icon to start the demonstration. Use the Lotus Screencam buttons to stop, restart, or quit the program.

Contact Information

PAVONE Informationssysteme GmbH,
Elsener Str. 95,
D-33102 Paderborn,
Germany
Telephone: (+49) 5251 3102-0
Fax: (+49) 5251 3102-99
E-mail: Info@pavone.de

Please direct all inquiries to:
www.pavone.de or www.notesware.com

Disclaimer

PAVONE Espresso is a product of PAVONE Informationssysteme Gmbtt.

Utility Program

Name	Folder on CD
WinBiff 3.6a	\Winbiff

WinBiff 3.6a

WinBiff is a Windows 95 mail notification program for use in conjunction with several mail systems, including Pegasus Mail, Eudora for Windows, Microsoft Mail, Microsoft Exchange, cc:Mail, Lotus Notes, FirstMail, Novell MHS, FSUUCP, sendmail (using PC-NFS), UUPC/extended, and Waffle. WinBiff also works as a POP3 and IMAP4 client using WinSock. WinBiff can display MIME-encoded headers for Internet mail.

Installing WinBiff

Copy the files WINBIFF.EXE and WINBIFF.HLP from the CD to any convenient directory. Users typically keep these files in a directory along with other small Windows utilities. Add WinBiff as a new Program item in Windows.

If you are using POP3 or IMAP4, your WinSock library, WINSOCK.DLL, must be available to WinBiff. If you are using cc:Mail or Lotus Notes, VIM.DLL must be available to WinBiff. A DLL file is available to WinBiff if the DLL's directory is in your DOS path, if the DLL is in the Windows or Windows System directories, or if the DLL is in the WinBiff Working Directory. Additionally, the Notes VIM.DLL itself appears to require other Notes DLLs. For Notes, add any directories that contain other Notes DLLs so they appear in your DOS path.

Installing WinBiff for Multiple Mailboxes

You may run multiple copies of WinBiff to monitor multiple mailboxes. For each mailbox to be monitored, you will need a separate configuration file.

With some mail systems, you may already have a directory for each mailbox; you can use these directories to store corresponding configuration files. For each mailbox, add a Program Item to a group in Program Manager and specify one of the directories just created as the Working Directory. WinBiff will create a WINBIFF.INI in each of these directories.

Otherwise, create a Program Item for each mailbox to be monitored and explicitly specify a configuration file in each command line. You may wish to name the configuration files after the accounts with mailboxes to be monitored. For example, if you have mailboxes for accounts fred and sally, you might use configuration files named FRED.INI and SALLY.INI.

For more detailed instructions and information, see the appropriate files for this program on the companion CD-ROM.

Contact Information

Paul Steckler
1720 Dryden Box 125
Houston TX, 77030
e-mail: winbiff@stecksoft.com
World Wide Web: http://www.stecksoft.com/winbiff.htm

Disclaimer

You use WinBiff at your own risk. All liability for damages, whether direct or consequential, is explicitly disclaimed by the WinBiff author, Sybex, and the authors of this book. All warranties expressed and implied arising out of the use or purchase of WinBiff are disclaimed by the WinBiff author, Sybex, and the authors of this book.

Except for those associated with the name WinBiff, all rights associated with names mentioned in this program and in the accompanying Windows help file, WINBIFF.HLP, are held by their respective companies. Other than the name WinBiff, all names and trademarks mentioned herein belong to their respective owners.

GLOSSARY

G

@ A character that must appear before a pre-defined Notes function. (See *function*.)

About This Database document (or Policy document) An optional document written by the designer or manager of a database to describe the purpose of the database. If a database has an About This Database document, it's automatically displayed the first time you open the database. To see it again, choose Help ➤ About This Database.

access control A security feature that specifies the tasks that each user of a Notes database can perform. Some users may have access to all activities, while others will be limited to specific operations.

access control list (ACL) A list of database users (individual users, Notes servers, and groups of users and/or servers) created and updated by the database manager. The ACL specifies which users can access the database and the activities that they can perform. To see the ACL for a selected or open database, choose File ➤ Database ➤ Access Control.

access levels Database usage controls assigned to users in a database's ACL. The levels are Manager, Designer, Editor, Author, Reader, Depositor, and No Access. In addition to access levels, a database designer can define more specific access roles.

access role A level of database access assigned to a user or group that specifies the user's ability to use specific forms and views or to access specific documents in the database.

Action The core element of any object because it determines what happens when users click the object. An Action adds automation to a form and speeds up repetitive tasks. Notes provides several Simple actions that are easy to create and don't require any programming knowledge. Actions that use @function formulas require knowledge of LotusScript.

Action bar Displays Actions that are associated with a specific form. Actions appear as buttons on the Action bar. The Action bar stays in place at the top of the screen even when the user scrolls down to read another screen of text.

active window The window in which you are working; the top window; the window with the insertion point. Up to nine windows can be open at once, but you can work in only one at a time.

Agents Macros that execute an Action or set of Actions. Agents perform automatic tasks on multiple documents and consist of a document selection formula, a trigger, and one or more Actions. Notes supports a variety of Agents for SmartIcons, for buttons, and for filtering documents. Like other design elements, Agents are stored with the database for which they are created.

You can set up an Agent to run in one of these ways:

- Manually, which allows users to run the Agent by highlighting the database icon and choosing Actions ➤ *<Agent name>*.

- As a hidden Agent, running from another Agent or from the Agent list using Actions ➤ Run.

- On a schedule in the background. (The On Schedule options create automatic Agents that run hourly, daily, weekly, or monthly.)

- When documents are new or modified. (A change-activated Agent runs only if documents that match the search criteria have been changed since the last time the Agent ran.)

- When documents are mailed to the database. (A mail-activated Agent runs on any documents that are sent to a user's mail database or a shared mail-in database.)

- When documents are pasted into the database. (A paste-activated Agent runs only if documents that match the search criteria have been pasted into the database since the last time the Agent ran.)

application A single Notes database or collection of databases that automate a business process.

article A newsgroup article is a note or message posted to one or more USENET newsgroups. Newsgroup readers post articles in a newsgroup, and other readers can post replies to that article.

attach Store a file with a Notes document. You can attach virtually any type of file, even an entire Notes database. The attached file, or *attachment*, is copied and stored in the Notes database and remains with the document until the document or the attachment is deleted and travels with the document if it is mailed. (See also *embedding*.)

attachment A file attached to a Notes document using File ➤ Attach. An attachment remains with the Notes document until either the attachment or the Notes document is deleted. Deleting an attachment requires at least Editor access to the document, or Author access if you created the document.

authentication A bidirectional authorization process that establishes a trusted communication relationship between a Notes client and Notes server or two Notes servers. During authentication, Notes checks that the user or Notes server trying to gain access to a particular Notes server has a trusted certificate in common with it.

background macro A macro that's executed on a regularly scheduled basis, often used in workflow applications. For example, a background macro could look in a course enrollment database daily and forward new enrollment applications to the course administrator. (See also *Agent*.)

bitmap A type of graphic format that appears as a pattern of dots—or pixels—in a certain sequence and color on screen or on paper. When you edit a bitmapped graphic, you do so by erasing or changing the color of the individual dots in the picture. Bitmapped graphics cannot be resized without a loss of quality, and in many cases, the edges appear jagged and the dots are easily seen.

You can prepare your own bitmaps for use as database icons or SmartIcons and to add to forms and documents. For a SmartIcon, create a drawing that is no larger than 22 × 22 pixels, save the drawing as a BMP file, and copy the BMP file to your Notes SmartIcons directory.

browser See *Web browser.*

bullet A graphical element that you use to identify items in a list. You can create a bulleted list automatically by adding bullets to paragraphs. Make sure the document is in Edit mode. Select the paragraph(s) you want to start with a bullet. Choose Text ➤ Bullets. You can also add bullets with the Bullet SmartIcon.

button A design element that is used in a form to invoke an Agent or Action. A button can be used to help users navigate through the application or to automate certain tasks within the application. A button is a time-saving tool because it performs repetitive actions automatically when the user is editing or reading a document.

C News A news software program that allows a computer to operate as a USENET news server.

category A name (word, phrase, number) used to group and sort documents in a view. For example, documents related to purchase orders might be grouped under the Purchasing category. To assign a document to a category in a view, the database designer must specify that the view's first column sorts by the Categories field. The database may let you create new categories, or it may restrict you to predefined categories. (Many views are sorted chronologically or by discussion topic and therefore don't use categories.)

cc:Mail Lotus cc:Mail is an e-mail system that can be connected to Notes by using the Lotus Notes cc:Mail MTA (messaging transport agent). This connection permits Notes servers and workstations to synchronize directories and exchange mail between Notes and cc:Mail.

certificate A unique electronic stamp stored in a User ID file. Certificates permit you to access specific Notes servers. Your User ID may have several certificates.

certifier A person, often the administrator of one or more Notes servers, who uses a special Certifier ID to create (or certify) User IDs.

checkbox A graphical way to present options for displaying keywords. Each keyword is displayed as a box; users click one or more keywords to fill in a field. Checkboxes have a frame and column options. The Allow Values Not in This List option is not applicable to checkboxes.

Clipboard A Microsoft Windows feature that allows you to cut or copy information from one application and paste the information in another application in a format that the application can edit. Together with DDE (Dynamic Data Exchange) or OLE (Object Linking and Embedding), the Clipboard also enables you to link data that you've transferred to its source, or original application, providing your applications can work with DDE or OLE.

CLS (Character and Language Services) files Files that let you convert characters like foreign currency symbols and accented letters to other characters when importing or exporting files. CLS files also control collation (the order in which characters are sorted). You select a CLS file by choosing Tools ➤ Setup ➤ User Preferences ➤ International.

collapsing Closing a section in a document or a folder in a view. To collapse a section in a document or a folder in a view, click its triangle when it's pointing down.

columns Design elements that help users find documents in views and folders by including at least one identifier per document, such as the contents of a Subject field, a customer or product name, or a document name. Columns contain instructions for what to display: either the contents of a field in a document, a simple function, or the results of a formula.

constants Data types for fields whose value, once set, cannot be altered. Notes formulas use three types of constants: text constants, numeric constants, and time/date constants.

Create menu Use the Create menu to add elements (e.g., views, forms, folders, or Agents) to the current database or to add elements to the current document (e.g., tables, pictures, or hotspots).

database A group of documents, and their forms and views, stored under one name and opened through a database icon on your Workspace. A database is always one—and only one file—with the .NSF extension. A database can be as small and simple as a workgroup telephone book, containing a few documents and a single view, or as large and complex as a customer service system.

database catalog A special Notes system database containing information about databases stored on a single Notes server, a group of servers, or all the servers in a domain. The database catalog (CATALOG.NSF) resides on a server and can hold an inventory of databases. Databases are listed in the catalog by default, but database designers and managers can deselect the Design Property list in the database directory to prevent them from appearing in the catalog. You can create replicas of the database catalog.

database icon Every database on your Workspace is represented by an icon. You open a database's views and access its documents by double-clicking the icon. Most icons will display a graphic that relates to the database and the information it contains.

database replication The process of making the main database that's stored on a server and a copy—a replica—that's stored on a workstation (or another server) identical over time. Changes that have been made to the replica are passed back to the main database; likewise, any changes made to the main database are passed back to the replica. (See also *replication*.)

data type A field is categorized by the type of data it can contain. The data type also determines how a user can enter data in a field.

DDE (Dynamic Data Exchange) A protocol that lets you share data between applications. DDE lets you link data from another application as an object in a Notes document. Notes can act as a DDE client application, but not as a DDE server application. Before you can create or activate a DDE link in Notes, both Notes and the DDE server application must be running. (See also *OLE*.)

debugger Allows you to step through a script a line at a time or to stop at preset breakpoints. You can examine and set the values of the script variables. The debugger window becomes available when you choose File ➤ Tools ➤ Debug LotusScript.

default form Documents composed with obsolete or deleted forms or documents copied from another database use the default form for display (although the information that is displayed may be different from the original). Only one default form is allowed per database; it is marked by an asterisk in the Forms list.

default setting An initial setting that Notes uses until you specify another setting.

default view The view displayed the first time you open a database. The default view is specified by the database designer in the Design View Attributes dialog box. Notes remembers which view is displayed when you close a database and displays that view, rather than the default view, the next time you open the database.

Design pane Occupies the bottom part of any window. You can use the design pane for writing formulas and scripts for specifying other Actions. (See also *LotusScript*.)

design template A feature that lets database designers share field definitions among forms within a database, share high-level design elements (fields, forms, views, macros) among many databases, and optionally store all database design elements with a template. Consequently, when someone changes the template, all databases created with that template reflect the change. (Compare with *template*.)

desktop A key concept behind any Windows graphical user interface (GUI) is the desktop metaphor. It refers to the screen background upon which the various windows and their contents are displayed.

detach Make a local copy of a file attached to a Notes document. The file remains attached to the document until the attachment icon is deleted (which requires Editor access to the document).

dialog box A graphical element that is used by any Windows application to request information from the user. Dialog boxes come in three flavors: those that simply present a message; those that ask the user to make a yes or no choice—for example, Save Changes Before Quitting?; and those that present an array of options, which in turn may include dialog boxes that bring up dialog boxes that bring up even more dialog boxes. (See also *InfoBox*.)

dial-up Notes See *Mobile Notes*.

distinguished names A method of ensuring that each Notes user is assigned a unique name that can never be confused with any other name in the system, no matter how large the Notes installation grows. When a hierarchical certifier registers a user, the name on the User ID inherits the distinguished name of the certifier. For example, if the certifier's name is Sales\Acme\US and he certifies Lisa Smith, her fully distinguished name is Lisa Smith\Sales\Acme\US. (See Release 4.0 specifications for more information.)

DNS (Domain Name System) A TCP/IP service that translates domain names to and from IP addresses. The DNS maps the domain name of every computer on the Internet to its IP address so that each computer can send and receive information on the Internet.

doclink (or Document Link) An icon representing direct access from one Notes document to another. The documents don't have to be in the same view or even in the same database. Click a doclink to go to its target document, or move to the doclink (in Read-only mode) using the keyboard arrow keys and then press the spacebar. Notes opens the target document without closing the document you branched from. A doclink is similar to a hypertext link.

document The default form type that's assigned to a form unless it's designated as a Response-type form. A document is created by using a form on the Create menu. A document can range from a short answer to a coworker's question to a multipage market analysis. Documents consist of fields containing text, numbers, graphics, scanned images, or even voice messages. (See also *form*.)

document preview The Document Preview pane lets you read the content of the selected document, or if Notes is set to preview document links, lets you read documents linked to the selected document.

document type Notes supports three document types: Document, Response, and Response to Response.

domain A group of Notes servers with the same public Name & Address book. Domains define the scope of a Notes Mail environment.

Domino (or Domino Web server) Domino is server technology that transforms Lotus Notes into an Internet applications server. Domino combines the open networking environment of Internet standards and protocols with the powerful application development facilities of Notes, enabling you to develop a broad range of business applications for the Internet and intranet. Using Domino, you can build applications that leverage access control to databases, views, pages, forms, and fields. This flexibility allows you to present information or commands differently to different users, even though all the information resides within one database or application.

Edit mode Edit mode lets you modify a document. A document is automatically in Edit mode when you first compose it. To put a document in Edit mode later, you must either have Editor access (or better) to the database or be the document's author. Open the document and then choose Actions ➤ Edit Document or highlight the document in a view and press Ctrl+E. (See also *Read-only mode*.)

embedding An embedded object is a copy of data from a source file. When data from the source file changes, the changes are *not* reflected in Notes. Because an embedded object's data is stored in Notes, users who need to edit an embedded object don't need access to the source file. Embedding makes it easy for users to share data from other applications in Notes. Embedded objects require more Notes database storage space than linked objects require.

encrypt (or encryption) Encryption encodes a field in a document so that only users who have the secret encryption key can read it. When a user with the key opens an encrypted document, the encrypted information is displayed. When a user without the key opens an encrypted document, the encrypted information is not displayed. Encryption is also used to protect transmission between a Notes client and its server on any port (modem or network).

Esc key Pressing the Esc key on the keyboard closes any open document or view. If you've made changes to a document, Notes asks if you want to save the document.

event A script executes in response to the occurrence of an event in an object. The scriptable Notes objects are Agents, Actions, forms (documents), fields, buttons, and hotspots. The event initiates execution of a predefined subprogram, which can be selected from a list.

Execution Control List (ECL) Choosing any one of the Execution Control List (ECL) options (by clicking the Security Options button in the User Preferences dialog box) enables you to protect your workstation by controlling access to it by people who execute Notes scripts or formulas—for example, through forms, documents, or mail messages—on your workstation. You can specify different types of execution access for different people or organizational certifiers. For example, you may give all types of execution access to your Notes administrator but allow no execution access to unsigned scripts or formulas.

expanding Opening a folder in a view or a section in a document. To open a folder in a view or a section in a document, click its triangle when it's pointing to the right.

export The process of saving a Notes document or view in a non-Notes format by using the File ➤ Export command. You can export data to other applications, such as word processors, spreadsheets, and graphics programs.

FAQ (Frequently Asked Questions) A file that contains commonly asked questions and their answers. Typically, each newsgroup has a FAQ that answers questions relating to that particular newsgroup. Some FAQs focus on questions that new users have about newsgroups in general.

field A named area on a form for entering a single type of information. A field is the smallest entity in Notes. Fields may contain formulas or data or both. Fields are also used to define view columns.

field exchange See *Notes F/X.*

file server A computer that stores and provides user access to shared files and printers on a local area network. (Compare with *Notes server.*)

firewall A collection of components, typically a computer with a network router, that filters incoming and outgoing network traffic (or packets) to create a secure environment.

flame When a newsgroup reader severely criticizes another reader by posting a follow-up article or sending a personal e-mail message.

flowchart A graphic representation of a business process. For applications that move information among people or databases, a diagram clarifies the elements that are vital to the process.

folders Folders let you store and manage related documents without putting them into a category, which requires a Categories field in the form used to create the documents. Folders are also convenient because you can drag documents to them. You can keep a folder private or share it with other users of a database. No one else can read or delete your private folders. To create private folders in a database, you must have at least Reader access to the database. To create shared folders in a database, you must have at least Designer access.

fonts You can use the Text Properties InfoBox to change the font, point size, style, and/or color of text. Make sure the document is in Edit mode. To format existing text, select the text. To format new text, click where you want to enter the text. Choose Text ➤ Text Properties. To format a section title or button label, select the section or button and choose Section ➤ Section Properties or Button ➤ Button Properties. Click the Font tab. Select a font, size, style, and/or color.

footers Footers display text at the bottom of a document as part of the margin. You can specify footers that appear when you print any document in a database or when you print a list of documents in a folder or view.

form The design element that controls how you enter information into Notes and how Notes displays and prints that information. To create a document, you fill in a form from the Create menu in a database. Forms contain fields and static objects (labels, graphics, etc.). Forms can be used to query information using the full text search engine. Database designers can create any number of forms for a database.

form type Each form in a database has a type associated with it. The type dictates the use of a particular form. Notes supports three form types: Document, Response, and Response to Response.

formula An expression used to select documents from a database, calculate values for display, validate and translate new entries, etc. Database designers are the most frequent users of formulas, but anyone can use formulas to write macros or create custom SmartIcons or buttons. Formulas are the proprietary language of Notes, and they are used for data transformations. Formulas combine Notes @functions and Notes fields.

forwarding mail You can forward messages from your mail database, and you can forward documents from nonmail databases. When you forward a message or document, you create a new message that contains the contents of the original message or document. You address this new message the same way you address any new message. You can forward a single message or document or forward multiple messages or documents as a single message.

FTP (File Transfer Protocol) A protocol used to transfer files from one computer to another over the Internet or intranet. Also refers to the actual application used to move files using the FTP protocol.

full text search A Notes feature that lets you search a database for words and phrases, as well as perform more complex searches using wildcards and logical operators. To perform a full text search, the database you want to search must have a full text index—a special file that lets Notes process searches within seconds.

function A predefined Notes formula that performs a specific type of calculation. @Functions are used in designing Notes applications and writing macros.

Gopher A popular Internet application that uses a menu system to search for and download information.

graphics Illustrations or drawings, such as bitmaps, logos, and scanned photographs, that you can import and add to database icons, SmartIcons, forms, documents, and views. Notes supports these graphic file formats on the PC: BMP, CGM, GMF, PIC, PCX, TIF, and Windows Metafiles. In all cases, you must import a graphic image into a rich text field.

group A named set of Notes users defined with the Group form in a Name & Address book (also called a user group or mailing list). Grouping users together facilitates sending mail to numerous users or assigning everyone the same access level in a database's access control list.

headers Headers display text at the top of a document as part of the margin. You can specify headers that appear when you print any document in a database or when you print a list of documents in a folder or view.

Help menu Use the Help menu to get guidance on your current task, open the Help database for more detailed information, find Release 3 menu equivalents (Release 3 Menu Finder), or see the Help ➤ About This Database and Help ➤ Using This Database documents for the current Notes database.

hiding You can hide (or display) a paragraph in a document when you preview, open, edit, print, or copy the document. You can also hide (or display) a paragraph when the results of a formula you specify are true.

hierarchy You can design views in Notes to present a hierarchical organization of documents, which gives the user a visual understanding of how documents relate to one another. This document relationship occurs between main documents and Response documents. Hierarchy also refers to hierarchical names, or distinguished names, which is a naming convention that allows unique names to be assigned to users, groups, and servers. Using this convention creates hierarchical certifiers (certificates using distinguished naming). When an ID is certified with a hierarchical certifier, the name takes on the distinguished name of the hierarchical certifier. If you are using hierarchical naming, the common name is adequate for the ACL, but entering the distinguished name (for example, Ken Brown/SecondWave/Atlantic Decisions) adds another level of security.

home server The server on which your Notes Mail file is stored.

home page Generic term for the hypertext document users see when they first access a World Wide Web server.

host name A term used to represent the name of an HTTP server.

hotspot Depending on its type, a hotspot may display pop-up text, switch to a linked destination, or perform a Notes Action. Click and hold the mouse over the hotspot. If the hotspot displays pop-up text, read the text. If the hotspot displays a link destination, click the hotspot to switch to the linked destination (another document, view, folder, or database). Otherwise, click the hotspot to perform a Notes Action. To display pop-up text, you must be in Read mode.

HTML (Hypertext Markup Language) The language used to write World Wide Web documents or pages. HTML is a subset of ISO's (International Standards Organization) SGML (Standard Generalized Markup Language).

HTTP (Hypertext Transfer Protocol) The protocol used by the World Wide Web to transfer documents between clients (or browsers) and WWW servers.

hypermedia The collective term for creating links to and from text, graphics, audio, and video within online documents.

hypertext Text within an online document that contains links to text within other online documents; selecting a link automatically displays the second document.

icon A graphical element that represents an object, command, or option on your computer screen. The word *icon* can refer to several different items in Notes. The most important is the icon on your Workspace that represents a database. One piece of information that can appear on a database icon is its picture icon. The database designer creates this icon to provide a visual identity for a database. *Icon* also refers to buttons or other active places on the screen that display small pictures, such as SmartIcons and the buttons in the Search bar.

IMAP The Internet Mail Access Protocol allows for the manipulation of mail in various modes. IMAP clients can retrieve messages from an IMAP server and store them locally (similar to POP3), access messages directly from the server, or copy messages for offline use and then later synchronize with mail on the server. IMAP clients can share mailboxes (the equivalent of Notes mail folders). The Domino IMAP server enables IMAP clients to access their messages but is not involved with sending or delivering messages (these functions are handled by SMTP and Domino mail routing). Some examples of IMAP clients are the Outlook Express Mail component of Microsoft Internet Explorer 4.0 and the Netscape Messenger component of Netscape Communicator 4.0.

import The process of bringing data and files into a Notes database from other applications by using the File ➤ Import command. You can import word processing, spreadsheet, graphic, ASCII, and rich text format files.

InfoBox Many Notes commands open InfoBoxes. InfoBoxes have tabbed pages that let you choose many options at one time. To change properties, click the appropriate tab. To change properties for another object, click the drop-down menu and select an object. To move the box, drag it by the title bar. To collapse the box to its title bar or to expand the box, double-click the title bar. To get Help, click the question mark. To close the InfoBox, click Close. Unlike dialog boxes, InfoBoxes can be left open while you work, and you don't have to click OK or Done to make Notes accept your changes. Changes to settings are made as soon as you click somewhere else in the box.

inheriting To save users from unnecessary typing or to keep related documents consistent, a document can inherit information from another document or from fields in the same form.

Internet A group of networks that are connected to each other and span the world. Through the Internet, users have access to services such as e-mail, file transfer, remote log in, USENET news, the World Wide Web, WAIS, and Gopher.

Internet Protocol (IP) The main protocol used to transfer information packets back and forth on the Internet.

Internet server A host computer on the Internet that runs a network protocol, such as HTTP, to allow other computers to access its local information.

Internet service provider (ISP) A commercial organization that provides Internet connections.

InterNetNews (INN) A news software program that allows a computer to operate as a USENET news server.

InterNotes News A Notes server add-on that allows users to participate in USENET newsgroups directly from the Notes environment.

InterNotes Web Navigator A Notes Release 4 feature that allows users to navigate through pages on the Web directly from their Notes environment. The Web Navigator is much more than a Web browser—it combines the features of a Web browser with the powerful capabilities of Notes. You access the Web through a central database called the Web Navigator database. This database resides on a Notes server that's connected to the Internet. Each time you retrieve a Web page off the Internet, the Web Navigator translates it into a Notes document and stores it inside the database. The next time you want to read that page, you can open it directly from the database instead of retrieving it from the Internet. All the capabilities of Notes are available for you to use with the pages inside the Web Navigator database.

keyword One of the predefined choices in a keyword field. A keyword can be one or more words. Keywords can be predefined by the database designer or added by the authors of the documents. Keywords are useful in creating views with meaningful categories. (See also *category* and *view*.)

launch If you have the application an attached file was created with, you can start the application directly from Notes and read the file.

LDAP The Lightweight Directory Access Protocol enables LDAP clients to access specific fields in Person and Group documents in the Public Address Book. This protocol accesses directory services over a TCP/IP connection. For example, clients and applications can retrieve e-mail addresses and telephone and fax numbers from the Domino Public Address Book (and cascading address books). LDAP clients can query these fields but they cannot edit them. Some examples of LDAP clients are Microsoft Internet Explorer and Netscape Communicator.

linked object A pointer to data in a source file; when data in the source file changes, Notes reflects the changes. (You can specify whether the linked data in Notes is updated automatically or manually when data in the source file changes.) Because a linked object's data is stored in the source file, users who need to edit (or update) a linked object need to have the server application, access to the source file on a file server, and the same directory mapping to the source file on the file server. Also, if a source file is moved or deleted, the linked object that points to it has to be re-created.

links Design elements that let readers switch to another document, view, folder, or database. To create a link to another document, select or open the document and choose Edit ➤ Copy as Link ➤ Document Link. To create a link to a view or folder, select or switch to the view or folder and choose Edit ➤ Copy as Link ➤ View Link. To create a link to a database, select or open the database and choose Edit ➤ Copy as Link ➤ Database Link. To use a link, you must have access to the database the link leads to and the database must be on a Notes server on your network.

Listserv Stands for list server, an automated mailing-list-distribution system. Listserv is a program that runs on IBM mainframe computers, responding to requests to add or delete names to and from hundreds of active discussion lists. You subscribe to a Listserv mailing list by sending e-mail to the computer on which Listserv is running. As a subscriber, you can exchange messages with other users on the list by addressing a message to the list. All other subscribers receive your message, as well as replies to your message.

local area network (LAN) A group of computers that can share devices, such as printers and file servers, and possibly communicate with each other. Since the connections are made over cable or dedicated lines, a local area network is often confined to one building. Notes uses the communication protocols of the LAN, but doesn't necessarily need the other devices (such as a printer or file server). (Compare to *wide area network*.)

local database A Notes database stored on your computer's hard disk or on a floppy disk.

LotusScript The full object-oriented programming language for Lotus Notes Release 4 that allows you to write programs—scripts—for objects. (You write formulas using the Notes formula language.) You cannot combine scripts with formulas or Simple actions. You attach scripts and formulas to various objects in Notes depending on need; the particular object determines what you can use. LotusScript includes predefined object classes and the properties and methods for the classes. Notes oversees the compilation and loading of user scripts and automatically includes the Notes class definitions.

macro (See *Agents*.)

Mailto A link within a Web page that opens into an e-mail system (such as Notes Mail) to allow the user to send e-mail to the person specified in the link.

Message Transfer Agent (MTA) A program called a gateway that is installed on a Notes server. The MTA enables you to send mail to and receive mail from users of other electronic mail systems. A gateway translates messages between the Notes Mail format and the mail format of the foreign system. An MTA can translate messages and/or send them in the native Notes format.

MIME (Multipurpose Internet Mail Extensions) This protocol enables users to send multiple kinds of binary data (e.g. video, sound files) as attachments to an Internet (SMTP) e-mail message.

Mobile Notes A Notes feature that allows you to access databases by calling Notes servers using a modem instead of using Notes on a local area network. It includes special functionality to reduce the amount of data transferred and stored on the local workstation.

modem From the term MODulator/dEModulator; a telecommunications device that listens to your computer and then translates computer data into analog data so that the computer data can travel over an ordinary telephone line. At the other end of the line, another modem translates the analog data back to computer data so that the computer to which yours is "talking," or sending the data, can understand what your computer "said."

Name & Address book A special Notes system database used to schedule replication between servers and to manage security. The public Name & Address book is a database containing the name of every Notes user, user group, and server in a domain. If you perform Notes Setup while you're connected to a local area network, Notes adds this database to your Workspace. The personal Name & Address book is a database containing the names and computer addresses of users and user groups. Unlike the public Name & Address book, this database contains only information that you enter yourself. Notes adds this database to your Workspace during Setup.

Navigators Design elements that provide a graphical way for users to find documents or take actions without having to maneuver through views or find menu commands. Notes provides standard Navigators called folders that appear in the left Navigation pane when you open a database. You can design your own Navigators for an application to perform specific functions, including those with formulas or LotusScript programs.

NCSA Mosaic A commercial Web browser that supports hypermedia.

Netscape Another commercial browser that provides an interface to the World Wide Web.

news feed Transferring news from one news server to another.

news reader A program that allows you to read newsgroup discussions from a news server.

news server A machine running news software such as C News or InterNetNews (INN) that allows news feeds. You can have a news server at your site, or you can subscribe to a commercial news server, known as an Internet service provider.

NNTP (Network News Transfer Protocol)
The standard protocol for exchanging newsgroup articles over TCP/IP network connections.

Notes client The client computer that runs the Notes client software.

Notes database See *database.*

Notes F/X A NotesFlow tool that uses OLE technology to enable Notes and OLE server applications to share field information. You can design forms so that field contents in an OLE server application file automatically appear in corresponding fields in a Notes document, and vice versa. Depending on the type of field, the contents can be updated from either Notes or the other application. To exchange data, a one-to-one correspondence between the shared fields must exist. Both the OLE server application file and the Notes form must contain the same shared fields.

Notes Mail database (or Notes Mail file)
A Notes database where you send and receive mail. Although your mail database is stored on a server, only you can open it. You can keep a local copy of your mail database, perhaps on a laptop or home computer, and use dial-up Notes features to exchange the local and server replicas to keep them in synch and to send your outgoing mail. (See also *database replication.*)

Notes server (or Domino server) A computer that stores Notes databases and allows users to share them. It communicates either through the network or by accepting incoming phone calls from mobile personal computers or laptops.

Notes workstation A personal computer running the Notes workstation software. The workstation contains the entire user interface for Notes. It can replicate, send mail, perform a full text index, and so on.

NOTES.INI A critical configuration file that defines how your Notes system runs.

.NSF extension Stands for Notes Storage File and describes regular databases created in Notes. If you do not include a file name extension when you enter a file name for a new database, Notes gives the file the .NSF extension by default.

.NTF extension Stands for Notes Template File and describes database templates created in Notes.

ODBC (Open Database Connectivity)
Standard that provides object classes, properties, and methods for accessing external databases using LotusScript.

OLE (Object Linking and Embedding)
A technology that lets you share data between applications and is supported for Windows and Macintosh. OLE lets you embed or link data, such as a 1-2-3 chart, Word Pro document, or Freelance Graphics presentation, as an object in a Notes document. You can embed or link part of a file or an entire file from another application as an object in a Notes document.

You can also embed a new object in a Notes document and use the object's application to enter data in Notes. For example, if you have 1-2-3, you could create a blank 1-2-3 worksheet object and enter 1-2-3 worksheet data in a Notes document.

OLE 2 OLE 2.0 is the latest version of OLE technology. You can use the following OLE 2 features in Notes: drag and drop, which enables you to create an OLE 2 object in Notes by dragging data from an OLE 2 server application and dropping it into Notes; edit in place, which lets you edit an OLE 2 object using the server application's commands without leaving the Notes window; link server, which allows you to create links to Notes documents, views, and databases in Notes documents and in other OLE 2 client applications; and storage server, which lets you embed an OLE 2 object in a Notes document and create links to the embedded data in Notes documents and in other OLE 2 client applications. OLE 2 enables you to use Notes to store data from other applications.

outgoing mail database A local repository for the mail you want to send when you use Notes with a modem rather than over a local area network. When you select Workstation-based mail in the Location Setup dialog box, Notes holds your outgoing mail in a file on your PC called MAIL.BOX until you route the mail to a Notes server.

packet A package of information (or data) that has been broken down by TCP in order to be transferred by IP. For example, if you post an article to a newsgroup, TCP breaks your article into small packets of information that IP then transfers over the Internet.

page breaks Notes treats documents as one continuous stream of data. However, you can deliberately insert hard page breaks in documents. Make sure the document is in Edit mode. Click where you want to insert the page break. Notes inserts the page break above the current paragraph. Choose Create ➤ Page Break. To see where pages will break, choose View ➤ Show ➤ Page Breaks. Notes displays a page break as a solid line across the screen. You can see where pages will break and words will wrap before you print a document.

passthru servers Your Notes administrator can set up one or more servers for you to use as "stepping stones" to connect to other servers. These intermediary servers are known as passthru servers. You can use passthru servers to connect to multiple servers through a single phone connection or to connect to a server on a local area network running a different network protocol.

Your Notes administrator can set up a passthru server so that it leads to additional passthru servers as well as target servers. Notes can "hop" from one passthru server to the next until it reaches the target server you want. You don't have to know how a passthru server reaches a target server; all you need to find out from your Notes administrator is which target servers you can reach from a passthru server.

Permanent Pen You can use Permanent Pen to add comments to a document in a different font. With Permanent Pen, you don't have to change the font as you move through a document. To turn on Permanent Pen, make sure the document is in Edit mode. Choose Text ➤ Permanent Pen. Enter text. To turn off Permanent Pen, choose Text ➤ Permanent Pen again. By default, Permanent Pen is red bold.

Personal Web Navigator The Personal Web Navigator provides you with easy access to information on the Internet right from your Notes workstation through its connection to the Internet. This database acts as a repository for Internet documents and files that you have retrieved. The Personal Web Navigator is your own personal database for surfing the Internet.

PING Utility A PING utility sends network packets to a remote computer and requests that server to return network packets. You use a PING utility to find out if a remote computer is available for a network connection.

plain text field A plain text field can't contain formatted data, whose appearance can be changed by using different attributes such as bold, italics, color, and so on. In other words, you can't alter the appearance of data in a plain text field.

POP (Post Office Protocol) An e-mail protocol for downloading mail from a mail server. The Domino server in Release 4.5 and above supports POP clients.

pop-up A Notes feature that lets you attach a block of text or a formula to a specific place in a document or form. A green rectangle usually indicates the presence of a pop-up.

portfolio database A portfolio database is a collection of databases that help organize your Workspace. A portfolio is usually a group of databases that are related or a group of databases that you use frequently. When opened, the Navigator pane contains buttons for each database in the collection. The first database in the collection is automatically opened. For example, the Favorites database is created when Notes 4.6 is installed. The portfolio contains buttons to your Mail file, the Calendar, the To-Do list, and your Personal Journal.

posting An article or response sent to a newsgroup.

PPP (Point-to-Point Protocol) A dial-up connection protocol that enables you to use a modem to connect to other modems on the Internet. PPP is similar to the Serial Line Internet Protocol (SLIP) but is the newer protocol. PPP, unlike SLIP, actually monitors and verifies Internet packets as they are sent.

preferences Notes settings that you can define by choosing File ➤ Tools ➤ User Preferences.

Preview pane Lets you read the content of the selected document, or if Notes is set to preview document links, lets you read documents linked to the selected document.

private key See *public key*.

private view A view that you design and save for your own use with a database. No one else sees a private view, and its name appears only on your own View menu. You can create a private view for any database for which you have at least Reader access. Choose Design ➤ Views to begin designing a private view.

Programmer's pane See *Design pane*.

proxy server A computer that provides access to information (such as URLs or network protocols) through a firewall server.

public key   Whenever a Notes client—that is, a workstation or a server—attempts to communicate with a Notes server for replication, mail routing, or database access, Notes activates two security procedures that verify that the client is legitimate. The first process, *validation*, establishes trust in the client's public key. If validation occurs successfully, the second process, *authentication*, begins. Authentication occurs by means of a challenge/response interaction that uses the public and private keys of the client and the server.

query   A search of a Notes database index for a specific term or topic. You enter a word or phrase that appears in a database's view in the Search bar or select the database in your Workspace and then choose Edit ➤ Find.

quick address   Notes helps you address messages by displaying names that contain the letters that you type in the To, cc, and bcc fields. You can select a name rather than type the entire name. In the To, cc, or bcc field of the message, type the first letter or two of the name of a person or group to whom you want to send the message. If the name that Notes displays is not the name you want, type additional letters in the name. If Notes displays the name you want, press ↵ to accept the name and then look for additional names. If you do not want to add more names to this field, press the down arrow to move to the next field. If Notes does not display the name you want, type the entire name and address. You can set up Notes to look for names in your Personal Address Book only or in both your Personal Address Book and in the Public Address Book. You can also turn off quick addressing. You make these selections in

the Recipient name type-ahead field in the Location document in your Personal Address Book.

radio button   A graphical way to present options for displaying keywords. Each keyword is displayed with a button; users click only one. Radio buttons have a frame and column options. The Allow Multi-values and Allow Values Not in This List options are not applicable to radio buttons.

Read-only mode   Read-only mode lets you read but not modify a document. To modify a document, you must have Editor access (or better) to the database or you must be the document's author. (See also *Edit mode*.)

refresh   You refresh a view or document to reflect changes that have been made to it after editing or making deletions. Refreshing also recalculates computations in fields. To refresh, press F9 or choose View ➤ Refresh.

Release 3 Menu Finder   Notes Release 4 can show its equivalent to any command you may be accustomed to using in Notes Release 3.*x*. Choose Help ➤ Release 3 Menu Finder. From the menu in the window that appears, choose the Release 3.*x* command you want to locate in Release 4.*x*.

remote server   A Notes server that you access using a modem and telephone lines rather than a local area network (LAN). A server is a local server if you're using it on a LAN; the same server is a remote server if you use a modem to connect to it (usually from off-site).

replica A copy of a database that is updated by exchanging information (or replicating) with the original database, either on a regular schedule or at will. Notes servers can connect to other Notes servers and periodically update all replicas of a database (or multiple databases) so that they become identical.

replication A process by which two replica databases are updated so that each contains the same information. Replication can be performed between two servers and between a server and a workstation (when the workstation initiates the replication).

Replicator The Replicator page is always the last page on your Workspace. The Replicator Workspace page lets you manage replication of your local databases in one place. With the Replicator page, you can replicate multiple databases with one or more servers with a single command. When you use the Replicator page, Notes replicates in the background so you can do other work while Notes replicates.

Response document A document created using a Response form, a typical component of a discussion database. In a view, Response documents are usually indented underneath the document to which they respond. Response documents typically inherit information from the parent document, which is the document highlighted when the Compose Response is invoked. (See also *form type*.)

rich text field Field that can accommodate formatted (bold, color, etc.) text. It can include pictures, tables, pop-ups, DDE and OLE objects, attachments, edition files, and other special data created in Notes, imported from other applications, or pasted from the Clipboard. Plain text, another data type, cannot accommodate styled text or special objects. Data validation and many other formula facilities won't work in a rich text field. (See also *plain text field*.)

right mouse button You can click the right mouse button to display a menu related to what you're doing in Notes. If you're using Windows or OS/2, you can also choose whether double-clicking the right mouse button closes the current Notes window. Choose File ➤ Tools ➤ User Preferences. Under Advanced options, select or deselect the Right Double-click Closes Window option. Click OK.

role See *access role*.

router A system that transfers data between networks using the same network protocol. You may connect to an Internet service provider through a router.

routing applications See *workflow automation*.

scheduled Agents Useful for running periodic workflow or maintenance tasks on selected documents. Select the database and choose View ➤ Agents. Double-click the Agent. Select one of the On Schedule options. Click Schedule to change the default schedule for the interval you've chosen or to change the server on which this agent runs. Specify the document selection and actions. Close and save the Agent.

script libraries A script library contains (Option), (Declaration), Initialize, Terminate, and User scripts. To create a script library, choose Create ➤ Design ➤ Script Library. To access a script library, choose View ➤ Design, click Script Libraries under Design, and double-click the name of the library. The script library appears as a Design pane. The scope of a script library is the current database. All scripts in a database can avail themselves of the code in a library in that database. However, the library is lost to scripts outside the database. For example, if a button in a document uses a script library and you mail the document to or paste it in another database that does not have the same script library, the script fails. If a script attempts to use a library not in the current database, you see the error message, "Error loading USE or USELSX module."

scroll bar You can scroll around a document when it's too large to display all of its contents on one screen. To move to a location in a document, drag the scroll box to the position in the scroll bar that corresponds to the desired location. To move up or down one screen at a time, click the scroll bar above or below the scroll box. To move up or down one line at a time, click the arrows at the top or bottom of the scroll bar. If you're using Windows or UNIX, you can hide or display the horizontal scroll bar in a document, in the View pane, or in the Preview pane. To hide or display the horizontal scroll bar, choose View ➤ Show ➤ Horizontal Scroll Bar.

Search bar Appears in a database view below the SmartIcons palette. Prior to doing a search, be sure the database is open to the view you want to search. If the Search bar is not visible, choose View ➤ Search Bar. If the database is not full text indexed, type the text that you want to find in the Search bar text box. Click Search. If the database is full text indexed, click Add Condition in the Search bar. Leave the default value, "Words and Phrases," in the Condition drop-down list. Finally, type the word or phrase you want to find in the first numbered text box. Click OK. Click Search in the Search bar.

sections You can use sections to collapse one or more paragraphs in a document into a single line. Sections make navigation in large documents easier. Readers can expand a section when they want to read its contents.

security If you have Manager access to a local database, you can secure that database to prevent someone with another User ID from accessing the database from the workstation or from a copy of the database made through the operating system. You can also change your user name by giving your certifier a disk that contains a modified version of your User ID and then by merging the recertified User ID (when you receive it) back into your User ID. Changing the user name removes all the certificates from the User ID, so after you change the name, you will need to acquire new certificates before you can use any shared databases.

selective replication With selective replication, you can save disk space, reduce the time and expense of remote replication, and display only the parts of databases you're interested in.

server See *Domino server, file server,* or *Notes server.*

Server Web Navigator The Server Web Navigator provides you with easy access to information on the Internet through a Notes server (the InterNotes server) connected to the Internet. This database acts as a repository for Internet documents and files that you or other users have retrieved. You can also use this database as an easy entry point for exploring the Internet. The Server Web Navigator is a collaborative database where you and your coworkers can explore the Internet together.

setting passwords To prevent unauthorized users from accessing databases, you can set a password, change an existing password, or clear a password at any time. To set or change your password, choose File ➤ Tools ➤ User ID. Enter your password in the text box. Click Set Password. If you are changing an existing password, type this password in the text box and click OK. If you did not previously have a password, skip this step. Enter a new password in the text box and click OK. Confirm the password by typing it again, exactly as you did the first time, and click OK. To clear your password, choose File ➤ Tools ➤ User ID. Click Clear Password. Enter your password in the text box and click OK.

shared database A Notes database that resides on a Notes server.

S-HTTP (Secure Hypertext Transfer Protocol) The proposed Internet protocol used for creating secure HTTP connections using public key technology.

sign Attach a unique electronic signature to a document or field when a document is mailed. The signature is derived from the sender's User ID. This security measure assures the recipient that the same user who wrote the document also sent it.

SLIP (Serial Line Internet Protocol) A dial-up connection protocol that enables you to use a modem to connect to other modems on the Internet.

SmartIcons Customizable buttons that choose one or more Notes commands or execute a Notes formula. To find out what a SmartIcon does, simply drag the mouse over it and balloon Help explains its function.

SMTP (Simple Mail Transfer Protocol) Part of the TCP/IP family of protocols and the standard used for formatting and sending e-mail on the Internet.

stacked icons You can set your Workspace to show all database replicas as stacked icons. Stacked icons conserve space in your Workspace and make it easier to act upon all replicas of a database at once. When you stack icons, the top-left icon appears at the top of the stack. To display icons as replicas, choose View ➤ Stack Replica Icons.

Startup Database You can set Notes to display a database instead of the Workspace at startup. This option is particularly convenient when you work with a specific database most of the time. You save time by having immediate access to the database instead of having to locate it on your Workspace (which may display many databases). Choose File ➤ Tools ➤ User Preferences. Click the Basics panel of the dialog box. Click the Startup Database button. Select the database that you want to open when Notes starts up. Click OK in the Startup Database dialog box. Click OK in the User Preferences dialog box.

static text Text that remains constant on every document created with a particular form, as opposed to fields in which you type information or Notes calculates information.

status bar The bar across the bottom of your screen that includes indicators and controls for disk and network access, messages, current typeface and point size, location settings, Notes Mail, and your access level to the active database.

stub (or replica stub) A new database replica that has not yet been filled with documents (or initialized). A stub is created when you choose File ➤ Replication ➤ New Replica and then select Initialize and Copy at First Replication. The database is no longer a stub once the first replication takes place.

subform A form-building shortcut that allows you to store regularly used fields and other form elements together. Instead of adding fields individually, you can place the subform on the form. You cannot add other fields to the form that have the same name as fields on the subform.

subscribe When users want to access a newsgroup, they first need to subscribe to that newsgroup.

table A design element for formatting information in multiple columns. To add a table, make sure the document is in Edit mode. Click where you want the table to appear. You must be in a rich text field to create a table. Choose Create ➤ Table. Specify the number of columns and rows you want in the table. Click OK. Notes adjusts the widths of the columns to fit the current window by default. However, you can set a column's width and specify other table settings in the Table Properties InfoBox. You can also create a table with the Create Table icon in the SmartIcons bar.

TCP (Transmission Control Protocol) One of the main protocols used on the Internet to break data into individual packets of information that can be transferred using the Internet Protocol (IP).

template A Notes database design that you can use as a starting point for a new database.

time zones You can set up location documents in your Personal Address Book that use different communication settings at different places where you work with Notes. You can update settings such as the area code and time zone for the current location. This setting is useful if you work with one location (such as Travel) in different places.

trash folder The trash folder contains mail messages that you want to delete. After placing messages in this folder, you can delete them later or remove them from the trash. You can specify how you want Notes to empty the trash folder in your mail database. You can also mark documents for deletion. Documents marked for deletion appear in the view with a trash can icon. To delete documents, select the document(s) you want to delete. Choose Edit ➤ Clear to mark the documents for deletion. When you are ready to delete documents, either close the database or refresh the view by pressing F9. Confirm that you want to permanently delete the marked documents. To change your mind about deleting marked documents, select the document(s) that you want to keep. Choose Edit ➤ Undo Delete to remove the deletion mark(s).

UNIX A very powerful and venerable operating system with simultaneous support of multiple users and multiple tasks built in, rather than added on as it is with other operating systems. UNIX can get files from and send files to any connected devices and lets programmers send output from one computing task to another task. UNIX has become the operating system of the Internet, and most other operating systems are customized to work with UNIX when they hook into the Internet (by emulating TCP/IP).

Unread marks You can mark documents Read or Unread (regardless of whether you have actually read them) to make a view easier to scan. You can mark either selected documents or all documents in the view. To mark documents Read, select the documents you want to mark. Choose Edit ➤ Unread Marks ➤ Mark Selected Read to mark only selected documents. Choose Edit ➤ Unread Marks ➤ Mark All Read to mark all the documents in the view. To mark documents Unread, select the documents you want to mark. Choose Edit ➤ Unread Marks ➤ Mark Selected Unread to mark only selected documents. Choose Edit ➤ Unread Marks ➤ Mark All Unread to mark all the documents in the view.

unsubscribe When users do not want to receive postings from a newsgroup, they unsubscribe to that newsgroup. After they unsubscribe, they will no longer be able to view and read postings in that newsgroup.

URL (Universal Resource Locator) The World Wide Web name for a document, file, or other resource. It describes the protocol required to access the resource, the host where it can be found, and a path to the resource on that host.

USENET A conferencing system that links discussion groups devoted to specific topics. USENET is accessible through most Internet service providers but technically is not part of the Internet. You read and post articles (i.e., messages) in newsgroups; then other users can read the messages on the topics that interest them and post their responses or comments.

USENET news server See *news server.*

USENET newsgroups USENET newsgroups are collections of discussion groups that reside on various servers on the Internet. USENET newsgroups resemble electronic bulletin boards where readers read, post, and reply to articles posted by other newsgroup readers.

user group See *group*.

User ID A file assigned to a user that uniquely identifies that user to Notes. All Notes users (and servers) must have a User ID. It is the "private" section of the public/private key Notes security system. ID files must be kept in a secure location and should be password protected.

Using Database document or Help document An optional document written by the designer of a database that explains how to use the database. If a database has a Using Database document, it's available when you choose Help ➤ Using This Database.

UUCP (UNIX-to-UNIX Copy Program) A standard protocol for exchanging newsgroup articles using asynchronous dial-up lines.

UUdecode and UUencode Programs that convert files from text to binary. You use these programs to send file attachments across the Internet; many e-mail applications automatically UUencode files when you send them and UUdecode files when you receive them. Both of these programs were developed as part of UUCP.

view A list of documents in a database that are usually sorted or categorized to make finding documents easier. A database can have any number of views. You can change to a different view from the View menu. Most views are created by the database designer, but you can create private views that only you can see. (A view can also look different to different users, or be altogether absent for some users, depending on their access roles.)

Web browser An application that provides an interface to the World Wide Web.

Web fill-out form A Web document in which users input information through option (radio) buttons, text input fields, checkboxes, and so on, and then submit that information to a Web server.

Web Navigator database The Notes database that resides on the InterNotes server and allows users access to the Web.

Web Navigator template The Notes template that contains all the design elements needed to create the Web Navigator database.

Web publisher Generic term for a tool or software package that converts documents to HTML so that they can be viewed on the World Wide Web.

Web server Stores the information accessible from a Web browser.

Web site The set of pages that comprise a person or organization's presence on the Web.

Webmaster A person who manages a Web site—similar to the network administrator.

wide area network (WAN) A group of computers that can communicate and share devices such as file servers. Unlike local area networks, wide area networks use telephone lines or dedicated leased lines. Notes servers can communicate across a wide area network (WAN).

workflow automation A method for supporting workgroup applications. Notes supports two basic workflow models: shared applications and routing applications. Shared applications are generally discussion databases where people contribute at different points and can check on the status of something at any point in time. Routing applications are mail-based databases, where information is passed from one person to another, with each person modifying it in some way.

Workspace The Notes desktop, which includes Notes windows, menus, SmartIcons, and the tabbed pages where you display database icons. You can organize your Workspace by naming the tabbed pages and by adding, moving, and removing icons.

World Wide Web (or Web) The World Wide Web, or Web (or WWW), is a wide-area hypermedia information retrieval initiative that gives universal access to a large universe of documents. To access the Web, you use a Web browser that provides hypertext links to jump to information on many Internet Web servers.

INDEX

NOTE: Page numbers in *italics* refer to figures or tables; page numbers in **bold** refer to significant discussions of the topic.

F

O

U

What's on the CD?

Database Applications

- **Da Big Library:** An electronic file cabinet that stores reference documents and enables members of a workgroup to access information easily.

- **RADD GUI Gallery:** A wealth of professional 3-D graphics you can copy and paste into your Notes Release 4 Navigators, layout regions, and forms.

- **US Zip Code Database:** Zip codes, city names, and state names for all zip codes in the United States as of 1994.

- **Employment Kiosk:** Use this sample database to practice the techniques you'll learn throughout the book.

Graphics Programs

- **Visio Express 4.0:** A graphic program which enables you to create diagrams, flowcharts, project timelines, workflow processes, and other business drawings by using task-specific stencils with hundreds of SmartShapes.

- **Paint Shop Pro v.5:** A complete windows graphics program for image creation, viewing, and manipulations. Features include painting with eight brushes, photo retouching, image enhancement and editing, color enhancement, image browsing, batch conversion, and scanner support.

- **Screen Thief for Windows v.1.01:** The ultimate screen capture system for Windows, with up to eight user-defined capture configurations.

Demonstration Programs

- **PAVONE Espresso:** A Notes workflow management system that automates routing and tracking key documents and information around your office or organization.

- **PAVONE Groupflow Movies:** A demonstration of a workflow management system that consists of a graphical editor, a configurable runtime system, and a workflow simulator.

- **NotesWare EIS:** A Notes information analysis program that allows you to analyze, in greater detail, information brought together from a variety of sources.

- **Adobe Acrobat Reader v.3.0:** A program that allows you to view the PAVONE product information summaries included on the CD.

Utility Program

- **WinBiff 3.6a:** 32-bit versions of the Windows 95 mail notification program.